McGraw-Hill Yearbook of Science and Technology 1974 REVIEW

1975 PREVIEW

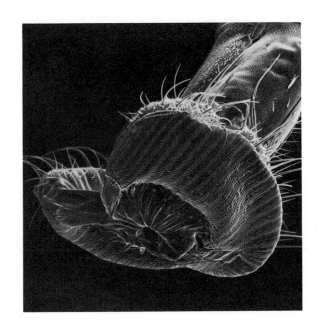

McGraw-Hill **Yearbook of**

McGRAW-HILL BOOK COMPANY

NEW YORK   MEXICO
ST. LOUIS   MONTREAL
SAN FRANCISCO   NEW DELHI
                            PANAMA
                            PARIS
AUCKLAND   SÃO PAULO
DUSSELDORF   SINGAPORE
JOHANNESBURG   SYDNEY
KUALA LUMPUR   TOKYO
LONDON   TORONTO

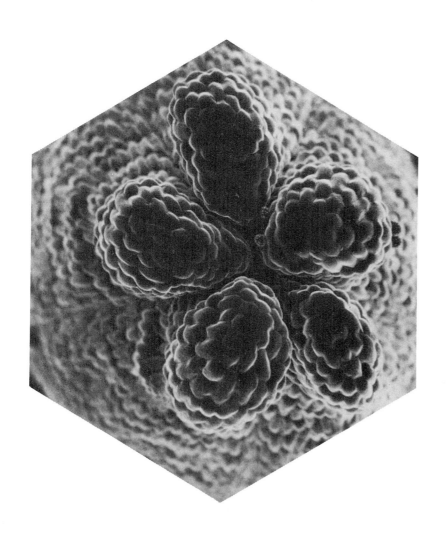

Science and Technology

COMPREHENSIVE COVERAGE OF

THE IMPORTANT EVENTS OF THE YEAR **1974**

AS COMPILED BY THE STAFF OF THE

McGRAW-HILL ENCYCLOPEDIA OF SCIENCE AND TECHNOLOGY

On preceding pages:

Left. Scanning electron micrograph of the tongue of a housefly; magnification 90X.

Right. Scanning electron micrograph of a daisy pistil fertilized with two pieces of pollen; magnification 105X.

Both specimens were photographed in the natural state without use of fixatives, preservatives, or stains. (Courtesy David Scharf)

McGRAW-HILL YEARBOOK OF SCIENCE AND TECHNOLOGY Copyright © 1975, by McGraw-Hill, Inc. All Rights Reserved. No part of this publication may be reproduced, stored in a retrieval system, or transmitted, in any form or by any means, electronic, mechanical, photocopying, recording, or otherwise, without the prior written permission of the publishers. Philippines Copyright, 1975, by McGraw-Hill, Inc.

Library of Congress Catalog Card Number: 62-12028

International Standard Book Number: 0-07-045342-X

The Library of Congress cataloged the original printing of this title as follows:

McGraw-Hill yearbook of science and technology. 1962—
  New York, McGraw-Hill Book Co.

    v. illus. 26 cm.
   Vols. for 1962— compiled by the staff of the McGraw-Hill encyclopedia of science and technology.

    1. Science—Yearbooks. 2. Technology—Yearbooks. I. McGraw-Hill encyclopedia of science and technology.

Q1.M13	505.8	62-12028
Library of Congress	(10)	

Table of Contents

Consulting Editors

Consulting Editors (continued)

Dr. Manley Mandel. *Section of Molecular Biology, M. D. Anderson Hospital, Houston.* MICROBIOLOGY.

Prof. Robert W. Mann. *Department of Mechanical Engineering, Massachusetts Institute of Technology.* DESIGN ENGINEERING.

Dr. Edward A. Martell. *National Center for Atmospheric Research, Boulder.* GEOCHEMISTRY.

Dr. Harold B. Maynard. *Chairman of the Board, Maynard Research Council, Inc.* INDUSTRIAL AND PRODUCTION ENGINEERING.

Dr. Howard Mel. *Associate Professor of Biophysics, Division of Medical Physics, Donner Laboratories, University of California.* BIOPHYSICS.

Dr. Bernard S. Meyer. *Professor and Chairman, Department of Botany and Plant Pathology, Ohio State University.* PLANT PHYSIOLOGY.

Dr. N. Karle Mottet. *Professor of Pathology and Director of Hospital Pathology, University of Washington.* ANIMAL PATHOLOGY.

Dr. Royce W. Murray. *Professor of Chemistry, University of North Carolina.* ANALYTICAL CHEMISTRY.

Dr. Harry F. Olson. *Staff Vice President, Acoustical and Electromechanical Laboratory, RCA Laboratories.* ACOUSTICS.

Dr. Jerry Olson. *Oak Ridge National Laboratory.* CONSERVATION; PLANT ECOLOGY.

Dr. Guido Pontecorvo. *Imperial Cancer Research Fund, London.* GENETICS AND EVOLUTION.

Prof. K. R. Porter. *Chairman, Department of Molecular, Cellular and Developmental Biology, University of Colorado.* CYTOLOGY.

Prof. C. Ladd Prosser. *Head, Department of Physiology, University of Illinois.* COMPARATIVE PHYSIOLOGY.

Brig. Gen. Peter C. Sandretto (retired). *Director, Engineering Management, International Telephone and Telegraph Corporation.* NAVIGATION.

William C. Schall. *Purcell, Graham and Company, New York.* COMPUTERS.

Dr. Bradley T. Scheer. *Head, Department of Biology, University of Oregon.* GENERAL PHYSIOLOGY.

Dr. Marlan O. Scully. *Department of Physics, University of Arizona.* ELECTROMAGNETIC RADIATION AND OPTICS.

Prof. Frederick Seitz. *President, The Rockefeller University.* SOLID-STATE PHYSICS.

C. Dewitt Smith. *Mining Consultant, Dewitt Smith and Company, Inc., Salt Lake City.* MINING ENGINEERING.

Dr. Mott Souders. *Formerly Director of Oil Development, Shell Development Company.* PETROLEUM CHEMISTRY.

Prof. William D. Stevenson, Jr. *Department of Electrical Engineering. North Carolina State University.* ELECTRICAL POWER ENGINEERING.

Dr. Earl L. Stone. *Department of Agronomy, New York State College of Agriculture and Life Sciences—Cornell University.* FORESTRY.

Dr. Horace W. Stunkard. *Research Associate, Invertebrate Zoology, American Museum of Natural History.* INVERTEBRATE ZOOLOGY.

Dr. E. L. Tatum. *The Rockefeller University.* BIOCHEMISTRY.

Dr. Craig S. Tedmon. *Manager, Surfaces and Reactions Branch, Physical Chemistry Laboratory, General Electric Company, Schenectady.* METALLURCIGAL ENGINEERING.

Gordon N. Thayer. *Technical Consultant.* TELECOMMUNICATIONS.

Dr. Garth Thomas. *Director, Center for Brain Research, University of Rochester.* PHYSIOLOGICAL AND EXPERIMENTAL PSYCHOLOGY.

Dr. C. N. Touart. *Senior Scientist, Air Force Cambridge Research Laboratory.* GEOPHYSICS.

Leonard Trauberman. *Managing Editor, "Food Engineering."* FOOD ENGINEERING.

Dr. Henry P. Treffers. *Professor of Pathology, Yale University School of Medicine.* MEDICAL MICROBIOLOGY.

Prof. William W. Watson. *Department of Physics, Yale University.* ATOMIC, MOLECULAR, AND NUCLEAR PHYSICS.

Contributors

A list of contributors, their affiliations, and the articles they wrote will be found on page 423.

Preface

The 1975 *McGraw-Hill Yearbook of Science and Technology*, fourteenth in the series, focuses on the outstanding scientific, engineering, and technological achievements of 1974. The articles report in detail and analyze developments in areas such as astrophysics, space technology, forestry, genetics, and energy production and utilization.

The Yearbook performs two functions. As an individual book it is a ready reference to the progress of science and technology. As part of a larger reference work it supplements the basic material in the *McGraw-Hill Encyclopedia of Science and Technology* with up-to-date information.

The format for the 1975 Yearbook follows the organization established in previous editions. The first part includes six major articles on subjects selected for their broad interest and growing significance. The second part, a selective pictorial section, features a number of the outstanding scientific photographs of the past 12 months. The third part consists of alphabetically arranged articles on advances, discoveries, and developments in science and technology during the past year.

The choice of the subject matter was the work of 67 consulting editors and the editorial staff of the *McGraw-Hill Encyclopedia of Science and Technology.* But most of the credit should go to the 193 eminent specialists who contributed to the present volume. Their interest, knowledge, and writing ability make them the real creators of the 1975 Yearbook.

DANIEL N. LAPEDES
Editor in Chief

Mammalian Fertilization

Benjamin G. Brackett holds doctorates in veterinary medicine and biochemistry and is presently a professor in the Department of Clinical Studies, School of Veterinary Medicine, and in the Department of Obstetrics and Gynecology, School of Medicine, at the University of Pennsylvania. He serves as a consultant to NICHD, as a member of the Scientific Advisory Committee for the NIH Primate Research Centers, and on the Editorial Board of the "Biology of Reproduction" journal.

Fertilization involves meeting of the sperm and egg, their interaction and combination with progression to complete union of the parental genetic moieties to form a zygote, which undergoes mitotic cleavage to form a two-cell-stage embryo. This process, which normally takes place in the upper (toward the ovary) part of the oviduct or fallopian tube, is initiated at varying intervals after mating according to the species. Fertilization takes place over an interval of several hours in mammalian species, for example, approximately 12 hr in the rabbit, 16–21 hr in the sheep, 20–24 hr in the cow, about 21 hr in the rhesus monkey, and somewhat less than 36 hr in the human.

The fertilization process provides the vital link which joins the end product of oogenesis, the egg, and the end product of spermatogenesis, the spermatozoon, to develop a new individual. Each identifiable event in

male and female germ cell development, formation of the zygote, and embryonic development may be thought of as a link in the reproductive chain. Much recent thought has been directed toward the goal of controlling fertility by breaking or strengthening one or more of the links in this chain of reproductive events. An ideal contraceptive agent might prevent sperm and egg from uniting. Discovery of a means for specifically blocking an essential reaction or a step to prevent gamete union (but without harmful side effects) would be of obvious advantage in face of the population explosion for use in humans, and also for use in animals, pet and pests, in order to curb their populations for humane or public health indications. On the other hand, strengthening of the link in the reproductive chain by enhancing gamete union should be beneficial in leading to more efficient production of animals for food and fiber and also for enabling subfertile couples to have children.

The purpose of this article is to review progress in understanding the process of mammalian fertilization, with emphasis on recently acquired knowledge made possible through the development of procedures for test-tube or extracorporeal fertilization.

SPERM CAPACITATION

Prior to penetration of an egg, a fertilizing sperm cell must undergo a process termed sperm capacitation. This involves a physiological change in the sperm cell and normally takes place within the female reproductive tract. Although in the strictest sense capacitation is considered a prerequisite of fertilization, it is appropriately included in any discussion of mammalian fertilization since the end point of sperm capacitation and the acrosome reaction is penetration into the ovum. Much information has been obtained in studies of sperm capacitation, and at the present time it is thought to involve the removal of seminal plasma components from the sperm surface and also increased metabolic activity of the sperm cell as it achieves the capacity to fertilize. In several species the increased metabolism has been described as resulting in a changed character of motility which becomes more propulsive. A fourfold increase in respiration by sperm cells following uterine incubation has been demonstrated concomitantly with this process in the rabbit.

The capacitation process has been studied in greatest detail in the rabbit, rat, hamster, mouse, and guinea pig. In these species it is now possible to capacitate sperm in culture media of defined composition and subsequently to accomplish extracorporeal fertilization with the treated sperm cells. Following this procedure in the mouse, rat, and rabbit, it has been possible to transfer the resulting embryos into reproductive tracts of female recipients and to obtain offspring. In the rabbit experiments in which sperm capacitation and fertilization were achieved outside the animal, the sperm cells were obtained following ejaculation; in the rodent experiments epididymal sperm cells were used.

FERTILIZATION PROCESS

Once sperm cells become capacitated, they are capable of undergoing the so-called acrosome reaction which enables them to enter the perivitelline space and activate the egg. Following penetration of the vitellus, the egg and sperm nuclei undergo a series of changes resulting in intermingling of the chromosomes and the initiation of cleavage.

Acrosome reaction. The acrosome reaction involves the vesiculation of the plasma membrane of the sperm cell with the outer acrosomal membrane and presumably enables release of enzymes that are of importance in penetration through the investments of the ovum, which include the cellular cumulus oophorus and corona radiata layers and the acellular zona pellucida (Figs. 1 and 2). By the time the sperm cell has reached the zona pellucida, the vesiculated membranes are completely lost, leaving the inner acrosomal membrane exposed (Fig. 3). It is generally held that the proteolytic enzyme responsible for digestion through the zona pellucida is tightly bound to the inner acrosomal membrane. Several enzymes have been detected in the sperm acrosome; and these include hyaluronidase, which allows penetration through the cumulus oophorus cell mass, and corona-penetrating enzyme, which enables the sperm cell to reach the zona pellucida where the acrosomal proteinase, or acrosin, allows the sperm cell to force its way into the periviteline space.

Egg activation. Once inside the perivitelline space, sperm cells generally are believed to penetrate the vitellus quite rapidly, at least in the case of the mouse and hamster. The rabbit might be an exception, since on occasion freely swimming sperm cells have been observed within the perivitelline space for one-half hour before penetration of the vitellus took place. A sperm cell in the process of penetrating the vitellus is shown in Fig. 4. No enzymes have been associated with sperm penetration of the vitellus, and from electron-microscopic studies the impression has been obtained that microvilli from the vitelline surface engulf the fertilizing sperm cell and play an active role in the initial contact of the sex cells.

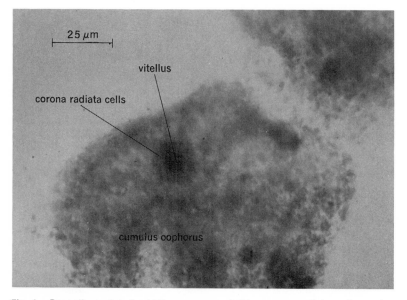

Fig. 1. Recently ovulated rabbit egg surrounded by corona radiata and cumulus oophorus cells; corona radiata cells adhere tightly to the zona pellucida, which is not visible.

Once contact is made between fertilizing sperm cell and the vitellus of the egg, rapid changes take place, collectively referred to as egg activation. The egg becomes activated to resume the meiotic process which is arrested in metaphase II in ovulated eggs of most mammalian species. Hence, the spindle rotates and the meiotic process culminates with extrusion of the second polar body, which leaves the haploid number of maternal chromosomes in the female sex cell vitellus along with the fertilizing spermatozoon. In addition to the meiotic changes, the cortical granules, at the periphery of the ooplasm, break down, thereby releasing their contents into the perivitelline space. This reaction has been associated with the block to polyspermy, which is a normal defense mechanism exhibited by the egg to prevent entry of additional sperm cells into the perivitelline space. In the rabbit, mole, and a few other species it is commonplace to find many sperm cells within the perivitelline space; and in these species the major block to polyspermy is at the level of the vitelline membrane.

Pronuclear formation and development. Following penetration of the vitellus, the sperm membranes rapidly change to release the nuclear material from the male parent into the ooplasm. The sperm nucleus then undergoes decondensation and at the same time the female chromosomes are becoming more closely associated. Both maternal and paternal chromosome groups, respectively, become enclosed by a membrane. These structures are properly termed "pronuclei." The male pronucleus is usually the larger of the two structures (Fig. 5). The pronuclei increase in size and migrate to the center of the egg during an interval of several hours. The two pronuclei normally come into close apposition and some fusion of the membranes takes place in the rabbit, although in the mouse internuclear communication of this sort has not been observed. Once in juxtaposition, the pronuclear membranes rapidly break down, releasing the chromosomes from the two parents (Fig. 6a and b).

Cleavage. The chromosome groups intermingle; and during an interval of approximately one-half hour from the pronuclear membrane breakdown to the beginning of cleavage, there is no discrete nuclear structure within the egg which is then nearing the completion of the fertilization process (Fig. 6c). The chromosomes align on the metaphase plate of the first mitotic division, and fertilization is followed by cleavage into the two-cell-stage embryo. The process of cleavage requires only about 8 min from the observation of initial flattening of the egg to what appears to be complete division into two blastomeres when viewed by light microscopy (Fig. 6c–g).

EXTRACORPOREAL FERTILIZATION

Beginning about 1878, scientists observed interactions between eggs and spermatozoa of the rabbit, guinea pig, mouse, and rat and attributed the resulting interaction to fertilization. This approach has, in general, been unacceptable since 1951, when a requirement for sperm to undergo capacitation in the female reproductive tract prior to fertilization was independently discovered by C. R. Austin and M. C. Chang. During the last quarter century, progress has been rapid and criteria for

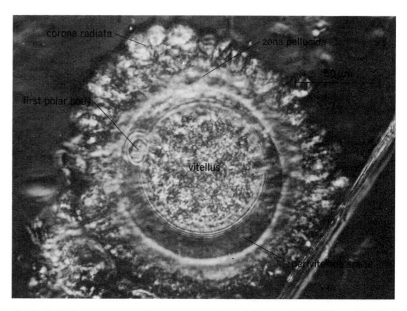

Fig. 2. Rabbit egg recovered from a mature preovulatory ovarian follicle and treated to remove cumulus oophorus and most of the corona radiata cells. The first polar body can be seen within the perivitelline space, indicating that the egg is mature and presumably ready to undergo fertilization. (*From B. G. Brackett, J. M. Mills, and G. G. Jeitles, In vitro fertilization of rabbit ova recovered from ovarian follicles, Fertil. Steril., 23:898, 1972*)

the documentation of fertilization in laboratory culture dishes have become more exacting.

Criteria for documentation. Soon after the discovery of sperm capacitation, French scientists, led by Charles Thibault, demonstrated the ability

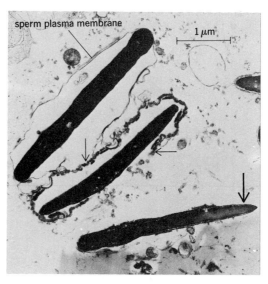

Fig. 3. Three rabbit sperm heads as seen by the electron microscope, showing consecutive steps in the acrosome reaction in the area of the corona radiata cells. The sperm in the upper left has an intact but swollen sperm plasma membrane. The sperm head in the middle is surrounded by the plasma membrane which is undergoing vesiculation with the outer acrosomal membrane (indicated by arrows). The lower sperm has already undergone the acrosome reaction and is presumably ready to penetrate the matrix of the zona pellucida. In this sperm the inner acrosomal membrane is exposed (large arrow). (*Courtesy of Y. K. Oh and B. G. Brackett*)

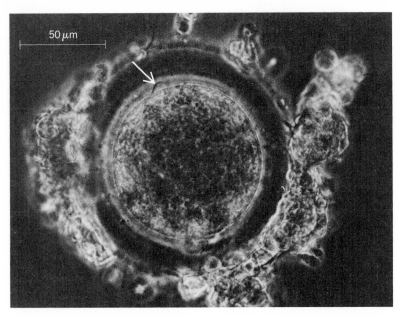

Fig. 4. Sperm penetration of the vitellus of a rabbit egg recovered from an ovarian follicle and exposed to capacitated sperm outside the animal 10 hr previously. The sperm head is in the vitellus and the tail (arrow) remains visible within the perivitelline space. *(From B. G. Brackett, J. M. Mills, and G. G. Jeitles, In vitro fertilization of rabbit ova recovered from ovarian follicles, Fertil. Steril., 23:898, 1972)*

of sperm recovered from the uterine environment of mated rabbits to fertilize ova recovered from oviducts of hormonally treated does under conditions in a test tube. The criteria used by these workers for the proof that fertilization occurred outside the animal consisted of histological observation of inseminated ova and demonstration of pronuclei and remnants of the sperm cell within the vitellus. The most convincing criterion of successful test-tube fertilization is the birth of young resulting from ova inseminated and cultured through early cleavage stages and then transplanted into foster mothers (Fig. 7).

Chang, in 1959, was the first to demonstrate the feasibility of such an experiment in a mammalian species, the rabbit. This criterion has been used in several additional experiments involving test-tube fertilization in the rabbit, mouse and, more recently, in the rat as well. In addition to successful development of test-tube-fertilized ova recovered following ovulation in these laboratory species, ova recovered from ovarian follicles of rabbits and mice have also undergone test-tube fertilization and subsequent development throughout gestation. When this approach is used for documentation of a claim for extracorporeal fertilization, care must be taken to allow cleavage to occur in the culture dish before the ovum transfer into the surrogate dam, in order to be sure that the fertilization resulting in young did not occur in the adult animal following the transfer. Also, young of both sexes should result, since there is the theoretical possibility that female offspring might be the result of parthenogenetic development. In experiments involving transfer before the end of the fertilizable life of either gamete, it is also important to use gametes which, following fertilization, will result in offspring genetically dissimilar to the recipient

animal in order to establish the origin of the gametes involved.

Ovum cleavage. The feasibility of embryo transfer has not been established for most mammalian species. An additional consideration for selecting criteria to support the accomplishment of extracorporeal fertilization is that not all ova that undergo fertilization and early development can be expected to have the potential for subsequent term development; and, even if they did, technical problems involved in surgical transfer of ova might be responsible for failures in attempts to observe development within the adult following test-tube fertilization. Ovum cleavage has been widely used to indicate that extracorporeal fertilization took place. However, simple cleavage alone is inadequate proof for the occurrence of fertilization since certain conditions induce degenerative fragmentation, and also parthenogenetic activation might result in ovum cleavage. Degenerative cleavage usually results in fragmentation with unequal-sized "blastomeres" and, furthermore, chromatin cannot be demonstrated in every "blastomere" following an appropriate staining procedure. Under ideal conditions ova should not undergo cleavage or fragmentation when incubated in the absence of sperm cells and when handled similarly to inseminated ova which do cleave following incubation.

Evidence of sperm involvement. Any claim for the accomplishment of extracorporeal fertilization should include some evidence that the sperm cells participated in the development observed. The production of male offspring resulting from transfer of test-tube-fertilized ova satisfies this requirement. Another way to show the involvement of the sperm cell would be to demonstrate the presence of the Y chromosome, which could be introduced into the ovum only by the sperm cell. A method has been described by which this criterion might be possible in human test-tube fertilization studies. Time-lapse microcinematography facilitates direct observation of sperm penetration and sequential development of the fertilization process. Extracorporeal fertilization has been documented in this way in the rabbit (Fig. 6) and, more recently, in the hamster as well. Sperm involvement can also be well documented by sequential observation of ova at increasing intervals following insemination. Motile spermatozoa within the perivitelline space and pronuclei at various stages of development can be observed. In addition to its larger size, the male pronucleus can be recognized by the proximity of the sperm midpiece or sperm tail remnants. This is best done by electron microscopy. The sperm midpiece has been observed by light microscopy in ova of the human, fowl, rat, and rabbit but is reported not to be distinctly visible in ova of the cow. In addition, the female pronucleus is reported to have an asymmetrical distribution of deoxyribonucleic acid (DNA) in several species, including the rabbit, cat, fowl, sheep, and cow. Near the end of the fertilization process, the pronuclei become very similar in many species and then are indistinguishable from pronuclei that result from parthenogenetic activation.

Ultrastructural evidence. Many of these morphological observations are easily made with phase-contrast or interference-contrast microscopy. Histological sectioning and staining of ova embedded in Epon provide a means of circumventing difficulties in evaluating progress of fertilization in live specimens. An advantage of this type of preparation is that it can also be sectioned for electron-microscopic examination. The cortical granules can be seen by electron microscopy in unfertilized ova, whereas their absence indicates that activation has taken place. This information, along with demonstration of sperm remnants within the vitellus, provides excellent ultrastructural evidence that the fertilization process is taking place. Ultrastructural details associated with fertilization have been described in the case of the hamster, mouse, and rabbit, and recently in the case of human ova that were inseminated in tissue culture dishes following recovery from ovarian follicles and preincubation to allow for completion of ovum maturation.

Conditions for fertilization. Much of the modern research on mammalian fertilization has involved efforts to define optimum conditions for extracorporeal gamete union. In the early experiments using capacitated sperm, fertilization rates were higher when media contained biological fluids such as follicular fluid, oviductal fluid, uterine fluid, and serum. Efforts have been made to duplicate conditions within the oviduct by using defined media. Gametes of several species can now undergo fertilization in simple, defined media. Although species variations have been noted regarding the ideal medium for test-tube fertilization, there are several features that appear to be desirable. These include the presence of crystalline bovine albumin, glucose, and pyruvate as energy substrates, and sufficient bicarbonate to maintain a pH of 7.8 at 38°C under a 5% carbon dioxide atmosphere. In addition, an oxygen tension of approximately 8%, which simulates that reported to occur in the oviduct, and high relative humidity surrounding the gamete-containing solutions are desirable conditions. Covering of the gamete-containing solution with paraffin oil or silicone oil has also been found to be desirable. More complete culture media containing additional ingredients are necessary for extracorporeal development through the blastocyst stage.

Efforts have been made to examine influences of calcium and pH on sperm penetration of mouse ova. Sperm motility was better and more eggs were penetrated by spermatozoa when calcium (0.02%) was present than when it was absent from the medium. Higher concentrations of calcium ions (0.05%) may be inhibitory to sperm penetration. The components of the buffered solution, that is, barbital acetate—HCl or citrate phosphate, seemed to affect capacitation of mouse sperm and the penetration of mouse ova to a greater degree than did the absolute pH value of the medium.

Use as an experimental tool. The development of media which enabled a consistently high proportion of gametes to undergo test-tube fertilization led to the development of experiments in which sperm or egg treatments or additives to the medium can be assessed in a controlled experiment (Fig. 8). Methods for test-tube fertilization are available for such use in the rabbit, mouse, hamster, guinea pig, cat, and rat. In the rabbit, ova for

test-tube fertilization can be obtained from three anatomical sites. These include the recovery of ovulated ova from the oviduct, recovery of them from the ovarian surface to which they cling by the surrounding cumulus oophorus mass when inaccessible to the fimbriated end of the oviduct, and recovery from the ovarian follicles just prior to their anticipated rupture. Using capacitated rabbit spermatozoa, recovered from the uterus of a mated doe, one can now expect with reasonable certainty to obtain test-tube fertilization of 80–100% of the most recently ovulated ova recovered from the ovarian surface, 60–70% of those recovered from oviducts, and 40–50% of those taken from preovulatory ovarian follicles.

The experimental design indicated by Fig. 8, in which gametes from the same sources are used under two sets of conditions and compared for proportions of ova fertilized in laboratory dishes, has been used extensively in our laboratory. In an early series of experiments the two gamete-containing dishes were identical and one dish was removed in each experiment at a successive interval following insemination. This allowed a comparison between light-microscopic evidence of fertilization during the process of fertilization with the proportion of ova that cleaved in the control dish, which was incubated for approximately 24 hr following extracorporeal insemination. From these experiments it was learned that penetration of the ovum took place by capacitated sperm before 3 hr after exposure to sperm; and the subsequent steps, including pronuclear formation and cleavage, occurred at time intervals similar to those following sperm penetration of rabbit ova in the animal body. Completion of each step in the sequence of events of the fertilization process was established when similar proportions of ova were found in each stage when compared with the proportion of control ova

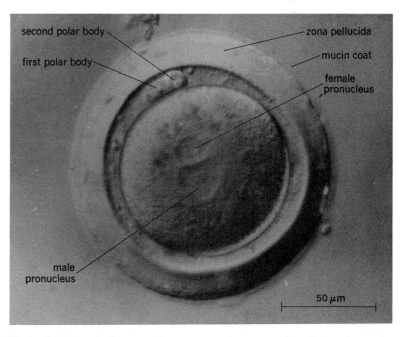

Fig. 5. Rabbit egg in the pronuclear stage; mucin coat was deposited on the egg by the oviduct. The first and second polar bodies can be seen within the perivitelline space of this rabbit ovum.

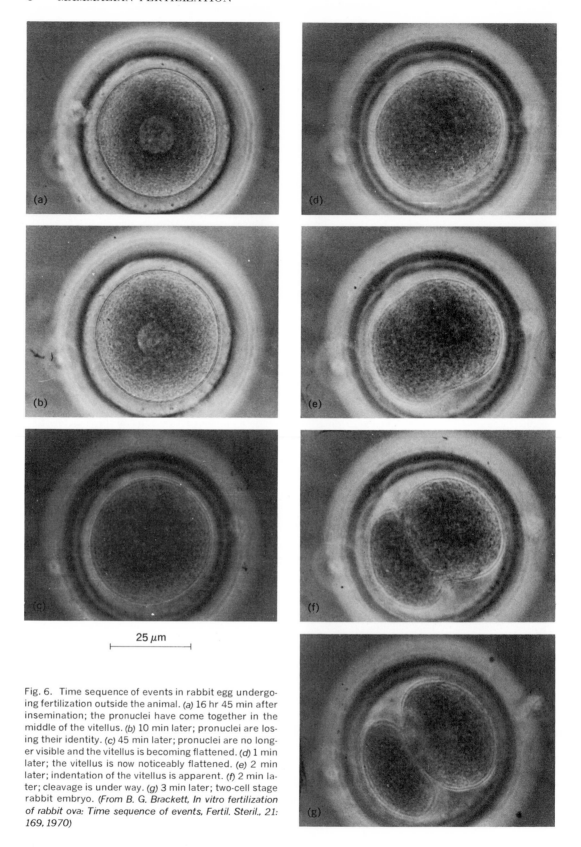

25 μm

Fig. 6. Time sequence of events in rabbit egg undergoing fertilization outside the animal. (a) 16 hr 45 min after insemination; the pronuclei have come together in the middle of the vitellus. (b) 10 min later; pronuclei are losing their identity. (c) 45 min later; pronuclei are no longer visible and the vitellus is becoming flattened. (d) 1 min later; the vitellus is now noticeably flattened. (e) 2 min later; indentation of the vitellus is apparent. (f) 2 min later; cleavage is under way. (g) 3 min later; two-cell stage rabbit embryo. (From B. G. Brackett, In vitro fertilization of rabbit ova: Time sequence of events, Fertil. Steril., 21: 169, 1970)

that cleaved following the prolonged incubation interval. Establishment of the apparent normality of the extracorporeal fertilization process provided encouragement for continued studies to assess various influences on the fertilization process.

Washing the gametes. Experiments in which rabbit ova and spermatozoa were washed prior to incubation together in a test tube revealed that washing of the capacitated sperm cells decreased the fertilization rate significantly while washing of the ovulated ova recovered from the oviducts of donor rabbits provided neither an enhancement nor a decrease in fertilization rate. From data of these experiments it was concluded that a soluble substance carried with the sperm cells from the female reproductive tract was beneficial to fertilization and that removal of this material by washing caused the observed decrease in fertilization rate; or, alternatively, interference with the oxygen and carbon dioxide tensions surrounding the sperm cells by the sperm washing procedure might account for the loss of fertilizing ability.

Enzyme inhibition. The rabbit fertilization process was found to be inhibited when soybean trypsin inhibitor (1.0 mg/ml) was added to the medium of the experimental dish. This inhibition of the trypsin-like sperm acrosomal proteinase provided support to the contention that the effect of this enzyme was to mediate passage of the sperm cell through the zona pellucida. Extracorporeal fertilization provides the means for examination of mechanisms for inhibition of discrete molecular events, and perhaps exploitation of this approach will be helpful in contraceptive development efforts.

Ultrastructural events. Extracorporeal fertilization has provided a means for making large numbers of penetrating sperm cells available for ultrastructural examination. With this approach it has been possible to describe the acrosome reaction in much detail for the hamster, a species in which extracorporeal insemination has led to excessive polyspermy. Experiments have been carried out in the rabbit and mouse involving the removal of the cellular investments surrounding the eggs prior to extracorporeal insemination. In these studies it has been observed that extracorporeal fertilization can take place following denudation of ova to the zona pellucida. In rabbit experiments, when the zona pellucida is removed by brief treatment with trypsin and the released vitelli are washed by passage through media and then incubated with spermatozoa, cleavage of the vitelli results. Since cleavage failed to take place when vitelli were incubated in the absence of sperm cells, the suggestion that fertilization occurs in this situation is strengthened. Interestingly, the cleavage of naked vitelli occurs following extracorporeal insemination with washed ejaculated sperm as well as with capacitated sperm recovered from uteri of mated does. This observation suggests the need for sperm capacitation might be equated with achievement by the sperm cell to penetrate through the cellular barriers and the zona pellucida of the ovum. Efforts are under way to discern the ultrastructural events that take place during this sort of experimental egg-sperm interaction.

Fertilizing capacity of sperm. Perhaps one of the most important uses to which extracorporeal fertilization has been employed is as an assay for the capacity of sperm to fertilize ova. By exposing recently ovulated rabbit ova to sperm cells recovered from uteri of mated does at increasing intervals following coitus, it was found that the fertilization rate increases with sperm recovered at increasing intervals up to 18 hr after mating. Additionally, rabbit spermatozoa have been seen to fertilize ova in test-tube conditions after as long as 30 hr had lapsed between the time of mating and the time of

Fig. 7. Three New Zealand White offspring that developed from test-tube-fertilized follicular ova after transfer to the Dutch Belted recipient. *(From B. G. Brackett, J. M. Mills, and G. G. Jeitles, In vitro fertilization of rabbit ova recovered from ovarian follicles, Fertil. Steril., 23:898, 1972)*

uterine sperm recovery.

In other experiments in which extracorporeal fertilization of rabbit ova was used to assay the fertilizing ability of sperm, rates of fertilization similar to those normally occurring in rabbits, or in the best extracorporeal fertilization conditions, were found to be possible following capacitation of sperm in does with no oviducts. A subsequent series of experiments revealed that capacitation could take place in the absence of ovaries or oviducts and optimal capacitation resulted when the ovariectomized and salpingectomized animal was treated with estrogen and a small amount of progestin in efforts to simulate the normal uterine environment. The hormonal treatments of capacitator does with no ovaries or oviducts afforded a uterine environment that enabled sperm to achieve the ability to fertilize 90% of the eggs. This level of fertilization compares favorably with that which normally occurs in the rabbit and with that observed following extracorporeal insemination of eggs by sperm recovered from intact capacitator does.

In addition to the use of extracorporeal fertilization as an assay for the ability of sperm that have been conditioned by the female reproductive tract to fertilize ova, this approach has also been employed in recent years as a means of assessing the fertilizing ability of sperm taken directly from males and treated in laboratory cultures in various ways. As mentioned above, test-tube capacitation of sperm has been achieved in several laboratory species, as evidenced by extracorporeal fertilization. In collaboration with G. Oliphant, it was found that capacitation of mouse sperm can be accelerated by the addition of NaCl to the medium. The mechanism involves a salt-mediated removal of seminal plasma components which normally coat the surface of sperm cells. The removal, or alteration, of these inhibitory factors prepares the sperm cells for the acrosome reaction and subsequent steps in the fertilization process. In our recent work it has also been demonstrated that rabbit sperm can undergo capacitation following similar treatments which presumably facilitate the dissociation of decapacitation factor or factors from the sperm surface. Basic information derived

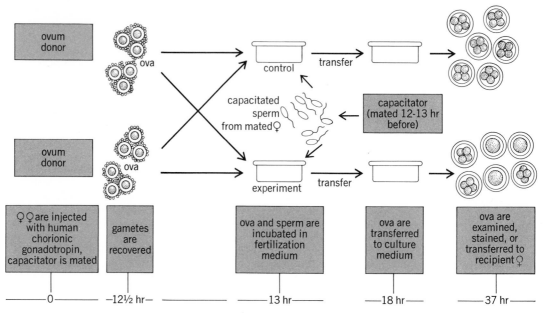

Fig. 8. Schematic diagram of a controlled laboratory fertilization experiment. (From B. G. Brackett, Effects of washing the gametes on fertilization in vitro, Fertil. Steril., 20:127, 1969)

from experiments such as these might have significant implications in studies of infertility and can be looked to as providing the basis for future clinical treatments.

Potential direct applications. Direct application of extracorporeal fertilization as a treatment of infertility caused by blocked oviducts can be predicted to receive future human clinical usage. At the present time the procedures for this approach to circumvent blocked oviducts (fallopian tubes) are not in a stage of development that could be applied on a widespread basis. More extensive animal experimentation is a desirable prerequisite for such efforts in humans, since many questions concerning risks involved, along with the anticipated incidence of success, must first come from animal experimentation.

The presently available data from animal experiments provide encouragement for continuation of these efforts but seem rather inadequate as a basis for immediate human clinical application. From the studies in rabbits and mice, only slightly more than 10% probability can presently be predicted for the success of obtaining an egg from an ovarian follicle, carrying out extracorporeal fertilization, and obtaining a live offspring from that egg after surgical transfer of the resulting embryo into the female reproductive tract of a surrogate dam. Under the best present conditions for extracorporeal fertilization and culture of rabbit ova to the four-cell stage, only 25 of 137 embryos that were transferred to recipient does developed into live offspring. These ova were obtained from ovarian follicles and from the ovarian surface after ovulation, and the original source of the eggs was found to have no bearing on the proportion of offspring developing from four-cell-stage embryos. Although higher proportions of embryos transferred directly from a donor rabbit into a recipient can develop, it is interesting that when rabbit eggs are recovered

after the initial stages of fertilization have taken place in the animal, then are cultured under test-tube conditions prior to transfer into recipients at the four-cell stage, the developmental potential for such embryos was similar to that observed for test-tube fertilized eggs. This observation points to the importance of the laboratory culture conditions and suggests the need for supplementation of the simple medium with additional factors in order to more closely simulate the environment provided by the female reproductive tract to the early embryo. Such modifications can be expected to greatly improve the presently pessimistic picture regarding feasibility of clinical application of this approach. Many more offspring must be obtained and examined before any generalization regarding normality can be made since only a few reports involving rats, mice, and rabbits are available.

Perhaps the most important potential direct applications of extracorporeal fertilization will be in the realm of veterinary medicine. A repeatable procedure for extracorporeal fertilization with gametes of large domestic species is not available at the present time. Nevertheless, the future applications of extracorporeal fertilization should be expected to receive greatest impetus in efforts to improve livestock production, since such efforts are exempt from the ethical and moral considerations involved in treatment of human patients. A consistent procedure by which cow eggs could be fertilized outside of the animal body would be of value in combining gametes from animals with desirable genetic traits. Resulting embryos could be transferred into female reproductive tracts of less valuable, but not less fertile, cows for development into desirable calves. Exploitation of the desirable genetic traits from the male through artificial insemination has already proved to have a profound impact, especially in the dairy industry. At least theoretically, exploitation of the female germ cells for extending desirable, maternally transmissible traits offers a similar possibility for potential development of the bovine species. Embryo transfers are presently being done on a limited scale in cattle to accomplish these ends. However, much additional research must be done before exploitation of the female genetic contributions can be put into widespread use. Among the most urgent needs are the development of easier ways to obtain eggs and replace embryos in the female reproductive tract, better methods for extracorporeal fertilization, and improved methods for embryo storage.

An additional direct, practical application of extracorporeal fertilization would be for the facilitation of early testing of the ability of bull sperm to penetrate eggs after frozen storage of the sperm. This application might allow early elimination from artificial insemination programs of bulls that yield sperm that cannot be successfully stored. Also along these lines, the use of extracorporeal fertilization for assessing sperm in questionable states of fertility for their ability to fertilize ova would be desirable. Such an application might be useful in development of a male contraceptive treatment designed to render sperm cells incompetent. By testing the ability of sperm from treated men to fertilize eggs recovered from ovarian tissue removed for surgical indications, it might be possible to avoid direct involvement of women in initial clinical studies.

Clinical application of procedures for extracorporeal fertilization can be predicted in human and veterinary medicine. Basic research in the important area of mammalian fertilization should receive even greater impetus with the approaching development of directly applicable procedures. Rapid technical improvements are anticipated in studies of extracorporeal fertilization, and these advances in knowledge of the mammalian fertilization process should enable industrious individuals to apply the resulting information in ways to better the life of humankind.   [BENJAMIN G. BRACKETT]

Comets

William Deutschman's interest in cometary astronomy grew out of his work in coordinating the many information sources for Comet Kohoutek and preparing data to be used by the Skylab astronauts in their observations of the comet. At the Smithsonian Astrophysical Observatory, he worked on Project Celescope, which mapped the sky in the ultraviolet from the orbiting astronomical observatory and cataloged the observations. In addition, he has studied short-lived Earth events with the Earth resources satellite. He is assistant professor of astronomy at Dickinson College, Carlisle, PA.

Lukos Kohoutek's discovery of the famous comet that bears his name on March 7, 1973, appeared to be a routine discovery of a comet similar to the one he had found earlier in the year—but it was not. Comet Kohoutek (Fig. 1) would be hailed as the "comet of the century" and later, after inflated press coverage, as the "flop of the century." It was neither. But it did provide a new stimulus to the study of comets; as much new information about the structure of comets was obtained from Comet Kohoutek and Comet Bradfield, which reached perihelion (closest approach to the Sun) 2 months after Comet Kohoutek, as had been obtained in the previous 5 and possibly 10 years. These advances were possible because new and more sensitive equipment—image intensifiers, television equipment, satellites, and the Skylab space station—were available to study the comets. In addition, Kohoutek's discovery 9 months in advance of perihelion allowed astronomers to plan experiments and schedule the necessary telescope time for observations.

But why all the interest in studying comets? Scientists usually study comets for one of three reasons: to understand what a comet is; to obtain information about the formation of the solar system; or to study the solar wind.

Comets are some of the most spectacular objects in the solar system. They are among the oldest astronomical objects recorded. Ancient civilizations believed they were signs from the gods; thus there is a long history of bright-comet sightings. Bright comets still evoke widespread interest when they appear. Astronomers reflect this interest by trying to learn what comets are and how they behave.

The study of comets as a source of information about the formation of the solar system arises from the belief that comets consist of the same primordial materials that originally made up the solar system. All of the material that scientists are able to study firsthand—material on the Earth, the Sun, meteorites, and even the other planets—has gone through many cycles of heating and cooling or has undergone other changes; it is no longer the original material. But comets, scientists believe, condensed from the original solar nebulae and have been frozen since then. The arguments for this theory will be discussed at length later.

Finally, solar-system astronomers study cometary gas tails to learn more about the interplanetary plasma and the solar wind. The solar wind is a hot ionized plasma that flows outward from the Sun. It has been measured in limited regions in space by experiments aboard spacecraft orbiting in the ecliptic plane. There are no spacecraft available now that can map and study the regions of space outside the ecliptic plane. Comets, therefore, may be the only means of obtaining information about these regions. The goal is to use the tails of comets as giant windsocks to map the direction of the solar wind—and other conditions

Table 1. Inferred diameters for some comets

Comet	Diameter, km	Observer
Tago-Sato-Kasaka	2.2	A. Delsemme and T. Rudd
Bennett	3.7	A. Delsemme and T. Rudd
Halley	1.5–4	Z. Sekanina, A. Orlov

such as the local velocity field—more comprehensively than is now possible.

This article will discuss what comets are and how they originated, and examine some of the many unanswered questions about them. Comets can be discussed with either a historical approach or an observational approach. This article will use the latter and review the known observational facts about each of the three parts of a comet: the nucleus, the coma, and the tail (Fig. 2). It will then consider a model that fits this data.

THE NUCLEUS

A cometary nucleus has never been directly observed because the surrounding coma shields it from view. The properties of the nucleus, therefore, must be inferred from other observations. Astronomers know the nucleus is very small, somewhere between one and a few tens of kilometers in diameter. Table 1 lists diameters calculated for Halley's Comet and two other recent comets. These diameters were measured by observing the brightness of the comet far from the Sun, where no appreciable coma has formed. Then, knowing the brightness of sunlight at the comet's position and assuming a reflectivity for the nucleus, astronomers can calculate the area of the comet necessary to reflect enough of the Sun's light to equal the observed brightness.

The mass of a comet nucleus is between 10^{15}

Fig. 1. Comet Kohoutek, photographed by Hawaii Baker-Nun Station, Smithsonian Astrophysical Observatory.

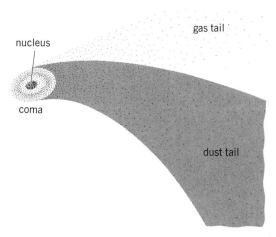

Fig. 2. A schematic diagram that illustrates the structural components of a comet.

and 10^{21} g, or about one-millionth the mass of the Earth. The structure and composition of the nucleus have not been measured and must be inferred from the material observed in the coma. The nucleus is generally believed to be composed of water and other volatile hydrocarbons. Water and methylcyanide are two of these compounds that have been identified in recent comets. The nucleus is believed to rotate and create the helical patterns observed in the tails of some comets. Changes in the orbit of the comet due to nongravitational forces have been ascribed to jets of water molecules emitted from a rotating nucleus.

THE COMA

The coma—or diffuse head—of the comet shown in Fig. 3 has been studied more than any other part of the comet. Its size, shape, spectrum, and brightness have been well measured. The spectrum (the intensity of the light emitted at various wavelengths) indicates that there are two physical components to the coma. One is a dust component consisting of micrometer- and submicrometer-sized particles ($1\ \mu = 10^{-6}$ m) similar to the dust particles found in interstellar space. These particles scatter the solar radiation and produce a slightly reddened solar-continuum radiation. Also present is a gas component consisting of atoms, molecules, and free radicals, each of which emit a unique set of wavelengths of light and can therefore be detected in the spectrum of the coma.

The relative amounts of dust and gas in the coma vary from comet to comet. In general, new comets that have experienced few perihelion passages are relatively dusty. Old comets have little dust in their comas. The molecules, atoms, and radicals detected in comets comprise H, C, C_2, C_3, OH, C^{12}, C^{13}, O, CH, NH, NH_2, CN, Na, Si, Ca, Cr, Fe, Mn, HCN, CH_3CN, H_2O, and H_2O^+. Most of the molecules are combinations of hydrogen, oxygen, carbon, and nitrogen. This composition provides an important condition on the model of the comet nucleus proposed later.

Coma size. The visible coma in Fig. 3 is about 10,000 km in diameter, or about the size of the Earth. The number of molecules in each cubic

centimeter is greatest near the nucleus—about 10^{14} per cubic centimeter or one ten-thousandth the density of the Earth's atmosphere—and decreases inversely with the square of the distance from the nucleus. The molecules and dust that form the coma are eventually blown away from the coma and form the tail. A hydrogen coma was discovered in 1969 by the orbiting astronomical observatory and, later that year, by one of the orbiting geophysical observatories. The size of this coma was totally unexpected, extending millions of kilometers into space. (In the case of Comet Kohoutek, the hydrogen coma was larger than the visible portion of the Sun.) The light radiated by the atomic hydrogen is in the far-ultraviolet at a wavelength of 1216 A (10 A=1 nm). Light of this wavelength is totally absorbed by the Earth's atmosphere, hence rockets or spacecraft are necessary to observe this part of a comet. Figure 4 shows two rocket photographs of Comet Kohoutek, both taken at the same scale. Figure 4a was taken with film that was sensitive to ordinary visible light; the picture is similar to what one could see from the ground. Figure 4b was taken with film sensitive to the light radiated by the hydrogen atoms. These two pictures show the huge size of the hydrogen coma relative to the visible coma.

Radio spectrum. Further recent discoveries resulted from studies of the radio spectrum of the comet. Before Comet Kohoutek, observers had looked unsuccessfully for radio emission in comets. As Comet Kohoutek brightened on its approach toward the Sun, radio telescopes began to detect it. Hydrogen cyanide, methylcyanide, and the CH radical were all detected. The methylcyanide was particularly exciting because it was one of the molecules that had been discovered in interstellar clouds deep in space and was the first direct

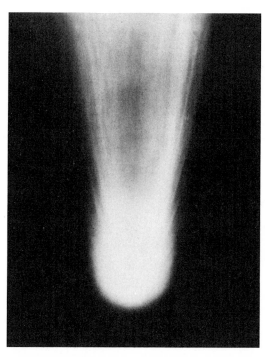

Fig. 3. An enlarged photograph of Halley's Comet showing the coma and the beginning of the tail.

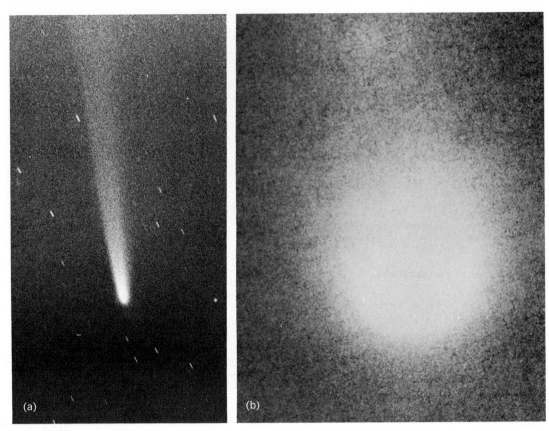

(a)

(b)

Fig. 4. Comet Kohoutek, photographed (a) in visible light by Johns Hopkins University in an Aerobee rocket flight on Jan. 4, 1974; and (b) in the far-ultraviolet light of atomic hydrogen by the Naval Research Laboratory in an Aerobee rocket flight on Jan. 7, 1974. The ultraviolet image, to the same angular scale as the visible light image, reveals that the hydrogen halo of Comet Kohoutek had a diameter of more than 5,000,000 km, nearly four times the diameter of the Sun.

Fig. 5. Comet Mrkos, with dust tail extending away from the coma in a gentle curve to the right and the gas tail pointing directly away from the Sun.

evidence that comets had complex organic molecules frozen in the nucleus. Several groups tried to find water in the spectrum but were unsuccessful. They were successful, however, with Comet Bradfield. The detection of these molecules, particularly the water molecule, provided vital confirmation for the icy conglomerate model of comets that will be described later.

Infrared emission. The infrared region of the spectrum has also been used recently to study the dust in the coma. In Comet Kohoutek, E. Ney and his collaborators at Minnesota were able to detect micrometer-sized dust particles in the coma and also to show that there were silicate grains by detecting the emission feature at 10 μ caused by these grains. This was the first direct indication of the composition of the dust particles in the coma. These new measurements mean that astronomers can now study comets in a range of wavelengths not available 5 years ago.

COMETARY TAILS

The tail of a comet is physically divided into two parts: a dust tail and a gas tail (Fig. 5).

Dust tail. The dust tail is composed of the dust particles that have been blown away from the coma by the Sun's radiation pressure. The dust extends from the coma in a long featureless curve that always points away from the Sun. Hence the tail follows the comet when it is approaching the Sun and precedes the comet as it recedes from the Sun. It may be between 2,000,000 and 10,000,000 km long and is extremely tenuous, having a density between 1 and 100 particles per cubic centimeter. The particles scatter the Sun's light, thus the dust tail is yellow-reddish in color. The dynamics of the tail are well understood and can be predicted by a theory developed by two MIT scientists, M. C. Finson and R. F. Probstein. The particles are acted on by the Sun's radiation, which pushes them away from it, and by the Sun's gravitational force, which pulls them inward. The resultant force depends on the size of the particles. Small particles have a relatively large ratio of surface area to mass and have large forces pushing them away from the Sun; larger particles have smaller net forces acting on them. Finson and Probstein showed that the shape and motion of the tail can be predicted by calculating the trajectory of particles emitted from the coma and acted on by the resultant force.

Antitail. A different aspect of the dust tail is occasionally observed in comets: an antitail that points toward the Sun. It was observed in Comet Arend-Roland in 1957 (Fig. 6) but was not observed again until Comet Kohoutek. Z. Sekanina predicted from the Finson and Probstein theory that an antitail would be visible for Comet Kohoutek in early January 1974, just after perihelion. The prediction was correct; the Skylab astronauts were the first to observe the antitail on December 30,

1974 (Fig. 7). In early January the antitail was visible to Earth-based observers as a very small spike.

The antitail consists of relatively large particles from 0.1 to 1 mm in size, released from the nucleus 2 to 3 months before perihelion. Their large size causes them to lag behind the smaller particles in the tail and, because of geometric projection, they appear to point toward the Sun. Sekanina's studies of the antitail of Comet Kohoutek have shown that the tail begins to form 50 to 100 days before perihelion.

Gas tail. The gas tail of a comet is created when the molecules in the coma are ionized and then blown away by the solar wind. Because the molecules are much lighter than the dust particles and the solar wind is much stronger than radiation pressure, the particles are blown away from the comet in nearly straight lines, in contrast to the curved path of a dust tail. The constituents of the gas tail are CO^+, CO_2^+, $N_2^+CH^+$, OH^+, and CN. The primary radiation is from the CO^+ bands, which cause the tail to have a bluish color. The gas tail has considerable structure and can change shape in as little as 2 hr. Figure 8, for example, shows photos of Comet Mrkos taken at intervals of 2 days; there is a pronounced change in the gas tail between the pictures.

Comet Kohoutek had features that appeared to move away from the Sun with velocities of 450 km/sec. It has not been determined whether these features are real mass motions of the gas moving at 450 km/sec or a shock wave moving outward with this velocity that causes the gas to radiate as the wave moves through it. Future comets should provide answers to these questions. When the nature of the general shape, direction, and changes of the tail are more fully understood, astronomers will be able to study the interaction between a comet and the solar plasma and eventually to study the solar plasma with comet tails.

COMET MODELS

All of these observed facts about comets can be used to create a physical model which, in turn, can be used to explain and to predict the behavior of comets in general.

Comets were originally thought to be atmospheric phenomena by the ancient cultures. Aristotle, for instance, said that they were meteorologic phenomena associated with storms and bad weather. It was not until 1577 that the atmospheric theory was abandoned, when the astronomer Tycho Brahe accurately measured the apparent position of a comet from several locations in Europe and showed that its distance was at least three times the distance from the Earth to the Moon. Several other theories — including one that comets were swarms of small meteoric particles all traveling in the same orbit — were proposed but later dismissed because they could not explain all of the observational data.

Dirty snowball model. In 1950 F. Whipple proposed a new theory for comets: that they are similar to a large dirty snowball. This model was proposed to explain nongravitational forces that act on the orbit of the comet and to explain the source of the material that forms the coma and the tail. The currently accepted model is an extension of Whipple's original model.

Fig. 6. Photograph of Comet Arend-Roland by Alan McClure of Hollywood, CA, showing the antitail.

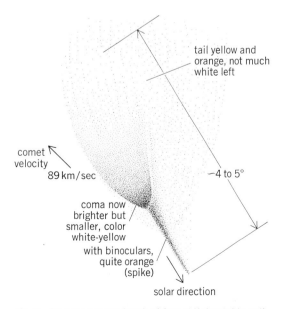

tail yellow and orange, not much white left

−4 to 5°

comet velocity
89 km/sec

coma now brighter but smaller, color white-yellow

with binoculars, quite orange (spike)

solar direction

Fig. 7. An astronaut's sketch of Comet Kohoutek's antitail as observed during the *Skylab 2* mission.

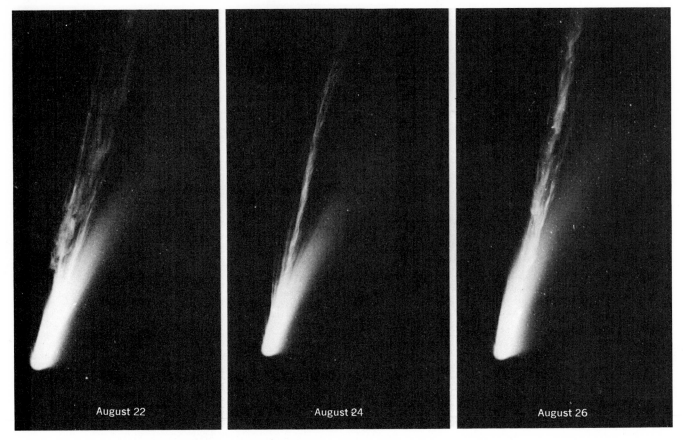

August 22   August 24   August 26

Fig. 8.   Sequence of photos of Comet Mrkos showing changes in gas tail that can take place within 2 days.

The nucleus of a comet is composed primarily of water ice and other organic compounds in a clathrate hydrate structure. (In a clathrate hydrate, one molecule of a gas is trapped between six water molecules in the ice.) Also included in the nucleus are the dust grains and smaller particles that form the dust coma, but there are no large solid chunks of rock or iron. The water ice controls the vaporization properties of the entire nucleus and explains why most comets start showing activity about 3 AU (an astronomical unit is equal to the mean distance between the Sun and the Earth, or 15,000,000 km) from the Sun. At this distance the Sun's radiation warms the comet enough to start vaporizing the water ice. These molecules then evaporate to form the hydrogen coma and release the dust and other molecules to form the visible coma and tail. Initially these molecules leave the nucleus with velocities near 1 km/sec, which is sufficient to remove the dust particles from the surface of the comet. As the comet becomes older, some of the larger particles stick to it, forming a mottled surface with patches of dust. As the patches grow, they shield the surface from the Sun's heat and lower the production of gas and dust. The relative amount of gas in the coma and tail then increases because the gas can escape through the dust layer but the dust cannot. Hence young comets have lots of dust in the coma and tail; older comets with a surface layer of dust have little.

Loss of mass. Studies of the coma and the tail indicate that the comet must lose between one-hundredth and one-thousandth of its mass at each perihelion passage. This loss implies that the short-period comets could not last more than 100,000 years and even a long-period comet could last only 80,000,000 years. Since the solar system is about 4,800,000,000 years old, all comets would have evaporated if there were no way to store them or to continuously make them.

Oort's Cloud. This problem was addressed by a Dutch astronomer, Jan Oort, when he discovered that a large fraction of the comets with long periods have semimajor axes between 25,000 and 75,000 AU. This indicated to Oort that there is a cloud of comets at distances of 50,000 to 150,000 AU from the Sun. He deduced that there are about 10^{11} comets in this region, which is now generally called Oort's Cloud. The comets in the cloud never come near enough to the Sun to melt and thus they do not lose any material. They would continue to travel in these orbital paths if it were not for the weak gravitational forces from nearby stars. All of the stars are slowly moving relative to each other, and occasionally a star will provide just the right pull on one of the comets in Oort's Cloud to change its orbit so that it passes near the Sun. As the comet approaches the Sun, its orbit is determined by the gravitational perturbations of the planets and by the jets of evaporating gases that escape the icy nucleus. The forces further modify the orbit and cause some comets to be captured by the Sun. These are the comets seen at regular intervals and which will eventually die in one of two ways.

Table 2. Relative abundance of types of material in the bodies of the solar system

Body	Gaseous	Icy	Earthy
Inner planets	—	—	1
Jupiter	0.9	0.1	—
Saturn	0.7	0.3	—
Uranus, Neptune, Comets	—	0.85	0.15

Death of comets. First, all of the material can finally evaporate from the nucleus and the comet will cease to exist. The remaining dust and small debris become visible when the Earth passes through the comet's orbit as the material melts in the atmosphere, forming a meteor shower. A number of these periodic showers are known, some of which are associated with current comets, including the Leonids (Comet 1886I), the Perseids (1962 III), and the Geminids (unknown).

The second way a comet can die is by forming a thick layer of dust on its surface. As a comet becomes smaller, it has less gas to vaporize and does not blow all the dust away from the surface. Thus a dusty layer slowly builds up on the surface. The dust is a good insulator and keeps the covered icy areas from warming up and vaporizing. Sekanina has studied a number of the Apollo asteroids' orbits and found that 5 of the 14 asteroids with Earth-crossing orbits produced streams of faint meteors detectable by radar. He postulates that the asteroids are nuclei of old comets that have thick dust layers and can no longer produce any gas, and that the meteors are debris from the comet traveling in the comet's orbit.

ORIGIN OF COMETS

To understand how comets were formed, one must examine how the solar system formed. Astronomers assume that the solar system condensed from a diffuse cloud of gas and dust similar to the interstellar clouds in other regions of this galaxy. The original cloud may have been 2 or 3 light-years in diameter. As it collapsed, the central region became warmer and eventually formed the Sun. The outer regions can be loosely grouped into three zones: the region of the inner planets—Mercury, Venus, Earth, and Mars; the region of Jupiter and Saturn; and the outer region of the solar system. These regions are progressively cooler, and different compounds condensed in each to form the planets. The differences are evident in the data in Table 2, compiled by Whipple. The table groups materials into three categories: gaseous, icy, and earthy. The earthy materials are composed of silicon, magnesium, and iron combined with oxygen. These are the rocklike minerals found in the Earth. They have a melting point of about 2000 K. Icy materials are compounds of carbon, nitrogen, oxygen, and hydrogen, such as methane, ammonia, or water with melting points near 0°C (273 K). Gaseous materials are primarily hydrogen and helium. They evaporate near absolute zero and are found in the liquid state only under conditions of high pressure or low temperature. The table shows that the terrestrial planets are composed of earthy materials; Jupiter and Saturn are composed of gaseous compounds; and Uranus, Neptune, and the comets are composed of icy compounds.

Formation and distribution. The data and other theoretical calculations show that comets are formed in the region outside of Saturn's orbit. Because Saturn is a fairly large planet, it swept up the comets that formed near it. This is why Saturn has a larger icy fraction than Jupiter. Uranus and Neptune are probably composed of the material from many small comets that collected into the two large planets. As the planets grew larger, they started to affect the orbits of the remaining comets. Some were changed so that they collided with the Sun, some collided with the outer planets, adding to their mass, and some formed Oort's Cloud of comets to be kept "in cold storage" until they were slowly sent back to become "new" comets.

Belt beyond Pluto. A number of comets must also have formed outside of the orbit of Pluto—in fact, beyond Pluto there may be a comet belt similar to the asteroid belt between Earth and Mars. However, because the comets there are too faint to be observed from Earth, their existence must be inferred by other techniques. B. Marsden and Whipple used Halley's Comet to study this region because at aphelion (the greatest distance away from the Sun) the comet's orbit would be perturbed by a cloud of comets in this region. They were able to show that if there are comets there, all of them must have a total mass less than that of the Earth. Therefore, any comet belt in the region beyond Pluto still remains unproved.

FUTURE STUDY

Further tests of the theory of the origin of comets will have to await more information about the comets themselves. Future bright comets, which occur about once every 10 years, should provide as much new information as Comet Kohoutek has, because by then new techniques and even more sensitive instruments will be available. However, a visit to a comet will be necessary to understand the structure of comets and to solve the problem of the origin of comets. Visits are already being planned and should occur within the next 10 to 15 years. First will be a "fly-by" space probe that will pass near a comet and study it briefly. Next will be a probe that will fly up to a comet and then accelerate to stay next to it for a considerable period of time. Finally, a remote station will be placed on a comet and will study its surface. Until these probes are ready, scientists will continue to rely on data acquired by conventional means to learn more about these objects that have fascinated man since the beginning of time.

[WILLIAM DEUTSCHMAN]

Earthquake Prediction

Christopher H. Scholz received his Ph.D. in geology from the Massachusetts Institute of Technology in 1967. He is an associate professor at Columbia University and on the scientific staff of the university's Lamont-Doherty Geological Observatory, where he is currently working on various aspects of the earthquake mechanism and earthquake prediction.

Among storms, droughts, and other natural hazards, earthquakes are the most feared and least comprehensible. Perhaps because of this, earthquakes are deeply interwoven in the ritual beliefs of almost all ancient peoples. The ancient Chinese, for example, believed in an underground fish which shook the earth. The early Indonesians believed that their god occasionally shook the earth to remind the people of his power.

Thousands of earthquakes occur every day, and have occurred for billions of years. A great earthquake strikes somewhere in the world only once every 2 or 3 years. However, human civilization has become more susceptible to earthquake damage as it has developed — as people have grouped together in cities for protection and for convenience. When a great earthquake occurs in a highly populated region, tremendous destruction can happen within a few seconds. In the Shensi province of China in 1556, 800,000 people were killed in a single earthquake. In 1755, Lisbon, one of the principal cities of that day, was utterly destroyed, with high loss of life.

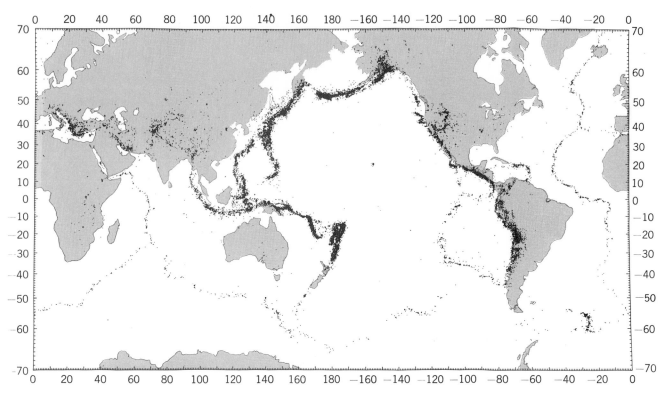

Fig. 1. Seismicity of the Earth from 1961 to 1967; depths to 700 km. The earthquake belts mark the plate boundaries. The number scales indicate latitude and longitude. *(From M. Barazangi and J. Dorman, World seis-* *micity maps compiled from ESSA, Coast and Geodetic Survey, Epicenter Data, 1961–1967, Bull. Seis. Soc. Amer., 59:369–380, 1969)*

In the 20th century, such cities as Tokyo and San Francisco have been leveled by earthquakes. In these modern cases much of the damage was not from the earthquake itself, but from fire started by the damage to gas and electrical lines and from the loss of fire-fighting capability which left the cities helpless to control the conflagration.

Increasingly, cities rest upon a delicate framework of continuous power and communication delivery—a dependency which has led to a greater hazard of disaster resulting from earthquakes. Today, no city in an earthquake-prone part of the world will be safe from such disasters until the mechanisms of earthquakes are fully understood

and until future earthquakes can be predicted with some certainty. Up to about 10 years ago, earthquake prediction was the province of soothsayers. More recently, it has been a reputable field of scientific study, as a result of enhanced knowledge of what causes earthquakes.

CAUSE OF EARTHQUAKES

Earthquakes are not distributed randomly over the globe but tend to occur in narrow, continuous belts of activity, as illustrated by a map showing the location of earthquakes between 1961 and 1967 (Fig. 1). The earthquake belts link up so that they encircle large seismically quiet regions, which are known as lithosphere plates. The plates move continuously with respect to one another at rates on the order of centimeters per year, and it is the motion of the plates which results in most geological activity, including earthquakes.

Plate motion occurs because the outer cold, hard skin of the Earth, the lithosphere, overlies a hotter, soft layer known as the asthenosphere. Heat from decay of radioactive minerals in the Earth's interior apparently sets the asthenosphere in thermal convection. This convection has broken the lithosphere into plates which move about in response to the convective motion (Fig. 2). The plates move apart at oceanic ridges. Magma wells up in the void created by the motion and solidifies to form new sea floor. This process, in which new sea floor is continuously created at oceanic ridges, is called sea floor spreading.

Since new lithosphere is continuously being

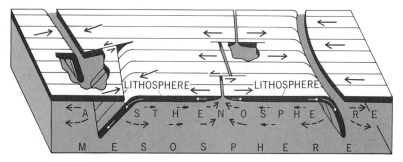

Fig. 2.   Movement of the lithosphere over the more fluid asthenosphere. In the center, the lithosphere spreads away from the oceanic ridges. At the edges of the diagram, it descends again into the asthenosphere at the trenches. *(From B. Isacks, Oliver, and L. R. Sykes, Seismology and the new global tectonics, J. Geophys. Res., 73: 5855–5899, 1968)*

N

W   +   E

0.5 mi

S

Fig. 3. Vertical view of the San Andreas Fault in central California. Note that the streams in the eastern side are offset southward. *(From C. R. Allen, The San Andreas Fault,* *Eng. Sci. Mon., California Institute of Technology, pp. 1–5, May 1957)*

created at the oceanic ridges by the process, a like amount of lithosphere must be destroyed somewhere. This occurs at the oceanic trenches, where plates converge and the oceanic lithosphere is thrust back down into the asthenosphere and is melted. Some of the melted material is thought to supply the magma for the volcanic arcs which occur behind the trenches.

Where two continents collide, however, the greater bouyancy of the less dense continental material prevents the lithosphere from being underthrust, and the lithosphere buckles under the force of the collision, forming great mountain ranges such as the Alps and Himalayas. Where the relative motion of the plates is parallel to their common boundary, slip occurs along the great faults which form the boundary, such as the San Andreas Fault in California.

The motion of the plates, according to the theory of plate tectonics, resembles the movement of ice floes in arctic waters. Where floes diverge, leads form (cracks open) and water wells up, freezing to the floes and producing new floe ice. The formation of pressure ridges where floes converge is analogous to the development of mountain ranges where plates converge.

Stick-slip friction and elastic rebound. As the plates move past one another, the motion at their boundaries does not occur by continuous slippage but in a series of rapid jerks. Each jerk is an earthquake. The jerky motion happens because — under the pressure and temperature conditions of the shallow part of the Earth's lithosphere — rock exhibits a property known as stick-slip, in which frictional sliding occurs in a series of jerky movements, interspersed with periods of no motion. In the geologic time frame, then, the lithospheric plates chatter at their boundaries. The time between chatters at any one place may be hundreds of years.

The period between major earthquakes is thus a period in which strain slowly builds up near the plate boundary in response to the continuous movement of the plates. The strain is ultimately released by an earthquake when the frictional strength of the plate boundary is exceeded. This pattern of strain buildup and release was discovered by H. F. Reid in his study of the 1906 San

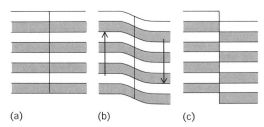

(a)   (b)   (c)

Fig. 4.   Schematic representation of the elastic rebound theory. (a) Unstrained rocks (b) are distorted by relative movement between the two plates, causing strains within the fault zone that finally become so great that (c) the rocks break and rebound to a new unstrained position. (*From C. R. Allen, The San Andreas Fault, Eng. Sci. Mon., California Institute of Technology, pp. 1–5, May 1957*)

Francisco earthquake. During that earthquake, a 250-mi-long (400 km) portion of the San Andreas Fault, from Cape Mendicino to the town of Gilroy south of San Francisco, slipped an average of 12 ft (3.7 m). When the area was resurveyed, it was found that the west side of the fault had moved northward with respect to the east side, but that evidence of the motion disappeared at distances of 20 mi (32 km) or more east or west of the fault (Fig. 3). Reid noticed, however, that measurements made about 40 years prior to the 1906 quake had shown that points far to the west of the fault were moving northward at a slow rate. From these clues he deduced his theory of elastic rebound in which unstrained rocks are distorted by the slow move-

ment of plates until slippage in an earthquake occurs, returning the rocks to an unstrained state (Fig. 4).

Features of earthquakes. Earthquakes vary enormously in size, ranging from tremors in which slippage of a few tenths of an inch occurs on a few feet of fault, to great events which involve a rupture many hundreds of miles long with tens of feet of slip. Accelerations as high as 1 g (the acceleration of gravity) can occur during the earthquake motion. The velocity at which the two sides of the fault move during an earthquake is only 1 to 10 mph (0.45 to 4.5 m/sec), but the rupture front spreads along the fault at a velocity of nearly 5000 mph (2235 m/sec).

Seismic waves. The earthquake's primary damage results from seismic waves—sound waves which travel through the earth, excited by the rapid movement of the quake. The energy radiated as seismic waves during a large earthquake can be as great as a trillion calories, and the power emitted during the few hundred seconds of movement can be as great as a billion megawatts.

Earthquake magnitude. The size of an earthquake is given by its magnitude on a scale based on the amount of seismic waves generated. Magnitude 2.0 is about the smallest tremor that can be felt. Most destructive earthquakes are greater than magnitude 6; the largest shock known measured 8.9. The scale is logarithmic; therefore a magnitude 7 shock is about 30 times one of magnitude 6, and 30×30, or 900, times more energetic than magnitude 5. Because of this rapid increase in size with magnitude, it is only the largest events

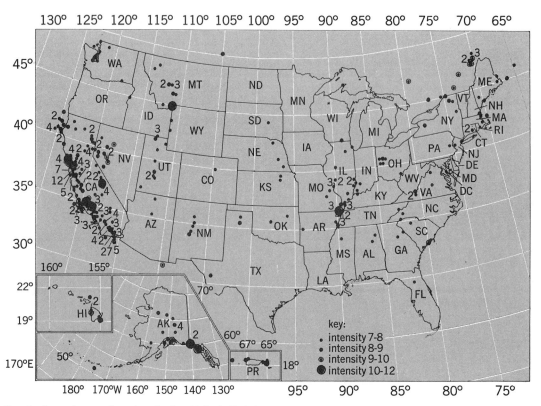

Fig. 5.   Damaging earthquakes in the United States through 1969. (*From M. L. Sbar and L. R. Sykes, Contempo-* *rary stress and seismicity in eastern North America, Geol. Soc. Amer. Bull., 84:1861–1882, 1973*)

(greater than magnitude 8) which contribute significantly to plate movements. The smaller events occur much more often, but are almost incidental to the plate movement process.

Intraplate earthquakes. Although most earthquakes occur on plate boundaries, they are known to occur infrequently within plates as well. The only earthquakes in the United States which can be directly related to plate motion are those on the Pacific coast. However, it can be seen from a map of past earthquakes in the contiguous area (Fig. 5) that earthquakes occur sporadically through other areas. Although such intraplate earthquakes are probably caused by the same convective forces that drive the plates, their immediate cause is not understood. Some intraplate earthquakes can be quite large. One of the largest earthquakes known to have occurred in the United States was part of a series in the Mississippi Valley, near New Madrid, MO, in 1811 and 1812. Another intraplate earthquake, in 1886, caused moderate damage to Charleston, SC.

EARTHQUAKE RISK EVALUATION

The risk of earthquake damage is clearly greatest in the immediate vicinity of plate boundaries. Even along plate boundaries, seismic activity varies considerably. It appears that convergent plate boundaries, such as island arcs, tend to have larger earthquakes than do other types of plate boundaries, such as oceanic ridges, where plates diverge, or transcurrent boundaries, exemplified by the San Andreas Fault in California, where the motion is parallel to the boundary. And among

members of a given type, the boundaries with higher rates of plate motion tend to have higher rates of seismicity as well. There have been numerous attempts to quantitatively describe these variations in seismicity in order to estimate seismic risk.

Statistical approach. One method which has been used for some time is to estimate seismic risk on the basis of past seismic activity. The method involves collecting all available information about past earthquakes in a region and collating the information in terms of a useful parameter such as felt intensity or seismic energy release. Plotted on a map, the data yield a picture of the geographical distribution of past earthquake activity. The distribution is interpreted as an indication of future seismic hazard. The map in Fig. 6, in which the United States is divided into seismic hazard zones, is based on this type of information.

There are methods of statistically analyzing the information on seismic risk maps in order to make more quantitative predictions of future activity. One such method utilizes the fact that the logarithm of the number N of earthquakes which exceed a magnitude M during any given period of time is almost inversely proportional to M. Therefore, there are about 10 times as many earthquakes greater than magnitude M as magnitude $M+1$, and 100 times as many as $M+2$. If one knows, then, the annual number of occurrences of events of some moderate size, one can predict the estimated recurrence interval of much larger events for the area covered.

One difficulty with statistical evaluation of

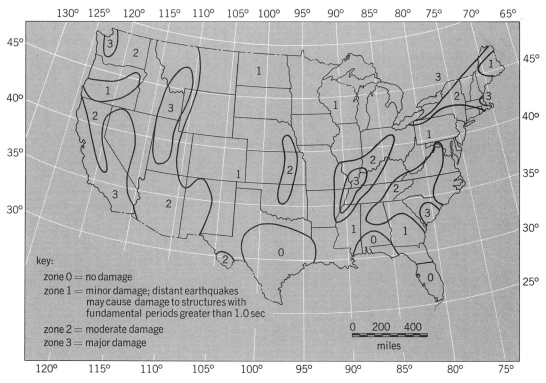

Fig. 6. Seismic risk map for conterminous United States. (From S. T. Algermissen, Seismic risk studies in the United States, Proceedings of the 4th World Conference on Earthquake Engineering, Santiago, Chile, vol. 1, pp. 14–27, 1969)

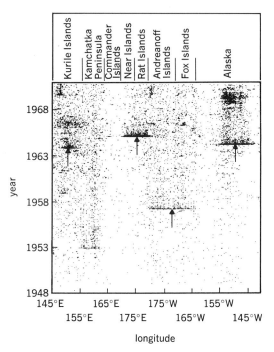

Fig. 7. Space-time plot of earthquakes in the northwestern basin of the Pacific shows major events and their aftershocks (arrows) preceded by gaps in major seismicity. The greater number of events in recent years reflects improved recording coverage and methods. *(From C. Kisslinger, Earthquake prediction, Phys. Today, p. 38, March 1974)*

seismic hazard is that of ensuring that the time sample for which data are available is long enough to be wholly representative of the seismicity. Good records on seismic activity in California, for example, are available for only about the last century. The largest earthquakes often have recurrence intervals (the time for a repeat of a large earthquake in a given place) of over 100 years so that a complete cycle of great earthquakes has not yet been observed in California. This means that

many areas of California which have historically been seismically quiet cannot be reckoned completely safe from future earthquakes solely on the basis of past activity.

Other parts of the world, of course, have much longer recorded histories. In Japan, for example, accurate coverage of seismic activity is available for the past 600 years, with poorer records going back a millennium before that. Two thousand years of recorded history in the Middle East have shown that seismic activity can show long-term variations, with periods of very high activity interspersed with times of near quiescence lasting several centuries. In Turkey, for example, a series of great earthquakes have occurred along the North Anatolian Fault from Iran to the Mediterranean since 1939, leaving tens of thousands of casualties. No activity of comparable severity had occurred in this region for 250 years prior to this latest episode. As long as such long-term variations in seismic activity remain poorly understood and unpredictable, seismic hazard evaluation based on statistical analysis of past activity will remain a chancy business.

Gap theory. Another method of earthquake risk evaluation is based on a combination of several elements of plate tectonics and the elastic rebound theory. Elastic rebound theory holds that great earthquakes on major plate boundaries should occur infrequently, separated by long intervals of seismically quiet times during which the continuing plate movements build up the strain until the frictional sliding resistance is again exceeded. Plate tectonics holds that such strain buildup rates should be fairly constant in time, because of the massive thermal inertia of the convection driving the major plates, and that each segment of the plate boundary must rupture periodically. This reasoning, therefore, indicates that the places near major plate boundaries which have the lowest risk of a great earthquake are those in which a major event has happened in the fairly recent past. The regions along major plate boundaries which have not experienced great earthquakes in many decades are the places where the next great earth-

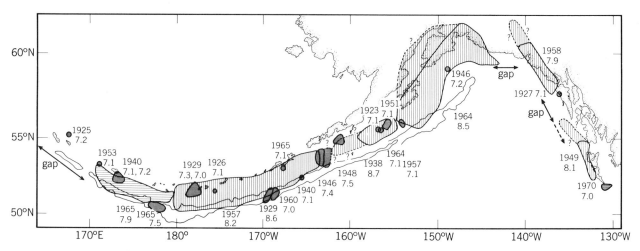

Fig. 8. Map of rupture zones (indicated by various shaded areas) of major earthquakes in Alaska and the Aleutians. Number below year indicates the magnitude of the quake. *(From J. Kelleher et al., J. Geophys. Res., 78:2547–2585, 1973)*

quakes are to be expected. Such high-risk regions are called seismic gaps.

Figure 7 is a space-time diagram of earthquakes along the plate boundary which runs from Alaska along the Aleutian Islands to Kamchatka and down the Kurile Islands. The linear groups of earthquakes are aftershocks which mark the rupture zones of great earthquakes, such as that of 1957 in the Andreanoff and Fox islands, that of 1964 in the Kuriles and Gulf of Alaska, and that of 1965 in the Rat Islands. The zones do not overlap and had almost no large earthquakes for many years prior to the major events. The map of the Aleutians in Fig. 8 shows the rupture zones of the large earthquakes which have occurred there since 1920. There are three noticeable gaps: in the eastern Gulf of Alaska, in southeastern Alaska, and in the far western Aleutians in the vicinity of the Commander Islands. Since this diagram was drawn, the southeastern Alaska gap has been filled by the Sitka earthquake, in 1972. On a broader scale, the map of the western Pacific Margin plate boundaries in Fig. 9 shows segments which have not ruptured in 30 years.

In many ways, the gap theory contradicts the older statistical seismic risk evaluation approach. Seismic risk maps which are not based on many hundreds of years of historical earthquake data may show regions of low seismicity which would be traditionally interpreted as regions of low risk but which, according to gap theory, might be interpreted as seismic gaps and hence areas of high risk. Gap theory, on the other hand, is applicable only to large earthquakes on major plate boundaries. It is not applicable, for example, to intraplate earthquakes or to the smaller plate boundary earthquakes.

PREDICTION METHODS

The methods of earthquake hazard evaluation can be considered to be a qualitative form of earthquake prediction. But what is really needed is a quantitative method of prediction whereby the place, time, and magnitude of an impending earthquake can be predicted with reasonable certainty.

This topic has become a reputable field of scientific research only in the last decade. In the early 1960s Japan began a national research program to discover means of predicting earthquakes. Several years later the Soviet Union followed suit, and although the United States has only just begun such a program, scattered research had been going on at a number of institutions on various aspects of the problem for some time.

Premonitory phenomena. Early research on earthquake prediction attempted to discover some phenomenon prior to an earthquake that could be used to warn of the coming of such a major event, affecting large volumes of rock in the Earth's crust.

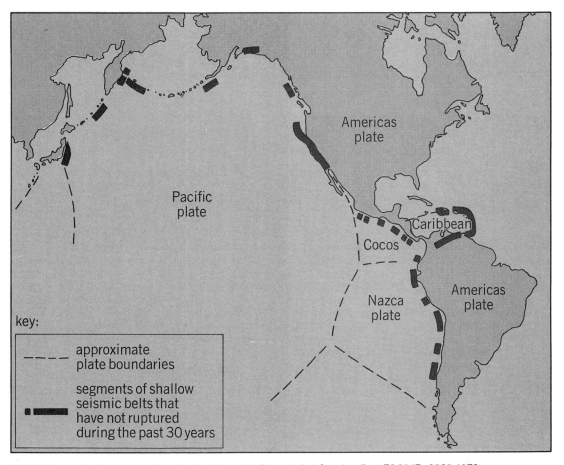

Fig. 9. Major seismic gaps, western Pacific. *(From J. Kelleher et al., J. Geophys. Res., 78:2547–2585, 1973)*

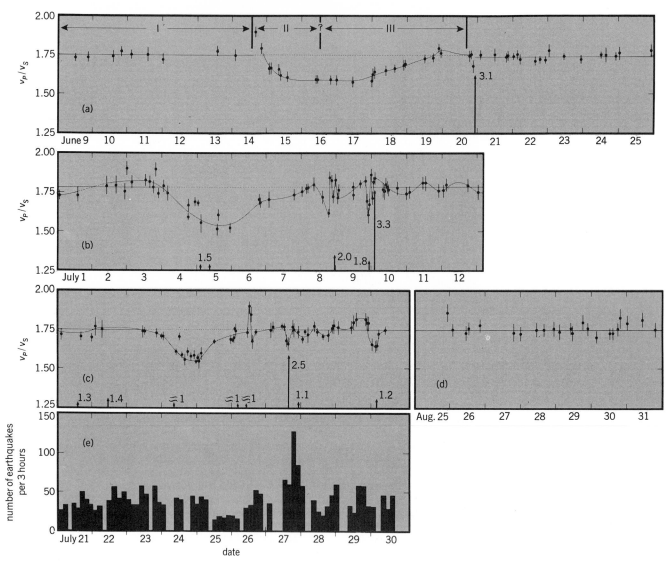

Fig. 10. (a–c) Diagrams of changes in the ratio v_p/v_s preceding three of the largest events in the Blue Mountain Lake, NY, earthquake swarm of 1971. All quakes of magnitude greater than 1 are shown as arrows. (d) A similar plot during a time when no large events took place. (e) A plot of the frequency of occurrence of small earthquakes in the swarm plotted on the same time scale as c. (From C. H. Scholz et al., Earthquake prediction: A physical basis, Science, 181:803–810, 1973)

The search for precursors in the last decade, carried out principally by researchers in the Soviet Union and Japan, has involved measuring many different physical properties in seismic areas to see if anomalous changes preceded earthquakes. As a result of these studies, a surprising number of allegedly precursory phenomena were observed. The effects included uplift of the ground surface preceding earthquakes, and anomalous changes in such diverse properties as electrical resistivity of the crust, velocity of seismic-wave propagation, ratio of large to small earthquake frequency, intensity and direction of the local magnetic field, and even the isotopic composition of deep well water. Many of the observations were fragmentary, since without knowing how to predict earthquakes, it is difficult to set up a proper monitoring system. For this reason, because the premonitory phenomena were so unexpectedly diverse, many earth scientists were dubious of their validity. As more and more examples of premonitory phenomena were reported, however, it became evident that the effects were real.

Wave velocity ratio. One of the most persistently observed precursors was a reduction of the ratio of the velocity of the seismic P wave, v_p, to the velocity of the S wave, v_S. Unlike sound waves in air, sound travels through solids in two modes: as the P wave, in which the direction of particle motion is parallel to the wave propagation direction, and as the S wave, in which the motion is transverse to the propagation direction.

One of the most universal properties of solids, rock included, is that the P wave travels faster than the S wave, the ratio, v_p/v_S, being 1.75. But Soviet seismologists working in the Garm area of the Tadzik S.S.R. of Central Asia found in numerous cases changes in the value of v_P/v_S a few months prior to moderate earthquakes there. They observed that v_P/v_S dropped to values as low as 1.60 several months before the earthquakes, then rose to its original value shortly before the quake occurred.

Confirmation of observations. The Soviet results were presented in detail to American seismologists for the first time at an international meeting in Moscow in 1971. At the time of the meeting, a swarm of small earthquakes beneath Blue Mountain Lake in New York's Adirondack Mountains was under intensive study by a group from Columbia University's Lamont-Doherty Geological Observatory. The earthquake swarm provided the first chance to check the Soviet observations. The results were positive. Each small-to-moderate earthquake at Blue Mountain Lake was preceded by a drop in v_P/v_S, and a return to normal just prior to the event (Fig. 10). Subsequently, a group at the California Institute of Technology studying old seismograph records found that a similar reduction of v_P/v_S had preceded the damaging 1971 San Fernando, CA, earthquake by 3 years. It thus became apparent that the v_P/v_S anomaly could occur in a variety of tectonic settings. It also appeared that the length of the anomaly seemed to increase with the size of the earthquake: it lasted 3 years for the San Fernando earthquake (magnitude 6.5), several months for the Garm events (magnitude 4 to 5), and only a few days for the small Blue Mountain Lake shocks (magnitude 2 to 3). This relationship turned out to be an important clue for understanding what caused the fluctuations.

Dilatancy theory. An explanation for these precursory seismic velocity changes, worked out by the Lamont-Doherty team and arrived at independently by a Stanford University researcher, lies in a rather obscure characteristic of rock known as dilatancy. A material exhibits dilatancy by expanding in volume when its shape or structure is altered under stress. Dilatancy was first discovered in the late 19th century by Osborne Reynolds, an Anglo-Irish engineer and physicist, in connection with his studies of the qualities of granular materials.

Dilatancy in sand. The essence of dilatancy is illustrated by wet beach sand. Anyone who has walked along the thoroughly wet, but not flooded, part of a beach near the water's edge has probably noticed that the sand surrounding the pressure point of the foot appears to dry out, then returns to its previous wetness when the foot is raised. The sand in the depression of the footprint, however, becomes wetter than it was before.

This phenomenon is explained in the following way. Under the pounding of the surf, the sand settles into a condition in which its grains are as closely packed as possible. Any subsequent change or deformation of the sand, as when it is walked upon, forces the grains upward and outward into a more open packing, thereby increasing the space between the grains and expanding the sand's total volume. The pore spaces in wet sand are filled with water. The new, increased pore volume immediately beneath the footprint becomes filled with additional water sucked in from adjacent areas. That displacement of water accounts for the partial drying of the region around the print. As the dried-out region gradually becomes saturated again by inflow from its surroundings, the entire area around the footprint will contain more water than it did before. That is why the sand in the footprint looks wetter once the foot has been lifted.

The expansion of the pore volume beneath the foot produces a partial vacuum. This causes the sand grains to cling more firmly together, and the sand thus becomes firmer. The strengthening of sand through a reduction of the pore fluid pressure is called dilatancy hardening and is the main reason why wet sand is firmer than dry sand.

Dilatancy in rock. Solid rock also exhibits dilatancy. When rock is strongly deformed, small cracks open up and grow in it, producing an increase in pore space. If the rock cracks are initially filled with a pore fluid such as water—as they normally are in the shallow parts of the Earth's

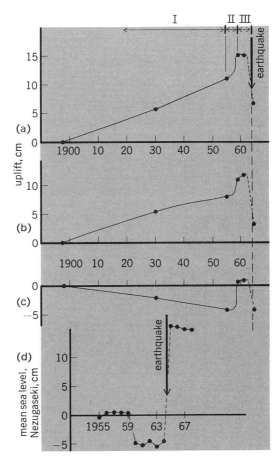

Fig. 11. Crustal uplift preceding the Niigata, Japan, earthquake of 1964 (magnitude 7.5). (*a–c*) Curves showing elevation changes of benchmarks in a leveling line along the coast, which had been resurveyed several times since 1898. Different phases of uplift are: I, due to slow elastic strain buildup; II, rapid uplift due to dilatancy; III, little movement after dilatancy has stopped. (*d*) Curve showing the drop in mean sea level, reflecting the uplift of the land, observed at a tide gage for the same time period. (*From C. H. Scholz et al., Earthquake prediction: A physical basis, Science, 181:803–810, 1973*)

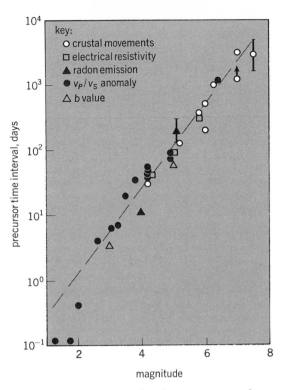

Fig. 12. Duration time of various precursory phenomena as a function of the magnitude of the following earthquake. Here *b* is a parameter that describes the ratio of small to large shocks. *(From C. H. Scholz et al., Earthquake prediction: A physical basis, Science, 181:803–810, 1973)*

crust—the increase in pore volume will produce the same effects as in beach sand.

The theory advanced to explain the changes in the velocity ratio of the P and S waves associated with earthquakes is that the stress that builds up before an earthquake ultimately becomes great enough to cause cracks to grow, resulting in dilatancy. If the dilatancy is extensive enough to cause the rock to partially dry up, there will be less difference between P- and S-wave speeds. The P-wave velocity depends on the average compressibility of the rock and the pore water in it (the greater the compressibility, the lower the velocity), whereas the S velocity depends on the average shearing resistance of the rock and pore water. Water is nearly incompressible compared with air, whereas both have a negligible shearing resistance. Therefore, if the pore material in rock changes from water to air because of dilatancy-induced drying, the P-wave velocity will drop, but the S-wave velocity will be unaffected.

Why, then, does the P-wave velocity return to normal just before the earthquake? For the same reason that the sand does not stay dry around a footprint: water flows in from adjacent regions to fill the voids.

Dilatancy before an earthquake is a naturally buffered process. The pore water at some depth in the Earth's crust is normally under considerable pressure from the weight of the water above it. Dilatancy must first reduce that pressure to zero

before it can begin undersaturating the rock. This reduction in pore pressure causes dilatancy hardening, which inhibits further dilatancy and also strengthens the fault, thus delaying the earthquake. After dilatancy has stopped, the influx of water from adjoining regions brings the pore pressure up to its original value, the P-wave velocity rises to normal, and the increase in pore pressure weakens the fault, thereby triggering the earthquake.

The dilatancy mechanism can be compared to a pump. Like a pump, dilatancy first reduces the fluid pressure (in the region where an earthquake is about to occur), then it allows the pressure to be built back up by the influx of fluid (from the surrounding rock).

The triggering of earthquakes by an increase in fluid pressure is a well-known occurrence; earthquakes are often caused by the impounding of deep reservoirs. Because of this phenomenon, earthquakes were created in the Denver area in the mid-1960s when fluid wastes were injected into the crust at the Rocky Mountain Arsenal 10 mi (16 km) from the city.

Application to other precursors. As the dilatancy theory was further developed, it became obvious that the same processes invoked to explain the v_p/v_s variations would also explain the diverse kinds of other precursors as well. Thus the increase of volume due to dilatancy would cause an uplift of the ground in the region surrounding the upcoming earthquake, almost exactly as was observed preceding the earthquake which destroyed the Japanese city of Niigata in 1964 (Fig. 11). Similarly, influx of water into the dilatant region would be expected to cause the decrease of electrical resistivity of the crust observed prior to a number of earthquakes, because water is more conductive than rock. Almost all of the various types of long-term precursors previously observed were found to be explicitly predicted by this one theory.

Duration of precursor. The relationship between the duration of the precursor and the size of the earthquake has also become clearer (Fig. 12). The time duration from the beginning of dilatancy to the earthquake largely depends on the time it takes for water to diffuse into the dilatant zone to recharge the pore pressure, and this depends on the size of the dilatant zone—and hence the size of the earthquake.

PROSPECTS FOR THE FUTURE

The relationship between the precursor time, dilatant zone size, and the magnitude of the impending earthquake is important because if either of the first two are known, the magnitude as well as the time and place of the impending earthquake can be predicted. In practice, then, if a monitoring system for detecting v_p/v_s changes, for example, were set up and a drop in v_p/v_s were observed, an earthquake could be expected. By finding the size of the region over which the v_p/v_s drop occurred, seismologists could predict the size of the impending earthquake as well as its approximate time of occurrence. When v_p/v_s returned to normal, a more precise time of occurrence could then be predicted.

At present this method of earthquake prediction is still in the research stage. It is not known if all earthquakes are preceded by such dilatancy-induced phenomena. Furthermore, the prediction time is still only approximate, involving possible errors of weeks or months. However, it appears that the major breakthroughs have been made and that real earthquake prediction may be a practical possibility in the not too distant future.

[C. H. SCHOLZ]

Fire Engineering

A. Murty Kanury has devoted nearly 15 years of his research efforts to the study of fires and explosions. In 1961 he joined the fire research team at the University of Minnesota. From 1969 to 1973 he was associated with the Basic Research Department of the Factory Mutual Research Corporation, where he was engaged in the study of ignition, fire spread, and flammability of various construction materials. He is presently with the Fire Research Group at Stanford Research Institute, where he has expanded his interests into the areas of physics of smoke and toxicity, forest fire management, and environmental impact of agricultural burning.

In over 3,000,000 fires nearly $3,000,000,000 worth of property is destroyed every year in the United States. More important, almost half a million people are injured annually; 12,500 of these lose their lives, and many of the others are left disabled, often with agonizing, life-long physical as well as psychological scars. Statistical breakdowns indicate that more than half of those who die in fires perish in ordinary dwelling fires.

In the recent report of the National Commission on Fire Prevention and Control this often avoidable tragic waste of resources and life has been brought to public attention. The important recommendations made by the commission include updating the fire services to cope with the modern challenges; establishing a national center to collect data on a uniform basis; educating the public in fire prevention and control; and furthering research into fire behavior. This article will consider the state of the art of the technology of fires and fire prevention and control. It will also examine the past contributions and future promise of science to this technology.

Inasmuch as a fire can occur nearly anywhere and as fires in different situations behave differently, scientific and technological strategies to understand, prevent, and control fires must be based on some generalities and the generalities then may be refined for the specific situations. This premise will be followed throughout this article.

Fires can be classified into the following categories: (1) rural structural fires; (2) forest and wildland fires; (3) transportation fires—railroad, marine, aircraft, highway (commercial vehicles, passenger vehicles); (4) urban fires—light industrial, heavy industrial, institutional (nursing homes, child-care centers, hospitals, schools), mercantile, storage, public assembly (churches, convention halls, sports arenas, airports, theaters, restaurants, clubs), one- or two-unit dwellings, multiple dwellings (hotels, motels, dormitories, apartments).

Rural structural fires. Inadequate water supplies, lack or inefficient enforcement of building codes, and antiquated fire services are among the principal characteristics of rural structural fires. Most fire deaths in rural areas occur at night. Attributable, perhaps, to the usually delayed arrival of the fire department, the death rate in rural fires exceeds that in urban fires, being 4.0 per 100,000 population for rural versus 2.7 for urban. A valuable short-term solution would be the adoption in rural areas of early-warning detection and alarm systems.

Forest and wildland fires. The U. S. Forest Service has performed extensive research into reliable prediction methods and fighting techniques for forest fires. A dismaying 90% of all forest fires are caused by human carelessness; the rest result primarily from lightning. A forest whose undergrowth and dead fuel are cleared is considered a fire-safe forest. Australians have been using the technique of controlled burning (also known as prescribed burning) of forest tinder for many decades. Their understanding of the dependence of fire spread through the forest tinder, based upon such variables as the magnitude and direction of wind, topography, ambient temperature and humidity, fuel bed composition and structure, and moisture, is so sophisticated that thumb rules, charts, and tables usable by even nontechnical personnel exist now.

In the United States, however, the situation is different, partly due to the vast differences in climate, species of vegetation, and geography. Prescribed burning is known to have been practiced by Indians centuries ago. A surprising fact is that a mere 1% of all forest fires in the United States cause over 60% of the total forest fire destruction.

Transportation fires. The table shows the number of fires and the loss of life and property in various categories of transportation fires. The glaring point is that even though transportation fires constitute only a fifth of the total number of all fires in the nation, they contribute over a third of the total life loss. Their contribution to property loss, however, is lower than might thus be expected. This heavy toll of motor vehicle highway fires points to the fact that the design of vehicles and the choice of construction materials leave much to be desired. Basic difficulties are encountered also in fighting transportation fires, especially highway fires, because the local fire department rarely knows the nature of the goods in transit.

Railroad fires usually involve hazardous goods in transit and cause local disasters. Fires in aircraft resulting in the most extensive property loss occur mainly in airports and hangars. Research and development are direly needed to reduce ignition causes, to improve survival, and to cut down time for detection and suppression. Toxicity and smoke are reputedly responsible for most of the in-flight fatalities. Reliable statistics to substantiate any speculations, however, are scarce. Considerable analysis also remains to be done in connection with the design of mass transit and subway systems, which will be increasingly prevalent in a future dominated by dwindling of energy supplies and fouling of urban environments.

URBAN FIRES

The rest of this article deals with urban fires, which, as indicated by the statistics, dominate the scene in number of fires, property loss, and deaths.

Statistics. In order to identify the areas begging for improvement, and to quantitatively assess the effectiveness of improvements, reliable data on the causes and consequences of accidental fires must be gathered on a rational, uniform, and consistent basis. The data available are sparse, the best-

Statistics on transportation fires in the United States*

Category	Fires		Life loss		Property loss	
	Number	% of total	Number	% of total	Amount, millions of dollars	% of total
Railroads, ships	20,000	0.7	185	1.5	27.60	1.0
Aircraft, aerospace vehicles	200	—	125	1.1	192.00	7.0
Motor vehicles						
Farm and construction	19,200	0.7	3950	33.3	16.12	0.6
Pleasure	482,400	17.7	—	—	96.54	3.5
Total transportation units	521,800	19.1	4260	35.9	332.26	12.1

*Data estimated for 1971 by National Commission on Fire Prevention and Control.

known source being the National Fire Protection Association (NFPA). The following are some of the implications of the known statistics.

Among 14 industrialized nations, the United States leads in the annual per capita fire losses. The direct property loss suffered by the United States in 1973 was over $2,750,000,000. Total cost of fire, including fire department operation, burn therapy, insurance expense, and loss of productivity, amounted to over 4.25 times the cost for direct losses.

Indications are that the direct loss due to fire is increasing annually at a rate of about 5%; thus, the present rate of increase is roughly $120,000,000 per year.

Nearly 40% of all fires in 1971 were in brush and grasslands, which pose little direct loss even though indirect costs add up considerably. The remaining fires—approximately 1,650,000 of them—occurred in the forests (6.9%), transportation equipment (32%), and structures (61.1%). Among transportation fires 93 out of 100 occurred in the automobile, usually following a collision. Of the structural fires, 70 out of 100 occurred in homes, and the rest occurred almost equally in industrial and commercial buildings.

Of all building fires, 19% are initiated by heating and cooking equipment, 14.3% by cigarettes and matches, 19.6% by electrical mishaps, 7.9% by flammable liquids, and 8.6% by children with matches.

In 1971 the direct loss was distributed as 31.9% residential, 21.1% commercial, 29.6% industrial, 4.4% forest, 7% aerospace and aircraft vehicles, 4.1% motor vehicles, and 1% railroads and ships.

Turning to life-loss distribution (of 11,850 in 1971), 56% of the victims died in residential fires, 8% in commercial and industrial structural fires, 0.2% in forest fires, 1.1% in aerospace and aircraft fires, 33.3% in motor vehicle fires, and 1.5% in railroad and ship fires.

The causes of fire deaths in one- and two-family residences are predominantly inhalation of fire gases (73.6%) and burns (23.6%). In multiple-dwelling structures the respective figures are 68.4% and 28%.

These statistics show that considerable property loss occurs in a relatively few types of fires, that the staggering high number of automotive fires cause insignificant property loss and disproportionately high loss of life, and that losses of both life and property are considerable in fires occurring in homes.

Gross features. Since the fundamental nature of fire is the same in all situations discussed in the preceding paragraphs, and since urban dwelling fires cause such a large loss of life and property, it is appropriate to discuss the science and technology of fire safety as related to these urban fires.

Consider the development of a fire in a typical urban enclosure such as a living room. After an accidental fire starts, it grows first slowly and linearly with time and then exponentially. Air from the room is induced into the flame to react with the fuel vapors which emanate from the construction and furnishing materials (Fig. 1). Heat and copious quantities of combustion products are

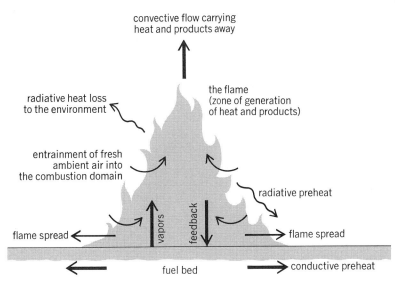

Fig. 1. Schematic of a growing fire.

evolved. Although most of the heat is carried away from the fire in hot product flow, some is fed back to the burning fuel bed to continue the vapor production. A considerable fraction of the heat that is convected and radiated away is usually fed forward, preheating the adjoining fuel surfaces and thus preparing them to receive the growing fire.

Figure 2 shows schematically the growth of a typical fire. The fire intensity may be expressed in many ways—for example, by the area covered by the fire, volume of the fire, the temperature at some neighboring location, or the velocity in the product flow. The figure shows an unrestrained fire as well as one which is suppressed at different stages of its growth. The initial linear growth and the following exponential growth are evident. As various structural components continue to be heated by the growing fire, energy and mass conservation in the room culminate in an eventual abrupt enhancement of the flame spread rate, termed "flashover." Upon flashover, the entire room is engulfed in fire and attains a steady state of burning, even if briefly. Beyond this stage, the fire can propagate and penetrate into the adjacent rooms to involve the entire structure.

Two important points are clear from this brief description of fire growth. First, chances of saving lives are minimal after the flashover occurs, for the flames and fire gases are too intense by then. Moreover, enough evidence exists in fire records to show that the deadly poisonous products of combustion reach remote areas of the structure even before flashover occurs in the room of origin. Second, in the entire episode of the birth and growth of fire, the time factor is crucial.

Control tactics. The various tactics used in fire prevention and control essentially involve modification of the fire characteristics to alter the time factor to save lives and minimize property damage. Such modifications include preventing fire by reducing possible ignition sources and increasing the ignition time to infinity; early detection of the fire and prompt sounding of the alarm;

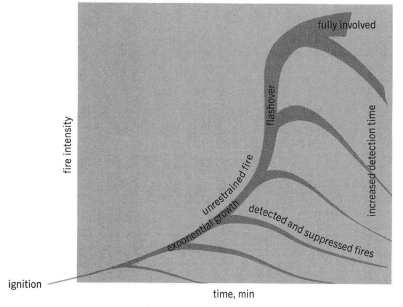

fire intensity

ignition

time, min

fully involved

flashover

increased detection time

unrestrained fire

exponential growth

detected and suppressed fires

Fig. 2. Schematic of fire growth and influence of suppressive action at various stages of growth.

reducing the fire department arrival time; facilitating quick attack, easy egress, and rescue; decelerating the fire growth; delaying the flashover; and enhancing structural fire endurance. As the NFPA points out, fire-safe construction starts on the drafting board, where careful attention can be given to such complexly interrelated factors as the selection of materials, details of architecture, proposed use of the structure, building codes, and legal requirements. All too often, fulfillment of the minimum safety requirements of the codes is no guarantee against a disaster, for what goes into the building changes with time and people.

Specific technological strategies to improve fire safety in an urban structure include the following items.

Location and exposure control. This requires placement (zoning) of structures in a community as well as placement of hazardous processes on the periphery of a structure or area. Factors to be taken into account include not only the combustibility of construction materials and the hazards of occupancy, but also the dangers of possible ignition of the building or its contents from exposure to a fire in an adjoining building or other exterior source of ignition.

Occupancy control. This strategy advocates either prohibition or restricted entry of certain materials into a structure with regard to their life hazard and combustibility.

Early detection and alarm systems. The sooner a fire is detected, the easier it is to put out and the less the threat to the occupants. There are basically two types of detectors: thermal and products-of-combustion (POC) detectors. Thermal detectors are comparatively sluggish and delayed in response. They are usually used in conjunction with automatic sprinkler systems. POC detectors are preferred for early detection. Among the currently

marketed POC detectors, smoke and ionization detectors are prevalent.

Fire loading control. This strategy could be a part of occupancy control. It involves limiting the maximum amount of combustible allowed per unit floor area of a structure. Fire loading does not tell much about the ease of ignition and speed of fire growth, but in conjunction with the geometry of the structure, it tells something about the severity of the fully involved fire. The quantity of fuel and its rate of burning determine the duration of a fire.

Regulation of materials. A structure built of steel, concrete, and brick is, of course, safer than one built of wood. When wood is used, application of gypsum or asbestos board improves the safety. The fire properties of building materials fall broadly into two categories: combustibility and fire resistance. Combustibility is further divided into ease of ignition, fire spread, fuel contributed, and smoke developed. The fire resistance of materials and assemblies is expressed in hours of endurance to the exposure from a standard time-temperature furnace.

Compartmentation, subdivision, and ventilation. An effective way of restraining spread of fire through a structure is to suitably seal off each unit of the structure with walls, ceilings, floors, windows, and doors which are impervious to fire. Such a practice is frequently followed in large modern buildings subdivided by fire walls and fire curtains.

In subdivision of buildings, factors must be considered such as the occupant population and the available modes of egress. Pressurized stairwells are under consideration to facilitate safe egress atmospheres. The concept of ventilation is related peripherally to compartmentation and subdivision in that the sealed atmosphere of a modern high-rise building requires, upon detection of a fire, automatic opening of certain vents and closing of others to keep smoke and toxic gases from entering the entire air circulation system.

Structural stability and fire integrity. Since a modern structure is a complex system of many interconnected components, and since a single weak link can defeat the purpose of the entire chain, it is necessary to examine the complex structure for its overall stability and integrity in a potential fire. An otherwise well-designed building and its occupants could, for instance, be placed in jeopardy by improper and inadequate installation of building service equipment.

Accessibility. The need for all-around accessibility of a structure often contradicts the need for security in nonfire situations. Basements, especially, offer some difficulty in accessibility. Exit facilities in accord with the Life Safety Code serve the dual function of providing means of exit from and access to the upper stories of buildings, especially those high-rises that are too tall for fire truck ladders.

Suppression. Advocates in the insurance industry give an all-embracing answer to most of the problems discussed above—automatic sprinkler protection. Many commercial and industrial properties are deemed uninsurable unless they are provided with automatically (thermally) actuated water sprinklers. Rigid inspection and maintenance of sprinkler systems are recommended, for insurance company records show that a building with no sprinklers and one with inoperative sprinklers are equally destructible by fire. Novel extinguishants such as surfactant foams and halocarbons are used in special situations.

Codes, standards, and laws. Codes are, of necessity, generalities, and since fire situations vary over a broad range, literal application of the codes in the design and maintenance of a structure seldom leads to guaranteed safety. Codes and laws are usually based on standards which themselves are deduced from the best available scientific and technological knowledge on fires. Unfortunately, the little available scientific and technological knowledge becomes obscured when filtered through standards to codes. Codes consequently vary widely from place to place in the United States and Canada, but there is a strong movement in the United States to bring uniformity. True uniformity is possible only when enough factual data are developed from science and technology.

The existing codes are of three categories. Life safety codes primarily concern exits—their adequate number and size and unrestricted approach. Building codes provide rules for safe construction. Most municipalities have their own codes, which are based largely on five model codes: National Building Code (NBC), Uniform Building Code (UBC), Southern Standard Building Code (SSBC), Basic Building Code (BBC), and National Building Code of Canada (NBCC). Finally, fire prevention codes exert an important influence on the occupancy and operation of a building by further refining the building codes.

TECHNOLOGY OF FIRES

What has science done for fire safety? Presented below are a few significant advances and a few direly needed solutions in fire prevention and control. The presentation is best done by considering the various stages of a fire.

Definition of a fire. A fire may be defined as a chemical reaction between a fuel and an oxidizer (which is usually the ambient air), resulting in release of energy (mostly thermal) and production of such inert and noxious chemical species as CO_2, CO, H_2O, soot, and smoke. A fire may be flaming (the exothermic reactions are predominantly homogeneous, involving the gas phase only), glowing (the reaction is heterogeneous, confined to the surface), or smoldering (the reaction is heterogeneous in the subsurface layers of a porous fuel bed).

To initiate a fire, fuel (vapor), oxidant, and heat have to be simultaneously provided in proper proportions. For persistence, the initiated fire must produce heat at a rate sufficient to exceed the loss rate (from combined conduction, convection, and radiation in addition to any other extraneous heat loss mechanisms). In order to grow, the persistent fire must feed heat back to the fuel yet to be burned; the larger the feedback, the greater the growth rate.

Smoldering ignition. From slow oxidation reactions, heat is generated in such porous solids as sawdust, food grains and flour, cotton linters, fiberboard, foam rubbers, and oil rags. If the generation rate is large enough to exceed the rate of dissipation through the solid boundary, the temperature in the body gradually builds to a sufficiently high level so that the reactions accelerate to self-ignition. Large volume-to-surface ratio of the body, low conductivity of the solid, and high ambient temperature are factors which reduce the heat loss rate. High reactivity and heat of oxidation are among those factors that increase the generation rate. If the ratio of heat generation rate to the heat loss rate is denoted by δ, the available theories show that the minimum value of δ for assured ignition is about 1, 2, and 3 for a slab, cylinder, and sphere, respectively.

Another phenomenon, somewhat related to self-ignition, is that of smolder spread. It is poorly defined in the literature but is common in residential fires. For example, materials which are extremely porous and spongy (such as a mattress, a bed of pine needles, or a layer of damp autumn leaves) can support an internally self-propagating combustion wave, once a nonflaming ignition has occurred at a spot from a source such as a cigar butt. Clearly, the wave propagation rate is determined by a combination of heat transfer processes and chemical reaction processes. Radiation and conduction are probably the controlling heat transfer processes. Among the chemical reactions, at least one endothermic process (for example, decomposition) and one exothermic process (oxidation) seem to be involved. The precise mechanism that governs smolder spread—and hence the variables that influence it—are not known at present.

Self-ignition and smolder spread probably pose greater toxicity hazard than gas-phase combustion does, because of the slowness of the oxidation process and incompleteness of the pyrolysis gas combustion. Thus, toxicity investigators should give

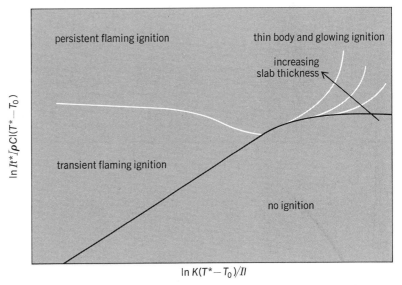

Fig. 3. Martin's ignition map. K, ρ, and C are the solid's thermal conductivity, density, and specific heat; T is temperature with * for ignition and subscript 0 for initial condition; t^* is time to ignition; l is specimen thickness; and capital I is radiant exposure. (*From S. B. Martin, Diffusion-controlled ignition of cellulosic materials by intense radiant energy, in 10th International Symposium on Combustion, The Combustion Institute, Pittsburgh, pp. 872–896, 1965*)

smoldering fires priority. Furthermore, it is widely acknowledged that when solids are "inhibited" by trace retardant additives, the tendency to flame is greatly discouraged, whereas the tendency to glow and smolder is enhanced. Investigations into this behavior are needed to cope with the toxicity problem effectively.

Flaming ignition. Ignition of cellulosic solids by radiative and convective heating received much investigatory attention in the last 2 decades, spurred by interest in fire prevention, burn protection, and firemen's apparel design. As the solid is heated, it chars; progressively deeper layers degrade in a time-dependent manner. Most of the pyrolysates transpire out of the solid into the gas phase to mix with air. If the resultant mixture is within the so-called flammability limits, it may be ignited by a pilot flame, heating coil, or glowing ember.

In the absence of a pilot heating source, the mixture requires additional heating to spontaneously ignite. The critical temperature for piloted and spontaneous ignition is known to be near 350 and 600°C respectively for most organic solids. Figure 3 delineates various regimes of spontaneous ignition of radiantly heated cellulosic solids. These delineations are predicted by simple transient conduction solutions (Fig. 4).

To establish the mechanism of ignition, N. J. Alvares and Martin measured spontaneous ignition times (from radiant heating) by varying the atmospheric total pressure, oxygen partial pressure, and the nature of the gas-phase inert species. Although predictions can be made by theoretical models, it still remains to similarly establish the mechanism of ignition of a wide assortment of construction and furnishing materials.

Fire spread. Once ignition has occurred, interest shifts to the process of spread and growth of the fire. Naturally, the faster the fire propagates to the neighboring fuel surfaces, the greater the hazard and the shorter the time available for escape or suppression attempts. The fire spread rate is determined by the rate at which heat is fed forward by the fire to the fuel ahead of it and the effectiveness with which the feedback heat raises the fuel to the state of ignition.

Essentially, if q (cal/cm²/sec) is the heat feed-forward rate and Q (cal/cm³) is the heat required to raise the fuel from the initial state to the state of ignition (which is indirectly characterized by an ignition temperature T^*), then the spread rate U (cm/sec) is given by q/Q. The feedback rate and the heat requirement themselves may, and often do, depend upon the spread rate itself, thus bringing nonlinearity into the analysis. In general, q is composed of various fluxes—conductive, convective, and radiative, in both the fuel bed and the gas phase. Q depends upon the fuel density, specific heat, ignition temperature, initial temperature, moisture content, internal conductive drain, and other factors.

Flashover. Once the initiated fire is allowed to spread in a confined space such as a typical room, a time will soon come when flashover occurs, that is, the fire spread abruptly increases to an extremely fast speed to engulf the entire room in flames. Prior to flashover, fuel surfaces ahead of the slowly propagating fire front release visible vapors, mainly perhaps from radiative heating. As

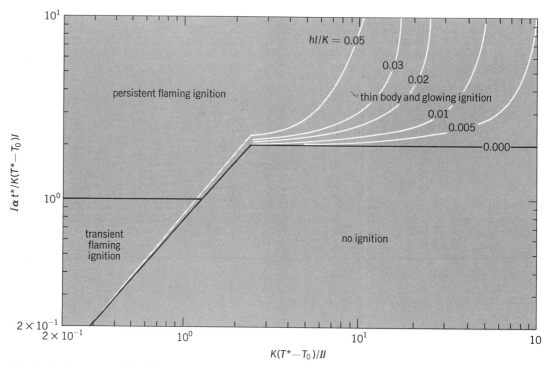

Fig. 4. Martin's map obtained from transient conduction solutions, where α is thermal diffusivity of the solid, and h is heat loss coefficient. (*From A. Murty Kanury, Ignition of cellulosic solids: A review, Fire Res. Abstr. Rev., 14:24–52, 1972*)

the surfaces get hotter, the radiant energy exchange between various surfaces is augmented while the relatively localized fire continues to release the combustion energy at a gradually but measurably increasing rate. The feedback to the unburned fuel is no longer solely from the propagating fire—all the enclosing surfaces contribute radiatively. Finally, almost like an explosion, flashover occurs.

From the standpoint of life safety in fires, flashover is obviously a process of utmost importance. However, flashover is such a newly recognized feature that no quantitative information pertaining to it is available in the literature; no definite mechanisms have been postulated.

Burning of solids and liquids. Regardless of the nature of the materials involved, the initiation of a fire in an enclosure, if unattended, is followed by spread, flashover, and then the fully involved steady-state phase of burning. The strength of the heat source resulting from steady maximum burning is an important characteristic—not only intrinsically but also with regard to the events in progress in the vicinity. Intrinsically, the heat source strength governs the self-burning rate. Extrinsically, it is significant in at least two ways: the radiation emitted by the flame outward contributes to the spread and growth; and the convective flow and heat and mass transfer patterns in the enclosure are profoundly affected by the heat release rate.

It is this rate, too, that determines the minimum extinguishant application rate to create the nonpositive heat balance—an absolute requirement to suppress the fire. The burning rate also determines the time of structural failure.

To solve the convectively controlled diffusion flame problem, the fluid dynamic part may be separated from the thermodynamic part. The burning rate may then be written as the product of a mass transfer coefficient and a function of the mass transfer number.

In Fig. 5, which shows the pattern of burning of a liquid fuel (methanol) on a 6-in. (15 cm) flat plate wick in different orientations, the boundary layer–type burning feature is clear. Sophisticated boundary layer theory has been used to quantitatively describe fires on isolated bodies with results as shown in Figs. 6 and 7, in which many of the currently available data on burning rates, $\dot{m}''$ (g/cm²/sec), are correlated as a function of size of the fire l (cm) for a variety of solid and liquid fuels. The figures show that while the small fire (one with low Grashof number) may be adequately predicted by the rules of laminar free convective heat transfer, larger fires are strongly affected by radiation—particularly if the fire is in a pool configuration. It is not known at present how best to compute the radiation characteristics across the participating medium of fire, not because the method is lacking but because data on the temperature and soot and composition properties are lacking.

Suppression. Any suppressive action taken against a roaring fire involves depriving it of its requirements to grow and to subsist. This means reducing or eliminating the feedback, rendering the heat balance negative, and taking the fuel, oxygen, or heat away.

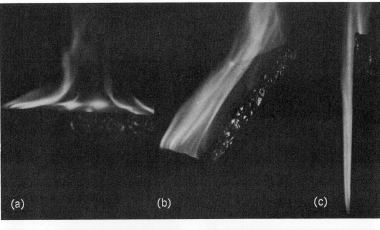

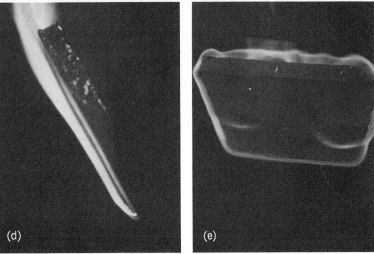

Fig. 5.   Alcohol burning on a ceramic wick. (a) $\theta = 0°$. (b) $\theta = 35°$. (c) $\theta = 90°$. (d) $\theta = 140°$. (e) $\theta = 180°$. (From P. L. Blackshear, Jr., and A. Murty Kanury, Heat and mass transfer to, from, and within cellulosic solids burning in air, in 10th International Symposium on Combustion, The Combustion Institute, Pittsburgh, pp. 911–923, 1965)

Feedback can be reduced by such measures as altering the geometry of the fuel array or diverting the hot gases away from the fuel yet to be involved in the fire. Increase in heat loss rate may be brought about by sprinkling water on the fire, by applying a high-heat-capacity inert gas to the environment, or by some other technique of extracting heat from the fire. For example, heat generation rate may be reduced by changing the atmosphere to an inert one (to eliminate the oxygen availability), blanketing the fuel by a foam or by a surfactant film, killing the reactive species of all sorts in the gas phase by reaction inhibitors, or modifying the fuel chemically to reduce its vaporization rate.

The most important question in connection with suppression is this: How effectively can a given agent put out a given fire? To answer this, experimental investigation is needed to answer the following preliminary questions: What is the best manner of applying the extinguishant? What is the critical minimum extinguishant application rate to ensure an end to the fire? What factors determine the fraction of delivered extinguishant reaching the fuel and fire? Is there any quantitative way of

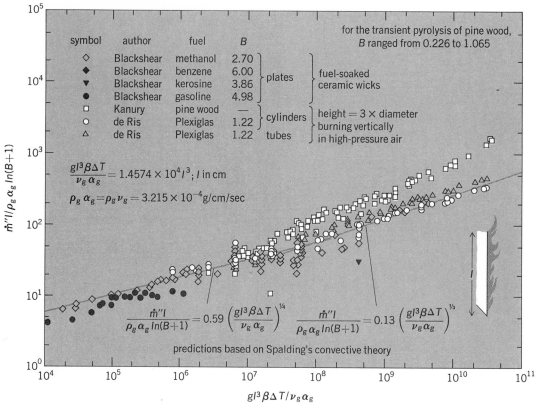

Fig. 6. Laminar and turbulent burning of various fuels on a vertical wall. Here $\dot{m}''$ is burning rate per unit area; l is the height of the wall; ρ_g, α_g, and ν_g are respectively the density, thermal diffusivity, and kinematic viscosity of the gas phase; g is the acceleration due to gravity; β is the volumetric expansion coefficient; ΔT is the temperature differential causing buoyancy; and B is the mass-transfer driving force. (From A. Murty Kanury, The science and engineering of hostile fires, Fire Res. Abstr. Rev., 15(3), 1974)

expressing the critical rate of heat (or active species) removal by the extinguishant? What exactly is the mechanism by which a fire is suppressed?

Flammability. Flammability is a term used in assessing the response of a given material to a given fire exposure. Materials noncombustible under conditions of test exposure may not necessarily be noncombustible under other conditions. To develop quantitative techniques of assessing the fire hazard of a given situation, it is first necessary to understand the behavior of real fires. Since nearly all materials degrade when subjected to severe enough thermal environments, a description of the fire-environment-exposure conditions must be made an integral part of flammability ratings. The present level of understanding of these conditions is so primitive that only recently have the component processes begun to be identified.

Smoke and toxicity. Even though smoke and toxic gases are purported to be responsible for a majority of dwelling fire deaths, very little useful quantitative knowledge is available on them. Test chambers are in existence to obtain comparative measures of the smoke potential of materials. However, it is not known how to extrapolate these measures to more realistic geometries, sizes, and arrangements of different materials present in an actual fire. The situation regarding toxic gas production and movement is even more obscure.

Modeling of fires. To conduct systematic observations on destructive fires, simulation is necessary, reproducing what is considered the essential picture of the real thing. Full-scale fire simulation tests require a large test facility, inherently pose the danger of going out of control, are difficult to instrument and observe, and are cumbersome to analyze because of the voluminous data. When a crucial measurement is found, full-scale tests are extremely costly to repeat, for the same and other reasons. Modeling offers an excellent tool to overcome the inconveniences of testing full-scale fires. Conceptually similar small-scale fires are easy to control, permit more accurate measurement, and are less expensive to study by repetitive experimentation.

Certain constraints and rules of modeling originate from the need to preserve several nondimensional numbers relevant to fire. Frequently, only partial modeling is possible. H. C. Hottel and F. A. Williams have done much work in this area. A promising new method for modeling free convectively controlled fires (by varying the ambient air pressure) has been developed by Kanury and colleagues J. de Ris and M. C. Yuen. Results of this modeling work on vertical wall burning and pool burning of various fuels are briefly presented in Figs. 8 and 9. The fluid dynamic, radiative, and chemical kinetic interactions that arise in pressure

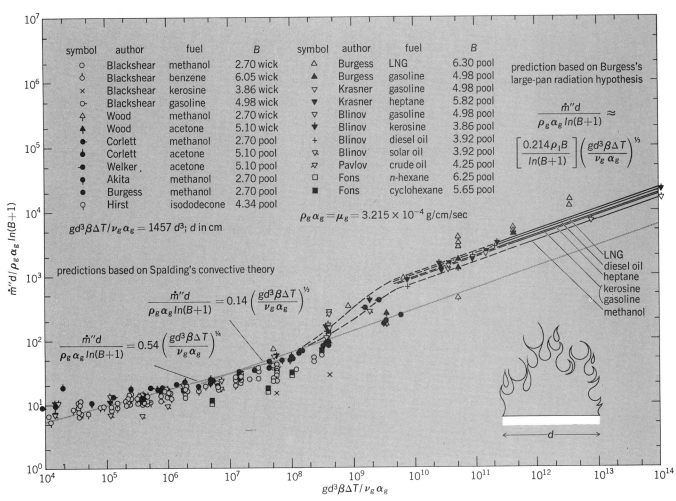

Fig. 7. Laminar and turbulent burning of various fuels on a horizontal surface. Here d is the pool diameter; ρ_l is the liquid fuel density. Other symbols are the same as in Fig. 6. (*From A. Murty Kanury. The science and engineering of hostile fires, Fire Res. Abstr. Rev., 15(3), 1974*)

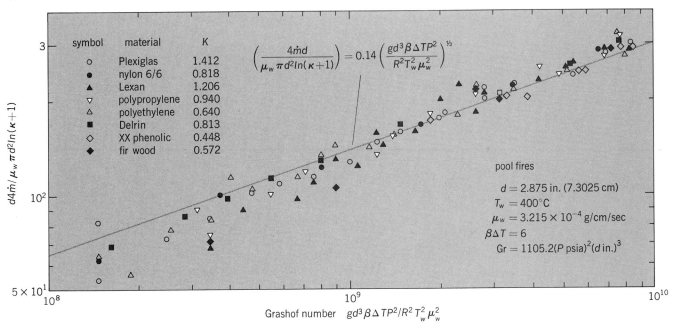

Fig. 8. Modeling of pool fires with a variety of polymers. Here $\dot{m}$ is burning rate; μ_w is gas-phase dynamic viscosity at fuel surface; T_w is fuel surface temperature; R is universal gas constant; P is ambient pressure; and κ is mass-transfer driving force modified for radiative feedback. (*From A. Murty Kanury, Modeling of pool fires with a variety of polymers, 15th International Symposium on Combustion, The Combustion Institute, Pittsburgh, 1975*)

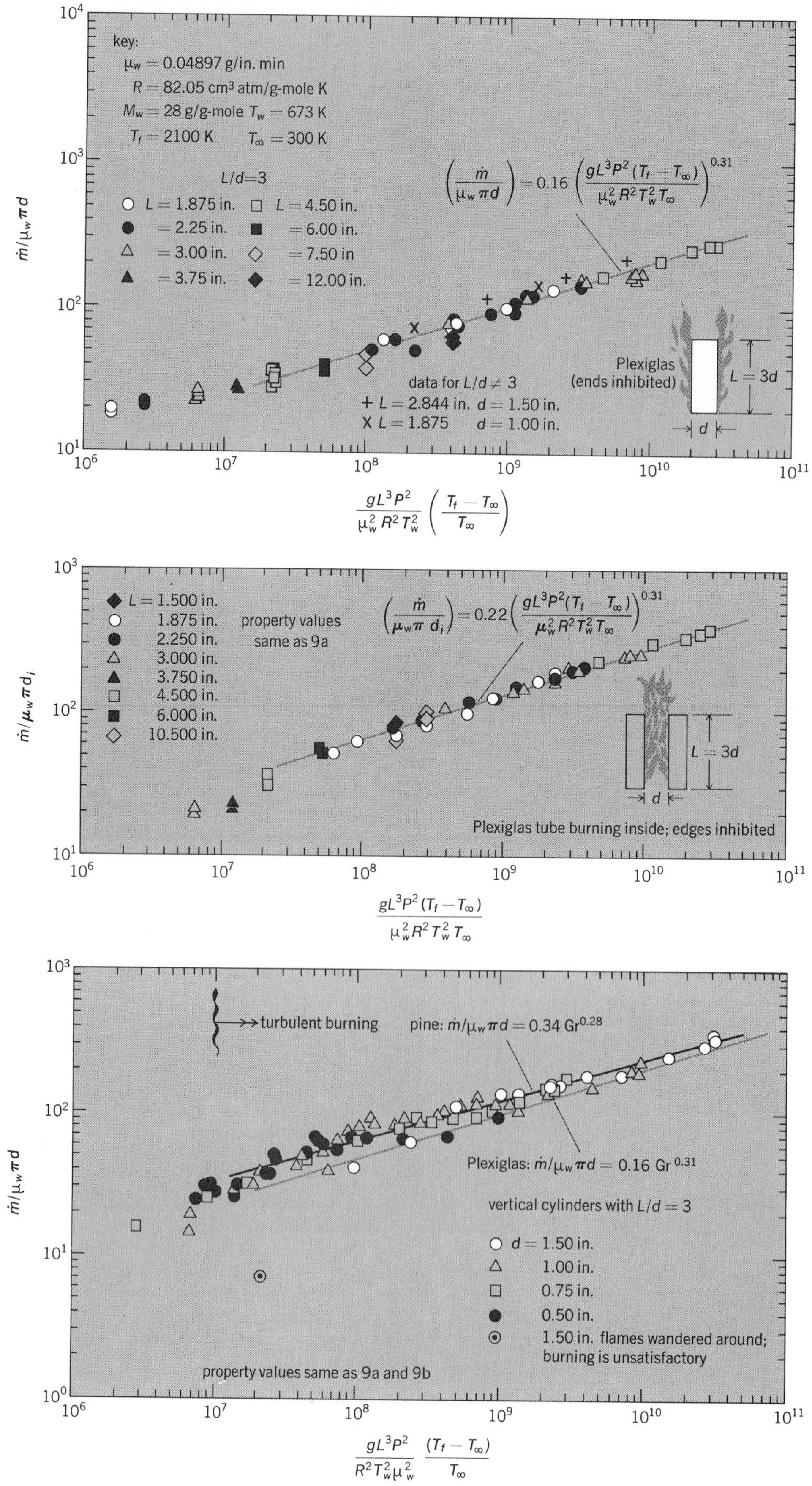

key:
$\mu_w = 0.04897$ g/in. min
$R = 82.05$ cm^3 atm/g-mole K
$M_w = 28$ g/g-mole $T_w = 673$ K
$T_f = 2100$ K $T_\infty = 300$ K

$L/d = 3$

○ $L = 1.875$ in.   □ $L = 4.50$ in.
● $= 2.25$ in.   ■ $= 6.00$ in.
△ $= 3.00$ in.   ◇ $= 7.50$ in
▲ $= 3.75$ in.   ◆ $= 12.00$ in.

$$\left(\frac{\dot{m}}{\mu_w \pi d}\right) = 0.16 \left(\frac{gL^3P^2(T_f - T_\infty)}{\mu_w^2 R^2 T_w^2 T_\infty}\right)^{0.31}$$

data for $L/d \neq 3$
+ $L = 2.844$ in. $d = 1.50$ in.
X $L = 1.875$ $d = 1.00$ in.

Plexiglas (ends inhibited) $L = 3d$ d

$\dot{m}/\mu_w \pi d$

$$\frac{gL^3P^2}{\mu_w^2 R^2 T_w^2}\left(\frac{T_f - T_\infty}{T_\infty}\right)$$

$L = 1.500$ in.
1.875 in.
2.250 in.
3.000 in.
3.750 in.
4.500 in.
6.000 in.
10.500 in.

property values same as 9a

$$\left(\frac{\dot{m}}{\mu_w \pi d_i}\right) = 0.22 \left(\frac{gL^3P^2(T_f - T_\infty)}{\mu_w^2 R^2 T_w^2 T_\infty}\right)^{0.31}$$

$L = 3d$ d

Plexiglas tube burning inside; edges inhibited

$\dot{m}/\mu_w \pi d_i$

$$\frac{gL^3P^2(T_f - T_\infty)}{\mu_w^2 R^2 T_w^2 T_\infty}$$

→ turbulent burning   pine: $\dot{m}/\mu_w \pi d = 0.34$ Gr$^{0.28}$

Plexiglas: $\dot{m}/\mu_w \pi d = 0.16$ Gr$^{0.31}$

vertical cylinders with $L/d = 3$

○ $d = 1.50$ in.
△ 1.00 in.
□ 0.75 in.
● 0.50 in.
⊙ 1.50 in. flames wandered around;
burning is unsatisfactory

property values same as 9a and 9b

$\dot{m}/\mu_w \pi d$

$$\frac{gL^3P^2}{R^2 T_w^2 \mu_w^2}\frac{(T_f - T_\infty)}{T_\infty}$$

Fig. 9. Modeling of vertical wall fires with Plexiglas and pinewood; 1 in. = 2.54 cm. (From J. de Ris, A. Murty Kanury, and M. C. Yuen, Pressure modeling of fires, 14th International Symposium on Combustion, The Combustion Institute, Pittsburgh, pp. 1033–1044, 1973)

modeling of realistic enclosure geometries have yet to be fully investigated.

CONCLUSION

Only with a thorough, unbiased understanding of the role played by a host of physical and chemical processes can experts successfully devise effective, efficient, and reliable schemes to assess, avoid, or minimize the deplorable destruction of life and property by fires. Current fire protection practice, as has been emphasized in this article, uses little scientific information—which itself is in a limited state of development. It is imperative to know in this matter of life and death whether devised practices are in fact the most efficacious ones.   [A. MURTY KANURY]

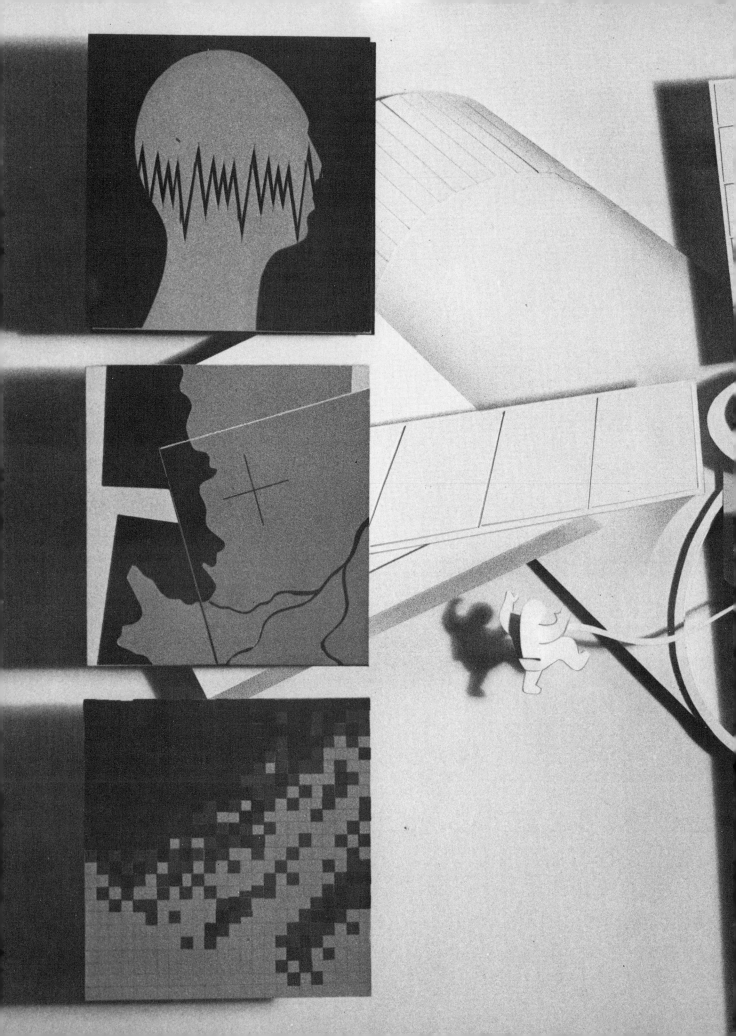

Skylab

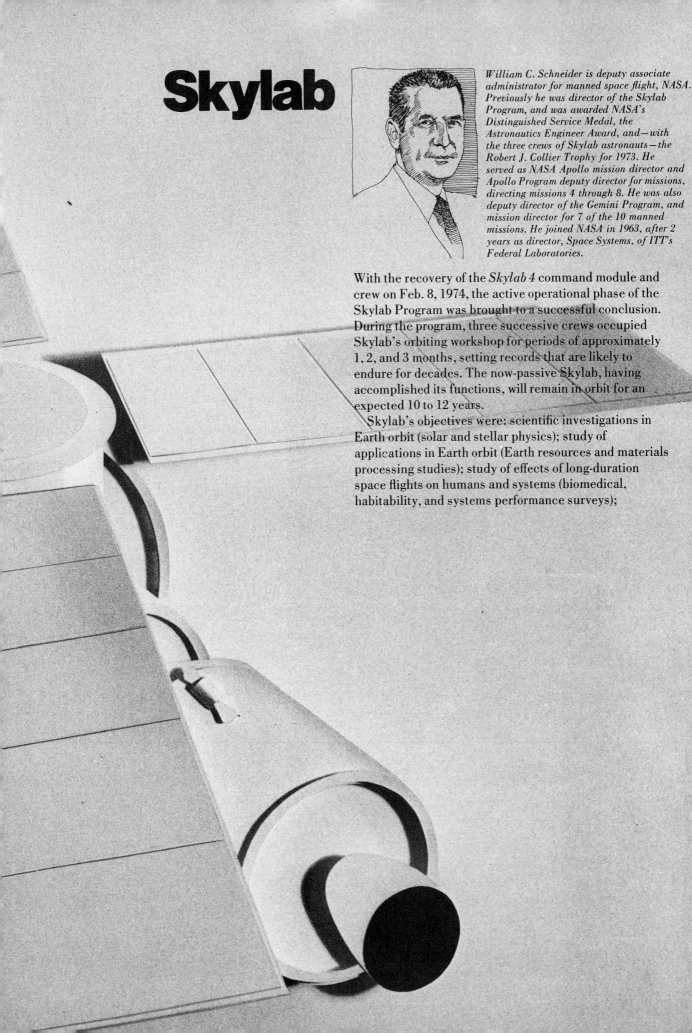

William C. Schneider is deputy associate administrator for manned space flight, NASA. Previously he was director of the Skylab Program, and was awarded NASA's Distinguished Service Medal, the Astronautics Engineer Award, and—with the three crews of Skylab astronauts—the Robert J. Collier Trophy for 1973. He served as NASA Apollo mission director and Apollo Program deputy director for missions, directing missions 4 through 8. He was also deputy director of the Gemini Program, and mission director for 7 of the 10 manned missions. He joined NASA in 1963, after 2 years as director, Space Systems, of ITT's Federal Laboratories.

With the recovery of the *Skylab 4* command module and crew on Feb. 8, 1974, the active operational phase of the Skylab Program was brought to a successful conclusion. During the program, three successive crews occupied Skylab's orbiting workshop for periods of approximately 1, 2, and 3 months, setting records that are likely to endure for decades. The now-passive Skylab, having accomplished its functions, will remain in orbit for an expected 10 to 12 years.

Skylab's objectives were: scientific investigations in Earth orbit (solar and stellar physics); study of applications in Earth orbit (Earth resources and materials processing studies); study of effects of long-duration space flights on humans and systems (biomedical, habitability, and systems performance surveys);

acquisition of data for design and development of future space programs (technology transfer to the space shuttle).

Skylab's success (documented in Table 1) did not come without its share of difficulty. Sixty-three seconds after lift-off of the unmanned Skylab cluster, the orbital workshop meteoroid shield and one solar array were torn off by the slipstream. A second solar panel was jammed by debris so that it could not deploy. This damage reduced electrical power production to about half of that planned. Thus, in a minute's time Skylab was confronted with a catastrophic situation. The meteoroid shield was intended to protect the workshop from penetration by small space particles, and to provide part of the workshop's thermal protection. Without the shield, the thermal protection system was thrown out of balance, thereby exposing the workshop to excessive solar heat to such a degree that it could not possibly support a manned mission.

Stopping temperature rise. The urgent need was to stop the rapid temperature rise which, if allowed to continue, would soon damage film, food, and medicines. The workshop was therefore reoriented so that it was no longer in its design attitude, broadside to the Sun. The abnormal attitude, however, caused an exceptionally high use of attitude control fuel and, in addition, reduced the already limited electrical power output by tilting the fully deployed solar panels on the Apollo telescope mount (a battery of instruments for solar observations) away from the Sun. Clearly, some kind of thermal shield had to be designed, fabricated, and deployed quickly if Skylab was to be saved.

Several excellent suggestions were rapidly formulated and narrowed down to three. The ability of the aerospace team to design and fabricate three different solar shields within 2 weeks, to transport them within the limited confines of the command module, and to deploy one of them in the unfavorable environment of space was in itself a notable achievement. The shield which was initially deployed consisted of a specially treated reflective cloth on a parasol-like mechanism, packed

Table 1.   Skylab mission accomplishments

| Workshop launch | 14 May 73 | | |
| Launch vehicle | Saturn V-513 | | |
Manned missions	I	II	III
Crew launches	25 May 73	28 July 73	16 Nov. 73
Launch vehicle	Saturn 1B-206	Saturn 1B-207	Saturn 1B-208
Command & service module	CSM-116	CSM-117	CSM-118
Crew splashdown	22 June 73	25 Sept. 73	8 Feb. 74
Flight duration (days:hr:min)	28:00:50	59:11:09	84:01:16 (new record)
Crew members			
Commander	Charles Conrad, Jr.	Alan L. Bean	Gerald P. Carr
Scientist pilot	Joseph P. Kerwin	Owen K. Garriott	Edward G. Gibson
Pilot	Paul J. Weitz	Jack R. Lousma	William R. Pogue
Experiment performance			
Earth resources passes	11	39	38
Solar observing man-hours	81	305	308
Comet observing man-hours	—	—	185
Other experiment man-hours	319	915	1198
Unmanned experiment hours	154	443	988
Extravehicular activities			
First EVA	7 June 73	6 Aug. 73	22 Nov. 73
Duration (hr:min)	3:30	6:31	6:30
Principal accomplishments	Freed and deployed workshop solar array.	Deployed twin-pole sunshade over parasol. Installed film in solar telescope.	Installed film in solar telescope. Repaired EREP antenna. Deployed experiment modules.
Second EVA	19 June 73	24 Aug. 73	25 Dec. 73
Duration (hr:min)	1:36	4:30	7:01 (new record)
Principal accomplishments	Film retrieval. Repaired charger battery regulator module.	Installed electrical connectors for rate-gyro package. Changed film in solar telescope.	Observed Comet Kohoutek. Changed film. Repaired cameras.
Third EVA		22 Sept. 73	29 Dec. 73
Duration (hr:min)		2:41	3:39
Principal accomplishments		Retrieved film and experiment data.	Changed film in solar telescope. Observed Comet Kohoutek.
Fourth EVA			3 Feb. 74
Duration (hr:min)			5:19
Principal accomplishments			Retrieved film and experiment modules.

into a canister originally made for storing and deploying instruments outside the workshop. The beauty of the system was that the canister was designed to be used in the workshop scientific airlock, and thus would allow the shield to be deployed from inside the workshop.

Restoring power. While efforts to solve the thermal problem were in progress, similar efforts were under way to solve the electrical problem. On the theory that the remaining workshop solar wing was restrained by debris from the meteoroid shield, a decision was made to provide cutting tools for the crew to use to free the wing. A fly-around in the command module by the first crew confirmed that the meteoroid shield and one solar wing were gone (Fig. 1) and that the second wing was indeed stopped from deploying by an aluminum angle (Fig. 2). Working in space suits through the command module hatch, the crew was unsuccessful in freeing the jammed wing. Now, however, the ground crew had a clear picture of the situation and began a major effort to release the wing.

Docking to Skylab was accomplished that day. The following day the crew entered the workshop and deployed the parasol thermal shield. The drop in temperature was dramatic. However, the power crisis remained. With only the telescope mount solar wings to supply power, the flight and ground crews learned to live with the reduced supply. Flight plans were adjusted to reduce power usage. Changes in attitude to photograph the Earth were shortened, and all nonessential equipment was turned off until needed. Meanwhile, on the ground, procedures to free the solar wing were thoroughly developed, tested, and then explained to the crew. With the work of the men on the ground behind them, the astronauts were able to free the panel while working outside the spacecraft (Fig. 3).

Other equipment problems. Subsequent Skylab missions proceeded almost as planned. Other equipment problems occurred, such as drift of the rate gyros, a leak in the coolant system, and a malfunction in one of the solar instruments. These were significant since they would have a large effect on the missions, and therefore required rapid solutions. The second crew took with them a replacement rate gyro package, which they successfully installed. They also deployed the twin-pole solar shield over the parasol to counter any degradation of the parasol due to ultraviolet radiation. The third crew took a reservicing kit to recharge the coolant system and performed work outside Skylab (extravehicular activity, or EVA) to fix an antenna. The discovery that the ground crew and flight crew can react rapidly to fix or work around crippling problems has been one of the bonuses of America's first space station.

A final malfunction—one that could not be repaired—was the failure of one of the three large gyros that controlled the attitude and stabilized the workshop. Although this was a serious failure Skylab never lost stability, since the system had been designed to work properly when only two gyros were functioning.

THE EXPERIMENTS

Once the workshop temperatures were reduced and Skylab became habitable, the main business at hand was the performance of experiments (listed in Table 2). One cannot select any single experiment area as providing the most important results of the Skylab missions. Skylab has, however, served almost every scientific and technological discipline that could benefit from its special characteristics: the broad view of Earth; the freedom from atmospheric interference in observing the Sun and stars; the absence of gravitational effects; the presence of trained men to make scien-

Fig. 1. Skylab in orbit, photographed from the command module. Meteoroid shield and one solar wing are missing. (*NASA*)

Fig. 2. Skylab's second solar wing, prevented from deploying by a metal part from the meteoroid shield. (*NASA*)

Fig. 3.   Repaired by crew, Skylab wears improvised shield and has second solar wing fully deployed. (*NASA*)

Fig. 4.   San Andreas Fault photographed from Skylab. San Francisco Bay is at center. The fault line runs along the left side of the bay at the juncture of the light and dark areas. Skylab photographs have revealed many previously undetected faults in the area. (*NASA*)

tific observations and to operate the complex equipment. In addition, Skylab has established a base of factual data on which to build future space systems and future manned space operations.

The harvest of benefits is just beginning, as hundreds of investigators in many fields analyze and interpret the results of their experiments. However, preliminary findings have already been made in some of the areas of investigation and are discussed in the following sections.

EARTH RESOURCES

From their vantage point far above the Earth, the Skylab crews acquired 40,000 photographs and 240,000 ft (73,120 m) of electronically recorded data with a complement of six advanced instruments which formed the Earth resources experiment package (EREP). Over 140 investigator teams from the United States and 20 other countries are evaluating the usefulness of the space-acquired data for studies of crop inventories, crop health, soil moisture, mineral potentials, coastal processes, land and water use, water and air pollution, sea state, ocean currents, fish productivity, and many other subjects that affect the life of all on Earth.

Crop studies. Photographs from a multispectral bank of six cameras and a high-resolution single-frame camera have been used to delineate crop acreage and to identify crop types. Studies for the State of Michigan classified the quantity of acreage devoted to bare soil, forest, grass, forage, and grains with an adjusted accuracy greater than 90%. With high-resolution photography (to about

Table 2. Skylab experiments

MEDICAL		SOLAR		MATERIALS SCIENCE/MANUFACTURING IN SPACE	
M071	Mineral balance	S052	White light coronagraph	M512	Material-processing facility
M073	Bioassay of body fluids	S054	X-ray spectrographic telescope	M518	Multipurpose electric furnace system
M074	Specimen mass measurement	S055	UV spectrometer (A)	M551	Metals melting
M078	Bone mineral measurement (B)	S056	Dual x-ray telescope	M552	Exothermic brazing
M092	In-flight lower body negative pressure	S082	UV spectrograph/heliograph	M553	Sphere forming
M093	Vectorcardiogram			M555	Gallium arsenide crystal growth
M111	Cytogenetic studies of blood			M556	Vapor growth of II-VI compounds
M112	Human immunity – in vitro aspects	**OPERATIONS**		M557	Immiscible alloy compositions
M113	Blood volume & red cell life-span			M558	Radioactive tracer diffusion
M114	Red blood cell metabolism	M487	Habitability/crew quarters	M559	Microsegregation in germanium
M115	Special hematologic effects	M509	Astronaut maneuvering equipment	M560	Growth of spherical crystals
M131	Human vestibular function	M516	Crew activities/maintenance	M561	Whisker-reinforced composite
M133	Sleep monitoring	T002	Manual navigation sightings (B)	M562	Indium antimonide crystals
M151	Time & motion study	T013	Crew/vehicle disturbance	M563	Mixed III-IV crystal growth
M171	Metabolic activity	T020	Foot-controlled maneuver unit	M564	Metal and halide eutectics
M172	Body mass measurement			M565	Silver grids melted in space
ESS	Experiment support system			M566	Copper-aluminum eutectic
		BIOSCIENCE			
EARTH RESOURCES		S015	Zero-gravity single human cell	**SCIENCE**	
		S071	Circadian rhythm – pocket mice		
S190	Multispectral photographic facility	S072	Circadian rhythm – vinegar gnat	S009	Nuclear emulsion
		T003	In-flight aerosol analysis	S019	UV stellar astronomy
S191	Infrared spectrometer	D008	Radiation in spacecraft	S020	UV/x-ray solar photography
S192	Multispectral scanner			S063	UV airglow horizon photography
S193	Microwave radiometer/ scatterometer & altimeter			S073	Gegenschein/zodiacal light
		TECHNOLOGY		S149	Particle collection
S194	L-band radiometer			S150	Galactic x-ray mapping (B)
ESE	EREP support equipment	D024	Thermal control coatings	S183	UV panorama
		M415	Thermal control coatings	S201	UV electronographic camera
		M479	Zero-gravity flammability (B)	S228	Transuranic cosmic rays
		T025	Coronagraph contamination measurement	S230	Magnetospheric particle composition
		T027	ATM contamination measurement	S232	Barium plasma observation
		T053	Earth laser beacon	S233	Comet Kohoutek observation

10 m), agricultural fields of 5 acres (1 acre = 4047 m²) and woodlots as small as 2 acres can be mapped. In California, the early summer acreage devoted to rice was correctly assessed with an 82% accuracy. In Texas, citrus-grove, sugarcane, or vegetable fields as small as 2 acres were identifiable. The techniques being developed for discern-

ing crop acreage and identifying crop types may eventually provide an accurate and convenient means for estimating world food production.

Geological studies. Space imagery has provided a new and useful tool for geological study of large areas. EREP photographs are being used to map large faults, fractures, and lithologic units (Fig. 4).

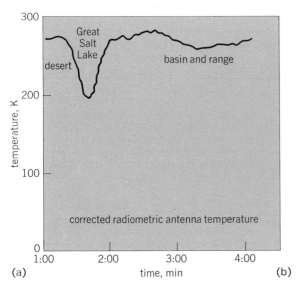

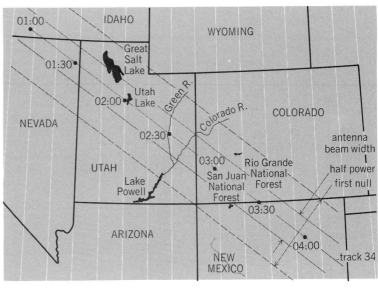

Fig. 5. The radiometer applications experiment indicates the presence of moisture in the upper soil by the lower brightness temperature between 3:00 and 4:00 min (in the Colorado—New Mexico region). (a) Graph of temperature data from (b) Skylab radiometric scan of western states. (NASA)

It appears that systematic exploration for major ore prospects in a large favorable region can be accomplished perhaps five times as rapidly at one-fifth the cost of conventional methods. The EREP data show many large geologic features genetically related to major ore deposits which cannot be seen in the field, on geological maps, or with aerial photography. EREP data are also being used to map strip mining acreage and to detect potential mine hazards. Thermal infrared imagery of northern California has been successfully correlated with geothermal sources located at the Geysers, an area where geothermal steam is being used to generate electricity for San Francisco.

Snow cover. Mapping of the extent of snow cover has been accomplished with space imagery more accurately than is possible from ground measurements or from most existing aerial survey techniques. Studies using data acquired with the EREP multispectral scanner show a remarkable reversal in the reflectance of snow between the visible and near-infrared bands. The sharp drop in reflectance is believed to be a result of meltwater on the snow surface.

Water quality, represented by chlorophyll concentration, for Conesus Lake and Lake Ontario has been derived from EREP photographic data and has been found to be in excellent agreement with aircraft measurements.

With the EREP L-band passive microwave radiometer, which penetrates a short distance into the Earth, a good correlation has been obtained between antenna temperature and soil moisture (Fig. 5). The data indicate that the technique could provide reliable estimates of soil moisture over a given region. Vegetation and other factors that affect emitted visual and infrared radiation do not degrade data collected by the radiometer.

Land-use mapping. Initial analyses of EREP photography indicate that detailed land-use map-

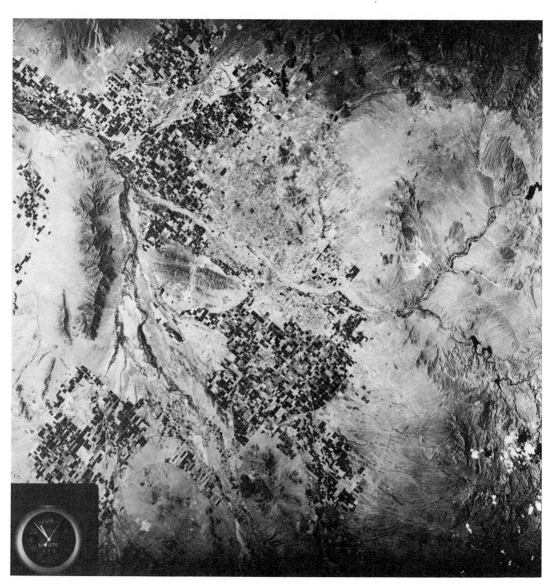

Fig. 6. Land-use mapping. Phoenix, AZ, is the light speckled area on the north side of the Salt River, in center of photograph; the cities of Tempe and Mesa lie on the south side. The darker checkerboard areas are agricultural. (NASA)

ping to a scale of 1:25,000 (Fig. 6) is possible with high-resolution camera systems. A computer-generated land-use recognition map was produced from EREP data with an overall accuracy of 85%.

The oceans. Optical and microwave data are demonstrating new techniques for understanding the oceans. Mapping shallow water features around the world is possible according to studies which show that multispectral data can delineate the shape and extent of shoals and reefs (Fig. 7) and the general trend of bottom bathymetry. Underwater linear features which are not discernible on existing maps are seen in the EREP data. Many geoidal variations, such as the surface depression over the Puerto Rico Trench, measured by Skylab's microwave altimeter, have been correlated with major subsurface topography variations. High-resolution sunlight enhanced photography has provided evidence of large (12 to 32 km) eddies associated with the known location of a current system. These eddies are believed to be cooler than the current and may be an important meteorological factor.

The results of the EREP investigations are bringing close the day when remote sensing from space will be used routinely in determining what actions should be taken in managing the world's resources.

SOLAR OBSERVATIONS

After only a few months of dedicated effort on data reduction and analysis, it is apparent that the Skylab solar data, together with data from associated ground-based observing programs, will revolutionize solar physics. A battery of instruments contained in the Apollo telescope mount (ATM) was designed to observe the solar chromosphere, transition region, and corona with good spatial, spectral, and temporal resolution. The primary

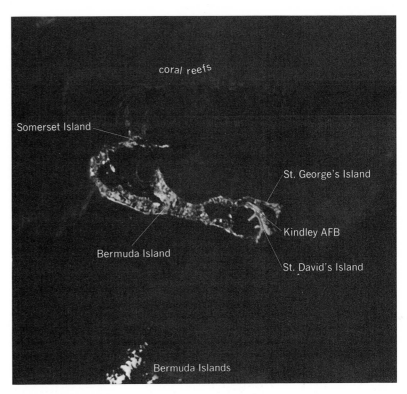

Fig. 7. Shoals and reefs near Bermuda are evident in the diagram made from multispectral data collected on Skylab. (*NASA*)

purpose of the instruments was to achieve understanding of the heating mechanisms, energy balance conditions, and plasma instabilities in the Sun's outer atmosphere. A summary of the individual instruments flown and of the specific solar regions observed appears in Table 3.

Table 3.   ATM solar instrument summary

Instrument	Sponsor	Spectral coverage, A*	Solar region observed	Spatial resolution, arc-seconds	Spectral resolution, A	Maximum picture rate, per min	Data form
X-ray telescope	American Science and Engineering Company	3–60	Corona	2	0–15	96	70-mm film 5 cameras 7000 frames each
X-ray telescope	NASA Marshall Spaceflight Center	6–33	Low corona	2–5	2–5	77	35-mm film 5 cameras 7200 frames each
XUV spectro-heliograph	U.S. Naval Research Laboratory	150–615	Chromosphere	5	0–13	1	35-mm film 6 cameras 200 strip frames each
UV spectro-heliometer	Harvard College Observatory	300–1400	Chromosphere	5	1–2	9 lines	Photoelectric, digital data
UV spectrograph	U.S. Naval Research Laboratory	970–3940	Chromosphere	3	0–08	4	35-mm film 4 cameras 1600 frames each
White light coronagraph	High Altitude Observatory	3500–7000	Outer corona	8	Broadband	4	35-mm film 5 cameras 8000 frames each
Hα telescope	Harvard College Observatory	6563	Low chromosphere	1	0–7	4	35-mm film 5 cameras 16,000 frames each

*10 A = 1 nm.

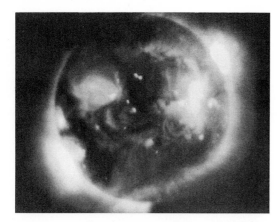

Fig. 8. X-ray photograph of solar corona showing numerous small bright points, closed-loop structures, large bright active region, and dark coronal holes. (*American Science and Engineering, Inc.*)

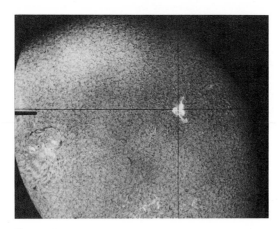

Fig. 9. Solar flare photographed from Skylab's Apollo telescope mount. (*Harvard College Observatory*)

Fig. 10. Balloon-shaped disturbance on the Sun, photographed from Skylab on June 10, 1973. (*High Altitude Observatory, National Center for Atmospheric Research, Boulder, CO*)

Bright points. A class of features observed for the first time in detail from ATM are x-ray and ultraviolet bright points. These features have been found to be more numerous than anticipated from previous sounding-rocket observations. It is estimated that as many as 1500 bright points emerge per day. They are small compared to major features on the Sun, and their mean lifetime is of the order of 8 hr. The most outstanding property of bright points—which distinguishes them from active regions—is that they are distributed uniformly over the entire solar disk. The magnetic field configuration associated with these features is unknown but is currently being investigated.

Bright points appear to be formed low in the atmosphere, and to have a temperature comparable to that of the quiet corona but a density two to four times larger than the quiet Sun density at that altitude. The bright points flare on time scales of the order of minutes. Since the structure of the points is so simple, these features may provide a unique tool for the investigation of flares.

The corona. Soft x-ray observations of the corona (Fig. 8) obtained from ATM destroy all vestiges of the concept of a homogeneous background corona which had served as a basis for much of modern solar physics. The new observations reveal the corona to be composed almost entirely of closed-loop structures which trace the form of the magnetic field lines. Active regions are seen as overlapping clusters of closed loops, the most compact and hottest of which are low in the atmosphere. Systems of large-scale loops, termed filament cavities, overlay quiescent filaments.

Finally, large-scale, apparently open features are present, devoid of any soft x-ray emission and surrounded by diverging boundary structures. These features are called coronal holes. Emissions from ionized helium exhibit anomalous behavior in these regions. In the quiet Sun, these emissions are about 10 times stronger than expected, while in coronal holes they are weaker. Several theoretical explanations of the anomaly are being considered. One explanation is the possible existence of a "transient ionization state" resulting from the extreme temperature sensitivity of the collisional excitation term for helium. Another explanation involves some unknown exciting force present in the quiet Sun but not in holes. Comparisons of the structure of the corona with that of the solar wind have verified that coronal holes are the source of recurrent high-velocity streams in the solar wind.

The study of flares from ATM (Fig. 9) was hampered by the fact that the instrument controls could not be manned at all times. However, interesting results on the time history of several flare events have been obtained, and analyses of these events as seen at both ultraviolet and x-ray wavelengths are in progress.

Some of the most interesting transient events observed from ATM took place in the outer corona. There was, on the average, a transient event every 72 hr during the first two Skylab missions. These coronal ejections typically took the form of expanding loops of magnetic field whose foot points remained anchored in the photosphere. Balloon-shaped disturbances, up to a solar radius in size (Fig. 10), were seen to expand outward from the solar surface with velocities ranging from 200 to 450 km/sec. In many cases, pressure waves could be seen distorting the surrounding coronal structures. In the majority of events, the transients were associated with eruptive prominences.

Additional studies are in progress on active region evolution, on the structure of quiescent prominences, and on the relationship between the corona and the solar wind. It is apparent that the true value of the ATM data will be realized only after several more years of dedicated and coordinated analysis.

COMET KOHOUTEK

Comet Kohoutek is a characteristic example of the family of comets that have periods of revolution around the Sun of many tens of thousands of years. As such, it demonstrated a brightness variation and tail structure similar to many other comets. What set Kohoutek apart from other comets is that its passage was subjected to more scientific observation than ever before. The attention resulted because Kohoutek was discovered while still very distant from the Sun, allowing ample time to organize observations by a variety of techniques. The comet was observed in many wavelengths of the electromagnetic spectrum, from the far-ultraviolet through the radio frequencies, and by observatories throughout the world. Skylab provided more observations than any other single observatory and conducted many unique experiments because it could observe objects close to the Sun from its orbit above the Earth's obscuring atmosphere (Fig. 11).

Kohoutek, along with other comets, may be among the oldest objects of the solar system and little changed by subsequent events since its creation. Therefore, knowledge of the structure and composition of this comet may provide insight into the solar system's evolution and the chemistry of objects from the system's outer fringes. At present, it is not known for certain what comets are made of or how they are put together. However, observations of Kohoutek are consistent with a model which assumes that the comet was formed out of material similar to that found in interstellar space. The materials of the comet seem to be hydrogen, carbon dioxide, and water, with a small amount of hydrogen cyanide and methyl cyanide in ice and clathrate form. The main body of the nucleus is probably composed of a porous material with extremely low strength, and was probably never heated above 100 K (−173°C).

Comet Kohoutek ejected more material before perihelion than after. This behavior suggests that the surface of the comet, which probably had never come close to the Sun before, may be much more fragile than that of comets that have repeatedly come close.

Since the nucleus cannot be observed directly and since most molecules such as water are fully ionized close to the nucleus, the observations of the comet and tail are of utmost importance. Observations of these regions from Skylab were made by photography, spectroscopy, and infrared photometry.

The observations from Skylab just after Comet Kohoutek swung past the Sun suggest that parti-

cles up to 1 mm in diameter were ejected from the nucleus. This is 100 times larger than particles that usually form the dust tails of comets. The Kohoutek particles were more numerous than previously believed and more volatile. Moreover, the gravity of the nucleus influenced their ejection. These larger particles probably form the meteor streams that periodically produce brilliant meteor showers in the Earth's atmosphere.

Skylab's extensive observations of Comet Kohoutek provide unique data to cometary science and will significantly improve understanding of what a comet really is.

MATERIALS PROCESSING IN SPACE

A group of experiments on Skylab evaluated how the conditions of space might affect the properties of materials processed in orbit. The experiments were performed in a materials processing facility installed in the multiple docking adapter (Fig. 12). The facility consisted essentially of a vacuum chamber, connected to the space vacuum outside the vehicle, a heat-treating apparatus, including an electron-beam gun, and a small electric furnace for processing samples of diverse materials inside the chamber.

The experiments were conducted to assess the potential of materials processing in space for industrial research purposes and eventual manufacturing operations on future space missions. All of these experiments involved processes in which materials were melted or evaporated and then resolidified, the objective being to determine how the weightlessness of the melted or vaporized materials could be exploited to control the formation of the final solid and thereby obtain various desirable properties. Control over such processes on Earth tends to be marginal, because of the force of gravity acting on the density differences that arise from temperature differences during cooling. The density differences generate turbulent convection

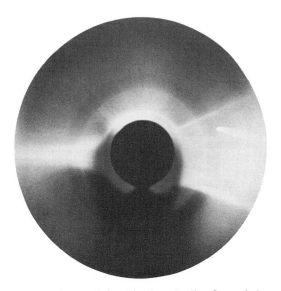

Fig. 11. Comet Kohoutek close to the Sun, photographed from Skylab on Dec. 27, 1973. (*High Altitude Observatory, National Center for Atmospheric Research, Boulder, CO*)

Fig. 12. The materials processing facility on board Skylab. (*NASA*)

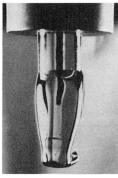

Fig. 13. Crystal grown from molten material at zero gravity. Facets of the crystal are optically flat over about 30% of their surface. (*NASA*)

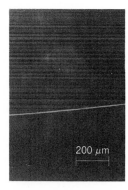

200 μm

Fig. 14. Sections of indium-antimonide crystal, Earth-grown (top) and space-grown (bottom). No dopant inhomogeneities are evident in the space-grown section. (*NASA*)

currents that make it difficult or impossible to control the exact composition of the material from which the solid is formed.

The Skylab experiments verified that melts and vapors remain quiescent under normal flight conditions even when applied temperature conditions are extreme. The most extreme conditions studied were produced in an experiment in which beads of pure nickel and three selected nickel alloys were melted by the electron beam and then allowed to freeze by free cooling. In all cases, motions of the material during solidification were entirely due to forces generated by the freezing process itself. The samples provided a uniquely detailed and informative record of all stages of the process.

Eleven experiments were performed in the electric furnace of the materials processing facility under more moderate and closely controlled conditions. They furnished quantitative data on solidification of convectionless melts and vapors, and yielded several results pointing toward the future feasibility of space processing of electronic materials. In three experiments on the formation of semiconductor crystals by controlled solidification of melts, the basic crystal structure formed in space was in all cases more perfect than could be obtained on Earth. In one of these experiments, crystals were formed from drops of molten material that hung without any other support from the ends

of single crystal "seeds." The crystals (Fig. 13) formed in this way had optically flat facets over about 30% of their surfaces, which has given rise to speculation that the forces intrinsic to solidification might eventually be controlled to produce crystals directly in the form of thin flat wafers such as are used to manufacture semiconductor components.

Uniformity of chemical composition can be as important in semiconductor applications as uniformity of crystal structure, because the electrical characteristics of semiconductors are controlled by intentionally added impurities. Two of the Skylab semiconductor crystal experiments verified that much more uniform composition is obtained by growth from convectionless melts in space than under conditions available on Earth. Figure 14 shows an example of the striking difference demonstrated in one of the experiments. It is expected that further development of ultrauniform semiconductor crystals may lead to significant improvements in technology for manufacturing integrated circuits for computers and other applications.

Dramatic results were also obtained in an experiment on the growth of semiconductors by vaporization and condensation. The experiment produced well-formed platelets of material with nearly perfect crystal structure. Most of the crystal platelets were of about the same order of magnitude in

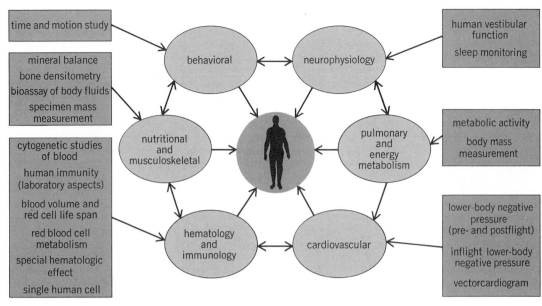

Fig. 15. Relationships between life science experiments conducted on Skylab. (*NASA*)

size as those used in transistors and integrated circuits, but one of them was approximately 10 times as large as the rest. Moreover, the total amount of crystal material produced in the experiment was about 10 times as large as had been theoretically predicted. Neither of these effects has been explained as yet, and it is expected that significant advances in crystal growth technology will result when they are fully understood.

BIOMEDICAL STUDIES

One of Skylab's primary objectives was to determine and evaluate the physiological responses and aptitudes of humans under long-duration zero-gravity conditions, and readaptation to the environment upon return to Earth.

A series of medical experiments were designed to study these responses, and comparisons were made between data collected before, during, and after the flight. The interrelationship of these studies is illustrated in Fig. 15. Baseline data were collected periodically on each crewman—including backup crewmen—commencing about a year prior to flight. Similar data were taken after each flight until the crew member regained his preflight baseline condition.

Trend data. During the flight, biomedical experiments were performed on a schedule of sufficient frequency to develop trend data as the flight progressed. For instance, in support of the nutritional and musculoskeletal studies, inflight data were collected daily on crewman weight, caloric intake, mass of fecal matter, fluid intake, urine output, and exercise levels. These data were transmitted to the ground for development of trend information and for evaluation of each crewman's physical condition. In addition, urine samples and fecal material were collected daily and preserved for postflight analysis. At approximately 3-day intervals, data were collected on heart rate, blood pressure, cardiac outputs, and metabolic activity while

the cardiovascular system was stressed at predetermined exercise levels. Vestibular tests were conducted on each crewman several times during a mission to measure the adaptation of his balance and movement-detection systems to weightlessness. The amount and depth of sleep were measured periodically on one astronaut of each Skylab crew to determine the effects of zero gravity on sleep (Fig. 16).

In all, 16 life science experiments were conducted on Skylab. To accomplish these studies, experiment hardware had to be developed that would meet the operational conditions and constraints of space flight, and could be operated without a great amount of training by crew members not normally involved in medical studies.

Weightlessness. In the three Skylab missions, many new things were learned about humans in

Fig. 16. Skylab astronaut Joseph Kerwin, in a sleep restraint, wears a sleep monitor cap. (*NASA*)

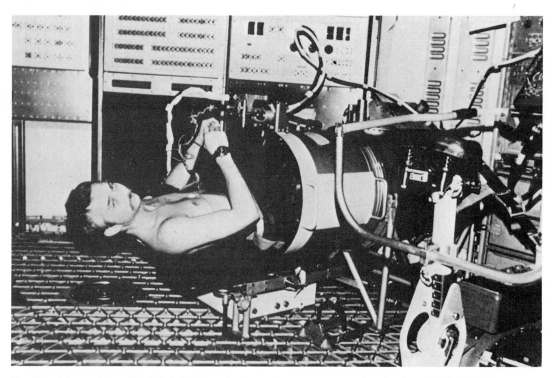

Fig. 17.   Astronaut Owen Garriott during lower-body negative-pressure experiment on board Skylab. *(NASA)*

weightlessness. The adjustment to weightlessness was found to be easier than the readjustment to Earth gravity upon return. After initial adaptive periods, all crewmen exhibited a marked increase in tolerance to motion sickness. A suction device (Fig. 17) that developed a negative pressure on the lower half of the crewman's body was used as an analog of gravity to challenge the astronaut's cardiovascular system. The negative pressure tended to pool the blood in the legs. The body's response was followed by measuring heart rate, blood pressure, and the swelling of the legs. While cardiovascular deconditioning was observed in flight, it did not impair the crew's health or their ability to function effectively. These changes appear to be adaptive and tend to stabilize after 3 or 4 weeks.

There were no significant decreases in work capacity or physiological responses to exercise. A regular daily inflight personal exercise program with appropriate dietary intake and adequate sleep appears essential for maintaining crew health. The eating and sleeping habits of the astronauts were about the same as on Earth. In general, the medical findings on Skylab showed that there were no physiological changes that would preclude longer-duration manned space flight.

Benefits of medical studies. The medical studies conducted on Skylab will benefit understanding of basic body physiology of humans on Earth. For example, in ground-based studies prolonged bed rest is used to simulate weightlessness, the effects of which are a drop in blood pressure and increase in heart rate on standing, calcium loss from bones, and loss of muscle mass. From Skylab data, these effects have been quantified, and countermeasures can now be developed to help hospital patients who are confined to bed for extended periods. In addition, understanding of the response of the heart and blood vessels to some pressure and volume changes induced by weightlessness will assist future ground studies of heart disease, heart failure, and hypertension. And the medical technology—both the equipment and the procedures—used to conduct the Skylab studies can be applied to health care on Earth.

SKYLAB'S IMPACT ON FUTURE SPACE OPERATIONS

If the potential of future space operations is to be fully realized, certain questions must be answered: Can humans function effectively in space over relatively long periods of time? Will the useful services humans can perform in space compensate for the added cost and complexity required to put them there? Are there worthwhile experiments, tasks, and services which can be accomplished only through manned operations? Is it important to develop a system capable of lifting very large and heavy payloads into Earth orbit?

Until Skylab, the answers could be assessed only by analyses, studies, and considerable extrapolation of data from the earlier manned space missions. Now, the Skylab missions have furnished concrete answers. The physiological effects of adaptation to orbital flight for periods up to 12 weeks and the subsequent readaptation to Earth gravity impose no limitations. Equally important, all nine crewmen found living in space enjoyable and exhilarating. They found they could work long and productive hours.

Even more to the point, Skylab showed clearly that there is important work for humans to do in space. The dramatic recovery from near-disaster early in the first mission and the steady routine that developed in the later missions provide strong endorsement for the full exploitation of human capabilities in space. The ability of men to react to unplanned events and to modify procedures, to improvise and to repair, was the key to the success of the Skylab missions.

The space programs now being planned for the 1980s—the space shuttle, the European-built spacelab, and hundreds of scientific and applications payloads that will use these vehicles—can move forward with assurance based on factual experience. Major program decisions as well as many specific details of design and operations will benefit from the wealth of data amassed from the Skylab missions.   [WILLIAM C. SCHNEIDER]

Sensors for Industrial Automation

*James Lawrence Nevins is division leader
of the Automation and Man-Machine
Systems Division of Charles Stark Draper
Laboratory, Inc. He is the principal
investigator for an applied research project
sponsored by the National Science
Foundation on an adaptable-programmable-
modular industrial assembly system. At the
Draper Laboratory, he has directed the
Space Nuclear Systems Office (SNSO)
project in support of the NERVA engine
instrumentation and control system, the
SNSO project to develop a multimode
remote manipulator system, and the design
and implementation of the human-machine
interfaces for the Apollo and Lunar
Excursion Module guidance, navigation,
and control systems.*

In recent years, research and development work in
automation has stressed the need for new and
imaginative approaches to sensors and sensing systems
—largely because it has now been recognized that the
need for new sensors and data-feedback systems is
common to a number of disciplines in which some form
of reliable automation is desirable. Developments in one
discipline can be applied to similar problems in others—
with benefit to all. Among the fields that stand to
benefit are medicine, for diagnosis and rehabilitation;
industry, with emphasis on manufacturing processes;
work performance in environments hostile to humans;
and distribution.

For example, bilateral benefits can result from the
synergistic coupling of automation with human-
rehabilitation engineering. This is not as disparate a
union as it might seem. Defense, aerospace, and

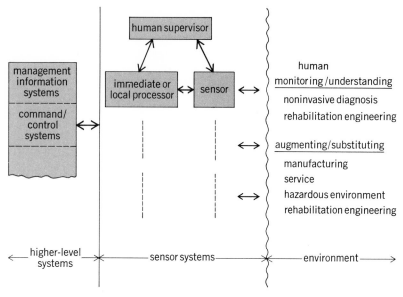

Fig. 1. A model of a sensor and associated subsystems. (*H. D. Nayar, ed., Proceedings of the NSF Research Workshop on Sensors for Automation, April 1973*)

industrial automation, there is a tendency toward viewing problems in a holistic frame in which various interdependent elements of a process or system are defined, along with the information requirements of each, in an integrated fashion.

It is important to remember, however, that manufacturing is more an experience-based industry than a science-based one. For this reason—and for obvious economic reasons—sensors, like other improvements, have evolved in the industry on an "add as you need it" basis. It is hardly economically feasible, for example, for a firm to throw out its existing equipment and start anew. Instead, individual sensors are tacked on as new needs arise.

As automation requirements for manufacturing become more complex, however, this type of solution becomes simplistic—particularly in a world that in other technical areas is thinking in terms of information loops and feedback systems. The new approach to solving these problems therefore includes the entire concept of computer-managed manufacturing (CMM): system and software architecture, high-level computer languages, computer-processor organization for multilevel systems, and, of course, sensors at the interface between the systems and the universe from which data are to be gathered and work to be controlled.

Figure 1 illustrates the concept which views the "environment" as a source of data to be utilized for accomplishing specific functions. (There is intentional distinction made in this article between the terms data and information. Data are understood to lack form and specification, while information is applicable to a specified end.) The functions, in turn, define the kinds of information needed and, therefore, the types of sensors (the sensor modality) required, including the associated processing and formatting of the information necessary to modify the specific process and, thus,

industrial applications have tended to emphasize the hardware through which the environment can be manipulated. Rehabilitation has been more concerned with the problems of generating meaningful artificial sensory inputs to the human and coupling the human's cognitive ability to an external manipulator. The fields, therefore, are complementary.

As logical and mutually beneficial as this direction of thinking may seem, it is not yet widespread enough to be implemented. In general, however, there is a trend toward perceiving the problems of sensor requirements somewhat differently than in the past. Within the area of

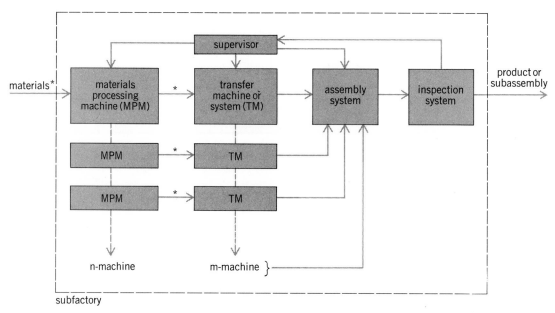

Fig. 2. A subfactory. Asterisks = quality-control monitoring points. (*Charles Stark Draper Laboratory, Cambridge, MA*)

to close the loop. The figure shows that defining requirements and seeking solutions in terms of information needs—rather than simply of sensors—enlarges the possibility of seeing similarities between the requirements of medicine for diagnosis, for example, and of industrial automation.

It is clear, then, that discussing sensors apart from the context of their use to perform a series of integrated functions has little meaning, except for the component specialist. For the types of advanced automation systems envisioned, it becomes necessary to define the application, possible ways of organizing the system (system architecture), and the kinds of information needed to make the system perform. The mention of performance further implies a need for specification of the information—both static and dynamic—needed to achieve system goals. All this must be done efficiently and economically.

With this broader view, sensors and sensory systems can be discussed as they apply to the automation of manufacturing discrete parts for the durable-goods industry. To begin, consider a subfactory where a small mechanism can be manufactured and where the parts are put together to form subassemblies. The mechanism itself can be a small element of a much larger mechanism; for example, a carburetor for an automobile, or a pump for a clothes washer. The subfactory (Fig. 2) contains all the processes—each of which is a system—required to perform manufacturing: (1) material processing (metal removal—that is, machining—or plastic forming); (2) internal transportation (parts and material); (3) assembly; (4) inspection. The subfactory needs additional systems for specifying what is to be manufactured, and how. It also needs systems for scheduling the manufacturing, the ordering of materials, warehousing, and whatever else is required to effectively manage the entire process. These systems can be loosely termed management information systems.

The rest of this article describes the present status of system organization for manufacturing, the information requirements (for example, the sensor system requirements), the apparent directions the manufacturing systems are moving toward, and the impact these directions will have on sensor system technology.

ORGANIZATION OF MANUFACTURING SYSTEMS TODAY

Systems for automating material processing, material transportation, and assembly have been constructed for commercial production based on the requirements of a particular process or product. Reproducibility has been obtained by rigidly controlling materials and jigging or positioning. Once designed, developed, and checked out, these systems can reproduce simple mechanisms indefinitely (if, of course, wear is ignored). Their success, however, depends on the absence of variation; every action and every operation must be precisely the same as every other—within, of course, some design tolerance. These requirements naturally limit flexibility of output. They limit, for example, the possibility of introducing changes to the mechanism, of mixing models, or of changing over to new products or new models.

Material processing. The manufacture of automobile engine blocks on transfer lines is an example of one of the more complex sequence of tasks carried out by an automated material-processing system. This type of manufacturing requires approximately 5 years for a proper return on investment for equipment, costing perhaps $5,000,000. To actually obtain this return, the product must not vary during the economic life cycle of the equipment. Should changes occur, expensive retooling will be necessary.

Assembly. Assembly systems for high-volume production operate under a set of ground rules similar to that of materials processing. However, since the tasks that can be handled by automated assembly systems are fairly simple, the equipment operates on payback cycles of 2 to 3 years and costs in the $50,000 to $250,000 range—an order of magnitude less than that for material processing. The limitations are similar, however. There is no model mixing, and operations are limited to fixed jigging or positioning.

Newer systems of even greater complexity that integrate both metal removal (machining) functions and assembly functions have been implemented for a number of subassemblies. Figure 3 shows an example involving washing-machine gear boxes.

In the system, a washing-machine transmission starts as a raw (preinspected) casting that is clamped in a fixture pallet, faced across a gasket

Fig. 3. System that both machines and assembles gear boxes for home clothes washers. (*American Machinist*)

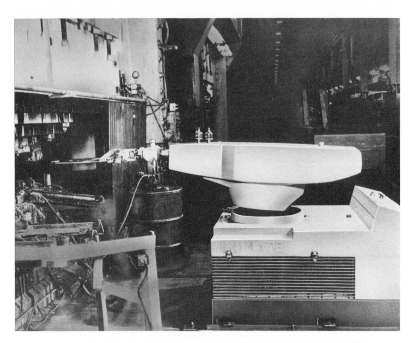

Fig. 4. Unimate loading and unloading a press. (*Unimation Inc., Danbury, CT*)

surface by a cross-feed milling center, drilled in several locations, hollow-milled and bored to produce a precision pocket, and then tapped. After passing through a washing unit that removes chips and trapped cutting oil, the part goes to mechanized inspection stations (for hole probing, pocket-diameter gaging, and other measurements) and then to assembly stations where a set of premachined gears and stub shafts are inserted, the assembly is greased, and a cover plate is added and bolted down. This processing is not fully automatic—because some of the loading and positioning operations are manual.

Material transport. Material transport systems have also been automated—again with similar limitations. They range from rigid systems such as conveyor belts to more flexible programmable systems such as stacker cranes, power- and free-conveyor systems, or stationary put-and-take machines such as Unimates (Fig. 4). The stacker crane systems and power- and free-conveyor systems also provide programmable temporary storage for items in process. In some factories, overhead conveyor systems also provide nonprogrammable circulating storage.

Open-loop positioning. Most of the systems just discussed can be classified as open-loop-control positioning devices. Open-loop control means that these machines receive no data (or very little data) from the work environment in which they function. Thus, they cannot respond in a reasonable and flexible way to such changes in the environment as variations of parts or materials. Should this type of machine become out of phase with interacting equipment, both it and the equipment could be severely damaged. One of the first, most important types of information incorporated into the controllers for these machines, therefore, is the discrete information necessary to properly sequence the machine (for example, such facts as whether parts

are pushed all the way in, or tools are present). Later discussions will describe more advanced systems that do receive the type of information that allows the machines to adapt and respond in a reasonable way, as a closed loop, to changes in environment.

MATERIAL-PROCESSING SYSTEMS

For material processing, the general problem involves gathering information for monitoring the metal-removal and the plastic-forming processes. The specific aspects of the problem for metal removal are three: monitoring and controlling the metal-removal process, positioning the tool and workpiece, and monitoring the machine (automatic diagnosis of machine failures). For plastic forming, the specific aspects are monitoring and controlling the temperature and pressure of the plastic—both statically and dynamically—and the feed rates of the materials.

Monitoring and controlling metal removal. The physical phenomenon of removing metal is awe-inspiring when observed closely. Relatively large forces are brought into play as the tool tears chips of metal from the workpiece. At present, the interaction of the tool and the workpiece cannot be measured directly. Thus arises the problem of interpreting what is going on by indirect measurements. The general approach is to try to characterize the metal-removal process by such indirect measurements as deflection of the tool, spindle motor loading (indicated motor current or power), and mechanical vibrations and sounds detected by microphones or accelerometers mounted at the base of the tool.

All these measurements are relatively remote from the metal-removal process. Therefore a great deal of research is required to interpret the measured information and to correlate it with the randomly varying physical process in order to establish controls and acceptable limits for the process.

Once the measurement signals have been interpreted, they can be used in feedback systems to change the spindle speed (or cutting velocity), the depth of cut, or the feed rate of the tool or workpiece so that a process will always cut metal at the maximum rate allowed by the momentary state of the tool and the workpiece. Such systems are called adaptive.

Adaptive-control system. Adaptive-control systems can be classified in two functional levels: completely optimizing systems (which at present do not exist), and adaptive-control constraint systems. Completely optimizing systems will seek the best combination of machining rates, at every instant of time, to satisfy some predetermined optimum value for metal removal and cost. The geometry of a workpiece is constantly changing, and both the width and the depth of cut vary greatly. Implementing a completely optimizing system, therefore, first requires experiments to determine wear-versus-time plots for both the tool and material for at least two different speeds. These are needed because the actual values can vary from the published values by as much as 200%. It is also necessary to determine criteria for tool life and devise a wear-rate sensor to measure how tool wear changes with such factors as time, and geometry of the cut. This information is used in the economic tool-life equation to automatically adjust the machining rates, thus providing the minimum cost per part. The economic tool-life equation is shown here. In the equation, T_e is the minimum economic

$$T_e = \left(\frac{1}{n} - 1\right)\left(t_c + \frac{60R}{C}\right)$$

tool life, n is the Taylor exponent, t_c is the minimum tool change time, R is the tool depreciation and regrind cost in dollars, and C is the hourly cost of the machine in dollars. The equation was first derived by W. Gilbert of General Electric, in 1954. It represents the correct balance between tool life and tool-change time to provide minimum cost.

At present, however, wear-rate sensors do not exist, and most manufacturers are unwilling to spend the time to obtain the necessary data for the tool-life equations. Several universities and laboratories are trying to develop practical tool-wear sensors.

Adaptive-control constraint system. The type of system currently in existence, the adaptive-control constraint system, differs from a fully optimizing system in that it changes machining rates within limited and predetermined bounds only. The magnitude of the machining rates depends on the process variables (for example, the depth and width of the cut, hardness of the material), and, of course, the minimum times for machining occur when the cut is most severe. A constraint system can control one, two, or more of the important process variables. Its cost and effectiveness depend on how many of the variables are sensed and controlled. It has been found by E. J. Pilafidis of Cincinnati Milacron that constraint systems can result in productivity gains that are within 15% of those of completely optimizing systems. But, as the table illustrates, the cost of contraint systems is significantly lower. The relative productivity gains in the table were determined by allowing one process variable to change at a time. The values represent the widest variation found; some changes in variables resulted in almost identical results for the three types of systems.

Choices of variables. Determining which process variables to control requires an economic feasibility study of all the relevant variables. For milling machines, for example, the two most important variables are the deflection of the tool and the

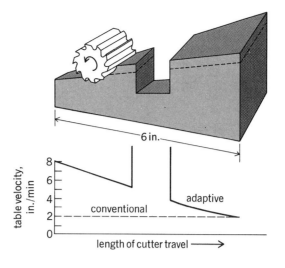

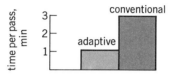

Fig. 5. Adaptive milling with gap elimination. *(From R. A. Mathias, Adaptive control of the milling process, Pap. 34CP67-716, IEEE National Tools Industry Conference, Cleveland, Oct. 9– 11, 1967)*

horsepower developed by the motor driving the workpiece feed mechanism. Measurement of tool deflection allows feed rates of the machine to be kept just below the point at which the cutter would break or at which the machine error exceeds some predetermined tolerance. Measurement of horsepower allows control of feed rate to keep the machine operating at its design-rated cutting capability. And when the cutting forces go to zero because the cutter is hitting air, a simple logic circuit can be triggered to speed up the feed rate until the tool is again cutting metal (Fig. 5). Typically, speed-up feed rates are 3 times the maximum rate used during the metal cutting.

During milling more than 30 variables can influence the efficiency of the metal-cutting process. The most important ones are: width and depth of the cut, tool wear, material hardness, and rigidity of the basic machine. Again, tool wear is important

Relative productivity and cost of adaptive control systems*

Type of adaptive control	Productivity gains	Cost of machine with adaptive control
Completely optimizing system (wear-rate sensor used)	100 units	$1.5M†
Sophisticated constraint system (a number of variables sensed and controlled); feed and speed rates change	95–97 units	1.2M
Simple constraint system (few important variables sensed and controlled); only feed changes	85–88 units	1.1M

*From E. J. Pilafidis, *Adaptive Control Systems and the Manufacturing Process,* Cincinnati Milacron Inc., May 1970.
†M is the basic cost of the machine without adaptive control.

because deflection forces for dull tools can be 2 to 10 times as great as for sharp tools. Maintaining the appropriate tool deflection over the lifetime of the tool may mean reducing the feed rates by factors of 2 to 20 over the lifetime of the tool.

For machining by numerical-control machines without adaptive controls, the value selected for feed rates must be conservative; thus, a feed rate corresponding to a dull tool must be chosen. Adaptive-control systems with deflection-limit control, however, permit machine feed rates up to 10 times the dullest-tool safe feed rate.

Figure 6 shows an adaptive-control system developed by the Japanese firm Makino. The system controls spindle speed by measuring spindle pressure, which is indicative of the spindle cutting force. The system also predicts tool wear based on time of usage.

Sensors for measurements. Typically, sensors for measuring tool deflection have been simple inductive pickups. Horsepower has been indicated by a wattmeter or inferred from motor-current measurements. Quartz multicomponent dynamometers for measuring cutting forces have also been recently developed. A simpler, more reliable new system that is employed for monitoring tool deflection uses measurements of the spindle drive-motor current.

For measuring tool wear, T. Sata of the University of Tokyo has used micrometers placed at the tool-cutter interface. When the tool is positioned, the micrometers touch both the worn and the un-cut edge of the tool. The output difference gives the flank wear of the tool. At the end of each pass of the tool, the tool is driven to a specific point, activating the electrical micrometers. Another tool-wear measurement system employs an electrically conductive device that wears at the same rate as the tool. Simple measurement of conductivity or resistivity of the device indicates the percent of tool wear.

Techniques for predicting tool wear have also been developed. They include analyzing vibrations measured by an accelerometer mounted at the base of the tool. The frequency components of the complex waveform from the accelerometer can be determined by fast-Fourier-transform processing. But, after the frequency components have been determined, their meaning can be interpreted only by the same experimental tests needed for the fully optimizing systems. Although systems have been developed on these principles, their general implementation on factory floors has been retarded by their high cost. They are used, however, in limited numbers in the aerospace industry and in certain precision-machine operations.

Presence or absence of the tool has been indicated by fluidic sensors that simply blow on the tool. If the tool is missing, the back pressure drops and a fluidic logic gate trips.

For grinding operations, Bendix has developed a trainable, adaptive-control system that measures the surface-finish quality of the workpiece and compares it with a quality measurement made by a

Fig. 6. Makino adaptive-control system introduced at 1970 Machine Tool Show. (*Prof. T. Sata, University of Tokyo*)

performance-measurement system (Fig. 7). Then, using the comparison, the training-system logic either reinforces the appropriate function in the performance-measurement system or modifies the function. A seismic-type vibration sensor is installed on the spindle housing; the optical head of a commercially available surface-quality comparator is installed on the grinding machine so that the workpiece passes beneath the probe immediately after each grinding stroke. The output of the comparator is then used to correct the performance-measurement function in such a way as to reduce the error.

Sensors for positioning. A variety of sensing devices are used to position machine tools and workpieces. They range from the simple lead screw with a mechanical indicator (resolution approximately 0.001 in.) to optical devices having engraved glass scales and ruled gratings, based on moiré fringe effects (error and resolution range from 0.001 to 0.00001 in., or 25.4×10^{-6} m to 0.254×10^{-6} m).

When one axis must interact with another, however, the squareness or parallelism of one axis to another or to a third must be considered. A new device combines the new technology of lasers with an old optical technique, interferometry. The device can make single-axis measurements to a resolution that ranges from 0.00001 to 0.0000001 in. (0.254×10^{-6} m to 0.00254×10^{-6} m). Accuracy for linear displacements is within ±0.5 part per million ± 1 count in the last digit (in metric, ±0.5 part per million ± 2 counts in the last digit). For two-axis measurements (Fig. 8), the system is accurate to ±5 microinches/foot ± 1 count in the last digit (±0.4 micrometer/meter ± 2 counts in the last digit). Squareness measurements are not often used, however, except in certain rare industries requiring extreme precision. At present, this technique is utilized mainly in calibration laboratories. It may find increasing use in checking machines at final inspection because of its simplicity and the quick readings it provides.

Plastic forming. Process instrumentation currently available for the plastic-molding industry can be categorized as simple process monitors, more complex process controllers, and computer-controlled systems that both monitor and control, or act as supervisors of multiple systems.

The process monitor is simply an electronic supervisor that watches selected variables of the process. Typical sensors are thermocouples to read plastic-melt temperature, or linear potentiometers to read pressure in the mold cavity or plastic injection pressure. This information is displayed to the operator by a variety of devices (such as meters and oscilloscopes) or recorded on strip-chart recorders. The recorders can be scanned to determine the long-term trends of the process. When out-of-limit conditions occur, the monitor can actuate alarms, reject the finished products affected, or possibly shut down the machine.

The process controller, on the other hand, automatically compensates the process and returns it to nominal values. For example, if the controller detects above-tolerance readings in cavity pressure, the system decreases the travel of the screw that controls the input pressure.

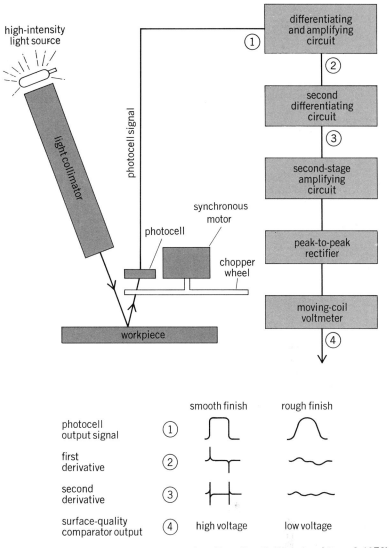

Fig. 7. Surface-quality comparator operation. (*From Bendix Tech. J., vol. 5, no. 2, 1972*)

Since the plastic-molding process is not as visible to the human eye as the metal-removal process, the sensor systems must be more sophisticated. Such systems have been only recently developed and applied. Among the incentives for developing these sensing systems, of course, is the need for consistency of products in a constantly growing market.

Among the more ambitious systems designed for full adaptive control of the molding process is AIM (adaptive injection molding) introduced by Cincinnati Milacron in 1971 (Fig. 9). Unlike most other systems—which control one to four variables—AIM not only operates the machine, but also adjusts for daily changes in temperature and humidity and compensates for nonuniformities of raw-material blending.

Currently, the thrust for the plastic-forming industry area seems to be toward developing software systems for designing parts (for example, number of cavities and press size required to mold a particular part) rather than on additional infor-

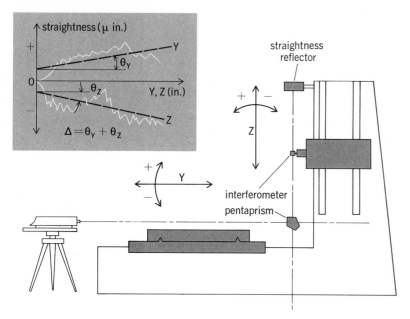

Fig. 8. Straightness and squareness calibration using the pentaprism. (*From David A. Harland, Total machine tool calibration with the laser interferometer, Conference on Dimensional Accuracy in Manufacturing, National Bureau of Standards, Oct. 31–Nov. 1, 1972*)

mation or sensor systems for implementing the process.

Diagnostics. The previous discussions stress the point made at the beginning of this article: at present, industrial automation consists mainly of individual systems with sensors added as the need arises to fulfill a particular requirement. Diagnostic systems for monitoring and indicating the status of the previously described machines, in particular, are characteristic of this trend. This approach is no longer viable, however, and, as single machines are integrated into higher-level computer-controlled manufacturing systems, automatic and efficient methods of diagnosing failures will be urgently needed to prevent long, unproductive hours of system downtime.

As practiced today, diagnostics are very rudimentary. The information given the operator is often fragmentary and inadequate. For single machines, this does not present a serious problem. However, for more complex machines such as transfer machines, maintenance can become a nightmare, with downtime approaching 30%. As stand-alone machines become integrated with other machines, system designers will face the same problems of inadequate information that beset today's transfer-machine designers.

Adequate diagnostic equipment requires sensor systems for monitoring and predicting the lifetime and current condition of, for example, spindle ball bearings, bearings for sliders, electric motors, hydraulic systems, sequencers, tool changers, and lubricants.

New techniques using discrete system analysis show much promise as design tools for synthesizing complex systems and as diagnostic tools for predicting the state (or specific machine sequence) that the machine has failed to attain. This information alone can go a long way in helping maintenance personnel to debug the system and

get it quickly back on line. Developing these techniques to a point at which they are broadly usable will require not only the sensor systems mentioned earlier, but monitoring systems that feed data to a computer, giving "visibility" to the status of all the relevant machine systems. The data can then be used not only to predict and prevent failures, but also to provide up-to-date status of in-process machining so that a truly efficient path can be plotted for the workpiece through all the machining steps necessary for completion.

Thus, information is now the key, and integration of the information is the tool, to the more efficient systems of the future.

MATERIAL TRANSPORT SYSTEMS

Moving things around automatically requires first identifying the object to be moved, then keeping track of the object as it moves along the path to its destination, and, finally, presentation—delivering the object to the next preselected work station on time and properly positioned. Proper presentation includes both accurate alignment and correct orientation.

Material transport systems now in use can be classified according to their ability to move either individual items or bulk parts. For moving bulk parts, systems range from fork-lift trucks with pallets and bins, to conveyor belts of many forms, to computer-controlled stacker cranes. For moving individual items, there are put-and-place machines (Fig. 4), automobile production lines, and computer-controlled pallets used in some of the advanced CCMS (computer-controlled machining systems, Fig. 10).

Information requirements. At the initial acquisition or entrance of the object onto the transport system, sensing information is needed on the method of presentation of the part, the method of its attachment to the system, and maintainance of a precise orientation or alignment with respect to the system. Much of this information is now handled by people. Once on the system, the object must be tracked and its arrival at a desired point in some specified time must be controlled. It must also be possible to move objects into temporary storage and to recall them as they are needed. For many continuous-conveyor systems storage does not present a problem, since such systems are often used for temporary storage. At the final destination, the object must be removed from the transport system and properly presented to the next work station. If orientation is maintained during the transition, it may be sufficient to switch or gate the object off the line by some simple trip mechanism, such as a microswitch. Gating works well for objects of simple shape, such as cubes. For those with complex shapes, the problem becomes more difficult, possibly requiring a put-and-place machine.

Material transport systems today are an interesting ad hoc combination of people, simple machines, and fairly complex systems controlled, sequenced, and monitored by computers. And it is not surprising to find examples of all three working side by side in the same factory. Perhaps the biggest limitation of today's systems is the inability to quickly and economically accept randomly oriented parts, orient them, and present them to some

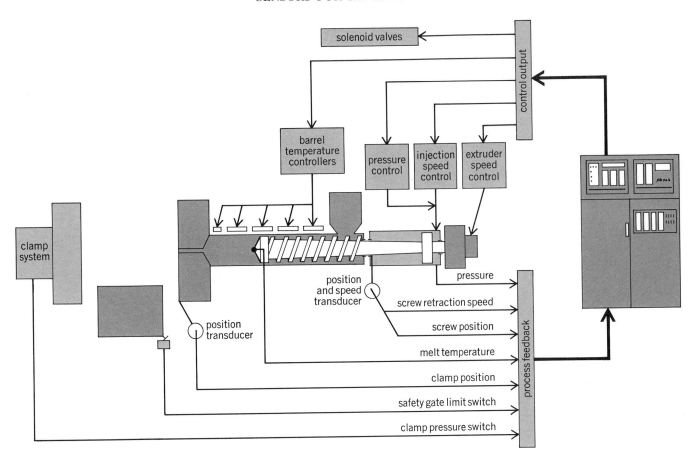

Fig. 9. Diagram of an adaptive injection-molding (AIM) control system. (*From Kirby L. Stone, Computers for process control, SPI National Plastics Conference, Chicago, Nov. 2–4, 1971*)

machine for processing (material processing, assembly, or inspection, for example). These systems require sophisticated visual and nonvisual imaging information of the object being presented (Fig. 11). Nonvisual imaging might be detailed range information on the object, obtained by scanning it with a modulated laser source, receiving data with collector lenses and photodiodes and processing the data through phase-comparator circuits to reconstruct the object's range image. Work is under way on systems that will, it is hoped, soon take their place in factories.

For the present, however, sensors for transport systems are largely restricted to simple limit switches for determining the presence or absence of a piece, and simple current- or power-overload detectors to shut down the system in case of difficulties. For power- and free-conveyor systems the required sequencing is usually done electromechanically.

Universal parts identification. Fully automating these systems requires that enough manufacturers agree upon and implement a universal parts-identification system to provide supplier industries with a sufficient market to produce economic systems. Agreement has already been reached in the food industry. In April 1973 an ad hoc group representing food processors, wholesalers, and retailers agreed to a code to be affixed to all processed foods. With this code, a hand-held or in-place optical scanner can determine what the product is, access the computer-stored price of the article,

deduct one from the inventory data storage for that item, and keep a running total of the units purchased. Similar codes have been developed for the railroad industry to allow automatic scanning of freight cars to determine contents, destination, and other facts.

Fig. 10. Prisma, integrated machine system for manufacture of prismatic parts, using computer-controlled pallets. (*VEB Werkzengmaschinekombiant, Leipzig, East Germany*)

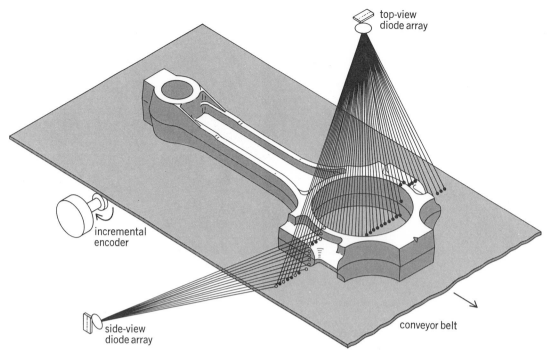

Fig. 11. Obtaining orthogonal views of a part moving on a conveyor belt by two linear diode arrays. (From C. Rosen et al., *Exploratory Research in Advanced Automation, Stanford Research Institute, 1973*)

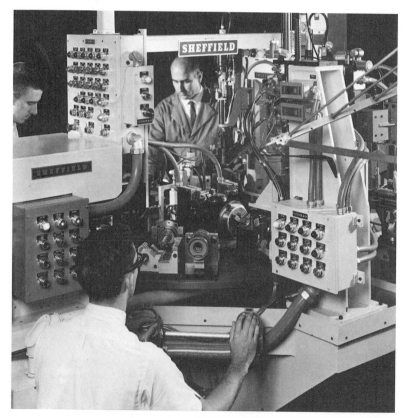

Fig. 12. Power-steering ball screw components are assembled at the rate of 300 assemblies per hour. The race diameters of the "worm" and "nut" are automatically gaged by a special electronic differential matching system after being loaded by operator no. 1. At the ball assembly station, 27 balls of the size computed in the gaging are automatically loaded into the worm-nut assembly after the ball count is verified. Subsequent operations automatically place the ball guide retainer strap and drive two retainer strap screws into place. Operator no. 2 loads the ball guides, and operator no. 3 unloads the completed assembly and makes the final inspection on a special torque-test gage. (*Bendix Automation and Measurement Division*)

Of course, food-processing and railroad industries are less difficult to cope with than the manufacturing industry. A significant difference, for example, is the various contaminants such as oil, grease, and dirt in a manufacturing environment. Another is the manufacturing industry's need for universal traceability—from the finished part right back through to the original melt for the billet used to make the part—in order to create manufacturing systems with minimum defects. For example, in manufacturing brake drums for automobiles, safety considerations require determining the cause of a failure; that is, one can determine whether the cause is a material defect or a processing and handling defect only if one can completely trace the material and the processing steps performed on the material.

ASSEMBLY SYSTEMS

As they exist today, systems for automatically assembling devices can be described as precision block-stacking machines in which fairly accurate, machined parts are pushed, pulled, or dropped into place in a sequence of steps that may or may not be synchronized. In general, assembly systems perform more operations than transfer machines. The operations range from automatically inserting electronic components to welding an entire car body. In some operations both machining and assembly are combined. As pointed out earlier, an example is the system that automatically machines and assembles gear boxes for clothes washers (Fig. 3). In general, parts to be assembled in this manner require closer tolerances than they would if assembled manually. Manual assembly, since it involves continuous inspection by the assembler (by sight, touch, and other senses), can get by with less strict tolerances. The mechanical assemblers, therefore, require extensive parts-gaging inspec-

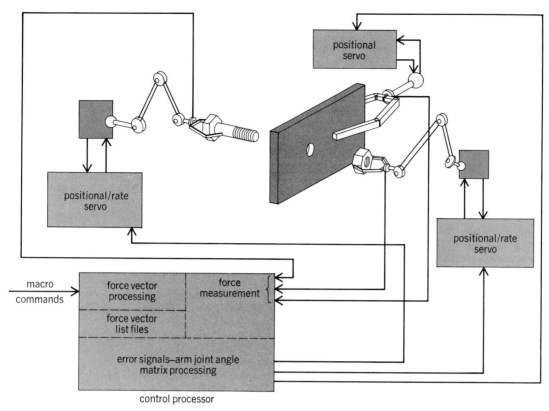

Fig. 13. Block diagram of a four-vector assembly system. (*Charles Stark Draper Laboratory, Cambridge, MA*)

tion in order to function well. An example of this class of machines is shown in Fig. 12.

Assembly machines are mainly single machines uniquely designed for each product. Thus, making them economical requires production rates of the order of 1,000,000 or 2,000,000 parts per year. The product should change not at all — or very little — throughout the useful lifetime of this special-purpose machine.

For high-volume assembly, without inspection, the prime need for sensors is in sequencing. Sequencing involves detecting parts absent or present at a station, full or empty bowl feeders for parts, and pieces not shifting or transferring properly to another station. All these operations are now usually indicated by simple sensors such as switches. Essentially, a task is accomplished by pushing or pulling something until it reaches a hard stop. The stop is simply detected by a switch.

New systems. Newer, more advanced systems now under development (Fig. 13) are highly organized and require large amounts of data from the assembly environment in order to function. These systems are both adaptable and programmable. Therefore, they require force- and tactile-sensor arrays (Fig. 14) and sophisticated control algorithms to monitor the processs and to properly respond to differences in the parts being assembled and to the imprecision of the system performing the assembly.

More advanced future systems will require visual and nonvisual imaging sensors to allow parts presentation to be less organized. This means that the systems will be able to receive disoriented parts and orient them, and to detect parts with

gross defects by visual means and reject them before the assembly process begins. (The defect-detection operation will be explored later in this article under Inspection Systems.)

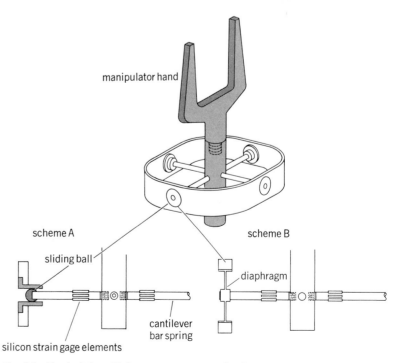

Fig. 14. Manipulator with force-sensor arrays. (*Charles Stark Draper Laboratory, Cambridge, MA*)

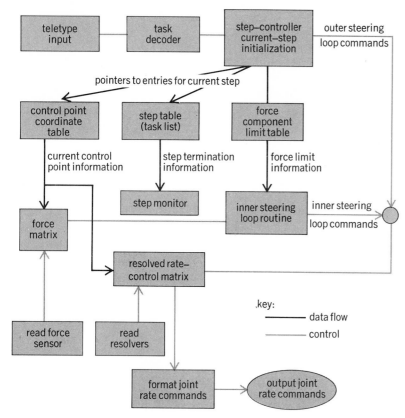

Fig. 15. Control law for automatic insertion machine. (*Charles Stark Draper Laboratory, Cambridge, MA*)

Since the more advanced assembly systems are programmable, they can be used for different products and for changed products. These systems are not being designed to replace machines for high-volume production of a single product. Instead, they are being designed to handle high or intermediate production volume with model mixing.

Sensor information. Assembly tasks in the advanced systems require sensors that can obtain multiaxis information from the environment to institute the proper control response. Force information can be obtained from the measured mechanical deformation of a four-beam structure (Fig. 14). The sensors shown in the figure are solid-state strain gages. With the appropriate vector transformation, the torques appearing at the end point or at some arbitrary radius can be easily determined. Other sensor systems to monitor the multiaxis mechanical deformation of a structure use either linear-variable-differential transformers (LVDT) or laser interferometry techniques. Laser interferometry offers the potential of a dynamic range (ratio of maximum force allowed to minimum force detectable) of approximately 10,000/1 with a force threshold of 5 g (0.176 oz).

With a limited-range strain gage array and a fairly simple control law (Fig. 15), a 0.5-in. (1.27-cm) diameter peg has been automatically inserted into a hole with a clearance of 0.0005 in. (0.0127 mm).

The assembly strategy for such tasks is similar to that used by blind people. That is, parts are presented at specific known locations and in the proper orientation so that the assembly sequence can be carried out in an efficient manner. Groping for

parts could be used, but would be slow and certainly not economical.

More complex systems will also involve tactile sensors, proximity sensors, and visual or nonvisual imaging systems. For example, a nonvisual imaging sensor system consisting of an array of sensors at the end of a manipulator hand would allow the orientation of a grasped object to be determined, or some salient feature of the object—such as a corner or an edge—to be recognized. With such sensors, assembly can be performed in a less "structured" environment. Since everything need not be known before the assembly process begins, parts can be fed randomly via a conveyor belt. With a visual system, the correct parts can be selected, and their orientation determined; they can then be properly grasped and presented to the assembly system. Of course, gross visual inspection would also be carried out during this process. However, whether these approaches are the appropriate ones (in an economic sense) for feeding and presenting parts for an assembly remains to be determined.

INSPECTION SYSTEMS

When automation is used to supplement people, one must not forget that in every job—even the most mundane, dirty, and dull—people are continuously performing inspection. They inspect the materials or parts as they receive them, as they handle them, and during the processing. Thus, to even partially supplement people's activities, a tremendous array of devices and sensor systems is needed to perform parts sizing, classifying, and segregating (Figs. 12 and 16), and electrical-function checking for everything from spaceships to washer machines (Fig. 17). Also needed are single-function devices that utilize x-rays or other radiation to gage thickness or to find internal flaws and computerized devices employing fluorescent-dye penetrants and ultraviolet light to recognize patterns on surface finishes.

Systems now under development will measure very small displacements using holographic interferometry (Fig. 18). Others will provide noncontact surface measurements using close-range photogrammetry. In addition, systems will use holographic or visual imagery for general inspection (Fig. 18).

Sensors for these systems cover a broad spectrum. At present, most sensors accept stimuli only from a single point, but with the more rapid measurements possible with computers there is a growing trend to construct arrays of sensors that accept multipoint data on complex structures, and process and integrate the data to provide meaningful displays easily interpreted by humans or by other computers. Figure 11 illustrates a way of gathering three-dimensional information on an object by linear diode arrays.

CONCLUSION

This article has described the needs for sensors and shown the rationale for their use in the broad context of manufacturing systems, rather than discussing specific sensors out of context of their use. An appreciation of the broader applications of sensor systems—not just those associated with manufacturing—may prove to be a stimulus for the re-

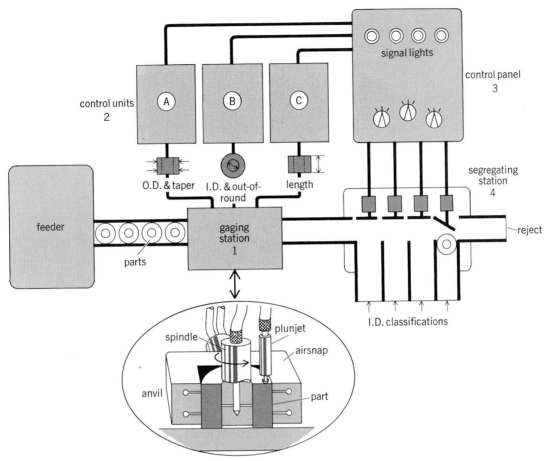

Fig. 16. Automatic gaging machines permit inspection of any and all dimensional features of each component part, ensuring total control of production quality. This machine checks the O.D. and taper, the I.D. and out-of- roundness, and the length. Parts are then segregated by I.D. classification. (*Bendix Automation and Measurement Division*)

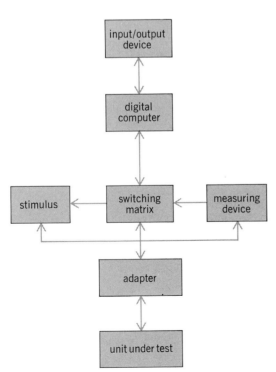

Fig. 17. Simplified computer-controlled test system. (*From Bendix Tech. J., vol. 5, no. 2, 1972*)

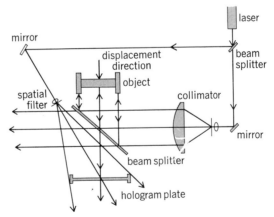

Fig. 18. Holographic interferometer schematic. (*Bendix Tech. J., vol. 4, no. 1, 1971*)

search required to develop more useful systems. The sensor systems that lend themselves to computer integration are particularly interesting because many problems can be solved efficiently only if many channels of information can be quickly scanned, processed, and interpreted.

Furthermore, integration of single "stand-alone" systems into the automated factories of the future will be possible when these lower-level systems can generate information quickly, in a way that allows it to be verified easily and in a manner that allows problems to be diagnosed by higher-level computer-controlled systems. It is important to keep in mind, however, that sensors and sensing systems are not the only consideration in developing automation for the future. Rather, they are only a part of broader issues of understanding very basic functions and of organizing them.

[J. L. NEVINS]

Photographic Highlights

These photographs have been chosen for their scientific value and current relevance. Many result from advances in photographic and optical techniques as humans extend their sensory awareness with the aid of the machine, and others are records of important natural phenomena and recent scientific discoveries.

Aerial view of belugas, or white whales *(Delphinapterus leucas)*, in breeding grounds at Cunningham Inlet, Somerset Island, Northwest Territories, Canada. Photograph taken at an altitude of 310 m with water-penetration color film made by Eastman Kodak Company. *(Quebec Wildlife Service)*

Coronagraph showing the solar corona surrounding an occulting disk, with Comet Kohoutek visible at upper right. View reproduced from a television transmission made by a camera aboard Skylab space station at 21:49 Greenwich mean time, Dec. 27, 1973. *(NASA)*

Above. Solar eruption photographed by an extreme ultraviolet spectroheliograph aboard the Skylab space station. *(NASA)*

Opposite. Cool (50,000 K) asymmetrical arch of helium sent 800,000 km into the solar corona by an enormous solar eruption. Photograph taken from Skylab space station by an extreme ultraviolet spectroheliograph. *(NASA)*

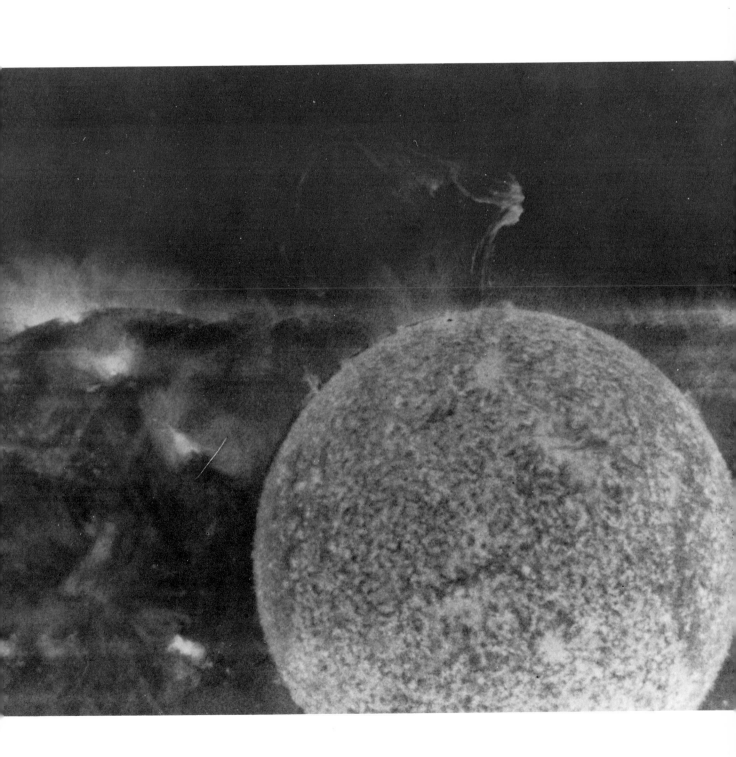

Opposite. Computer-enhanced photograph of Venus taken by *Mariner 10* from 720,000 km. *(Jet Propulsion Laboratory)*

Below. Series of pictures of Venus taken at *(a)* 10 A.M., *(b)* 5 P.M., and *(c)* midnight Pacific daylight time 2 days after *Mariner 10* flew past the planet. Arrows point to feature measuring about 1000 km. *(Jet Propulsion Laboratory)*

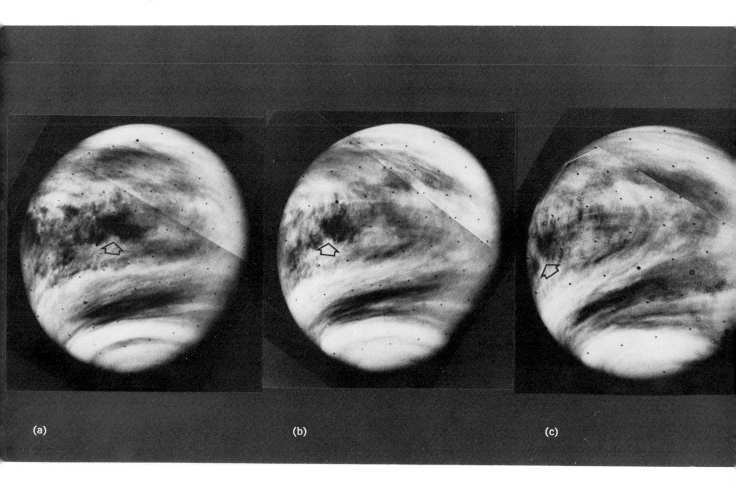

(a)   (b)   (c)

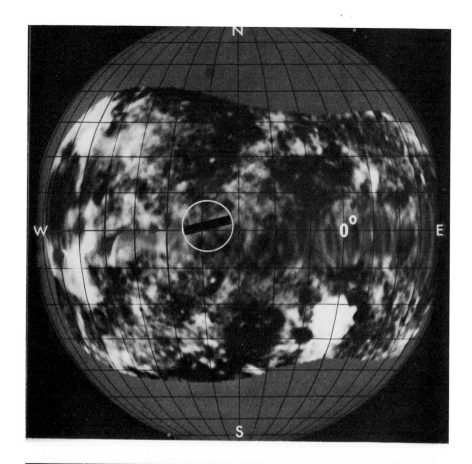

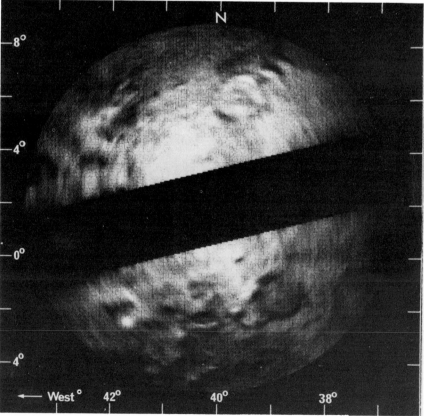

Top. Radar map of Venus showing relative location (circle) of area where large shallow craters have been detected. *(Jet Propulsion Laboratory)*

Bottom. Area enclosed by circle in photograph at top; black belt is an area that cannot be accurately mapped. *(Jet Propulsion Laboratory)*

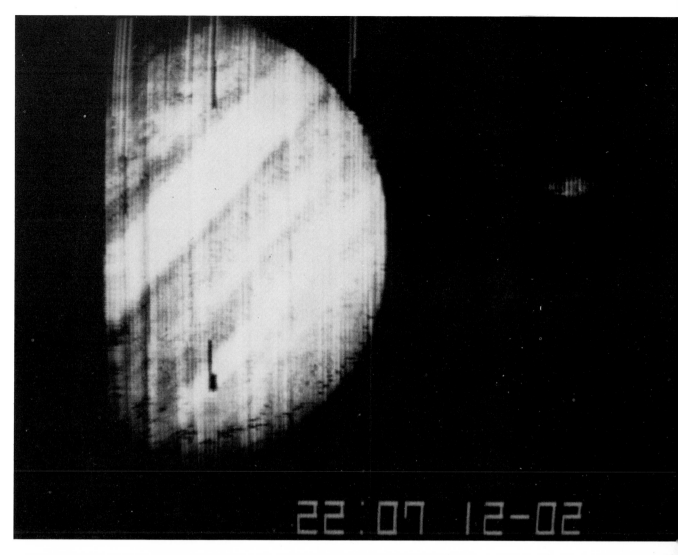

22:07 12-02

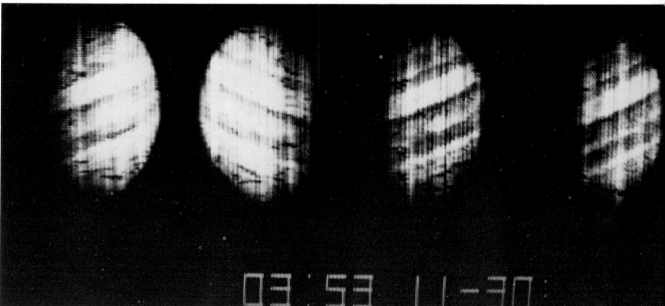

03:53 11-30

Top. *Pioneer 10* photograph of Jupiter with its moon Ganymede seen to the upper right; true round shape of Ganymede is distorted by imaging instrument. *(NASA)*

Bottom. Views of Jupiter taken by *Pioneer 10;* viewing angle causes cloud bands to appear slanted. *(NASA)*

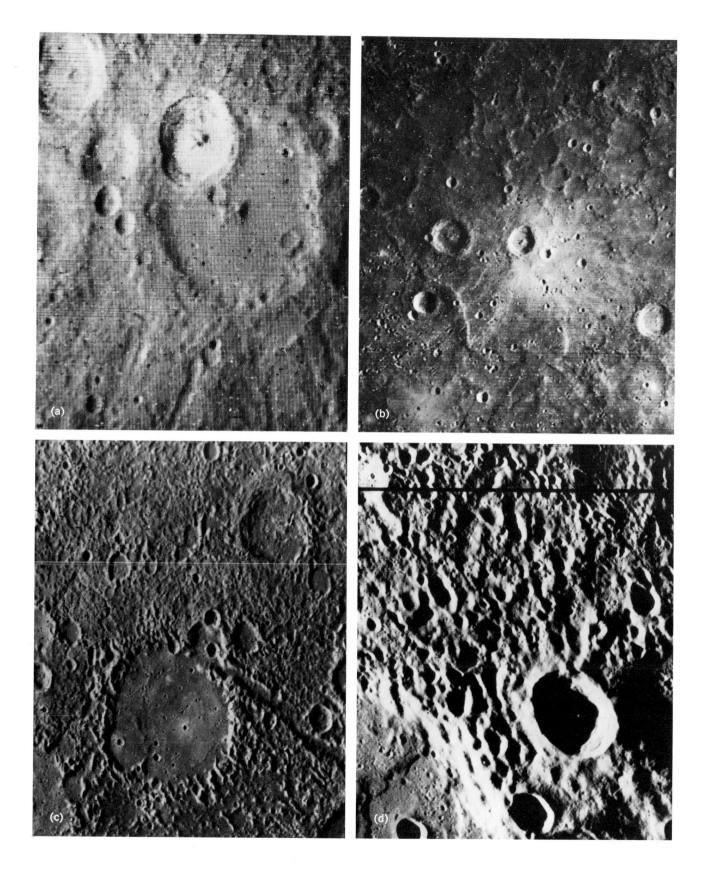

(a)

(b)

(c)

(d)

Above. Computer-enhanced *Mariner 10* photomosaic of Mercury showing prominent bright-rayed craters; north pole is at top. Picture is composed of 18 photographs taken at 42-sec intervals. *(Jet Propulsion Laboratory)*

Opposite. *Mariner 10* photographs of Mercury. *(a)* Kuiper (top center), a bright-floored crater. *(b)* A dark area with relatively few craters; the Sun is from the right. *(c)* A heavily cratered area with many low hills; the valley on the right is 7 km wide and more than 100 km long. *(d)* Densely cratered surface of the planet. *(Jet Propulsion Laboratory)*

Above. View of Hurricane Carmen nearing Yucatan Peninsula, Sept. 1, 1974, with winds at 150 mph (67 m/sec), as seen by the Synchronous Meteorological Satellite *(SMS-1)*. *(NOAA)*

Right. Picture of Hurricane Carmen taken by *SMS-1* on Sept. 7, 1974, as the hurricane moved northward toward New Orleans. *(NOAA)*

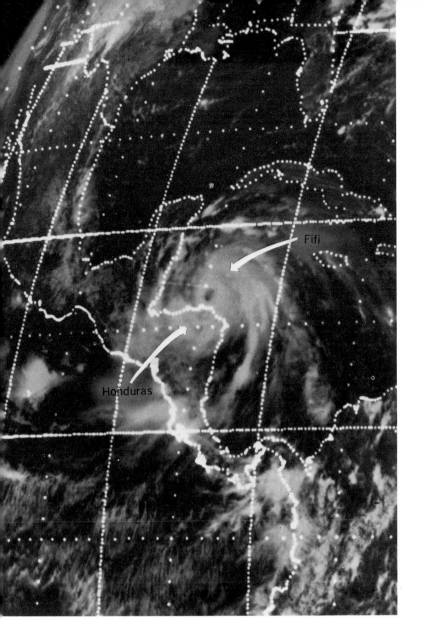

Fifi

Honduras

Above. Visible spectrum shot of Hurricane Ione taken by the orbiting *NOAA-3* satellite on Aug. 26, 1974, over the eastern Pacific Ocean; the form is considered a classic shape. *(NOAA)*

Left top. Synchronous Meteorological Satellite *(SMS-1)* photo of Hurricane Fifi moving westward off the coast of Honduras on Sept. 18, 1974. *(NOAA)*

Left bottom. Hurricane Fifi as seen by *SMS-1* on Sept. 18, 1974; the eastern top of Cuba is in the upper right corner, and the northern tip of the Yucatan Peninsula is above and to the left of the hurricane eye. *(NOAA)*

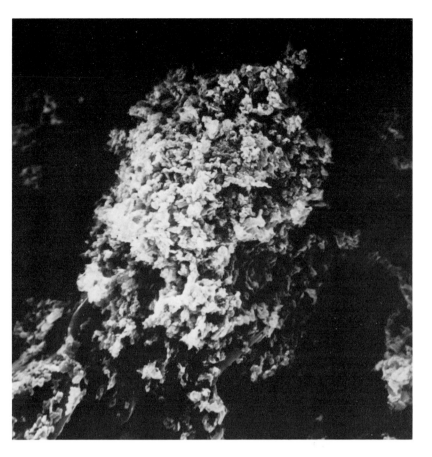

Spheroids and filaments, two morphologically simple types of microorganisms, have been found in the sedimentary rocks of the Upper Onverwacht Group. They may represent the oldest microfossils on Earth.

Left. Spheroid recovered from rocks lying stratigraphically above the Middle Marker Horizon (dated at 3.355×10^9 years) of the Kromberg Formation.

Below. Small hollow filament seen in the etched chert of the Kromberg Formation.

From J. Brooks, M. D. Muir, and G. Shaw, Chemistry and morphology of Precambrian microorganisms, Nature, 244:215–217, 1973

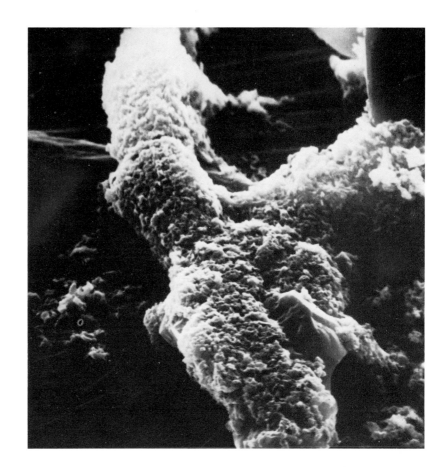

Right. Spheroid partly etched out of the chert from the Swartkoppie Formation.

Below Filament from the Swartkoppie Formation; it is shown etched out of the chert in which it was found.

From J. Brooks, M. D. Muir, and G. Shaw, Chemistry and morphology of Precambrian microorganisms, Nature, 244:215–217, 1973

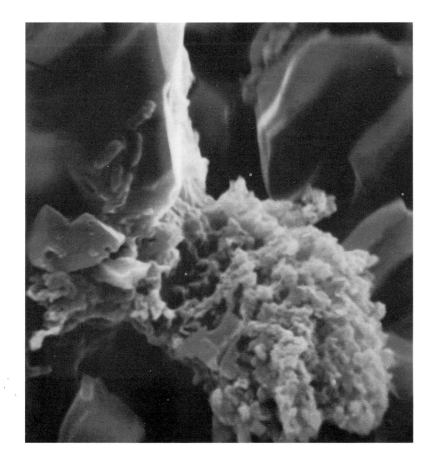

Above. Photograph of the surface of a nearly vertical scarp inside the Rift Valley of the Mid-Atlantic Ridge taken with Naval Research Laboratory's Light Behind Camera (LIBEC) System. The vaned compass suspended above the scarp determines the magnetic orientation of features on the sea floor. *(Naval Research Laboratory)*

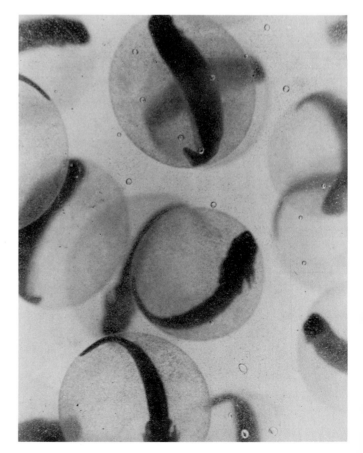

Right. Salamander *(Ambystoma maculatum)* embryos about 9 mm in length surrounded by thin gelatinous envelopes. The envelopes appear darkened due to the presence of *Oophilia ambystomatis*, a mutualistic algae which increases survivorship and rate of embryonic development.

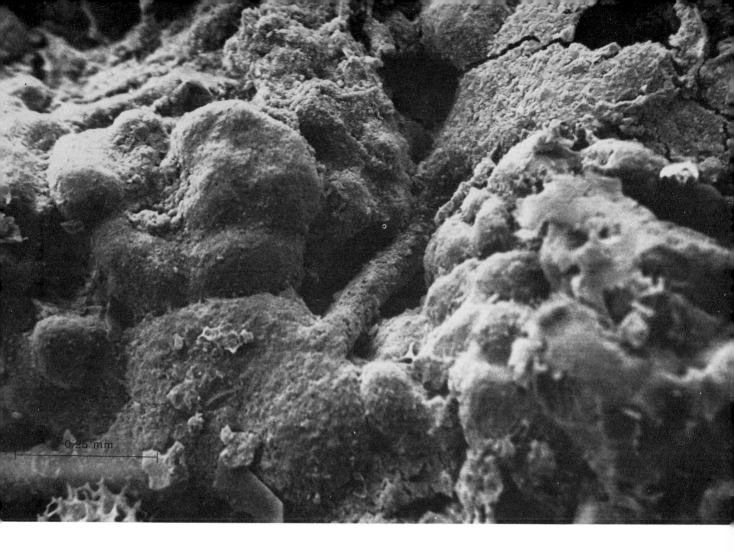

0.25 mm

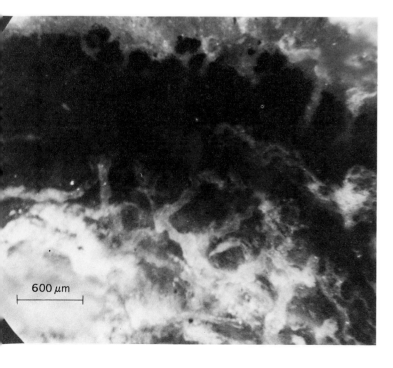

600 μm

Above. Micrograph of surface of a manganese nodule from the deep ocean floor showing biological tubular and domelike structures. *(J. Greenslate, Scripps Institution of Oceanography)*

Left. Photomicrograph of cross section of biological tubes in the interior of a manganese nodule. They have been exposed by leaching; leached material appears white. *(J. Greenslate, Scripps Institution of Oceanography)*

Following page. Three members of *Lycospora* spore tetrad from a *Lepidostrobus* cone found in coal balls about 310,000,000 years old in Indiana. *(Science magazine cover, June 28, 1974; Joan M. Courvoisier, Florida State Museum, Gainesville)*

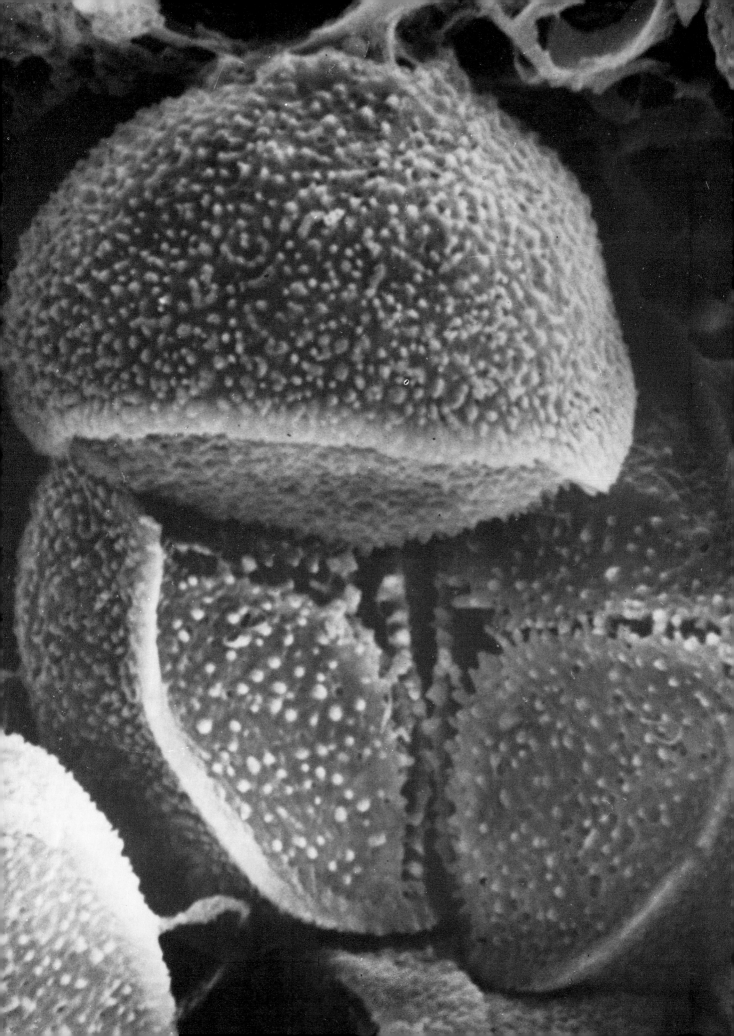

A-Z

Acid and base

It has recently become possible to determine the acidities of a variety of Brønsted acids in the gas phase and, thus, in the absence of solvent.

The Brønsted acidity of a molecule or ion is a measure of its ability to transfer a proton to another species (a Brønsted base). Correspondingly, Brønsted basicity is a measure of ability to accept a proton. For many years chemists have used acidities and basicities measured in solution as an aid in understanding intrinsic molecular and ionic properties. (For example, the relatively strong acidic behavior of trifluoroacetic acid has been associated with the electron-withdrawing property of fluorine, which helps to stabilize the trifluoroacetate anion inductively.) Although such explanations have been very important in understanding chemical properties, they do not take into account the role of solvent. Until recently, this was necessary since all measurements were made in solution. Now, with gas-phase data available, the effects of intrinsic properties and of solvent can be separated. J. I. Brauman and L. K. Blair were able to demonstrate the importance of solvent in determining acidity orders by showing that the acidity order of the aliphatic alcohols in the gas phase is t-butyl alcohol > isopropyl alcohol >

ethanol > methanol, an order exactly reversed from that in solution. This finding had substantial importance, because explanations of the solution order had previously assumed it to be a property of the alcohols and not of the solvent. Similarly, the anomalous basicity order of amines (ammonia < methylamine < dimethylamine > trimethylamine) was shown to result from solution effects rather than being an intrinsic molecular phenomenon. Subsequently, a variety of techniques have been brought to bear on problems of this type.

Direct measurements. The most straightforward methods for determining relative acidities or basicities in the gas phase involve studying reactions such as (1) or (2). The reason is that the energy required for simple dissociation $AH \rightleftharpoons A^- + H^+$ is far too large to permit direct measurement of ion

$$AH + B^- \rightleftharpoons A^- + BH \qquad (1)$$

$$CH^+ + D \rightleftharpoons C + DH^+ \qquad (2)$$

concentrations. The experimental techniques use mass-spectrometric determinations of ion concentrations; either equilibrium or kinetic measurements can be made. Thus the equilibrium constant K can be determined directly, or it can be inferred by measuring the rate constants for the forward and backward reactions, or the magnitude of K can be ascertained by determining whether the forward or backward reaction is faster. Three different techniques have been applied extensively: high-pressure mass spectometry, the flowing afterglow method, and ion-cyclotron resonance spectrometry.

The high-pressure mass-spectrometric method, used extensively by P. Kebarle, involves generation of ions with the neutral molecules present at a pressure of about 1 torr. The ions and neutrals come to equilibrium, as in reaction (1) or (2); the ions then escape and are analyzed. The flowing afterglow method, used extensively by D. Bohme, involves generation of ions in a rapidly flowing gas with neutrals present at a pressure of about 1 torr. Further reactants are introduced downstream; the ions are analyzed at the end of the tube. The time during which initial neutrals and reactant ions are in contact is determined by the flow rate and length of the tube. From these experiments, rate constants for reaction (1) or (2) can be determined. The ion-cyclotron resonance method, used extensively by J. L. Beauchamp, M. T. Bowers, Brauman, and R. T. McIver, Jr., among others, allows ions to be trapped in magnetic and electric fields for relatively long times (up to seconds) and permits the observation of reactions, even at neutral pressures as low as 10^{-7} torr. The ions are detected with a marginal oscillator detection system, similar to that used in other magnetic resonance experiments. Both kinetic and equilibrium determinations can be made. Each of these very different methods has given the same results when applied to the same systems. Compounds whose relative acidities have been studied include alcohols, phenols, carboxylic acids, carbon acids, and simple binary hydrides. Basicities of amines, alcohols, and ethers have been studied as well.

Indirect determinations. An alternative method for determining acidities makes use of the thermochemical cycle shown here. This cycle permits an

$AH \rightarrow A + H$	Bond dissociation energy (DH^0)
$A + e^- \rightarrow A^-$	$-$ Electron affinity ($-EA$)
$H \rightarrow H^+ + e^-$	Ionization potential (IP)
$AH \rightarrow A^- + H^+$	ΔH^0

absolute determination of the acidity of AH if the bond energy in AH and the electron affinity of A are known. In the past, this method has been severely hampered by the lack of available electron affinities. However, electron affinities, obtained primarily from photodetachment thresholds $A^- + h\nu \rightarrow A + e^-$, where $h\nu$ is the minimum energy of a photon which is required to detach an electron from A^-, are just now becoming available for a variety of neutrals. Use of this method has made it possible to estimate the acidities of cyclopentadiene and of a number of binary hydrides including ammonia. Thermochemistry combined with direct determination provides consistency checks, absolute calibration points, and even a way of determining bond energies when enough other data are available.

Results. Determination of gas-phase acidities and basicities for a variety of types of molecules has, for the first time, isolated these molecular properties from solvent effects. Among the important developments has been the demonstration that, in general, larger molecules are both more basic and more acidic than smaller ones of similar structure. From a classical viewpoint this behavior can be regarded as a result of internal stabilization of charged species by polarization. This effect does not appear to be nearly as important in solution as in the gas phase. A variety of other effects, including resonance, electronegativity, dipole effects, and hybridization effects, have been shown to be important when model systems are chosen properly. In solution, hydrogen bonding can play a critical role. This has been demonstrated by the observation that the hydrocarbons toluene and propylene are stronger acids than water in the gas phase.

Recent measurements by E. M. Arnett on the thermochemistry of ion solvation have led to a great advance in understanding the details of acidity and basicity in solution. Arnett's data, coupled with quantitative gas-phase results, have made it possible to isolate and examine the components of solution reactions, including intrinsic molecular effects, solvation of neutrals, and solvation of ions. This has already been accomplished for solution amine basicities, formerly a major area of confusion.

Future prospects. The wide variety of techniques recently brought to bear on the problem of determining and understanding acidity and basicity in the gas phase have had a far-reaching impact on chemistry. It is now clear that, ultimately, both the details of intrinsic effects and the details of the interaction of solvents with ions will be known. Thus, ionic behavior will be understood, and predictions for unknown systems will be possible.

For background information *see* ACID AND BASE; BASE (CHEMISTRY); HYDROGEN ION in the McGraw-Hill Encyclopedia of Science and Technology.   [JOHN I. BRAUMAN]

Bibliography: D. K. Bohme, R. S. Hemsworth, and H. W. Rundle, *J. Chem. Phys.*, 59:77, 1973; R. T. McIver, Jr., and J. H. Silvers, *J. Amer. Chem. Soc.*, 95:8462, 1973; J. H. Richardson, L. M. Stephenson, and J. I. Brauman, *J. Chem. Phys.*, 59:5068, 1973; R. Yamdagni and P. Kebarle, *J. Amer. Chem. Soc.*, 95:4050, 1973.

Agricultural science (plant)

Reports of recent research on unconventional sources of plant protein have been concerned with the production of edible seeds with higher protein content, extraction processes for seeds that have toxic constituents, extraction of protein from those leafy crops not normally eaten, and the growth of microorganisms on molasses, sewage, and so on.

The term "protein source" will be restricted to foods containing more than 20% protein because it is only with the help of such foods that a diet containing 10% protein can be assembled that contains enough sugar and fat to be palatable. Of the seeds that can be eaten with no more processing than can be carried out in the kitchen, a few cereals and many legumes qualify as protein sources. Other seeds need some form of processing or protein extraction before they are acceptable. Protein can also be extracted from the leaves of forage crops. The natural growth of blue-green algae in saline lakes is being exploited. Various agricultural by-products are used for the cultivation of edible microorganisms.

Edible seeds. Recent research has resulted in the production of barley, oats, sorghum, triticale, and wheat varieties containing 20–25% of protein in bulk samples and still larger percentages in individual grains. Beans, lentils, and peas containing this amount of protein are familiar, as is the idea of using cereal seeds as food. The only unfamiliar aspects in the use of these protein sources as food arise from a difference in cooking quality (the flour made from protein-rich cereals differs from conventional flour) and from the unusual appearance of some of the beans.

Seeds that need processing. In spite of the toxicity of some varieties, *Lathyrus* has been traditionally used as food, especially when other food is scarce. The discovery that the toxic constituents are removed by boiling seems to be recent. Soya, and protein extracted from it, is also a traditional food; modern methods of preparation are so widely known that they can no longer be considered unconventional. Rape was originally grown for almost exclusive use as a source of oil because the meal contained toxic thioglucosinolates, which have now been largely eliminated by breeding and by extraction. The protein-rich residue is used as a fodder and will probably soon be accepted as a food. Similarly, there are varieties of cotton that contain little gossypol, which can be separated from the ground seed mechanically. The product is eaten—but not extensively. With the waning of a somewhat hysterical fear of aflatoxin (which can contaminate any food that is ineptly stored), groundnuts are becoming more important as a food in India. For obscure reasons, the practice, common in the United States, of making peanut butter from groundnuts is seldom followed.

The seeds discussed in the preceding paragraph contain more than 20% protein initially; processing is needed only to remove or inactivate toxic or unpleasantly flavored components. Protein concentrates have been separated from low-protein cereal seeds by wet or dry processes for many years. The "meat" in coconuts contains about 10% protein on the defatted DM (dry matter); this is accompanied by so much fiber that it can satisfy only a small part of the protein requirement for a day. In the South Pacific it is traditional to make "coconut cream" by extracting grated meat with warm water. Several organizations are trying to develop this method into an industrial process that will separate the oil from the protein in the cream. The most difficult phase of the operation seems to be the extraction of the meat from the shell without drying it and thus making much of the protein insoluble.

Leaf protein. Leafy crops are potentially the most abundant source of protein because they grow in a wide range of climates and yield more protein, per hectare and year, than other crops do. Protein is extracted by pulping the fresh forage and pressing (see illustration). The extract is then coagulated, and the protein is filtered off and washed if necessary. In the extractor, the leafy crop is fed into the pulper; the pulp flies out under

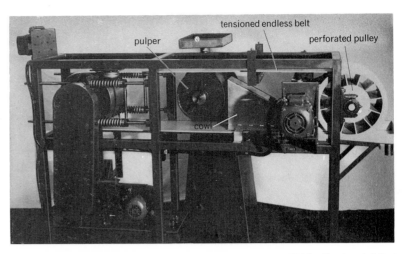

Laboratory-scale extraction unit for leaf protein; as much as 100 kg (fresh weight) of leaf per hour is pulped.

the cowl and is then pressed between the tensioned endless belt and the perforated pulley. The extract is pressed into the pulley and flows over its edges into a tray. Material made in laboratories has been used in human feeding experiments and demonstrations in Britain, India, and Nigeria. Less refined leaf protein, cheap enough for use as pig and poultry feed, is made commercially in Hungary and the United States. Commercial production is starting in France, and active research is being carried out in New Zealand. There are only small differences in the amino acid composition of the protein of many different species. The protein is of greater nutritional value than any seed protein available in bulk; it has as much nutritional value, when used as a supplement to most diets, as meat or fish, although not as much as milk or eggs. The main by-product is leaf fiber containing 1.5–2% nitrogen. Because of extraction and pressing, leaf fiber contains three to four times as much DM as the original crop and is therefore more economically dried for use as cattle fodder. This economy is the main reason for the interest the process has elicited in most countries.

The leaves best suited to extraction are soft, lush, and neither acid nor glutinous. Toxicity is of little importance because most of the toxic components are removed from both protein and fiber during extraction. Water weeds, and leaves that are by-products from other crops, are obvious sources, but crops grown especially for the purpose are likely to be the main source. There is no advantage in extracting protein from leaves normally eaten as vegetables; it would be better to publicize the very large yields of edible material given by leafy vegetables, the fact that they contain 20–35% protein on the DM, and the advantages of eating more of them.

Algae. Organizations in several countries have studied green algae as a possible source of food protein and then become disillusioned. Commercial production of pharmaceutical and flavoring products from green algae continues in Japan, but there has never been commercial production of a cheap foodstuff from this source. Blue-green algae *(Spirulina)* grow naturally in alkaline and saline lakes in North Africa and Mexico. It is a traditional food; tests involving human beings and animals have shown that it has good nutritive value. It is being harvested commercially from a lake in Mexico, where the natural yield is 10 tons (DM) per hectare and year. Greater yields are claimed from artificial cultivation in tanks. The unfractionated product contains 64–70% protein of good nutritive value. The salinity and alkalinity of the water in which *Spirulina* grows restrain the growth of other, possibly harmful, microorganisms and ensures the presence of abundant carbon dioxide. Furthermore, the lakes in which there is natural growth are in arid regions that have food shortages, and the water is of little use for agriculture. The advantages of growing *Spirulina* in expensive artificial tanks are less obvious.

Microorganisms. All the protein sources discussed so far depend on photosynthesis and atmospheric carbon dioxide. Bacteria, fungi, and yeasts do not photosynthesize and so must be supplied with carbon compounds that are already in a reduced state. The range of possible sources is enormous, for example, molasses, petroleum, sewage, straw, and the effluents from vegetable processing. The main commercial product is yeast grown on petroleum for use as animal fodder. Petroleum, however, is becoming a less attractive substrate, and the technique is so difficult that it is unlikely to be adopted in the countries most in need of increased protein supplies. There is commercial interest in the cultivation on sewage of a mixture of algae and bacteria because the mixture can be used as a fodder and the effluent is more suitable than the original sewage for use as irrigation water. It is more difficult to recover yeasts and bacteria from a culture fluid than to recover the mat of fungus mycelium. There is, therefore, commercial interest in cultivating *Aspergillus*, *Fusarium*, and *Paecilomyces* on molasses and on the effluent from papermaking. The large-scale production of leaf protein also yields a suitable effluent, for 10–20% of the DM of the crop is soluble. Experiments involving animals suggest that these products would be valuable foods, but they are not yet in use.

For background information *see* AGRICULTURAL SCIENCE (PLANT); FOOD ENGINEERING; YEAST in the McGraw-Hill Encyclopedia of Science and Technology.   [N. W. PIRIE]

Bibliography: M. Milner (ed.), *Nutritional Improvement of Food Legumes by Breeding*, Protein Advisory Group of the United Nations, 1973; N. W. Pirie (ed.), *Food Protein Sources*, 1975; N. W. Pirie (ed.), *Leaf Protein: Its Agronomy, Preparation, Quality, and Use*, 1971; J. W. G. Porter and B. A. Rolls (eds.), *Proteins in Human Nutrition*, 1971.

Aircraft testing

Since the advent of the missile age, the complexity and associated cost of aircraft testing have increased by several orders of magnitude. Technological advance coupled with the "fly-before-buy" concept which is prevalent on recent programs has led the aerospace community to place greater demands on the prototype model and to simultaneously attempt to obtain verification of the design performance early in the flight-test program. The task of testing the new generation of development aircraft has grown to the extent that a typical test article will require from 300 to 2000 individually sampled measurements which are examined from only once to more than 5000 times per second. This massive amount of available information far surpasses human ability to comprehend and react in a timely manner. Stated from a different viewpoint, the human element had once again become the limiting factor in the technological process.

This article examines recent advances made in the area of aircraft flight testing through the application of third-generation computer technology. Desirable attributes of an integrated systems approach are included, as is a practical example of an operating system.

System organization. The development process can basically be visualized as a closed loop consisting of three fundamental elements: design, test, and analysis. As in any closed-loop situation, feedback (in this case answers to the query: is this design satisfactory, or are changes required and should the cycle be reinitiated?) plays a critical part in the final satisfaction of the objective. In the area of development testing, analysis and the associated feedback commonly proved to be the pacing item for completion of a program.

Traditionally, the data reduction cycle was performed in time-consuming serial operation, referred to as batch processing. This procedure sometimes took as long as 2–4 weeks to supply the results required to continue the test sequence. The entire area of data management (airborne data acquisition, batch processing, and distribution of results) thus became a prime candidate for optimization and improvement.

Initial advances were made in the area of airborne data acquisition. Improvements in transducer design (a transducer is a device that transforms a physical stimulus such as heat, pressure, or acceleration into a proportional electrical output), coupled with the introduction of digital sampling, increased reliability and provided the means for obtaining the vast amount of data currently available. The introduction of telemetry (packaging of the information provided by the airborne system onto a carrier wave for transmission to the ground) proved to be the final step necessary for closing the loop and allowing the ground-based test team to interact with the pilot-aircraft in the real-time environment.

The next logical step in the evolutionary process was to provide an analysis tool that would supplement the abilities of the flight-test engineer by performing the arduous task of converting the raw information into meaningful engineering results. The engineer is thus freed of the routine procedure involved in obtaining the result and, instead, is able to concentrate on the effect of the answer on his test objectives.

To obtain the goals discussed above, the system in question must, to some degree, be capable of performing the following functions:

Unpackaging the information provided by the airborne acquisition system.

Converting the transducer inputs back into meaningful engineering terms.

Converting the raw engineering inputs into meaningful answers by means of analysis routines.

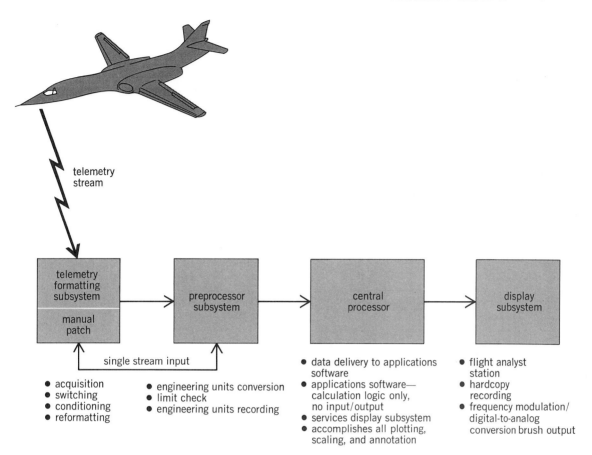

Fig. 1. Automated telemetry station configuration.

Providing the answers to the flight-test engineer on a media that can be readily understood.

Providing a cost-effective system capable of supporting vehicles with different acquisition schemes.

The final success of any system that proposes to operate in the real-time environment is directly proportional to its ability to fully perform these functions.

Automated telemetry system. In recent years there have been a number of systems constructed for operation within the real-time environment. The diversity of the objectives is indicated by examples of the test articles they have supported: the Sikorsky UTTAS helicopter entry, the McDonnel Douglas DC-10 airliner, and the Grumman Corporation F-14 fighter.

The system that perhaps best exemplifies the goals outlined in the preceding section is the automated telemetry station (ATS) developed by the Grumman Data Systems Corporation of Long Island, NY. The ATS has been used in a production environment for the past 4 years. It has supported the Navy's F-14 flight-test program and numerous other Grumman projects. The approach taken by Grumman in planning the ATS was unique in that the system was designed from the user's point of view. An intensive human engineering study was performed to determine the necessary person-machine interactions so that the completed installation would function as a true aid to the engineer, rather than as an additional hindrance to be over-

come in the performance of his duties. The true power of the integrated approach is fully realized in the ATS as demonstrated by an examination of its functional components (Fig. 1).

Telemetry formatting subsystem. Traditional telemetry hardware is utilized to unpackage and prepare the incoming telemetry data stream for transmittal to the next functional unit. The entire complement of equipment is under the control of the central computer subsystem, which makes possible automatic configuration as well as continuous monitoring of the performance of the unit. Sufficient equipment is provided to support three simultaneous flight-test efforts.

Preprocessor subsystem. The electrical input supplied by the transducers is converted to meaningful engineering terms in the specially designed hardware unit by applying up to a fifth-order polynomial expansion to the incoming data. The information is then limit-checked (high, low, or delta) and passed to the central computer subsystem for additional processing. An additional capability is then presented to the flight engineer so that he can, at his option, record the converted engineering measurements on computer-compatible tape suitable for additional processing. Three preprocessor units are available with this system.

Central computer subsystem. A third-generation multiprocessing computer performs additional analysis on the raw engineering information and provides results that the engineer can readily identify and utilize (that is, drag, lift, handling quali-

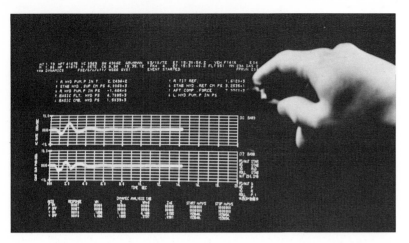

Fig. 2. Sample of cathode-ray-tube output. (*Courtesy Grumman Data Systems Corp.*)

ties, and propulsion information). This subsystem also serves as the master "traffic cop" of the operation. It interprets and implements the engineer's requests in real time and thus provides an interactive environment.

Display subsystem. Extensive utilization of human visual comprehension has been achieved by teaming a cathode-ray tube, on-line hard copy, and 35-mm microfilm in an interactive graphics subsystem. This unit provides the engineer with a direct input to the system and presents the results in a format that can be readily interpreted. Three of these units are available for use.

Operational aspects. In operation, the engineer receives cross-plotted or tabulated answers (see Fig. 2 for a sample of the cathode-ray-tube output) and information on critical measurement limit violations (for example, engine overheating) and is afforded the ability to select alternative flight objectives from the computer's mass storage units. The system flexibility permits three simultaneous flight-test efforts or allows all three data-reduction streams to be concentrated on a single test article. The ability to compare test results with predicted values in real time makes possible a reduction in the total test cycle and an improvement in flight safety. The monetary savings realized by the reduction in the test cycle are further increased when the method is applied to multiple-discipline test articles. This universal application is illustrated by two recent developments concerning the Grumman ATS concept:

An aerospace firm will flight-test its entry in the U.S. Army helicopter competition while utilizing the identical system that supported the F-14 effort.

The U.S. Air Force has purchased a system similar in design to that described above to support flight-test programs at its Edwards Flight-Test Center in California. The system will provide real-time results to the upcoming B-1 bomber program as well as to the multitude of other projects being tested at the center.

Conclusion. Real-time acquisition and processing systems have proved to be a valuable addition to the inventory of flight-analysis tools. New advances in computer and instrumentation technology are widening the scope of possible applications. The combination of new hardware, flexible operating systems, and human ingenuity will assure efficient, timely processing of the massive amounts of available information, providing not only data but the necessary answers in real time.

For background information *see* AIRCRAFT TESTING; SYSTEMS ENGINEERING; TELEMETERING in the McGraw-Hill Encyclopedia of Science and Technology.   [LYNN S. WILSON]

Air-cushion vehicle

In the past 2 years the surface effect ship (SES) has received the most attention of any air-cushion vehicle for marine use. The SES is supported on a cushion of air that is contained at the ship's ends by flexible seals and at the sides by solid sidewalls, unlike a hovercraft that has flexible seals around the entire periphery. High speed is possible because little of the hull is immersed in the water.

SES test craft. During 1973 and 1974 the U.S. Navy conducted test and evaluation of two 100-ton (1 long ton = 1016 kg) SES craft. The SES-100B (Fig. 1), designed and built by Bell Aerospace Company, achieved a speed of over 80 knots (41 m/sec). The SES-100A (Fig. 2), designed by the Aerojet-General Corporation with many different technical approaches from the SES-100B, reached a speed of 76 knots during testing.

The principal difference between the two craft is the propulsion plant. The SES-100A has a waterjet propulsion system employing high-powered water-jet pumps that shoot large columns of water astern. The SES-100B uses propellers—supercavitating because of the high speeds involved, and semisubmerged because only half of the propeller blades are submerged beneath the hull at any one time.

Tests of these craft have validated the technology base which led to their design. Testing emphasized speed and drag resistance relationships, maneuverability, dynamic behavior in a seaway, water-jet and propeller propulsion efficiency, operation of the lift system which supplies air to the air cushion, structural loading, and seal performance.

Four other solid sidewall craft were used in test-

Fig. 1. SES-100B air-cushion vehicle. (*Bell Aerospace Company*)

Fig. 2. SES-100A air-cushion vehicle. (*Aerojet-General Corporation*)

Fig. 4. Artist's rendition of the preliminary design of a 2000-ton SES for the U.S. Navy. (*Rohr Industries*)

ing in the past 2 years: the 20-ton HM-2, constructed in the United Kingdom for commercial use; the 18-ton XR-1, operated by Rohr Industries for propulsion plant testing; the 3½-ton XR-5, constructed by the Naval Ship Research and Development Center at Carderock, MD, to investigate the effects of SES with high ratios of length to beam (6 or greater) in comparison with conventional ratios of 2 to 3; the 2½-ton XR-3, in research use at the U.S. Naval Postgraduate School at Monterey, CA.

2000-ton SES. The major thrust of the U.S. Navy's SES development efforts has been oriented toward the design of a 2000-ton surface effect ship. This ship would be a developmental test bed to demonstrate the practicality and utility of a high-speed oceangoing ship in naval applications. Its approximate dimensions—length 250 ft (76.2 m), beam 105 ft (32 m), cushion height 18 ft (5.5 m)—represent a scaling increase of about three times those of the 100-ton test craft.

Progress. From November 1972 to August 1973

Fig. 3. Artist's rendition of the preliminary design of a 2000-ton SES for the U.S. Navy. (*Bell Aerospace Company*)

preliminary design of the 2000-ton SES was conducted by Aerojet-General Corporation, Bell Aerospace Company, Litton Industries, and Lockheed Missiles and Space Corporation. After additional technical work and program reformulation, contracts were awarded in June 1974 to both Bell Aerospace and Rohr Industries (the latter having replaced Litton as prime contractor) for a large program of SES subsystem development and ship design.

Artists' concepts of the Bell and Rohr preliminary designs are shown in Figs. 3 and 4.

Technical challenge. The design of the 2000-ton SES represents a significant challenge in many areas of technology. The Navy's program contains development work in all of the critical areas where the scale jump from 100 to 2000 tons requires extension of the state of the art. A brief discussion of some of these areas of technical challenge follows.

Propulsion. The 2000-ton SES will be propelled by four water-jet pumps driven by four LM2500 gas turbine engines, each rated in excess of 20,000 shaft horsepower (14,900 kW). Water-jet pumps of nearly this rating have been used in large hydrofoil applications. The principal area of new development in propulsion is in the design of the water-jet inlet (which is flush with the bottom of the sidewall) so as to minimize cavitation, to provide proper water flow conditions to the pump over the entire speed range, and to reduce any adverse effects which may result from intermittent broaching (unwetting) of the inlet in rough water.

Seals. Flexible seals at the bow and stern of an SES help contain the air cushion, but at the same time must deform so that waves can pass under the ship. The principal problems in developing seals so much larger than those used on 100-ton test craft include the requirements for higher strength and durability of the elastomeric seal material.

Structure. The aluminum structure of an SES generally weighs more than 25% of the gross weight of the ship. Accordingly, it must be designed for high efficiency. One of the most important developmental problems associated with SES structures is the definition of the imposed loading because of impact with waves at the bow at high speed.

Lift system and ride quality. The lift system of an SES consists of gas turbines, large fans, and associated ducting and controls. It provides air to maintain the air pressure of the cushion against losses from leakage under the sidewalls and the seals, and losses due to "wave pumping" (wave-induced leakage). It also can provide means for regulating variations in the cushion pressure which directly control the vertical accelerations experienced by the crew. The definition of acceleration limits for crew comfort is an associated technical problem which is receiving increased emphasis.

Stability and control. The unusual hydrodynamic characteristics of an SES, and the problems of safety and controllability at high speed, dictate a comprehensive program of analysis and testing to ensure satisfactory operation of a large SES. Operations with the 100-ton test craft have demonstrated that the technology exists to meet such an objective.

Other technical challenges. The engineering of a large Navy ship which is part aircraft and part ship obviously entails new challenges to the naval architect. One of the most critical problems is weight reduction in all facets of the ship design without adversely affecting the reliability of ship operation. Another problem is providing protection against fire without excessive weight penalty since aluminum can lose its strength if exposed to high temperature. Also, an SES contains a very-high-power generation capability for propulsion and lift system operation, and providing suitable acoustic insulation from these gas turbines is important to the well-being of the crew.

Revolutionary potential. If development of a 2000-ton SES is successfully accomplished, a vehicle with revolutionary new military potential will be at sea by the end of the decade. Larger sizes can then be designed with confidence for naval missions where the ability to transit long distances at very high speeds is important. Commercial applications may also emerge where the payload requirements exceed the payload which can be carried by aircraft and where the speed requirements exceed the speeds achievable by conventional displacement ships.

For background information *see* AIR-CUSHION VEHICLE in the McGraw-Hill Encyclopedia of Science and Technology.   [MICHAEL C. DAVIS]

Bibliography: Four papers presented by M. C. Davis, C. L. Forrest, P. Kaplan and S. Davis, and N. L. Werner and F. P. Burke, at the American Institute of Aeronautics and Astronautics/Society of Naval Architects and Marine Engineers Conference, San Diego, February 1974; R. McLeavy (ed.), *Jane's Surface Skimmers: Hovercraft & Hydrofoils,* 1973.

Air-pollution control

Air-pollution control is practiced by government and private agencies to limit the emission and formation of air pollutants and thus reduce the deleterious effects upon humans and their environment. The U.S. Environmental Protection Agency (EPA) performs a regulatory function to control air pollution by using a control cycle that requires identification and study of pollutant sources, pollutant transport processes and transformations, and health and economic effects on pollutant receptors. EPA also requires setting standards and taking enforcement actions to limit emissions from sources in order to reduce pollutants to socially acceptable levels.

Monitoring provides a vital link in all phases of the control cycle, from the qualitative and quantitative identification of source emissions, to the collection of data on biological and health effects, to the continuous measurement of ambient pollutant concentrations for long-term trend information, and to determining compliance with emission standards. Monitoring techniques for air-pollution control are developed in the laboratory, applied to measurement of emissions from stationary and mobile sources, and used to measure pollutants in the ambient air.

This discussion deals with some outstanding recent advances in techniques for monitoring air-pollutant concentratons. The methodology is broadly divided into contact- and remote-sensing techniques. With contact techniques, the polluted air sample is brought into intimate contact with the sensing device. Remote techniques are used to measure average pollutant concentrations over an extended path in air or to measure the pollutant at a given location with a remotely located sensor. Contact techniques discussed below apply chemiluminescence and fluorescence in measuring pollutant gases, and x-ray fluorescence in elemental analysis of airborne particulates. Remote techniques apply infrared absorption in gas-phase measurements and laser scattering in measuring inversion layers and mapping pollutant clouds. These techniques do not include all recent developments, but do represent significant trends in modern monitoring activities.

Contact monitoring techniques. In the earliest air-pollutant measurement procedures, pollutants were isolated from large volumes of air and measured by classical and complex wet chemical procedures. By contrast, advanced techniques used today are instrumental in nature and employ sensing devices that continuously and directly measure pollutant concentration.

Chemiluminescent techniques. In the typical chemiluminescent detector, an air sample is mixed in a reaction chamber with a reagent chemical (Fig. 1). Reaction between the reagent and the pollutant of interest produces a characteristic emission of light known as chemiluminescence. The light is viewed by a photomultiplier tube through an optical filter that is used to isolate a given spectral region and eliminate interfering chemiluminescent emissions. The photomultiplier output is amplified to produce a photocurrent that is a linear function of pollutant concentration. Chemiluminescent detectors are capable of measuring pollutant concentrations on the order of 1 part per billion (ppb).

Ozone (O_3) was the first pollutant to be routinely monitored by chemiluminescent techniques. In the detector, O_3 reacts with ethylene gas to produce a characteristic chemiluminescence. This is the preferred technique of the EPA and is widely applied today.

More recently chemiluminescence has been applied to the measurement of nitric oxide (NO) and nitrogen dioxide (NO_2) in the atmosphere and in the emissions from automotive and industrial sources. The basic chemiluminescent reaction is between NO in air and a concentrated stream of O_3 as reagent. The reaction between NO and O_3 results in light emission in the near-infrared region. The basic reaction is applicable only to the detection of NO. The typical instrument, however, contains a high-temperature inlet device that quantitatively converts any NO_2 present to NO before the air sample enters the reaction chamber. When the air sample passes through the converter, the detector output is proportional to the concentration of total oxides at nitrogen ($NO_x = NO + NO_2$). A parallel instrument channel without a converter is used to measure the concentration of NO. The difference between the NO_x measurement and the NO measurement yields the concentration of NO_2.

Advanced chemiluminescent detectors are available only for the measurement of O_3 and NO_x. Several laboratory investigations have recently been made on chemiluminescent reactions, and they may be applied in the future to the detection of carbon monoxide (CO), peroxyacetyl nitrate (PAN), sulfur compounds, and certain hydrocarbons.

Fluorescence techniques. Several pollutant molecules absorb light in the ultraviolet or visible region of the spectrum. When molecules absorb light, a portion of this absorbed energy is reemitted as light of longer wavelengths. As with chemiluminescence, this fluorescent emission can be used to monitor the concentration of the absorbing pollutant molecule.

In the fluorescent detector, a high-intensity light source irradiates a flowing airstream and induces fluorescence from the pollutant of interest. A photomultiplier tube monitors the fluorescent emission. The fluorescent emission can be isolated from the incident light by the use of optical filters.

Fluorescence techniques have been applied more recently than chemiluminescence methods have, and are at a much less advanced stage of development. Fluorescence methods employ radiant energy rather than chemical energy to induce light emission. In both cases, the emission intensity is monitored with a photomultiplier, the output photocurrent is linearly related to pollutant concentrations, and detection limits are on the order of a few parts per billion. In comparison to chemiluminescence, fluorescence offers some simplification of detector design. The external addition of chemical reagent is not required, and the air sample flow rate need not be critically controlled.

To date, fluorescence detectors have been developed for sulfur dioxide (SO_2) and NO_2. The SO_2 detector is available commercially, and the NO_2 detector is at an advanced engineering stage. Laboratory work has shown that it is feasible to detect NO by ultraviolet-induced fluorescence. In controlled laboratory experiments, CO has been monitored by vacuum ultraviolet fluorescence techniques. Other candidates for fluorescence detec-

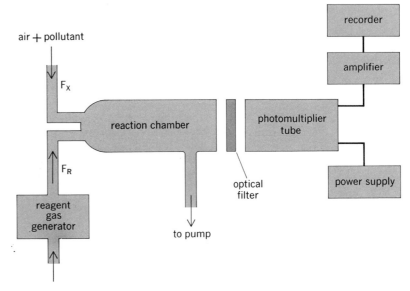

Fig. 1. Chemiluminescence detector. *(From J. A. Hodgeson, W. A. McClenney, and P. L. Hanst, Air pollution monitoring by advanced spectroscopic techniques, Science, 182:248, 1973)*

tion are formaldehyde and chlorine gas.

X-ray fluorescence techniques. Concentrations of specific elements in ambient air particulates are normally too low to be determined by continuous techniques. Particulate matter must therefore be collected and concentrated on an air filter prior to analysis. In the usual procedure, the air filter is returned to the laboratory, and the particulate matter is dissolved by an ashing procedure. The resultant solution is analyzed for elemental composition by complex laboratory procedures.

X-ray fluorescence is a nondestructive technique that can be applied to the automated, elemental analysis of a heterogeneous surface. A number of elements can be determined within a few minutes without sample preparation. Recently, this technqiue has been applied to the direct elemental analysis of particulate matter on air filters.

In the x-ray technique, the air filter is irradiated with a beam of high-energy x-rays. The elements within the sample are excited and emit fluorescent x-ray photons. The energy of the photon is characteristic of the element, and the intensity or rate of photon emission is proportional to elemental abundance. Two types of x-ray fluorescence spectrometers are available. In the wavelength-dispersive type, x-ray photons from different elements are separated by a grating. The alternative technique, energy-dispersive x-ray fluorescence, employs an energy-sensitive solid-state detector and associated electronics to separate x-rays from different elements.

Both systems can be used for the multielement analysis of air filter samples. The energy-dispersive device offers some advantages in terms of compactness, analysis time, and adaptability to automated field operation. Recently a prototype energy-dispersive analyzer was used to obtain semiautomated analysis for up to 25 elements on air filter samples collected during an EPA field program.

Remote monitoring techniques. Significant advances have been made recently in applying remote sensing to pollutant measurements. Research and development efforts are presently accelerating because of potential benefits to be derived from remote measurements, for example, mapping of large geographical areas (especially by airborne sensors); validation of networks employing contact sensors; measurements at inaccessible locations; and monitoring of pollutant sources for possible emission violations.

Infrared techniques. The majority of remote-sensing techniques employ the interaction of infrared (IR) radiation with pollutants. Virtually all molecules possess absorption bands in the IR region. These bands serve as a very distinct fingerprint by which pollutant molecules can be identified. Pollutant concentrations down to a few parts per billion can be measured over moderate path lengths of a few kilometers by IR techniques.

IR absorption techniques for remote sensing employ an IR source, a long optical path through the atmosphere, and a detector. Several configurations can be employed in a remote IR absorption experiment. In passive sensing, the Sun is used as the source, and pollutant bands appear in the solar background spectra observed through the Earth's atmosphere. In active sensing, an artificial source, for example, an IR laser, is employed. Some remote measurements are made horizontally across the Earth's surface. Others are made vertically, from the Earth looking upward or from an airborne sensor looking downward.

The most advanced technique today for remote pollutant monitoring is called differential absorp-

tion. Two or more closely spaced laser emission lines are simultaneously transmitted across a long optical path. A resonance line coincides with the wavelength of a pollutant absorption band. The nearby reference laser line is used to correct the effects of interfering absorption bands and of scattering from suspended particles. A schematic representation of a differential absorption system employing a retroreflector is shown in Fig. 2. Prototype differential absorption systems are now being applied by EPA to measure O_3 and ethylene in the atmosphere.

Differential absorption measurements yield the average pollutant concentration along the optical path. The differential absorption and scattering (DAS) technique is a new approach that may yield the spatial distribution along the optical path. Like differential absorption, DAS employs pulsed laser operation both on and off a characteristic absorption band. However, DAS measures the backscattered pulses from ambient atmospheric particulates and molecules, which are used as distributed reflectors along the optical path. Time resolution of the laser pulses backscattered to the detector yields information on the range of measurement as well as pollutant concentration. At present, DAS is still in an experimental stage.

Measurements have recently been made of several minor atmospheric constituents by passive IR sensing with the Sun as source and an interferometer spectrometer as detector. This spectrometer is an instrument that can be used to collect and store a portion of the solar infrared spectrum. Characteristic IR absorption bands in the solar spectrum are used to identify and measure the concentration of trace atmospheric species. Aircraft-flown interferometers have measured nitrous oxide, NO, NO_2, CO, and methane. Most of these measurements are preliminary in nature and are unconfirmed by independent observations.

Lidar techniques. Lidar (light detection and ranging) devices measure the presence and range of atmospheric aerosols. Aerosols are micrometer- or submicrometer-diameter particles formed by reactions occurring in photochemical smog or emitted directly by pollutant sources.

A pulsed laser beam is directed upward from the ground or downward from an aircraft. Some of the laser photons are scattered back toward the source by aerosol particles and detected by a photomultiplier tube. The output of the photomultiplier tube is time-analyzed to yield a measure of the aerosol concentration as a function of distance from the laser source. The application of lidar systems is analogous to detecting clouds and rain by radar (radio detection and ranging). A radar's microwaves match the size of airborne water particles detected, just as lidar's wavelength matches the size of aerosol particles.

The primary importance of lidar lies in its ability to map the height and boundary of air inversions (an inversion is a layer of warm air above cool air). Air pollutants are boxed in by the inversion and cannot disperse normally. At the height of the inversion layer, the number of backscattered photons from a given laser pulse decreases dramatically. With lidar techniques, inversion boundaries can be measured more completely and quickly

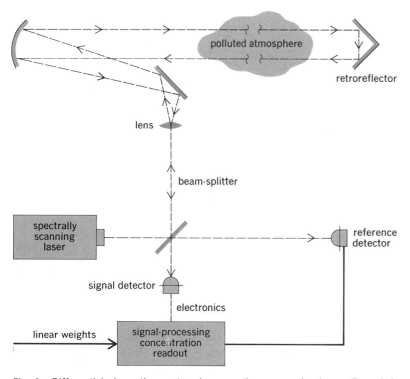

Fig. 2. Differential absorption system incorporating a scanning laser. (*From J. A. Hodgeson, W. A. McClenney, and P. L. Hanst, Air pollution monitoring by advanced spectroscopic techniques, Science, 182:248, 1973*).

than they can with the conventional method of temperature soundings with weather balloons.

Airborne lidar systems are also capable of yielding detailed information on the structure of the pollutant cloud below the inversion. As an aircraft traverses an urban area, a series of downward-looking lidar soundings are made to obtain vertical profiles of aerosol scattering. By combining a series of vertical profiles along a transverse coordinate and drawing contour lines along constant scattering points, a two-dimensional map showing the dispersion of the pollutant cloud is obtained.

Lidar techniques are being applied in field demonstrations and research studies. Lidar will be useful in research studies on the transport and dispersion of pollutant clouds. Future applications call for the mapping of air inversions in their early stages, before they become visible, thus making it possible for air-pollution-control officials in smog-prone areas to take prompt preventive action.

For background information *see* AIR-POLLUTION CONTROL; LASER; X-RAY FLUORESCENCE ANALYSIS in the McGraw-Hill Encyclopedia of Science and Technology.   [J. A. HODGESON]

Bibliography: J. A. Hodgeson, W. A. McClenney, and P. L. Hanst, *Science*, 182:248, 1973; Instrument Society of America, *Proceedings of the 2d Joint Conference on Sensing of Environmental Pollutants*, Washington, D.C., Dec. 10–12, 1973; R. K. Stevens and W. F. Herget (eds.), *Analytical Methods Applied to Air Pollution Measurements*, Ann Arbor Science Publishers, 1974.

Air-traffic control

Recent developments in air-traffic control include the use of an automated radar terminal system (ARTS) and the development of an integrated communications-navigation-identification (ICNI) system.

ARTS. An automated radar terminal system, ARTS III, has been installed at 61 of the high-traffic-density airports in the United States. This new automation system accepts inputs from the airport surveillance radar (ASR) and the air-traffic control radar beacon system (ATCRBS). Radar video, representing aircraft targets, is presented on the air-traffic controllers' displays. The automation system automatically tracks controlled aircraft which are equipped with ATCRBS transponders and presents alphanumeric information adjacent to these targets. Tracking is automatically initiated on aircraft equipped with discrete beacon code capability (4096 codes). When received, discrete codes are correlated with a stored list of codes representing controlled aircraft. Controlled aircraft equipped with older transponders with limited code capability (64 codes) are tracked automatically; however, track initiation requires controller manual entries to associate the proper aircraft identification with the nondiscrete code. Once tracking is initiated, aircraft identification, altitude determined in the aircraft and reported to the ground, and aircraft ground speed are presented in a data block located adjacent to each controlled aircraft target.

Altitude is determined in the aircraft by using a barometric altimeter which digitally encodes the information for transmission by the aircraft transponder. This transmission is initiated in response to a coded request for altitude received from the ground. The discrete transponder code is assigned to the pilot as a part of the air-traffic control (ATC) procedure. The pilot, in turn, sets this information into code wheels in the transponder. This code is transmitted each time a request for assigned identity codes is received from the ground ATCRBS interrogator. Ground speed is computed on the ground as a part of the tracking process.

System components. The basic ARTS III system represents a capability which can be added to existing radar approach control facilities, utilizing present ASR and ATCRBS systems. The system consists of a programmable digital computer, a beacon digitizer, and an improved ASR display system. The system interfaces with an air route traffic control center for the transfer of flight data and control handoff messages. (Control handoff is a procedure which consists of identifying the radar target on the controller's display at the receiving ATC facility and the transfer of control responsibility for an aircraft from the controller in one facility to the controller in another facility.) In addition, data on aircraft departing from the airport without an ATC clearance are entered manually into the system through the use of an alphanumeric keyboard and a radar position entry device. A preview display area is provided on the display for validating messages prior to entry into the system.

The display used by the controller presents primary radar target information, ATCRBS target information on targets replying on codes selected by the controller, and alphanumeric data. These data include airway map information, data blocks on controlled aircraft, numeric readout of transponder altitude data on uncontrolled aircraft within a band of altitudes selected by the controller, arrival aircraft lists, and departure aircraft lists for aircraft arriving and departing from airports within the controller's area of responsibility. Radar controller positions located in the approach control facility include those for arrival and departure. ARTS III assists the controllers at these positions by automatically maintaining the identity of video targets representing controlled aircraft; by providing automatic readout of transponder-reported aircraft altitude to greatly reduce the number of air-ground communications required for terminal control; and by providing ground speed to facilitate the sequencing and spacing of arrival aircraft.

Capabilities and automation. The basic ARTS III system as currently installed provides tracking and alphanumeric data only on transponder-equipped aircraft. The design of the system is modular, however, and subsequent expansion of the basic system will include provision of additional capabilities. These capabilities include tracking of non-transponder-equipped aircraft using primary radar data with display of full data blocks on controlled aircraft; generation of digital mosaic displays using inputs from more than one radar; and automation of additional air-traffic control functions. These functions include conflict prediction and controller warnings when aircraft are predicted to violate minimum separation standards; computerized control of aircraft flow into the terminal area and computer assistance to the terminal controller in sequencing and spacing aircraft to achieve maximum arrival rates at high-traffic airports; and final-approach altitude monitoring to detect unsafe approaches and to warn the controller when aircraft are below the safe approach path.

Expansion of the basic ARTS III system to handle increased traffic as well as increased functions is made possible through the use of a multiprocessing type of computer. The smallest computer configuration includes an input-output processing unit and separate memory unit. The largest configuration, capable of handling 500–600 aircraft, consists of four input-output processing units, three central processing units, and up to twelve memory units. Another feature of the larger configurations is the incorporation of a fail-safe capability to protect the air-traffic control system performance against failure of computer units. The larger systems will include one additional unit of each type (that is, input-output processor, central processor unit, or memory). A failure detection and reconfiguration unit monitors system operation to detect failures, switch inoperative units out of the on-line configuration, and switch in the redundant spare elements. This method of operation results in very high levels of system reliability. Implementation of the ARTS III expansion functions is scheduled to start within a year.

Automation is also scheduled for 72 lower-density terminals using an automation system similar to ARTS III in that it includes all basic ARTS III functions except beacon tracking. This system, called ARTS II, is also expandable to accommodate growth in traffic and automation of additional functions. The system is modular, and functions such as beacon tracking may be added to the basic ARTS II system by addition of computer units, such as memories, and new computer programs.

Introduction of the ARTS type of automation into terminal air-traffic control facilities has resulted in significant advantages to the system in reducing control workload through presentation of alphanumeric data on the controller's scope; increasing safety through display of altitude data on both controlled and uncontrolled aircraft to facilitate detection of potential conflict situations; and reducing training time as controller trainees no longer have to depend solely on manual correlation between radar targets and flight identities. Future expansion of the ARTS capabilities will serve both to increase control system capacity and to limit controller manning requirements, which in turn will result in the gradual reduction of system operating costs.   [NEAL A. BLAKE]

ICNI. The integrated communications-navigation-identification (ICNI) concept is an attempt at the unification of the multiple subsystems that currently provide these functions for the civil and military avionics community into a single integrated system. In the past year some significant progress toward this goal has been made. It is expected that ICNI will help civil air-traffic control by the addition of digital data links to the voice communications now used as a primary control method.

Historical background. The formalized concept to integrate the basic CNI functions into a single system can be traced to the Radio Technical

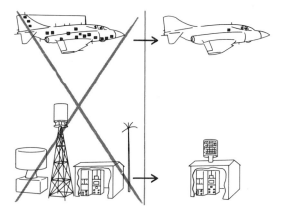

Fig. 1. Simplification through integration.

Commission for Aeronautics Special Committee 31 (RTCA-SC31) Final Report, issued in 1948: "In the interest of national defense and national welfare, an integrated system of air traffic control is a vital necessity." ". . . Indeed, the RTCA system consolidates into a single equipment all the services required for navigation and instrument landing, radiocommunications for traffic control, . . ." Only in the past several years has significant progress toward this goal been made. Both the Federal Aviation Administration (FAA) and the Department of Defense have ICNI systems in various stages of development.

Driving factors. Several driving factors are behind the developments leading to the current activities in ICNI. In civil aviation a major concern is flight safety. As the number and frequency of flights increase, the burden on the existing air-traffic control (ATC) system is increased. The primary control medium for both in-flight and terminal ATC is inefficient voice communications. The major thrust of the current systems work is the addition of digital data links.

In the military application of ICNI cost reduction is an especially important goal. The military inventory includes hundreds of different types of basic CNI equipments. The associated cost penalties that these separate systems impose on a typical military aircraft and on the ground-based support function are enormous.

Other important benefits of the proposed ICNI system are significantly higher levels of system performance, interference protection (antijamming), and security.

Figure 1 shows the substantial reductions envisioned in airborne and ground-based CNI hardware through integration. Comparative studies on representative military aircraft have shown that the weight and volume savings achieved by the integrated system are on the order of 30–40%. Comparable cost savings are also achieved with ICNI.

Major considerations. The analytical work and systems definition developed to date in ICNI have considered several key items. First is a recognition that radio-frequency spectrum is a scarce commodity. The choice of a suitable spectrum for an ICNI system is further limited by atmospheric propagation properties, line-of-sight limitations, and hardware design considerations. The major emphasis is currently on the uhf portion of the spectrum, especially the $960-1215$ MHz, L_x band, orginally identified by RTCA-SC31 for common use. This L_x band has historically been allocated internationally to aeronautical radio functions. It also offers very attractive features in the areas of commonality to civil and triservice military users, desirable propagation characteristics, and a low utilization factor which provides a compatible growth potential. In the shared use of this spectrum it is recognized that any new ICNI system to be introduced must not interfere with the tactical air navigation/distance-measuring equipment (TACAN/DME) and identify friend or foe/air-traffic control radar beacon system (IFF/ATCRBS) currently using the band. The new ICNI system must also have a high tolerance level to the signals that are presently being transmitted by the TACAN/DME and IFF/ATCRBS systems to prevent undesirable interference effects.

This requirement leads to another important element of ICNI system design, namely, signal structure. The signal structure selected for the ICNI system must possess inherent characteristics, such as bandwidth, modulation, dwell time (the duration of a signal exchange on a particular carrier frequency), and duty cycle (the product of pulse width and pulse rate), that make it suitable for the performance levels required, while at the same time having the essential compatibility features with the current users to allow for common utilization of the band. The selection of suitable signal structure has been simplified by recent advances in signal-processing techniques. In addition, the advanced state of development and ready availability of integrated circuits has enabled digital communication to become economically feasible for ICNI applications. The utilization of matched filters, such as surface acoustic wave (SAW) devices, charge coupled devices (CCD), and digital matched filters (DMF), as correlation elements has brought the powerful technique of spectrum spreading into the forefront of the military ICNI applications and has reduced the cost of these techniques for civil application. Although the technical details of spread spectrum techniques as

applied to military ICNI are currently classified for national security, a general description may be given. *See* FILTER, ELECTRIC.

The spread spectrum modulation technique achieves its enhanced performance by producing a signal whose rf bandwidth is intentionally expanded to be much wider than the basic information bandwidth. In order to receive these signals a correlation process is applied to remove the spread spectrum modulation. The major benefits afforded to an ICNI system by the use of the proper combination of time hopping, frequency hopping, and spread spectrum techniques are that the signals transmitted by the ICNI system have none of the predictability and exploitability features that would allow an enemy jammer to compromise performance. Additionally, through the use of these signaling techniques, an increased measure of compatibility with narrow-band signals is provided since in many instances the spread spectrum signal appears as background noise to the narrow-band receivers.

Current ICNI programs. Current ICNI program developments for civil application are the Digital Data Broadcast System (DDBS) and Discrete Address Beacon System (DABS). The DDBS is a development of FAA contracts with ITT Avionics, Nutley, NJ, a division of International Telephone and Telegraph Corporation, and the EDMAC Company, Rochester, NY. The DDBS will provide for a ground-to-air digital data link on the current VOR/TACAN (VORTAC) channels. The data will be of a preprogrammed broadcast nature and will carry information on the geographic location, elevation, magnetic variation, and related data of the particular VORTAC station being received.

The DABS concept is an important element of the FAA's next-generation air-traffic control system. It will result in an improved aircraft surveillance system by providing for the unique addressing of identification-interrogations to specific aircraft. It will also add a new ground-to-air digital data link for routine ATC information and flight control. A feature calling for all ground-based DABS elements to operate in a synchronized manner has led to Synchro-DABS, which can provide a relatively simple air-to-air collision avoidance ser-

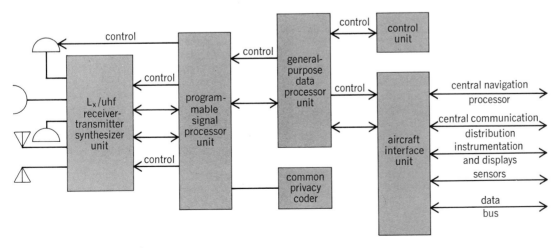

Fig. 2. Typical ICNI block diagram.

vice in addition to the basic DABS functions. DABS and Synchro-DABS will operate compatibly with the conventional ATCRBS ground-based interrogators. The system design and analysis were performed for the FAA by Lincoln Laboratory, Lexington, MA.

For military applications of ICNI there are several on-going programs. The USAF, under the auspices of the Electronic System Division and MITRE Corporation, Bedford, MA, has initially developed the communication elements of an ICNI system known as SEEK BUS. The first application of the system is expected to be on the airborne warning and control system (AWACS) platform being developed by the Boeing Company, Seattle, WA. The U.S. Navy currently has two related ICNI programs under development by the Naval Air System Command, Washington, D.C., and the Naval Air Development Center, Warminster, PA. One, which initially addresses improved navigation for Navy ships and aircraft, is the Integrated Tactical Navigation Subsystem (ITNS). The system, designed and built by the Singer-General Precision Company, Little Falls, NJ, is currently undergoing evaluation testing.

The second of these is the Integrated Tactical Air Control System (ITACS), an ICNI concept that incorporates ITNS and further addresses the entire range of communication navigation and identification functions. The current status of ITACS is the advanced engineering evaluation of two terminals designed and built by the ITT Avionics Division. Figure 2 shows a typical block diagram of an ICNI system operating in both the uhf 225–400 MHz and L_x 960–1215 MHz bands. The major elements are a receiver/transmitter unit and associated antennas, a programmable signal processor, and a general-purpose digital computer which is used as the data processor and overall control element. A control unit, privacy coder or scrambler, and associated interface with other aircraft systems are shown. A major element of the typical interconnection shown in Fig. 2 is the time-shared utilization of programmable hardware elements to perform the various CNI functions.

Future. The outlook for ICNI systems looks promising. The technology in digital devices, high-speed microprocessors, analog and digital matched filters, and related areas promises to deliver a continuing base of high-performance low-cost devices. The driving factors of current equipment proliferation and the need for improvements in performance will also provide necessary impetus for future developments.

For background information *see* AIR-TRAFFIC CONTROL in the McGraw-Hill Encyclopedia of Science and Technology.   [JACK RUBIN]

Bibliography: R. L. Asher, *J. Inst. Navig.*, 18(4): 425–432, Winter 1971–1972; C. R. Cahn, *Spread Spectrum Applications and State of the Art Equipment*, Magnavox Research Labs, MX-TM-3134-72, Nov. 22, 1972; Department of Transportation, Federal Aviation Administration, *ARTS III System Description*, SPO-MD-600, 1970; P. J. Klass, *Aviat. Week Space Tech.*, pp. 44–51, July 23, 1973; Radio Technical Commission for Aeronautic Special Committee 31, *Final Report Paper*, 27–48/DO-12, May 12, 1948.

Alloy

Amorphous metallic alloys have been investigated for more than a decade. During the last 3 years these materials have assumed particular importance because of their potential application in two widely different areas of industry. In one case they offer the potential of simple and inexpensive materials for storage in computers, and in the other, of replacements for materials requiring high strength and corrosion resistance, or of materials with low acoustic losses.

Amorphous alloys are solids that have no crystal structure. The atoms are packed together; their positions can be described in terms of a dense but random packing. One of the principal advantages of a dense random packing is the ability to vary the composition of a large number of amorphous alloys without undue concern for phase equilibria as given by phase equilibrium diagrams that show the composition ranges of crystal stability. This extra degree of freedom in amorphous alloys has enabled investigators to "tune in" the required properties. For example, the magnetic properties of the amorphous alloys have caused them to become early and strong candidates for magnetic bubble technology.

Magnetic bubble applications. Magnetic bubbles are cylindrical magnetic domains occurring in thin films, the easy axis of magnetization being perpendicular to the plane of the film. Information is stored by the presence or absence of bubbles. The bubbles form the zeroes and ones of binary information storage in a computer. An advantage of magnetic bubbles in storage arises from the low cost of bubble devices. They have the potential of replacing disks by a solid-state store. Magnetic bubbles also offer an incredibly high density of information packing. The smallest bubble is of the order of 1000 A (10 A=1 nm); with this size the density of information storage is of the order of a billion bits per square centimeter, which is several orders of magnitude larger than current commercially available densities in disk storage.

Magnetic bubbles were traditionally thought to be useful only in single-crystal materials. After it was discovered that they could be produced in amorphous films, prototype devices using magnetic bubbles have been built. Their advantage, apart from the ability to tune magnetic properties, lies in the ease of manufacture of large-area films by sputtering techniques.

In this technique a cathode made of the desired composition is used as a target. For example, in the case of magnetic bubbles, the target may consist of a gadolinium-cobalt-molybdenum (Gd-Co-Mo) alloy that has been arc-melted on a refractory plate. The melting is done in an inert atmosphere to avoid oxidation of the constituent species. Targets can also be made by using powder metallurgical techniques. This process ensures uniformity over the target area. In fact, commercially available targets use this process. An inert gas—usually argon—is ionized, and these ions move toward the cathode. The argon ions bombard the surface of the target and sputter off the target atoms, which consist, in this case, of Gd-Co-Mo. The atoms deposit on the substrate, giving rise to a film. The area of the substrate over which a uniform film can be deposited is determined by several factors. However, the ratio of the size of the target and the distance between the target and the film are particularly significant. With an 8-in. (20-cm) target, films with a uniformity variation of only a few percent can readily be grown over a several-inch-diameter substrate. In contrast, the single-crystal approach has so far yielded good-quality films that have a diameter of less than 2 in. (5 cm). The advantages of manufacturing large-area substrates are inherent to the bubble technology, which lends itself to full-wafer processing. This ability increases the yield, with a subsequent savings in cost per bit of information.

The magnetic properties of the amorphous metallic films are qualitatively similar to those of their crystalline counterparts. The principal reasons for this similarity lie in the atomic arrangement of an amorphous solid and the origin of the magnetism of metallic systems. The short-range order in amorphous alloys is quite similar to that of their crystalline counterparts, and as a result, those physical properties that rely on nearest-neighbor interaction are similar. Magnetic phenomena in metallic alloys are an example. Although qualitative understanding of magnetism in these materials is quite good, a quantitative theory is still lacking. Despite this shortcoming, amorphous materials show very good potential in the area of storage for computers.

Bulk application. Within the last few years the rapid cooling required to obtain amorphous materials has been developed in a form that makes available thin strips or wires of amorphous materials. The process was developed by Allied Chemical; the material is available under the trade name Metglas. This development has opened up several possible applications of amorphous metallic alloys. All rely on properties of amorphous materials that are directly relatable to the absence of long-range atomic order.

The amorphous alloys that have been made in strip or wire form are iron- or nickel-based alloys with various amounts of phosphorus, carbon, boron, and silicon. The iron or nickel atoms form the base alloy, and the four elements added in various combinations stabilize the amorphous state. They are frequently called glass formers, and it is generally accepted that they impart stability to the atomic arrangement characteristic of the amorphous state by occupying small holes that are generated when larger atoms are packed together in a random but dense fashion. Some of the properties of these alloys that make them commercially interesting are discussed below.

Crystalline metallic materials generally have a low yield stress at which plastic flow sets in. Dislocations can move easily in crystalline materials; hence the yield strength is determined by the stress required to nucleate mobile dislocations and move them through the crystal. Virtually all high-strength materials, including the steels, achieve their high strength by blocking either the nucleation or the motion of dislocations. In an amorphous material, a dislocation cannot be defined with respect to a crystal lattice, for the structure does not exist. Thus, a more general definition of a

dislocation must be adopted. In the absence of long-range order the local order determines the strength of the material. As this order fluctuates over the average value, it is clear that any defect that traverses this value is constrained to move at a value determined by the stronger regions. It is therefore to be expected that metallic glasses will show high yield stresses, and this is indeed observed. Combined with this high strength is hardness. It has therefore been suggested that amorphous materials can be used as the hardening fibers in composite materials, as tip materials for tools, and in cutlery, in which resistance to wear and corrosion is an important criterion. Also, in the absence of mobile dislocations, which are characteristic of most crystalline solids, damping losses or attenuation associated with the propagation of elastic waves are small. Hence it is possible that amorphous metallic materials may be useful in producing acoustic delay lines.

Two other properties that arise from the presence of atomic disorder are temperature independence of electrical conductivity and corrosion resistance. Electrical conductivity in crystalline metallic solids is determined by the number of electrons and their mean free path. At low temperatures, the mean free path is determined by defects, but with increasing temperatures it is limited by the thermal motion of the atoms about their mean position, defined by the lattice. In an amorphous material, there is no lattice, and the electrons are scattered by the randomly packed atoms. The mean free path of the electrons is then comparable to atomic dimensions. Amorphous metallic alloys therefore have a high electrical resistivity. However, the fact that the resistivity is only weakly temperature-sensitive, owing to the dominant disorder scattering events, makes them interesting. It has been proposed that this effect be taken advantage of in making resistors that are used as standards.

Amorphous materials are, in principle, isotropic and homogeneous. These two properties in combination imply that an exposed surface of an amorphous solid does not contain sites that are energetically different from each other, and this is so, when the sites are not of the order of atomic dimensions. Since a cell cannot be generated, galvanic corrosion is anticipated to be relatively small. In most commercial crystalline materials the potential for such cells is invariably present owing to well-defined dislocations or grain boundaries.

For background information *see* ALLOY; ALLOY STRUCTURES; CORROSION; ELECTRICAL CONDUCTIVITY OF METALS; FERROMAGNETISM; METAL, MECHANICAL PROPERTIES OF; SPUTTERING in the McGraw-Hill Encyclopedia of Science and Technology.   [PRAVEEN CHAUDHARI]

Bibliography: P. Chaudhari, J. J. Cuomo, and R. J. Gambino, *IBM J. Res. Develop.*, 17:66, 1973.

Animal morphogenesis

One of the most important problems in biology is how the genetic information in the egg becomes expressed in terms of pattern and form. It is possible to think of this problem in terms of a program: the egg contains a program for making the animal, with the genetic information playing the major role; in fact, the genetic information constitutes the program. The nature of the program for making, for example, the eye or the five fingers of the hand is not known, but it is becoming possible to see what kinds of processes are involved by considering what the cells have to do in order to make such structures. A very important feature is pattern formation, that is, the spatial localization of different cell types. For example, the main difference between a developing arm and a leg is not in the types of cells composing them—muscle, cartilage, connective tissue—but in their spatial organization. It is a question of the right type of cell being at the right place. A characteristic of many developing systems is their ability to regulate, or adjust, when they are perturbed. For example, if the region that will normally form the eye is removed from an early amphibian embryo, a normal animal will nevertheless develop. This regulative ability is particularly clear in animals that have good powers of regeneration, such as hydras and newts.

French flag problem. The problem of pattern formation and regulation can be illustrated by the French flag problem. Consider a line of cells, each of which can become blue, or white, or red. What sort of patterning process is required so that the line of cells will form a French flag, that is, so that the left-hand third will be blue, the middle third white, and the right-hand third red? One answer is that the position of the cells is specified with respect to the ends, and that they use this positional information to decide what type of cell they will form. The specification of position might be achieved by a chemical concentration gradient such as that postulated by many workers, in particular, C. M. Child. It has been suggested by L. Wolpert that such a mechanism may provide the basis for pattern formation in a variety of developing and regulating systems, the pattern being primarily due to different cellular responses to the gradient.

Morphogen effect. Evidence that diffusion of a morphogen may play some role in specification of positional information comes from studies both on *Hydra* and the insect epidermis. P. A. Lawrence has summarized much of the evidence for gradients in the insect epidermis. The concentration of the postulated morphogen may determine what sort of cuticle is formed. In addition, the polarity of structures in the epidermis, such as hairs and bristles, may be specified by the way in which the gradient slopes. A local reversal of the gradient following grafting can lead to a local reversal of polarity. In *Hydra*, regeneration can be viewed as the reestablishment of the boundary region and gradient and involves the interaction between two gradients. The presence of a head can prevent the regeneration of another head. Wolpert, M. Clarke, and A. Hornbruch have investigated the transmission of this inhibitory signal along the axis of *Hydra* and have found it to be consistent with a mechanism based upon diffusion. In a rather different system (the egg of the leafhopper) K. Sander has also obtained good evidence for a gradient that spreads during early stages and that operates even before cell walls form. This gradient apparently determines the main segmental pattern of the insect.

Chick wing pattern. The development of the pattern of the skeletal elements in the chick wing requires, in terms of positional information, a three-dimensional coordinate system. Mechanisms for the proximodistal axis and the anteroposterior axis have been proposed largely on the basis of the work of J. W. Saunders. D. Summerbell, J. Lewis, and Wolpert suggest that there is a region at the tip of the outgrowing limb bud (the progress zone) in which the cells undergo an autonomous decrease in "positional value" with time. Since the width of the zone is constant, and all the cells in it are dividing, cells are continually overflowing; when they leave the zone, the change in positional value ceases. Thus the first cells to leave, which will form proximal regions like the humerus, will have a higher value than those that leave later. Insofar as the anteroposterior axis is concerned, there appears to be a gradient set up by a region at the posterior edge of the progress zone, known as the polarizing region. These two parameters may be interpreted by the cells to give the pattern of the cartilaginous elements and to control their later growth. The autonomy of the progress zone is demonstrated when, for example, a young progress zone is grafted in place of an older one. In this case a composite limb, made up of humerus, radius and ulna, humerus, radius and ulna, wrist, and hand may result (see illustration). The activity of the polarizing region is demonstrated when the region is grafted to the anterior edge of the progress zone; mirror-image duplication of the limb, particularly clear for the hand, results. The model of a progress zone may be applicable to epimorphic regeneration, in this case the progress zone being equivalent to an early blastema.

Genetic mosaics. A different approach to pattern formation, which shows great promise of revealing how genetic information is used, takes advantage of genetic mosaics with appropriate markers and can reveal the behavior of cell lineages. A. Garcia-Bellido has shown that in *Drosophila* there are well-defined developmental compartments that separate, for example, the anterior and posterior regions of the wing. Cell lineages be-

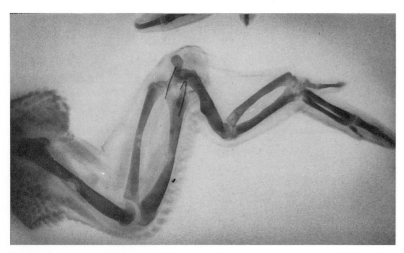

Composite limb resulting from grafting a young progress zone of a developing limb in place of that of an older progress zone. (*Courtesy of Dr. Dennis Summerbell*)

come determined as members of one or another compartment and, thereafter, do not cross compartment boundaries. These studies, together with S. Kauffman's suggestions as to how positional information may be interpreted by genes in combinatorial fashion, make it possible to begin to construct simple programs for the development of complex patterns.

For background information *see* ANIMAL MORPHOGENESIS; CELL LINEAGE in the McGraw-Hill Encyclopedia of Science and Technology.

[LEWIS WOLPERT]

Bibliography: Ciba Foundation Symposium, *Cell Patterning*, 1975; P. Lawrence, in S. J. Counce and C. H. Waddington (eds.), *Developmental Systems: Insects*, vol. 2, p. 152, 1973; L. Wolpert, A. Hornbruch, and M. Clarke, *Amer. Zool.*, 14:647, 1974.

Antigen

Reports of some recent research in antigens have been concerned with solubilizations and immunogenicity of tumor-specific transplantation antigens (TSTAs). Antigens stimulating the response to homograft rejection are called transplantation antigens or histocompatibility antigens. The classical procedure for the study of transplantation antigens has been based on assessing their ability to elicit rejection of an allograft. In addition, antisera containing antibodies to transplantation antigens have been used as reagents for the study of transplantation antigens by means of laboratory serological tests. TSTAs have been demonstrated in many experimental neoplasms. They are capable of inducing a rejection response in syngeneic animals. This immune reaction can vary considerably; it is weak for spontaneous tumors of unknown origin, moderate to strong for tumors caused by cancerinducing viruses or chemicals. In general, it can be stated that immunity to TSTAs parallels immunity

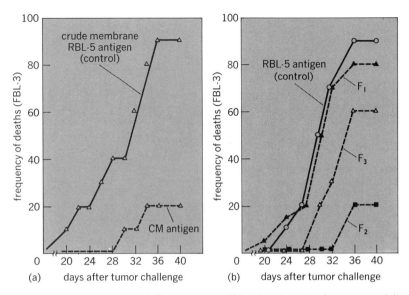

Fig. 2. Inhibition of growth of FBL-3 leukemia. CBF$_1$ mice 12 weeks of age were recipients. All challenge inoculations, 5×10^5 and 1×10^6 FBL-3 cells, made 2 weeks after the last immunization, intraperitoneally (TD50 of FBL-3 = 10^4 cells). Antigen doses used: CM = 400 μg $\times$ 2, and F$_1$, F$_2$, F$_3$ = 100 μg $\times$ 2; (a) comparison of 400 μg of CM antigen in complete Freund$_1$ adjuvant with controls; (b) comparison of F$_1$, F$_2$, F$_3$ fractions with controls. (*From L. W. Law and E. Appella, Immunogenic properties of solubilized tumor antigen from an RNA virus-transformed neoplasm, Nature, 243(5402): 83–87, 1973*)

to transplantation antigens. This similarity is of some relevance since it is hoped that sooner or later TSTAs will be used for immunotherapy and prevention of neoplasms.

Manipulation of immune response. Allograft rejection is an immunological phenomenon. It can be related to the immune response of the transplantation antigens present in the graft but absent in the recipient. From a large number of experiments, it can be concluded that cell-mediated immunity rather than humoral immunity is primarily responsible for the rejection of solid tissue allograft. The humoral response in many cases leads to immunological enhancement. The position of balance between the two types of response determines whether the antigenic tissue is rejected or not. Under natural conditions it seems rather easy to shift the balance toward enhancement and quite difficult to shift the balance toward rejection (Fig. 1). To be able to manipulate at will this point of balance implies that there is some way of handling the immune response more precisely. Solubilization and purification of TSTA and a study of the factors controlling its immunogenicity could reveal some information as to whether the immune response can be manipulated effectively.

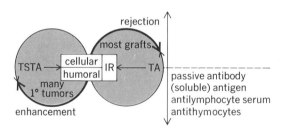

Fig. 1. Schematic representation of the immune response (IR) to TSTA and normal histocompatibility antigens (TA). (*From D. A. Blumenstock et al., Transplant. Proc., 3(3):1148, 1971*)

Table 1. Test for specificity of RBL-5 tumor antigen in C57BL mice immunized with RBL-5 crude membrane antigen, challenged with polyoma-specific neoplasm no. 89

Group	Treatment	Number of polyoma tumor cells inoculated	Number with tumor / Number in group	Mean tumor diameter (mm) at day: 14	28	35	50
1	Crude membrane, 400 μg	5×10^4	5/5	7.2	8.3	12.3	16.2
		1×10^4	4/5	6.7	6.2	7.9	11.5
2	Freund's adjuvant only (controls)	5×10^4	5/5	8.3	8.1	13.3	18.3
		1×10^4	4/5	7.4	6.6	6.8	11.4

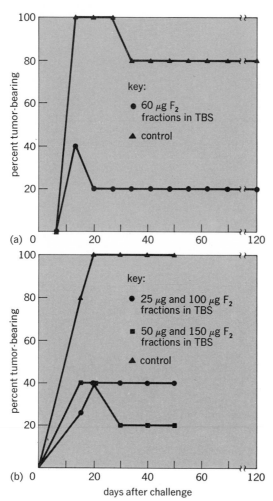

Fig. 3. Inhibition of growth of mKSA fibrosarcoma. BALB/c synegeneic mice were recipients. All challenge inoculations, 1×10⁴ mKSA-ASC cells, made 2 weeks after the last immunization; (a) comparison of effect of 60 μg F₂ fractions in TBS (tris-HCl, pH 7.4, 0.005 *M*; MgSO₄, 2 × 10⁻⁴ *M*; NaCl 0.85%) with controls (TBS alone); (b) comparison of effect of 25 μg and 100 μg F₂ fraction in TBS and 50 μg and 150 μg F₂ fraction in TBS with controls (TBS alone). (*From M. Drapin, E. Appella, and L. W. Law, Immunogenic properties of a soluble tumor-specific transplantation antigen induced by simian virus 40, J. Nat. Cancer Inst., 52(1):259–265, 1974*)

Purification of antigens. Solubilization of transplantation antigens is a rather difficult procedure. Successful attempts using limited proteolysis with papain have been reported. Most transplantation antigens are proteins, and the antigenic determinants are within the polypeptide chain. Solubilization and partial purification of two TSTAs, one from a Rauscher virus−induced leukemia (RLV), designated RBL-5, and the other an SV40 virus−transformed BALB/c mouse embryo line (mKSA), have been obtained. The RBL-5 system has been intensely studied recently. RBL-5 cells are immunogenic and provide immunity against other leukemias of the Freund, Maloney, Rauscher (FMR) type. RBL-5 is also a good target cell and is easily lysed in the laboratory by sensitized syngeneic lymphocytes or by anti-RBL-5 antiserum. The method for extraction and partial purification principally involves the use of ascites cells, the disruption of the cell by a sonifier or nitrogen bomb, and collection of the membrane by high-speed centrifugation at 55,000 *g*. Pellets obtained were suspended in 0.05 *M* tris buffer, pH 8.4, and solubilized with papain. The papain-solubilized material was concentrated by ultrafiltration and chromatographed on a column of Sephadex G-150. A peak of approximately 50,000 mol. wt containing immunogenic material was recovered. The immunogenic activity recovered here was specific; challenge with a syngeneic tumor no. 89 containing a polyoma virus−specific surface antigen did not reveal inhibition of the growth of this neoplasm. Data are reported in Fig. 2 and Table 1.

Soluble TSTA has also been obtained from dissociated tumor cells of the ascitic or tissue culture SV40-transformed BALB/c lines (mKSA). These lines are non-virus-producing. The methods used have been exactly the same as those reported for the isolation of TSTA from RBL-5 or mouse H-2 histocompatibility antigens. Immunogenic activity as assayed by tumor rejection was recovered in at least 20% yield, and this activity was specific (Fig. 3 and Table 2).

The solubilized fractions from both RBL-5 and mKSA, containing the major titers of immunogenic material, chromatographed in a manner similar to that reported for the mouse H-2 alloantigens derived from normal lymphoid cells. This suggests

Table 2.   Specificity of immunity induced by SV40 antigen*

	Tumor challenge dose			
Animal group	mKSA-ASC			Mouse plasmacytoma, induced by intraperitoneal mineral oil (Adj-PC-5, 4.6 × 10⁴)
	10⁴	10⁵	Total	
Control	4/5†	5/5	9/10	8/9
Immune (mKSA-ASC CM)	0/4	1/5	1/9 (P < 0.002)	9/9

*BALB/c mice immunized with two weekly sc inoculations of 1 mg each mKSA-ASC CM (mKSA ascites crude membrane) in TBS (tris-HCl, pH 7.4, 0.005 *M*; MgSO₄, 2 × 10⁻⁴ *M*; NaCl 0.85%); control animals received TBS only. Challenge with viable mKSA-ASC or Adj-PC-5 tumor cells subcutaneously 2 weeks after last immunization.

†Numerator = number of animals with progressively growing sc tumors resulting in death. Denominator = total in group.

that transplantation antigen on a variety of normal or transformed cells is similar in physical-chemical characteristics. Indeed, the approximate molecular weight (50,000) for these antigens has also been reported for a skin-sensitizing antigen from rat tumor. Both TSTAs described here showed good biological activity; however, attempts have been made to demonstrate reactivity with specific cytotoxic antisera. With the RBL-5 system, when a high-titered anti-Maloney sarcoma virus antiserum or antiserum produced in syngeneic mice after repeated immunization with a crude membrane preparation was used, inhibition of lysis was observed using RBL-5 target cells labeled with ^{51}Cr. However, titer decreased drastically as the purification was carried through the chromatography on Sephadex G-150, probably because of lability of the antigen. Thus, the usefulness of this method for monitoring further steps in purification is not without limitations. For the mKSA system, mKSA tissue culture cell lines did not react with specific cytotoxic antiserum, although these cells could be lysed by an H2-4 alloantiserum, showing the presence of H-2 antigen specificity. Other laboratory methods for following purification of these antigens are being investigated; among them are microcomplement fixation, anti-immunoglobulin assay, and inhibition of macrophage migration.

Antigenic polymorphism. Like allotypes and blood groups, transplantation antigens show polymorphism within the species. There are several different systems of transplantation antigens, at least 20 in mice, which are inherited independently and have different strengths. The major murine histocompatibility antigens are controlled by the H-2 locus. Within the H-2 system there is further antigenic polymorphism, in that about 30 antigenic determinants have been reported. Tumors induced by DNA viruses (SV40, polyoma, adenovirus) usually do not release infective virus and have TSTA on transformed cell surfaces. They usually share a cross-reactive type-specific TSTA regardless of histogenesis or the species of origin. Since tumors induced by RNA viruses do release appreciable amounts of infective virus, the complication arises as to how to determine whether these TSTAs are virus structural proteins or cellular components. However, with an RBL-5 neoplasm that arose in a C57BL/6 mouse infected with RLV, solubilized preparations that were shown to be immunogenic did not contain any infectious virus. Moreover, a syngeneic antiserum prepared in C57BL/6 mice by immunization with a mixture of crude membrane and complete Freund's adjuvant did not have any neutralizing activity against RLV. The same antiserum in a microtiter complement-fixation test was shown capable of detecting nonvirion antigens that were concentrated in a highly immunogenic fraction.

Tumor immunity. The TSTAs of chemically or physically induced neoplasm are tumor-specific. Non-cross-reactive TSTAs, distinctly different in each tumor, are found in many neoplasms of different species. Very little is known about the activity of solubilized fractions from these tumors in terms of immunogenicity. The aminoazo dye–induced rat hepatomas have been shown to produce antisera that react in membrane immunofluorescence tests only with cells of the immunizing tumor. A heterogeneous preparation, solubilized by limited papain digestion and fractionated by diethylaminoethyl cellulose chromatography, retained tumor-specific antigenicity by the immunofluorescence test, but no biological or chemical characterizations have been reported recently. Although immunization with the antigen could provoke a specific humoral response, tumor rejection was not elicited. Other studies with methylcholanthrene-induced tumors in guinea pigs revealed delayed cutaneous hypersensitivity with soluble potassium chloride extracts. However, multiple immunization with such antigens has not convincingly demonstrated tumor immunity.

In summary, solubilization and partial purification of immunogenic TSTAs from different sources have been obtained. Chemical and biological analyses on purified materials should provide important information as to the mechanisms of tumor immunity. This information will be essential in helping individuals to become immune to their own TSTAs.

For background information *see* ANTIGEN; TRANSPLANTATION BIOLOGY in the McGraw-Hill Encyclopedia of Science and Technology.

[ETTORE APPELLA]

Bibliography: R. W. Baldwin, *Nat. Cancer Inst. Monogr.*, 35:135–139, 1972; M. S. Drapkin, E. Appella, and L. W. Law, *J. Nat. Cancer Inst.*, 52:259–265, 1974; L. W. Law and E. Appella, *Nature*, 243:(5402)83–87, 1973; E. J. Leonard et al., *Nat. Cancer Inst. Monogr.*, 35:129–134, 1972.

Archeological chemistry

When exposed to ionizing radiation and subsequently heated, many transparent crystalline solids emit a faint light (in addition to the ordinary incandescence) called thermoluminescence, the intensity of which is proportional to the amount of the previous irradiation. The date of firing of archeological ceramics can be determined by measuring the thermoluminescence from appropriate minerals in them and determining the yearly radiation dose from their radioactive elements, uranium, thorium, and potassium. This dating method has recently been used on many archeological ceramic samples and is being extended to older, Paleolithic sites by using burnt flint samples.

Bronze Horse. Thermoluminescence dating has been used to show that the famous Bronze Horse of the New York Metropolitan Museum of Art was made in antiquity and is not a modern forgery as had been charged several years ago. For many decades the 15-in.-high (38 cm) statue enjoyed a reputation as one of the finest examples of classic Greek sculpture. However, its authenticity became suspect because of questions that were raised about its construction after the discovery of a "mold line," or "casting fin," circumscribing the sculpture and indicating a modern piece-mold casting technique. Although the mold line was subsequently found to be only a superficial line in a wax coating, doubts about the authenticity of the sculpture remained, and it was not placed back on display.

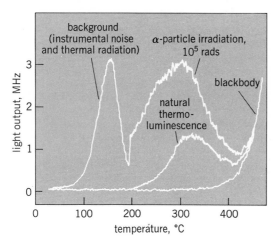

Thermoluminescence glow curves from a single zircon grain from the Bronze Horse.

Thermoluminescence measurements were made on material from the ceramic core of the horse, which contained suitable mineral grains. Conventional thermoluminescence measurements, which are made on the bulk ceramic material or a major component of it, such as quartz or feldspar, would not have been conclusive in this case because the statue had been extensively exposed to x-rays and gamma-rays during previous analyses. The dosages from these irradiations could have masked the naturally accumulated doses. Instead, the measurements were made on single grains of the mineral zircon, about 50–100 μm in size. The zircon grains form a very small fraction of the core material but are typically 100 times higher in radioactivity than the rest of the material. As a result, the x-ray and gamma-ray dosages were negligible compared to the large, internal, naturally accumulated alpha-particle doses in the zircon grains. The figure shows the natural glow curve (light output as a function of temperature the first time the grain is heated) and the thermoluminescence from a subsequent alpha-particle irradiation of 10^5 rads. A comparison of the two curves (at temperatures above ~300° C, at which the stored thermoluminescence has been thermally stable) shows that the natural dosage is about 6×10^4 rads, a very large value that could be accumulated only over thousands of years. The table summarizes the dating results, which indicate that the horse is between 2000 and 3500 years

Results of thermoluminescence measurements and radioactivity determinations of zircon grains separated from the ceramic core of the Bronze Horse*

Grain number	Natural dose, rads	Uranium content, ppm	Dose rate, rads/yr	Age, yr B.P.
6	7.0×10^4	139	37	1900
9	6.3×10^4	106	28	2250
11	16.6×10^4	174	49	3400

*From D. W. Zimmerman, M. P. Yuhas, and P. Meyers, Thermoluminescence authenticity measurements on core material from the Bronze Horse of the New York Metropolitan Museum of Art, *Archaeometry*, 16:19–30, 1974.

old, an age consistent with that of a classical Greek sculpture.

T'ang dynasty ceramics. Thermoluminescence dating measurements have been made on an extensive range of T'ang dynasty (A.D. 618–906) ceramics. This important class of Chinese ware has received extensive examination by art historians during the past 60 years, and the 37 pieces examined by thermoluminescence were believed to be genuine. The authenticity of 29 of the wares was confirmed, but 8 were found to be modern forgeries. A criterion for authentication judgment commonly used on these ceramics, that of glaze crazing, or craquelure, was found to be of only limited reliability.

Preceramic datings. For the dating of older, preceramic archeological sites, thermoluminescent measurements of burnt flint, a common artifact at Paleolithic sites, appear promising. Thermoluminescent dating has been reported on a series of 10 flints from a site at Carigüela, in southern Spain, ranging from 12,000 to 50,000 years before present (B.P.), and on one Bronze Age flint. The thermoluminescent date of the Bronze Age sample (4500 ± 400 years B.P.) agreed well with the known age of the sample (4000–4500 years B.P.), and the series of 10 older flints gave reproducible results in agreement with the approximate ages expected. The method, if proved reliable, should be usable to 200,000 or 300,000 years B.P. before being limited by saturation effects. It could become an important dating method for the period 50,000–200,000 years B.P.—older than the limit of C-14 dating and younger than the minimum ages generally datable by the postassium-argon method.

Volcanic rock dating. Although most successful thermoluminescent dating has been carried out on archeological ceramics, the method can, in principle, be applied to recent geologic samples that have been sufficiently heated, such as volcanic rocks. A study has recently been made of the thermoluminescence from eight Hawaiian basalt flows, ranging in age from 12,000 to 17,000 years. After normalization for sensitivity and dose rate, the thermoluminescent peak heights of plagioclase tholeiitic basalt showed a good linear correlation with the known ages. However, plagioclase from two alkalic basalts did not correlate well. Another difficulty in dating lavas, called anomalous fading, has been reported. Over a period of hours or days following irradiation there is a gradual loss of the stored thermoluminescence in some lava minerals even at high temperatures in the glow curve (> 350° C), where the stored energy was expected to be thermally stable for thousands of years, as it apparently is in ceramic minerals. However, it may be possible that the method can be developed for reliable dating of certain types of lavas.

For background information *see* ARCHEOLOGICAL CHEMISTRY; THERMOLUMINESCENCE in the McGraw-Hill Encyclopedia of Science and Technology.   [DAVID W. ZIMMERMAN]

Bibliography: A. L. Berry, *J. Geophys. Res.,* 78: 6863–6867, 1973; S. J. Fleming, *Archaeometry,* 15: 31–52, 1973; H. Y. Göksu et al., *Science,* 183:651–654, 1974; A. G. Wintle, *Nature,* 245:143–144, 1973.

Arthritis

Although the etiology of rheumatoid arthritis (RA) is unknown, the prevailing view is that the disease is initiated by an exogenous infectious agent. Animal models indicate that a variety of known microorganisms, including bacteria or their cell walls, mycoplasma, and viruses, are arthrotropic and can induce an acute and chronic arthritis. The special feature of interest here is that chronicity with joint destruction may develop thereafter; inability to recover the causative organism at this time implicates immunologic mechanisms as the main factor in perpetuating the disease, as in human RA. In RA the antigen, or antigens, to which the host responds is unknown, for no pathogenic agent has been recovered with any consistency, and none has as yet been implicated in the etiology.

Synovial joints in RA. The surfaces of the two bones in apposition for articulation are covered by hyaline cartilage that forms the actual contact surface. Synovial fluid plays a role in the nutrition and lubrication of the cartilage. On the internal surface of the capsule and enclosing the joint is the synovial membrane, composed of delicate fibrous tissue, blood vessels, and a surface layer of specialized lining cells. In RA the synovial membrane appears to be the first site involved; the lining cells proliferate, and the vessels become engorged and produce a protein-rich exudate that increases the volume of fluid in the joint. Deeper in the synovial membrane there is an infiltration of immunocompetent cells (plasma cells and lymphocytes), and local immunoglobulin production (especially antigammaglobulins), immune complex formation, and complement consumption occur. The synovial membrane proliferates as a pannus ("apron") over the cartilages and erodes them. Fibrous adhesions across the joint limit the range of motion, and, in a small proportion of cases, disability and crippling occur.

Animal models. Arthritis occurs naturally in a wide range of animals, such as horses, pigs, calves, lambs, mice, and rats, and various infectious agents have been identified. Studies of the course of spontaneous infectious arthritis of animals have been extended to the laboratory to provide a comparative model for RA. The table lists some of the

microorganisms that have been identified in natural joint infections or that have been used for experimental production of chronic arthritis by intraarticular or systemic injection.

The relevance to human RA of animal joint disease produced by these agents in their respective hosts may be summed up as follows: the initial synovitis is usually more pyogenic (that is, polymorphonuclear leukocytes predominate) than is observed early in RA, and the pathogenic organism can be recovered from the joint fluid of the animal. Later, however, many of the pathological features resemble those of RA, including proliferation of the synovial lining cells, infiltration of plasma cells and lymphocytes, pannus formation, and cartilage erosion. Frequently, the organism cannot be isolated despite chronicity of the arthritic process. That nonviable cell wall components of many bacteria also produce acute and chronic arthritis, as C. Pearson, in studies involving the rat, first showed with the Wax D fraction of mycobacteria, is evidence that an immunologic response of the host to microbial components may activate and perpetuate arthritis.

Intraarticular injection of herpes virus or rubella virus produces chronic synovitis in rabbit joints. Following systemic inoculation of pregnant rabbits with rubella virus, the highest concentration of virus is found in fetal cartilage, and long-term embryonic rabbit chondrocytes maintain a persistent rubella virus infection.

Clinical studies. A heterogeneous group of diphtheroids has been isolated with somewhat greater frequency from rheumatoid than from control joints. Small-colony *Mycoplasma arthritidis* has been isolated by one group, and *M. fermentans* by another, but a substantial number of other studies have failed to confirm isolation of mycoplasma. A virus has not yet been isolated from rheumatoid tissues by means of passage to a variety of cell types or by animal injection. Electron microscope studies of synovial membrane from rheumatoid joints have failed to reveal virus structures, but "tubular" inclusions resembling the nucleocapsid of paramyxovirus have been observed in the vascular endothelium and lymphoid cells. Similar findings have been reported in lupus erythematosus. In view of the known arthrotropic nature of rubella virus, a report of higher antibody titers to rubella virus in juvenile patients with RA is of interest. An antigen termed rho, identified as a protein component of normal plasma, rises as a phase reactant in association with known rubella virus infection, and in association with other conditions, such as pregnancy and RA.

Laboratory studies. Since bacteria and mycoplasma have not been isolated with any consistency from rheumatoid joint tissue, it is thought that a persistent virus localized in the synovial membrane may be implicated in the etiology of RA. The failure to isolate a virus could be attributed to its inability to replicate and produce progeny in a titer sufficient for isolation. These concepts have gained theoretical support from several sources:

(1) As discussed above, animal models of arthritis exist in which active disease persists despite the inability of investigators to recover a known

Microorganisms associated with natural and experimental animal arthritis

Organism	Natural host	Animal model
Erysipelothrix rhusiopathiae or *E. insidiosa*	Pig	Pig
Corynebacterium rubrum	—	Rat
Mycoplasma hyorhinis	Pig (3–10 weeks)	Pig
M. hyosynoviae	Pig (3–6 months)	Pig
M. pulmonis	Mice	—
M. arthritidis	—	Mouse, rat
Chlamydia psittaci	Lambs, calves	Lambs
Chlamydia (human isolates)	? Man	Monkey, rabbit
Herpes simplex virus	Man	Rabbit
Rubella virus	Man	Rabbit

microorganism or identify it in the tissues. (2) The immunologic response in the rheumatoid joint could be attributed to persistence of antigenic components derived from an infectious agent or from cellular changes induced by such an agent. (3) Types of virus-host cell relationships exist in which known viruses persist in cells without replication and in which the cells may appear unaffected, undergo transformation ("oncogenic" virus), or demonstrate slowly developing and progressive dysfunction ("slow" virus). In many of these cases, special methods are needed to "rescue" the virus. (4) Fibroblastic (synovial) cells have been derived from rheumatoid synovial membranes and have been perpetuated in long-term culture which demonstrate metabolic properties that are persistently different from those of cells obtained from normal membranes. One consistent difference has been increased levels of hyaluronate in the rheumatoid synovial cell cultures. Another difference of greater potential importance is the finding that cells derived from rheumatoid synovial membranes, but not normal fetal synovial cells, develop cytopathic changes after exposure to antirubella serum plus complement. However, rubella antigen has not been detected in cultured rheumatoid synovial cells by immunofluorescent methods. Nor has the use of a number of indirect means succeeded in identifying or "rescuing" a latent virus from rheumatoid synovial cell cultures. When fed labeled uridine or thymidine, the cells do not liberate labeled material with the buoyant density of virions into the fluid phase of the culture; nor has infectious virus been obtained when synovial cell cultures are incubated with halogenated pyrimidines or fused by Sendai virus with a variety of cell lines. Developments in the area of viruses and RA will be awaited with interest.

For background information *see* ANTIGEN; ARTHRITIS; BACTERIA in the McGraw-Hill Encyclopedia of Science and Technology.

[DAVID HAMERMAN]

Bibliography: R. Cappel et al., *J. Exp. Med.*, 139:497, 1974; R. Patterson et al., *Clin. Res.*, 21: 878, 1973.

Aspirin

It is quite fascinating that millions of tons of aspirin have been taken, and will be taken, even though there is little if any experimental proof for its clinical superiority. During the past decade, more than 60 years after its introduction into the pharmacopeia, R. K. S. Lim made innovative attempts to design laboratory assays for the various alleged functions of the drug. He identified nociceptors in skin and mucosa as kinin receptors and demonstrated that "minor analgesics" that block peripheral pain are kinin inhibitors. After Lim's death, interest flagged, but his ingenious experiments appear to have stood the test of time.

During the past 5 years, interest in aspirin, which has been shown to have a number of startling and hardly expected actions, has been reactivated. Some of the new information is based on the discovery that it acts on prostaglandins; some on a reinterpretation of its side effects.

Historical background. Aspirin, though known to everyone, deserves a brief introduction. In 1874, after Lister's use of carbolic acid for surgical disinfection, H. Kolbe introduced salicylic acid—synthesized by reacting CO_2 with phenol—as a possible "internal disinfectant"; 1974 was thus an anniversary year. Physicians discovered rapidly that, although the new drug had no effect on the natural course of infections, it reduced their major symptoms, fever, swelling, and pain. Twenty-four years later, F. Hoffmann prepared acetyl salicylic acid for the relief of his father's arthritis. H. Dreser named the compound aspirin: "a" for acetyl, "spirin" for the spiric acid of the willow tree.

During the century that followed the discovery of aspirin, its mode of action remained unknown. Certain clinical facts emerged: aspirin was a superior analgesic, but its effect on inflammation or fever was about the same as, and certainly not more than, that of sodium salicylate.

Inhibition of prostaglandin synthesis. Prostaglandins (PG) are oxygenated cyclic C_{20} fatty acids derived mainly from arachidonic acid. PGE is a β-hydroxyketone, PGF a 1,3-diol. Changes on the cyclopentane ring and degrees of unsaturation determine their biologic function.

Prostaglandins are ubiquitous; they participate, in a manner that is not yet understood, in a variety of biological reactions; they are synthesized on demand and released—it is generally assumed that synthesis equals release. Aspirin, indomethacin, and other peripheral analgesics inhibit prostaglandin synthesis; and it appears that the effectiveness of analgesic drugs and their ability to inhibit prostaglandin synthetase parallel each other. The inhibition has been demonstrated in cell-free enzyme systems from guinea pig lungs and in single cells (platelets). Analgesics that act centrally and corticosteroids have no effect on prostaglandin synthesis.

Although it is certain that aspirin blocks the synthesis of prostaglandins under laboratory conditions, it is difficult to prove what it does to systems within the organism. Prostaglandins have been classified as mediators of inflammation. Where, then, does aspirin interfere? First, there are obviously several ways of controlling inflammation; the effect of corticosteroids, for instance, is not blocked by aspirin. Second, prostaglandins are only one of several mediators of inflammation; and their specific role is not clear. The carrageenin-induced inflammation of the rat's paw, for instance, has an initial histamine-serotonin phase, a secondary kinin phase, and a late prostaglandin (mainly PGE_2) phase; the presence of multiple mediators that are inhibited by different inhibitors complicates the interpretation of experimental results. A similar situation exists in the lung: PGE_1 and PGE_2 (prevalent in the bronchus) dilate bronchial muscle; PGF_2 (found in parenchymal tissue) constricts it. In the laboratory, aspirin blocks the prostaglandin-induced constriction of the tracheal chain. In the organism, it is difficult to differentiate the effect of aspirin on coexisting prostaglandins that have opposite effects on tissue components.

Side effects. The side effects of aspirin have been subjected to closer scrutiny than before. Shortly after the introduction of aspirin, death from small doses of aspirin was reported in the literature. Intolerance to aspirin is not uncommon; it has been estimated to occur in more than 300,000 individuals in the United States. It tends to develop in middle age; in a classical pattern, it occurs as a "triad" that includes formation of nasal polyps and intermittent (but occasionally progressive) bronchial asthma; some patients have urticaria. Death rarely ensues, because patients rapidly become aware of their intolerance.

The clinical symptoms are almost identical with symptoms encountered in clinical allergy and anaphylaxis; consequently, reactions caused by aspirin have been thought to represent an aspirin "allergy," that is, an antibody-mediated sequence. The allergic hypothesis was strengthened by the finding of P. Minden and R. S. Farr that aspirin acetylates human serum albumin and that some patients who take aspirin form antibodies which react with acetylated serum albumin. A. L. DeWeck has proposed that a reactive contaminant of aspirin, aspiryl anhydride, leads to the formation of aspiroyl- or salicyloyl-substituted proteins that become antigenic after conjugation. Such anticipated immunological responses probably occur, but they do so in aspirin-sensitive patients and in normal controls, and the correlation of their titer with clinical symptoms is poor. Moreover, laboratory tests usually demonstrate that such antibodies also react with sodium salicylate, which can be taken with impunity by aspirin-sensitive patients. It has been proposed by J. A. Phills and coworkers that urticaria might differ from respiratory forms of aspirin intolerance, but the evidence, for example, for specific mast cell degranulation in patients with aspirin urticaria, is at best suggestive.

Because of the discrepancies in the reported findings, M. Samter and associates concluded in 1968 that evidence for an immunological pathogenesis of reactions to aspirin is unconvincing, and that intolerance to aspirin represents a specific disease, probably one that alters the connective tissue component of nociceptors. They emphasize that "aspirin-sensitive" patients do not react only to aspirin but to many other peripheral analgesics and to a food color, F.D. & C. yellow #5, or tartrazine, which is a pyrazolone derivative. Surprisingly, they do not react to phenacetin and phenacetin derivatives. Samter and coworkers find it unlikely that such a series of structurally unrelated compounds should cross-react with the same antibody but prefer the hypothesis that the common denominator is the altered nociceptor.

Other observations seem to support this hypothesis. Aspirin-sensitive patients react to the administration of minimal doses of aspirin and aspirin-like compounds with marked prolongation of bleeding time even though platelets obtained from aspirin-sensitive patients behave in the laboratory precisely like platelets from normal controls.

The suggestion that aspirin produces its side effects (as well as its effects) by acting on prostaglandins has been made but has not yet been substantiated by the available evidence. Current intensive investigations will clarify this point—an important issue, for recent discoveries have widened the therapeutic potential of the drug, for example, for the inhibition of clotting and, therefore, for possible prevention of myocardial infarction. Unfortunately, it will probably be years before the insights gained in the laboratory can be applied to clinical problems.

For background information *see* ASPIRIN in the McGraw-Hill Encyclopedia of Science and Technology.   [MAX SAMTER]

Bibliography: A. L. DeWeck, *Int. Arch. Allergy,* 41:393, 1971; P. Montegazza and E. W. Horton (eds.), *Prostaglandins, Peptides and Amines,* 1971; J. A. Phills et al., *8th Int. Congr. of Allergol.,* Tokyo, Abstract no. 184., 1973; P. W. Ramwell (ed.), *The Prostaglandins,* 1973; M. Samter, *Hosp. Pract.,* 8:85–90, 1973.

Atmospheric pollution

Recent studies of atmospheric pollution have focused on particle emissions in automobile and smokestack exhausts, but more than 90% of the aerosol (dust) particles in air are contributed by wind erosion of soil. Such erosion is greatly accelerated by land cultivation for cropping, because natural vegetation and surface-lying stones in deserts provide considerable protection to natural soil from wind erosion. Over millions of years, wind erosion of naturally disturbed arid land soils and global wind trajectories have led to deposition of aerosol fine-silt particles not only on continents but also on mid-oceanic islands, and of pelagic sediments on ocean bottoms thousands of miles from land. An analysis of mineral dusts provides a form of historical record of climatic (atmospheric) changes resulting from the latitudinal drift of the continents over hundreds of millions of years.

Kinds of contaminants. The nature and pathways of dust have been of interest for centuries. The insoluble, inorganic aerosol portion of dust on a global scale arises through wind erosion of soil, volcanic eruptions, and fall of extraterrestrial mat-

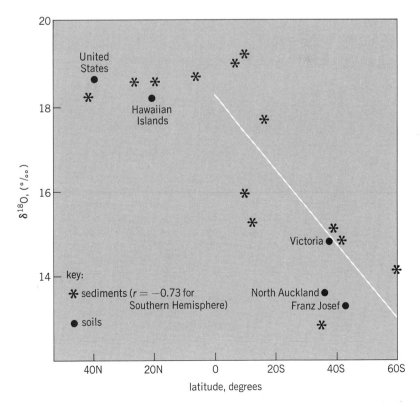

Oxygen isotope abundance ($\delta^{18}O$) of eolian-derived quartz as a function of latitude of fine silt in pelagic sediments and soils. (*From M. L. Jackson et al., Global dustfall during the Quaternary as related to environments, Soil Sci., 116:135–145, 1973*)

ter. According to an emissions inventory made by G. M. Hidy and J. R. Brock in 1970, volcanic and extraterrestrial contributions are negligible compared with the effect of the soil-wind erosion, which amounts to 5×10^8 metric tons per year according to E. D. Goldberg. Human-made air pollution accounts for 6% of aerosol emissions, approximately 3% from the sulfur cycle and 3% by direct particle emissions. Other sources of aerosols include sea salt emanations, production from gaseous atmospheric constituents in the sulfur and nitrogen cycles, and biologically produced particles such as spores and terpenes. Among the minerals in soil-derived aerosols are quartz (silica, SiO_2), carbonates of calcium and magnesium, feldspars, and phyllosilicates such as micas, vermiculite, montmorillonite, kaolinite, and chlorite. The phyllosilicates seed clouds and initiate rain and hail.

According to a report by J. K. Syers and associates, the micaceous vermiculite component of dusts carries the radioactive element cesium, produced in bomb testing. Depending on the locality and time of deposition, the specific activity of cesium-137 varied from 0 to 264 picocuries per gram in aerosolic dusts collected from snow, glacial ice, mud rains, and the atmosphere in worldwide localities. Eolian soils and Pacific pelagic sediments exchange-fixed appreciable amounts of added cesium. Fixation of cesium by dust in air greatly decreases the health hazard, for dust is easily washed from the skin of animals. Aerosolic dusts carry organic pesticides and heavy metals. They supply plant nutrients to organic soils occurring in marshes, and nutrients to aerial portions of plants.

Tracing soil aerosols. The oxygen isotopic ratio of the tracer mineral quartz has been used by R. N. Clayton and associates to identify the global distribution of long-range aerosolic dusts carried by winds. The particle size is mainly in the 1- to 10-μm range. Weathering of rocks and fluvial mixing during deposition in major shale reservoirs give a characteristic cross section of quartz origin from igneous-metamorphic rock materials (low isotopic ratio, which reflects high-temperature origin) mixed with authigenic quartz in cherty sediments (high isotopic ratio, which reflects low-temperature origin). According to work in progress by G. J. Churchman, Clayton, K. Sridhar, and M. L. Jackson at the University of Wisconsin and University of Chicago, further mixing occurs during soil formation, and still further mixing occurs in the eolian processes; these processes remove dust from arid lands and deposit it on land and sea.

Meteorological conditions required to dislodge dust in the hot, dry regions such as the Southwestern states of the United States have come under intensive study by the U.S. National Center for Atmospheric Research, under the direction of E. F. Danielsen. According to a report by Jackson, D. A. Gillette, Danielsen, R. A. Bryson, and Syers, an upper-level jet (300-mb level) moving from Japan over the Gulf of Alaska, and descending and deflecting to the right along the British Columbian coast, converges with a large heated, mixed volume of air over Arizona and adjacent states. The heated air rises and is rapidly replaced by the cold-front jet in downward motion. The resulting strong gusts of wind transfer downward momentum that is important in breaking up the soil so that the fine particles become airborne. Dust is lifted by compensating ascending air plumes. Mean wind speeds of 30–50 knots (1 knot $= 5.14 \times 10^{-1}$ m/sec) are maintained by cold-front pressure gradients. Dust storms of tens of thousands of square miles ensue. Some radioactive debris from the stratosphere is injected into the troposphere as a portion of the tropopause is drawn under the jet. According to Danielsen, such dust storms have been found to coincide with groups of tornadoes and may relate to their generation.

Global dust distribution. The oxygen isotopic ratio of quartz in dusts deposited as pelagic sediments in the North Pacific Ocean, expressed relative to that of standard mean ocean water, ranges from 18 to 19 ‰, that is, per thousand (see illustration), whereas values decrease to 13 ‰ and below with latitude to 60°S. Soil silts and deep-ocean sediments at comparable latitudes have similar isotopic ratio numbers. The dust accretion rate in the ocean basins is 0.6–10 m per million years, according to reports of Goldberg and H. L. Windom. However, according to a report of Jackson and associates, the dust accretion rate may be 100–1000 times as fast during glacial ages. The dust content of air, up to 600 μg per cubic meter of air and reaching altitudes of 4–10 km, can effect diabatic cooling of the mid-troposphere, possibly increasing subsidence and aridity, according to Bryson. Vertical fluxes of soil material during dust storms reach 10 μg per square centimeter per second, according to Gillette. According to a report by Jackson to the International Congress of Soil Science in Moscow, circumpolar westerly winds carry the dusts eastward over the oceans in each hemisphere. Some backflow occurs as easterlies pick up a component of the westerlies at west coasts of the continents. The Caribbean area, including islands and the coastal states, receives long-range aerosolic dusts from the Sahara by means of the easterlies, with quartz of intermediate ratios of about 16.3 ‰. The main reservoirs of intermediate isotopic-ratio quartz are detrital mixtures of high-ratio (24–32 ‰ for cherts) with low-ratio (5–14 ‰ for igneous and metamorphic rocks) materials in shale deposits and soils formed on shale-derived materials such as glacial tills, loess, and alluvium.

The latitudinal variation (see illustration) arises from global tectonics. Paleomagnetic data summarized by A. Cox and R. R. Doell show that a northward movement of Laurasia (North America and Eurasia) has, since the Precambrian, carried these continents from the Southern Hemisphere through tropical and equatorial regions which are characterized by warm climates and intense mobilization of silica from soils and rocks. This leaching process is currently evidenced by the accumulation of desilicated weathering products rich in kaolin and aluminum and iron oxides in landscapes presently in such latitudes. As part of what is believed by R. Siever to be a steady state of the Earth's crust, oceans, and atmosphere, silica is carried in solution by rivers into lagoons, estuaries, and seas. Such silica is not only adsorbed by constituents of muds but also absorbed by planktonic organisms for use as skeletal material. The skeletal material collects in lagoons (where it forms chert of marls and dolomite) and in equatorial ocean bottom muds (where it forms cristobalitic and subsequently quartzose bedded cherts). Crystallization of the silica to quartz is accelerated in warm, alkaline environments of tropical and equatorial lagoons. Such siliceous marker beds have been traced by the National Science Foundation deep-sea drilling project (JOIDES) as the abyssal plains have been moved by plate tectonics to the North Pacific latitudes, for example, and subsequently have been buried by the red muds of pelagic sediments now identified as aerosolic dust sediments.

Earlier episodes of uplifting enormous areas of chert-bearing, shallow marine sediments, including limestones, dolomites, and argillaceous shales and siltstones, into enlarged Laurasian continental great plains and mountain belts of the Northern Hemisphere have supplied the quartz of low-temperature origin in these rocks for recycling by glacial, fluvial, and eolian processes and soil formation. The higher chert content gave higher oxygen isotopic ratios to quartz in the detrital mixture in shales, soils, and dusts of the Northern Hemisphere silts resulting from erosion of these deposits. The Southern Hemisphere continents are known to be relatively poorer in limestones and chert-bearing silts because the southern portions of these continents have not crossed the chert-forming tropical and equatorial environments since the Precambrian. Their silts in shales, soils, and dusts have been derived from a higher proportion of igneous and metamorphic rocks and therefore have lower quartz oxygen isotopic ratios, according to current studies in an International Consortium for Interinstitutional Cooperation in the Advancement of Learning (ICICAL) by Jackson, Clayton, Churchman, Gillette, R. W. Rex, J. W. Hawley, J. S. Creager, S. Y. Lee, Sridhar, M. Sayin, and others.

For background information see ATMOSPHERIC POLLUTION in the McGraw-Hill Encyclopedia of Science and Technology.   [MARION L. JACKSON]

Atomic absorption spectroscopy

During the past few years several important developments have occurred in atomic absorption spectroscopy. Perhaps the most significant has been the nonflame atomization systems. With the development of these devices, sensitivities and detection limits (minimum detectable concentrations or amounts) for many elements were improved by about two orders of magnitude in comparison with the usual chemical flame atomization of samples. This greatly increased sensitivity, and the ability to work with very small sample sizes, opened up many new avenues of investigation, particularly in the environmental and biomedical areas.

Types of systems. Most of the nonflame atomization systems consist of resistively heated graphite tube furnaces of various sizes or of heated graphite rods or tantalum (Ta) strips on which the sample is placed. One system, a notable exception, was developed about the same time and is used exclusively for mercury (Hg) determination. The sample is treated with a reductant, such as stannous chloride ($SnCl_2$), and a gas stream, bubbled through the solution, that carries the Hg vapor through a quartz-windowed absorption cell. If organically bound Hg is present in the sample, it can be released by treatment with an oxidant (for example, $KMnO_4$ or H_2O_2) prior to the reduction to elemental Hg. To some extent Hg is an ideal case in that it has an appreciable vapor pressure at room temperature and exists as atoms in the gas phase. The tremendous increase in analytical sensitivity obtained with this technique permitted the investigation of the Hg content of a variety of samples. One side effect was the recent "great tuna fish scare," and similar cases of mild hysteria, for Hg now appeared to be in everything. Additional research has revealed that this Hg has apparently always been there; and data now indicate how it is concentrated and passed up the food chain. The next problem is, of course, to investigate the role of Hg in these minute amounts in biological systems, particularly those important in humans. This sensitive analytical technique will play an important role in this investigation.

The heated graphite furnaces and Ta strip atomizers have been utilized for the determination of many elements and have demonstrated detection limit improvements of two or three orders of magnitude over chemical flame atomization. When the Ta strip and graphite rod or filament atomizers are used, the sample is placed on the rod or strip and subsequently atomized. The atomizers have not proved to be as popular as the tube furnace varieties, for although they are more simple and convenient, the fact that the sample is vaporized away from the highest temperature region and experiences a rapid temperature falloff, causing possibly more serious matrix effects in some cases, is a disadvantage.

The most popular nonflame atomization systems are thus the heated graphite tube furnaces. Several versions are available commercially, and although they have various names, such as L'vov-type, Woodriff-type, Massmann-type, and mini-Massmann furnaces, they are essentially all heated graphite tube furnaces of various sizes. Perhaps the two most popular versions are those of

Typical absolute detection limits, in nanograms

Element	Graphite atomizer	Flame
Ag	0.003	2
Al	0.03	20
Au	0.08	10
Bi	0.1	25
Cd	0.001	0.2
Co	0.04	10
Cr	0.05	3
Cu	0.01	1
Fe	0.03	5
Mn	0.01	2
Ni	0.1	2
Pb	0.06	10
Sb	0.2	40
Si	0.08	20
Tl	0.14	30
Zn	0.0006	1

Perkin-Elmer (HGA series) and Varian-Techtron (Models 61 and 63). The essential difference between these two is size; the Varian has a smaller internal volume than the Perkin-Elmer. The smaller volume should allow a greater sensitivity for a given amount of sample, but it should permit a smaller range of allowable sample sizes (that is, the usable range should be smaller). There are perhaps few really significant differences between the two furnaces in most analytical situations.

Sensitivities. A battle—known as the "war of detection limits"—seems to be going on among the various manufacturers of atomic absorption instruments. Despite claims and counterclaims, one fact is clear: the nonflame atomization systems are clearly superior in terms of sensitivities and detection limits, by two or three orders of magnitude for most elements. Some typical detection limits are given in the table. These data compare the detection limits of 16 elements on an absolute basis (smallest detectable amount) for a heated graphite atomization system and for chemical flames (air-acetylene or nitrous oxide—acetylene, as the case may be). For the computation of the flame detection limits, which are usually reported in concentration rather than in absolute units, a sample solution volume of 1 ml was selected as the minimum amount necessary for a determination. These data clearly indicate the superior powers of detection of nonflame atomization, of two or three orders of magnitude.

Limitations. Nonflame atomization systems are not without limitations. However, they do overcome, or almost overcome, some of the more important limitations of chemical flames, notably compound formation (atomization efficiency), and they can utilize very small samples. Typically, a flame requires about a milliliter of sample solution for a determination. The chemical environment experienced by the sample is reactive and not readily controlled. The temperature can be varied only over a relatively small range. The sample atoms are relatively dilute in the flame, and their residence time in the optical path is relatively short. The graphite furnaces, on the other hand, have neutral (for example, N_2 or Ar) atmospheres, reducing conditions (for example, from the hot graphite), and relatively small volumes and long residence times, and they utilize very small samples (0.5–100 μl). The principal limitations of these devices, at least as presently designed, are as follows: Although small samples are desirable in sample-limited cases, present devices *must* use small samples to achieve reasonable linearity and reproducibility. Because of the transient temperature conditions during the atomization step, matrix effects are frequently more serious. The reproducibility of measurement is generally not as good as with flames. Some elements react with the graphite to form stable carbides. Graphite elements have relatively short lifetimes, requiring replacement and, thus, recalibration. Recently a methane pyrolysis treatment was used to coat the graphite with pyrolytic graphite, and greatly increased the useful lifetime.

Most of these limitations are outweighed by the improved sensitivity. Developments will be forthcoming in the near future that will remove, or diminish, some of the limitations. Many matrix effects, for example, have not yet been investigated in detail, and investigations will undoubtedly suggest means of overcoming them. In short, these devices are not ideal atomization systems, but they are a step in the right direction.

Applications. Nonflame atomizers, with their high sensitivity and small sample requirements, are finding increasingly wide application in a variety of areas. Among the most important uses are biomedical applications (blood, urine, tissue, and so forth) and related environmental studies (natural waters, waste water, air, and so forth). Another important area of application is agricultural (foods, soils, and so forth). Recent reviews describe the many applications of these devices in atomic absorption analyses more fully. Nonflame atomization is also being used increasingly in atomic fluorescence spectrometry, in which the high atomization efficiency and low background emission are used to advantage.

For background information see SPECTROSCOPY in the McGraw-Hill Encyclopedia of Science and Technology.   [CLAUDE VEILLON]

Bibliography: M. D. Amos, *Amer. Lab.*, 4(8):57, 1972; M. K. Murphy and C. Veillon, *Anal. Chim. Acta*, 69:295, 1974; C. R. Parker et al., *Amer. Lab.*, 5(8):53, 1973; J. D. Winefordner and T. J. Vickers, *Anal. Chem.*, 46(5):192R, 1974.

Atomic physics

In the collision of two atoms with atomic numbers Z_1 and Z_2, the nuclei may approach each other so closely that, for a very short time, the atomic electrons arrange themselves as if they belonged to an atom of atomic number $Z_1 + Z_2$. This is true even for $Z_1 + Z_2$ up to 200, for collision energies up to 7 MeV per nucleon in the center-of-mass system. Two important uses of such "quasiatoms" have been proposed recently. First, if $Z_1 + Z_2$ is sufficiently large, W. Greiner and coworkers have pointed out that quasiatoms provide an opportunity to study behavior of matter in the presence of extremely high electric fields. Second, x-ray emission spectra from quasiatoms can yield detailed information about the atomic collision process.

Central to these investigations is a knowledge of the electronic energy levels of two-nucleus quasimolecular systems, a subject pioneered by D. R. Bates and coworkers through studies of the hydrogen molecular ion. This work has been extended by K. Helfrich and H. Hartmann to the general nonrelativistic, one-electron quasimolecule, and by B. Müller and coworkers to the general relativistic, one-electron quasimolecule. Only isolated calculations have been made for many-electron systems.

Overcritical electric fields. The interaction between two charged particles, classically treated, is given by Coulomb's law, if the particles are at rest with respect to one another, and by Maxwell's electrodynamic equations, if the particles are in relative motion. The inclusion of quantum effects has led to a more general theory, called quantum electrodynamics (QED). Many refined calculations and predictions have been made with QED and have been found to be in agreement with experiment. Yet, the search continues for possible limitations of the theory, in order to develop it further.

Consider the following thought experiment. Assume that a nucleus of charge $Z(e)$ exists in free space, not surrounded by electrons or any other matter. (Technically, the nucleus is spoken of as being in a "vacuum.") QED calculations by J. Rafelski and coworkers have shown that if Z is less than a critical value Z_{cr} ($\sim$173), the system under consideration is stable, but for Z exceeding Z_{cr}, an electron-positron pair would be created spontaneously, that is, without the expenditure of any energy. The electron of the pair would be captured into the lowest orbit (called $1s$ or K) around the nucleus, and the positron would be ejected with a kinetic energy $B - 2mc^2$, where B is the binding energy of the K-electron, m the electron rest mass, and c the speed of light. The critical value of Z is that value which causes B to be just equal to $2mc^2$ ($= 1.02$ MeV). For $Z > Z_{cr}$ it can be said that the (overcritical) electric field of the nucleus is so strong that the "vacuum breaks down."

The detection of positrons from overcritical electric fields would constitute an important test of QED. Although the production of nuclei with $Z > 173$ presently seems impossible, electric fields of overcritical magnitude can be produced in the collision of two atoms with atomic numbers Z_1 and Z_2 such that $Z_1 + Z_2 > 173$. Figure 1 shows the lowest electronic state of the U + U quasimolecule ($Z_1 = Z_2 = 92$, $Z_1 + Z_2 = 184$) as a function of the internuclear separation R. Normally the lowest state ($1s\sigma$) is filled with two electrons. But, if only one electron occupies this state, that is, if there is a $1s\sigma$ vacancy during the collision, a situation similar to the preceding thought experiment may occur. If the nuclei come close enough together, so that the binding energy B_1 of the $1s\sigma$ state exceeds $2mc^2$, the electric field becomes overcritical. An electron-positron pair is created spontaneously, the electron filling the $1s\sigma$ vacancy and the positron being emitted (see process 1 in Fig. 1). Unfortunately, positron-electron pairs can also be created in the collision before the electric field becomes overcritical, that is, for $B_1 < 2mc^2$, because energy is available from the nuclear motion (see process 2 in Fig. 1). Only a detailed examination of the positron spectrum can distinguish the spontaneously produced positrons, which provide the important test for QED, from the positrons induced by the nuclear motion. Several laboratories are making preparations to generate U beams of sufficient energy (600–1600 MeV) in order to search for the predicted positrons.

K x-rays from quasiatoms. Two important atomic physics questions must be investigated before the foregoing test of QED can be made. Do vacancies form in the $1s\sigma$ state during the collision of two heavy atoms (not necessarily U + U) and, if so, by what process? Do electrons have sufficient time to fill vacancies during the collision itself? The second question is pertinent, because it can be estimated that a $1s\sigma$ vacancy in a heavy quasimolecule exists for times of the order of 10^{-16} sec, whereas typical collision times are of the order of 10^{-19} sec. Hence the probability that a $1s\sigma$ vacancy will be filled during a collision is only of the order of $10^{-19}/10^{-16} = 10^{-3}$.

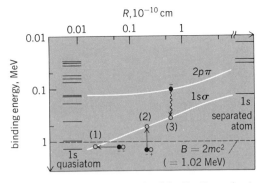

Fig. 1. Electronic energy levels of the U + U quasimolecule as a function of the internuclear separation R. Three possible ways of filling a $1s\sigma$ vacancy are illustrated: (1) by spontaneous electron-positron creation, (2) by induced electron-positron formation, and (3) by electron transition from the $2p\pi$ level. Processes 1 and 2 are accompanied by positron emission, 3 by x-ray emission. (*After B. Müller, J. Rafelski, and W. Greiner, Solution of the Dirac equation with two Coulomb centres, Phys. Lett., 47B:5–7, 1973*)

The filling of a $1s\sigma$ quasimolecular vacancy, just like the filling of an atomic $1s$ vacancy, will normally occur with an electron from a higher-lying electronic state (see process 3 in Fig. 1). The electronic transition is accompanied by x-ray emission. If the final electron state is a $1s\sigma$ or $1s$ state, the x-rays are called K x-rays. In U + U collisions at high energy, K x-ray emission and positron emission compete with each other in the $1s\sigma$ vacancy filling. In the collision of lighter atoms, only x-ray emission is important.

Inner-shell vacancy formation. Since the filling probability of a $1s\sigma$ vacancy during a collision is only of the order of 10^{-3}, most $1s\sigma$ vacancies are filled when the collision partners have already separated after the collision. Hence the atomic x-rays of the collision partners can serve as a tool for the study of vacancy-formation processes in quasimolecular states.

Basically, electron ejection from an atom or a quasimolecule is due to the time-varying electric field acting on the electron as the collision partners pass each other. If the projectile atomic number is much less than the target atomic number, one can assume that the orbit of the target electron to be ejected is unaffected by the projectile before the ejection occurs. If the collision partners have comparable atomic numbers, it must usually be assumed that the electrons in both adjust their orbits so as to form quasimolecular states from which an electron will be removed. Depending on the availability of vacancies in the higher-lying quasimolecular states, various processes of electron removal can be distinguished.

Quasimolecular K x-rays. The filling of a $1s\sigma$ vacancy during a collision from a higher-lying state (see process 3 in Fig. 1), even though rare, can take place at any internuclear separation. Hence one expects to observe beyond the atomic K x-ray lines of the projectile (Z_1) and the target (Z_2) a weak continuous band of quasimolecular K x-rays extending up to the K x-ray energies of the quasiatom $Z_1 + Z_2$. Such quasimolecular x-ray bands were first

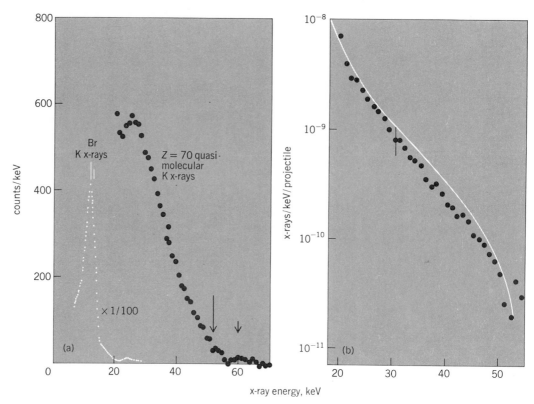

Fig. 2. X-ray spectrum from the bombardment of solid Br by a 30-MeV Br beam. (a) Raw spectrum after subtraction of room background. Arrows mark energies of quasiatomic *Kα* and *Kβ* x-rays near which the quasimolecular *K* x-ray spectrum is expected to terminate. (b) Experimental spectrum corrected for absorber effects and detection efficiency, compared with absolute theoretical curve for quasimolecular *K* x-ray spectrum. (*After W. E. Meyerhof et al., Molecular-orbital K x-ray formation in heavy-ion collisions, Phys. Rev. Lett., 32:1279–1282, 1974*)

observed by F. Saris and coworkers and P. Mokler and coworkers in Ar + Ar collisions (*L* x-rays) and I + Au collisions (*M* x-rays), respectively. J. R. McDonald and coworkers made the first observation of a quasimolecular *K* x-ray band in C + C collisions at 20–240-keV bombarding energy.

Figure 2a shows observations of a continuum x-ray spectrum from collisions of a 30-MeV Br beam ($Z_1 = 35$) with a thick solid target of pure Br ($Z_2 = 35$) deposited on a refrigerated backing. The spectrum was observed with a 17-cm³ Ge(Li) solid-state detector. A $\frac{1}{16}$-in.-thick (1.587 mm) Al filter was inserted between the target and the detector to eliminate unwanted, low-energy radiation. Beyond the unresolved atomic *K* x-ray lines of Br, a weak continuum can be seen that melts into room background near the *K* x-ray energies of the quasiatom with $Z = Z_1 + Z_2 = 70$. Although the time-varying nature of the collision process, among other factors, causes the end point of the spectrum to be broadened, it has been shown the "practical" end point does not vary appreciably with bombarding energy. This is expected if the bombarding energy is sufficient to bring the colliding nuclei to separations much smaller than the quasiatomic *K* orbit radius.

The identification of the continuum spectrum shown in Fig. 2a as a quasimolecular *K* x-ray spectrum can be assured only after a detailed comparison with theory. In making such a comparison, it must first be shown that all sources of background are either well understood or are small in the x-ray energy region of interest. Furthermore, the raw spectra must be corrected for the distorting effect of the absorbing filter and the detector. In the case of 30-MeV Br-Br collisions, all backgrounds such as electron and nuclear bremsstrahlung are indeed small. Figure 2b gives the corrected experimental spectrum and a theoretical curve computed without any adjustable parameters but not including end point broadening. Theory and experiment are in sufficiently good agreement that one can be confident about the identification of the quasimolecular *K* x-ray spectrum, especially since other target and projectile combinations have also been examined experimentally and well fitted with the same theory.

Outlook. It is desirable to detect quasimolecular *K* x-ray spectra from atomic collisions of even higher *Z*. Unfortunately, since at a given bombarding energy the yield varies approximately proportional to Z^{-6}, experiments become progressively more difficult as *Z* increases. On the other hand, since the yield also varies roughly as the third power of the bombarding energy, as higher-energy, heavy-ion beams become available, these experiments can be extended. Indeed, quasimolecular *K* x-ray bands have been observed from $Z_1 + Z_2 = 106$ in 82-MeV I + I collisions and from $Z_1 + Z_2 = 114$ in 115-MeV La + La collisions.

Recently, coincidence experiments between the scattered projectile and the continuum x-ray spectrum have been attempted. Also, the angular anisotropy of the continuum spectrum with respect to the beam direction has been determined. These experiments promise to give a refined understanding of quasimolecular K x-ray spectra.

As techniques improve, attempts will be made to detect the positrons from energetic U + U collisions, and, in addition, new uses to which superheavy quasiatoms can be put will be considered. For example, it has been suggested that the study of M x-rays from superheavy quasiatoms may aid in the identification of superheavy elements, but difficulties may be encountered in this area. It is also possible that other tests of QED that make use of inner-shell vacancy formation in heavy-atom collisions can be attempted.

For background information *see* QUANTUM ELECTRODYNAMICS in the McGraw-Hill Encyclopedia of Science and Technology.

[W. E. MEYERHOF]

Bibliography: B. Crasemann (ed.), *Atomic Inner-Shell Processes*, 1975; J. D. Garcia et al., *Rev. Mod. Phys.*, 45:111–177, 1973; W. E. Meyerhof et al., *Phys. Rev. Lett.*, 32:1279–1282, 1974; J. Rafelski, in R. L. Robinson et al. (eds.), *Proceedings of the International Conference on Reactions between Complex Nuclei*, vol. 2, 1974.

Aurora

Two satellite systems have provided the first large-scale photographs of the aurora. A much broader view is obtainable from the satellites than from the ground. Satellite photographs have led to the discovery of several new features in the global pattern of auroral displays and the direct verification of many other features that had been painstakingly deduced from pictures obtained from ground-based networks of auroral All-Sky cameras. When more fully analyzed, the data from these satellites may provide the answers to some key questions regarding the magnetospheric interactions that cause the aurora.

Satellite characteristics. The two satellite auroral imaging systems differ markedly in detail; however, both generate pictures electronically by systematically scanning the Earth from side to side as the satellite moves along in its orbit. The satellite motion causes successive scans to be displaced geographically from one another, making it possible to combine the data from these individual strips into a composite picture that is very similar in resolution and information content to a high-quality television picture. The data from an entire satellite pass are required to obtain a single such picture. Continuous satellite television pictures of the aurora will probably not be available for several years.

The joint Canadian-American satellite *ISIS-2* (International Satellite for Ionospheric Studies) was launched in April 1971. It contains two instruments that image the aurora at three specific wavelengths prominent in the auroral spectrum. It also contains a complement of particle and plasma experiments, including a topside ionospheric sounder. At an altitude of 1400 km, the satellite is in a nearly polar orbit, and it provides a very broad view of the auroral zone at a limiting resolution of about 10 km with the high-resolution 5577 A/3914 A instrument.

The U.S. Air Force DMSP (Defense Meteorological Satellite Program) satellites are also capable of

auroral imagery. Although intended primarily for meteorological purposes, these satellites have proved to be sufficiently sensitive to detect auroras. Pictures shown publicly have dated from December 1971, although it is probable that one or more satellites were operational before then. The program is an ongoing one involving several satellites, and data from 1973 onward are available from the U.S. Environmental Data Service.

The detector used in the DMSP satellites is a sensitive silicon photodiode that has a wavelength response which covers the spectral range from 4500 to 1100 A (10 A = 1 nm). It is therefore sensitive to a broad range of auroral emissions, although perhaps chiefly the near-infrared emission bands of molecular nitrogen. Angular resolution of the instrument is somewhat better than that of the high-resolution scanner on *ISIS-2*. The improved angular resolution, together with a lower-altitude orbit (800 km), gives better spatial resolution (about 3–6 km) but narrower coverage of the auroral zone on any given pass. A beautifully detailed picture obtained from one of the DMSP satellites is shown in Fig. 1. The complex structure exhibited by both the discrete (center and lower left) and diffuse (right) aurora is quite apparent.

The picture in Fig. 2 was obtained with the 5577 A (auroral green line) instrument on *ISIS-2*. The data have been transformed by computer onto a modified polar grid in order to avoid the geometrical distortions inherent in the original scanning pattern. The two pictures in Fig. 2 are identical except that, on the upper one, major continental boundaries around the northern polar cap are shown, with Hudson Bay at the bottom, Greenland on the right, and Alaska-Siberia at the upper left. The geographic pole is shown as a cross near the top. Jagged boundaries at the left and right edges of the pictures represent the limits of scan of the instrument.

Morphology of aurora. The aurora in Fig. 2, as seen from the vantage point of the satellite, is both familiar and startling from the standpoint of auroral morphology. It contains features that are prominent in many satellite pictures. The large-scale pattern, or "morphology," of the aurora is impor-

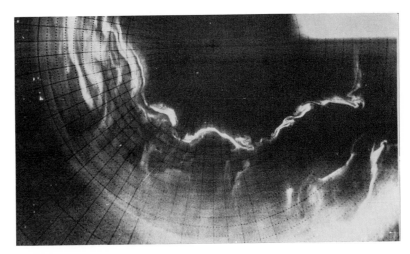

Fig. 1. The nighttime polar region as seen from the DMSP satellite. All the bright features are the aurora, except for some bright dots on the left, which are cities. (*Courtesy of E. Rogers, Aerospace Corp.*)

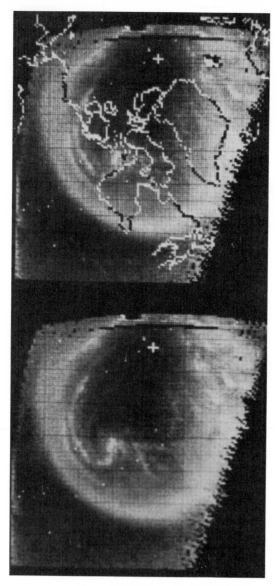

Fig. 2. The auroral distribution around the northern polar cap as seen on Dec. 22, 1971, by *ISIS-2*. The upper picture is the same as the lower, except that major continental boundaries are superimposed. Midnight is at the bottom, and noon at the top. (*Courtesy of W. Sawchuk, University of Calgary*)

tant because the upper atmosphere gives off auroral light in response to incoming fluxes of energetic charged particles that have traveled great distances along the Earth's magnetic field lines. The geographic patterns of these auroral emissions, arranged into complex narrow arcs and broader diffuse regions, are often observed to extend for thousands of kilometers around an oval-shaped region centered on the Earth's magnetic pole. The auroral pattern is linked by the Earth's magnetic field to magnetospheric regions where magnetic and electric field interactions and discontinuities that energize the auroral particles occur. Auroral observations, particularly when made from a satellite, provide the only known technique for remote sensing of these processes on a global basis.

Many of the characteristic features of what S. I.

Akasofu has termed "auroral substorms" are apparent in Fig. 2. Substorms consist of a characteristic sequence of auroral intensifications and movements around midnight, where a rapid poleward movement of arcs produces a "bulge." The spectacular bulge associated with the intense substorm shown in Fig. 2 (lower part of the picture) extends well north of Hudson Bay. A bright auroral arc connects to this bulge and extends around and through the evening sector at the left of the picture and out over the Arctic Ocean north of Alaska. The great length of this arc, and the fact that a faint extension of it appears to continue around into the noon sector at the top of the picture, supports the idea that the "auroral oval," proposed by Y. Feldstein, is not merely a statistical average of auroral positions. The satellite pictures show that the instantaneous pattern of auroral arcs can be described as following the Feldstein oval.

Another feature of the bright arcs in Fig. 2 is their tendency for the abrupt discontinuities, both in intensity and direction, that are especially apparent on the right-hand side of the midnight bulge and along the bright evening arc. Such effects are difficult to understand but are probably fundamentally related to the mechanisms that produce the arcs. The satellite pictures also show many fascinating cases of auroral arcs cutting across the polar cap in a noon-to-midnight direction, often connecting with the midnight aurora. Some faint examples are evident in Fig. 2. Arcs with this alignment are not easy to explain on the basis of current auroral theories.

Perhaps the most suprising aspect of the satellite pictures has been the prominence, one might even say dominance, of the diffuse aurora. Outside the discrete auroras described above is a ring of diffuse aurora surrounding the polar cap. Because this type of aurora is widespread and relatively uniform, it has been overlooked in most ground-based studies. Although it is usually less intense than in the example shown here, the diffuse aurora is always present. It does not appear to participate in the poleward motion of the discrete auroras during substorms, but it does undergo substantial intensification at these times. In the case shown here, some of the patches in the morning sector (upper right of Fig. 2) rival the brightest parts of the discrete aurora in the midnight bulge.

Although the noon sector is not covered fully in the illustrations, it is currently of great interest. A high-latitude region has been discovered that is thought to connect directly (by means of magnetic field lines) to the outermost regions of the magnetosphere on the day side and, perhaps, to the interplanetary field itself. The atmosphere at the foot of these field lines emits relatively intense radiation in the red part of the spectrum at 6300 A. G. G. Shepherd discovered this region of emission by using a special photometer on *ISIS-2* that isolates this particular wavelength.

For background information *see* AURORA in the McGraw-Hill Encyclopedia of Science and Technology.   [CLIFFORD ANGER]

Bibliography: C. D. Anger and G. G. Shepherd, in B. McCormac (ed.), *Proceedings of the Conference on Earth's Particles and Fields*, Sheffield, England, 1973, in press; A. T. Y. Lui and C. D.

Anger, *Planet. Space Sci.*, 21:789–809, 1973; C. P. Pike and J. A. Whalen, *J. Geophys. Res.*, 79(7): 985–1000, 1974; E. H. Rogers, D. F. Nelson, and R. C. Savage, *Science*, 183:951–952, 1974; G. G. Shepherd and F. W. Thirkettle, *Science*, 180:737–739, May 18, 1973.

Bark

Transport of organic substances in the phloem is still far from being understood. At present, research not only concerns sieve elements themselves but extends to those cells that are anatomically and functionally intimately connected with the sieve elements. These cells are the companion cells of angiosperms and the albuminous cells, or Strasburger cells, of the gymnosperms. Recent research on the Strasburger cells is the subject of this article.

Recent enzyme-cytochemical studies succeeded for the first time in localizing the remarkably increased respiratory and phosphatase activity of Strasburger (albuminous) cells in the phloem of conifers. This increased enzyme activity was clearly restricted to those Strasburger cells that were in contact with fully differentiated and obviously conducting sieve cells. Since enhanced metabolic activity of the conducting phloem as a whole has been documented by numerous physiological studies, its precise localization at the cellular level is of interest, particularly because loading and unloading of sieve elements along the translocation path, as well as long-distance translocation itself, are believed to involve metabolic activity.

Strasburger cells. One remarkable characteristic of differentiating sieve elements is that, even in the enucleated state, they remain in close association with specialized parenchyma cells. Although the lack of a nucleus in the mature sieve elements of some species has been questioned, according to recent reports by R. F. Evert and coworkers, the sieve elements must be considered to be not only enucleated but also devoid of ribosomes in their functional stage. These characteristics have been repeatedly confirmed by ultrastructural studies. Whether, and to what extent, synthesis of enzymes and of nucleoside triphosphates identified in mature sieve elements by several scientists can be achieved without nuclei and ribosomes seems to be more doubtful than ever before. In this respect, the nucleated cells associated with the mature sieve elements certainly are most important and, probably, important for the process of long-distance translocation itself.

Sieve elements of angiosperms are accompanied by "companion cells" that remain in close ontogenetic association with the sieve elements, whereas gymnosperms lack such developmentally related phloem cells. Nevertheless, in 1891, E. Strasburger described highly specialized cells that were anatomically, though not ontogenetically, in intimate contact with the sieve cells of gymnosperms and that were believed to be analogous in function to the companion cells. Strasburger named these cells *eiweisshaltige Zellen*, that is, "albuminous cells." It has recently been suggested that albuminous cells be referred to as "Strasburger cells," for the former term is a misnomer. Strasburger called these cells albuminous not because of their high protein content but because he believed that they received the contents of the sieve cells for further distribution among other parenchyma cells (see illustration), and because, at that time, the content was thought to be proteinaceous in nature. The term Strasburger cells is also more appropriate because the unusually high protein content that is implied in the term albuminous cells has not been confirmed in more recent reports. The identification and physiology of Strasburger cells are still quite ambiguous, but investigations carried out during the last few years have provided new insights.

Occurrence. The occurrence of Strasburger cells in the phloem of gymnosperms differs according to the taxonomic family, and their classification sometimes remains a matter of definition. They form part of the axial parenchyma system, such as in members of Cycadinae, Ginkyoinae, Taxaceae, Araucariaceae, and Gnetales, or part of the radial parenchyma system (the phloem rays), as in Pinaceae, or even part of both, as in most Cupressaceae and Taxodiaceae. That this is only a rough classification has been demonstrated in an extensive study by R. W. Den Outer. He also distinguished three evolutionary stages in the Strasburger cell–sieve cell association that probably precedes the formation of genuine companion cells. The fact that these cells have also been found in the rays and in the axial system of larch indicates the imprecision of the above classification. The information about Strasburger cells observed in some angiosperms is still scanty in contrast to the recently acquired information on albuminous cells in conifers.

Cytological characteristics. Wherever Strasburger cells occur, their most consistent characteristic is their connection with the sieve cells by one-sided sieve areas and their premature death, which occurs when sieve cells cease to function. The question of whether they contain starch or not seems to be solved now. Although some scientists distinguished Strasburger cells by their lack of starch, others found that the cells did contain starch. Results from studies on larch have clearly proved that young Strasburger cells and those in contact with immature sieve cells are able to form starch, but that they regularly lose this starch as the contiguous sieve cell matures. Thus, at the height of their function at least, the Strasburger cells are always free of starch; this is certainly more than an accidental parallel to the companion cells in angiosperms that are always free of starch, too.

High protein content is another feature frequently attributed to these cells. However, recent cytochemical studies by Den Outer and by F. J. Alfieri and Evert do not confirm any particular protein richness. Similarly, in larch, active Strasburger cells were found to show little increase in protein content if they were compared with adjacent ordinary ray cells; protein levels were not higher when they were compared with Strasburger cells of the cambial zone. The protein richness of these cells thus remains questionable. Of considerable interest, however, is the detection of both proteinaceous slime and slime bodies in Strasburger cells at the light microscopic and the

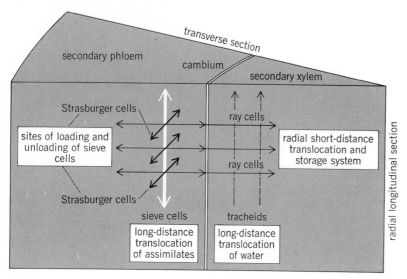

Diagram illustrating the main translocation pathways in a stem section of a gymnosperm.

electron microscopic level by Evert and coworkers. The significance of this finding must be elucidated, for this substance is most characteristic for sieve elements; indeed, it is the focus of present research on the functioning of sieve elements. Another interesting characteristic is the much-increased metabolic activity of Strasburger cells, ascertained by cytochemical methods at the cellular level.

Metabolic activity and function. New information on the physiology and the possible role of Strasburger cells in translocation of assimilates was obtained recently with cytochemical methods. These procedures make it possible to observe, at the cellular level, the activity of individual dehydrogenases involved in aerobic and anaerobic respiration and of phosphatases indicating phosphorylating-dephosphorylating steps. Since Strasburger cells, in contrast to companion cells, can be studied in a whole sequence of different physiological stages, even within one tissue section, this new information takes on added significance. The advantage for the interpretation of the cytoenzymatical results is obvious.

The Strasburger cells of larch and pine have been found to have highly increased levels of activity of respiratory enzymes and acid phosphatases, and to differ greatly in these features from other parenchymatous phloem cells. The most striking observation, however, was that it was not the young and almost meristematic Strasburger cells of the cambial region that exhibited greatly increased respiratory and phosphatase activity, nor those contiguous with young and still-differentiating sieve elements, but only those cells that were in contact with mature, enucleated sieve elements. Furthermore, the enhanced metabolic activity was found to be restricted to those periods of the year during which accumulation or mobilization of starch in the parenchyma system, and therefore loading or unloading of sieve elements, was taking place. Both results strongly indicate the relevance of this metabolic activity for translocation. The common view that conducting phloem is a site of increased metabolic activity is thus supported

once again; in addition, in this case it is demonstrated that increased activity is located in the nucleated cells associated with mature sieve elements.

Yet, whether this high metabolic activity of Strasburger cells at the border of mature sieve cells is caused exclusively by the loading or unloading of sieve cells, or by a supply of energy or energy-rich substances for long-distance translocation within sieve cells themselves, or by both events at the same time, still cannot be decided. The first interpretation would be supported by the fact that the energy-dependent processes of uptake and secretion of assimilates must be carried out anatomically via Strasburger cells (see illustration). The second interpretation would be supported by the results of recent years that indicated energy-dependence of long-distance translocation within sieve elements themselves. Such conclusions were drawn from quite different kinds of experiments and recently have been supported substantially by the work of F. A. Qureshi and D. C. Spanner and of D. C. J. Gardner and A. J. Peel. Since, as mentioned above, mature sieve elements are devoid of nucleus and ribosomes, it must be assumed that energy is furnished by the nucleated cells associated with them. In any case, the activity of these cells certainly must be taken into consideration when the mechanism of translocation is considered.

For background information *see* PHLOEM in the McGraw-Hill Encyclopedia of Science and Technology.

[JÖRG J. SAUTER]

Bibliography: J. J. Sauter, *Z. Pflanzenphysiol.*, 66:440–458, 1972.

Binaural sound

Results of recent studies indicate that the mechanism of binaural sound location depends on differences in phase and intensity of sound. Phase appears to be important up to 1000 Hz, and intensity appears to be important above 1000 Hz. Phase and intensity are both involved in the frequency between 500 and 1000 Hz.

Binaural hearing is an innate physical property of the human hearing mechanism that provides the means for determining the directional location of a sound source. The property of binaural hearing supplies the physical mechanism that enables the listener to place the location of a group of independent and different original sound sources in auditory perspective according to the geometrical configuration of the listener and the original sound sources. The main feature of stereophonic sound reproduction is auditory perspective. In stereophonic sound reproduction, as in firsthand listening, the subjective location of the reproduced sound sources corresponds to the location of the original sound sources under geometrically corresponding conditions. Quadriphonic sound reproduction provides, in addition to auditory perspective, the acoustic ambience or reverberation envelope and all manner of spatial effects that depend upon the properties of binaural hearing.

Binaural hearing. Binaural hearing is the directional localization characteristic of human hearing. The lateral direction of a source of sound in the

BINAURAL SOUND

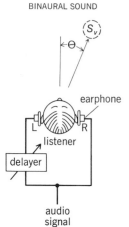

Fig. 1. An experiment illustrating the binaural phase effect; S_v is virtual sound source.

horizontal plane containing the line joining both ears can be determined to a high degree of accuracy. For example, a source of sound that originates on the right of the median plane (the plane bisecting and normal to the line joining the two ears) can be recognized and accurately localized on the right. Furthermore, the accuracy of directional localization becomes very great when the sound source is in a direction very close to the median plane and in front of the listener. Binaural hearing provides the facility of listening to a particular speech sound source while discriminating between that source and others. Binaural hearing also makes it possible to discriminate between noise and a desired sound. The lack of binaural hearing is particularly evident, and annoying to, the hard-of-hearing who employ a single hearing aid and thereby lose the effect of binaural hearing. The net result is a loss of the localization of sound sources and thus an inability to discriminate between noise and desired sounds.

In the directional localization of a sound source by means of binaural hearing, a difference in the phase of the sound and a difference in the intensity of the sound at both ears of the listener are the determinants, either separately or together.

Binaural phase effect. An experiment for determining the binaural effect of the phase difference between the sound at each ear is shown in Fig. 1. The same audio signal is applied to both ears. The intensity of the sound is the same at both ears. A delayer in the left channel makes it possible to delay the audio signal applied to the left ear. If there is no difference in phase between the audio signal applied to both ears, the virtual source of the audio signal will appear to be in a direction directly in front of the listener in the median plane. When the audio signal to the left ear is delayed, the virtual sound source will appear to the right of the median plane. Experiments have shown that the angular displacement of the virtual sound source of Fig. 1 is given by Eq. (1), where Θ is the

$$\Theta = \frac{\phi}{0.0034f + 0.8} \qquad (1)$$

angle between the median plane and the direction of the virtual sound source, in degrees; ϕ is the phase difference between the audio signal at the two ears, in degrees; and f is the frequency, in hertz. In general, the binaural phase effect ceases at about 1000–1500 Hz.

Binaural intensity effect. An experiment for determining the binaural effect of the difference in intensity between sound at each ear is shown in Fig. 2. The same audio signal is applied to both ears. The phase of the sound at both ears is the same. An attenuator makes it possible to reduce the intensity of the audio signal applied to the left ear. If the intensity of the audio signal is the same at both ears, the virtual sound source will appear to be in a direction directly in front of the listener in the median plane. When the audio signal to the left ear is attenuated, the virtual sound source will appear to the right of the median plane. Experiments have shown that the angular displacement of the virtual sound source of Fig. 2 for 250–1000 Hz is given by Eq. (2), where Θ is the angle between the median and the direction of the virtual sound

source, in degrees; P_L is the sound pressure at the left ear, in microbars; P_R is the sound pressure at the right ear, in microbars; and f is the frequency in hertz. In general, the binaural intensity effect occurs over the entire audio-frequency range.

$$\Theta = \frac{2000}{\sqrt{f}} \log_{10} \frac{P_R}{P_L} \qquad (2)$$

Sound localization. The preceding considerations and experiments provide an insight into the phenomena involved in binaural hearing. The experiments show that both phase and intensity play a part in binaural hearing. The experiments of Figs. 1 and 2 can be translated to actual acoustic field conditions, as depicted in Fig. 3, in which there is a real sound source and a listener. When the real sound source is directly in front of the listener, that is, $\Theta = 0$, the phase and intensity at each ear of the listener are the same. The result is that the real sound source appears to be directly in front of the listener. When the real sound source is at an angle Θ greater than zero, there is a difference in phase at each ear of the listener. For frequencies up to about 1000 Hz, this phase difference plays the most important part in determining the location of the real sound source. In the low audio-frequency range, the sound pressure for a real sound source at a distance of 1 m or more is practically the same at each ear. In the frequency range above 300 Hz, there will be a difference in sound pressure at each ear owing to diffraction for an angle Θ greater than zero. The difference in sound pressure at both ears will now be discussed.

The diffraction of sound by the head produces a difference in the sound pressures at both ears that is a function of the angle of incidence of impinging sound. The directivity characteristics depicting the difference in sound pressure at both ears as a function of the angle of incidence for 125, 250, 500, 1000, 2000, 4000, 8000, and 16,000 Hz are shown in Fig. 4. These characteristics show that the difference in sound pressure at each ear increases with frequency. The difference in sound pressures at each ear rises from 0 dB, at $\Theta = 0°$, to a maximum at $\Theta = 90°$, when one ear faces the sound source, and then decreases to 0 dB at $\Theta = 180°$.

From the preceding discussion, it can be seen that diffraction produces a difference in pressure at each ear which is essentially a function of the angle from the median plane. This difference in pressure provides the binaural directivity characteristic in the high audio-frequency range.

In summary, a consideration of the preceding exposition and Figs. 1–4 indicates that phase plays the most important part in the binaural directional localization up to about 1000 Hz. Above 1000 Hz, intensity plays the most important part; and in the frequency range 500–1000 Hz, both phase and intensity play a part.

An experiment was performed to determine the angular accuracy of binaural hearing under free field conditions. The test was conducted in an anechoic room, and the speech and music were reproduced on a loudspeaker. A light-opaque sound-transmitting dark-colored screen was placed on the arc of a circle so that the observer could not see the loudspeaker. A vertical white rod was sup-

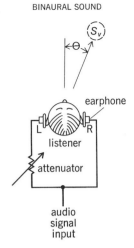

Fig. 2. An experiment illustrating the binaural intensity effect; S_v is virtual sound source.

Fig. 3. Field experiment on sound source (S_0) localization.

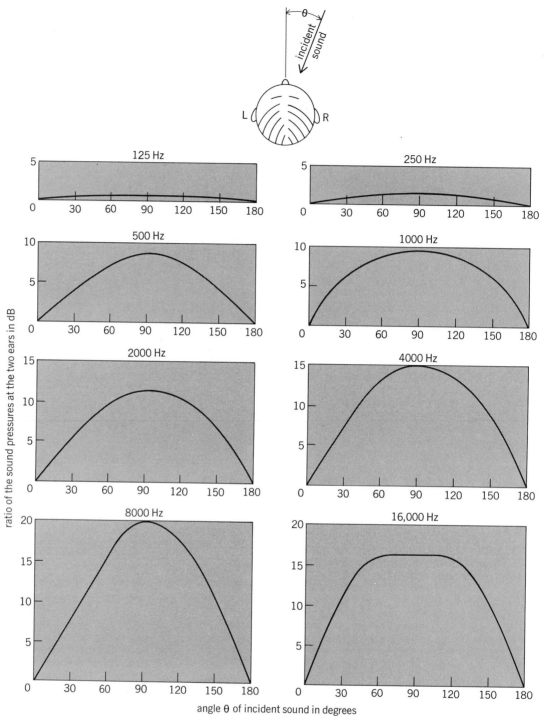

Fig. 4. The ratio of the sound pressures at both ears as a function of the angle of the incident sound.

ported on a toy electric locomotive running on a track on the arc of a circle. The locomotive was operated by the listener. The head of the listener was always directed along the angle $\theta = 0$. The listener moved the vertical rod by proper actuation of the locomotive until he thought that the location of the rod coincided with that of the hidden sound source. The results of the experiment are shown in Fig. 5. The error angle was practically the same for

speech and music. The data of Fig. 5 show that the angular accuracy of binaural hearing is indeed quite good. For the larger angles, the accuracy can be improved by slight movement of the head.

The localization experiments described above have been confined to the front quadrants. For live auditory perspective and stereophonic sound reproduction, the localization of sound in the front two quadrants is the most common. In the case of

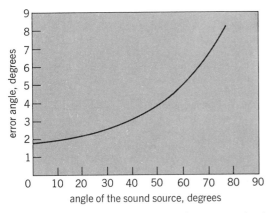

Fig. 5. Data from an experiment on the error angle of localization of a sound source as a function of the angle of the sound source from the median plane $\theta = 0$.

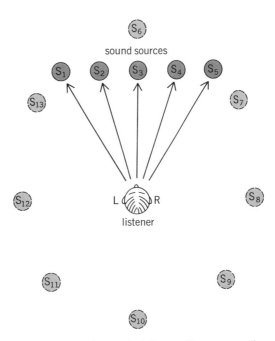

Fig. 6. An experiment depicting auditory perspective and acoustic ambience of a group of different and independent sound sources.

quadriphonic sound reproduction, the directional localization by binaural hearing in all four quadrants may be of interest. In an experiment for determining the angular accuracy of binaural hearing in all four quadrants, there were nine loudspeakers spaced 22.5° apart on a semicircle. A light-opaque sound-transmitting screen was placed in front of the loudspeakers so that the listener could not see the loudspeakers. The head of the listener was always directed along the angle $\Theta = 0$. Speech and music were used as the audio signal. The selection of the particular loudspeaker was random. The listener was asked to identify, by number, the loudspeaker that was reproducing the audio program, that is, speech or music. To assist the listener in identifying the one loudspeaker that was reproducing the program, a sketch depicting the angular locations of the loudspeakers, numbered 1 to 9, was provided. The results of this experiment, given in the table, show that the localization accuracy is very good in all four quadrants. Therefore, sound reproduction that requires a sense of directivity in all four quadrants can be used with good results.

Auditory perspective and acoustic ambience. The binaural nature of the human hearing mechanism attributes a directional sense to the sound that is received. Because of this mechanism, a source of sound can be angularly localized. Consequently, when there is a group of different and independent sound sources, the binaural hearing mechanism provides the means for placing the

sound sources in auditory perspective.

A group of different and independent sound sources, S_1, S_2, S_3, S_4, and S_5, and a listener are shown in Fig. 6. The results of the experiment shown in Fig. 5 indicate that a source of sound may be localized to within 3° for the configuration of Fig. 6. Therefore, the sound sources of Fig. 6 can be localized to within 3°. This means that sound sources are localized by the binaural human hearing mechanism and placed in auditory perspective corresponding to the geometrical configuration of the sound sources and the listener.

When a source of sound operates in a room, the sounds reflected from the boundaries provide the reverberation envelope or acoustic ambience. The reflected sounds arrive from all directions. Some of the reflected sound sources, S_6, S_7, S_8, S_9, S_{10}, S_{11}, S_{12}, and S_{13}, are depicted in Fig. 6. An experiment carried out to determine the accuracy of localization of a sound source in the second and third quadrants indicated that the hearing mechanism can detect the direction of these sound sources. In addition, the experiment showed that discrete sound sources can be positioned all around and their location identified by the listener.

For background information *see* BINAURAL SOUND; HEARING (HUMAN) in the McGraw-Hill Encyclopedia of Science and Technology.

[HARRY F. OLSON]

Bibliography: M. B. Gardner, *J. Acoust. Soc. Amer.*, 44(3):797, 1968; L. A. Jeffries and R. W. Taylor, *J. Acoust. Soc. Amer.*, 33(4):482, 1961; A. W. Mills, *J. Acoust. Soc. Amer.*, 30(4):237, 1958; T. T. Sandel et al., *J. Acoust. Soc. Amer.*, 27(5):842, 1955; J. C. Steinberg and W. B. Snow, *Bell Syst. Tech. J.*, 13(1):245, 1934; G. W. Stewart, *Phys. Rev.*, 15(5):425, 1920.

Angular accuracy of binaural hearing in all four quadrants

Loudspeaker	Angle, degrees	Score, %
1	0	99
2	22.5	98
3	45	98
4	67.5	95
5	90	90
6	112.5	85
7	135	79
8	157.5	71
9	180	87

Blood groups

Animal blood-typing laboratories in the United States and other countries provide a variety of services that relate to practical matters such as the solution of problems of questionable parentage that arise in the breeding of livestock. Of current interest, particularly in the horse-breeding industry, is the potential use of blood typing as a permanent means of identification. Identification of stolen animals and those fraudulently substituted for others, particularly at racetracks, constitutes a serious problem. The key to the success of such programs depends largely upon the development and maintenance of tests that are capable of detecting a sufficient variety of genetic markers in the blood so that the blood types can serve in lieu of fingerprints for purposes of identification. Such tests have recently been developed for use with horses and have long since been used with such domestic species as cattle, pigs, and sheep.

Genetic markers. There are two distinctly different classes of genetic markers. One involves the numerous isoantigenic determinants that characterize the surface of the membrane which surrounds red blood cells, or erythrocytes. These antigenic markers are detectable only when antibodies are used that combine with them and produce some visible manifestation of the reaction, such as clumping or agglutination of the red cells, or dissolution (lysis) of the red cells in the presence of another component (complement) of the blood. These genetic markers alone characterize the "classical" blood groups of man and animals, and they are the subject of this article. The other type of genetic marker is made up of the so-called electrophoretic markers that become discernible when protein solutions such as blood serum and lysates of the blood cells are electrophoresed in gels and the gels are appropriately stained.

The antibodies used in animal blood typing are produced mainly by injecting red cells from one individual into another of the same species, in a process known as isoimmunization. Whenever the red cells of the donor possess one or more antigenic determinants not present in the red cells of the recipient, those red cells are recognized as foreign. The immunocompetent cells of the recipient begin to manufacture antibodies that will promote the destruction not only of the donor's red cells but also of those of any other individual that possesses the same antigenic determinant or determinants. Very useful blood-typing antibodies can also be produced by injecting red cells from one species into another, as, for example, red cells from horses and cattle into rabbits.

Horse blood typing. Consequently, maintaining an adequate battery or panel of blood-typing antibodies for use in blood typing any domestic species is a constant challenge because such antibodies are not commercially available. However, this problem has some positive aspects, for almost every year antibodies are discovered that permit the detection of some hitherto unrecognized antigenic determinant and thus, in turn, permit an expansion of the knowledge of blood groups in the species under study. Of particular interest in horse blood typing are new developments relating to the D system, which was discovered in 1964. When it was originally described, the D system was made up of four groups, D+J+, D+J−, D−J+, and D−J−, analogous in several respects to the four ABO groups of humans. It is now, however, known to be a closed system (that is, no longer is there a "negative" group like D−J−), and many more groups have been discovered. There have also been some recent developments relating to the blood groups in the A system, but reports about these discoveries have yet to be published.

Neonatal isoerythrolysis. Horse blood groups are of considerable interest in the etiology, prognosis, prevention, and treatment of a disease in newborn foals that is akin to erythroblastosis, or hemolytic disease of the newborn human infant. Clinically, the disease in horses is known as neonatal isoerythrolysis (N.I.). As in humans, it is brought about by leakage of red blood cells from the developing fetus into the bloodstream of the mother. Whenever the red cells from the fetus possess one or more antigenic determinants inherited from the paternal parent alone, they are recognized as foreign by the mare, which produces isoantibodies that will lead to their destruction. Unfortunately, these isoantibodies become concentrated in the colostrum, or new milk, of the mare, along with all the other antibodies so necessary for maintaining the health of the newborn foal. The foal is healthy at birth. However, the picture changes after it feeds on the mother's milk. The antibodies in the colostrum are absorbed unaltered from the gut and proceed into the bloodstream of the foal, where the offending isoantibodies attack the foal's red cells, causing an acute anemia characterized by jaundice. Such foals often die if unattended. In humans, the offending isoantibodies are passed from the mother to the fetus across the placenta. Consequently, the newborn baby manifests hemolytic disease.

Data being accumulated on N.I. in horses, particularly in the United States and Great Britain, now indicate that the antigenic determinants responsible for most cases of the disease are members of the A and Q systems. In contrast, determinants in one system alone, namely, the Rh-Hr system, account for more than 90% of the human cases.

N.I. is not a naturally occurring disease in cattle. In fact, there were no recorded cases until 1970. However, in that year two papers appeared coincidentally, one in an Australian journal and the other in an American journal, in which the first cases were described.

In the Australian report the offending isoantibodies were traced to the use of a babesiasis vaccine that is prepared from cattle blood and that was developed in 1966. Blood typing, along with appropriate serodiagnostic tests, was used not only in the diagnosis of N.I. but also in the identification of the offending isoantibodies.

In the American report the finger was pointed at an anaplasmosis vaccine that had been on the market since 1965. It is prepared from the blood of cattle infected with *Anaplasma marginale*, the causative organism of anaplasmosis, which is a serious disease of cattle. Although that vaccine, considering its source, was certainly a likely candidate, there was no direct evidence in that report, and those which followed, that the vaccine was capable of producing isoantibodies. Independent studies in two blood-typing laboratories have now conclusively shown that the anaplasmosis vaccine gives rise to powerful isoantibodies when administered according to instructions. The hallmark of that vaccine is its capacity to give rise to antibodies of specificities anti-A, anti-F, and anti-V in vaccinated animals that lacks one or another of the corresponding antigenic determinants. It also gives rise to isoantibodies specific for numerous additional antigenic determinants on cattle red cells, but the antibodies for those determinants do not usually rise to such high titers as those directed toward A, F, and V. Another characteristic is that the isoantibodies engendered by the vaccine persist month after month following the final injection. Hence, N.I. is still a problem in those herds in which the vaccine is no longer used.

Many calves have already died as the result of the use of these blood vaccines. However, since N.I. is not classified as a communicable disease, the losses are not reported. Nevertheless, it is estimated that they are now in the millions of dollars.

It is of some interest to recall that a similar epidemic of N.I. occurred in pigs in the late 1940s and early 1950s. The cause of that epidemic was also traced to the use of a blood vaccine, the so-called crystal violet vaccine, which was then being used to vaccinate animals for hog cholera or swine fever. When that vaccine was removed from the market, the disease disappeared. However, recent studies indicate there might be a few cases of N.I. in pigs that have been caused by transplacental isoimmunization, as in horses and humans.

Economic factors and blood groups. Studies concerned with the correlation between blood groups and economic factors such as milk production, rate of growth, fertility, and longevity are still very much in vogue. A recent report provides statistical evidence that the degree of heterozygosity or homozygosity for blood-group genes in cattle is correlated with production characteristics. In other words, the animals that perform best appear to have the highest degrees of heterozygosity for their blood-group genes. If this is so, the selection of cattle for high milk production, rate of gain, fertility, and so on could help account for the maintenance of large numbers of allelic genes at such blood-group loci as B and C, a problem that has challenged population geneticists for years.

For background information *see* ANTIBODY; BLOOD GROUPS in the McGraw-Hill Encyclopedia of Science and Technology.   [CLYDE STORMONT]

Bibliography: H. C. Hines et al., in *Proceedings of the Sixth National Anaplasmosis Conference,* pp. 82–85, 1973; K. Sandberg, in *Animal Blood Groups and Biochemical Genetics,* vol. 4, pp. 193–205, 1973; W. Schleger, G. Mayrhofer, and F. Pirchner, in *Animal Blood Groups and Biochemical Genetics,* vol. 5, 1974; C. Stormont, in *Advances in Veterinary Science and Comparative Medicine,* vol. 19, 1975; C. Stormont, in *Proceedings of the California Anaplasmosis Conference,* Sacramento, pp. 35–38, 1972; C. Stormont, in *Proceedings of the Federation of American Societies for Experimental Biology,* 31:761, 1972.

Brain (vertebrate)

During the past decade a primary interest of neurobiologists has been the neuronal circuitry of the cerebellum, a part of the brain involved in the fine control of movement. The cerebellum became a focus for investigation because of the remarkably regular and beautiful organization of the intrinsic neurons, first revealed by light microscopy at the turn of the century. The advent of the microelectrode led to a sequence of electrophysiological investigations of the neuronal circuitry of the cat cerebellum by J. C. Eccles and coworkers. These studies were soon extended to the cerebellums of several lower vertebrates by R. Llinás and colleagues. The progress in electrophysiology in turn led to a demand for more structural information, and, here again, a new technological tool, the electron microscope, provided the needed information. A pioneer in this area is S. L. Palay, whose work, on the rat cerebellum, together with the studies of other electron microscopists such as J. Szentágothai, C. Fox, and D. E. Hillman, has provided the necessary anatomical basis for the interpretation of recent electrophysical findings, in a wide variety of species. The structure, interconnections, and function of all the neuronal elements of the cerebellum can now be discussed and an insight gained into the evolution of the circuit from comparative studies.

Basic cerebellar neuronal elements. Using suitable neurohistological impregnation techniques, such as the Golgi method, the anatomist S. Ramón y Cajal and his contemporaries were able to reveal all the neurons of the mammalian cerebellum by the end of the 19th century. In the discussion that follows, it will be helpful to refer to the illustration, which shows the cerebellar neuronal elements. By far the most striking element is the Purkinje cell, the geometry of which is unlike that of any other nerve cell discovered to date. The immensely complex fronds composing the candelabra-like dendrites (region of the cell that receives most of the incoming neuronal connections) are largely confined to a plane, with the dendrites of each cell lining up parallel to one another. The dendrites are covered with tiny "thorns" that electron microscopy reveals to be the site of postsynaptic terminals of the cell. Synapses are junctions between nerve cells and are specialized for transferring neuronal information between cells, usually through the mediation of minute quantities of chemical transmitter. The transmitter release is triggered by electrical signals in the presynaptic terminal. At the postsynaptic site the transmitter can either produce new electrical activity or inhibit ongoing activity, depending on the type of synapse. One of the major achievements of electron microscopy has been the clear identification of synapses, and a major achievement of electrophysiology has been to distinguish between excitatory and inhibitory contacts.

A typical Purkinje cell dendritic tree is 300–500 μm square, and in mammals there may be many thousands of synaptic thorns. In lower animals the numbers of synaptic contacts are less, but the remarkable geometry of the Purkinje cell dendrite is evident in fishes, amphibians, reptiles, and

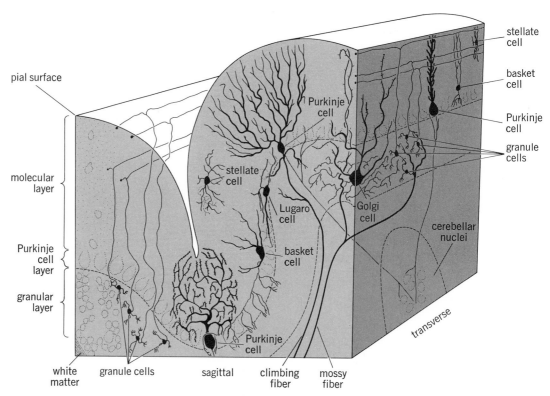

The neurons of the cerebellar cortex. *(From S. L. Palay and V. Chan-Palay, Cerebellar Cortex, Springer-Verlag, 1974)*

birds. In fact, in one type of electric fish, the African mormyrid, the Purkinje cell attains a geometrical regularity unparalleled in any other cell. The cell body, or soma, of the Purkinje cell gives rise to an axon, or nerve fiber, that leaves the cerebellar cortex to terminate in the cerebellar or vestibular nuclei. As the Purkinje cell axon leaves the cerebellum, it emits collateral fibers that terminate on other cells within the cerebellum. Electrophysiology has revealed that the synapses formed by Purkinje cell axons are inhibitory.

The synaptic input to the dendritic thorns of the Purkinje cell is excitatory and comes from thousands of parallel fibers that are the T-shaped axons of the granule cells which run at right angles to the plane of the Purkinje cell dendrites. The volume containing the parallel fibers and Purkinje cell dendrites constitutes the molecular layer of the cerebellum.

The granule cells are probably the smallest neurons in the vertebrate nervous system and are located below the Purkinje cells. Granule cells receive their excitatory input from the mossy fibers, which contribute one of the two input systems to the cerebellum. The mossy fiber–granule cell–Purkinje cell circuit is a consistent feature of the cerebellum throughout evolution.

Inhibitory interneurons. Among the granule cells is a much larger type of neuron, the Golgi cell. The dendrites of this cell extend into the molecular layer, where they are contacted by parallel fibers; the cell also receives direct mossy fiber contacts. The axon of the Golgi cell branches profusely within the granule cell layer and contacts the dendrites of granule cells within a specialized neuronal structure, the glomerulus, which is also the site of the mossy fiber–granule cell contact. It has been shown that the Golgi cells inhibit the electrical activity of the granule cells; consequently they constitute a negative feedback circuit that acts on information arriving by way of the mossy fibers.

Two other types of inhibitory cells occur within the cerebellum; both have dendrites in the molecular layer and receive an input from parallel fibers, that is, granule cells, and both synapse predominantly on the Purkinje cells. One of the cells is known as the stellate cell; its body and axons are in the molecular layer, and it synapses onto the Purkinje cell dendrites. The soma of the other type of cell, called the basket cell, is located near the Purkinje cell body. The axon of the basket cell forms a basketlike structure around the soma and initial axonal segment of the Purkinje cell. These two cell types tend to reduce the electrical output of the Purkinje cell.

During the past few years there has been considerable discussion as to whether the inhibitory interneurons (Golgi, basket, and stellate cells) are present in all lower vertebrates. Anatomical studies have now shown that Golgi and stellate cells are present in all species studied so far but that basket cells are found only in birds and mammals. It is possible that one effect of evolution has been to increase the sophistication of the inhibitory circuits of the cerebellum.

Lugaro cells. Palay and V. Chan-Palay have confirmed the existence of another type of neuron within the cerebellum, the Lugaro cell, which appears to receive its input largely from Purkinje axon collaterals and parallel fibers. The destination of the Lugaro cell axon is presently unknown. It is interesting that in the African mormyrid fish a class of cells exists that have inputs similar to those now established for the Lugaro cells. This finding will undoubtedly be the subject of further research.

Climbing fibers. The second input system to the cerebellum is the climbing fiber, which branches a few times and then makes extensive synaptic contact with the Purkinje cell, which it strongly excites. Recent work by Palay, Chan-Palay, and others has shown that the climbing fibers also contact most of the other neuron types of the cerebellum and thus can also activate the inhibitory circuits. Climbing fibers have been found in amphibians, reptiles, birds, and mammals. It has not been easy to demonstrate these fibers in fishes, however, and it remains to be shown whether this input has become more significant with evolutionary advancement.

Neuronal interactions. There remains considerable speculation on how all the above neuronal machinery interacts. Eccles, in experiments with cats, and Llinás, in work with frogs, have noted that nearly adjacent Purkinje cells may have very different electrical behavior in response to a physiological stimulus. This finding indicates that, despite the apparent anatomical regularity of the cerebellum, the microcircuitry can exhibit very complex behavior. This conclusion is reinforced by the demonstration that Purkinje cell dendrites in some reptiles and birds can produce action potentials that interact in complex ways instead of simply summing inputs and producing an action potential at the cell body and axon. In order to better understand the functional implication of cerebellar structure, investigators are now beginning to focus on the patterns of information entering and leaving the cerebellum. This trend is likely to continue in the near future.

For background information *see* BRAIN (VERTEBRATE); NERVOUS SYSTEM (VERTEBRATE) in the McGraw-Hill Encyclopedia of Science and Technology.   [CHARLES NICHOLSON]

Bibliography: J. C. Eccles, *J. Physiol.*, 229:1, 1973; R. Llinás, *Physiologist*, 17:19, 1974; R. Llinás (ed.), *Neurobiology of Cerebellar Evolution and Development*, American Medical Association, 1969; S. L. Palay and V. Chan-Palay, *Cerebellar Cortex*, 1974.

Bridge

One of the measures used by bridge engineers in judging the structural significance of a bridge is the span, or unsupported length. Although the span of the Verrazano-Narrows Bridge (4260 ft; 10 ft = 3.048 m) has not yet been exceeded, construction was begun in 1973 on a suspension bridge over the Humber River in England that will have a main span of 4626 ft. Even this great span will be exceeded if the suspension bridge planned to connect the islands of Honshu and Shikoku in Japan is built; its main span will be 4995 ft.

The longest cantilever bridge in the world is the Quebec Bridge over the St. Lawrence River, which was completed in 1917 and has a span of 1800 ft. The second-longest is the old Firth of Forth railroad bridge in Scotland, which was completed in 1890 and has main spans of 1710 ft. The third-longest in the world, and the longest in the United States, is the Commodore John Barry Bridge, over the Delaware River at Chester, PA. This is a six-lane highway bridge with a vertical clearance of 188 ft over the main channel. It was opened to traffic in February 1974.

Built in 1931, the longest arch bridge in the world, with a main span of 1652 ft, is the Bayonne Arch, over the Kill van Kull, which connects Staten Island, NY, and Bayonne, NJ. This record arch span will be exceeded when the bridge crossing New River Canyon east of Charleston, WV, is completed in 1976. The span will be 1700 ft, and the deck will be 873 ft above the river. It is a highway bridge, as is the Bayonne Arch.

Cable-stayed bridge. A type of bridge that has gained increasing recognition in recent years is the cable-stayed bridge. Its increasing use for substantial spans derives logically from its economy and its suitability for locations where poor foundation conditions exist. It has generally been used for spans intermediate between those of the suspension type and the long girder type. In the cable-stayed bridge, the deck is supported by diagonal steel ropes connected to the tower tops, whereas in a suspension bridge, the deck is supported by vertical suspenders hanging from the main cables (see Figs. 1 and 2). The advantage of the cable-stayed bridge with respect to poor foundation conditions arises from the absence of anchorages, the deck, in effect, being a pair of cantilevers extending from each tower.

In the cable-stayed bridge, the stiffening element, which minimizes vertical distortions of the deck under unbalanced vehicular loads, is usually in the form of a box. In Fig. 2 the box is the heavy member at deck level. It may be of either steel or reinforced concrete, with the choice of the material usually dictated by availability. Steel is likely to be used in the industrially developed countries, and concrete elsewhere. However, another factor that may result in the selection of concrete is its economy of maintenance in exposed locations, for, unlike steel, it does not suffer from corrosion.

Although early cable-stayed bridges have remained in use for many years, the number of bridges of this type has increased dramatically since 1950. In the early years of the 19th century, there were a number of collapses of this type of bridge, and construction of them virtually ceased for several decades.

Because the structural action of a cable-stayed bridge is complex, and its design requires fairly advanced analysis, there had been a reluctance to use the type until the analytical tools were available. The first modern cable-stayed bridge, which was designed by a German engineer, F. Dischinger, is the Stromsund Bridge in Sweden, which was completed in 1955.

It is apparent in Table 1 that a substantial number of these bridges have been built, are under construction, or are in the planning stage in various parts of the world. As of 1974, the record for span length is held by the Duisburg Bridge, which was completed in 1970; but this record will soon be broken by the Calcutta Bridge, which is under

Table 1. Recent cable-stayed bridges

Bridge	Crossing	Year completed	Main span, ft	Country
Duisburg	Rhine River	1970	1148	West Germany
Wadi Kuf	A dry valley	1971	940	Libya
Frankfurt	Main River	1972	485	West Germany
John O'Connell Memorial	Sitka Harbor	1972	450	United States (Alaska)
Bratislava	Danube River	1972	994	Czechoslovakia
General Manuel Belgrano	Paraná River	1973	803	Argentina
West Gate (Melbourne)	Lower Yarra River	Under construction	1102	Australia
Calcutta	Hooghly River	Under construction	1500	India
Zárate-Brazo Largo	Paraná River	Under construction	1116	Argentina
Pasco-Kennewick	Columbia River	Planning	981	United States (Washington)
East Huntington	Ohio River	Planning	900	United States (West Virginia)
Le Havre	Seine River	Planning	1600	France

Table 2. Recent box girder bridges

Bridge	Crossing	Year completed	Main span, ft	Country
San Mateo–Hayward	San Francisco Bay	1967	750	United States (California)
San Diego–Coronado	Coronado Bay	1969	660	United States (California)
Queen's Way	—	1970	500	United States (California)
—	Urato Bay	1971	754	Japan
Santo Domingo	Rio Higuano	1973	623	Dominican Republic
Presidente Costa e Silva	Rio Harbor	1974	984	Brazil
—	Yukon River	Under construction	410	United States (Alaska)

Fig. 1.   Verrazano-Narrows suspension bridge.

construction; and its record, in turn, will be broken by a bridge in the planning stage at Le Havre, France (scheduled opening date 1980).

The largest bridge in South America is of the cable-stayed type and is unusual in having a stiffening system of reinforced concrete. Called the General Manuel Belgrano Bridge, it crosses the upper Paraná River in Argentina and has a span of 803 ft (see Fig. 2). It was opened in May 1973 and is a toll bridge.

With increasing understanding of the structural action of cable-stayed bridges and growing confidence from their continued use, this type may ultimately challenge the suspension bridge for very long spans.

Long-span box girder. Another recent trend in bridge engineering has resulted from an intensive restudy of the structural theory necessary for the safe design of long-span box girders. A girder is a structural member designed to carry a load applied at right angles to its length. A simple example would be a wooden plank placed across a small stream. For greater lengths and heavy loads, as in bridges, a steel member built up of plates and angles is used. In the simpler cases the cross section is in the form of an I. For greater strength and stiffness the cross section can be rectangular or trapezoidal—hence the name "box."

In spite of the great success of the first large box girder bridge, which was built in 1850, the type fell into neglect for almost 100 years because of its high cost of construction when compared with trusses. However, with the increasing need for highway bridges in the 1930s, and in an effort to reduce the dead load arising from the use of concrete roadway slabs, experimental designs, using steel plates with sheet asphalt riding surfaces, were initiated. This so-called orthotropic design was fully developed in Germany during the period following World War II, when many destroyed bridges had to be replaced. As spans increased, the plate girders that initially supported the steel plate decks gave way to the stiffer box girders. An early example is the Düsseldorf-Neuss Bridge, which was completed in 1951 and has a main span of 676 ft.

The stimulus for the intensified study of the design and erection of long-span box girders arose from the failure during construction, in two consecutive years (1970 and 1971), of four bridges of this type. These were the Fourth Danube Bridge in Vienna, Austria, the Milford Haven Bridge in Wales, the West Gate Bridge in Melbourne, Australia, and the Koblenz Bridge over the Rhine River in Germany. All were steel box girder bridges.

It should be noted that all four failures occurred during erection, when, occasionally, a set of loading conditions occurs that is quite different from the conditions that would exist in finished structures. Unfortunately, in several instances there was a large loss of life. Following the failure of the Milford Haven Bridge and the West Gate Bridge, the British government appointed a committee under the chairmanship of A. W. Merrison to study the basis of design and method of erection of steel box girder bridges. In addition to mathematical analyses, much time and effort have been expended in testing to destruction quarter-scale models of the box girders. As a result, there is now emerging

Fig. 2. General Manuel Belgrano cable-stayed bridge.

a large body of data that will ultimately give rise to design specifications that, when properly applied, will produce box girder bridges that will be as safe as any of the other time-tested types.

In Table 2 the long-span box girder bridges that have been recently constructed in various parts of the world are listed.

For background information *see* BRIDGE in the McGraw-Hill Encyclopedia of Science and Technology.   [NOMER GRAY]

Bibliography: A Lally, Steel box girder bridges, *Eng. J. Amer. Inst. Steel Const.*, Fourth Quarter, 1973; F. Leonhardt and W. Zellner, Cable-stayed bridges: Report on latest developments, *Canadian Structural Engineering Conference*, 1970.

Cell differentiation, senescence and death

Experimental gerontology is concerned with identifying the primary causes of aging. Recent studies at the molecular level have evolved in two major directions: proposing and elucidating possible mechanisms of aging; and defining various expressions of this aging phenomenon.

The available evidence has enabled a characteristic profile of cellular aging to be built up, but the fundamental question—the etiology of the aging process—remains unanswered.

The aging process is complex and involves a succession of changes in structure, metabolism, and function at the cellular level. These alterations, as pointed out by H. P. von Hahn, characteristically are deleterious and progressive and lead to an increased probability of death. They are, however, by no means general or uniform and, at the biochemical level, have a highly selective effect on certain cells and specific activities. The term senescence, defined by S. Goldstein as a progressive loss in the individual of physiological adaptability to the environment culminating in death, therefore relates to alterations in the control mechanisms that regulate functional activity within and between cells, rather than to generalized or regional death itself.

On a molecular level, interference with the flow of cellular information anywhere in the sequence from DNA to RNA to protein and other macromolecular biosynthesis and degradation could initiate the decline that leads to aging. Information may be lost or modified in at least two ways, which need not be mutually exclusive: by means of a genetic program related to normal differentiation and development; and by means of a random deterioration due to the accumulation of damage or errors. These two concepts form the basis for the proposed primary mechanisms of aging.

Theories of aging. According to the first concept, called programmed senescence, the aging process is a genetic expression occurring as a consequence of differentiation or development or both. It is an inherent, specific property of each differentiated cell, and its effect is to place a definite limit on the life-span of a cell or organism.

Details of the control mechanisms that guarantee senescence and ultimately ensure the mortality of a species at the appropriate time, however, remain speculative. W. S. Bullough, who considers that cellular homeostasis is based on mitotic control governed by the production of a tissue-specific "chalone," has, however, suggested that a chalone may control the turnover of pacemaker cells, which limit the total life-span. Probably the best evidence in favor of this theory of aging comes from L. H. Hayflick's demonstration that, in cell culture, the number of potential generations or cell cycles seems to be species- and organ-specific and related to donor age. However, more recent observations have called into question the original interpretation of these data. R. J. Hay, A. Macieira-Coelho, and V. J. Cristofalo have shown that life-span can be extended by the use of conditioned or fortified medium or by the addition of hydrocortisone. On the other hand, L. M. Franks believes that the presence of certain cell types may be essential for survival, and that their absence leads to death. This apparently conflicting evidence has, however, highlighted the practical problem of measuring accurately the true relationship between donor age and life-span.

In the second concept, called random or stochastic error accumulation, the primary aging event is considered to be governed only by laws of chance. L. E. Orgel originally proposed that the enzymes responsible for regulation of protein synthesis and the replication of chromosomes were the group most critically susceptible to random errors. He postulated that an accumulation of such errors might reduce the fidelity of protein synthesis and cause a lethal "error catastrophe." However, this basic theory has subsequently been modified and extended, first, according to the work of H. J. Curtis and F. M. Burnett, to include errors due to somatic mutation, whose contribution to aging cannot readily be separated from those involving faulty transcription, and errors due to translation; and second, to take into account the views of Orgel which stress that extracellular and intracellular mechanisms of aging are tightly coupled in whole animals. For example, the deterioration of extracellular components is likely to alter the intracellular environment and could reduce the fidelity of macromolecular synthesis, which in turn could exert a feedback effect on the extracellular components.

This hypothesis of random deterioration has enabled several predictions to be made and then tested experimentally. For example, under conditions of starvation, protein turnover is greatest, and therefore the rate of accumulation of abnormal error proteins should decrease. A correlation has been shown between prolongation of life and restrictive growth conditions. Also, in aging cells there should be a mixture of normal and abnormal proteins, the latter being heterogeneous owing to the introduction of random errors by faulty amino acid substitution. Clonal senescence of human fibroblasts has been shown by R. Holliday and G. M. Tarrant to be accompanied by the accumulation of qualitatively different heat-labile enzymes; recent studies, however, have been unable to confirm this finding.

An interesting and far-reaching corollary of Orgel's theory is that the increase in error frequency might not inevitably lead to a catastrophe. For example, since most tissues have an excessive number of cells to perform their functions, compensation processes capable of countering the adverse effects of defective proteins may exist and may function under altered experimental conditions and with aging. Therefore, the balance between synthesis and degradation becomes important in determining whether the altered protein is accumulated or eliminated. It is, therefore, essential in assessing enzyme activity to determine not only the specific activity but the maximal reserve capacity, since it may be called upon under conditions of stress or with increasing age. In addition, protective processes to guard against the accumulation of errors or mutations may exist. For example, the mutation itself may inactivate the gene at the initiation of transcription or cause premature termination during chain elongation. The observed redundancy of essential genes may also serve as a genetic protective mechanism by ensuring that a minimum degree of essential information remains free over a given length of time. Reiteration of genes would also provide a novel mechanism by which each new generation could be rejuvenated and begin life with a mutation-free genome. However, R. G. Cutler has not been able to show experimentally any clear correlation between the overall percentage of reiterated nucleotide sequences on the genome or the amount of ribosomal gene redundancy and aging rate. He has, however, demonstrated that there is a general decrease in the percentage of usage of ribosomal and transfer RNA genes as a mammalian species' aging rate declines and that, in the human brain, genes involved only in transcribing messenger RNA are redundant in the longer-lived mammalian species.

Furthermore, protection may be afforded by the preferential accumulation of damage in chromosomal sectors that may not be transcribed actively, allowing preservation of active genes, which are more subject to homeostatic repair in differentiated cells, since inactive DNA is less physically accessible to repair enzymes except during limited periods of the cell cycle. However, no universal correlation between DNA repair and aging has yet been established.

The concept of accumulation of unrepaired damage in the section of the genome with limited accessibility would be consistent with the observation that cells will replicate in culture for a finite

Some biological expressions of aging

Type of expression	Target site	Experimental observation	Possible end result
Functional	Immunological systems	Decreased response to extrinsic antigens	Deterioration of immune competence
	Central nervous system	Accumulation of degenerative lesions, for example, age-associated inadequacies in polyribosomal RNA synthesis that may be concerned with memory transfer	Deterioration of mental performance
	Hormonal regulation	Impaired sensitivity to hormones	Impaired homeostatic control
		Age-dependent delay in response to a proliferative stimulus	
	Cell cycle	Prolongation of cell cycle time with increasing age	Altered division potential
Structural	Postmitotic cells (for example, brain and heart)	Accumulation of pigment lipofuscin	Impaired cellular function
		Accumulation of amyloids in brain, heart, and aorta with increasing age	
	Collagen	Decreased susceptibility to enzymatic digestion and increased stability due to cross-linking	Loss of plasticity
	Chromosomes	Age-dependent increase in aberrations	Faulty gene expression
Molecular	DNA	Accumulation of single-strand breaks in DNA of postmitotic cells of mouse brain and heart muscle with age	Faulty repair, leading to accumulation of un-repaired damage
		Increased amount of satellite-like fraction of DNA with highly repetitive sequences with increasing age	DNA deterioration leading to faulty gene expression
		Decline in size of DNA-containing species in cerebellum of dogs with increased age	
		Presence of repetitious genes as age increases	Protection against accumulation of mis-coded information
		Increased template activity of nuclear DNA for DNA polymerase with age	Consistent with strand breakage or separation
		Decreased ability with age of the DNA to function as a template for RNA polymerase	Faulty transcription
		Alteration in composition of DNA-protein complexes, with reduced rate of histone acetylation with increasing age	
		Decreased levels of DNA methylation in postmitotic tissues	Degenerative changes in ribosomal RNA synthesis
	RNA	Selective loss of genes coding for ribosomal RNA with age in the brain	Degenerative changes in regulatory but not in structural genes
		Differences in transfer RNA and associated acylases and methylases with age	Altered translational control
		Increased incorporation of cytidine into nuclear and cytoplasmic RNA with age	
	Protein	Alteration in total activities of many enzymes, some increasing and others decreasing with age	Faulty protein synthesis
		Altered enzyme composition, with increased proportion of a thermolabile component of, for example, glucose-6-phosphate dehydrogenase protein with age	Error accumulation leading to faulty protein synthesis

period and then die, since the cell would become increasingly restricted in its potential to utilize its inactive gene pool.

Therefore, experimental evidence is now available to lend support both to the aging program and to the error-accumulation hypotheses of aging. However, it is probably more realistic to consider aging as resulting not from a single particular cause or mechanism but, rather, from a summa-tion of the interaction of the many factors discussed above.

Expressions of aging. Many different biochemical, biological, and physiological parameters show regular alterations that can be correlated statistically with chronological age, but it is important to remember that the evidence is only conjectural. Some of the specific changes occurring with age are listed in the table. However, it is difficult to determine whether certain processes, for example, immunological mechanisms and the deterioration of extracellular material, are independent of errors of macromolecular synthesis, coupled to them, or a consequence of them. Furthermore, it is important to distinguish between the progressive changes in a whole organ or organism that accompany the aging of mitotically competent cells and those generalized repercussions on the function of the organ occurring as a result of individual cell death.

Thus the basic questions concerned with the cause of the aging process remain unresolved. Is it a normal universal process of a physiological nature or an accumulation of lesions that should be considered pathological? Is maximal life-span genetically determined and species-specific, or is it a result of accidental events that may be subject to biochemical manipulation? Some of the controversy surrounding these questions might be resolved if it were remembered that the ability to measure a factor and associate it with a phenomenon does not necessarily imply causality. Therefore, these are the main problems facing the researcher in attempting to determine the causes of senescent deterioration of biological form and function.

For background information *see* CELL DIFFERENTIATION, SENESCENCE AND DEATH; DEOXYRIBONUCLEIC ACID (DNA); PROTEIN; RIBONUCLEIC ACID (RNA) in the McGraw-Hill Encyclopedia of Science and Technology.   [BRIDGET T. HILL]

Bibliography: L. Hayflick, *J. Amer. Geriat. Soc.*, 22:1, 1974; L. E. Orgel, *Nature*, 243:441, 1973; G. B. Price and T. Makinodan, *Gerontol.*, 19:58, 1973; K. L. Yielding, *Perspect. Biol. Med.*, vol. 201, Winter 1974.

Chromosome

The giant polytene chromosomes found in larval tissues of dipteran flies have long intrigued cytogeneticists. They possess an aperiodic pattern of

transverse bands of different thicknesses that, in the fruit fly *Drosophila melanogaster*, number more than 5000, taking all chromosomes together. The genetic significance of this band organization was noted by C. B. Bridges, who stated explicitly his belief that "each of the . . . crossbands . . . corresponds to one (gene) locus." Several early workers had estimated the number of sex-linked loci as being between 500 and 1280. These numbers compared favorably with the number of bands that Bridges drew for the X chromosome: 725 in his original 1935 map and 1012 in his revised 1938 map. Thus, the one gene–one band hypothesis gained credence.

Saturation experiments. However, the various estimates of number of genes differed considerably and were of doubtful validity; thus within the past 2 or 3 years renewed efforts have been undertaken to provide clear evidence, one way or the other, relating to the one gene–one band hypothesis.

The most ambitious efforts were the recent "saturation" experiments of B. H. Judd and associates. These studies attempted to produce a mutant for every gene in a specific region of the X chromosome, encompassing a known number of bands. In brief, Judd and coworkers concluded that in a delimited region of the X chromosome extending from the locus of *giant* (*gt*, located in band 3A1) to *white* (*w*, in band 3C2), a region in which Bridges drew 15 bands, there were exactly 15 different genetic functions; but this apparent identity in gene band numbers may have been fortuitous because electron-microscopic (EM) analysis of the region now shows certainly one and possibly two "extra" bands in 3B. Moreover, in 3A the double band 3A3-4 of Bridges was shown to be, in actuality, a double-double band (four bands); but EM analysis did not reveal another of Bridges's bands, 3A5. Nonetheless, Judd's work has been taken to provide strong support for the one gene–one band hypothesis.

Further evidence of this kind in support of the one gene–one band hypothesis is provided by the briefly reported studies of R. E. Rayle on the *stubarista* (*sta*) region. Here, in a short interval near the tip of the X chromosome (1E-2A), the number of complementation groups and the number of bands appear to be in perfect agreement. In addition, B. Hochman and collaborators, during a number of years, have studied mutations in the small chromosome 4, containing only about 50 bands. In his latest report, Hochman states that he has identified a total of 43 different loci, 37 vital and 6 recessive visible (having no lethal alleles). He calculates, however, that saturation has not yet been achieved and that the total number of different lethal and visible loci may reach 60 before complete saturation is achieved. Achieving this total would constitute "supersaturation," and the one gene–one band hypothesis would suffer a serious blow, unless EM studies identify several submicroscopic bands that have so far escaped detection with the light microscope.

Two possible objections to the saturation studies described above can be made: the regions studied have been short and may not be representative of the genome as a whole; and mutants that do not

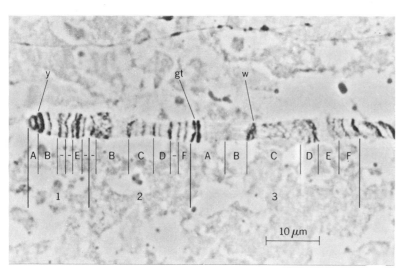

The left end of the *Drosophila melanogaster* polytene X chromosome, shown in a well-stretched condition. Note the banding patterns in the first three numbered sections and in their lettered subdivisions. Regions 1B and 3A-D have been studied intensively. The cytological locations of the genes *yellow* (*y*), *giant* (*gt*), and *white* (*w*) are indicated.

produce readily detectable effects on viability or external phenotype may not have been included in the sample of mutants utilized in the saturation studies; that is, many genetic functions may exist in addition to those that mutate to readily detectable lethal and visible phenotypes. S. J. O'Brien has emphasized this problem.

More recently, G. Lefevre has extended the analysis of gene band relationships to several new regions of the X chromosome. One finding revealed that certain regions, including section 1B at the tip of the X chromosome, are clearly supersaturated. In 1B, 20 or more genetic functions exist where Bridges drew only 14 bands. By contrast, the 17 bands just to the right of the *w* locus (3C2-3D6) are strangely "empty." Only four genetic functions have been identified there, even though the 15 bands just to the left of the *w* locus (which Judd studied) are virtually all associated with identified genetic functions. The banding patterns in these regions are shown in the illustration.

Register of genes and bands. A consideration of these regions and others whose genetic content has been evaluated leads to the conclusion that significant differences exist in the concentration of readily identifiable genetic functions in different parts of the X chromosome. In addition, of course, an unknown number of difficult-to-recognize genetic functions may also be present. In some regions, such as 1B and 3AB, identified functions are as numerous as, if not more numerous than, bands. In others, such as 3CD, few functions have been identified in an equally intensive search. Overall, sex-linked genes and polytene chromosome bands may be about the same in total number, but it can no longer be maintained that the two are in perfect register, one gene for each band. It is unfortunate that a concept so attractive and intellectually satisfying as the one gene – one band hypothesis may have to be abandoned, because there is no other evident explanation for the pattern of organization exhibited by polytene chromosomes.

For background information *see* CHROMOSOME in the McGraw-Hill Encyclopedia of Science and Technology.

[GEORGE LEFEVRE, JR.]

Bibliography: B. Hochman, *Cold Spring Harbor Symp.*, 38:581, 1973; B. H. Judd, M. W. Shen, and T. C. Kaufman, *Genetics*, 71:139, 1972; G. Lefevre, Jr., *Annu. Rev. Genet.*, vol. 8, in press; S. J. O'-Brien, *Nature New Biol.*, 242:52, 1973; R. E. Rayle, *Genetics*, 71(suppl.):s50, 1972.

Clinical pathology

Clinical pathology has traditionally used laboratory methods to examine materials and fluids from patients to aid in diagnosis. Now a new method has been added by which physical studies of the external urine stream tell of problems in the lower urinary tract. An electrooptical system, the urinary drop spectrometer, provides pulse trains as the urine drops pass through a thin sheet of light. The statistical properties of the pulse trains, as well as progressive changes in them during a urination, provide information which can be related to common disorders. Of particular value is the physical and psychological noninvasiveness of the method, in contrast to previous methods for diagnosing out-

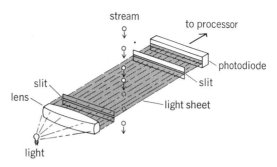

Fig. 1. Schematic representation of transducer for urinary drop spectrometer. (*From G. Aiello et al., The urinary drop spectrometer, Phys. Today, 27:23–30, 1974*)

let-tract obstructions. The patient only urinates and need not know he or she is being studied at that time.

Principle of method. The method is based upon the instability of a liquid jet in air which leads to the formation of discrete drops of fluid from the initially continuous stream. The details of the jet breakup are influenced by the microscopic fluid motions within the jet. These motions in turn are affected by geometric and elastic variations within the urethra. Thus the patterns embedded in the sequence of drops are characteristic of urethral function. In addition, abnormal urinations such as those caused by spastic sphincters or unusual bladder contractions lead to sequences which are clearly distinguishable. In the latter usage the method avoids inherent fluctuations in the collection methods of standard flowmeters which are often used to observe such abnormalities.

Instrumentation. Instrumentation consists of a transducer for converting the drop sequence to a sequence of electrical pulses, analytical circuitry to extract patterns from the pulses, and recording equipment to plot the analyzed pattern for immediate use, as well as the recording (on magnetic tape) of the raw electrical signal for future, more detailed analysis by computer.

The transducer (Fig. 1) consists of a light source, collimating lens and slits, light-sensitive receiver, and preamplifier. When a fluid drop passes through the thin light sheet, a portion of the light is interrupted, giving an electrical pulse. The shape of the pulse corresponds accurately to the time sequence of the obstruction of the light. Thus the height and width of the pulse is related to the drop size and velocity. Refraction of light, even by transparent water, is sufficient to preclude distortions from direct transmission except for a miniscule fraction of the drops.

Drop size and velocity analysis. Analysis of the amplitudes of the pulses gives information closely related to the drop size. Analysis of time intervals between pulses gives information of another type, largely independent of the drop sizes. The latter analysis has been most used thus far in the clinical application of the method.

The average voiding by a normal adult contains about 280 cm³ of urine and has a duration of 13 sec. The mean flow rate is about 21 cm³/sec. The stream breaks into drops of various sizes, but usu-

Summary of parameters and deviation from normal values with obstruction

	Time interval histogram		Frequency	Average drop volume	Average flow rate
	Peak	Width*	magnitude		
Normal urination	4–6 msec	9–11 msec	150–200/sec	0.10–0.12 cm³	15–25 cm³/sec
Distal obstruction	Shorter time interval	Narrower	Higher	Reduced	Normal or reduced
Proximal obstruction	Longer time interval	Broader	Lower	Normal or reduced	Reduced

*Measured at ¼ peak height.

ally falling into a main group, of mean volume 0.12 cm³, and "satellites," much smaller drops. The main group of drops most nearly represent standard meatus conditions, and these drops have been selected for analysis thus far. Their number is about 170/sec and the velocity is about 200 cm/sec.

These figures are roughly consistent with a theory of jet breakup given by Lord Rayleigh in 1879. In this theory, the drop diameter is about 1.9 times the jet diameter. A jet of 3.7-mm diameter having the above velocity and flow rate would break up into drops of 6.9-mm diameter having a volume of 0.17 cm³. Consequently the drops can

provide a rough estimate of meatus size and, potentially, meatal compliance.

The time interval distributions, as expected, relate to these quantities. The mean interval is approximately the reciprocal of the drop frequency, or about 5.9 msec. The distribution about the mean reflects a number of things, most obviously the spread in time interval correlating with variations in instantaneous drop frequency.

Method consistency. Figure 2 shows representative time interval distributions for a normal subject and two patients with the two most common types of obstructions. The normal patterns are highly consistent. Under computerized discriminant analysis these have been capable, with 98% accuracy, of detecting each normal subject out of a group of three, each giving 50 urinations.

The obstruction patterns are highly consistent in character. Patients with proximal obstructions always have broad distributions and patients with meatal obstructions have sharp, narrow ones. The ranges of these and other parameters are shown in the table.

Method sensitivity. By employing time interval analysis, the sensitivity of the method to diametral change has been tested with models. Changes of 0.3 mm in the diameter of an obstructing orifice in a 3.25-mm tube are clearly distinguishable and repeatably identifiable, even in the presence of pressure changes up to 40%.

Clinical use. Clinical use of the method has thus far been restricted to urological patients with well-developed symptoms. These patients usually have significant obstructions. A potential future use of the method, in screening, is obvious because of its noninvasiveness and ease of performing. In particular, the early detection of patients at risk with developing prostatic hypertrophy seems possible.

For background information *see* CLINICAL PATHOLOGY; TRANSDUCER in the McGraw-Hill Encyclopedia of Science and Technology.

[ROGERS C. RITTER]

Bibliography: G. Aiello et al., *Phys. Today*, 27: 23-30, 1974; R. C. Ritter, N. R. Zinner, and A. M. Sterling, *Phys. Med. Biol.*, 19:384, 1974; N. R. Zinner et al., *Proceedings of Western Sections, American Urological Association*, San Francisco, 1974.

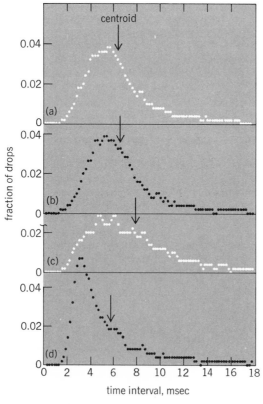

Fig. 2. Time interval distribution for four male adult voidings. (*a*) Normal subject. (*b*) Same subject one day later. (*c*) Patient with slight proximal obstruction. (*d*) Patient with moderate distal obstruction. (*From R. C. Ritter et al., Analysis of drop intervals in jets modeling obstruction of the urinary tract, Phys. Med. Biol., 19:161, 1974*)

Combustion

Recent advances in studies of the combustion products from materials have taken place on two levels. In a purely analytical sense, the studies have concentrated on the basic mechanisms of combustion product release, whereas, in the medical area, the studies under way are aimed at defining the true hazard these combustion products present to life safety.

Historical approach. The chemical literature is well endowed with a variety of articles on the combustion products from natural and synthetic products. Historically (and universally) the approach to combustion product analysis has been to generate the combustion products by some thermal method and then analyze those combustion products using a variety of analytical methods. Much of the past interest has been directed toward a definition of the types of combustion products formed from the thermal exposure. Much more emphasis was placed on the qualitative than on the quantitative nature of the combustion products. The problem with much of the early work is that the results from the varied studies are not relatable owing to the fact that different investigators exposed their materials to very different thermal conditions and environments. In early 1973 E. A. Boethner, G. L. Ball, and B. Weiss at the University of Michigan published a report that brought a great sense of unification to the study of combustion product formation. In that program, more than 19 polymers and finished products were studied under identical conditions with the most advanced analytical instrumentation. A quantitative and qualitative analysis of the combustion products from these materials offers an excellent background for understanding the types and relative quantities of combustion products involved during the thermal destruction of materials. Among the polymers (and their atomic composition) studied were polyethylene, polypropylene, and polystyrene (C, H); polymethacrylonitrile (C, H, N); polysulfone (C, H, S); polycarbonate, phenol formaldehyde, polyphenylene oxide, and polyester (C, H, O); polyurethane, polyimide, and acrylonitrile-ethyl acrylate copolymer (C, H, N, O); and polyvinyl chloride (C, H, Cl). Some of the finished products are Dacron, Orlon, Lopac, Barex, and nylon; the natural products are wood and wool.

Mechanistic studies. The more recent trend in analytical combustion analyses has been to emphasize the basic mechanism of combustion product formation. In December 1973 W. D. Woolley of the Fire Research Station, Boreham Wood (Great Britain), published work on small-scale and large-scale studies involving rigid polyvinyl chloride and polyurethane flexible foams. His investigation of polyurethane is of current interest because of the conflicting reports in the literature relating to the release of hydrogen cyanide during the combustion of this material. Woolley noted that, during decomposition, toluene diisocyanate (TDI) based flexible urethanes (polyether and polyester derivatives) evolved a yellow smoke early in the temperature cycle. For example, at 300°C, with only a 25–30% weight loss recorded, nearly 100% of the original nitrogen in the polymer had evolved as a yellow smoke. There was no evidence of free TDI, which is highly toxic. Studies were then directed toward the yellow smoke that had been isolated from the burning polyurethane foams. Surprisingly, the yellow smoke was found to be thermally

stable up to 800°C. At higher temperatures, the yellow smoke degraded and yielded hydrogen cyanide and a number of other nitrile compounds. At exposure conditions near 1000°C, about 70% of the nitrogen in the yellow smoke could be accounted for as hydrogen cyanide. Similar experiments with the original polyurethane foams yielded comparable results.

These findings are extremely significant in terms of the mechanism of hydrogen cyanide formation and may well explain the conflicting reports relating to the formation of this decomposition product. It can be surmised that, in those studies in which the polyurethane was slowly heated, no hydrogen cyanide was found because of the formation of the yellow smoke and its evolution away from the heat source. On the other hand, when heating conditions are much more severe and combustion product residence times much longer, it can be seen that a path is present for hydrogen cyanide formation by means of the intermediate yellow smoke and its subsequent decomposition. Woolley's work not only provides additional insight into the chemistry involved in combustion product formation, but it also demonstrates the complexities of combustion processes.

During the past 5 years, a number of researchers have spent considerable effort on developing a method for assessing smoke development from materials during combustion. The National Bureau of Standards (NBS) smoke chamber, which currently is being evaluated by a number of regulatory and code bodies, has evolved from this work. The results of the application of the NBS smoke chamber, coupled with specific methods of analysis to generate and measure combustion products, have recently been published by M. M. O'Mara. In this study, a number of wood products were exposed to

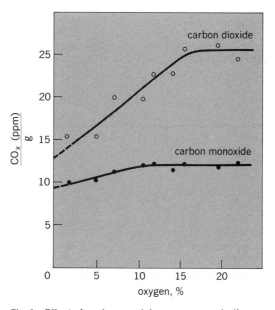

Fig. 1. Effect of environmental oxygen concentration on carbon monoxide formation under NBS smoldering conditions. (*From M. M. O'Mara, J. Fire Flammability, 5:34, January 1974*)

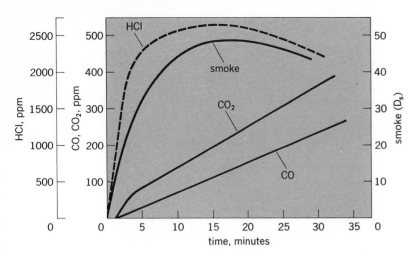

Fig. 2. Generation of combustion products from PVC under NBS smoldering conditions.

Rate of carbon monoxide generation for selected woods under NBS (smoldering) smoke chamber conditions

Wood	Rate, ppm/min
Masonite	208
White pine	232
Plywood	267
White oak	276

2.5 W/cm² of radiant heat. Smoke, carbon monoxide, carbon dioxide, oxygen, and nitrogen were monitored as a function of time. It was found that, under these fuel-lean conditions (only about 6% of the available oxygen was consumed), carbon monoxide generation was essentially a zero-order process. A summary of carbon monoxide rate data for the products investigated in the study is shown in the table.

In terms of the mechanism of carbon monoxide formation from wood, this study revealed that in reduced oxygen atmospheres the yield of carbon monoxide was not significantly altered, thereby suggesting that a major part of the carbon monoxide develops from the pyrolysis of the wood structure (Fig. 1).

In a continuation of this study, more recent information has been generated by O'Mara on the combustion of polyvinyl chloride (PVC). In this work, thermal exposures have been expanded to encompass both flaming and smoldering conditions. Concentration-time profiles for PVC under NBS smoldering and flaming conditions are shown in Figs. 2 and 3. Significantly different evolution profiles are seen under these two conditions. Un-

der smoldering conditions (Fig. 2), hydrogen chloride and smoke evolve at relatively slower rates than under flaming conditions (Fig. 3). The rather rapid decay of hydrogen chloride and smoke under flaming conditions is not completely understood at this time. It may be due to gas-phase coagulation caused by the more humid conditions that are present under flaming conditions. This study shows that hydrogen chloride does act as a "warning gas" when PVC becomes involved in a fire, for the gas is evolved rather early in the time cycle and before significant quantities of carbon monoxide are present. In light of recent statistical data that show that most deaths in fires are caused by carbon monoxide inhalation (where no "warning" exists), this concept is important.

Assessment of the hazard. Probably the most complex feature of combustion product evolution lies in assessing the actual life hazard under real fire conditions. It should be pointed out that, although the above studies are worthwhile scientific investigations directed toward an improved understanding of a very complex process, they are, in fact, very poor models of an actual fire. An attempt to extrapolate from small-scale laboratory experiments to large-scale fires, the scaling factors of which are unknown, must end in failure.

In a recent symposium on fire safety, B. Zikria revealed the outcome of an in-depth investigation of fire deaths that involved clinical analyses of fire deaths, analytical studies of combustion products, and animal exposure studies. It revealed that aldehyde evolution from burning wood may play a key role in many fire deaths. Zikria's conclusion is based on a series of experiments that started with the clinical analyses of fire victims. In this way, he was able to assess ultimate cause and effect. Probably the only viable approach to assessing the life hazard created by burning materials, these types of investigations, coupled with in-depth analytical studies, will lead to a better understanding of combustion and the hazard created by it.

For background information see COMBUSTION WAVE MEASUREMENT; FIRE; POLYMER PROPERTIES in the McGraw-Hill Encyclopedia of Science and Technology.   [MICHAEL M. O'MARA]

Bibliography: E. A. Boettner, G. L. Ball, and B. Weiss, *Combustion Products from the Incineration of Plastics*, U. S. Environmental Protection Agency, February 1973; M. M. O'Mara, *J. Fire Flammability*, 5:34, January 1974; M. M. O'Mara, *Recent Advances in Flame and Smoke Retardance of Polymers*, Polymer Conference Series, University of Detroit, May 20–24, 1974; W. D. Woolley, *Plast. Polym.*, 41(156):280, 1973; B. A. Zikria, *3d Annual Combustibility Symposium*, Rosemont, Ill., April 18–19, 1974.

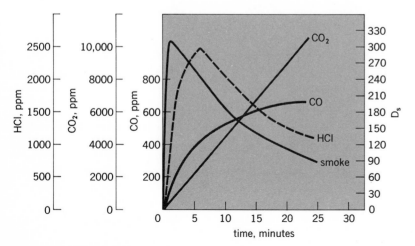

Fig. 3. Generation of combustion products from PVC under NBS flaming conditions.

Communications systems (traffic) design

The Bell System has made plans to inaugurate a new private-line Dataphone Digital Service (DDS) for customers who need to transmit data signals at 2.4, 4.8, 9.6, or 56 kilobits per second. In the past, medium-speed data transmission by the Bell System has been achieved primarily by transmission over regular 4-kHz telephone circuit facilities and modems (modulator-demodulators); however, the new system will be carried entirely by digital means and will not require digital-analog conversion prior to transmission. The data terminals at the customer's premises condition the signal for transmission over the Bell network. Wire facilities provide the connections from the customer's data terminal to the "serving central office" of the local telephone company. The lines can be similar to those used in the voice telephone plant; the length of the lines from the customer to the telephone building can be upward of several miles in some cases. Connection from the serving office to a "hub office," the gateway to the DDS long-haul network and a central test access point, is by a digital carrier known as T1. The T1 pulse-code-modulation system over which this connection is made operates at a line rate of 1.544 megabits per second and uses wire pairs in conventional telephone cables. Since 1962 the Bell System has built a vast network of T1 carriers for interexchange applications, and this facility is well suited for data transmission. Either radio or coaxial cable channels can be used from one hub office to another, depending upon the needs and the availability of facilities in a given area. The arrangement by which the DDS signal is applied to radio facilities, along with telephone voice-grade circuits, is reasonably straightforward and quite efficient in bandwidth usage, as will be shown below.

Combined telephone and data signal. Radio systems today can carry typically 1200–1800 telephone circuits on each radio channel. The telephone circuits are multiplexed together on a frequency-division basis in the toll office and are handled in blocks of 600 circuits for convenience of interconnecting and restoring on coaxial cable or other radio routes. A block of 600 circuits is called a master group (MG). Figure 1 shows the preemphasized spectrum of the baseband (the band of frequencies occupied by the signal before it modulates the carrier frequency) of a radio system carrying 1800 voice-grade circuits in MG1, MG2, and MG3, along with a data signal. The low-frequency end of MG1 starts at 564 kHz in the baseband spectrum, an important point to remember because the portion of the band below 564 kHz is the part that is used to transmit the 1.544-megabit digital signal of DDS. This signal, as shown in the figure, is under the voice circuits in the spectrum, hence the name of the arrangement, "data under voice," or DUV.

When the T1 data signal from the serving central office is received at the hub office, the signal format is in bipolar form; that is, alternate signals are positive and negative in polarity. Such a signal at 1.544 megabits per second could not be transmitted in the 500 kHz of bandwidth as shown in Fig. 1; substantial energy would spread well up into MG1 and interfere with telephone circuits in that master group. Signal processing of the digital bit stream is therefore required to compress the bandwidth to substantially less than 500 kHz. This is done in the 1A radio digital terminal, known as the 1ARDT.

Radio digital terminals. The block diagram of the 1ARDT unit is shown in Fig. 2. Figure 3 shows three such terminals on a single bay mounting. It should be noted that these terminals perform both transmitting and receiving functions and that, therefore, one terminal is needed at each end of a two-way facility.

Considering for the moment only the transmitting portion of the 1ARDT, the 1.544-megabits-per-second input signal is processed in such a fashion

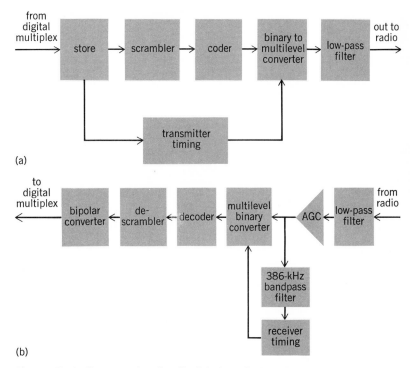

Fig. 2. Block diagrams of a 1A radio digital terminal. (*a*) Transmitter. (*b*) Receiver.

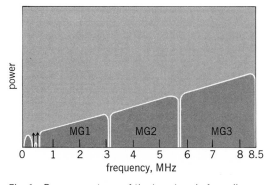

Fig. 1. Power spectrum of the baseband of a radio system carrying both telephone and data signals. Telephone circuits are in three blocks of 600 circuits called master groups, labeled MG1, MG2, and MG3. Data signals are at lower end of spectrum.

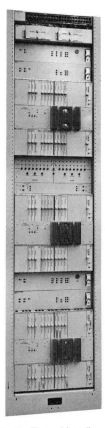

Fig. 3. Three 1A radio digital terminals on a single-bay mounting.

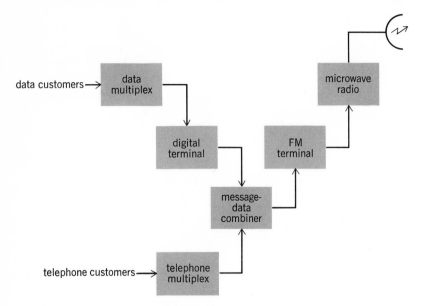

Fig. 4. Block diagram of equipment that combines message and data signals, and of its connection to the radio.

that the bipolar signal is converted into a seven-level signal whose spectral bandwidth is compressed by a factor of 4. The baud rate of the DUV signal is 772 kilobits per second, with 2 bits per baud and a bandwidth equal to one-half the baud rate. It should be remembered that when such techniques are used to reduce bandwidth, some penalty in error performance in the presence of noise must be accepted. In other words, a seven-level DUV signal requires a better signal-to-noise ratio for a given error rate than does the three-level signal such as that used in T1.

The 1ARDT also includes a signal scrambler to modify the spectrum so that it will be more like the one of a random noise signal or like the telephone signals that lie above it in the baseband spectrum. The scrambler modifies the pulse pattern so that essentially no repetition of pulse sequence can occur, regardless of the information content of the input information. This is important because the Bell System cannot control the nature of the signal that the customer might apply. If the digital pattern had a repetitive character, the spectrum would then contain discrete tones that could interfere with the telephone circuits on the radio channel under certain conditions and produce undesirable cross talk for the telephone customers using that radio channel.

The signal from the processing circuits in the 1ARDT contains energy spread over a band of frequencies with a null in the spectrum at direct current and at 386 kHz. It is necessary only to faithfully transmit the amplitude and phase of that portion of the spectrum below 386 kHz to be able to satisfactorily detect and recover the signal at the receiver end. By using a fairly sophisticated low-pass filter, energy above about 450 kHz is very greatly attenuated, and at 500 kHz and above, no measurable data signal exists.

In order to synchronize the receiver with the transmitter, it is necessary to have a receiving "clock" running at the same rate as the one used in the transmitter. Since the null in the spectrum at 386 kHz is caused by the specific coding used in the transmitter, adding a 386-kHz signal at the transmitter that is derived from that clock introduces a precise timing signal that is conveyed along with the digital information. By properly extracting this component from the composite data signal at the receiving end of the system and appropriately adjusting its phase, synchronization can be achieved.

Combining circuits. Figure 4 shows how the digital signal is added to the telephone circuits and how the combination is connected to the radio. The data multiplex accepts customers at the various speeds mentioned earlier and combines them on a time-division basis into the 1.544-megabits-per-second digital stream of a T1 system. This signal is connected to the 1ARDT and then to the message-data combiner. Another input to the combiner receives the signals from the telephone customers via the telephone multiplex.

The message-data combiner consists of a high-pass filter in the message path and a resistive bridge circuit that combines the message and data signal for connection to the frequency modulator and the microwave radio. Figure 4 shows the layout of the transmitting direction; the receiving direction is essentially the inverse.

Radio interferences. In the dense networks that exist in many places in the Bell System, a number of radio routes, using the same radio frequencies, converge at a single station. At some stations, as many as eight routes are beaming signals into eight highly directional antennas that connect to radio receivers in the station. Since it is necessary to reuse frequencies, a desired signal can also contain interference of essentially the same frequency from one or more undesired distant transmitters. This is called cochannel interference, even though the frequencies from the two sources are only nominally the same; they are not coherent. Only the directivity of the antennas keeps this interference under control to allow the reuse of frequencies at a merge point or junction station of the type that is described here.

The frequency band below about 500 kHz is less desirable for telephone circuits than is the spectrum above 500 kHz because of the tones that can be generated by the cochannel carriers heterodyning or beating together in the receiver mixer. Because of the noncoherent nature of these carrier frequencies, the difference frequency shows up directly as a tone, or tones, in the baseband. As an example, assume that the desired carrier signal at a given instant is actually 125 kHz higher than its assigned value and that a single cochannel interfering carrier signal entering into the same receiver is 100 kHz lower than the same assigned value. The beat tone would then be 225 kHz. If the interference levels are not kept low by good antenna design and route engineering, these undesired products in the receiver can disturb telephone circuits in this band. On the other hand, tests have shown that the DUV signal is immune to tone interference until the tone level is quite high — much higher than could be tolerated by telephone circuits in the same band. The microwave frequencies used by the Bell System are in the 4-, 6-, and

11-GHz common carrier bands, which can be used by all common carriers on a license basis. Cochannel interference into Bell System channels could emanate from transmitters of other carriers in the vicinity using these same frequencies.

The spectrum below 564 kHz has been used for telephone circuits in the past, subject to the tone problems already described, but it has been possible, and previously determined desirable, to rearrange the baseband spectrum of MG1 so as to retain the same number of telephone circuits on the radio facility. By so doing, the Bell System has been able to give the long-distance telephone customer better telephone circuits at no increase in cost.

Atmospheric fading. Radio systems, unlike coaxial cable or other wire facilities, are subject to selective atmospheric fading, and provisions are made for automatically protecting the working radio channels with a spare channel when the fading becomes severe and the noise rises substantially. The system is adjusted to permit the noise to increase to a predetermined limit value during a fade, at which point the protection switch is initiated and a switch is made to a radio channel that is not being disturbed at the time. At this noise level on the radio, the DUV signal is still essentially free of errors, but, if switching were not provided and the channel faded still further, errors would result.

Equipment malfunctions. Equipment malfunctions can affect the error rate of a data facility if the disturbances are such that the transmission path is momentarily interrupted. In this respect the data signal is more sensitive to short interruptions than the telephone circuits are. The data user will notice such an interruption as an error on a printed copy, or his data equipment will be called upon for retransmission of the block of data in error. In the analog telephone circuits, the interruption might be only a brief click in the handset. To avoid excessive error rates, very reliable electronic equipment is required for data transmission. This requirement applies to any transmission facility carrying data signals and is not unique to the DUV technique.

System growth. The growth of the DDS network by DUV on radio can be rapid because of the highly standardized nature of the Bell System radio routes. The DUV arrangement has been fitted into long-distance, heavy trunk routes that interconnect large metropolitan areas. It has also been adapted to tributary routes that use radio facilities with relatively small cross sections, which have been termed short-haul or light routes. By using a basic digital rate of 1.544 megabits per second, 460 circuits at a 2.4-kilobit speed can be accommodated on each radio channel. In some areas of the United States, as many as 11 or 12 radio channels are available at 4 GHz, and an additional 6 channels are available at 6 GHz. If all channels were equipped with 1ARDTs, a total digital capacity of about 25 megabits per second could be provided on such a route. However, only as many radio channels as necessary would be equipped for the DUV signal. The arrangement described here provides for gradual and graceful growth so that large quantities of bandwidths or facilities will not lie idle if the growth rate is small. By using

DUV on radio facilities, the Bell System can provide reliable DDS without relinquishing or displacing any telephone circuits from the radio channels now in service.

For background information *see* COMMUNICATIONS, ELECTRICAL; COMMUNICATIONS SYSTEMS (TRAFFIC) DESIGN in the McGraw-Hill Encyclopedia of Science and Technology.   [U. S. BERGER]

Bibliography: C. C. Kleckner, Technical aspects of the Bell System Data System, *Conference of the Georgia Architectural Engineering Society*, November 1973; L. R. Pamm, The Bell System's Digital Data System, *IEEE Convention Session Record*, March 28, 1974; C. S. Stuehrk, The Bell System's Dataphone Digital Service, *International Conference on Computer Communications*, Stockholm, Sweden, Aug. 13, 1974.

Composition of type

The proofing of copy prior to the actual printing operation was one area that initially did not benefit from the incorporation of the computer into the composition procedures of newspapers and commercial typesetting shops. However, a number of different system approaches are now being tried to efficiently couple the required human element into a proofing procedure that is compatible with computer composition procedures.

Hard-copy proofing. Proofing from hard copy produced by a high-speed (500–2200 characters/sec) electrostatic line printer is one of the new methods that has evolved, and it is is becoming the most economical approach to this problem. Other techniques involve the use of visual display terminals (VDT) or optical character readers. A recent development in the electrostatic writing technique that has further supported the hard-copy approach has been the high-density, dual-array writing head that prints overlapping dots at up to 200 dots per linear inch (80 dots per centimeter), or 40,000 dots per square inch. This new writing head produces print quality that is comparable to typewriter output in both character definition and contrast.

The Matrix Electrostatic Writing Technique (MEWT) as developed by Versatec, Inc., is an all-electronic printing method that utilizes few moving mechanical parts and has a reliability factor more than 10 times higher than that of a mechanical printer. Its silent operation and low power requirements are additional benefits. The writing is accomplished by varying the voltage applied to a linear or dual array of closely spaced writing nibs embedded in a stationary writing head. The voltage is controlled by information obtained directly from a computer or contained on punched paper tape or magnetic tape, and during operation, minute electrostatic charges are placed on the electrographic paper by the nibs. The paper is then exposed to a liquid toner (Fig. 1) to produce a permanent visible image of the data. In this process, characters are made up of individual dots within a 16×16 matrix, as indicated in Fig. 2. As the paper emerges, it is immediately ready for proofing or editing. No special handling is required, and it has the look, feel, and writing characteristics of any good-quality paper. It is not sensitive to light and is reproducible on office copying machines.

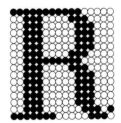

Fig. 1. In the Matrix Electrostatic Writing Technique process, individual characters are formed by using a 7×9 or 16×16 dot matrix. Each character is made up of selected dots within the matrix.

Fig. 2. Entire 128-character set formed by using a 16 × 16 dot matrix with a dot density (resolution) of 200 dots/in.

On-line system. In using the hard-copy approach, two modes of operation are possible. The on-line system is used if a stand-alone computer is available for direct connection to the line printer. Normally this would be the case with medium- to large-size daily newspaper companies or large commercial typesetting companies. The off-line approach is used by smaller daily and weekly newspapers as well as most commercial typesetters.

In the on-line system, a copy of the text stored in the computer is sent to the line printer (in American Standard Code for Information Interchange, or ASCII) for printout and distribution to the proofreaders. The readers indicate the corrections to the input keyboard operator, who transmits them directly to the computer. The computer then makes the indicated changes in its stored copy.

Since the computer now contains proofed copy, neither its output to the phototypesetter nor the phototypesetter's output requires further proofing. This permits taking the print from the phototypesetter directly to the composition room for full-page paste-up and subsequent production of the newspaper.

Off-line system. The off-line system does not use a computer; however, a VDT is required for the correction step. In this approach paper tape punched in either ASCII or TTS (Teletype System) code is taken from the original input keyboard to the line printer in order to obtain the hard-copy proofing material. The copy from the printer then goes to the proofreader, who, after correcting the text, gives the marked-up copy and its corresponding paper tape to the VDT operator.

At this point, the original paper tape is used to put the copy on the VDT; the errors noted on the hard copy are corrected on the VDT; and the corrected text is punched out on a new paper tape. This new tape is then put on the phototypesetter, and no further proofing is required.

The economical justification of the off-line approach is this: a computer is not required; and proofreaders do not require their own VDT since they read from hard copy and since a single VDT is used only for the correction process.

Future developments in hard-copy proofing are likely to be in the area of the ability to print out one-to-one representations of classified advertise-ments in different type size, exactly as they would appear in the newspaper; full-size newspaper page proof copy; and a variety of font styles and sizes for use by the commercial typesetter.

For background information see COMPOSITION OF TYPE; COMPUTER; ELECTRONIC WRITING in the McGraw-Hill Encyclopedia of Science and Technology.　　　　[NORMAN MITCHELL]

Bibliography: P. J. Hartsuch, Graphic Arts Mon., November 1973; N. Mitchell, Proceedings of Compcon 74, IEEE Computer Society International Conference, pp. 237–239, February 1974; J. W. Seybold, The Primer for Computer Composition, Printing Industries of America, 1971.

Computer design

Virtual memory systems increase the effective memory space available to a computer operating system and simplify the memory allocation process in multiprogramming systems. Virtual memory is a mechanism which maps one or more virtual address spaces into a single, finite real memory space. The virtual spaces are described to the hardware by breaking them up into pages of a fixed size and by defining a page table, consisting of an entry for each page which may be marked invalid or with an associated real memory address. Hence, an address space is defined for which associated real pages can be scattered throughout real memory and whose effective memory is extended by high-speed direct-access storage devices. Pages marked invalid can be made valid by paging them in from an external storage device. Any program reference to a page will either result in a page fault to notify the operating system that the page is required in core, or result in an implicit translation within the hardware to access the virtual address at its real location (see illustration).

Advantages of virtual memory. Each virtual address space may be treated by the operating system, for the purposes of execution, as if it were entirely core-resident, and different address spaces can coexist in main storage without any need for the partitioning of memory. The disadvantage of partitioning storage by nonvirtual memory systems is that to place an address space in a partition requires the cumbersome relocation of all internal address references by a constant relocation factor to enable the program to run in different real address spaces. This is a high-overhead procedure that cannot be done realistically more than once, at program load time. From then on, the program must be swapped in and out of the same real address space, a constraint that particularly affects time-sharing systems which need to allocate core in quick response to rapidly changing demands.

Another advantage is that programs can be written with little or no attention to core residency requirements. Programs which are larger than the total real address space available do not have to resort to overlay techniques in which the same blocks of storage are repeatedly used for different routines during different stages of a problem. Some operating systems take advantage of this: OS/VS1 runs all jobs in a single virtual address space of 16 megabytes, while OS/VS2 allocates an independent 16-megabyte virtual region to each job.

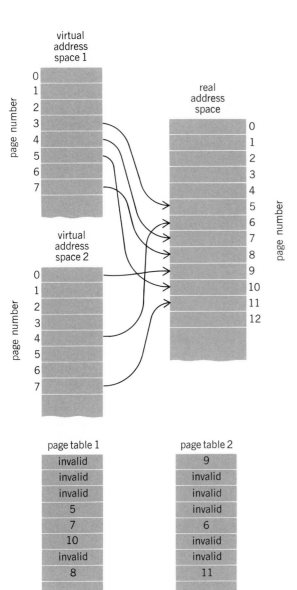

Two virtual address spaces mapped into real storage.

I/O to avoid this problem, and MULTICS goes to the logical extreme of avoiding I/O altogether. MULTICS handles all files within its immense virtual memory. Programs see files as core-resident.

Paging techniques. Techniques have been developed to handle paging in an efficient manner. Operating systems keep track of working sets needed to run a virtual address space effectively. A working set is that part of virtual memory which is core-resident at a given time. Working-set size is of critical importance. Typical virtual programs will run in real memory of about one-third of the virtual memory size, a tremendous savings. However, the amount of real storage allocated must be carefully controlled. If not enough space is allocated, the program will thrash; that is, it will generate a high number of page faults with little or no program execution.

Modern systems use LRU (least recently used) techniques. Core is allocated as needed, and the working set is continually scanned to catch any in-core pages which have not been referenced for a period of time. Thus pages are deallocated to reduce the working-set size. Current LRU scanning techniques are expensive, and one would expect to see more progress in this area, possibly with the help of hardware timers in each page which would cause a hardware exception to notify the operating system that a page can be released.

For background information *see* DIGITAL COMPUTER; DIGITAL COMPUTER PROGRAMMING in the McGraw-Hill Encyclopedia of Science and Technology.   [ROBERT M. JAY]

Bibliography: P. A. Franaszek and P. J. Wagner, *J. ACM*, 21(1):31–39, 1974; G. Ingargiola and J. F. Korsh, *J. ACM*, 21(1):40–53, 1974; G. J. Popek and R. Goldberg, *Commun. ACM*, 17(7):412–421, 1974; D. R. Slutz and I. L. Traiger, *Commun. ACM*, 17(10):563–565, 1974.

Congenital anomaly

The Ehlers-Danlos syndrome is a clinically heterogeneous group of related conditions characterized by hyperextensible and fragile skin, hypermobile joints, and easy bruisability. Friability and premature rupture of fetal membranes (of fetal origin) often lead to precocious delivery. Affected infants are often floppy, have retarded motor development, and are frequently misdiagnosed as having amyotonia congenita. Skin lacerations are common, and wound healing is poor and often delayed. The resulting scar is frequently thin ("cigarette paper" or "papyraceus" scar) and poorly retracted ("fish mouth" scar). Other affected structural tissues may lead to dislocated joints, flat feet, hernias, and floppy heart valves. Recent biochemical evidence suggests that molecular abnormalities of collagen, the major structural protein of the body, may explain certain forms of the Ehlers-Danlos syndrome.

Clinical heterogeneity. P. Beighton reported a clinical study of 100 patients with Ehlers-Danlos syndrome and classified them into five subtypes on the basis of clinical presentation and inheritance (see Table 1). Recent biochemical data have allowed an additional two groups to be recognized. Four subgroups show a dominant inheritance pattern, one group is X-linked, and the two disorders

In today's security-oriented systems, virtual memory techniques offer a memory protection mechanism which is much more difficult to breach than the older keyed protection systems. Keys try to protect storage which is otherwise visible to all programs being run by an operating system. If a program manages to change its run key, it can get access to otherwise protected storage. Virtual memory provides impenetrable boundaries if an operating system is designed with that type of security. In general, virtual machine operating systems such as VM offer a high degree of security.

Input/output. The only major disadvantage of virtual memory management is the complexity of handling input/output (I/O). Input/output channels are not capable of dynamic address translation. They must be programmed with real memory addresses. Data which must be read across page boundaries is complex to handle. Many virtual operating systems are evolving toward page-based

Table 1.   Clinical features in Ehlers-Danlos syndrome*

Type	Inheritance	Skin extensibility	Joint mobility	Skin fragility	Bruising	Major features
I, gravis	Dominant	Gross	Gross	Gross	Moderate	Musculoskeletal deformity Prematurity
II, mitis	Dominant	Moderate	Moderate	Moderate	Moderate	
III, benign hypermobile	Dominant	Variable Usually gross	Gross	Minimal	Minimal	
IV, ecchymotic	Dominant	Minimal	Minimal	Moderate	Gross	Arterial rupture Intestinal perforation
V, X-linked	X-linked	Moderate	Limited to digits	Minimal	Minimal	
VI, hydroxylysine-deficient collagen disease	Recessive	Gross	Gross	Moderate	Moderate	Musculoskeletal deformity
VII, procollagen peptidase deficiency	Recessive	Moderate	Gross	Minimal	Moderate	Short stature Dislocated hips

*Modified from P. Beighton, *The Ehlers-Danlos Syndrome*, London: William Heinemann, 1970.

in which biochemical abnormalities have been demonstrated are recessively inherited.

Of the various subtypes of Ehlers-Danlos syndrome, the most important clinical subtype to recognize is the ecchymotic variety. These patients have an unusual tendency for excessive bruisability and often die suddenly from arterial rupture or intestinal perforation. Joint hypermobility is essentially limited to digits, and skin hyperextensibility is minimal. The skin is thin and pale, and a prominent venous network is frequently apparent. Perhaps if these patients could be accurately recognized, prophylactic measures could be instituted to minimize the risk of such catastrophes.

Hydroxylysine-deficient collagen disease. The first biochemical abnormality of human collagen was described by S. Pinnell and coworkers in two sisters, ages 9 and 12, with a form of Ehlers-Danlos syndrome and hydroxylysine deficiency. The girls were born as floppy infants, had delayed motor development, and suffered from severe, progressive kyphoscoliosis. Their joints were lax, and easily dislocated, and their skin was thin, velvety, and hyperextensible. Subsequently recognized patients, in addition, have had marked skin fragility with poor wound healing and retinal hemorrhage.

Amino acid analyses of tissue collagens from these patients have revealed a marked reduction in hydroxylysine. Hydroxylysine is a unique amino acid in the body, being found only in collagen, and its presence is important for proper function. Covalent cross linking between molecules of collagen, so necessary for structural stability, occurs via aldimine bonds involving lysyl and hydroxylysyl side chains. Because hydroxylysine is diminished in hydroxylysine-deficient collagen disease, hydroxylysine-derived cross links are diminished, leading to increased solubility of tissue collagens and reduced structural stability of collagen-containing structures. Reduced collagen cross linking presumably then leads to the features found in the disease.

In addition, carbohydrate is covalently attached to collagen through hydroxylysine side chains. Its function is not entirely clear, but it may be important in controlling hydroxylysine-derived cross linking or may be important in stabilizing hydroxylysine-containing cross links.

Hydroxylysine occurs in collagen as a post-ribosomal modification involving hydroxylation of certain lysyl residues by the enzyme lysyl hydroxylase. Lysyl hydroxylase activity can be measured in cultured human skin fibroblasts, and its activity was found to be diminished to 5% normal levels in patients with hydroxylysine-deficient collagen disease. Lysyl hydroxylase levels were found to be intermediate in fibroblasts derived from the presumptive heterozygote parents of the affected patients. Both biochemical and genetic evidence suggests that the condition is inherited as an autosomal recessive disorder.

Procollagen peptidase deficiency. A second form of Ehlers-Danlos syndrome with abnormal collagen has been recently described by J. Lichtenstein and coworkers. The patients had hyperextensible skin, hypermobile joints, short stature, and dislocated hips. Skin collagen was more soluble in aqueous solvents, and analysis by polyacrylamide disc gel electrophoresis revealed collagen polypeptide chains that were longer than normal chains.

Collagen is normally secreted by fibroblasts as procollagen, a more soluble form of collagen with an additional amino-terminal extension piece. An enzyme, procollagen peptidase, specifically cleaves off the amino-terminal extension piece, leaving collagen. Studies utilizing skin fibroblast cultures from patients with this form of Ehlers-Danlos reveal decreased levels of procollagen peptidase which would lead to a defect in conversion from procollagen to collagen. The larger abnormal collagen in the extracellular space cannot form normal collagen fibrils and might interfere with collagen cross linking, leading to poor structural strength.

The specificity of procollagen peptidase is unfortunately uncertain since the procollagen-to-collagen conversion can be mediated by a number of proteolytic enzymes. The major portion of the collagen molecule is resistant to proteolytic attack

Table 2. Biochemically distinct collagens

Type	Molecular designation*	Present in
I	$[\alpha 1 (I)]_2 \alpha_2$	Bone, tendon, skin
II	$[\alpha 1 (II)]_3$	Cartilage
III	$[\alpha 1 (III)]_3$	Skin, blood vessel, lung, intestine but not bone or tendon
IV	$[\alpha 1 (IV)]_3$	Basement membrane

*Subscripts refer to the number of individual chains present in the molecule.

because of its stable triple helical conformation. Nonetheless, tissue from patients with this type of Ehlers-Danlos appear to contain an enlarged molecular species of collagen, and their fibroblasts are lacking in an enzymatic activity for producing collagen from procollagen.

Heterogeneity in collagen. Until recently collagen has been perceived as a single species of molecule containing two $\alpha 1$ chains and one $\alpha 2$ chain. Primary structure analysis of soluble skin collagen utilizing cyanogen bromide cleavage, amino acid analysis, and amino acid sequence studies has clearly revealed the $\alpha 1$ and $\alpha 2$ chains to be chemically similar but clearly different. E. Miller, using similar techniques, showed that cartilage contains its own chemically unique species of collagen composed of three identical α chains which are chemically distinct from $\alpha 1$ and $\alpha 2$ chains.

E. Epstein and Miller subsequently have isolated a third collagen type by proteolytic digestion of insoluble connective tissues. This treatment cleaved cross links located in carboxy- and amino-terminal protease susceptible areas of the molecules, thus freeing the helical core polypeptide chain which is impervious to this proteolytic attack. Primary structure analysis of the isolated helical core polypeptide chain revealed a new, distinct molecular species of collagen composed of three identical α chains different from previously described chains. Basement membranes clearly contain a fourth, although less well characterized, form of collagen. This work has led to a classification of biochemically distinct collagens, as shown in Table 2.

This new understanding of the degree of heterogeneity of collagen may explain why in some forms of Ehlers-Danlos a particular tissue is affected more than others. For example, in the ecchymotic type of Ehlers-Danlos syndrome where blood vessels and skin are primarily involved and bone and tendon are spared, one might suspect an abnormality in type III but not type I collagen.

Now that it is certain that forms of Ehlers-Danlos syndrome can result from abnormal collagen, a careful study of collagen in all patients with Ehlers-Danlos syndrome should be rewarding.

[SHELDON R. PINNELL]

Bibliography: P. Beighton, *The Ehlers-Danlos Syndrome*, 1970; J. Lichtenstein et al., *Science*, 182:298, 1973; V. McKusick, *Heritable Disorders of Connective Tissue*, 1972; S. Pinnell et al., *New Eng. J. Med.*, 286:1013, 1972.

Connective tissue

Elastin is a protein that confers rubberlike elasticity on many vertebrate tissues such as arteries, skin, lung, and ligaments. In aging, and in certain diseases (for example, atherosclerosis), elasticity is impaired, often with serious consequences. Recent studies on the structure and function of elastin at the molecular level are providing insights into its normal behavior, and how its behavior can change under different conditions.

Like all rubbers, elastin consists of a network of molecular chains held together by cross-links. In this case the individual chains are protein molecules of approximately 70,000 mol. wt (850 amino acids); cross-links are derived from the side chains of the amino acid lysine, which occurs about 38 times. The cross-linking process is an oxidative one, employing a copper-containing enzyme known as lysyl oxidase. Under conditions of extreme copper deficiency, animals may fail to cross-link their elastin, and also their collagen, which is another important structural protein. This results in very fragile connective tissue, with death frequently occurring owing to rupture of major blood vessels. Pigs raised on copper-deficient diets have provided a limited supply of monomeric elastin, the chemical structure of which is now being elucidated.

Chemical structure of elastin. Amino acid analysis of elastin shows some notable resemblances to collagen: approximately one-third of the residues of both proteins is glycine, and both contain relatively large amounts of proline and alanine. The ordering of the amino acids in elastin is, however, quite unlike that in collagen and results in completely different molecular properties. Sequence analysis of the elastin monomer is being carried out at the University of Utah by W. R. Gray, L. B. Sandberg, and colleagues. They have discovered that two distinct types of sequence alternate with each other in the molecule. In the first type, there is a very marked clustering of Ala (alanine) and Lys (lysine) residues, the latter occurring in pairs separated by two or three alanines; the sizes of the clusters have not been determined. The second type of sequence is made up mostly of Gly (glycine), Pro (proline), and Val (valine) residues; often a short pattern is repeated several times in succession, sometimes with slight variations. In contrast, it is now well established that, in most of the collagen chain, Gly occurs strictly in every third position. Typical sequences from the two proteins are shown in Fig. 1.

Folding of protein chains. The regularly occurring glycines in collagen have a well-defined function—they allow three chains to wind closely around each other, forming thin rod-shaped molecules that are virtually inextensible. These molecules pack in a ropelike fashion, creating macroscopic fibers of high tensile strength. On the basis of their sequence analysis, Gray, Sandberg, and J. A. Foster proposed a model for the structure and function of elastin that involves two general types of folding in the protein chain. It was proposed that the type 1 sequences, rich in Ala and Lys, take up the well-known α-helical configuration; in this state the pairs of lysine side chains are in close

-Ala.Ala.Ala.Ala.Lys.Ala.Ala.Ala.Lys.Ala.Ala.Glu.Phe-

-Ala.Ala.Ala.Ala.Lys.Ala.Ala.Lys.Tyr.Gly.Ala.Ala.Gly.Ala-

(a)

-Val.Pro.Gly.Ala.Pro.Gly.Phe.Gly.Pro.Gly.Val.Gly.Val.Pro.Gly.Val.Gly.Val.Pro.Gly.Val.Gly.Val-

Gly.Gly.Val.Pro.Gly.Ala.Val.Pro.Gly.Val.Pro.Gly.Gly.Val.Phe.Phe.Pro.Gly.Ala.Gly.Leu.Gly-

(b)

-Gly.Leu.Asp.Gly.Ala.Lys.Gly.Asn.Thr.Gly.Pro.Ala.Gly.Pro.Lys.Gly.Glu.Pro.Gly.Ser.Pro.Gly-

(c)

Fig. 1.　Representative sequences in elastin: (a) type 1; (b) type 2; (c) collagen.

proximity, sticking out from the same side of the rigid helical rod. Such an arrangement appears favorable for directing the formation of the very complex cross-links that are derived from four lysines after lysyl oxidase has converted three of them to aldehydes.

For the type 2 sequences it was suggested that the chain folds in an orderly fashion dictated by the short-range repetitive nature of these sequences. The type of structure proposed is one in which the large hydrocarbon side chains of Pro and Val are buried in the center of a broad coil, around which winds the much more polar peptide backbone; Gly residues provide the needed flexibility and have no large side chain to create steric hindrance or unfavorable interactions with water. This type of structure was termed an oiled coil. In

a sense it is a transition between an extended chain and the globular structure typical of most proteins. Figure 2 shows how each molecule is thought to be made up of alternating segments of oiled-coil and α-helical regions, with various molecules cross-linked to each other, forming a network.

The most interesting feature of the oiled coil is that it should be capable of a novel type of rubber elasticity. When the flexible coil is stretched, the hydrocarbon side chains are increasingly exposed to water, which permeates the elastin fibers in the living body. Such interactions are energetically unfavorable, largely because they lead to a much more ordered water structure, which causes a decreased entropy of the system. When the stretching force is removed, the coils shorten to their original size, thus burying the hydrophobic groups away from contact with water.

At the molecular level, then, this model of elastin resembles a mattress spring made up of a system of coils linked by inextensible sections.

Thermodynamic measurements on elastin. There is a well-developed theory of rubber elasticity that successfully describes the behavior of most rubbers. The essence of the theory is that the molecular chains are highly flexible and that a lack of bonding interactions (other than occasional cross-links) leaves the chains highly mobile so that the whole network assumes a state of maximum entropy. Deformation, by preferentially aligning the chains along the direction of stretching, decreases the entropy of the network; the driving force behind contraction is the diffusion of the chains back to a more disorganized state. In 1970 T. Weis-Fogh and S. O. Anderson of Cambridge University published the results of delicate measurements of the heat changes that accompany stretching and contraction of elastin. They concluded that the heat changes were severalfold larger than could be accounted for by the usual rubber elasticity theory. On the basis of measurements in several different solvents, they proposed that hydrocarbon-water interactions were the main source of elasticity and developed a "liquid-drop" model for elastin. Their data are compatible with those of the oiled-coil model. The main difference between the models is that the protein subunits are envisioned as globular in one (liquid-drop) and fibrous in the other. Certainly the measurements seem to exclude the purely diffusive "classical rubber" model.

Electron microscopy of elastin. At the macroscopic level, elastin is clearly fibrous, but under most conditions of observation in the electron microscope, it appears amorphous. One of the major problems in interpreting such studies is the drastic nature of the procedures used for sample preparation, and the ease with which elastin undergoes changes in molecular shape. Using ultrasonic disruption of elastin fibers and negative staining techniques, L. Gotte of the University of Padova has obtained evidence of a fibrillar structure extending to the molecular level (Fig. 3). Analysis of such pictures using densitometry and optical diffraction techniques indicates that the fibers have diameters of 30–40 A (3–4 nm); there also appears to be some periodicity along the fibers, with approximately a 40-A repeating distance. Existence of fibers at this degree of resolution argues against

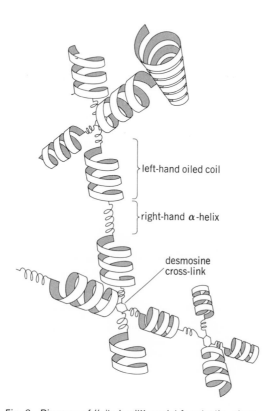

left-hand oiled coil

right-hand α-helix

desmosine cross-link

Fig. 2.　Diagram of "oiled-coil" model for elastin, showing parts of several cross-linked molecules, each containing alternating sections of coil and helix. (From W. R. Gray, L. B. Sandberg, and J. A. Foster, A molecular model for elastin structure and function, Nature, 246:461, 1973)

Fig. 3. Electron micrograph of sonicated elastin, which has been negatively stained with uranyl acetate. (*From* *L. Gotte, et al., On the ultrastructural organisation of elastin fibres, J. Ultrastruct. Res., 46:23, 1974*)

the liquid-drop model, since individual molecular gobules would have diameters of about 55 A (5.5 nm).

Mobility of peptide chains in elastin. Clearly, when elastin is stretched, the peptide chains move to new positions. D. A. Torchia and K. A. Piez of the National Institute of Dental Research have recently studied the extent to which the chains are mobile in the resting state, using the techniques of ^{13}C nuclear magnetic resonance. Their results showed clearly that the chains are moving around quite rapidly, even in "solid" tissue such as ligamentum nuchae. In this respect they resemble classical rubbers, but they differ from collagen, whose molecules are rigidly fixed in position.

Environmental effects on elastin. It has long been known that elastin's properties change drastically on drying or on immersion in various solvents. When dry, elastin is brittle and inextensible; swollen with dilute alcohol solutions, it becomes more easily stretched; in strong alcoholic solutions, it becomes much tougher. Many of the physical measurements described above have also been carried out on elastin under these conditions. Overall, the results support the idea that hydrophobic interactions are a major contributing factor to the rubbery behavior of elastin. Thus, in 20% ethanol, which should greatly reduce the strength of hydrophobic interactions, there is about a 50% decrease in the force needed to stretch a piece of elastin; at the same time the abnormally high heat exchanges on stretching are eliminated, and the peptide chains become more mobile, indicating greater freedom of movement. These environmental effects may be of more than academic significance. In atherosclerosis, for instance, deposition of lipid in the arterial walls takes place. This could lead to an increasingly nonpolar environment in which the delicately balanced structure of elastin becomes deranged, and elasticity lost.

Conclusions. In some respects elastin behaves like a conventional rubber, having flexible molecular chains that are cross-linked to each other but that retain considerable mobility in the solid material. In other respects, however, it seems as though interactions between water and the protein chain provide the main driving force for recovery after stretching. Probably the best model at present is one in which the chains vibrate and twist around a series of preferred conformations in which there is an average minimum exposure of hydrocarbon groups to water. On stretching, a new state is reached, with the chains oscillating around a new average position in which there is increased exposure of these groups.

For background information *see* COLLAGEN; CONNECTIVE TISSUE in the McGraw-Hill Encyclopedia of Science and Technology.

[WILLIAM R. GRAY]

Bibliography: W. R. Gray, L. B. Sandberg, and J. A. Foster, *Nature*, 246:461, 1973; L. Gotte et al., *J. Ultrastruct. Res.*, 46:23, 1974; D. A. Torchia and K. A. Piez, *J. Mol. Biol.*, 76:419, 1973; T. Weis-Fogh and S. O. Anderson, *Nature*, 227:718, 1970.

Control systems

One of the most significant developments in control systems that has occurred during the last few years is the increasing use of dynamic displays as the person-machine interface in computer-supported interactive systems. These displays have generally used cathode-ray tubes (CRTs) as the display medium, in conjunction with large-area displays that present one-line schematic diagrams of the system under control. These displays are generally referred to as mimic boards and have

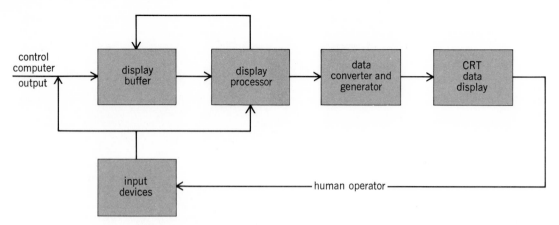

Fig. 1. Functional block diagram of CRT console.

varying amounts of dynamic capability. Special-purpose and general-purpose computers dedicated to the control operation are also central to these systems and are used as the means for sorting and computing the data to be presented to the operator for decision making and control. Areas of application include supervisory control, centralized energy-control and dispatching centers, and direct control of generation and transmission. In addition, these types of systems are being increasingly used in large petrochemical plants and in a variety of pipeline distribution systems. Other applications are evolving at a rapid pace, and it can be anticipated that dynamic display systems will become a commonplace of industrial control in the near future.

The primary advantage of dynamic displays for control systems is their ability to present rapidly the state of the system under control, upon demand and in a graphic form, so that the operator or dispatcher can use the information in a most expeditious and effective way. As a result, dynamic displays have become an essential element in the control of the large interconnected grids that constitute a modern power network, for they permit rapid response to potential crisis conditions. This development is being used worldwide and can be found in Europe, in Eastern as well as Western countries, and throughout the Americas.

CRT console. The CRT console is a major component of this new approach to the control of energy and a large number of industrial processes. The console contains the circuit elements that enable it to accept inputs from a central control computer and convert them into visual images on the face of the CRT. A basic functional block diagram of such a console is shown in Fig. 1, including the input devices that complete the loop through the human operator. The display buffer accepts these computer outputs and stores them for use by the display processor, which formats and otherwise modifies the information so that it can be operated on by the data converter and generator. The computer, in turn, accepts its information from various data sources and operates on them to provide the inputs to the CRT console in a coded form that directs the character- and symbol-generation functions of the CRT console so as to produce the one-line diagrams and tabular alpha-numeric displays

that constitute the most common formats for the display of this information. Both monochromatic and multicolor displays are available, with up to seven colors readily achieved. In general, television-type displays are used, resulting in the type of imagery shown in Fig. 2, although there are also examples of nontelevision images, which are commonly referred to as vector types and do not use the fixed-scanning format characteristic of television displays. The vector units may be capable of higher-quality imagery and greater data density, and the choice of one or the other of these types is dependent on such factors as cost, amount and type of data to be presented, and the number of colors that are desired or needed. The television types tend to be lower in cost because of benefits derived from mass production of entertainment television, whereas the vector types are more suited to applications requiring higher image quality and more complex formats than can be satisfactorily shown in television units. Thus both types have advantages and disadvantages, and both can be used effectively in control systems.

Input devices. In order for one to enter into the person-machine loop, one must have the means to input commands and requests for information, the results of which will then be shown on the display device. These means are the input devices shown in Fig. 1. In general, they may consist of no more than some type or types of keyboard units, but they usually include more sophisticated devices, such as a light pen. The keyboard may have the standard typewriter format, or it may contain numbers of special-function keys that designate particular operations to be performed. The keyboard can also be used to position a cursor on the CRT and thus act as an editing and control element. However, for involved operations, it has become customary to include a light pen as one of the input devices. This device senses the light output of a display at a specific position of the electron beam as it traverses the face of the CRT, and therefore can be used to identify parts of a display and enter commands and queries, in much the way the keyboard is used, but more rapidly and flexibly. Other input devices such as the track ball and joy stick, to name only the most common, have also been tried but have not achieved the popularity of the light pen.

Large-area mimics. Static mimic boards have been a fixture in dispatch and control centers for many years, and they are gradually being replaced by new boards with varying amounts of dynamic capability and compatibility with the control computer. The types range from the simplest addition of lights at selected locations to displays in which all variable visual elements can be changed dynamically by computer or other remote command. These displays have been constructed with assemblies of CRTs, as shown in Fig. 2, as well as with special television projectors and the reflective matrix system shown in Fig. 3. The reflective matrix system is of particular interest in that it embodies an approach that may be the forerunner of the flat-panel matrix systems of the future. The present system consists of assemblies of electromagnetically actuated reflective disks that can be rotated on command so that one or the other side is exposed to view. If the sides of the disks are painted with different colors, a two-color display is achieved; and if other assemblies are made up of different color pairs, a multicolor system results.

An example of such a system in current use is shown in Fig. 3. This mimic is capable of responding in a fully dynamic way, as are the CRT and projection systems. As can be seen in Fig. 2, the CRT system consists of a bank of 10 CRT units that contain the total mimic diagram in mosaic form. The television-type systems still suffer somewhat from limitations in light output and data density and thus may not suit all applications. However, they do represent the most fully dynamic approach to mimic board displays, at least until the all-electronic mimic board is achieved, and therefore are probably the trend of the future.

Application examples. From the large number of dynamic control systems that have been put into service in recent years, a few examples that embody the features discussed above can be selected. First, there is the very elaborate system installed by the Philadelphia Electric Company, which is used to centralize control of the total generation and distribution system. It consists of a large number of CRT consoles as operator stations and is particularly noteworthy in that it uses the bank of CRTs shown in Fig. 2 as a fully dynamic four-color mimic board. It represents a total computer-controlled concept, with the displays as the means for the human operator to interact with the system and maintain constant and effective surveillance and control.

Next, there is the Cleveland Electric Illuminating Company system, which uses the large-matrix mimic board shown in Fig. 3 as an integral part of the total control complex. It is another example of a fully integrated system that combines CRT consoles and the dynamic mimic board with a centralized computer to attain a flexible dynamic capability.

Fig. 2. Mimic board consisting of bank of CRT units. (*Courtesy of Aydin Controls and Philadelphia Electric Co.*)

Fig. 3.   Matrix mimic board. (*Courtesy of Ferranti-Packard, Inc., and Cleveland Electric Illuminating Co.*)

Finally, the multiconsole system used by the Bonneville Power Authority, combining more than 30 separate, seven-color CRT consoles in various ways to achieve control of generation and transmission in its hydroelectric system, should be mentioned. This very extensive use of color CRTs is noteworthy as demonstrating the value of CRTs and the many ways in which they can be used in such applications. Although these three examples by no means indicate all of the types of usage of CRTs found in power control, and although none of them typifies the process-control applications that are developing in the petrochemical and fluid transmission systems, they are still sufficiently representative of the large and complex installations which are becoming more evident in these industries.

Future developments. The main developments to be expected in the future will be those based on the use of color CRT consoles for on-line control, coupled with greater dependence on centralized control computers for data manipulation and computation. In addition, there is a high probability that improved matrix displays using light-emitting diodes or liquid crystals will come to the fore, thus extending the ways in which dynamic, large-area mimic boards can be used and achieving results not yet possible with the CRTs, light valves, or electromagnetic rotating disks. Once the

fully dynamic, large-area mimic is combined with the versatile, multicolor CRTs, the revolution in on-line control through dynamic displays will be complete.

For background information *see* COMPUTER; COMPUTER GRAPHICS; CONTROL SYSTEMS in the McGraw-Hill Encyclopedia of Science and Technology.   [SOL SHERR]

Bibliography: J. E. Braun and H. G. Stewart, *SID J.*, 1(2):16–23, 1972; T. Di Liacco, *IEEE Proc.*, 62(7):884–891, 1974; R. G. Rice, *IEEE Intercon Sess.*, 20(2):1–10, 1973; S. Sherr, *Automatisme*, 19(5):227–283, 1974.

Cosmic rays

The study of isotopic abundances in cosmic rays is important because it can resolve basic questions on the origin and propagation of cosmic rays and can tie together the fields of high-energy astrophysics, cosmic-ray physics, and nuclear physics. Among the questions that might be answered through the study of isotopes are the following: Are cosmic rays generated near supernovae by acceleration of nuclei newly formed by nucleosynthesis, or are they derived from old interstellar gas? Does the source composition of cosmic rays require processes of nucleosynthesis different from those that gave rise to the material of the solar system? How long are cosmic rays confined by the magnetic fields in the Galaxy? Are they confined principally to the galactic disk, or to a low-density galactic halo? To what extent are cosmic rays decelerated by the outflowing solar wind? How steep is the interstellar cosmic-ray energy spectrum prior to solar modulation? The tentative answers that are already available to some of these questions are discussed below, and crucial experiments for resolving the remaining questions are outlined.

Propagation and path length traversed. About half of the cosmic rays that are heavier than helium have suffered collisions with the tenuous interstellar gas, fragmenting into lighter nuclei. Hence, elements and isotopes that were present in the sources of cosmic rays have become depleted by a factor of about 2, whereas the abundances of some rare nuclides have been greatly enhanced, sometimes by several orders of magnitude. (Some nuclides in nature are rare, their buildup by nucleosynthesis in stars being inhibited, but their rate of production in high-energy nuclear spallation reactions is appreciable.) The rare isotopes of hydrogen and helium ^2H and ^3He are thus built up in cosmic rays, as are the isotopes of the light elements Li, Be, and B. Also, the abundance of elements with atomic numbers $17 \leq Z \leq 25$ and $61 \leq Z \leq 75$ is considerably enhanced in cosmic rays owing to fragmentation. From the ratio (Li, Be, B)/(C, N, O) $= 0.25 \pm 0.02$ one can deduce that cosmic rays have passed through 6 g/cm^2 of material (mostly hydrogen). This amount of material is equivalent to that in a 2-ft-long (0.6 m) hydrogen bubble chamber.

As a result of nuclear breakup reactions, the isotopic composition of cosmic rays is different from that of normal stars like the Sun. In Fig. 1 the calculated isotopic abundances of cosmic-ray Li, Be, C, N, S, and Ar are compared with those of the solar system. Both sets are normalized to unity for each element. The results in Fig. 1 are due to C. H. Tsao and coworkers at the Naval Research Laboratory. The data of W. R. Webber and coworkers for elements from Li to N are shown in Fig. 2. The agreement between these values and the predicted ones of Fig. 1 is good.

Cosmic-ray "age." Among the breakup products are certain isotopes of Be, Al, Cl, and Mn with radioactive half-lives of nearly a million years, for example, ^{10}Be, which has a half-life of 1.6×10^6 years. From the degree of survival of such nuclei the "age" of cosmic rays, that is, their confinement time in the Galaxy, can be calculated. The NRL group, in a report by F. W. O'Dell, M. M. Shapiro, R. Silberberg, and C. H. Tsao, has found that the Be/B ratio in cosmic rays has a value of 0.38 ± 0.02, which favors the survival of ^{10}Be over its decay (by two standard deviations). Observations of the relative fluxes of relativistic Be and B arriving at the Earth, and comparison with calculations by Shapiro and Silberberg, give an upper limit to the cosmic-ray confinement time of 10^7 years. Preliminary—and very scant—data on the isotopes of Be suggest that cosmic rays have a dwell time consistent with 3×10^6 years, within a factor of 2. Such an age estimate is supported further by the absence of the effects of synchrotron and inverse Compton losses on the energy spectrum of cosmic-ray positrons and electrons.

From the path length traversed (6 g/cm^2 of interstellar gas) and the confinement time of 3×10^6 years, the mean density of the medium traversed by cosmic rays can be calculated. The result, 1 atom/cm^3, is the mean density of gas in the galac-

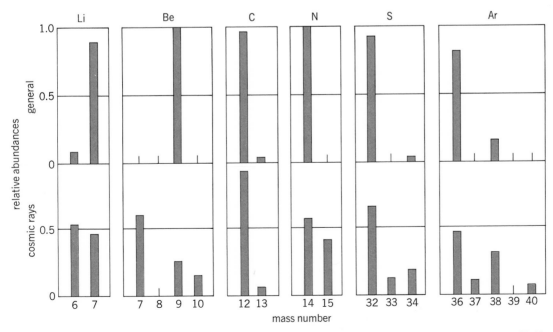

Fig. 1. A comparison of the calculated isotopic abundances of Li, Be, C, N, S, and Ar in cosmic rays with the observed abundances in the matter of the solar system. The ordinates are adjusted so that the total for each element is normalized to unity. (From C. H. Tsao, M. M. Shapiro, and R. Silberberg, Cosmic-ray isotopes at energies > 2 GeV/amu, in R. L. Chasson, ed., 13th International Cosmic Ray Conference, Denver, vol. 1, p. 107, 1973)

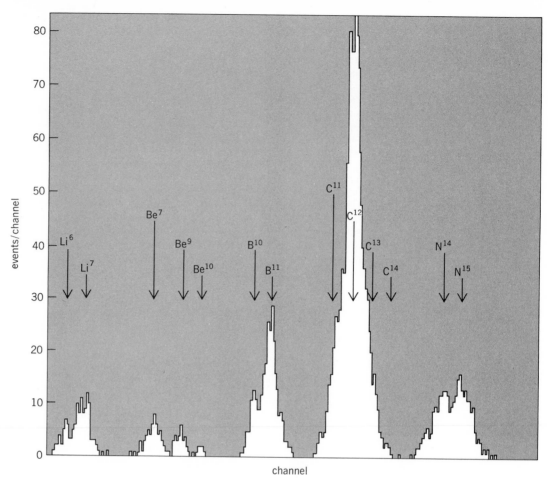

Fig. 2. The isotopic abundances of elements Li to N in cosmic rays. *(From W. R. Webber et al., The relative abundance of the isotopes of Li, Be, and B and the age of cosmic rays, Astrophys. Space Sci., 24:17, 1973)*

tic disk. Cosmic rays thus are largely confined to the galactic disk rather than to the exceedingly tenuous halo.

Deuterons, ^{3}He, and the energy spectrum. The energy dependence of the ratios ^{3}He/^{4}He and ^{2}H/^{4}He (both are ratios of secondary nuclei to primary ones) is rather sensitive to the shape of the cosmic-ray energy spectrum in interstellar space (prior to solar modulation) and to the deceleration of cosmic rays by the outflowing solar wind. At energies near 100 MeV/nucleon, the above ratios are about 0.11 ± 0.02 and 0.2 ± 0.1, respectively, as measured by the groups at NRL, University of Chicago, and Goddard Lab (NASA). Near solar minimum, the same ratios are only about one-fifth as large at 20 MeV/nucleon. From these measurements it has been deduced that, at very low energies, cosmic rays can enter the solar system without much deceleration and that the spectrum prior to solar modulation is steep or, otherwise, interstellar ^{4}He is accelerated by the solar wind.

Cosmic-ray deceleration by solar wind. Several elements have isotopes that normally decay by electron capture but survive in cosmic rays, if positron decay is prohibited by energy conservation. These nuclides, for example, ^{7}Be, ^{37}Ar, ^{41}Ca, ^{49}V, ^{51}Cr, ^{53}Mn, and ^{55}Fe, survive because the orbital electrons of the atoms have been fully stripped. At low energies, an electron will be captured and the nucleus will decay. The group of scientists at Orsay has shown that by measuring the surviving fraction, in cosmic rays near the Earth, one can learn about the extent of deceleration by the solar wind. If deceleration is appreciable, the nuclei will survive even below their normal decay energy, for the time they spend in the solar system is too brief to allow substantial decay.

Cosmic-ray origin and nucleosynthesis. If cosmic rays are derived from recent galactic supernovae, there should be very little thorium in them. The chain of heavier r-process nuclides that would decay into ^{232}Th is stopped at the long-lived species ^{244}Pu and ^{236}U. Thus, the ratio of Th/U would be about 0.1, and transuranic nuclei should be present in cosmic rays. If, however, heavy cosmic rays are extragalactic, or are derived from the acceleration of old interstellar gas, thorium would be more abundant than uranium. Present experimental data are slightly in favor of a recent origin, but experiments during the coming years will have to resolve this problem.

It has been proposed by R. M. Kulsrud and co-workers that cosmic rays are accelerated within a few years after the supernova explosion by the interaction of waves from the pulsar with the nebula of the supernova remnant. In this case, the isotope of titanium, ^{44}Ti, should be present in cosmic rays. Normally this nuclide decays by electron capture, with a half-life of 48 years, but it should survive at high energies. It is generated during nucleosynthesis by explosive silicon burning. Only a minute amount of the titanium that is formed subsequently by spallation will be ^{44}Ti; hence the primary ^{44}Ti should be discernible.

Investigations of isotopic abundances of cosmic rays have provided valuable information about high-energy processes in astrophysics and are likely to continue to do so in the future.

For background information see COSMIC RAYS in the McGraw-Hill Encyclopedia of Science and Technology.   [REIN SILBERBERG]

Bibliography: F. W. O'Dell et al. (p. 490), C. H. Tsao, M. M. Shapiro, and R. Silberberg (p. 107), and W. R. Webber, J. A. Lezniak, and J. Kish (p. 120), in R. L. Chasson (ed.), *13th International Cosmic Ray Conference, Denver*, vol. 1, 1973; W. R. Webber et al., *Astrophys. Space Sci.*, 24:17, 1973.

Cryobiology

Recent work in cryobiology and cryosurgery has demonstrated that, through carefully controlled freezing procedures, it is possible to preserve or to selectively destroy increasingly complex tissue masses and other biological materials. Both mouse and sheep embryos have been frozen to below −320°F (−196°C) and stored for up to 1 month in liquid nitrogen. After thawing and transferring to foster mothers, these embryos have developed into apparently normal newborn mice and lambs. Cryosurgical procedures have been successfully used in the extirpation of malignant tumors presenting special surgical difficulties, although the existence of a cryoimmune response in clinical cases involving the repeated freezing of such tumors remains controversial.

Spermatozoa and blood. Twenty-five years have now passed since the discovery of the cryoprotective action of glycerol in preserving spermatozoa and red blood cells. Bovine spermatozoa have for some time been routinely preserved through freezing in cryoprotective media containing glycerol, but only recently have frozen red blood cells come into increasingly widespread usage. Such frozen red cells not only provide a valuable hospital resource but may also provide a means of decreasing the possibility of the transmission of hepatitis to blood recipients. It is now thought, however, that the decrease in hepatitis transmission may be due to the cleansing effect of washing procedures used to remove glycerol from the thawed blood rather than to the freezing process itself. The only apparent drawback to the use of such blood is the added processing cost, which currently amounts to approximately $25 per unit.

Other biological materials. Techniques have been developed for the viable freezing and storage of an ever-increasing variety of other biological materials, including white blood cells, eye corneas, skin, and developing embryos. Banks of frozen skin now exist and have been used in the treatment of victims of severe burns. Larger tissue masses, however, including whole organs such as kidneys, cannot presently be frozen without the destruction of their biological function. A considerable amount of research aimed at the preservation of such large tissue masses is in progress.

Cryoprotective agents. For small biological materials, such as individual cells, very rapid freezing has sometimes been found to minimize freezing damage. For larger masses, however, high cooling rates cannot be achieved because of the relatively low thermal conductivity of biological materials. The preservation of larger tissue masses apparently can be achieved only through the use of cryoprotective agents. In the case of sheep embryos, for example, freezing is currently carried out in a phosphate-buffered salt solution containing dimethyl sulfoxide. After suspension in the solution, the embryos are first cooled to 21.2°F (−6°C), and then ice growth is initiated by using ice crystal seeds. Final freezing is accomplished in liquid nitrogen at −320°F (−196°C). Related processing steps involving the use of cryoprotective substances such as dimethyl sulfoxide and glycerol will almost certainly be required for the successful freezing and viable preservation of all large tissue masses and organs.

Although the action of cryoprotective suspension or perfusion agents is undoubtedly complex and may involve a variety of membrane, adsorption, and micromolecular effects, a substantial part of their influence is due to their effect on the low-temperature phase relationships that exist while the total system, consisting of the biological material and the cryoprotective agent, is frozen. Of particular importance is the influence of cryoprotectives on the degree of concentration of salts, especially sodium chloride and potassium chloride, in the remaining liquid phase during initial freezing. Recently, physical scientists have begun to contribute to the development of cryoprotective procedures by investigating low-temperature phase relationships in relevant systems containing cryoprotective agents, such as the ternary system water–salt–dimethyl sulfoxide.

Cryosurgery. Neurosurgeons and ophthalmologists were the first to realize the advantages that could be obtained in surgery by means of a well-controlled discrete area of tissue destruction. Use could also be made of the adhesive properties of cold probes for manipulation of tissues. In the removal of cataracts, for example, cryoextraction is now a preferred surgical technique. By placing the cryosurgical probe against the cataract lens and then lowering the temperature of the tip of the probe to −22°F (−30°C), an ice mass that encompasses the cortex and a portion of the nucleus of the lens is produced. The cataract is then firmly attached to the probe, and extraction can readily be carried out. In ophthalmology, cryosurgical methods are also used in the treatment of retinal detachment and advanced glaucoma. In the neurosurgical treatment of parkinsonism and several other involuntary movement disorders, the controlled freezing of portions of the thalamus by means of a cryosurgical cannula inserted through the cerebral cortex is now used routinely in many cases.

Malignant tumor. Cryosurgery has also recently been carried out successfully on patients with inoperable lung metastases of malignant tumors. Animal experiments indicate that cryosurgical le-

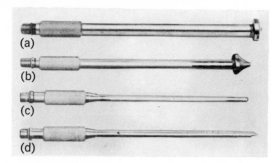

Types of cryosurgical probes: (a) cervix probe tip; (b) cone probe tip; (c) general probe tip; (d) microcondyloma probe tip. (*Courtesy of Frigitronics, Inc.*)

sions in the lung are reabsorbed relatively rapidly. Therefore, a favorable state might exist for the induction of tumor immunity by means of sequential freezing treatments. In one study reported at the 11th Annual Meeting of the Society for Cryobiology held in London on Aug. 4–8, 1974, half the cases of inoperable lung metastases treated by cryosurgery showed that progression of the tumor was stopped for up to 18 months, and, in the case of one patient, a single metastasis in the left lung was found to be eliminated after cryosurgery was carried out on multiple metastases of a malignant teratoma in the right lung.

In many cases head and neck cancers are small and contained close to their site of origin. Because these cancers are often resistant to radiotherapy or surgical treatment, there is increasing interest in their treatment by cryosurgical methods. Results announced in 1974 suggest that some small tumors of the tongue margin or palate might be cured painlessly, rapidly, and without deformity by freezing. Large vascular, bleeding, and ulcerating carcinomas of the mouth or postnasal space have been treated palliatively by repeated freezing.

Prostate. Cryosurgical methods have also been used with increasing success in the treatment of prostatic obstruction. The advantages of the cryosurgical method over conventional surgical procedures arise primarily from the fact that the cryosurgical method is bloodless, requires only local anesthesia, permits early ambulation, and is in general a mild operative procedure tolerated well by elderly patients. Cryosurgical methods have also been used in the treatment of prostatic cancer. The results of one recent study suggest that there is an immunothermic response following cryotherapy in patients with prostatic cancer. This augmentation of host immunity may be a significant factor in resistance to neoplasia. The development of a cryoimmune response in clinical cases involving the repeated freezing of malignant tumors remains controversial, however.

Rectum. There have been recent reports on the use of cryorectal surgery for the destruction of hemorrhoids. These operations were carried out with a hand-held apparatus designed to achieve cooling by means of the Joule-Thompson effect; the refrigerant gas was nitrous oxide. The treatment failure rate was less than 1%.

Instruments. Each of these surgical procedures preferably requires freezing probes of special de-

sign (see illustration). The probe itself may be cooled with liquid or gaseous nitrogen or with gaseous nitrous oxide or carbon dioxide. In ophthalmologic procedures, probes cooled by means of a thermoelectric effect have also been used. The design of such probes is a particularly favorable field for the cooperation of engineers and surgeons.

For background information *see* CRYOBIOLOGY in the McGraw-Hill Encyclopedia of Science and Technology.

[FRANKLIN H. COCKS]
Bibliography: E. O. Gursel, M. S. Roberts, and R. J. Veenema, *Urology*, 1:392–396, May 1973; H. Haschek (ed.), *Latest Developments in Cryosurgery*, 1972; A. U. Smith (ed.), *Current Trends in Cryobiology*, 1970; D. G. Whittingham, S. P. Leibo, and P. Mazur, *Science*, 181:288, July 20, 1973.

Cyprinodontiformes

Nearly three dozen all-female species have been identified among the reptiles, amphibians, and fishes. Current studies are directed toward determining their origins, methods of reproduction, and significance to evolution. Among unisexual vertebrates, fishes, especially live-bearers in the order Cyprinodontiformes, are the most easily reared and, hence, readily lend themselves to experimentation into the causes and significance of all-femaleness.

The most popular theory emerging from such studies is that hybridization between normal species leads to the formation of unisexual species and that unisexuality in turn leads to polyploidy. Polyploidy involves an increase in chromosome number and, therefore, an increase in the amount of hereditary information available. Major steps in evolution from simple to complex organisms may depend upon the addition of enough genetic material to code for increased complexity.

Population structure. All-female species have been verified from three genera of fishes, *Carassius* (goldfish), *Poecilia*, and *Poeciliopsis* (the last two are Mexican live-bearers in the family Poeciliidae). The unisexual goldfish ranges in distribution from Japan across the Soviet Union and into Europe. Centuries of association with the fish culture industry mask its origin and obscure its role as part of a natural phenomenon. The two Mexican live-bearers, on the other hand, originated in the wild and constitute a significant part of natural communities.

The first all-female species to be identified was *Poecilia formosa*, discovered by C. Hubbs and L. Hubbs in 1932. It lives in the Gulf coastal streams of northwestern Mexico, ranging a short distance into Texas. Having no males of its own species, it utilizes those of other species; it is in a sense, then, a sexual parasite. In the northern part of its range, it lives with *P. latipinna*, whereas in the southern part it associates with *P. mexicana*. Males of both species provide sperm, which is essential for the activation of eggs into development (gynogenesis), but none of the father's characters typically enter into the formation of young. Instead of the offspring having 23 chromosomes (hereditary units) contributed by the female through the egg, plus a paternal set of 23 contributed through the sperm, the fertilized egg has twice the normal chromosome number, a result of a doubling of the maternal set. The offspring, consequently, are all females and identical to their mothers. Recently it was discovered that some specimens of *P. formosa* from Mexico have an extra set of chromosomes. Apparently, the eggs of *P. formosa* females, which usually carry two maternal sets, for a total of 46 chromosomes, on rare occasions have actually been fertilized. Rather than the sperm providing only the stimulus to development, then, a third set of chromosomes, or third genome, as it is also called, is added. Offspring carrying this extra set of chromosomes (making 69 chromosomes) are called triploids. They, too, are all females that have become established in nature and now reproduce their own triploid kind gynogenetically, utilizing the same males as the *P. formosa*.

In the fresh-water streams of northwestern Mexico, *Poeciliopsis* has evolved a similar but slightly more complex unisexual-bisexual series. Two unisexual species were originally described in 1959, one living with *P. occidentalis* in the Río Mayo and the rivers north of it nearly to the border of the United States, the other living with *P. lucida* in the three rivers south of the Río Mayo, the Ríos Fuerte, Sinoloa, and Mocorito (see illustration). Lines of these unisexuals collected in 1961 are still maintained in the laboratory and, after 35 generations of matings to males of *P. lucida*, still consistently produce only female progeny. More than 70 different lines of unisexuals have been tested for 2–35 generations without a breakdown of the unisexual mechanism.

Origin. After nearly 20 years of studying unisexual *Poeciliopsis* in the laboratory and field, it was clearly established that they are of hybrid origin. Living in the headwaters of the Ríos Mayo, Sinoloa, and Fuerte is a solitary species of *Poeciliopsis*, *P. monacha*, which comes into contact with *P. lucida* at only a few restricted places. In these narrow zones of overlap they have hybridized. Although many hybrids are sterile, these are not; by mating back to males of *P. lucida*, the hybrid offspring have built up extensive populations. One might expect the *monacha* traits to be diluted by many generations of backcrossing with *lucida*, and normally they would be, were it not for an unusual mechanism that operates at the time the hybrid produces eggs for the next generation. Instead of the male *(lucida)* and female *(monacha)* traits mixing and being randomly distributed to the eggs, no mixing occurs; only the maternal *(monacha)* traits are deposited in the eggs, and the male *(lucida)* traits are lost. Each generation, then, consists of a *monacha* × *lucida* F₁ hybrid, but only the *monacha* chromosomes are passed on to the next generation, and the *lucida* chromosomes must be replaced. This mechanism, called hybridogenesis, differs from the gynogenesis of *Poecilia formosa* in that both the maternal and paternal traits of each generation are expressed, whereas, in gynogenesis, only the maternal traits are present.

The original *monacha-lucida* unisexual has given rise to a series of unisexual species. The process has involved additional hybridization with other species. The *monacha* traits that in *mona-*

Poeciliopsis lucida (female top left, male below) and the unisexual forms associated with its populations (gynogenetic triploid above right, hybridogenetic diploid below). *(From W. S. Moore and F. E. McKay, Behavioral aspects of population dynamics in unisexual-bisexual Poeciliopsis (Pisces:Poeciludae), Ecology, 52(5):779, 1971)*

cha-lucida are typically held intact and passed through the egg to the next generation are combined with sperm from other species. One of these species, *Poeciliopsis latidens*, is dramatically different from both *monacha* and *lucida* in appearance and in way of life. It has bold black bars and spots on the body and lives in shallow riffles, whereas *monacha* and *lucida* are uniformly gray, like guppies, and live in quiet pools. The *monacha-latidens* unisexual has the spots plus a liberal mixture of other *latidens* and *monacha* characters. At no locality are *monacha* and *latidens* known to live together; thus it appears that *monacha-lucida* hybrids have served as a go-between, transferring the *monacha* genome from its solitary headwater residence to a broad distribution and a radically different way of life. A similar process has transported the *monacha* genome northward several hundred miles out of its normal range, this time as a sexual parasite on *Poeciliopsis occidentalis*. In the form of a *monacha-occidentalis* unisexual, it has reached abundance levels of 0.1–10 times those of its host species in various parts of its range.

The *monacha-lucida* hybrid has also served as a stepping-stone to polyploidy in somewhat the same way that *Poecilia formosa* has. Normally, *monacha-lucida* produces eggs with a single set of *monacha* chromosomes. Rarely, however, the *lucida* set is retained in the egg; thus, when fertilization by *lucida* sperm occurs, an offspring made up of two doses of *lucida* and one of *monacha* (*P. monacha-2 lucida*) is produced. Similarly, retention of *monacha* and *lucida* chromosomes and fertilization by *monacha* sperm have resulted in triploids with two doses of *monacha* and one of *lucida* (*P. 2 monacha-lucida*). The unisexuals are named according to the parental dose contributed; *P. 2 monacha-lucida* lives and mates with *P. monacha*, which it closely resembles, and *P. monacha-2 lucida* lives and mates with *lucida*, which it closely resembles. Reproduction has shifted to gynogenesis; thus, the three sets of chromosomes (three genomes) present in their eggs require sperm only for stimulation of development; the offspring are identical to their mothers. All five forms, *P. monacha*, *P. 2 monacha-lucida*, *P. monacha-lucida*, *P. monacha-2 lucida*, and *P. lucida*, are abundant in the Río Fuerte; the last three are also widespread and highly successful in the Ríos Sinoloa and Mocorito.

Synthesis of a unisexual. The role of hybridization in evolution has long been open to question. The belief that it originated unisexual species is based on morphological, chromosomal, and biochemical analysis. By these methods the parental species for many unisexual animals have been identified, but attempts to "create" unisexual species in the laboratory have, until recently, been unsuccessful. Since circumstantial evidence indicated that one of the *Poeciliopsis* unisexuals was a *monacha* × *lucida* hybrid, numerous attempts were made to hybridize the two species in the laboratory. Of 67 such crosses, 5 were successful; they resulted in all female offspring. Two lines of the original five were maintained in the laboratory for four generations, and one for seven generations, by matings to males of *P. lucida*. More than 500 offspring have since been born to laboratory-produced *monacha-lucida* females. All have been females that are indistinguishable from a wild *P. monacha-lucida*. Thus, 40 years after the discovery of the first unisexual vertebrate, hybridization of a unisexual species has been accomplished in the laboratory.

For background information *see* CYPRINIFORMES in the McGraw-Hill Encyclopedia of Science and Technology.   [R. JACK SCHULTZ]

Bibliography: M. C. Cimino, *Evolution*, 26:294–306, 1972; W. S. Moore and F. E. McKay, *Ecology*, 52(5):791–799, 1971; E. M. Rasch and J. S. Balsano, *Copeia 1973*, pp. 810–813, 1973; R. J. Schultz, *Science*, 179:180–181, 1973; R. C. Vrijenhoek and R. J. Schultz, *Evolution*, 28:306–319, 1974.

Cytochalasins

Ten years ago the cytochalasins, a new class of antibiotics produced by fungi, were discovered. The cytochalasins (from Greek *cytos*, cell; *chalasis*, relaxation) elicit in animal and plant cells a puzzling diversity of responses. Examples of cytochalasin effects, usually reversible on removal of the antibiotic, are given in the table. The tenth anniversary of discovery of these compounds is marked by the appearance of radio-labeled cytochalasins, a development which greatly enhances the analytical power of this family of research tools and opens the way toward elucidation of its modes of action, which presently appear to be at least twofold.

Cell membrane. Evidence is accumulating that numerous chemicals, including cytochalasins, interact directly with plasma membrane components, modulate activity of membrane-bound enzymes, and often produce changes in membrane structure which are detectable by using high-resolution electron microscopy. Labeled cytochalasins, applied to a variety of animal cells, attained maximal binding within 1 to 5 min. Dissociation on transfer to cytochalasin-free medium was equally rapid, but as much as half the cytochalasin remained associated with the cells. Both whole cells and fractioned cell components have been used to establish cytochalasin binding to plasma membranes. Red blood cells, for instance, each have 3×10^5 high-affinity cytochalasin binding sites, all in the plasma membrane. Binding is competitively inhibited by D-glucose; treatments which inactivate glucose-transport-related binding sites also eliminate cytochalasin binding; the estimated number of glucose binding sites, $2-5 \times 10^5$, corresponds well with the number of cytochalasin B (CB) binding sites. Most of these CB-binding sites appear therefore to be glucose transport sites. Similar results from other mammalian cells help to account for the potent inhibition of glucose uptake often observed with cytochalasins. Does the resulting glucose starvation explain the rapid "freezing" effect on cell motion that is the most universal of cytochalasin responses? Apparently not. Cellular motion is arrested long before glucose starvation occurs, and "freezing" occurs even in cells whose glucose uptake machinery is immune to cytochalasin.

The first evidence for direct cytochalasin action on a membrane-bound enzyme is the inhibition of (Na^+-K^+) ATPase. It appears that changes in the cell surface, and in cytochalasin sensitivity, are correlated with the stage of the cell cycle. For instance, mammalian cells in G1 (the period during interphase just prior to DNA synthesis) show maximal sensitivity, as determined by rapid morphological responses. Such cells, treated during G1, also fail to acquire the ability during the synthesis (S) phase to transport thymidine, a DNA precursor. In contrast, CB treatment during the S phase failed to inhibit thymidine uptake.

Actin microfilaments and myosins. Evidence, accumulated using electron-microscopic, biochemical, and biophysical techniques, seems to point to the conclusion that the bundles of microfilaments (6–8 nm in diameter) associated with protoplasmic movements in plant and animal cells are constructed of actin subunits, closely related to muscle actin. Microfilaments tend to abound in the peripheral cytoplasm, near the plasma membrane. Microfilaments, like actin filaments from muscle, can be "decorated" along their length with "arrowheads" of myosin fragments, visible by electron microscopy. Arrowheads on a microfilament all point in the same direction, indicating filament polarity. In cell regions where microfilaments appear attached to the cell membrane (such as at the tips of intestinal epithelial microvilli), all arrowheads of the microfilament point away from the membrane, just as the arrowheads in muscle actin point away from the attachment zone, the Z band. Since muscle contraction is achieved by an energy-dependent ratchetlike interaction between parallel actin and myosin filaments, it is assumed that actin microfilaments in nonmuscle cells may generate streaming by interaction with myosin.

Myosins are more difficult to study than actins—more difficult to recognize using electron microscopy, and more difficult to characterize biochemically, since they are larger molecules and seem to be far more heterogeneous. Indeed this variation in myosins may dictate the type of movement generated by different actin-myosin systems. The presence of myosin-like proteins on cell organelles and vesicles suggests that movement of such cell

Cytochalasin effects on animal and plant physiology*

Membrane phenomena		Cellular and intracellular movement		Miscellaneous effects	
Animal	Plant	Animal	Plant	Animal	Plant
Inhibits: 1. Uptake of small molecules (for example, glucose, deoxyglucose, glucosamine, thymidine, uracil) 2. Secretion (for example, alpha-amylase, dopamine hydroxylase, norepinephrine, growth hormone, lymphotoxin) 3. Osmotic water movement stimulated by vasopressin or cyclic AMP 4. Potential difference development and fluid transport *No inhibition of:* 1. Leucine uptake 2. Immunoglobin secretion *Inhibits/stimulates:* Glucose-induced insulin secretion, depending on concentration	*Inhibits:* 1. Uptake of glucose 2. Synthesis and secretion of cellulose in *Achyla* without inhibiting overall protein synthesis 3. Establishment of cell polarity in fucoid brown algae *No inhibition of:* Alpha amylase or extensin secretion	*Inhibits:* 1. Cytokinesis 2. Embryonic morphogenesis 3. Cell movement 4. Phagocytosis 5. Axoplasmic transport of melanin granules *Inhibits/stimulates:* Chemotaxis in leukocytes, depending on concentration	*Inhibits:* 1. Cytoplasmic streaming 2. Tip growth 3. Mitotic rate in roots without affecting phragmoplast formation 4. Chloroplast movement in the green alga *Mougeotia*	*Inhibits:* Lymphocyte-mediated cytolysis *Induces:* Nuclear extrusion	*Inhibits:* 1. Root growth in onion and soybean 2. Recovery of normal protoplasm distribution after centrifugation 3. Establishment of cell polarity in fucoid brown algae *Induces:* 1. Cell sphering in onion roots 2. Phloem translocation: two reports based on different plants are contradictory; one reports no effect, the other inhibition by cytochalasin B

*Where effects of cytochalasin on animal cells have been indicated, similar results on plants have not yet been reported but may be forthcoming.

inclusions in contact with microfilaments may be due to musclelike shearing forces generated between actin and myosin. Cytoplasmic streaming is frequently arrested by cytochalasins, suggesting the possibility of interaction with actin microfilaments or with myosin.

Electron-microscopic evidence for such cytochalasin effects is conflicting. Different workers describe modification of microfilaments in terms of disruption, hypercondensation, or detachment from an anchoring site. Others find no evidence of microfilament changes, and studies using isolated actin and myosin fragments revealed no inhibition of arrowhead formation. However, cytochalasin B did decrease the viscosity of an actin-myosin mixture and inhibited the ATPase of the myosin moiety. *See* MUSCLE (BIOPHYSICS).

Radio-labeled cytochalasins have now been used to determine whether or not cytochalasins bind to "contractile" proteins. Results using cytochalasin D (CD) show binding to myosin, not actin, and suggest that actin and CD may compete for a binding site on myosin. Other results using CB report binding both to actin and to myosin.

Applications. The great value of the cytochalasins as research tools, in spite of present ignorance of their precise mode of action, is that they appear to achieve their reversible impact on cell behavior with a minimum of undesirable side effects such as inhibition of respiration or protein synthesis. Cytochalasin is extensively applied as a chemical "scalpel" to enucleate mammalian cells rapidly, precisely, and efficiently in studies of nuclear-cytoplasmic relations and in cell hybridization and nuclear transplant work. Another major application is in examining the consequences of arrested cytoplasmic movement. For instance, plant cells with complete CB arrest of streaming have been found to show only mild inhibition of transport of the hormone auxin, supporting the conclusion that auxin transport within a cell depends more on diffusion than on cytoplasmic streaming.

Challenges for the future. Research has emphasized one cytochalasin, CB. The research potential of other natural cytochalasins and of synthetic analogs remains to be determined. Most workers use the supposedly inert solvent dimethyl sulfoxide (DMSO) as a primary solvent for cytochalasins before diluting in the treatment medium. Work in the laboratory of P. Emmelot showed that doubling the DMSO concentration from 0.6 to 1.2% increased CB response by 45%. Since DMSO is a chelator of Ca^{++}, important in regulating membrane structure and function, the effects of this compound may seriously confound experiments with cytochalasins, and urgently require evaluation.

Many cytochalasin-related questions remain unanswered. Do they actually penetrate beyond the plasma membrane? Do cells inactivate or metabolize them? Do cells use their own brands of cytochalasin-type molecule to regulate their development? What benefits, if any, do they confer on the fungi that produce them? Why do they sometimes give conflicting results in different laboratories, or sporadic results in a single laboratory?

Cytochalasin responses, since they involve membranes, are of necessity complex. To begin to understand them, more information will be needed on key biological problems such as the regulatory role of membrane configuration, and the roles of actins, myosins, and related proteins in cellular mobility.

For background information *see* ANTIBIOTIC; CELL MEMBRANES; MUSCLE (BIOPHYSICS) in the McGraw-Hill Encyclopedia of Science and Technology. [DONOVAN DES S. THOMAS]

Bibliography: C. J. Bos and P. Emmelot, *Chem. Biol. Interact.*, 8:349, 1974; P. K. Hepler and B. A. Palevitz, *Annu. Rev. Plant Physiol.*, 25:309, 1974; S. Lin, D. V. Santi, and J. A. Spudich, *J. Biol. Chem.*, 249:2268, 1974; E. and S. Puszkin, L. W. Lo, and S. W. Tanenbaum, *J. Biol. Chem.*, 248: 7754, 1974.

Digital computer usage

Progress in the measurement and evaluation of computer system performance has been so rapid during the 1970s that computer performance evaluation (CPE) is already a nearly separate discipline of the computer sciences. The tools and techniques of this emerging discipline are described in this article.

Background. The invention of a new tool is soon followed by a search for useful methods of measuring the performance of the tool. Mark I, the first computer, had no more than two programs in operation before programmers began inserting "check flags," or special codes, that would enable the programmers to determine how far their program had progressed before the program or the computer ceased operation. This was a valuable measure; if it were known that some specific amount of the program's work had been completed before a failure, then a facility to save intermediate results at each check flag would allow the completed work to be saved. In the early computers this was an adequate performance criterion for increasing the efficiency of a system.

The growth in size and complexity of both the computing equipment and the programming methods has been matched by the growth in the complexity of the questions that must be answered to adequately assess the performance of contemporary computer systems. CPE has become a field that is as necessary as, and complementary to, internal auditing for all but the smallest of present computer installations. CPE addresses the efficiency of an installation; that is, it is aimed at ensuring that a minimum amount of effort, expense, and waste is incurred in the production of data-processing services. Internal auditing, on the other hand, addresses the effectiveness of an installation; that is, it is aimed at ensuring that all necessary and no unnecessary data-processing services are produced. Together, CPE and internal auditing have become the indispensable tools of the "control" function of management. This article deals only with the first of these fields.

Tools of CPE. The specialized CPE tools fall into two broad categories: measurement tools and predictive tools. Accounting packages, source program optimizers, software monitors, and hardware monitors are all measurement tools. The principal predictive tool is simulation. Bench marking is primarily a predictive tool, but it is also used as a measurement tool during some phases of a CPE project. Table 1 shows the relationship of these tools to the life cycle of a computer system.

Accounting packages. Nearly every manufacturer now supplies a set of special routines that allow collection of information about the usage level of various system components by each production program. These special routines are an evolution of programs developed to determine what cost should be billed to each user of a computer system. Current accounting packages are used to help in the day-to-day management of the operation of computer installations. They provide detailed information that is useful in scheduling the workload of the installation and in analyzing the degree of usage of existing equipment. Recent innovations in the use of accounting packages include the development of commercial products that accept data collected by the accounting package and produce special reports in simplified formats that facilitate the use of the information in the operation and management of the computer installation. A few of these recent products are capable of producing computer users' bills. Of course, the variety of additional products that are available go far beyond the production of bills for services rendered.

Accounting packages are typically system-dependent and are usually a part of the control program or operating system that is supplied by the computer manufacturer. Accounting packages are often referred to as a "free" tool for CPE, as there is seldom any extra charge for them as a part of the control program. The recent products for report generation from accounting package data are sold separately by numerous "software companies." Nearly all are available only for computers of the IBM 360 and 370 lines but are relatively independent of specific models within these lines.

Source program optimizer. This CPE tool is commercially available for examining the source code of programs written in either of the two major "high-level" languages: FORTRAN and COBOL. Program optimizers are modules of code that are usually written in the language of the program that is to be examined and compiled along with the target program. During execution of the program, information about use of the various portions of the code is accumulated for later reporting to the programmer. Analysis of this information enables the programmer to modify those sections of the target program that are most heavily used in order to improve performance of the final, operational pro-

Table 1. Life cycle of a computer system related to computer performance evaluation tools*

Phase	Activity	Simulation	Bench marks	Accounting data	Software monitors	Hardware monitors
Selection	Conceptual workload design	X				
	Detailed workload specification	X	X			
	Equipment specification	X	X			
	Request for proposals (RFP)	X	X			
	Reviewing RFP responses	X	X			
	Selecting equipment		X			
Adaptation	Tailoring workload to equipment		X	X	X	X
	Configuring the equipment		X	X	X	X
	Installation and checkout		X			X
	Acceptance testing		X		X	X
Operation	Workload implementation			X	X	X
	Program reviews	X		X	X	X
	Configuration enhancement	X		X	X	X
	Adding workload	X	X	X	X	X
	Projecting workload growth	X		X		
	Predicting system saturation	X		X		X
Preselection	Review of new systems	X				
	Review of potential data-processing needs	X				
	Conceptual design of foreseeable workload	X				
	Reuse analysis of owned equipment	X	X			

*Adapted from M. F. Morris and P. F. Roth, *Computer Performance Evaluation,* New York: Petrocelli Books, to be published.

gram. This tool is most useful in a test or development environment, in which new programs must be checked thoroughly prior to their release to a production environment.

Software monitor. The software monitor is closely related to accounting packages. Nearly all information collected by accounting packages can also be collected by software monitors. However, monitors are typically able to collect more data concerning usage of the various components of a computer system than an accounting package can. Software monitors are also usually a part of the control program, but they are not supplied "free" by manufacturers along with the control program. They are available only for IBM 360 and 370 series equipment on a commercial basis. Users of other equipment may locate software monitors that will operate on their equipment through the users group for their brand of computer.

Hardware monitor. This CPE tool is an electromechanical device that is a descendant of the oscilloscope. Hardware monitors attach to the circuitry within a computer by means of special "probes" that sense changes in the voltage levels at their point of attachment. The monitor unit collects information on the number of times or length of time that the monitored signal occurred. This information is either displayed immediately or saved on some medium that can be fed to a special data-reduction program after the monitoring has been completed. Hardware monitors in their basic form are completely system-independent.

The singular advantage of the hardware monitor over all other measurement tools is that it causes no performance degradation while it is collecting data on the target system. However, once the data are collected, the data-reduction program must be run to assemble the information in a usable form. Data reduction can be regarded as the overhead associated with a hardware monitor.

Recent hardware monitors include minicomputers that can be used to reduce monitor data as they are collected. In addition, the memory of the minicomputer can be used to increase the amount of information that can be measured simultaneously. Some of these recent hardware monitors are especially adapted to monitor any one type of computer. Although this adaptation allows these monitors to collect virtually any desired piece of information about the computer or its workload, it also makes the hardware monitor system-dependent.

Simulation. The most important use of simulation as a CPE tool is in the prediction of performance of either equipment or programs that do not exist or are not available for direct measurement. Simulation is the one CPE tool that is also used widely outside the field of CPE. The use of simulation requires that mathematical models of the system to be studied be created and exercised to test the likely outcomes of some particular design or alternative within a design. Simulation allows an entire system to be examined before a major investment is committed to either constructing or purchasing the system.

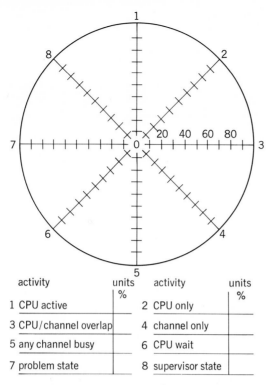

activity	units %	activity	units %
1 CPU active		2 CPU only	
3 CPU/channel overlap		4 channel only	
5 any channel busy		6 CPU wait	
7 problem state		8 supervisor state	

Fig. 1. Format for plotting eight variables on a Kiviat graph.

Simulation is certainly the most expensive CPE tool in that it not only requires the purchase or lease of a suitable language or simulation package but also demands extensive training and a dedication of personnel on a continuing basis. The high cost of simulation is typically repaid severalfold

through savings made by not electing alternatives that would be inappropriate but that might be chosen were it not for the predictive power of simulation.

Simulation languages are generally used to address CPE problems that are concerned with very small time increments, say, from seconds to microseconds or nanoseconds. Simulation packages are special sets of computer programs that are designed to examine typical problems encountered in data-processing installations. These packages are most useful in addressing problems that involve much longer time increments, say, from hours or shifts through weeks or even months. The very significant area between seconds and hours may be addressed by either languages or packages on the basis of the merits of each individual problem. The examination of the merits of such problems is, in itself, a difficult exercise that requires in-depth knowledge of both the problem and the flexibility of simulation languages and packages.

Bench marks. The final major CPE tool is the bench mark. A bench mark is a program or set of programs that represent a real workload that is in operation or is planned to be implemented on some computer equipment configuration. Bench marks are both measurement tools and predictive tools. The primary use of bench marks occurs during the selection phase of the life cycle of a computer system. The bench mark programs serve as a measure of the comparative capability of the equipment of several manufacturers to predict the value of each set of equipment as it might operate in the customer's environment. Bench marks are also useful when a system is operational, as a point of reference for checking the merit of changes suggested by the application of other CPE tools.

There is no known commercial source for bench

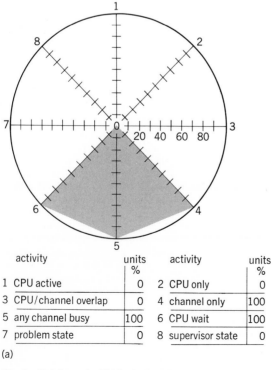

activity	units %	activity	units %
1 CPU active	0	2 CPU only	0
3 CPU/channel overlap	0	4 channel only	100
5 any channel busy	100	6 CPU wait	100
7 problem state	0	8 supervisor state	0

(a)

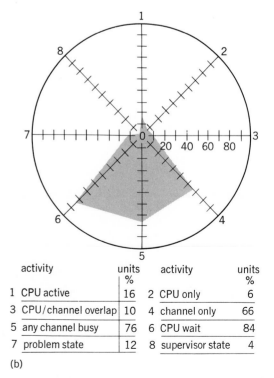

activity	units %	activity	units %
1 CPU active	16	2 CPU only	6
3 CPU/channel overlap	10	4 channel only	66
5 any channel busy	76	6 CPU wait	84
7 problem state	12	8 supervisor state	4

(b)

Fig. 2. Kiviat graph of (a) limit of I/O boundedness, and (b) actual data showing an I/O wedge.

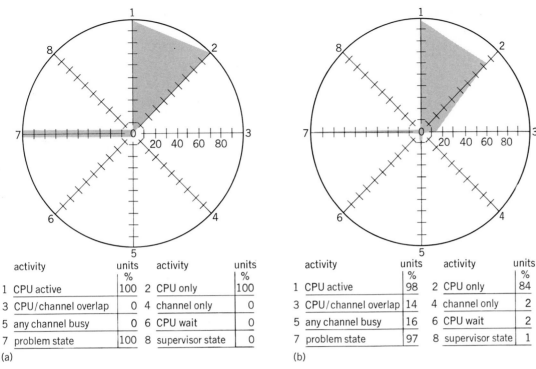

activity	units %		activity	units %
1 CPU active	100		2 CPU only	100
3 CPU/channel overlap	0		4 channel only	0
5 any channel busy	0		6 CPU wait	0
7 problem state	100		8 supervisor state	0

(a)

activity	units %		activity	units %
1 CPU active	98		2 CPU only	84
3 CPU/channel overlap	14		4 channel only	2
5 any channel busy	16		6 CPU wait	2
7 problem state	97		8 supervisor state	1

(b)

Fig. 3. Kiviat graph of (a) limit of CPU boundedness, and (b) actual data showing a CPU sailboat.

mark programs. Each installation typically selects those programs or portions of programs that define its major workload and creates some smaller program that will represent this workload. The degree of representativeness of any bench mark is the key to the successful application of bench marks. It is therefore wise to develop bench marks with great reliance upon all the other CPE tools that are available.

Presentation technqiues. The abundance of specialized CPE tools has produced something of a dilemma: what does one do with "all that data"? Most reduction programs associated with the measurement tools produce either tabular listings of figures or histograms. These are excellent outputs for detailed analysis by CPE technicians. However, the important part of most CPE projects is the communication of the results or expected re-

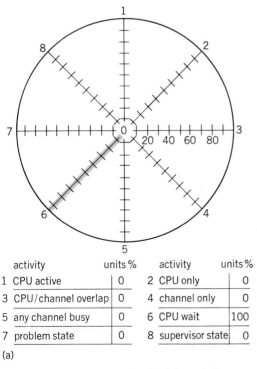

activity	units %		activity	units %
1 CPU active	0		2 CPU only	0
3 CPU/channel overlap	0		4 channel only	0
5 any channel busy	0		6 CPU wait	100
7 problem state	0		8 supervisor state	0

(a)

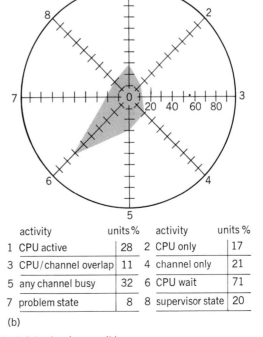

activity	units %		activity	units %
1 CPU active	28		2 CPU only	17
3 CPU/channel overlap	11		4 channel only	21
5 any channel busy	32		6 CPU wait	71
7 problem state	8		8 supervisor state	20

(b)

Fig. 4. Kiviat graph of (a) limit of wait boundedness, and (b) actual data showing a wait leg.

Table 2. Groups with special interests in computer performance evaluation

Group	Contact	Publications
SIGMETRICS (Special Interest Group on Measurement and Evaluation/ACM)	Philip J. Kiviat Chairman, SIGMETRICS Dept. of Air Force FEDSIM/CA Washington, DC 20330	Quarterly newsletter and periodic proceedings
SIGSIM (Special Interest Group for Simulation/ACM)	Harold J. Highland Chairman, SIGSIM State University of New York Agricultural and Technical College Farmingdale, NY 11735	Quarterly newsletter and periodic proceedings
CPEUG (Computer Performance Evaluation Users Group)	William Letendre Chairman, CPEUG ESD/MCIF L. G. Hanscom Field Bedford, MA 01730	Periodic proceedings
CM&E Project (Computer Measurement and Evaluation Project/SHARE)	Dennis Chastain Manager, CM&E Project U.S. General Accounting Office Washington, DC 20548	Periodic newsletter

sults of the project to management, which is typically neither interested in nor trained in the details of computer operation. Therefore, the detailed outputs that have been the norm in CPE work are not really useful as a medium of communication outside the immediate computer environment.

One technique that has been developed recently is the use of Kiviat graphs, which are circular diagrams that are useful for displaying several variables simultaneously. Figure 1 shows a format for a Kiviat graph. Eight typical IBM system variables have been selected and shown on this format. There is no reason to be constrained to the particular variables, or to the eight axes, shown here. Kiviat graphs of up to 20 axes have been used to good purpose.

The only conventions that should be followed are, first, that an even number of axes be used and that the axis numbered 1 be at the top of the graph with the others numbered in sequence around the graph; second, that each variable be plotted in percentage, with 0% at the origin of the circle and 100% at the circumference; and, third, that those variables which are "good" as they approach 100% are plotted on odd-numbered axes, and those variables which are "bad" as they approach 100% are plotted on the even-numbered axes.

Following these conventions, the system referred to as I/O bound has as a limit the Kiviat graph shown in Fig. 2a. Figure 2b shows an actual system that is approaching complete I/O boundedness. This characteristic shape is called an I/O wedge. Figure 3a shows the limit of a CPU-bound system, and Fig. 3b displays actual data in a characteristic CPU-sailboat shape (CPU refers to the central processing unit). A third category became apparent during the early application of Kiviat graphs. Figure 4a shows the theoretical limit of such a system. Figure 4b is a wait leg that was plotted from real data on a wait-bound system. A Kiviat graph of a well-balanced system is shown in Fig. 5. This characteristic star shape, which results whenever a well-tuned system is plotted on a Kiviat graph, following the conventions outlined above, is referred to as a Fedsim star, after the organization that carried out the principal development work on Kiviat graphs.

The aim of displaying information using the new Kiviat graph technique is to see at a glance how well distributed the workload is over the existing equipment configuration. Kiviat graphs have recently been adapted for a different purpose—showing what amount of computing power or capacity remains in an operational configuration. This adaptation of Kiviat graphs is shown in Fig. 6. It is called Hesser's variation. With this approach, all variables are arranged so that their plots ap-

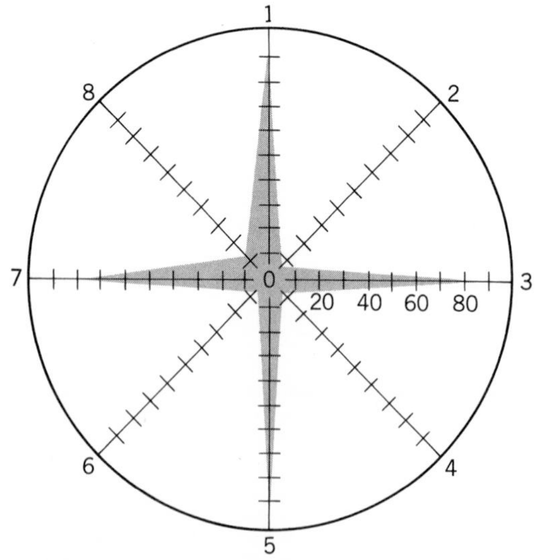

activity	units %		activity	units %
1 CPU active	91		2 CPU only	6
3 CPU/channel overlap	85		4 channel only	7
5 any channel busy	92		6 CPU wait	7
7 problem state	78		8 supervisor state	13

Fig. 5. Kiviat graph of actual data from a well-tuned system showing a Fedsim star.

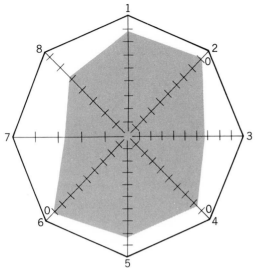

axis	activity (axis range)	plot origin	units %
1	CPU active (0–90)	cntr	78
2	CPU only (0–100)	edge	9
3	CPU/CH overlap (0–100)	cntr	69
4	CH only (0–100)	edge	15
5	any channel busy (0–100)	cntr	84
6	CPU wait (0–100)	edge	8
7	problem state (0–50)	cntr	27
8	supervisor state (0–75)	cntr	51

Fig. 6. Hesser's variation of a Kiviat graph showing actual data from a computer system nearing "saturation."

proach the circumference of the graph as the system approaches "saturation." The scales on the various axes may be in units other than percent, or they may be in percent, but not covering the full 0–100% range.

Kiviat graphs can be used to plot whatever parameters are of interest at the individual installation, just as histograms or Gantt charts can be used. The value of the Kiviat graph is that easily recognized geometric patterns made up of several variables are shown in a single "picture."

Activities in CPE. Because CPE is still a new and dynamic field, it is useful for various groups with continuing special interest in the field to cooperate to ensure that the latest information and techniques are known to the installation. Table 2 lists four of the principal sources for such information. These sources also provide periodic write-ups of CPE projects and general articles on new or innovative CPE techniques.

For background information see DIGITAL COMPUTER; DIGITAL COMPUTER PROGRAMMING in the McGraw-Hill Encyclopedia of Science and Technology.   [MICHAEL F. MORRIS]

Bibliography: T. E. Bell, *Computer Performance Analysis: Measurement Objectives and Tools*, RAND Corporation, R-584-NASA/PR, February 1971; *Computer Measurement and Evaluation Newsletter*, SHARE, May 1974; R. F. Dunlavey, *Inside Hardware Monitoring*, Tesdata Systems Corporation, 1972; A. Hesser, *Proceedings of the Computer Performance Evaluation Users Group*, *May 1974*, unpublished; K. W. Kolence, *Performance Evaluation Review*, SIGMETRICS, June 1973; M. F. Morris, Performance evaluation: An emerging discipline of the computer sciences, *Proceedings of the Jerusalem Conference on Information Technology*, August 1974; *Proceedings of the Symposium on the Simulation of Computer Systems*, SIGSIM, June 1973 and June 1974.

Diplopoda

The locomotion of most millipedes consists of slow, powerful pushing movements. Detailed studies of these locomotory patterns were made by S. M. Manton, who also showed that some millipedes can run moderately fast, particularly members of the order Nematophora. Recently, some west African species of fast-running Nematophora have been seen to jump short distances. This is a highly unusual activity for a millipede and is regarded with some astonishment by most zoologists.

Jumping millipede. The jumping millipede studied by M. E. G. Evans and J. G. Blower was *Diopsiulus regressus* Silvestri (suborder Stemmiuloidea). Several very similar species of *Diopsiulus* were collected by Blower in Sierra Leone, and he noticed that all could perform a succession of four or five short hops. In fact, these observations were a rediscovery, for 80 years ago O. F. Cook reported that some neotropical Stemmiuloids would "frequently throw themselves several inches when disturbed," and he pointed out that *D. ceylonicus* could also jump.

The jump of *D. regressus* is an escape reaction that is provoked when the millipede is touched. Its response is to run forward a short distance, jump 2–3 cm, land, run forward, jump again, and so on, all in the same straight line. Evans and Blower filmed the jump using a high-speed motion picture camera operated at up to 2000 frames per second. Study of the film revealed that the jump is initiated by a rapid humping of the body about one-quarter of a body length behind the head. This hump becomes a vertical loop that is thrown forward and upward, the hind part of the body being dragged after it (see illustration). The head and front legs remain stationary on the ground until they are overtaken by the rapidly moving body loop, when they are also dragged forward and upward.

Jumping mechanism. A 2.3-cm-long *D. regressus* specimen can run at 5.6 cm/sec, a high speed for a millipede. In a rapidly running nematophoran, the approximation of the sliding sternites causes a

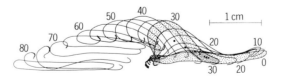

Side view of a jump of the millipede *Diopsiulus regressus*. Every tenth frame of a film taken at 2000 frames/sec is shown; figures are in milliseconds. The initial position (at 0 msec) and the position at lift-off (30 msec) are shaded. The successive positions of the centers of gravity of each profile shown between the 0- and 30-msec positions are indicated by large black dots. (*From M. E. G. Evans and J. G. Blower, A jumping millipede,* Nature, *246: 427–428, 1973*)

slight dorsal hump to form over those legs that are moving forward off the ground. This may be the mechanism that initiates the jump, but since the millipede stops running momentarily before jumping, the mechanism must operate in a stationary animal. Once the hump has started to form, the body muscles that normally cause spiraling are probably responsible for the formation of the vertical body loop. Just behind the head, several front-leg segments remain turned forward to maintain a grip upon the ground so that the front limb of the loop can be swung forward about a fixed point. When the main part of the body reaches lift-off speed for a particular jump, both the front and back ends of the millipede are dragged off the ground.

The jump is caused by the rapid upward and forward movement of the millipede's center of gravity. In a typical jump, the center of gravity of a 2.3-cm-long millipede was accelerated obliquely upward at an angle of 27° to the horizontal over a distance of 0.72 cm in 0.03 sec. This gave the millipede a lift-off speed of 48 cm/sec, and a ground-level-to-ground-level displacement of its center of gravity of about 2.5 cm. The average acceleration during the jumping action was equivalent to 1.6 g. The changes in position of the center of gravity were estimated roughly by cutting cardboard profiles of the position of the millipede at successive 0.005-sec intervals. They showed that accelerations apparently fluctuated between 0 and 4 g. However, when a smoothed distance-time curve was used, acceleration estimates were closer to the 1.6 g average, and maximum accelerations were probably no greater than 2–3 g.

Many small arthropods use a catapult mechanism to produce the high accelerations they need for reasonably sized jumps. The mechanism normally involves a stationary prejump period during which the contracted jump muscles can store sufficient energy for the jump. In *Diopsiulus* the pause between stimulation and jumping is only 0.03–0.04 sec. This is obviously sufficient for the jumping reflex, but it would allow very little time for a catapult mechanism to store much energy. However, since the maximum acceleration involved is relatively small, such a mechanism may be unnecessary.

After jumping, the millipede normally lands in a U-shaped position; even if it descends vertically, it usually falls onto its side. It recovers very rapidly; the body is turned onto its legs, and the head is turned forward, in about 0.05 sec after landing. It then runs forward for a short distance before the next jump.

Spiraling. A characteristic defensive reaction of many millipedes is a rapid body spiraling to enclose the head and legs. This movement proceeds while the millipede is lying on its side. If this movement were restricted to the front half of the body, and the head and front legs remained turned forward to maintain their grip upon the ground, a loop would be formed in the vertical plane and the millipede would jump. It appears, therefore, that the unusual escape reaction of jumping could have evolved from the normal Diplopodan defensive reaction of spiraling.

For background information *see* DIPLOPODA in the McGraw-Hill Encyclopedia of Science and Technology. [M. E. G. EVANS]

Bibliography: O. F. Cook, *Amer. Natur.*, 29: 1111–1120, 1895; M. E. G. Evans and J. G. Blower, *Nature*, 246:427–428, 1973; S. M. Manton, *J. Linn. Soc. (Zool.)*, 42:299–368, 1954, and 43:487–556, 1958.

Doppler radar

In the past few years microwave pulse Doppler radar facilities have become increasingly available to researchers in the field of meteorology. This article discusses the most recent developments in the application of a dual Doppler radar system for the observation and study of the kinematics of convective storms.

Radar operating techniques. Pulse Doppler radars are capable of sensing and measuring the velocity of targets and are therefore useful tools for the observation of the movements of precipitation particles. This capability of Doppler radar relies on the fact that a receding or approaching target produces continuous variations in the phase of the backscattered radar signal. These variations can be interpreted as a virtual increase (approaching motion) or decrease (receding motion) with respect to the transmitted frequency of the radar signal. The Doppler frequency shift is proportional to the velocity with which the target is approaching or receding in the direction of the radar beam (radial velocity).

The Doppler frequency shift associated with the velocity of atmospheric targets, such as precipitation particles or artificial chaff, is always a very small fraction (10^{-6}–10^{-8}) of the radar operating frequency. The observation and measurement of such small frequency shifts require excellent radar system frequency-stability characteristics that are not usually found in conventional radars but can be added without a drastic increase in equipment cost. It must be noted that pulse Doppler radar effectively samples the backscattered signal at the radar pulse repetition rate and can therefore provide unambiguous Doppler frequency observations only in the frequency range allowed by the sampling rate. The Doppler frequency shift for the radial velocity of a given target increases with the transmitted frequency. Decreasing the radar operating frequency thus increases the effective velocity coverage for the same sampling rate. Since the need for increasing velocity coverage would otherwise require an increase of the pulse repetition rate (which reduces the radar maximum range), it is advantageous to use the longest possible wavelength. The choice of wavelengths is limited, however, to centimetric waves if production of narrow radar beams with antennas of reasonable size is desired.

Since Doppler radars can observe and measure the radial velocity of targets, they are well suited for the observation of the motion of raindrops (precipitation). However, precipitation has the form of a "distributed" target; that is, there are numerous independent scatterers distributed in space. The backscattered signal that is selected at any given time after the transmitted pulse by a sampling circuit called a range gate is therefore due to the contribution of a finite scattering region that is determined by the radar beam cross-section area and half the radar pulse length in space (pulse volume). The backscattered signal sampled by the range gate is thus composed of a large number of separate scattering amplitudes, each having a Doppler frequency shift associated with the radial velocity of a particular scatterer. Therefore, a spectrum of frequency shifts (Doppler spectrum) is observed. This Doppler spectrum constitutes the basic velocity information acquired by the Doppler radar when it is used for the observation of precipitation systems.

At each range gate, a Doppler spectrum can be evaluated by processing the signal sampled at that range. The basic processing operation is a Fourier transform of the sampled signal. In order to take advantage of the radar resolution, the processing must be done at a large number of range gates, with the only limitation being that the gates must be spaced by more than one radar pulse width. The signals obtained at successive range gates can be digitized by analog-to-digital converters operating at high speed, with the digitized signals stored in a memory and then processed by a fast arithmetic system. Fast Fourier transform techniques are used for greatest computing efficiency. Although these systems are capable of processing several thousand spectra per second, they require large input memories and produce a volume of information that is difficult to handle.

Mean Doppler. The amount of information can be reduced by considering only the first moment of the Doppler spectrum (mean radial velocity, or mean Doppler) and the spectrum width. Although the mean Doppler can be evaluated directly from the Doppler spectra, it can be more easily obtained by use of mean-frequency estimators that do not involve the computation of the whole spectrum through the Fourier transform operation. One of the most efficient estimators uses the complex autocovariance $\mu_{12} = \overline{C_1 C_2}^*$ of the signal C sampled at a given range gate. C_1 and C_2 are successive samples obtained at the pulse repetition rate, and the asterisk denotes complex conjugate. It can be shown that the argument α of the complex expression μ_{12} is equal to $\alpha = 2\pi f_0 T$, where T is the time between successive samples at the same range gate. If the spectrum is narrow or symmetrical, or both, f_0 is the mean frequency. It can also be shown that the complex autocovariance estimator is not biased by receiver noise and therefore can operate at small signal-to-noise ratios.

With this technique, the mean Doppler can be easily processed simultaneously at a large number of range gates with relatively simple digital circuits. The spectrum variance can be measured by a slightly different approach.

Probing motion in convective storms. It can be assumed that precipitation particles move with the air in their environment and are therefore good tracers for air motion if appropriate corrections are made to eliminate the influence of particle terminal velocity on the Doppler measurements. Observing the motion of precipitation particles inside convective storms therefore offers a unique technique for the study of kinematic processes in storms. However, it should be noted that the use of a single radar beam to scan the three-dimensional structure of a storm is of limited value, since only the radial velocity of precipitation particles can be observed. However, even though this technique is limited, it has in some cases revealed well-organized structures in the radial velocity fields that have suggested the presence of strong, persistent vorticity and convergence.

A more complete study of three-dimensional storm structure can be made by the simultaneous use of several scanning radars. For example, two Doppler radars installed at different locations, and operating independently with intersecting beams, will provide two different radial velocity components at the region where the beams intersect. These two components can be used to evaluate the two-dimensional velocity in the tilted plane that is common to the two radar beams and the base line between the radars. Also, if two radar beams are allowed to scan the same tilted plane simultaneously, as shown in Fig. 1, two different radial velocity fields are independently observed and can be mapped in that plane. The two radial velocity fields can be expressed at rectangular grid points. The samples are subsequently combined so that, at any grid point where radar observations are available, a motion vector that would produce two radial velocity components identical to those observed can be evaluated.

The method, which is illustrated in Fig. 1, involves the sequential scanning of planes of different tilts so that the three-dimensional structure of the motion fields in storms can be observed. For small plane tilts, the contribution due to the vertical velocity is negligible, and the estimated velocity is essentially the horizontal air motion. For larger tilts, the contribution due to particle terminal velocity must be assessed and removed. When this is done, the velocity presented in a tilted plane is the three-dimensional air velocity projected onto that plane.

An example of the observations of motion fields inside a convective storm by use of this method was first presented a few years ago. Recently, such observations were made inside convective storms

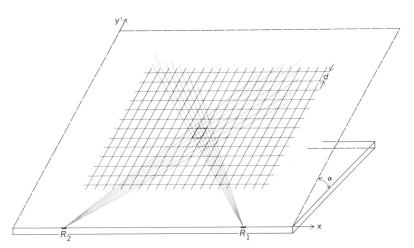

Fig. 1. Scanning a common plane by two radars installed at different locations (R_1 and R_2). The radar data are originally obtained in polar coordinates and are then mapped in rectangular coordinates (grid spacing, d) common to the two radars. Here α is the plane tilt.

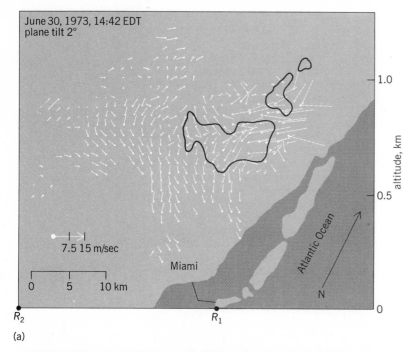

(a)

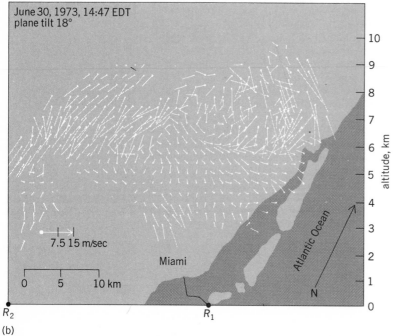

(b)

Fig. 2. Presentation of the motion fields in planes of (a) tilt 2° and (b) 18°, each scanned by radars at positions R_1 and R_2. The motion is displayed in the form of vectors showing the air velocity away from the dot, thus indicating the origin of the vector and the geographical position of the estimates. The altitude variation in the tilted plane is also indicated. The solid line outlines the storm region where the estimated precipitation intensity exceeds 10 mm per hour. At large wind speeds, the vectors appear as broken lines; these breaks are produced by the display and have no significance.

deflection by the storm) can be clearly seen in the 2° tilt plane. Also, note the inflow to the storm, which takes place at higher altitude. At the highest altitude (about 8 km), which is reached with the plane of larger tilt, velocity gradients are large and suggest a strong interaction between the dominant northwesterly synoptic-scale flow and the storm circulation. Each plane can be scanned by the two radar beams in less than 30 sec, and a vector field such as that shown in Fig. 2 can easily be evaluated and presented a few seconds after the plane has been scanned. Clearly, this method offers excellent capability for real-time monitoring of the kinematics of precipitation systems.

Estimating and evaluating velocity fields. The horizontal convergence of the velocity field in any tilted plane can be computed, and the velocity normal to that tilted plane can be evaluated, from the application of the equation of continuity of mass for an incompressible fluid, $\nabla \cdot \vec{V} = 0$. If this equation is applied to the velocity data observed in tilted planes, the equation shown here results,

$$\frac{\partial w'}{\partial \alpha} = -v' + y'\left(\frac{\partial u'}{\partial x'} + \frac{\partial v'}{\partial y'}\right)$$

where u' and v' are the velocity components along the rectangular coordinates x' and y' in the tilted plane; w' is the velocity component normal to the plane; and α is the plane tilt. Integrating $\partial w'/\partial \alpha$ will then provide measurement of the component normal to each plane.

For convenience in meteorological analysis, the velocity components evaluated from the method outlined above must ultimately be converted into horizontal and vertical motion components. These data can then be expressed in a cartesian coordinate system of horizontal planes at different altitudes.

To accomplish this, it may be more appropriate to first project the velocity data onto horizontal planes. This procedure eliminates the contribution of vertical shear, which is present in the tilted planes, and permits the three-dimensional structure of the motion fields to be more clearly shown. If the maximum tilt of the plane is small (<15°), and if the contribution due to particle's terminal velocity is removed, the original data obtained in the tilted planes can be identified with the horizontal u, v components of velocity. A first estimate of horizontal convergence in the horizontal planes can be computed and followed by a first evaluation of the field of vertical velocity. These results can then be used to correct the first estimate of the velocity fields.

The dual Doppler radar method outlined here offers a unique opportunity for real-time mapping of the motion fields inside precipitation systems. Motion fields can be sampled at grid points spaced by less than 1 km, thereby allowing the observation and monitoring of the storm microstructure. These measurements can be extended to the storm environment if airborne radar-reflecting targets are introduced there.

For background information *see* DOPPLER RADAR; WEATHER FORECASTING AND PREDICTION in the McGraw-Hill Encyclopedia of Science and Technology.   [ROGER LHERMITTE]

Bibliography: R. Brown and K. Crawford, *Preprints of the 15th Radar Meteorological Confer-*

developing under sea breeze conditions in the area of Miami, FL. Selected examples, which are presented in Fig. 2, illustrate the capability of the method. The velocity data are displayed in two selected planes of very different tilts (2° and 18°) to reveal the three-dimensional structure of the storm. The low-level sea breeze inflow (and its

ence, American Meteorological Society, Boston, pp. 16–21, 27–34, 1972; H. Groginsky, *Preprints of the 15th Radar Meteorological Conference*, American Meteorological Society, Boston, pp. 233–236, 1972; R. Lhermitte, Real-time processing of meteorological Doppler radar signals, *Preprints of the 15th Radar Meteorological Conference*, American Meteorological Society, Boston, 1972; R. Lhermitte, *Atmospheric Technology*, no. 6, National Center for Atmospheric Research, in press; R. Lhermitte, *Science*, 182(4109):258–272, 1973; R. Serafin, *Atmospheric Technology*, no. 6, National Center for Atmospheric Research, in press.

Earth, heat flow in

Observations of heat flow through the ocean floor are being successfully interpreted in terms of the cooling of aging lithosphere, and continental heat flow can be interpreted as the additive effect of heat from the mantle and heat generated at a high level from crustal concentrations of radiogenic elements. Most of the high heat flow areas of the world that are being expressed as active volcanoes are associated with extremes of topography and are concentrated close to active plate margins. *See* EARTH, INTERIOR OF; OCEANIC ISLANDS.

Hot spots are a group of volcanic features that occur in both continents and oceans. They possess characteristics that cannot be explained in the above three ways. Hot spots can be defined as topographically high areas of volcanic activity distinct from those commonly developed at plate margins. Interest in hot spots has developed because they might help to show how lithospheric plates are driven across the surface of the Earth and because of a hope, since shown to be unfounded, that they might provide a fixed frame to which plate motions could be referred. Studies of hot

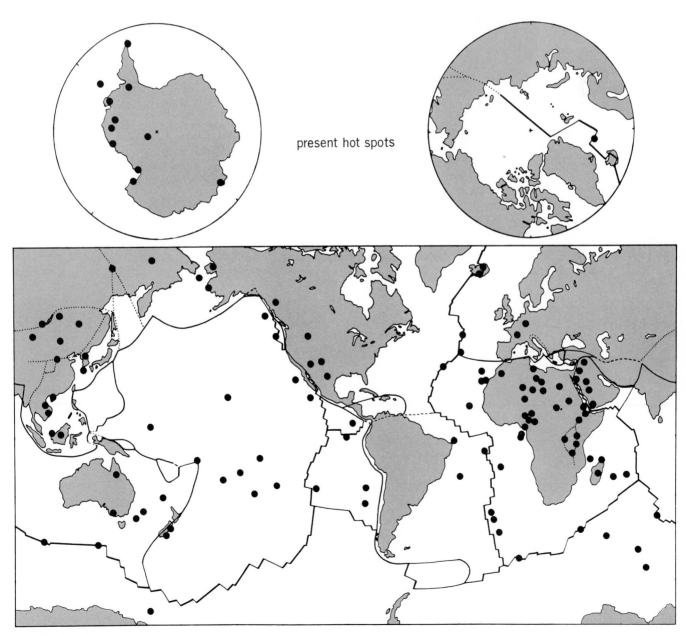

present hot spots

Fig. 1.   World distribution of 120 hot spots where volcanic activity has occurred within the last 10,000,000 years.

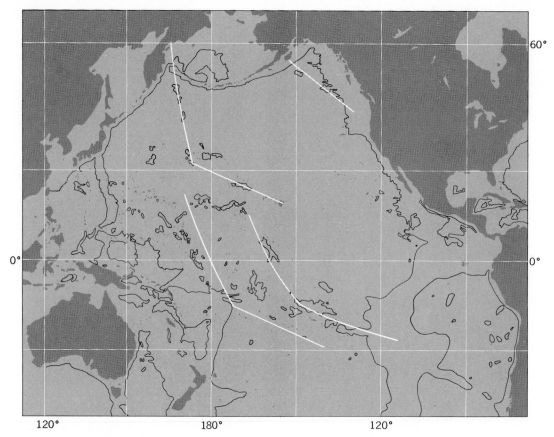

Fig. 2. Hot spot trajectories constructed by rotating the Pacific plate 34° about a pole at 67°N73°W and then 45° about a pole at 23°N110°W. (*From W. J. Morgan, in R. Shagam, ed., Studies in Earth and Space Sciences, Geol. Soc. Amer. Mem. 132, pp. 7–22, 1972*)

spots formed during the last 2,000,000,000 years are providing evidence of how continents rupture and of how long the rigid lithosphere has been breaking up and moving about in the complex interwoven cycles of ocean opening and closing that result in continental drift.

Present hot spots. A striking feature of hot spots of the world is their uneven distribution (see Fig. 1). This inhomogeneity is partly, but cannot be entirely, due to the difficulty of successfully recognizing all hot spots, especially in extensive oceanic areas such as the Pacific. Hot spots like Iceland are concentrated along the axes of spreading oceanic ridges, where they are readily recognized by their anomalously high topography as well as by the distinctive chemistry of the lavas they erupt. W. J. Morgan pointed out that a majority of this group of hot spots lie close to triple junctions, places where three plate boundaries meet (for example, the Azores and Bouvet Islands in the central and South Atlantic). Concentrations of hot spots within plates are very uneven. A major concentration lies in the northern half of the African plate. Volcanism within this plate started roughly simultaneously in a number of widely separated areas about 25,000,000 years ago and coincided with the beginning of an episode of rifting that has led to the separation of Arabia from Africa along the Red Sea and the Gulf of Aden and to the development of the East African Rift Valley. A similar episode of rifting and volcanism in Africa

marked the breakup of Gondwanaland between 100,000,000 and 200,000,000 years ago.

More than 10 years ago, J. T. Wilson showed that aseismic ridges and lines of islands in oceans could be explained as products of the passage of rigid oceanic lithosphere over underlying hot spots. Morgan produced supporting evidence for this hypothesis by showing that three L-shaped ridges in the Pacific (Fig. 2) could be described by two successive rotations of the rigid Pacific plate over three hot spots which had been fixed with respect to each other during the last 70,000,000 years. Deep-sea drilling close to the Line Islands (the upper arm of the middle of the three L-shaped ridges of Fig. 2) during 1973–1974 has shown that more complicated relations between hot spots and plate motions are needed to account for the aseismic ridges of the Pacific. In this respect, Pacific Ocean hot spots are being shown to resemble those of the Atlantic and Indian oceans, which are known to erupt intermittently and to move with respect to each other in complex and irregular ways at velocities at times as high as 6 cm/yr.

Atlantic hot spots have also been shown to have lives ranging from 200,000,000 to 20,000,000 years, although some may be even shorter-lived. The spectacular development of hot spots on the African plate during the last 25,000,000 years, and during the breakup of Gondwanaland, has shown (Fig. 4) a characteristic sequence of development from uplift and volcanism through the develop-

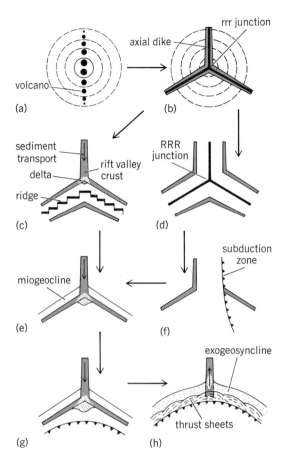

Fig. 3. Schematic origin and evolution of plume-generated triple junctions: (a) uplift develops over plume with crestal alkaline volcanoes; (b) three rift valleys develop, meeting at an rrr (rift-rift-rift) junction; (c) two rift arms develop into a single accreting plate margin (ridge), and continental separation ensues; (d) three rift arms develop into accreting plate margins that meet at an RRR junction, where three spreading ridges meet; (e) Atlantic-type continental margin evolves with growth of delta at mouth of a failed arm and miogeoclines; (f) one arm of RRR system of d begins to close by marginal subduction; (g) Atlantic-type continental margin with miogeoclines and failed rift arms approaches a subduction zone; (h) continental margin collides with subduction zone, collisional orogeny ensues, sediment transport in the failed arm reverses polarity, and failed arm is preserved as an aulacogen striking at a high angle into an orogenic belt. (From K. Burke and J. F. Dewey, Plume generated triple junctions: Key indicators in applying plate tectonics to old rocks, J. Geol., 81:406–433, 1973)

ment of crestal rifts on uplifts and three-armed rift junctions to continental rupture (Figs. 3a–d and 5). The most common sequence of events (Fig. 3c) is for two rift arms at a triple-rift junction to spread, and thus create a new ocean, and for the third to survive as a failed rift arm striking at a high angle into the continent. The characteristic irregular shapes of continental margins (Fig. 5) are thus seen as a normal consequence of rupture along lines joining triple-rift junctions over hot spots. The major deltas, such as those of the Niger and the Mississippi, which lie at the mouths of failed rift arms, are places where exceptional accumulations of petroleum are commonly found.

Aulacogen patterns. One of the main results of the application of the principles of plate tectonics

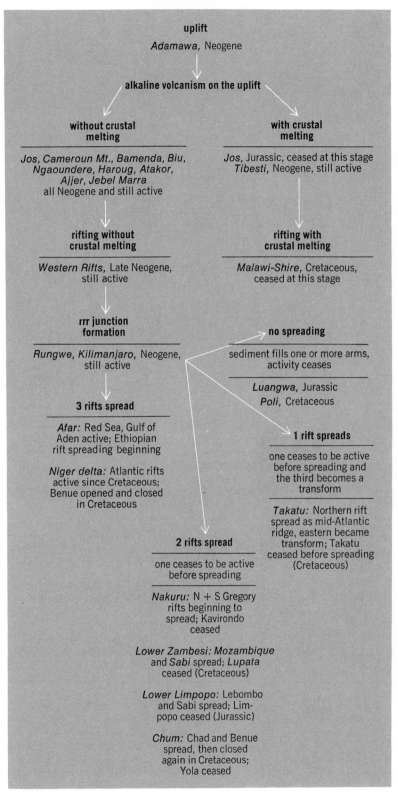

Fig. 4. Sequences of African structural development, (From K. Burke and A. J. Whiteman, Uplift, rifting and the break-up of Africa, in D. H. Tarling and S. K. Runcorn, eds., Implications of Continental Drift to the Earth Sciences, Academic Press, vol. 2, pp. 735–755, 1973)

to the interpretation of continental geology has been the recognition that orogenic belts mark places where oceans have first opened and then closed (the so-called Wilson cycle, after J. T. Wil-

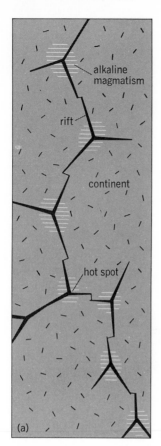
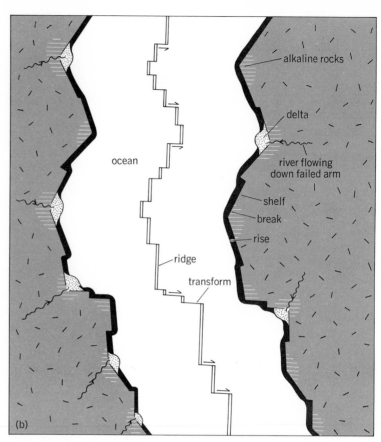

Fig. 5. Sketch maps representing early stages of Wilson cycle. (a) Continental crust starting to rupture along rifts that meet at rrr junctions over hot spots characterized by alkaline magmatism. Major irregularities in continental margins mark sites of former rrr triple junctions; minor irregularities mark misfit connections between propagating rifts. (b) Ocean in advanced Atlantic stage. Rivers flow down failed arms to feed deltas at reentrants on continental margins. Shapes of continental margins retain pattern of continental rupture. Alkaline rocks with ages dating rupture are concentrated at projections and embayments. Shapes of deltas and interdelta miogeoclinal sediment wedges are more variable than shown and are controlled by such factors as wind direction, transform strike, salt tectonics, and currents both at surface and at oceanic depths. (From J. F. Dewey and K. Burke, Hot spots and continental break-up: Implications for collisional orogeny, Geology, 2:57–60, 1974)

son). The irregular continental margins formed by ruptures that linked lines of hot spots during ocean opening can be recognized where the oceans have later closed as bends in mountain belts, some having failed arms leading away at high angles into cratonic areas (Fig. 3h). This relationship between failed rift arms and mountain belts was first recognized more than 25 years ago by N. Shatsky in the Soviet Union. Shatsky coined the word aulacogen for the failed rifts. It was not recognized that the junction of an aulacogen with a mountain belt marks the site of a former hot spot until mountain building was interpreted in terms of ocean opening and closing.

Because the pattern formed by an aulacogen and its junction with a mountain belt is so distinctive (as in Fig. 3h), the sites of old hot spots have proved readily recognizable, and during 1974 it was shown that hot spots have formed a distinctive feature of the Wilson cycle throughout the last 2,000,000,000 years. Prior to that time, more complex patterns prevailed, and it has been inferred that, because of greater rates of radiogenic heat generation, the thick rigid lithosphere that characterizes the plate tectonic regime had not developed.

Source of volcanic materials. Although much has been learned in recent years about hot spot distribution in space and time, no correspondingly clear picture has emerged of the source of the volcanic materials in the hot spots. There is some geochemical evidence that indicates a source at a depth greater than the 100 km or so that is sufficient to produce most hot spot volcanic material. Among the hypotheses of hot spot origin currently under consideration are: production of hot spots along propagating fractures in the lithosphere; origin by partial melting at the abraded base of the lithosphere, leaving a dense root in the mantle that serves as an anchor to keep the hot spot fixed; and an origin from deep-mantle plumes. Seismic evidence has revealed the existence of an area of anomalous density just above the core-mantle boundary beneath the Hawaiian Islands. This anomalous mantle is compatible with the last two hypotheses.

For background information see EARTH, HEAT FLOW IN; EARTH, INTERIOR OF; RIFT VALLEY; VOLCANOLOGY in the McGraw-Hill Encyclopedia of Science and Technology.

[KEVIN BURKE; W. S. F. KIDD]
Bibliography: K. Burke and J. F. Dewey,

J. Geol., 81:406–433, 1973; K. Burke, W. S. F. Kidd, and J. T. Wilson, *Nature*, 245:133–137, 1973; S. R. Hart, J. G. Schilling, and J. L. Powell, *Nature Phys. Sci.*, 246:104–107, 1973; E. R. Kanasewich et al., *J. Geophys. Res.*, 78:1361, 1371, 1973.

Earth, interior of

The acceptance of the concept of continental drift has revolutionized the earth sciences. Although the mantle of the Earth is a solid, on geological time scales it must behave like a fluid. One of the most important unanswered questions concerns the mechanism that causes continental drift.

Energy and motion in surface plates. The surface of the Earth is broken up into a number of plates that move with respect to one another. Plates apparently are created from mantle rock at ocean ridges and descend into the mantle at trenches. Lateral motion between plates results in great faults such as the San Andreas in California.

Relative motion between plates is responsible for most mountain building, earthquakes, and volcanism. The energy source for plate motions is also the energy source for these secondary phenomena. The only energy source of sufficient magnitude is the heat generated by the decay of radioactive elements within the Earth. Principal sources of heat are uranium-235, uranium-238, thorium-232, and potassium-40. The concentration of these elements within the Earth can be estimated from the measured heat flow to the Earth's surface and the relative concentrations of these elements in surface rocks.

Once the energy source is found, it is necessary to determine the mechanism that converts heat into motion in order to explain the relative motion of the surface plates. This can be done if the solid mantle of the Earth behaves like a fluid on geological time scales. Such behavior is in accord with present understanding of the physics of mantle rocks. At high temperatures crystalline solids under low stresses deform because of diffusion of atoms and dislocations within the crystals. This deformation is strongly temperature-dependent; only at temperatures near the melting temperature does significant deformation occur. Studies of the subsidence due to glaciation and the subsequent uplift have supplied quantitative values for the fluidlike properties of the solid mantle.

Mantle convection. A fluid that is heated from within and cooled on the upper surface is subject to thermal convection. The interior of the Earth is hot, and the uncompressed density of the interior rocks is less than that of the cool, near-surface rocks. In the gravitational field of the Earth, the cool near-surface rocks tend to sink, and the hot interior rocks rise. Numerical calculations of the resultant flows have been made by D. L. Turcotte, K. E. Torrance, and A. T. Hsui. A typical flow pattern is shown in Fig. 1.

The near-surface rocks are cold and brittle and form the rigid surface plates of plate tectonics. Deformations of the surface rocks cause fractures that result in earthquakes. The surface plates are created from hot ascending mantle rocks at ocean ridges. During the ascent of the mantle rocks, partial melting of the basalt component occurs owing to the reduction of pressure. The liquid basalt is light and mobile and rises to the surface, causing volcanism at ocean ridges and forming the ocean crust above the Moho.

As the near-surface rocks convect away from the ridge, they cool by conduction of heat to the surface. It is deduced from the topography of the ocean ridges that the thickness of the surface plates increases as the square root of their age. This is the expected relation for a cooling plate, and it is concluded that the lower boundary of the plate is defined by the temperature at which the plate significantly deforms under stress (about 1000°C).

Because of thermal contraction the uncompressed density of the cool surface plate is greater than that of the underlying hot mantle. As the plate thickens, it becomes gravitationally unstable and plunges into the mantle at an ocean trench. The gravitational body force on the dense plate pulls it down like a stone in water, and the surface plate is pulled with it; this is a primary mechanism causing continental drift.

It has been deduced from seismic observations

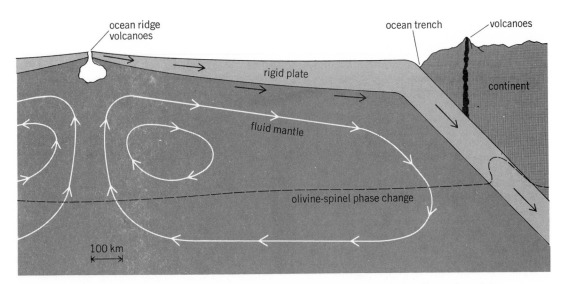

Fig. 1. Illustration of two-dimensional mantle convection and the body forces (arrows) on the surface plate.

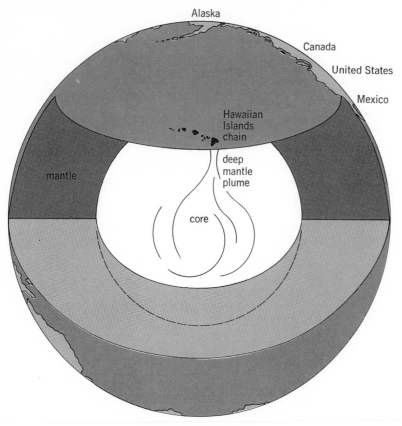

Fig. 2. Proposed deep mantle plume beneath Hawaii.

and laboratory studies that there is a primary phase change in the mantle at a depth of about 400 km. Pressure causes the olivine component of mantle rock to compress to the denser spinel structure. Laboratory measurements of this phase change show that it occurs at a shallower depth in the cool descending plate, thus increasing the density of that plate. The result is an additional body force that also pulls the plate down into the mantle.

The surface plates in the Pacific Ocean have extensive trench systems, and it has been observed that they have relatively high plate velocities, almost 10 cm/year. However, the surface plates in the Atlantic Ocean have significant relative motion, although they have almost no trench systems to drive their motion. The velocities are small, however, almost 2 cm/year. The ocean ridge system has an average elevation above the ocean basins of about 3 km. This elevation is a surface expression of the horizontal pressure gradient associated with thermal convection in the Earth's mantle. If molasses is poured on a table, its thickness will increase until the component of gravity is sufficient to spread the molasses out. An ocean ridge behaves similarly.

A third body force that may be significant in driving the surface plates is the viscous traction forces on the base of the rigid surface plates. If the fluid upper mantle is convecting faster than the surface plates are, the traction forces will tend to drag the surface plates along.

Mantle plumes. Although the relative movement between plates explains the linear features

associated with the margins of the plates, there are also volcanoes, earthquakes, and mountain building in the interior of plates. An example is the Hawaiian Islands, which are the end of an island and seamount chain that extends to the Aleutian Islands. *See* OCEANIC ISLANDS.

In order to explain this and other examples of extensive volcanism within the interior of plates, W. J. Morgan has proposed another form of mantle convection, in addition to the two-dimensional form of mantle convection illustrated in Fig. 1. His suggestion is that cylindrical plumes of hot mantle rock rise from near the core-mantle boundary. The Hawaiian island chain is the result of the motion of the Pacific plate over the fixed mantle plume (see Fig. 2). Other proposed deep mantle plumes would be beneath Iceland, Tristan da Cunha (including Gough Island), Easter Island, the Galapagos Islands, and Reunion Island.

Kimberlite geotherms. Much of what is now known about the interior of the Earth has been inferred. Detailed studies have been carried out to determine the distribution of seismic wave speeds within the Earth. These studies place constraints on the composition of the mantle but give little information on the dynamic processes that are occurring.

During the past 5 years it has been accepted that mantle rocks are exposed at the surface of the Earth. One source of mantle rocks is kimberlite pipes. Kimberlite pipes are small regions of broken rock which extend deep into the crust. They are caused by kimberlite eruptions which transport diamonds and other well-preserved mantle rocks to the surface. Because of the rapid vertical velocities in these eruptions, the mantle mineralogy is preserved. By studying the composition of the mantle rocks, F. R. Boyd has been able to determine the depth at which they originate, and the temperature at that depth. By studying a series of rocks which originated from different depths in the mantle he has been able to deduce a temperature profile to a depth of 250 km. Since temperature is a sensitive function of transport processes, these studies have produced important information on material transport and forces in the upper mantle.

For background information *see* CONTINENT FORMATION; EARTH, INTERIOR OF; OCEANIC ISLANDS in the McGraw-Hill Encyclopedia of Science and Technology.   [DONALD L. TURCOTTE]

Bibliography: F. R. Boyd, *Geochim. Cosmochim. Acta*, 73:2533–2546, 1973; W. J. Morgan, *Bull. Amer. Ass. Petrol. Geol.*, 56:203–213, 1973; D. L. Turcotte, K. E. Torrance, and A. T. Hsui, *Methods Comput. Phys.*, 13:431–454, 1973.

Electrical utility industry

The year 1974 was an extremely critical one for electrical utilities. It began with imported fuel oil, used extensively by East Coast and West Coast generating stations, virtually shut off, and with sharply rising fuel prices for generating stations across the nation. Unable to get relief, in the form of rate increases, fast enough to counter this sharp rise in operating costs, many utilities encountered extreme difficulty in raising money to pay for major additions already under construction to supply an expected increase in the demand for electricity. And there was great uncertainty about how the new energy conservation movement and rising electricity costs would affect future demand.

Fuel and the oil embargo. In large degree, this problem with fuel stemmed directly from the oil embargo imposed in November 1973 by the Arab nations, acting as a group through the Organization of Arab Oil Exporting Countries. As a result, the supply of oil to the United States was curtailed by an amount estimated at 6 to 10%. The United States government had promptly launched a campaign for the voluntary conservation of all remaining energy resources, setting as a goal the complete independence from foreign sources by 1980. Imports of Arab oil did not return to normal until May 1974, and then at a price level 300 to 400% above the previous level.

The impact on electrical utilities was extremely severe, because 86% of their total generating capability consumes fossil fuel—oil, gas, coal, or lignite—and 15% of their total output during preembargo 1972 was fueled with oil. During 1973, prior to the embargo, oil-fueled generation had climbed to 16.8% of the industry's total output as efforts to conserve natural gas for higher-priority uses spurred many utilities to convert gas-burning stations to oil. In one year's time, the dependence on natural gas had dropped to 18% from the 1972 level of nearly 21%; but this move to conserve gas boosted the dependence on oil and sharply increased operating costs for utilities that had been buying natural gas at very low prices on long-term contracts.

An additional disadvantage was that only certain oils could be burned, under the air-pollution restrictions prescribed by the Environmental Protection Administration (EPA) to satisfy the Clean Air Act. In many areas this required using oil imported only from low-sulfur fields, mostly in Africa, or oil that had been specially processed at one of the few refineries that were equipped for desulfurizing oils.

Prior to the Arab embargo, most of the generating stations on the East Coast had already converted from coal to imported oil to meet environmental restrictions, while those on the West Coast had switched from gas to imported oil to conserve natural gas. Hence the sudden shutdown of the largest source of imported low-sulfur oil sparked a frantic scramble for acceptable fuel, and the prices soared 300 to 400% in a few weeks. Fuel oil soon became almost unavailable at any price.

The United States government moved promptly by setting up the Federal Energy Office (FEO), later to become the Federal Energy Administration after Congress passed enabling legislation. The FEO, assuming coal to be in adequate supply, promptly urged reconversion to coal for a long list of electric generating stations, but many of the reconversions were blocked by EPA's insistence that emergency reconversions be accompanied by commitments to retrofit antipollution facilities on a crash basis.

Another FEO directive, that East Coast utilities procure electricity via transmission linkages from coal-burning stations in the Midwest, failed to recognize limitations on the capability of the transmission grid, weakened as it was by environmentalist opposition to the construction of certain key sections. The directive also failed to assure Midwestern utilities that they could obtain the additional

coal for this "coal-by-wire" scheme. Finally, the FEO promoted wide-scale conservation of energy by the residential, commercial, and industrial sectors of the economy, thereby achieving a nationwide drop of about 10% in the use of electricity.

This series of events was detrimental to the nation's electrical utilities in at least four ways. First, it curtailed their use of natural gas, which gave the lowest generating cost because, under long-term contracts, it provided cheap fuel for stations that were the least costly to build and operate. Second, it forced utilities to spend many millions of dollars to convert gas-burning stations to oil, and oil-burning stations to coal. Third, it forced utilities to use alternative fuels at a cost that was not covered by their rates, and which could be covered only after lengthy hearings before regulatory agencies. And last, by promoting conservation of electricity, it deprived utilities of the revenue necessary to pay for the conversions and the more costly fuels required, as well as to finance the building of facilities necessary to serve future demands for electrical service.

Nuclear power plants. Nuclear power plants are the long-range key to easing the pressures of fuel shortages and inflated fuel prices. According to a survey of 27 modern steam stations completed by *Electrical World* late in 1973, three nuclear stations, comprising nearly 20% of the total capability covered, had total power costs averaging 10.4% below those of the fossil-fueled stations. The difference was attributable entirely to savings in fuel costs, which averaged 34% lower for the nuclear stations than for the fossil-fueled stations. The investment cost per kilowatt for these three nuclear stations was very nearly the same as that of coal-burning stations that had some of the costly antipollution facilities that are prescribed for burning coal.

The cost of fossil fuels has risen far more than that of nuclear fuel since the conclusion of *Electrical World*'s survey. Unfortunately, however, only about 5% of the total generating capability of United States utilities during 1974 was nuclear, and some of that was out of service for modifica-

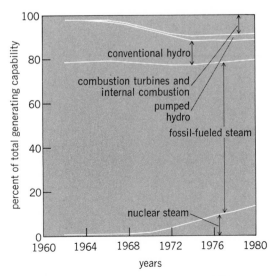

Graph of percent of total generating capabilities supplied by five types of power stations from 1962 to 1980.

tions and repairs (see illustration). The approximately 20,000,000 kW of nuclear generation that remained in service should be credited with saving the equivalent of nearly 200,000,000 bbl of fuel oil, which is a very important step toward the projected self-sufficiency in fuels.

Generating additions. The electrical utility industry entered 1974 with 418,904,000 kW of generating additions under construction or planned to the early 1980s. Of this total, 43,607,000 kW were scheduled for completion in 1974, at a cost of about $12,000,000,000. They were to serve an expected gain of 33,100,000 kW in summer-peak demand and to provide a modest margin for retiring obsolescent units (over 40 years old) and for boosting the reserve for reliability. Delay in completing a few units cut the year's net additions to 37,180,000 kW. But the conservation program and cool summer weather slashed the increase in peak demand to 3,500,000 kW. Consequently the reserve margin soared to 30%, far higher than could possibly be supported financially by revenues that had been cut by the conservation program (see table).

By mid-1974 many utilities had invoked austerity and started postponing or canceling generation additions planned for future years. Additions under construction for 1975, of course, were too nearly completed (it takes about four years to build a fossil-fueled station, six years for nuclear) to afford much advantage from delaying completion. But those planned for completion during 1976 and several years thereafter were cut as much as 40% to save about 27.5% during the remainder of the decade. These savings, of course, are based on the premise that the energy conservation ethic will remain in effect until 1980, the first year in which energy self-sufficiency seems remotely possible.

Some 9,751,000 kW of the generation additions during 1974 were nuclear, about 26% of the total additions, and 12,236,000 kW are scheduled for 1975. Thus the additions during just 2 years will

exceed the total nuclear capability on line at the end of 1973. By 1980, nuclear generation is scheduled at a total of 86,626,000 kW, 13.6% of the 638,918,000 kW total generation in service. And this nuclear generation should supply upward of 25% of all the nation's electricity while saving more than 800,000,000 bbl of fuel oil in 1980 alone and holding down the average price of electricity by nearly 10%.

During 1974 some 21,081,000 kW of fossil-fueled generation was completed and put in service. Of this, about 2,372,000 kW replaced 40-year-old stations that are too obsolescent for continued economical operation or too costly to retrofit with antipollution devices. Generating units in these new stations are designed to burn fuels as follows: coal, 17 units; oil, 20; and natural gas (in gas-producing areas), 8. Most of them are prepared to burn alternative fuels if necessary. Additions nearing completion for 1975 total 23,819,000 kW, of which 2,497,000 kW will replace obsolescent generation. Of these 1975 additions, 18 units will burn coal, 22, oil, and only 2, natural gas. Thus the trend away from gas as boiler fuel will have become almost complete, as far as new electric generating stations are concerned.

After 1975, fossil-fueled generation additions are slated lower each year until at 9,276,000 kW (after retirements) in 1980, they will be, for the first time, less than nuclear. Moreover, as nuclear capability becomes more ample, the fossil-fueled generation will be used increasingly to supply the additional energy required on week days, and be shut down nights and weekends; this type of operation, commonly known as cycling, consumes considerably less fuel than continuous, or base-load, operation. Both trends reflect the electrical utility industry's effort to conserve fuels that are expected to remain in short supply.

EPA regulations. The major problem for fossil-fueled stations today is compliance with air- and water-pollution regulations. The only fuels that seem likely to remain in ample supply are coal and, in some areas, lignite. Thus essentially all new installations, and many of the existing ones, require high-efficiency electrostatic precipitators to capture 99% or more of the particulates in the combustion gases. In addition, unless the coal is extremely low in sulfur content, they could be required by the EPA to add sulfur-removal equipment in the gas stream. These facilities add as much as 45% to the cost of the station and consume up to 5% of its electrical output. In addition, EPA has decreed that most steam stations have cooling towers for the water used to condense the exhaust steam; if these towers are of the evaporative type, they add another 3 to 4% to the station investment and further reduce its net output.

Gas turbine. Combustion, or gas, turbines reached a new peak of 6,593,000 kW in 1974 additions, many of them linked by heat-recovery boilers to steam turbines in an arrangement known as combined cycle. This arrangement, by using part of the heat that is discharged in the exhaust of conventional combustion turbines, achieves a substantial improvement in fuel economy for a reasonable increase in investment cost. The greatest disadvantage is that present designs require either

United States electric power industry statistics for 1974*

Parameter	Amount	Increase over 1973, %
Generating capability, kW ($\times 10^3$)		
Total	475,672	8.5
Conventional hydro	53,997	0.6
Pumped-storage	9,317	22.5
Fossil-fueled steam	337,066	5.9
Nuclear steam	30,821	46.2
Combustion turbine and		
internal combustion	44,471	17.7
Energy production, kWhr ($\times 10^6$)	1,888,500	0.3
Energy sales, kWhr ($\times 10^6$)		
Total	1,707,501	0.3
Residential	557,000	0.5
Commercial	393,000	−1.0
Industrial	694,000	1.0
Miscellaneous	63,501	−2.1
Revenue, total ($\times 10^6$)	$39,500	24.8
Capital expenditures, total ($\times 10^6$)	$19,198	2.5
Customers ($\times 10^3$)		
Residential	70,700	1.8
Total	79,800	1.7
Residential usage, kWhr (average)	7,970	−1.3
Residential bill, ¢/kWhr (average)	2.88	20.9

*From *Elec. World*, Sept. 15, 1974, and extrapolations from Edison Electric Institute monthly data.

gas or distillate oil for fuel, both of which are likely to remain in short supply. Efforts today are directed toward developing simple gasifiers to produce suitable combustion-turbine fuel from coal or residual (heavy) oil. Until such devices become available, however, the construction of combustion-turbine stations is expected to decline to 2,354,000 kW in 1975 and to even lower levels thereafter.

Hydroelectric stations. Conventional hydroelectric additions dropped to a very low 330,000 kW in 1974, but are scheduled to return to a more normal 1,860,000 kW in 1975 as the first of three 600,000-kW units goes on line at Grand Coulee. With these additions, conventional hydro capability will rise to 55,857,000 kW, some 10.8% of the total generating capability of United States electrical utilities. But it should be recognized that most of the added capability stems from converting existing stations to part-time, or cycling, operation or, as at Grand Coulee, to harness additional water flows made available by new upstream storage. Actually, very few sites remain where it would be feasible to build new hydro stations, and the best of these, in the Snake River canyon, has been blocked by special-interest groups for 20 years and appears to be a lost cause.

Pumped-storage hydroelectric stations. Pumped-storage hydroelectric stations are a very desirable complement to nuclear generation in that they use the surplus of low-fuel-cost generation late at night to pump water into high-level reservoirs. The stored water is then used during heavy-load periods of the day to generate additional electricity in a hydroelectric station, thus functioning much like a giant storage battery. This generating cycle recovers about 65% of the energy used for pumping, and at a time when the energy is needed to serve customers. Some 3,495,000 kW of such additions were completed in 1973, followed by 1,704,000 kW in 1974. The growth will slacken somewhat during the remainder of the decade, however, because of the austerity programs forced on the investor-owned utilities, but the total pumped-storage capability in service by 1980 is slated at 15,639,000 kW, 2.5% of the industry's total generating capability.

Transmission circuits. A record construction program during 1974 added about 13,000 mi (20,900 km) of transmission circuits to the grid. These were needed to connect the 39,574,000 kW (about 2,000,000 replaced obsolete units) of new generating capability to load areas and to strengthen interconnections among load areas. About 23% of this added mileage was in overhead circuits for operation at upward of 345,000 V, hence with carrying capabilities of 600,000 kW or more per circuit. Nearly 24% of these extra-high-voltage (EHV) additions were in the heavily industrialized East North Central Region of the country. But the Pacific Region had 18%; the Mountain Region, 17%; the West South Central Region, 16%; and the remaining 25% was spread among all five other regions.

Lower-voltage circuits, mostly in the 115,000- to 230,000-V range, accounted for 77% of the total mileage added, but only about one-third of the total carrying capability. Of these, about 28% of the mileage was built in the South Atlantic Region, which has been somewhat slow to use EHV circuits. But substantial additions were built in the West South Central Region (18%) and in the Mountain Region (13%), with the remaining 41% spread among the other six regions.

Only 1.4% of the transmission mileage added during 1974 was underground, with nearly 80% of the total in the metropolitan areas of the Middle Atlantic, South Atlantic, and East North Central regions. Of the total mileage, only 40% was for operation at 230,000 V or higher.

Transformer capability. Substation capability for stepping up generating-station outputs to transmission voltage levels, and for stepping the voltage back down at load centers, required the addition of 130,000,000 kVA in transformer capability during 1974. Of this total, about 35% was at new generation additions, and 45% at major substations to interconnect transmission systems operating at different voltage levels. The remaining 20% was placed in load-area industrial and distribution substations; this portion was below normal, however, because of the near-zero growth of industrial and distribution loads attributable to the energy conservation effort.

Distribution load growth. Largely because of energy conservation, distribution load growth lagged far behind the rate of recent years, with the average residential customer usage, 7970 kWhr, dropping slightly below the 1973 level. In addition, 40% fewer new customers were connected during 1974. Consequently, the total kilowatt-hour sales to residential customers gained only 0.5% in 1974, versus 8.4% in 1973, and commercial consumption, largely served from distribution facilities, dropped about 1%. (During 1974, residential sales totaled 557,000,000,000 kWhr, and commercial sales, 393,000,000,000 kWhr.) Both factors contributed to a sharp 30% drop in distribution expenditures below 1973 levels, and the drop approaches 35% if 1973 spending is adjusted for a year's inflation.

Industrial sales also gained at far less than the historical annual growth rate, reflecting the energy conservation ethic. Despite continuing growth in usage by the aluminum industry, and by the Atomic Energy Commission for enriching nuclear fuel—two important industries which, combined, account for nearly 18% of electricity sales to the industrial sector of the economy—total industrial sales of 694,000,000,000 kWhr showed a gain of only 1% over the 1973 level.

Combining these three major sales categories with sales to a miscellaneous group that includes street and highway lighting and electric traction brought the total for 1974 to 1,707,501,000,000 kWhr, up only 0.3% over the 1,703,203,000,000 kWhr sold during 1973.

Construction budget. As a consequence of this near-zero growth, the electrical utility industry found itself saddled with a $21,173,000,000 construction budget intended to serve a 7 to 8% annual increase in demand, and an income (revenues) held down by the 0.3% increase in kilowatt-hour sales. The situation was further aggravated by fuel costs rising far faster than the industry could cover with rate increases, and by uncertainty about how long the energy conservation ethic would persist. But the industry did invoke strict austerity to hold 1974 capital spending nearly 10% under budget, and it delayed the completion of additions planned for service in 1975 and later years to match a slower probable load growth rate. The latter move deferred up to 30% of the heavy annual expenditures that had been scheduled for later years. Of the $86,740,000,000 (in 1974 dollars) now projected for the remainder of the decade, 56.7% will go for generation additions, 11.0% for transmission, 27.5% for distribution, and 4.8% for such items as control centers, load control systems, operating headquarters, and a wide variety of construction and transportation devices.

Electric rates. Rates charged for electric service climbed steeply in 1974, reflecting an increase of about 0.37¢/kWhr in fuel cost adjustments, and 0.12¢/kWhr from a record $2,220,000,000 per year of rate increases authorized by various regulatory agencies. These increases boosted the average cost for residential service during 1974 to 2.88¢/kWhr, commercial service to 2.79¢/kWhr, industrial service to 1.66¢/kWhr, and the average for all ultimate customers to 2.35¢/kWhr. With these increases, the industry's total revenues for 1974 climbed to $39,500,000,000, up 24.8% over the 1973 level. Even this sharp increase, however, leaves the industry short of funds for paying the sharply higher fuel costs and for financing continuing expansion that cost $19,198,000,000 in 1974 and is projected at $18,010,000,000 (1974 dollars) for 1975.

For background information *see* ELECTRIC POWER GENERATION; ELECTRIC POWER SYSTEMS; NUCLEAR POWER; TRANSMISSION LINES in the McGraw-Hill Encyclopedia of Science and Technology.   [LEONARD M. OLMSTED]

Bibliography: Edison Electric Institute, *Statistical Yearbook of the Electric Utility Industry*, 1974; Eighteenth Steam Station Cost Survey, *Elec. World*, 180(9):39–54, 1973; Federal Power Commission, *The 1970 National Power Survey*, pts. 1 and 4, 1972; 1974 Annual Statistical Report, *Elec. World*, 181(6):35–66, 1974; Summer peak oozes up only 1%, *Elec. World*, 182(8):86–87, 1974; 25th Annual Electrical Industry Forecast, *Elec. World*, 182(6):43–58, 1974.

Electrode

Conduction in thin films has been studied for many years and remains a subject of active research. Only recently, however, has conduction in thin-film electrodes been investigated. This work is proving significant from two points of view, namely, from that of surface solid-state physics and from that of electrochemistry. The conductance is a measure of the ease with which electrons are transported along the film; it is the reciprocal of the electrical resistance. Resistance arises from several sources, including thermal motion of the atoms in the film, impurities and other imperfections in the structure of the film, the scattering of conducting electrons by the surface, and low electron population.

Thus, if conduction electrons near the surface make up a measurable fraction of the electron population in the film, resistance measurements will be sensitive to surface changes. These

changes will occur in an electrode-electrolyte system whenever the electrode potential is changed. Changes may also occur when the chemical environment of the film is changed. There is a powerful advantage, however, in being able to change the chemical potential of the electrons by merely adjusting the film potential, which is possible if the film is an electrode in an electrochemical cell. This is the main advantage of electrochemical studies over gas-phase or vacuum studies. The conductance is an extremely sensitive probe of the double-layer region of an electrode-electrolyte system. It is sensitive to double-layer charging and strongly affected by changes in the chemical species bound to the electrode. Therefore, conductance monitoring of thin-film electrodes constitutes a powerful new approach to the study of surface chemistry and physics.

Setup to study conduction. The thin-film electrode (metal or semiconductor) is made the working electrode in a cell and is also part of a resistance-measuring circuit. Figure 1 shows one possible arrangement. The bridge off-balance gives the resistance change during electrochemical manipulation. This is only a very simple setup. If air is to be eliminated, for example, the cell must be closed and purged. A more sophisticated bridge circuit is useful for highest sensitivity, and an ac bridge offers advantages. The ac bridge eliminates errors due to coupling with the electrochemical currents in the electrode but introduces problems because

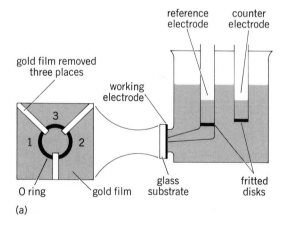

(a)

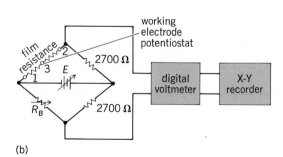

(b)

Fig. 1. Experimental arrangement for studying conduction in thin-film electrodes. (a) Electrochemical cell and gold film electrode. (b) Electronic circuitry for monitoring gold film conductance. (*From W. J. Anderson and W. N. Hansen, Observing the electrochemical interphase via electrode surface conductance, Electroanal. Chem. Interfacial Electrochem., 43:329–338, 1973*)

of the finite ac conductance of the electrolyte. With care, both ac and dc measurements can be made.

Double-layer charging. The simplest case to interpret is that involving only double-layer charging, that is, when there is no significant change in the chemical species bonded to the electrode. This case is illustrated by Fig. 2, in which the relative change in conductance $\Delta c/c$ is superimposed on a current-voltage plot. The potential was varied linearly with time between the end points, a complete cycle taking 9.2 sec. The electrode current and conductance change were recorded simultaneously, and the cycle was repeated many times without change. The cyclic voltammogram (current-voltage curve) indicates that, except for the slight deviations near the end points, the current was purely capacitive. For this case the simplest theory would suggest that $\Delta c/c = \Delta n/n$, if nothing changes but n, the free electron population per unit area of the electrode. This simple theory seems to hold in this case. The curve A . . . B was calculated from $\Delta c/c = \Delta n/n$.

In other cases it is found experimentally that $\Delta c/c = \alpha(\Delta n/n)$, where α is some constant and may even be negative. Linearity is preserved, but either the added electrons are not equivalent to those already present or the surface is altered somewhat for all of the electrons. The added electrons would not be equivalent to those already present, for example, if hole and electron conduction were present together, since the added electrons might shift the electron-hole ratio. The surface would be altered for all electrons if the film boundary shifted slightly with surface electron concentration, or if the effective mass of the electrons depended on surface population density. In another experiment, $\Delta c/c$ remained linear at hydrogen evolution potentials where the faradic current was orders of magnitude larger than the charging current. This result shows that $\Delta c/c$ is due to charging and is insensitive to the flow of electrons across the electrochemical interface. It provides a new way of separating charging and faradic currents. Investigations with semiconductor films have also shown $\Delta c/c$ to be proportional to $\Delta n/n$.

Adsorption and other phenomena. The addition of iodide ion to a cell with a gold film electrode increases the effect by an order of magnitude or more. From Fig. 3 it is clearly seen that this increase is due to iodide adsorption. At relatively positive electrode potentials, iodide is adsorbed on the gold electrode surface, and conductance is low compared to that at the right side of the figure, where there is no iodide adsorbed, probably because the adsorbed iodide ions cause the free electrons in the electrode to be more diffusely scattered, thus decreasing the film conductance. A very high sensitivity is indicated. Behavior with a positive adsorbed ion is illustrated in Fig. 4. Here the ion is adsorbed at negative potentials and desorbed at the left. Again, adsorption decreased conductance. It can be seen that the effect of Cs^+ adsorption on conductance is opposite to the effect of charging but completely dominates. The conductance curve shows hysteresis because of the different potentials at which adsorption and desorption occur, as shown by current density.

Three cases of conduction in thin-film electrodes have been discussed and illustrated: (1) the

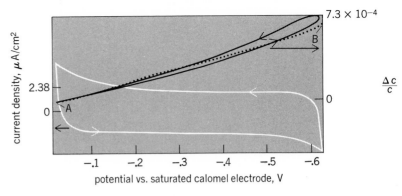

Fig. 2.   Voltammetric electrochemical curve for 16.0-nm silver electrode in 0.1 M Na$_2$SO$_4$ solution with pH = 5.6. Potential sweep is linear between end points. Curve is traversed every 9.2 sec.

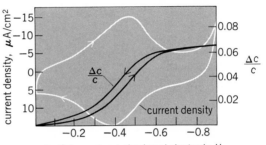

Fig. 3.   The cyclic voltammetry and conductance curves showing I⁻ adsorption and desorption on a 6.1-nm gold electrode. The electrolyte is 0.1 M Na$_2$SO$_4$ and 0.01 M NaI at pH = 4.0. (*From W. J. Anderson and W. N. Hansen, Electroreflectance and conductance, Electroanal. Chem. Interfacial Electrochem., 47:229–243, 1973*)

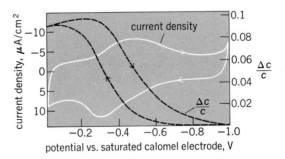

Fig. 4.   The cyclic voltammetry and conductance curves showing Cs⁺ adsorption and desorption on a 6.1-nm gold electrode. The electrolyte is 0.1 M Na$_2$SO$_4$ and 0.0184 M Cs$_2$SO$_4$ at pH = 8.5. (*From W. J. Anderson and W. N. Hansen, Electroreflectance and conductance, Electroanal. Interfacial Electrochem., 47:229–243, 1973*)

ideal double-layer region, in which only charging occurs, with no electrons crossing the metal-electrolyte interface and no significant change in adsorption; (2) the same as case 1 but with a large faradic current crossing the interface; and (3) strong specific adsorption, which changes with potential. Other cases could be illustrated. Any reaction with the electrode to form a new compound such as its oxide will certainly change its conductance, if for no other reason than that the thickness will change. Restructuring of the surface would also have some effect. As the double layer is charged, very large fields are established at the electrode surface that penetrate into the electrode only a fraction of an atomic spacing in the case of metal electrodes. Besides changing the electron population, the field might also change the electron mobility and the effective boundary at which the electrons are reflected.

The experiments of K. Niki and T. Shirato showed a complicated behavior. When n-amyl alcohol was added to the electrolyte, the resistance of a gold film electrode increased at all potentials, but the increase was at a minimum near the point of zero charge for gold. When benzoic acid was added instead, the increase in resistance was at a maximum near the point of zero charge.

Theory. These experiments have identified and clarified several aspects of thin-film electrode conduction. However, no theory exists at present to explain the effects in detail. Even when only charging occurs, the resultant change in conductance depends on the sign of the dominant charge carriers; that is, α may be plus or minus. When oxide layers are present, the effects of specific adsorption will be dampened. Clearly, more work is needed to understand these effects in detail.

For background information see ELECTROCHEMICAL TECHNIQUES; ELECTROCHEMISTRY in the McGraw-Hill Encyclopedia of Science and Technology. [WILFORD N. HANSEN]

Bibliography: W. J. Anderson and W. N. Hansen, *Electroanal. Chem. Interfacial Electrochem.*, 43:329–338, 1973, and 47:229–243, 1973; K. Niki and T. Shirato, *Electroanal. Chem. Interfacial Electrochem.*, 42:7, 1973.

Electron spectroscopy

Significant advances in surface physics and chemistry have been made due to the recent development of two distinct but interrelated and complementary analytical techniques: Auger electron spectroscopy (AES) and x-ray photoelectron spectroscopy, more commonly known as ESCA (electron spectroscopy for chemical analysis). Both techniques are capable of providing surface analysis, in-depth profile analysis when combined with in-situ ion sputtering, information on chemical bonding due to Coulomb and exchange interactions, and quantitative analysis by the use of homogeneous standards. Vacuum requirements are in the range of 10^{-5} to 10^{-10} torr, depending on the application. For surface analysis, ultra-high vacuum (10^{-10} torr) is needed to prevent contamination from residual gases in the vacuum chamber.

The fundamental mechanisms leading to Auger and photoelectron emission are illustrated in Fig. 1. In ESCA (Fig. 1a) a monochromatic photon source (such as Al Kα) of known energy $h\nu$ is used to eject photoelectrons from core energy levels. The photoelectron kinetic energies E_k are given by $h\nu - E_b - \Phi$, where E_b is the binding energy of the ejected core level electron with respect to the Fermi level, and ϕ the work function of the spectrometer used to detect and energy-analyze the emitted photoelectrons. AES (Fig. 1b) is based on the emission and energy analysis of Auger elec-

trons produced when an excited atom relaxes by a radiationless process after ionization by a high-energy electron (3–5 KeV) or x-ray beam. The energy released is transferred to an electron at a higher energy level, which is ejected with an energy characteristic of the excited atom. The characteristic kinetic energy of the ejected Auger electron of Fig. 1b can be estimated by $E_K - E_{L_1} - E_{L_2}$, where E_K, E_{L_1}, and E_{L_2} are the binding energies of the K, L_1, and L_2 levels with respect to the Fermi level. Note (Fig. 1b) that as many as three energy levels can be involved in the Auger process, but only one energy level is involved in ESCA (Fig. 1a). This makes chemical bonding information from energy shifts in the AES and ESCA spectra theoretically more interpretable in ESCA than in AES.

Surface analysis. The escape depths of Auger (d_A) and photoelectrons (d_p) are in the range of 5–30 A (10 A = 1 nm) with $d_p \sim 2d_A$ due to the lower kinetic energy of Auger electrons. These low escape depths make surface analysis by both AES and ESCA possible for all elements, excluding He and H for AES and H for ESCA. Higher spatial (x,y) resolution is obtained in AES surface analysis since electron beams can be easily focused down to the submicron range compared to ~1 cm for x-rays. In addition, the Auger image, obtained by scanning a finely focused primary electron beam and intensity-modulating a cathode-ray tube (CRT), provides a two-dimensional map of the distribution of surface impurities with a lateral resolution in the micron range. Beam-induced surface damage effects during surface analysis are believed to be more pronounced in AES, where electron-beam-assisted desorption, diffusion (to and away from the surface), polymerization of organic surface contaminants, adsorbate dissociation, and possible temperature increases have been observed, particularly at high electron current densities.

The surface analysis provided by AES and ESCA has found important applications in fields such as micro-electronics, catalysis, corrosion, thin-film and bulk metallurgy, and basic surface chemistry and physics. Some recent examples include studies of the poisoning of catalyst surfaces used in oxidation reactions, localized corrosion on metallic surfaces, grain boundary segregation in fractured surfaces, and the charge transfer and energy levels involved in chemical bonding at solid surfaces.

In-depth profile analysis. The combination of Auger and ESCA analysis with simultaneous in-situ ion sputtering, used to gradually erode the sample, has made possible the monitoring of the distribution of impurities with depth (that is, composition profiles) from the surface into the bulk of the sample. Depth resolution is in the range of 5–10% of the thickness of the sample removed by sputtering (for example, 100 A for a removed thickness of 1000 A) in the absence of sputtering artifacts such as preferential sputtering for alloy samples, misalignment of the electron or x-ray beam and the sputtering ions, "knock on" phenomenon whereby lattice atoms are pushed deeper into the solid, and surface roughness. The simultaneous detection of as many as six preselected Auger peaks can be accomplished by interfacing a multiplexer into the electronic detection scheme.

Information on impurity distribution with depth is of particular importance since the quantitative analysis provided by the more conventional analytical techniques such as the electron microprobe, x-ray fluorescence, and spark source analysis assume a uniform (homogeneous) distribution of the impurities, which is often not the case. Ion sputtering combined with AES or ESCA can also be used to monitor the thickness of multilayer thin-film systems.

Chemical bonding. Information on chemical bonding due to surface reactions can, in principle, also be obtained from ESCA and AES chemical shift data, that is, shifts (≤ 10 eV) of the characteristic Auger or photoelectron energy positions due to chemical environment. As previously mentioned, chemical shift data interpretation is more difficult in AES than ESCA. In addition, energy resolution with ESCA is superior (0.1–0.5 eV) to AES since Auger line widths are broader (several electron volts) than photoelectron line widths, especially when valence band electrons are involved in the Auger transition. The magnitude of shift (2–10 eV) necessary to obtain reliable chemical information from valence level Auger spectra can sometimes occur in oxidation, as when Si forms SiO_2 (a shift of ~ 8 eV). Characteristic changes in the Auger spectra also occur when metal surface oxides such as TiO_2 are formed. ESCA shift data can often be used to identify submonolayer adsorbate-substrate chemical reactions, and ultraviolet-excited photoelectron spectroscopy (UPS) is particularly well suited to the study of valence electrons involved in chemical bonding at solid surfaces with good energy resolution (<0.2 eV). *See* SILICON.

Auger and photoelectron peak shape changes (line width and height) can also influence Auger and ESCA quantitative analysis. Quantitative AES and ESCA analysis is briefly discussed in the next section.

Quantitative analysis. Quantitative analysis without the use of standards is not yet possible with Auger or ESCA, but should be possible once parameters such as electron and photon flux density, escape depths, backscattering corrections, and ionization cross sections are known or easily measured. The effect of surface roughness and surface contaminants such as oxygen and carbon on Auger and ESCA signal intensities are, perhaps, the most severe limitation to quantitative surface analysis. Quantitative surface analysis, however, is further complicated by the fact that surface impurities are often nonhomogeneously distributed within the x,y plane of the surface and within the depth z of the surface region (≤ 100 A).

Despite these limitations and others (such as chemical effects, electron-beam-induced artifacts), quantitative analysis by the use of standards of known and uniform composition has been demonstrated. Standards of doped silicon and metals prepared by the use of ion implantation and reactive sputtering, known coverage chemisorption, and thin-film alloys have been used to obtain calibration curves of a type shown for P and B doped silicon in Fig. 2. These data have also been used to establish the detectability limits of AES to be be-

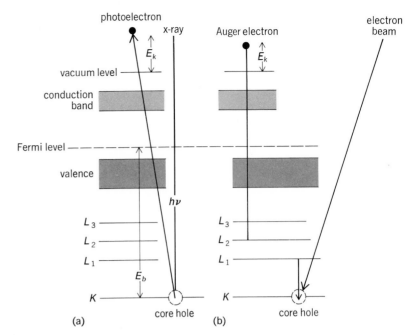

Fig. 1. Mechanisms leading to photoelectron and Auger electron emission: (a) electron spectroscopy for chemical analysis; (b) Auger electron spectroscopy.

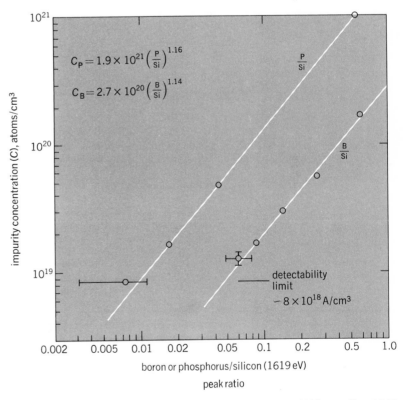

$$C_P = 1.9 \times 10^{21} \left(\frac{P}{Si} \right)^{1.16}$$

$$C_B = 2.7 \times 10^{20} \left(\frac{B}{Si} \right)^{1.14}$$

Fig. 2. Auger calibration curves for B and P in silicon. *(From J. H. Thomas III and J. M. Morabito, Detectability limits for boron and phosphorus in silicon by Auger electron spectroscopy (AES), Surface Sci., 41:629, 1974)*

tween 0.1 and 1% of a monolayer. Detectability limits fo ESCA are in the same range, but ESCA analysis times are considerably longer for the same detection limit due to the lower transmission of ESCA spectrometers. A detection limit of 0.1%

of a monolayer corresponds to ∼ 10^{-14} g of material.

Future trends. The increased use of instrumentation capable of providing both Auger and ESCA analysis is expected in the future. ESCA is the preferred technique for the study of polymer surfaces and for cases where information on the chemical state of the element is of interest. Continued advances in the monochromatization of x-ray and synchrotron radiation will increase the signal-to-background ratio and resolution possible in ESCA. Advances in AES are expected in the areas of spatial resolution, data reduction, and theoretical models for standardless quantitative analysis which include corrections for backscattering, spectra overlap, and peak shape change due to chemical effects. The quantitative models developed for AES should be applicable to ESCA data.

For background information *see* AUGER EFFECT; ELECTRON SPECTROSCOPY; PHOTOEMISSION in the McGraw-Hill Encyclopedia of Science and Technology.   [J. M. MORABITO]

Bibliography: J. M. Baker and D. E. Eastman, *J. Vac. Sci. Tech.*, 10:223, 1973; N. C. MacDonald, in D. Beaman and B. Siegel (eds.), *Eelectron Microscopy: Physical Aspects*, 1974; J. M. Morabito, *Anal. Chem.*, 46:189, 1974; J. M. Morabito and J. G. C. Tsai, *Surface Sci.*, 33:422, 1972; S. P. Wolsky and A. W. Czanderna (eds.), *Methods of Surface Analysis*, 1975.

Element 104

In 1973 an isotope of element 104 was positively identified from study of characteristic x-rays of its product. Further investigations with characteristic x-rays, a method of identification developed by H. G. J. Moseley about 1912, may help resolve the controversy between G. N. Flerov and A. Ghiorso over priority in the discovery of element 104 and may also aid in determining the atomic numbers of other transuranium isotopes.

Discovery controversy. The first reported claim to the synthesis of an isotope of element 104 was made by Flerov and coworkers at the Joint Institute for Nuclear Research, Dubno, U.S.S.R., in 1964. The isotope of element 104 with mass number 260 was reported to decay by spontaneous fission with a half-life of 0.3 ± 0.1 sec, as produced in the bombardment of plutonium-242 with neon-22 ions. Comparative chemical studies with

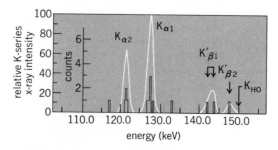

Identification of element 104. The theoretical K-series x-ray spectrum of nobelium (element 102) is shown as the continuous curve. The histogram gives the Oak Ridge National Laboratory experimental x-ray spectrum counted in coincidence with alpha particles emitted in the energy range 8.5–9.1 MeV.

the 0.3-sec activity were subsequently performed in 1966 by the Dubno group using a chloride volatility technique. On the basis of these studies, the name kurchatovium (symbol Ku) was suggested for the new element.

In 1969 researchers at the Lawrence Berkeley Laboratory under the direction of Ghiorso reported that they were unable to produce the 0.3-sec spontaneous fission activity of element 104 first announced in 1964 by the Dubno group. Although they did not duplicate the Dubno experiments exactly, they tried to produce 104-260 in the bombardment of a target of curium-246 with oxygen-18 ions, in the bombardment of a target of curium-248 with oxygen-16 ions, and in the bombardment of einsteinium-253 with boron-10 and boron-11 ions, all with negative results. All these possible nuclear reactions were claimed to be at least as effective in producing 104-260 as the Dubno method, using plutonium-242 targets and neon-22 ions, was.

The Berkeley group did claim success in 1969 in the synthesis of three other isotopes of element 104, all of which undergo radioactive decay by the emission of alpha particles. These three isotopes of element 104 are mass number 257 with a half-life of 4.5 sec; mass number 259 with a half-life of 3.5 sec; and a surprisingly long-lived isotope, mass number 261 with a half-life of about 1.2 min. They were produced by bombarding targets of californium-249 with ions of carbon-12, carbon-13, and oxygen-18 and were assigned the atomic number of 104 because of the establishment of a genetic link between the alpha decaying parent nuclide and the daughter product of the decay, which is an isotope of element 102. Comparative chemical studies using the 1.2-min half-life isotope 104-261 were performed by R. Silva and coworkers at Berkeley, and it was shown that the chemical behavior of element 104 is similar to that of hafnium, the expected homolog in the chemical periodic table. The Berkeley group suggested the name rutherfordium (symbol Rf) for element 104 on the basis of their studies. As of 1974 no official name had been adopted for element 104 because the conflicting claims of the Soviet and Berkeley groups had not been resolved.

Element identification from x-ray spectra. The synthesis, identification, and study of the isotopes of elements greater than fermium ($Z = 100$) is extremely difficult, for these isotopes can be produced only at a rate that might be as low as one atom per hour, even when the most intense ion beams available are used. Some of the difficulties experienced in the studies of these short-lived isotopes can be overcome if a unique detection and identification technique, that can establish the atomic number unequivocally, even though the decay of only a few atoms is observed, is used. This technique is the x-ray identification method first developed by Moseley. Since characteristic x-ray energies have a unique functional relationship with the atomic number Z, it is not surprising that Moseley was able to unravel the mysteries of the ordering of the rare-earth elements (La to Lu) in just a few days, a task that classical chemists had labored over for about 20 years.

Positive identification of element 104. In 1973, using an adaptation of the Moseley x-ray method, C. Bemis and coworkers from the Oak Ridge National Laboratory confirmed the Berkeley experiments on element 104 using the mass number 257 isotope. The nuclear reaction used by the Berkeley group was also used by the Oak Ridge scientists to synthesize element 104, namely, the bombardment of a californium-249 target with carbon-12 ions. The alpha particles and x-rays from the decay of the reaction products were observed with high-resolution semiconductor radiation detectors. The x-rays, observed in time coincidence with the alpha particles, can arise following an alpha decay if the alpha decay proceeds to excited nuclear states in the daughter nucleus. In this case, characteristic x-rays of the daughter nucleus with atomic number $Z = 2$ are observed in time coincidence with the alpha particles ($Z = 2$); thus the x-ray experiments can unequivocally establish the atomic number Z of the parent nuclide.

The experimental x-ray spectrum obtained by the Oak Ridge group by using this technique in their studies of the 104-257 isotope is shown in the illustration, together with the expected theoretical spectrum. All the indicated peaks $K\alpha_1$, $K\alpha_2$, and so forth, constitute the characteristic K-series x-ray spectrum of nobelium ($Z = 102$), and because the spectrum was observed in coincidence with alpha particles, an unequivocal determination of the parent atomic number, $Z = 104$, is obtained. This experiment confirms, in a unique way, the work of the Berkeley group on the nuclide 104-257.

Although the element 104 discovery controversy has not been resolved, it may be possible to investigate the Dubno discovery isotope, 104-260, by using a similar x-ray technique. Thus x-ray methods may again be instrumental in resolving the problems of placing elements in the periodic table as they were about 1912, in Moseley's time.

For background information *see* ACTINIDE ELEMENTS; ELEMENT 104; TRANSURANIUM ELEMENTS; X-RAY POWDER METHODS in the McGraw-Hill Encyclopedia of Science and Technology.   [CURTIS E. BEMIS, JR.]

Bibliography: C. E. Bemis et al., *Phys. Rev. Lett.*, 31:647, 1973; A. Ghiorso, in W. O. Milligan (ed.), *Proceedings of the Thirteenth R. A. Welch Foundation Conference on Chemical Research: The Transuranium Elements — Mendeleev Centennial*, p. 107, 1970; A. Ghiorso et al., *Phys. Rev. Lett.*, 22:1317, 1969.

Endocrine system (invertebrate)

Some years ago it became apparent that new insecticides were required to replace DDT and other potentially hazardous and persistent chlorinated hydrocarbons. The replacements would have to be biodegradable and highly specific toward the target insect. The observation that insect metamorphosis was regulated by two relatively simple compounds, the molting hormone (Fig. 1) and the juvenile hormone (Fig. 2), led to the suggestion that these compounds, or compounds closely related to them, might be employed as insecticides. After many hundreds of compounds based on the structure of insect juvenile hormone were tested, a small group of potent insect growth regulators was developed. Two such insect growth regulators are ZR-512 (Fig. 3) and ZR-515 (Fig. 4).

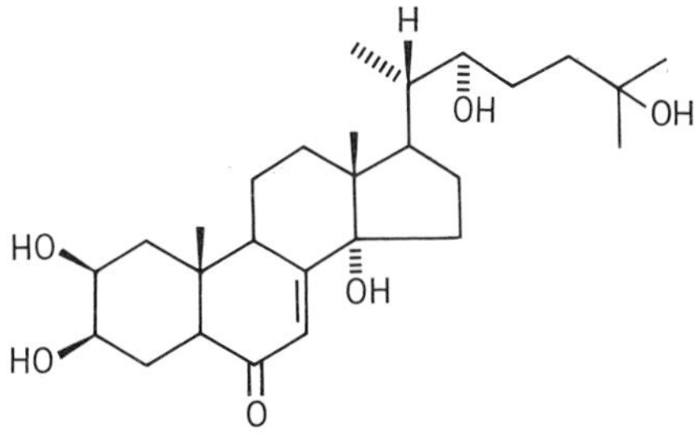

Both insects and crustaceans are members of

Fig. 1. Structural formula of ecdysone.

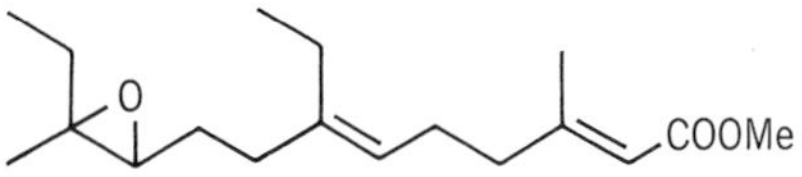

Fig. 2. Structural formula of a juvenile hormone.

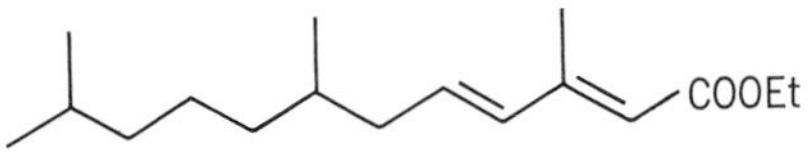

Fig. 3. Structural formula of ZR-512, an insect growth regulator. (*From E. D. Gomez et al., Juvenile hormone mimics: Effect on cirriped crustacean metamorphosis, Science, 179:813–814, 1973*)

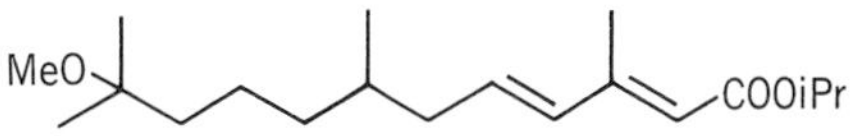

Fig. 4. Structural formula of ZR-515, an insect growth regulator. (*From E. D. Gomez et al., Juvenile hormone mimics: Effect on cirriped crustacean metamorphosis, Science, 179:813–814, 1973*)

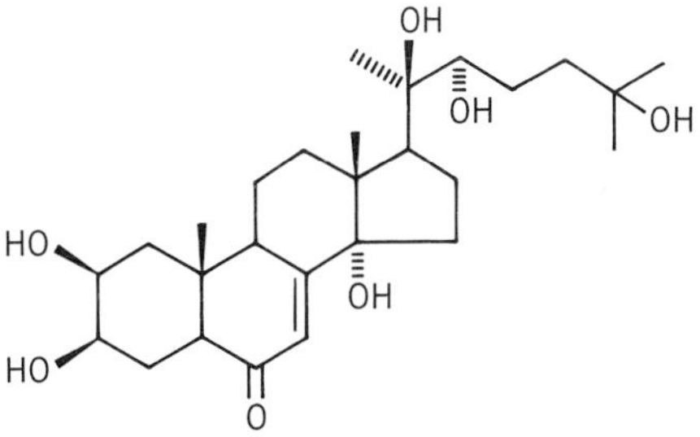

Fig. 5. Structural formula of crustecdysone.

the phylum Arthropoda, and thus one might expect to observe some similarities in their developmental biology and biochemistry. For example, the molting hormone from the crayfish *Jasus lalandei*, called crustecdysone (Fig. 5), is almost identical to ecdysone, isolated from the silk moth *Bombyx mori*. The similarity of the two molting hormones pointed to the possibility that insect juvenile hormone or closely related compounds could have a role in crustacean metamorphosis. It therefore became important to investigate the action on

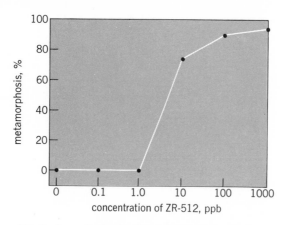

Fig. 6. A graph showing the percentage of metamorphosis of the cyprid larva of the acorn barnacle exposed to different concentrations of ZR-512. *(From E. D. Gomez et al., Juvenile hormone mimics: Effect on cirriped crustacean metamorphosis, Science, 179:813–814, 1973)*

crustaceans of the newly developed insect growth regulators before they were widely employed in coastal regions.

Acorn barnacle experiment. It is somewhat fortuitous that the first experiments by E. D. Gomez and coworkers were an investigation of the effects of ZR-512 and ZR-515 on the acorn barnacle *Balanus galeatus*, for no more striking results have since been observed. The acorn barnacle spends its adult life on a gorgonian coral and has not been found elsewhere. The adults release eggs that hatch into larvae called nauplii. The nauplii feed on phytoplankton and develop through six naupliar stages to the cyprid form. The cyprid does not feed but "swims" in search of the gorgonian on which it must settle. When the cyprid locates a suitable substrate, it attaches and undergoes metamorphosis into an adult. Laboratory-reared cyprids, isolated from their gorgonian substrate, continue to search for 4 to 6 weeks, until they are exhausted.

When exposed to sea water containing more than 10 parts per billion (ppb) of ZR-512, most of the cyprid barnacles underwent precocious metamorphosis to an adult form that was not attached to a substrate. Lacking attachment, they were unable to attain the correct position for feeding and soon died. A graph of the percentage of metamorphosis versus ZR-512 concentration (Fig. 6) shows a threshold concentration at 1–10 ppb. At concentrations above 500 parts per million (ppm), both ZR-512 and ZR-515 were toxic to barnacle nauplii and cyprids. Despite its close chemical relationship to ZR-512, ZR-515 did not show any metamorphic activity against barnacle cyprids.

ZR-512 also caused precocious metamorphosis in other species of barnacles *(Balanus amphitrite, B. pacificus, B. glandula)*; but as yet no activity against other subclasses of crustaceans has been reported. Other insect growth regulators, as well as insect juvenile hormone itself, have shown activity in the *B. galeatus* assay, but none is as active as ZR-512. From these results it is anticipated that insect growth regulators will prove far less harmful to nontarget organisms than the insecticides they could replace.

Other uses of ZR-512. Attempts were made to test ZR-512 as an antifouling component in marine paint, but the test panels became covered with other organisms, and barnacles were able to settle on calcareous deposits. These results demonstrate how difficult it will be to control fouling by using selective regulators. A more profitable use of ZR-512 was found in the study of the developmental biology of barnacles. Gomez showed that, in the commensal barnacle *B. galeatus*, the ratio of hermaphrodites to males was genetically determined, for he obtained approximately the same sex ratios when metamorphosis was induced either by a substrate or by ZR-512.

For background information *see* CRUSTACEA; ECDYSONE; ENDOCRINE SYSTEM (INVERTEBRATE); INSECT CONTROL, BIOLOGICAL; THORACICA in the McGraw-Hill Encyclopedia of Science and Technology.   [D. JOHN FAULKNER]

Bibliography: E. D. Gomez et al., *Science*, 179: 813–814, 1973; E. Sondheimer and J. B. Simeone (eds.), *Chemical Ecology*, 1970.

Endodermis

The endodermis has long been considered to act as some form of barrier to the movement of water and nutrient ions from the cortex into the conducting elements of the stele of vascular plants. Although this belief was to some extent substantiated by the experiments of botanists during the early years of the 20th century, only recently have joint physiological and structural studies provided a closer understanding of how endodermal cells may affect the inward flow of water and solutes.

Endodermal wall development. The endodermis is a single-layered sheath of cells strategically situated between the cells of the cortex and those of the xylem and phloem of the vascular strand. Whereas the cells of the cortex commonly have intercellular spaces between them, those of the endodermis are close-packed. A characteristic, and physiologically important, feature of the endodermis is the specialized development of the walls of its cells. Four stages are recognized: proendodermis, the young cells just cut off from the meristem and showing no peculiar features; Casparian band (state I), a heavy deposition of suberin- and lignin-like material occurring in the longitudinal and transverse radial (anticlinal) walls; suberin lamella (state II), a thin layer of suberin-containing material deposited around the whole internal boundary of the cell wall; thick cellulosic wall (state III), a heavy, lamellated wall of cellulose laid down internal to the suberin lamella (Fig. 1).

Casparian band. With the possible exception of the Lycopodiaceae, the production of a Casparian band in the anticlinal walls appears to be universal in the roots of vascular plants. It has been known for a very long time that, if endodermal cells are plasmolyzed, the plasmalemma remains tightly bound to the Casparian band. Electron-microscopical evidence shows that this is a direct, and very close, binding between the cell membrane and the wall material of the band. In many plants the endodermis does not develop beyond this (state I) condition. However, other roots may go on to produce state II and state III endodermal cells, a process that seems to occur somewhat asynchronously. The state III cells can have an even thickening of cellulose (O type) or a much greater thickening of cellulose on the inner tangential walls than on the outer ones (C type). All endodermal states are well represented in the roots of grasses, and for this reason, and others, the roots of graminaceous cereals have been successfully used in experiments relating to endodermal function. In some species a few endodermal cells may remain in state I while all the cells around them have progressed to state III; such cells have been termed passage cells. In some cases (such as Iridaceae) permanent passage cells may be formed, whereas in others (such as barley, *Hordeum vulgare*) they may be temporary phenomena that will also eventually develop to state III.

Plasmodesmata. A striking feature of endodermal cells that has been revealed by electron-microscope examination is the degree to which the walls are perforated by plasmodesmata. These thin (60-nm) cytoplasmic threads are usually grouped into pit fields on all walls and are commonly present in quantities of the order of 1,000,000/mm².

Apoplastic and symplastic pathways. It is important to understand that water and solutes can travel through the cells of the root either via the cell walls and intercellular spaces external to the cell membranes (apoplastic pathway) or from cytoplasm to cytoplasm via plasmodesmata (symplastic pathway). The endodermis acts as a strong barrier to the passage of apoplastically transported ions.

If "tracer" solutions are fed to plants so that electron-opaque material becomes bound within the root (uranyl acetate, lanthanum hydroxide, and other solutions have been used), it is possible to establish where barriers exist in the apoplastic pathway. The proendodermis does not seem to be a barrier to movement through the walls, but whether it permits gross leakage in the translocatory system is in question, for the xylem-conducting elements are not fully formed at that stage (usually within the first millimeter or so behind the meristem). However, as soon as the Casparian band is formed on the radial walls, it can be seen that the inward movement of the electron-opaque material through the walls is totally blocked (Fig. 2).

In Fig. 2 it can be seen that in the state I cells the crystals of the uranyl complex are present in the cell wall up to the Casparian band, which blocks their further inward progress. In the cell that has developed to state III, the suberin lamella completely blocks access of the tracer solution to the plasmalemma of the endodermal cell. Such experiments demonstrate the way in which the Casparian band prevents apoplastic movement of water or ions from the cortex into the stele, and how the formation of the suberin lamella prevents solutes in the cortical apoplasm from gaining access to the endodermal symplasm. The tight binding between plasmalemma and Casparian band is clearly important in this context.

Two other lines of evidence point to the effectiveness of the Casparian band barrier. First, when barley roots were fed with labeled calcium (⁴⁵Ca)

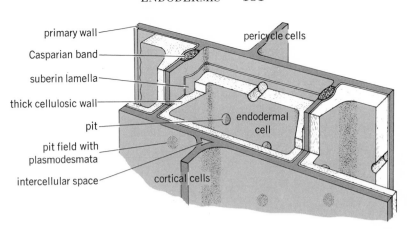

Fig. 1. Diagram illustrating the structure of an endodermal cell of barley that clearly shows all three states of wall development. The pits pass through the thick cellulosic wall and most of the suberin lamella; the thin membrane that remains between the endodermal cells and their neighbors is traversed by plasmodesmata.

and subsequently allowed to exchange with unlabeled calcium chloride solution, it was found that, although 50–60% of the label was removed from the whole root, the exchange was principally within the epidermal and cortical cells; thus the ⁴⁵Ca that had penetrated beyond the endodermis had become unavailable for free exchange. Second, if the cortex of barley roots is stripped from the stele, the radial walls of the endodermal cells are the sites of fracture, and water uptake is considerably increased until the root has time to construct repair mechanisms; further, the normal ability for ion discrimination appears to be lost. The indication is, again, that removal of the barrier of the

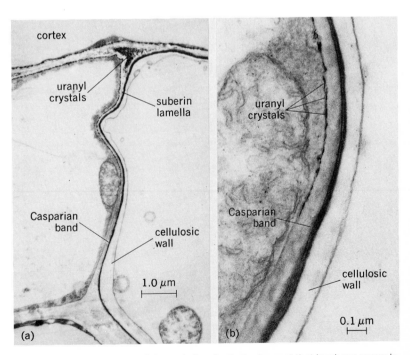

Fig. 2. Transverse section of the endodermis of a barley root that has been grown in a solution of uranyl acetate, showing (a) blockage of uranyl acetate crystals by Casparian band in state I cell; (b) blockage by suberin lamella in state III cell of access of uranyl acetate to plasmalemma. (*From A. W. Robards and M. E. Robb, Uptake and binding of uranyl ions by barley roots, Science, 178:980–982, 1972*)

Casparian band normally limits inward movement of water.

As the development of the endodermis moves from state I to state II, there is (in barley and marrow) a strongly correlated reduction in the amount of water and calcium moved into the stele. Phosphorus and potassium, however, do not show such a decline. These results are interpreted as indicating that the formation of the suberin lamella blocks the route for the uptake of much of the water and most of the calcium; that is, it stops the direct absorption by endodermal cells from the free space. Phosphorus and potassium must travel symplastically via the plasmodesmata; these ions, therefore, are little affected by suberin lamella formation. Considerable interest is thus focused on the plasmodesmata and, although most recent calculations show that they probably can account for observed rates of flow, much work remains to be carried out on the structure and function of these tiny intercellular connections.

These recent results thus show that, contrary to earlier beliefs, roots do not have "absorbing zones" that are uniform for all ions and that are completely blocked by suberin lamella formation. For ions that enter the stele via the symplast, the state II and state III stages of development are of little significance, and, although the rate of uptake may be lower in the older parts of the root, the overall contribution from such regions to the aerial parts of the plant may still be considerable.

For background information *see* ENDODERMIS in the McGraw-Hill Encyclopedia of Science and Technology.   [A. W. ROBARDS]

Bibliography: D. T. Clarkson, *Ion Transport and Cell Structure in Plants*, 1974; D. T. Clarkson and A. W. Robards, in J. G. Torrey and D. T. Clarkson (eds.), *The Development and Function of Roots*, 1975; A. W. Robards et al., *Protoplasma*, 77:291–312, 1973; A. W. Robards and M. E. Robb, *Science*, 178:980–982, 1972.

Ethology

The Northern bluejay (*Cyanocitta cristata*) and other closely related members of the family Corvidae have been observed to use nonfood objects to secure or manipulate food objects. Regular observation of such behavior has been confined largely to the laboratory, but instances of the behavior in the wild have been reported.

Tool using. The use of any object (food or nonfood) as an implement, instrument, or utensil for digging, cutting, hitting, raking, luring food or penetrating physical boundaries to obtain food is defined as tool using. The object used extends the organic integrity of an organism and is therefore considered a tool. Specialized appendages or organs which are specifically suited to have utility in an organism's niche are not to be considered tools. The bill of nectar-feeding birds, the hand of *Homo sapiens*, and the tongue of anteaters are specialized appendages that are best limited to a metaphorical use of the word tool. In accordance with the above definition of tool using, the bluejay uses tools.

Northern bluejays use paper clips, pieces of straw, plastic bag ties, pieces of feces removed from the bottom of their cage, feathers, or pieces of paper ripped from newspaper beneath their cage to maneuver food pellets to within reach of their beak. Factors influencing the use of these objects as tools by an experienced bluejay are whether or not food pellets are present, and the amount of time elapsed since last eating. Food pellets in view but unattainable with the beak alone set the occasion, and hunger level determines the frequency of attempts.

Information about the stimulus qualities controlling tool-using behavior affords some insight into the adaptiveness and generality of the behavior, but information about its acquisition should be available in order that it might be placed in a more comparative perspective. Some important considerations are: Does tool using develop through experience? Or, is it an expression of a genetic predisposition or preadaptation? If the use of one object to manipulate another object is developed through experience: Is it the result of trial-and-error learning? Is it the result of social facilitation or observational learning? Or, is it an instance of insightful learning? If the use of one object to manipulate another object is an expression of the genes: How did it develop phylogenetically? Finally, what is the significance of tool using toward extending the range of adaptability of an organism?

There are numerous anecdotal accounts of tool using by avian species. Unfortunately, such reports are not conducive to answering these types of questions. However, research at the University of Massachusetts provided data to answer some of these questions regarding tool use by the Northern bluejay.

Tool-use behavior. Both learning and a predisposition to manipulate and hoard food as well as nonfood objects are implicated in the development of tool-use behavior. Bluejays both in the wild and in the laboratory are notorious hoarders. Between bouts of pecking and wrenching objects such as a piece of paper or a food pellet between beak and feet, the bluejays are continually worrying objects in and out of every nook and cranny in their cage. The only objects that escape this activity cycle are those that come to rest beyond the reach of the bluejay's beak or that are eaten. If the bluejays are given free access to food or large quantities of food all at once, quite a few food pellets accumulate. The accumulation of food pellets that cannot be reached and the happenstance occurrence of a newly placed nonfood object displacing one of the food pellets sets the stage for learning. This experience of accidentally moving food pellets resting beyond the reach of the beak can be cumulative. If previously unattainable food pellets are accidentally moved a few times, especially if one of the food pellets is moved within reach, the thrusting of nonfood objects in the vicinity of food pellets increases in frequency. If the frequency of thrusting increases enough, the behavior is deemed intentional.

Preliminary evidence indicates that observation of successful tool use by another bluejay may increase the general level of manipulatory behavior, thereby facilitating the occurrence of food pellets being moved by nonfood objects. In the illustration, curves *a*, *c*, and *d* show an increase in general level of frequency that occurred after a

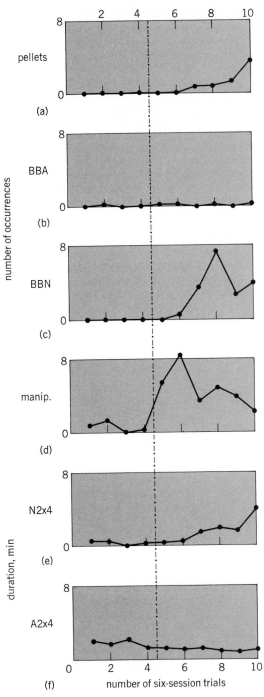

Six behavioral measures represented for a single blue-jay: (a) the number of pellets obtained; (b) the number of thrusts between the bars of the cage away from the pellets on the 2×4 board (BBA), and (c) near the pellets on the 2×4 (BBN); (d) the number of manipulatory episodes (manip.); (e) the amount of time spent near the 2×4 (N2×4); and (f) the amount of time spent away from the 2×4 (A2×4).

number of pellets obtained (curve *a*). The increase in manipulatory behavior preceded increases in both number of pellets obtained and number of thrusts. The rise in number of thrusts slightly preceded the rise in number of pellets obtained, but no more than would be anticipated, given that thrusting had to have occurred before the first pellet was obtained or even moved. However, the rate of increase in thrusting behavior was greatly accelerated by the moving and obtaining of the first few pellets.

Idiosyncratic components. Learning based on experience continues to exert influence on the development of tool-use behavior. Early tool-use behavior can be described as being idiosyncratic, with individual birds exhibiting different modes or distinct topographies of the behavior. One bluejay thrusts the piece of paper back and forth, confining lateral movement, if it occurs, to between two or three vertical bars of the cage; a second bluejay places the piece of paper to the extreme left of any pellets on the 2 × 4 ledge and by progressive steps moves the paper to the right (the direction of movement was usually from left to right); a third bluejay puts the piece of paper against a vertical bar of the cage and, by grasping the paper to either side of the vertical bar and pulling, causes the piece of paper to swing in an arc; a fourth bluejay thrusts the paper through at a position 1–2 in. (2.5–5 cm) above the 2 × 4 ledge on which the pellets rest and lets the paper fall.

Extraneous components. During the incipient stages of development, a number of components are inefficient as far as obtaining food pellets is concerned and therefore could be considered extraneous. Some of the idiosyncratic components fall in this category. As an example, one bluejay evolved the fairly elaborate ritual of approaching the front of the cage to obtain the piece of paper, hopping to and resting momentarily on the perch, hopping to the food cup where it might or might not insert the paper, hopping back to the perch, and then hopping to the front of the cage and inserting the paper between the bars of the cage. The entire sequence of behavior was repeated prior to each thrust of the paper between the bars of the cage. The paper was often thrust at a point too distant from the pellets to be successful, and the bluejay nearly always returned to the perch with the piece of paper and engaged in paper manipulating behavior before taking notice whether a pellet had been dislodged or not.

As individual bluejays gain more and more experience, the idiosyncratic and extraneous components begin to disappear and the tool-use behavior increases in efficiency. In the illustration, if a comparison is made between curves *e* and *f*, the amount of time spent away from the 2 × 4 with pellets on it can be considered a rough index of the amount of extraneous activity engaged in. Not only does the amount of time away from the 2 × 4 decrease, but a reciprocal relationship is apparent between this measure and the amount of time spent near the 2 × 4. When the tool-use behavior is less efficient or nonexistent, the amount of time spent away from the 2 × 4 is greater than the amount of time spent near it. As tool-use behavior becomes more efficient, the inverse is true. In

previously tool-using-naive bluejay was allowed to observe a model successfully using a tool prior to being given pieces of paper (trials to the right of the vertical broken line representing the twenty-fifth session). Increase in frequency was relatively dramatic for thrusts in the vicinity of pellets and manipulation (curves *c* and *d*), but subdued for curve *b* the number of thrusts between bars of the cage occurring away from the 2 × 4 (BBA) normally shows a general tendency to decrease as a bluejay becomes more and more successful in obtaining pellets. This is considered to be a second parameter that is indicative of the level of efficiency. However, in this particular instance the initial occurrence of this behavior was low in frequency, and therefore the decrease in occurrence is not easily discernible in the graph.

Experienced bluejays. The role of experience in tool-use acquisition by the bluejay is further evidenced by the degree to which different sizes of paper are modified by experienced bluejays. All bluejays will tear, crumple, and otherwise modify a piece of paper, but this activity takes on a special significance when observed in tool-using-experienced bluejays. If experienced bluejays are given two different sizes of paper, one of which approximates the size used successfully by experienced tool users, the piece of paper that approximates the most successfully used size is manipulated 25% more of the time than a larger piece of paper is manipulated. This difference in manipulation time is quite consistent. The time of manipulation is that elapsed time from when the bluejay takes the piece of paper offered between the bars of the cage to when the bluejay first *attempts* to thrust the paper back through the bars. Differences in the degree to which different sizes of paper are manipulated can be considered a behavioral expression of an awareness that there is an optimal size for a tool.

In addition to using a piece of paper as a means to maneuver food pellets into reach, bluejays will crumple and moisten a piece of paper and then run it about the inside of their food cup. Loose food particles and dust adhere to the moistened paper. The food particles are then either picked off the moistened paper, or paper and all are ingested bit by bit.

Comparative adaptations by avian species. The use of tools by avian species falls broadly into two classes: the wielding of objects such as twigs, pieces of paper, or leaf segments as a direct extension of the body; or, the heaving or dropping of objects such as rocks or dirt clods. In a majority of these cases, the development of tool-use behavior is probably a stepwise alteration of already existing behavior patterns that are influenced in varying degrees, depending upon the species, by the experience of each individual. If tool-use is adaptive, experience could play less and less of a role in the development of the behavior. Such is probably the case for the Galapagos woodpecker finch (*Cactospiza pallida*), which uses twigs or cactus spines to startle or pry prey from crevices. The behavior which was once altered by learning is gradually shaped by evolutionary processes until very little altering by learning is required for tool-use behavior to develop. Such tool-use behavior would become, as the woodpecker finch's has, much more stereotyped or species-typical.

Without ethological information the behaviors upon which the tool-using behavior might have developed cannot be specified. However, in most instances of tool use, the species involved exhibits enough behaviors such as nest building and food gathering that could conceivably, with minor alteration through experience, result in a form of tool using. However, the tool-use behavior of some green herons (*Butorides virescens*) poses a special problem.

The green heron places pieces of bread on the surface of water, and then waits for a fish to nibble at the bread. Any fish that accepts the green heron's invitation to dinner rapidly becomes the dinner himself. The behavior is deliberate on the part of the green heron. If the bread is about to be picked up by another bird such as a coot, the bread is retrieved by the heron and the intruder driven off. The bread is then placed back on the surface of the water. If water embroiled by the activity of a school of fish indicates fishing might be better elsewhere, the green heron promptly moves the bread to the new location. What previously existing behavior could have been elaborated upon?

As is probably the case in mammals, the number of observed instances of tool use by avian species is probably much less than the actual number of occurrences. Many species of both birds and mammals manipulate, as an expression of a genetic predisposition, objects found in their environment. The elaboration of manipulatory behaviors through learning could potentially lead to the development of tool using by individuals in any one of these species.

For background information *see* ETHOLOGY in the McGraw-Hill Encyclopedia of Science and Technology.   [THONY B. JONES]

Bibliography: J. Alcock, *Evolution*, 26:464–473, 1972; H. B. Lovell, *Wilson Bull.*, 70:280–281, 1958; G. C. Millikan and R. I. Bowman, *The Living Bird*, 6th Annual of the Cornell Laboratory of Ornithology, 1967; R. Sisson, *Nat. Geogr.*, 145:142–147, 1974; J. Van Lawick-Goodhall, in D. S. Lehrman, R. A. Hinde, and E. Shaw, *Advances in the Study of Behavior*, vol. 3, 1970.

Evolution, organic

Extinctions have been of major importance in the history of life and are attracting increasing attention from paleontologists, evolutionary biologists, and ecologists. The fossil record indicates that there have been episodic waves of mass extinctions, but as yet no single general explanation of these phenomena has been widely accepted. However, recent work has shed light on a new hypothesis, that mass extinctions in the sea were due to a loss of genetic variability in lineages that inhabited stable environments.

This hypothesis is based on the assumption that species which inhabit variable environments require large pools of genetic variability to cope with the variations, whereas species that inhabit more stable environments require only small genetic variability. It has long been observed that lineages which appear to have been the more specialized were particularly hard hit during mass extinctions. Perhaps when wide regions of the oceans were stable for long periods of time, their populations became highly specialized and genetically depauperate. Subsequently, during times of either increasing instability or of large environmental changes, those lineages would lack the genetic resources necessary to maintain their adaptations and would mostly be swept away in a wave of mass extinction.

Trophic resource variability. Although it is not possible to gain information about the genetic variabilities of extinct organisms directly, this hypothesis can be tested by investigating its major assumption, that genetic and environmental variabilities are directly correlated. To design such a test raises the issue of which environmental parameters should be associated with genetic variability. Insofar as evolutionary strategies for adaptive flexibility or specialization are concerned, the trophic resource regime seems to be of major importance: where productivity is most stable, specialization is particularly favored; on the other hand, where productivity fluctuates on the scale of seasons, flexibility is favored and many species are generalists. Therefore it is reasonable to study genetic variability in populations from environments with markedly different trophic resource variabilities, and it is possible to do so by investigating protein polymorphisms. Variability in the gene loci coding for enzymes and other soluble proteins is estimated by studying variations in the proteins themselves as measured by techniques of gel electrophoresis. Only relatively few loci can be studied, but the results can be extrapolated to the entire genome, since the loci studied are selected at random with respect to their variabilities. Nevertheless these estimates must be regarded as only first approximations.

The more stable marine trophic resource regimes lie in the tropics, where primary productivity varies little seasonally, and in the deep sea, where detrital resource supplies appear to be relatively constant. The species studied from these environments prove to have unusually high genetic variability. Studies involving large numbers of individuals have shown that, of the loci studied, a tropical marine clam has an average individual heterozygosity of more than 20%, whereas five species of echinoderms and a brachiopod from the deep sea average about 17%. Less stable resource regimes are found in temperate latitudes. The heterozygosity of marine species from these regions (two echinoderms, one arthropod, and one phoronid) ranges from just over 1% to about 9% for an average individual. High-latitude resource regimes are even more unstable. A brachiopod from Antarctica has just under 4% average heterozygosity.

From these new data it is clear that there is no positive correlation between genetic stability and environmental stability as measured by trophic resource regimes. Indeed, there is a distinct tendency for these factors to be negatively correlated. Furthermore, levels of genetic variability and other environmental parameters such as temperature or hydroclimates do not have the same patterns of variability; for example, heterozygosities are both high and low in thermally stable regions (tropical regions and Antarctica, respectively). Accordingly, a different hypothesis relating environmental and genetic variability is required.

Hypotheses of genetic variability. The following model has been suggested. In trophically unstable environments, average fitness is at a premium and individuals tend to be phenotypically flexible and generalized. Such wide functional range is attained by a harmoniously coadapted genotype that codes for the more generalized functional responses. In order to prevent destruction of optimal genotypes by recombination, the gene pool becomes depauperate; even though some alleles may enhance some special function, they are selected against. In more trophically stable environments, genetic variability that enhances specialization is permitted to accumulate and is employed to improve adaptation to spatial environmental variations. Genetic variability becomes large, and many genotypes permit many functionally specialized individuals.

An alternate hypothesis is that the protein variations detected electrophoretically are adaptively neutral. In this event, environmental patterns of genetic variability would not be expected, and the correlation suggested above would be spurious. However, observations of allele frequencies and patterns do not correspond well to the expectations under a neutrality hypothesis, which is thereby weakened.

In summary, present understanding of environmental patterns of genetic variabilities does not support the hypothesis that mass extinctions are caused by genetic depauperation. On the contrary, highly specialized lineages may possess the highest genetic variabilities, and yet they are most frequently the sorts of species that are swept away in waves of extinction, leaving genetically relatively invariant but ecologically flexible organisms as survivors. Therefore, extinctions may deplete the total genetic variability of the biosphere to an extent that is disproportionate to their severity. It appears that theories involving the evolution of genetic variability and its preservation in variable environments should be reevaluated.

For background information *see* EVOLUTION, ORGANIC in the McGraw-Hill Encyclopedia of Science and Technology.   [JAMES W. VALENTINE]

Bibliography: F. J. Ayala et al., *J. Paleontol.,* vol. 48, 1974; F. J. Ayala and J. W. Valentine, *Mar. Biol.,* vol. 14, 1974; P. W. Bretsky and D. M. Lorenz, *North American Palentology Convention, Chicago, 1969, Proceedings E,* pp. 522–550, 1970; J. W. Valentine, *Evolutionary Paleoecology of the Marine Biosphere,* p. 511, 1973.

Eye (invertebrate)

Students of the visual process are confronted with two major problems. First, how does the capture of a photon by the visual pigment in a primary photoreceptor result in the electrical response generated by that cell's membrane? Second, the capture of photons by a population of visual pigment molecules results in ambiguous information for the cell; that is, it cannot discriminate between the number of incident photons (intensity) and their wavelength (color) or, in the special case, their plane of orientation if the light is polarized. How, then, is the nervous system able to extract complex information from a large number of ambiguous inputs? In a general sense, the answer is that a retina is composed of receptors of different sensitivities or capabilities, or both, and that their responses must be compared at some higher level. Different information channels must therefore be isolated at the level of the photoreceptors. Recent studies on the visual organs of invertebrate species, especially within the arthropod group, have added to the understanding of these fundamental questions.

Interreceptor coupling. The compound eyes of arthropods are composed of many subunits called ommatidia. Each consists of a lens, a photoreceptor organelle (rhabdom), and a number of photoreceptors (retinular cells). Portions of the retinular plasma membranes are modified microvillar structures which, in the majority of species, are fused with the similar modifications of other cells of the ommatidium to form the rhabdom. Much evidence has accumulated to suggest that individual retinular cells can function independently even when they are excited through such a common organelle. This implies that, if receptor cells are electrically coupled to others in the same ommatidium, they must share common physiological properties.

A recent study of the crayfish retina by K. Muller has shown this to be the case. Retinular cells in the ommatidium of this crustacean are more sensitive to polarized light aligned parallel to their microvillar axis than to light orthogonal to it. Within each ommatidium there are two sets of cells that have orthogonal microvillar axes and therefore orthogonal polarization sensitivity maxima. In addition, these cells also fall into two spectral classes, one more sensitive to orange light, the other more sensitive to blue light. Muller studied pairs of receptors in single ommatidia with intracellular recording techniques and found that, when cell pairs had the same angle of maximum sensitivity to polarized light, they were electrically coupled. The exception occurred when the cells had similar polarization sensitivities but different spectral sensitivities; in this case, they were not coupled. Cell pairs having different polarization sensitivities were never coupled. Thus it appears that electrical coupling is present when it enhances the sensitivity of the eye to a particular stimulus modality but that this increased sensitivity is sacrificed so that channels carrying information about different stimulus modalities will be isolated.

Phototransduction. The process of phototransduction can be separated into three distinct parts. The first is obviously the interaction of the visual pigment molecules with incident photons, and the last is an alteration in the membrane conductances of the cells that results in a depolarizing receptor potential. Recent evidence suggests that these events are coupled by a third event, which probably consists of several stages.

The visual pigments of the invertebrates are rhodopsins, as in vertebrates, but they differ in that they exist in two stable states. Irradiation of the native pigment converts it to a stable metarhodopsin, usually with a shorter wavelength of maximum absorption, which is photoconvertible back to the native rhodopsin. Recently P. Hillman and colleagues have observed electrophysiological signs of this process in cells of the barnacle ocellus. The temporal characteristics of the receptor potential are dependent upon the state of adaptation. Illumination of the cell with a high-intensity red light after a period of adaptation with blue light results in a prolonged afterdepolarization of the cell membrane that persists for up to 30 min after the red stimulus is removed. Essentially the cell

does not "turn off." A blue light presented to the cell during this period of afterdepolarization reverses the effect. The spectral maxima for this phenomenon are coincident with the spectral maxima of two stable pigment states. Adaptation paradigms that place the pigment in the native state (absorption maximum 532 nm) result in the prolonged afterdepolarization with red stimuli. Adaptation paradigms that place the pigment in the stable metarhodopsin state (absorption maximum 495 nm) either prevent or reverse that event. The resulting model for the phototransduction process proposed by this group supposes that irradiation of pigment in the native state produces an "excitor substance" that in turn acts upon the plasma membrane to increase its conductance to certain ions. H. M. Brown and coworkers have shown that in this cell the ions are predominantly sodium and calcium. The model further proposes that the photoconversion of the stable metarhodopsin back to the native state releases an "inhibitor substance" that does not act upon the membrane but neutralizes the "excitor substance." These antagonistic processes are thought to be in equilibrium under the normal illumination conditions encountered by the animal.

A different approach is the study of phototransduction mutants of *Drosophila* that are obtained by a behavioral screen for blind animals. A class of mutants obtained by this procedure do not produce a receptor potential. The effect appears to be the alteration of a single gene that in turn results in the alteration of a single protein in a manner dependent upon the location of the lesion in the cistron. A temperature-sensitive variety produces normal receptor potentials at 17°C that are abolished if the temperature is quickly raised to 34°C. The effect is instantaneous and reversible, providing the animals are not held at 34°C for more than a few minutes. If the temperature is raised to 25°C, the receptor potential is present but altered in that the response is temporally prolonged, persisting long after the stimulus light is removed. The cell does not turn off, and the situation is reminiscent of that described above for the barnacle. Two lines of experimentation suggest that the genetic lesion is in the coupling mechanism between photon absorption and membrane depolarization.

First, the visual pigment appears to be normal in this mutant. Measurements of the early receptor potential suggest that the *Drosophila* visual pigment also exists in two stable states and that the conditions for conversion and reconversion in the mutant whose receptor potential has been altered or abolished by temperature changes are similar to those in the wild-type fly. Second, the mechanism of altering membrane permeability also appears normal. This was determined by studying the characteristics of the unitary membrane responses, or "quantum bumps," at very low light intensities. These events were similar in time course and amplitude to those observed in normal animals, even though the latency in response to a light flash was markedly prolonged. Since these two features of the phototransduction process appear normal in this mutant, W. L. Pak has concluded that the mutant protein has affected the coupling between them, possibly causing the release of an intracellular transmitter. It appears that the genetic approach to the study of phototransduction will be particularly fruitful in the near future.

For background information *see* EYE (INVERTEBRATE); PHOTORECEPTION in the McGraw-Hill Encyclopedia of Science and Technology.   [MICHAEL I. MOTE]

Bibliography: M. C. Deland and W. L. Pak, *Nature New Biol.*, 244(136):184, 1973; S. Hochstein, B. Minke, and P. Hillman, *J. Gen. Physiol.*, 62:105, 1973; K. Muller, *J. Physiol.*, 232:573, 1973.

Ferromagnetism

The decades-old problem of the origin of ferromagnetism in iron (Fe), cobalt (Co), and nickel (Ni) at last appears to be resolved. The understanding of the behavior of hyperfine fields (the magnetic fields produced at nuclei by the electrons) in Fe alloys led to the resolution of the problem. These fields were measured by nuclear magnetic resonance and Mössbauer experiments.

Early theories and experiments. In Fe, Co, and Ni the *d*-electrons are not completely paired off and are thus responsible for the magnetism. Since the early 1930s, when quantum mechanics was first applied to the problem of ferromagnetism, two schools of thought about the nature of the *d*-electrons have developed. The first was the "localized" school, which assumed that the *d*-electrons were attached to individual atoms. The atoms were assumed to be close enough to one another that they were directly influenced by the spin direction of the unpaired *d*-electrons. The second was the "itinerant" school, which proposed that all the *d*-electrons were free to move from atom to atom and that, by some mechanism, they developed an excess spin and aligned with one another. Over the years, many different types of experiments were also performed to elucidate the nature of the *d*-electrons. Some experiments indicated that the *d*-electrons were quite localized, whereas others showed that some *d*-electrons were itinerant. To the present time the itinerant school has never been able to find a mechanism that gives rise to stable ferromagnetism, and in the early 1960s computer calculations showed that the direct interactions were much too weak to cause Fe to be magnetic.

Indirect alignment of d-electrons. Meanwhile, during the 1950s, in anticipation of the difficulties of the direct theory, a new model was proposed that assumed that the *d*-electrons were localized but were indirectly aligned by the polarization that they induced in the *s* conduction electrons, which are present in all metals. With the demise of the direct interaction model, this indirect model became the most likely explanation of ferromagnetism. It was soon tested by measuring the hyperfine fields in Fe alloys, which gave the polarization of the *s* conduction electrons. As shown in the illustration, the *s*-electrons in Fe are negatively polarized at first- and second-neighbor distances (solid curve), and thus, if this interaction were dominant, it would lead to antiferromagnetism. The spin of the localized *d*-electrons can be considered at the origin, as shown by the heavy arrow. The *s*-electrons are negatively polarized at the near-neighbor distances because there are too

many of them; fewer would give rise to a polarization curve, as shown by the dashed curve in the figure. Thus, as a result of these measurements, the proposed model claimed that there were very few (~ 0.3 per atom) itinerant *d*-electrons that provided the ferromagnetic coupling between the mainly localized *d*-electrons. The existence of a small number of itinerant *d*-electrons was strongly supported by a reexamination of the many different experiments of earlier years. Also, recent de Haas–Van Alphen measurements and band structure calculations on Fe have indicated rather directly that there is about 0.3 itinerant *d*-electron per Fe atom. Further, it has been shown recently that the moment perturbations on Fe atoms caused by alloying Fe with other transition elements are a direct result of the polarization of the itinerant *d*s. These moment perturbations directly reflect oscillations in the itinerant *d* polarization such as those indicated in the figure.

This model not only explains the ferromagnetism of Fe, Co, and Ni but, from the systematics of the behavior of the polarization curve, gives the correct behavior for the rest of the first transition series; namely, Mn is antiferromagnetic, and Cr, V, Ti, and Sc show no atomiclike magnetism.

Conclusion. Thus the mechanism that produces magnetism in transition-series metals is an alignment of the mainly localized *d*-electrons by the well-known intraatomic exchange interaction (Hund's rule). The local moments then polarize the *s* and *d* conduction electrons. Since the two types of *d*-electrons have the same orbital symmetry, the interaction between them is much stronger than that between the *s*- and localized *d*-electrons, and

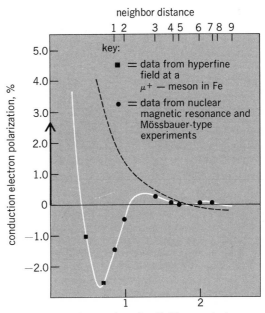

Measured polarization of the *s* conduction electrons in Fe (solid line). The dashed line shows proposed polarization of the itinerant *d*-electrons in Fe. Heavy arrow at origin represents spin of localized *d*-electrons. (*From M. B. Stearns, On the origin of ferromagnetism and the hyper-fine fields in Fe, Co, Ni, Phys. Rev., 8B:4383, 1973*)

it is this interaction that determines the magnetic behavior.

For background information *see* BAND THEORY OF SOLIDS; FERROMAGNETISM in the McGraw-Hill Encyclopedia of Science and Technology.

[MARY BETH STEARNS]

Bibliography: A. V. Gold et al., *Int. J. Magn.*, 2: 357, 1971; C. Herring, Exchange interactions among itinerant electrons, in G. T. Rado and H. Suhl (eds.), *Magnetism*, vol. 4, 1966; F. Mott, *Advan. Phys.*, 13:325, 1964; M. B. Stearns, *Bull. Amer. Phys. Soc.*, 19:230, 1974; M. B. Stearns, *Phys. Rev.*, 8B:4383, 1973.

Field-emission microscopy

Field-emission microscopy and field-ion microscopy have remained productive avenues in surface science in the last few years. Field-emission microscopy, as the older technique, is more matured and a subject of refined interpretation made possible by advances in the electron theory of metals. Field-ion microscopy of metal surfaces at the atomic level has benefitted from two instrumental developments, the general use of channel plate image intensification, and the employment of the atom probe as a microanalytical tool of ultimate sensitivity. A more detailed mechansim of the image formation process is emerging.

Field-emission microscope. The field-emission microscope either is used by itself as an imaging device in order to display and measure crystallographic anisotropies of work functions of clean and adsorption-covered metals and changes in surface shapes due to thermal equilibration and surface migration, or is used as a part of an experimental set-up for the study of the mechanism of field emission as a tunneling effect. The relatively low fields of 0.2 to 0.6 V/A (10 A = 1 nm) represent a minor perturbation of the electronic condition at the surface, and the 20-A limit of resolution washes out complicating atomic details, so that many theoretical problems can be treated one-dimensionally. A considerable degree of understanding has been achieved: Experimental data on total energy distribution, particularly those of E. W. Plummer, have led to gradually more comprehensive theories of electron tunneling, involving band structure effects, surface states, many-body effects, and chemisorption. The theories of resonance tunneling due to chemisorption, and of adsorbate-enhanced inelastic tunneling, are now well established. The subject of spin polarization of field-emitted electrons is attracting greater interest. Reports of polarization of up to 50% obtained from a europium sulfide emitter, somewhat less from ferromagnetic metals, and even from tungsten in a high magnetic field, are stimulating more research.

Field-ion microscope. Just as in the field-emission microscope, the specimen in the field-ion microscope (both developed by E. W. Müller) is a sharply pointed wire tip opposite to a phosphor screen. However, atomic resolution is obtained by imaging at cryogenic temperature with gas ions rather than electrons. A sharper tip, of 200 to 1000 A radius, and a higher voltage of 10 to 30 kV provide a field strength between 2 and 6 V/A and produce an image, magnified a million times, of the atomic arrangement at the tip cap. This surface, being the specimen and the imaging "projection lens" at the same time, must be perfectly rounded by the prior application of a somewhat higher voltage, which causes "field evaporation" of all excessive protuberances. Controlled field evaporation at cryogenic temperatures is subsequently employed for removing material from the specimen, atom layer by atom layer. By this unique sectioning technique, details within the bulk structure of the specimen are brought to the surface for inspection. Lattice imperfections such as vacancies and interstitials, the structure of dislocations and grain boundaries, the size and distribution of precipitates, and the order in alloys have been the main subjects of observations, which are mostly beyond the range of conventional electron microscopy. Experimentation with single atoms or a few atoms planted on a perfectly clean crystal plane has yielded data on the surface self-diffusion of single atoms, the interaction between adjacent adatoms, and the nucleation of the first atomic layer in vapor condensation. Surprisingly, the interaction between adatoms as seen by the thermal stability of clusters turned out not to be pairwise, and T. T. Tsong found the first direct evidence of a strongly correlated motion when two or more adatoms are within an interaction range of several lattice spacings.

Study of nonrefractory metals. The constraints imposed by the yield strength of the tip material under the mechanical stress $F^2/8\pi$ exerted by the high field F, particularly during the preparation of the specimen surface by field evaporation, as well as the low image brightness, had limited the application of field-ion microscopy mostly to study of the refractory metals and to helium as an imaging gas. Using external intensification of neon images, metals as soft as iron, gold, and copper had been marginally imaged a decade ago. With the availability of the channel plate electron multiplier, originally developed for photoelectronic night viewing, the weak images of the field-ion microscope can now be brightened by a factor of 1000 or more with the conversion of the primary ion image into an electron image. Field-ion microscopy of metals with melting points down to 1000°C is now quite routine, preferably using more easily ionized neon as the imaging gas. By careful field evaporation procedures with hydrogen promotion the evaporation field may also be kept low. Studies of precipitation-hardened steels and numerous other alloys have been performed, the most successful being those of the group under B. Ralph at Cambridge University. Going to still lower imaging fields by using argon as the imaging gas turned out to be difficult for routine metallurgical work. There is no longer a safety margin between the ionization field of the imaging gas and that of contaminating residual gases which may cause severe field-induced specimen corrosion and atomic rearrangement at the surface. Tedious ultrahigh vacuum techniques have yielded satisfactory argon ion images of aluminum, but the broader application to the study of aluminum alloys is still unlikely.

Atom probe. The chemical nature of a single atom or a small surface area selected by the observer of a live field-ion microscope image can be identified by manipulating the tip direction so that the image of the desired area falls onto a probe hole in the screen. Subsequent removal of surface

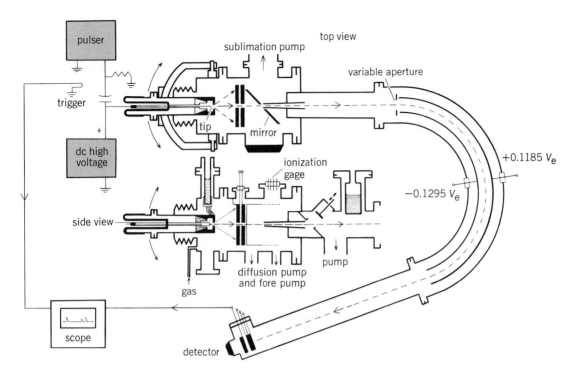

Schematic of a time-of-flight atom probe with a 163° toroidal deflector system for energy focusing. The 250-cm drift path and oscilloscopic time readout to 2 ns gives a mass resolution > 1000 even if the ion energy is uncertain by ±3%. V_e = evaporation voltage (sum of dc and pulse voltage supplied to tip). (*From E. W. Müller and S. V. Krishnaswamy, Energy deficits in pulsed field evaporation and deficit compensated atom-probe designs, Rev. Sci. Instr., 45:1053, 1974*)

particles by nanosecond pulsed field evaporation sends the selected atoms in ionic form through the probe hole and a time-of-flight mass spectrometer of single-ion sensitivity. Since the inception of the atom probe by Müller in 1967 there are now three such instruments in use, and a dozen under construction. In addition, a magnetic sector atom probe, in which the mass spectrometer separates ions by deflecting them in a magnetic field, has also been introduced. Metallurgical applications of these uniquely sensitive microanalytical instruments by S. S. Brenner at U.S. Steel and by P. Turner and coworkers at Cambridge University were centered on determining the composition of nuclei of precipitates in steel and other alloys, which are often too small to be visible under an electron microscope. Using Müller's recently successful concept of a field-desorption microscope, in which the tip specimen is imaged by ions that are field-desorbed or field-evaporated directly from the surface rather than by ions obtained from an externally supplied gas, J. F. Panitz produced an overall view of the entire tip surface in the "light" of one ion species. The quite limited mass discrimination is achieved by "opening" the channel plate viewing screen by means of a gating pulse voltage for only a few nanoseconds after a predetermined time-of-flight gap following the desorption pulse. The shortness of the 10-cm drift path limits the resolution $M/\Delta M$ (where M is the ion mass and ΔM is the minimum difference in mass of ions which can be separated by the spectrometer) to about 15. Atom probe discoveries of a more basic nature are the unexpectedly high charge of field-evaporated metal ions, with up to four electrons removed from

refractory metal atoms, the adsorption due to field-induced dipole bonding of He and Ne up to a temperature of 150 K, and the field evaporation of metal ions in the form of helium and even neon compound ions. The latter phenomena, initially only reluctantly accepted because of a limited resolution and the occurrence of artifacts, are now definitely established since the introduction by Müller of a new energy-focused time-of-flight atom probe (see illustration) and the magnetic atom probe. Both types exceed a mass resolution $M/\Delta M$ of 1000, an improvement by at least an order of magnitude, and in addition the time-of-flight version is completely free of artifacts. These new instruments are seen as promising tools for the study of catalysis, adsorption, and field-induced surface reactions at the atomic level. While a definite theory of field evaporation is still outstanding, the process of field ionization by tunneling through the noble gas adsorbate seems to be a reasonable mechanism.

For background information *see* FIELD-EMISSION MICROSCOPY in the McGraw-Hill Encyclopedia of Science and Technology.

[ERWIN W. MÜLLER]

Bibliography: J. W. Gadzuk and E. W. Plummer, *Rev. Mod. Phys.*, 45:487–584, 1973; E. W. Müller and S. V. Krishnaswamy, Energy deficits in pulsed field evaporation and deficit compensated atom-probe designs, *Rev. Sci. Instr.*, 45:1053, 1974; E. W. Müller and T. T. Tsong, in S. G. Davison (ed.), *Progress in Surface Sciences*, vol. 4, pt. 1, pp. 1–139, 1973; L. W. Swanson and A. E. Bell, in L. Marton (ed.), *Advances in Electronics and Electron Physics*, vol. 32, pp. 194–309, 1973.

Filter, electric

Surface acoustic-wave (SAW) filters for the frequency range 10^7–10^9 Hz have made dramatic advances in design, performance, reliability, and cost reduction in the last few years. SAW bandpass filters now have no serious commercial competitors for achieving intermediate Qs (10 to 100), particularly in the ultrahigh-frequency band. New products include frequency discriminators, selective frequency multiplexing networks, frequency synthesizers, reflective-array devices, and, most importantly, stable oscillators.

Basic design. The basic bandpass filter consists of a piezoelectric bar with a polished upper surface on which two interdigital transducers (IDT) are deposited. Each transducer consists of a series of photolithographically defined, interleaved metal electrodes, each a few hundred nanometers thick, fed from two bus-bars (Fig. 1a). The simplest IDT has a periodicity (indicated by p on Fig. 1a) of one SAW length in the propagation direction. Also, the overlap between adjacent electrodes (the length w on Fig. 1a) is constant throughout. The designer can control the characteristics of the filter by varying the overlap between adjacent electrodes, a technique termed apodization (Fig. 1b), or by grading the periodicity (Fig. 1c).

Design advances. In contrast with conventional LC filters, SAW filters are members of a class of nonminimum phase networks having the property that linear phase response can be achieved independently of the amplitude response. Further, SAW filters are transversal filters in which the signal is repetitively delayed and added to itself, as in antenna arrays and digital filters. This analogy has been identified by R. H. Tancrell. He has applied the optimization procedures of digital filters in the synthesis of SAW filters with equiripple bandpass response. Another basic design procedure, due to C. S. Hartmann, is to compute the inverse Fourier transform of the prescribed filter response, giving the impulse response, which is the spatial image desired of the electrodes in the IDT. Due to finite piezoelectric substrate lengths, the infinitely long time-duration impulse response is not realizable. This has necessitated use of weighting functions to multiply and truncate impulse response.

A vital factor in SAW filters is amplitude weighting, that is, alteration of the amplitude-frequency response, in order to improve the filter's selectivity. A popular method of achieving this, due to ease of design and relative insensitivity to fabrication errors, has been apodization of the input IDT. However, an apodized IDT generates a spatially nonuniform SAW. This necessitates an output IDT of constant electrode overlap and few electrodes to reproduce faithfully the apodized IDT response. Undesirable consequences are high loss and poor selectivity for the filter.

Figure 2a shows the solution of Tancrell and H. Engan. It embodies a multistrip coupler (MSC) due to F. G. Marshall and E. G. S. Paige. The MSC has the property of converting the spatially nonuniform SAW generated by one apodized IDT into a spatially uniform SAW received by an identical apodized IDT, with additionally a high rejection of spurious bulk acoustic modes. The apodized transducers, particularly when fabricated on lithium niobate, incorporate special electrodes to reduce SAW impedance mismatch between the unloaded and metallized substrate surface. An alternative approach due to Hartmann, shown in Fig. 2b, obtains amplitude weighting by selective withdrawal of electrodes from identical and constant-overlap IDTs arranged in nondispersive combination. In this arrangement the electrodes to the right of both IDTs in Fig. 2b are spaced by a large amount (that is, low frequencies are excited), whereas those to the left of both IDTs are spaced by a small amount (that is, high frequencies are excited). Thus, both low- and high-frequency components of the excitation travel exactly the same distance before being received, so that the nondispersive characteristics of the SAW are preserved. Additionally, phase weighting, that is, production of a controllable nonlinear phase response, introduced by grading the IDT periodicities, allows the filter bandpass width to be traded off optimally against the loss.

Technology advances. Dominant piezoelectric substrates to emerge are ST-cut, X-propagating quartz for temperature stability, lithium niobate, bismuth germanium oxide, and bismuth silicon oxide for fabricating color television filters. The IDT remains the cornerstone of SAW filter designs. In the photolithographic technique of fabricating IDT patterns, optical masks containing the required patterns are used to suitably expose by light the photoresist overlaid on the completely metallized piezoelectric substrate. New tech-

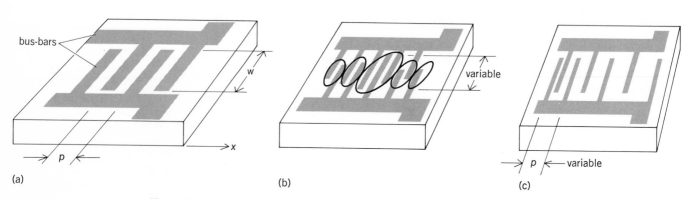

Fig. 1.   Transducers. (a) Interdigital construction. (b) Apodization technique. (c) Graded periodicity technique.

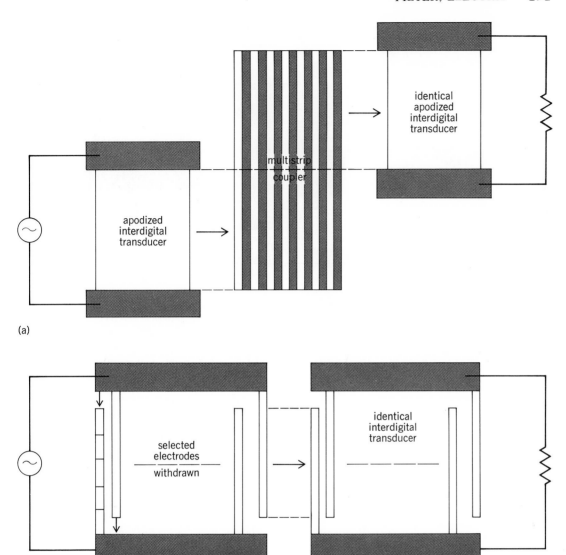

(a)

(b)

Fig. 2. Surface acoustic-wave bandpass filter geometries. (a) Apodized-amplitude weighted interdigital transducers interconnected through a multistrip coupler (Tancrell and Engan configuration). (b) Graded periodicity phase–weighted interdigital transducers, incorporating selective withdrawal of electrodes in nondispersive combination (Hartmann configuration).

niques utilized in defining the IDT electrode patterns include conformable optical masks (optical masks made on a flexible glass substrate so that they can be pulled down under vacuum into intimate contact with the piezoelectric substrate for accurate IDT fabrication) and x-ray lithography, both due to H. I. Smith, coupled with sputter etching by radio-frequency and ion-beam methods for submicron resolutions. These techniques allow frequency filters to be fabricated up to 2×10^9 Hz.

SAW reflective-array frequency filtering, due to R. C. Williamson, has also been demonstrated. This technique aids the rejection of spurious bulk acoustic modes. Ion-beam etching is necessary to form the grooves which act as the SAW reflectors. The bandpass response is tailored by adjustment of the length or depth of the grooves. This procedure is an alternate to those of Tancrell and Engan and of Hartmann.

SAW bandpass filter capabilities. Current and projected performance are shown in the table. Sidelobe rejection specifies the magnitude of the loss of sidelobes, that is, unwanted but necessary responses close to but outside the bandpass, with respect to that at the center of the bandpass. Ultimate rejection specifies the greatest magnitude of the loss at frequencies far removed from the bandpass region with respect to that at the center of the bandpass. Linear phase deviation expresses the undesired deviation in the response of the filter from a linear phase change with frequency. The majority of the data in the table are not obtainable simultaneously. Rather, performance for specific parameters must be traded off. Examples are given below.

The lower limit on a 3-dB bandwidth is dictated by size of practical piezoelectric substrates. The upper limit is set by interference from spurious

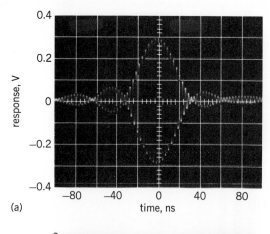

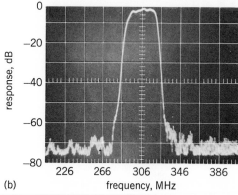

Fig. 3. Surface acoustic-wave bandpass filter performance, showing oscillograms of (a) impulse response and (b) bandpass response. (*Texas Instruments*)

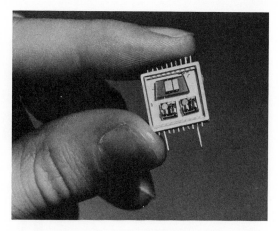

Fig. 4. Photograph of a 2×10^8 Hz SAW oscillator. (*Royal Radar Establishment, U.K.*)

bulk acoustic modes. The minimum loss of 6 dB assumes a three-IDT configuration in which the outer IDTs are connected electrically in parallel. This removes half the 6-dB bidirectionality loss. The remaining 3 dB is composed of resistive losses in the IDTs and matching networks; propagation, beam steering, and diffraction losses on the piezoelectric; and losses associated with apodization. The projected minimum insertion loss is dependent on the development of practical unidirectional IDTs.

The minimum transition bandwidth data given in the table are an important indicator of the maximum selectivity inherent in SAW filters. The transition bandwidth must exceed the inverse of the impulse response length of the IDT. Hence, a minimum transition bandwidth is equally applicable to narrow-band and wide-band filters. This implies that low shape factors cannot be achieved for filters with extremely narrow bandpass widths.

The major sources of undesired sidelobe responses in SAW bandpass filters are spurious bulk acoustic modes and direct electrical feedthrough. The major sources of undesired amplitude ripple and linear phase deviation are electroacoustic regeneration and reflections at the IDT electrode edges. Figure 3 shows both the impulse response in the time domain and the bandpass response of an SAW filter made by Texas Instruments, having 3.06×10^8 Hz center frequency and a sidelobe rejection of 60 dB.

The smallest SAW filters built to date are 0.02 in.³ (0.3 cm³). Unfortunately, high performance as indicated in the table demands complex SAW structures, thus increasing both substrate size and cost. This dilemma presents a considerable challenge for applications in the consumer market.

SAW oscillators. Two classes of oscillators are in common use, the quartz crystal oscillator and the LC oscillator, including the resonant cavity type. The former is of high stability ($Q > 10^4$) but suffers from a number of disadvantages, including mechanical fragility, low fundamental frequency operation ($<5 \times 10^7$ Hz), and limited frequency modulation (FM) capability (500 parts per million, ppm). In contrast, the LC is much less stable ($Q \ll 10^4$), but has superior FM performance. Recently the SAW oscillator, due to M. F. Lewis, has demonstrated an intermediate stability and modulation capability, with practical advantages over both. These properties seem destined to make the SAW oscillator significant commercially as a local oscillator in radar and communication systems, frequency synthesizers, telemetry, and strain gages, over the frequency range 2×10^7 to 2×10^9 Hz.

The basic SAW oscillator comprises a SAW delay line with a transistor amplifier as the feedback element. Figure 4 shows a 2×10^8 Hz SAW oscillator in a microelectronic flat pack.

The frequency of operation is determined by the IDT pattern and *not* by a dimension of the quartz

Surface acoustic-wave bandpass filter capabilities

Parameter	Current	Projected
Center frequency, f_0 (Hz)	$10^7 - 10^9$	$10^6 - 2 \times 10^9$
3-dB bandwidth (Hz)	$5 \times 10^4 - 0.4\, f_0$	$2 \times 10^4 - 0.8\, f_0$
Minimum loss (dB)	6	1.5
Minimum shape factor (ratio of bandpass width at 3 dB and 40 dB)	1.2	1.2
Minimum transition width from bandpass to bandstop (Hz)	5×10^4	2×10^4
Sidelobe rejection (dB)	55	65
Ultimate rejection (dB)	65	80
Amplitude of bandpass ripple (dB)	0.5	0.2
Linear phase deviation (degrees)	5	2

crystal. Hence, the crystal is rugged and can be firmly bonded to the encapsulating package. This good thermal contact allows output powers up to 1 W. Current performance figures for the SAW oscillator are: frequency deviation up to 2%; short-term stability of <1 in 10⁹ for 1 sec; medium-term stability of 100 ppm for temperature excursion of ±40°C; and single-sideband FM noise of −138 dB per hertz, 10 kHz away from carrier. Limits to the long-term stability still need establishing, but ±1 ppm per month is achievable. Research is now being directed to circumventing aging by improved quartz substrate preparation, and reducing migration of the IDT metallization.

For background information *see* FILTER, ELECTRIC; MICROCIRCUITRY; OSCILLATOR; PIEZOELECTRIC CRYSTAL; PIEZOELECTRICITY in the McGraw-Hill Encyclopedia of Science and Technology.

[J. H. COLLINS]

Bibliography: IEEE Trans. Microwave Theory Tech., Special Issue on Microwave Acoustics, no. MTT-21, April 1973; *IEEE London Conference Proceedings*, no. 109, September 1973; R. H. Tancrell, *IEEE Trans.*, Sonics and Ultrasonics, no. SU-21, pp. 12–22, January 1974; *Ultrasonics Symposium Proceedings*, IEEE Cat. no. 73 CHO 807-8 SU, 1973.

Flame photometry

Flame spectrometry, traditionally a single-element technique, has been advanced recently to include multielement analysis. To perform simultaneous multielement analysis, a multichannel device, that is, a device capable of measuring intensities at different wavelengths, is necessary. Two general categories of such detection systems are temporal and spatial multichannel devices. Temporal multichannel detection systems include scanning spectrometers, scanning detectors such as image-dissecting photomultipliers, and rotating filter photometers. Spatial multichannel devices employ multiple detectors in which each channel is separated in space. Typical examples include photographic detectors, direct-reading spectrometers, mosaics of photodiodes, and television camera tubes.

Vidicon flame spectrometer. The most promising developments within the past year involve the use of silicon diode vidicon television tubes as detectors for flame photometry. A typical vidicon flame spectrometer consists of a flame excitation source, a grating monochromator from which the exit slit has been removed, a vidicon tube detector, and an optical multichannel analyzer. Removing the exit slit from the monochromator and mounting the vidicon detector at the focal plane make it possible for a range of wavelengths to be dispersed across the light-sensitive tube target by the grating. A typical commercial vidicon tube has a target width of 0.5 in. (1.27 cm). The extent of the wavelength range or spectral window simultaneously covered by the tube depends upon the focal length of the monochromator and the grating ruling selected.

Figures 1 and 2 are schematic diagrams of two commonly used vidicon detectors, the image vidicon and the silicon-intensified target (SIT) vidicon. At one end of the vidicon tube is an electron

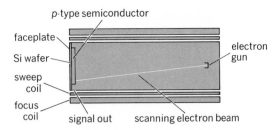

Fig. 1. Silicon diode image vidicon detector for multielement analysis. *(From K. W. Busch and G. H. Morrison, Multielement flame spectroscopy, Anal. Chem., 45(8):712A, 1973)*

gun that emits a beam of electrons. Focusing coils surrounding the tube focus the electron beam on the tube target. Deflection coils controlled electronically by the optical multichannel analyzer permit the electron beam to scan the target in a raster pattern of 500 vertical sweeps, producing 500 electronic channels. The spectral lines dispersed by the monochromator are focused on the tube target as vertical images that can be aligned with the vertical channels of the detector. The tube target consists of an array of *p*-type semiconductor islands grown on an *n*-type silicon wafer to form a mosaic of photodiodes. Radiation absorbed in the *n*-type silicon wafer results in a charge pattern that is produced in the neighboring *p*-type islands and is read off in 500 electronic channels by the scanning electron beam. This charge pattern is stored by the target until it is read by the electron beam, and it continues to accumulate as long as light strikes the target.

The SIT tube is approximately 2 orders of magnitude more sensitive than the image vidicon, owing to the presence of an image-intensifier stage prior to the silicon target. Radiation focused on the fiber optic faceplate causes photoelectrons to be emitted from the photocathode surface. These photoelectrons are collimated by the curved photocathode surface and internal focusing electrodes to produce an electron image on the silicon target that corresponds as closely as possible to the optical image focused on the faceplate of the tube. The emitted photoelectrons are accelerated toward the

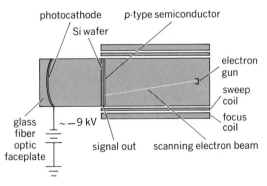

Fig. 2. Silicon-intensified target (SIT) vidicon detector. *(From K. W. Busch, N. G. Howell, and G. H. Morrison, Simultaneous determination of electrolytes in serum using a vidicon flame spectrometer, Anal. Chem., 46(9):1231, 1974)*

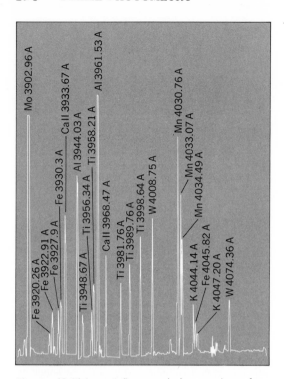

Fig. 3. Multielement flame emission spectrum from 3886 to 4086 A (10 A = 1 nm). *(From K. W. Busch, N. G. Howell, and G. H. Morrison, The vidicon tube as a detector for multielement flame spectrometric analysis, Anal. Chem., 46:575, 1974)*

target, where they are absorbed; and, as in direct photon absorption with the image vidicon, they produce a charge pattern on the target. Accelerated photoelectron absorption produces a target change pattern more efficiently than direct photon absorption. For this reason the SIT tube is more sensitive than the image vidicon.

The ability to perform simultaneous multielement analysis with the vidicon flame spectrometer depends not only on the use of the vidicon detector but also on the use of an associated optical multichannel analyzer, which controls the vidicon tube. Current optical multichannel analyzers have two separate memories to allow the storage of both a data spectrum and a blank spectrum. Since the vidicon tube is less sensitive than a photomultiplier, the optical multichannel analyzer is capable of accumulating the signal from a preset number of frame scans of the electron beam into either memory. In this way, weak signals can be built up in memory by signal averaging. This feature is also important in integrating time-varying signals. To allow the operator to view the spectrum, the contents of either memory can be displayed on an oscilloscope. An arithmetic unit is provided so that channel-by-channel subtraction of one memory from the other is possible. The blank spectrum can thus be subtracted from the data spectrum so that the spectrum of the analyte alone is available. Finally, the optical multichannel analyzer digitally displays the contents of any given channel and is capable of summing the contents of any number of adjacent channels to obtain peak area.

Simultaneous multielement flame analysis. Simultaneous multielement analysis using the vidicon flame spectrometer is based on a "window" concept. Thus, the number of elements that can be determined simultaneously depends on the extent of the wavelength window and the number of spectral lines emitted by various elements in that particular wavelength region. A typical portion of a spectrum of a sample containing eight elements obtained with a 20-nm window and a nitrous oxide–acetylene flame is shown in Fig. 3. For complex samples, the spectral window monitored cannot be increased more than 40 nm, if spectral interferences are to be avoided. Under certain circumstances the effective wavelength window may be increased without loss of resolution by monitoring overlapping orders. The choice of the wavelength window for a given analytical sample depends on the available lines for the given elements, and on their concentrations in the sample. After an appropriate window has been selected, the analytical flame conditions must be determined.

In single-element flame-emission determinations, the operating conditions are optimized for the given element according to its spectrochemical properties, which include the excitation potential of the analytical line, the ionization potential of the element, and the tendency for the element to form compounds in the flame. This optimization is conventionally carried out by optimizing the flame zone sampled by the spectrometer and by adjusting the fuel-to-oxidant ratio of the flame. For simultaneous multielement analysis, individual optimization is not possible, and a compromise must be reached. This compromise flame condition may be obtained by observing the variation of signal with flame height and fuel-to-oxidant ratio for each element. For some samples, the conditions producing the most intense signals for all the given elements may be chosen. In other cases, it may be desirable to select the excitation conditions that favor certain elements and not others. In this way, samples in which the elements of interest are present in varying amounts can be analyzed simultaneously without saturating the detector.

Once the spectral window and compromise flame conditions have been selected for the sample, the analyte spectrum is accumulated in memory A by aspirating the sample into the flame for a sufficient number of frame scans to provide a signal of adequate intensity. A blank or background spectrum is then obtained by aspirating distilled water into the flame under the identical experimental conditions for the same number of frame scans and storing the result in memory B. The A minus B mode is selected to display the analyte spectrum, and the intensities of the selected analytical lines are determined and compared with calibration curves to obtain the concentrations of the given elements.

Applications. To date, the vidicon flame spectrometer has been applied to the multielement analysis of a geological sample and the simultaneous determination of serum electrolytes. Because of the advantages of flame analytical techniques, the further development of the vidicon flame spectrometer will be readily applied to clinical, metallurgical, geological, and environmental samples, as well as a variety of other samples.

For background information *see* FLAME PHOTOMETRY in the McGraw-Hill Encyclopedia of Science and Technology.

[G. H. MORRISON; K. W. BUSCH]
Bibliography: K. W. Busch, N. G. Howell, and G. H. Morrison, *Anal. Chem.*, 46:575, 1974, and 46(9):1231, 1974; K. W. Busch and G. H. Morrison, *Anal. Chem.*, 45(8):712A, 1973.

Flower

Flowers exhibit a tremendous diversity of morphological forms. An important element of this diversity is the development of compound organs as a result of fusions between individual organs. Some of these fusions are known to involve the union of free surfaces on the fusing organs with a subsequent adhesion of the organs into the compound structure. Similar unions also occur between separate tissues or separate cells. It has recently been demonstrated that, in some cases of fusion, the mechanism is an actual modification of the cell walls by a profuse deposition of newly synthesized cell wall substances into the regions of cell contact. The manner and control of this deposition are especially remarkable since the areas of contact, the external cell walls, are nonliving and the living protoplasts of the cells are spatially removed from the region that effects the binding.

Types of plant tissue fusions. It is possible to distinguish at least four categories of tissue fusions in higher plants. The first type is a union of protoplasts in which the plasma membranes of two cells combine with an intermingling of cytoplasmic components. In higher plants such fusions are restricted largely to the fertilization process. The second type is the union of cells to effect a wound closure or grafting response; this kind of fusion occurs between the scion and stock of a horticultural plant graft. It can be considered anomalous in that it is a traumatic response by the tissues and does not occur during the normal ontogeny of a plant organ. In contrast, the last two types of fusion not only are widespread within higher plant tissues, especially floral tissues, but are also normal ontogenetic events that occur in these tissues. Congenital fusion and postgenital fusion are adnations of cell walls rather than unions of cytoplasmic components; that is, cells of separate origin become part of a homogeneous tissue, but a cell wall continues to separate the cell protoplasts.

Although the ultimate appearance of the tissues produced by a congenital and a postgenital fusion may be quite similar, the unions arise by two drastically different mechanisms, as explained diagrammatically in Fig. 1. In congenital fusion (also called phylogenetic fusion and zonal growth), cells are fused because they arise united from the activity of a basal meristematic zone. The organs are "phylogenetically" fused because it is presumed that the ancestral condition was one of separate entities but that the individuality of the organs was lost through evolution. The mechanism of congenital fusion is therefore the establishment of a basal meristem to replace the apical growth that is responsible for the formation of separate organs. The physiological explanation for this spatial shift in meristematic activity has not yet been elucidated. In contrast, postgenital fusion (also called ontogenetic fusion) involves the contacting of organs that have already developed as individual entities. The outer tangential walls of the surface cells of the separate organs become physically appressed, and adhesion of the organs follows. In many cases the anatomical appearance of tissues arising from either congenital or postgenital fusion

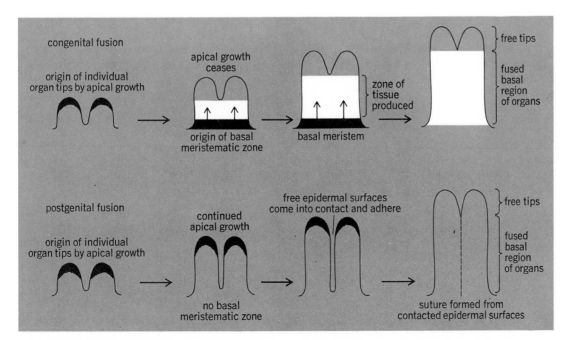

Fig. 1. Diagrammatic explanations of the developmental processes of congenital fusion and postgenital fusion, both of which serve to unite plant organs into compound structures. Darker shading indicates meristematic regions.

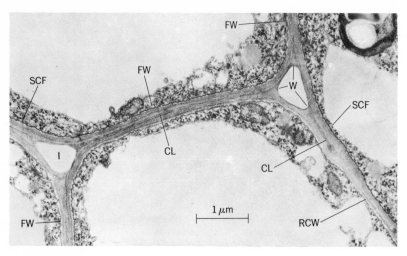

Fig. 2. Postgenital union between epidermal cells in carpel tips of the garden periwinkle. The abbreviations are explained in the text.

may be practically identical and has led to considerable confusion in floral interpretations.

Mechanism of postgenital fusion. There are various degrees of adhesion between fused organs. Some organs are barely connected anatomically and can be pulled apart by using very little force; others are extremely intimate anatomically, and the binding is correspondingly firm. The intimate cases of fusion are very interesting developmentally because the cells on the two fusing surfaces experience cell divisions and altered pathways of development which suggest that the postgenital fusion process is an active metabolic response by the cells involved and not merely a physical interlocking. Such a response leads one to ask some important questions concerning the regulation and control of extracellular developmental processes in higher plant tissues. For instance, are the cells that will subsequently unite programmed for the fusion response in advance of cell contact, or does the contact induce the response of itself? Since the contact is established between the nonliving, largely carbohydrate walls of the cells, do these walls become modified to effect the adhesion and, if so, in what manner and through what cellular processes? Recently, answers to some of these questions have been pursued by D. B. Walker in an attempt to elucidate the cytological and physiological mechanisms of postgenital tissue fusion.

The postgenital fusions investigated are those occurring in the carpels (the female organs of the flower) of the garden periwinkle *Catharanthus roseus* (also known as *Vinca rosea*). Two different and easily identifiable examples of postgenital fusion routinely occur within the carpels of this plant. One example is the apical union between the two separate carpels to form a united stigma and style, thus forming a compound gynoecium. The second example is the union of the infolded wings of each basal ovary (similar in appearance to a horseshoe that is bent inward to form a closed circle) to form a tubular pocket, called the locule, in which the ovules develop. Each of these examples of fusion can be found in many plant families, and both examples were studied in the periwinkle

to determine the events occurring during a postgenital fusion.

In the periwinkle, although the time necessary to complete a postgenital fusion is different for different tissues, the anatomical details ultimately appear similar in both cases. Prior to cell contact, a distinctive epidermis can be recognized on the fusion surfaces, evidenced by the exclusive occurrence of anticlinal cell divisions (divisions forming cells in the surface cell layer only), the convex outer cell wall characteristic of epidermal cells, and a thin but detectable cuticle on the outer cell surfaces. No cytological evidence could be found to indicate that these epidermal cells are programmed in advance for postgenital fusion. Apparently, the developmental pathway of postgenital fusion is independent of and superimposed upon the normal pathway of epidermal cell development.

However, with cell contact, dramatic changes are produced in the participating epidermal cells. In the most rapid fusion response, cell contact results in an almost immediate dedifferentiation (reversal of development to a less specialized state) of the epidermal cells, indicated by a reorientation of cell divisions, loss of the distinctive cellular morphology, and immediate cessation of cuticle deposition. Although such a developmental reversal in the contacting cells can be regarded as an indication of a postgenital union, other cases of fusion have been observed in which no dedifferentiation but only a union of the cell walls occurs. It is this union of cell walls that appears to be the ultimate criterion for a postgenital fusion. The mechanism of this union involves a modification of the cell walls by the deposition of new wall material that acts as an intercellular glue.

Figure 2 is an electron photomicrograph of the fused cell walls in the apical carpel tips of the periwinkle. Two regions of wall fusion can be identified: the fused walls (FW) between the opposing epidermal cells of the two carpels, and the short segments of fused wall between sister cells (cells within the same carpel that are adjacent and share a common radial cell wall) that have become appressed during cell expansion. The fusion mechanism is identical in both of these regions, and since such sister-cell fusion is probably a common phenomenon in many tissues of higher plants, some degree of postgenital union between cells may prove to be ubiquitous in higher plant tissues. It is not an interlocking of cells but the confluence of certain regions of the contacting cell walls that establishes the union (Fig. 2). These fused cell walls are distinctive in this tissue because they are twice as thick as the nonfused radial cell walls (RCW) and because the previously formed cuticle remains trapped within the fusion line (CL = cuticular layer, which consists of the two appressed cuticles with narrow, darkly staining bands on each side). The special modification of these fused cell walls is particularly evident in the regions of wall adjacent to an intercellular space (I). The spaces are partially filled in by a profuse deposition of cell wall material (W) outside the boundaries of the cuticles. This newly added wall material serves as the intercellular glue. An ontogenetic study of the deposition of this material strongly implicated the rough endoplasmic reticulum and the Golgi apparatus in the synthesis or transport, or both, of this material, but further research is required to define adequately the precise role of these two organelles in the fusion process.

The position of the newly deposited wall material, beyond the limits of the original cell wall and cuticle, suggests the probable nature of the material. The higher plant cell wall can be regarded as elongate fibrils of cellulose embedded in an amorphous, but chemically bound, matrix of (noncellulosic) carbohydrate material and protein. Since current evidence indicates that cellulose fibrils are deposited only adjacent to the plasma membrane of the cell, the intercellular glue added during fusion must be of the amorphous matrix variety, for deposition is throughout and beyond the existing wall.

The temporally coordinated deposition of this intercellular wall material by the fusing cells plus the well-coordinated development of the two fused portions of the tissue following union are quite remarkable since no protoplasmic connections (called plasmodesmata) are formed between the fused cells. Some cellular coordination of activities must occur during the fusion; however, whether the process is strictly a contact response or whether some growth regulator passes across the fusion boundary as a messenger is unknown and awaits further investigation.

For background information *see* FLOWER in the McGraw-Hill Encyclopedia of Science and Technology.   [DAN B. WALKER]

Bibliography: D. B. Walker, *Amer. J. Bot.*, in press; D. B. Walker, *Protoplasma*, in press.

Food

Development of a new technology for providing food additives leashed to nonabsorbable polymer molecules offers the promise of safer ingredients, with enhanced functionality in foods.

Demand for processed and fabricated foods has increased dramatically in recent years. This accelerating change in eating patterns is attributable to a number of social forces, including the population concentration in urban centers, the changing role of women in many societies, and the shortages and price rises among traditional commodity foods.

Processed and fabricated foods depend upon food additives to enhance palatability by imparting color, flavor, and texture; and to preserve their quality, through processing, distribution, and storage, by preventing rancidity or other chemical change and microbial contamination. Because they impart such desirable properties to foods, additives have an essential role in assuring an adequate food supply.

Animal studies in which toxicity resulted from feeding large doses of certain food additives led to the removal of many ingredients from the market. Suspicion then arose among scientists and consumers that other food additives may present an unacceptable risk-to-benefit ratio.

Safer food additives. Most additives perform their function in the food before it is consumed. Others merely make contact with the taste buds or olfactory receptors. There is no need for these food additives to act inside the body.

When toxic effects are caused by additives, they invariably occur in internal organs—principally the liver, kidney, and bladder. To reach these organs, the additive must be absorbed through the walls of the gastrointestinal tract and enter the systemic circulation. The gastrointestinal tract itself is protected against harm by a one-cell-thick envelope, the mucosal layer, that is replaced every few days. Continuous replacement of this lining is a natural mechanism of renewal and defense by the body.

Developments in the past year have aimed at eliminating the toxicities of food additives, while retaining or enhancing their benefits, by preventing the additive molecules from being absorbed into the body through the walls of the gastrointestinal tract. To achieve nonabsorption, the small additive molecules are leashed, or chemically attached through covalent chemical bonds, to a much larger, food-compatible polymer that is unable to pass through the gastrointestinal lining (see illustration). By proper selection of the polymer, the leash, and the additive, absorption can be blocked and desirable functional properties maintained or even enhanced.

"Polymer" is a broad term for a natural or synthetic compound with a high molecular weight, composed of repeated linked units. Not all polymers are acceptable for providing useful, nonabsorbable food additives. Four characteristics of the polymer are important.

(1) It must be of sufficiently high molecular weight to be nonabsorbable. Minimum molecular weight for nonabsorption will vary from polymer to polymer due to secondary and tertiary structural characteristics which cause variation in molecular volume for a given molecular weight. Molecular volume, rather than molecular weight, is the important determinant of passive transport through the walls of the gastrointestinal tract.

(2) In synthesizing polymers, a product with a range of molecular weights is typically obtained. Because low-molecular-weight polymers can be absorbed, a criterion is that the polymerization reaction not produce a product containing polymer of too low a molecular weight or that the polymer be carefully fractionated to remove the low-molecular-weight components.

(3) Many polymers, even of high molecular weight, can be broken down by the acids, alkalis, digestive enzymes, and bacterial flora of the gastrointestinal tract to yield absorbable fragments. Proteins and carbohydrates are well-known examples of biologically unstable polymers and, in fact, their nutritional value is dependent upon this instability. Polymers can also be unstable under the thermal, enzymatic, and pH conditions employed in food processing operations. It is important that the polymer not be degraded either during food processing or after ingestion.

(4) Prior criteria relate to assuring the nonabsorption of the polymer-leashed food additive. The fourth relates to its usefulness in food. The chemical composition of the polymer must be such as to permit active food additive molecules to be attached to many (preferably, virtually all) of its repeated linked units. When only a few additive molecules are attached to a high-molecular-weight

FOOD

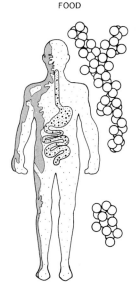

Food additives of small molecular size (represented by small dots in the digestive track) are readily absorbed (and so are shown throughout the body), while polymer-leashed additives (represented by larger dots in the track) are too large to pass into systemic circulation. Models of both molecules are shown. *(From Polymeric leashing explored to improve food additive safety parameters, Food Prod. Dev., 8(4):18, May 1974)*

polymer, the desired activity of the additive, on a unit weight basis, has been found to be low. However, when a large number of active molecules are repeated along the polymer chain, unit activity can be high. This has been achieved in the past year with two important classes of food additives—colors and antioxidants.

In addition to the criteria described above, proper selection of the polymer can impart desirable physical properties to the final product. These include solubility characteristics, food affinity, and nonvolatility. This permits engineering, at the molecular level, of food ingredients with specifically desired properties.

Leashes for bonding the food additive to the polymer must be covalent chemical bonds. The additive can be bonded directly to the polymer or indirectly through a chain of atoms. As with the polymer itself, it is important that the covalent bonds of the leash be stable to food processing conditions, as well as to the environment of the gastrointestinal tract. Some chemical groups otherwise useful as leashes can diminish the effectiveness of the food additive (for example, in the case of colors, an inappropriate leash can cause undesirable shifts in spectral properties) and are to be avoided. And, of course, the point of attachment of the leash to the additive molecule must not be at a site essential to its activity in food, for that can reduce or even eliminate the desirable properties of the ingredient.

Progress with this new technology during the past year can be illustrated by developments with food colors and antioxidants.

Food colors. Three water-soluble food colors now account for about 85% of usage in the United States. These are Sunset Yellow (FD&C Yellow #6), Tartrazine (FD&C Yellow #5), and Amaranth (FD&C Red #2). In the past year W. Leonard and coworkers at Dynapol in Palo Alto, CA, have succeeded in making three polymeric food colors with spectral properties identical to these FD&C dyes by chemically leashing chromophore molecules to high-molecular-weight hydrophilic polymers. Of these, the polymeric color comparable with Sunset Yellow has received the most attention to date and is more fully described below.

In pure powdered form without diluents, this polymeric food color is deep red. However, the shade of the pure powdered material can be altered somewhat by adjusting its particle size.

The polymeric food color is water-soluble and 20 to 30% solutions can be prepared by using simple agitation. In solution, the dye color varies from a faint yellow-orange at low concentrations to an intense blood red at high concentrations. In the coloring of foods, it can serve as a direct replacement for Sunset Yellow. Use levels in foods can range from about 20 parts per million (ppm) in clear beverages to 1000 ppm in solid comestibles.

In biological experiments the intact polymeric food color has been shown to be virtually nonabsorbed from the gastrointestinal tract following oral administration of carbon-14 radio-labeled materials. Acute toxicity tests in mice show that ingestion of 10 g of dye per kilogram of body weight is tolerated without untoward effects.

The range of usefulness for the polymeric color in foods has been demonstrated in still and carbonated beverages; dry beverage bases; gelatin desserts; baked goods; confections; dairy products such as yogurt and ice cream; oil and water emulsions, including mayonnaise, salad dressings, and sauces; and various systems containing protein, fat and carbohydrate.

In addition to these properties it shares in common with Sunset Yellow, the polymeric food color exhibits certain unique and unexpected characteristics, including an increased tinctorial strength, nondiffusion in gel systems, and enhanced stability in the presence of bisulfite. It is especially useful in the preparation of insoluble alumina lakes showing exceptional nonbleeding characteristics in a variety of media (for example, strong acids, chlorides, or sulfates).

By providing a greater margin of safety and improved functionality in food systems, as well as compatibility with current food processing techniques and equipment, nonabsorbable food colors are expected to have an important impact on the food industry.

Antioxidants. Foods become rancid through oxidation, which can be retarded by incorporation of an antioxidant such as butylated hydroxytoluene (BHT) or butylated hydroxyanisole (BHA). Shelf life of food packaging materials, along with indirect protection of the food, is obtained by adding antioxidants to the packaging material.

Recently, T. Furia and coworkers at Dynapol have successfully leashed active antioxidant molecules to high-molecular-weight, oil-soluble polymers. The resulting polymeric antioxidants have been tested for efficacy in a variety of fat and oil systems under conditions including frying and broiling. Test methods included the usual oxygen bomb, active oxygen method, accelerated oven tests, and new techniques simulating processing conditions.

Surprisingly, the researchers discovered that their polymeric antioxidants were much more effective on a weight basis than either BHT or BHA in preventing the oxidative deterioration of fats, oils, and foods containing fats and oils. In a representative test, samples of cottonseed or soybean oil containing 200 ppm of the antioxidant were placed in a controlled air draft at 80°C and the time to rancidity (defined as 70 milliequivalents of peroxide per kilogram of oil) measured. The results of this accelerated test were: control, 68 hr; BHT, 82 hr; BHA, 87 hr; polymeric antioxidant, 164 hr.

Additionally, because of the nonvolatility of the polymeric antioxidants, they will not be steam-distilled from foods in cooking, as are conventional materials.

Biological tests, using carbon-14 radio-labeled polymeric antioxidants, have shown that they are stable to the biological environment and are not absorbed through the walls of the gastrointestinal tract. Thus, they are expected to be nontoxic.

Polymer-leashed food additives require additional testing, including longer-term animal toxicity studies, before they may be expected to go into general usage. Results to date with colors and antioxidants are encouraging and it is expected that this innovative technology will provide safer, more effective food ingredients. With enhanced performance in foods and reduced toxicity, these new ingredients should have far better risk-to-benefit ratios than do conventional additives. This approach, of engineering food additives at the molecular level, is applicable to other fields too. Already, the technology is being extended to nonnutritive sweeteners.

For background information *see* FOOD; POLYMER in the McGraw-Hill Encyclopedia of Science and Technology.

[STEVEN GOLDBY]

Bibliography: *Food Prod. Dev.*, 8(4):18, May 1974; C. H. Havighorst, *Food Eng.*, 46(6):46, June 1974; Panel on Chemicals and Health of the President's Science Advisory Committee, *Chemicals and Health*, September 1973.

Food engineering

In an effort to reduce the cost of merchandising grocery items, improvements are being made in the areas of food distribution, packaging, and retailing practices.

Economical food distribution. The soaring cost of energy has made it necessary to reevaluate food distribution patterns and concentrate on distribution changes which will reduce the energy expended to bring a calorie of food from the farm to the table. These changes include improvements in the utilization of available transportation space, reductions in in-transit damage and nonproductive weight, and the reduction of refrigeration losses in storage and transit.

Energy consumption. The magnitude of the energy problems associated with food and its distribution was spelled out in a study by J. S. Steinhart and C. E. Steinhart. The study calculated total United States energy use in the food system as 2172×10^{12} kcal (Fig. 1). This was 12.8% of the total United States energy use. The data for the study covered the period from 1940 to 1970.

By 1970 energy consumed for transportation fuel (trucks and trailers) had grown to 14.8% of total food-associated energy consumption. Presumably the skyrocketing cost of fuel in 1974 significantly increased the fuel component of food-associated energy consumption. Certainly the energy crisis was felt most critically in this area. At one point protests by truckers idled some 250,000 workers and even forced one supermarket chain to charter a plane to move meat to the East Coast to alleviate a critical shortage.

Reevaluating food distribution in terms of energy cost also highlighted some distribution diseconomies which are not readily apparent from a normal economic analysis. For example, food from the sea is commonly thought of as the eventual solution to the food shortage problems of the future. However, in terms of energy cost, this source of food can be one of the highest if the food comes from a distant ocean.

Even exporting American food technology to alleviate the distribution cost is not necessarily an energy conserver. In many countries the "green revolution" requires irrigation, which is one of the greatest energy consumers.

Therefore, energy conservation in food distribution will most likely revolve around efficiency improvements in American methods of distributing food. Certainly this is a most practical direction for the near future.

Packaging efficiency. A step toward more efficient food distribution was made by the National Association of Food Chains when they instituted a study of modular packaging. A Neilson survey showed that there are 2400 package sizes in use in the American food industry. This compares with as few as 75 in one European country that has a standard packaging program. It is not expected that the American level could reach that low, but it is expected that a nationwide system of modular containers could achieve new efficiencies in transportation and warehousing. Advantages would include better automation of warehouses, reduced in-transit damage, improved space utilization, and a higher degree of mechanization of automation and materials handling.

Reducing in-transit damage and thereby increasing transportation efficiency has put new emphasis on unitizing. One manufacturer has developed a new polystyrene pallet. The pallet weighs only 4 lb (1.8 kg) but will support a 2000-lb (906 kg) load, thereby reducing excess weight as well as decreasing damage. Other companies have emphasized the shrink-wrapped unitized load, with new systems to reduce heat energy consumption. An infrared unit that uses only 13.6 kW per hour was introduced. It is said to cost less than 11¢ per hour to operate. Another company has eliminated the heat requirement entirely by developing a stretch film that is applied without heat. Finally, a user reduced energy consumption even more by demonstrating that only the last load of pallets need be shrink-wrapped for transport by ships. These end pallets were found to be stable enough to contain the remainder of the load.

Another approach toward reducing energy consumption in food distribution is to reduce the energy content of the package. One technical study indicated that flexible packaging for beverages and heat-processed foods will begin to take over in the future, as the energy consumption is less than for current packages. However, there was evidence that current packages will also change as a result of the new energy economics. For example, a unique German lightweight-glass process has been

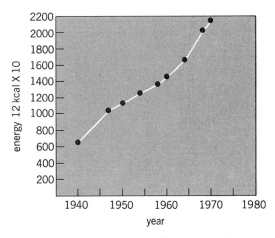

Fig. 1. Energy use in the United States food system.

receive
merchandise

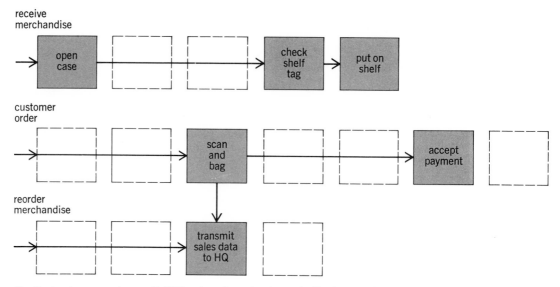

customer
order

reorder
merchandise

Fig. 2. In-store procedures with UPC automation, showing reduction in procedures.

developed and will soon be available in the United States. This process produces a lightweight narrow-mouth nonreturnable bottle. These bottles are reported to have less breakage than conventional bottles when run at speeds as high as 1000 per minute. The bottle has a unique narrow-neck press and blow which overcomes wall thickness inconsistencies and improves bottle strength. The process reduces glass amount and weight by 25%, thereby increasing payload. In addition, less energy is consumed in manufacture as well as handling and shipping. The bottle can also be recycled.

Conserving refrigeration energy. Several developments designed to decrease refrigeration requirements in food distribution have been emphasized. Included in this area is a unique application of sprayed foam or urethane to reduce warehouse refrigeration loss. In one instance an old warehouse was coated with 4 in. (10 cm) of urethane to reduce heat loss in the 1,500,000-ft³ (42,000 m³) building. The application cost less than 10% of the cost of replacing the building. Another approach to conservation of refrigeration energy was a new orange juice concentrate announced by one package equipment manufacturer. By aseptically filling this product into a new paper container, it is possible to completely eliminate the refrigeration requirement in storage and handling.

Carrier space utilization. The biggest steps toward energy conservation in food distribution will be in better utilization of the cube of existing vehicles. Little progress was made in this area by most modes of transportation. Surprisingly, one of the few exceptions is in the rail transport of grain: A new covered hopper car was introduced and became an immediate success. The car is capable of carrying 100 tons of grain. It can be loaded in 12 min and unloaded in 3 min. Nearly 15,000 of these cars were bought during 1973.

The problem in the shipping industry was highlighted by the head of the Federal Maritime Commission when she asked ocean carriers to reduce speed and utilize all available space. Predicting a 30–35% fuel consumption cut, she nevertheless estimated that all product requirement could be met by filling up available space.

On land, a leading distribution magazine received great industry support when it called for changes in the law which would permit double bottoms (tractors pulling two trailers) to operate fully loaded in all states. The magazine observed that the increased use of plastics and aluminum, as well as improved packaging, has created a trend toward lighter freight and has increased the space required to transport a given volume of freight. The interior capacity of a 65-ft (19.5 m) double unit is more than 900 ft³ (25.2 m³) greater than a comparable, uninsulated 40-ft (12 m) semitrailer. This could mean a 35% increase in cargo with very little increase in energy requirement. However, little action has been taken in these areas, and it appears that these kinds of energy savings will not be realized for several years.

[DUANE S. MALM]

Universal Product Code. There are now over 1100 member companies in the Uniform Grocery Product Code Council, Inc., which directs the entire Universal Product Code (UPC) program. These firms represent $60 billion of the $100 billion annual retail grocery volume. Over 90% of the dollar volume capable of being symbol-marked at the source is already under consideration for UPC adoption. It was estimated that by the end of 1974 over 50,000 products, or 50% of the items moving through the retail grocery stores, would be source-marked. Scanning systems began to appear in late 1974 in various stores throughout the country. These stores will be in a test phase of the program initially. Depending upon the results of initial installations, others will follow—perhaps more quickly than some observers may anticipate.

Many stores are currently using electronic cash registers, some tied into computers performing administrative functions automatically. The addition of an automatic package recognition system—the scanner—is all that is needed to complete a total system. Most recent systems and those currently being sold have anticipated UPC and have

receive
merchandise

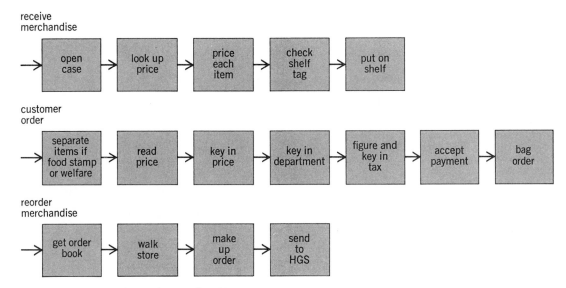

Fig. 3. In-store procedures of conventional type.

provision for adding the scanner whenever a store desires (Fig. 2).

Background. The UPC is an effort on the part of grocers, supported by both manufacturers and suppliers, to reduce the high cost of checking, inventorying, and packaging the thousands of items normally sold in supermarkets (see Fig. 3).

At the heart of the system is an optical scanner which reads a symbol printed on the product as it is passed over a slit in the checkout counter. A computer, which reacts to the symbol with a price printout and an inventory adjustment, and if desired a mechanical bagging device, is associated with the scanner.

In 1974 various guidelines were developed by package suppliers in an effort to aid food processors in converting to UPC. A description of these suggestions will follow; however, it is important to note that the initial information needed to effect conversion must originate from the package printer. Proper printing of the UPC symbol begins with the procurement of a film master produced in accordance with UPC specifications, with certain details prescribed by the printer. These details include a general description: positive or negative; emulsion up or down (copy reading right); and two numerical factors — magnification, and line width reduction.

It is recommended that magnification and line width reduction be applied by the film master suppliers in producing the original masters. It is also recommended that symbols be printed in the nominal size — 1.0 magnification, whenever possible. Reduced-size symbols should be used only when space limitations demand it. Symbol printing tolerances are tighter and scanner reliability is reduced with less than nominal symbols. For this reason, the prescription above will generally call for 1.0 magnification (nominal-size symbols) with a line width correction only.

Specifications. A printability gage is a standard pattern of lines with graduated spaces between them, from relatively far apart to very close together. Graduations are lettered from A through K. The

gage is used by the printer to determine the size of symbol he can print with fidelity and to measure the amount of spread in the width of printed lines inherent to his process. Finally, it is used as a quality-control tool when printing the symbol.

The printability rating is determined by observing where the lines in the printability gage pattern first touch and is defined by the letter of the alphabet at that point, such as E or J. The printability rating may be defined as a range if the point where the lines touch varies, such as H–J or I–J.

The percent of increase or decrease from the nominal symbol size is the magnification factor. A range from 0.80 to 2.00 is provided for in the UPC specifications to accommodate the capabilities of the various printing processes serving the grocery industry.

The amount of reduction in the width of the lines in the symbol master and in the printing cylinder or plate corrects for the inherent tendency of line widths to be greater.

A table in the UPC specifications lists "printability ratings" and corresponding "magnification factor" and "line width reduction." For example, the three values might be H–I, 0.90, and 1.5 respectively. This means that the process can print symbols reduced to 90% of nominal and that a line width reduction of 0.0015 in. (3.8 mm) should be planned to compensate for spread. Although the capability of printing a smaller symbol is illustrated in the example, it would generally be recommended that a magnification of 1.0 (no reduction) be used. The line width reduction of 0.0015 in. would still apply, however.

The example is typical of the kind of results observed in printing tests. The printability rating has invariably indicated the possibility of reducing the symbol size — the minimum size depending upon the job and the substrate. This will be apparent to some by the small line width reduction specified.

Can label printing. The importance of orienting the UPC symbol in the press direction for printability must be stressed. Printability in the context of UPC as measured by the gage is the most obvious advantage. The printability rating is at least one gage letter better when the symbol lines are parallel to the press direction compared with the lines across the web.

More important, however, is the difference of the effect of the various factors that influence quality while printing. Lines in the press direction are much less affected by ink flooding, slurs, lines, chatter, and cylinder wear. The importance of cylinder wear has become especially obvious to food processors who are assessed the cost of a spare when their symbol is oriented contrary to the preferred direction.

Can-label customers are particularly prone to orient their symbols with the lines parallel to the axis of the can, which is across the gravure printing direction. Lines going around the can are preferred for printability and for scannability—in spite of the fact that the only illustration in the original *UPC Symbol Guidelines Manual* showed the lines parallel with the can.

The manual has recently been revised, specifically stating that symbols properly oriented enhance the (scanning) equipment performance. The original misleading illustration has been changed so it now presents the symbol in the preferred direction.

For background information *see* FOOD ENGINEERING in the McGraw-Hill Encyclopedia of Science and Technology.   [STANLEY SACHAROW]

Bibliography: J. R. Gottlieb, The Universal Product Code, *Gravure*, February 1973; *Packascope—USA*, vol. 18, no. 4, 1973; J. S. Steinhart and C. E. Steinhart, *Science*, 184(4134):307–316, 1974; *UPC Symbol Specification*, May 1973; D. E. Whitehead, Modular packaging: Key to distribution savings, *Food Eng.*, vol. 46, March 1974.

Forage crops

The quality of forage materials is of primary concern in livestock management. Recent studies attribute poor performance and high death rates among grazing livestock to such factors as fescue toxicity, the occurrence of alkaloids in certain grasses, and reduced availability of dietary magnesium.

Although most of the chemical compounds in forage plants are either nutritional or inert when consumed by livestock, some are harmful. These harmful components, called antiquality substances, are the concern of allelochemistry.

Allelochemicals. The prefix "allelo" is of Greek origin, meaning "of each other." Allelochemistry, then, is defined as the science of compounds that are synthesized by one organism and stimulate or inhibit other organisms. For example, allelochemicals in forage plants are compounds synthesized by a plant and in turn affect other plants, insects, fungi, bacteria, nematodes, or higher animals. Implied in this definition is the concept that allelochemicals participate in defense mechanisms that aid in the survival of the species.

Biosynthetic origin. In plants, allelochemicals are present as secondary metabolites, that is, side products of pathways leading to the synthesis of primary metabolites. Secondary metabolites, in contrast to primary metabolites, are not utilized in cellular structure, energy production, protein assembly, or RNA or DNA synthesis. Secondary metabolites have been classified on the basis of their biosynthetic origin into five major groups: terpenes, steroids, acetogenins, phenylpropanes, and alkaloids.

Direct effects on animals. The effect of allelochemicals on animals can be somewhat predicted according to species. For example, ruminants and nonruminants have different absorption and metabolism rates of specific compounds, and allelochemicals have different effects on their tissues. Other factors that affect animal tolerance of allelochemicals are age, sex, body size, nutritional status, and general health of the animal. The physiological status (for example, lactation versus gestation of dairy cows) also may determine whether a stimulation or inhibition will result from ingestion of allelochemicals. Also, the genetic potential of the animal, as well as the environment, may influence its level of tolerance to certain compounds.

Examples of allelochemicals. A number of plant chemicals have been identified as antiquality components in forages and may be classified as allelochemicals. In some instances, these compounds are potentially useful for improving forage quality because of their physiological effects on animals.

Tannins are responsible for the astringent or bitter taste of many plant tissues. They have been implicated in reduced intake and apparent poor digestibility of sericea lespedeza and bird-resistant sorghum. These effects may be caused by the inhibition of cellulolytic and pectinolytic enzymes. In contrast, tannins may aid in reducing bloat in cattle by inactivating bloat-producing proteins. Genetic differences for tannin levels suggest that selection for improved forage quality is possible.

Cyanogenic glycosides occur naturally in many plants and are hydrolyzed when two plant enzymes are released as a result of mechanical injury (such as mastication). The first enzyme, a β-glycosidase, removes the sugar component to yield a nitrile compound that is converted by a second enzyme, an oxynitrilase, to the aglycone and toxic hydrogen cyanide (HCN). Cyanogenic compounds can occur at certain times in several forages (sorghum, sudangrass, and white clover); some have been identified, and their chemical structure has been determined. Although there appears to be genetic control of these compounds, more research is necessary before significant progress can be made in controlling HCN production.

Animal reproduction may not take place in the presence of estrogenic isoflavones such as genistin, formononetin, biochannin A, and daidzein. The flavonoid coumestrol has also been identified as estrogenic in clover. Moreover, some evidence suggests the presence of antiestrogenic compounds in forages.

The presence of teratogens in forages may easily pass unnoticed. These substances, if ingested by an animal at a certain time during gestation, alter normal fetal development and result in a malformed fetus. Such occurrences are likely to be accepted as random birth defects and often are not regarded as being caused by dietary constituents. As an example, congenital cyclopian-type malformations in 1% of lambs occurred in the western

United States during the first half of this century. Three steroidal alkaloids, cyclopamine, cycloposine, and jervine, have been identified as the teratogens in the range forage veratrum.

Coumarin has been identified as the hemorrhagic agent in sweetclover responsible for a bleeding disease of cattle. This compound is found in the plant as a glycoside, but is converted by a β-glycosidase to coumarin. Not toxic itself, it is converted to the toxic principle dicoumarol by fungi present in spoiled forage.

Newly discovered allelochemical. Crownvetch is a forage legume used to a limited extent in the northeastern United States for beef and dairy cattle. This forage has no adverse effects on cattle or other ruminants, but recent cooperative studies by the Pennsylvania State University and the Agricultural Research Service of the U.S. Department of Agriculture have shown that it may be toxic when consumed by monogastric animals. Experiments with the meadow vole have established that when these animals are fed crownvetch forage, they lose weight because of low food intake and within 3–6 days die from the presence of a toxic factor. Using this animal in a bioassay procedure, scientists have isolated the toxic factor and identified it as β-nitropropionic acid (BNPA). This compound is one of three aliphatic nitro compounds known to occur in nature. The pure compound has been shown in feeding trials not to be toxic to ruminants at the levels found in crownvetch (0.3–3.5% of dry weight), but is toxic to meadow voles, chicks, and pigs (all monogastric animals).

Importance of allelochemicals. Identifying or anticipating the presence of allelochemicals in forages has several important results in forage production: Breeding programs to improve forage quality can reduce the amounts to insignificant levels. Such programs could also introduce new problem allelochemicals and thus these programs must test for allelochemicals, whenever feasible. Allelochemicals can positively aid in controlling plant disease and pest resistance. Allelochemicals undoubtedly are involved in taste or odor stimulation in animals and so influence the acceptance of a forage for food.

[R. F. BARNES; D. L. GUSTINE]

Fescue toxicity. Fescue toxicity includes the animal syndromes of poor summer performance, fescue foot, and fat necrosis. The alkaloid perloline accumulates in the forage in late summer and inhibits digestibility and utilization of the forage by the animal. Microflora associated with fescue have been used to induce fescue foot in cattle, but the specific substances responsible for inducing fescue foot have not been isolated. The fat necrosis syndrome occurs only in female cattle over 2 years of age that graze fescue pastures receiving extremely large amounts of plant nutrients.

In the United States, fescue toxicity has been associated primarily with tall fescue (*Festuca arundinacea* Schreb.). Many different symptoms have been observed in cattle affected by fescue toxicity. These symptoms are the result of different causative agents, and the best understood of the causative agents are alkaloids produced by tall fescue and toxins produced by fungi associated with tall fescue. The symptoms of fescue toxicity usually include a reduced rate of weight gain, reduced milk production, a rough dull hair coat, or all three. The symptoms may also include lameness; dry gangrene on the tail, legs, and ears; open sores on the legs; emaciation; and increased body temperature, respiration rate, and heart rate. Some cattle also accumulate hard masses of abdominal fat. If only reduced weight gain is observed, it usually occurs in the summer; whereas lameness and dry gangrene usually occur in animals grazing tall fescue in fall and winter. Fescue toxicity symptoms occur more frequently and more severely in cattle grazing pastures fertilized with large amounts of plant nutrients.

Because of the seasonal occurrence, and many different animal symptoms, at least three different conditions or pathologies of cattle have been identified with fescue toxicity: poor animal performance; fescue foot; and fat necrosis.

Poor animal performance. Poor animal performance, lack of weight gain or lack of milk production, results in the greatest economic loss caused by fescue toxicity. Poor performance by cattle grazing tall fescue does not occur each grazing season or necessarily for a full grazing season. More animals can be maintained on an acre of tall fescue than on other cool-season grasses because tall fescue grows better in summer and fall. However, production per animal is variable and, as indicated, very low weight gains or milk production frequently are obtained. Poor performance most often occurs in late summer. Often associated with poor animal performance are rough hair coat, diarrhea, rapid respiration rates, and high rectal temperatures.

The cause of this poor performance is substances on or in tall fescue, and most noted of these are the alkaloids produced by tall fescue. Perloline is the principal alkaloid in tall fescue forage. Greatest accumulation of alkaloids in tall fescue occurs in late summer, corresponding in time to the poorest animal performance (Fig. 1). The alkaloids inhibit digestion in the rumen of cattle by inhibiting the function of the microflora in the

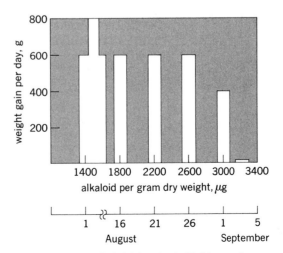

Fig. 1. Influence of alkaloid content of tall fescue forage on cattle weight gain per day.

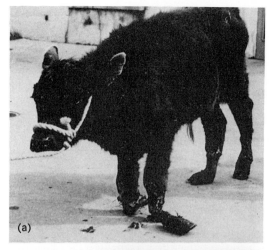

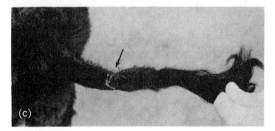

Fig. 2. Extreme symptoms of fescue foot. (a) Emaciated animal showing general condition and loss of digits. (b) Necrotic line and loss of digits. (c) Necrotic line on tail that may result in loss of the switch.

rumen. Poor animal performance results from the subsequent decrease in energy and nutrient availability to the animal. As the rate of digestion decreases, the rate of the grass passing through the animal decreases, and the intake of the grass by the animal then decreases. Consequently, as the animal consumes less forage and has less nutrients and energy available for growth, the rate of growth decreases, and in some instances the animals even lose weight while grazing tall fescue pastures.

Fescue foot. The first signs of fescue foot are general stiffness and soreness. Necrosis of the tail with loss of the switch may occur with or without signs of lameness. Lameness is usually in the hind-

quarters; cattle become listless, refuse to graze, and lose weight (Fig. 2). The causal agent of fescue foot is not known. However, recent work has shown that when cattle are dosed with fungi known to be associated with tall fescue, the cattle develop symptoms of fescue foot. Researchers have been unable to induce fescue foot by treating the animals with substances isolated from the grass; consequently, most researchers now consider that fescue foot is caused by fungi or their metabolites.

Fat necrosis. Fat necrosis develops in cattle grazing tall fescue pastures fertilized with very high levels of plant nutrients. Abdominal fat lesions range in size from small, 1-cm-diameter loci, to large, 30-cm-diameter masses. The necrotic fat lesions are most common in the mesenteric fat surrounding the intestine and are found anywhere along the intestinal tract. The larger hard masses can cause constriction of the small intestine. The disease has not been reported in bulls, steers, or in animals under 2 years of age, and is associated with an imbalance in fat metabolism in females. Encasement and constriction of the small intestine are associated with digestive upset, deterioration of body condition, and death.   [LOWELL P. BUSH]

Reed canarygrass alkaloids. The recent discovery of alkaloids in reed canarygrass (*Phalaris arundinacea* L.) helps explain why grazing sheep and cattle often find this high-producing grass to be unpalatable and why these animals sometimes perform poorly when they are forced to eat it. Establishment of a repeatable negative correlation between total basic alkaloid concentration and palatability (preference when a choice is offered) by ruminants for genotypes of reed canarygrass has prompted more research to determine the significance of these alkaloids to animal health and performance. Also, plant scientists have determined the influence of botanic, climatic, and soil variables on alkaloid concentration in this species. Plant geneticists have investigated the heritability of alkaloid type and concentration, leading to information necessary to breed low-alkaloid cultivars that will permit wide acceptance and use of this agronomically desirable grass.

Alkaloid occurrence. Agronomists, biochemists, and pharmacologists have reported the presence of eight specific alkaloids in reed canarygrass (Fig. 3). Two of these alkaloids (*N,N*-dimethyltryptamine and 5-MeO-*N,N*-dimethyltryptamine) have been claimed to be responsible for two diseases in sheep and cattle grazing *Phalaris aquatica* L. (= *P. tuberosa* L.) in Australia. One of these diseases is "phalaris staggers," which causes chronic disorder of the central nervous system. The other is "sudden death," characterized by sudden collapse, ventricular fibrillation, and cardiac arrest. Parenteral administration of these two tryptamines has proved them toxic to both ruminants and nonruminants.

The tryptamines of reed canarygrass and their derivatives are of great interest to pharmacologists, because these alkaloids cause hallucination when consumed by humans.

Individual plants of reed canarygrass may contain only gramine, only specific tryptamines, or a combination of the eight alkaloids known to occur in the species. No reports exist of genotypes completely free of alkaloids, but ranges in total alkaloid concentration from 0.01 to 2.75% of tissue dry matter have been reported within groups of plants treated uniformly.

Palatability and animal performance. Relative palatability of reed canarygrass genotypes to sheep and cattle is negatively correlated to total basic alkaloid concentration. This relationship was repeatable in experiments in Minnesota, Indiana, and Iowa. Studies reported in 1974 show that lambs, ewes, and ponies grazing relatively unpalatable reed canarygrass perform poorly during the times of the year when alkaloid concentration is greatest (midsummer). These animals perform better if pastured on more palatable orchardgrass or smooth bromegrass which are alkaloid-free, but otherwise of comparable nutritive value to reed canarygrass. Lambs and ewes develop severe diarrhea when grazing reed canarygrass. However, cattle often perform well when grazing this species and do not usually contract diarrhea, indicating that they are less sensitive to the problem.

Unpalatable genotypes of reed canarygrass containing high tryptamine levels are rejected by grazing lambs to the point of causing reduced nutrient intake and weight loss when no other feed is available. Lambs grazing relatively palatable, low-tryptamine genotypes continue to gain weight.

Botanic factors. Leaf blades contain most of the alkaloids in reed canarygrass, with very small amounts occurring in leaf sheaths, stems, inflorescences, rhizomes, and roots. Alkaloid *concentration* in the herbage declines as the plant matures, but absolute *content* per plant part increases somewhat with time. Dilution of the still-forming alkaloids by more rapidly accumulating fiber components and other substances during maturation probably accounts for this situation.

Climatic factors. Climatic conditions that enhance alkaloid concentration in reed canarygrass include moisture stress and low light intensity. More than a twofold increase in alkaloid concentration may result from lack of rainfall even though wilting does not occur. This probably explains why alkaloids peak during the often dry midsummer growing conditions. Temperature and day length during growth do not consistently influence reed canarygrass alkaloid concentration, although these factors sometimes cause minor alkaloid accumulation changes in specific genotypes.

Soil factors. Nitrogen fertilizer causes increased alkaloid concentration in reed canarygrass, especially in those genotypes having inherently high alkaloid potential and especially when nitrogen rates are high (greater than 200 kg/ha). Recent hydroponic studies revealed that the source of nitrogen amendments has even greater influence on alkaloid concentration than does the amount applied; alkaloid enhancement was greater from ammonium-N than from nitrate-N fertilizers (Fig. 4).

Reed canarygrass alkaloids are usually not affected when individual deficient elements other than N are applied to the soil (including P, K, Ca, Mg, S, Mn, and Cu). However, supplying combinations of these elements to infertile soils may cause reduced alkaloids in the herbage.

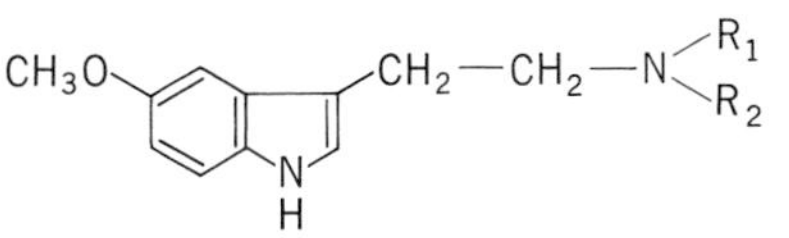

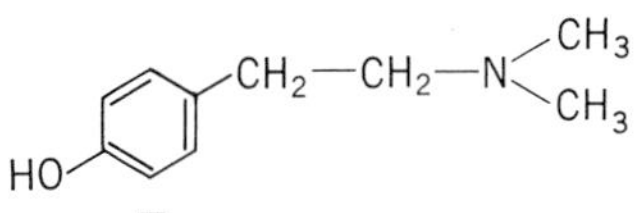

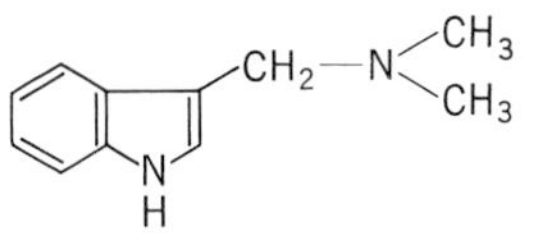

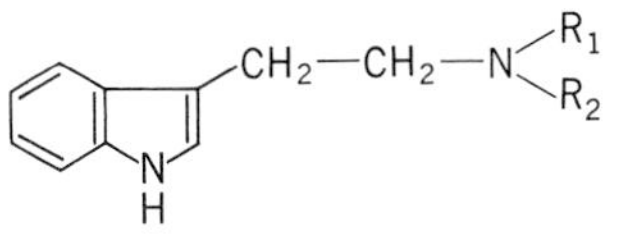

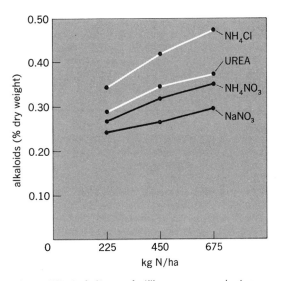

Fig. 3. Structures of alkaloids found in reed canarygrass: Ia, 5-methoxy-*N*-methyltryptamine; Ib, 5-MeO-*N,N*-dimethyltryptamine: II, hordenine; III, gramine; IVa, *N*-monomethyltryptamine; IVb, *N,N*-dimethyltryptamine; Va, 2,9-dimethyl-6-methoxy-1,2,3,4-tetrahydro-β-carboline; Vb, 2-methyl-6-methoxy-tetrahydro-β-carboline. (*From G. C. Marten, Alkaloids in reed canarygrass, in A. G. Matches, ed., Anti-quality components of forages, Crop Sci. Soc. Amer. Spec. Publ. no. 4, pp. 15–31, 1973*)

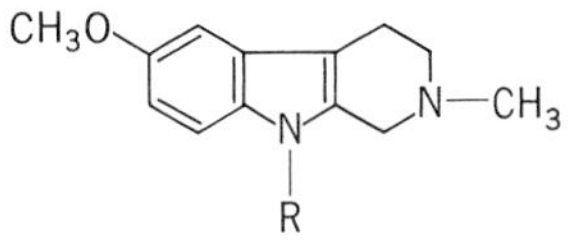

Plant breeding. Total basic alkaloid concentration in reed canarygrass is highly heritable, indicating favorable possibilities for breeding low-alkaloid cultivars. Other recent studies also indicate that some of the specific indole alkaloids are simply inherited. The breeding of low-alkaloid or alkaloid-free cultivars will aid the task of determin-

Fig. 4. Effect of nitrogen fertilizer sources and rates on alkaloid concentration in reed canarygrass. (*From G. C. Marten, A. B. Simons, and J. R. Frelich, Alkaloids of reed canarygrass as influenced by nutrient supply, Agron. J., 66: 363–368, 1974*)

ing the total biological significance of alkaloids in reed canarygrass. New semiquantitative quick tests for these alkaloids will hasten the screening process necessary to enable breeding improved cultivars.

Results of current experiments suggest a strong possibility of more efficient production of ruminant animals if reed canarygrass alkaloids can be reduced via breeding or pasture management.

[GORDON C. MARTEN]

Grass tetany. Grass tetany is a magnesium (Mg) deficiency in cattle and other ruminants that has caused many livestock deaths in the United States and throughout the world. The occurrence of grass tetany depends greatly on forage constituents that reduce the availability of dietary Mg. Recent research findings are increasing our understanding of this difficult nutritional problem.

Forage low in Mg. When cattle are grazing forage containing less than 0.2% Mg, grass tetany may occur. The type of forage eaten by the animal is very important. For example, grasses and legumes contain an average of 0.14 and 0.26% Mg, respectively. Mature timothy hay may contain as little as 0.07% Mg. However, hay is less likely to lead to tetany than is fresh forage because the Mg in hay is more available to cattle.

Forage Mg levels vary because of cultural practices that affect the actual amount of soluble Mg in the soil or its availability to plants. Fertilizing with high levels of potassium (K) often depresses Mg uptake by plants, but fertilizing with nitrogen (N) may increase Mg uptake and concentration. However, fertilizing grass-legume pastures with N may increase the proportion of grass. Thus the Mg concentration in the overall forage mixture may decrease, since grasses generally contain much lower Mg concentrations than do legumes.

Acid soils should be limed for optimum forage yields. Continued application of calcitic limestone, however, causes a gradual depletion of soil Mg sources and may ultimately lead to lower forage Mg levels and to increased incidence of grass tetany. Calcium (Ca) ions may depress Mg uptake by plants if soil Ca concentrations greatly exceed those of Mg. This effect on Mg uptake may also be observed in calcareous soils.

Organic manuring also may affect forage Mg concentrations. Poultry manure, for example, may contain 3.6% N, 1.5% K, and only 0.35% Mg. Fertilizing with poultry manure increases forage Mg concentrations. However, applying more than 4 metric tons of poultry manure (dry-weight basis) per hectare-year to pastures would be expected to greatly reduce the Mg availability to ruminants because of the high forage N and K levels produced. Thus, applying large amounts of animal litter or inorganic N and K fertilizer increases the tetany hazard.

Magnesium uptake and subsequent concentrations in grasses are temperature-related. Perennial ryegrass, when grown at constant K and Mg levels, contained 0.13% Mg when exposed to a day-night temperature of 20–14°C. At a higher day-night temperature of 26–23°C, the forage contained 0.24% Mg. Temperature may also control the type of forage available for grazing. Cool-season grasses grow better at lower temperatures than do most legumes. Thus forage in a mixed grass-legume pasture may consist primarily of grasses during the early spring when tetany usually occurs.

Reduced availability of forage Mg. The reduction in dietary Mg availability is most often associated with rapidly growing grass forage. High concentrations of K in the forage may reduce dietary utilization of Mg by cattle. Tetany has often occurred in pastures where the forage K concentration is 3% or greater, and values approaching 4% K should certainly cause concern. The incidence of tetany increases greatly when the forage K/(Ca + Mg) values exceed 2.2 on an equivalent basis. Magnesium in forage having high N levels also is less available to cattle (Fig. 5).

Availability to livestock can also be reduced when the Mg is complexed with certain organic compounds. Such tricarboxylic acids as citric and *trans*-aconitic may complex Mg, but these acids are not likely to be the most important factor in reducing Mg availability to animals. Long-chain fatty acids may also complex with Mg, forming water-insoluble soaps that are excreted in the feces. The concentration of long-chain fatty acids in forage is directly proportional to the N concentration. Therefore, the decreased Mg availability attributed to N (Fig. 5) may be partly due to the effect of organic complexing agents whose levels are associated with forage N concentrations.

A high ratio of N to soluble carbohydrates in the forage may be related to reduced Mg availability. Forage N values may increase under conditions of rapid forage growth and N fertilization. Soluble carbohydrates are reduced by N fertilization, and

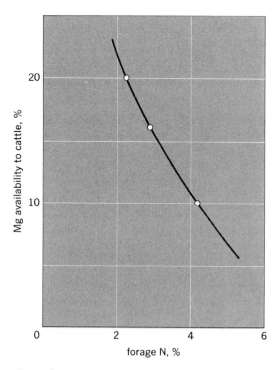

Fig. 5. Relationship between total nitrogen content of forage and "availability" to cattle of forage magnesium. *(From A. J. Metson et al., Chemical composition of pastures in relation to grass tetany in beef breeding cows, N. Z. J. Agr. Res., 9:410–436, 1966)*

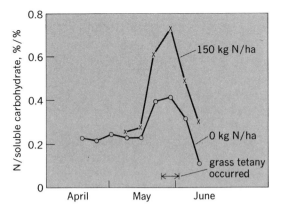

Fig. 6. Grass tetany coincided with an increase in ratio of nitrogen to soluble carbohydrate in forage. Fertilizing with 150 kg N/ha amplified the ratio increase and would likely increase the tetany hazard. (*H. F. Mayland and D. L. Grunes, unpublished data*)

concentrations are greatly decreased during rapid plant growth. Thus, environmental conditions conducive to rapid forage growth have coincided with the occurrence of grass tetany (Fig. 6).

The Mg in forage produced under low solar radiation levels may be less available to cattle. For example, when the average daily radiation levels for three consecutive spring tetany periods were 437, 547, and 551 langleys per day, the incidence of grass tetany was severe, light, and a trace, respectively.

Alternatives to reduce tetany. Several agronomic management alternatives are available for reducing the incidence of grass tetany. Pastures can be renovated to include a larger proportion of legume. Dusting forage with 30 kg/ha MgO will provide temporary protection from tetany, until the Mg is lost from the forage by wind or rain. A spray of a Mg-bentonite clay-water slurry will adhere more to the foliage and last somewhat longer than the dust. Either the dust or spray will provide Mg to the animals as they graze the treated forage.

Magnesium fertilization will increase the Mg concentration of forage grown on coarse-textured acid soils, but responses, if any, will be much smaller on fine-textured soils. Using dolomitic limestone, rather than calcitic sources, will assure some replenishment of Mg in acid soils. The dolomite solubilizes more rapidly if mixed into the soil.

Another helpful practice is to apply only a portion of the N and K fertilizer in early spring and apply the remainder later in the season. Soil test recommendations should be followed to avoid excessive N and K fertilization. Where soils are to be limed, or Mg fertilization is economical, maintenance of a balance of soil nutrients should be attempted. For Mg this includes sufficient exchangeable soil Mg to give 10 to 15% of the cation exchange capacity, Mg/K values of 2 or greater, and Mg/Ca values of 0.2 or greater (all values on an equivalent basis).

Alternatives in livestock management should also be considered in reducing the severity of grass tetany. Grazing of forage likely to produce tetany should be postponed until the danger passes. Or,

such forage might be grazed by livestock having lower Mg requirements, that is, nonlactating animals. The more direct method of reducing Mg tetany is to supplement the animals with Mg. This should decrease the incidence of grass tetany, although some cases may still occur if some animals do not accept the Mg supplement.

For background information *see* ALKALOID; FESCUE; GRASS CROPS; LEGUME FORAGES in the McGraw-Hill Encyclopedia of Science and Technology.   [H. F. MAYLAND; D. L. GRUNES]

Bibliography: R. E. Barker and A. W. Hovin, *Crop Sci.*, 14:50–53, 1974; R. F. Barnes and D. L. Gustine, L. P. Bush and R. C. Buckner, D. L. Grunes, and G. C. Marten, in A. G. Matches (ed.), *Anti-quality Components of Forages*, Crop Sci. Soc. Amer. Spec. Publ. no. 4, 1973; L. P. Bush et al., *Crop Sci.*, 12:277, 1972; D. L. Gustine et al., *Agron. J.*, 66:636–639, 1974; G. C. Marten and R. M. Jordan, in *Proceedings of the 12th International Grassland Congress, Moscow, 1974*, in press; G. C. Marten, A. B. Simons, and J. R. Frelich, *Agron. J.*, 66:363–368, 1974; H. F. Mayland et al., *Agron. J.*, 66:441–446, 1974; H. F. Mayland and D. L. Grunes, *J. Range Manage.*, 27:198–201, 1974; J. A. Stuedemann and S. R. Wilkinson, *1974 Beef Cattle Short Course Proceedings, Athens, GA*, 1974; R. H. Whittaker and P. P. Feeny, *Science*, 171:757–770, Feb. 26, 1971; S. R. Wilkinson et al., *International Symposium on Livestock Wastes*, ASAE Publ. Proc., 271:321–324, 328, 1971.

Force, weak and electromagnetic

It has been conjectured for many years that two of the basic forces of nature—electromagnetism and the weak or Fermi interaction—may be intimately related. These forces share certain important characteristics but appear to differ profoundly in others. One significant difference has been the apparent forbiddenness of certain weak scattering processes, such as the scattering of a neutrino by a nucleon, leading to a neutrino and one or more hadrons in the final state, particularly when compared with the allowed nature of the corresponding electromagnetic scattering, in which an electron, for example, scatters off a nucleon into a final state consisting of an electron and one or more hadrons. Until recently, allowed neutrino scattering by a nucleon seemed always to involve a charged lepton (electron or muon) in the final state, but never a neutral lepton (neutrino). In 1974, however, two experiments utilizing rather different techniques have provided evidence which strongly suggests that the scattering of a neutrino into a neutrino ($\nu \to \nu$) does in fact occur, and at a rate which is a substantial fraction of the rate for neutrino scattering into a charged lepton ($\nu \to \ell^{\pm}$).

CERN bubble chamber experiment. One of the experiments was carried out at the European Organization for Nuclear Research (CERN) in Geneva, Switzerland, by a collaboration involving 55 scientists from eight countries. They used a liquid freon (CF_3Br) bubble chamber, which served as both the target and detector of the neutrino interactions. The chamber was cylindrical in shape, with a length of 4.5 m and a diameter of 1.8 m. The density of the heavy freon was 1.5×10^3 kg/m³, and the total detector weight was about 10 tons (9072

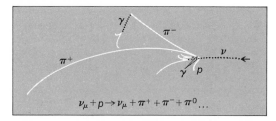

Fig. 1. Tracing of an example of a candidate for an interaction involving a neutral current in the CERN experiment. The neutrino enters from the right, and no charged lepton emerges from its interaction with a proton. All the observed tracks can be identified as strongly interacting particles by measuring their curvatures and observing their range in the heavy liquid and their subsequent interactions. *(From Physics at Bonn and Aix, CERN Courier, vol. 13, no. 10, October 1973)*

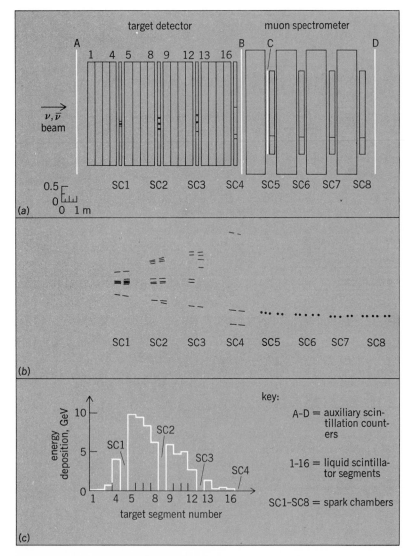

Fig. 2. NAL experiment. *(a)* Plan view of experimental apparatus. *(b)* Rendering of an enlarged spark chamber photograph of typical inelastic neutrino event with an associated muon. *(c)* Graph of energy deposition in each segment during the event. *(From A. Benvenuti et al., Observation of muonless neutrino-induced interactions, Phys. Rev. Lett., 32:800, 1974)*

kg). The chamber was located in a magnetic field of 2 tesla. The collision of protons of energy 28 GeV from the CERN proton synchrotron with a metal target yielded, among other particles, charged pions and kaons that were focused by a magnetic horn and then decayed in flight. These decays produced either a beam of neutrinos (ν_μ), with the same lepton number as the negative muon through the decays (π^+, $K^+ \rightarrow \mu^+ + \nu_\mu$), or a beam of antineutrinos ($\bar{\nu}_\mu$), with the same lepton number as the positive muon through the decays (π^- $K^- \rightarrow \mu^- + \bar{\nu}_\mu$), depending on the sign of the particles focused by the magnetic horn.

The analysis was based on 8.3×10^4 pictures taken with the neutrino beam and 2.07×10^5 pictures taken with the antineutrino beam. In the film 102 neutrino events without muons and 428 neutrino events with muons were found; for antineutrino events the corresponding numbers were 64 and 148. Events were classified as muonless if all the particles emitted in the interaction were identified as hadrons through measurement of the curvature of their tracks and observation of either their subsequent interaction or characteristic decay in the chamber. The observed distributions in energy in space and in angle of events with and without muons were essentially the same. An example of a muonless event is shown in the tracing in Fig. 1.

The principal source of background in this experiment arose from the interaction of neutral hadrons, primarily neutrons, produced by neutrino interactions outside the visible volume of the chamber. Background due to low-energy neutrons was eliminated by the requirement that the total hadronic energy in all accepted events be greater than 1 GeV. A semiempirical correction was made for spurious events produced by higher-energy neutrons.

Additional small corrections for impurity of the neutrino and antineutrino beams and for misidentified pions (as muons) were made, resulting finally in the cross-section ratios shown in Eqs. (1) and (2), in which the errors are statistical.

$$R^\nu = \frac{\sigma(\nu_\mu + \text{nucleon} \rightarrow \nu_\mu + \text{hadrons})}{\sigma(\nu_\mu + \text{nucleon} \rightarrow \mu^- + \text{hadrons})}$$
$$= 0.21 \pm 0.03 \quad (1)$$

$$R^{\bar{\nu}} = \frac{\sigma(\bar{\nu}_\mu + \text{nucleon} \rightarrow \bar{\nu}_\mu + \text{hadrons})}{\sigma(\bar{\nu}_\mu + \text{nucleon} \rightarrow \mu^+ + \text{hadrons})}$$
$$= 0.45 \pm 0.09 \quad (2)$$

NAL ionization calorimeter experiment. The other experiment was carried out by a collaboration of 14 physicists from three universities at the National Accelerator Laboratory (NAL) in Batavia, IL, where collisions of 300-GeV protons with a target produced the secondary hadrons that decayed to provide the incident neutrino and antineutrino beams. *See* PARTICLE ACCELERATOR.

The target-detector of the neutrino interactions in this experiment was a large ionization calorimeter consisting of 16 optically separated segments, each of which was 3.5 m high, 3 m wide, and 0.46 m long and filled with liquid scintillator of density 0.87×10^3 kg/m³. Each segment was viewed by 12 photomultiplier tubes; the summed output measures the ionization energy deposited by the products of a neutrino or antineutrino interaction. One segment was about 0.6 collision length of a strongly interacting particle, and about 1 radiation length for electromagnetic particles. Hence most of the energy in the hadronic-electromagnetic cascade from a neutrino interaction was contained within the total volume of the ionization calorimeter. Interspersed between every four segments of the calorimeter were optical spark chambers that gave a visual display of the secondary particle cascade. Immediately downstream of the ionization calorimeter was a muon detector and spectrometer to identify muons and to measure the momentum of a subsample of muons. This consisted of large-area scintillation counters and four magnetized iron toroids, the axes of which coincided with the beam line; each toroid was followed by a narrow-gap spark chamber.

The experiment was triggered by the deposition in the target-detector of energy greater than a preset minimum value of a few gigaelectron-volts. Following a trigger signal, the electrical outputs of all segments of the ionization calorimeter were recorded individually, as were the outputs of the muon identifier counters, and all the spark chambers were fired. A diagram of the apparatus and a reproduction of an event are shown in Fig. 2.

In a run with a mixed neutrino-antineutrino beam, 1484 triggers were obtained, yielding 169 useful events in a restricted fiducial volume, of which 76 events showed no final-state muon and 93 events exhibited a muon. The principal correction to the raw data of this experiment was for wide-angle muons that miss the muon identifiers. A semiempirical correction was made using the measured muon angular distribution. The final result of that experiment was $R = 0.23 \pm 0.09$, where R is related to R^ν and $R^{\bar\nu}$ by $R = \alpha R^{\bar\nu} + (1 - \alpha) R^{\bar\nu}$ and α is a measure of the corrected admixture of interacting neutrinos and antineutrinos observed in those events with a muon.

Conclusions. The primary conclusion from these experiments is that, unlike earlier neutrino scattering experiments, they show a significant number of neutrino- and antineutrino-induced events without final-state charged leptons (muons). It is important to note that this positive signal is obtained in both experiments even though the experimental methods are so different. It is also of interest that the average energy of events observed in the two experiments is quite different; in the CERN experiment the average was about 3 GeV, in the NAL experiment, roughly 40 GeV.

Ultimately, the precise values of $R^{\bar\nu}$ and R^ν will be vital parameters in any interpretation of the effect. For example, $R^{\bar\nu} \approx 3R^\nu$ would suggest that the neutrino and antineutrino cross sections that give rise to muonless events might be approximately equal. This would follow from the experimentally known fact that the neutrino and antineutrino cross sections for events with muons, in the energy region of these experiments, are in the ratio of about 3:1. Alternatively, the Weinberg-Salam gage model of the weak interactions, in which neutral weak currents as well as charged weak currents make a natural appearance, suggests a

different value for $R^{\bar\nu}/R^\nu$. Still other interpretations, based on variations of the Weinberg-Salam model, or more phenomenological, are also possible.

Finally, it should be mentioned that a search for reactions of the type $\nu_\mu + e^- \rightarrow \nu_\mu + e^-$ has also been initiated at CERN. If that process is shown to exist, it will play a decisive role in the choice of interpretations of neutral weak current phenomena. Further work on neutrino- and antineutrino-nucleon scattering, aimed also at clarifying the nature of the matrix element of the effective neutral weak current, is continuing at CERN and NAL.

For background information *see* ELEMENTARY PARTICLE; SELECTION RULES (PHYSICS) in the McGraw-Hill Encyclopedia of Science and Technology.   [A. K. MANN]

Bibliography: E. S. Abers and B. W. Lee, *Phys. Rep.*, 9C:1, 1973; A. Benvenuti et al., *Phys. Rev. Lett.*, 32:800, 1974; F. J. Hasert et al., *Phys. Lett.*, 46B(121):138, 1973.

Forest and forestry

Prescribed burning, or the intentional ignition of grass, shrub, or forest fuels for specific purposes, has long been a recognized land-management practice. The objectives of such burning are varied: reducing the fire hazard after logging, exposing mineral soil for seedbeds, eliminating hardwoods from forests of southern pines, controlling insects and diseases, thinning dense stands of saplings, improving yields and quality of forage, improving wildlife habitat, and modifying the composition of species in different plant communities.

Today there is a new, additional role for fire on some wildlands. More than 3,000,000 acres (1 acre = 4047 m²) in the United States are being managed by the National Park Service and the U.S. Department of Agriculture Forest Service so that wildland fires may play a more nearly natural role in forests. In many areas, fires now are allowed to burn under observation, and are not automatically suppressed. Fire management zones have been established in national parks and in wildernesses, from the Everglades in Florida to the High Sierras in California. This new fire management policy is being applied on lands that in the past received the same high level of fire protection as commercial forests.

More than 60 years of fire protection have sharply reduced the diversity of life forms in wilderness ecosystems. The absence of roads has not prevented an increasingly sophisticated technology of fire detection and fire control from being brought to bear on wilderness fires. The lookout towers and foot trails of the 1930s have gradually been supplanted by patrol planes, some equipped with infrared scanners, and airplanes and helicopters that can deliver fire fighters, equipment, and fire-retarding chemicals to even the most remote fire. The impacts of advanced fire control systems are least pronounced in sparsely vegetated high-elevation forests and most apparent at lower elevations where mosaics of different age classes, species, and life forms are gradually becoming less discernible.

Fig. 1. The 1200-acre lightning-caused fire in the Selway-Bitterroot Wilderness in northern Idaho, August 1973. (*Photograph by R. W. Mutch, USDA Forest Service*)

Fire-dependent plant communities are highly flammable; thousands of years of evolutionary development in the presence of periodic wildfires produced plant species well adapted to recurrent fire. The routine extinguishing of wildfires in recent times has caused organic fuels to accumulate, perhaps contributing to wildfires of unnatural size and intensity. Fire statistics compiled for a large portion of the Northern Rockies reveal an increase in the proportion of acres burned during the 1960s as compared with the 2 preceding decades. This may be an early clue that modern fire control technology cannot indefinitely reduce acres burned because fuels are continuing to accumulate on a greater and greater number of contiguous acres.

Thus, an emerging rationale suggests that fire be restored to wilderness ecosystems—ecosystems which by law (Wilderness Act of 1964) are to be managed to perpetuate areas that are "affected primarily by the forces of nature." Such restoration provides scientific, educational, and esthetic opportunities regarding the role of fire in wilderness ecosystems and allows procedures more in harmony with nature. As O. Loucks observed, per-

turbations such as fire tend to recycle the system and maintain a periodic wave of peak diversity. He concluded that any modifications of the system that preclude random perturbation and recycling would be detrimental to the system.

Wilderness fire management. The basic knowledge to return fire to wilderness is available. But because over 50 years of fire protection have altered these ecosystems and caused unusually high accumulations of fuels on some sites, one must proceed very carefully.

To develop procedures for allowing fires to play a more nearly natural role in wilderness, in 1970 the Forest Service launched a study on the Bitterroot National Forest in the Selway-Bitterroot Wilderness of northern Idaho. Called the White Cap Study, this work has provided the necessary data on fuel, vegetation, and landforms to identify and establish a series of fire management zones. The fire potential in each management zone was determined by processing fuel inventory data in a mathematical model for fire spread. Fire spread and fire intensity parameters, derived from the fuel inventory data, were used to help prepare fire management prescriptions applicable to the specific zones.

Discovered fires are carefully observed and are suppressed when necessary to protect human life and property, or to contain fires within the management area. Wilderness fire management is not a policy of simply letting fires burn; fire suppression measures backed by modern fire control technology are still necessary.

A lightning fire that started in August 1973 in the ponderosa pine savanna zone provides an example of the wilderness fire management concept (Fig. 1). A portion of the fire was suppressed to contain it within the management area. But much of the perimeter was allowed to burn free, covering an area of 1200 acres during a 43-day period. The fire, which was rained out in late September, amply demonstrated the significant effects of even a single naturally spreading fire on the wilderness ecosystem. In 6 weeks' time it burned almost as much acreage as 216 fires had burned during the preceding 47 years.

Specific effects of this fire were many. In the dry, cool climate of the Northern Rocky Mountains, the process of decomposition barely functions; thus, forest fuels accumulate over time and nutrients are tied up in dead woody materials and duff. The table shows the percent of change of fuel

Change of fuel components after the Fritz Creek Fire, White Cap Fire Management Area*

Dead fuel category	Ponderosa pine stand, lb/acre†			Douglas fir stand, lb/acre			Young Douglas fir stand, lb/acre		
	Prefire	Postfire	Change, %	Prefire	Postfire	Change, %	Prefire	Postfire	Change, %
Branchwood									
0–1/4 in. diam.	86	49	−43	102	40	−61	189	40	−79
1/4–3/4 in. diam.	308	173	−44	398	294	−26	237	42	−82
3/4–4 in. diam.	2515	448	−82	570	211	−63	2506	1092	−56
>4 in. diam.	4512	0	−100	911	683	−25	52,761	32,239	−39
Litter	1339	1052	−21	630	658	+5	612	1594	+160
Duff	5001	324	−94	7162	3262	−54	110,343	0	−100

*From R. W. Mutch, I thought forest fires were black!, *West. Wildlands*, 1(3):16–22, 1974.
†Equals 0.454 kg/4047 m².

components after the 1200-acre fire in the White Cap Fire Management Area. Fuel inventories, 3 weeks after the fire, indicated that needle litter was already near or above prefire levels. The rapid reestablishment of litter resulted from scorched needles and natural needle cast. But the significant reduction in weight of all other fuel categories suggests that fire may be the agent in the Northern Rockies that serves a vital role in fuel reduction and nutrient cycling.

Redstem ceanothus, an important browse species for deer and elk, was stimulated by the burn. Fire triggered germination of the redstem seed, which may lie dormant in the soil and duff for 100 to 200 years. Nine thousand redstem seedlings per acre occurred in an area burned by a low-intensity ground fire. Nearby, a high-intensity crown fire resulted in 80,000 redstem seedlings per acre.

Morel mushrooms were abundant on the burn in May 1974, in areas where the ground fire was hottest.

Fire management strategies. Prescribed burning can restore fire to lower-elevation forests where fuel accumulations hold the potential for fires of unnaturally high intensities. B. Kilgore reported that fire is closely linked to the life cycle of giant sequoia, and low-intensity fires probably burned under sequoias about every 10 to 20 years. After longer periods of fire exclusion, fuel buildup may support crown fires that will kill mature trees. In Sequoia and Kings Canyon national parks, the National Park Service is deliberately burning the understory vegetation and downed trees and litter to return the sequoia groves to more nearly natural conditions (Fig. 2).

Fire can also be restored by allowing lightning-ignited fires to burn within predetermined zones. This practice is operational today in Saguaro National Monument, the Everglades, Grand Teton, Yellowstone, Rocky Mountain, Sequoia and Kings Canyon, Yosemite, and North Cascades national parks, and the Selway-Bitterroot Wilderness.

Lightning fires have played an important role in the natural history of Sierra Nevada forests. Fire scars, charred bark, and charcoal in the soil show that fire is common in the High Sierras. Recognizing the need to return fire to these forests, land managers in Sequoia and Kings Canyon national parks have placed 71% of the parks in a high-elevation fire management zone, where lightning-caused fires are allowed to burn. Of the 80 lightning fires occurring in this zone between 1968 and 1973, 80% have gone out naturally at less than $\frac{1}{4}$ acre.

Natural ecosystems. Regardless of the method of restoring fire to wilderness, whether prescribed burning or allowing lightning fires to burn, perpetuation of natural ecosystems is the management objective. However, imposing traditional prescribed burning methodology on wilderness ecosystems carries the danger of also imposing human values and controls on biotic communities that should be regulated by natural and random events. A random lightning discharge igniting fuels on a wilderness mountainside and the resulting fire sprawling ameba-like over the landscape in an unplanned manner for days or even weeks is in harmony with the mystique of wilderness.

Fig. 2. Prescribed burning in Sequoia and Kings Canyon national parks is returning fire to fire-adapted sequoia groves. (*Photograph by B. M. Kilgore, National Park Service*)

This is not to discount the important role prescribed burning might play under certain conditions, or the need to bring a wilderness fire under control at some point in time. But, ideally, a wilderness fire should be a random event that produces dynamic ecosystem change: killing some trees but leaving others, removing undergrowth in places but also leaving unburned areas, exposing mineral soil, producing open-grown forests or dense stands of lodgepole pine, converting dead organic material to ash, recycling nutrients, restricting some plants and favoring others. Not only are fire-dependent communities well adapted to such change, but also the diversity of plants and animals that follows fire contributes to ecosystem stability.

There is much that is not understood about the functioning of natural ecosystems — and fire is a fundamental force in many biotic communities throughout North America. Fire management programs that are operational in national parks and in wildernesses today provide unique opportunities to appreciate the responses of plant and animal populations to fire in areas not subject to man's overt influence. Studies are already under way to determine the natural habitat preferences of terrestrial and aquatic insects and deer and elk populations following the 1200-acre fire in the Selway-Bitterroot Wilderness in 1973. Other studies are documenting water quality and successional relationships of vegetation and forest fuels on this same area. Such wilderness-oriented research programs will one day assist forest management outside wilderness as well.

For background information *see* FOREST AND FORESTRY; FOREST FIRE CONTROL in the McGraw-Hill Encyclopedia of Science and Technology.

[ROBERT W. MUTCH; JAMES R. HABECK]

Bibliography: J. R. Habeck and R. W. Mutch, *Quaternary Res.*, 3(3):408–424, 1973; B. M. Kilgore, *Nat. Parks Conserv. Mag.*, 44(277):16–22, 1970; B. M. Kilgore and G. S. Briggs, *J. For.*, 70(5): 266–271, 1972; O. L. Loucks, *Amer. Zool.*, 10:17–25, 1970.

Forest management and organization

Improved management of the forest and its resources depends heavily upon minimizing the impact of road construction on the environment. Any alteration of the landscape, such as road building, brings an environmental response.

Erosion, subsurface failure, and esthetic degradation constitute the major environmental threats of road construction. Research to control erosion, slope stability, and esthetic impact is usually designed to produce the quantitative data needed for complete analysis. Attempts to construct models to represent the system and predict responses have generally failed for lack of quantitative data. Research under way or planned will help provide the necessary data.

Surface and subsurface stability. The detachability of soils and the forces imposed upon a soil mass or soil particle determine erodibility. Water-related erosion can best be visualized by illustrating the principal forces causing detachment and transportation (Fig. 1). The detachability of soil particles is dependent upon their size, the water depth, and shear forces. Soil transport is influenced by water velocity induced by slope. A unique combination of these forces produces maximum erosion, shown by the interception of the transportation and detachment rate surfaces in the figure. Recent research results show that wind is also an important erosive force on steep road-fill slopes.

In the absence of treatment, erosion rates are 10

to 20 times greater the first year after road construction than in any succeeding year and tend to stabilize after the second or third year. Erosion rates in excess of 100 tons/day/mi² (3488 kg/day/km²) have been recorded during this critical period on roads built in the unstable soils of the Idaho batholith. Preventing surface erosion by either water or wind is primarily accomplished by controlling slope, compacting soil, and planting vegetative cover. Reducing the degree of slope also reduces flow velocities and gravitational forces on soil particles. Vegetation helps minimize rainfall splash forces and retards overland flow. It also breaks up wind patterns on long, steep slopes. On certain soils, chemical additives such as Gelgard and Orzon A form a tenacious gel that can help prevent detachment of soil particles on loose road-fill slopes for the first year after construction.

To ensure success, vegetative treatments must be matched carefully to the climate and soils of the area. In Montana alone, more than 150 species of grass and shrubs have been tested for landscaping and controlling erosion along highways. Grass is usually planted along with a cellulose mulch and is often fertilized to ensure better results. Grass planted on slopes greater than 1:1 (100%) seldom stabilizes the slope. If stabilization is imperative, transplanted shrubs will do the job except on the very harshest sites. The most successful mulch to use on the harshest, driest sites is straw compacted into the top 2–3 in. (5–7.5 cm) of soil by a modified sheep's-foot roller.

Both subsurface stability and structural stability are influenced primarily by the topography, geology (soils), and climate. Slope failures, caused by unstable subsurface conditions, are common in forest roads, and standard methods of analysis have been employed for studying and predicting failures. Most failures can be prevented by collecting and analyzing geologic, soil, and hydrologic information. Recent research results of W. S. Hartsog and G. L. Martin and of M. J. Gonsior, Hartsog, and Martin have improved infinite slope analysis by refining soil pressure calculations. Hartsog and Martin developed expressions for the normal and tangential stresses for the active and passive states of stress, with the angle of the investigation α being one of the variables. This permits calculation of stresses on any plane.

A further refinement of infinite slope analysis was presented by Gonsior, Hartsog, and Martin. The infinite slope theory is based on the assumptions that a conjugate relationship exists between the pressures acting on vertical planes and that stress conditions at any two points of equal depth are identical. In the conventional analysis, the difference in end conditions (uphill and downhill) are ignored. Gonsior and coworkers extended the theory to include stress conditions on the uphill and downhill ends of infinite slope failures, thereby improving the analysis.

In studies under way in northern Idaho and Montana, experimental roads are being built that incorporate design features hypothesized to reduce environmental and esthetic impacts and still serve traffic needs. The principal design features involve reducing the width of the finished road prism to minimize esthetic, hydrologic, and erosion im-

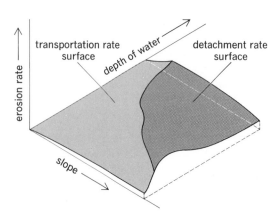

Fig. 1. Surface of maximum erosion rate as formed by a unique combination of the transportation and detachment rate surfaces. (*From D. L. Rowlison and G. L. Martin, Rational model describing slope erosion, ASCE Proc., J. Irrig. Div., vol. 97, no. 1RI, March 1971*)

Fig. 2. Conventional forest road (lower center) and experimental road (upper center) in a northern Montana forest.

pacts. Significant width reductions are possible when B horizon bedrock conditions are sufficiently competent to support 10:1 back slopes. These conditions are identified by seismic surveys of the road locations. Sections in which velocities are above 4000 ft (1220 m) per second will support these back slopes. Other advantages are reduced interception of groundwater flows, less open rock slope for air slacking and spalling, and increased tree cover to screen raw slopes. The economic impact of reducing both width and the number of turnouts on logging and log hauling will be analyzed and incorporated in the overall analysis of optimum management alternatives. Tradeoffs between economic values and environmental values will be resolved on the basis of study data.

Esthetics. Ecological damage constitutes the public's major objection to resource use and the attendant road systems. In recent years, many forest users have come to regard the appearance of the forest to be as valuable as the forest products. Protection or enhancement of esthetic values has been a slow process because of the difficulty of measuring and appraising these qualities. Not only has the forest many different values to visitors, but many values cannot be measured in common terms, such as dollars. Nevertheless, managers are now attempting to include esthetic values in management plans. One method is through meetings at which the public can express their esthetic desires. Other techniques are being developed by social scientists. R. Boster and T. C. Daniel have developed a method of evaluating esthetics that involves a degree of "like" or "don't like" impressions from random photographs shown to the raters. The values are based on a 0−9 ranking, with 0 = strong dislike, 9 = strong like, and so on. This method will be used to evaluate the esthetic impact of the experimental roads constructed in Montana and Idaho.

In Fig. 2 a conventional road crosses the forest in the upper half of the photograph. Immediately above the old road, the clearing for the experimental road, designed to reduce impacts, is just barely

visible. It is hypothesized that the esthetic impact of the less visible new road will be judged as relatively insignificant.

Near the upper end of the experimental road, another experiment in dampening or eliminating esthetic impact is being tried. Road cuts through rock, which are very difficult to revegetate, are being serrated (stepped) to promote plant growth. The small benched areas will retain both seed or shrub plantings and more moisture. This method shows considerable promise, especially in areas with relatively high annual precipitation. Although this type of treatment is relatively expensive, the cost must be evaluated in terms of its esthetic benefit. Complete evaluation of ecological and social impacts will be made for these roads.

For background information *see* ECOLOGY; FOREST MANAGEMENT AND ORGANIZATION in the McGraw-Hill Encyclopedia of Science and Technology.   [R. B. GARDNER]

Bibliography: R. B. Gardner, *USDA Forest Serv. Res. Note INT-145*, 1971; W. S. Hartsog and M. J. Gonsior, *USDA Forest Serv. Res. Pap. INT-5*, 1973; W. S. Hartsog and G. L. Martin, *USDA Forest Serv. Res. Pap. INT-149*, 1974; W. F. Megahan and W. J. Kidd, *USDA Forest Serv. Res. Pap. INT-123*, 1972.

Fusion, nuclear

Thermonuclear fusion by laser-driven compression, commonly called laser fusion, is a new approach to nuclear fusion, utilizing inertial confinement rather than conventional magnetic confinement. The basic idea is to utilize a high-power pulse of radiation to ablate the outer surface of a fusion pellet and thereby implode it to achieve

Fig. 1. Photograph of a 100-micrometer CD_2 pellet irradiated by the Sandia Laboratories four-beam laser.

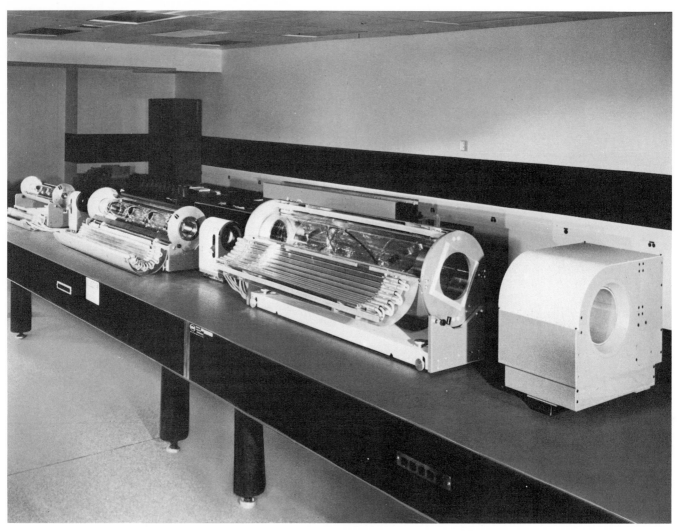

Fig. 2. Photograph of one of the large laser amplifiers presently under construction at the Lawrence Liver-more Laboratory for use in their 10,000-joule multiple-beam laser facility.

thermonuclear conditions. In the case of laser fusion, the pellet is imploded by an array of high-power, short-pulse lasers.

The fusion goals in laser fusion are the same as those in magnetic confinement fusion: to produce a high-temperature plasma possessing conditions such that the combination of temperature, density, volume, and containment time provide an environment in which fusion energy is released in excess of that required to produce the plasma. In the case of magnetic confinement fusion, the plasma density is required to be relatively low in order that it be contained by the magnetic field for a long time (seconds). In the case of laser fusion, since the process begins with a solid density pellet which is subsequently imploded, the densities involved in the fusion plasma are exceedingly high while the containment time may be exceedingly short (of the order of 10^{-9} sec).

Process of laser fusion. The basic concept for laser fusion is one in which a small solid pellet of fusionable material (deuterium and tritium) is uniformly irradiated by a high-intensity array of lasers such that the outer surface of the pellet is instantaneously vaporized. This high-temperature

vapor then provides a spherically symmetric impulse to the remaining material, which causes that material to implode. The net result is a situation in which approximately 90% of the pellet is vaporized by the laser beams and approximately 10% of the original material is imploded to densities and temperatures at which fusion reactions can occur (typical densities required are 1000–10,000 × solid density, and temperatures of the order of 100,000,000 K).

Under these conditions the assembled material must remain inertially confined for a time of only a few nanoseconds (1 ns = 10^{-9} sec) in order for enough fusion reactions to occur that net energy is produced. Hence, this approach is not subject to the requirement that the plasma remain free of instabilities for long periods of time, as is the case in magnetic confinement fusion. On the other hand, it is necessary in this approach to reach plasma densities which are exceedingly high. It is only by virtue of the unique features of high-power lasers that this approach to fusion appears feasible. Finally, the basic concept for a laser fusion reactor is one in which a continuing sequence of pellets is dropped into the center of a fusion reactor chamber and sequentially imploded by an array of rapidly firing lasers timed to irradiate each pellet as it reaches the center of the chamber.

Research activities. The research activities in laser fusion are presently directed primarily toward development of large, high-power lasers and toward first-generation experiments to study the dynamics of laser-driven compressions. The most important considerations in the laser-driven compression studies relate to the absorption of the laser light, the vaporization of the outer surface of the pellet, and the subsequent implosion of the remaining pellet material. Based on recent experience with large lasers, with laser-plasma experiments, and with detailed computer calculations, it appears likely that fusion can be achieved by this process if the laser absorption proceeds as expected and the initial conditions are established properly for implosion of the final material. Figure 1 is a photograph of a laser-imploded pellet obtained from a four-beam laser system at Sandia Laboratories in Albuquerque, NM. It is typical of data being obtained in experiments of this type at several laboratories in this country and abroad.

The important pacing technology for laser fusion is that of large high-power, short-pulse lasers with which to implode the small pellets of fusion fuel. One of the most advanced lasers being developed at this time is at the Lawrence Livermore Laboratory in Livermore, CA, a 20-beam subnanosecond 10,000-joule laser (Fig. 2). This laser is called a Nd^{3+}:glass laser since it utilizes transitions in Nd^{3+} ions which are integral constituents of a glass medium. The efficiency of this laser is relatively low (of the order 0.1%), but since it is the most highly developed laser available, a 20-beam system is being assembled in order to provide a useful research capability for near-term fusion experiments. Large CO_2 laser amplifiers are also being developed for similar experiments at the Los Alamos Scientific Laboratory in New Mexico. Although the CO_2 laser technology is not as highly developed as Nd^{3+}:glass laser technology, it does offer potential for applications to larger laser fusion experiments since it inherently possesses higher efficiency. In order to reach the long-range goal of producing a fusion power reactor from laser-driven compression of pellets, it is necessary to develop still better lasers which possess both high power capability and high efficiency. Consequently, laser development is an integral part of the laser fusion program.

For background information *see* FUSION, NUCLEAR; LASER in the McGraw-Hill Encyclopedia of Science and Technology.

[EVERET H. BECKNER]

Bibliography: T. J. Burgess, *Plasma Science*, PS-2:26, 1973; J. S. Clarke, H. N. Fisher, and R. J. Mason, *Phys. Rev. Lett.*, 30:89, 1973; R. E. Kidder, *Nuclear Fusion*, 14:53, 1974; J. Nuckolls et al., *Nature*, 239:139, 1972.

Gallstones

The recent finding that gallstones in humans can be dissolved has stimulated great interest in gallstone research. A better understanding of the physical chemistry of gallstones and the metabolic abnormalities associated with gallstone formation has been achieved.

Cholesterol metabolism. The most common variety of gallstones are composed predominantly of cholesterol, a highly insoluble lipid substance that is excreted almost exclusively by the liver through the biliary tract. Because of the insolubility of cholesterol in aqueous solutions, special mechanisms are required to remove it from the body. In the liver, for example, cholesterol is partly converted into bile acids. These water-soluble sterols not only serve as a pathway for removal of body cholesterol but also participate in the solubilization of cholesterol itself. The mechanism of solubilization involves the formation of molecular aggregates, called mixed micelles, with the phospholipid lecithin. Micellar solutions of bile acids and lecithin normally provide for complete solubilization of biliary cholesterol. However, recent work has shown that the stability of mixed micelles is dependent on the relative amounts of cholesterol present. When cholesterol constitutes less than 5% (on a molar basis) of the total biliary lipids (cholesterol + bile acids + lecithin), it is held completely in solution. When the cholesterol content increases to 5–9%, micelles are in a metastable state, and cholesterol will crystallize out of solution after prolonged periods or in the presence of nucleating agents. At higher percentages of cholesterol, bile is highly supersaturated, and crystallization occurs rapidly. The likelihood of gallstone formation seems to be largely dependent on the degree of cholesterol saturation, but nucleating factors that are as yet undefined may also play an important role in stone formation at intermediate percentages of cholesterol.

Lithogenic bile. Bile that is highly saturated or supersaturated with cholesterol has been called lithogenic bile because of the tendency for gallstones to form under these conditions. Theoretically, lithogenic bile could develop either from a deficiency of solubilizing lipids (bile acids and lecithin) or from an excess of cholesterol in bile. Bile acids are normally confined to a pool consisting of the liver, gallbladder, and intestinal tract. Since bile acids that are secreted into the intestine by the liver are reabsorbed almost entirely, they circulate more or less continuously within this enterohepatic system. Early studies strongly suggested that patients with cholesterol gallstones have a deficiency of bile acids in the enterohepatic circulation, a deficiency that is generally considered to be of paramount importance in the production of lithogenic bile. Since secretion of lecithin into bile is dependent on rates of bile acid secretion, reductions in bile acid pools apparently cause decreases in biliary lecithin as well. Therefore, both of these solubilizing lipids are probably reduced in the bile of gallstone patients.

Chenodeoxycholic acid. The concept that a bile acid deficiency contributes to gallstone disease has been reinforced by the observation that oral feeding of bile acids can dissolve cholesterol gallstones. The recent finding that one of the primary bile acids, chenodeoxycholic acid, dissolves gallstones when fed orally represents a significant advance in the understanding of both the cause of gallstones and their possible treatment. An important study has shown that most patients with cholesterol stones show partial or complete dissolution following 6–12 months of oral administration of chenodeoxycholic acid. If future clinical trials can prove that chenodeoxycholic acid is safe as well as effective, medical treatment of gallstone disease could become a reality.

Overproduction of cholesterol. Although a deficiency of bile acids apparently plays a significant role in the production of lithogenic bile, recent clinical studies have also demonstrated that abnormal bile can be due to an excess of cholesterol. In most cases, increased amounts of cholesterol in bile are related to an overproduction of cholesterol by the body. Since the biliary tract is the major route of cholesterol excretion, an overproduction of cholesterol leads to an increased hepatic secretion of cholesterol into bile. The most common cause of an increase in biliary cholesterol is obesity. Obese persons produce considerably more cholesterol than normal persons do, and this excess of newly synthesized cholesterol is ultimately secreted into bile. Thus, an increase in biliary cholesterol may well account for the common clinical association between obesity and gallstones.

These considerations indicate that two factors are important in the formation of lithogenic bile: a deficiency of solubilizing lipids, especially bile acids, and an overproduction of cholesterol. Although bile acid deficiency may be corrected by oral administration of bile acids such as chenodeoxycholic acid, a reduction in biliary cholesterol might best be achieved by weight reduction so as to decrease cholesterol synthesis. In fact, recent investigations indicate that the high lithogenicity of bile found in obese persons can be decreased significantly by weight reduction.

For background information *see* BILE ACID; CHOLESTEROL; GALLSTONES in the McGraw-Hill Encyclopedia of Science and Technology.

[SCOTT M. GRUNDY]

Bibliography: R. G. Danzinger, *J. Clin. Invest.*, 52:2809–2821, 1973; S. M. Grundy and A. L. Metzger, *Gastroenterology*, 62:1200–1217, 1972; R. T. Holzbach et al., *J. Clin. Invest.*, 52:1467–1479, 1973; J. L. Thistle and A. F. Hofmann, *N. Engl. J. Med.*, 289:655–659, 1973.

Gamma-ray astronomy

In 1974 scientists at Los Alamos, NM, announced the detection by Vela satellites of brief, intense bursts of cosmic gamma rays. Discovery of the bursts, which are not obviously associated with any known class of astronomical objects, has aroused great interest in the possible origin of gamma-ray events having such high intensities and short durations. The discovery has once again underlined the tendency in astronomy for exploration of new time scales in new regions of the electromagnetic spectrum to reveal entirely unexpected phenomena, as well as the important role of serendipity in such discoveries.

The Vela satellites were developed to monitor the Nuclear Test Ban Treaty. In 1967, with an improved detection and analysis system, project scientists sought to demonstrate that no natural sources of gamma rays existed that might be confused with nuclear tests. One can imagine their shock and surprise when examination of satellite data for July 2, 1967, clearly showed that a gamma-ray burst characteristic of nuclear debris had been detected. Subsequent analysis of the event and of similar later events showed, however, that they did not come from any object in the solar system. And thus what could potentially have been a grave political problem has become an exciting scientific one.

Los Alamos Laboratory scientists I. Strong, R. Klebesadel, and R. Olson have now reported the detection of a total of 23 soft gamma-ray bursts through the end of 1973. The omnidirectional monitoring capability and nearly continuous coverage in time, together with the possibility of coincident detections by more than one satellite, were vital to the discovery and verification of events that occur only four or five times a year at a level exceeding the Vela detector thresholds. Subsequent observations by many other satellites, among them the *IMP-6, OSO-7,* and *Uhuru,* have confirmed the bursts and have provided valuable additional information on the temporal and spectral characteristics of the bursts.

Character of the bursts. The soft gamma-ray bursts typically last 1–10 sec; however, some are as short as 100–300 msec, and the longest burst observed so far had a duration of about 80 sec. Most of the bursts exhibit multiple (nonperiodic) pulses with significant structure occurring on time scales of 100 msec. Some even show variations on a time scale as short as the 16-msec resolution of the Vela detectors. Such short time scales imply a source size less than 10^{10} cm (10^8m) or a highly relativistic emission process. Figure 1 shows the temporal structure of the event 71-5 (the fifth event in 1971 cataloged thus far).

Because the individual Vela satellites lack directional sensitivity, directional information has come primarily from time-of-flight measurements between the satellites (typically about 0.8 sec). All the Vela satellites, however, lie in a single orbital plane approximately perpendicular to the galactic plane. Consequently, detection by a pair of satellites provides a circle of position on the celestial sphere, but detection by three or more satellites reduces this circle only to a pair of directions that are mirror-symmetric with respect to the orbital plane and that lie at approximately the same galactic latitude. At present the error boxes for the two possible directions are as large as $10° \times 10°$ owing to uncertainties in the time-of-flight measurements.

Figure 2 shows in galactic coordinates the possible directions of the 10 events for which moderately complete directional information is available. In a few cases the direct detection of a burst by another satellite, or the failure of another satellite to detect a burst, has indicated that one of the pair of possible directions is the more likely. A concentration of sources close to the galactic equator would provide unambiguous evidence that the soft gamma-ray-burst sources lie within the Galaxy. The distribution of possible directions shown in Fig. 2, however, is consistent with a uniform distribution in both galactic latitude and galactic longitude. This suggests that the sources either lie rather nearby, with a characteristic distance of about 100 parsecs or less (1 parsec equals approximately 3 light-years, or 3×10^{16} m) or are extragalactic, with distances greater than about 10 Mparsecs. If the factor-of-10 increase in sensitivity potentially obtainable by combining present data from a number of satellites can be realized, the results might distinguish between the local and extragalactic hypotheses by revealing a concentration of sources near the galactic equator.

The soft gamma-ray bursts have typical fluxes of approximately 10^{-5} erg cm^{-2} sec^{-1} (10^{-8} joule m^{-2} sec^{-1}) and integrated fluxes of about 10^{-4} erg cm^{-2} (10^{-7} joule m^{-2}). An estimate for the total energy of a burst can be derived from these flux values by using the two characteristic distances mentioned above. This energy is approximately 10^{38} ergs (10^{31} joules) for a source distance of 100 parsecs, or about 10^{46} ergs (10^{39} joules) if the distance is 10 Mparsecs. Information on the spectral characteristics of the soft gamma-ray bursts has been gleaned from data provided by satellites which, of course, were not designed to study the bursts. Almost all the data are contaminated by the effects of secondary particles that the gamma rays produce through interactions with the matter in the satellite. Consequently, there are substantial uncertainties in the spectral data, and the general spectral characteristics described below should be viewed with caution.

Using data from the *IMP-6* satellite, T. Cline and U. Desai have reported evidence indicating that the gamma rays that make up a burst may have a characteristic energy of about 150 keV. Results reported by the *OSO-7* group at the University of California at San Diego (W. Wheaton and colleagues) suggest that the multiple pulses observed in most bursts have rather hard spectra and are superimposed on a softer background that grows and decays in intensity on a longer time scale. Similar evidence comes from *OSO-6* observations reported by G. Palumbo, G. Pizzichini, and G. Vespignani. These observations also suggest that, at least in some bursts, the energy contained in x-rays is comparable to that observed in soft gamma rays.

Models. About 6 years ago S. Colgate suggested that type I supernovae explosions might produce a burst of gamma rays. However, the predicted gamma-ray energies were much higher and the burst durations were much shorter than those observed in the Vela events. Following discovery of the bursts, Colgate has suggested that type II supernovae involving massive stars (M $\gtrsim$ 30 M$\odot$) with extended hydrogen envelopes might be the sources of the observed events. This model postulates that, in the supernovae explosion, photons are Compton-scattered to energies that are approximately equal to the rest mass of the electron (0.5 MeV). A gamma-ray burst lasting typically about half a second is then produced as the photons break through the surface of the relativistically expanding envelope. At present, this is the only extragalactic model that has been elaborated in detail.

The gamma-ray-burst temporal time scales lie in the range that is characteristic of the dynamical time scales (10^{-4} to 1 sec) associated with degenerate dwarfs, neutron stars, and black holes. There are believed to be a large number of such compact objects within the 100-parsec distance already mentioned as possibly characteristic if the gamma-ray-burst sources lie within the Galaxy. Such distances also imply source luminosities of about 10^{37} ergs sec^{-1} (10^{30} joules sec^{-1}), which is typical of the

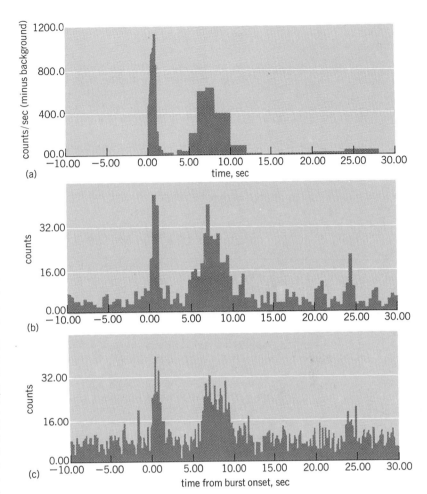

Fig. 1. Temporal structure of gamma-ray burst 71-5 as revealed by detectors aboard satellites. (a) *Vela 6B* satellite. (b) *Uhuru* satellite FWHM (full width at half maximum) 5° collimated detector. (c) *Uhuru* satellite $\frac{1}{2}$° FWHM collimated detector. (*From D. Koch et al., Gamma-ray bursts seen by Uhuru, in I. Strong, ed., Proceedings of the Conference on Transient Cosmic Gamma Ray and X-Ray Sources, Los Alamos Lab. Rep. LA-5505-C, 1974*)

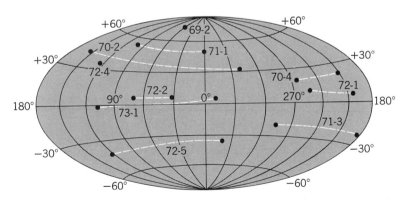

Fig. 2. Distribution in galactic coordinates of the 10 gamma-ray-burst sources for which moderately complete directional information is available. Events 69-2 and 72-4 were detected in the field of view of the *OSO-6* and *OSO-7* satellites, respectively; consequently, only the single directions consistent with this data are plotted for these two events.

luminosities encountered earlier in the compact x-ray sources. These considerations led D. Lamb, F. Lamb, and D. Pines to suggest accretion onto nearby compact objects as the source of the Vela events. They pointed out that if the compact object were a member of a close binary system, solarlike flaring of the companion star could provide the $10^{17}-10^{19}$ g ($10^{14}-10^{16}$ kg) of accreting material needed to produce the observed integrated fluxes. M. Harwit and E. Salpeter earlier suggested that a cloud of comets might exist around neutron stars as they do around the Sun. They proposed that the gamma-ray bursts might thus originate from the accretion of cometary material onto the neutron star following tidal disruption of a comet in a close encounter with the neutron star. See GRAVITATIONAL COLLAPSE.

Among other proposed models is the suggestion of F. Stecker and K. Frost that nearby stellar "superflares," involving energies as much as a billion times greater than those of the largest solar flares, could be the source of the gamma-ray bursts. In a modification of this model, K. Brecher and P. Morrison have postulated that relativistic beaming of photons emitted by electrons streaming along magnetic field lines might narrow the cone of flare-produced gamma rays to perhaps 10^{-4} sterad. This would reduce the required energy of the flares by such a factor, while increasing the required frequency of flares by the same factor. Perhaps the most imaginative idea has been put forth by J. Grindlay and G. Fazio, who have suggested that the bursts are produced by relativistic iron grains entering the solar system. In this model the gamma rays originate from the absorption and reemission of ordinary sunlight, which, in the rest frame of the relativistic iron grains, is blue-shifted to gamma-ray energies.

For background information see SUPERNOVA in the McGraw-Hill Encyclopedia of Science and Technology.

[D. Q. LAMB]

Bibliography: R. Klebesadel, I. Strong, and R. Olson, Astrophys. J., 182:L85, 1973; D. Lamb, F. Lamb, and D. Pines, Nature Phys. Sci., 246:52, 1973; I. Strong (ed.), Proceedings of the Conference on Transient Cosmic Gamma Ray and X-Ray Sources, Los Alamos Lab. Rep. LA-5505-C, 1974; I. Strong, R. Klebesadel, and R. Olson, Astrophys. J., 163:L1, 1974.

Gene action

Reports of some of the recent research in gene action have been concerned with (1) the isolation of the lactose operator in Escherichia coli, analysis of its sequence, and analysis of the sequences of two mutant operators, and (2) advances in the understanding of the molecular mechanism of gene regulation in bacteriophage lambda.

E. coli lactose operator. At the lactose operator site of the E. coli genome, the lactose repressor protein binds to the DNA to prevent transcription of the lactose operon. Since the repressor chooses this one region from the entire E. coli chromosome, clearly there must be some unique features of the operator DNA that determine this specific interaction. Efforts to identify these features have turned on learning the structure of the operator in the greatest possible detail.

Control of lactose operon. There are three structural genes in the lactose (lac) operon: z, y, and a, coding for β-galactosidase, lactose permease, and transacetylase, respectively. Lac permease transports lactose into the cell, and β-galactosidase cleaves the disaccharide into glucose and galactose; the physiological role of transacetylase, if any, is not known. In the absence of an "inducer" — a substrate or substrate analog for β-galactosidase — lac repressor, the product of the neighboring gene i, binds to the operator (o) to prevent RNA polymerase from transcribing z, y, and a. When an inducer is added, repressor binds the inducer and releases the operator DNA. Then polymerase, aided by a general positive control factor, CAP (catabolite activator protein), recognizes the promoter site (p) on the DNA and transcribes z, y, and a into a single polycistronic message. The order of genes and controlling sites is i, p, o, z, y, a. Induction results in a 1000-fold increase in the cellular level of β-galactosidase. Mutations in the operator ("operator constitutive," or o^c) or in the repressor protein allow transcription of the lac genes in the absence of an inducer.

Lac repressor has been purified and shown to be a tetrameric protein of 150,000 mol. wt, composed of four identical subunits. In the test tube purified lac repressor binds tightly and specifically to purified DNA containing the lac operator region; the dissociation constant for binding is 10^{-13} M. Purified repressor also binds to inducers of the lac operon, in particular, to the synthetic inducer IPTG (isopropyl-β,D-thiogalactoside) and, in the presence of IPTG repressor, will not bind the operator region.

Isolation of lac operator. To isolate the operator, W. Gilbert took advantage of the unique ability of lac repressor to bind the operator. He used repressor to fish out fragments of DNA that contained the operator and to protect the operator from DNase digestion. He first incubated repressor with DNA fragments about 1000 base pairs long, produced by sonicating lambdoid transducing phage (about 50,000 base pairs long), which carry the lac operon as a replacement for part of the phage genome. Repressor binds only to those DNA fragments that contain the lac operator. These repressor-operator complexes were separated from free DNA by filtration through a nitrocellulose filter—free DNA passes through the filter, and protein-DNA complexes are trapped. The filter was washed with IPTG to release repressor from operator and effect a purification of operator-containing DNA fragments. Gilbert incubated these operator-containing fragments with repressor once again and, during this incubation, added DNase. The DNase cleaves expose DNA, but the tight interaction with repressor protects the operator from digestion, and it remains intact. The protected fragment is double-stranded DNA, 27 base pairs long, and it retains operator activity; that is, it binds repressor and is released by IPTG.

Operator sequencing. To determine the operator sequence, Gilbert and A. Maxam transcribed the operator into RNA and sequenced this RNA. They used denatured operator as template for E. coli RNA polymerase to copy with α-^{32}P-labeled triphosphates. With denatured template for a sufficient time (16 – 18 hr), polymerase can transcribe even such short pieces of DNA, initiating at random sites and copying both strands of operator. Using

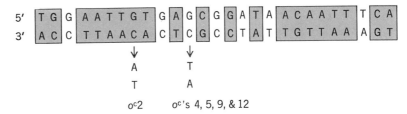

Fig. 1. The *lac* operator sequence, and the sequences of five *o*ᶜ mutants. Symmetric regions in the operator are boxed. A= adenine, C= cytosine, G= guanine, T= thymine.

standard RNA sequencing techniques, and fitting complementary sequences on opposite strands, Gilbert and Maxam arrived at the sequence shown in Fig. 1. They verified its correctness by examining RNA copied from one of the two strands of operator. They used oligonucleotide primers to force polymerase to initiate transcription at specific sites on the template and thus to generate long RNA molecules that copied a single strand of operator.

There is a second technique for sequencing the *lac* operator. N. Maizels has shown that the operator is copied into the mRNA synthesized in the test tube from template containing a CAP-independent promoter mutation, called UV5. Sonic fragments of DNA, 1000 base pairs long and purified as described above to contain the operator, served as template; synthesis was designed to produce the correct *lac* operon messenger from the UV5 DNA. Figure 2 shows the sequence of the first 63 bases of this message, which includes the *lac* operator sequence copied into bases *1* and *24*, and the triplets coding for the first 7 amino acids of β-galactosidase beginning with the AUG codon at position *39*.

Two operator mutations. A single mutation in the operator can decrease repression 50- to 200-fold and weaken repressor-operator binding in the laboratory 10- to 100-fold. Clearly, such a mutation destroys a feature that is essential for repressor to recognize or bind operator efficiently. By sequencing a series of operator mutants, one would hope to learn what characteristics of operator determine its interaction with repressor. One cannot sequence mutant operators by isolating a sequence of repressor-protected DNA and copying it into RNA; repressor does bind *o*ᶜ operator, but not well enough to protect it efficiently from DNase digestion. One can sequence operator mutants by transcribing the 1000-base-pair UV5 *o*ᶜ DNA fragments and then sequencing the RNA product.

Gilbert, Maizels, and Maxam isolated five independent spontaneous *o*ᶜ mutants in a strain with the UV5 promoter mutation and sequenced their *lac* messages. In one of the mutants, UV5 *o*ᶜ2, there is a transition from G to A at position *5* of the message. The other four mutants turned out to be identical; they have a G to U transversion at position *9* of the mRNA. Figure 1 shows the DNA sequences corresponding to these two mutant operators. More mutations exist in strains with the wild-type *lac* promoter; their sequence analysis awaits the sequencing of the wild-type *lac* message.

Repressor-operator interaction. The most striking feature of the operator sequence is that 20 of the 27 base pairs are symmetrically arranged.

(They are boxed in Fig. 1.) On a random basis, one of four base pairs would be symmetric, or 7 in a 27-base-pair sequence. Earlier genetic data of J. Sadler and T. Smith had hinted that such symmetries might be found in the operator. The symmetric regions in the operator and the tetrameric structure of *lac* repressor suggest that operator and repressor could interact on a twofold axis of symmetry, with either two or four subunits of the protein interacting with the DNA. The *o*ᶜ2 mutation is readily interpreted in terms of symmetry, since *o*ᶜ2 introduces a change in a major symmetry region. However, the transversion in the other *o*ᶜ mutants actually increases the overall symmetry, creating a region of three symmetric bases between the two main blocks of symmetry.

DNA protein recognition models. In general, there are three classes of models for DNA protein recognition: (1) the protein reads a DNA sequence, specific amino acid residues forming contacts with the DNA bases or phosphates, or both; (2) the protein interacts mainly with the phosphate skeleton, whose fine structure is in turn dictated by the sequence or base composition of the DNA strands; (3) symmetric regions in the DNA allow it to contort itself into an unusual secondary structure, DNA strands unwinding and self-complementary regions in a single strand binding to one another to form a stem from which the unpaired bases protrude as "ears." Unfortunately, the sequences of the *lac* operator and the two known *o*ᶜ mutants fit easily into all three models. Since the first model requires of an *o*ᶜ only that it change something, the model cannot be tested by simply analyzing mutations.

The second model is especially interesting in light of a claim that A·T-rich regions of DNA (like the *lac* operator, particularly its symmetric regions) have a more flexible structure than the G·C-rich regions do, and thus might have more potential for DNA protein interaction. Both *o*ᶜ

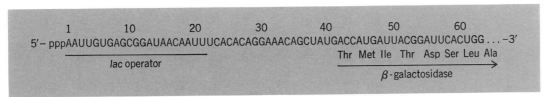

Fig. 2. The first 63 bases of the mRNA transcribed from the UV5 *lac* promoter showing *lac* operator sequence copied into bases *1* to *24* and the triplets (beginning with position *39*) coding for the first amino acids of β-galactosidase.

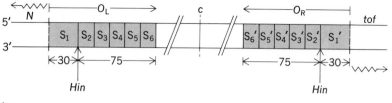

key:

〜〜〜＞ shows direction of transcription of repressor-
←〜〜〜   controlled genes N and tof

――――＞ indicates order of repressor binding from preferred
←――――   sites (S₁ and S₁') to final sites (S₆ and S₆')

Hin   indicates cutting sites in O_L and O_R and number of base pairs
         within the operators on either side of *Hin* cut

Fig. 3. Schematic representation of the λ operators and adjacent genes.

mutants could then be interpreted as loosening the operator structure by substituting A · T for G · C base pairs. The third model would view o^c2, which disrupts overall symmetry, as weakening the structure of a stem, and the other o^c as collapsing an "ear" at the end of the stem. However, this model seems energetically unlikely, since it requires that the run of G · C pairs in the middle of the operator break apart to form ears, whereas the base pairing occurs mainly in the energetically less favorable A · T-rich region. Any strong conclusions about repressor-operator interaction must await sequencing of more o^c mutants or even, perhaps, more operators.   [NANCY MAIZELS]

Bacteriophage lambda. In 1974 remarkable advances were made in the understanding of the molecular mechanism of gene regulation in bacteriophage lambda. The operators, the sequences to which the repressor binds, have been isolated and characterized. These regions of double-stranded DNA are more complex than had been anticipated. Moreover, the relationship of these operators to the λ promoters, the sites to which RNA polymerase binds, has been described, and the mechanism of action of the repressor clarified. Finally, the sequence of the DNA bases binding a repressor has been determined. This sequence has interesting features that suggest new principles governing certain DNA-protein interactions.

Repressor action in phage λ. Repressor, the structure of which is coded in the phage cI gene, binds to two operators, O_L and O_R, thereby directly blocking "leftward" transcription of gene N and "rightward" transcription of the gene termed *tof* or *cro*. The product of gene N is required to depend on other λ genes. For this and other reasons, repressor bound to the two operators turns off all of the (about 50) phage genes except cI. Repression at O_L is independent of that at O_R, and if the appropriate operator mutants are used, events at either operator can be studied independently.

Monomeric repressor protein has a molecular weight of 27,500. Monomers are in concentration-dependent equilibrium with dimers and possibly tetramers. Repressor initiates binding as an oligomer, probably a dimer. The apparent dissociation constant describing repressor-operator interaction ($10^{-14} M$) signifies very tight binding indeed.

Structure of λ *operators.* The current picture of

the λ operators is presented in Fig. 3, the main features of which are as follows. Each operator contains about 105 base pairs and consists of about 6 nonidentical repressor binding sites (S_1 to S_6, and S_1 to S_6 in Fig. 3). These sites have a gradient of repressor affinity such that repressor preferentially binds to the terminal site S_1, or S_1', and subsequent repressor molecules add to adjacent sites in sequence. The first site covered by repressor is about 30–35 base pairs long, the other sites about 15 base pairs long. Near the junction of first and second repressor-binding sites there is a sequence specifically broken by a restriction endonuclease (*Hin*) isolated from *Haemophilus influenzae*. Finally, although these features are common to O_L and O_R, the two operators differ in base sequence and affinity for repressor.

Relationship of operator and promoter. The promoter is defined as the site to which RNA polymerase binds preparatory to initiating transcription of an operon. Thus in λ there must be two promoters, P_L and P_R, concerned with leftward and rightward transcription. Consider two simple alternatives for the mechanism of repression. Operator and promoter could share common sequences, in which case repressor would compete with polymerase for binding to DNA. Alternatively, the operator might be located between the structural gene and the promoter, in which case repressor would block the movement of polymerase. In λ the first model holds.

Two classes of mutations (sex and x) in λ have been described which, on the basis of their effect on transcription in the test tube and in the intact bacterium, have been called promoter mutations. The sex mutations decrease transcription of gene N, and the x mutations decrease transcription of gene *tof*. Using specific DNA fragments, it was found that RNA polymerase binds tightly to the promoters unless the promoter (in this case O_L) bears the mutation sex l. Thus sex l is located in the promoter. It was then discovered that the sex l mutation altered the *Hin* cutting site in O_L, and that an x mutation similarly altered the *Hin* cutting site in O_R. From these and other experiments, it was concluded that polymerase binds to a site within O_L and to another site within O_R. Moreover, these sites must be recognized by three different proteins: repressor, *Hin*, and RNA polymerase.

Repressor binding site sequence. The base sequence between the *Hin* site in O_L and gene N has been determined (the region includes the repressor-binding site S_1 in O_L) as follows: A denatured specific-restriction endonuclease fragment was annealed to the appropriate (1) single strand of λ DNA to produce a structure in which the full-length strand served as template and the fragment as a primer for addition of labeled nucleotides. The region immediately adjacent to the 3'-OH end of the primer was S_1, followed by gene N. The primer chain was extended by DNA polymerase I in a mixture containing three deoxynucleoside triphosphates (one of which was labeled in the α position with ^{32}P) and either ribocytosine triphosphate or riboguanosine triphosphate. In the presence of Mn^{++}, DNA polymerase will insert ribonucleotides into DNA, thereby greatly aiding sequence analysis. The synthetic products were released from the

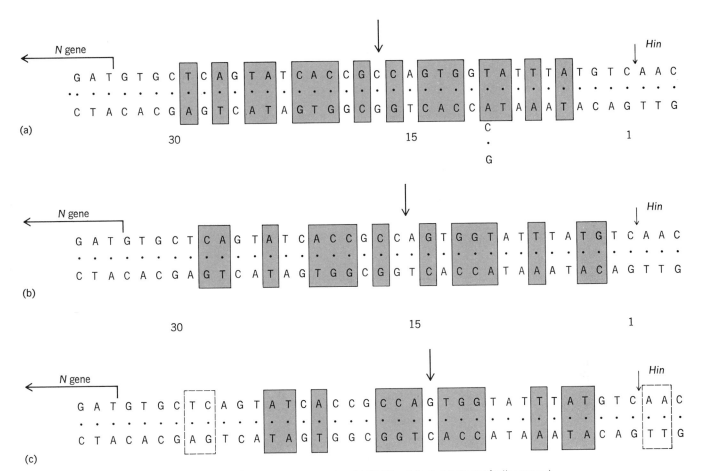

Fig. 4. Symmetries in the region between the *Hin* site in O_L and gene *N*. The bases in boxes are symmetric about twofold rotational axes indicated by vertical arrows. An operator mutation at position *10* is indicated. (*a*) Of 24 residues, 16 are perfectly symmetric, and 6 of the remaining 8 show pyrimidine-pyrimidine or purine-purine symmetry. (*b*) Of 26 residues, 14 are perfectly symmetric, and 6 of the remaining 12 show Py-Py or Pu-Pu symmetry. (*c*) Of 30 residues, 16 are perfectly symmetric, and 10 of the remaining 14 show Py-Py or Pu-Pu symmetry.

template-primer complex by cleavage with *Hin*, and the sequence determined by the methods developed by F. Sanger and coworkers and reported in 1973.

The sequence between the *Hin* site in O_L and gene *N*, which includes S_1, is shown in Fig. 4. Note the following: (1) the sequence recognized by the *Hin* enzyme is 5′ GTCAAC 3′ and 3′ CAGTTG 5′; (2) an operator constitutive mutation, which decreases the affinity of S_1 for repressor, changes the base pair AT at position *10* to GC; (3) axes of extensive symmetry are located in nucleotide 17, between residues 15 and 16, and at residue 14. It has been calculated that a region containing the symmetry properties of configuration *a* or *c* in Fig. 4 appears by chance in a sequence of 35 base pairs less than 1% of the time; for configuration *b* the probability is perhaps a few percent.

It is not surprising that an axis of twofold rotational symmetry appears in the sequence of Fig. 4. Repressor initiates binding to DNA as an oligomer, probably a dimer, and it is not unreasonable to expect the active site of the oligomer to be twofold symmetric. But what is the significance of the presence of three such axes? One possibility is that one axis, or more, is present by chance. A

more intriguing conjecture is that these overlapping symmetries are recognition sites for different regulatory proteins. The requirement that a control region in DNA contain interdigitating symmetries (one might call it "multiplexing") would explain the presence of hyphenated (that is, imperfect), as opposed to perfect, symmetries; it is difficult, if not impossible, to construct nontrivial examples of multiple overlapping perfect symmetries. It remains to be determined whether the conjecture that the various symmetries are recognized by different regulatory proteins is true, and whether this pattern of DNA protein recognition holds in other cases.

For background information *see* BACTERIOPHAGE; GENE; GENE ACTION in the McGraw-Hill Encyclopedia of Science and Technology.

[MARK PTASHNE]

Bibliography: W. Gilbert, *Polymerization in Biological Systems*, Ciba Foundation Symposium (ASP, Amsterdam), 7:245, 1972; W. Gilbert, N. Maizels, and A. Maxam, in *Cold Spring Harbor Symposium on Quantitative Biology*, 1973; W. Gilbert and A. Maxam, *Proc. Nat. Acad. Sci. USA*, 70: 3581, 1973; N. Maizels, *Proc. Nat. Acad. Sci. USA*, 70:3585, 1973; T. Maniatis et al., Sequence of a repressor binding site in the DNA of bacteriophage λ, *Nature*, 1974; T. Maniatis and M. Ptashne, *Nature*, 246:133–136, 1973; R. Maurer, T. Maniatis, and M. Ptashne, *Nature*, 249:221–224, 1974; J. R. Sadler and T. F. Smith, *J. Mol. Biol.*, 62:139, 1971; F. Sanger et al., *Proc. Nat. Acad. Sci. USA*, 70:1209, 1973.

Geosynclines

The year 1973 marked the centenary of the definition of the word "geosynclinal" by James Dwight Dana as referring to an area subsiding as deposition progressed. The past decade has been marked by the advent of theories of plate tectonics that have brought revisions in the concepts of geosynclines. The original paper of Dana referred to many regions, such as the early Mesozoic red beds of the Connecticut Valley, the Cretaceous of the Laramie Plains of Wyoming, and the Tertiary lake beds of Utah. The most widely known example was the Paleozoic subsiding basin of the region of the Allegheny Mountains, where James Hall had proposed 15 years earlier that a trough of greater depression became the site of the Appalachian Mountains.

In the past half century, as knowledge of the rocks of the continents increased from the study of surface exposures and drilled wells, the multiplicity of types of subsiding basins that were broadly geosynclinal was recognized. The basic separation proposed by the German geologist Hans Stille (1876–1966) distinguished between linear geosynclinal belts, which he called orthogeosynclinal, commonly forming linear mountain systems such as the Alps, and the basins developed within the continental shields (or "cratons" in his terminology), which he called parageosynclinal. Subsequently, the linear geosynclinal belts were differentiated by M. Kay and Stille into volcanic geosynclinal belts (eugeosynclinal) and miogeosynclinal belts ("little volcanic"). The parageosynclinal structures were separated into several

classes, principally, elliptical isolated basins (autogeosynclines) and fault-bounded rift troughs (taphrogeosynclines). There was some uncertainty concerning the sometimes foredeep linear geosynclines (exogeosynclines), as originally propsed by Hall; although they are intracratonic and thus parageosynclinal, some investigators preferred to associated them with the orthogeosynclinal belts.

Plate tectonics. The most significant developments in the past few years have been in relating the types of geosynclines to modern analogs, particularly to the concepts of plate tectonics and global tectonics that have emerged in the past decade. Until the 1970s the general view was that the ocean basins were floored by dense mafic rocks that had been the fundamental crust of the Earth from which the continental blocks had been derived. This view was not universally accepted, but it was the dominant dogma. The theory of continental drift, proposed more than a century ago by A. Snider-Pelligrini, came about more from inferences than from data based on specific observations. Most support had come from observations of similarities in the geology of facing continents that seemed to indicate greater original proximity, particularly where coastal or continental margins showed some parallelism. Similarity in continental margins was, in fact, the original reason for suggesting drift. But the mechanisms that were proposed were quite inadequate to convince the skeptics. *See* EARTH, INTERIOR OF.

A succession of observations and discoveries led to a reappraisal of the nature of ocean basins and, ultimately, to a recognition of analogs in the geosynclinal belts. R. Dietz and J. Holden identified the gently seaward-thickening wedges of sediments such as the Mesozoic-Tertiary of the Atlantic Coastal Plain of the Carolinas as miogeoclines. The term miogeosynclinal was related to nonvolcanic areas, regardless of whether the basement floor was a tilted plane or trough—or an assemblage of troughs and basins, as was the case with

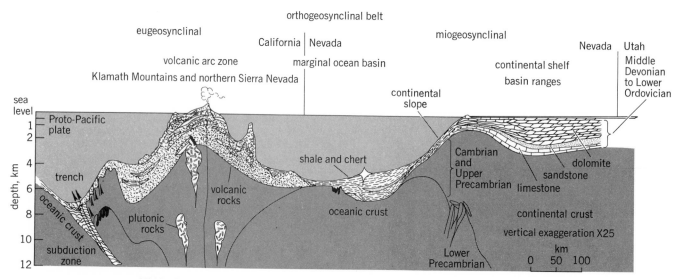

Middle Paleozoic reconstruction of western margin of North America showing relation of ancient geographic features in a geosynclinal belt. (*From Michael Churkin, Jr., in R. H. Dott, Jr., and R. H. Shaver, eds., Modern and Ancient Geosynclinal Sedimentation, Soc. Econ. Paleont. Mineralog. Spec. Publ. no. 19, 1974*)

Stille's original miogeosynclinal belt in the Cordilleran region of North America (see illustration).

Aulacogens. N. S. Schatsky had proposed that the major fault-bounded troughs, such as the Dnieper-Donetz Graben, be termed aulacogens. E. S. Belt showed that the conceptual deep downfolds that had been defined as epieugeosynclines were fault-bounded, and hence also taphrogeosynclines. It was further suggested, by J. M. Bird and J. F. Dewey, that the original opening of ocean basins took place along such rift belts, as in the Red Sea. And recently, aulacogens have been considered to be one part of a three-rayed fault system on the domes above mantle hot spots, the other two rays opening as proto-ocean basins.

Intraplate basins. The intracratonic basins that were termed autogeosynclines seem to relate to the stability of continental plates, for they are present in the North American Paleozoic craton but apparently not in the European Paleozoic plate. The European plate moved over the mantle toward the North American plate in closing the ancient ocean (the Protacadic Ocean) that was deformed in the early Paleozoic, Taconian, Caledonian, and Acadian orogenies.

Volcanic belts. The main developments in recent years have been in the understanding of the eugeosynclinal belts, which were characterized by the presence of volcanic and intrusive rocks. In the 1940s they were recognized as having had geographic lava-floored troughs, volcanic island arcs, and tectonic lands (lands composed of older rocks). According to the theory of plate tectonics, oceans are floored by basaltic lavas that have been extruded along the flanks of a midoceanic rift. Some of the rocks found within the eugeosynclinal belts contain sequences that seem to correspond to rocks which have been identified, from geophysical evidence and from dredge hauls, as oceanic crust. Thus, in a broad sense, the original distinction between low cratons or ocean basins and eugeosynclines in orthogeosynclinal belts was erroneous; ocean basins were in themselves eugeosynclinal. However, the term was originally applied to rocks in mobile belts, where they are associated with volcanic, hypabyssal, and plutonic rocks. The volcanic rocks are commonly of types now found in volcanic island arcs, so the eugeosynclinal belts have bands of oceanic rocks that were subducted, that is, descended beneath island arc crust. Tectonic lands are now seen as welts raised by processes within the eugeosynclinal belts, associated with intrusions of more silicic rocks, granites, granodiorites, and similar rocks. In some instances, they are attributed to slabs of continental rocks ("microcontinents") isolated during the processes of continental drift and separated from the parent continents by interarc basins of oceanic rocks; the analogies are Japan and the Japan Sea, although the scale may not have been as great. *See* OCEANIC ISLANDS.

Thus the orthogeosynclinal belts of Stille and Kay have come to be understood as an assemblage of crustal features related to continental shelf subsidence, subducted ocean floor, associated island arc or continental margin arc volcanism, and intrusion into island arc assemblages—and perhaps some continental fragments.

For background information *see* CONTINENT FORMATION; GEOSYNCLINE; OROGENY; TECTONIC PATTERNS in the McGraw-Hill Encyclopedia of Science and Technology.

[MARSHALL KAY]

Bibliography: R. H. Dott, Jr., and R. H. Shaver (eds.), *Modern and Ancient Geosynclinal Sedimentation*, Soc. Econ. Paleont. Mineralog. Spec. Publ. no. 19, 1974; J. A. Jacobs, R. D. Russell, and J. T. Wilson, *Physics and Geology*, 1973.

Gestation period

Reports of recent research on the termination of the gestation period have been concerned with the chain of endocrine factors that appear to signal the beginning of labor.

The beginning of pregnancy is a fixed point; its end is indeterminate. The onset of labor determines the length of gestation, which varies greatly from one mammalian species to another, as does the concatenation of circumstances that finally causes the uterus to expel its contents. The onset of human labor is probably the most special case of all. In spite of the fact that this event has been under scrutiny almost since the race began, less is known about the onset of labor in the human being than in many other species. Much of what can be said about it has been inferred from observations of other animals.

One central fact about the onset of labor is clearly established. It might be thought that the maternal organism somehow determines the appropriate moment at which to relieve itself of its parasitic burden. Not so; the signal comes from the conceptus within the uterus, either from the fetus or the placenta. In the human being, as in many other mammals, this signal is dispatched by the fetal adrenal gland, although its origin lies in the fetal brain. One of the first clues to the role of the adrenal gland was found in a strain of Guernsey cattle that exhibited a curious trait of greatly prolonged pregnancy associated with a defective development of the adenohypophysis in the fetal calf. In this context sheep are more amenable to experimentation, and it was soon found that destruction of the pituitary of the fetal lamb in the uterus, or of the effector end of the endocrine arc (the fetal adrenal), leads to a failure in the onset of labor in the ewe. It is hardly feasible to test the role of the pituitary or the adrenal in the human fetus by such direct methods, but some experimental evidence has been provided by the human fetal anomaly of anencephaly. In this condition, the development of the fetal brain is defective, and the hypothalamus and its associated pituitary gland may be aplastic.

Although there are mechanical factors such as uterine distension or cervical stimulation from the pressure of the fetal head, the main component of the fetal signal for the ending of gestation is endocrine in nature. During the last 3 decades too much time was devoted to a futile search for the single chemical entity that precipitates labor. It is becoming increasingly clear that there is no single critical compound which determines the event. At best, labor results from a chain of events, the individual links of which are different endocrines. None of the links has been shown to be essential;

at most, they cause the change in the *milieu intérieur* which makes it likely that the next endocrine event in the sequence will happen. Although the chronology is by no means established, it seems best to consider, hormone by hormone, the endocrine changes that cause labor.

Corticosteroids. Once the fetal adrenal was identified as the point from which the fetal signal emerged, it seemed likely that the hormone involved would be cortisol or some related adrenal steroid. In the case of sheep, the experimental findings fit neatly. The injection of cortisol into the fetal lamb precipitates premature labor, as does stimulation of the lamb's own adrenals by the injection of corticotrophin into the fetus. In the sheep, the first endocrine event leading to the onset of labor at term is a rise of plasma cortisol in the fetal circulation. Many other mammals, notably the human being, do not fit this model so well. The only evidence that cortisol will induce labor in the human being arises from the finding that the injection-delivery interval for postmature women administered an intraamniotic injection of betamethasone is shorter than that of controls given a placebo. It is, of course, tempting to surmise that the anencephalic fetus is unable, by virtue of its incompetent pituitary-adrenal axis and relatively atrophic adrenal glands, to raise plasma cortisol and that such pregnancies are postmature for want of a fetal signal.

Estrogens. The fetal adrenal signal need not be cortisol in every species. Androgens, such as dehydroepiandrosterone, are the precursors of fetoplacental estrogens. It may be that a surge of androgen from the fetal adrenal leads to an increased synthesis of estrogen by the placenta. Indeed, in some species, such as the goat, there is a sharp rise in the estrogen concentration in the fetal circulation and in the maternal uterine vein about 48 hr before the onset of labor. Attempts have been made to determine whether similar rises of estrogen levels occur in the maternal circulation before the onset of labor in the human being, but convincing evidence has never been found. Nor does the administration of estrogen in late pregnancy hasten the onset of labor. It cannot, however, be assumed that estrogens play no part in the onset of labor. The change in estrogen concentration may be short-lived and confined to the uterine circulation. Although 27 estrogens have been identified in the urine of pregnant women, the relationship of only two or three of them to the onset of labor has been examined.

Progesterone. This steroid is purely a placental product. If it is involved in the onset of labor, the signal would be placental, not fetal, in origin. Progesterone lowers the contractility of smooth muscle by dampening the transmission of the contractile impulse. There is a body of evidence which suggests that its presence in high concentration in the uterine muscle is a restraining influence on uterine contraction. But it is a long jump from this suggestion to the conclusion that a decline of placental progesterone precipitates labor. Whether a consistent decline in plasma concentration of progesterone takes place before the onset of labor is a matter of controversy. The advocates of the progesterone withdrawal theory have been obliged to claim that the definitive changes in progesterone that affect the transmission of the contractile impulse take place in the maternal blood of the retroplacental space; it is not possible to investigate this compartment under suitable experimental conditions. In short, a fall in progesterone concentration has some bearing on the onset of labor in women, but it is unlikely to be a dominant factor.

Oxytocin. This peptide hormone produced by the posterior pituitary causes contraction of the pregnant uterus. Every day, all over the world, hundreds of women are put into labor by the infusion of oxytocin. It might be supposed, therefore, that one need look no further than the release of oxytocin from the maternal pituitary for the cause of labor. Oxytocin is very rapidly removed from the circulation, and only very small quantities can be detected during its evanescent existence in plasma. Until recently, reliable measurements of plasma oxytocin before and during labor were not possible. The development of radioimmunoassay techniques has demonstrated that oxytocin is released in short bursts from the pituitary with increasing frequency as labor becomes established. It is likely that the function of oxytocin is not to initiate labor but to reinforce the expulsive contractions of the second stage.

Prostaglandins. These tissue hormones are widely distributed throughout the body, and a number are released by the decidua vera. They have, like oxytocin, the property of causing the uterine muscle to contract and can be used to induce labor. Evidence increasingly suggests that, whatever the preceding events, the final act in the onset of labor is the local release of prostaglandins in the uterus.

Integrated endocrine activity theory. Much remains to be done to clarify the details, but it can be accepted that the concerted action of the hormones mentioned is a major element in the onset of labor. The chain of events probably starts in the pituitary-adrenal axis of the fetus, resulting in the release of corticosteroids and an alteration in the rate of biogenesis of other fetoplacental steroids. Estrogen production increases, and progesterone production declines. This alteration in steroid levels has two effects: the uterus becomes increasingly sensitive to the action of oxytocin, and prostaglandins, released from the endometrium, cause myometrial contractions.

For background information *see* ADRENAL CORTEX; ESTROGEN; PROGESTERONE in the McGraw-Hill Encyclopedia of Science and Technology.

[ARNOLD KLOPPER]

Bibliography: G. Dawes (ed.), *Proceedings of Sir Joseph Barcroft Centenary Symposium*, Cambridge, 1974; A. Klopper and J. Gardner (eds.), *Endocrine Factors in Labour*, 1973; M. Liggins, *Clin. Obstet. Gynecol.*, 16:148–165, 1973; C. G. Pierrepoint (ed.), Endocrinology of pregnancy and parturition, in *Studies in Sheep*, 1972.

Glaciology

The launch of the first Earth resources technology satellite (*ERTS-1*) late in 1972 was soon followed by the use of images from the satellite to monitor glacier behavior in a way never before thought possible. Although normal glacier variations are so gradual that observations only once a year are required, certain classes of glaciers may move so swiftly that valleys may be dammed and the resulting lakes released as devastating floods before the change in the glacier is noticed by mankind. These surging glaciers must be monitored at time intervals of weeks or months, and it has not been possible to do so with conventional aircraft or ground-based techniques (because of cost and inaccessible locations) or with meteorological satellites (resolution is too poor for the task). ERTS images permit identification of surge-type glaciers anywhere on Earth, prediction of imminent surges and measurements of their motion, and monitoring of other dangerous glacier situations such as changes in tidal glaciers (those which calve icebergs into the sea).

Surging glacier. Surging, or "galloping," glaciers have highly contorted surface moraines that result from periodically alternating intervals of near stagnation (up to 50 years) and brief intervals (1–3 years) of extremely high flow rates when the ice may flow as fast as 2–5 m/hr. Thus surge-type glaciers can be distinguished from normal glaciers in high-resolution satellite images. The causes of glacier surges—and why some glaciers surge while others do not—are questions of great scientific interest; the "stick-slip" coupling to the glacier bed in the presence of a varying water film is a type of periodic but sudden response common to many other phenomena in nature, perhaps even to the mechanism of earthquakes.

Tweedsmuir Glacier, 70 km in length and the largest glacier in British Columbia, Canada, is shown in Fig. 1, ERTS image 1417-19531-4, taken on Sept. 13, 1973. At that time it was undergoing a typical surge. The glacier, situated astride the British Columbia–Yukon Territory boundary 256 km northwest of Juneau, Alaska, flows out of the St. Elias Mountains into the Alsek River valley, where it spreads out in a large terminal lobe 13 km across. The lobe forces the river into a narrow gorge along the margin of the glacier.

In the past, surges of Tweedsmuir Glacier closed off the Alsek River, forming a lake up to 20 km long. A surge was again closing off the river, and a lake was being impounded in the winter of 1973–1974. Sudden—perhaps repeated—releases of the lake when the ice dam fails may cause hazardous flooding in downstream channels and in Dry Bay, Alaska. Thus, it is important to monitor the behavior of the glacier and to measure the changing rate of ice flow in order to determine the maximum volume and probable time of release of the glacier-dammed lake.

Changes have been observed on Tweedsmuir Glacier from ERTS imagery by L. R. Mayo and others. The ice velocity was calculated from ERTS images by measuring the changing positions of medial moraine loops during the intervals between Apr. 15, July 22, Sept. 13, and Nov. 7, 1973; these results closely match the advance of the terminus as measured on the ground.

Study of a sequence of ERTS images of the surging Tweedsmuir Glacier reveals other interesting features. Most important is the existence of a "shock wave"—a steplike feature on the glacier that also marks the downglacier limit of intense

Fig. 1. Portion of ERTS image 1417-19531-4, Sept. 13, 1973. The width across this portion of the image is 80 km. The Alsek River flows from north to south down the center of view, passing close to the termini of Lowell, Tweedsmuir, and other surging glaciers.

crevassing (although actual crevasses are rarely seen on ERTS images, regions of intense crevassing appear distinctly darker because of the shadows within the crevasses). This shock wave advanced in mid-glacier about 8.8 km from April 15 to July 22, an average of 88 m/day, at least an order of magnitude faster than the actual ice velocity. Other features could be seen on the ERTS images, including the increasingly steep ice margins along the valley walls, the spreading of zones of intense crevassing, and the deformation of medial moraines. Perhaps most interesting, the region of intense crevassing was seen to spread upglacier at a rate of about 200 m/day, clearly showing the point of origin and spread of the surge.

ERTS images have thus been shown to be useful in recording important glacier dynamics data in inaccessible, rarely visited areas. Also, ERTS images can be used to produce maps and quantitative displacement data for large surging glaciers far more quickly and efficiently than conventional aerial photography or ground surveys can. For instance, the Lowell Glacier (which has dammed the Alsek Glacier in the past), surged in 1968–1970. A map of the medial moraine pattern had been made before the surge, by means of the laborious procedure of mosaicking and rectifying many aerial photographs. A new map was made from the ERTS image, it was compared with the old map, and the ice displacement vectors were measured—in just 1.5 hr.

Surge-type glacier. The ERTS images have also been used to identify surge-type glaciers and to predict surges in regions for which few records or

Fig. 2.   ERTS image 1057-19542-4, Sept. 18, 1972, showing the coast of Alaska off Glacier Bay. The width across the image is 180 km.

aerial photographs exist. For instance, an image of the Pamir Mountains, in Tadzhik S.S.R., was taken during July 1973, at which time the destructive surge of the Medvezhii (Bear) Glacier was coming to an end. American glaciologists were thus enabled to search for evidence of surging glaciers in a relatively unknown area. Six other glaciers on this image show the unmistakable contorted moraines that indicate periodic surges; sixteen show probable surge features, and one (Bivachnyi) appears to be ready for a surge of about 2 km in the next year or so.

Tidal glacier. Tidal glaciers, which discharge icebergs when they terminate in deep water, may be inherently unstable and thus may change position rather suddenly. ERTS images have proved to be invaluable in monitoring several tidal glaciers in Alaska, such as the Hubbard Glacier, which is advancing and threatening to close off Russell Fjord near Yakutat, and the Columbia Glacier, which may retreat and cast increasing numbers of icebergs into Prince William Sound.

Glacial sediment. In other ERTS images, sediment plumes from Alaskan coastal glaciers, extending more than 50 km into the Pacific Ocean, could be clearly identified. Although it was known that large amounts of sediments are carried to the sea from glaciers, the overall view provided by the satellite images is the first to show visually the extent. Especially striking is the amount of glacial sediment in the surface water along the coast northwest of Glacier Bay in the Alaskan Panhandle, as seen in Fig. 2 (ERTS image 1057-19542-4). A visible plume from the Lituya Bay glaciers extends 54 km away from the coast. Also noteworthy are the larger plumes from the Alsek River and from Brady Glacier. A better understanding of glacier hydrology is becoming increasingly important because of the potential of glaciers as sources of wa-

ter supply, but the sediment concentration in glacier runoff is a problem. ERTS images also demonstrate that glacier sediment is an important aspect of the offshore environment of the northeast Pacific Ocean.

For background information *see* GLACIOLOGY in the McGraw-Hill Encyclopedia of Science and Technology.   [MARK F. MEIER]

Bibliography: G. Holdsworth, *Ice*, vol. 43, 1973; M. F. Meier, *Symposium on Significant Results Obtained from ERTS-1*, New Carrollton, MD, vol. 1, pp. 863–875, March, 1973.

Gravitational collapse

According to the general theory of relativity, the end point of gravitational collapse is a black hole, perhaps the most exotic object in theoretical astrophysics. Scientists have long sought to confirm this prediction of Einstein's theory, but with typical radii of a few kilometers and with no inherent luminosity, black holes have presented a seemingly impossible challenge to observers. Now, thanks to recent developments in x-ray astronomy and to progress in the theory of mass accretion by compact objects, it seems very likely that a black hole has been identified in the compact x-ray source Cygnus X-1. *See* X-RAY STAR.

Black hole identification. The search for black holes has rested on two observational phenomena associated with them: (1) A black hole might reveal its presence by its effect on the motion of a companion star in a binary system, and (2) the compressional heating of gas falling into a black hole could produce observable radiation. An astrophysical structure, then, that could lead to the detection of black holes is a binary system in which the outer layers of a normal star stream onto a close black hole companion. Model calculations suggest that temperatures generated by such a system would give rise to radiation in the x-ray range. Although such systems would provide a likely candidate for a black hole identification, a complicating ambiguity arises in the fact that neutron stars and black holes (both extremely condensed, both essentially nonluminous) should give rise to x-ray signals with the same general properties. Once a close binary x-ray source is found, the task remains to distinguish between the neutron star and black hole possibilities.

Until the advent of x-ray astronomy by satellite, insufficient data existed to search for a candidate for such a system. The launching of the *Uhuru* satellite rectified this situation and provided astronomers with several new compact x-ray sources, a number of which had regular variations in their output with a period (presumably due to eclipses) of several days indicating an underlying binary structure. It was, however, the improved data on Cygnus X-1, a previously known compact source with no periodic variations (no eclipses), that were of greatest importance in the search for black holes. From the x-ray data alone it is not possible to come to a reasonable understanding of any of the x-ray sources. Optical identifications are very important but very difficult in general due to the low resolution of x-ray telescopes. For example, for Cyg X-1 the uncertainty in angular position is about 30 seconds of arc.

Black hole or neutron star? In the cases of the sources showing periodic variation it is simple in principle to look for an optical binary with the same period within the resolution box of the x-ray observations. In this way, for example, the star HZ Hercules can be positively identifed with the x-ray source Hercules X-1. For Cyg X-1 the identification had to be less direct: In the spring of 1971 the x-ray intensity of Cyg X-1 fell by a factor of 3, and at roughly the same time a radio source appeared within the x-ray resolution box. By the end of 1971 the position of the radio source had been measured with the radio interferometer at the National Radio Astronomy Observatory to an uncertainty of a fraction of a second. The only star compatible with this radio source was the 25 $M_\odot$ ($M_\odot$ = solar mass) supergiant star HDE 226868. An optical study showed this star to be a single line binary with a period of 5.607 days.

The identification of single line binaries with such compact x-ray sources gave credence to the idea of the infall of hot gases onto a dark condensed companion. It remained to be established whether any of the condensed companions could be demonstrated to be a black hole. Two of the binaries could immediately be ruled out. The x-ray emission from Herc X-1 and Centaurus X-3 is in the form of rapid regular pulses reminiscent of the radio emission from pulsars. The rapid periodicity of the pulses, as in the case of pulsars, is almost certainly associated with the rotation of a condensed object. Black holes can rotate, but they have no surface features to drive the clock mechanism in these x-ray pulsars. Neutron stars rather than black holes are probably the condensed objects in Herc X-1 and Cen X-3.

For the other *Uhuru* binaries no short periodic pulsations exist, so no a priori distinction between neutron stars or black holes is possible on this basis, but there is a criterion for the distinction. Studies of the structure of neutron stars strongly suggest that the maximum mass of a neutron star is less than about 2 $M_\odot$. This is a probable but not a strict upper limit because the behavior of matter at the supernuclear densities in the center of neutron stars is uncertain. Despite this, a strict upper limit of around 3 $M_\odot$ for nonrotating neutron stars can be derived, independent of the unknown behavior at high densities. If rotation of the neutron star is also considered, the limit moves up to about 4 $M_\odot$. Black holes, on the other hand, have no such mass limit. To find a likely candidate for a black hole system, it is necessary to find an x-ray binary with a secondary more massive than about 3 or 4 $M_\odot$.

For a single line binary the dynamics as manifested in the curve of Doppler shift versus time gives the mass function $(M_2^3 \sin^3 i)/(M_1 + M_2)^2$, a combination of the mass of the visible primary (mass M_1), the dark companion (M_2), and the inclination of the orbital plane i. For the HDE 226868 system this mass function is measured to be around 0.2. With the assumed identification of the primary as a 25 $M_\odot$ star, this predicts that the dark secondary has a mass that is probably around 8 $M_\odot$ but is in any case significantly larger than the neutron star limit. For this reason many astrophysicists now believe that Cyg X-1 contains a black hole.

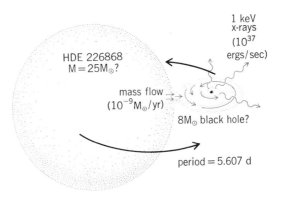

The disk accretion model with appropriate parameters for Cyg X-1.

Disk accretion model. The model for a close x-ray binary is the result of calculations by several groups of theorists in England, the Soviet Union, and the United States. The basic feature of the model (see illustration) is that the envelope of the primary expands until it is extended enough to be pulled across to the secondary (that is, the primary fills its Roche lobe). Since the system is rotating, the flowing gases possess angular momentum, and rather than flowing directly into the black hole the infalling gases form a relatively thin accretion disk. Turbulence and magnetic fields produce viscosity in the differentially rotating disk so that the gas in the disk slowly spirals inward, where it is compressed in the gravitational field of the black hole, to higher and higher temperatures. Once the gas gets too close to the black hole, the spiraling is unstable and the gas quickly falls into the hole. Radiation from gas which has fallen into the hole is necessarily swallowed by the hole; furthermore, radiation from gas *just* outside the hole is enormously red-shifted, but at a distance of several times the Schwarzschild radius of the hole, $R_s = 3$ km ($M_2/M_\odot$), red shifts are not overwhelming and radiation can escape.

For the proposed black hole in Cyg X-1, the radiation would be predominately generated in the region of the disk around 100 km ($\approx 5 R_s$). Since the gas spirals slowly into the black hole, losing energy by radiation, almost all the gravitational potential energy gained by the gas infalling into 100 km is converted to x-ray luminosity. From the observed luminosity (10^{37} ergs/sec) a mass flow rate of $10^{-9} M_\odot$/yr can be inferred, so the model system has a long enough life to be observationally important. The 100-km radius is also appropriate as the characteristic size for a region radiating 10^{37} ergs/sec at a temperature of 10^7 K corresponding to the 1-keV radiation of Cyg X-1. Other features of Cyg X-1 also fit this model, at least qualitatively. In particular, the x-ray emission shows rapid nonperiodic variation on all time scales down to the resolution time of the x-ray detectors (on the order of milliseconds). This is understood as a consequence of the turbulence in the inner regions of the disk. Other compact x-ray sources which are considered possible black hole candidates (especially Circinus X-1) share this rapid fluctuation feature.

Evolution of binary system. At first the existence of a 8-$M_\odot$ black hole plus 25-$M_\odot$ supergiant seems paradoxical. The fact that more massive stars evolve more quickly seems to require that the more highly evolved black hole should be the more massive component. According to the calculations of E. P. J. Van den Heuvel and others, however, the scenario for evolution of stars in a close binary should be greatly modified by mass exchange. The envelope of the initially more massive, more quickly evolving star expands during its helium-burning stage and transfers mass to its initially less massive companion. The remaining core subsequently undergoes a supernova explosion (without disrupting the binary system!), leaving a black hole or a neutron star. The direction of mass transfer then reverses, producing, according to this model, the compact x-ray sources now being observed.

Probably the weakest link in the chain of reasoning that associates a black hole with Cyg X-1 is the identification of the primary in HDE 226868 as a 25-$M_\odot$ supergiant. If this identification were changed and the mass were lowered to 10 $M_\odot$, the secondary mass inferred from the mass function could be 3 $M_\odot$. Van den Heuvel and J. P. Ostriker have argued that it is risky to apply normal stellar criteria to a supergiant star in a close binary system since the structure of the star's envelope can be changed dramatically by its companion.

Other models for Cyg X-1. The black hole and disk accretion model is not the only explanation that has been offered to account for the observed properties of Cyg X-1. A. C. Fabian and colleagues and J. N. Bahcall and colleagues have suggested a neutron star which orbits a more massive dim star, which in turn orbits the primary supergiant. Although there are no irregularities in the observed motion of the system to suggest this model is true, neither are the data sufficiently accurate yet to rule it out. Another model suggested by Bahcall and colleagues is based on the magnetic field pulsations in a binary star consisting of two highly magnetized rotating stars. Both these suggestions, however, seem somewhat contrived, compared to the disk accretion model, so astrophysicists find themselves in the strange position of having a black hole explanation as the establishment viewpoint.

For background information *see* BINARY STARS; GRAVITATIONAL COLLAPSE; PULSAR; X-RAY ASTRONOMY; X-RAY STAR in the McGraw-Hill Encyclopedia of Science and Technology.

[RICHARD H. PRICE]

Bibliography: H. Gursky, and I. D. Novikov and K. S. Thorne, in C. DeWitt and B. S. DeWitt, eds., *Black Holes*, 1973; J. E. Pringle and M. J. Rees, *Astron. Astrophys.*, 21:1, 1972; K. S. Thorne, *Sci. Amer.*, 231:32, 1974; E. P. J. Van den Heuvel and C. Deloore, *Astron. Astrophys.*, 25:387, 1973.

Human genetics

Chromosome loss and segregation at a mitotic level are fundamental processes in the methods of genetic analysis by means of somatic cells, insofar as they allow genes to be assigned to chromosomes and their linkage relationships to be established. These chromosome changes occur spontaneously in cultured cell populations, but they are rare and hard to control. It would therefore be desirable to have some physical or chemical agents that would increase their incidence. The use of x-rays and bromodeoxyuridine followed by visible-light exposure has been used for inducing the directional loss of chromosomes in hybrid cells obtained by artificial fusion of cells from different species. Colchicine has also been used to induce aneuploidy in cultured cells. Griseofulvin, an antifungal antibiotic isolated from *Penicillium griseofulvum* and widely used in dermatology, seems to be a promising agent for genetic research with somatic cells.

Cytological effects of griseofulvin. A multinucleate condition and mitotic abnormalities have been described in the fungus *Basidiobolus ranarum* grown on media containing 5 to 10 μg/ml griseofulvin. Multinuclearity and cell giantism are most evident in mammalian cells cultured in the presence of the antibiotic (Fig. 1). The frequency of cells with two or more nuclei depends on the drug concentration and on exposure times; 90% of the cells were found to contain more than one nucleus in cultures of human embryonic epithelium (EUE), a human cell line, treated for 60 hr with 40 μg/ml griseofulvin. In these cultures, cells with more than a dozen nuclei of varying size were frequent. The multinucleate elements originate from cells arrested in mitosis. In actively proliferating cultures, an accumulation of cells, mostly in metaphase, is observed. Individual chromosomes show a morphology similar to that caused by c-mitotic agents such as colchicine and *Vinca* alkaloids.

In some other respects, however, griseofulvin seems to have a different action. In a few cells, anaphase takes place, although the migration of chromosomes appears grossly irregular owing to delays and to the presence of multipolar arrays. In most metaphases the chromosomes appear to be

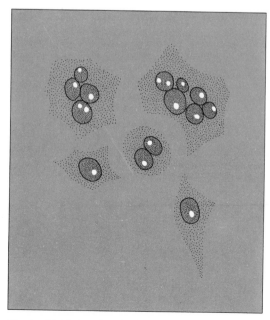

Fig. 1. Multinucleate cells in a culture of the human heteroploid EUE line treated with 40 μg/ml griseofulvin for 60 hr (a drawing from a microphotograph).

associated in groups of different sizes from which presumably separate resting nuclei will be reconstructed. These groups seem to be the most probable origin of the multinucleate cells. In the electron microscope the cells inhibited in metaphase by griseofulvin show normal microtubules. Therefore, it has been assumed that some function of these structural elements, rather than their actual assembly, is affected by the drug. Such a function would be essential for the proper separation of chromosomes during mitosis. The actual mode of action of griseofulvin at a molecular level is at present not completely understood.

Changes in number of chromosomes. In view of its unique effects on the distribution of the nuclear material, griseofulvin has been investigated as a potential agent of chromosome segregation in cultured cells. The variations in the chromosome complements induced by the drug have been analyzed both on primary cultures of diploid cells and on permanent cell lines. Although a considerable variation in chromosome number spontaneously occurs in permanent cell populations, the range and distribution in chromosome number is fairly constant under given culture conditions. Therefore, even small changes in the distribution of chromosome numbers caused by a modification in the chemical composition of the medium can easily be detected. The chromosome counts of the griseofulvin-treated cells were performed in all cultures at the end of a 3-day treatment and after various periods of subsequent growth in a medium without the antibiotic. In phytohemoagglutinin-stimulated cultures of peripheral blood from normal individuals, a large proportion of cells with more than 46 chromosomes were observed immediately after griseofulvin treatment and after 3 days of growth in the absence of the antibiotic. Among the deviating complements, those with 92 chromosomes predominated (Fig. 2a–c).

On cultures of the EUE line, the effect on the distribution of the chromosome number is more striking: the modal chromosome number of 62 is doubled in most of the cells at the end of treatment. Further culture of the same cells in a medium without griseofulvin reveals a further increase in variability of chromosome numbers (Fig. 2d–f).

A similar pattern of chromosome variation was evident in hybrids produced between clonal cell progenies of the same EUE line, which could be distinguished by biochemical variant characters.

In almost all griseofulvin-treated cell cultures, both diploid and heteroploid, the cells with double chromosome complements persisted for several generations in the absence of the drug. The other sets that deviated from the original ones tended to disappear, probably because they are at a selective disadvantage. Maximum chromosome variability occurs between the end of the treatment and the following 3 days of growth in the absence of the drug. However, the actual effective treatment period may vary according to cell type and generation time.

Chromosome structural damages. In addition to alterations in chromosome number, chromosomal structural abnormalities were found in griseofulvin-treated cells. Among these abnormalities

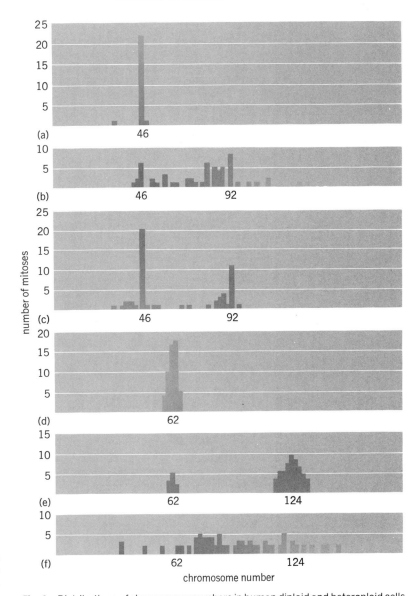

Fig. 2. Distributions of chromosome numbers in human diploid and heteroploid cells treated with 40 μg/ml griseofulvin for 3 days and grown for 3 additional days in absence of the drug. Chromosome complements of lymphocytes (a) before treatment, (b) after treatment, and (c) after recovery in medium without griseofulvin. Chromosome complements of EUE cells (d) before treatment, (e) after treatment, and (f) after recovery in medium without griseofulvin.

were both chromatid and chromosome breakages and rearrangements such as dicentric chromosomes, rings, and chromatid exchanges. So far, these effects have been revealed only in lymphocytes stimulated by phytohemoagglutinin and have not been detected in other types of cells. The reason for the differential response of cells with different origin to the mutagenic action of griseofulvin has not been clarified.

Griseofulvin and human cell genetics. The chromosome variability caused by griseofulvin may be of use in somatic cell genetics. The loss or gain of chromosomes may allow recessive mutations to be expressed, or it may lead to changes in gene dosages, thus facilitating the production and isolation of genetic variants in populations of human cultured cells. Since griseofulvin has been proved to be effective in work with cellular hybrids, it may also be helpful in activating the dynamics of chromosome complements and, in particular, reductional processes, when these processes are excessively slow or absent, as in homospecific hybrids. Chromosome loss is a necessary prerequisite for gene assignments and linkage studies of hybrid systems. To date, only a few interspecific hybrids such as human-mouse and human-hamster have been exploited for mapping genes on human chromosomes. The use of agents such as griseofulvin would make available a larger variety of hybrids suitable for this purpose and would make the method based on chromosome reduction more efficient and controllable. Another process that can be enhanced in cell cultures by griseofulvin is the mitotic segregation of cell characters in the heterozygous state by way of polyploidy and subsequent division by multipolar mitoses.

For background information *see* CHROMOSOME; GRISEOFULVIN; HUMAN GENETICS in the McGraw-Hill Encyclopedia of Science and Technology.

[LUIGI DE CARLI]

Bibliography: L. De Carli et al., *Mutat. Res.,* 21: 27, 1973; L. Grisham, L. Wilson, and K. G. Bensch, *Nature,* 244:294, 1973; K. Gull and A. P. J. Trinci, *Nature,* 244:292, 1973; G. Pontecorvo, *Nature,* 230: 367, 1971.

Hydride, metal

One of the chief developments in the field of metal hydrides has concerned the chemistry and reactions of potassium hydride (KH). Long known, this saline (saltlike crystal structure) hydride has recently been demonstrated to have considerable utility in organic and organometallic chemistry. KH is markedly more reactive both as a base, as in reaction (1), and as a hydriding agent, as in reaction (2), than either sodium hydride (NaH) or lithium hydride (LiH). In these relations, R is any organic group of C and H atoms only.

$$ROH + KH(s) \rightarrow RO^-K^+ + H_2 \uparrow \quad (1)$$
$$R_3B + KH(s) \rightarrow [R_3BH]^-K^+ \quad (2)$$

Reactivity. Reactions of KH appear to occur at the surface of the KH crystal; no solvent is known that dissolves KH without reacting with it. Thus reactivity reflects the strength of the crystal binding forces (lattice energy); the weaker the crystal, the faster the reactions. The reactivity for reaction (1) or (2) is KH $\gg$ NaH $\gg$ LiH; the lattice energy for these reactions is KH $\ll$ NaH $\ll$ LiH. Potassium hydride is stable to hydrocarbon solvents, ethers (diethylether, tetrahydrofuran, and glymes), and tertiary (3°) amines. Tetrahydrofuran has proved especially useful as a reaction solvent.

$$\begin{array}{c} CH_2—CH_2 \\ | \quad\quad | \\ CH_2—CH_2 \\ \backslash \quad / \\ O \end{array} \qquad \begin{array}{c} CH_3—O—(CH_2CH_2—O)_n—CH_3 \\ \text{Glymes } (n = 1, 2, \ldots) \end{array}$$

Tetrahydrofuran (THF)

Handling and use. KH is normally prepared and stored in mineral oil suspension; the oil can be removed by washing with a purified hydrocarbon (for example, pentane), for the KH is substantially more dense and settles rapidly. KH protected by the oil matrix can be handled safely in air; however, finely, powdered pure KH may ignite when it comes in contact with air, especially under conditions of high humidity, and must be kept under an argon or nitrogen gas atmosphere. Reaction of KH powder with water [reaction (1), R=H] is violent; the hydrogen that is liberated will ignite. Waste KH is normally decomposed by carefully treating a suspension with isopropyl alcohol. When there is no solvent, and thus substantial friction, powdered KH has been observed to react with, and produce carbonization of, polytetrafluoroethylene (for example, Teflon). As a base, KH possesses several attractive features: It is relatively inexpensive, easily stored, and indefinitely stable. The by-product of its reaction with an acid is an inert gas (H_2). Since it is insoluble in all nonreacting solvents, any excess can be removed readily. KH is also highly active.

Reaction with O—H, N—H. KH reacts rapidly with weakly acidic O-H and N-H bonds. The reaction provides an exceptionally simple method for preparing pure solutions of the potassium salts of organic acids, alcohols, and so on in various solvents. Reaction (1) proceeds smoothly even when O—H and N—H are hindered (crowded) by large bulky groups in the molecule. For example, KH reacts rapidly with THF solutions of 2,6-di-*tert*-butylphenol and bis-(trimethylsilyl)-amine to replace H by K. Such bases have important uses in organic synthesis.

2,6-Di-*tert*-butylphenol   Bis-(trimethylsilyl)-amine

Reaction with C—H. Weakly acidic C-H bonds are also readily metalated by KH suspended in THF, as illustrated by the reaction of KH with a sulfoxide, shown in relation (3), and a ketone, shown in relation (4). These potassium salts are

$$R—\overset{\displaystyle O}{\underset{\displaystyle \|}{S}}—CH_3 + KH \rightarrow R—\overset{\displaystyle O}{\underset{\displaystyle \|}{S}}—CH_2^-K^+ + H_2 \uparrow \quad (3)$$
Sulfoxide

$$R—\overset{\displaystyle O}{\underset{\displaystyle \|}{C}}—CHR'R'' + KH \rightarrow$$
Ketone

$$[R—\overset{\displaystyle O^-K^+}{\underset{\displaystyle |}{C}}=CR'R''] + H_2 \uparrow \quad (4)$$
Enolate ion

highly useful in organic synthesis both as reagents for building carbon structures and as bases. Surprisingly, as shown in reaction (5), no reduction of

$$\overset{\backslash}{\underset{/}{C}}=O + KH \,/\!\!\!\!\rightarrow\, H—\overset{|}{\underset{|}{C}}—O^-K^+ \quad (5)$$

$\overset{\backslash}{\underset{/}{C}}=O$ occurs, although this is a major reaction with many other hydrides, such as $NaBH_4$ and $LiALH_4$. The potassium salt of the ketone enolate is exceptionally active in reactions with alkyl halides, reacting even at dry ice temperatures; thus KH provides a simple, direct route for carbon-carbon bond formation, as illustrated in reaction (6).

$$[R\overset{\overset{\displaystyle O^-K^+}{|}}{C}{=}CR'R''] + CH_3I \xrightarrow{-78°}$$

$$R\overset{\overset{\displaystyle O}{\parallel}}{C}{-}C(CH_3)R'R'' + KI \downarrow \quad (6)$$

Formation of K alkamides. KH reacts with alkylamines to form the salts potassium alkamides, otherwise prepared only with considerable difficulty. In these cases, excess amine must be utilized as the solvent, for ethers are rapidly attacked by the strongly basic alkamides. One alkamide, in particular, the potassium salt of the diamine 3-aminopropylamine (1,3-diaminopropane), shown in reaction (7), has proved exceptionally reactive

$$\text{3-Amino-propylamine} + KH \rightarrow \text{Potassium 3-aminopropyl-amide (KAPA)} + H_2 \uparrow \quad (7)$$

as a catalyst for isomerization reactions of unsaturated hydrocarbons involving proton transfers, as illustrated in reaction (8). Some of these rapid isomerization reactions, carried out on acetylenic compounds, provide new direct routes to structures used in species-specific control of insects.

$$\underset{\text{C=C-C-H}}{} \xrightarrow[<1\text{ min, }0°]{KAPA} \underset{\text{H-C-C=C}}{} \quad (8)$$

Hydride transfer. KH reacts as a hydride transfer reagent, reaction (2), as well as a strong base. Hydride transfer occurs to organometallic compounds such as alkyl borates, mono-, di-, and trialkylboranes, and dialkyl magnesium, as well as to the much more reactive trialkylaluminum. Reaction of KH proceeds rapidly even with boron compounds, which are essentially inert toward NaH or LiH, as illustrated in reactions (9) and (10). These

$$[CH_3CH_2CH(CH_3)]_3B + KH \rightarrow$$
$$[CH_3CH_2CH(CH_3)]_3B\text{-}H\,K \quad (9)$$
$$\text{Potassium tri-}sec\text{-butyl borohydride }(A)$$

$$[(CH_3)_2CHO]_3B + KH \rightarrow$$
$$[(CH_3)_2CHO]_3B\text{-}H\,K \quad (10)$$
$$\text{Potassium triisopropoxy borohydride }(B)$$

borohydrides are very useful in organic synthesis, for they reduce cyclic ketones to produce the less stable of the two possible products, as shown in reaction (11). Although A is an extremely powerful reducing agent for many organic functional

groups, B is very selective, reducing only aldehydes and ketones.

$$(95-99\%) + \quad (1-5\%) \quad (11)$$

The lithium salt corresponding to A has been prepared by indirect means but is less specific for formation of the less stable isomer.

The alkyl and alkoxy borohydrides transfer hydride rapidly to alkylboranes and alkyl borates, as shown in reaction (12). The position of the equilibrium lies increasingly to the right as the ratio of the size of R to R' increases, and as the Lewis acidity of R'_3B increases.

$$R_3BH\text{-}K^+ + R'_3B \rightleftharpoons R_3B + R'_3BH\text{-}K^+ \quad (12)$$

For background information *see* HYDRIDE, METAL in the McGraw-Hill Encyclopedia of Science and Technology.   [CHARLES A. BROWN]

Bibliography: C. A. Brown, *J. Amer. Chem. Soc.*, 95:982, 1973; C. A. Brown, *J. Org. Chem.*, 39:1324, 1974; H. C. Brown and S. Krishnamurthy, *J. Amer. Chem. Soc.*, 94:7159, 1972, and 95:1669, 1973.

Hydrofoil craft

During the early 1970s there was a strong surge of interest in the military hydrofoil. This was primarily the result of more than 2 decades of development of fully submerged foil-type craft by the U.S. Navy.

NATO/PHM. Three countries, the United States, the Federal Republic of Germany, and Italy, jointly underwrote the construction of a missile-equipped hydrofoil ship designated the NATO/PHM (Fig. 1). Two lead ships are being built by the Boeing Company in Seattle, WA, with the first scheduled for launch in late 1974. Characteristics of the NATO/PHM are shown in the table.

Foil-borne propulsion is achieved by means of a single water-jet pump that discharges through a nozzle at the stern. The pump, driven by a gas turbine engine at 16,000 hp (11,840 kW), delivers about 90,000 gal (340 m³) of water per minute.

The crew of the PHM will consist of 4 officers

Characteristics of NATO/PHM

Length	132.8 ft (40.5 m)
Width	28.2 ft (8.6 m)
Hull-borne draft (foils up)	6.2 ft (1.9 m)
Hull-borne draft (foils down)	23.2 ft (7.1 m)
Weight	230.8 long tons (235 metric tons)
Speed, hull-borne	12 knots (22.2 km/hr)
Speed, foil-borne	40+ knots (74.1 + km/hr)

Fig. 1 The NATO/PHM. *(U.S. Navy)*

Fig. 3. The U.S.S. *Plainview* (AGEH-1). *(U.S. Navy)*

and 17 enlisted men. Armament will vary according to the country. Most versions will carry the Italian-built Oto Melara 76-mm gun. Among the types of surface-to-surface missiles to be carried are the U.S. Harpoon, the Italian Otomat, and the French Exocet.

P-420 hydrofoil gunboat. Another military hydrofoil that has resulted from technology developed by the U.S. Navy program is the Italian P-420 hydrofoil gunboat. The P-420, called the "Swordfish," was constructed by Alinavi, an Italian-based company owned principally by Boeing. It is essentially an improved version of the *Tucumcari* (PGH-2), a 57-ton hydrofoil gunboat built by Boeing and delivered to the U.S. Navy in 1968. (It might be noted that the NATO/PHM program received much of its early impetus from a successful tour of the *Tucumcari* throughout NATO nations.) The *Tucumcari* met a premature end in September 1972, when it ran aground on a submerged reef off the coast of Puerto Rico during night exercises with the fleet. The 67-ton *Flagstaff* (PGH-1), sister ship of the *Tucumcari*, designed and built by the Grumman Corporation and also delivered in 1968, continues to operate with the fleet, based in San Diego, CA.

The Italian Navy initiated trials of the P-420 in

1973. It displaces 64.5 metric tons and is propelled by a water-jet pump driven by a 4500-hp (3330 kW) gas turbine engine. It employs retractable, fully submerged foils in a canard arrangement much like that of the PHM.

Other U.S. Navy hydrofoil ships. Development of future military hydrofoil ships is being continued by the U.S. Navy. The thrust is toward ships of larger size, 1000 tons or more, and higher speeds, 80–90 knots (128+ km/hr). The 130-ton *High Point* (PCH-1) (Fig. 2), having undergone major modifications and overhaul in 1973, is being primarily employed to test various mission suites for the NATO/PHM. The 320-ton *Plainview* (AGEH-1), the world's largest hydrofoil ship (Fig. 3), entered Todd Shipyard in Seattle in early 1974 for its first overhaul since delivery to the U.S. Navy in 1969. Upon completion of the work early in 1975, this ship will be employed in studies to continue extension of the technology to larger sizes. Both platforms are operated by the Hydrofoil Special Trials Unit of the Naval Ship Research and Development Center as part of the Navy's development program.

Soviet commercial hydrofoil. In the Soviet Union, application of the hydrofoil to military purposes has not, thus far, been very significant; in

Fig. 2. The U.S.S. *High Point* (PCH-1) firing Harpoon missile. *(U.S. Navy)*

Fig. 4. Supramar PT-150, the *Expressan*. *(Supramar AG)*

contrast, the commercial hydrofoil has been widely used. Many hundreds of hydrofoil craft of a variety of sizes operate in commercial passenger service over the extensive waterways in the Soviet Union. Further, the Soviets are making strong bids to export their craft throughout the world. In June 1974, for example, two Soviet hydrofoils of the Raketa type were introduced in passenger service in London on the Thames River. Three more are expected shortly to join the first two in a fast passenger service between Charing Cross and Thamesmead.

A large number of different types of Soviet passenger hydrofoils have been developed, primarily at the Krasnoye Sormova shipyard at Gorki. These include the Kometa, a seagoing variant of the Raketa that is capable of carrying as many as 100 passengers; the 130–150-passenger Meteor; and a new 250-passenger Tsiklon. Until recently, the Soviets have used only variations of the surface-piercing foil system. Their first hydrofoil of the submerged-foil type is the *Taifun*, or *Typhoon*, which is designed to carry 89–105 passengers at a cruising speed of about 44 knots (82 km/hr).

Supramar hydrofoil. Elsewhere in the world the commercial hydrofoil market is dominated by hydrofoils of the Supramar type. More than 100 Supramar hydrofoils are in operation. The largest is the 250-passenger, 165-ton PT-150 (Fig. 4). This design was developed by Baron Hanns von Schertel, technical director of Supramar in Lucerne, Switzerland, and built by Westemoen Shipyard in Norway. Work on improving stabilization and control, utilizing air piped to foil-lifting surfaces, is currently under way.

U.S. commercial hydrofoil. Based on experience derived from military hydrofoil development, the Boeing Company has ventured into the commercial hydrofoil market with its model 929-100 Jetfoil. This ship is 90 ft (27.4 m) long, displaces 106 tons, and is capable of carrying up to 250 passengers at speeds of 45 knots, even in rough water. It employs retractable, fully submerged foils of stainless steel and is propelled by two water-jet pumps each driven by a gas turbine engine rated at 3300 hp (2442 kW).

The first of several Jetfoils currently under construction at Boeing in Seattle was launched in March 1974. One is to be delivered for operation on a commuter-tourist run between Hong Kong and Macao. Additional units are planned for this run as well as in the Hawaiian Islands beginning in late 1974. *See* SHIP, FERRY.

It has been proposed that a hydrofoil passenger service be established between Baltimore and Annapolis, MD, and Norfolk and Williamsburg, VA, as part of the nation's bicentennial in 1976. Transit time between Annapolis and Norfolk is estimated to be about 3 hr.

For background information *see* HYDROFOIL CRAFT in the McGraw-Hill Encyclopedia of Science and Technology.

[WILLIAM M. ELLSWORTH]

Bibliography: I. I. Baskalov and V. M. Burlakov, A seagoing vessel on automatically controlled submerged foils, in *Hovercraft Hydrofoil*, October 1972; K. M. Duff, CDR, USN, The NATO/PHM program, *AIAA Advanced Marine Vehicles Symposium, Annapolis*, July 1972; W. M. Ellsworth, Hydrofoil development: Issues and answers, *AIAA/SNAME Advanced Marine Vehicles Conference, San Diego*, February 1974; Roy McLeavy (ed.), *Jane's Surface Skimmers, Hovercraft and Hydrofoils*, 1973.

Hydroponics

Water culture systems that closely simulate the nutrient environment of soils are being used by plant and soil scientists to determine the factors governing the absorption of nutrients by plants from soils. It has been shown that plants can absorb nutrients from extremely low concentrations and that, if these concentrations are maintained, the growth and chemical composition of the crop are comparable to those of a crop grown in a fertile soil or conventional culture. These dilute culture techniques have also been used to evaluate nutrient uptake-concentration relationships, the influences and magnitude of internutrient competitions, and the effects of mineral nutrition on the growth and ecological distributions of different plant species and cultivars.

Flow cultures. In flowing cultures, the nutrient solution is continuously renewed or flowed past the plant. This hydroponic method has been widely and variously adopted as a means of maintaining the chemical composition of the culture. The procedure has several serious limitations, but is an effective method of controlling culture composition when properly used.

The environment of plant roots in soils is both highly variable and dynamic. The root-soil interface is a region of variable dimensions which cannot be completely characterized directly. Estimates of the concentrations of nutrient elements in this zone, made from analysis of displaced soil solutions, show nutrient levels that, with the exception of nitrate-nitrogen, are quite low and not appreciably influenced by crop growth. A number of solution culture systems simulating this condition have been devised. The most generally successful and commonly used have employed continuous additions of all or a part of the culture. The use of continuous renewal techniques is complicated by the large amounts of pure water required and by the problems associated with quantitative measurements for monitoring of the low concentrations of the several nutrient elements involved.

The enormity of the problem is best illustrated by considering the absorption of potassium. The experiments of D. E. Williams have demonstrated that barley grows well in cultures supplying as little as 0.01 ppm of the nutrient. One-month-old plants absorbed 24 mg of potassium per day from 0.01 ppm cultures, or the amount of the element contained in 2400 liters of solution. If absorption by the plant is allowed to drop the potassium content of the solution by only 10%, then 24,000 liters of culture would need to be flowed past a single plant each day. The problem has been solved by using the large volumes of solutions required, by combining smaller volumes of solutions with frequent analysis and additions, and by fixed fraction depletion—the latter being accomplished by varying the rate at which culture is supplied to conform to the rate of absorption of nutrients by the crop.

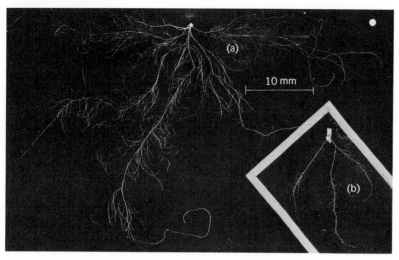

Fig. 1. The influence of nutrient culture concentration on roots of wheat seedlings. The tops of these plants were the same size. (a) Plant grown in a dilute culture; (b) Plant grown in a concentrated culture.

At best, maintaining the composition of dilute cultures within the narrow limits required for meaningful experiments is difficult, and for this reason relatively few experiments have been reported.

Required nutrient concentrations. Plants have the unique ability to absorb nutrient elements over wide ranges of concentrations, and to absorb one nutrient, such as potassium, at low concentrations and in the presence of high concentrations of another element, such as calcium. Plants grow well in fertile soils; in culture solutions such as Hoagland's solution that have total cation concentrations of over 18 millequivalents per liter; and in dilute cultures supplying less than 1/50 that amount of salts. The mechanisms by which plants adjust to these wide differences in root media environments are not well understood; however, changes in both the extent and nature of their root systems contribute. The extent by which the root system of wheat seedlings may be modified by culture concentration is illustrated in Fig. 1. The extensive root system of the plant grown in the very dilute culture had a total length of 2000 cm, while that of the plant from the concentrated culture was less than 100 cm.

Although root extension contributes to the plant's ability to compensate for differences in

nutrient levels, it is not sufficient to allow for maximum growth rates under all conditions. Thus for each essential element there are concentrations that limit plant growth either through nutrient deficiency or toxicity. This has been demonstrated repeatedly in culture solution experiments and is evidenced by the many increases in yields that have resulted from fertilizer and lime applications to field crops. Some of the deficiency concentrations are in the table.

Nutrient interrelationships. The uptake and utilization of nutrients by plants is influenced by factors in addition to root media concentration, and in some cases the effects of these other factors exceed that of concentration. Significant differences in nutrient requirements exist between plant species and cultivars within a species, and result from differences in growth rates, in the chemical form of the element supplied, in the pH of the system, and from interactions among nutrients, temperature, and other factors.

The influence of one of these factors, the form of nitrogen supplied, on the growth of wheat is shown in Fig. 2. Ammonium supplied alone and at low concentrations produced yield increases equal to those from nitrate, but when supplied with adequate nitrate gave an additional 50% increase in growth rate. This increase is of potentially great economic importance; however, the details of its application to commerical agriculture are yet to be worked out. Plants growing in soils are supplied both nitrate and ammonium nitrogen. Whether or not the supply of ammonium is adequate or toxic can be determined only after methods for the characterization and control of ammonium nutrition have been developed. Levels of ammonium only slightly higher than those associated with maximum growth rates are toxic and reduce growth. Toxicity results when the rate of ammonium absorption exceeds the plant's ability to utilize this form of nitrogen. Thus both the external ammonium concentration and the rates of reactions inside the plant must be considered.

Dilute culture techniques have also been utilized to evaluate the sensitivity of different plants to nutrient levels. Species differ in their response

Root media nutrient concentrations below which growth is limited

	Nutrient	Plant	Limiting concentration, ppm
Nitrogen	(nitrate)	Wheat	1.4
	(ammonium)	Wheat	0.4
Phosphorus		(Several)	0.05–0.7
Potassium		Barley	0.01
		(Several)	0.3–0.9
Calcium		Wheat	0.4–4.0
		(Several)	0.1–4.0
Sulfur		Wheat	0.2
Zinc		Wheat	0.001

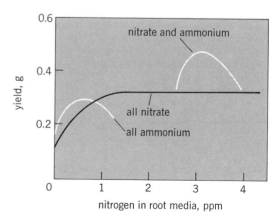

Fig. 2. The effect of source and concentration of nitrogen on growth of wheat. Different amounts of ammonium were supplied with 2.8 ppm of nitrate nitrogen for the "nitrate and ammonium" treatments.

to nutrient level, and these differences are related to their ability to grow and compete in different soils.

Conclusion. Low-concentration solution cultures provide plant and soil scientists an invaluable tool for study of soil-plant interrelationships. Experiments utilizing these techniques will improve understanding of the reactions and fluxes of nutrients at the root-soil interface, and thus aid and improve utilization of soils and the production of the food and fiber required by the world's people.

For background information *see* FERTILIZING; HYDROPONICS; PLANT, MINERAL NUTRITION OF in the McGraw-Hill Encyclopedia of Science and Technology. [H. M. REISENAUER]

Bibliography: E. W. Carson (ed.), *The Plant Root and Its Environment*, 1974; W. J. Cox and H. M. Reisenauer, *Plant Soil*, 38:363–380, 1973; J. F. Loneragan, *9th International Congress of Soil Science, Adelaide*, vol. 2, pp. 173–182, 1968; D. E. Williams, *Plant Soil*, 15:387–399, 1961.

Hypertension

Recent studies describe the risk factors involved in the development of essential hypertension as inheritance (which acts as a predisposing factor) and environment. The environmental factors are poorly understood, but they appear to include dietary salt intake and possibly psychogenic stress and obesity. Long-term use of oral contraceptives is associated with increase in blood pressure. High plasma renin levels appear to aggravate and accelerate the degree of hypertension; however, whether low plasma renin activity is associated with protection against vascular damage remains the subject of controversy.

Among the factors that increase the risk of developing complications in a hypertensive patient, the most important is the level of blood pressure—the higher the level the greater the risk. Other risk factors include male sex, young age, and black race, the latter being the most significant. Patients whose blood pressures do not return to normal with relief of psychic stresses have an increased risk of developing major complications as compared to patients with labile hypertension. The presence of hypercholesterolemia or diabetes mellitus in a hypertensive patient further increases the risk of heart attacks and other atherosclerotic complications.

Inheritance. The view of G. Pickering, that hypertension results from a mixture of inherited and environmental influences, is now generally favored, although it has not been proved. Essential hypertension apparently is not transmitted as a dominant trait. Rather, it is a predisposition to hypertension that appears to have a polygenic basis. For example, by selective breeding L. Dahl developed two strains of rats, one hypertension-prone, the other hypertension-resistant. Surgical intervention, such as constricting a renal artery; administering drugs to create, for example, an excess of certain adrenal cortical hormones; or changing the environment, for example, to increase the oral salt intake, all resulted in a higher incidence and more severe degree of hypertension in the prone strain than in the resistant one.

In humans the data on identical twins are especially impressive with respect to the importance of inherited factors. Despite separation at an early age several pairs of hypertensive monozygotic twins were found to have nearly identical levels of blood pressure. If one monozygotic twin has hypertension, the other twin will also have it. Such a complete correlation holds only in monozygotic and not in dizygotic twins. It is well known that American blacks have higher levels of blood pressure and a greater incidence of hypertension than American whites do. Is this difference due to inherited or environmental factors? The importance of environment rather than inheritance is suggested by the observations made during the National Health Survey. The blood pressures of urban blacks were nearly the same as those of urban whites, but the incidence of hypertension in rural blacks, particularly in the Southeast, was markedly higher than that of any other group.

Recently E. Bertrand surveyed approximately 10,000 West African blacks, both rural and urban. The incidence of hypertension, as defined by a blood pressure level of 160/95 mm Hg or higher, and the distribution of blood pressure were insignificantly different from that found among American whites in the National Health Survey and considerably below that found in American blacks. Since American blacks are predominantly of West African heritage, it appears that some environmental influence is operating in the black American to produce an abnormally high incidence of hypertension.

Salt. Among the various environmental factors that might influence the development of hypertension, salt appears to be very important. In man, salt has been demonstrated to be critical in the development of hypertension, but only in a limited range of salt intake. It is well known that if the salt intake of hypertensive patients is severely curtailed, to a level of less than 0.5 g per day, the blood pressure will fall in many cases. Accompanying the fall in blood pressure is a modest reduction of extracellular fluid and plasma volume. The effect is exactly the same as that which follows the administration of thiazide diuretics.

There are primitive populations whose salt intake is apparently very low. However, only meager data as to quantitative estimates of salt ingestion exist. For obvious reasons 24-hr urine collections for purposes of measuring salt excretion are difficult to obtain from primitive peoples. These people do not use salt as such, and their diet is primarily vegetarian. With this type of diet, salt intake should approximate the critical level of 0.5 g per day. In such primitive peoples the blood pressure is characteristically low and does not rise with age.

F. W. Lowenstein studied two neighboring tribes in the Amazon Basin. One tribe lived in the manner of their ancestors, whereas the other had been partially civilized by missionaries, and had grown accustomed to table salt. In members of the more primitive tribe, blood pressure stayed low throughout life, whereas among the somewhat civilized tribe, blood pressure rose with age, with some members becoming hypertensive. It is impossible to say, of course, that salt is the culprit, but this study and many other lines of evidence tend to implicate salt as an important environmental influence in the development of hypertension in congenitally predisposed individuals.

Whereas diets very low in salt reduce and possibly prevent hypertension, the corollary that high salt diets will raise blood pressure above the level achieved with normal salt intakes (by American standards) has not been established in humans. In some regions of Japan the average daily salt intake is approximately 30 g. It is said that these populations show a higher incidence of hypertension and more cerebral hemorrhage than is seen in other parts of Japan. In Great Britain and the United States, however, surveys by J. E. Evans and by T. R. Dawber did not indicate any relationship between salt intake and blood pressure. In a study using spontaneous hypertensive rats S. Spector and others have shown that a high salt intake increases the severity of the hypertension. The evidence in man, however, is too fragmentary and inconclusive to permit acceptance of the conclusion that the higher the salt intake the higher the blood pressure, except at very low levels of salt intake.

Body build, smoking, and stress. Both longitudinal and cross-sectional surveys have consistently demonstrated a correlation between body build and blood pressure. Heavier individuals tend to have higher levels of blood pressure. In the Framingham study W. B. Kannel also found that blood pressures tended to fall in those individuals who lost weight. However, Dahl found that blood pressure fell with loss of weight only when salt was also severely restricted.

Whereas smoking a cigarette may temporarily raise blood pressure, no correlation has been found between cigarette smoking and the general level of blood pressure. For example, in the Framingham study Dawber found no more hypertension among smokers than among nonsmokers. Cigarette smoking, however, has been found to be a risk factor in the development of coronary artery disease; thus the combination of smoking and high blood pressure carries an especially bad prognosis. Obviously, hypertensive patients should not smoke cigarettes.

No evidence has been found that definitely implicates emotional stress as an important factor in the development of hypertension. Psychic stress will raise blood pressure acutely, but the level returns to normal when the stress has passed. Investigation in this area has been hampered by the obvious difficulty of quantitating psychic stress.

Oral contraceptives. Oral contraceptives raise blood pressure in some women. J. Laragh believes that this rise is due to an increase in renin substrate, but this relationship has not been proved. In a controlled prospective trial R. J. Weir found that over a 4-year period women taking estrogen-progesterone mixtures showed an average increase of 14.2 mm Hg systolic and 8.5 mm Hg diastolic blood pressure. Blood pressures fell to pretreatment levels within 3 months after the contraceptives were stopped. The increase was not associated with the progesterogenic potencies of the preparations used but, rather, with the estrogen.

Renin. Ever since its discovery in renal extracts in the 19th century, renin has been implicated in the pathogenesis of hypertension. Despite a great volume of work, however, renin has not been firmly established as the etiological agent in essential hypertension. Recently Laragh and associates found a relationship between plasma renin levels and cardiovascular damage. Patients who have high renin values exhibit more vascular damage than others. Patients with low renin values are protected from vascular damage.

Other investigators such as A. Amery, W. J. Mroczek, and D. C. Kem, while agreeing that high plasma renin is associated with advanced hypertensive disease, do not find that patients with low plasma renin levels exhibit fewer vascular complications than patients with normal renin levels do. It is the low plasma renin group that is most controversial. Considerable evidence supports the implication of elevated renin and angiotensin in the pathogenesis of the vascular changes in malignant hypertension. An excellent review of this subject has been written by J. Giese.

Laragh has constructed an elaborate hypothesis to advance his views on the renin-aldosterone system in hypertension. The system is a positive feedback one in which an excess of aldosterone suppresses the secretion of renin. Laragh believes that low renin hypertensives have increased plasma volume relative to their vascular tree and will respond therapeutically to diuretic treatment. High renin hypertensives, on the other hand, have constricted blood vessels and therefore develop more severe vascular damage. They will respond therapeutically to agents that block the secretion of renin from the kidney, such as propranolol. These concepts must await further experimental verification.

Age, race, and sex. The influence of age, race, and sex on the course of hypertension was recently reviewed by E. Freis. Strangely, the younger the patient, the greater the risk of mortality in hypertension. Life insurance statistics indicate that the reduction in life expectancy of hypertensives as compared to normal individuals of similar age is significantly greater for men in their thirties as compared to men in their fifties.

The sex difference is not great; women exhibit a moderately reduced risk as compared to men. The actuarial data indicate that with a blood pressure of 150/100 mm Hg at age 45 life expectancy was reduced from normal by an average of 8.5 years in women and 11.5 years in men.

Of all these risk factors, race is the most important; blacks have a considerably poorer prognosis than whites do. For example, the vital statistics for 1967 indicate a death rate of 66 per 100,000 for hypertension in black men as compared to 16 per 100,000 in white men. This represents a 4:1 ratio of black men to white men in mortality from hypertension. A similar ratio is found in black women as compared to white women.

Lability of blood pressure. In addition to these factors of sex, race, and age Freis also emphasized the importance of the lability of the blood pressure. Although blood pressure fluctuates over a wide range during 24 hr in all individuals, there are some in whom the fluctuations are unusually wide. In such individuals, marked temporary rises of blood pressure are more easily provoked by moderate emotional stress that would have little influence on more stable individuals. A variety of studies have indicated that the risk of developing major cardiovascular complications is considerably lower in patients exhibiting a labile blood pressure.

H. S. Mathison divided hypertensive patients into two groups, those whose blood pressure fell to normal after 24 hr in the hospital (the labile group) and those whose blood pressures remained above normal (the stable group). During a 16-year follow-up he observed that the mortality in the labile group was only one-third that of the stable group.

M. Sokolow used a portable semiautomatic blood pressure recorder to obtain records for a 24-hr period of a group of patients during normal activities. For many of the patients the average pressures recorded on the portable recordings were considerably lower than the pressures recorded in the office. These patients showed less evidence of cardiovascular disease than the patients exhibiting similar levels of blood pressure both in the office and in their normal daily activities. Sokolow found that the average of the blood pressures recorded throughout the day correlated much more closely with the degree of vascular damage present than did the blood pressures recorded in the doctor's office.

The importance of inheritance in the development of hypertension has already been indicated. R. Platt describes identical twins who developed malignant hypertension within 18 months of one another. He indicates that the middle-aged sibling of a patient with severe essential hypertension has an eight times greater risk of developing hypertension than an individual selected at random. Nevertheless, although the risk is increased, the presence of hypertension in one or both parents does not necessarily mean that all of the offspring will have hypertension.

Level of blood pressure. With respect to the development of major complications of hypertension such as stroke, heart failure, and renal failure, the most important risk factor of all is the level of blood pressure. By far the most extensive data on this subject have been reviewed by E. Lew. Mortality increases linearly with either systolic or diastolic blood pressure. Men with low blood pressures have a lower mortality rate than those with pressure levels in the midnormal range. A slight rise to only 140/90 mm Hg is associated with an excess of mortality of 75% in men under 40 and 45% in men over 40 years of age. In a follow-up study of 3300 individuals with higher levels of blood pressure the excess mortality at a diastolic of 98–107 mm Hg increased to 340% at a diastolic of 108–117 to 440%, and at 118 mm Hg or higher to 780%. A similar rise in percentage mortality ratios was observed with systolic blood pressures in the range of 158 to 198 mm Hg or above. A similar correlation between levels of blood pressure and risk of developing such complications as stroke and heart failure was observed by Kannel in the Framingham study.

Hypercholesterolemia and diabetes mellitus. Patients with both high serum cholesterol and diabetes mellitus have an increased risk of developing atherosclerotic complications, particularly myocardial infarction. Patients with hypertension also exhibit an increased incidence of myocardial in-

farction. As shown by Kannel, if two or more of these risk factors are present, such as hypertension plus high serum cholesterol or diabetes, the incidence of myocardial infarction is considerably higher than in the presence of either condition alone.

For background information see CHOLESTEROL; DIABETES; HYPERTENSION; LIPID METABOLISM in the McGraw-Hill Encyclopedia of Science and Technology.   [EDWARD D. FREIS]

Bibliography: E. D. Freis, Age, race, sex, and other indices of risk in hypertension, *Amer. J. Med.*, 55:275, 1974; J. Giese, Renin, angiotensin, and hypertensive vascular damage: A review, *Amer. J. Med.*, 55:315–332, 1974; E. A. Lew, High blood pressure, other risk factors, and longevity: The insurance viewpoint, *Amer. J. Med.*, 55:281, 1974; R. J. Weir et al., Blood pressure in women taking oral contraceptives, *Brit. Med. J.*, 1:533–535, 1974.

Immunoglobulin

Immunoglobulins are proteins present in the blood serum of vertebrates that either possess antibody activity or are related to antibodies in chemical structure and biosynthetic origin. In humans and most higher animals there are three major classes of immunoglobulins, designated IgG, IgA, and IgM. Although IgG is the most abundant, IgM has special biological significance because it is the first antibody formed in the newborn animal and in the primary immune response. IgM is also the only immunoglobulin formed by lower vertebrates; hence, it is deemed the more primitive antibody. Most antibodies that agglutinate bacteria or cause hemolysis of red cells are of the IgM class. IgM antibodies are involved in certain autoimmune diseases such as rheumatoid arthritis. Although most IgM antibodies are heterogeneous, consisting of a family of structurally related molecules, a homogeneous IgM immunoglobulin is produced by patients with the lymphoma (plasma cell tumor) called macroglobulinemia in an amount up to 100 times the normal blood level of IgM. Recently the complete amino acid sequence (the order of the amino acids) and the carbohydrate composition of an IgM immunoglobulin from a patient with macroglobulinemia were determined by F. W. Putnam and coworkers. The results serve as a model for the structural study of IgM antibodies.

Structure. All immunoglobulins are composed of a pair of heavy polypeptide chains (so called because of their molecular weight of 50,000–70,000) and a pair of light chains of molecular weight 23,000. The four chains are disulfide-bonded together to give the basic monomeric unit of molecular weight ranging from 150,000 to 190,000, according to the class of the immunoglobulin. The light chains are of two types, kappa and lambda, and are akin to the Bence-Jones proteins excreted in the urine of patients with multiple myeloma and macroglobulinemia. The three major classes of immunoglobulins common to higher vertebrates (IgG, IgA, and IgM) all have antibody activity and are distinguished by their heavy chains, which differ in structure and are named gamma, alpha, and mu, respectively. In each class the light chains may be kappa or lambda, but hybrid combinations are not formed because each antibody-forming cell is committed

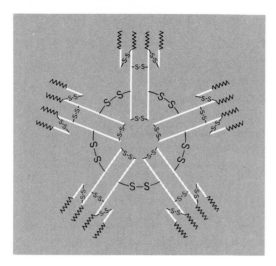

Fig. 1. Schematic diagram of the pentameric structure of human IgM immunoglobulin. Zigzag lines denote the variable regions that determine the antibody-combining sites. S—S indicates disulfide bonds. *(From F. W. Putnam et al., Ann. N.Y. Acad. Sci., 190:83–103, 1971)*

to the synthesis of a single class of heavy chain and a single type of light chain. In man, there are two minor or less abundant classes, IgD and IgE, which have delta and epsilon heavy chains, respectively. Although the function of IgD is unknown, IgE antibodies are responsible for reaginic hypersensitivity reactions. IgA and IgM form polymers. The size of IgM (it is the largest immunoglobulin) explains its affinity for linking cells in the agglutination reaction. IgM is a pentamer with a molecular weight of almost 1,000,000. The schematic structure is given in Fig. 1.

Homology regions. All immunoglobulin polypeptide chains are divided into a series of homology regions, or domains, each made up of from 110 to 120 amino acid units and containing one intrachain disulfide bond joining about 60 amino acid units. These regions are homologous in amino acid sequence and in three-dimensional structure and are responsible for the strong interactions among the chains that are the basis of their biological functions. Figure 2 shows the schematic structure of the half-monomer of IgM, consisting of one light chain and one mu heavy chain. A similar minimal subunit is characteristic of all immunoglobulins. Each light chain has two homology regions, a V or variable region (V_L), and a C or constant region (C_L). Although the gamma heavy chain of IgG (and probably the heavy chains of other immunoglobulins) has four homology regions, the mu chain of IgM has five, making it the longest heavy chain.

Amino acid sequence analysis of IgM. The amino acid sequence in human IgM was determined by Putnam and associates by the conventional techniques of protein chemistry and by the use of the new automatic protein sequencer. Since IgM has a molecular weight of about 1,000,000, it is the largest covalent structure yet determined. The work was simplified by the fact that IgM contains 10 identical mu heavy chains and 10 identical light chains. However, just the mu heavy chain alone, which has 578 amino acids of 20 different kinds, is the longest continuous amino acid sequence yet determined.

Variable and constant regions. Analysis of the sequence of the amino acids in light chains and in IgG and IgM immunoglobulins has shown that all immunoglobulin polypeptide chains are divided into V and C regions. The C region is invariant in amino acid sequence within each class or subclass

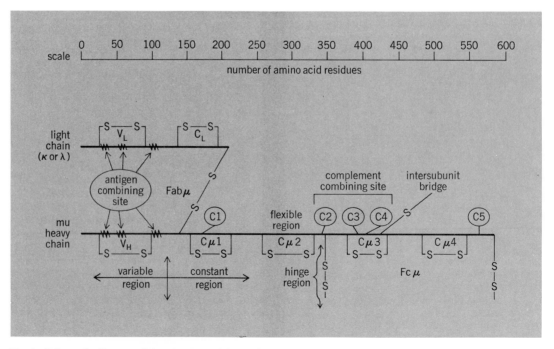

Fig. 2. Schematic diagram of the structure of the half-monomeric subunit of human IgM immunoglobulin. C1 to C5 are carbohydrate groups; other symbols are explained in the text.

of heavy chain or light chain except for minor inherited variations of an allotypic nature that are under Mendelian genetic control. The C region sequence is different for each class of chain and is unique for the class or type. The variable region is that portion at the beginning or amino terminus of the immunoglobulin polypeptide chain that undergoes multiple amino acid substitutions which are independent of the class, subclass, or allotype of the chain. For example, the mu chains from the IgM proteins of five different patients with macroglobulinemia that were sequenced by G. Florent and associates are identical in amino acid sequence in the C regions, each containing about 450 amino acid units.

Yet, the V regions at the beginning of the chains have amino acid substitutions in from 30 to 70 positions when the chains are compared with one another. In the V region, the mu chain of normal IgM antibodies cannot be sequenced because of the multiple substitutions, but the sequence of the C region of the normal IgM and that of the IgM from the patients appears to be identical. According to the theory of the genetic code, each such amino acid substitution must represent a difference or mutation in the corresponding codon. The abnormal human hemoglobins generally represent single amino acid substitutions that convey deleterious effects owing to change in a single codon. No human immunoglobulin light chain studied thus far has had the same amino acid sequence as any other. The almost infinite variability in sequence of immunoglobulins presents a paradox for genetic theory: either an enormous number of immunoglobulin genes, representing a significant fraction of the total DNA, is inherited by each individual, or some novel, unknown mechanism for generating somatic mutation and antibody diversity must exist.

Sequence variability and antibody specificity. Much evidence indicates that the variability in the amino acid sequence of immunoglobulins is the basis of antibody specificity and diversity. Antibodies such as IgM undergo limited proteolytic cleavage to yield two fragments, designated Fab and Fc. The Fc fragment of IgM contains 10 identical Fc segments of the mu chain joined in circular array by disulfide bonds. Fc prepared from IgM antibodies by tryptic cleavage at 60°C lacks antibody activity but has a twentyfold increase in ability to bind the first component of complement (Clq), as has been shown by A. G. Plaut and associates. In the normal antigen-antibody interaction, binding of one molecule of Clq by one molecule of IgM (or by five molecules of IgG) initiates the complement cascade, an important mechanism of immunity. In contrast, the Fab fragment lacks the ability to combine with complement but retains all the original specificity and affinity for combination with antigen.

The V regions of both light chains and heavy chains contain three short hypervariable regions that conjointly make up the antigen-combining site, as has been shown by Florent, D. Lehman, and Putnam. Amino acid sequence analysis showed that this is true for mu heavy chains (Fig. 2). The hypervariable regions are also the sites labeled by affinity-labeling reagents that mimic

specific antigens. X-ray diffraction analysis of the Fab fragment of an IgG myeloma globulin by R. Poljak and associates has given the three-dimensional structure at a resolution of 2.8 A (2.8×10^{-10}m). In their model, the three hypervariable portions of the V regions on each chain cooperate to shape a shallow depression believed to be the antigen-combining site. Precisely how the complementary site is determined for each different antigen is unknown, but the variability in amino acid sequence would permit many different configurations.

Studies of the amino acid sequence of IgG and IgM proteins produced by different patients, and of IgG and IgM proteins produced by the same patient, give a clue to the mechanism of the switch from IgM to IgG antibodies of the same specificity that occurs in the transition from the primary to the secondary immune response during normal antibody formation. This switch could occur if the IgM and IgG antibodies were to contain the same light chains and were to have heavy chains with identical V regions but different C regions. Such conditions might be brought about by repression of the gene for the C region of the mu chain and derepression of the gene for the C region of the gamma heavy chain. Continued study of the amino acid sequence of IgM and IgG immunoglobulins produced by patients with plasma cell tumors should provide the key to the understanding of the relationship between amino acid sequence and antibody specificity and the solution to the genetic control of antibody diversity.

For background information see AMINO ACIDS; ANTIBODY; GAMMA GLOBULIN in the McGraw-Hill Encyclopedia of Science and Technology.

[FRANK W. PUTNAM]

Bibliography: G. Florent, D. Lehman, and F. W. Putnam, *Biochemistry*, 13:2482, 1974; A. G. Plaut, S. Cohen, and T. B. Tomasi, Jr., *Science*, 176:55, 1972; R. J. Poljak et al., *Proc. Nat. Acad. Sci.*, 70:3305, 1973; F. W. Putnam et al., *Science*, 182:287, 1973.

Immunopathology

The possible role of viruses in the connective-tissue ("autoimmune") diseases has been the subject of recent research reports in immunopathology. These diseases affect all ages and vary in severity and outcome but are more often disabling than fatal. They are characterized by chronic inflammation in various organs; joints are often involved, with resulting arthritis. The most common connective-tissue disease is rheumatoid arthritis; rarer ones are systemic lupus erythematosus, polyarteritis nodosa, scleroderma, and polymyositis.

Viral hypothesis. Current thinking has focused on the possibility that chronic (latent, slow) virus infection may be an initial and probably persisting stimulus to the immunological events directly responsible for tissue damage in these diseases. The scientific basis for this opinion rests primarily on animal models of immunologically mediated disease caused by chronic virus infection. The most important such disease is New Zealand mouse disease, which has many features resembling human lupus—autoimmune hemolytic anemia, progressive glomerulonephritis, and presence of antinuclear antibody, the development of which correlates with various virologic events due to chronic infection with a murine oncornavirus (C-type or leukemia virus). Extrapolating to the human diseases, the hypothesis is that a virus infection occurring in genetically or otherwise predisposed individuals becomes chronic; that is, the virus or its antigens persist. Little cell damage may be caused by the virus directly, but persistence of viral antigens induces an immunologic response in the host. The foreign antigens may include host cell constituents altered enough by the virus infection (neoantigens) that antibodies cross-reacting with normal host cells (autoantibodies) are formed against them. Immune complexes of antibody and circulating neoantigens are deposited and lead to inflammation, as in lupus nephritis. Antibody may also combine with neoantigens on tissue cells, and cellular immunity may react with neoantigens on or in cells, so that inflammation results in various tissues.

The form of disease in an individual would depend on the distribution of viral neoantigens (for example, they are usually localized in joints in rheumatoid arthritis, but widespread in lupus and polyarteritis); the distribution may be a function of the nature of the virus, host factors, or other environmental factors, possibly in combination. Other unknown variables regarding the virus are whether infection is common or rare; how long infection antedates appearance of disease, or if transmission occurs vertically (parent to offspring); whether the virus persists during expression of disease and, if so, whether its replication continues or whether the viral genome (complete or incomplete) is present in a repressed form.

Polyarteritis and lupus. The first actual evidence of chronic virus infection causing immunologic disease in man was the discovery of persistent serum hepatitis virus infection in certain patients with polyarteritis, with evidence that suggested that deposition of circulating immune complexes of hepatitis B (Australia) antigen and antibody caused the arteritis. This finding has aroused more interest in viruses as the possible cause of other connective-tissue diseases. Excitement has been particularly intense regarding lupus, because of the electron-microscopic discovery of tuboloreticular ("viruslike") structures in lupus tissues. The nature and significance of these structures remain unclear because they occur in many other diseases, because they do not look identical to any known virus, and because of the failure to identify them by virologic means. Unlike viruses, the structures are not nucleoprotein but, rather, phospholipid and glycoprotein. Thus, rather than being viral components, they more likely are a cellular response to injury, among the causes of which may be viral infection. The structures are frequently found in lupus peripheral blood lymphocytes, and some of them carry an antigen recognized both by antibody in some lupus sera and by an antiserum against an oncornavirus from a murine tumor induced by material from a case of dog lupus. Oncornaviruses have been implicated etiologically in New Zealand mouse disease and have been isolated from the mice, from both spleen and embryonic tissues, and have been seen in normal human pla-

centas as well. The accumulated data suggest that an oncornavirus may be involved in human lupus, but attempts at virus isolation have been unsuccessful, although newer virus detection methods have been little used to date.

Antibody levels to specific viruses have been extensively studied in lupus blood in an effort to find a single striking elevation such as that which led to the implication of measles virus in a chronic neurologic disease, subacute sclerosing panencephalitis. However, it soon became apparent in lupus that antibodies to many viruses were somewhat increased. The increases are in part due to hypergammaglobulinemia and thus have not yet implicated a specific virus in lupus.

Rheumatoid arthritis and polymyositis. Rheumatoid arthritis has been extensively investigated from various microbiologic aspects. Bacteria and mycoplasma have been isolated from rheumatoid tissues, and viruslike effects have been found. Such reports have not been confirmed, and to date no specific microorganism has been etiologically implicated. Some of the newer virologic methods have been included in recent virus isolation studies but have been unsuccessful. However, metabolic differences between cultured rheumatoid and nonrheumatoid joint tissue cells have long been recognized and have been thought to result from chronic virus infection of the rheumatoid cells. Such infection could make them resistant to other viruses added in the laboratory; evidence that this is so has been presented but not generally confirmed. However, the original workers recently reported transferring the resistance to rabbit joint cells both in the animal and, by cell fusion, in tissue culture. Others have found evidence for the presence of a neoantigen, possibly viral, in cultured rheumatoid cells, as detected by lymphocytotoxicity. Taken together, these findings indicate that further attempts to isolate viruses from rheumatoid tissues should be made.

Studies of virus antibody levels in adult rheumatoid arthritis have, as in lupus, failed to implicate a specific virus. However, in juvenile rheumatoid arthritis, higher German measles antibody titres have been reported. A controlled study failed to confirm this finding but did show higher Epstein-Barr virus antibody titres. The causal implications of these findings are unclear. Similar studies in polymyositis have shown markedly increased antibodies to toxoplasma (a protozoa) in some patients, but again the causal implications are unclear.

Predisposing genetic factors. A major obstacle in causal studies of the connective tissue diseases is their heterogeneity, both in clinical presentation and probably in cause. For instance, only about one-third of polyarteritis cases are associated with hepatitis B virus infection. A better definition, either clinically or of predisposing factors, of subgroups within a given connective-tissue disease would aid causal investigations. In juvenile rheumatoid arthritis, clinical subgroups have long been recognized; recently an increased prevalence of the inherited histocompatibility gene HL-A 27 has been found. The very high prevalence of HL-A 27 found in ankylosing spondylitis suggests that HL-A 27 in juvenile rheumatoids may predispose to later development of spondylitis. The increased prevalence of HL-A 27 in adults with eye inflammation suggests that this gene may also be a marker for eye involvement in juvenile rheumatoids. Another adult rheumatic disease, Reiter's syndrome, which has long been thought to be a venereally transmitted infection, occurs almost exclusively in individuals with the HL-A 27 gene. Thus, possession of this gene, or a closely linked one, may be a necessary predisposing factor for the development of these rheumatic diseases. Presumably the gene is responsible for an aberrant immunologic response to as yet unknown infectious agents, and thus it should prove to be a useful marker in future studies.

Possible role of cellular immunity. Cell-mediated immunity (CMI) to specific viruses has not been studied extensively in the connective-tissue diseases. Viral infections in man and animals are known to suppress CMI to other antigens, such as tuberculin, and CMI to such antigens is frequently depressed in the connective-tissue diseases. Factors from the thymus are important in the development and maintenance of CMI, and they disappear prematurely in both human lupus and New Zealand mouse disease. In the latter the early occurrence of an autoantibody capable of killing thymus cells has been shown; its appearance might be in response to a viral neoantigen, perhaps caused by viral replication in the thymus. Since CMI appears to be essential for the elimination of viruses from the host, resulting thymic dysfunction and depressed CMI might allow abnormal persistence of the oncornavirus that has been implicated in New Zealand mouse disease; by analogy, the situation may be similar in human lupus.

Conclusion. Virus causation of the connective-tissue diseases remains largely hypothetical, except for some polyarteritis cases. Research in these cases has been hindered by the lack of laboratory culture systems and of an animal model, problems that may be overcome in the near future. The isolation of more easily studied causative viruses from the more common connective-tissue diseases will eventually lead to a better understanding of disease mechanisms. This would set the stage for the development of specific treatment and perhaps prevention, the human benefits of which would be enormous.

For background information *see* ANIMAL VIRUS; ANTIBODY; ANTIGEN; IMMUNOPATHOLOGY; INFLAMMATION; LUPUS ERYTHEMATOSUS in the McGraw-Hill Encyclopedia of Science and Technology.　　　　　　　[PAUL E. PHILLIPS]

Bibliography: C. L. Christian and P. E. Phillips, *Amer. J. Med.*, 54:611, 1973; D. C. Dumonde (ed.), *Proceedings of the International Symposium on Infection and Immunology in the Rheumatic Diseases*, London, March 19–21, 1974, in press; D. A. Person, J. T. Sharp, and W. E. Rawls, *Arthritis Rheum.*, 16:677, 1973; M. Siegel and S. L. Lee, *Seminars Arthritis Rheum.*, 3:1, 1973.

Integrated circuits

Continuing advancements in the processing of monolithic integrated circuits are facilitating the development of relatively low-cost and high-accuracy four-quadrant multipliers in building-block module and integrated-circuit form. These multipliers are devices that produce an output voltage or current that is proportional to the product of two or more independent input voltages or currents, a task that formerly required a large number of circuit components at considerably more cost, when using discrete-transistor or vacuum-tube components.

Four-quadrant multipliers are devices that accept all four product combinations of a pair of signal inputs (for positive and negative signals) and provide outputs of appropriate polarity—for example, one negative and one positive signal giving a negative output, and a pair of negative signals giving a positive output. While multipliers can also be used to square, divide, and take the square root of two or more input variables (the last two functions by simple external feedback connections), four-quadrant multipliers are best suited for applications involving multiplications only, since dividing and taking the square root of two or more input variables involves ratio computations which restrict the denominator to a positive quadrant. For the squaring function, the output is always a positive number, hence no four-quadrant operation can be considered here.

Multiplier techniques. A variety of four-quadrant multiplication techniques exist. The two most popular ones are the variable-transconductance (see illustration) and the pulse-width/pulse-height modulation techniques, the former being the recipient of most of the monolithic integrated-circuit processing advancements. The variable-transconductance technique predominates and the heart of it is the matched monolithic transistor pair. In fact, the recent availability of low-cost matched monolithic transistor pairs in discrete packaging has allowed circuit designers to put together their own multipliers with moderate output accuracies within 2 to 5% at extremely low costs.

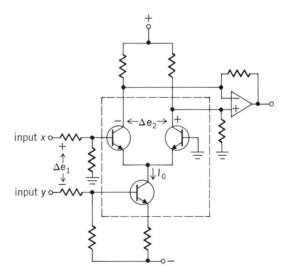

The variable-transconductance multiplier technique is the most popular circuit in four-quadrant multipliers. The Gilbert circuit (in dashed box) made this technique the most economical and widely used. Here Δe_1, $\Delta e_2 =$ differential voltages; $I_0 =$ offset current. *(From Roger Allan, EDN Mag., pp. 34–41, Feb. 20, 1974)*

Basic to the variable-transconductance technique is the simple differential transistor pair, where one variable input to the base of one transistor controls the device's gain or transconductance. One transistor amplifies the other's variable input, applied to the common emitter point, in proportion to the control input. This very simple concept has been well known, and various attempts to use it for multiplication with discrete transistors or vacuum tubes met with little or no success. Stability and accuracy parameters were usually poor. Not until the advent of the monolithic integrated circuit, with its inherent feature of having all its components on the same chip drift together due to temperature changes (thereby canceling out any errors due to drift), did the transconductance technique catch on. However, even the best transconductance integrated circuit had its limitations. Its multiplication properties were limited to small signal dynamic ranges, and it suffered from nonlinearities and temperature instabilities that required additional compensating components. This all but eliminated any economic advantage that such units had, due to the fact that they were made in monolithic form.

The Gilbert cell (see illustration), invented by B. Gilbert, was to be the answer. By using the logarithmic properties of diodes and transistors (connected as diodes), the Gilbert circuit allowed for the compensation of nonlinearities and instabilities in the basic monolithic variable-transconductance circuit. Multiplier designs were now possible with less than 1% errors of accuracy, over 100-MHz bandwidths, and all with the low cost inherent in the monolithic integrated-circuit technique. Actually, a single differential-transistor pair is only sufficient for two-quadrant multiplication. By adding a second differential-transistor pair in parallel, four-quadrant performance results.

It should also be pointed out that the technological breakthrough about 2 years ago of being able to trim a monolithic multiplier's resistive element by a laser beam, while it was still on the chip, has greatly contributed to producing four-quadrant monolithic multipliers, in packages no larger than those of discrete transistors, with accuracies within 0.1% at very low prices (in the $20 to $30 range versus $80 to $100 for similar-performing units, the size of a cigarette pack, produced without the benefits of laser trimming on the chip).

Two factors, both functions of the monolithic integrated-circuit process, are critical to the performance of the variable-transconductance circuit: the current unbalance or offset-voltage mismatch between individual transistors of a pair, and the difference between them as to how much current gain (known as beta) each has. These sources of error give rise to low-accuracy performance in a multiplier. The most advanced processing techniques allow monolithic transistor-pair matching of offset voltages (between the base and emitter) to within approximately 250 μV. Such matching allows multiplication performance to within 0.1% accuracy levels. To get some idea how this offset-voltage mismatch affects accuracy levels, a simple doubling of this close matching to 500 μV results in a tenfold degrading of accuracy levels to 1%. While there is every reason to believe that match-ing to within 50 μV or less may be accomplished (in large-production quantities for low-cost advantages) in one or more years, it may not necessarily be needed as far as four-quadrant multipliers are concerned, since the bulk of their applications lie in the accuracy range within 0.5 to 1%.

With the higher speeds of newer multiplier designs (larger bandwidths), newer error sources that heretofore have been negligible at lower frequencies have taken on new importance. The most important of these is a certain amount of resistance found in the base of each transistor, known as base-spreading resistance, again a function of the monolithic process. This resistance, which acts in series with the base, is generally a few ohms in value and can affect accuracy adversely. With the latest processing techniques, it is possible to keep base-spreading resistance under 1 ohm (referred to the emitter) for possible accuracy levels of multiplication within 0.1%. It is easier to minimize this source of error in discrete-transistor pairs than in monolithic pairs.

Multiplier applications. One of the earliest uses of the multiplication technique in electronic circuitry was in a modulator. Here, one signal was multiplied by another which modulated it, a technique that was largely used in communications circuitry with large and bulky vacuum tubes. What the monolithic and modular four-quadrant multiplier has done is allow the implementation of scores of multiplication applications in measurement and control circuits that were only possible on paper, but were either impractical in reality due to large costs or due to unrealized performance parameters.

Four-quadrant multipliers are useful for applications involving power measurements, rms (root mean square) computations, phase detection, dynamic gain setting as well as signal modulation. However, the real power of a four-quadrant multiplier can be appreciated when it is combined with other operational circuit elements such as transcendental-function, logarithmic, multiplexer, and sample-and-hold units. Exponential as well as correlation-function calculations are then possible.

The rms value of a signal is a useful quantity in most circuit calculations. Prior to the advent of the multiplier, accurate rms calculations were only possible with expensive thermal-converter techniques. Since the rms value is equivalent to the square root of an averaged quantity squared (rms $= \sqrt{\bar{X}^2}$), one multiplier used in the squaring mode, followed by an averaging circuit, then another multiplier to take the square root, can do the same job at far less cost.

Designers working with prototype circuitry often wish to calculate such quantities as instantaneous power through a transistor's collector circuit quickly and least expensively. By inserting one input of a multiplier in the collector circuit to sense the load current and the other input at the load to sense the collector voltage, accurate and rapid instantaneous measurement of power can be achieved at very low costs.

As more analog function circuit elements become available, so does the number of potential circuit applications for four-quadrant multipliers. The few applications mentioned represent only a handful of the many possible applications, limited only by the user's imagination.

For background information *see* ANALOG COMPUTER; INTEGRATED CIRCUITS in the McGraw-Hill Encyclopedia of Science and Technology.

[ROGER ALLAN]

Bibliography: B. Gilbert, *IEEE Proceedings of Solid State Circuits Conference*, pp. 166–167, February 1971; G. Papadopoulos, *IEEE J. Solid State Circuits*, SC-8:453, December 1973; D. Sheingold, *Nonlinear Circuits Handbook*, pp. 203–269, February 1974.

Intermolecular forces

The knowledge of forces between molecules is basic to the understanding of the properties and behavior of matter. In view of this, both experimental and theoretical techniques have been developed over the years to determine intermolecular forces. The most direct method to derive information about intermolecular forces is from experiments on molecular beams, but these become tedious with the increasing complexity of molecular structure, as do calculation methods developed from first principles. Therefore, in recent years considerable effort has gone into determining these forces by other methods, such as through experimental data on transport properties of fluids, and through the structure and properties of van der Waals molecules.

Transport properties of fluids. The successful determination of intermolecular forces from transport properties of fluids requires accurate experimental data and a sufficiently reliable theoretical formulation of these properties. The latter has been achieved only for dilute gas systems, and the theoretical description of a dense fluid is not yet satisfactorily developed. The intermolecular potential enters into the description of the molecular trajectories during collision, which are then utilized to specify the collision cross sections, and finally these appear in the expression of the transport property as a collision integral. Consequently, the Chapman-Enskog kinetic theory of dilute monatomic gases, in which only binary elastic molecular encounters determine the transport and classical mechanics is adequate for the description of the process, is employed in conjunction with the experimental data on viscosity, thermal conductivity, diffusion, and thermal diffusion to determine the molecular interaction potentials.

It is important to point out that if the gas is uniform, that is, there are no gradients of velocity, composition, and temperature in the gas, the molecular velocity distribution function is exactly known as determined by J. C. Maxwell a long time ago. On the other hand, when the gas is not in equilibrium, the distribution function is given only as a solution of the Boltzmann integrodifferential equation. S. Chapman and D. Enskog obtained a perturbation solution which is valid only when these gradients are small and under such conditions that the flux vectors are linearly proportional to the corresponding driving gradients, so that the usual definition of transport coefficients as proportionality constants results. Whenever such a condition is not satisfied in the gas system, it is only artificial to talk about the transport properties of such a gas.

C. S. Wang Chang, G. E. Uhlenbeck, and N. Taxman have given a similar formal kinetic theory for polyatomic gas systems which has been simplified by E. A. Mason and L. Monchick under well-defined approximations and which is cast in a form that can be employed to determine intermolecular forces for systems composed of polyatomic gases. It has been known for some time, and has been shown by the theory for polyatomic systems, that the viscosity and diffusion coefficients are not much influenced by the presence of internal degrees of freedom, but thermal conductivity and thermal diffusion are quite sensitive to molecular rotations and vibrations. Consequently, in recent years these properties are being determined with added incentive as probes for the determination of molecular mechanisms for translational-rotational and translational-vibrational energy transfer in a polyatomic molecule.

Determining the force law. Briefly, the procedure of determining the intermolecular force law from measurements on transport properties involves choosing an interaction potential form a priori and computing transport properties and collision integrals for this form. If on the basis of these integrals the experimental data on different transport properties over a temperature range can be successfully correlated, the assumed potential may be close to the correct one. It is to be stressed that theoretical investigations of intermolecular forces assist in making a choice for the potential and that experimental data of sufficient accuracy over a wide temperature range must be employed in such an analysis. Under such conditions the procedure provides a crucial test of the potential form, and realistic values of potential parameters are derived. This approach thus draws considerably from the theory of intermolecular forces in choosing an appropriate semiempirical analytical form for the potential. One practical advantage of such a derived intermolecular potential from data on a few properties over a limited temperature range lies in its use to predict a large variety of properties (even those which were not used while determining potential parameters) and over wider ranges of temperature and composition. This is particularly attractive to design engineers who need data on properties in temperature, composition, and pressure regimes where direct measurements may not be available.

The nature of the intermolecular force field between two nonpolar spherical molecules is an attractive one at large intermolecular separations (which explains why the molecules do not fly apart) and a repulsive one at small separations (which saves the two molecules from collapsing into one under ordinary conditions). J. E. Lennard-Jones suggested the following (12–6) intermolecular potential: $V(R) = 4\epsilon[(\sigma/R)^{12} - (\sigma/R)^6]$. Here $V(R)$ is the interaction potential at a molecular separation distance R, and ϵ and σ are called the potential parameters, with the following significance: ϵ is the depth of the potential well or the maximum energy of attraction, and σ is that value of R where the potential energy is zero. Various forms for the attractive and repulsive parts of the interaction potential have been used, and additional terms are added if the molecules are polar and have permament electric moment. Collision integrals have been computed for such a priori assumed semi-empirical potential functions.

Measurements of transport coefficients. In recent years accurate measurements of viscosity have been made by J. Kestin and coworkers using an oscillating-disk viscometer, and by E. B. Smith and coworkers using a capillary-flow viscometer. Kestin, S. T. Ro, and W. Wakeham have employed these and other reliable experimental data to develop a law of corresponding states for monatomic gases and their mixtures. S. C. Saxena and coworkers and G. S. Springer and coworkers have developed a modified hot-wire column technique to determine thermal conductivity of gases at high temperatures. S. H. P. Chen and Saxena reported thermal conductivity of nitrogen in the temperature range 100–2200°C at 1 atm. They have outlined the role such data play in determining the mechanism of energy transfer by the internal modes of a polyatomic molecule. W. F. Ahtye has suggested an expression for the calculation of thermal conductivity of a polyatomic gas in which molecular rotations and vibrations contribute significantly, and has computed the diffusion coefficient for the transport of vibrational energy, D_{vib}, on the basis of thermal conductivity data. This suggestion in conjunction with the accurate data of thermal conductivity of polyatomic gases being produced by Saxena and coworkers will lead to the knowledge of D_{vib} for polyatomic gases. Such data are almost totally unavailable at the present time. S. Weissman and coworkers have exploited the principle of observing the rate of transport of a gas contained in a bulb into another gas confined in a second bulb for the measurement of diffusion coefficients, and a trennschaukel apparatus consisting of 20 suitably interconnected tubes, the top and bottom ends of each being maintained at temperatures T_1 and T_2 (where $T_1 > T_2$), for the determination of the thermal diffusion factor of gases and gas mixtures. W. L. Taylor and Weissman have demonstrated the ability of thermal diffusion data in discriminating and assessing the appropriateness of various semiempirical potential functions for neon.   [SATISH C. SAXENA]

Van der Waals molecules.

Van der Waals molecules are held together, not by chemical bonding, but by intermolecular forces. Studies in the past several years have provided for the first time the structure and properties of a number of van der Waals molecules. This recent work not only represents the discovery of a new class of molecules but also contains detailed information on the intermolecular forces that bind them together.

The properties of solids or liquids, for example, solid argon, liquid oxygen, or water, are determined by the intermolecular forces that hold the molecules in place. Above the condensed phase, the vapor consists principally of Ar, O_2, or H_2O molecules rebounding off the walls of the container or occasionally off each other. However, a small fraction of the gas phase contains Ar_2, $(O_2)_2$, or $(H_2O)_2$. These weakly bound complexes, called van der Waals molecules, are stabilized by the same type of intermolecular forces that are present in the condensed phase. These molecules are named after J. D. van der Waals, who showed 100 years ago that intermolecular forces between atoms or molecules can quantitatively account for liquefaction of gases under the appropriate conditions of pressure and temperature. Van der Waals molecules can be expected to be found, at least in small concentrations, in most gaseous systems. It is the recent determination of the structure and properties of these van der Waals molecules, particularly by molecular-spectroscopic techniques, that is providing new information on intermolecular forces.

Argon van der Waals molecule. Gaseous argon at the temperature of the boiling liquid (−186°C) consists of about 98% Ar atoms and the remaining 2% are Ar_2 van der Waals molecules. At higher temperatures the concentration of Ar_2 becomes exceedingly small. The ultraviolet electronic spectrum of the gas at low temperatures obtained by Y. Tanaka and K. Yoshino reveals strong absorption by atomic Ar and weaker features associated with molecular Ar_2. Details of the Ar_2 absorption reflect vibrational motion of the two Ar atoms against the weak intermolecular interactions that bind this van der Waals molecule. From measurements of this vibrational energy it is possible to construct the intermolecular potential energy curve of the Ar_2 molecule. A combination of these spectroscopic experiments and studies of the dynamics of colliding Ar atoms reveals the intermolecular energy $V(R)$ as a function of the atom separation R in the Ar_2 van der Waals molecule, as shown in Fig. 1. (It is often more convenient to describe intermolec-

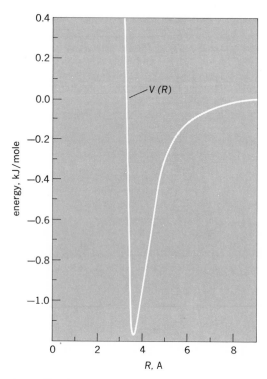

Fig. 1. The intermolecular energy of the Ar_2 van der Waals molecule. The potential energy is zero for the atoms far apart. *(From J. M. Parson, P. E. Siska, and Y. T. Lee, Intermolecular potentials from cross-beam differential elastic scattering measurements, IV: Ar + Ar, J. Chem. Phys., 56:1511, 1972)*

ular *energies* rather than intermolecular *forces*.)

The dissociation energy of the Ar_2 molecule (the energy needed to pull the atoms apart) is about 1 kJ/mole; this is hundreds of times smaller than the dissociation energy of a typical chemically bonded molecule like O_2, for example, where it is 490 kJ/mole. The bond length, 3.8 A (0.38 nm), is the distance between the Ar atoms at the bottom of the Ar_2 intermolecular energy curve. This is considerably longer than a chemical bond length where, for example, in O_2 it is only 1.2 A (0.12 nm). All this reflects the weak bonding in van der Waals molecules in contrast to the strong tight bond found in chemically bonded molecules.

H_2-Ar van der Waals molecule. The van der Waals molecule H_2-Ar is formed—together with Ar_2 and trace amounts of $(H_2)_2$—when H_2 is added to gaseous argon near −200°C. The infrared vibrational absorption spectrum of H_2-Ar reported by A. R. W. McKellar and H. L. Welsh reveals that while H_2 is weakly bound to Ar it is undergoing rotation within the H_2-Ar molecule. The arrows in the H_2-Ar structure in Fig. 2a are meant to suggest the internal rotation of H_2 in this van der Waals molecule. This H_2-Ar structure might be contrasted with that of a triatomic molecule like N_2O, for example, where all the atoms are locked into a linear configuration by strong chemical bonds. Attempts to force internal rotation of N_2 within N_2O would require heating the gas thousands of degrees Celsius and would principally result in dissociation of the entire molecule.

N_2-Ar van der Waals molecule. The infrared spectrum of N_2-Ar by G. Henderson and G. Ewing in a cold gaseous mixture of N_2 and Ar suggests that this molecule favors a T configuration, shown in Fig. 2b. The intermolecular interaction then not only binds N_2 to Ar but also tends to direct the N_2 molecule into a preferred orientation. These directional intermolecular forces are weak, however, and at temperatures where small concentrations of this van der Waals molecule are stable (near −190°C), only 20% of the N_2-Ar maintains the T configuration. In the remaining 80%, N_2 undergoes rotation within N_2-Ar in a manner somewhat analogous to the internal rotation of H_2-Ar. The determination of the properties of a molecule like N_2-Ar therefore implies information on the intermolecular forces which hold the molecules together. It has been possible for N_2-Ar to construct an intermolecular energy surface, analogous to Fig. 1 except that it is a function of the angle of the N_2 orientation as well as its distance from Ar.

Ar-HCl van der Waals molecule. Microwave and radio-frequency spectra monitor molecular rotational energies and can provide quite accurate structure determinations of van der Waals molecules. S. Novick, S. Harris, and W. Klemperer have studied gaseous mixtures of HCl and Ar and obtained the spectrum of the Ar-HCl van der Waals molecule. They find it has a linear (or near linear) structure, shown in Fig. 2c. However, the intermolecular forces which depend on orientation are weak, as they are in N_2-Ar, and HCl within the Ar-HCl molecule makes large-amplitude bending vibrational excursions from its linear equilibrium geometry. The structures of N_2-Ar and Ar-HCl represented in Fig. 2 are therefore static represen-

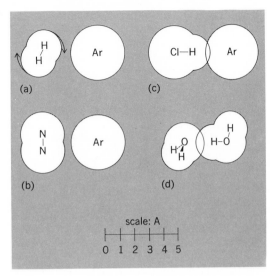

Fig. 2. The structures of some van der Waals molecules. (a) H_2-Ar (from A. R. W. McKellar and H. L. Welsh, *Anisotropic intermolecular force effects in spectra of H_2– and D_2–rare-gas complexes. J. Chem. Phys., 55:595, 1971*). (b) N_2-Ar (from G. Henderson and G. Ewing, *Infrared spectrum, structure and properties of the N_2-Ar van der Waals molecule, Molec. Phys., 27:903, 1974*). (c) HCl-Ar (from S. Novick et al., *Determination of the structure of ArHCl, J. Chem. Phys., 59:2273, 1973*). (d) $(H_2O)_2$ (from T. R. Dyke and J. S. Muenter, *Microwave spectrum and structure of hydrogen bonded water dimer, J. Chem. Phys., 60:2929, 1974*).

tations of very floppy molecules.

Hydrogen bonding. The hydrogen bond involves relatively strong intermolecular interactions. The energy of the hydrogen bond in water, about 20 kJ/mole, is intermediate in magnitude between the intermolecular bonding in Ar_2 and the chemical bonding in O_2. The recent structure determination of $(H_2O)_2$ by T. Dyke and J. Muenter is particularly interesting because hydrogen bonding in water is responsible for so many of its unique properties. The $(H_2O)_2$ was taken from water vapor and its microwave and radio-frequency spectrum analyzed. The structure that results is shown in Fig. 2d. The linear hydrogen bond (the O H-O angle) and the relative orientation of the two H_2O molecules agree with crystal structure determinations of ice. However, the distance between the H_2O molecules differs somewhat. Close comparisons of the theory of hydrogen bonds with crystal structure determinations and gas-phase structures will guarantee a deeper understanding of this important class of intermolecular interactions.

Outlook. The structures discussed here and presented in Fig. 2 represent only a small fraction of the van der Waals molecules studied in the past few years. Rare-gas diatomic van der Waals molecules such as Ne_2, HeNe, Kr_2, KrAr, and Xe_2 have been investigated. Small polyatomic van der Waals molecules such as $(H_2)_2$ and $(D_2)_2$, as well as H_2 and D_2 bonded by intermolecular forces to various rare-gas atoms, have been examined. The structure and properties of O_2-Ar, Ar-HF, Ar-FCl, $(N_2)_2$, $(O_2)_2$, and $(NO)_2$ have been discussed. With more and more of these van der Waals molecules being examined, the understanding of intermolecular forces may someday approach the understanding of forces associated with chemical bonds. Provided the experimental work inspires a comparable theoretical interest in van der Waals molecules, this time may not be too distant.

For background information *see* BOLTZMANN TRANSPORT EQUATION; CHEMICAL BINDING; CONDUCTION, HEAT; DIFFUSION IN GASES AND LIQUIDS; INTERMOLECULAR FORCES; VISCOSITY OF GASES in the McGraw-Hill Encyclopedia of Science and Technology.   [GEORGE EWING]

Bibliography: W. F. Ahtye, *J. Chem. Phys.*, 57: 5542–5555, 1972; S. H. P. Chen and S. C. Saxena, *High Temp. Sci.*, 5:206–233, 1973; S. Harris, S. Novick, and W. Klemperer, *J. Chem. Phys.*, 60: 3208, 1974; J. Kestin, S. T. Ro, and W. Wakeham, *Physica*, 58:165–211, 1972; C. Long and G. Ewing, *J. Chem. Phys.*, 58:4824, 1973; A. R. W. McKellar and H. L. Welsh, *Can. J. Phys.*, 52:1082, 1974; Y. Tanaka, K. Yoshino, and D. E. Freeman, *J. Chem. Phys.*, 59:5748, 1973; W. L. Taylor and S. Weissman, *J. Chem. Phys.*, 60:3684–3689, 1974.

Interstellar matter

The study of molecules in the giant clouds of gas and dust which inhabit the spiral arms of the Galaxy is beginning to tell scientists much about the evolutionary cycle which the Earth is part of. The Sun is a middle-aged star (4.5×10^9 years old) which is very quiescently living out its life on the main sequence. But what happened during the very early years of the solar system and how will it all come to an end? These are questions for which one must look to other stars and molecular clouds for an answer. In the process one crosses back and forth between the interstellar and stellar parts of the Galaxy.

From molecular clouds to stars. For about 6 years there has been an intensive amount of re-

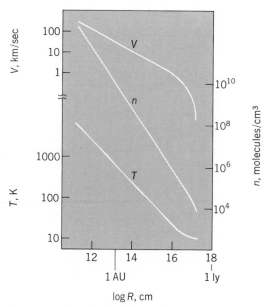

Fig. 1. Velocity *V*, density *n*, and temperature *T* in a 1-M$_\odot$ protostar (at 10^5 years) when half of the mass has accumulated into the central core. *(From R. B. Larson, Mon. Notic. Roy. Astron. Soc., 157:132, 1972)*

Molecular excitation and observed sizes of molecular emission

Molecule	Temperature, K	H$_2$ density per cubic centimeter	Radius*
H$_2$CO†	10	10^3	10 ly
CO	6	10^4	5 ly
HCN	4	10^6	2 ly
H$_2$CO‡	7	10^7	1 ly
OH	100	10^8	10 AU
H$_2$O	600	10^{10}	1 AU

SOURCE: From D. Buhl, Molecules and evolution in the galaxy, *Sky Telesc.*, 45(3):156, 1973.
*1 light-year (ly) = 10^{18} cm; 1 astronomical unit (AU) = 1.5×10^{13} cm.
†6-cm transition.
‡2-mm transition.

search directed toward detecting and identifying the various complex molecules which make up the dust clouds located along the inner edges of the spiral arms of the Galaxy and in the galactic nucleus. There are now known to be about 30 molecules, of which the latest to be discovered are SO and $(CH_3)_2O$. In addition, the various spectral lines of these molecules have been used to deduce the temperature, density, velocity, and quantity of molecular hydrogen (H_2) in these clouds.

Molecular hydrogen is not directly detectable in the dense molecular clouds (> 100 molecules/cm³). This is due to the fact that molecular hydrogen has lines only in the ultraviolet portion of the spectrum, and the dense clouds have so much dust that ultraviolet light does not penetrate these clouds. However, one may infer the amount of molecular hydrogen present from the densities required to excite other molecules which are detectable in the radio spectrum. This is illustrated in the table, showing the density and temperature of molecular hydrogen necessary to have the collision rate equal to the radiation rate for several common molecules which have been studied. The radius given in the table is obtained by mapping the size of the area in the sky over which the molecule appears in the Orion Nebula (for OH and H_2O this requires very-long-baseline radio astronomy). The first thing that is evident from examining this table is the increase of molecular hydrogen density as one proceeds in toward the center of a cloud. The second point is that even at the lowest density in the table (10^3/cm³) the cloud has a free-fall collapse time of 10^6 years which is derived from the H_2 densities.

Scientists are inevitably led to the conclusion that what is buried inside the dark molecular clouds are stars and planets in the process of contracting onto the main sequence. A comparison of the observations in the table with the theoretical studies of collapsing protostars by R. B. Larson results in some startling coincidences. Figure 1 shows a plot of the velocity, density, and temperature as a function of distance from the center of a 1-solar-mass star which has partially condensed from a uniform cloud. The densities and temperatures at a distance comparable to the measured radius given in the table for OH and H_2O are remarkably similar to those required to excite these molecules. In addition, the velocities observed for OH and H_2O show a spread similar to what would be predicted by the protostar model. Recently a

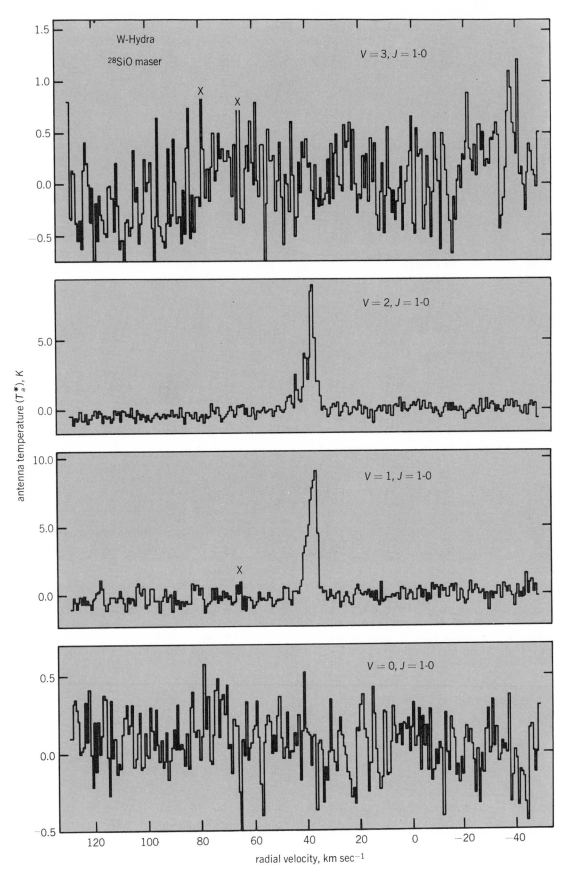

Fig. 2. Silicon monoxide (SiO) maser emission from the red giant star W-Hydra. The *V* quantum numbers refer to the vibrational state and the *J* quantum numbers refer to the rotational transition. The velocity is that of the star with respect to the local standard of rest. The 7-mm wavelength spectra were made with the National Radio Astronomy Observatories 36-ft telescope at Kitt Peak, AZ. *(From D. Buhl et al., Silicon monoxide: Detection of maser emission from the second vibrationally excited state, Astrophys. J., 192, L97, 1974)*

number of theoretical models have been proposed by F. O. Clark, D. Buhl, and L. E. Snyder, as well as P. Goldreich and J. Kwan, to account for the excitation of other molecules in protostellar clouds.

S. E. Strom and K. M. Strom have made infrared observations of several dust clouds, and they have detected a number of highly reddened stars which have not yet reached the main sequence. These are very young stars with dust shells around them. They apparently are still surrounded by some of the dust and gas from the cloud out of which they were born. Again, the observations of these stars seem to compare quite closely with theoretical studies of contracting stars.

Observations by J. F. Drake, E. B. Jenkins, D. C. Morton, J. B. Rogerson, L. Spitzer, and D. G. York, done with the Copernicus satellite, added a new puzzle to the question of evolution in a molecular cloud. They observed a number of atomic absorption lines in the ultraviolet spectrum of reddened stars which gave data on the abundances of the atoms in the intervening low-density ($<100/cm^3$) interstellar material. What they found was that the heavy atoms (such as C, N, O, Mg, P, Cl, and Mn) were depleted relative to hydrogen when the results were compared with abundances in this solar system. J. M. Greenberg has suggested that some of this depletion may be due to the build-up of heavy atoms on grains, and some due to large molecules in the cloud which have not been detected yet. A dust grain is thought to consist of a silicon or carbon core with a mantle of organic ices which are possibly the sites of the interstellar chemistry that produces all the complex molecules observed in dust clouds. Hence the depletion of the heavy atoms observed by Copernicus may just be evidence of the consumption of raw materials in the process of chemical evolution within the molecular clouds.

Death of a star. When a star has reached the point where it has exhausted all of its hydrogen, it will explode in a supernova if it is a very massive star. If it is a star like the Sun, it will probably become a red giant, expanding its envelope and decreasing its temperature to 2000–3000 K. This is the stage at which the star begins to burn helium. It also may become a variable star, changing its luminosity with time and throwing off gas and dust into the interstellar medium. This type of star has been found to exhibit peculiar maser emission from several molecular species. A. H. Barrett, P. R. Schwartz, and W. J. Wilson have found both OH and H_2O maser lines. The most recent discovery by D. Buhl and L. E. Snyder of maser emission from vibrationally excited SiO was particularly interesting because of the extremely high energies required to excite the vibrational states of SiO. Radio emission at 7 mm was detected from both the first and second vibrational levels; however, the ground and third vibrational levels are apparently not excited (Fig. 2). The excitation of the levels observed requires 1800 and 3600 K, or photons of 8 and 4 μ respectively. Infrared observations by D. D. Cudaback, J. E. Gaustad, R. F. Knacke, F. C. Gillett, W. A. Stein, and P. M. Solomon have shown absorption lines at 4 and 8 μ in these stars. What this means is that the star has a shell of gas and dust around it which is being expelled into the

interstellar medium. Some of the molecules in this shell are being excited by energy from the star, giving rise to maser emission at a number of wavelengths. Here is seen the end of a star's life and the recycling of its material back into the interstellar medium, where it will be used to make the next generation of stars.

For background information *see* INTERSTELLAR MATTER; STELLAR EVOLUTION in the McGraw-Hill Encyclopedia of Science and Technology.

[DAVID BUHL]

Bibliography: B. J. Bok, *Sci. Amer.*, 227:49, August 1972; D. Buhl, *Sky Telesc.*, 45(3):156, 1973; M. A. Gordon and L. E. Snyder (eds.), *Molecules in the Galactic Environment*, 1973; S. E. Strom and K. M. Strom, *Sky Telesc.*, 45:279, 359, 1973.

Invertebrate pathology

Élie Metchnikoff's investigations of invertebrate pathology about 80 years ago led to basic understanding of phagocytosis as a protective mechanism, but the subject of pathology in invertebrates other than insects was thereafter strangely neglected. In the 1970s interest in the responses of invertebrates to infection and injury has been renewed and is accelerating.

Immunity. Since among the invertebrates there is a vast array of different animals with many different physiological specializations, many different protective mechanisms have probably been developed; among them, phagocytosis, release of antibiotic or lytic substances, cellular and extracellular clotting, formation of mucus by specialized coelomic cells, and autointerference have been identified. Whether two or more reactions are analogous (having a separate evolutionary origin) or homologous (having a similar evolutionary origin) has not been determined in most cases. Recent work on sea stars (echinoderms), which are in direct evolutionary line with the prevertebrate ascidians, has shown that small molecules (30,000 molecular units) extractable from the amebocytes participate in several basic lymphocyte-mediated reactions in vertebrates. However, no substance that mimics the memory and specificity of the vertebrate system has yet been described in the invertebrate. There are substances in the body cavity of larval insects that destroy invading bacteria and that increase in amount after inoculation of avirulent bacteria, protecting the larva against otherwise lethal infection. However, memory and specificity are lacking. When the marine invertebrate coelomate *Sipunculus*, studied extensively by the Rumanian pathologist Jean Cantacuzène, is injected with foreign material, it releases a highly active lytic substance from its coelomic fluid (blood) cells. This activity is most effective against potentially pathogenic ciliates, which it destroys within 5 min of contact, but there is no evidence of increased response on subsequent inoculation. A variety of agglutinins of different red cells have been described, including some that occur in prevertebrates (ascidians). It has been suggested that all these substances be called "antisomes," to distinguish them from antibodies.

Phagocytosis, the basic protective mechanism, functions in all invertebrates at all levels, and its very importance has inhibited the search for other mechanisms of protection, or reaction to injury. Phagocytosis involves three major steps. First, recognition, usually manifested by the adherence of host cells to the foreign substance; second, ingestion of the foreign substance; and third, disposal, which may be by migration from the animal if the substance is indigestible. Specific ways in which phagocytosis operates in insects have been summarized by G. Salt, including the details of the mechanisms that parasites have developed to combat this host reaction. Recent emphasis has been placed on specific organs or areas of the animal in which phagocytosis is concentrated. Such analogs of the reticuloendothelial system of vertebrates have been described in insects, mollusks, and ascidians. They are probably similar to the *organes phagocytaires* described by early French zoologists. Despite the importance of phagocytic action, there has been no study of the mechanism during active infection with a natural pathogen comparable to the original work of Metchnikoff on the water flea *Daphnia*. Rejection of foreign tissue that has been engrafted onto another species or individual is a phenomenon commonly used in studies of immunological relationships among invertebrates. It is also a powerful tool in the search for self and nonself; but, as yet, the phenomenon of recognition is unrelated to the anamnestic response of vertebrates. *See* PHAGOCYTOSIS.

Clumping of circulating amebocytes following the formation of a wound is the usual mechanism of hemostasis. However, in some animals *(Limulus)*, extracellular clotting seems to predominate, and in some parasitic crustaceans *(Sacculina)*, the entire process of clot initiation by endotoxin or foreign material is independent of circulating cells. Cellular clotting has two phases. The first is the initiation of adherence of amebocytes to the wounded surface, and of other amebocytes to these activated cells. This process leads to the formation of a loose clump of amebocytes, which then contract individually to form a tight firm clot. Extracellular clot formation may occur around this cellular clot, creating a tight seal that prevents further fluid leakage. The combined cellular and fibrinlike clotting reaction of *Limulus* to gram-negative endotoxin is an exquisitely sensitive mechanism, and probably an ancient one, that prevents loss of blood in the marine environment in which these gram-negative organisms predominate and, at the same time, prevents the organisms from entering the wounded animal. This sensitivity to endotoxin has been used, by J. Levin and others, as the basis of a specific test for minute amounts of endotoxin in biological fluids.

Virus diseases. A great variety of insect virus diseases have been identified. Among marine invertebrates there have been many recent discoveries of such agents, most of them the result of electron-microscope examination of tissues and fluids of diseased oysters, octopuses, and crabs. Morphologically, agents belonging to the poxviruses, herpesvirus, and papovaviruses have been found in many parts of the world. When methods for working with these agents in tissue culture have been developed, there will be rapid advances in this branch of virology.

An agent that affects the amebocytes of the

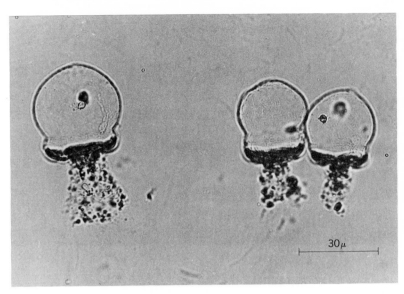

Fig. 1. Urn cells from a 4-day culture. The tails of mucus are short, as when the cells are normally scavenging noninfectious debris from the coelomic fluid. Cilia do not show because the ciliary motion is too rapid. *(From B. G. Bang and F. B. Bang, Amer. J. Pathol., 68 (2), 1972)*

shore crab *Carcinus* has been found in high titer in the blood of the animal. The disease is recognized by the loss of the ability of the amebocytes to form tight clots in the presence of cell extract. Infected animals recover from the disease, but they may continue to carry the agent. Although autointerference has been demonstrated in the blood of animals that have been infected for several days, its relationship to recovery from the illness is unknown.

Mucus secretion. The association of mucus secretion and its transport by cilia in a directional pattern of flow is a fundamental mechanism in a number of marine invertebrates that usually serves the purpose of collection of food or cleansing of surfaces. This mucociliary mechanism is fundamental to the cleansing (and protection against infection) of the respiratory mucosae of vertebrates. It has been specialized in a unique way in the "urn cells" of *Sipunculus*, which originate in the epithelial lining of the coelomic cavity, detach, and swim freely in the fluid, acting as scavengers of foreign particles. The urn consists of two cells, the anterior transparent one acting as a buffer against contact with other cells, and the posterior one secreting large streamers of mucus to which foreign material adheres, its collar of cilia throwing this material onto the mucus (Fig. 1). The numerous normal cells of the animal, including red cells, quiescent amebocytes, and gametes, do not stick to the mucus. Thus a degree of recognition of self and nonself is present within the mucus tail itself. Cantacuzène first showed the tremendous effectiveness of these cells in cleansing the body fluid of bacteria, and he followed the progress of recovery from infection within individual animals. Since this mucus-secreting cell system has no connection with the central nervous system, and the cells can be maintained in culture for as long as 2 weeks, the mucociliated urns offer a unique model for a study of the factors that

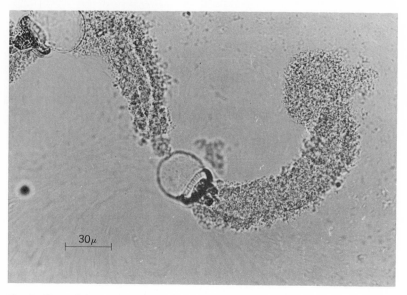

Fig. 2. Urn cell from a 4-day culture to which has been added one drop of filtered heated (90°C) serum from a *Sipunculus* that was injected with a marine vibrio that stimulated hypersecretion of the mucus of the urns in the injected host. *(From B. G. Bang and F. B. Bang, Amer. J. Pathol., 68 (2), 1972)*

initiate and maintain mucus secretion.

Mucus secretion in the living *Sipunculus* is greatly stimulated by infection with certain marine bacteria, but when the same bacteria are added to cultured urn cells, they usually fail to produce mucus. However, a powerful stimulus to mucus secretion in the laboratory was found to be present in the body fluid of acutely infected animals. This substance is heat-stable, withstanding boiling (Fig. 2). The increase in activity of the substance observed in laboratory tests may relate to the presence of an inhibitor within the body fluid of the normal animal; under normal conditions urns secrete very small mucus tails.

The poorly understood phenomenon of inhibition of ciliary motion of oyster gill fragments by sera from patients with cystic fibrosis, a disease of humans in which mucus secretion is inhibited, may have some connection. However, the possible usefulness of this urn cell system to the study of human pathology has not been explored.

For background information *see* ANTIBODY; IMMUNITY; INVERTEBRATE PATHOLOGY; PHAGOCYTOSIS in the McGraw-Hill Encyclopedia of Science and Technology.   [FREDERIK B. BANG]

Bibliography: F. B. Bang, *BioScience*, 23:584, 1973; F. B. Bang, *Bull. Johns Hopkins Hosp.*, 98: 325, 1956; R. G. MacFarlane (ed.), *The Haemostatic Mechanism in Man and Other Animals*, 1970; G. Salt, *The Cellular Defense Reactions of Insects*, 1970.

Invertebrate zoology

Some years ago there appeared in the textbooks the names of some animals of "unknown affiliation." Among these, a rare and little known organism, called *Trichoplax adhaerens*, was tentatively classified as a modified planula larva (phylum Cnidaria). In the last few years sufficient material was obtained from the Mediterranean Sea and the Red Sea to establish clones, and the organism has also

been found in Western Samoa. It has recently been studied in detail and has been placed in a phylum of its own, the Placozoa.

Characteristics of Trichoplax. The adult *Trichoplax* has a flat, pancake shape with a lobate outline (Fig. 1) and measures about 0.3 mm in diameter in juvenile specimens to about 2 mm in adults. Microscopic examination (Fig. 2) reveals an upper ciliated layer of cells, the upper epithelium or ectoderm, distinguished by the presence of many cells containing shining droplets, called Glanzkulgeln, and a lower ciliated layer, the lower epithelium or endoderm, with many glandular cells. Between these two layers there are mesenchyme cells, called fibroblasts. There are no organs, no differentiated muscle or nerve cells, and no specialized sense cells. The animal moves about in a random ameboid fashion without showing any polarity.

Trichoplax feeds principally on algae. Feeding behavior has been observed in individuals gliding about on the walls of an aquarium. The animal may be seen to glide about on the glass surface, now and then stopping to form a hump or invagination on the lower surface. This hump is a sort of temporary gastrulation and is thought to act as a temporary digestive cavity.

K. G. Grell and K. Marschall have both observed asexual reproduction in *Trichoplax* in the form of repeated fissions of the adult animal, producing many small individuals. Grell also reported cultivation of two strains of *Trichoplax*, one from the Mediterranean Sea and the other from the Red Sea. He put representatives of the clones of these two strains together and described development of eggs through cleavage into 2, 4, and 8 cells, and ultimate disintegration of the adults, liberating the embryos. Sperm cells were not seen. The occurrence of apparent sexual reproduction was attributed to putting the two strains together, which explains why no sexual reproduction has been observed among the individuals of only one strain.

Phylogeny and taxonomy. The place of *Trichoplax* in the phylogenetic scheme is in doubt; tentatively it is assigned to the new phylum Placozoa (Grell). In 1940 L. Hyman noted that *Trichoplax* and *Treptoplax*, having the construction of planulae, were actually modified planulae of Hydroidea. This was based on acceptance of the work of T.

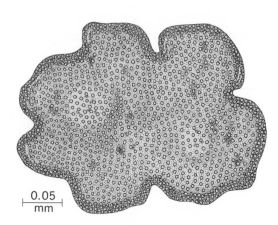

Fig. 1. *Trichoplax adhaerens*, small specimen. *(From K. G. Grell, Ency. Cinematogr., Film, E-1920, Gottingen, 1973)*

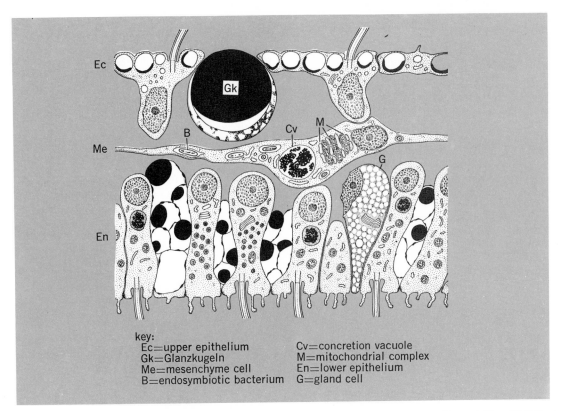

key:
Ec=upper epithelium
Gk=Glanzkugeln
Me=mesenchyme cell
B=endosymbiotic bacterium

Cv=concretion vacuole
M=mitochondrial complex
En=lower epithelium
G=gland cell

Fig. 2. Diagrammatic cross section showing the structure of *Trichoplax*. (From K. G. Grell, Einbildung und Furchung von Trichoplax adhaerens, Z. morph. Tiere, 73:297–314, 1972)

Krumbach, who attributed the "modified planula larva" to the hydromedusan *Eleutheria krohni* Krumbach. However, F. E. Schultz, who named the creature *Trichoplax adhaerens*, rejected Krumbach's statement; H. Schubotz also refuted this affiliation. In 1971 R. L. Miller reported that an animal which agrees in every detail with the published descriptions of *Trichoplax* was found on the walls of marine aquariums at Temple University. He described the animal as not being a coelenterate and as lacking all flatworm characteristics except the dorsoventral flattening.

While some workers consider the mesozoans as degenerate flatworms, Hyman took the position that they are a well-defined group with definite and rather remarkable characteristics which entitle them to the status of a phylum, and placed the phylum between Protozoa and Porifera—for want of exact knowledge as to where to place it. The mesozoans are all parasitic and have complex life cycles, making it difficult to know what the original free-living mesozoans would have been like, and to be certain of their phylogenetic affiliations. Because the Placozoa have two distinct specialized cell layers, it seems that they should certainly be placed above the Protozoa, and, assuming that the Mesozoa are not degenerate flatworms, above the Mesozoa. It is generally agreed that the Porifera diverged from the rest of the animal kingdom so early in evolution that they deserve their status as Parazoa. The Placozoa seem closer to, and very near the bottom of, the main line of metazoan evolution.

For background information *see* ANIMAL KINGDOM; ANIMAL SYSTEMATICS; TAXONOMY in the McGraw-Hill Encyclopedia of Science and Technology.

[RALPH BUCHSBAUM]

Bibliography: K. G. Grell, *Ency. Cinematogr., Film, E-1920*, Gottingen, 1973; K. G. Grell, *Zeitschr. morph. Tiere*, 73:297–314, 1972; K. G. Grell and G. Benwitz, *Cytobiologie*, 4:216–240, 1971; R. L. Miller, *Biol. Bull.*, 141:374, 1971.

Irrigation of crops

Recent research has provided new knowledge on managing irrigation water to decrease the degrading effects of irrigation on the mineral quality of drainage water and to increase crop yield and quality by effective use of sprinkler irrigation.

In sprinkler irrigation, water is exposed to the atmosphere, which enhances evaporation. The evaporation process cools the droplets, increases the heat absorbed by the droplets from the air through which they pass, and adds water vapor to the atmosphere. It has also been determined that the plant as well as its environment can be cooled with water applied by sprinklers.

Drainage water quality. The quality of drainage water from irrigated lands is influenced by the quality of the applied water, the leaching fraction (the fraction of the water infiltrating the soil and passing through it to become drainage water), the dissolving and precipitating of salts and minerals in the soil, soil properties, chemical amendments and fertilizers applied to the soil, and the removal of salts and minerals in crops. Recent research has increased the understanding of these factors. All natural irrigation waters contain some salts, and the quality of these waters for irrigation depends upon the total concentration and composition of the salts they contain.

Part of the water infiltrating the soil is removed in a pure state by evapotranspiration. Thus, the salts once contained in that fraction of the water are left behind and, except for the small quantity absorbed by plants, are concentrated in the water remaining in the soil. Much of this remaining water with its increased salt load will subsequently become drainage water reaching either ground or surface waters. Therefore, irrigating to produce crops increases the salt or mineral concentration in water and thus degrades the quality of water for subsequent uses.

Quality of applied water. The salt concentration in the irrigation water is a major factor influencing the salt concentration in drainage water that has percolated through the soil. Researchers at the United States Salinity Laboratory, Riverside, CA, have shown that the salt concentration of drainage water may vary about tenfold when a soil is irrigated with waters with a salt concentration range representative of typical western United States rivers. Concentrations of specific ions in drainage waters are also influenced by the concentrations of these same ions in the irrigation water.

When sufficient irrigation water was applied so that 0.1 of it passed from the soil as drainage water (leaching fraction = 0.1), the salt concentration in the drainage water was about six times that in the original irrigation water as measured by electrical conductivity, or EC (Table 1), except for the purest irrigation water (EC = 0.10) for which the increase was much greater. Much of the drainage water from irrigated lands returns to rivers and, after mixing with river water, is reused to irrigate lands downstream. Each time water is reused for irrigation, its salt concentration is greater than when it was used before, and each time more salt is picked up as the water passes through the soil and the salt concentration increases in the drainage water. Thus, in irrigated areas the mineral quality of river waters decreases downstream from the first irrigation project. In the lower reaches of some rivers, the quality of the water is so poor that the water is not suitable for irrigation.

Leaching fraction. The fraction of water infil-

trating the soil and appearing as drainage water is known as the leaching fraction. It approximates the amount of water applied in excess of evapotranspiration requirements. Some leaching is required to avoid salt accumulation to a concentration harmful to growing plants. The leaching fraction influences both the salt concentration in the drainage water and the total salt output from irrigated land. When the leaching fraction is increased from 0.1 to 0.3, the salt concentration in the drainage water is decreased (Table 1). However, the threefold increase in the leaching fraction results in less than a threefold decrease in the drainage water salt concentration. This means that the total salt output from irrigated land generally increases as the leaching fraction increases. For a 203,000-acre irrigated tract in southern Idaho with a leaching fraction of 0.5, the salt concentration in the drainage water was 2.26 times that in the irrigation water. If the increase in salt concentration had resulted only from evapotranspiration, the increase would have been 2.0 times. The additional increase of 0.26 times arises from dissolving minerals in the soil, and perhaps other factors.

Recent research results indicate that the leaching fraction should be kept as low as possible to prevent salts from concentrating in the soil and harming plants, because the lower the leaching fraction, the lower the total salt outflow and the less the subsequent mineral quality degradation of surface and groundwaters.

Salts and minerals in soil. Some soils contain deposits of soluble salts resulting from geologic and climatic processes. When irrigation water flows through soil with such salt deposits, large quantities of salts dissolve, and drainage water from such soils has an extremely high salt concentration. Also, many soils in arid areas contain enough soluble salt so that drainage waters during the first few years of irrigation contain high salt concentrations. Later, as these salts are leached out of the soil, the salt concentration in the drainage water decreases.

Some salts such as sodium chloride (NaCl) are highly soluble, others such as gypsum (CaSO₄ · 2H₂O) are sparingly soluble, and still others such as lime (CaCO₃) are only slightly soluble. Also, some soil minerals are more soluble than others. Therefore, large quantities of salt are leached from some soils and only small quantities from others. For example, 12 tons of salt per acre each year is carried by drainage water into the Colorado River from a study area in the Grande Valley, CO. In contrast, only 1 ton per acre per year was leached from a large tract in southern Idaho.

Soil properties. Many processes take place in irrigated soils, including exchange reactions involving salinity ionic components, oxidation and reduction reactions, and pH changes. These processes all influence the salt concentration in drainage water. Some soils contain CaCO₃, which controls pH and many soil reactions in the soil, which in turn influence the quality of drainage water.

Chemical amendments and fertilizers. The application of chemical amendments, such as lime or gypsum, can markedly influence the salt concentration and composition of drainage water. Apply-

Table 1. Influence of the salt concentration in irrigation water and the leaching fraction on the salt concentration in drainage water of soils containing CaCO₃*

Irrigation water†	Leaching fraction	Drainage water†
0.10	0.1	1.84
0.10	0.2	1.45
0.10	0.3	1.17
0.91	0.1	5.66
0.91	0.2	3.12
0.91	0.2	2.65
1.27	0.1	7.27
1.27	0.2	4.56
1.27	0.3	3.59
3.26	0.1	17.72
3.26	0.2	9.63
3.26	0.3	8.30

*Data from J. D. Rhoades et al., in *Proc. Soil Sci. Soc. Amer.*, 37:770–774, 1973.

†Salt concentration is measured by electrical conductivity in mmhos/cm.

ing such amendments can increase water infiltration, change soil aeration, and supply ions for exchange processes. All of these factors influence the quality of drainage waters. Similarly, fertilizers can influence drainage water quality, although their effects are usually small because relatively small quantities are applied. Nitrogen fertilizers can influence the nitrate concentration in drainage water if sufficient water is applied to leach some of the fertilizer through the soil. *See* SOIL.

Removal of salts and minerals in crops. Growing plants absorb small amounts of various minerals supplied by the soil, the irrigation water, or applied fertilizers. In most irrigated areas, the amount of mineral salts removed by plants represents such a small fraction of the total salt in the soil that its influence on drainage water quality can be neglected. Only when irrigation water contains an unusually low salt concentration does this factor have a significant effect, which would be lowering the salt concentration in the drainage water.

[DAVID L. CARTER]

Changes in plant microclimate. The increase in atmospheric vapor pressure and decrease in air temperature in sprinkler irrigation are of interest in crop production, because significant changes in these microclimatic variables could either benefit or retard plant growth, depending on existing weather conditions and plant environmental requirements. Under warm weather conditions, growth of cool-season crop might be improved, but growth of a warm-season crop might be retarded. Changes in air temperature above the crop will not be large, however, usually less than 1°C downwind from a sprinkler line.

Evaporation processes. Changes in vapor pressure and air temperature just above the crop surface depend directly on the amount of water evaporated. Generally, the total evaporation includes the evaporation from the spray plus that from the wetted foliage and transpiration. Wetted-foliage evaporation under sprinkler irrigation has been studied with fully established forage crops under arid conditions. The results showed that evapotranspiration from the wetted foliage was approximately equal to that from nonwetted, actively growing foliage when the crop had adequate soil moisture. Therefore, the influence of sprinklers on air temperature and vapor pressure over a well-watered crop would be mainly from spray evaporation.

The relatively short time of flight of the water droplets from nozzle to crop surface (usually less than 2 sec) and the very small volume of air in contact with the disintegrating jet severely limit the amount of heat that can be absorbed. Thus, a relatively small amount of evaporation occurs. Both I. Seginer and F. Robinson found that under arid conditions spray evaporation loss was less than 5% of the water discharged from standard agricultural sprinklers. At wind speeds of 2 to 3 m/sec, a 6% evaporation loss should reduce temperature 1°C or less and increase vapor pressure about 0.5 mb in the 1- to 2-m zone above the crop.

Downwind effects. R. Kohl and J. Wright measured the changes in air temperature and vapor pressure downwind from an operating sprinkler lateral under the semiarid conditions of southern

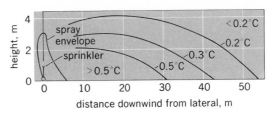

Fig. 1. Dry-bulb temperature depression downward from an operating sprinkler lateral. (*From R. A. Kohl and J. L. Wright, Air temperature and vapor pressure changes caused by sprinkler irrigation, Agron. J., 66(1):85–87, 1974*)

Idaho. They found that the air temperature was generally reduced less than 0.6°C. Figure 1 illustrates the degree of cooling found downwind from an operating sprinkler lateral.

The reduction in atmospheric cooling with elevation and distance downwind results from rapid vertical mixing by eddy diffusion. The magnitude of the changes in the horizontal direction is not expected to increase much with reduced wind speed, since strong vertical mixing exists under such conditions during the summer daylight hours.

For the most part, the addition of evaporated water vapor to the air passing through the spray is an adiabatic process. Adiabatic evaporation reduces the dry-bulb temperature and increases the vapor pressure, but does not change the wet-bulb temperature. Experimental data indicated that the wet-bulb temperature did not change significantly since the increase in vapor pressure due to spray evaporation was less than 0.8 mb.

As a rotating sprinkler applies water from a jet, at a given instant the droplets contact a very small portion of the air volume in the first 2 m above the crop. Therefore, a large change in temperature and vapor pressure from a single operating lateral cannot be expected.

Usually the magnitude of these changes is less than the modification in temperature and vapor pressure near the ground as dry air passes over an actively growing, well-watered crop. D. DeVries and J. Birch, comparing irrigated and dryland pastures in Australia, found temperatures 1 to 2°C lower, and vapor pressures 0.7 to 2.0 mb higher at the 1.25-m height 1 to 5 km inside the irrigated land. Thus, an actively transpiring crop significantly changes the microclimate in its vicinity because of the evaporative cooling process taking place over a large area.

Since the effect of an operating sprinkler lateral is dissipated downwind by vertical mixing, evaporative cooling within an irrigated area has a greater influence on air temperature and vapor pressure than a few sprinkler laterals. However, the effect of evaporative cooling resulting from sprinkler water evaporating from plant foliage is another subject and can be significant. [R. A. KOHL]

Changes in plant temperature. Significant advances have been made in predicting changes in plant, air, and soil temperature that result from evaporative cooling. Some reported increases in yield and quality attributed to lowering plant temperature by mist irrigation may not have been directly due to cooling, but to improved irrigation water management. Some studies in moderate climates show that misting and consequent lowering of plant and soil temperatures lowered yield and quality of some crops.

Mathematical models. Mathematical models are available to predict the change in plant temperature under various environmental conditions. Except for short periods of time, plants exposed to full sunlight seldom are at the same temperature as the ambient air. The plant temperature is in balance with the dissipation of heat energy that is absorbed. Plant surfaces gain heat from solar radiation and lose it by long-wave radiation to the atmosphere and the soil surface, by evaporation which converts sensible and radiant heat energy to latent heat, and by photosynthesis which converts a small amount of radiant energy to chemical energy. Mathematical models of leaf temperature show that leaf temperatures increase as the direct angle of the sun increases, and decrease with the square root or $\frac{2}{3}$ power of wind speed and the rate of transpiration. The temperature of the wetted portion of the plant cannot decrease below the psychrometric wet-bulb temperature, which is related to relative humidity and air temperature (Table 2).

Leaf temperature. Under arid conditions with low relative humidity when the saturation deficit (the difference between saturation vapor pressure and the actual vapor pressure in the air) is high, leaf temperatures tend to be lower than air temperature for several days after a thorough irrigation. As soil moisture decreases, the difference between leaf temperature and air temperature decreases. When most of the soil water has been depleted, leaf temperature may exceed air temperature. Under humid conditions the saturation deficit is usually relatively low. Under these conditions leaf temperatures are often 5 to 10°C above ambient air temperature and increase as available soil moisture decreases. The temperature of leaves drops very rapidly when wetted. Potato and cotton leaves decrease 10 to 12°C when wetted, but within 10 to 15 min generally return to the original temperatures as the water on the leaf surfaces evaporates. Since leaves of most farm crops are very thin, they have a large surface area per unit of mass. Heat gained from solar radiation is lost by transpiration, reradiation, and convection. Convection is closely related to wind speed and tends to dominate leaf temperatures when soil moisture is adequate.

Bud temperature. Plant components such as the buds on fruit trees and small stems have a relatively small surface area per unit mass. When they are wetted by sprinklers, they tend to approach the wet-bulb temperature, especially in the spring when solar radiation is low. J. Alfaro and coworkers used automatic sprinklers which operated when air temperature exceeded 5°C to keep the buds wet during the daytime hours. The wetted buds remained below air temperature and near the wet-bulb temperature during the day. By wetting the buds, their development is delayed and the probability of damage due to late spring frost when the trees would normally be in full bloom is reduced.

Cooling fruit. Overhead sprinkler irrigation has been used for many years to cool fruit such as apples, pears, and avocados. C. Unrath found that apples exposed to the sun in North Carolina often reached temperatures 8 to 11°C higher than air temperature, when air temperature exceeded 30°C. Misted fruit was 3 to 5°C cooler than air during the same period. Automatically activating the sprinkler system when temperatures exceed 30°C improved the quality of the apples by increasing the area of solid red color. Misting pears decreased their core temperature about 8°C. Prunes exposed to the sun were cooled 6 to 8°C when sprinkled, but shaded fruit was not affected as much.

Vineyards. Air temperatures often exceed 30°C and may reach 40 to 45°C in the San Joaquin Valley of California. Sprinkling vineyards using solid set sprinklers when temperatures exceed 30°C lowered air temperatures 4 to 6°C. The bulk of the temperature decrease occurred within the first 3 min. In about 15 min, leaf temperatures were about the same as before sprinkling. Leaf petiole temperature was decreased 8 to 14°C by sprinkling, and grape berry temperature was decreased 6 to 11°C. Sprinkling tended to lower the sugar content and increase the total acid, which suggested that sprinkling delays maturity and harvest date.

Effect on potatoes. In Minnesota, mist irrigation on potatoes decreased air temperatures within the canopy as much as 5 to 10°C in the upper part and 15 to 20°C in the middle part. The effect on growth and development, however, resulted in more small tubers of lower quality.

Optimum temperatures. Results to date indicate that evaporative cooling has been used to reduce apparent temperature stress when the plant may not have been adversely affected by the moderate temperatures under some conditions. Studies by K. Krogman and W. Torfason indicate that, if potatoes are adequately irrigated, misting the plant to lower the leaf temperatures has no beneficial effect. Optimum plant growth temperatures are needed, as are temperatures at which detrimental effects may occur within the leaf, flower, fruit, or other portions of the plant. Recent studies by C. Tanner and S. Goltz indicate that very high temperatures can occur in seed onion umbels. Excessively high temperatures produce sun scald, with desiccated and aborted florets on the sunlit side of the umbels. An umbel has few stomata, and consequently, its temperature is strongly regulated by convective heat transfer. In Wisconsin, umbel temperatures may exceed air temperature by as much as 25°C at wind speeds between 50 and 100 cm/sec, but only about 10°C at wind speeds of 250 to 350 cm/sec.

Table 2. Relationship of relative humidity to air temperature and wet-bulb temperatures for wetted portions of plant

Relative humidity, %	Wet-bulb temperature, °C, at air temperature of:		
	20°C	30°C	40°C
20	9	16	22
40	12	20	28
60	15	24	33
80	18	27	37

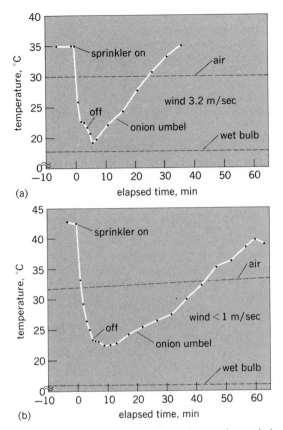

Fig. 2. Temperature of open florets in an onion umbel that has been wetted by sprinkler-applied water in Kimberly, ID. (a) Temperature changes that occur with moderate wind speeds; (b) changes that occur with low wind speeds. (*Unpublished data of J. L. Wright, J. L. Stevens, and M. J. Brown, ARS, Kimberly*)

Figure 2 shows that because of the ability of the seed head to retain water, sprinkling the onion umbel can reduce floret temperatures as much as 20°C and their temperatures will remain below air temperatures for about 20 to 40 min. With moderate wind speeds, the temperature of open florets was 5°C above air temperature and sprinkling lowered it 15°C. The temperature returned to ambient air temperature in about 25 min. With low wind speeds, open floret temperature was about 10°C above air temperature and the misted umbel remained below air temperature for about 40 min.

Evaporative cooling to enhance the quantity and quality of crop production has many possibilities. However, optimum temperature must be delineated and maintained relative to other microclimate conditions. Also economic systems must be developed to automatically control and supply small amounts of water frequently throughout the day when air temperatures exceed critical levels.

For background information *see* IRRIGATION OF CROPS; LAND DRAINAGE (AGRICULTURE); PLANT, WATER RELATIONS OF in the McGraw-Hill Encyclopedia of Science and Technology.

[MARVIN E. JENSEN]

Bibliography: J. F. Alfaro et al., *Preventive Freeze Protection by Preseason Sprinkling to Delay Bud Development*, ASAE Pap. 73-2531, 1971; C. A. Bower, in J. van Schilfgaarde, ed., *Drainage for Agriculture*, chap. 17, 1974; D. L. Carter, C. W. Robbins, and J. A. Bondurant, *Agricultural Research Service Publ. ARS-W-4*, 1973; D. A. DeVries and J. W. Birch, *Austr. J. Agr. Res.*, 12:260–262, 1961; R. A. Kohl and J. L. Wright, *Agron J.*, 66(1): 85–87, 1974; K. K. Krogman and W. E. Torfason, *Amer. Potato J.*, 50(4):133–137, 1973; J. D. Rhoades et al., in *Proc. Soil Sci. Soc. Amer.*, 37: 770–774, 1973; F. E. Robinson, *Agron. J.*, 65:130, 1973; I. Seginer, *Agr. Meteorol.*, 4:281–291, 1966; G. V. Skogerboe and W. R. Walker, *J. Environ. Qual.*, 2:377–382, 1973; C. B. Tanner and S. M. Goltz, *J. Amer. Hort. Sci.*, 97(1):5–9, 1972; C. R. Unrath, *J. Amer. Hort. Sci.*, 97(1):58–61, 1972.

Isotope (stable) separation

Laser techniques offer the promise of a new class of isotope separation processes with the capability of large separation factors and high capacity. The application of laser photoseparation to the enrichment of uranium is of great interest and is presently under investigation in several laboratories.

Laser photoseparation can, in principle, be used for the isotopes of any element. For many isotopes, laser processes may be inexpensive compared with more conventional isotope separation processes, although research is, at this time, too preliminary for reliable economic estimates to be made.

The earliest suggestions for the photochemical separation of isotopes appeared shortly after the discovery of the spectroscopic isotope effect. Several early processes were demonstrated on a laboratory scale but showed little commercial promise because of the lack of suitable light sources. Renewed interest in the photoseparation of isotopes has resulted from recent progress in the development of tunable lasers. During the past few years the stability, line width, and intensity of these sources have advanced to the point that a chosen isotope in an isotopic mixture of atoms or molecules can be excited by the selective absorption of light. Furthermore, the development of lasers with the power required for the separation of isotopes on a commercial scale now appears feasible.

Physical basis for laser photoseparation. There are many possibilities for laser photoseparation processes. All photoseparation schemes, however, are based on the spectroscopic isotope effect. The excited states of any atom, or molecule, can assume only certain allowed energy values, which depend upon the nuclear isotopic mass. In the illustration the energy levels for two isotopes of a given atom, or molecule, containing different isotopes Is_1 and Is_2 are shown schematically. Some of the allowed energy levels are different for Is_1 and Is_2. The energy difference between corresponding energy levels, or isotope effect, in atoms can be as large as $1:10^4$, although, more generally, it is of the order of $1:10^6$. The isotope effect for the vibrational and rotational levels of molecules is generally larger and may be greater than $1:10^3$.

If the isotope effect shifts an absorption line of one isotope, or isotopic molecule, to a spectral region in which the other isotopes do not absorb light, the selective excitation of that isotope is possible. The possibility for selective excitation is the

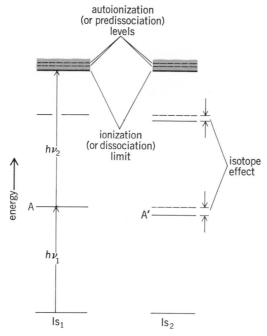

Schematic energy-level diagrams for two isotopes of a given element, Is_1 and Is_2, showing the spectroscopic isotope effect.

key to laser photoseparation, although several other conditions must be met as well.

These conditions will be briefly summarized. The widths of the chosen absorption lines for the various isotopes must be narrow enough that the lines from the different isotopes do not overlap. In addition, the selectively excited atom, or molecule, must remain in the excited state long enough for a subsequent process to occur that results in the extraction of the excited isotope. After extraction, the interaction between the feed stream and the enriched product must be such that isotopic remixing, or scrambling, does not occur.

Lasers used in photoseparation processes must also have certain characteristics. Obviously the wavelength of the laser must coincide with that of the absorption line corresponding to the isotope to be excited. The spectral width of the laser must be less than the isotope effect. The stability of the laser must be such that it can be locked to the absorption line of one isotope. These conditions generally require a tunable laser, since coincidence between fixed-wavelength lasers and isotopic absorption lines is very rare.

Following the isotopically selective excitation, the excited isotope must be extracted. The method of extraction varies according to the photoseparation process. The simplest extraction method is the two-step photoionization process. After the selective excitation of an intermediate energy level, by the absorption of a photon with energy $h\nu_1$ — level A in the illustration, for example — subsequent absorption of a photon with energy $h\nu_2$ will ionize Is_1. Isotope Is_2, however, is unaffected by either $h\nu_1$ or $h\nu_2$, since neither photon coincides with the characteristic absorption lines of Is_2. Is_1 ions can then be separated from the neutral Is_2

atoms by an electric field, or by a combination of electric and magnetic fields.

Two-step photoionization can also be used with isotopic mixtures of molecules. In this case the isotopically selective step could be the excitation of a molecular vibrational state rather than an excited electronic state, as in the atomic example. Processes of this type are not as attractive for molecules as the two-step photodissociation process described below is, because the energy required to remove an electron is generally greater than that required for photodissociation.

Another possible way to extract the excited atom or molecule is to cause it to undergo a sensitized chemical reaction while in state A. The reaction must yield a product having chemical or physical properties that are different from those of the feed stream. Although such processes have not been reported for laser photoseparation, a reaction between mercury and water vapor induced by the absorption of a single photon has been studied in detail and has been used to produce enriched mercury on a small scale.

In molecular systems the dissociation limit can play the role filled by the ionization limit in the atomic case. Separation processes can involve the absorption of one or two photons. In a two-photon process, absorption of the first photon $h\nu_1$ is the isotopically selective step. A photon of energy $h\nu_2$ dissociates molecule Is_1 but leaves Is_2 unaffected. If the dissociation products have vapor pressures that are different from that of the feed, the isotopically enriched product can be extracted by condensation.

A variant of this process, involving selective excitation and simultaneous dissociation by a single photon, is also possible. In this case the excited state is a discrete level lying above the dissociation limit, a so-called predissociation state. Some molecules, formaldehyde, for example, have predissociation states that meet the criteria laid down above for selective excitation and can be used in photoseparation processes.

Results of photoseparation experiments. Of principal interest in the early reports of laser photoseparation are those of C. B. Moore and V. S. Letokhov, which deal respectively with the photoseparation of hydrogen and nitrogen isotopes.

In Moore's experiments, the ultraviolet (second-harmonic) output of a ruby laser was used to excite formaldehyde to a predissociation state. Molecules containing deuterium were selectively excited and yielded a dissociation product that was enriched.

Letokhov demonstrated the separation of nitrogen isotopes by using isotopically selective excitation of ammonia by a CO_2 laser. The selectively excited ammonia was dissociated with ultraviolet light from a spark source to yield enriched nitrogen.

The laser photoseparation of the isotopes of calcium, bromine, boron, and barium were reported for the first time at the 8th International Conference on Quantum Electronics.

Several groups have reported success in the photoseparation of uranium isotopes; for example, a selective two-step photoionization process was described recently by S. A. Tuccio and coworkers. In this experiment a tunable dye laser was used to excite ^{235}U atoms in a beam of natural uranium. After ionization of the excited atoms by ultraviolet light, the ^{235}U ions were separated by an electric field.

Although the technical feasibility of the laser photoseparation of isotopes has been demonstrated for at least seven elements, the early experiments have not demonstrated the high-throughput, low-cost aspects of the process, for which there is great hope. Research on laser photoseparation, particularly as applied to uranium, is increasing very rapidly. Answers to economic and scaling questions will surely be forthcoming during the next few years.

For background information *see* ISOTOPE (STABLE) SEPARATION in the McGraw-Hill Encyclopedia of Science and Technology.

[BENJAMIN B. SNAVELY]

Bibliography: V. S. Letokhov, *Science*, 180:451, 1973; S. A. Tuccio et al., Two-step selective photoionization of ^{235}U in uranium vapor, Paper Q.14, *8th International Quantum Electronics Conference*, June 1974; E. S. Yeung and C. B. Moore, *Appl. Phys. Lett.*, 21:109, 1972.

Jupiter

The encounter with Jupiter by the space probe *Pioneer 10* has provided new knowledge of the giant planet. The preliminary results of the encounter were presented in a series of papers by C. F. Hall and the Pioneer investigators.

Jupiter is the largest planet of the solar system. Its mass is 318 times the mass of the Earth, and its diameter is 11 times the Earth's diameter. Jupiter moves in an orbit with a mean distance from the Sun of 5.2 astronomical units. Because of its great distance from the Earth, only the planet's directly sunlit face can be seen from ground-based telescopes. The features that can be seen from the Earth are continually changing; and strong, sporadic radio emissions indicate that violent physical processes are occurring in the atmosphere and magnetosphere.

Magnetosphere. Decimetric-wavelength radio emissions from Jupiter have been interpreted as synchrotron radiation from relativistic energy electrons trapped in a strong magnetic field. These observations, made in 1954 and 1955, were the first evidence that Jupiter possessed a magnetic field. Synchrotron radiation provides information on the combined effect of the electron energy flux and the magnetic field strength. It does not provide separable data on the individual parameters, nor does it give information on the presence of nonrelativistic energy electrons or of protons of any energy. With this fact in mind, the instruments for *Pioneer 10* were selected to measure individually the parameters of the Jovian magnetosphere (see illustration).

The first direct measurements of the Jovian magnetic field were made when *Pioneer 10* crossed the Jovian bowshock (the shock wave set up by the interaction of the supersonic solar wind with Jupiter's magnetic field) near 108 Jovian radii (R_j; 1 Jovian radius equals 70,850 km). The spacecraft approached Jupiter from 14° south latitude at a Sun-planet-spacecraft angle of 35°, and it exited at an angle near 100°. This trajectory was selected to carry *Pioneer 10* through the most intense region of the trapped radiation belt. At the bowshock the magnetometer observed an increase in the magnetic field from 0.5 to 1.5 gammas (1 gamma equals 10^{-5} gauss). The magnetosheath was observed at 96 R_j and again at 50 R_j during the inbound pass. When the spacecraft entered the magnetosphere proper at 94 R_j, the field rose to 5 gammas. When the bowshock swept over the spacecraft at 50 R_j, the field dropped to 1 gamma, and it remained near this value into nearly 25 R_j. The field retained a configuration similar to that in the Earth's magnetospheric tail. At about 25 R_j the field took on the form of a dipole field, and it began increasing until it reached a strength of 18,500 gammas at the point of closest approach to the planet (130,000 km above the cloud tops). This corresponds to a surface field of about 4 gauss. For comparison, the Earth's field at this latitude would be about 0.35 gauss.

The Jovian dipole magnetic field appears to be inclined 10.6° to the planet's axis of rotation, and it is offset from the center of the planet about 0.11 R_j toward latitude 16° and longitude 176° in system III, which is the coordinate system based on the location of the radio emissions. The plane of the dipole lies in the meridian plane of 222°, also in system III. The Jovian magnetic field measurements are somewhat at variance with the strength derived from radio data, but agree in tilt angle. The Jovian field observed by Pioneer is approximately half the moment determined from radio data. Several radio models have also predicted an offset of several tenths of a Jovian radius, which Pioneer has disproved. The trajectory at which *Pioneer 11* was to approach Jupiter was selected to give a latitudinal cut through the radiation belt and magnetic field. The *Pioneer 11* data should provide information to resolve unquestionably the strength and configuration of Jupiter's magnetic field.

On the outbound pass of the spacecraft, the magnetospheric bowshock appeared to pass back and forth over the spacecraft. Seventeen bowshock crossings were observed by the plasma analyzer, the last at a distance of 240 R_j. This has led several of the Pioneer investigators to conclude that the Jovian magnetosphere is inflated with a thermal energy plasma, which is highly responsive to small changes in the velocity and density of the solar wind.

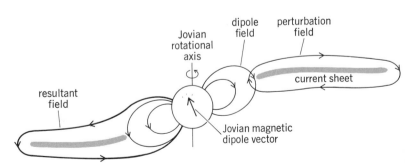

The system of Jovian magnetosphere currents as deduced from instruments of *Pioneer 10*. The electric current system (current sheet) created by drift of ions and electrons in the magnetic field creates the perturbation field. The resultant field is the vector sum of the perturbation and dipole fields. (*Courtesy of E. J. Smith, Jet Propulsion Laboratory*)

The high-energy charged-particle detectors on *Pioneer 10* observed electrons and protons in the million-electron-volt (MeV) energy range inside the magnetosphere. The particles were observed in a flat disklike distribution from 96 R_j to 25 R_j. The particles were modulated with a distinct 10-hr period, which corresponds closely to the 9 hr 55 min rotational period of the planet. At approximately 25 to 27 R_j a transition region was observed similar to the change in magnetic field observed by the magnetometer. Within about 20 R_j the charged particles were in stable trapped orbits, similar to the Earth's Van Allen radiation belts. Electrons with energies greater than 3 MeV had a peak flux of 5×10^8 electrons/cm² sec, and for energies greater than 50 MeV, 1×10^7 electrons/cm² sec. The peak intensity of electrons was observed at the point of closest approach to the planet (2.8 R_j from the center of the planet). Protons with energies greater than 30 MeV reached a maximum flux of 4×10^6 protons/cm² sec. The protons peaked near 3.5 R_j, that is, before the electrons peaked. It is not possible with the present Pioneer data to determine whether this separation of peak intensities is a characteristic of the Jovian radiation belt, or whether it is an anomaly resulting from a disturbance of the magnetosphere by the Sun during the encounter. *Pioneer 11* should provide the data necessary to answer this question. The present analysis of the Jovian magnetic field data, plasma data, and charged-particle data has resulted in a preliminary configuration of the Jovian magnetosphere similar to the system shown in the figure.

Planetary atmosphere. The clouds of Jupiter have been a subject of strong scientific interest for many years. Earth-based pictures have shown a continuously changing cloud structure. The Great Red Spot has been of particular interest. The Red Spot is oval-shaped, 40,000 km in length and 13,000 km wide. As the diameter of the Earth is 12,756 km, three Earths would fit comfortably into the Great Red Spot. The Red Spot has been seen to appear and disappear and also to change coloration since its discovery in 1665. The pictures of Jupiter taken by *Pioneer 10* have shown that the Red Spot is not a unique feature of Jupiter. There are many smaller red spots distributed over the surface. The red spots appear to be areas of dark clouds that are rising and falling through the atmosphere. The Pioneer pictures also show a fine structure of cells and rings in the clouds, indicative of a highly turbulent atmosphere. A comparison of cloud motion between successive images has shown the existence of a jetstreamlike cloud formation moving at a speed of over 360 km/hr relative to the surrounding clouds.

Another major unknown of Jupiter has been its heat balance. Earth-based observations of the front face of the planet showed that Jupiter is radiating back into space more heat energy than it is receiving from the Sun. The most plausible explanation of the heat excess is that the planet is still undergoing gravitational contraction and it is emitting heat through this process. The infrared radiometer on Pioneer made the first measurements of the thermal radiation on the dusk and dark sides of the planet. The instrument continued to observe a heat output of about 2.25 times the solar input as it

passed around the planet. There were no temperature changes observed at the cloud top altitude as the spacecraft passed from the illuminated to the nonilluminated hemisphere.

Jupiter has a very complicated atmospheric structure, and more detailed spectroscopic measurements from future spacecraft will be required to resolve the thermal structure of the planet. The infrared radiometer determined a cloud top temperature of 130 K. The temperature derived from the radio occultation observations is much higher than this. The most likely explanation for this discrepancy is that an invisible cloud of aerosols exists above the visible cloud tops, and the radiometer and radio occultation measurements were actually taken at different altitudes.

Jovian satellites. Jupiter posesses 12 satellites. They can be divided roughly into the inner 5 and the outer 7. The 4 largest of the inner group were discovered by Galileo Galilei in 1610, after the invention of the telescope in 1608, and they are called the Galilean satellites. They range in distance from the center of Jupiter as follows: Io 5.9 R_j, Europa 9.4 R_j, Ganymede 15 R_j, Callisto 26.4 R_j.

Io is particularly interesting among the satellites. Sodium emissions have been observed by R. A. Brown and F. H. Chaffee from Io, and nitrogen may also be present in its atmosphere. An ionosphere has been detected from the radio occultation data. A density of 6×10^4 electrons/cm³ at an altitude of about 100 km has been detected on the day side of the satellite, and a density of 9×10^3 electrons/cm³ on the nightside. This corresponds to a neutral surface number density, that is, the density of neutral atoms at the surface of the satellite, of 10^{10} to 10^{12}/cm³. Io also appears to have a hydrogen torus associated with its orbit. This torus consists of ultraviolet radiation (hydrogen glow) emitted by a cloud of hydrogen atoms surrounding the satellite. The *Pioneer 10* ultraviolet photometer detected the presence of a hydrogen glow around Io, extending about 60° in front and 60° in back of Io. The charged-particle investigators have also observed the apparent sweeping out by Io of charged particles that have large pitch angles. The source of the hydrogen torus has been suggested as the emission of hydrogen from the surface under the bombardment of high-energy charged particles. Another unusual feature of Io is its density. The celestial mechanics experiment yielded a density for Io of 3.5 g/cm³. This is much higher than the density of Jupiter, but is quite close to the density of the Earth's moon and of Mars. The densities of the other Jovian satellites decrease progressively with their distance from Jupiter, similar to the decrease in density of the planets from Mercury outward to Jupiter.

Pioneer program. *Pioneer 10* was the first of two nearly identical spacecraft. It carried 11 scientific instruments to investigate the interplanetary medium, the asteroidal belt, and the near environment of Jupiter. In addition, a celestial mechanics experiment and a radio occultation experiment were carried out, using the S-band radio transmissions from the spacecraft.

The Pioneer spacecraft weighs 260 kg, of which 33 kg is devoted to scientific instruments. The

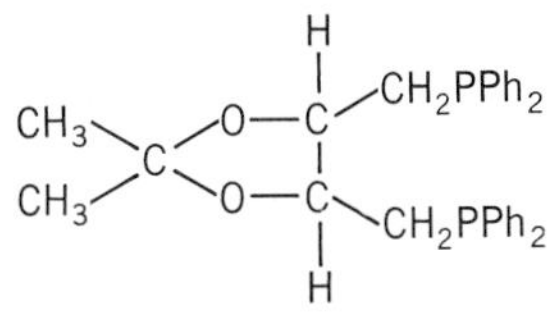

Fig. 1. Chelating diphosphine diop with asymmetry at carbon centers. Ph represents phenyl.

remainder is taken up by the spacecraft power supply, telecommunications system, spacecraft structure, and support systems. The Pioneers are powered by four SNAP-19 radioisotope thermoelectric generators, which provide about 140 W of power at Jupiter. Both spacecraft were launched from the Eastern Test Range in Florida aboard Atlas-Centaur TE-M-364-4 three-stage rockets. *Pioneer 10* was launched on March 3, 1972, and it reached its point of closest approach to Jupiter on Dec. 4, 1973. It is continuing outward, gathering scientific data. *Pioneer 10* will cross the orbit of Uranus in 1980 and will become the first artificial object to leave the solar system. *Pioneer 11* was launched on April 6, 1973, to encounter Jupiter in December 1974. *Pioneer 11* was planned to approach Jupiter from a high latitude, swing past the planet on the dawn side and approach to within about 0.6 R_j above the cloud tops, swing sharply around the planet, and depart in the direction of Saturn. If *Pioneer 11* survives, it will reach Saturn in September 1979. *See* SPACE PROBE.

For background information *see* JUPITER; MAGNETOSPHERE; SPACE PROBE in the McGraw-Hill Encyclopedia of Science and Technology.

[ALBERT G. OPP]

Bibliography: R. A. Brown and F. H. Chaffee, *Astrophys. J.*, 187:L125, 1974; C. F. Hall and Pioneer investigators, *Science*, 183(4122):301–324, Jan. 25, 1974; J. H. Wolfe and Pioneer investigators, *J. Geophys. Res.*, 79(25):3489–3700, Sept. 1, 1974.

Kinetics, chemical

The activation of molecular H_2 and molecular O_2 (increasingly referred to as "dihydrogen" and "dioxygen") by metals and metal complexes continues to be a research area of much interest. Recent developments in H_2 activation include the use of metal coordination compounds in solution for asymmetric hydrogenation, Eq. (1), and asymmetric hydroformylation, Eq. (2), where R_1, R_2, and R_3 are various functional groups and C^* represents a chiral carbon center. In addition, the attachment of certain metal complexes to polymers or inert resins has led to the development of supported (or heterogenized) homogeneous catalysts, which have considerable potential for commercial exploitation. Some supported catalysts (for hydrogenation as well as other catalytic reactions) preserve the high selectivity and activity of the homogeneous catalysts and operate at the same mild conditions. Detailed kinetic and mechanistic studies on these systems, in which homogeneous catalysis and heterogeneous catalysis appear to merge, and more meaningful comparison of the two kinds of catalysis, are beginning to appear.

$$R_1CH{=}CR_2R_3 + H_2 \rightarrow R_1CH_2{-}C^*HR_2R_3 \quad (1)$$

$$R_1CR_2{=}CH_2 + CO + H_2 \rightarrow R_1C^*HR_2{-}CH_2CHO \quad (2)$$

A major development in O_2 activation is the synthesis of several protein-free models for the active site of the oxygen-transporting proteins myoglobin and hemoglobin. Kinetic and thermodynamic studies of the reversible oxygenation equilibrium for the models are important so that the models can be compared with the protein systems to de-termine the role of the protein and other factors contributing to the stability of the oxyglobins.

Dihydrogen activation. In reaction (1), the addition of H_2 to the unsaturated precursor produces a chiral carbon center. Such a synthesis usually forms a DL-racemate product. However, by using a rhodium catalyst containing chiral phosphine ligands (designated L), some important α-amino acids, $R_1CH_2C^*H(NH_2)CO_2H$, have been synthesized with optical purities as high as 90%. The rhodium catalysts, effective at 1 atm H_2 and room temperature, have generally been prepared in situ in alcohol or benzene-alcohol media by adding the phosphine (L) to a labile rhodium (I) complex such as [Rh(diene)Cl]$_2$. Effective phosphines may have chirality on the phosphorus as in *o*-anisylmethylcyclohexylphosphine, or may have asymmetry in the side chain as in neo-menthyldiphenylphosphine or the chelating diphosphine (L$_2$) known as diop (Fig. 1).

The actual catalysts are probably cationic such as [Rh(diene)L$_2$]$^+$, which readily loses diene, or solvated RhClL$_2$ species. The hydride complex HRh [(+)diop]$_2$ is slower but otherwise equally effective. Kinetic and mechanistic studies on catalysts of the first two types, but with nonchiral phosphines such as triphenylphosphine, show that hydrogenation occurs via a rhodium(III) octahedral dihydrido-olefin intermediate with *cis*-phosphines, $H_2Rh(olefin)L_2X$, where X is Cl or solvent. Successive intramolecular hydrogen transfer steps give first a hydrido-alkyl intermediate and then a saturated product, with regenerated catalyst. Preliminary kinetic studies of the HRh(diop)$_2$ catalyst indicate a different mechanism, one which involves hydrogenolysis of an alkyl intermediate, shown in Eq. (3).

$$\text{HRh} + \text{Olefin} \rightarrow \text{HRh(olefin)} \rightarrow$$
$$\text{Rh(alkyl)} \xrightarrow{H_2} \text{HRh} + \text{Product} \quad (3)$$

Asymmetric hydroformylation of styrenes under mild conditions to give aldehyde products with up to 25% optical purity has been accomplished with reaction (2) with a catalyst prepared in situ by adding the diop ligand to the well-known hydroformylation catalyst HRh(CO)(PPh$_3$)$_3$.

These asymmetric syntheses must depend on the stereochemical rigidity of the intermediates. An important feature of the diop system is the rigid structure of the five-membered acetonide ring, whereas in the *o*-anisylmethylcyclohexylphosphine hydrogenation systems, hydrogen bonding from substrate to the phosphine methoxyl—as well as hindrance to free rotation of the *cis*-phosphines—is thought to be important. Detailed mechanistic studies should reveal information on the stereochemical pathways of these fascinating processes.

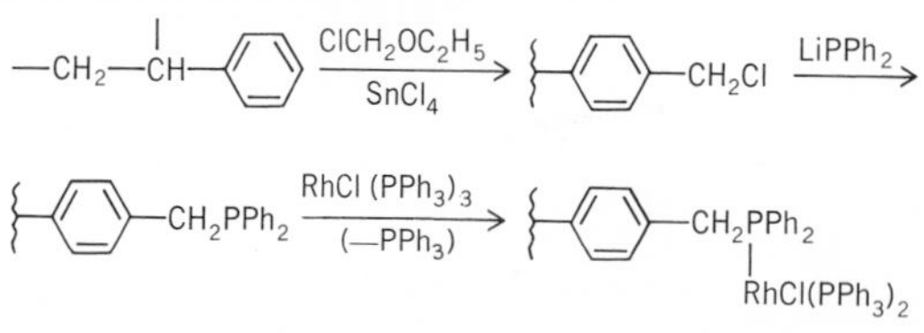

Fig. 2. Heterogenization of rhodium phosphine complex.

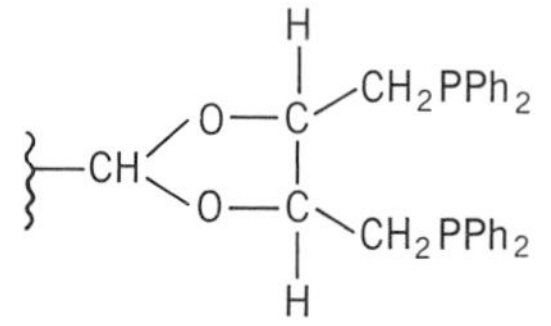

Fig. 3. Chiral phosphinated polymer used to develop a polymer-supported rhodium complex.

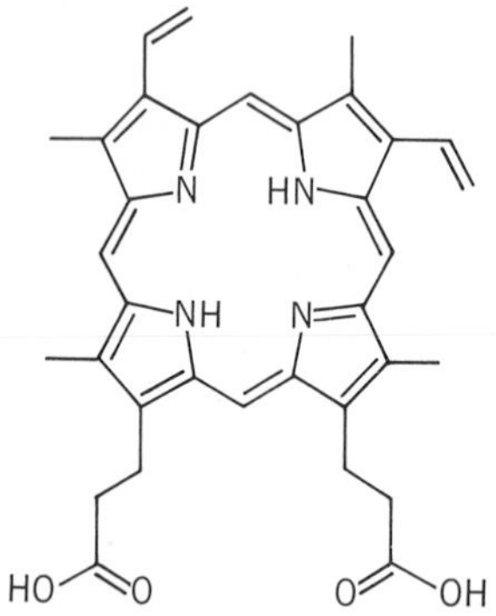

Fig. 4. Protoporphyrin IX. PpIX represents the dianion formed by loss of the two nitrogen-bonded protons.

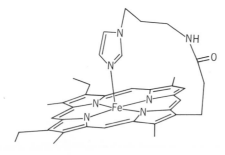

Fig. 5. Five-coordinate (imidazole)Fe(porphyrin) complex.

Supported catalysts. An obvious advantage in binding homogeneous catalysts to polymers is that after reaction the catalyst can be simply filtered off from the product solution and be ready for further use. Rhodium phosphine complexes of the type mentioned above have been heterogenized, for example, by coordination to diphenylphosphinomethyl resins prepared via chloromethylation of polystyrene cross-linked with divinylbenzene

(Fig. 2). The deep red beads of the product, suspended in benzene, were efficient for reduction of mono-olefins under 1 atm H_2 at 25°C. Hydrogen uptake plots fitted the same rate expression found for the well-studied homogeneous $RhCl(PPh_3)_3$ catalyst, and the same mechanism appears to operate (via the dihydrido-olefin intermediate mentioned above). An interesting selectivity based on olefin size was noted in the relative reduction rates: 1-hexene > cyclohexene > octadecene > cyclooctene > cyclododecene > Δ^2-cholestene. The reduction rate decreases as the olefin size increases, since reduction takes place inside the polymer bead. A model has been developed for calculating the change in effective catalyst concentration caused by changing the olefin size.

A similar polymer-supported rhodium complex has been developed using a chiral phosphinated unit closely related to diop. Treatment of the phosphinated polymer (Fig. 3) with $[RhCl(C_2H_4)_2]_2$ displaces the ethylene to give a heterogeneous analog of the soluble Rh-diop catalyst. The insoluble system suspended in benzene was, however, slower at ambient conditions than the soluble system for asymmetric hydrogenation of α-ethylstyrene and methyl atropate. The insoluble system also gave lower optical purities.

Dioxygen activation. In deoxymyoglobin the metal center is five-coordinate, high-spin Fe(II) with square-pyramidal coordination [(imidazole) Fe(PpIX)], the iron being some 0.7A (0.07 nm) out of the porphyrin ligand plane. The imidazole ring is that of a histidine residue in the globin protein chain, and PpIX is the dianion ligand formed from protoporphyrin IX (Fig. 4). On oxygenation a six-coordinate, low-spin $[FeO_2]$ complex is formed in which the iron fits into the porphyrin plane.

A problem in designing a model for myoglobin has been the difficulty of synthesizing a suitable high-spin, five-coordinate Fe(II) complex. Low-spin, six-coordinate complexes such as L_2Fe (porphyrin), where L is a nitrogen-base ligand, usually result, and reaction with O_2 generally leads to irreversible oxidation to Fe(III). In myoglobin the protein plays an important role in retarding the oxidation at body temperature. Both bimolecular and unimolecular processes have been proposed for this effect.

Iron(II) complexes. The synthesis of a protein-free five-coordinate (imidazole)Fe(porphyrin) complex (Fig. 5) has now been described, however. The solid complex binds O_2 reversibly at room temperature, although solutions of the complex show this property only at low temperature (−45°C). The complex is a pyrroporphyrin derivative with the axial imidazole held in the "correct" position via a seven-atom link (a substituted amide) to a pyrrole ring of the porphyrin. The crystal structure of a related complex (1-methylimidazole)Fe(L)O_2 − where the ligand L is a derivative of a readily synthesized tetraphenylporphyrin—has shown for the first time that iron porphyrins bind dioxygen in the bent, end-on fashion (shown as I) as opposed to the alternative side-on manner (II). Although kinetic studies have not yet appeared, thermodynamic data (from spectrophotometry) show that the complex in Fig. 5 binds O_2 at least 3800 times more strongly than does a similar complex with an axially held pyridine. The binding strength is attributed to the stronger π-donor ability of imidazole which serves to make the iron back-bond more strongly with the empty electronegative antibonding orbitals of oxygen. In myoglobin the histidine base must serve the same function.

$$\left(\begin{array}{c} Fe-O \\ \searrow \\ O \end{array} \right) \qquad \left(\begin{array}{c} O \\ Fe-\| \\ O \end{array} \right)$$

$$(I) \qquad\qquad (II)$$

Cobalt(II) complexes. Cobalt(II) is a $3d^7$ (seven electrons in the $3d$ shell) system and, unlike a $3d^6$ iron(II) system, readily forms five-coordinate, low-spin complexes of the type LCo(porphyrin), where L is a nitrogen ligand. These complexes also exhibit reversible oxygen binding, but low temperatures are required for 1:1 adduct formation since essentially irreversible oxidation to the trivalent state occurs at room temperature. Cobalt-substituted myoglobin and hemoglobin (coboglobin), which are also five-coordinate, low-spin complexes, exhibit reversible oxygen binding at 20°C. These cobalt systems also appear to bind O_2 in the end-on fashion, and to mimic the corresponding iron systems quite closely, although coboglobin's affinity for oxygen is 10 times less than that of hemoglobin. Preliminary kinetic data (from the temperature jump relaxation method with spectrophotometry) indicate that the rate constant for deoxygenation of a protein-free (1-methylimidazole)Co(PpIX) complex is considerably larger at 20°C than that for cobalt-myoglobin. This difference is ascribed to the protein controlling the oxygen dissociation directly (for example, by formation of a hydrogen bond) or indirectly (for example, by the cage effect). Thermodynamic data indicate that the reduced oxygen affinity for the protein-free system is a result mainly of a more negative entropy change which was attributed to unfavorable solvation of the O_2 adduct. In the protein system the O_2 fits into a hydrophobic pocket and solvation is less important.

Myoglobin and many other biological systems can be considered to operate as metal complexes "supported" on a large, semiordered protein polymer, and the advances being made in supported homogeneous catalysts and asymmetric synthesis suggest that studies toward improved model systems for metalloenzymes generally (with their well-known stereospecificity) will be intensified.

For background information *see* KINETICS, CHEMICAL in the McGraw-Hill Encyclopedia of Science and Technology.

[BRIAN R. JAMES]

Bibliography: C. K. Chang and T. G. Traylor, *J. Amer. Chem. Soc.*, 95:8477, 1973; J. P. Collman, R. R. Gagne, and C. A. Reed, *Chem. Eng. News*, p. 20, Jan. 21, 1974; W. R. Cullen, A. Fenster, and B. R. James, *Inorg. Nucl. Chem. Lett.*, 10:167, 1974; W. Dumont et al., *J. Amer. Chem. Soc.*, 95:8295, 1973; H. Yamamoto, F. J. Kayne, and T. Yonetani, *J. Biol. Chem.*, 249:691, 1974.

Laser, tunable

Lasers whose ouput frequencies can be continuously tuned through a wide range are now available from the vacuum ultraviolet to the far-infrared. These lasers are receiving increasing use in basic and applied research.

Available sources. Dye lasers are probably the most extensively used and most convenient of the currently available tunable lasers. They are pumped optically by other lasers or by flashlamps. Laser action takes place between the first excited and the ground electronic states, each of which comprises a broad vibrational-rotational continuum. Typically, the gain bandwidth of a dye laser is about 1000 cm^{-1} or larger, and without frequency-selective feedback, lasing occurs at the gain peak with a width of about 100 cm^{-1}. By incorporating frequency-selective elements such as gratings, prisms, or filters in the cavity, the dye laser output can be narrowed, without loss of power, and continuously tuned. One recent innovation has been a new type of mirrorless resonator: distributed feedback (DFB), which consists of a periodicity of the gain or reflective index (or both) throughout the laser medium. Significant progress has also been made in obtaining single longitudinal-mode operation, in controlling transverse-mode structure, and in improving frequency stability. Pulsed dye lasers are presently available, using a variety of dyes, in the spectral range from about 0.42 to about 0.7 μm. They are pumped by powerful flashlamps or pulsed lasers and have outputs up to several megawatts, with pulse widths from a few nanoseconds to around a millisecond. Using both ultraviolet and visible lines from an argon laser and the red line of a krypton laser, CW (continuous-wave) dye lasers have been operated from 0.31 to about 1.2 μm with a maximum power output of several watts. Up to 0.5 W of single axial mode output has also been obtained. A number of new, highly efficient laser dyes have been developed. Another recent achievement has been the mode-locking of the rhodamine 6G CW dye laser, to produce continuous trains of picosecond pulses as short as 0.5 ps.

Obviously, it would be extremely desirable to have dye lasers pumped directly by an electrical discharge. An important advance in this direction has been the achievement of (optically pumped) vapor-phase dye lasers. The scintillator dye PO-POP, heated in an oven to a vapor pressure of about 10 torrs (1.3 kilopascals), when pumped with 400 kW of ultraviolet light from a nitrogen laser, has produced 30 kW of tunable laser output. Importantly, it has been found that, as in liquid dye lasers, the spectral width of the output could still be narrowed without loss of power. This result was not fully expected. A number of other dyes have also been made to lase in the vapor phase, and this field is currently very active.

The spin-flip Raman laser uses a fixed-frequency laser to pump a semiconductor crystal at low temperature in a high magnetic field. In the crystal the electron spins are aligned either along or opposite the magnetic field, resulting in a splitting of the energy levels. The pump laser photons are scattered off these electrons and are down- or up-shifted in energy by an amount equal to the magnetic field splitting between the two spin states. Tuning of the resulting laser output is thus achieved by changing the magnetic field strength. For the indium antimonite spin-flip laser, the amount of tuning is approximately 2.25 cm⁻¹/kG ($1kG = 0.1$ tesla). There exists, however, a critical field strength below which no laser emission occurs. For InSb this has been recently lowered to below 1 kG, allowing the use of conventional, rather than superconducting, magnets. Peak output powers of tens of kilowatts have been obtained in pulsed operation, pumped with both 5- and 10-μm sources. For photon energies near the semiconductor band gap (5 μm for InSb) the resonance dramatically lowers the lasing threshold, allowing CW operation with several watts of continuous output. Clearly, the tuning range of the spin-flip Raman laser is limited to within a few hundred cm⁻¹ of the pump frequency. Very recently, an InAs spin-flip laser has been reported which extends the covered wavelength range to the region around 3 μm. This material is pumped near its band gap with an HF (hydrogen fluoride) laser at 3385 cm⁻¹. Above the critical magnetic field of 55 kG the tuning rate was 0.57 cm⁻¹/kG. Conversion efficiency in excess of 10% has been obtained, with a pump threshold of 10 W. An important feature of the spin-flip laser is its narrow line width (less than 1 kHz for InSb)—an advantage for a number of applications.

Semiconductor lasers work by stimulated recombination of electrons and holes across an energy gap. Population inversion is achieved by a current in a *p-n* junction structure, by electron beam excitation, or by pumping optically similar to a dye laser. These devices can be composition-tuned by selecting a material with an appropriate band gap. In particular, ternary lead-salt diode lasers of $Pb_{1-x}Sn_xTe$, $PbS_{1-x}Se_x$, and $Pb_{1-x}Cd_xSe$ cover the range from 3 to 32 μm by varying x. An individual laser has a gain bandwidth of about 40 cm⁻¹, and the output can be tuned over that range by varying the temperature or applying a variable pressure or magnetic field. Recently, DFB semiconductor lasers have been achieved. Semiconductor lasers are low-power devices with CW outputs of the order of a few hundred milliwatts.

Molecular lasers have operated in the infrared on a large number of individual rotational-vibrational lines. Increasing the gas pressure broadens the line width, and at a pressure of several atmospheres the individual lines overlap. A wide gain region is thus obtained, and the laser could be tuned in a manner similar to a dye laser. Research is in progress along these lines. Optically pumped CO_2 and N_2O lasers have been operated at pressures of 33 and 42 atm (3.3 and 4.3 megapascals) respectively. Some technological problems are yet to be solved for the full tuning range to be realized.

Another potentially useful tunable source in the near-infrared has been recently demonstrated by the achievement of CW laser action in a Li-doped KCl crystal, containing $F_A(II)$ color centers, pumped by the red line of a krypton laser. This laser has a low (50 mW) threshold, and the output is continuously tunable from 2.6 to 2.8 μm. Other alkali halides are known to produce color centers, and research is in progress to extend the wavelength range covered.

Optical parametric oscillators are based on the nonlinear optical properties of certain crystals. A pump laser field is applied to the crystal which is placed in a resonant cavity. Due to the nonlinear susceptibility of the material, sum and difference frequency generation between two optical fields can take place. In the parametric device only one pump field is input, and oscillations build up from noise at two other frequencies ω_s (signal frequency) and ω_i (idler frequency) such that $\omega_i + \omega_s = \omega_p$. In order to obtain substantial buildup of power at the new frequencies, the phase-matching criterion must be met. This requires that the propagation vectors of the three fields must satisfy conservation of momentum, just as their frequencies satisfy conservation of energy; thus, $\mathbf{k}_i + \mathbf{k}_s = \mathbf{k}_p$. Nonlinear crystals are also anisotropic and the phase-matching requirement can be satisfied, by proper choice of polarization of the fields, at a certain temperature and crystal orientation. Tuning of the parametric oscillator is accomplished by changing the temperature or rotating the crystal. Parametric oscillators have been operated with $LiNbO_3$, $LiIO_3$, KDP (potassium dihydrogen phosphate), ADP (ammonium dihydrogen phosphate), CdSe, and Ag_3AsS_3 (proustite). Although CW parametric oscillation has been achieved, most practical parametric oscillators are pulsed devices. Peak powers as high as 10 MW have been generated in high-optical-quality ADP. Presently, the wavelength range covered by these devices extends from 0.42 to 11 μm. Under development as materials for parametric oscillators in the infrared, to about 20 μm, are the $I-III-VI_2$ and $II-IV-V_2$ semiconductor compounds with the chalcopyrite structure such as $AgGaSe_2$ and $CdGeAs_2$. These materials have excellent nonlinear properties. At this time their application is limited by crystal quality, and considerable effort is being put into crystal growth.

Extension of the tuning range. Nonlinear optics makes possible the extension of the frequency range of tunable lasers to frequencies where primary sources are not available. Actually, the parametric oscillator is a special example of nonlinear techniques; it results in tunable laser output with a single, fixed-frequency pump source. In many situations, however, the losses in the material are too high, or the gain is too low, to allow parametric oscillation. In such cases it is possible to generate new frequencies by the application of two or more optical beams to a nonlinear medium. The resulting sum or difference frequency generation (doubling is simply a special case of sum frequency generation) is a means of obtaining tunable laser radiation at new frequencies, provided at least one of the input beams is from an existing tunable laser. As with the parametric oscillator, the phase-matching criterion must be fulfilled. All the nonlinear crystals used in parametric oscillators, plus some additional ones, have been used in this manner, to obtain tunable laser light from 217 nm in the ultraviolet to the far-infrared. The particular systems are too numerous to list in detail. A few recent advances are: frequency doubling of dye lasers in potassium pentaborate, wavelength range 217–234 nm; difference frequency mixing of the signal and idler outputs from a proustite parametric oscillator in CdSe, wavelength range 10–25 μm; mixing the output of an InSb spin-flip laser with that of the CO_2 pump laser in InSb itself for far-infrared tunable laser light in the region of 100 μm.

An exciting recent development is the generation of tunable coherent radiation in the vacuum ultraviolet. Two dye laser sources were used in a three-wave sum mixing process ($\omega_s = 2\omega_1 + \omega_2$) in Sr vapor. The efficiency of this nonlinear interaction was aided by strong resonance enhancement when $2\omega_1$ was tuned to double quantum-allowed transitions from the ground state of Sr. Using various combinations of four different dyes in the two dye lasers, the resulting output could be tuned from 158 to 196 nm. Extension of this method to other vapor systems and other dye lasers should produce coherent light from about 100 to 230 nm.

Applications. In addition to their tunability, these lasers have the important advantage of narrow spectral width and high brightness compared with conventional thermal sources. Due to these properties they are revolutionizing the field of spectroscopy. Classical spectroscopic methods, as well as new techniques peculiar to laser sources, are being used. Recently, scores of experiments in high-resolution absorption spectroscopy have been reported. Those performed with molecular beams have resulted in resolutions as high as a few parts in 10^{10}. In the last few years the new method of saturation spectroscopy with tunable lasers has been widely used, from the ultraviolet to the infrared. Notable is the improved accuracy determination of the fundamental Rydberg constant. A very recent advance is the novel technique of two-photon absorption spectroscopy using two counter-propagating dye laser beams. This technique, like saturation spectroscopy, eliminates Doppler broadening and carries ultrahigh-resolution spectroscopy to higher frequencies. *See* RYDBERG CONSTANT.

A combination of spectroscopy and detection of various atmospheric pollutants has been the goal of a number of recent experiments. In particular, properties and concentration of hydroxyl (OH) radicals in the atmosphere and in flames have been studied with a tunable ultraviolet laser. In another ambitious effort an entire spin-flip Raman laser experiment was launched in a balloon to study the photochemistry and resulting changing concentrations of stratospheric NO and H_2O.

Still another application receiving considerable attention of late is isotope separation. A number of techniques have been proposed and demonstrated. Examples are laser deflection of an atomic beam, and selective excitation followed by either photoionization or by photodissociation and subsequent photochemistry. Tunable dye lasers are the preferred sources for these experiments. *See* ISOTOPE (STABLE) SEPARATION.

For background information *see* LASER; OPTICS, NONLINEAR in the McGraw-Hill Encyclopedia of Science and Technology.

[ANDREW DIENES]

Bibliography: R. L. Byer, Optical parametric oscillators, in H. Rabin and C. L. Tang (eds.), *Treatise in Quantum Electronics*, 1974; D. C. Hanna et al., *Appl. Phys. Lett.*, 25:142, 1974; R. T. Hodgson, P. P. Sorokin, and J. J. Wynne, *Phys. Rev. Lett.*, 32:343, 1974; C. K. N. Patel, E. G. Burkhard, and C. A. Lambert, *Science*, 184:1173, 1974; F. P. Schäfer (ed.), Topics in applied physics, *Dye Lasers*, vol. 1, 1973.

Liver disorders

Although no single unifying concept has emerged that would provide a molecular basis for the neoplastic transformation, there is a growing body of evidence that points to a common molecular aberration in cancer, an anomaly of gene expression, manifested by a misprogramming of protein synthesis. Evidence for this concept derives from the ectopic production of polypeptide hormones, such as ACTH, by nonendocrine tumors; and by loss of normal tissue antigens and acquisition by tumors of neoantigens not present in the normal tissues of origin. These aberrations of gene expression have been extended in scope and given a functional significance by experimental studies during recent years on a series of transplantable hepatomas of the rat.

Liver-type isozyme. Several well-characterized enzymes that play key roles in the carbohydrate metabolism of liver exist in multimolecular forms called isoenzymes or isozymes, which can be detected and assayed separately by differences in chemical and kinetic properties. Studies of the activity levels of these enzymes have revealed a common pattern of isozyme expression in these hepatomas. Those isozymes that are preponderant in normal adult rat liver and have specific hepatic functions are retained to varying degrees in hepatomas that grow slowly, requiring 6 months or more for a transplant generation, and that, by usual histologic criteria, are highly differentiated. Tumors that grow somewhat more rapidly, requiring 3–6 months for a transplant generation, and that are somewhat less, but still well differentiated, lose the liver-type isozymes to varying degrees; in some instances there is an increase of isozymes that are normally low or absent in the adult liver. With progressive dedifferentiation to the poorly differentiated state and rapid growth, there is not only a complete, or nearly complete, disappearance of the liver-type isozymes but a virtually complete replacement by the nonhepatic forms, sometimes in extremely high activity compared with the original total enzyme activity in liver. In nearly every instance studied thus far, the isozyme patterns of the poorly differentiated hepatomas resemble those of fetal liver. Well-studied examples of this phenomenon are the loss of such key hepatic isozymes as glucokinase, aldolase B, and L-type pyruvate kinase and their replacement in each instance by isozymes that are low or absent from the adult liver. Similar alterations of isozyme composition in experimental hepatomas have been observed for glutaminase, branched-chain amino acid aminotransferases, fructose-1,6-diphosphate phosphohydrolases, thymidine kinases, adenylate kinases, fructose-6-phosphate-glutamine aminotransferases, and glycogen synthetases.

Isozyme composition alteration. Alterations in the composition of isozymes accompany the dedifferentiation of hepatomas. Glycogen phosphorylase, an enzyme that exists in multiple forms that can be separated by isoelectric focusing, is a typical example. Skeletal and heart muscle phosphorylase gives a sharp peak at pH 6.2, and the liver isozyme focuses at pH 5.9. In contrast, rapidly growing, poorly differentiated hepatomas have a third isozyme, which focuses at pH 5.6 and is distinguishable chemically, kinetically, and immunologically from the other two isozymes. Hepatomas, like normal tissues, also have kinases and phosphatases that interconvert the a and b phosphorylases. Hepatomas of intermediate growth rate and degree of differentiation contain both the liver and hepatoma isozymes. The sole or predominant isozyme of fetal muscle and liver, and of whole early embryos, is identical with that of the hepatoma. Phosphofructokinase, which exists in four molecular forms, is an apparent exception to the general pattern found for other enzymes, in that the sole liver isozyme is retained as a major form, not only in poorly differentiated hepatomas but also in other nonhepatic tumors whose tissues of origin do not contain this isozyme. In the tumors, the liver isozyme is always accompanied by one or two other phosphofructokinase isozymes.

Although lactate dehydrogenase isozyme patterns in cancer have been studied exhaustively, no clear, consistent pattern has emerged. Another interesting example of embryonic isozyme expression is the so-called Regan isozyme of alkaline phosphatase, which is identical with the normal human placental isozyme and is found in some human hepatic, pulmonary, ovarian, and other tumors. It is also present in the serum of some cancer patients, but the diagnostic significance is somewhat clouded, for it is present also in some noncancerous conditions.

For background information *see* ANTIGEN; ENZYME; GENE; MOLECULAR PATHOLOGY in the McGraw-Hill Encyclopedia of Science and Technology.   [SIDNEY WEINHOUSE]

Bibliography: W. E. Criss, *Cancer Res.*, 31:1523, 1971; F. Schapira, *Advan. Cancer Res.*, 18:219, 1973; S. Weinhouse, *Cancer Res.*, 32:1007, 1972; S. Weinhouse and T. Ono (eds.), *Gann Monograph 13*, University of Tokyo Press, 1972.

Lung disorders

Serum alpha$_1$ antitrypsin (AAT), a protein whose levels are determined primarily by genetics, was first shown to be related to pulmonary emphysema by C. Laurell and S. Eriksson in 1963. Since then it has been established that there is a high incidence of pulmonary emphysema among individuals with a severe deficiency of serum AAT and that the symptoms of this disease may begin at a relatively young age. Recent work in this field has centered upon the significance of an intermediate deficiency of serum AAT and on how a deficiency of this protein, which is an antiprotease, leads to destruction of the pulmonary parenchyma. Controversy still exists as to whether an intermediate level of serum AAT is a factor in the development of emphysema, although the evidence is beginning to indicate that it may play a contributing role. Studies on the relationship between the levels of leukocyte lysosomal proteases and serum AAT suggest that it is the ratio between the protease and its inhibitor (serum AAT) that may determine whether tissue injury and emphysema will occur.

Pi system. Levels of serum AAT can be measured by several methods. In addition, the genotype of an individual's AAT can also be determined. Patients who have a severe deficiency of AAT and pulmonary emphysema have AAT levels of only about 20% of normal, and their genotype shows the ZZ variant of AAT. Normal individuals usually have the MM genotype. Intermediate levels of AAT may be due to the heterozygous state in which the individual has inherited the M variant from one parent and the Z variant from the other to give the MZ genotype. There are also other variants of AAT, labeled with other letters. The S variant is relatively common, and the MS and SS genotype both cause intermediate levels of AAT. The different variants of AAT protein have been collectively termed the "Pi system"; the abbreviation stands for protease inhibitor. In the case of the Z variant it has been shown that the decreased AAT levels are due to a failure of release of the protein from the liver, which is the site of production. Some of these patients develop liver disease, possibly because the liver retains serum AAT. Some variants result in normal AAT levels, whereas others do not. Only the ZZ variant has been definitely linked with severe emphysema. Whether it is the absolute level of antiprotease activity or the genotype that leads to tissue damage is an unanswered question.

Intermediate deficiency state. Controversy still exists as to whether there is an increased incidence of pulmonary emphysema in persons with an intermediate level of serum AAT. In some populations of emphysema patients it has been found that the incidence of intermediate levels of serum AAT was more than would be expected in the general population. In another study there was no evidence of an increased incidence of emphysema among the parents of patients with the ZZ genotype. More recent data have led investigators to propose that it is not an intermediate level of serum AAT by itself, but the combination of cigarette smoking, and possibly other forms of air pollution, and moderately reduced AAT levels that lead to emphysema. Thus the 5% of the population with an intermediate level of serum AAT might be at risk only if they are cigarette smokers. This is an important issue to resolve. If intermediate levels do predispose to disease, then it would be worthwhile to screen the population to determine what individuals are at a greater risk if they are cigarette smokers, since preventive medicine is all that is available at this time.

Protease inhibition. The lysosomes of neutrophile leukocytes and alveolar macrophages contain proteases which, when released by these cells, can cause tissue damage. Depending on the site of action, these proteases are termed elastases or collagenases. Other forms of proteases with different sites of action are also present. M. Galdston and colleagues recently suggested that it is the ratio between these proteases and their inhibitors which determines whether or not tissue damage will occur. Serum AAT has the ability to inhibit most elastases and collagenases. Thus an individual with weak leukocyte proteases may not develop emphysema even in the presence of severely decreased serum AAT levels. In other recent studies the alveolar macrophages obtained by lung lavage from both smokers and nonsmokers have been compared. In the smokers, not only could more macrophages be obtained but the protease content of the smokers' macrophage had more potent proteases than that of nonsmokers. Thus, if the hypothesis that emphysema is the result of an excessive amount of proteases in the lung as compared with AAT, which inhibits these enzymes, is correct, then the high incidence of emphysema in patients who have a long history of cigarette smoking would be explained. However, these investigations are in progress, and no conclusions can be made at this time.

For background information *see* EMPHYSEMA; LUNG DISORDERS in the McGraw-Hill Encyclopedia of Science and Technology.

[RICHARD E. KANNER; ALFRED E. ABAUNZA, JR.]

Bibliography: M. Galdston et al., *Amer. Rev. Resp. Dis.*, 107:718–727, 1973; D. C. S. Hutchison, *Brit. J. Dis. Chest*, 67:171–196, 1973; R. E. Kanner et al., *Amer. J. Med.*, 54:706–712, 1973; F. Kuepper et al., *Amer. Rev. Resp. Dis.*, 110:176–194, 1974; C. Mittman (ed.), *Pulmonary Emphysema and Proteolysis*, 1972.

Lysin

Autolysis is self-lysis or lysis that occurs because of the presence in the cell, or the production by the cell, of some factor or factors that attack the components of the cell. Such factors are usually enzymes, and when the cells are bacterial cells, these enzymes are termed bacterial autolysins. This process of self-digestion is similar to the process observed, for example, when meat is "hung until tender," that is, to allow the intracellular enzymes to partially digest the cellular structure. The enzymes are potentially lethal for the cell but must have a role in normal cell growth and metabolism. Recent investigations of bacterial autolysins have, therefore, been concerned with the activation of the process, the nature of the enzymes involved, and the components of the bacterial cell that are attacked.

Bacteria are surrounded by a rigid cell wall that gives the characteristic shape (rod, coccus) to the particular bacterial species. Differences exist between gram-positive and gram-negative bacteria in the overall composition and number of layers making up the cell wall. However, in all normal bacterial cells (except wall-less forms) the rigidity is conferred by the presence of a macromolecular structure that surrounds the cell in a cross-linked network. This macromolecule is referred to by the synonymous terms murein, peptidoglycan, mucopeptide, or glycosaminopeptide, depending upon the national origin of the author. Breakage of the peptidoglycan allows lysis of the bacterial cell owing to the difference in osmotic pressure between the inside of the cell and the external environment.

Peptidoglycan structure. In a schematic generalization of the peptidoglycan structure (see illustration) the backbone of the macromolecule (glycan strand) is invariably composed of alternating β-1,4-linked *N*-acetyl-D-glucosamine and *N*-acetyl muramic acid. The *N*-acetyl muramic acid is attached to a tetrapeptide that in many, but not all, bacteria is composed of L-alanine, D-glutamic acid, D,L-(meso)diaminopimelic acid (or L-lysine), and D-alanine. Cross-linkage of peptidoglycan units is often established through peptide bridges

between the D-alanine carboxyl of one unit and the α-amino group on the lysine residue of a neighboring chain. In the illustration the interpeptide bridge is composed of five glycine residues, but many variations in composition are known.

Autolysins. The bacterial autolysins so far characterized fall into three classes of enzymes that attack the peptidoglycan structure. (1) Glycosidases are specific for bonds between amino sugars in the backbone. An enzyme attacking at site A is an endo-*N*-acetyl muramidase; one that attacks at site B is an endo-*N*-acetyl glucosaminidase. (2) Amidases specifically cleave the tetrapeptide side chain from the glycan strand (site C). Such an enzyme is *N*-acetyl muramyl-L-alanine amidase. (3) Endopeptidases attack the peptide bonds in the interpeptide bridge (sites D and E).

Soluble autolysins. Purification of bacterial autolysins has proved difficult because of problems involved in separating these enzymes from cell wall material, but recent advances have made it possible to characterize soluble autolysins. In *Bacillus licheniformis* and *B. subtilis*, both an *N*-acetyl-muramyl-L-alanine amidase and an endo-β-*N*-acetyl glucosaminidase are present. In *Streptococcus faecalis* the autolysin is present in a latent form that is activated by proteolytic enzymes, after which the *N*-acetyl muramidase activity is revealed. Pneumococcal autolysin contains *N*-acetyl-muramyl-L-alanine amidase activity. It is not unusual to find more than one autolytic activity associated with a bacterial cell. For example, *Staphylococcus aureus* strain Copenhagen has been reported to contain endo-β-*N*-acetyl glucosaminidase, *N*-acetyl muramyl-L-alanine amidase, and glycine endopeptidase activity. This is not surprising in view of the many functions during bacterial cell growth and division that require splitting of the

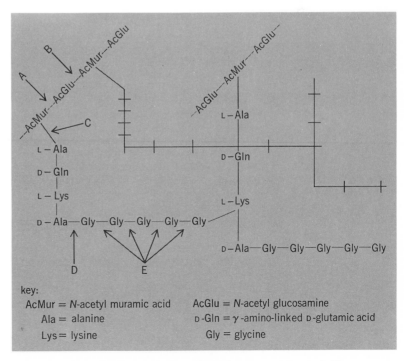

Fragment of peptidoglycan structure of *Staphylococcus aureus* strain H.

peptidoglycan molecule. Thus autolysins could be required for cell separation, to open up new sites in the peptidoglycan layer so that it could increase in size during cell growth, and, possibly, to allow remodeling of the peptidoglycan by relative movement of units of the polymer. Whether autolysins are located at specific anatomical sites or in an organelle such as the mesosome is not yet known. Mutant strains lacking one or more autolysins have been isolated, and the cells often show aberrant properties in terms of shape or ability to separate daughter cells. The fact that antibiotics which exert their effect by interfering with the process of cross-linking the peptidoglycan strands (for example, penicillin) are less effective against nonautolytic mutant strains suggests a role for the autolysins in the final lethal action of the antibiotic.

For background information see BACTERIA; LYSIN in the McGraw-Hill Encyclopedia of Science and Technology.

[HARRY GOODER]

Bibliography: C. W. Forsberg and H. J. Rogers, J. Bacteriol., 118:358–368, 1974; L. V. Howard and H. Gooder, J. Bacteriol., 117:796–804, 1974; H. M. Pooley et al., J. Bacteriol., 109:423–431, 1972; A. Tomasz, A. Alvino, and E. Zanati, Nature, 227:138–140, 1970.

Magnetism

A striking achievement in the field of magnetism during 1973–1974 was the observation of nuclear ferromagnetism in the submicrodegree temperature range. This observation was made on the system of fluorine nuclear moments in calcium fluoride, in which the interactions occur between the nuclear magnetic dipoles. This experiment follows those on the production and study of nuclear antiferromagnetism in the same system, which were carried out during the preceding years. Experimental evidence for the occurrence of a ferromagnetic structure with domains, predicted by theory, has been obtained in a spherical sample of CaF_2 by observing the nuclear magnetic resonance (NMR) of the low-abundance isotope calcium 43, as described below.

Production of nuclear magnetic ordering. Both the production and the observation of nuclear magnetic ordering are based on the techniques of NMR. The production of magnetic ordering among nuclear spins subjected to dipolar interactions requires exceedingly low temperatures, typically a fraction of a microdegree, because of the smallness of these interactions. This problem is solved by cooling the nuclear spins only, with all other degrees of freedom of the crystal, referred to as the lattice, remaining at a temperature of a fraction of a degree. The nuclear cooling is achieved by a two-step process.

In the first step, which takes place in a high magnetic field (25–50 kG or 2.5–5 T), the nuclear polarization is enhanced well above its thermal equilibrium value. This process can be shown to be equivalent to a cooling. To achieve nuclear polarization, which requires the presence of a small concentration of electron paramagnetic centers in the sample, mutual-flip transitions are induced between nuclear and electronic spins by a microwave irradiation of typically 2-mm wavelength in a

suitably adjusted magnetic field. Nuclear polarizations in excess of 90% result. Known as the solid effect, this method of nuclear dynamic polarization is also widely used for preparing polarized targets for nuclear and high-energy physics experiments, a quite different field of physics.

The second step in the nuclear cooling is an adiabatic demagnetization of the nuclear spins. This can be done in two different ways, either by slowly decreasing the magnetic field to zero or by the less obvious method of adiabatic demagnetization in the rotating frame. In the second method, the sample is irradiated with a radio-frequency magnetic field H_1 of a few tens of milligauss (a few microtesla), perpendicular to the main dc field H_0, and rotating at a frequency such that H_0 is several tens of gauss (several millitesla) off-resonance. The magnetic field is then swept slowly until the resonance condition is met. It can be shown that, when the nuclear system is viewed from a reference frame rotating around H_0 at a frequency equal to that of the radio-frequency field H_1, its evolution is the same as if it were in an "effective" field different from H_0 and subjected to "effective" interactions between spins distinct from the normal dipolar interactions. The effective field is the vector sum of the field H_1, which looks static in the rotating frame, and the field difference between the off-resonance and the resonance values of the dc field. The effective dipolar interactions are the part of the actual dipolar interactions that is time-independent when viewed from the rotating frame.

Under such conditions, it has long been assumed as a working hypothesis and more recently well verified by experiment, that the system evolves toward a state of internal equilibrium characterized by a temperature in the rotating frame, that is, by a Boltzmann distribution of populations among the energy levels of its effective interactions. The sweep of the external field toward the resonance value corresponds to a decrease in the effective field. It is the rotating-frame counterpart of the usual adiabatic demagnetization and, like this demagnetization, leads to a cooling of the nuclear spin system. The cancellation of the external magnetic field, in the rotating frame, is analogous to the cancellation of the gravitational field experienced by astronauts in a spacecraft.

Once cooled in the manner described, the nuclear spin system will eventually heat up to the lattice temperature. The characteristic time for this heating can be very long, however—from minutes to hours—so that the nuclear spin system is practically isolated for a substantial time, long enough to allow the observation of its low-temperature properties.

Two points are of importance. First, since the effective dipolar interactions in the rotating frame depend on the orientation of the external magnetic field with respect to the crystalline axes, the ordered structures expected at low temperature depend also on this orientation. Second, the temperature imparted to the nuclear spin system can be made positive or negative at will, whereas in the usual thermodynamic systems it can be only positive. At positive temperature, the lower the energy of an energy level, the larger its population; the converse is true at negative temperature. The nu-

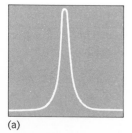

(a)

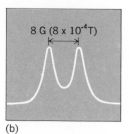

8 G (8 x 10⁻⁴ T)

(b)

Calcium-43 magnetic resonance signals in calcium fluoride when the fluorine spin system is either (a) paramagnetic or (b) ferromagnetic. Signal intensity is plotted against magnetic field strength.

clear-ordered structures are different at positive or negative temperatures.

As an example, consider the case when the fluorine spins of CaF_2 are cooled at negative temperature in the rotating frame. If the external field is along a fourfold crystalline axis, theory predicts the occurrence of an antiferromagnetic structure (its existence has been experimentally verified through the characteristic behavior of the magnetic susceptibilities). If, on the other hand, the field is along a threefold axis, theory predicts the occurrence of a ferromagnetic structure, with domains made of thin slices perpendicular to the external field and carrying magnetizations alternatively parallel and antiparallel to that field. The experiments that verify this prediction will now be described.

Observation of nuclear ferromagnetism. In addition to fluorine nuclei, the magnetic ordering of which has been investigated, calcium fluoride contains calcium nuclei, most of which belong to the nonmagnetic isotope ^{40}Ca. However, the magnetic isotope ^{43}Ca is also present, but at such a low natural abundance (0.13%) that it does not appreciably perturb the ordering among the fluorine nuclei. In spite of the low abundance of the ^{43}Ca spins, it is still possible to observe their magnetic resonance by cooling them by means of a technique (described at the end of this article) for measuring the temperature, and to use them as a probe of the properties of the fluorine spin system.

When the fluorine spins are demagnetized in the rotating frame, at negative temperature and with the dc field along a threefold axis, the calcium resonance signal is observed to split into two lines. This proves that the fluorine magnetic structure is made up of two kinds of domains whose different magnetizations create different dipolar fields at the sites of ^{43}Ca. The figure displays the calcium resonance signals, observed when the state of the fluorine system is either paramagnetic or ferromagnetic. Furthermore, it can be seen that the relative intensities of the calcium lines vary continuously as a function of the effective field applied to the fluorine spins, which reflects the variation of the relative sizes of the fluorine magnetic domains.

These two observations prove unambiguously that the structure of the fluorine system is ferromagnetic, that is, it consists of magnetized domains of macroscopic size with respect to the interatomic spacing, and that the size of these domains changes through the motion of the domain walls when the magnetic field is varied. The variation of the dipolar fields and of the relative domain sizes as a function of energy and field agrees semiquantitatively with theoretical expectation.

Another use of the calcium magnetic resonance is in measuring the fluorine spin temperature. When one applies to the sample a radio-frequency irradiation of frequency close to the ^{43}Ca resonance frequency, the ^{43}Ca spins acquire a magnetization that is a known function of the off-resonance distance and of the fluorine spin temperature and that affords the measurement of the fluorine spin temperature. The extreme temperature measured to date is −0.32 microdegree. From the variation of fluorine dipolar energy as a function of temperature, a Curie temperature for the ferromagnetic transition of about −0.5 μK, which is of the order expected from theory, could be deduced.

The field of nuclear magnetic ordering is still under active development.

For background information *see* FERROMAGNETISM; LOW-TEMPERATURE PHYSICS; MAGNETIC RESONANCE; MAGNETISM in the McGraw-Hill Encyclopedia of Science and Technology.

[MAURICE GOLDMAN]

Bibliography: M. Goldman et al., *Phys. Rev.*, 10B:226, 1974; J. F. Jacquinot et al., *C. R. Acad. Sci.*, 278B:93, 1974; J. F. Jacquinot et al., *Phys. Rev. Lett.*, 32:1096, 1974.

Mediterranean Sea

Since it is known that the northwest Mediterranean Sea is a region of deep-water formation in winter, many experiments (so-called MEDOC, from Mediterranée Occidentale) have been run in this area, particularly from 1969 up to the present. In 1969 and 1970 the experiments produced the first evidence of deep convection and subsequent deep-water formation occurring in very localized places called chimneys (Fig. 1). The data were the

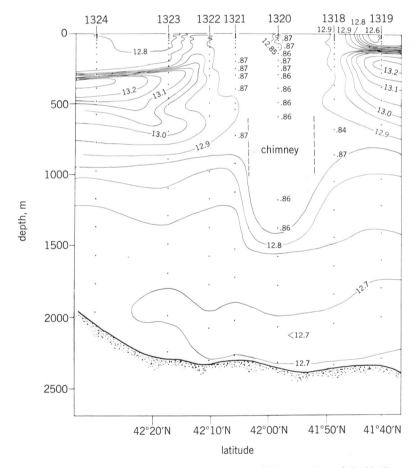

Fig. 1. Vertical distribution of potential temperature (°C) in a section of the Mediterranean occupied by the United States research vessel *Atlantis II*, longitude 5°20′E, on Feb. 10, 1969 (MEDOC 69), showing a typical configuration of a chimney. Numbers represent an identification code for hydrological stations. (*From D. Anati and H. Stommel, The initial phase of bottom water formation in the North West Mediterranean during MEDOC 69 on the basis of observations made by Atlantis II, 25 January–12 February, 1969, Cah. Oceanogr., 22(4), 1970*)

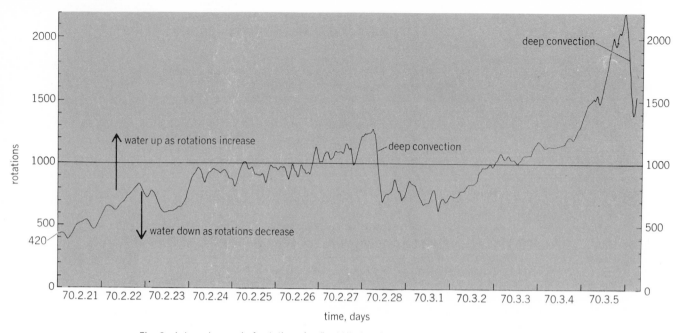

Fig. 2. Internal record of rotations for float VI showing two events of deep convection superimposed on a wave-like vertical motion. Instrument rotates approximately once per meter of water displaced vertically. Initial off-set (420) is caused by the 420 rotations of the meter as it sank to its equilibrium depth of approximately 400 m. *(From H. Stommel, A. Voorhis, and D. Webb, Submarine clouds in the deep ocean, Amer. Sci., 9(6):716–722, 1971)*

result of accurate hydrographic observations and current measurements using the most elaborate instruments, such as a bathysonde for the determination of potential density from electrical conductivity measurements, and vertical current meters for the determination of the vertical component of the current velocity. Large convective motions were found to exist, with very intense upward and downward vertical velocities, up to 10 cm/sec. These large convections coincided with a strong dry and cold wind, the mistral, blowing for several days (Fig. 2). From these experiments a quite detailed picture developed of the hydrological structure of this source region and some elements of the dynamics of the deep vertical convection.

In any season the area is characterized by a large cyclonic gyre (divergence), and the density stratification is weaker in the center than on the edge. In summer, in the presence of a strong stratification, the mechanical energy of winds, essentially transient, acts on the mixed layer from the surface to the thermocline and generates strong inertial currents. In winter, surface cooling occurs, leading to a very small reserve of buoyancy in the center of the gyre and generating vertical mixing in the surface layer. The evolution of the hydrological structure during wintertime can be split into three phases according to the MEDOC group (1970): the preconditioning phase, the violent mixing phase, and the sinking and spreading phase.

Preconditioning phase. The first phase has been studied in detail by many scientists, including H. Lacombe and P. Tchernia, H. Stommel, and J. C. Swallow and G. F. Caston. The initial processes of vertical mixing which takes place in the central area of the cyclonic circulation are essentially due to the intense loss of heat from the sea to the atmosphere, depending mainly on the effect of cold northwest winds (the mistral). The density of

the surface mixed layer increases up to the value of the warm and salty underlying intermediate water layer. Then the vertical potential density contrast between surface and bottom is a few parts per million and even less, which is at the limit of bathysonde sensitivity, instead of a thousand parts per million for usual conditions in the open ocean. However, it has been observed that the patches of dense surface water due to these initial processes of vertical mixing are small-scale compared to the large-scale area affected by the mistral winds. Swallow and Caston have suggested the influence of a preexisting feature, such as bottom topography, in the general circulation of the same small scale.

Violent mixing phase. The second and third phases are not as well known as the first one, and they are the subject of more recent experiments. For the present time, experiments are focusing on the second phase in order to gain a more precise understanding of the mechanisms involved in deep convection. It is uncertain whether the essential part in the processes of homogenization of the Mediterranean waters is thermal loss intensified by the winds as suggested by Lacombe and Tchernia, or dynamical effects of winds on the sea.

In order to observe natural deep convection during the violent mixing, researchers are concentrating on measurements of motions both vertically in, and horizontally in, and out of, the chimneys. Vertical motions are measured with neutrally buoyant rotating floats designed by D. C. Webb, D. L. Dorson, and A. D. Voorhis at the Woods Hole Oceanographic Institution. These floats are cylindrical bodies half as compressible as sea water and equipped with tilted vanes fixed around the cylinder. Ballasted, the float sinks to a depth where it is in static equilibrium, the axis of the cylinder being vertical. If there is vertical motion, it rotates be-

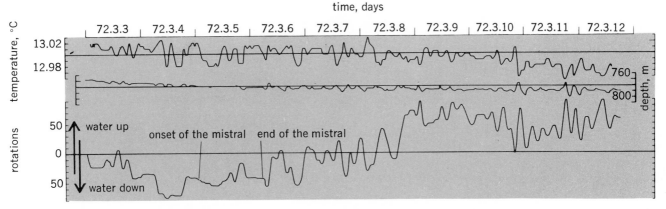

Fig. 3. Internal records of temperature, depth, and rotations for float I, which shows wavelike vertical motions (internal stability waves) occurring just after a gust of the mistral (MEDOC 72). *(From J. C. Gascard, Vertical motions in a region of deep water formation, Deep-Sea Res., vol. 20, 1973)*

cause of relative vertical flow past its vanes. In a sense, it can be considered as a propeller without bearing, and that makes it very sensitive.

From recent measurements (Fig. 3) in the winters of 1972, 1973, and 1974, it appears that the motion is governed by internal-waves dynamics since data show, in the Coriolis-Brunt-Väisälä frequency range of the energy spectrum, equipartition between the potential energy computed from vertical motion and horizontal kinetic energy computed from the horizontal current. Furthermore, a lot of energy concentrated in stability waves ranges near the Brunt-Väisälä frequency. Those are inertial gravity waves that are more or less influenced by Earth rotation as the Brunt-Väisälä frequency is close in order of magnitude to the pendular frequency. Coriolis frequency or pendular frequency is imposed by the Earth rotation Ω and is a sinus function of the latitude, and characterizes free inertial oscillations of a particle moving horizontally. Brunt-Väisälä frequency is due to the vertical potential density gradient, and characterizes free oscillations of a particle moving vertically through this gradient. In other words, in conditions of weak density stratification, the dominant carriers of energy are these stability waves, probably induced by gusts of wind at the surface.

In summertime conditions, when the main thermocline is near the surface, the dominant carriers of internal-wave energy in deep waters are inertial waves, more or less influenced by the stratification. Under these conditions the level of energy is two orders of magnitude smaller than before. From these observations there is good reason to think that internal stability waves may play a major role in the deep mixing and formation of bottom Mediterranean waters. This assumption must be validated, and what must be precisely determined is the relative part of the thermodynamical effects caused mainly by cooling and evaporation at the surface, and pure dynamical effects induced by the mistral for instance, both effects generating internal waves which in turn could trigger deep convection.

Sinking and spreading phase. The third phase must be considered in order to evaluate the quantities of deep waters formed each year through these mechanisms in order to be able to balance the Gibraltar outflow of deep Mediterranean water into the northern Atlantic. It is possible that some marginal phenomena produce additional deep waters such as the cascading of dense water from the shelf down to the deep canyons situated on the edge of the continental shelf of the Gulf of Lions.

Finally, it might be expected that part of the results obtained in the Mediterranean apply to some other regions of formation of deep water, particularly in the Labrador Sea, since hydrological situations are quite similar in some of these regions.

For background information *see* MEDITERRANEAN SEA in the McGraw-Hill Encyclopedia of Science and Technology. [JEAN-CLAUDE GASCARD]

Bibliography: H. Lacombe and P. Tchernia, *Ann. Inst. Oceanogr. Monaco*, 48:1, 1971; B. Saint-Guily, *Tellus*, 24(4), 1972; J. C. Swallow et al., in *Deep-Sea Res.*, vol. 20, 1973.

Membrane, gas separation by

Membrane separation processes are fundamentally attractive because they are passive and, in some cases, may have a relatively low energy requirement. A mixture is simply fed to a suitably packaged membrane from which separated components flow; no regeneration or replacement of any constituents is required. In spite of these inherent advantages, membrane gas separation has been little more than a laboratory curiosity because commercially available membranes do not have adequate permeability and selectivity for practical separations. This article describes recent advances in a silicone-base material that may become the basis for practical gas separation processes.

Much attention has been directed to silicone rubber for gas separation processes because, for most gases, it is the most permeable of all polymers. In 1967 W. Robb developed a method of producing a defect-free, 25-μ (1 $\mu = 1 \times 10^{-6}$ m) silicone rubber membrane that was 2.2 times as permeable to oxygen as to nitrogen, and he discussed a number of applications of the membrane, including the production of oxygen-enriched or oxygen-depleted air. Production of 1 ton/day (1 ton $= 9.072 \times 10^2$ kg) of 30% O_2 at atmospheric pressure from air fed at 10 atm (1 atm $= 1.013 \times 10^5$ N/m²) to this 25-μ membrane requires approximately 1000 ft² (1 ft² $= 9.3 \times 10^{-2}$ m²) of membrane.

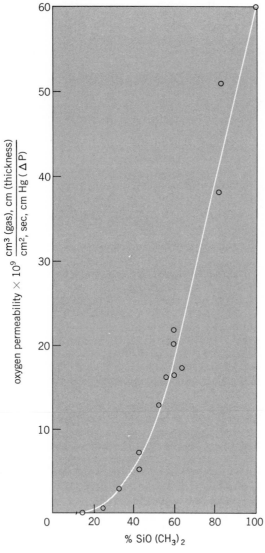

Fig. 1. Oxygen permeation coefficient versus percentage of silicone rubber.

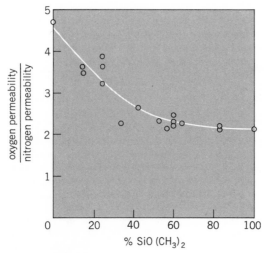

Fig. 2. Oxygen-nitrogen separation factor versus percentage of silicone rubber.

At a cost of membrane installment of at least $5/ft², the plant investment is excessive. Furthermore, without a power-recovery turbine, the power requirement is five times that of making the mixture with pure oxygen from a low-temperature air separation plant.

A number of other membrane gas separations have been analyzed from an economic standpoint, for example, by S. Stern. The result of these and other analyses is that membrane gas separations based on commercially available membranes are economically unreasonable. A silicone-like membrane that is orders of magnitude thinner than the 25-μ membrane previously available alters this situation.

Silicone-polycarbonate copolymer. The formation of membranes of the order of 0.1 μ requires that the polymer be solvent-castable. The material Robb worked with was not castable. However, H. Vaughn has developed a solvent-castable silicone-base material that is a copolymer of dimethyl siloxane and bisphenol A-polycarbonate and has excellent film-forming properties.

The oxygen permeabilities and the oxygen-nitrogen separation factor of a wide range of silicone-polycarbonate copolymers are shown in Figs. 1 and 2. For copolymers with the same overall composition but with different block size, ranging from 10 to 40 siloxane units per block, there was no significant variation in permeation properties. Copolymers containing greater than 70% dimethyl siloxane are too weak to form practical membranes. On the basis of this information and the data of Figs. 1 and 2, which show the rapid decline of permeability and only slight increase in separation factor with decreasing dimethyl siloxane content, 50–60% dimethyl siloxane was selected as optimum. A copolymer designated P-11 was used in most of the subsequent work. It contained 57% dimethyl siloxane and had an average of 20 siloxane units per block.

Techniques have recently been developed to produce and handle silicone-polycarbonate membranes as thin as several hundred angstroms (10 A=1 nm). To determine the thickness, quality, and uniformity of the ultrathin membranes, and to explore their utility for separation processes, the permeation properties of supported membranes were investigated. This was done by measuring the flux of oxygen and nitrogen at controlled pressures through supported ultrathin membrane samples mounted in a standard filter holder. The effective thickness was calculated by using the results of gas flux measurements on the supported ultrathin membrane and the permeation coefficient measured for the P-11 copolymer, determined with a thick (25-μ) membrane. In general, the effective thickness differed from the actual thickness of the ultrathin membrane because the support material offered some resistance to gas flow. The actual ultrathin membrane thickness could be calculated if the support resistance were evaluated. The thickness measured in this way agreed within 20% with that calculated from the concentration and volume of solution used, and samples taken from different sections of an ultrathin membrane did not show significant variations in thickness.

When Selectron B-13 with 0.005-μ pores was used as a support, a composite consisting of three layers of ultrathin membrane, each approximately 0.024 μ thick, could be routinely fabricated. The supported membrane composite had an effective thickness of 0.1 μ and could tolerate a transmembrane pressure differential of 270 psi (1 psi = 6.895×10^3 N/m²). Thinner membranes could be supported at lower pressure differentials.

Oxygen-enriched air. There are a variety of medical and industrial applications of oxygen-enriched air. It is now used for oxygen therapy, with the enriched air delivered to the patient by means of a nasal cannula or a small mask covering the nose and mouth. Alternatively, oxygen-enriched air can be provided to an entire room by a membrane system. This is not considered a fire hazard at oxygen concentrations up to 28%. Membrane systems are attractive for medical applications because the gas delivered is more humid than the available feed air, owing to the high permeability of water vapor in P-11 copolymer, and because the patient is protected from particulates, including viruses or bacteria that may be present in the feed air. In industrial applications, oxygen-enriched air could, for example, be used in fermentation and partial oxidation processes and in combustion systems in which the resultant increase in flame temperature and burning velocity would enhance radiant and convective heat transfer.

The two major costs in the production of oxygen-enriched air with membrane systems are electrical power for pumping and investment cost for the membrane package. In the most economical system based on the 0.1-μ P-11 membrane, a large excess of atmospheric-pressure air is fed to the system, and a vacuum is maintained on the low-pressure product side of the membrane. More membrane area is required in this case than when the feed gas is at high pressure, but the vacuum system is more efficient because only product gas is pumped. Furthermore, maximum enrichment is obtained because a large excess of feed air can be provided since it is virtually free at atmospheric pressure.

The degree of oxygen enrichment possible with a one-stage membrane system to which a large excess of feed air is supplied is shown in Fig. 3 as a function of the ratio of pressures on either side of the membrane. The data for Fig. 3 can be derived by writing the expression for the flux of each component, O_2 and N_2, through the membrane, and

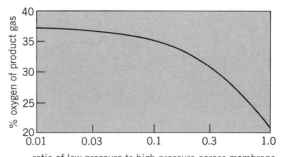

Fig. 3. Oxygen enrichment versus pressure ratio across silicone-base membrane.

then solving for the percentage of O_2 in the product gas. It is evident that a practical system could produce up to approximately 35% O_2.

The table summarizes the system parameters for producing 10,000,000 ft³/day (1 ft³ = 2.832×10^{-2} m³) of 30 and 35% oxygen with a one-stage 0.1-μ P-11 membrane system. It is notable that less energy is required to produce 30% oxygen with the membrane system and commercially available vacuum pumps than is required by the most efficient low-temperature air separation plant. For production of 500,000 ft³/day of 30% oxygen, which is the equivalent of 2.5 tons/day of added oxygen, the membrane area required would be 3900 ft². The power requirement, based on that used by a commercially available vacuum pump, would be 0.19 kWhr/100 ft³ (1 kWhr = 3.6×10^6 joule). An estimate of the size of the membrane system can be made, assuming a packaging density of approximately 300 ft² of membrane per cubic foot.

The cost of producing oxygen-enriched air with a P-11 membrane system is speculative at this point, since large systems have not yet been built. However, the economics appear attractive even for an installed membrane cost of $10/ft² and a lifetime of 3 years. This cost is an upper limit, and the life of 3 years is probably a lower limit, since the P-11 copolymer is chemically stable to all constituents of normal air.

For background information *see* OXYGEN in the McGraw-Hill Encyclopedia of Science and Technology.   [WILLIAM J. WARD, III]

Bibliography: W. L. Robb, *Ann. N.Y. Acad. Sci.*, 146:119, 1967; S. A. Stern, Gas permeation processes, in R. E. Lacey and S. Loeb (eds.), *Industrial Processing with Membranes*, 1972; H. A. Vaughn, *Polymer Lett.*, 7:569, 1969.

Metric system

Although the Metric Conversion Act of 1973 did not become law, conversion to the metric system is continuing in the United States, and education and training in metrics are moving forward at a rapidly accelerating pace. American industry is proceeding with conversion to the metric system at a pace directly related to economic need. Boards of education in all 50 states have assigned committees to prepare recommendations for metric curricula for all educational levels. General public conversion to the metric system is proceeding, with various programs designed to help the average American to "think metric."

System parameters to produce 10,000,000 ft³/day of 30 and 35% O₂-enriched air with 0.1-μ P-11 membrane

Parameter	30% O₂	35% O₂
Membrane area	78,000 ft²	55,000 ft²
Feed gas pressure	1 atm absolute	1 atm absolute
Pressure of permeated gas	0.35 atm absolute	0.1 atm absolute
Temperature	25°C	25°C
Power required to deliver permeated gas at 1 atm	0.15 kWhr/ 100 ft³	0.48 kWhr/ 100 ft³
Power requirement if O₂ is supplied from low-temperature air separation plant (basis: 1.4 kWhr/100 ft³ pure O₂)	0.16 kWhr/ 100 ft³	0.25 kWhr/ 100 ft³

Metric conversion in industry. The National Bureau of Standards, through its metric information office and the American National Metric Council, is proceeding with programs and services to assist the private sector to organize for metric usage. In general, the coordinating groups will survey key industries, such as the fastening industry, and will report to other industries, thus enabling them to plan their own conversion in an orderly, coordinated way. Standards for screws, gears, and structural materials, for example, will be formulated by the coordinating organizations, which will also establish goals and monitor the progress of industries during conversion. Priorities and timetables will be recommended. The establishment of minimum-cost strategy will be the responsibility of coordinating committees on building and construction, consumer products, education, training, industrial products, and primary materials.

Metric training programs. In general, metric training programs put more emphasis on thinking in metric terms than in memorizing conversion factors. Pocket-size conversion tables are readily available in a variety of shapes; there is a miniature slide-rule type with conversions from metric to Customary given on one side, and from Customary to metric on the other. The National Council of Teachers of Mathematics has a representative collection of metric training aids at its library in Reston, VA, including colorful plastic blocks, rulers, measuring cups, and beakers designed to provide visual and kinesthetic experience in metric dimensions for kindergarten and primary-grade students. These training aids will first supplement, and eventually replace, similar equipment in Customary dimensions. Films and sound-slide presentations on metrics are available on many levels of cost and sophistication, from fully sound-synchronized color films to simple hand-held slide viewers with the text in pocket-size booklets, most of which present an overview of the basic International System (SI) units and how they are related to Customary units. Some of the more sophisticated presentations contain information on the Customary system of measurement and on why the United States is converting to metrics. Metric training programs developed by industry for internal use employ films, booklets, posters, converters, and metric measuring instruments, and emphasize the company's products and needs. The Beloit Tool Corporation's metric program, which focuses on screw thread systems, taps, and gages, is typical.

Typical metric learning activities in a large city's public school system, grades 1 through 8, are as follows: grades 1, 2, and 3 learn decimals and use metric measuring instruments; grades 4 and 5 learn metric vocabulary, deal with Celsius temperatures, and work problems in metric units including area measurements. Films orient 6th, 7th, and 8th grade students to the SI units as a system of measurement.

Although national interest in metric education and training is currently more intense in some areas than in others, it can be expected to increase dramatically when the Metric Conversion Act becomes law.

For background information *see* METRIC SYSTEM; UNITS, SYSTEMS OF in the McGraw-Hill Encyclopedia of Science and Technology.

[DUANE C. GEITGEY]

Bibliography: F. Donovan, *Prepare Now for a Metric Future*, 1971; Pittsburgh Public Schools Department of Curriculum and Instruction, *Curriculum Bulletin*, 3(3), 1973; U.S. Department of Commerce, National Bureau of Standards, *A Metric America*, Spec. Publ. no. 345, 1971; U.S. Department of Commerce, National Bureau of Standards, *Some References on Metric Information*, Spec. Publ. no. 389, 1973.

Microprocessor

Significant jumps in technology occur when separate technologies that have been strong on their own are merged into one. The advent of the microprocessor system, or computer-on-a-few-chips,

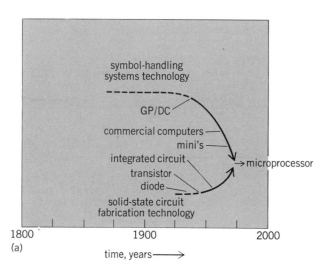

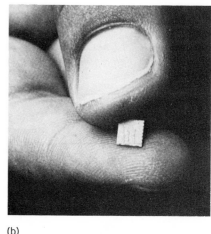

Fig. 1. Development of the microprocessor. (*a*) Historical interpretation of the microprocessor indicates that it represents the marriage of digital computer technology (upper arrow) and semiconductor circuit fabrication technology (lower arrow). (*b*) Microprocessor or "chip" dimensions are 1/5 in. (5 mm) square and 1/100 in. (0.25 mm) thick (*American Microsystems, Inc., Santa Clara, CA*).

during the past year represents such a jump. It is the happy marriage of computer systems technology and integrated-circuit-manufacturing technology (Fig. 1). The familiar electronic pocket calculator represents a special case of this marriage, in which a portion of a computer system is put on one integrated-circuit chip.

To this marriage, computer technology brings the concept of a standard machine that can be readily programmed to do any definable behavior. For example, it has been standard practice for many years for computer manufacturers to sell (or rent) the same computer to many different users, each of whom programs that computer for a unique application. The type of computer under discussion is the general-purpose digital computer, or GP/DC.

To this marriage, integrated-circuit technology brings the ability to put thousands of electronic circuit elements on a single chip of silicon about $\frac{1}{5}$ in. (5 mm) square and about $\frac{1}{100}$ in. (0.25 mm) thick (Fig. 2). This is called large-scale integration, or LSI. What counts is not the miniaturization achieved, but the economics of manufacture. As these chips can be produced for costs as low as $5 apiece, it becomes economically feasible to apply the resulting computers to a much wider range of end products.

During the past year the first microprocessor chips have been selling at prices of hundreds of dollars. They have been designed into end products such as computer terminals that sell for thousands of dollars. During coming years it is expected that there will be the same progressive price drops in the microprocessor chips as in other similar LSI chips. When the semiconductor manufacturers start mass-producing them in volume, the prices will drop to tens of dollars. Then they will appear in end products with price tags under $1000. As proof that lower prices are possible, some of the calculator chips that have similar complexity now sell at under $5 apiece when purchased in large volumes (hundreds of thousands per year), and the end calculator products sell for $20.

Thus it can be expected that end products that sell for hundreds of dollars will incorporate full-blown GP/DC's. Examples of the types of products that might soon (before 1980) contain GP/DC's are office typewriters and telephones, automobiles, residential comfort systems, and the whole span of industrial machine tools and automation appliances. Before the end of this century it is likely that more persons will own personal GP/DC's with substantial memories than now own pocket calculators.

Implementation of a GP/DC with LSI. The general-purpose digital computer consists of four subsystems, as shown in Fig. 2. At this level of discussion, the GP/DC's "architecture" has essentially remained unchanged over the past 30 or more years. The arithmetic subsystem does the basic processing of the data. The memory subsystem stores both the instructions to be executed and the data involved. The control subsystem continuously fetches the instructions from the memory one by one and directs the rest of the system to execute these instructions. Finally, the input/output subsystem allows the computer to usefully communi-

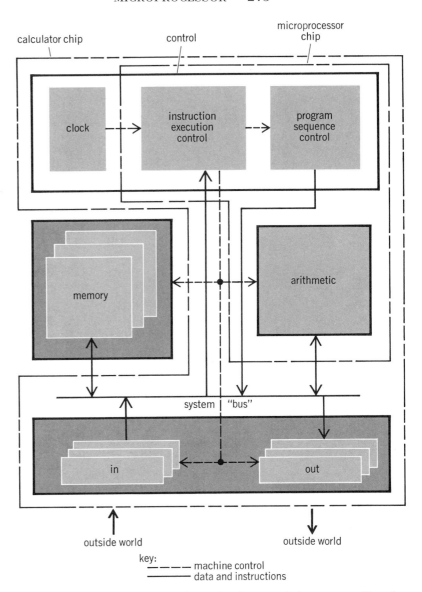

Fig. 2. The GP/DC is made up of four subsystems: control, memory, arithmetic, and input/output. Calculators can encompass everything but extensive memory on one chip, as the phantom outline for their chip indicates. Microprocessors do not include as much on their chips, but they have the all-important ability to work with extensive external memory and input/output chips.

cate with the outside world.

The outlines of the LSI chips superimposed on Fig. 2 show how semiconductor fabrication technology has reduced the GP/DC from a large roomful of equipment to a handful of chips that will comfortably fit upon a printed-circuit board the size of this page. The calculator chips are able to encompass practically all of the functions on just a single chip. However, they do not have enough memory, or the ability to control external memory, so they cannot be programmed to automatically do the long strings of calculations that one expects of a full GP/DC. Also, since they only need to keep up with human operators, they tend to be quite slow—often taking as long as $\frac{1}{10}$ sec to complete some commands.

The current microprocessor chips (Fig. 2) take in just the arithmetic and control functions. But—most important—they have the ability to address

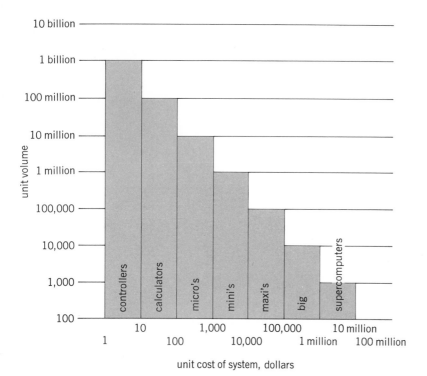

unit volume

unit cost of system, dollars

Fig. 3. Crude model for the market for LSI-GP/DC products predicts that it will extend from small $5 single-chip systems that will sell in the billions, all the way up to expensive supercomputer systems that will sell at much lower volumes. The significance of the current microprocessors is that they are leading the way to these new markets.

operated on 4 binary bits in parallel at a time and all their data paths and storage registers were this width. (A word of just 4 bits is considered narrow in modern GP/DC's, which typically have words 16 or more bits wide.) They were intended to be bridges between the inflexible architecture of calculator chips and the universality of a true GP/DC. The second-generation LSI microprocessors are the 8-bit-word-width machines that have appeared or been announced in the past year. The next generation will probably be 16-bit-word-width machines that incorporate the full architecture of the minicomputers. (The terms "micro-," "mini-," and "maxi-" loosely describe the relative size and physical cost of GP/DC's.)

But the above machines have all been manufactured with MOS (metal-oxide semiconductor) technology, and MOS technology is not suited for the largest and fastest maxicomputers such as the well-known IBM 360 family. A new wave of bipolar transistor LSI microprocessors is just starting to come out. These parts will permit the LSI manufacturing technology to be extended to top-of-the-line large computers.

Figure 3 models the market spectrum that appears to be evolving. It assumes that there will be application needs for LSI-GP/DC technology ranging all the way from small one-bit-word-width machines up to 64-bit supercomputers. The 4-, 8-, and 16-bit-word-width microprocessors of today are in the middle of this broad spectrum.

Figure 3 divides this spectrum into dollar decades and shows in simple bar-graph form the number of units that might be sold in each price decade at some time in the future when the full potential of this market is reached. It is assumed that the numbers of units in each price decade will be inversely proportional to the price level in that decade. Thus the descending-staircase appearance of Fig. 3. Each bar multiplies out to a billion-dollar market (units times maximum price), the very uniformity of these values reminding one that Fig. 3 is but a crude model.

The Fig. 3 model agrees with the widespread belief among leaders of the electronic industry that the electronics technology is ripe for a much wider penetration into all areas of the world economy. The microprocessor itself is the ideal tool for such a penetration, as it is low cost, very capable, and readily adapted to many different end uses. Figure 3 makes the commonsense observation that it will not be just one type of microprocessor, but a different type for each end market that has sufficient sales potential.

Not surprisingly, one does not need a very fast or powerful microprocessor to automate kitchen appliances, but one does need very low cost. The whole microprocessor, including its program and data memory, must be on one chip and sell for no more than a few dollars (leftmost bar of Fig. 3). And indeed, such chips have been made during the past year by reprogramming calculator chips. Their potential sales unit volume is in the hundreds of millions of units — as big as that of the appliances they can be used on.

On the other end of the marketplace (rightmost bar of Fig. 3), one needs the fastest and most powerful microprocessor possible when constructing

large amounts (65,000 words) of external memory, and large numbers of input/output ports. It is difficult for outsiders to comprehend that these little $\frac{1}{5}$ in. (5 mm) square chips of silicon can single-handedly supervise such large jobs as the control of all the cash registers in a large department store or of a complete factory automation line. In many instances, the cost of the external system elements such as sensors, actuators, and wiring far outweighs the cost of the microprocessor itself.

The memory is typically implemented with LSI chips also. Two basic types of memories are used: read-only memory (ROM), which is like this printed page, and random-access memory (RAM), which is really used to mean read-write memory, and is like a scratch pad or blackboard. The ROMs contain the instructions, and the RAMs contain the data. Many of the microprocessors now existing or under development are intended to use the same standard ROMs and RAMs that are being sold by more than one semiconductor manufacturer for regular "mini" and "maxi" computers — for example, the new "4K," or 4000-bit, RAMs.

There is now a sizable effort on the part of the microprocessor manufacturers to develop special LSI input/output chips. The goal is to have these "peripheral" chips so matched to the central microprocessor that users can assemble the total system in a simple building-block fashion.

Projected uses of microprocessors. The very first LSI microprocessors were the narrow-word-length machines such as the Intel MCS-4 and the Rockwell PPS-4 developed at the beginning of this decade. They had 4-bit-wide words, meaning they

the maxicomputers that government and large corporations use. Here the economies and increased performance achievable through LSI will be used to build yet more "cost-effective" large computers. Companies such as Four-Phase Systems and Amdahl, both near San Francisco, have used LSI technology to compete with the large IBM-class machines.

However, there will be a number of restraining factors that will in the next few years temporarily hold back the expected widespread use of microprocessor-type components. First, it takes a semiconductor manufacturer at least 2 or 3 years to conceive and put into mass production these complex devices. Second, there will be delay while design engineers are getting familiar with the art of using GP/DC architectures in their products. With microprocessors, the designer achieves the desired behavior by choosing the hundreds of instructions that constitute the program for the microprocessor. This is in marked contrast to designing by wiring logic gates together, as has been done in the past. The new approach can be learned, but it takes about a year, according to the experiences of designers reported on the first microprocessors. Fortunately, once a designer has made the transition from "hardware" design to "software" design on one microprocessor system, he has relatively little difficulty from then on in extending this knowledge to other microprocessors.

For background information see DIGITAL COMPUTER; INTEGRATED CIRCUITS; PRINTED CIRCUIT in the McGraw-Hill Encyclopedia of Science and Technology. [ROBERT H. CUSHMAN]

Bibliography: R. H. Cushman, Monthly series of reports on microprocessors, EDN Mag., p. 42, Nov. 20, 1973; p. 48, Jan. 20, 1974; p. 24, Feb. 20, 1974; p. 30, May 5, 1974.

Microscope, electron

The standard transmission electron microscope (TEM) of today, offering easily accessible resolution of several angstroms (10 A = 1 nm) and an ever-increasing range of applications in many fields, is usually operated at voltages in the range of 40–100 kV. Extensions to accelerating voltages as high as 3 MV have been realized during the last decade in France, Great Britain, the United States, and Japan with very encouraging results that have confirmed theoretical expectations and have aided in the study of materials and metals. Applications to biological problems were very limited during this period, and only during the last few years have activities become more systematically aimed at exploring whether high-voltage electron microscopy can be put to good use in biological research.

Electron microscopes in the megavolt range are several stories high and weigh tens of tons; they are also complicated and costly. Therefore, experimental activities in this field are most frequently carried out on a limited guest basis at few existing installations. About two dozen such installations exist throughout the world, four of which are located in the United States. Biological researchers in the United States presently have access to the 1-MeV unit at the U.S. Steel Research Center in Monroeville, PA, and greater access to two national facilities established for biological research by the National Institutes of Health at the end of 1972 at the University of Colorado in Boulder and at the University of Wisconsin in Madison.

Characteristics. Unlike the novel mechanism introduced by the scanning electron microscope (SEM), interest in the high-voltage electron microscope (HVEM) derives mostly from advantageous extrapolation of features already present in the TEM and from many useful consequences of the interaction of electrons with matter at higher energies. Thus the beneficial aspects of high-voltage operation are reduced specimen damage under beam exposure, increased specimen penetration and, hence, improved visibility of compact structures and thicker sections, better theoretical resolution, and more efficient dark-field operation. In a more technological vein, the advantage of increased versatility deriving from more column space available for special attachments, stages, or experimental devices should perhaps be added to this list.

Applications. In the short time since a more concerted effort toward exploring the usefulness of high-voltage electron microscopy in biological research was begun, various questions have been investigated and certain findings have emerged as to the potential and the limitations of this new approach.

Thick sections. In perhaps the most easily accessible and obvious consequence of increased specimen penetration at higher energies, sections of hitherto inaccessible thicknesses of 1 μm or more (instead of about 0.1 μm in the standard TEM) prove to be useful even when fine structure is required. Since micrographs of thicker sections represent superimposed two-dimensional projections of three-dimensional components, the optimum thickness for observation in the HVEM is largely determined by the complexity of the structures being studied. Because of the increased thickness, it is thus possible and meaningful to take stereoscopic micrographs by means of which larger or more complex structures appear whole and intact through three-dimensional viewing.

Serial sections. In cases of more extended complexity, in which the only available option has been to resort to tedious thin-serial sectioning and painstaking reconstruction, the use of thick sections reduces the overall effort as much as 10 or 20 times, not to mention the reduction in the distortion caused by cutting and handling. Not only does this process become more expeditious and reliable, but larger tissue fractions or systems can thus be morphologically analyzed, especially if all sections are viewed stereoscopically.

In such cases, when large amounts of data are to be stored, manipulated, and correlated, it is helpful to have recourse to the speed and versatility of a computer. In spite of the apparently insurmountable difficulty of automatic pattern recognition in micrographs of biological structures, hybrid methods are now being pursued, for example, by L. D. Peachey, that combine human selectivity with computer capability for data handling and in which the composite results appear either as graphic printouts or, more effectively, as images on interactive graphics display terminals.

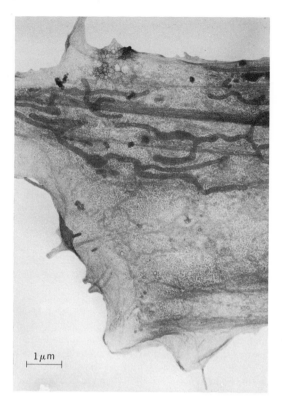

Fig. 1. Portion of a whole rat embryo cell, maintained undistorted by critical-point drying and viewed with a 1-MeV high-voltage electron microscope. Fine structures are still visible within the cytoplasm, and the organization and distribution of organelles within the cell can be directly analyzed. (*Courtesy of I. K. Buckley and K. R. Porter*)

Whole cells. If interest is focused on the overall organization of components within entire cells and their changes under controlled experimental conditions rather than in segments of tissues, cultured cells prove to be of incomparable value. The overall relationship of structures within the cell is maintained almost intact through critical point drying, and also through the absence of any embedding matrix, for unaltered exposure in the vacuum of the electron microscope. As shown in studies by I. K. Buckley and K. R. Porter, denser areas or components become transparent to the high-energy beam, and the resolution remains capable of revealing new domains of fine structures within the cytoplasm (Fig. 1).

Global morphological patterns can thus be identified in normal cells, and their changes can be followed in cells transformed under the influence of certain drugs or viral agents. It has even been possible, as demonstrated by J. W. Shay and Porter, to view the same area in the same cell with both the HVEM and the SEM, thereby clearly correlating surface features with underlying structures within the cell (Fig. 2).

Since micrographs of whole cells represent two-dimensional projections of all structures within them, much of this superimposed information cannot be unscrambled even by stereo viewing. In a different approach, used by M. Fotino, the grids containing whole cells can be tilted in the high-voltage beam by as much as ±60° with respect to the normal, and the micrographs taken at a number of angular positions can then be translated by computer processing into rotating images on graphics display terminals.

Autoradiography. The technique of tracer labeling and identification of active sites within tissues through autoradiography with thin sections and thin emulsion layers has been similarly extended in the HVEM to sections and emulsion layers of increased thickness. Even at the expense of some possible loss of resolution, the advantage in this case comes mainly from substantial increases simultaneously in the number of radioactive decays within the specimen and in the number of sensitive grains. K. Murti has shown that the exposure periods are then as much as 20–50 times shorter than those required for similar results under standard circumstances.

Isolated cell components. The limitation in usefulness of densely packed thick sections can be removed to a considerable extent by extracting selected cell components, such as whole nuclei or fragments of cell membranes, through biochemical and mechanical means. Entire mitotic spindles have thus been prepared by J. R. McIntosh, and their structure has been studied morphologically without the disruption deriving from thin sectioning.

Selective staining. Perhaps more than in standard electron microscopy, access to only certain cell components through selective staining is a valuable method for reducing the number of superfluous details projected and amassed on micrographs of balky specimens taken with HVEMs. The use of tannic acid—bismuth staining or peroxidase is currently being investigated by several researchers and appears promising.

Chromosome structure. In view of the great benefit from the penetrating power of high-voltage electron beams, H. Ris is systematically investigating the more detailed organization and structure of various chromosomes (*Drosophila* salivary glands, *Euplotes*, dinoflagellates, human leukocytes, Chinese hamster cells, *Blepharisma*, *Daphnia*) and attempting to resolve questions concerning the prevalence of coils or supercoils and the dependence of structural regularity on water content.

Image analysis. For the complex problems of intricate image analysis involved in many of the applications of high-voltage electron microscopy described above, methods are being developed and perfected for acquiring and handling the corresponding unavoidably large amounts of data by computer. Examples of such problems are three-dimensional reconstruction of highly complex structures, assembly and evaluation of cellular systems requiring serial sectioning, and enhancement of information content in high-resolution micrographs.

Ultrastructure by dark field. It has been possible to obtain more contrast and better resolution by dark-field operation, from very thin specimens such as macromolecule preparations, than could be obtained by bright-field operation because of the favorable combination of reduced specimen damage and higher forward-scattered intensities at higher energies.

Unprepared and wet specimens. The early hopes of, and attempts at, observing biological speci-

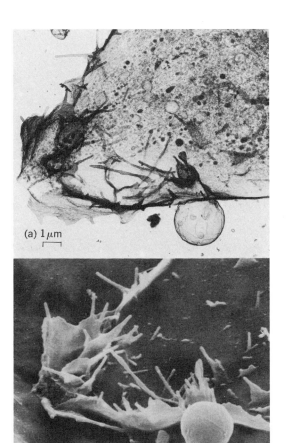

(a) 1 μm

(b)

Fig. 2. Portion of a whole Balb/3T3 mammalian cell, preserved undistorted by critical-point drying. (a) Viewed with a 1-MeV high-voltage electron microscope and (b) with a scanning electron microscope after gold coating. Although the tilt angle is not the same in both micrographs, surface features can easily be correlated. (*Courtesy of J. W. Shay and K. R. Porter*)

mens unaltered by preparation artifacts and in a natural environment instead of the normally unavoidable microscope vacuum have been bolstered by favorable conditions for improved hydration chambers prevailing in electron microscopes operating at high energies. Diffraction patterns of wet, unstained, and unfixed catalase crystals, and images of unprepared and wet whole cells, have been obtained in a dynamic environmental chamber at room temperature by D. F. Parsons and V. Matricardi. Human red blood cells and bacteria were observed unfixed and in a wet buffer environment by A. J. Salsbury, P. R. Ward, and J. A. Clarke. If some remaining difficulties are eliminated, the use of environmental chambers can be extended to many areas of biological and nonbiological research.

Scanning HVEMs. Based on slightly different aspects of electron optics and designed for applications not normally accessible in the transmission mode, two scanning developments are under way in the United States in the million-volt range, one by J. M. Cowley at the University of Arizona and the other by A. V. Crewe and E. Zeitler at the University of Chicago. It is expected that biological

applications, in particular, will benefit from advantageous features of scanning HVEMs, mostly in terms of contrast and resolution.

For background information *see* AUTORADIOGRAPHY; CHROMOSOME; MICROSCOPE, ELECTRON in the McGraw-Hill Encyclopedia of Science and Technology. [MIRCEA FOTINO]

Bibliography: K. Hama, in J. K. Koehler (ed.), *Advanced Techniques in Biological Electron Microscopy*, pp. 275–297, 1973; K. R. Porter and M. Fotino, in J. V. Sanders and D. J. Goodchild (eds.), *Electron Microscopy 1974: Abstracts and Papers Presented to the 8th International Congress*, Canberra, 1974; H. Ris, in C. Arceneaux (ed.), *Proceedings of the 32d Annual Meeting of EMSA*, Baton Rouge, 1974; P. R. Swann, C. J. Humphreys, and M. J. Goringe (eds.), *High-Voltage Electron Microscopy: Proceedings of the 3d International Conference*, 1974.

Molecular orbital theory

Molecular orbital theory is a quantum-mechanical theory of the electronic structure of molecules and is used to understand qualitatively and quantitatively the geometry, properties, and behavior of molecules. Recently there have been significant advances in the methodology for quantitative numerical calculation of molecular orbitals, in the production of molecular orbital wave functions for polyatomic molecules, and in molecular orbital calculations on the geometry of small molecules. Descriptive molecular orbital theory has emerged as a powerful qualitative tool for understanding molecular geometry and chemical reaction mechanisms. Molecular orbital calculations are beginning to be used in conjunction with statistical mechanics to describe the structure and properties of fluids.

Mathematically, molecular orbital theory involves the approximation of a many-electron molecular wave function as a product of one-electron functions or molecular orbitals. The theory was developed shortly after the discovery of quantum mechanics. R. S. Mulliken was awarded the Nobel Prize in 1966 for participation in the development and application of molecular orbital theory to problems in molecular structure and spectra. Two aspects of Mulliken's early work, the classification of molecular orbitals on the basis of their group theoretical symmetry properties and the construction of molecular orbital energy correlation diagrams, have been very influential in recent important developments in molecular orbital description of molecular structure and chemical reactions.

Numerical calculation of orbitals. The formulation of molecular orbital theory for numerical calculations stems from the matrix Hartee-Fock self-consistent field methodology set forth by C. C. J. Roothaan in 1951. A molecular orbital calculation for an n-electron molecule involves the linear expansion of individual molecular orbitals in a basis set of atomic orbital functions, the calculation of $\sim n^4$ multidimensional integrals over the atomic functions and the kinetic energy, electron-nuclear attraction and electron repulsion operators, and an iterative matrix eigenvalue procedure for the linear expansion coefficients. In early molecular orbital calculations, certain of the atomic integrals were systematically approximated or neglected to reduce the problem to tractable form. With the advent of third-generation digital computer equipment, *ab initio* molecular orbital calculations for polyatomic molecules have become feasible. Large digital computer programs such as POLYATOM, IBMOL, and GAUSSIAN-70 have been prepared for these calculations and widely distributed through the Quantum Chemistry Program Exchange at the University of Indiana. The capabilities and limitations of the various atomic orbital basis set alternatives have been explored and extensively documented by J. A. Pople and coworkers in recent years. A comprehensive bibliography of all *ab initio* molecular orbital calculations to date has been prepared by W. G. Richards and includes references to calculations on 311 different molecules.

Molecular structure. The results of molecular orbital calculations on small polyatomic molecules have been recently used to reexamine current ideas on the nature of molecular geometry. In 1953 A. D. Walsh proposed a general description of molecular geometry, based on molecular orbital theory, orbital symmetry, and intuitive ideas about the appearance of orbital energy correlation diagrams, wherein the molecular orbitals for a molecule in one geometry are related to the orbitals for another geometry. The energy of an individual molecular orbital is related to the binding energy of the electron therein, and the manner in which the orbital energies of a molecule change with geometry is one of the factors influencing the overall molecular geometry. Walsh devised a simple prescription for qualitatively predicting the behavior of molecular orbital energies with geometry and demonstrated a method using the sum of occupied orbital energies for predicting molecular geometry on this basis. The results are consistent with experiment in a preponderant number of cases. A number of recent studies involving *ab initio* molecular orbital calculations on polyatomic molecules have attempted to develop a quantitative account of Walsh's rules. R. J. Buenker and S. D. Peyerimhoff, who in recent years have carried out a number of quantitative studies of individual systems, have collected and critically evaluated all recent research on this topic and prepared a comprehensive review. It is clear that the sum of orbital energies used by Walsh is not a sufficiently reliable quantitative indicator of molecular geometry, but other elements of the Mulliken-Walsh–type correlation diagrams, such as the individual orbital energy curves, can be used to predict differences in geometry within the same molecular family. It is encouraging to note that the results of elaborate numerical calculations can be condensed to a qualitative account of molecular geometry accessible to scientists in areas outside theoretical chemistry.

Chemical reaction mechanisms. Molecular orbital symmetry and molecular orbital energy correlation diagrams have also figured in a major breakthrough in the theoretical description of both organic and inorganic chemical reaction mechanisms. From the collaboration of R. B. Woodward and R. Hoffman and independent work by K. Fukui, it has become clear that a primary factor which determines the pathway of chemical reaction is the necessity of maintaining maximum bonding throughout the reaction. The nuclei of reaction components may undergo extremely complicated coordinate motions to provide low-energy pathways. An inspection of the symmetry properties of the molecular orbitals of reactants and putative transition states for a reaction can lead to predictions in which mechanisms feature maximum bonding and are symmetry-allowed. These ideas have already stimulated extensive experimentation in mechanistic organic chemistry and in design of reaction sequences for the synthesis of new and novel compounds. Orbital symmetry control of inorganic reactions has been reviewed by R. G. Pearson. Orbital symmetry control of chemical reactions is now considered so pervasive that, according to Pearson, "in the future *any* postulated reaction mechanism must be examined to see if the symmetry properties of the molecular orbital involved will allow the reaction to proceed."

Supermolecular structure. Molecular orbital calculations up to now have been used mainly to study individual molecules. The properties of bulk matter depend not only on constituent molecules but on the energetics and properties of molecular assemblies as described by statistical mechanics. The molecular orbital formalism can be used directly to carry out calculations on small clusters of molecules, and recent studies on interacting water molecules by J. W. Moscowitz and coworkers and on the hydrated electron by M. D. Newton illustrate the use of molecular orbital theory in treating problems on condensed phases of the molecular level. The results of Moscowitz were used by F. H. Stillinger in constructing effective pairwise potential functions for a statistical mechanical calculation on aqueous fluids, and work in this area on fluids and solutions is being initiated by E. Clementi and coworkers. With the basic formalism and computational techniques now well in hand, it can be expected that molecular orbital theory will be used in diverse ways in conjunction with theory from allied disciplines for the description of the electronic structure of molecular systems.

For background information *see* MOLECULAR ORBITAL THEORY; MOLECULAR STRUCTURE AND SPECTRA in the McGraw-Hill Encyclopedia of Science and Technology.   [DAVID L. BEVERIDGE]

Bibliography: R. J. Buenker and S. D. Peycrimhoff, *Chem Rev.*, 74:127, 1974; K. Fukui, *Account. Chem. Res.*, 4:57, 1970; W. J. Hehre, R. F. Stewart, and J. A. Pople, *J. Chem. Phys.* 51:2657, 1969 et seq.; R. G. Pearson, *Chem. Eng. News*, 48:66, 1970; W. G. Richards, T. E. H. Walker, and R. K. Hinkley, *A Bibliography of ab initio Molecular Wave Functions*, 1971; R. B. Woodward and R. Hoffman, *The Conservation of Orbital Symmetry*, 1970.

Mollusca

Recent discoveries of uncommon fossils have provided new information that bears on the early history of two classes of mollusks, Cephalopoda and Monoplacophora, and has suggested a theory as to their relationships.

Cephalopoda. Living cephalopods are abundant; among them are the cuttlefish, squids, and octopuses. They are generally considered the most advanced mollusks, in part because their excellent eyesight, complex nervous system, and rapid movement by jet propulsion have allowed them to compete successfully with many groups of marine fish. With the exception of *Nautilus*, living cephalopods have an internal shell reduced in size or, more commonly, are completely shell-less.

Nautilus has a chambered shell, with partitions (septa) each of which is secreted inside the shell by the posterior part of the animal. Each septum is pierced by a tube (siphuncle). Studies of living *Nautilus* have demonstrated that the siphuncle acts like a blotter to draw liquid from the chambers. In this way, shell buoyancy can be controlled, and the animal can migrate vertically through the water.

There is an extensive record of fossil shelled cephalopods extending back about 450 million years (m.y.). Most have a coiled, bilaterally symmetrical shell like *Nautilus*, although there are many variations in shell profile and in shape of septa. During the Paleozoic, and especially the earlier Paleozoic, straight cephalopods were common.

A few authorities believe that straight cephalopods first occurred in the Early Cambrian (575 m.y. ago), but this conclusion is based on a misinterpretation of fossils. The oldest fossil that authorities generally agree is a cephalopod *Plectronoceras*, from the Late Cambrian of China (Fig. 1). The shell is oval in cross section, is slightly curved, and has few widely spaced septa, pierced by a large siphuncle along the interior concave side of the shell. In very slightly younger rocks, straight-shelled *Plectronoceras* occur, followed first by a host of other straight cephalopods and then by the most common coiled forms.

Monoplacophora. In contrast to the cephalopods of today, monoplacophorans are very rare; only a handful of specimens have been dredged from the deep sea. Their shell is simple and spoon-shaped, with the apex overhanging the front (anterior) margin much like that of some rock-clinging snails (Gastropoda). However, the soft parts are those of a bilaterally symmetrical animal with a number of pairs of gills, nerve connections, paired muscles, and other paired organs. In all gastropods the soft parts are twisted, and only one pair of gills — at most — is present. It is generally agreed that monoplacophorans are the most primitive of living mollusks.

Monoplacophorans have a fossil record ranging from Cambrian to Mid-Devonian (about 350 m.y. ago) but are unknown from then until the present day. Indeed, the group was first established and known for many years only from fossils. The multiple paired muscle scars seen in a few fossils indicated that this was a molluscan group fundamentally different from the gastropods.

Fossil monoplacophorans are rare but diverse. Some have spoon-shaped shells; others have an almost central apex; and still others are elongate cones that may be curved. Few preserve the muscle scars, and when muscle scars are not present, it is difficult to determine which part of the shell is the anterior part. Conventionally, it has been assumed that shells curve toward the anterior. However, *Kirengella* (Fig. 2), a low conical, slightly curved shell from the Late Cambrian of Siberia, has well-preserved muscle scars — one large pair

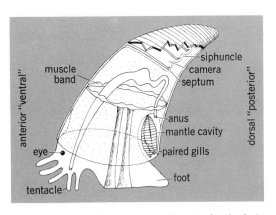

Fig. 1. Reconstruction of some soft parts for the Late Cambrian cephalopod *Plectronoceras*. (From E. L. Yochelson, R. H. Flower, and G. F. Webers, The bearing of the new Late Cambrian monoplacophoran genus Knightoconus upon the origin of the Cephalopoda, Lethaia, 6:275–310, 1973)

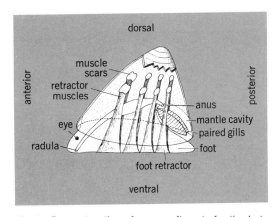

Fig. 2. Reconstruction of some soft parts for the Late Cambrian monoplacophoran *Kirengella*. (From E. L. Yochelson, R. H. Flower, and G. F. Webers, The bearing of the new Late Cambrian monoplacophoran genus Knightoconus upon the origin of the Cephalopoda, Lethaia, 6:275–310, 1973)

and three small pairs; from these muscle scars it can be deduced that the shell curved toward the back (posterior). Thus, some fossil monoplacophorans that do not show muscle scars might also have curved posteriorly.

The key feature for identifying a fossil monoplacophoran is paired muscle scars; as noted, clinging gastropods develop shells that look similar externally. The key feature for identifying a fossil cephalopod is the siphuncle. Some mollusks that are not cephalopods have a bilaterally symmetrical coiled shell. Some gastropods and pelecypods have septa; indeed, septa occur in animals, such as corals, that are unrelated to the mollusks.

Knightoconus from the Late Cambrian of western Antarctica is a monoplacophoran with a curved, moderately high, conical shape. It lacks muscle scars, but it is similar to *Kirengella* in having an oval cross section. In *Kirengella* the widest part of the oval is toward the front. If *Knightoconus* is oriented the same way, the curved cone points in the same direction as in *Kirengella*, that is, posteriorly.

In addition, in *Knightoconus* there are several internal septa that form chambers in the smallest part of the shell. As in the cephalopods, these septa were deposited by the posterior part of the animal as it moved a short distance forward in the shell at irregular intervals. This is the first known septate monoplacophoran. Because the conical shell is so high, the soft parts were strongly bent. Septa may have been deposited to limit the length of the soft parts.

Plectronoceras is smaller and more slender than *Knightoconus*, but both have the same degree of curvature and, presumably, the same direction of curvature and same oval cross section. The major difference between them is the large siphuncle in *Plectronoceras*. To form a septum, the posterior part of the soft parts must be completely free from the shell. If the animal were unable to free all the soft parts from the apex, the septum would have a hole to accommodate a tissue still attached behind it. Each succeeding septum would then have a similar hole as the attached tissue was pulled forward like a stretched rubber band.

This hypothesis suggests that the increased height of some monoplacophoran shells was responsible for the formation of septa and that the development of a siphuncle was a consequence of poor septum formation. If this explanation is correct, the gap between these two classes of mollusks is bridged. Once the system of chambers pierced by a siphuncle was developed, the cephalopods could then begin to regulate the buoyancy of their shells. With this new adaptation, they were able to evolve rapidly and in a variety of ways.

For background information *see* CEPHALOPODA; MOLLUSCA; MONOPLACOPHORA in the McGraw-Hill Encyclopedia of Science and Technology.

[ELLIS L. YOCHELSON]

Bibliography: E. L. Yochelson, R. H. Flower, and G. F. Webers, *Lethaia*, 6:275–310, 1973.

Muscle (biophysics)

In voluntary muscle the onset of contraction is very rapid: in some twitch fibers full tension is developed within milliseconds of excitation of the plasmalemma. Understanding of the mechanisms involved in this finely tuned and very fast control of muscle activity is a basic problem in muscle physiology, in which efforts of the past few years have produced rewarding results.

Excitation-contraction coupling involves the following steps: An action potential is transmitted along the fiber by the plasmalemma. Depolarization spreads to the fiber's interior along the transverse (T) tubules, whose walls are continuous with the plasmalemma (Fig. 1). A signal from the T tubules is transmitted to a separate system of membranes, the sarcoplasmic reticulum (SR), at specialized junctional areas, the triads and dyads (Fig. 1). Calcium is released from SR to fibrils and troponin, a component of the actin filaments, binds calcium and activation of actomyosin occurs. Relaxation is a result of calcium uptake by the SR. Thus the membranes of muscle play a number of roles in the cycling of calcium and regulatory proteins allow the effect of varying concentrations of calcium to be felt by the fibrils.

Spread of excitation along T tubules. The T tubules' diameter (800 A, or 80 nm) is too small to allow measurement of electrical properties. However, T tubules are a necessary link between excitation of the plasmalemma and contraction, so that the latter can be used as an indication of effective T tubule depolarization. Several ingenious experiments, based on this premise, have shown that spread of depolarization along the T tubule is a sodium-dependent action potential. The experiments involve either recording the mechanical output of a fiber, or monitoring the spread of contraction from periphery to interior by optical means. A failure of the centrally placed fibrils to contract can be interpreted as a failure of the central T tubules to depolarize sufficiently. Requirement for sodium and the existence of active sodium channels are established by the use of either low concentrations of sodium or of tetrodotoxin, the puffer fish poison, which is known to specifically block sodium channels.

Problem of transmission at the triad. T tubule depolarization is converted into a signal causing release of calcium from the SR. A possible initial link may be a voltage-dependent movement of charge which occurs across the walls of the T tubules. How this or other electrical events in the tubules affect the SR membrane is not understood. Basically, there are two mechanisms by which membranes can influence each other across a junction: (1) Ionic current may be able to flow from the lumen of one system to that of the other by way

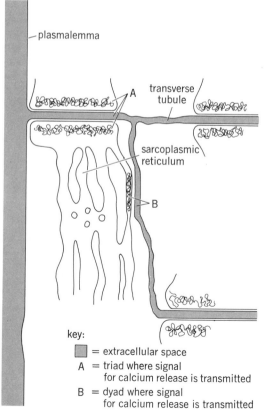

plasmalemma

A

transverse tubule

sarcoplasmic reticulum

B

key:

▨ = extracellular space

A = triad where signal for calcium release is transmitted

B = dyad where signal for calcium release is transmitted

Fig. 1. Schematic drawing of membranes involved in excitation-contraction coupling. The plasmalemma invaginates into the fiber to form the transverse tubules.

of a relatively low-resistance pathway. In cases where this occurs, electron microscopy of freeze-fracture surfaces shows that "particles" in matching arrays occupy the junctional membranes and it is assumed that channels directly join the two lumina. (2) A transmitter, released by one of the membranes, diffuses across the junctional gap and interacts with receptors located in the postjunctional membrane.

In the case of the triads, relevant information has been obtained by freeze-fracture, a technique of electron microscopy which puts in evidence the inner architecture of membranes. In fracturing frozen specimens, membranes are split along the hydrophobic interior and cytoplasmic and luminal leaflets are separated. Proteins which penetrate into the membrane are visible on the exposed fracture faces as small particles. The architecture of triads is quite different from that of low-resistance junctions in that the junctional surfaces of SR and T tubules do not show matching arrays of particles (Fig. 2). The possibility remains that transmission at triads occurs by the second type of mechanism. There are, however, two difficulties: identity of the transmitter or "trigger" and its storage sites which are nowhere to be seen. A small amount of calcium enters the fiber at the moment of excitation and this calcium has been a favorite candidate for the "trigger." Recently, however, fibers were induced to twitch in the absence of calcium and this leaves the identity of a possible trigger still open to investigation.

Release of calcium. There is now some evidence that a change in potential across the SR membrane is responsible for calcium release. In skinned fibers, a sudden change in chloride concentration of the medium bathing the SR induces release of calcium. Once the T tubules are excluded as mediators of the effect, it can be concluded that a change in SR polarization precedes release. A similar interpretation is given to the fluorescence changes which accompany excitation in muscles stained with Nile Blue, a dye which associates with membranes and is sensitive to the electric field across them.

A controversy remains on one detail of the calcium release mechanism. On one hand, release is considered to be a regenerative process, in which calcium itself induces further release of calcium. On the other hand, it has been shown that release may be graded, at least under experimental conditions.

Control of actomyosin interaction. At the molecular level one intriguing facet has been added to the knowledge of troponin's regulatory function. The "turn on" signal given by troponin in the presence of calcium affects seven actin monomers for each troponin. It is thought that troponin's regulation is mediated by tropomyosin molecules which occupy the grooves of the actin helix and cover the length of seven actin monomers.

Calcium pump. Calcium is accumulated within the SR by an active transport mechanism requiring ATP as an energy source. A proteolipid complex showing a calcium-activated ATPase has been isolated and it is a major component of the SR membrane. Lipids are an integral part of the complex and necessary for the maintenance of its activity.

Biochemical, x-ray diffraction, and electron mi-

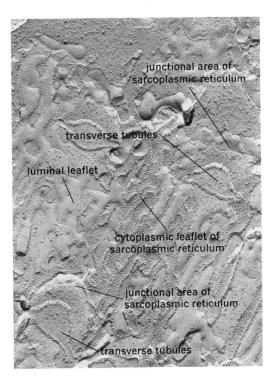

Fig. 2. Freeze-fracture of membranes in muscle. The cytoplasmic leaflet of the sarcoplasmic reticulum shows the particles of the calcium pump, the luminal leaflet is smooth. Particles in transverse tubules and sarcoplasmic reticulum at the junction do not match in disposition. (*From C. Franzini-Armstrong, Freeze fracture of skeletal muscle from the tarantula spider: Structural differentiation of sarcoplasmic reticulum and transverse tubular system membranes, J. Cell. Biol., 61:501, 1974*)

croscopical evidence suggest the following relationship between the calcium pump and the membrane. The pump consists of a hydrophobic globular portion embedded in the membrane and of a hydrophilic extension projecting outside the SR. The hydrophilic extension is digested by trypsin, is visible in negatively stained preparations and can be tagged by ferritin labels. The hydrophobic region is visible in freeze-fracture. The most striking feature of the density profile calculated from x-ray diffraction of stacks of SR membranes is a strong asymmetry, indicating location of most of the protein within the outer leaflet. In freeze-fracture the asymmetry of the SR is strikingly evident (Fig. 2): the cytoplasmic leaflet is covered by numerous particles, the luminal leaflet is smooth.

In the interior of the SR calcium is able to attain a fairly high concentration by binding to an acidic protein, calsequestrin.

For background information *see* BIOPOTENTIALS AND ELECTROPHYSIOLOGY; MUSCLE (BIOPHYSICS) in the McGraw-Hill Encyclopedia of Science and Technology.

[CLARA FRANZINI-ARMSTRONG]

Bibliography: J. Bastian and S. Nakajima, *J. Gen. Physiol.*, 63:257, 1974; J. M. Murray and A. Weber, *Sci. Amer.*, p. 59, February 1974; M. F. Schneider and W. K. Chandler, *Nature*, 242:266, 1973; P. S. Stewart and D. H. McLennan, *J. Biol. Chem.*, 249:985, 1974.

Nobel prizes

Twelve men received Nobel prizes in 1974. In awarding the Physics prize, the Nobel Committee for the first time cited achievements in astronomy.

Medicine or physiology. There were three recipients, all working in cellular biology. Albert Claude, who heads the Jules Bordet Institute in Brussels, pioneered in application of electron microscopy to cell studies and in use of the centrifuge to separate cell components. Christian de Duve, who holds appointments at Rockefeller University in New York City and at the University of Louvain, and George E. Palade, of the Yale University School of Medicine, refined these techniques in studying cell components, discovering lysosomes and ribosomes respectively.

Chemistry. Paul J. Flory, Professor of Chemistry at Stanford University, was honored for his extensive work in developing analytic techniques to explore the properties and molecular structures of long-chain molecules.

Physics. Martin Ryle and Antony Hewish, Professors at the Cavendish Laboratory of Cambridge University in England, were named for the Physics award. Dr. Ryle devised the aperture synthesis method in radiotelescopy and has gained much information about objects in the universe. Dr. Hewish led in the discovery of pulsars, through use of radiotelescopes.

Literature. The corecipients in this category were Eyvind Johnson and Harry Edmund Martinson, both well-known authors in their native Sweden.

Economics. This award was shared by Gunnar Myrdal, Visiting Professor at the City University of New York, and Friedrich A. von Hayek, Visiting Professor at Salzburg University. The Nobel Committee cited "their pioneering work in the theory of money and economic fluctuations and . . . analysis of the interdependence of economic, social and institutional phenomena."

Peace. Recipients of the Peace prize were Eisaku Sato, former Premier of Japan, for his policies leading to his nation's pledge to forego development of nuclear weaponry; and Sean McBride of Ireland, who as United Nations Commissioner of South-West Africa supervised the UN effort to gain independence for this area from South Africa.

Noise control

Traffic noise is man's most widespread form of audio pollution, and year by year the problem is becoming more acute. Schools, recreational areas, and even homes are subjected to this irritating invasion. Much has been done to reduce traffic noise at the source, but because of practical limitations, these efforts have been only partly successful, and other means must be found.

Trees, shrubs, and other forms of vegetation have been used to screen objectionable traffic from view, but no thought has been given to their noise-reducing ability. Recent experiments have demonstrated that wide belts of tall, dense trees can significantly reduce traffic noise. Sound levels have been cut up to 10 dB—a reduction in noise of approximately half—although 5–8 dB is more typi-

cal for the average 50–70 ft-wide belt (10 ft = 3 m). Frequently, this reduction is sufficient to bring the noise level down from "objectionable" to "not objectionable," so that normal outdoor activities can proceed undisturbed. Unfortunately, the time required to develop a tree barrier of the size required may be prohibitive, and some additional barriers may be necessary.

Combinations of trees and solid barriers. A natural combination of trees and landforms provides an effective noise screen that has pleasing esthetic qualities (Fig. 1). This combination retains the desirable features of the single solid barrier without some of its esthetic drawbacks. The solid barrier provides some immediate relief, and the plant materials soften the profile and increase protection as they mature. Recent experiments show that the combination of trees and solid barriers results in more uniform control for a greater distance than when either method of sound reduction is used separately. Sound reductions of 10–15 dB (that is, the noise is one-third to one-half as loud) are common for 12-ft-high landforms combined with wide belts of moderately tall, dense trees (Fig. 2).

Relative placement of the barrier between the noise source and the protected area is of great importance. Generally, a barrier placed close to a noise source is more effective than one placed midway between source and receiver. Furthermore, screening is effective only when the noise source is hidden from the receiver's view, and the effectiveness gradually increases as the height of the screen is increased. A 10-ft-high landform should be close to optimum height for level terrain, so that it will screen the exhaust stack of a large truck from view.

Natural hills, cuts, and other topographic features can be used to advantage when rest areas and other noise-sensitive sites are being located along highways. If trees and shrubs are already present, they should be undisturbed, and additional ones planted to achieve the best results. Elevated highways have undesirable acoustic qualities, for generated noise may pass over the tops of adjacent trees or terrain, depending on the elevation of the highway.

Physical considerations in noise control. The mechanisms by which plant materials and landforms reduce noise are quite complex. Among them are diffusion, or scattering, of the sound by leaves, branches, and solid surfaces, and absorption of the sound energy within the cavities and over the surfaces of the plants, especially if they support large amounts of heavy foliage.

Altering the shape and direction of propagation of the wave front profoundly affects sound levels. Sound projected upwind decreases rapidly with distance, whereas sound projected downwind carries much farther. Fortunately, tree structures have been found to be most effective in blocking downwind projections, where the need is greatest.

Variations of temperature with elevation tend to "bend" the wave front upward or downward, producing some rather surprising "shadow zones" and unusually long-distance projections. In summer, a band of cooler, high-density air within a belt of trees may offer some resistance to sound penetration; this effect has not been investigated thoroughly.

The variables encountered in studies of this nature are formidable. Trees in most plantings vary greatly in size and shape, and their foliage characteristics change from season to season. Atmospheric phenomena, already mentioned as affecting sound transmission, vary hourly. Landforms also vary in size, shape, and placement. Because of the large number and range of variables, a statistical analysis is indicated, and the conclusions stated in this article are based to a large extent on such analysis.

Continuous forest propagation. The attenuation (diminishing) of sound through a continuous forest is an entirely different phenomenon from that previously described, in which structures of trees, shrubs, and solid barriers are interposed between a source and a receiver. In a forest the noise source originates within the medium rather than outside of it. Furthermore, the objectives of research studies are usually related to "foreign" noises that are brought into the natural forest environment and that are therefore considered intrusive. The results of such studies are usually given as "excess attenuation" (in excess of the amount calculated theoretically for a point source emission) in decibels per 100 ft, whereas barrier studies yield a more complicated relationship; usually a cubic equation is required. Formerly, studies within a forest used fixed-frequency (continuous-tone) noise sources. Quite recently, however, a group of 11 typical forest noises, both natural and foreign, were used as the noise source. Natural forest noises were those made by hand saws, axes, picks and shovels, rock drills and sledges, pistol and rifle fire, a man shouting, and trail crews at work. Noises made by a pickup truck, motorcycle, small internal combustion engine, and chain saw were judged to be foreign. Results of the studies indicate that the density of the plant materials plays an important part in the attenuation of sound and that, for a rather open type of forest, containing bare tree trunks for a considerable height, the excess attenuation is small. Other studies that have compared the attenuation through forests with that over surfaces of varying degrees of hardness—from tall grass to pavement—indicate that tree-covered surfaces provide greatest attenuation.

Expectations for the future. Natural phenomena and practical limitations largely govern the extent of outdoor noise control. The "open" nature of the outdoors and the requirement of full enclosure of a noise source for complete control are diametrically opposed. Some sound will always pass over and around a barrier of reasonable size. The hard-surfaced roadways and building walls that are found in urban areas are incompatible with the softness required for absorption of sound; reflection from these surfaces often increases the noise level beyond that expected. Recent awareness by landscape architects and community planners of the need for quieter environments will no doubt result in a greater use of plant materials in the form of landscaped malls and parking areas, but because of the expense of modification, urban areas are likely to be noisy for some time to come.

In new developments, and in suburban and rural

Fig. 1. Scientists measuring highway traffic noise behind bare and tree-covered landforms. (*Courtesy of the University of Nebraska Agricultural Experiment Station*)

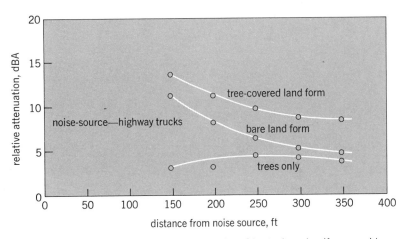

Fig. 2. Comparison of noise-reducing properties of trees, bare landform, and tree-covered landform. Attenuation is relative to a level, mowed grass surface. (*Courtesy of the U. S. Forest Service Rocky Mountain Forest and Range Experiment Station*)

areas, the picture is somewhat brighter. Surveys along major arterials have shown that sound levels below 68 dBA are acceptable for outdoor daytime activities, although most authorities favor somewhat lower levels—below 65 dBA for daytime and below 50 dBA for nighttime in residential areas. Traffic noise produced by passenger cars—not trucks—traveling at 35–40 mi (56–64 km) per hour reaches about 70 dBA at 33–66 ft (10–20 m) from the traffic lane, and a modest reduction of 5 dB by the use of soft surfaces—trees, shrubs, and grass—is often sufficient. Under more severe conditions the addition of solid barriers is indicated. Many common noises can be brought below the disturbing level by the tree belts and landforms suggested, because a 10-dB reduction, which is often sufficient, is not too difficult to obtain.

For background information *see* NOISE CONTROL

in the McGraw-Hill Encyclopedia of Science and Technology.

[DAVID I. COOK; D. F. VAN HAVERBEKE]
Bibliography: D. I. Cook and D. F. Van Haverbeke, *Tree-covered Land-forms for Noise Control*, Univ. Neb. Coll. Agr. Exp. Sta. Bull. 263, 1974; R. T. Harrison, *Sound Propagation and Annoyance under Forest Conditions*, Equip. Devel. Test Rep. 7120-6, U.S. Dep. Agr., Forest Serv. Equip. Develop. Ctr., San Dimas, CA, 1974.

Nuclear fuels

The enrichment of uranium in its U-235 content, a major step in the nuclear fuel cycle, is receiving increasing attention as nuclear power continues to grow and the projected demand for enriched uranium begins to exceed available enrichment capacity. New methods of uranium enrichment are being studied as possible alternates to the gaseous diffusion process used in the three plants owned by the U.S. Atomic Energy Commission. Rapid advances have been made in the development of gas centrifuges for large-scale commercial isotope separation. Very recently, laser isotope separation has been demonstrated in small-scale laboratory experiments. *See* ISOTOPE (STABLE) SEPARATION.

The three gaseous diffusion plants located near Oak Ridge, TN, Paducah, KY, and Portsmouth, OH, are being improved and uprated in power to help meet the new demand, but additional enrichment capacity will be needed by as early as 1984. Government and industry in the United States and in other countries are mounting intensive development efforts in enrichment technology to assure that new economically competitive plants will be in operation by this time.

Demand for enriched uranium. The demand for enriched uranium is tied to the installation schedule for new nuclear power stations. The near term growth of nuclear power in the United States has been revised downward in a recent AEC forecast because of delays in power plant construction and national policies encouraging energy conservation. Even so, the predicted growth remains large, start-

ing with an installed nuclear generating capacity of 24,000 megawatts of electric power in 1973, increasing to 102,000 MW(e) in 1980, 475,000 MW(e) in 1990, and reaching 1,090,000 MW(e) by the year 2000. Foreign installed nuclear capacity is forecast to exceed 2,000,000 MW(e) by the year 2000. *See* ELECTRICAL UTILITY INDUSTRY.

Forecasts of enrichment requirements depend not only on expected rate of installation of nuclear power capacity but also on estimates of average percentage of full-capacity operation (presently assumed 75%) and the type of power reactor installed. The light water reactor, the type installed or on order for most American plants, is fueled with uranium enriched to 2 to 4% U-235 (natural uranium contains 0.7% U-235). A 1000-MW(e) light water reactor operating in equilibrium requires about 100,000 separative work units (SWU) of enrichment per year. (The separative work unit is a fundamental measure of the work required to separate a quantity of isotopic mixture into two component parts, one having a higher percentage of concentration of the desired isotope and one having a lower percentage. Separative work depends only on the initial and two final concentrations and the quantity of material processed. It is independent of the separation process used. It is common practice in the enrichment of uranium to give the SWU the dimension of kilograms of uranium.)

The AEC's estimate of "most likely" annual separative work requirement of the world through 2000, where "most likely" falls about midway in a range of possible cases, is shown in Fig. 1. The projections of annual separative work demand assume a 0.3% U-235 content in the enrichment plant waste stream, power plants operating at an average of 75% of full capacity, recovery and recycle as fuel of some of the plutonium produced, and, by 1988, the introduction of breeder reactors which do not require enriched uranium. The scale on the right of Fig. 1 is the number of new enriching plants that would be required to produce the indicated demand if each plant were to have a nominal capacity of 8,750,000 SWU/yr. The three present American gaseous diffusion plants will have a combined capacity of 27,700,000 SWU/yr when improved and uprated. The projected United States share of the demand curve exceeds this capacity in 1982, but preproduction and stockpiling will permit production from new plants to be delayed until 1984.

New plants. Estimates of construction costs, in 1973 dollars, of a new 8,750,000 SWU/yr enrichment plant range from $1,400,000,000 to over $2,000,000,000, depending to some extent on the process selected. Ten such plants are projected to be completed in the United States over a 15-year period starting in 1984, about 1 every 18 months. It requires as long as 8 years to construct a plant and to get it into operation. Thus, the type of process to be used in new plants must be selected at an early date. The gaseous diffusion process has been in use in large-scale plant operation for over 25 years and offers minimal technological risks, but it consumes large quantities of electric power, requiring 2400 MW for each 8,750,000 SWU/yr plant. In comparison, the gas centrifuge process requires only about a tenth as much power and can likely be

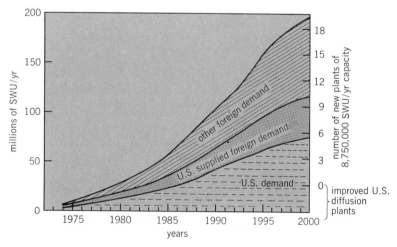

Fig. 1. Projections of annual separative work demand based on the "most likely" growth in nuclear power. (*From U.S. Atomic Energy Commission, Nuclear Power Growth 1974–2000, Rep. WASH-1139(74), February 1974*)

built on a considerably smaller scale than the 8,750,000 SWU/yr minimum size required for diffusion plants without substantial economic penalty. Even at the present stage of development, the gas centrifuge appears to be economically competitive with gaseous diffusion, and since centrifuge technology is relatively new it offers greater potential for technological gains which can reduce the costs of separative work even further. It is therefore likely that at least some of the new United States enrichment plants will be gas centrifuge plants.

Plans for new enrichment plants are being developed by a number of other countries. There are the Tripartite Centrifuge Group, URENCO Ltd. (United Kingdom, Federal Republic of Germany, and the Netherlands); and the Eurodiff diffusion group (France, other European countries, Japan, and Australia). The Federal Republic of Germany has an independent development program for the jet nozzle method. South Africa has an undisclosed enriching process. The U.S.S.R. is presently the only major existing source of supply of uranium enrichment services outside of the United States.

Gas centrifuge. The operation of a gas centrifuge is illustrated in Fig. 2. Uranium hexafluoride (UF_6) having a molecular weight of 352 is used as the process gas. The rotor, a long cylindrical tube containing the process gas, is spun a high rotational speed, creating a high centrifugal field in the rotor. The heavier UF_6 molecules containing U-238 are concentrated near the periphery by the centrifugal field while the lighter molecules containing U-235 are concentrated near the axis. A countercurrent flow moving up near the axis and down along the periphery effects a net transport of heavy isotopes toward the bottom and light isotopes toward the top, thereby establishing an axial concentration gradient. Thus gas removed from the top of the rotor is enriched in U-235 (product) while the gas removed from the bottom is depleted in U-235 (waste). The process can be made continuous by feeding new gas at the center of the rotor.

In practice the rotor is operated at such a high peripheral speed, 400 m/sec or above, that most of the UF_6 is compressed into a thin layer near the periphery, much like the atmosphere is held close to the surface of the Earth by gravity. This leaves a near vacuum along the axis, and hence very little gas is lost from the rotor through the central opening in the top end cap. The gas is fed into and extracted from the rotor through stationary tubes inserted through this opening. The gas is collected from near the periphery by impact tubes called scoops. In addition to extracting the gas, the scoops may also drive the countercurrent flow by removing angular momentum from the gas through drag. In Fig. 2, the bottom scoop pumps the gas radially inward, forcing it up along the axis and pulling it down along the periphery. The top scoop is shielded by a rotating baffle so that it will not drive the countercurrent flow in the reverse direction. The countercurrent flow can also be driven by cooling the top and heating the bottom of the rotor, much like thermal gradients drive the winds at high altitudes in the Earth's atmosphere.

Because of the high surface speed, the rotor must be surrounded by a vacuum to reduce drag

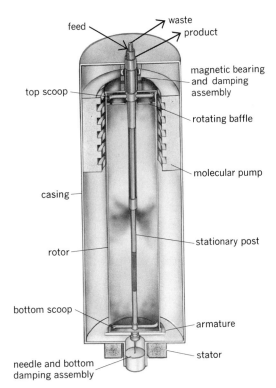

Fig. 2. Schematic of a gas centrifuge, based on a model developed by G. Zippe. (*Courtesy of Union Carbide Corporation*)

and heating. The rotor is supported at the bottom by a low-friction bearing mounted in a damping system while the top is supported by a frictionless magnetic bearing. Once the rotor has been accelerated to speed, very little power is required to keep it running. The rotors are expected to run unattended for as long as 10 years.

The maximum theoretical separative capacity of a gas centrifuge is proportional to its length and the fourth power of the peripheral speed but independent of the diameter. Thus it is the peripheral speed that is important, not the rotational speed. The peripheral speed is limited by the strength-to-density ratio of the rotor material. For a given rotor material the rotor can be large in diameter, spinning at a low rotational speed, or small in diameter, spinning at a high rotational speed. The appropriate length-to-diameter ratio for a rotor is determined by mechanical vibration considerations. The rotor sketched in Fig. 2 is 7.6 cm in diameter and 38 cm long. A separative capacity of 0.4 SWU/yr is obtained with this rotor at a peripheral speed of 350 m/sec. The exact dimensions and speeds of proposed production-type rotors have not been disclosed. However, available information indicates that an 8,750,000 SWU/yr plant would require from tens of thousands to hundreds of thousands of centrifuges, corresponding to individual machine separative capacities ranging from 10 to 100 SWU/yr.

For background information *see* ISOTOPE (STABLE) SEPARATION; NUCLEAR FUELS in the McGraw-Hill Encyclopedia of Science and Technology.

[RALPH A. LOWRY]

Bibliography: D. G. Avery and E. Davies, *Uranium Enrichment by Gas Centrifuge*, 1973; J. J. Christie (ed.), *Nucl. Ind.*, 21(5):15–19, May 1974; E. P. Muntz and B. B. Hamel, *Proceedings of the 9th International Symposium on Rarefied Gas Dynamics*, 1:B.1.1–B.1.10, 1974; U.S. Atomic Energy Commission, *Nuclear Power Growth 1974–2000*, Rep. WASH-1139(74), February 1974.

Nuclear magnetic resonance (NMR)

During the past few years a variety of nonlanthanide reagents have been developed. One group that is noteworthy in terms of its potential is made up of species characterized by the presence of metal or metalloid porphyrin or porphyrin-like ring systems (Fig. 1). During the same time, a number of lanthanide shift reagents have also been developed.

All the members of this promising group function in the same general fashion. They all bind the substrates or the significant portions of the substrates to their ring centers by forming, as appropriate, addition or condensation bonds with them. Similarly, they all shift the protons brought under their influence by enveloping them in nonhomogeneous local ring-current generated fields (in the functioning reagents there are no paramagnetic atoms).

These reagents are used in one or both of two ways. Some are used to spread and simplify the spectra of substrates, that is, as ordinary shift re-

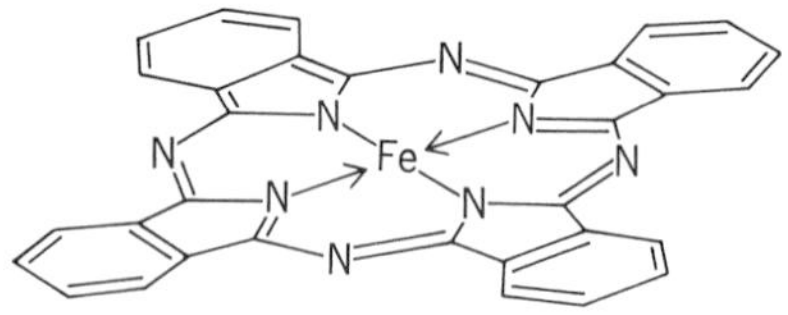

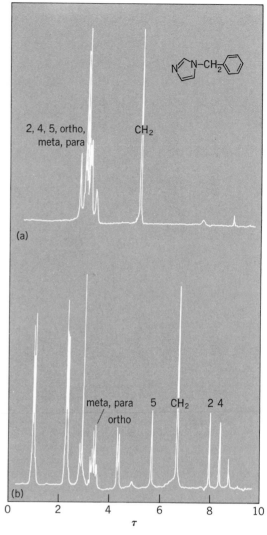

(a)

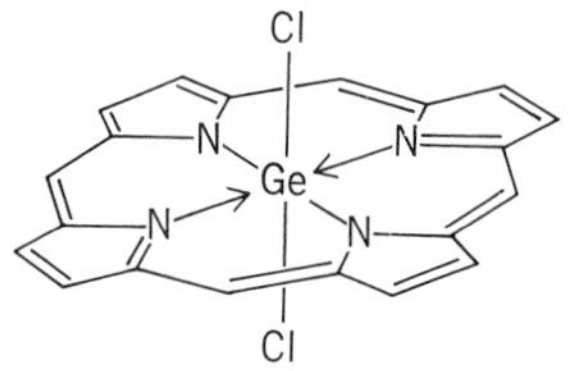

(b)

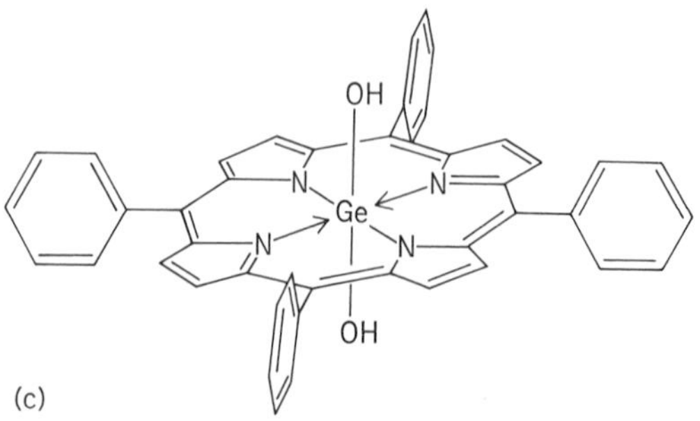

(c)

Fig. 1. Three typical macrocyclic shift reagents. (a) Iron(II) phthalocyanine; (b) dichlorogermanium(IV) porphine; and (c) dihydroxygermanium(IV) tetraphenylporphine.

Fig. 2. The ordinary and shifted spectra of benzylimidazole (the numbers identify positions of the imidazole hydrogens). (a) The ordinary 100-MHz spectrum. (b) The spectrum as shifted by the reagent PcFe(ND$_2$C$_6$D$_5$)$_6$ (the solvent used was CDCl$_3$). (*Courtesy of Clement K. Choy*)

agents. The others, as well as two of those used as ordinary shift reagents, are used in work that has as its objective the determination of substrate bond parameters.

Spectral simplification. The reagents used to simplify spectra are best classified according to the atoms in their ring centers. Those of current interest have iron, cobalt, silicon, or germanium as ring center atoms.

Iron reagents. One of the most important reagents that has iron as a central atom is iron(II) phthalocyanine, PcFe. This reagent is applicable to unhindered amines. In use it is typically reacted with the amine of interest under moderate conditions in ordinary apparatus. The resultant compound is then dissolved in a suitable solvent, such as deuteriochloroform, and a spectrum is obtained. In general the reagent-substrate reaction proceeds as in Eq. (1), with the product being trans octahedral and diamagnetic. (Occasionally the reaction proceeds differently and gives a product not suitable as a shift compound.)

$$\text{PcFe} + 2\text{B} \rightarrow \text{PcFeB}_2 \qquad (1)$$

Another reagent that has iron as a central atom is bis-n-deuteriobutylamineiron(II) phthalocyanine, $\text{PcFe}(\text{ND}_2\text{C}_4\text{D}_9\text{-}n)_2$. It is also applicable to unhindered amines. However, it is more convenient to use because, in general, it is reacted with the amine of interest directly in the NMR tube. For many amines the main reagent-substrate reaction is that given in Eq. (2).

$$\text{PcFe}(\text{ND}_2\text{C}_4\text{D}_9\text{-}n)_2 + 2\text{B} \xrightarrow[\text{solvent}]{\text{NMR}}$$
$$\text{PcFeB}_2 + 2\,\text{ND}_2\text{C}_4\text{D}_9\text{-}n \qquad (2)$$

A third reagent that has iron as a central atom is the aniline analog of the butylamine reagent, $\text{PcFe}(\text{ND}_2\text{C}_6\text{D}_5)_6$ (the extra amine in this reagent is presumed to be free of direct association with the iron of the reagent). This reagent is applied in the same way as its butylamine analog and is particularly easy to use (Fig. 2).

An important feature of these iron reagents is their considerable specificity. Experience shows that they are particularly suited for application to heterocyclic amines, such as imidazoles and pyridines, and to primary aliphatic amines.

Cobalt reagent. Cobalt is the central atom of another reagent used for simplification, bromocobalt(III) tetraphenylporphine, TPPCoBr. Like its iron analogs, it is applicable to unhindered amines, Eq. (3). Well-simplified spectra are obtained with it.

$$\text{TPPCoBr} + 2\text{B} \rightarrow (\text{TPPCoB}_2)\text{Br} \qquad (3)$$

Silicon and germanium reagents. One of the important reagents of the silicon and germanium classes is dihydroxygermanium(IV) tetraphenylporphine, TPPGe(OH)_2. It is applicable to alcohols, phenols, and carboxylic acids. In use, it is reacted with the substrate of interest under moderate conditions in ordinary apparatus. The product is then dissolved in a suitable solvent such as deuteriochloroform, and a spectrum is obtained. For phenols the reagent-substrate reaction is that given in Eq. (4). Generally the reagent gives well-resolved spectra.

$$\text{TPPGe(OH)}_2 + 2\,\text{ROH} \rightarrow \text{TPPGe(OR)}_2 + \text{H}_2\text{O} \qquad (4)$$

A closely related reagent is dichlorogermanium(IV) tetraphenylporphine. Like the analogous dihydroxide, it is applicable to alcohols and phenols. However, the reaction chemistry involved in using it with these substrates is less direct. It can also be used with Grignard and organolithium reagents.

Other reagents used for simplification and closely related to the above two reagents are dichloro- and dihydroxygermanium(IV) porphine and dichloro- and dihydroxysilicon(IV) phthalocyanine. The ranges of applicability of these reagents, insofar as they are known, are similar to those of the analogous tetraphenylporphines.

A desirable feature of all these group IV reagents is their specificity. For the two porphine

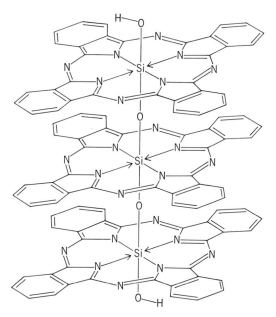

Fig. 3. The trimeric shift reagent $\text{HO(PcSiO)}_3\text{H}$.

reagents an attractive feature is the simplicity of their ring resonances. For the tetraphenylporphine and phthalocyanine reagents a feature of substantial importance is the ease with which they can be prepared.

Bond parameter determination. The reagents to which most of the attention has been given in the bond parameter work are dihydroxysilicon phthalocyanine, PcSi(OH)_2, and the four closely related oligomeric oxygen-bridged hydroxy silicon phthalocyanines, $\text{HO(PcSiO)}_{2-5}\text{H}$ (Fig. 3). Some attention has been given to iron(II) phthalocyanine.

The ring-current equation upon which the work has been based is of the superconducting loop type. This equation was developed with the aid of data pertaining to some oligomeric siloxysilicon phthalocyanines and some siloxymethylsilicon phthalocyanines.

A procedure that has been followed when one parameter is being sought involves, as an initial step, the determination of induced shifts for appropriate protons of the shift compounds being used. Then, by estimation, a value is set for the parameter being sought. Next, induced shifts for the proton under consideration are calculated (using literature data or specially determined data for the remaining needed parameters). Finally, by iteration, a best set of induced shifts is obtained, and the value of the parameter yielding this set is taken as the best value for the parameter.

In one bond parameter determination effort of this type, the reagents used were $\text{HO(PcSiO)}_{1-5}\text{H}$, and the shift compounds were $(\text{CH}_3)_3\text{SiO(PcSiO)}_{1-5}\text{Si(CH}_3)_3$. It was assumed that the Si_{Pc}—O—Si_{Me} bond angle common to the compounds was the same in all five compounds, and on this basis the value of this angle was sought. Four induced shifts, the monomer-dimer, the dimer-trimer, the trimer-tetramer, and the tetramer-pentamer induced shifts, were used in the calculation. With

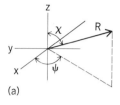

(a)

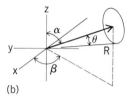

(b)

Fig. 4. Pseudocontact interaction.
(a) Coordinates.
(b) Coordinates, with free rotation about the lanthanide substrate bond.

the assumption of many equally occupied and rapidly interconverting conformers about the O—Si$_{Me}$ bond, the angle obtained was 162(3)°. This angle is in reasonable agreement with the angle found by x-ray crystallography for PcSi(OSi(CH$_3$)$_3$)$_2$, 157.2(8)°.

Since the reagents used in macrocyclic shift reagent work of this type are quite unlike those used in the corresponding lanthanide reagent work, the kinds of problems met in using them are different. Thus, substantially different sets of advantages and disadvantages are associated with the two types of reagents. For example, the sizes of the induced shifts produced by the macrocyclic reagents are smaller than those produced by the lanthanide reagents. On the other hand, the orientations of the local nonhomogeneous magnetic fields produced by the macrocyclic reagents are clear, whereas this is not the case with the lanthanide shift reagents.   [MALCOLM E. KENNEY]

Lanthanide shift reagents. The usefulness of lanthanide complexes as NMR shift reagents is a consequence of a favorable combination of chemical and magnetic properties; advances in this area of chemical research can be classified accordingly. The scope of application of these reagents has continued to increase as new classes or compounds have been found to associate with the lanthanide complexes. A deuterium isotope effect that is a consequence of subtle chemical differences has been observed. Structural analyses of organic compounds, based on new insights into the nature of lanthanide-induced shifts, have been demonstrated to have broad applications.

Organometallic and coordination compounds. Recently, T. M. Marks has demonstrated that many organometallic compounds will associate with lanthanide chelates and that proton resonances associated with the compounds are shifted. Sites of coordination between the organometallics and lanthanide chelates are unique. For instance, metal complexes containing halides and pseudohalides such as F, Cl, N$_3$, and CN were found to interact with the shift reagent, whereas complexes containing Br, I, and NCS did not. In metal carbonyls, CO groups are sites of association with bridging carbonyls more basic than terminal groups. Substantial lanthanide-induced shifts were observed in spectra of the complexes (C$_5$H$_5$)$_2$WH$_2$ and (C$_5$H$_5$)$_2$Sn. These results represent the first evidence for metal-lanthanide bonds.

Isotope effects. A deuterium isotope effect in lanthanide-induced shifts has been observed when a deuterium atom is substituted for a hydrogen atom near the site of coordination on the organic substrate. Proton resonances of the deuterium-substituted substrate are shifted 1–3% further than those of the unsubstituted form. The effect is most readily observed in lanthanide-shifted spectra when 50:50 mixtures of substituted and unsubstituted molecules are studied, and is seen as a doubling of peaks as one set of resonances is shifted away from the other. The effect has been observed in studies of appropriately substituted alcohols, amines, ethers, and aldehydes.

Deuterium substitution near these functional groups increases the basicity of the compounds. The greater fractional association of the deuterium-substituted compound with the lanthanide complex results in a greater observed shift for the associated proton resonances. Since the deuterium atom is not directly involved in the interaction between lanthanide and substrate, the effect is classified as a secondary isotope effect. In the simplest case, the ratio of shifts for the substituted, Δ_D, and unsubstituted, Δ_H, substrates is equal to the ratio of association constants, $\Delta_D/\Delta_H = K_D/K_H$. A 3% difference in shifts, through the above reaction, represents only a 20 cal/mole difference in the free energies of association for the two cases. This phenomenon offers a unique tool in the study of secondary isotope effects.

Pseudocontact interaction. A central concern in lanthanide shift reagent research has been the analysis of molecular structure using lanthanide-induced shifts. Pseudocontact interactions are dipolar magnetic interactions. The pseudocontact interaction is the principal contributor to the shifts observed, which are given by Eq. (5), where Δv_i is the shift induced in the resonance assigned to the ith nucleus at a resonance frequency; v_o, K_a, and K_n are dependent upon magnetic susceptibilities, R_i is the distance from the paramagnetic metal to the ith nucleus; and χ and ψ are angles measured from axes centered on the metal (Fig. 4a). Values of K_a and K_n are dependent upon the particular metal, but the form of the equation is a function only of symmetry. Equation (5) is written for the most general case of total magnetic anisotropy. The angles χ and ψ and the distance R are parameters of molecular structure and form the basis for the study of molecular structure in solution. Application of Eq.(5) is in principle, however, not immediate. The principal axes from which the angles χ and ψ are measured require specification.

$$\frac{\Delta v_i}{v_o} = K_a \frac{(3\cos^2 \chi_i - 1)}{R_i^3} + K_n \frac{\sin^2 \chi_i \cos 2\psi_i}{R_i^3} \quad (5)$$

In 1970 it was found in a study of norborneol that the induced shifts could be calculated using only the first term of Eq. (5) and, further, that the principal axis was defined by the lanthanide-substrate bond. This meant that the complexes between lanthanide chelate and substrate could be considered axially symmetric. This simplification was successfully applied in a wide variety of systems and firmly established on an empirical basis for many classes of substrate. It was not clear, however, why the axial form of the pseudocontact equation applied. X-ray crystallographic studies of both lanthanide chelate complexes and lanthanide chelate-substrate complexes show that they are in each case nonaxial. On that basis, pseudocontact shifts should in general be given by both terms of Eq. (5).

Recently E. W. Randall and coworkers derived a relationship that explains the paradox in many instances. They found that if the substrate can rotate freely about the lanthanide-substrate bond, the pseudocontact shift for the ith resonance is given by a relation of the type shown in Eq. (6), where the

$$\frac{\Delta v_i}{v_o} = \frac{1}{2} \left[K_1(3\cos^2\alpha - 1) + K_2 \sin^2\alpha \cos 2\beta \right]$$
$$\cdot \frac{(3\cos^2\theta_i - 1)}{R_i^3} = K_3 \frac{(3\cos^2\theta_i - 1)}{R_i^3} \quad (6)$$

angles α and β orient the axis of rotation and θ is measured from the rotation axis (Fig. 4b). In this instance, the shifts are *effectively* axial. Equation (6), and the insight its derivation provides, not only supplies theoretical foundation for a commonly observed situation, but also suggests approaches to the analysis of those cases in which free rotation does not obtain and the greater complexity of total anisotropy must be faced.

Contact shifts in ^{13}C NMR. The contact interaction is an alternative paramagnetic shift mechanism. Shifts in resonances due to this interaction are called contact shifts. Magnetic polarization is transferred from the paramagnetic metal through the electronic framework of the substrate molecule and depends upon parameters of electronic structure rather than molecular structure. There are no methods for calculating a priori contact shift contributions, and, therefore, if this interaction contributes, it represents a confusing complication in pseudocontact shift analyses of molecular structure. In proton spectra, contact shifts can usually be ignored, but in ^{13}C spectra, they must be considered. Significant contact interactions have been observed in lanthanide-shifted ^{13}C NMR spectra for resonances assigned to carbon nuclei near sites of association. Fortunately, not all lanthanides induce large contact shifts. Contact contributions to shifts induced by ytterbium are relatively small, and molecular structure studies based on ytterbium-induced pseudocontact shifts in ^{13}C NMR spectra have been successful in a number of cases.

Other directions. Work with the lanthanides has stimulated a general reexamination of paramagnetic phenomena in NMR. Use is being made of paramagnetic complexes other than those of lanthanides. Relaxation phenomena have been effectively applied to supplement shift data. Techniques for the analysis of molecular structure in solution using paramagnetic metal complexes continue to be an active area of research.

For background information *see* NUCLEAR MAGNETIC RESONANCE (NMR) in the McGraw-Hill Encyclopedia of Science and Technology.

[C. C. HINCKLEY]

Bibliography: M. Gouedard, F. Gaudemer, and A. Gaudemer, *Tetrahedron Lett.*, 25:2257, 1973; J. E. Maskasky and M. E. Kenney, *J. Amer. Chem. Soc.*, 93:2060, 1971, and 95:1443, 1973; J. E. Maskasky, J. R. Mooney, and M. E. Kenney, *J. Amer. Chem. Soc.*, 94:2132, 1972; J. R. Mooney, Ph.D. Thesis, Case Western Reserve University, 1973; J. Reuben, in J. W. Emsley, J. Feeney, and L. H. Sutcliffe (eds.), *Prog. NMR Spect.*, vol. 9, pt. 1, 1973; R. E. Sieners (ed.), *Nuclear Magnetic Resonance Shift Reagents*, 1973.

Ocean currents

During the spring of 1973, at a site 600 km southwest of Bermuda, about one hundred scientists from several dozen institutions engaging in oceanographic research conducted a large-scale deepwater cooperative physical experiment called MODE-I, for Mid-Ocean Dynamics Experiment One. The object of the experiment was to find and instrument one or more of the mesoscale, or MODE, eddies first discovered in the late 1950s and since thought to be of central importance in the physics of ocean circulation.

MODE eddies are probably densely packed, irregularly oval (see Figs. 1 and 2) high- and low-pressure centers roughly 400 km in diameter in which current intensities are typically manyfold greater than the local means. The pressure centers move at rates of a few kilometers a day. These scales of motion require an experimental approach quite different from approaches in traditional use. To study them, new instruments would have to be developed: some with the capability of being deployed, left in place to record data, and then recovered at a later time; others freely floating and unattended; still others sinking untethered to the bottom and returning to the surface with a ship nearby, to list only a few. New methods for handling and storing large quantities of data would be required, as would direct-dial ship-to-shore communications, and overall an air of intense scientific cooperation and conciliation. All the pieces were assembled in MODE-I when a large number of scientists and technicians took their instruments in ships and airplanes to the same location in the ocean at the same time to launch a systematic coordinated attack on the eddy problem. Although some experiments continued to produce data for more than a year after launching, the most intense period of measurement ended in the summer of 1973. New and significant results are already beginning to appear. First synthetical reports are scheduled for circulation in late 1974, and it is anticipated that they will continue to evolve and enlarge for some years to come.

Swallow-Crease discovery. Gyres are the natural subdivisions of ocean basins for analyses of wind-driven circulation. They usually occupy from 5 to 20° of latitude and extend from shoreline to shoreline in longitude. To a first approximation, mean flows within a gyre are asymmetric and wind-driven (anticyclonic in the subtropical North Atlantic) above the main thermocline (roughly the upper kilometer of water), and conjectured to be similarly asymmetric but thermally driven and reversed below the main thermocline. Except for narrow and intense regions of return flow on the western side (the Gulf Stream in the North Atlantic subtropical gyre), the flow over most of the gyre and especially in the deep water had been thought to be steady and quite sluggish at about 1 cm/sec.

Accordingly, J. C. Swallow and J. Crease set out in 1959 aboard the research vessel *Aries* with a new neutrally buoyant mid-depth float of their own design to measure the deep circulation. The floats sink to a preset depth and thereafter move passively with the water on an isobaric surface. Weak acoustic signals from the floats can be detected at a nearby research ship, which can then compute the position of the floats relative to the ship. It was planned to collect field data on the magnitude and direction of the supposed sluggish deep mean circulation. Instead, Swallow and Crease discovered that the deep flow was neither steady, uniform, nor weak. Floats originally deployed on a nearly east-west line moved off in irregular directions at speeds up to 10 times faster than anticipated, and the experiment had to be abandoned due to the difficulties of tracking the rapidly dispersing floats with a slow, short-range research vessel. With it was abandoned the notion of purely slow, steady uniform gyres in favor of the

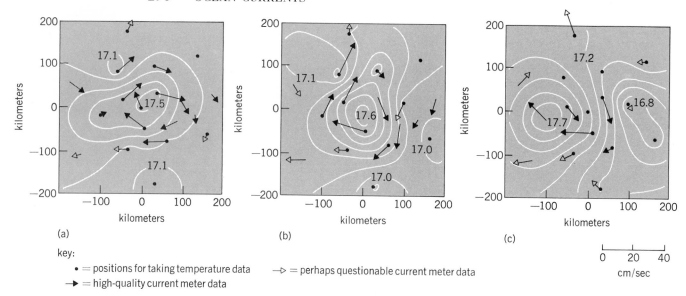

key:

• = positions for taking temperature data   ⇨ = perhaps questionable current meter data

➤ = high-quality current meter data

Fig. 1. Successive 4-day mean isotherms at a depth of 418 m from temperature-pressure gages with 4-day mean current meter vectors superimposed. Isotherms are drawn at 0.1°C intervals and vary smoothly without inversions between indicated extremes. Axes are paral- lel to longitude and latitude; origin is at 28° N 69°40′ W. Day 1 is Jan. 1, 1973. (a) Days 101–104. (b) Days 129– 132. (c) Days 157–160. (Contributors to temperature data are N. Hogg, J. Richman, C. Wunsch; to current meter data, N. Fofonoff, J. Gould, W. Schmitz, and J. Swallow)

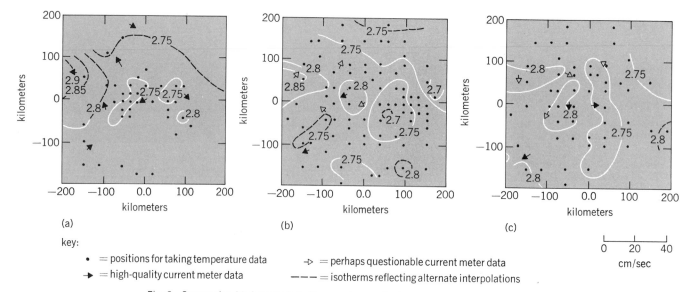

key:

• = positions for taking temperature data   ⇨ = perhaps questionable current meter data

➤ = high-quality current meter data   – – – = isotherms reflecting alternate interpolations

Fig. 2. Successive 12-day mean isotherms at a nominal depth of 3000 m from conductivity-temperature-depth (CTD) data with 12-day mean current meter vectors superimposed. Day 1 is Jan. 1, 1973. (a) Days 93–104. (b) Days 129–140. (c) Days 153–164. (Contributors to tem- perature data are J. Crease, L. Dantzler, A. Leetmaa, R. Mil- lard, W. Sturges, R. Scarlet, and T. Sankey; to current meter data, N. Fofonoff and W. Schmitz)

idea that the ocean, like the atmosphere, has su- perimposed upon the mean flow smaller scales of variability—the eddy scales—which are energeti- cally at least as important as the mean flow. In- deed, the atmospheric high- and low-pressure sys- tems which dominate the daily weather provide a familiar example with which to compare ocean eddies. The two are (nondimensionally) compara- ble in length and time scales, but ocean eddies are by far the more energetic, being 10 to 100 times more energetic than the mean flow compared with atmospheric pressure systems, which are about comparable to the mean flow. Further, there is

evidence (gathered for the first time during MODE-I) that the eddy field is close-packed, which is generally so only in mid-latitude belts for the atmospheric system.

Dynamically, the eddies produce a perturbation on the mean flow, and although the flow perturba- tions may themselves average to zero, their dy- namical effects generally do not, due to the non- linearities inherent in fluid flows. Perturbations from the mean correlate and, if amplitudes are adequate, can produce significant transports of physically important quantities such as heat, momentum, and energy, in addition to salt, oxygen, nutrients, and other chemical constituents of the water. Nearly all data that have been analyzed indicate that MODE eddies are in the dynamical range where such correlations are significant. Hence, the phenomenon is a difficult one to understand theoretically.

The Swallow-Crease discovery was met with both excitement and frustration. If the eddies were sufficiently densely distributed, as they now appear to be (that is, not just isolated local effects), then they must be of central importance to circulation dynamics. However, most oceanographic research instrumentation available at the time of discovery was suited only for the hypothetical slow, steady, uniform flows and were wholly inadequate for eddy experiments. The main attack on the eddy problem had to be postponed until ocean engineers and technologists could produce reliable, suitably designed instrumentation for eddy experiments. The accumulation process that followed was massive and international, and culminated in the MODE experiment.

MODE experiment. The collected records from each of the specific MODE experiments constitute a formidable data base on the eddy time and space scale. Briefly, every measurement technique capable of resolving eddy signals saw a major westward-propagating, warm (depressed isotherms at a fixed depth), anticyclonic (clockwise), baroclinic eddy pass through the MODE region.

Main moored array. The main MODE-I moored array used 100 current meters, including the new vector-averaging, temperature-reading current meters developed at the Woods Hole Oceanographic Institution by R. Koehler and J. McCullough and 60 temperature-pressure recorders (developed by C. Wunsch and R. Dahlen, both of MIT) on 25 moorings closely spaced in an inner circle of 100-km radius (the zero crossing of pilot experiment correlation functions), and less densely spaced moorings in a circumscribing annulus of 300-km outer radius. Data from the inner circle would be used for local dynamical analysis of a single eddy, while data from the larger circle could be used for pattern recognition of several eddy centers. Data from this array shows (Fig. 1) the horizontal scale of the "MODE eddy" by depressions of the isotherm at a nominal depth of 418 m and the corresponding flow speeds by 4-day averaged current meter vectors at 1-month intervals. Note that flow speeds are typically 20 cm/sec and that the eddy is positioned fortuitously near the center of the MODE array.

Conductivity and temperature. The data for Fig. 2 is primarily from a newly developed (by N. Brown of the Woods Hole Oceanographic Institution) and highly accurate, continuously reading conductivity-temperature-depth (CTD) instrument and partly from more traditional hydrographic instruments. The CTD senses the conductivity, temperature, and depth of the water around it and continuously transmits this data up the cable by which the instrument is lowered into the water. It provides evidence that eddy scales below the main thermocline (3000 m) may be smaller than those above and that the two motions may be at least partially uncoupled. Averaged current meter speeds at this depth are a few centimeters per second, although gusting can occur at all depths. The eddy field at 1500 m is erratic and confused. Other eddy centers are visible in Fig. 2 and in almost all other synoptic maps of density-determining variables, strongly supporting the idea of a closely packed eddy field.

The main eddy dynamical balance appears to be nearly geostrophic (to within ±20%) with radial pressure gradients balancing radial Coriolis accelerations. The eddies, however, are not perfectly geostrophic and are clearly not steady in time. Deviations arise from a combination of propagation, advection, growth, and interaction (linear and nonlinear) with surrounding eddies and the mean field. In 1974 ongoing studies included: theoretical and numerical investigations of ageostrophic affects, multiple Rossby-wave fits to the data (Rossby waves are constant kinetic energy oscillations in a rotating fluid system with spatial variations in vertical rotational rate and/or depth), and several searches for major sources of eddy energy. The latter include a promising baroclinic instability model (a fundamental and meteorologically important instability of density-stratified shear flows), and models testing a wide variety of geophysical phenomena which could generate eddies such as direct effects of the wind, meanders in the path of the Gulf Stream, effects of topography, and energy radiation from Gulf Stream rings (large meanders which break away from the Gulf Stream and seem to migrate slowly to the southwest as isolated entities). Theoretical investigations were to be summarized in the MODE Dynamical Group Report appearing in late 1974.

SOFAR floats. About 20 SOFAR floats, developed by H. T. Rossby of Yale University and D. Webb of Woods Hole Oceanographic Institution, were deployed in the MODE area. These are large aluminum cylinders carefully ballasted to float with the surrounding water at a predetermined (about 1500 m) fixed depth. The floats periodically emit accurately timed acoustic signals, detectable at shore listening stations, from which float locations can be determined to within a few hundred meters by arrival delay times. Where they can be compared, the floats have corroborated velocity information obtained from moored instruments. But, because they are free to disperse wherever the flow will carry them, the SOFAR floats have supplied evidence that the eddy field is anisotropic with a general diffusion to the south and west at about 1 km per day with significant southward elongation of the float cluster but with little to no east-west dispersal. There appear also to be temporal variations in total field kinetic energy by factors of as much as 2 over 2-month time intervals. Correspondingly, total averages over all current meter and float (including historical) data indicate a general decline in mean and eddy kinetic energy in the deep water (4000 m nominal, ±100 m) with distance from a maximum at the Gulf Stream to a first zero-crossing about 1000 km to the southeast.

Velocity shears. Velocity shears top to bottom are given by a free-falling electromagnetic profiler developed by T. Sanford and R. Drever of the Woods Hole Oceanographic Institution. The instrument measures minute voltages induced by the flow of sea water in the Earth's weak magnetic field. It provides evidence that throughout the MODE area there are strong inertial motions (oscillations at the frequency $2\Omega \sin\Theta$ where $\Omega = 2\pi/24$ hr is the angular velocity of the Earth, and Θ is latitude) over the entire water column with vertical wavelengths of 100 to 200 m. To the west of the MODE region over the smooth abyssal plane, the profiles indicate primarily the first baroclinic mode (an oscillation in which the entire water column heaves up and down with maximum vertical excursions at the main thermocline rapidly diminishing to zero both above and below) with intense shears of 15–20 cm/sec over the upper 1000 km but little variation thereafter. However, over the rough topography to the east there is little surface intensification. What shear does exist is most evident in the deep water. These results were confirmed by Swallow float measurements (with an updated model of the 1955 instrument). An acoustic profiler developed by T. Pochapsky of Lamont-Doherty Geological Observatory produced similar results.

Minimode. Swallow, Crease, J. Gould, and T. Sankey, all of the Institute of Oceanographic Sciences in England, conducted a smaller-scale experiment within MODE using an updated version of the 1955 neutrally buoyant floats, moored current meters, and hydrographic and bathymetric equipment. They concentrated on horizontal scales from 5 to 20 km and depths from 500 to 4000 m. Floats at the same depth and initially 5 km apart separated at only 0.7 cm/sec or less, whereas mean speeds of floats initially 20 km apart could differ by as much as 8 cm/sec at 500 m and half that at 4000 m. Marked topographic influences were observed.

Tow fish. One of the most synoptic large areal coverage measurements was made with the E. Katz–R. Nowak (both of WHOI) tow fish, which continuously monitors the depth of a preselected isotherm by towing at about 5 knots (2.57 m/sec) two depth-controlled instrument packages which bracket an isotherm (12°C in MODE). Besides sampling structures on a spatial scale of a few to several hundred kilometers, the instrument revealed mean deviations up to 10 m in isotherm depths on retraced records separated by as little as 48 hr.

Inverted echo sounder. The inverted echo sounder (IES) is a new bottom-mounted instrument (developed by Rossby and D. R. Watts of Yale University) which measures transit time of an acoustic pulse from the instrument to the sea surface and back again. Because sound speed is density-dependent, transit time is related to average density of the water column, and that depends primarily on the vertical position of the main thermocline. Overall dynamic height (a measure of horizontal pressure anomalies associated with tilting isopycnals) variations averaged in four-day segments compared well with those independently determined from CTD and other hydrographic data. At higher frequencies the rms (root-mean-square) excursions of the main thermocline were confirmed to be about 5 m. However, in the bandwidth from 11 to 14 hr, containing the semidiurnal internal tide, the IES found excursions of the main thermocline of about 10 m with occasional bursts of as much as 30 to 40 m. Aliasing from such bursts (the introduction of error into a time series by phenomena whose frequencies are greater than sampling frequency) could help account for the confused eddy picture in temperature at 1500 m. Other bottom-mounted instruments from Scripps Institute of Oceanography, Atlantic Oceanographic and Meteorological Laboratory of the National Oceanographic and Atmospheric Administration, and Harvard University were designed to measure eddy-scale pressure anomalies. Thus, they must have the overall heft to withstand 500 atm of pressure, the delicacy to measure one part in a million, and the stability to hold constant over durations of several months. A successful low-frequency residual pressure measurement (tides, inertial-internal wave, and other large high-frequency fluctuations filtered) was made from several instruments at both small (10 km) and large (100 km) separations. Records do not differ significantly over these scales, nor do they differ from simulated bottom-pressure records at Bermuda some 600 km away. Thus, although amplitudes are of the anticipated order for MODE eddies, the length scales are too large, and a convincing interpretation of these exciting measurements has yet to emerge.

Significance of MODE-I. Although results are only preliminary, it is clear that the MODE-I experiment has (1) established the amplitudes and scales of the mesoscale motions, and (2) obtained the first complete four-dimensional synoptic maps of the eddy field, including synoptic measurements throughout the water column of all components of velocity, temperature, and salinity, as well as the first Lagrangian measurements of an eddy field, and the first direct residual bottom pressure measurements. These findings provide the first three-dimensional case history of an oceanic eddy for dynamical analysis, including strong documentation of the close-packed nature of the eddy field. These, together with the new revelations from the data and explanations from the theory which continue to appear, have contributed substantially to understanding of the nature of mesoscale eddies, their dynamics, and their role in the general circulation of the world's oceans.

For background information *see* OCEAN CURRENTS; OCEANOGRAPHY; THERMOCLINE in the McGraw-Hill Encyclopedia of Science and Technology.

[WILLIAM SIMMONS]

Bibliography: W. Brown et al., MODE bottom experiment, *J. Phys. Oceanogr.*, in press; J. Gould, W. Schmitz, and C. Wunsch, Preliminary field results for a mid-ocean dynamics experiment (MODE-O), *Deep Sea Res.*, in press; A. R. Robinson and J. McWilliams, The baroclinic instability of the open ocean, *J. Phys. Oceanogr.*, in press; H. Stommel, *The Gulf Steam*, 1965; J. C. Swallow, The *Aries* current measurements in the Western Atlantic, *Phil. Trans. Roy. Soc. London*, A., 270–451–460, 1971.

Oceanic islands

Geological thought over the past decade concerning the origins and distributions of volcanic structures within the oceans has been dominantly concerned with how the structures fit into kinematic models of plate tectonics.

Kinematic concepts. The kinematic models have mainly emphasized concepts of time and position, not the processes and systems of forces that cause tectonic motions; plate tectonic theory relies heavily on geometrical concepts at the present

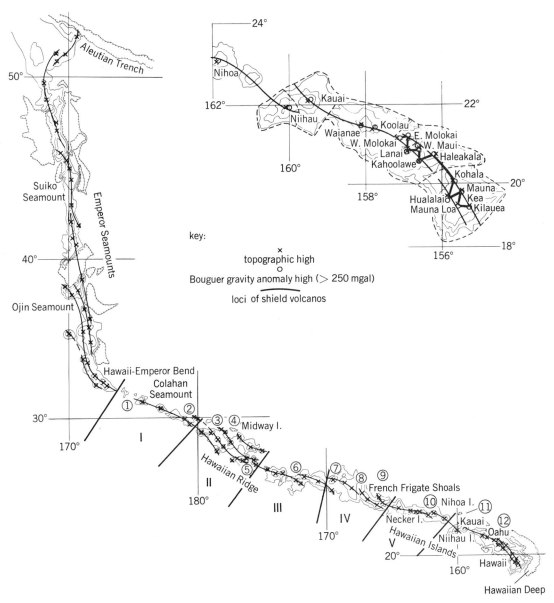

Fig. 1. Map of the Pacific showing the structure of the Hawaiian and Emperor chains of volcanism with tentative subdivisions used for calculation of volumes in Fig.

2. (From H. R. Shaw, Mantle convection and volcanic periodicity in the Pacific: Evidence from Hawaii, Geol. Soc. Amer. Bull., 84:1505–1526, 1973)

largely because of the paucity of age data. Conspicuous volcanic activity located in central regions of the oceanic plates, such as in Hawaii, did not fit easily into the idea that volcanism occurred primarily at plate boundaries, such as centers of ocean floor spreading at the Mid-Atlantic and East Pacific rises, and in island arc systems above zones of subducted oceanic lithosphere. The initial kinematic assumption was to consider melting anomalies in Central plate regions to be "hot spots" that gave rise to lines of volcanic islands as the rigid lithosphere plate passed by in the ordinary course of sea floor spreading. This idea was first offered by J. T. Wilson, and later was systematized by W. J. Morgan (one of the principal founders of kinematic descriptions of plate motions), who proposed that several such anomalies have retained constant synchronous positions relative to one another even though they have propagated long traces of volcanism across the ocean floors. The

seeming constancy of this pattern led to the idea that all such "hot spots" were fixed relative to the deep mantle (that is, the mantle at depths exceeding a few hundred kilometers). Morgan proposed that island chain patterns could be explained by a system of plumelike convection currents rising up through the mantle from the vicinity of the core-mantle boundary (at a depth of nearly 2900 km) and that such a system was not only responsible for "hot spots" of anomalously high volcanic activity, but that the traction on the bottom of the lithosphere as the plumes spread out constituted the main driving force of plate motion. As of 1974 the "thermal plume" or "plume" hypothesis has permeated the literature on plate tectonic theory and has given rise to elaborate classifications and kinematic reconstructions of plume sites and their histories. Originally, about 20 plume sites were postulated, but this number has grown to as many as 150 terrestrial sites in recent discussions. Few of these

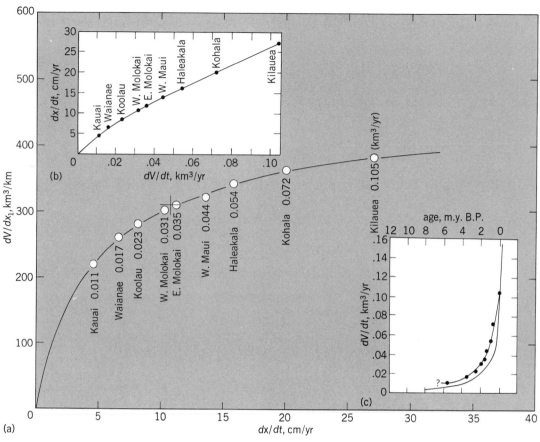

Fig. 2. Graphs showing various relationships established for volcanic loci in the southeastern Hawaiian Islands: (a) between average volume per unit length of volcanic loci and propagation rates determined on basis of radiometric dating of lavas; (b) between propagation rates and the rate of lava production; (c) rate of lava production and radiometric age. (From H. R. Shaw, Mantle convection and volcanic periodicity in the Pacific; Evidence from Hawaii, Geol. Soc. Amer. Bull., 84:1505–1526, 1973)

postulated plume sites are well documented as to age sequences and chemical composition of volcanic rocks. It is possible that the subsequent history of geological concepts will show that the current population of "plume sites" is an artifact of geometrical emphasis, and that there are a number of origins for melting anomalies. The period has nonetheless been significant as the harbinger of an increasing attention to dynamical rather than kinematical concepts of volcanism.

Dynamical concept. In the 19th century J. D. Dana deduced that the Hawaiian Archipelago and other chains of volcanism in the Pacific consisted of more than one line of volcanic loci arranged in en echelon patterns. E. D. Jackson and others (Fig. 1) found that recent mapping and geochronology of volcanic chains have confirmed Dana's deductions. This combination of studies, spanning more than a century, has shown unequivocally that the idea of plates simply moving over a "hot spot" to form a row of volcanoes is not correct. Figure 1 illustrates the structure of the Hawaiian and Emperor volcanic chains. The volcanic loci used in Fig. 1 were defined by Jackson and coworkers in 1972. Further minor revisions of the loci and refinements of the lava volumes have been made by K. E. Bargar and Jackson. Age data indicate that volcanic

loci were developed in a sequence of episodes that varied in volumes of lava extruded and rates of propagation. These relations for the southeastern Hawaiian Islands are shown in Fig. 2. The detailed structures of composite volcanic chains therefore indicate a need for modification of theories founded primarily on geometric constructions. See GEOSYNCLINES.

A dynamical theory proposed by H. R. Shaw in 1973 (see Fig. 2) suggested that the positions and episodic character of oceanic volcanism might be explained in terms of processes of deformation in the asthenosphere (the soft layer underlying the rigid plates) related to gravitationally induced sliding of plates away from spreading centers. One objection to this theory was that it did not fit previous ideas of approximately fixed positions of the melting anomalies through time. Subsequently it was discovered by Shaw and Jackson that the residual materials left after melting below anomalous sites such as Hawaii were sufficiently dense as to tend to sink into the deeper mantle (Fig. 3). This discovery suggested that the Hawaiian melting anomaly is not actually "hot" relative to regional patterns of heat flow. The lack of an anomaly of heat flow is a paradox not previously explained by the plume model. Shaw and Jackson's general

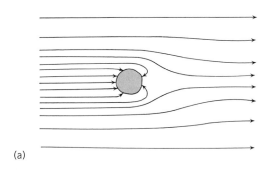

(a)

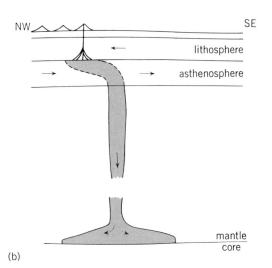

(b)

Fig. 3. Schematic diagram illustrating the relationship between melting anomalies in the asthenosphere and growth of "gravitational anchors" in the deep mantle: (a) plan view; (b) vertical section. (From H. R. Shaw and E. D. Jackson, Linear island chains in the Pacific: Results of thermal plumes or gravitational anchors?, J. Geophys. Res., 78(35): 8634–8652, 1973)

dynamical theory indicates that anomalies of melting in the asthenosphere are not necessarily to be considered as sharply defined spots and therefore are not necessarily fixed relative to the deep mantle. A few melting anomalies, however, may become roughly fixed and sharply defined, depending on the rate of growth of "gravitational anchors" of sinking residua from melting. It can be seen from Fig. 3 that as partial melting proceeds in the asthenosphere, lava is extruded at the Earth's surface through volcanic conduits and dense refractory minerals continuously accumulate until the entire residual mass begins sinking into the deeper mantle. This sinking in turn influences the lateral supply of new material to the site of the melting anomaly in the asthenosphere, which continues to add more of the refractory phases to the density current. This feedback cycle between melting rate and sinking rate of dense residua provides an anchoring effect for the melting anomaly because flow of the rheid materials in the asthenosphere is continually pulled toward the position of the sinking mass as though that position were an orifice or "hole" in the bottom of the asthenosphere. More typically the orifice (Fig. 3a) may be elongated parallel to the net direction of transport in the asthenosphere.

Late in 1973 it was discovered by a drilling expedition of the *Glomar Challenger* (Leg 33 of the Deep Sea Drilling Project) that one of the chains of propagating volcanism supposedly created as the Pacific plate passed over a "hot spot" or "thermal plume" has virtually the same age over most of its length, hence was produced by some other form of melting anomaly.

At the present it is considered promising that dynamical theories can systematically explain discrepancies of plate kinematics and the relationships of midocean, spreading ridge, and island arc volcanism, but the requisite research in geochronology, geochemistry, and geology of oceanic islands represents a frontier that is only just beginning to furnish geological facts that will be constraints on the imaginative ideas of previous decades. See EARTH, INTERIOR OF.

For background information *see* OCEANOGRAPHY: TECTONIC PATTERNS in the McGraw-Hill Encyclopedia of Science and Technology.

[HERBERT R. SHAW; EVERETT D. JACKSON]

Bibliography: K. E. Bargar and E. D. Jackson, Volumes of individual shield volcanoes along the Hawaiian-Emperor chain, *U.S. Geol. Surv. J. Res.,* in press; J. M. Bird and B. Isacks (eds.), *Plate Tectonics: Selected Papers from the Journal of Geophysical Research,* 1972; J. D. Dana, *Geology,* vol. 10 of *United States Exploring Expedition During the Years 1838–1839, 1840, 1841, 1842*; E. D. Jackson, E. A. Silver, and G. B. Dalrymple, Hawaiian-Emperor chain and its relation to Cenozoic circumpacific tectonics, *Geol. Soc. Amer. Bull.,* 83:601–617, 1972; S. O. Schlanger et al., *Geotimes,* 19:16–20, 1974.

Oil and gas, offshore

There is little doubt that the petroleum industry will experience significant increases in offshore exploratory, developmental, and production activities during the next several years. Major oil companies as well as groups of large independent companies are planning on investing a large portion of their exploration and development dollars in offshore leases. It is estimated that this investment may amount to well over a trillion dollars in the next 10 years. It is estimated that, by 1982, 2500 exploratory holes will be spudded, as compared to about 500 in 1973.

Just as certainly as activity will increase, the water depth in which holes will be drilled will increase. Projections are that between 11 and 15% of the wells drilled in the North Sea during the next 2 years will be in water depths of 500 ft (100 ft = 30.5 m) or more; 2½% of the wells in the Gulf of Mexico are expected to be in similar water depths. In addition, well depth is expected to increase, though not as dramatically as water depth. The average depth of offshore wells drilled in these areas in 1972 is about 9700 ft. A vast majority of the wells are drilled in the 7500–12,500-ft range. By 1975 this average is anticipated to be just over 10,000 ft.

Drilling operations. To date, ocean bottom formations have been penetrated to 3334 ft from the dynamically positioned drill ship *Glomar Challenger*, in water depths of 20,000 ft. Also from this unit, a drill hole was reentered from the ocean surface in 13,000 ft of water. Exploratory oil and gas wells that are operated under somewhat different conditions have been drilled safely in water depths to 1497 ft in the Santa Barbara Channel. These experiences have resulted in a consensus that oil and gas wells can be drilled safely in water depths to 3000 ft. Meanwhile, engineering and technical advances are continuing at an accelerated pace to provide drilling capability at sea in practically unlimited water depths.

In 1975 about 520 mobile and platform-mounted offshore rigs will drill about 2000 wells. Figure 1 shows the increase in the number of offshore mobile drilling rigs since 1959 and the projected unit construction through 1975. As shown in Fig. 1, there are three types of mobile drilling rigs. Jackups are self-elevating mobile platforms; the legs are lowered to the sea floor, and the platform is jacked above the wave height. Submersible platforms are towed to a location and then submerged to the sea bottom. Semisubmersibles are a variation of the submersibles and can function as bottom supporter units or, in deep water, as floaters.

The estimated increase in the size of the mobile rig fleet during the next 10 years ranges from about 250 to 400 units. In a recent report it was predicted that by 1982 the mobile rig fleet will total 620 units—more than double the current fleet.

Most of the exploratory drilling is accomplished by means of mobile drilling units that are either bottom-supported while drilling (submersibles and jackups) or moored floaters (drill ships and semisubmersibles). A current mobile rig summary lists 222 active rigs, 13 inactive rigs, and 132 rigs under construction. The value of the mobile rigs under

construction is approximately $2.9 billion, almost 1½ times the original construction value of the current worldwide mobile rigs (about $1.9 billion). At current prices and projected cost increases, much more than $6.5 billion may be spent in rig construction by 1982.

Of the 222 mobile rigs currently in service, 127 are bottom-supported. However, the number of floaters is increasing. They constitute 71% of the mobile rigs under construction; at present, only about 43% of active units are the floater type.

Furthermore, in the recent past, the ratio between shipshaped and semisubmersible units has changed, the proportion of semisubmersible units under construction being greater than those in service. The greater stability of semisubmersibles makes them ideal all-weather development rigs, whereas the higher transit speed of shipshaped vessels makes them more useful as wide-ranging exploratory rigs. Although there are currently 54 semisubmersibles and 41 shipshaped vessels in service, only 19 of the 94 floating rigs under construction are shipshaped vessels. However, there is some evidence that this trend will reverse in the near future as oil companies continue examining plans for deep-water exploration. By 1975 orders for drill ships are expected to equal or exceed those for semisubmersibles.

Offshore production systems. With few exceptions, all of today's offshore oil and gas production has been from platforms located in water depths ranging up to 400 ft. However, in 1975 a number of fixed platforms under construction for use in the North Sea will extend this means of production to water depths of 500 ft. Within the next 5 years fixed structures made from steel, concrete, and a combination of steel and concrete will further extend the limit to 1000 ft. However, the costs of producing oil from such surface facilities become prohibitively high, increasing exponentially as a function of depth, size, and complexity of platforms. Worldwide steel shortages and increasing prices for the materials and labor required to construct large platforms have escalated the cost of using conventional fixed surface facilities for oil field development. Therefore, interest in subsea production systems is intensifying.

The technology required for underwater completions has been available to the industry for more than 10 years, and to date approximately 89 such completions have been installed in water depths ranging from 50 to 375 ft. The wellheads of all but one of these completions are exposed to sea water (wet trees), and most of them were installed with the assistance of deep-sea divers; the one wellhead that is encapsulated (dry tree) is in 375 ft of water in the Gulf of Mexico.

Theoretically, the wet tree has unlimited water-depth capability, but in practice its use is directly dependent on drilling capability, which is in the range of 3000 ft of water. Dry trees are currently limited to a 2000-ft depth range because of the limitations of presently available diving bells or utility capsules. Concept development studies have already indicated the feasibility of extending the capability of this system to the 6000-ft depth range.

Over the years a number of systems, ranging

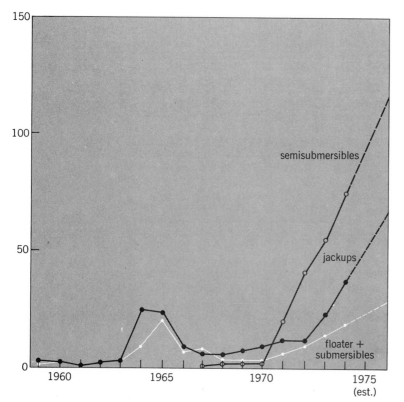

Fig. 1. Mobile rig construction by type.

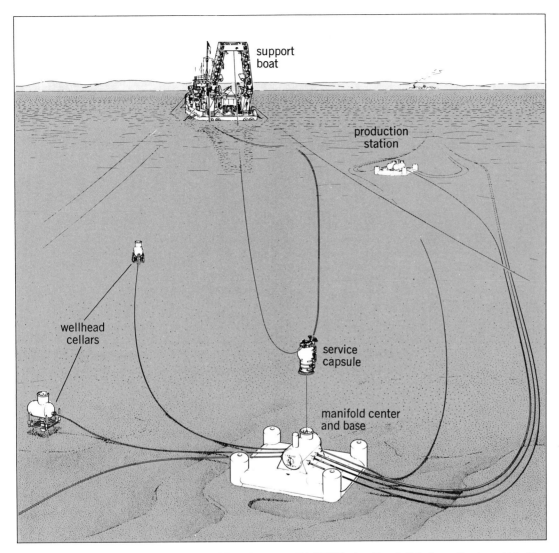

Fig. 2. The component units of the Lockheed Petroleum Services System. *(From The LPS System, Tech. Broch. no.* 5M-107301, *Lockheed Petroleum Services Ltd., New Westminster, B.C.)*

from relatively exotic subsea chambers to more traditional equipment that can be modified to permit its installation and maintenance on the sea floor, have evolved. The single dry tree in use today is a type of subsea chamber. Basically, this production system, shown in Fig. 2, is built around subsea chambers that provide a normal atmospheric environment. The wellhead cellars are 1-atm pressure chambers that contain the Christmas tree and its necessary connections. Oil and gas from several wells are received at the manifold, commingled, and piped to the production station. Here the gas is compressed and then pumped, along with the oil, to onshore facilities. Oil field technicians wearing ordinary clothing can be lowered from a surface vessel in the service capsule, which can be latched to any one of the basic units. Equipment such as flow lines, wellheads, and controls can then be installed, inspected, or repaired in a dry atmosphere with the same tools that would be used ashore.

As mentioned above, a portion of the system has been installed in the Gulf of Mexico in 375 ft of water. The remaining modules are scheduled to be completed and tested by 1975. The entire system is expected to be commercially available by 1977.

An approach that illustrates to a certain extent the adaptation of traditional equipment to subsea use incorporates a tension-leg platform (TLP) and a subsea production system. The system, shown in Fig. 3, consists of a tension-moored, triangular-shaped semisubmersible vessel located directly above a sea floor drilling template. Wells are drilled through the template, with the casing and tubing in a wellhead on the ocean floor. The cost of the TLP, unlike that of the fixed platform, is essentially unrelated to water depth; the initial capital cost is affected only by the cost of the additional wire rope and production riser.

Since the platform buoyancy exceeds its weight, the anchor cables remain in tension at all times. This tension prevents the platform from heaving and acts as a restoring force when weather causes the platform to move sideways (surge). Thus, the cable tension prevents heave, roll, and pitch and attenuates surge.

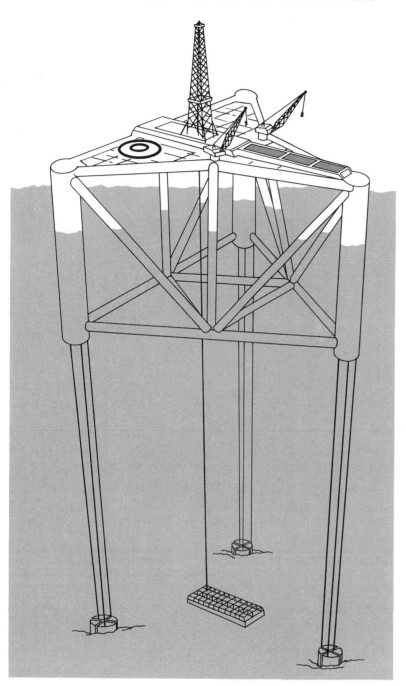

Fig. 3. Tension-leg platform. *(From J. H. Brewer and S. J. Shrum, Tension-leg platform will get at-sea test next year, Oil Gas J., 71(41):88–91, 1973)*

Oil and gas production travels through a riser or pipeline to a central onshore or offshore production facility. Well servicing is carried out and pipeline connections are made by using manual manipulators on a manned atmospheric chamber lowered from a surface vessel. Prototypes of the template, wellheads and controls, and atmospheric chamber have been built and tested in shallow water.

A consortium has been formed to build and conduct sea tests, scheduled for completion in July 1975, of a scaled-down model of a TLP designed for use at a depth of 600 ft. The purpose of the tests is to establish the feasibility of the concept for worldwide application. One mobile rig construction firm claims that it has completed model testing of a TLP and that it plans to have a production unit of this type for water depths of 3000 ft by 1977.

Pipeline technology. Two limiting factors in extending oil production capability to a depth of 3000 ft are the availability of hardware for installing pipelines and the means for repairing damaged pipelines. The installation capability of conventional lay barges utilizing an articulated stinger and a tensioning system is currently limited to pipelines 24 in. (61 cm) in diameter in 1500 ft of water. A dynamically positioned semisubmersible lay barge now in the development stages is expected to lay pipelines of up to 30 in. (76 cm) in diameter in 3000 ft of water.

The technology to repair subsea pipelines damaged by corrosion, storms, earth movement, or other factors does not presently exist for water depths beyond the practical reach of divers (currently estimated to be 1500 ft). Such a capability will be necessary, however, before future deepwater production can be begun. More efficient and economical methods of repairing lines in shallower waters are also needed.

Current research is focusing on the development of a "total-package" solution to repair problems for pipelines in water depths up to 4000 ft. The package includes locating the damage, removing a damaged section, preparing the pipe, replacing or repairing the damage, and testing the repair.

For background information *see* OIL AND GAS, OFFSHORE in the McGraw-Hill Encyclopedia of Science and Technology.

[W. R. MC LEOD; G. R. SCHOONMAKER]

Bibliography: J. H. Brewer and S. J. Shrum, *Oil Gas J.*, 71(41):88–91, 1973; Forecast issue, *Offshore*, 33(13), 1973; H. B. Leeton et al., *World Oil*, 177(1):82–94, 1973; Lockheed's new underwater wellhead system, *Oil Gas J.*, 70(32):67–70, and 70(43):64–66, 1972; Offshore drilling, *Oil Gas J.*, 71(53), 1973; Subsea production, *Oil Gas J.*, 71(44), 1973; *World Oil*, 177(7), 1973.

Oil and gas well drilling

In spite of the increase in the depth of wells (the deepest is below 30,000 ft; approx. 9140 m), higher labor and operating costs, and the hostile environments of ocean and arctic locations, the rise in drilling costs has been held below that of industrial commodities in general. Research and engineering efforts have concentrated on ways to drill faster and to minimize interruptions caused by unstable boreholes. A significant factor in the success of the program has been the development of drilling fluids designed to improve hole stability and rate of penetration. Laboratory research has contributed to this development through studies with miniaturized drilling machines.

Laboratory drilling machine. Downhole conditions of pressure, temperature, and circulation of drilling fluid have been simulated in laboratory equipment (Fig. 1). A drilling machine designed to operate at pressures up to 15,000 lb/in.² (1 lb/in² = 6.895×10^3 N/m²) and temperatures up to 500°F (260°C) makes possible the independent control of

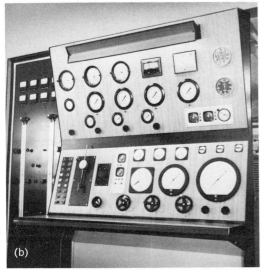

Fig. 1. Laboratory drilling machine. (*a*) Pressure chamber in which tests are made. (*b*) Control panel for operation of machine. (*Courtesy Baroid Division, N L Industries, Inc., Houston*)

forces corresponding to overburden pressure, pressure in the pores of the rock, and the pressure of the drilling fluid being circulated. Drilling tests are made on rock specimens 3 9/16 in. (1 in. = 2.54 cm) in diameter and 8 in. long, using a two-core bit 1¼ in. in diameter. Force on the bit is applied by a hydraulic cylinder that moves the core down upon the rotating bit. The arrangement is shown schematically in Fig. 2. Drilling-rate studies are usually made on cores cut from blocks of sandstone or limestone obtained from quarries.

Problems of unstable borehole are usually associated with shales. Because cores of shales are not common and usually are not suitable for repetitive tests, shale "cores" are prepared by expressing water from a slurry of powdered shale. In this way, modification in the shale core corresponding to changes in ionic environment and depth of burial can be simulated. Studies of borehole stability in the laboratory drilling machine are made by pumping the drilling fluid through a predrilled hole in the shale core (Fig. 3). Numerous tests have been made with various drilling fluids under constant conditions of overburden pressure, pore pressure, and drilling fluid pressure. Most of the tests were made at 5000 lb/in.², pumping 3.5 gal (1 gal = 4.55 liters) of drilling fluid per minute for 6 hr at a temperature of 175°F (79°C). After circulation and heating had been stopped, the cores were allowed to remain in the chamber for 16 hr before they were removed and examined.

Effect of drilling fluid on drilling rate. Early studies showed that drilling rate decreased when the pressure exerted by the drilling fluid exceeded the pressure in the pores of the rock. The decrease was attributed to the formation of a layer of cuttings and mud solids held in place on the rock surface by the pressure differential. The use of thin, low-solids drilling fluids has markedly increased drilling rate. In low-solids drilling fluids, organic polymers are substituted (wholly or in part) for the bentonite normally used to furnish suspension and sealing qualities. A distinct advantage in the maintenance of such systems comes in the avoidance of the usual dispersing agents, such as causticized tannins and lignite, and the lignosulfonates. Polymers suitable for use in drilling fluids can be produced by modification of naturally occurring cellulose, gums, and starches, by the action of bacteria on carbohydrates, and by chemical synthesis from selected acrylic monomers. If the degree of

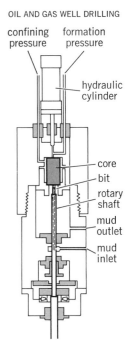

Fig. 2. Diagram of pressure chamber of drilling machine. Core is lowered by hydraulic controls to contact the drill bit. (*Courtesy Baroid Division, N L Industries, Inc., Houston*)

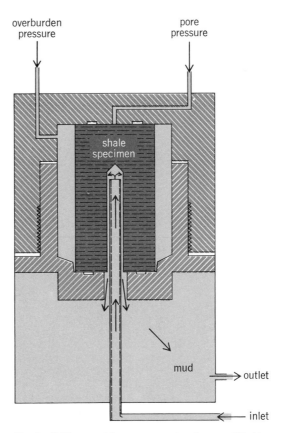

Fig. 3. Drilling machine pressure chamber, modified so that borehole stability of shale specimen can be studied. (*Courtesy Baroid Division, N L Industries, Inc., Houston*)

Fig. 4. Shale specimens sectioned to show borehole enlargement. (a) Shale not exposed to drilling fluid. (b) Shale exposed to polymer–potassium chloride drilling fluid. (c) Shale exposed to fresh-water, bentonite, and chrome-lignosulfonate drilling fluid. (d) Shale exposed to oil-base drilling fluid containing emulsified calcium chloride solution. (*Courtesy Baroid Division, N L Industries, Inc., Houston*)

hydrolysis and the molecular weight are varied, acrylic polymers can be prepared that will flocculate drill cuttings, with or without an effect on the bentonite fraction of the drilling fluid. Although useful polymers vary widely as to their source and composition, they are similar in certain properties; specifically, they are strongly absorbed by clays. Some polymers are particularly effective in hole stabilization in shales.

Borehole stability. Problems of borehole stability often can be identified with the effect of water on the clay constituents of the shale formations. Two forces are involved in the imbibition of water by clays: surface hydration and osmosis. The surface hydration force is directly related to the difference between the compacting force that has been applied by the overburden and the pressure of the fluid in the pores of the shale. The osmotic hydration force depends on the difference between the concentration of the ions in the water associated with the shale and the ion concentration of the drilling fluid in contact with the shale. Adsorption of water by confined shale produces internal stresses that are relieved by spalling, fracturing, and reduction in compressive strength. Some shales fail by plastic deformation when they come in contact with fresh water. High concentrations of dissolved salts in the water cause the separation of relatively firm fragments and, thus, the failure of such shales.

Adsorption of certain polymers by shale retards the imbibition of water. Salt solutions can be thickened by some polymers. Accordingly, attempts to improve borehole stability have involved the testing of various salt solutions and polymers together. As an example, Fig. 4 shows the significantly greater stability of a borehole after exposure to a water-base drilling fluid containing a polysaccharide polymer and potassium chloride (Fig. 4b) in comparison with a borehole in which a commonly used composition containing bentonite, chrome lignosulfonate, and causticized lignite was circulated (Fig. 4c). Tests have shown that potassium salts are more effective than other salts at the same ionic concentration. This preferred behavior is thought to be due to the favorable size of the potassium ion in relation to the lattice structure of the clay and also to the low hydrational energy of the potassium ion.

An obvious solution to problems arising from the imbibition of water by shales would appear to be the use of a drilling fluid having oil as the liquid phase. Experience has shown, however, that some water is always incorporated in the oil-base drilling fluid and that this water sometimes affects hole stability. By raising the salinity of the water to a concentration substantially above that of the water in the shale, and by maintaining the salt solution as a stable emulsion in the oil, advantage can be taken of osmotic forces to transfer water from the borehole wall into the drilling fluid. The shale is thereby made stronger. The effect on the borehole of circulating an oil-base drilling fluid containing emulsified calcium chloride solution is shown in Fig. 4d. The shale was actually hardened by prolonged contact with this oil-base drilling fluid.

Because of the cost of oil-base drilling fluids and the potential for surface pollution, research is continuing so that water-base drilling fluids that can provide the properties needed in drilling all types of shales can be developed.

For background information *see* OIL AND GAS WELL DRILLING; PETROLEUM GEOLOGY in the McGraw-Hill Encyclopedia of Science and Technology.   [GEORGE R. GRAY]

Bibliography: G. R. Gray, *World Oil*, pp. 84–86, May 1973 (36 references); G. R. Gray and F. S. Young, Jr., *J. Petrol. Tech.*, pp. 1347–1354, December 1973 (50 references); T. C. Mondshine, *Oil Gas J.*, pp. 120–130, April 1974; D. E. O'Brien and M. E. Chenevert, *J. Petrol. Tech.*, pp. 1089–1100, September 1973.

Oncology

Dimethylnitrosamine (DMNA) has a potent toxic and carcinogenic effect and occurs in small amounts in many foods and in tobacco. The first clinical and pathological description of the toxic effect of DMNA was presented by H. A. Freund in 1937. Two chemists were industrially exposed to DMNA, and one died from the toxic effect. Liver cirrhosis after industrial exposure to DMNA, fatal in one out of three patients, was reported from Great Britain in 1954 by J. M. Barnes and P. N. Magee. The acute hepatic damage in humans and laboratory animals described by these authors received scant attention compared with the extensive investigation of the unexpected carcinogenic

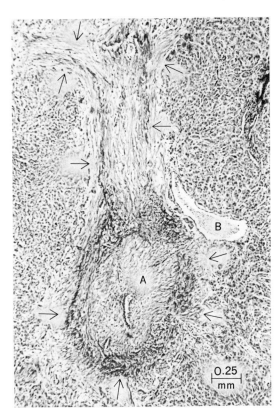

Fig. 1. Liver from calf exposed to 0.54 mg DMNA per kilogram of body weight per day that died after receiving 25 mg DMNA per kilogram of body weight. Sublobular vein A (inside arrows) is partly occluded, and a new vein B formed proximate to the occluded one.

activity of DMNA initiated by their 1956 paper.

Sources of DMNA. A hepatotoxic compound in fish meal produced from nitrite-preserved herring was discovered by bioassay in Norway in 1962 and identified as DMNA. After these results were reported, there was great concern about nitrosamines in the food supply of human beings and their possible link to human cancer. When present in food, nitrosamines are found in concentrations of parts per million, or even parts per billion. Thus very careful, well-developed methods of analysis are necessary. Nitrites are added to food for preservative purposes. They undoubtedly inhibit the growth of clostridia bacteria and hence prevent outbreaks of botulism; but they may interact with amines present in food and tissues, and under certain conditions nitrosamines are formed. The extent to which added nitrite is responsible for nitrosamine formation is not clear. Nitrosamines may also be formed in natural, untreated food, such as mushrooms and salted dried fish, in cigarette smoke, and in the gastrointestinal tract as a result of chemical interaction between various amine precursors and nitrites. At various sites, nitrosamines occur as a result of synthesis by bacteria, some of which are pathogenic to humans.

Recent government action in reducing the maximum level of nitrite that can be used as a curing agent will at best reduce nitrosamines rather than eliminate them from the environment. Nitrites or nitrates, or both, are present in several kinds of vegetables and also in drinking water, partly as a result of the heavy use of fertilizer with high nitrogen content. S. R. Tannenbaum has noted that human saliva contains a significant amount of nitrite as well as thiocyanate, which, as shown by E. E. Boyland and coworkers, catalyzes the formation of nitrosamines from nitrite and secondary amines. W. Lijinsky pointed out that many drugs and pesticides contain tertiary amino groups that may interact with nitrite in the mammalian stomach to produce varying amounts of carcinogenic nitrosamines.

Toxic and carcinogenic effect. The relevance of small amounts of nitrosamines in food and environmental sources to human cancer is difficult to evaluate. However, with regard to DMNA, one of the most potent carcinogens among the nitrosamines, some comparative conclusions can be drawn. Freund's description of the clinical symptoms and pathological changes in the two chemists exposed to DMNA transmitted by air relates to the picture seen in cows, sheep, and dogs continually exposed to DMNA. It has been proved experimentally that the toxic and carcinogenic effects of DMNA vary among species, depending on the dose per kilogram of body weight and time of exposure. The median lethal dose (LD_{50}) varies from species to species; within the same species there are individual variations that to some degree may depend on age, sex, and feeding habits. Alimentary or parenteral exposure usually has the same effect.

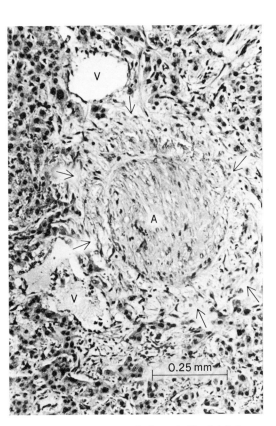

Fig. 2. Liver from same calf shown in Fig. 1; totally occluded hepatic vein A (inside arrows) with two newly formed veins V.

Mink, sheep, and cows are especially susceptible to DMNA; the LD$_{50}$ for these animals is in the range of 7 mg DMNA per kilogram of body weight; for blue foxes, 14 mg DMNA per kilogram of body weight; and for dogs, 15 mg DMNA per kilogram of body weight. After a single dose which approximates the LD$_{50}$ for the species, some of the animals will recover after 2–4 weeks, but they may die later of liver cirrhosis or hemangiosarcomas. Feeding sheep, cows, mink, blue foxes, and dogs with daily doses of ≧ 0.15 mg DMNA per kilogram of body weight will cause liver toxicosis and death after a total dose of 16–70 mg DMNA per kilogram of body weight is administered. Cows kept on a level of about 0.1 mg DMNA per kilogram of body weight for 490 days remained healthy, and autopsy did not reveal any gross liver changes. A group of blue foxes kept on the same level of DMNA (0.1 mg per kilogram of body weight) have reproduced normal offspring and have not shown any symptoms of disease for an experimental period of 3½ years. Then one died of hemangiosarcomatous liver tumors after receiving 125 mg DMNA per kilogram of body weight, but the others still remained healthy after a 4-year experimental time period. In feeding experiments with mink on a daily level of about 0.1 mg DMNA per kilogram of body weight, all the mink died within a period of 7½–22 months of hemangiomatous tumors, many with metastasis to omenta and lungs, after receiving 40–65 mg

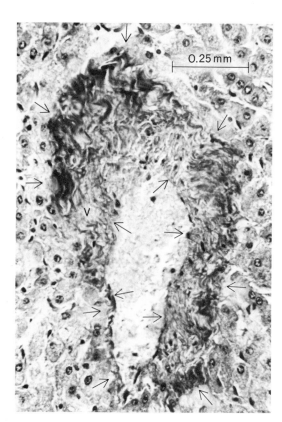

Fig. 4. Liver from same cow shown in Fig. 3. Note thickening of wall of sublobular vein V (inside arrows).

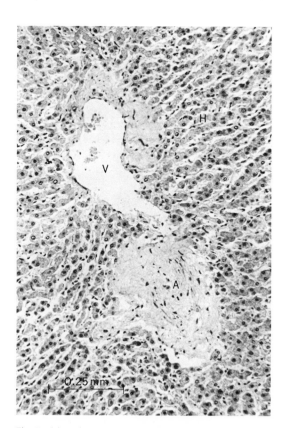

Fig. 3. Liver from cow exposed to about 0.1 mg DMNA per kilogram of body weight in 490 days; total DMNA dose 39 mg per kilogram of body weight. Liver architecture, H, is normal, but some central veins are occluded, A, and new veins formed, V.

DMNA per kilogram of body weight. If the daily DMNA dose is lowered to 0.05 mg per kilogram of body weight, the exposure time will be longer; hemangiomatous lesions occur in the liver when the mink has received 40–65 mg DMNA per kilogram of body weight. In mink, which have a short life-span, the hepatotoxic and carcinogenic doses of DMNA are the same. A daily exposure of ≧ 0.2 mg DMNA per kilogram of body weight will cause toxic hepatosis; a lower dose may be carcinogenic. In other domestic animals, such as cows and pigs, an experimental time of about 2 years with an intake of 57 and 210 mg DMNA per kilogram of body weight respectively did not produce tumors or any gross lesions. Together with results in studies with blue foxes these results indicate that, in animals with a long life-span, the carcinogenic dose of DMNA is most likely higher than the hepatotoxic dose.

Pathomorphologic observations. Liver necrosis in animals exposed to a single LD$_{50}$ dose is well known. In animals recovering after these lesions, the liver cells may regenerate quite well. The injury in the hepatic veins, however, may be worse, producing obliterative processes that may lead to liver cirrhosis. Vessel changes primarily caused by DMNA have been observed in the livers of sheep, cows (Figs. 1 and 2), blue foxes, and mink; even if they are exposed to doses below the hepatoxic threshold value, an obliterating endophlebitis occurs in the central and sublobular veins without any liver necrosis after a longer or shorter time of DMNA exposure (Figs. 3 and 4). Observations in mink indicate that the hemangiomatous tumors arise from these altered vessels. In pigs exposed to DMNA, generalized vascular changes occur, as they do to a lesser degree in cows.

Both the oncogenic and vascular effects of DMNA are of great interest and warrant further study.

For background information *see* ONCOLOGY in the McGraw-Hill Encyclopedia of Science and Technology.

[NILS KOPPANG]

Bibliography: N. Koppang, *Amer. J. Pathol.*, 74: 95–106, 1974; N. Koppang, *J. Nat. Cancer Inst.*, 52:523–528, 1974; W. Lijinsky, *Cancer Res.*, 34: 255–258, 1974; J. G. Sebranek and R. G. Cassens, *J. Milk Food Technol.*, 36:76–91, 1973.

Particle accelerator

Recent advances in the use of particle accelerators include the operation of the accelerator at Fermi National Accelerator Laboratory, producing proton beams with energies of 300 GeV and more, and the exploitation of synchrotron radiation produced in electron synchrotrons and storage rings to carry out research in a variety of disciplines.

Fermi National Accelerator Laboratory. The research facilities at the Fermi National Accelerator Laboratory (Fermilab) in Batavia, IL, are nearly complete and are being used extensively. The accelerator operates routinely at 300 GeV, and occasionally at 400 GeV. It provides a proton beam into all experimental areas simultaneously and reaches an intensity of about 10^{13} protons per pulse. Data taking for over 50 experiments is complete, and research results are regularly reported in the scientific literature.

From the groundbreaking in December 1968 until a 200-GeV beam was available in March 1972, a dedicated group of workers (scientists, engineers, technicians, laborers, and others) worked day and night to bring into existence this major scientific instrument. Working like a giant microscope, the accelerated beam probes the inner workings of the nucleus, and even the particles within the nucleus. The probes are protons derived from the ionization of hydrogen gas and accelerated to high energies by four cascaded accelerators. After reaching full energy the protons are deflected from the accelerator and directed into the experimental areas, where they collide with matter and allow the trained physicist to "see" the inner structure of the nucleus, and the forces that hold the nucleus together.

As shown in the background of Fig. 1, the dominant feature of the site is the 1¼-mi (2 km) diameter large circle containing the main accelerator. It receives the beam from the injector accelerator at 8 GeV and accelerates it in a few seconds to 300 GeV. At full energy the beam is removed from the accelerator and directed toward the experimental

Fig. 1. Aerial photograph of Fermilab site taken from experimental areas. (*Fermi National Accelerator Laboratory*)

Fig. 2. Central Laboratory area with the injector accelerators in the foreground and the main accelerator in the background. (*Fermi National Accelerator Laboratory*)

areas that are shown in the foreground of the photograph.

Injector accelerator. The injector consists of three accelerators located near the Central Laboratory. Figure 2 shows how they are arranged in a tight cluster. In the foreground is the linear accelerator leading to the circular booster accelerator that surrounds the cooling pond. The protons originate in an ion source fed by compressed hydrogen gas. The gas is ionized by separating the

Fig. 3. Photograph taken within the main-ring tunnel showing the magnets bending the proton beam to the right. (*Fermi National Accelerator Laboratory*)

negatively charged electrons from the positive nuclei called protons. The protons are then pushed and accelerated from the ion source into the front end of the linear accelerator by 0.75 MeV on the dome of the ion source. Electric fields generated by high voltages give rise to the acceleration of the protons in all accelerators. The linear accelerator is 500 ft (150 m) long and carries the protons from 0.75 MeV to 200 MeV in one straight push. The push is provided by the electric fields within the linear accelerator.

At the end of the linear accelerator the protons enter a booster accelerator that increases the energy of the protons to 8 GeV. This is accomplished by bending the protons into a 500-ft (150 m) diameter circle so that they can go repeatedly through the same electric field. The bending is accomplished by a series of magnets that deflect the particles without changing their energy. As the particles achieve higher energies, the magnetic fields must be increased to keep them within the circular vacuum chamber. The complete booster cycles rapidly, providing 15 bursts of 8-GeV protons per second for injection into the main accelerator.

Main accelerator. The main accelerator accepts 12 bunches of the booster protons and accelerates them to 300 GeV. The acceleration is the same as in the booster accelerator except that it takes several seconds to reach final energy. The components of the main accelerator are located in a tunnel that has a circumference of nearly 21,000 ft (6400 m) and is 20 ft (6 m) below ground level. Within this tunnel are located 1400 magnets and 14 accelerating cavities, as well as numerous beam monitoring and control devices. A photograph taken within a typical segment of the tunnel is shown in Fig. 3. Here can be seen many of the 20-ft-long magnets that bend the protons in the gentle curve. In addition to the 800 bending magnets (dipoles), there are many other magnets (quadrupoles) that concentrate the beam and keep the protons from leaving their track in the vacuum chamber.

Accelerator cycle. Figure 4 displays the manner in which the beam is accelerated to high energy. There are two traces shown; the lower one represents the number of protons accelerated, while the upper one represents the increasing energy of the circulating protons. When the magnetic field of the main-ring magnets is low, the bunches of protons from the injector are inserted into the main accelerator. This leads to the increase of intensity as each booster bunch is added to the circulating proton beam. When the main-ring vacuum chamber is filled, the accelerating cavities are turned on and the magnetic fields slowly increased. The proton beam increases in energy as it goes around the main ring 50,000 times per second. This is represented by the gentle slope on the upper curve as the beam is brought to 300 GeV. Finally, at peak energy, the beam circulates without further acceleration, and is available for experimental use. In most cases the protons are removed from the accelerator during the "flat top" and directed to the experimental areas. Typically, the beam is extracted slowly for counter experiments and rapidly for the bubble chamber. The main accelerator operates as a pulsed device providing a burst of beam of 1-sec duration every 6 sec, and then repeating itself day and night for steady use.

Experimental areas. The extracted proton beam is a pencil-thin stream of particles that leaves the accelerator and passes into the switchyard area. There the proton beam is divided and directed into individual experimental areas. This must be done with considerable care because the beam has over 100 kW of power associated with it. The beam splitting must be efficient so that little beam is lost and will not contribute to induced radioactivity.

The proton beam is usually focused into metallic targets producing other particles that are formed into secondary beams and transported onto the experimental detectors. In one of the experimental areas, the meson area, there are five secondary beams used by 10 or more research groups. Here beams of pi mesons, *K*-mesons, neutrons, antiprotons, and other particles are used in experimental research. In another research area, neutrinos and muons are the particles primarily available, while the third and fourth experimental areas use protons directly.

Experimental detectors and research. Research has been carried out using all these beams with a variety of detectors. The primary visual detectors are bubble chambers. Figure 5 shows a very-high-energy interaction in the 30-in. (76 cm) diameter bubble chamber. Most chamber research has been done with this small chamber, and it has taken over 1,200,000 pictures of particle interactions at Fermilab. Examination of these pictures has shown that a remarkable number of particles are produced in the nuclear collisions at high energies. Recently, the 15-ft (4.6 m) bubble chamber containing 30,000 liters of liquid hydrogen began operation. *See* BUBBLE CHAMBER.

The other major class of detectors are electronic. They do not leave a visual picture, but the signals are recorded on magnetic tapes to be analyzed by physicists with the aid of computers. Electronic detectors are used for a variety of ex-

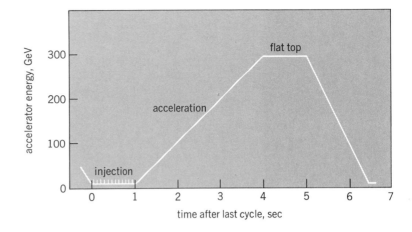

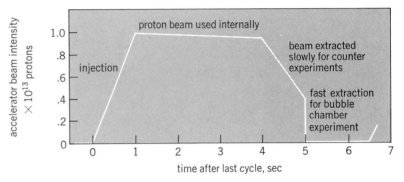

Fig. 4. Curves representing the energy and intensity of the circulating protons during a cycle of the main accelerator. (*Fermi National Accelerator Laboratory*)

periments ranging from search and survey experiments to studies of more complex processes. Among the former have been searches for fractionally charged particles called quarks, and magnetically charged objects referred to as monopoles. Unfortunately none was found. More complex pro-

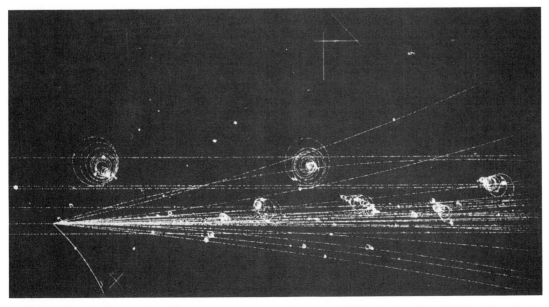

Fig. 5. Nuclear collision which was initiated by an incoming 300-GeV proton within the 30-in. (76 cm) diameter bubble chamber. (*Fermi National Accelerator Laboratory*)

Table 1. Number of experiments completed, under way, and remaining to be done at Fermilab as of July 1, 1974

Experiments	Completed	Under way	To be done
Hadron experiments in electronic detectors			
Search and survey experiments	11	6	7
Total cross-section experiments	1	1	0
Elastic scattering experiments	1	6	5
Inelastic scattering experiments	3	6	4
Multiparticle experiments	3	3	4
Hyperon and neutral kaon experiments	0	2	1
Hadron experiments in bubble chambers			
30-in. (76 cm) bubble chamber	13	1	10
15-ft (4.6 m) bubble chamber	0	1	0
Neutrino experiments in electronic detectors	1	2	1
Neutrino experiments in bubble chambers	0	2	5
Muon/electron/photon experiments in electronic detectors	1	2	4
Emulsion experiments	21	0	10
Miscellaneous experiments	2	3	3
TOTALS	57	35	54

cesses consist of measuring the frequencies of collisions (cross section) and the patterns of scattering after collisions (elastic and inelastic scattering). Other experiments compare the interactions of muons and those of electrons, while the weak interaction is probed by the neutrino beams. *See* FORCE, WEAK AND ELECTROMAGNETIC; QUARKS; SCATTERING EXPERIMENTS, NUCLEAR.

Table 1 indicates the overall scope of the research at Fermilab. Many experiments are now complete, while other researchers are eagerly awaiting their chance to use this unique facility.   [JAMES R. SANFORD]

Synchrotron radiation. The emission of light by electrons in circular motion guided by celestial magnetic fields has long been known to astronomers and is responsible, for example, for the beautiful background light in the Crab Nebula. Very powerful terrestrial sources of this same synchrotron radiation are now being exploited at electron synchrotrons and storage rings in more than a dozen laboratories in England, France, Italy, Japan, the Soviet Union, the United States, and West Germany, opening new horizons in ultraviolet and x-ray research in many disciplines.

Types of research. The unique properties of this radiation (high intensity, high polarization, natural collimation, and broad spectral bandwidth) have, in only a few years of use, made a significant impact on research in atomic, molecular, and solid-state physics, particularly in the energy region below 100 eV (corresponding to wavelengths greater than 10 nm). With more energetic radiation now available (up to 20 or 30 keV) this work is being extended and new research areas are being ex-

plored: for example, structural biology using x-ray diffraction. At the Cambridge Electron Accelerator (CEA) in Cambridge, MA, focused synchrotron radiation has been used to operate a novel scanning x-ray microscope with 1-μm resolution, 2-mm depth of field, and capable of making stereoscopic, element-discriminating photographs of hydrated thick specimens in an atmospheric environment.

Synchrotron radiation may be used in studies of reflection and photoemission from freshly cleaved or deposited surfaces; transmission through thin samples of solids, liquids, and gases; x-ray fluorescence; photoionization and photodissociation; and x-ray Raman and Compton scattering. On some machines the time structure of the radiation (for example, sub-nanosecond bursts separated by 0.8 μsec in the SPEAR storage ring) is favorable to studies of short-duration luminescence or other time-constant measurement.

The high intensity of synchrotron radiation enables users to monochromatize to very narrow bandwidths ($\Delta E/E \approx 10^{-3}$ or 10^{-4}) and still have very high flux for experiments. The tunability of the source is particularly important to certain studies, such as x-ray absorption edge fine structure.

Sources of synchrotron radiation. Synchrotron radiation sources are either electron synchrotrons, in which the electron energy varies (typically at 50–60 Hz) as electrons are accelerated to peak energies of about 10–20 times the injection energy, or storage rings, in which electrons are stored at constant energy. Storage rings have the advantages of a constant synchrotron radiation spectral distribution, essentially constant intensity (the electron current decays with a lifetime of several hours), very stable source size and position, and high-vacuum environment.

Synchrotrons, however, can reach higher electron energies more easily and hence provide higher-energy synchrotron radiation. The reason is that the critical energy, which characterizes the spectrum of emitted radiation, and above which the intensity falls off exponentially, is proportional to the cube of the electron energy. (Its value in kilo-electron-volts is 2.2 E^3/R, where E is the electron energy in giga-electron-volts, and R is the radius of curvature in meters.)

At most laboratories synchrotron radiation research programs are secondary efforts on machines designed, built, and operated for high-energy physics research. One or two beam ports are installed, and radiation is made available to synchrotron radiation users, who have little or no control over scheduling time or beam energy and intensity. At these laboratories synchrotron radiation research may terminate with high-energy physics programs, as happened in 1973 at the CEA and is expected to happen in 1978 at the NINA synchrotron in Daresbury, England. A plan view of the synchrotron radiation facility at Daresbury is shown in Fig. 6.

In a few cases (notably at the 240-MeV storage ring at the University of Wisconsin) the laboratory is dedicated to synchrotron radiation research. Here many ports are installed on the machine, viewing a larger fraction of the curved orbit, and the machine parameters are controlled by synchrotron radiation users.

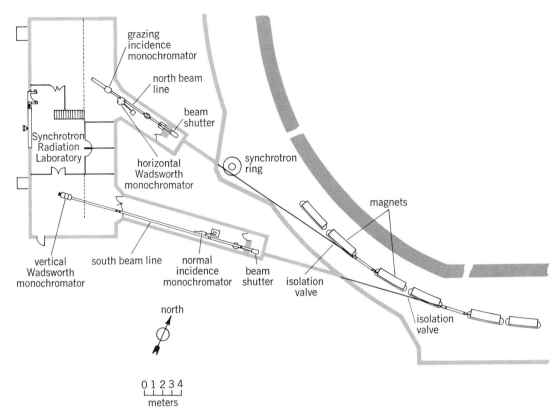

grazing
incidence
monochromator

north beam
line

beam
shutter

Synchrotron
Radiation
Laboratory

synchrotron
ring

magnets

horizontal
Wadsworth
monochromator

vertical
Wadsworth
monochromator

south beam line

normal
incidence
monochromator

beam
shutter

isolation
valve

isolation
valve

north

0 1 2 3 4
meters

Fig. 6. Synchrotron Radiation Facility at the NINA synchrotron, located in Daresbury, England. (From Daresbury Nuclear Physics Laboratory, Science Research Council, 1971 Annual Report, 1972)

Higher-energy storage rings are being proposed
as dedicated synchrotron light sources in many
parts of the world. Since the synchrotron radiation
spectral distribution and intensity depend only on
the electron energy and radius of curvature (Fig. 7),
local regions of high magnetic fields (as high as 50
kG if superconductors are used), alternating in
polarity to produce no net deflection, may be inserted into the ring to control and enhance the
synchrotron radiation. Such "wiggler" magnets
have been proposed for use in dedicated synchrotron radiation facilities.

Although high-energy physicists make some use
of synchrotron radiation in controlling and monitoring the cross section of circulating beams, for
the most part they regard this radiation as an unfortunate by-product of circular motion of electrons. In fact, sychrotron radiation imposes a very
severe economic and technical limitation on the
energy attainable in these machines because the
power radiated by a current in circular motion with
fixed bending radius increases as the fourth power
of the energy. (Its value in kilowatts is 88 E^4I/R,
where E is the electron energy in giga-electron-
volts, I is the current in amperes, and R is the radius of curvature in meters.)

Synchrotron radiation facilities. Table 2 lists
the major synchrotron radiation facilities and their
chief characteristics. The most powerful synchrotron radiation sources now in operation are the
new storage rings SPEAR at the Stanford Linear
Accelerator Center (SLAC) at Stanford University, and DORIS at Hamburg, West Germany. Both
machines are primarily used for high-energy phys-

ics studies of colliding electron positron beams.
SPEAR is in routine operation, now storing up to
50 mA at 2.5 GeV. By late 1974 both SPEAR and
DORIS are expected to be capable of storing currents of $\geq$100 mA at energies of ~4 GeV, producing hundreds of kilowatts of synchrotron radiation.
At SPEAR, the Stanford Synchrotron Radiation
Project is already in operation with one port capable of serving six or seven simultaneous experiments. At DORIS, synchrotron radiation from both

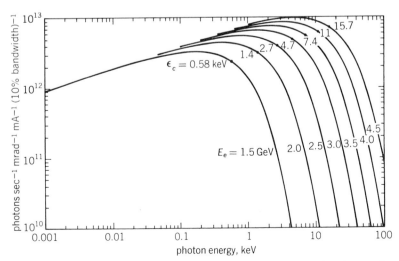

Fig. 7. The spectral distribution of synchrotron radiation from the storage ring
SPEAR is given; ϵ_c is the critical energy and E_e is the stored electron beam energy;
bending radius is 12.7 m.

Table 2. Synchrotron light facilities

Laboratory	Storage ring or synchrotron	Energy, GeV	Current, mA	Bending radius, m	Critical energy ϵ_c, keV	Remarks
DORIS, Hamburg	S. R.	3.0	~500	12.4	4.8	Initial capability; to be completed in late 1974 or 1975
		4.0	~250		11.4	
SPEAR, Stanford	S. R.	2.5	50	12.7	2.7	Present capability; to be completed in late 1974 or 1975
		4.0	100		11.1	
CEA	S. R.	3.5	50–100	26.3	3.6	Closed in 1973
Cambridge, MA	Synch.	5.5	20		14.0	
DESY, Hamburg	Synch.	7.5	10–30	31.7	29.5	
Arus, Erevan	Synch.	6.0	20	24.6	19.5	
VEPP-3, Novosibirsk	S. R.	2.25	200	6.0	4.2	
VEPP-2M, Novosibirsk	S. R.	0.67	100	1.22	0.54	
NINA, Daresbury	Synch.	5.0	40	20.8	13.3	
Bonn I	Synch.	2.3	30	7.65	3.5	
Bonn II	Synch.	0.5	30	1.7	0.16	
INS-SOR, Tokyo	Synch.	1.3	30	4.0	1.22	
INS-SOR, Tokyo	S. R.	0.3	100	1.0	0.059	Dedicated to synchrotron radiation
Frascati, Italy	Synch.	1.1	10	3.6	0.82	
ACO, Orsay	S. R.	0.54	100	1.1	0.32	
DCI, Orsay	S. R.	1.8	500	3.8	3.4	In construction
Tantalus I, Wisconsin	S. R.	0.24	20	0.54	0.057	Dedicated to synchrotron radiation
Moscow	Synch.	0.68	–	2.0	0.35	
NBS, Washington	Synch.	0.18	1	0.83	0.016	Being converted to synchrotron radiation

electron and positron beams will be utilized with two ports and two synchrotron radiation research areas. Even larger colliding beam storage rings are being proposed in several parts of the world. For example, the PEP (Positron-Electron-Proton) colliding beam complex proposed at SLAC is designed to store 100 mA of electrons at 15 GeV, providing large fluxes of synchrotron radiation up to ~ 200 keV.

Extraction and use of radiation. High flux densities on small targets are possible with synchrotron radiation sources because relativistic effects cause all the radiation to be folded forward into a narrow cone with vertical opening angle given approximately by the ratio of the electron rest mass energy to its kinetic energy ($mc^2/E = 2 \times 10^{-4}$ rad for $E = 2.5$ GeV). The radiation is thus emitted tangentially from all curved parts of the electron orbit in a flat pancake. By comparison, conventional light and x-ray sources emit radiation in all directions, and only a small fraction of the total radiation strikes small targets at some distance from the source. In use the radiation from a small arc of the electron orbit (typically 10 millirad) travels down an evacuated pipe equipped with valves, gages, pumps, and beam-splitting mirrors.

When possible, windows (for example, thin beryllium foils) are used to separate the experimental apparatus from the machine vacuum. In some parts of the spectrum, transmitting windows are unavailable and the experiment must be connected directly to the ring vacuum. Since storage rings operate at high vacuum (~10^{-9} torr), experiments that couple to the ring must be compatible with these requirements or be isolated from the ring by conductance limitations and differential pumping.

Low-energy synchrotron radiation (up to ~4 keV) may be deflected through small angles by grazing incidence reflection on smooth surfaces. In this manner beam splitters can be made, enabling several users to share a single port. Since the higher-energy part of the spectrum is not reflected, these mirrors act as low-pass filters. Furthermore, by working at an angle to the direct tangential synchrotron radiation beam, radiation hazards are reduced, simplifying access to experimental equipment. By figuring the mirror surface the reflected radiation can be focused, greatly increasing the flux density on small samples.

For background information *see* ELEMENTARY PARTICLE; PARTICLE ACCELERATOR; SYNCHROTRON in the McGraw-Hill Encyclopedia of Science and Technology. [HERMAN WINICK]

Bibliography: F. C. Brown, Ultraviolet spectroscopy of solids with the use of synchrotron radiation, in H. Ehrenreich, F. Seitz, and D. Turnbull (eds.), *Solid State Physics*, vol. 29, 1974; P. Horowitz and J. Howell, *Science*, 178:608, 1972; S. Kapitza, *Proceedings of the 9th International Conference on High Energy Accelerators*, SLAC, May 2–7, 1974, publication pending; I. Lindau et al., *Nature*, 250:214–215, July 19, 1974; G. V. Marr and I. H. Munro (eds.), *International Symposium for Synchrotron Radiation Users*, Daresbury, DNPL/R26, Jan. 4–7, 1973; G. V. Marr, I. H. Munro, and G. C. C. Sharp, *Synchrotron Radiation: A Bibliography*, DNPL/R24, 1972; *Proceedings of the 17th International Conference on High Energy Physics*, London, July 1974; E. M. Rowe, *IEEE Trans. Nucl. Sci.*, NS-20(3):973, June 1973; T. E. Toohig, *Design Description of the External Experimental Areas at the Fermi National Accelerator Laboratory, Batavia*, 1974; R. R. Wilson, *Sci. Amer.*, 2:72–83, February 1974; H. Winick, *IEEE Trans. Nucl. Sci.*, NS-120(3):984, June 1973.

Petroleum processes

Since 75% of the energy used in the United States comes from petroleum and natural gas, and domestic production of both materials is leveling off, the high cost of imported oil to meet the rising energy demand and the drive to minimize United States dependence on foreign sources are combining to accelerate development of alternate energy sources and of alternate raw materials—coal, shale oil, tar sands. Much of the technology involved has been under development, mostly by the petroleum process industry, for many years but was not economically competitive in the past, when low-cost crude oil and gas were plentiful.

These matters have been the subject of many recent economic and technical studies by government agencies, universities, research foundations, industries, financial groups, and professional societies. Federal funding on energy research and development programs—conversion of energy and its resources, production of oil and gas, and production and utilization of coal, nuclear energy, and other sources—is expected to be about $10,000,000,000 during the next 5 years. Industry research and development are expected to include $4–5,000,000,000 for oil and gas, and $3,000,000,000 for coal. Similar studies are under way in Western European countries and Japan.

Many of these studies are in substantial agreement that projected costs on an energy-supplied basis—and in consideration of environmental protection costs—for synthetic crude from oil shale, tar sands, or coal or for methanol, substitute natural gas, or H_2 from coal may be in the acceptable range in comparison with the cost of materials from imported petroleum and natural gas. For the near future, a guiding factor will be the continuing need for portable liquid fuels for cars, trucks, planes, and trains, which use about 25% of the total United States energy, and for agricultural machinery.

Raw-materials supply problems, in combination with environmental controls, have become major influences on petroleum processes. Significant recent developments include changes in petrochemical economics, conservation of energy as a major item in refinery and petrochemical plants, more sophisticated pollution control in these plants, and accelerated development of stack gas clean-up processes in electric power plants, as well as substantial improvements in conventional refining processes. These developments arise principally from markedly better catalysts and process configurations that make more gasoline-range aromatics and olefins, that increase conversion process capacity and selectivity to desired products, and that reduce sulfur content of products. As shown in the table, there was a 6% increase in American crude refining capacity from 1973 to 1974, the result mostly of debottlenecking and reactivation of existing equipment; no new refineries were built.

Environmental controls effect. Environmental controls on American automobiles are affecting refining processes in two ways. First, controls are causing a significant increase in fuel consumption per mile. Second, the Environmental Protection Agency (EPA) is requiring annual reductions in tetraethyllead content of gasoline; especially significant is the EPA ruling that an unleaded grade must be supplied in 1974 to help prevent deactivation of exhaust catalytic converters on new cars. To provide the high-octane components needed for good antiknock performance of low-lead and, especially, of unleaded gasolines, refining processes must be made more severe; it is desirable that the octane number be kept high enough so that automobile engine compression ratios do not have to be reduced, which would cause a further decline in fuel economy.

Catalytic reforming. This process, which produces about 23% of crude capacity, supplies more than 30% of the gasoline used in the United States and is the principal way to make antiknock quality directly. The process does not essentially change molecular size but reforms the lower-octane paraffins and cycloalkanes to aromatics—benzene, toluene, xylenes—which have very high unleaded octane numbers; but, in terms of severe operation, the cost in gasoline yield is significant.

Reforming catalyst, typically 2-mm-diameter pellets in fixed reactor beds, has usually been an activated alumina on the extended surface of which a small amount of platinum is finely dispersed. Recently, almost half of the United States reforming industry has begun to use newly developed bimetallic catalysts, such as platinum-rhenium; these materials inhibit coke formation on the catalyst and therefore permit operation at higher temperature and lower pressure, where the reaction equilibrium favors aromatics production. Another important aid to severe operation has been the development of semicontinuous regeneration and of systems in which a portion of the catalyst is circulated continuously through a regenerator; units installed and under construction for continuous regeneration now total more than one sixth of all United States reforming capacity.

Severe reforming also makes the additional by-product H_2 much in demand in all the hydrogenation and hydrodesulfurization processes in the refinery.

Isomerization. This procedure converts *n*-pentane and *n*-hexane to higher-octane-number branched paraffins. The need for such components, plus major improvements in the process, may cause isomerization to be more widely used in the future. The improved process uses molecular sieves—crystalline materials selective for molecular shape—to concentrate the high-octane components in the product.

United States refining process capacity in 1974*

Process	Barrels per day × 10³	% of crude capacity	% over 1973
Crude distilling	14,800	100	6.2
Catalytic reforming	3,360	23	2.6
Catalytic cracking†	4,620	31	2.4
Hydrocracking	860	6	—
Other hydroprocesses	5,780	39	10.6
Alkylation	850	6	4.6
Aromatics and isomerization	350	2	4.3

*From L. R. Aalund, *Oil Gas J.*, p. 76, April 1, 1974.
†Fresh feed.

Catalytic cracking. This process, the principal way to convert heavier components to lower-molecular-weight products, represents 31% of crude capacity and provides 37% of the gasoline consumed in the United States. Most cracking units employ a powdered catalyst that is rapidly circulated through a fluidized-bed reactor and regenerator vessel. In recent years there has been an impressive technology revival in this mature process. The most important advance has been the marked improvement in activity and selectivity of catalyst by inclusion of molecular-sieve or zeolitic components—highly ordered crystalline silica-alumina structures. Interacting with this development has been another major one, riser cracking, in which extensive use is made of computer-aided process models and calculations; the units are redesigned so that most of the cracking occurs in the transfer line, and the vaporized feed carries the freshly regenerated catalyst up into the reactor vessel. This short contact time at high temperature, and with more active catalyst, gives much better conversion, and much less coke is formed on the catalyst. The capacity of many units that were limited by regenerator coke-burning ability is thereby increased. Also, the method produces greater gasoline yield directly, of improved unleaded octane number, as well as more light olefins, some of which can be alkylated, that is, chemically combined with isobutane, to make additional high-octane isoparaffin components. The olefins are also valuable as petrochemical feedstock.

Another important development is hydrogenation of fresh and recycle feed for cracking units, which improves gasoline yield and reduces coke make. It also removes considerable sulfur from feed, helping to produce a low-sulfur gasoline and to minimize the amount of SO_2 emitted in regenerator stack gas.

Because of such developments, gasoline-producing capacity is increasing more rapidly than intake capacity of cracking units.

Hydrocracking. Catalysts and process details are being improved so that the potential of hydrocracking as a way of converting aromatic feedstocks to gasoline-range aromatics will improve; hydrocracking can be used with straight-run gasoil feedstocks, or it can operate on the aromatic gas-oil stream produced from catalytic cracking.

Petrochemical refinery. Several years of intensive research and development have resulted in a major commercial process combination in which refinery gas-oil streams are steam-thermal-cracked to produce very large amounts of ethylene, propylene, butadiene, and so on for the petrochemical industry, and by-product streams containing aromatics and other pyrolysis gasoline components are returned to the refinery system. Application of the process to crude oil feed is under development. The naphtha or other light components, which would otherwise have to be used for pyrolysis feed, are made available for refinery processing to gasoline and other products.

Residual fuel desulfurization. Many refinery streams are desulfurized by hydrogenation processes, and the H_2S recovered is converted to solid sulfur for commercial sale; there has been steady improvement in the sulfur recovery processes. As the table shows, there has been a substantial increase in the capacity of hydroprocesses (including hydrodesulfurization), mostly by extending application of well-known technology. An important exception is residual fuel, which poses very difficult technical problems because it contains resins, asphaltenes, and organometallic compounds (especially Ni and V) that deactivate hydrodesulfurizing catalyst.

Because of high-severity processing of light products, the residual fuel yield of United States refineries averages only 6% of crude oil intake; much of the fuel oil for United States electric power plants is imported from refineries in the Caribbean area.

To meet SO_2 emission limits, power plants need fuel well below 1% sulfur—in some areas well below 0.5%. Major efforts have been made in developing a variety of processes to desulfurize typical 2–4% sulfur stocks down to this range. Some of the large-scale units in operation and under construction are designed for an indirect processing scheme; by vacuum distillation, mild thermal cracking, or deasphalting, a high-sulfur pitch or asphalt is separated out (thus removing many compounds harmful to catalyst) for disposal by some means (refinery fuel, gasification, or asphalt sales), and the heavy distillate is deeply desulfurized over an improved hydrodesulfurizing catalyst. This low-sulfur stream may be blended with feed material to make 1% sulfur fuel.

A number of direct processes (that is, feeding residue directly) are in advanced development stages, including ebullating-bed systems using hydrocracking-type catalysts, and catalyst regeneration systems, all of which employ high-pressure H_2. A much different process, potentially capable of 0.1% sulfur product, involves low-conversion fluidized-bed catalytic cracking.

Because of complexity and high cost, it may be several years before very large volumes of low-sulfur fuel are available from the use of these processes.

Flue gas desulfurization. Processes to remove SO_2 from power plant stacks are of indirect importance to petroleum processors because they reduce requirements for desulfurizing fuel; they are of direct interest to refineries in which some sulfur-containing fuels may have to be burned.

Substantial progress has been made with both wet and dry processes, and a considerable number of commercial plants are in operation. However, for some of these plants, those using limestone as a scrubbing medium, there may be serious disposal problems with resulting calcium sulfate sludges. To avoid such problems, a number of regenerative processes are under development. In a particularly promising example of a dry process, the flue gas passes through a grid containing an acceptor, believed to be $Cu-Al_2O_3$, which removes SO_2 by an oxidation-reduction regenerative cycle; this process is undergoing commercial trials in Japan, where there is very strong effort in desulfurization process development.

Of considerable potential importance is the development of combined-cycle power plants that utilize a gasification step to convert residual fuel oil or coal to a flue gas that can be cleaned up to remove sulfur (as H_2S) and nitrogen compounds as well as fly ash; this gas is burned in a special power turbine whose hot exhaust is used in a waste-heat boiler to raise steam driving a conventional turbine. Both turbines generate electric power for an overall efficiency of about 50% compared to the conventional 40%, and the stack gas is clean. By making coal-burning power plants acceptable for air-quality standards, such gasifying systems, used for clean combustion of coal, or stack gas scrubbers, indirectly increase the availability of hydrocarbon for conversion to portable liquid fuels and reduce dependence on imports.

Energy recovery in refineries. For a typical refinery producing 50–60% gasoline, energy equivalent to about 10% of the crude oil intake is consumed for fuel, steam, and electricity to operate process equipment. Intensive efforts are being made by refiners to conserve or recover as much of this energy as possible. Many modern catalytic cracking units recover energy by operating a turbine on the hot gases from the regenerator; heat is recovered in a waste-heat steam boiler or feed preheater furnace. Other measures include installing supplementary heat exchange, maintaining optimum efficiency of process heaters and boilers by computer-guided control systems, and installing power-recovery turbines on refinery liquid and gas streams flowing from higher to lower pressure. By employing all of these measures, a savings of about 10% of energy, that is, 11% of crude intake, can be expected.

Alternate raw materials. From pilot-scale results with oil shale and tar sands, confirmed by the early commercial experience of Great Canadian Oil Sands, Ltd., with Athabasca tar sands, it appears that the processing of these materials yields synthetic crude oil of very good quality, with sulfur and other undesirable compounds removed, and heavy residual materials mostly converted to lighter components; planned installations could bring tar sands synthetic crude production to 800,000 barrels per day by 1985.

Among the coal processes of most relevance to the petroleum industry are conversion to a synthetic crude by extraction or hydrogenation, or to gasoline by more intensive hydrogenation. Coal can also be converted by reaction with steam to a low-Btu producer-gas mixture of CO and H_2, or by hydrogenation to form substitute natural gas, essentially methane. Some of these are very elaborate processes or are not yet technically perfected for very-large-scale operations. For these and other reasons, such as environmental protection, very high equipment costs, and strained capabilities of major construction contractors, it will be several years before products from these processes are likely to be available on a major scale.

Alternate fuels. Methanol (CH_3OH) has been proposed as a gasoline supplement on the basis of studies indicating advantages in octane number, reduced exhaust emissions, and fuel economy. Large quantities of methanol might be imported from overseas sources where the raw material for its manufacture—natural gas—is plentiful. Methanol might be made on a large scale from coal, as a readily transportable, clean fuel, by currently available technology. Since there are a number of potential disadvantages and difficulties to be overcome before methanol would be fully practical in the United States gasoline distribution system, among the alternatives under study are to use it as a clean fuel for special industrial purposes or for petrochemicals, depending on economics, thereby releasing corresponding amounts of conventional fuels for transportation use.

Also under intensive study are a number of technological systems for generation of hydrogen and its distribution on a large scale as a clean fuel; however, such use of hydrogen appears to be some time in the future and thus would have little impact on petroleum processes in the short term.

For background information *see* ATMOSPHERIC POLLUTION; COAL; CRACKING; ELECTRIC POWER GENERATION; GASOLINE; HYDROCRACKING; HYDROGEN; ISOMERIZATION; OIL SHALE; PETROLEUM PROCESSES; PETROLEUM PRODUCTS; REFORMING IN PETROLEUM REFINING in the McGraw-Hill Encyclopedia of Science and Technology.

[N. L. MORSE]

Bibliography: J. J. Blazek, *Oil Gas J.*, pp. 65–70, Oct. 8, 1973; A. L. Conn, *Chem. Eng. Progr.*, 69(12):11–17, December 1973; H. Hoffman et al., *Hydrocarbon Processing*, pp. 73–105, May 1974; J. Vandeven and J. Mackey, *Oil Gas J.*, pp. 116–118, Sept. 24, 1974.

Petroleum reservoir models

The localized depletion of light-oil reserves, combined with international political developments, has resulted recently in shortages and sharply higher prices of oil in many industrialized nations. This in turn has focused increased attention on vast heavy-oil reserves which have been untapped in the past due to the cost and lack of proved technology required for recovery. At reservoir conditions, light-oil viscosities are generally less than several centipoises while heavy oils in Venezuela, California, and Alberta exhibit viscosities from 500 to more than 100,000 centipoises (1 cp = 10^{-3} newton second per square meter).

The relatively high cost of recovering heavy oil reflects the necessity of heating the reservoir formation to reduce the oil viscosity. This heating may be achieved by in-place combustion or by steam injection. The effect of increased temperature on oil viscosity is dramatic, as indicated by Cold Lake (Alberta) oil viscosities of 100,000 cp at 55°F (13°C) and 6 cp at 400°F (204°C).

Prediction of steamflood performance. A large number of field pilot tests have been conducted in California and Alberta to evaluate the feasibility of steamflooding heavy-oil reservoirs. The resulting performance data provide insight into the nature of the oil displacement and heat flow in those particular pilots. However, difficulties arise in attempts to extrapolate or scale the data to estimate commercial-scale field performance under altered operating conditions. Numerical modeling offers an inexpensive (relative to field pilot costs) approach to the problem of designing an optimum commercial operation. A mathematical model can be validated by obtaining good agreement between calculated and observed field pilot flood data. The model can then be used to study the effects of changes in those factors or conditions at the control of the op-

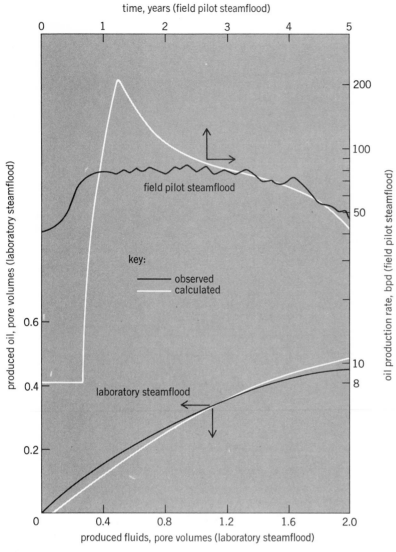

time, years (field pilot steamflood)

produced fluids, pore volumes (laboratory steamflood)

Fig. 1. Comparison of observed and model calculated oil recovery by steamflood. (*From K. H. Coats et al., Three-dimensional simulation of steamflooding, Soc. Petrol. Eng. J., vol. 14, no. 4, 1974*)

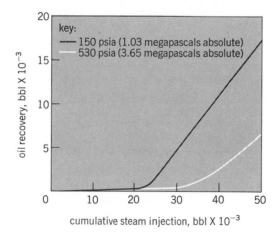

cumulative steam injection, bbl X 10⁻³

Fig. 2. Effect of pressure level on linear steamflood oil recovery. (*From K. H. Coats et al., Three-dimensional simulation of steamflooding, Soc. Petrol. Eng. J., vol. 14, no. 4, 1974*)

erator. These include well pattern and spacing, injection-production intervals (steam is injected at the top or bottom of the sand formation and oil is recovered from the bottom, or vice versa) and rates, quality of injected steam, and optimum steam bank size—if a bank is found preferable to continuous steam injection. A steam bank is a finite quantity of injected steam followed by an injection of cold water.

Steamflood model. A recent steamflood model consists of Eqs. (1) through (5), which describe the three-dimensional, transient flow of steam, oil, water, and heat energy through heterogeneous reservoir formations. In differential form, the mass balances—continuity equations are (1), (2), and (3); the energy balance equation is (4); and the equilibrium equation is (5).

$$-\nabla \cdot (\rho_w \mathbf{u}_w) + q_c - q_w = \frac{\partial}{\partial t} (\phi \rho_w S_w) \qquad (1)$$

$$-\nabla \cdot (\rho_s \mathbf{u}_s) - q_c - q_s = \frac{\partial}{\partial t} (\phi \rho_s S_s) \qquad (2)$$

$$-\nabla \cdot (\rho_o \mathbf{u}_o) - q_o = \frac{\partial}{\partial t} (\phi \rho_o S_o) \qquad (3)$$

$$-\nabla \cdot (\rho_w H_w \mathbf{u}_w + \rho_s H_s \mathbf{u}_s + \rho_o H_o \mathbf{u}_o)$$
$$+ \nabla \cdot (K\nabla T) - q_w H_w - q_o H_o - q_s H_s$$
$$= \frac{\partial}{\partial t} [\phi(\rho_w U_w S_w + \rho_o U_o S_o + \rho_s U_s S_s)$$
$$+ (1-\phi)(\rho c_p)_R T] \qquad (4)$$

$$T = T_s(p) \qquad (5)$$

Subscripts w, o, and s denote water, oil, and steam, respectively. The volumetric velocities (volume/area-time) $\mathbf{u}_w$, $\mathbf{u}_o$, $\mathbf{u}_s$ are representable through Darcy's law as Eq. (6), where $m = w$, o, or

$$\mu_m = -k k_{rm} (\nabla p - \gamma_m \nabla z) / \mu_m \qquad (6)$$

s. Formation (rock) permeability k is a function of spatial position (x, y, z); relative permeability k_{rm} is a function of fluid saturations (S_w, S_o, S_s); and specific weight γ_m and viscosity μ_m are functions of temperature T and pressure p. Molar densities (moles/volume) ρ_w, ρ_o, ρ_s are dependent upon temperature and pressure. Water saturation S_w is the fraction of pore space filled with water; thus $S_w + S_o + S_s = 1.0$, and only two of the three saturations are independent. The term q_c is steam condensation rate (moles/time-unit volume) and q_w, q_o, q_s are sink terms (moles/time-unit volume) representing production wells. Porosity ϕ is a known function of pressure and spatial position. In Eq. (4), H and U are specific enthalpy and internal energy, respectively, K is formation thermal conductivity, and $(\rho c_p)_R$ is volumetric rock specific heat. In Eq. (5), $T_s(p)$ is steam saturation temperature, a function of pressure given by the steam tables. Equation (5) applies if steam is present; if temperature T is less than $T_s(p)$, then Eq. (5) is replaced by $S_s = 0$.

Results of the model. Equations (1)–(5) are equations in the five unknowns q_c, S_w, S_o, T, and p. All other variables or coefficients are expressible as known functions of one or more of these five unknowns. The equations are expressed in finite-difference form and solved by a numerical method. Model results consist of fluid saturations, pressure, and temperature as functions of spatial position and time, and oil, water, and steam production rates versus time for each production well.

Figure 1 illustrates the agreement obtained between model calculated and observed oil recovery curves for both laboratory and field pilot steamfloods. The laboratory steamflood was conducted in a sandpack with a permeability of 200 darcy (2×10^{-8}m), 12 in. (305 mm) square, and 6.4 in. (163 mm) thick. The field pilot was a $2\frac{1}{2}$-acre (10^4 m²) five-spot in a 65-ft-thick (20 m) California formation. A five-spot is a set of four producing wells located on the corners of a square pattern with a steam injector in the center. In both cases, oil viscosity exceeded 2000 cp at original reservoir temperature and declined to about 8 cp at the 300°F (149°C) temperature corresponding to the flood pressure level of about 80 psia (550 kilopascals). The volume unit designated "pore volume" in Fig. 1 corresponds to a fluid volume equal to the total pore space of the sandpack. The barrels-per-day (bpd) oil production rate unit is equivalent to 5.6146 ft³/day or 0.1590 m³/day. The early disparity between calculated and observed field pilot oil rates is caused by the fact that the calculations did not model the stimulation of the pilot production wells. This production well stimulation consisted of repeated cycles, each cycle consisting of steam injection, a shut-in soak period during which the steam condensed, and a production period. The production wells were placed on continuous production after breakthrough of steam from the injection well, which occurred about 1 year after start of the pilot flood.

The cumulative ratio of steam injected (cold water equivalent volume) to oil recovered at the end of the field pilot was about 4.4. At current oil prices, ratios less than 5 in general make steamflooding economically attractive.

The mathematical model has been used to evaluate alternate design conditions for a number of different types of heavy-oil reservoirs. Results have shown that steam injection at the bottom of the reservoir formation generally increases the ratio of oil recovered/steam injected. This effect is small in thin formations where the ratio of injection-production well distance to formation thickness exceeds 4. The effect is large in thick reservoirs where the ratio approaches 1. Results also indicate a strong effect of flood pressure level on oil recovery. For a given amount of steam injection, oil recovery generally increases with decreasing flood pressure level. Figure 2 indicates this effect in a linear steamflood conducted at 150-psia (1.03 megapascals absolute) and 530-psia (3.65 megapascals absolute) pressure levels. The effect occurs primarily due to the higher specific volume of steam at lower pressure which results in greater volumes of steam (for the same mass of steam) displacing the oil.

For background information see FLUID-FLOW PRINCIPLES; PETROLEUM RESERVOIR ENGINEERING; PETROLEUM RESERVOIR MODELS; PETROLEUM SECONDARY RECOVERY in the McGraw-Hill Encyclopedia of Science and Technology.

[K. H. COATS]

Bibliography: K. H. Coats et al., Soc. Petrol. Eng. J., vol. 14, no. 4, 1974.

Phagocytosis

It is now more than three-quarters of a century since Élie Metchnikoff proposed his "theory of phagocytes." This thesis assigns to the phagocyte a central role in the body's defense against infecting organisms. Since then, the functionality of the polymorphonuclear (PMN) leukocyte in the acute inflammatory response has become increasingly clear. Recently, however, new approaches have given a new vitality to the field of PMN leukocyte research. These new developments relate to both the mechanics of phagocytosis and the microbicidal metabolism directed against the engulfed organism.

Engulfment and degranulation. Upon contact with opsonized bacteria or particulate material, the PMN leukocyte invaginates and engulfs the particle, forming a phagocytic vacuole. Subsequent to engulfment, granules disappear from the cytoplasm of the PMN leukocyte. The leukocyte contains two chemically distinct types of cytoplasmic granules. One is relatively large (800 mμ; 1 m$\mu = 1 \times 10^{-9}$m), dense, and azurophilic. This granule contains myeloperoxidase, acid phosphatase, and acid hydrolytic enzymes and is referred to as the primary, azurophilic, or A-type granule. The other major type of granule is smaller, less dense, and contains alkaline phosphatase, lactoferrin, and lysozyme; it is referred to as the specific, secondary, or B-type granule.

Using cytochemical techniques with electron microscopy, D. Bainton observed that the specific granules empty into the phagocytic vacuoles first. This fusion occurred within 30 sec after engulfment. It was not until 3 min after phagocytosis that significant fusion of primary granules was observed. These findings correlate with the temporal decrease in pH within the phagocytic vacuole. Because of the neutral pH requirements of the enzyme complement of specific granules, the initial fusion of these granules ensures at least temporary conditions of optimal activity. After 3 min the intervacuolar pH drops to 6.5, and fusion of primary granules containing acid pH optima enzymes occurs. There is a continuing decrease in pH to 3.5–4.0 within 7–15 min.

Cytophilic antibodies and tetrapeptides. It has been demonstrated that leukokinin, a highly specific leukophilic α-globulin, is necessary for the attainment of full phagocytic function in the PMN leukocyte. Furthermore, V. Najjar and coworkers have presented evidence that a tetrapeptide (tuftsin) is bound to this globulin in an ester linkage and that it in some way causes the PMN leukocyte to phagocytize. The spleen appears to be the major organ responsible for the production of tuftsin. The involvement of this tetrapeptide in phagocytosis is supported by the increased susceptibility to infection in cases of familial tuftsin deficiency. Splenectomy also causes diminished phagocytic capacity.

Research involving leukokinin and tuftsin systems might lead to a physiologically sound method for treating individuals who have recurrent or persistent infections that do not adequately respond to antibiotic therapy.

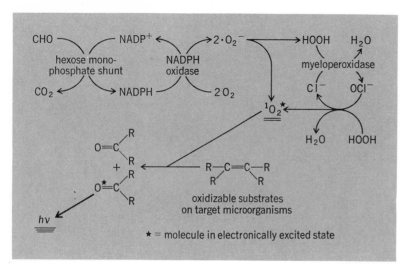

Microbicidal metabolism of the PMN leukocyte.

Microbicidal metabolism.

Microbicidal metabolism. The function of the PMN leukocyte is to destroy microorganisms. Microbicidal activity is linked to certain metabolic alterations involving the mobilization and transduction of reducing potential (see illustration). Subsequent to engulfment there is a "respiratory burst"; that is, there is an increase in glucose oxidation via the hexose monophosphate (HMP) shunt and an increase in nonmitochondrial O_2 consumption.

Both metabolic alterations can be fully explained by the activation of a granular-bound NADPH (reduced nicotinamide adenine dinucleotide phosphate) oxidase. Activation of this oxidase results in a shift in the NADPH/NADP$^+$ ratio. The increase in HMP shunt reflects the attempt by the cells to reestablish this ratio. Increased O_2 consumption reflects the reduction of O_2 by this enzyme.

It should be noted that the leukocyte also contains an NADH oxidase; however, its Michaelis constant (Km) appears too high to be physiologically significant.

Superoxide anion. It has been postulated that oxygen is univalently reduced by NADPH oxidase to the superoxide anion ($\cdot O_2^-$). Recent experiments by B. M. Babior, R. S. Kipnes, and J. J. Curnutte have lent direct support to this explanation of the generation of this free radical. Using superoxide dismutase (erythrocuprein), a copper-containing enzyme responsible for the disproportionation (that is, the interaction of like reactants in such a manner that one is oxidized and the other reduced) of 2 $\cdot O_2^-$ to HOOH and ground-state oxygen, these workers were able to prevent superoxide-dependent cytochrome c reduction. They were also able to demonstrate defective $\cdot O_2^-$ production by PMN leukocytes from patients with chronic granulomatous disease. On the basis of their research, they concluded that $\cdot O_2^-$ is responsible for microbicidal activity.

However, in the presence of an acid pH, such as that found in the phagosome (phagocytic vacuole), $\cdot O_2^-$ is highly unstable and disproportionates spontaneously. (Spontaneous disproportionation occurs in the presence of an adequate proton [H$^+$] source.) This nonenzymatic disproportionation has been demonstrated to result in the generation of electronically excited singlet multiplicity molecular oxygen, $^1O_2$ (1 refers to the spin multiplicity of the oxygen molecule). As discussed below, this species is in itself microbicidal.

Myeloperoxidase system. Probably the most significant enzyme of the PMN leukocyte with regard to direct microbicidal activity is myeloperoxidase (MPO). This heme-containing green protein is responsible for more than 5% of the dry weight of the leukocyte, and, when provided with HOOH and an oxidizable (anionic) halide (X$^-$) cofactor, it gives evidence of its antimicrobial activity. The enzyme requires an acid pH and is capable of oxidizing a number of substrates.

The microbicidal mechanism of the MPO-X$^-$-HOOH system involves the oxidation of the halide to a halogonium-type species (any oxidized form of halogen, such as X$^+$, OX$^-$, or X$_2$). In the case of iodide, the oxidized halide is capable of direct electrophilic halogenation of an adequate substrate.

However, in the presence of oxidized chloride or bromide, the most likely microbicidal candidate is again $^1O_2$. In fact, the classical chemical reaction for the generation of $^1O_2$ is as shown. Cl_2, OBr$^-$, and Br$_2$ can be substituted for OCl$^-$ in this reaction.

$$OCl^- + HOOH \longrightarrow Cl^- + H_2O + {}^1O_2$$

Electronic excitation and $^1O_2$. Thus, there are two potential methods for the generation of $^1O_2$ by the PMN leukocyte: first, the nonenzymatic disproportionation of $\cdot O_2^-$, and second, the reaction of a halogonium species with HOOH. Once generated, $^1O_2$ is a potent electrophilic reactant with a relatively long lifetime (as electronically excited states go). It is capable of reacting with a wide spectrum of molecules, including unsaturated lipids, nucleic acids, and amino acid residues.

The products of singlet oxidation are in many cases dioxetanes or other $^1O_2$ reaction intermediates capable of disintegration to form electronically excited carbonyl groups that can relax by means of photon emission. Furthermore, it is possible that such an excited carbonyl group might itself react in a microbicidal manner.

Photon emission resulting from relaxation of electronically excited molecules is demonstrated as the chemiluminescence observed from PMN leukocytes subsequent to phagocytosis of an oxidizable substrate. This emission is expressed as $h\gamma$, where h is Planck's constant, and γ is the frequency of radiation. The integral of chemiluminescence (counts per unit of time) is proportional to the integral of glucose oxidation via the HMP shunt and is also correlated with nonmitochondrial oxygen consumption. There is also an absence of chemiluminescent response from patients with chronic granulomatous disease.

The MPO-X$^-$-HOOH system has also been demonstrated to function through the generation of electronically excited states, and the chemiluminescence observed from this system correlates with microbicidal activity. Furthermore, the chemiluminescent response also shows a dependence on halide concentration and pH.

Demonstration of the functional, metabolically linked generation of an electronically excited molecule in the microbicidal activity of the PMN leukocyte is of significance in explaining the enigmatic nature of the microbicidal agent. On the more general theoretical scale, electronic excitation opens a new dimension with regard to the energy transduction capabilities of mammalian systems.

For background information *see* GLOBULIN; PHAGOCYTOSIS in the McGraw-Hill Encyclopedia of Science and Technology.   [ROBERT C. ALLEN]

Bibliography: R. C. Allen et al., *Biochem. Biophys. Res. Commun.*, 47:679–684, 1972; J. Curnutte et al., *N. Engl. J. Med.*, 290:593–597, 1974; M. S. Jensen and D. F. Bainton, *J. Cell Biol.*, 56: 379–388, 1973; T. H. Maugh II, *Science*, 182:44–45, 1973; V. A. Najjar and A. Constantopoulos, *J. R.E.S.*, 12:197–215, 1972.

Phloem

Although ultrastructural studies have provided much valuable information on the phloem of higher vascular plants, until recently the electron microscope has barely been used in the study of the phloem tissue in lower vascular plants (such as the ferns and club mosses). With the aid of this powerful tool, investigators are just now beginning to gain an understanding of ontogeny and structure of sieve elements and of the relation of sieve elements to parenchymatous elements in this diverse group of plants. Such information is essential to a critical evaluation of the various hypothetical phloem transport mechanisms presently being considered by investigators, and to the establishment of trends of evolutionary development of sieve elements in lower vascular plants.

As of June 1974, less than a dozen articles concerned with ultrastructural studies on the phloem of lower vascular plants have been published, and five of them (by M. Liberman-Maxe) deal with the phloem of the fern *Polypodium vulgare*.

Sieve-element protoplast. The most distinguishing feature of the protoplast of the sieve elements of most lower vascular plants is the presence of highly refractive, proteinaceous granules called refractive spherules (Figs. 1 and 2), which were once thought to be similar to the plastids of monocotyledonous sieve elements or, possibly, related to the proteinaceous substance known as slime or P-protein in sieve elements of flowering plants.

Liberman-Maxe first demonstrated that refractive spherules are single, membrane-bound entities distinct from plastids. Since then she, W. Sakai, and C. Lamoureux have implicated the endoplasmic reticulum (ER) in the origin of refractive spherules in the polypodiaceous ferns *Polypodium vulgare* and *Microsorium scolopendria*, respectively. Apparently, refractive spherules develop in dilated portions of the ER. Results of a recently completed study strongly implicate the Golgi apparatus in the accumulation of the granular material that makes up the refractive spherules in *Platycerium bifurcatum* and *Phlebodium aureum*. In these species and two other polypodiaceous ferns, *Polypodium schraderi* and *Microgramma lycopodioides*, the delimiting membranes of the refractive spherules eventually fuse with the plasmalemma and, very late in cellular differentiation, discharge

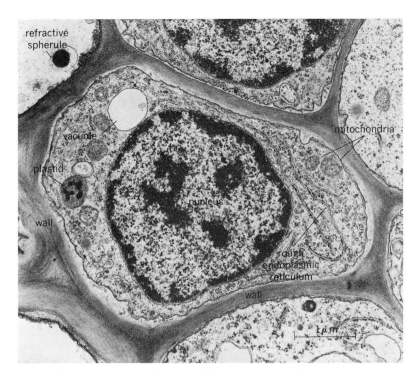

Fig. 1.   Transverse section of immature *Platycerium bifurcatum* sieve element, showing many of the protoplasmic components characteristic of immature fern sieve elements. Nacreous wall formation had just begun in this element.

their contents into the region of the cell wall. The function of refractive spherules remains to be determined.

Although refractive spherules have been report-

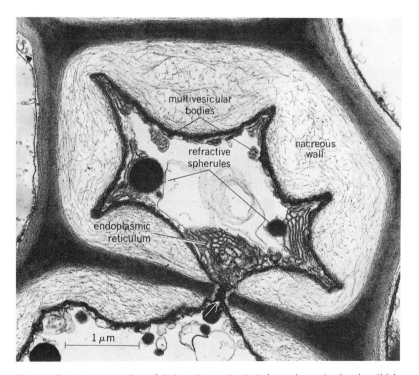

Fig. 2.   Transverse section of *Polypodium schraderi* sieve element, showing thick nacreous wall and peripherally distributed, smooth endoplasmic reticulum. Two multivesicular bodies can be seen. The round, dense bodies are refractive spherules. The unlabeled arrow points to a pore that is occluded with endoplasmic reticulum.

ed in sieve elements of the Lycopsida (club mosses), recent ultrastructural studies indicate that they do not exist in *Lycopodium, Selaginella,* and *Isoetes.* However, large quantities of crystalline and fibrillar proteinaceous material occur in numerous small vacuoles of *Selaginella kraussiana* and in cisternae of the rough ER of *Isoetes muricata.* In *Isoetes,* the dilated portions of ER enclosing the proteinaceous substance become smooth-surfaced and migrate to the cell wall, where they fuse with the plasmalemma, discharging their contents to the outside. The role of the proteinaceous substances in *Selaginella* and *Isoetes,* like that of the refractive spherules, remains a mystery.

The nucleus. Among the ferns, only the metaphloem sieve elements of *Ceratopteris cornuta* have been reported to contain intact, although obviously degenerated, nuclei at maturity. Little is known about the manner of nuclear degeneration in ferns. During her study of the sieve elements in *Polypodium vulgare,* Liberman-Maxe reported that, in advanced stages of nuclear degeneration, the chromatin forms a very dense mass that occupies almost all of the (by then) smaller nucleus. In the final stages of degeneration, the nucleus fragments. In *Platycerium bifurcatum* and *Phlebodium aureum* no apparent increase occurs in the quantity of the chromatin during the development of sieve elements. In the final stages of nuclear degeneration, the nuclear envelope ruptures and releases the contents of the nucleus into the cytoplasm.

The condition of the nuclei in mature sieve elements of the Lycopsida is quite varied. There are no nuclei in mature sieve elements of *Lycopodium lucidulum.* In *Selaginella kraussiana* the nucleus persists in mature elements as a mass of tubules. At maturity, the nuclei in sieve elements of *Isoetes muricata* leaves persist as extremely long, dense aggregates of chromatin partly delimited from the protoplast by remnants of the nuclear envelope.

Remnants of the nuclear envelope and of chromatin material have been found in mature sieve elements of *Psilotum nudum,* but stages in the degeneration of the *Psilotum* nucleus have not been observed.

Other protoplasmic components. At maturity the sieve elements in most lower vascular plants are apparently lined by a plasmalemma and a parietal, anastomosing network of smooth ER. Immature fern sieve elements contain an extensive system of rough ER (Fig. 1). In the polypodiaceous species examined by R. F. Evert and S. E. Eichhorn, most of these membranes form multivesicular bodies (Fig. 2) and are eventually deposited outside the plasmalemma in the region of the wall. M. Kruatrachue and Evert observed a similar phenomenon in *Isoetes* sieve elements. In *Platycerium bifurcatum* large arrays of ER accumulate outside the plasmalemma, where they eventually disappear.

Both plastids and mitochondria occur in mature sieve elements of lower vascular plants. Whether plastid ultrastructure will prove to be useful for taxonomic and phylogenetic considerations in lower vascular plants remains to be determined. Interestingly, the plastids in mature sieve elements of *Lycopodium* and *Selaginella* are more similar in appearance than those in *Selaginella*

and *Isoetes* (*Lycopodium* is homosporous; *Selaginella* and *Isoetes* are heterosporous). Considerable difference exists in the appearance of the plastids of the sieve elements of polypodiaceous ferns. For example, the mature sieve elements of *Polypodium schraderi* and *Microgramma lycopodioides* contain chloroplasts with grana and intergrana lamellae similar to those of adjacent parenchyma cells, whereas those of *Platycerium bifurcatum* and *Phlebodium aureum* contain plastids whose thylakoids are never organized into grana.

P-protein apparently is lacking in the sieve elements of lower vascular plants.

Sieve-element wall. Investigators have long been interested in the so-called nacreous wall thickenings (Fig. 2) of sieve elements. Nevertheless, only one ultrastructural study on nacreous walls has been published. One of the exciting revelations to come from recent studies on the phloem of some polypodiaceous ferns is the relation that exists between the nacreous wall and the endomembrane system of the sieve element. During early stages of nacreous wall development, numerous dictyosome vesicles are deposited in the extracytoplasmic space between plasmalemma and wall. Later, numerous elements of ER are discharged into the region of the wall. By the time all this activity has ended, the nacreous wall itself has all but disappeared. At the height of activity, the nacreous wall may be so thick that it almost occludes the lumen of the cell. Thus, nacreous wall development is correlated with the discharge of numerous endomembranes from the protoplast of the sieve elements into the region of the wall. This relation strongly suggests that the nacreous wall in polypodiaceous ferns is a lysosomal compartment—a site of autophagic activity. It will be necessary to demonstrate the presence of hydrolytic enzymes in the wall in order to confirm this theory.

Sieve-area pores. The connections, or pores in sieve areas, between contiguous sieve elements in lower vascular plants are very narrow; for example, in *Lycopodium lucidulum* they range in diameter from 0.07 to 0.86 μm. As in higher plants, the pores are derived from plasmodesmata through widening of the plasmodesmatal channels. In mature sieve elements of *Lycopodium, Selaginella,* and *Isoetes,* and of at least some ferns, the plasmalemma-lined pores apparently are normally unoccluded by membranes or cytoplasmic components. One interesting problem, concerning the sieve elements of certain ferns, exists. When first formed, the pores are occluded with ER (Fig. 2). Are such cells involved in long-distance transport, or do they become involved in such transport only after all or most of the ER has disappeared from the pores? Studies with labeled assimilates may be useful in answering this and other important functional questions.

For background information *see* PHLOEM in the McGraw-Hill Encyclopedia of Science and Technology.

[RAY F. EVERT]

Bibliography: F. A. Burr and R. F. Evert, *Protoplasma,* 78:81–97, 1973; M. Kruatrachue and R. F. Evert, *Amer. J. Bot.,* 61:253–266, 1974; W. S. Sakai and C. H. Lamoureux, *Protoplasma,* 77:221–229, 1973; R. D. Warmbrodt and R. F. Evert, *Amer. J. Bot.,* 61:267–277, 1974.

Photosynthesis

Recent experiments have led to the discovery of multiple pathways for photosynthetic CO_2 fixation in higher plants. In a broad examination, higher plants can be grouped into at least three categories on the basis of their primary pathway of leaf CO_2 fixation. These categories are reductive pentose phosphate (pentose), C_4-dicarboxylic acid (C_4), and Crassulacean acid metabolism (CAM). A plant can be characterized not only by a specific CO_2 assimilation pathway but also by a number of other unique characteristics, some of which have been collated in Table 1. Interestingly, these categories of higher plants do not conform to standard taxonomic classifications in that a genus may have species in one, two, or all three categories; for example, *Euphorbia corollata* is pentose, *E. maculata* is C_4, and *E. grandidens* is a CAM plant. Examination of the characteristics listed in Table 1 makes it evident that plants with these pathways of CO_2 assimilation differ not only in the metabolic sequence used for CO_2 assimilation but also in the rates of CO_2 assimilation, rates of growth, and ability to utilize H_2O to produce dry matter. Thus, these important economic and ecological factors of plant productivity and plant water utilization are intimately associated with the variations in the biochemical pathways whereby higher plants assimilate net quantities of CO_2.

Reductive pentose phosphate pathway. The pentose pathway was essentially elucidated 2 decades ago through the efforts of M. Calvin and A. Benson, who outlined a complete CO_2 fixation cycle including CO_2 reduction and generation of the initial substrate, ribulose-1,5-diphosphate (RuDP). A significant modification of the pentose pathway came about recently with the discovery of an additional activity of the initial CO_2-fixing enzyme, RuDP carboxylase, namely, a cleavage of RuDP by the enzyme in the presence of oxygen (see equation). Thus, the initial carboxylase for CO_2 assimi-

$$RuDP + O_2 \xrightarrow[\text{Oxygenase}]{\text{RuDP}}$$

3-Phosphoglyceric acid + 2-Phosphoglycolic acid

lation can also function as an oxygenase. Since the atmospheric O_2 level is ~21%, this reaction can be strongly competitive, relative to CO_2 fixation, and can result in a decrease in net CO_2 assimilation. In addition, the 2-phosphoglycolic acid can serve as the substrate for photorespiration, whereby additional CO_2 is released by plants. Hence, much research effort currently is directed at understanding and controlling RuDP oxygenase and RuDP carboxylase activity.

The presence of the pentose pathway appears to be a universal feature of the known CO_2 assimilation pathways used by plants. Thus, as CO_2 enters a plant, it may pass through the various metabolic pathways that will be considered below, but ultimately it enters the pentose pathway for reduction to the level of sugars that can be utilized by the plant or eaten by animals. Hence the enzyme for carbon reduction in photosynthesis, the NADP-dependent (nicotinamide adenine dinucleotide phosphate) glyceraldehyde, 3-phosphate dehydrogenase, is also present in all plants. In the other two major groups of plants, C_4 and CAM, pro-

Table 1. Unique characteristics for three categories of higher plants*

Characteristic†	Primary pathway of CO_2 assimilation		
	Pentose	C_4-dicarboxylic	CAM
Major leaf carboxylation sequence in light	RuDP carboxylase	PEP carboxylase; then RuDP carboxylase	Both PEP and RuDP carboxylase
Theoretical energy requirement for CO_2 fixation (CO_2:ATP:NADPH)	1:3:2	1:5:2	1:6.5:2
Maximum rate of photosynthesis (mg of CO_2 fixed/dm² of leaf surface/hr)	15–40	40–80	Generally 1–4; highest reported ~12
Transpiration ratio (g of H_2O used/g of dry weight produced)	450–950	250–350	50–125
Maximum growth rate (g of dry weight produced/dm² of leaf surface/day)	0.5–2	4–5	0.015–0.018
Optimum day temperatures for net CO_2 fixation	15–25°C	30–47°C	~30–35°C
Leaf anatomy in cross section	Diffuse distribution of organelles in mesophyll or palisade cells with similar or lower organelle concentrations in bundle sheath cells, if present	A definite layer of bundle sheath cells surrounding the vascular tissue, which contains a high concentration of organelles; layer, or layers, of mesophyll cells surrounding the bundle sheath cells	Spongy appearance; mesophyll cells have large vacuoles with the organelles evenly distributed in the thin cytoplasm; generally lack a definite layer of palisade cells

*From C. C. Black, in W. R. Briggs (ed.), *Ann. Rev. Plant Physiol.*, 24:253–286, 1973.
†These characteristics apply to healthy and mature leaf photosynthetic tissues growing in normal atmospheres of ~21% O_2 and ~0.03% CO_2 and in full sunlight. References, discussions, and additional characteristics are given in Black, 1973.

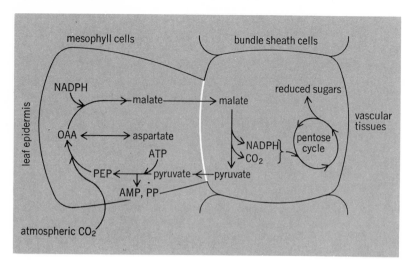

The C_4-dicarboxylic acid pathway of photosynthetic CO_2 assimilation in crabgrass leaves.

cedures have apparently evolved, in addition to the pentose cycle for trapping or concentrating CO_2 or both, so that their growth rate or their capacity to use CO_2, O_2, H_2O, sunlight, or heat can be varied (Table 1).

C_4-dicarboxylic acid pathway. Beginning in 1965, with the research of H. Kortschak followed by the work of M. Hatch and R. Slack, plant biologists began to realize that another pathway of CO_2 assimilation was present in sugarcane, the C_4 pathway. Then, as this research was expanded to additional plants, it was realized that other C_4 pathways are present in other plants. Today the generally accepted biochemical route for most ($\sim$85–90%) of the CO_2 assimilation in C_4 plants is that outlined for crabgrass in the illustration. The initial accumulating products of C_4 photosynthesis are malate and asparate, since oxaloacetate (OAA) is unstable in aqueous solutions. After the original C_4 pathway that had been proposed for sugarcane was subjected to intensive research, it was modified several times.

One of the major biochemical modifications re-

sulted from the discovery that all C_4 plants have a characteristic leaf cell anatomy in which two major green cells, mesophyll and bundle sheath, exist. When these leaf cell types were successfully isolated from crabgrass and other C_4 plants, it was established that C_4 photosynthesis involved a compartmentation of phosphoenolpyruvate (PEP) carboxylase into mesophyll cells and of RuDP carboxylase into bundle sheath cells. Thus, as CO_2 enters the internal leaf cavities of C_4 plants and penetrates the mesophyll cell, it is rapidly used to carboxylate PEP to form OAA. The OAA then can be subject to reduction by NADP-malic dehydrogenase to form malate, or it can be reversibly transaminated to temporarily form aspartate. In crabgrass the malate is translocated to an adjacent bundle sheath cell, where it is oxidatively decarboxylated by malic enzyme to form pyruvate, NADPH (reduced NADP), and free CO_2. The free CO_2 is then fixed by RuDP carboxylase, and the carbon passes into the pentose cycle to be reduced to sugars. The NADPH can be used in this pentose carbon reduction cycle in bundle sheath cells. The pyruvate is translocated to the mesophyll cells and converted by pyruvate phosphate dikinase plus adenosinetriphosphate (ATP) to PEP to complete the regeneration of the CO_2-accepting substrate in the mesophyll cells (see illustration).

Although this route of CO_2 assimilation is used by some C_4 plants such as crabgrass, it is modified in others. Some biochemical variations that occur in C_4 photosynthesis are outlined in Table 2. A particular site of variation is the decarboxylase in the bundle sheath cells. In plants such as *Panicum maximum* the decarboxylase in bundle sheath cells is PEP carboxykinase, which, in the presence of ATP, decarboxylates OAA to form PEP plus adenosinediphosphate (ADP). In plants with PEP carboxykinase, pyruvate phosphate dikinase is not involved in the regeneration of PEP, since pyruvate would not be an intermediate in the pathway. In plants such as *Atriplex* the decarboxylase is a newly discovered NAD-malic enzyme that catalyzes the oxidative decarboxylation of malate to pyruvate, NADH (reduced nicotinamide adenine dinucleotide), and CO_2. Thus, several variations in the

Table 2. Biochemical variations in CO_2 assimilation pathways in C_4 photosynthesis*

C_4 plants	Crabgrass, corn, sugarcane	*Panicum maximum, P. texanum*	*Atriplex spongiosa, Panicum miliaceum*
Primary photosynthetic $^{14}CO_2$ fixation product accumulating (<10-sec exposures to $^{14}CO_2$)	Malate	Aspartate, 3-PGA†	Aspartate
Active intermediate translocated (?) from MC to BSC†	Malate	OAA or aspartate	Aspartate
Decarboxylation enzyme in BSC	NADP-dependent malic enzyme	PEP carboxykinase	NAD-dependent malic enzyme†
Active intermediate, or or intermediates, translocated (?) from BSC to MC	Pyruvate or alanine and 3-PGA	PEP	Pyruvate or alanine
Level of pyruvate phosphate dikinase in MC	Equals photosynthesis	<30% of photosynthesis	Equals photosynthesis

*From C. C. Black, in W. R. Briggs (ed.), *Ann. Rev. Plant Physiol.*, 24:253–286, 1973.
†MC = mesophyll cells; BSC = bundle sheath cells; 3-PGA = 3-phosphoglyceric acid; NAD = nicotinamide adenine dinucleotide.

pathway of CO_2 assimilation within C_4 photosynthesis have been found, and it is likely that others will be discovered. One could speculate from these results that C_4 photosynthesis now is in an active stage of evolution.

Crassulacean acid metabolism pathway. CAM plants often grow in deserts and other dry areas of the world. Cactus, pineapple, and orchids are common CAM plants. Biochemically, they assimilate their net CO_2 at night, when their stomata are open, by means of PEP carboxylase. The three carbons that form PEP originate in starch. The nighttime pathway from starch to PEP is not known but is the subject of active research. The OAA formed is reduced to malate or transaminated to form asparate and is stored, presumably in the vacuole of green mesophyll leaf cells.

During the following day CAM plants close their stomata to conserve H_2O (see the transpiration ratios in Table 1) and then release free CO_2 inside the green cells either through PEP carboxykinase in some plants (pineapple) or through malic enzyme in other plants (cactus). The free CO_2 is carboxylated by RuDP carboxylase and enters the pentose cycle, in which it is reduced to form sugars and starch. The PEP or pyruvate formed in the light decarboxylations may return to sugar by means of a reversal of glycolysis during the day.

In CAM plants, therefore, the entire pathway for CO_2 assimilation is present in each green leaf cell, with net CO_2 fixation occurring at night and final reduction to sugars occurring during the day. Individual green cells are completely responsible for carrying out CAM, with part of the pathway being functional at night and part during the day. In contrast, C_4 photosynthesis follows a somewhat similar pathway of CO_2 assimilation, but it occurs only during the day, and the carboxylations and decarboxylations are spatially divided into the two adjacent green cells, mesophyll and bundle sheath. Functionally, CAM seems to be an adaptation to conserve H_2O, whereas C_4 seems to be an adaptation to concentrate CO_2 in the bundle sheath cells so that photosynthesis and growth are more rapid in these plants than in any other known plant types.

For background information *see* PHOTOSYNTHESIS in the McGraw-Hill Encyclopedia of Science and Technology. [CLANTON C. BLACK, JR.]

Bibliography: C. C. Black, in W. R. Briggs (ed.), *Ann. Rev. Plant Physiol.*, 24:253–286, 1973; T. M. Chen et al., *Biochem. Biophys. Res. Commun.*, 51: 461–467, 1973; M. D. Hatch and T. Kagawa, *Arch. Biochem. Biophys.*, 160:346–349, 1974; M. L. Salin, W. H. Campbell, and C. C. Black, in G. Cocks (ed.), *Proc. Nat. Acad. Sci.*, 70:3730–3734, 1973.

Phylogeny

Paleobiologists have long sought to formulate general laws to explain the patterns of origination, diversification, and extinction of plant and animal groups. During 1974 two quite different approaches to this problem were published. In the first, L. Van Valen proposed a "law of extinction" on the basis of his analysis of the geologic records of about 25,000 groups of fossil organisms. In the second, a team of three paleontologists and a biologist presented a computer program that simulated

some aspects of phylogeny using a purely random system and Monte Carlo methods. Neither of these approaches can be considered proved yet, but both offer intriguing possibilities for the reinterpretation of evolutionary data.

Van Valen's law. In its simplest form, the law states that extinction in any adaptive zone occurs at a stochastically constant rate. This means that all species (or higher taxa such as genera and families) living in a given ecological setting have the same probability of extinction. It further implies that an evolving group does not go through "stages" that differ from one another in likelihood of extinction. The law suggests, in effect, that extinction is like radioactive decay and that each group of organisms has a "half-life" subject only to the vagaries of chance. The extinction of a species is thus thought to be analogous to the decay of one atom of a radioactive isotope.

Van Valen used the survivorship curve, common in population ecology, as the principal vehicle for documenting constant extinction. Figure 1 shows an example. The ordinate is the number of taxa (genera, in this case) surviving at least as long as the duration shown on the abscissa. Because the plot uses a logarithmic scale for the ordinate, the points will fall approximately on a straight line under the condition of constant extinction probability. For the group shown in Fig. 1 (extinct mammalian genera) the "half-life," assuming constant extinction rate, is about 3,000,000 years.

The main question to be answered with regard to Van Valen's law is whether the survivorship curves are actually straight. Statistical tests are available and are being applied to the data to determine the conditions under which the "law" holds and whether modifications are necessary.

Computer simulation of phylogeny. A program being tested at the University of Rochester's Computing Center evaluates the proposition that some elements of the phylogenetic process behave like stochastic or random variables. The simulation itself is extremely stylized and does not attempt to replicate the actual processes of evolution. It starts with a hypothetical lineage (species or other group) in an arbitrary time system. The lineage is

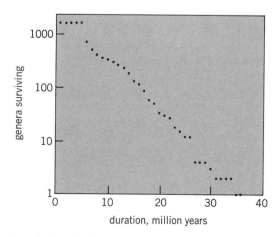

Fig. 1. Survivorship curve for extinct mammals based on the geologic ranges of fossil genera. (*From L. Van Valen, Evol. Theory, 1(1), 1973*)

made to progress through time, and as it moves, it may either terminate (become extinct) or persist.

For each new time interval, termination or persistence is determined by Monte Carlo techniques, controlled by a random number generator in the computer and preset probabilities. If the lineage persists, it may branch to form a second lineage (speciation); this event is also signaled by random numbers. When a new lineage is formed by the branching process, it is also subject to probabilistic development; that is, it may become extinct, persist without branching, or persist with branching. After this process has been repeated many times over a long time sequence, the result is a complex phylogeny of originations and extinctions

of lineages, all of which have a common ancestor (the starting lineage). Some typical output is shown in Fig. 2. If the probability of extinction is the same for all lineages and is constant through time, the resulting phylogeny inevitably conforms to Van Valen's law; but many other scenarios are possible with the program.

Each lineage in the simulated phylogeny has a "morphology" defined by up to 20 imaginary characters or traits. Each trait is expressed as an integer—which may increase or decrease by one unit at each branch point. This morphologic change is also controlled by random numbers and preset probabilities; that is, whether or not a given character changes with the formation of a new lineage (and whether it increases or decreases) is controlled by chance. Each of the 20 characters is independent of the others.

Typical runs with the simulation program yield 200–500 descendant lineages, each characterized by a coded morphology. When the full 20 characters are used, the probability of two lineages having precisely the same morphology is very low; rarely are they identical. Similarly, evolutionary sequences of morphologic change rarely repeat themselves.

After the full phylogeny has been generated, the program subjects the mass of data to a taxonomic routine in order to subdivide the array of lineages into "genera," "families," or higher categories. This can be done either cladistically, using only the information of branching and persistence of lineages, or phenetically, using the morphology of the lineages to arrive at a classification, in which case the standard methods of computerized numerical taxonomy are used.

As noted above, the simulation does not attempt to replicate the true biologic processes. Rather, it asks: What would the evolutionary record look like if origination, extinction, and the modification of morphology were determined solely by chance? When the results resemble the real world, it may be suggested that the stochastic model is a good approximation of nature. When the resemblance is not good, there is evidence for nonstochastic or deterministic processes at work in the real world. Thus, the similarities and differences between computer-produced and natural data are used to explore the prevalence of random processes in nature.

Not surprisingly, the simulated phylogenies appear unreal in several regards. For example, if extinction and branching probabilities are held constant through time, mass extinctions such as those that occurred at the end of the Paleozoic and again in the Cretaceous are not evident. This result substantiates the view of many workers that the observed mass extinctions are probably the result of special, largely nonrecurring events in the history of life. On the other hand, a rather large number of the characteristics of the computer phylogenies are disturbingly similar to their real-world counterparts. For example, each monophyletic subgroup of lineages tends to be characterized by a persistent set of morphological traits, and the several characters are often biometrically correlated with one another. Both phenomena are often encountered in the real world

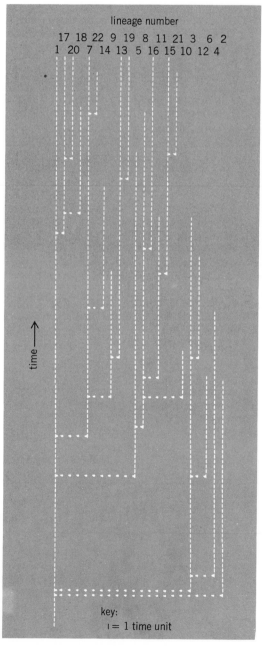

Fig. 2.   Sample output of computer program. (From D. M. Raup et al., J. Geol., 81(5), 1973)

and are interpreted as being the result of adaptation. But natural selection and adaptation are not included in the computer logic.

Explanations for the unexpected similarities between the simulated and actual phylogenies are still tentative. At this stage, the computer program is an exploratory tool that is being used primarily to determine which aspects of phylogeny are good candidates for a stochastic interpretation.

For background information see PHYLOGENY in the McGraw-Hill Encyclopedia of Science and Technology. [DAVID M. RAUP]

Bibliography: D. M. Raup et al., *J. Geol.*, 81(5), 1973; D. M. Raup and S. J. Gould, *Syst. Zool.*, 23(4), 1974; L. Van Valen, *Evol. Theory*, 1(1), 1973.

Pisces (zoology)

Reports on some recent research on the physiology of fish have been concerned with the function of red and white muscle and with the central heat-exchange system.

The red and white muscle fibers of fish are segregated into distinct regions of the myotome. Normally the red fibers are located just under the skin along the side of the fish and increase in concentration toward the tail. The red muscle usually makes up a small amount of the muscle mass, frequently much less than 20%, the white muscle more than 80%.

Muscle function and features. The function of the two kinds of muscle can be inferred from the behavior of various fish. Pike, for example, which lie still, wait for their prey to swim by, and then dart after it, have almost entirely white muscle fibers, whereas fish that swim continuously, as tunas do, have a large amount of red muscle. Red muscle is adapted for continuous activity; white muscle is specialized for sprints. Distinctive features of the two types of fibers strengthen this conclusion. The most noticeable gross difference is the color; red fibers contain myoglobin, the white do not. Closer inspection shows other differences: Red fibers are small, less than one-half the size of the white fibers, and their nuclei are peripheral; the white muscle nuclei are distributed throughout the cytoplasm. Red muscle fibers are rich in mitochondria and are supplied by many blood vessels; white muscle fibers have few mitochondria and few associated capillaries. Associated with the difference in abundance of mitochondria are high levels of oxidative enzymes in the red fibers; there is a greater activity of glycolytic enzymes in the white fibers.

Muscle metabolism. In the red muscle the well-developed blood supply brings in oxygen, and the high myoglobin concentration probably facilitates diffusion of oxygen within the fiber. This assures an adequate oxygen supply for the abundant mitochondria, which rapidly oxidize substrates, usually fat, and supply the energy for continuous activity. The white muscle is used for brief periods of rapid contraction during which glycogen reserves are decreased and lactic acid formed. The energy released by this fermentative process is not dependent upon the oxygen supply, and, in fact, it appears that the blood flow to the white muscle is reduced or stopped during activity. If a fish is exercised vigorously, by being chased, for example,

lactic acid builds up in the muscle but does not appear in the blood until exercise has ceased. After exercise, when blood flow through the white muscle is restored, blood lactic acid levels rise and remain elevated for a long time as the muscle slowly recovers.

Fish that can swim continuously for days at a steady cruising speed can be exhausted within minutes if they are chased at their maximum speed. The continuous swimming utilizes the red muscle, which does not tire, but the white muscle, which supplies a burst of power, can be quickly exhausted and must recover at rest. Electrophysiological recordings from dogfish by Q. Bone and from skipjack tuna by M. Rayner show that the white fibers do not fire (contract) during steady-state swimming but only during vigorous contractions. The white muscle is specialized for rapid twitchlike contractions and is used for feeding and escape reactions when speed is required. Increasing speed requires an exponential increase in power, and to achieve a significantly higher speed, a large bulk of white muscle is needed. Thus, even though the small volume of red muscle propels the fish most of the time, the white muscle forms the major portion of the axial musculature. See MUSCLE (BIOPHYSICS).

Heat-exchange mechanism. The active metabolism of the red muscle produces heat, which is usually carried off by the blood to be lost to the water through the gills. Tuna and lamnid sharks, however, have evolved a countercurrent heat-exchange mechanism that retains this heat in the tissues to produce a high body temperature. The main heat exchanger is a rete mirabile, or mass of small, parallel arteries and veins in the blood supply to the red muscle. The presence of this structure and the importance of preventing heat losses result in some unusual arrangements of the red muscle of these fish. Instead of being concentrated on the lateral surface of the body near the tail, the red muscle is located within the white muscle in the bulkiest region of the body. The axial muscle of a fish is arranged in segments separated by a connective tissue myoseptum that in certain regions is prolonged into a tendon. In the warm-bodied fish, these tendons from the red muscle are arranged so as to produce motion of the vertebral column well posterior to the level at which the muscle is located. The muscle mass is loosely connected to the adjacent white muscle and is free to move relative to it, so that the normal swimming motion does not require the stretching and compression of the inactive white muscle.

In the warm-bodied fish, the location of the red muscle deep within the white muscle provides some isolation from the effects of surface cooling. In those fish with laterally located heat exchangers, such as bluefin tuna and lamnid sharks, the bulk of the red muscle is some distance lateral to the vertebral colum, whereas, in the skipjack, which has a central heat exchanger, the thickest red muscle is close against the vertebral column.

A good description of the central heat-exchange system in the black skipjack (*Euthynnus lineatus*) has been published by J. Graham. The main axial blood vessels in fish are the dorsal aorta and the postcardinal vein, which lie just beneath the vertebral column in the hemal canal. The skipjack tunas (*Katsuwonus* and *Euthynnus* species) have a particularly large hemal canal that contains a major heat-exchange system. In the black skipjack the dorsal aorta is embedded in the dorsal side of the postcardinal vein so as to be surrounded by venous blood. Many ranks of small vessels arise from the vein and artery and run vertically, filling the hemal canal with a rete mirabile that acts as a countercurrent heat exchanger. The location of the dorsal aorta within the postcardinal vein and the countercurrent flow of the blood in the two vessels should allow additional heat transfer to take place between this large artery and vein, and it probably increases the overall efficiency of the system. Most of the blood flow through the rete goes to the red muscle, and temperature profiles through cross sections of these fish show that the warmest temperatures occur in the red muscle along the vertebral column. In contrast, in the bluefin, the vertebral region may be cooler than the mass of red muscle adjacent to it. In the bluefin the vertebral region is supplied with cold blood from a dorsal aorta without heat-exchange structures. The heat exchangers for the muscle of this fish are laterally located retia mirabilia that arise from large cutaneous vessels. The correlation between the location of the retia and the temperature distribution in the muscle confirms the heat-exchange function of these retia.

E. D. Stevens and W. H. Neill have pointed out that the countercurrent heat-exchange system in tunas effectively slows the rate of cooling of a tuna when it enters cold water. When operating at high efficiency, the countercurrent system essentially halts the convective transfer of heat by the circulatory system from the interior of the fish to the environment. In a large fish, heat loss by conduction is slow compared to convective losses due to the circulatory system, and by reducing the convective losses, tuna have insulated themselves against temperature change. This thermal lagging achieved by the heat-exchange system may be an aid in thermoregulation and in damping the effects of rapid changes in environmental temperature.

For background information *see* MUSCLE (BIOPHYSICS); PISCES (ZOOLOGY) in the McGraw-Hill Encyclopedia of Science and Technology.

[FRANK G. CAREY]

Bibliography: Q. Bone, *J. Mar. Biol. Ass. U.K.*, 46:321–349, 1966; J. B. Graham, *Proc. Nat. Acad. Sci. U.S.*, 70:1964–1967, 1973; W. H. Neill and E. D. Stevens, *Science*, 184:1008–1010, 1974; M. D. Rayner and M. J. Keenan, *Nature*, 214:392–393, 1967.

Plant, water relations of

An explanation for the perennial puzzle of xylem sap ascent in plants was propounded in 1896 by H. H. Dixon and J. Joly as the cohesion theory. It has gained acceptance rather slowly due to the great difficulty in studying negative sap pressures. They are usually so negative as to be well below true zero (vacuum). This fact, coupled with the intricate anatomy of the essentially porous conduction system, gave rise to many uncertainties. Many of these have now been resolved, and the water relations of plants are in the process of quantization

with the use of instruments that have been developed in the last decade and are continuously refined. To a considerable extent, the flow of water through the soil-plant-atmosphere continuum can be likened to the flow of electrons, and instrumentation required for water relations studies is closely analogous to measurements of voltage (water potential differences), amperage (rate of sap flow) from which conductance is calculated (hydraulic conductivity), and also capacitance of the components of the system (representing their water balance). Instrumentation is therefore a key to the newer developments, and current techniques will be outlined, with a summary of some recent interesting discoveries.

Pressure bomb measurements. Water potential (WP) is a measure of the Gibbs free energy of water with respect to free water at atmospheric pressure (WP = 0). Strictly, it should be measured in energy units, but pressure units (atm or bar) are convenient and reasonably legitimate. Water potentials are related to other colligative properties of water. Thus in the plant, the hydrostatic sap pressure and the osmotic potential (OP) of solutes dissolved in it are of critical importance. Once, osmotic techniques were the only way to measure water potentials. However, the pressure "bomb" introduced by P. F. Scholander and coworkers in 1965 is now used to measure the sap-pressure component directly. In essence, the plant tissue, enclosed in a bomb, is compressed by gas until xylem sap begins to exude from vascular xylem projecting from the bomb. The positive pressure so measured corresponds with the tension (or negative pressure) which held the sap in the intact sap-filled system. It is important to prevent transpiration of water prior to detachment by enclosing the organs to be sampled so that the living cells equilibrate with the xylem and not partially with the atmosphere.

Pressure bomb measurements of xylem sap tensions are now routine and have been made on many plants in differing environmental conditions. Bomb techniques can be extended to study the water relations of living cells adjoining the vascular system and also to measure the osmotic potential of the cells. In this technique the pressures are increased to expel water from tissues to the point of incipient wilting when only osmotic forces retain water without the interaction with cell wall compression. Furthermore, J. S. Boyer and several others found that plant tissues often grow after detachment from the plant, consuming water in so doing. Thus in an excised shoot protected from water loss, sap tensions increase, as may be measured at intervals with a pressure bomb, giving an interesting measure of the growth capacity of the organ.

Psychrometer and hygrometer techniques. Pressure techniques require removal of samples from the plant and provide only intermittent measurements. Ideally, more continuous records of changes in water potential are needed. One useful technique is the thermocouple psychrometer, which measures the humidity of the air in contact with the plant tissue investigated. However, humidities in proximity with living tissues are often in the difficult range 97–100% relative humidity.

Thermocouple psychrometers measure humidity by the difference in cooling between wet and dry thermocouples, or even with the same probe wetted and dried in sequence. However, serious errors are caused by minute temperature gradients, and the need for thermal stabilization to 0.001°C has limited their usefulness. Additionally insulation interferes with respiratory gas exchange, which is enhanced considerably if the tissues are injured. Further complications arise from growth effects and localized heating through respiration. A common procedure is to freeze and thaw the sample to kill it and destroy the pressure components; in this way the osmotic potential of the cell sap may be measured. Recently a new dewpoint-depression hygrometer has been developed by E. Campbell and coworkers, using rapid electronic scanning of a probe to hold it at equilibrium with a tissue by alternately heating and cooling it to dewpoint. Such advances should overcome many of the technical objections to thermocouple psychrometers and make them rapid in response, portable, and less vulnerable to "drift." In addition, several other devices such as the piezoelectric and neutron probes have been developed.

Thermoelectric and electromagnetic techniques. Sap flow through small potted plants can be determined simply by weighing them or fitting potometers. In-place measurements on trees and other plants raise special problems which, so far, have only partly been overcome with hygrometers or meteorological measurements to estimate water loss. Instruments for measuring flow through tree trunks are severely hampered by the anatomical complexity of the xylem, which consists of numerous discrete units that to some extent overlap and interweave. Pipes transport sap at different velocities depending on their diameters; ideally, the average velocity must be measured. A favorite technique to determine sap flow, now used for many years, is the thermoelectric detection of a heat pulse carried by the moving sap. Refinements in the technique have been made, but the instruments require careful calibration, which tends to limit their usefulness. Two more recent developments may resolve these problems. D. W. Sherriff used electromagnetic flowmeters; these measure the distortion of a magnetic field by the flow of sap. However, thus far the system has found application only to small seedlings. Another promising technique is the detection of a small electrical current produced by the flow of sap (Delta I technique). Promising results have been obtained from trees by M. T. Tyree, but the sophisticated instrumentation required has probably prevented its general adoption to date.

Cavitation detection. The old idea that the sap system could not withstand tensions beyond vacuum gave way, with the adoption of the cohesion theory, to the view that sap could withstand very great tensions without cavitation, that is, the development of a gas phase in the conduits. Satisfactory techniques to verify this were lacking, for the preparation for microscopic examination itself produced disruption, and only a small part of the vascular system could be examined thus.

Over the last decade cavitation has been monitored acoustically by detecting the vibrations produced when the stress in xylem conduit walls, produced by sap tension, is released by cavitation. The microphonic probe is essentially a micro-seismograph and the "micro-quakes" (clicks) are transmitted for considerable distances through plant tissues to a single probe.

Summary of developments. Though the ascent of sap was originally conceived as a problem of tall trees, it has become apparent that the extraction of water from dry soil, or from sea water as performed by mangrove trees, is often more demanding in terms of sap cohesion than mere elevation. Thus the tallest trees, 100 m tall, require about 10 bars of tension to raise sap, whereas the desalination of sea water by mangroves requires about 30 bars of tension. Trees normally undergo diurnal changes in sap tension, reaching a maximum roughly coincident with peak solar radiation (Fig. 1). In deciduous trees and pines the tensions range commonly from about 2–5 bars at night to 15–20 bars by day. Since the normal sap has an insignificant osmotic potential, the water potential measurements closely accord with the tension measurements. However, the xylem tensions may exceed 40 bars in some species, and stomatal regulation must protect the plant from the development of excessive sap tensions.

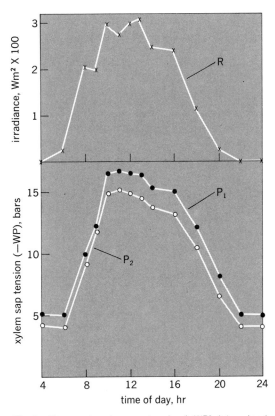

Fig. 1. Changes in xylem sap tension (−WP) determined by a pressure bomb from two clones of pine (*Pinus sylvestris*, P₁ and P₂) throughout the day. Irradiance (R; 400–700 nm) closely matches WP. Sap tension = negative pressure = −WP. (*Redrawn from J. Hellkvist, The water relations of Pinus sylvestris, II: Comparative field studies of water potential and relative water content, Physiol. Plant, 29:271–279, 1973*)

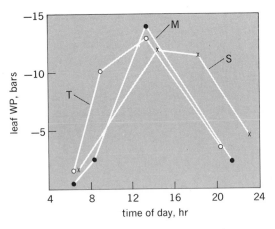

Fig. 2. Water potential in the upper leaf canopy throughout sunny days determined by pressure bomb in maize (M), sorghum (S), and tobacco (T). Leaf water potentials are probably slightly more negative than the corresponding xylem tensions. Soil water was abundant. (*Drawn from data of N. C. Turner and J. E. Begg, Stomatal behavior and water status of maize, sorghum and tobacco under field conditions. Physiol. Plant, 29:371–379, 1973*)

What has proved more surprising is the fact that crop plants and small herbs develop tensions which are of much the same order as tall trees, even when well watered (see Fig. 2), and which become even greater during drought. Since these plants are often less than a meter tall, very consid-

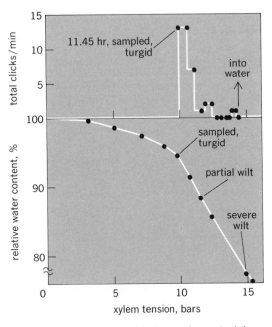

Fig. 3. Cavitation detected in leaves from plantain, a small herbaceous weed. When the leaf was sampled early on a sunny day, some cavitation had already taken place. After cessation of click production the leaf was restored to full turgidity with water. Next a pressure bomb was used to express sap so that leaf weight could be related to sap tension and hence the tension at which cavitation occurred. Cavitation took place before wilting was evident at about 10 bars sap tension.

erable WP gradients have been found in their xylem. Similarly, J. B. Passioura has calculated very high velocities of sap flow through xylem of wheat roots. A high root resistance may curb excessive use of limited water supplies, which may be an important defense mechanism to combat drought. Furthermore, some herbs have been found by J. A. Milburn and M. E. McLaughlin to cavitate before and during the onset of wilting (Fig. 3). Many small herbs wilt diurnally in this way, yet recover each night without obviously adverse effects. Apparently there is a difference in water conservation strategy. Tall trees, lacking the means to refill cavitated conduits, avoid cavitation; but small herbs seem capable of accommodating cavitation damage by refilling the embolized conduits by night through the operation of root pressure. It remains to be seen how widely these recent findings apply to the plant kingdom in general. Seemingly, therefore, the original doubts expressed about the capacity of sap to withstand tensions have some foundation, but through natural selection plants have developed the capacity to tread a dangerous course to maximize assimilation at the risk of cavitation and so exploit their environment efficiently without endangering survival.

For background information *see* HYGROMETER; PLANT, WATER RELATIONS OF; PSYCHROMETER in the McGraw-Hill Encyclopedia of Science and Technology.   [JOHN A. MILBURN]

Bibliography: G. S. Campbell and M. D. Campbell, *Agron. J.*, 66:24–27, 1974; J. A. Milburn and M. E. McLaughlin, Studies of cavitation in isolated vascular bundles and whole leaves of *Plantago major* L., *New Phytol.*, 73:861–871, 1974; D. W. Sherriff, *J. Exp. Bot.*, 23:1086–1095, 1972; M. H. Zimmermann, Conceptual developments in plant physiology 1924–1974: Long-distance transport, *Plant Physiol.*, 54:472–479, 1974.

Plant disease

Recent findings by phytopathologists suggest the occurrence of new groups of microorganisms that may be significant plant pathogens. Two groups which have received considerable attention are certain mycoplasma-like organisms and species of the fungal genus *Rhizoctonia*.

Plant-inhabiting mycoplasma-like organisms. The discovery 8 years ago by Y. Doi, T. Y. Ishiie, and colleagues of wall-less prokaryotic microorganisms in diseased plants opened a new area of plant pathology and gave a fresh approach to the study of diseases of unsolved cause. The morphology and ultrastructure of these organisms closely resemble those of the mycoplasmas (as the term is used to refer to members of the class Mollicutes), already known to be associated with and to induce certain diseases in humans and animals. These mycoplasma-like organisms in plants also bear intriguing differences compared with organisms presently classified with the mycoplasmas, however. For example, the plant-inhabiting mycoplasma-like organisms multiply intracellularly, in contrast to the extracellular habitat of human and animal mycoplasmas; and the plant mycoplasma-like organisms multiply in and are transmitted by insect vectors, whereas vectors are unknown for mycoplasmas that infect humans or animals. It is possible that these differences in habitat may reflect fundamental aspects of structure and physiology by which the plant-inhabiting organisms may eventually be characterized. This concept is strengthened by the recent finding that at least some mycoplasma-like organisms in plants are unusual wall-less, motile, helical prokaryotes, previously unknown in plants, and for which the term spiroplasma has been proposed by R. E. Davis and J. F. Worley. The discovery of spiroplasmas and recent progress in their cultivation in artificial media constitute an important step in the development of this new area of plant pathology.

Spiroplasmas. During the past 6 or 7 years, a considerable amount of thin-section electron microscopy has been devoted to the study of plant diseases with which mycoplasma-like organisms are associated. In the case of corn stunt, as in other diseases, organisms interpreted as closely resembling mycoplasmas have been found both in diseased plants and in infected insect vectors. Recently, however, the organisms associated with corn stunt disease, and subsequently those associated with stubborn disease of citrus, have been shown to be unusual helical, motile microorganisms now termed spiroplasmas (Fig. 1).

The first occurrence of a helical microorganism in plants was reported in corn *(Zea mays)* infected by the Rio Grande strain of the corn stunt disease agent. This new, cell-wall-less organism produces helical cells of about 250 nm in diameter and about 3 to 12 μm in length, to which may be attached one or more spherical bodies about 400 to 600 nm in diameter. This morphology, confirmed by freeze-etch and thick-ultramicrotome-section electron microscopy, was previously undescribed for the organisms reportedly associated with plant diseases. Moreover, it is unreported for mycoplasmas and apparently unknown among named cell-wall-deficient organisms of any type. The association of this unusual organism with corn stunt disease development led to the suggestion that it may represent the causal agent itself.

The helical organisms associated with corn stunt disease were observed by phase-contrast microscopy and by dark-field optical microscopy of extracts and juice freshly expressed from infected corn plants. The spiroplasma was found only in juice from corn-stunt-infected plants and was absent in juice from corn-stunt-free plants, even after corn-stunt-free leafhopper vectors had fed on the latter. The organism could be detected only after an incubation period following inoculation of plants with the corn stunt agent, but could be found several days before symptoms appeared. Organisms were most numerous in juice from the leaves of a given plant in which symptoms of corn stunt were most severe, and treatment of inoculated plants with tetracycline antibiotics inhibited both the development of corn stunt symptoms and the development of the organism. Spiroplasmas have also been detected in juice expressed from plants of a related host, teosinte *(Euchlaena mexicana* Schrad.), infected by the Rio Grande strain of the corn stunt agent. Experience with phase-contrast or dark-field microscopy thus suggested that direct observation of this organism in juice expressed from plants might be a useful aid in diagnosis of

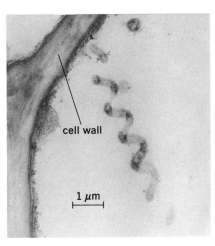

Fig. 1. Electron micrograph of a thick ultramicrotome section (cut at about 0.3 μ) of phloem tissue from a corn-stunt-infected corn plant showing helically coiled filament of the spiroplasma associated with corn stunt disease. *(From R. E. Davis and J. F. Worley, Spiroplasma: Motile, helical microorganism associated with corn stunt disease, Phytopathology, 63:403–408, 1973)*

corn stunt disease. Studies incorporating maize dwarf mosaic virus (MDMV) gave further support for this contention and indicated that the helical filaments did not represent structures simply produced by plant cells under the stress of virus infection. In such studies, both MDMV and the corn stunt disease agent could be recovered by transmission tests (mechanical transmission of MDMV and vector transmission of corn stunt agent) from doubly infected corn plants, and helical spiroplasmas could readily be found in juice expressed from such plants. No helical filaments could be detected, however, in juice from plants infected by MDMV alone. The findings confirmed the consistent association with corn stunt disease of an organism producing helical filaments and indicated that corn stunt disease may be diagnosed by optical microscopy in cases of mixed infection with virus.

The work on corn stunt disease discussed so far, however, had dealt with only one isolate of a single strain of the corn stunt disease agent that had been maintained in laboratories for several years. This left open the possibility that the helical organism studied might be associated with only this strain, or even with only this one isolate, and might be unrelated to naturally occurring corn stunt disease. Therefore, corn plants with naturally occurring disease in Mexico were examined for spiroplasmas. Spiroplasmas were detected in all cases of plants possessing symptoms typical of corn stunt disease. While providing the first diagnosis by optical microscopy of naturally occurring corn stunt disease in the field, these findings gave additional support to the hypothesis that the spiroplasma is the corn stunt disease agent itself.

Much attention has thus been devoted to the susceptible plant, but the preceding investigations omitted close examination of an important element—the insect vector. The significance of the leafhopper vector, still essential for transmission of the corn stunt disease agent to plants, prompts the question: Are spiroplasmas also to be found in corn-stunt-infected insects? More recent work has provided the response. Spiroplasmas have also been detected in corn-stunt-infected (but not in corn-stunt-free) individuals of the leafhopper vector (*Dalbulus maidis* DeL. W.).

These lines of evidence provide impressive support for the hypothesis that the spiroplasma observed is the causal agent of corn stunt disease. Nevertheless, accepted proof of the etiology awaits isolation and purification or cultivation of the organism in an artificial medium and fulfillment of Koch's postulates.

Motility. The ability of the presumed corn stunt disease agent to form helical filaments in infected plants and insect vectors can be recognized as an indication of important structural differences compared with the filaments formed by known mycoplasmas. Although formation of helical filaments by mycoplasma-like organisms possibly may be influenced by environment and stage of growth, no information is available to indicate that any present member of the class Mollicutes is capable of forming helical filaments under any circumstances. This difference supports the contention that the plant-inhabiting mycoplasma-like organisms will probably give rise to new genera and possibly new, higher taxa as well. The motility exhibited by the helical filaments is yet another characteristic divergent from members of the class Mollicutes. In liquid media, the filaments appear to whirl or spin rapidly about the long axis of the helix and exhibit flectional movements but are incapable of significant translational migration. The apparent rotational movements may be an illusion, however, for in semisolid media the spiroplasmas are capable of applying what appear to be waves of contractile movement in order to achieve a significant migration, during which they course through the semisolid surroundings.

Filaments are formed by a number of mycoplasmas in culture, but motility of mycoplasma filaments has not been reported. Motility thus suggests the possibility of important differences in structure and function of filaments and makes increasingly apparent the divergence of the spiroplasmas from present members of the class Mollicutes.

The presumed corn stunt disease agent provided the first recognized example of a wall-less, helical, motile microorganism inhabiting plants. Subsequently, the mycoplasma-like organism associated with citrus stubborn disease was found to possess a helical morphology and to exhibit a motility similar to those of the corn stunt spiroplasma, thus providing the second recognized example of spiroplasmas in plants. One other possible example of a spiroplasma is the "spirochete-like" organism associated with the sex ratio condition in the fly *Drosophila.*

Cultivation in artificial media. Because the mycoplasmas that inhabit humans and animals are cultivable in artificial media, considerable effort has been devoted over the past several years to attempts to isolate and cultivate the mycoplasma-like organisms found in diseased plants. To date, most reports of cultivation of plant-inhabiting

mycoplasma-like organisms remain unconfirmed. The case of stubborn disease of citrus, however, is a notable exception.

The remission of stubborn disease by tetracycline antibiotics and the observation of mycoplasma-like bodies in phloem of diseased plants prompted independent attempts at isolation and cultivation of the presumed mycoplasma-like agent by A. A. Fudl-Allah and colleagues and by P. Saglio and colleagues. The organism obtained in culture forms "fried egg" colonies on agar media (a colony form typical for mycoplasmas), possesses an optimum temperature of about 32°C for growth, and in culture forms motile helical filaments strikingly similar to those that had been described for the corn stunt spiroplasma. Work by Saglio and colleagues revealed the guanine-plus-cytosine content of the deoxyribonucleic acid of the organism to be close to 26 mole %, a value within the range known for established species within the class Mollicutes, but serological tests indicated that the organism from citrus stubborn disease is serologically distinct from recognized species in the class. Based on an extensive characterization of this organism, Saglio and colleagues proposed the recognition of a new genus, *Spiroplasma* (following the suggestion by Davis and Worley for use of the term spiroplasma), having as type species *Spiroplasma citri*, the spiroplasma associated with and presumed to be the causal agent of stubborn disease of citrus.

Proof of pathogenicity. The successful cultivation in artificial media of the presumed citrus stubborn disease agent opened the door for fulfillment of Koch's postulates for proof of pathogenicity. Unfortunately, although it had long been suspected that the citrus stubborn disease agent was transmitted from plant to plant in nature by an insect vector, this presumed vector had not yet been found. It was thus that the first transmission of cultivated *S. citri* to plants was, intriguingly, to plants of clover by a leafhopper, *Euscelis plebejus* (Fall.), of temperate regions, and not by a normal part of the insect fauna on citrus. Organisms of *S. citri* isolated from citrus plants with little-leaf disease were injected by M. J. Daniels and colleagues into individuals of *E. plebejus*, which were then held for several weeks on plants of clover at 25 to 30°C. These plants subsequently developed symptoms of stunting and chlorosis; helical spiroplasmas were found in ultrathin sections of phloem; and *S. citri* could be reisolated from the infected plants. Thus, the first demonstration that cultivated *S. citri* is plant-pathogenic was obtained with a host other than citrus. The transmission of cultivated *S. citri* to plants of citrus, and the consequent development of stubborn disease in the plants, however, has recently been reported by Daniels, B. M. Meddins, P. G. Markham, R. Townsend, and colleagues. E. C. Calavan and associates have recently reported the first isolation and cultivation of *S. citri* from field-collected specimens of a leafhopper, *Circulifer tenellus* (Baker), a natural feeder on citrus and a likely vector of the citrus stubborn disease agent in nature.

Summary. New findings in plant pathology are beginning to suggest the existence of entirely new groups of plant-inhabiting microorganisms. Certain of these organisms may closely resemble, in morphology and physiology, established members of the class Mollicutes; others may soon be included in the class Mollicutes under the new genus *Spiroplasma*. Prior to 1967, no mycoplasma-like organisms were known to occur in plants. Whether or not certain of the plant-inhabiting mycoplasma-like organisms truly fit within current concepts for members of the genera already present in the class Mollicutes [genus *Mycoplasma* (mycoplasmas), *Acholeplasma* (acholeplasmas), *Ureaplasma* (ureaplasmas)] is yet to be demonstrated. What has been established during the past few years, however, is that certain plant diseases have associated with them organisms entirely new to pathology—the spiroplasmas—and that at least some of these organisms are cultivable in cell-free culture media, transmissible by leafhoppers, and pathogenic to plants.   [ROBERT E. DAVIS]

Rhizoctoniosis of aquatic plants. Species of the fungal genus *Rhizoctonia* are ubiquitous soil inhabitants. Many of them are facultative parasites on a large number of terrestrial plants. Species belonging in the *Rhizoctonia solani* complex by virtue of possessing a common perfect state, *Thanatephorus cucumeris*, are especially notable as plant pathogens. They cause disorders ranging from root rots, to crown and stem necrosis, to aerial blighting of the foliage. Tomes have been written concerning these fungi and the diseases they cause in cultivated plants. Considerably less attention has been directed toward rhizoctoniosis of uncultivated plants, especially those living in a nonterrestrial environment. In fact, until recently only a few scattered reports existed of *Rhizoctonia* infection on aquatic plants.

Workers in Japan recognized in the early 1930s that paddy rice was affected by *Hypochnus sasakii*, a species now considered synonymous with the perfect state of *R. solani*. This fungus was also found to be pathogenic to water hyacinth *(Eichhornia crassipes)*. A few years earlier, the destruction of large acreages of wild-duck food plants in the Currituck Sound area of North Carolina and Virginia was attributed to *R. solani*. Affected plants included *Potamogeton pectinatus*, *P. perfoliatus*, *Ruppia maritima*, *Vallisneria spiralis*, and *Najas flexilis*. However, these reports went virtually unnoticed, and aside from brief notes of *Corticum solani* (probably *R. solani*) attacking water hyacinth in India and alligator weed in Louisiana, the potential of *R. solani* as a destructive force on aquatic plants was unexplored.

In 1970 plant pathologists at the University of Florida embarked upon a study of the utilization of plant pathogens as biocontrols for noxious aquatic species. Foremost among these noxious plants was the beautiful but prolific water hyacinth. In less than 100 years after its introduction from Latin America, this pest infested more than 200,000 acres (91,000 hectares) of waterways in Florida alone and cost taxpayers there more than $15 million annually for control efforts.

RhEa fungus. While in search of diseases on water hyacinth, a blight of its relative, the anchoring hyacinth *(E. azurea)*, in Panama was found to be caused by a species of *Rhizoctonia*, which was tentatively identified as *R. solani*. An isolate of the

Fig. 2. Disease damage caused by RhEa isolate of *Rhizoctonia* on (a) water hyacinth, (b) water lettuce. Uninoculated healthy plant on left. *(From B. G. Joyner and T. E. Freeman, Pathogenicity of Rhizoctonia solani to aquatic plants, Phytopathology, 63:681– 685, 1973)*

fungus from Panama (designated RhEa) was found to be extremely pathogenic when the water hyacinth was inoculated with it. The same fungus was later isolated from water hyacinth in Panama and Puerto Rico. Symptoms on affected plants consisted of irregular leaf lesions that were tan in color and surrounded by a dark brown border. Under ideal conditions for disease development, the entire aerial portion of the plant became blighted (Fig. 2a). Severely diseased plants eventually died and sank to the bottom. Thus, the potential of the Panama isolate of *Rhizoctonia* as a biocontrol was established.

The RhEa isolate was found to parasitize several species of emersed plants, that is, those that rise above the water surface, and free-floating aquatic plants. Those affected were alligator weed *(Alternanthera philoxeroides)*, pennywort *(Hydrocotyle umbellata)*, frogbit *(Limnobium spon-*

gia), duckweed *(Lemna minor),* pickerel weed *(Pontederia lanceolata),* salvinia *(Salvinia rotundifolia),* water lettuce *(Pistia stratioties;* Fig. 2*b),* anchoring hyacinth *(E. azurae),* and water hyacinth *(E. crassipes).* It was especially severe on the last three species listed. Submersed plants (those remaining below the surface) affected were hydrilla *(Hydrilla verticillata),* Eurasian water milfoil *(Myriophyllum spicatum),* vallisneria *(Vallisneria species),* and parrotfeather *(Myriophyllum brasiliense).* Two other submersed plants, Brazilian elodea *(Elodea densa)* and coontail *(Ceratophyllum demersum),* were not infected. The latitude of this host range is evident by the fact that the 11 affected species belong to 9 different plant families. Isolate RhEa also affected a wide range of terrestrial crop plants. In fact, its host range and symptoms on these crop plants were similar to terrestrial isolates of *R. solani.*

The RhEa isolate was most pathogenic to water hyacinth in the temperature range of 28–30°C, with a marked decrease in severity as the temperature was increased above 32°C. Such a decrease was not evident in its pathogenicity to cucumber seedlings. However, the growth of RhEa in culture was not drastically decreased at 32°C. Therefore, the decrease in disease severity at elevated temperatures was considered to be the result of a host-pathogen interaction. RhEa infects aquatic plants primarily through the stomates after the formation of infection cushions over these structures. This fact probably accounts for its inconsistency in infecting submersed portions of water hyacinths and submersed species of aquatic plants.

Culturally, RhEa was similar to other isolates of *R. solani.* It formed a buff-colored mycelium and produced sclerotia (resting bodies) abundantly. These sclerotia were brown, pitted, and 1–3 mm in diameter. The mycelium branched at right angles, had doliform septa, and was multinucleate. These facts prompted the placing of the fungus into the *R. solani* group. However, recent unpublished studies by C. C. Tu indicate that the perfect stage of RhEa differs somewhat from *T. cucumeris.* He considers the fungus to have become adapted to an aquatic environment and proposes to establish a new genus to accommodate the perfect stage of this species of *Rhizoctonia.* It certainly cannot be denied that the fungus is adapted to survival in an aquatic environment. Sclerotia of RhEa survived submersion in lake water for a period exceeding 26 months with no apparent loss in viability or pathogenicity. This longevity of submersion in water is considerably more than that recorded for *Rhizoctonia* species attacking paddy rice.

Other Rizoctonia isolates. A comparison of RhEa with isolates of *R. solani* from other hosts in regard to pathogenicity and symptomatology on aquatic plants showed them to be similar in many respects. Isolates of *R. solani* from such widely divergent hosts as bean, cotton (American type culture collection no. 14011), kenaf, palm, Natal plum, and *Rhododendron* species affected the same host range of aquatic plants as RhEa and caused similar symptoms on them. The isolates differed somewhat in their optimum temperature for infection, in severity of infection, and in their ability to infect submersed portions of aquatic

plants. Ironically, the isolate from cotton infected submersed portions of water hyacinth more readily than did RhEa. The cotton and the bean isolates were equal to RhEa in their pathogenicity to aquatic plants, and the symptoms they caused were strikingly similar to those caused by RhEa. The isolate from kenaf also caused similar symptoms, especially on water hyacinth.

During the course of studies at the University of Florida, an additional *Rhizoctonia* species has been consistently isolated from aquatic plants. It apparently does not belong in the *R. solani* group, because of the difference in nuclear conditions (binucleate as opposed to multinucleate) of the cells. It also differs in sclerotial characteristics, having small black sclerotia rather than brown to buff ones, as formed by *R. solani.* Thus far, it has not been demonstrated to be pathogenic, and its association with aquatic plants is apparently not a parasitic one.

Assessment of pathogenicity. The implications of these recent findings concerning pathogenicity of *Rhizoctonia* on aquatic plants are several-fold. First, a notorious pathogen of terrestrial crop plants has been firmly established as having pathogenic capabilities on plants endemic to an aquatic environment. Second, if the RhEa isolate of *Rhizoctonia* does indeed belong to a new genus, a possible precedent has been established for the evolution of a plant pathogen from a terrestrial to an aquatic form, or vice versa—with the probability favoring the former. Third, the occurrence of a disease with biocontrol potential for noxious aquatic species, especially the water hyacinth, has been established. But fourth, this potential cannot be realized until the full impact of *Rhizoctonia*-caused disease on desirable aquatic plants has been fully assessed, and any hazard to crop plants generated by its use evaluated.

For background information *see* PLANT DISEASE in the McGraw-Hill Encyclopedia of Science and Technology.

[T. E. FREEMAN]

Bibliography: M. J. Daniels et al., *Nature,* 244: 523–524, 1973; R. E. Davis and J. F. Worley, *Phytopathology,* 63:403–408, 1973; T. E. Freeman, *Plant Dis. Rep.,* 57:601–602, 1973; T. E. Freeman and F. W. Zettler, *Phytopathology,* 61:892, 1971; B. J. Joyner and T. E. Freeman, *Phytopathology,* 63:681–685, 1973; I. M. Lee et al., *Calif. Agric.,* 27:14, 1973; P. Saglio et al., *Int. J. Syst. Bacteriol.,* 23:191–204, 1973; C. C. Tu, Ph. D. Dissertation, University of Florida, 1974.

Plant virus

Since some plant viruses are among the most readily available sources of natural messenger ribonucleic acids (RNAs), the recent achievement of accurate translation of plant virus RNAs under conditions of cell-free protein synthesis will benefit the study both of plant viruses and of the mechanism of protein biosynthesis. For example, cell-free systems derived from plant tissue or from animal cells can synthesize the coat protein of a plant virus, brome mosaic virus (BMV), under the direction of the viral RNA. In both cases, the fact that the product appears to be identical to the authentic viral coat protein provides further evidence for

first dimension ⟶

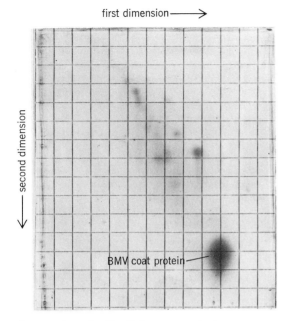

second dimension

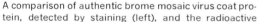

BMV coat protein ⟵

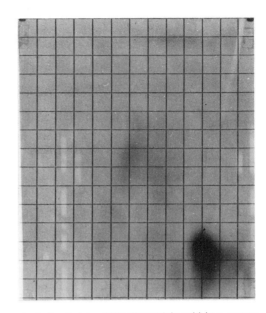

A comparison of authentic brome mosaic virus coat protein, detected by staining (left), and the radioactive product directed by BMV ribonucleic acid in a mouse cell-free system, detected by autoradiography (right).

the universality of the genetic code and of the processes by which peptide chain initiation and termination sites are recognized.

Cell-free protein synthesis. Lysates of bacterial, plant, and animal cells can carry out active protein synthesis under the direction of appropriate messenger RNAs. Such systems have contributed greatly to the elucidation of the genetic code and to the present understanding of the mechanism of protein synthesis. More recently, cell-free systems have been used to identify specific messenger RNAs on the basis of the proteins for which they code. However, the task of purifying a cellular messenger RNA, even from highly specialized cells producing predominantly one type of protein, is usually very difficult. In many cases, the most convenient source of messenger RNA is one of the small viruses that contain single-stranded RNA as their genetic material, for example, the bacterial viruses f2 and Qβ, the mouse virus encephalomyocarditis virus, and the plant viruses BMV and satellite tobacco necrosis virus (STNV). It is relatively easy to purify these viruses; then, the pure viral RNA can be extracted for translation in the laboratory. STNV and BMV are particularly convenient, for they can be purified in large amounts and contain fairly small RNA molecules that direct the synthesis of a simple pattern of protein products.

Translation of STNV RNA. There are several examples of the accurate translation of viral RNAs by extracts of cells that, in their intact state, would not have been susceptible to infection by the virus itself. Thus the RNA of STNV, which probably codes only for the viral coat protein, can be translated in extracts of bacterial cells as well as in a cell-free system derived from wheat embryos. In each case the product closely resembles the authentic viral coat protein, although it appears to be slightly smaller, perhaps because of premature

termination of the nascent peptide chain. However, there is a significant difference between the products of the prokaryotic and eukaryotic systems. The N-terminal amino acid sequence of the protein synthesized in the bacterial cell-free system is formyl-methionine-alanine-lysine- . . . , whereas that of the product made in the wheat embryo system (and that of the authentic STNV coat protein) is alanine-lysine- . . . . . J. M. Clark, Jr., and colleagues have shown that this difference is due to the fact that, in the bacterial system, the initiating amino acid, formylmethionine, survives as the N-terminal residue of the protein product, whereas in the wheat embryo system the initiating amino acid, methionine, is incorporated only transiently before being cleaved from the nascent peptide chain. The absence of cleavage in the bacterial system is due to inactivation of the cleavage enzyme during preparation of the cell-free system.

Translation of BMV RNA. BMV is a more complex virus than STNV is, and it contains sufficient information to code for about eight proteins. This information is divided among four RNA molecules, the smallest two of which each contain a copy of the gene for the single viral coat protein. The four RNA species are encapsidated in three separate viral particles, two of which each contain one of the two larger RNA molecules, and the third contains the two smaller species. Thus infection requires the cooperative action of three viral particles. It is not clear what selective advantages accrue to viruses like BMV that have fragmented genomes distributed among multiple-component particles, but the occurrence of such genomes is a common phenomenon among plant viruses.

The presence of the coat protein gene on two different molecules of BMV RNA makes it possible to study the influence of the structure of a message on its translation. In the wheat embryo cell-free system the smallest RNA directs the efficient synthesis of BMV coat protein. However, when the same nucleotide sequence is part of a larger RNA, it is a relatively inefficient messenger for coat protein synthesis. It has been suggested that the larger RNA is folded in such a way as to partially obscure the site to which ribosomes bind at the start of the coat protein message. The need for rapid synthesis of the viral coat protein is greatest late in infection, and it is thought that the small, efficient messenger RNA is produced at this stage by a cleavage of the larger, inefficient messenger RNA.

BMV RNA also directs coat protein synthesis in extracts of mouse cells, although the intact virus cannot infect mice. The identity of the product with authentic viral coat protein has been established by various methods. For example, the size and charge of the two molecules can be compared by electrophoresis in two dimensions on a slab of polyacrylamide gel (see illustration). In the first dimension, the protein molecules migrate according to their charge, whereas in the second, they migrate according to their size. The coincidence of the spots shown in the illustration demonstrates that the cell-free product has the same charge and size as the authentic viral coat protein. A more rigorous test of identity is to compare the peptides produced at the time of enzymatic digestion of the proteins by a specific protease. Trypsin, which cleaves polypeptide chains at each arginine and lysine residue, cuts BMV coat protein into about 26 specific fragments. Comparison of these fragments with the peptides resulting from digestion of the protein synthesized in the mouse cell-free system shows that the synthesized protein is indistinguishable from the authentic coat protein. Clearly, the processes of peptide initiation, elongation, and termination in plants and animals have many important features in common.

TMV RNA translation. Not all plant virus RNAs that have been tested can be translated to yield protein products as simple as those of BMV and STNV RNAs. Several attempts have been made to demonstrate the accurate synthesis of tobacco mosaic virus (TMV) coat protein in a variety of cell-free systems, but the results have been disappointing. Recently B. E. Roberts and colleagues used the RNA from a mutant strain of TMV as a messenger in a cell-free extract of wheat germ. The mutant they chose carried a methionine residue in place of the threonine residue at position 107 of the coat protein. When ^{35}S-methionine was used as the radioactive label for the cell-free products, a tryptic peptide was revealed that contained this residue in the digest of wild-type RNA-directed products. This result shows that the virus RNA strand is the messenger strand (rather than being complementary to the messenger strand) and that it is translated in the correct phase in the wheat germ cell-free system. However, no material of the correct size for TMV coat protein could be detected among the undigested cell-free products. At present it is not clear whether the lack of TMV coat protein is due to incorrect initiation, defective termination, or, perhaps, failure to cleave a larger precursor polypeptide.

Conclusions. The successful translation of plant virus RNAs in cell-free extracts of bacterial, plant, and animal cells will therefore contribute to knowl-

edge about plant virus and protein biosynthesis in two ways. First, the elucidation of the detailed mechanism of protein synthesis will be facilitated by the availability of large amounts of messenger RNAs that can be translated into simple proteins; second, cell-free systems will help in locating specific viral genes among the RNA components of split genome viruses.

For background information *see* PLANT VIRUS; RIBONUCLEIC ACID (RNA) in the McGraw-Hill Encyclopedia of Science and Technology.

[L. ANDREW BALL]

Bibliography: L. A. Ball et al., *Nature New Biol.*, 246:206–208, December 19–26, 1973; W. H. Klein and J. M. Clark, *Biochemistry*, 12:1528–1531, 1973; B. E. Roberts et al., *J. Mol. Biol.*, 80:733–742, 1973; D. S. Shih and P. Kaesberg, *Proc. Nat. Acad. Sci. U.S.A.*, 70:1799–1803, 1973.

Porphyrin

The structures of porphyrin derivatives are of interest because of the relationship of these metal complexes to several biological systems. The iron porphyrins are central to the function of the oxygen-carrying family of hemoproteins; chlorophyll, a magnesium porphyrin derivative, is present in all organisms that carry out photosynthesis. Important advances in both iron and magnesium porphyrins have occurred recently. Also, manganese porphyrins continue to be of particular interest since a detailed description of their unique physical-chemical properties will enhance the understanding of metalloporphyrins in general and of the iron porphyrins in particular.

Molecular structure. Porphin, the basic skeleton of a porphyrin, is a cyclic tetrapyrrole in which four five-membered rings are joined by methine carbon atoms to form a macrocycle (Fig. 1). Porphyrins are formed from porphin by adding substituents on the pyrrole carbon atoms (C_{b_1}-C_{b_8} of Fig. 2) or the methine carbon atoms (C_{m_1}-C_{m_4}). These macrocycles bind a large variety of metal ions to form metalloporphyrins. Additional ligands can then be complexed to the central metal ion.

The structures of several metalloporphyrins, further coordinated by the small molecules nitric oxide (NO), carbon monoxide (CO), and dioxygen (O_2), are of interest as models of the prosthetic group of the oxygen-carrying hemoproteins and hence further the understanding of the bonding of O_2 in these systems.

Geometry of the molecule. The molecule shown in Fig. 2 is a good model of the coordination group of the nitric oxide complex of hemoglobin; the sixth ligand in the hemoprotein is an imidazole from the amino acid residue histidine. The iron-

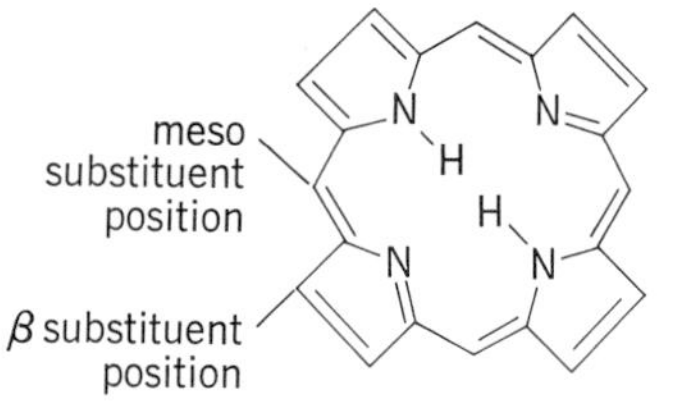

Fig. 1. Structure of a porphin molecule.

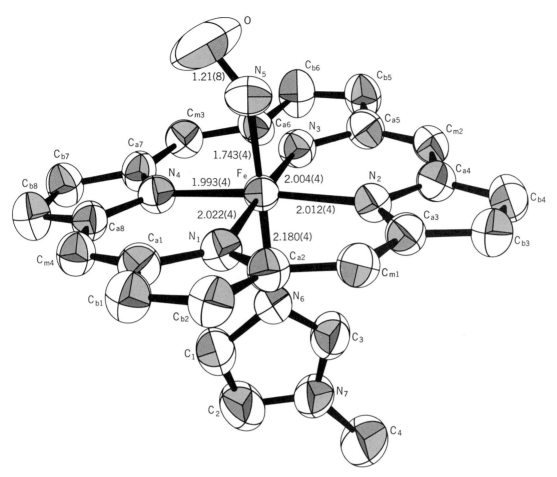

Fig. 2. A computer-drawn model of the NO adduct of iron(II) tetraphenylporphyrin; the four phenyl groups which are bonded to the methine (C_m) carbon atoms have been omitted for clarity; the sixth ligand is 1-methylimidazole. (*From P. L. Piciulo, G. Rupprecht, and W. R.*

Scheidt, Stereochemistry of nitrosylmetalloporphyrins: Nitrosyl-α,β,γ,δ-tetraphenylporphinato (1-methylimidazole) iron and nitrosyl-α,β,γ,δ-tetraphenylporphinato (4-methylpiperidine) manganese, J. Amer. Chem. Soc., 96:5293, 1974)

porphin nitrogen bond distances average 2.008 A (10 A = 1 nm), a value typical of low-spin iron(II) porphyrins. The geometry of the FeNO group is of special interest; the bond angle is 142°, intermediate to the limiting values of observed MNO angles of 180° and ~120°. The iron-imidazole nitrogen bond length is ~0.2 A longer than normal; this is attributed to the influence of the nitric oxide ligand. This observation may be of use in understanding some of the fine points of the behavior of the nitrosylhemoglobin molecule. The structure of the closely related five-coordinate molecule ONFeTPP (the abbreviation for the NO adduct of iron(II) tetraphenylporphyrin) reveals that the effect of removing the sixth ligand is small. The largest change in the molecular geometry is an increase in the FeNO bond angle to 149°.

The effect of removing one d electron is shown by the structure of ONMnTPP(MPip) (MPip = 4-methylpiperidine, the sixth ligand). The MnO group becomes linear and the Mn-NO bond distance is 0.1 A shorter than the Fe-NO bond distance. The effect of adding one d electron relative to the iron complex is shown by the structure of the five-coordinate cobalt porphyrin, ONCoTPP.

The major structural changes are a decrease in the CoNO angle to ~128° and an increase in the Co-NO bond length by ~0.1 A, to 1.82 A. It has been pointed out by W. R. Scheidt and J. L. Hoard that the cobalt complex is isoelectronic with the corresponding FeO_2 complex and should represent a good structural model of the oxygenated hemoproteins. Structural study of two ruthenium(II) porphyrins in which one of the axial ligands is carbon monoxide has demonstrated that the RuCO linkage is linear; it is a natural presumption that the isoelectronic iron(II) complexes have a similar structure.

The characterization of a reversibly oxygenated iron(II) porphyrin has been recently reported by J. P. Collman and coworkers. The complex has four aryl groups (pivalamido) on one side of the porphyrin to form a hydrophobic pocket to enclose the dioxygen ligand. The sixth ligand is 1-methylimidazole. The dioxygen molecule coordinates end-on as suggested by L. Pauling in 1948. The FeOO angle is ~135°, the Fe-O_2 bond length is 1.75 A, and the Fe-N(imidazole) bond length is 2.07 A. Figure 1 is thus a good picture of the molecular geometry. This structure clearly represents a sig-

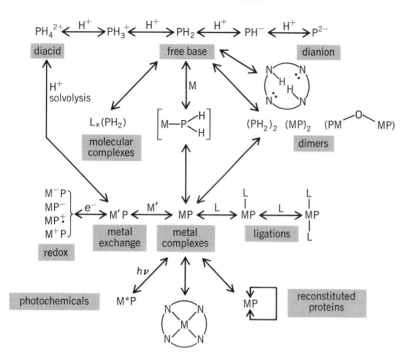

Fig. 3. Interactions between metal ions and porphyrin molecules. The free base form, PH_2, is represented by the circle with protons, and the metalloporphyrin, MP, by the circle enclosing a metal (M) ion.

nificant advance in the understanding of these systems.

Electronic configuration and crystal structure. C. E. Strouse has succeeded in crystallizing ethyl chlorophyllide *a* dehydrate (this molecule is derived from chlorophyll *a* by replacing the phytol side chain with ethanol) and has determined the crystal and molecular structure. One molecule of water is coordinated to the magnesium, giving it a coordination number of five. A second molecule of water is used for cross-linking to form a sheetlike structure. Strouse has suggested a model of chlorophyll aggregation to account for the light-harvesting capacity (a model for the transmission of

light energy from the chlorophyll molecule absorbing light, to the reaction center) of chlorophyll in the living plant.

The structures of several cobalt porphyrins have demonstrated the importance of the electronic configuration on the structure. The structure of the low-spin cobalt(III) complex, bis(piperidine)tetraphenylporphinatocobalt(III), has cobalt-porphin nitrogen bond distances of 1.978 A; the bond lengths to the axial piperidine ligands are 2.060 A. The addition of one electron to give the low-spin d^7 cobalt(II) complex, wherein the added *d* electron occupies the d_{z^2} orbital pointing directly at the two axial ligands, has axial bond distances of 2.436 A. Thus the unpaired electron causes a lengthening of the axial bonds of almost 0.4 A. The effects of the unpaired electron are not as pronounced in the five-coordinate derivatives. Thus the 1-methylimidazole adduct of cobalt(II) tetraphenylporphyrin has an axial bond length of 2.16 A.

[ROBERT SCHEIDT]

Metalloporphyrins. Interstellar dust may be rich in magnesium (Mg) benzoporphyrins, nickel (Ni) and vanadium (V) derivatives are found in oil shale, and lunar samples have been specifically analyzed for porphyrin material. The major advances in this field are coming from investigations on model synthetic porphyrins having favorable properties such as systematic side chain and metal ion variations, and complete water solubility. The structure-function relationships established with the synthetic complexes clarify aspects of the behavior of porphyrins in nature.

Porphyrins are macrocyclic tetradentate coordinating agents (Fig. 3) differing from noncyclic multidentate ligands which can wrap around and unravel from a metal center. Both x-ray crystal structures and the preparation of sterically strained derivatives indicate that the porphyrin nucleus is fairly flexible; deformation modes rather than dissociative modes are the central themes of metalloporphyrin interactions.

With the exception of the lanthanides and actinides, most metals in the periodic table (Fig. 4) form metalloporphyrins. Many of these complexes are made by simply heating the porphyrin with a metal salt in a common solvent, such as dimethylformamide. Recent preparative methods for difficult cases use metal carbonyls, hydrides, and organometallics as substrates, or the reactions are run at high temperatures in molten imidazole or phenol.

In aqueous solution, metals probably incorporate into metalloporphyrins by a sterically controlled, dissociative interchange process, as in Eq. (1). The metal and porphyrin rapidly come together

$$ML_6 + PH_2 \leftrightarrow [L_6M \underset{(I)}{\cdots} PH_2] \leftrightarrow$$
$$[L_4M \underset{(II)}{=\!=} PH_2] \rightarrow MP + \cdots \quad (1)$$

to form an outer sphere complex (I), and at least two ligands from the metal must dissociate to provide vacant positions for the porphyrin nitrogen atoms to occupy as in (II). The slow step in the majority of complex formation reactions is the dissociation of the first ligand (L) from the metal ion (ML_6). The cyclic porphyrin framework positions the nitrogen lone pair electrons inward toward the

H																	He
Li	**Be**											B	C	N	O	F	Ne
Na	**Mg**											**Al**	Si	P	S	Cl	Ar
K	**Ca**	**Sc**	**Ti**	**V**	**Cr**	**Mn**	**Fe**	**Co**	**Ni**	**Cu**	**Zn**	**Ga**	**Ge**	**As**	Se	Br	Kr
Rb	**Sr**	**Y**	**Zr**	**Nb**	**Mo**	**Tc**	**Ru**	**Rh**	**Pd**	**Ag**	**Cd**	**In**	**Sn**	**Sb**	Te	I	Xe
Cs	**Ba**		**Hf**	**Ta**	**W**	**Re**	**Os**	**Ir**	**Pt**	**Au**	**Hg**	**Tl**	**Pb**	**Bi**	Po	At	Rn
Fr	Ra																

	La	Ce	Pr	Nd	Pm	Sm	Eu	Gd	Tb	Dy	Ho	Er	Tm	Yb	Lu
	Ac	Th	Pa	U	Np	Pu	Am	Cm	Bk	Cf	Es	Fm	Md	No	Lr

Fig. 4. Periodic table of the chemical elements; metal ions that have been incorporated into porphyrins are denoted by the boldface symbols.

central cavity, and the porphyrin nucleus must deform to force these pairs in an outward, coordinating direction. Thus the first $[L_5M—PH_2]$ bond breaks many times before the porphyrin nucleus has deformed enough to allow a second bond $[L_4M=PH_2]$ to form. The low probability of a correct orientation between the deformed porphyrin and a metal ion with empty coordination positions accounts for the fact that complex formation with porphyrins is millions of times slower than with related, more flexible, open-chain ligands. While the product metalloporphyrin has lost the two free base (PH_2) protons, adducts have been isolated which contain a ligated metal, and a porphyrin with one or two central protons still attached.

Demetallation. Metal ions are more firmly bonded to porphyrins than to almost any other multidentate ligand. The ease of demetallation by acids is proportional to the charge and electronegativity of a metal ion, and inversely related to its radius. Many complexes can be sublimed unchanged at 500°C, and it requires weeks for the Zn/ZnP isotopic exchange reaction, in Eq. (2), to occur. The

$$*Zn^{2+} + ZnP \rightarrow *ZnP + Zn^{2+} \qquad (2)$$

Cu/ZnP reaction is much faster, and probably involves a copper entering the porphyrin from one side as the zinc leaves from the other. Porphyrins containing two metal atoms on opposite sides of the porphyrin plane have been characterized.

Acid-catalyzed removal of metals is a stepwise process, usually requiring three protons. As each of the metal-porphyrin bonds dissociate, an N-H linkage forms, which blocks the return of the metal ion, and causes deformation of the macrocycle. The addition of the third proton breaks the stabilizing chelate effect, and the resulting one-coordinate metal is readily removed.

Binding of nitrogenous bases. Many porphyrins and metalloporphyrins form dimers in aqueous solution with association constants around $10^4 M^{-1}$, and very rapid formation rates near $10^7 M^{-1} sec^{-1}$. Such species are held together by pi cloud polarization forces, and differ from the recently discovered oxybridges which bind iron porphyrin dimers. Depending on the metal, one or two nitrogenous bases can occupy the two axial positions in a metalloporphyrin. For ionic metals like zinc, the stability constants for 1:1 complexation are proportional to ligand basicity and decrease with porphyrin basicity. The opposite trend is found for Fe^{2+}, where covalent bonding is important. Cr^{3+} and Co^{3+}, which exchange their first coordination sphere ligands slowly in aquo complexes, are less basic and more labile metals when coordinated to porphyrins. This is a reflection of the ease of delocalization of metal electrons into porphyrin orbitals.

Divalent cobalt porphyrins in solution bonded to one nitrogenous base can carry (not reduce) molecular oxygen, and when reconstituted with proteins, such cobalt species behave in almost the same manner as natural iron-containing hemoglobin or myoglobin. Iron(II) porphyrins have been synthesized which allow a nitrogen base to occupy only one axial position, and in this form, they mimic the oxygen transport and CO binding properties of myoglobin. These models are important means of elucidating the role of metal ions and proteins in respiration pigments.

Oxidation-reduction reactions. Electrons can be added to or removed from either the porphyrin molecular orbitals, or the metal center in metalloporphyrins. Spin resonance work on Mg porphyrins oxidized on the ring or iron porphyrins involving both ring and metal oxidation to Fe(IV) oxidation have contributed to the delineation of the photochemistry of chlorophyll, and the catalytic properties of certain peroxidases and catalases.

The mechanisms of oxidation-reduction reactions in solution are being probed by rapid kinetic techniques. With the reductant Cr^{2+} and $Cl-Fe^{3+}P$ in nonaqueous media, the observed product is $CrCl^{2+}$. This could arise only if the bridged inner sphere intermediate $[Cr—Cl—FeP]$ is the electron transfer pathway, where the transfer is mediated by an axially coordinated chloride. Dithionite reacts with bis-pyridine Mn^{3+} porphyrins by an outer sphere mechanism, in which the electron transfer could be via the edge of the porphyrin ring. Cytochrome *c* contains an Fe^{3+} porphyrin that is partially exposed on the protein edge. With Cr^{2+}, both an adjacent attack at the iron atom (which involves an opening of the protein crevice leading to the face of the porphyrin) and a remote pathway at the exposed porphyrin edge have been found.

Radioactive metalloporphyrins themselves are now being used as selective lymph node irradiation agents to facilitate organ transplants, and as imaging chemicals for tumor cells.

[PETER HAMBRIGHT]

Manganese porphyrins. The biological significance of manganese porphyrins is not yet clear. Although the requirement of manganese for oxygen evolution in green plant photosynthesis is generally agreed to, even a qualitative characterization of the manganese-containing redox catalyst is not available at present. While a naturally occurring manganese porphyrin remains an attractive candidate here, no materials of this type have been isolated from green plants, nor has any conclusive evidence pro or con been found for the natural occurrence of such a compound. Of possible relevance are the recent observations which offer strong circumstantial evidence for the existence of a biosynthesized manganese porphyrin in mammalian erythrocytes. The hemolysate was prepared from blood withdrawn from a rat 6 days after the injection of radioactive manganese(II) chloride. The biological function of the manganese-porphyrin-containing protein, which is identical in size to hemoglobin, is not known. A number of recent reports have appeared which include the synthesis and characterization of several new manganese(III) and manganese(II) porphyrins as well as oxidation-reduction properties of some known complexes. These works generally deal with a variety of metalloporphyrins, and the manganese porphyrins are not systematically examined as a group. The results complement and extend previous observations and do not break significant new ground with respect to manganese porphyrins. However, several papers have appeared which do add substantially to the understanding of

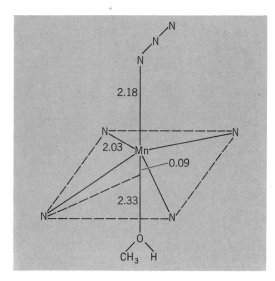

Fig. 5. Coordination sphere showing bond distance in angstroms (10 A = 1 nm) around the manganese atom in (methanol) azide (α, β, γ, δ-tetraphenylporphin) manganese(III). The dashed lines between nitrogens signify the plane of the porphyrin monocycle which is not shown.

manganese(III) porphyrins, particularly from the point of view of stereochemistry, molecular and electronic structure, and possible catalytic activity in the important biological process photosynthesis.

Stereochemistry. Preliminary results of a single-crystal x-ray structure study of a new six-coordinate complex (methanol)azide(α,β,γ,δ-tetraphenylporphin) manganese(III) have appeared. The distorted octahedral coordination polyhedron for [Mn(TPP)N$_3$(CH$_3$OH)] is shown in Fig. 5. Unlike many other metalloporphyrins, the porphin skeleton (Fig. 1) is nearly planar with the manganese(III) atom displaced 0.09 A toward the coordinated azide. While the manganese-porphin nitrogen bond lengths are normal, the axial bond lengths are substantially lengthened, by 0.2−0.3 A, from that expected for a manganese-azide nitrogen and manganese-methanol oxygen bond. Only one other manganese-porphyrin solid-state structure has been determined, for [Mn(TPP)Cl]. In contrast to the azide complex, this complex is five-coordinate and shows a square pyramidal stereochemistry. The bond structure (C—C, C—N) of the porphin skeleton is not planar but distorted (ruffled) in such a way that the C and N atoms are alternately above and below the hypothetical plane of the porphin. The manganese atom is displaced from the basal plane by 0.27 A toward the axial chloride ion. The chloride ion manganese(III) bond length is normal, that is, the sum of the ionic radii. Thus salient structural features for five- and six-coordinate stereochemistry for manganese porphyrins emerge: complexes that are crystallized from noncoordinating solvents give five-coordinate square pyramidal complexes, with the metal atom substantially out of the plane of the porphin macrocycle, and a normal metal ion−axial anion bond length. Conversely, complexes crystallized from coordinating solvents give six-coordinate com-

pounds with the metal ion more nearly in the plane of the porphin macrocycle and long bonds to the axially bound groups. It is significant that these stereochemical changes occur without spin pairing of the four unpaired d electrons of manganese(III). In contrast to this the iron(III) porphyrins show spin pairing concomitant with a similar change in stereochemistry.

Bonding. Characterization of the unusual electronic absorption spectrum of [Mn(TPP)Cl] has been carried out by observation of visible-ultraviolet absorption and magnetic circular dichroism spectra, and by theoretical molecular orbital calculations. The observed electronic transitions have been quantitatively accounted for by invoking configuration interaction of porphin triplet and singlet (π,π^*) states and porphin to metal charge transfer (π,$d\pi$) excited states. The theoretical calculations support the notion that appreciable delocalization of the metal $d\pi$ electrons into the empty porphin π^* orbital occurs. Qualitatively the manganese-porphin bonding can be described as synergic, that is, strong sigma donation from the porphin to the metal and substantial back π bonding from the metal to the porphin.

Catalytic activity. The chemical oxidation of hydroxo(hematoporphyrin-IX) manganese(III) in strong base with aqueous hypochlorite ion yields a species which has not been fully characterized, but is postulated to be a manganese(IV) complex, [Mn(Hpor)(OH)$_2$]. It must be pointed out that electrochemical measurements on nonaqueous aprotic solvent solutions of manganese(III) porphyrins have shown that the porphyrin ligand is oxidized first and that there is no evidence for the formation of a manganese(IV) species. Nonetheless, the hypochlorite oxidation product converts to the original manganese(III) complex with the production of hydrogen peroxide. The formation of oxygen in this reaction has not been proved. The pH-rate profile, which shows an increasing rate with decreasing pH, indicates that four uncharacterized species, which are related by rapid proton equilibria, are involved in the reaction. The results show that the so-called manganese(IV) porphyrins can effectively oxidize water at pH 9 or below. This work is of some relevance to the possible function of a manganese porphyrin in photosynthesis since it is the first demonstration that a higher oxidation state of a manganese porphyrin can function as a redox catalyst. However, the structure of the catalyst is not yet determined.

For background information *see* CHLOROPHYLL; HEMOGLOBIN; PORPHYRIN in the McGraw-Hill Encyclopedia of Science and Technology.

[LAURENCE J. BOUCHER]

Bibliography: A. Adler (ed.), *Ann. N.Y. Acad. Sci.*, vol. 206, 1973; J. P. Collman et al., *Proc. Nat. Acad. Sci., U.S.*, 71:1326, 1974; V. W. Day et al., *J. Amer. Chem. Soc.*, 96:2650, 1974; P. Hambright, in K. B. Smith (ed.), *Porphyrins and Metalloporphyrins*, vol. 2, 1975; P. Hambright and P. B. Chock, *J. Amer. Chem. Soc.*, 96:3123, 1974; R. G. Hancock and K. Fritze, *Bioinorganic Chemistry*, 3:77, 1973; H. Kobayashi et al., *Bull. Chem. Soc. Jap.*, 46:1471, 1973; P. L. Piciulo, G. Rupprecht, and W. R. Scheidt, *J. Amer. Chem. Soc.*, 96:5293, 1974; W. R. Scheidt, *J. Amer. Chem. Soc.*, 96(84):90, 1974; C. E. Strouse, *Proc. Nat. Acad. Sci., U.S.*, 71:325, 1974; I. Tabushi and S. Kojo, *Tetrahedron Lett.*, vol. 1577, 1974.

Printing plate

Magnesium printing plates have been used in the graphic arts industry for many years. During the past 3 years, the use of magnesium has increased to such an extent that it is currently the principal metal in the letterpress plate industry. This rapid growth has been due to a number of production and environmental requirements that have recently become significant. These requirements are speed of reproduction, pollution control, and, of course, economics.

Photocomposition, the production of entire pages photographically, has substantially replaced the traditional "hot-type" method using Linotype. This shift in operations created unforeseen demands in page production. Speed in producing the original engravings was the key requirement, if production demands were to be met. It was achieved by combining a new high-speed chemistry for etching magnesium that was introduced by Mona Industries, Inc., with a uniform-quality, ultraviolet-light-sensitive coated magnesium plate produced by the Dow Chemical Company.

New high-speed ultraviolet exposure units and automated developing units that "print" the actual characters and pictures on the metal surface also added the capability needed for plate production. The equipment and the chemistry made it possible for engravings to be produced at from two to four times the former rate without substantially increasing the labor force.

Environmental restrictions. Environmental regulations had to be considered, and pollution-abatement methods put into effect, if the engraving method was to be feasible. Prior to the shift to magnesium, zinc was the principal metal used for photoengraving. Zinc, however, causes pollution, for the quantities of the salt produced by the reaction of nitric acid (the actual etchant) and zinc are far above acceptable effluent levels. The salt had to be removed by a precipitation method, and separate, costly disposal effected, to solve the problem. This is not the case for magnesium. Neither the metal nor its salt, magnesium nitrate, is considered a pollutant.

Another aspect of pollution revolved around the fact that all previous chemicals used in photoengraving zinc and magnesium plates contained substantial concentrations of a petroleum hydrocarbon solvent. This solvent is considered a serious pollutant and must be removed prior to disposal. Again, the industry was faced with a costly disposal problem. The new high-speed, high-quality magnesium etching additives do not contain any polluting solvents; since they are biodegradable, they do not contribute to pollution.

Economics. As expected, the final consideration in the conversion from zinc to magnesium was economy. The need to have a better product at an equal cost—or, at least, a product of equal quality at a lower cost—was a major factor in evaluation.

Magnesium plates or sheets cost the same as or less than zinc plates. The new high-speed, nonpolluting chemistries, however, produce better results at a considerable reduction in cost.

Further economic advantages manifest themselves in a variety of unforeseen ways. The stability of the chemical system allows three to four times the number of pages to be engraved without resetting the system. The higher operating speed results in a greater output in an equal time. The nonpolluting aspects eliminate separation or treatment processes for either the metal or the chemicals. And finally—an immeasurable but vastly important consideration insofar as labor is concerned—the fact that magnesium is four times lighter than zinc influences the output of the workers and results in increased productivity.

Production sequence. A typical sequence in producing a single newspaper page is described below, in order to illustrate the importance of speed in the production of the engraved plate.

A story or advertisement is received in the editorial department, and a determination of its news value is made. A decision is made concerning the size of the article and the lead or caption size, page, and position on the page. Then, in the production department, the editorial information and the text are "typed" onto a punch tape or computer tape. In the newest systems, a video screen flashes the "typing" so that corrections can be made prior to entering the information into the computer.

The computer then "reads" the tape and converts the information into electronic signals to a phototypesetter that exposes each character of the story onto a photographic paper in the size that it will be in the newspaper. The computer also hypenates words and spaces each line of each column as it sends its signals. The exposed photographic paper is then developed, trimmed, and pasted onto a board equal in size to the newspaper page. When all the stories, advertisements, and pictures have been pasted in place, the full page is reproduced in negative form on a "copy" camera. The negative is then processed, placed on top of an ultraviolet-light-sensitive coated magnesium plate, and "printed" onto the surface of the metal. The printed magnesium sheet is developed, etched in the high-speed chemistry, and trimmed to actual page size. It can then be used directly on the press or duplicated by casting lead semicylinders from a matrix obtained from the original engraving. The matrix and lead casting system is generally used when hundreds of thousands of copies of a page must be printed. The entire process from editorial entry to printed page is accomplished in less than 2 hr.

For background information *see* MAGNESIUM; PRINTING PLATE in the McGraw-Hill Encyclopedia of Science and Technology.

[HAROLD J. MESSERSCHMIDT]

Printing press

The use of printing inks with volatile solvents requires that the printed paper pass through a gas-fired hot-air dryer to dry or set the ink. About 30% of the solvent in the ink is exhausted through the

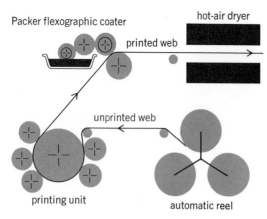

Fig. 1. Press coating arrangement on a hoe five-color letterpress.

stack of the dryer and contributes to atmospheric pollution. With the energy crisis, the use of gas for the drying process has also become a problem. Printing technologists have therefore been studying other ink formulations and other methods of setting the ink on the paper. A recent development, called press coating, is a printing system that appears to be both nonpolluting and energy-conserving.

Available technology. One approach to the problem is to use a conventional ink with an abatement device such as an afterburner; energy shortages make this approach unfeasible. Low-solvent-content heat-set inks are a possible answer to reducing the amount of emission to the atmosphere. Low-odor, low-smoke inks emit less objectionable fumes. Thermally catalyzed inks are being used; but they are costly, some effluent is generated, and the dried ink film may not de-ink.

Finally, ultraviolet-cured ink (uv ink) has been tried by a fairly large number of printers (approximately 43 web printers as of July 1, 1974). The uv inks do not liberate materials to the atmosphere. They are essentially monomethyl methacrylates, which dry by polymerization. The source of energy that causes this curing or polymerization is a high-pressure, high-uv lamp. The wet ink is dried instantaneously as it passes beneath the lamps. To date, the method has been used only on offset presses. The uv inks are several times the cost of conventional inks; lamp installation and replacement costs are high; and some problems have been encountered in recycling the printed paper.

In addition to the changes described above in the nature of the inks, attempts have been made to remove the exhaust fumes generated by drying conventional heat-set or solvent-type inks. One method is to absorb the fumes in a large bed of activated carbon. To accomplish this, the exhaust from the dryers must be cooled to 200°F (93°C), or lower. This cooling may be done by air or by water. The carbon can be recycled periodically, and the absorbed exhaust solvents can be sold or used as fuel. One disadvantage is that the cost of cooling the large volumes of exhaust might be prohibitive.

Another method being tried is to spray chemicals in the exhaust stack, thus causing the fumes to conglomerate or dissolve. They are removed as a caustic sludge that is neutralized before it goes to the sewer.

A third method for removing the exhaust is to pass the "cooled-down" stack gases through an electrostatic precipitator. Trials using this method have been fairly successful. There is no visible emission from the precipitator, but there is some odor that is not detectable at the property line.

A system has also been discussed that is similar in many respects to uv drying in that it involves the conversion of a monomeric ink to a polymeric ink. The system uses an electron beam or a large radio tube. The printed paper is bombarded by electrons supplied by an accelerated emission cathode; both sides of the web can be cured at the same time.

Press coating. In this printing system all the ink components are retained on the paper instead of being released into the atmosphere (Fig. 1). In 1954 J. P. Costello obtained a patent for a method to protect wet ink films on printed surfaces, and in 1965 Inmont Corporation developed an aqueous sealer for wet ink called Project GROW. These two processes did essentially what press coating is attempting to do, but for different reasons, for at that time there was little or no thought given to environmental-control measures.

Calling "press coating" a printing system means that there are a number of parts that must work together to produce on paper a desirable film of ink that can be handled immediately after printing and that will enhance the quality of the print rather than detract from it. The parts of the system are paper, ink, coating, press, coater, and coating drying mechanism.

The paper used in the press coating system should have a smooth surface and should be cap-

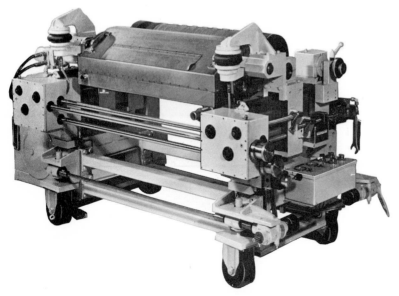

Fig. 2. The Packer flexographic coater, which applies coating over the ink.

able of good runability and printability in the process used (letterpress or offset lithography). Experiments with uncoated paper have been unsuccessful, for press coating makes the finished product look like a coated paper.

Inks used in the press coating process should contain a minimum amount of hydrocarbons. Successful recent experiments have used oxidative oil-type inks containing no hydrocarbons. The inks should contain no waxes, oils, or silicones, which would disturb the bond of the coating material. In addition, the inks should produce good dot formation, trap well, and contain no ingredients that would bleed or be leached out when the coating is applied.

The press coating should be applicable to a wet film of ink without causing it to bleed or mark, and it must protect the wet ink as the web of paper travels through the press, impression, and folder. The press coating should impart protection, attractiveness, and gloss (if desired) to the overall page, both the printed and nonprinted areas, without adding excessive weight to the paper. It should be economical and repulpable so that the paper can be recycled. A number of coatings, water-based and solvent-based, have been tried. One very promising material is a cellulose derivative (alcohol-soluble propionate) manufactured by Eastman Chemical Company. A completely different approach being considered is to use a uv-cured coating over conventional inks and to cure the coating with uv lamps.

Several types of coaters have been tried so that the coating can be applied over the wet ink without disturbing it. The Packer flexographic coater (Fig. 2) has been used most often. However, an Inta-Roto gravure-type coater and a Dahlgren liquid application system have also been tried with some success. Web speeds have been as high as 1600 ft (488 m) per minute in the test runs on the coaters, and the film thickness of about 0.05 mil (0.127×10^{-5} m) seems adequate.

In conclusion, the economic feasibility of developing press coating with the goal of reducing air pollution must still be proved. Tests on printing presses at Meredith Printing have shown that, in principle, the printing press–press coating system can work; however, much remains to be done in perfecting the process.

For background information see INK; PRINTING in the McGraw-Hill Encyclopedia of Science and Technology.

[WILLIAM A. ROCAP, JR.]

Bibliography: W. A. Rocap, Jr., in G. A. Mattson (ed.), Proceedings of the 1973 Printing Industries of America Web-Offset Section, pp. 28–34, May 1973; W. A. Rocap, Jr., Print. Manage. Mag., 104(1):32–33, 1973, and 104(8):46–48, 1974; W. A. Rocap, Jr., in H. Spencer (ed.), The Penrose Annual, p. 199, 1973.

Quarks

The constituents of heretofore "elementary" particles have been termed quarks. Although theories using the quark concept have been generally successful in predicting many properties of these proposed particles, experiments have thus far failed to detect them. Now, three new quark-search experiments at the highest-energy particle accelerators have again given negative results.

Background. In 1961 physicists noted that many properties of hadrons, or strongly interacting elementary particles, could be understood if it were assumed that they were made up of internal constituents named quarks. M. Gell-Mann and G. Zweig independently conceived of quarks as particles of electrical charge $\pm^{1}/_{3}$ or $\pm^{2}/_{3}$ on an electron that, in combinations of two or three, would form all known baryons (the proton, neutron, excited nucleons or nucleon isobars, and hyperons) and mesons (pions, kaons, as well as the rho, eta, omega, and others). In the late 1950s and early 1960s a bewildering array of elementary particles were discovered, totaling more than 50 mesons and more than 100 baryons. Gell-Mann, K. Nishijima, and others observed that these particles could be arranged logically into multiplets, with each multiplet possessing a common set of characteristics but with different members of each multiplet possessing different electrical charge or different values of hypercharge (or strangeness) or both. This symmetry scheme could be given physical substance if it were assumed that there exist three kinds of quarks, together with their respective antiquarks, with quantum numbers as noted in the table. Protons and other baryons were then understood as combinations of three quarks; antiprotons and the corresponding antibaryons were each made up of three antiquarks; and the various mesons were each composed of a quark-antiquark pair.

Partons. In 1968 experiments carried out at the Stanford Linear Accelerator Center on the deep inelastic scattering of electrons on protons (scattering during which mesons are produced) were interpreted in terms of the scattering not on the proton as a whole, but on internal constituents of the proton that R. P. Feynman and J. D. Bjorken referred to as "partons." Results of later experiments on inelastic muon-proton scattering and on proton-proton collisions were also consistent with this parton concept of proton structure.

It was natural that quarks and partons should be interpreted as different manifestations of the same fundamental entity—the constituents of protons (and other hadrons). Interpretation of the deep inelastic scattering data suggested that there might be more than three partons in the proton. These observations are still self-consistent with the quark model if virtual quark-antiquark pairs are also present in the proton. The outstanding mystery remains: why are quarks not observed as free objects in high-energy collisions? Their fractional electric charge should render them easily detect-

Postulated quark properties

Property	Quarks			Antiquarks		
	u	d	s	$\bar{u}$	$\bar{d}$	$\bar{s}$
Electric charge	$+^{2}/_{3}$	$-^{1}/_{3}$	$-^{1}/_{3}$	$-^{2}/_{3}$	$+^{1}/_{3}$	$+^{1}/_{3}$
Baryon number	$^{1}/_{3}$	$^{1}/_{3}$	$^{1}/_{3}$	$-^{1}/_{3}$	$-^{1}/_{3}$	$-^{1}/_{3}$
Strangeness	0	0	-1	0	0	$+1$
Spin	$^{1}/_{2}$	$^{1}/_{2}$	$^{1}/_{2}$	$^{1}/_{2}$	$^{1}/_{2}$	$^{1}/_{2}$

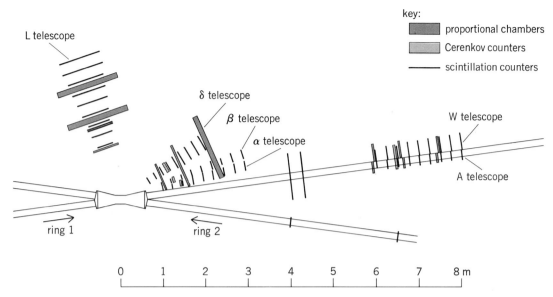

key:
proportional chambers
Cerenkov counters
scintillation counters

Fig. 1. A schematic plan view of the CERN quark experiment at the intersecting storage rings showing six counter "telescopes." *(From M. Bott-Bodenhausen et al., A search for quarks at the CERN intersecting storage rings, Phys. Lett., 40B:693, 1972)*

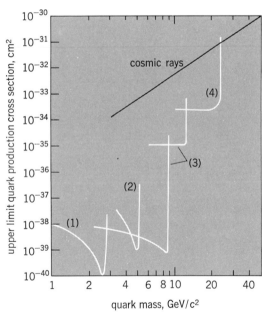

Fig. 2. The upper-limit cross section for production of quarks of charge $-\frac{1}{3}e$ as a function of quark mass from experiments at various particle accelerators and cosmic rays. The particle accelerators are indicated by numbers: (1) CERN 28-GeV proton synchrotron; (2) Serpukov 70-GeV proton synchrotron; (3) 400-GeV synchrotron of the Fermi National Accelerator Laboratory; (4) CERN intersecting storage rings.

able. The reason is that the ionization, and hence the signal, produced by a charged particle of very high energy passing through a detector is proportional to the square of the electric charge. A quark would then give a signal of $\frac{1}{9}$ or $\frac{4}{9}$ that from an electron, proton, meson, or any other known charged particle.

One possible explanation for the failure of experiments to detect quarks would be that their rest mass is so great that searches at particle accelerators have failed to reach the threshold for their production. Alternatively (or in addition), they might be produced so rarely that the quark production cross section might be very low.

Sensitive searches have been made at all high-energy particle accelerators and with cosmic rays. In 1969 positive evidence for quarks was reported from cosmic rays by C. B. A. McCusker of Sidney, Australia, and by some other cosmic-ray groups. Subsequent, more sensitive cosmic-ray experiments have, however, failed to confirm those observations.

Recent accelerator experiments. There have been three recent experiments at particle accelerators. In an experiment at the intersecting storage rings (ISR) of the European Organization for Nuclear Research (CERN), several "telescopes" of scintillation counters, Cerenkov detectors, and multiwire proportional chambers were assembled to search for particles of fractional charge emerging from the proton-proton (p-p) intersection region (Fig. 1). These p-p collisions at 52 GeV in the center of mass (equivalent to a proton of 1500 GeV striking a proton at rest) would be energetically above threshold for the production of quarks in pairs of up to 23-GeV rest mass. No quarks were seen in a flux of 6×10^8 charged secondaries, corresponding to an upper-limit quark production cross section of 2×10^{-34} cm². (The interpretation of the flux data in terms of a cross-section limit depends somewhat on the production model assumed. The lowest-limit cross sections are quoted here.)

The other two experiments were carried out at the synchrotron of the Fermi National Accelerator Laboratory (NAL) near Chicago. Here protons of up to 300 GeV strike a beryllium target, and beams of secondary particles are detected emerging from it. In the first experiment, a Yale University–Brookhaven National Laboratory group used a telescope of scintillation counters to search for particles of fractional electric charge. No quarks were found among 1.4×10^9 negative particles (mesons) corresponding to an upper-limit production cross section of about 10^{-35} cm². With 300-GeV protons incident, this search was sensitive to quarks of up to 12-GeV rest mass. *See* PARTICLE ACCELERATOR.

The second search was made with similar beams over a somewhat longer period of time and with additional detectors. A group of physicists from NAL, Cornell University, and New York University have reported that no quarks were detected in an upper-limit production cross section of 10^{-39} cm² for 9 GeV/c^2 rest mass quarks of $-\frac{1}{3}e$ charge (where e is the magnitude of the charge on an electron, 1.6×10^{-19} coulombs) and 10^{-38} cm² for 11 GeV/c^2 quarks of $-\frac{2}{3}e$ charge.

These recent searches, together with accelerator and cosmic-ray searches reported earlier, are summarized in Fig. 2 for quarks of charge $-\frac{1}{3}e$. In this figure, the area of production cross section–quark mass to the lower right of the curves represents still possible quark production. As quarks are not observed even at very high energy, physicists are now inclined to believe that they may not be heavy objects after all but may have a mass of only $100-500$ MeV/c^2 and that they cannot be observed as free particles. It has also been suggested that they interact through a long-range force that increases with the separation between two quarks. For whatever reason, physicists now generally believe that free quarks will not be found, although each new advance in accelerator energy or intensity will stimulate a new search for quarks.

The puzzle of the internal structure of the proton–and of all other elementary particles–is among the essential challenges on the frontiers of modern science. Quarks may indeed be the essential internal constituents of all hadrons, but without more direct physical evidence for their existence, these theories must remain tenuous. The puzzle persists.

For background information *see* BARYON; ELEMENTARY PARTICLE; MESON; QUARKS; SYMMETRY LAW (PHYSICS) in the McGraw-Hill Encyclopedia of Science and Technology.

[LAWRENCE W. JONES]

Bibliography: M. Bott-Bodenhausen et al., *Phys. Lett.*, 40B:693, 1972; R. P. Feynman, *Science*, 183:601, 1974; L. W. Jones, *Phys. Today*, 26(5):30, 1973; L. B. Leipuner et al., *Phys. Rev. Lett.*, 31:1226, 1973; T. Nash et al., *Phys. Rev. Lett.*, 32:858, 1974.

Radar

Lasers have been used in radar-type applications to precisely measure the range from the Earth to the Moon. They have also provided precision range, velocity, and angle tracking to microwave radars. Lasers have been utilized at a variety of wavelengths, from the ultraviolet at the short-wavelength region of the electromagnetic spectrum, to the far-infrared at the long-wavelength region of the optical spectrum.

Although a large number of lasers with wave-

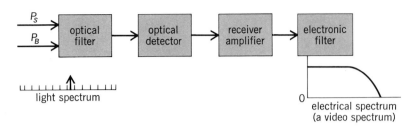

Fig. 1. Block diagram of an incoherent detection receiver.

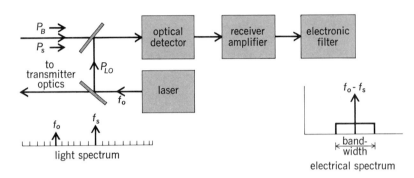

Fig. 2. Block diagram of a coherent detection receiver.

lengths spanning virtually this entire optical spectrum have been invented, laser radar systems commonly have been designed to utilize those wavelengths where the atmosphere tends to be more transparent and where significant laser output energy exists. Atmospheric transmission bands include the ultraviolet (10^{-4} to 0.4 micrometer), visible (0.4 to 0.7 μm), near-infrared (0.7 to 2.5 μm), mid-infrared (3 to 5 μm), and far-infrared (8 to 14 μm).

Detection techniques. Early laser radars were designed to be operated in the visible wavelength region and utilized the argon gas laser (0.5 μm) and the ruby laser (0.7 μm). Present-day systems tend to operate in the infrared radiation band, and popular laser sources are the gallium arsenide semiconductor laser (0.9 μm), the yttrium-aluminum-garnet (YAG) solid-state laser (1.06 μm), and the carbon dioxide gaseous laser (10.6 μm). Detection techniques utilized with these lasers are similar to those developed in the microwave portion of the electromagnetic spectrum. Both incoherent and coherent detection techniques, illustrated in Figs. 1 and 2, are employed. In the incoherent detection system (Fig. 1) a desired signal P_s is received from a target along with a noise signal due to some background noise radiation P_B, such as the Sun or other undesired noise-type source. These two signals are passed through an optical filter to allow optical discrimination of the undesired background source. Energy is then optically detected in a square-law detector. The output of this detector is a video-type spectrum signal, that is, one having a response extending from a low value up to some high value. This is the signal which is observed in the receiver output. The coherent detection receiver (Fig. 2) utilizes a portion of the transmitting source to provide a reference signal P_{LO} at the detector. The transmitted signal f_o is propagated to the target, where it may be Doppler-shifted in fre-

Comparison of Doppler-shift frequencies for conventional and laser radars

Transmitter	Wavelength, cm	Frequency, GHz	Doppler shift/fps, Hz
Radar	1	30	61
CO_2 laser	1.06×10^{-3}	28,300	57,500
YAG laser	1.06×10^{-4}	283,000	575,000
Ruby laser	0.6943×10^{-4}	431,800	878,000

quency by a target velocity. This results in a signal P_s at the receiver, having a frequency f_s dependent upon the target's motion, in addition to the undesired background noise P_B. The three signals P_s, P_B, and P_{LO} are then mixed in an optical detector to yield a signal $(f_o - f_s)$ corresponding to the target's velocity.

Laser radar capabilities. The ability of laser systems to operate in radar-type system applications is dependent upon the laser's potential capability to provide ranging, angle tracking, and velocity measurement. These are the facilities which are normally required of microwave systems.

Angle tracking. The diffraction limited beam width θ of a transmitting source with an aperture diameter D and a wavelength λ is $\theta \approx \lambda/D$. If an antenna with an aperture diameter of 1 ft (30 cm) is operating at a wavelength of 1 cm, the radar will have a beam width of approximately 2°. Operating in the optical spectrum results in the same aperture size providing beam widths 1/1000 to 1/10,000 times smaller than that of the microwave system. This resultant smaller beam width is utilized to

provide increased angular tracking precision capability. However, because the laser beams are so narrow, long acquisition time is required if search volumes are large. Because of this limitation, laser sensors are coupled to acquisition systems in order to reduce search times to practical sizes.

Target velocity. The ability of a radar system to sense target velocities by use of the Doppler principle may be expressed by the equation shown,

$$F_D = \frac{2V}{\lambda} \cos \gamma$$

where V = relative target velocity, λ = transmission wavelength, γ = angle between the propagation vector and target velocity vector. Because of the shorter operating wavelengths associated with lasers, the Doppler-shift frequency F_D from a target is significantly increased and, as a result, there are more cycles of Doppler shift for each foot per second (fps) of target motion (see table). As a result of this increased accentuation of the Doppler shift, target velocities may be measured instantaneously with more accuracy.

Ranging. Range measurement capability is directly related to the pulse width of the source. Pulse widths of laser sources tend to be very short, and typical values are in the order of 30 nanoseconds; as a result, range measurement precision to 1-m accuracy is common.

System description. From the foregoing evaluation, one may observe that laser radar systems are employed in those areas where more accurate ranging information is required, where better velocity measurements of target motion are necessary, or where more precision is required to locate a target in direction. To this end, a number of laser

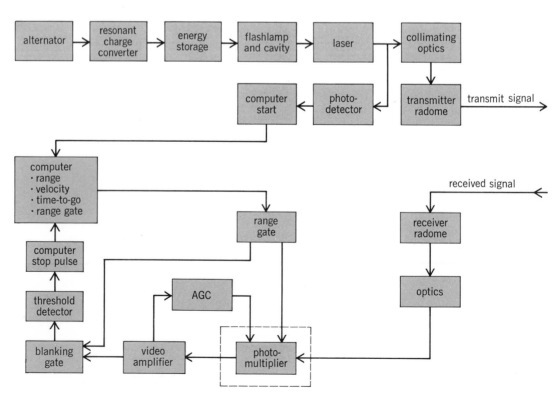

Fig. 3. Block diagram of a typical laser range finder.

Fig. 4. Laser radar mounted to a microwave radar acquisition and tracking system. (*Raytheon Company Equipment Division, Sudbury, MA*)

radar systems have been built employing any or all of these features. A block diagram of a typical laser range finder is shown in Fig. 3. Here energy stored in a charging network is utilized to trigger a flashlamp inside a laser cavity. The light emitted by the flashlamp in turn causes the laser to emit radiation. A small portion of the laser energy is detected by a photodetector, which is utilized to start an elapsed-time computer. Most of the energy emitted from the laser, in the form of photons, is directed through the optical system, propagated to the target and back, and collected by a receiving telescope. The collected photons are then applied to an optical detector, where the light energy is converted to an electrical signal. After suitable processing, the electrical signal is detected and utilized to generate a computer stop pulse. Inasmuch as the computer counting capability is accurately known, the time between start and stop of laser signals is used to provide an accurate range indication.

Figure 4 illustrates an incoherent detection laser system. It appears in the foreground, mounted to a microwave radar acquisition and tracking system. In this configuration, the microwave radar searches through a large volume to acquire and track targets of interest. When additional precision is required, the range and angle measurement capability of the laser system is employed to search out the footprint of the microwave radar beam. In this way, the antenna size of the microwave system remains a practical size, and the wavelength advantages that laser beams provide are utilized to improve the performance of existing microwave pointing and tracking systems.

Meteorological applications. Continuous-wave and pulse Doppler laser radar systems, utilizing the high efficiency and coherence of the 10.6 μm CO_2 lasers, have been designed to remotely measure atmospheric turbulence and wind velocities. In these systems a beam of 10.6-μm radiation is propagated into the atmosphere containing aerosols, or particulate matter. The illuminated particles shift the frequency of the laser beam, by the Doppler effect, and scatter energy back to a receiving telescope. The collected backscatter energy is then coherently detected, as illustrated in Fig. 2, to produce a Doppler frequency spectrum having a mean value proportional to the wind velocity and a Doppler spectrum width proportional to the turbulence level. Optical focusing or electronic modulation is employed to determine the range to the atmosphere being sampled. Future systems are envisioned which can be utilized to augment weather radar capabilities.

For background information *see* LASER; RADAR in the McGraw-Hill Encyclopedia of Science and Technology.

[ALBERT V. JELALIAN]

Bibliography: D. W. Coffey and V. J. Norris, *Appl. Optics*, 11(5):1013–1018, May 1972; A. V. Jelalian, IR laser Doppler radar systems for the remote detection of atmospheric turbulence, *Conference Proceedings of the Optical Society of America*, Spring 1974; C. G. Lehr et al., *Appl. Optics*, 12(5):946–947, May 1973; M. Ross, *Laser Applications*, vol. 2, 1974.

Radioactive waste disposal

The current policy of the U.S. Atomic Energy Commission is to assume custody of all commercial high-level radioactive wastes and to provide containment and isolation of them in perpetuity. This policy requires that the high-level wastes from nuclear fuels reprocessing plants be solidified within 5 years after reprocessing and then shipped to a federal repository within 10 years after reprocessing.

Ultimate disposal sites or methods have not yet been selected and are not expected to be ready when waste deliveries begin about 1983. Therefore the AEC is studying the use of an interim storage facility, called the Retrievable Surface Storage Facility, to store and isolate the waste from humans and their environment until the suitability of the permanent repository is demonstrated and public acceptance has been established.

During 1974, initial results of AEC studies of options to manage high-level waste from commercial nuclear power operations were released. These studies, still in progress, define a broad range of options for long-term management.

Fuel discharged from the nuclear reactor is reprocessed to recover uranium and plutonium by chemical dissolution and treatment. Current processes form high-level waste as an acidic aqueous stream. Other processes being considered would produce high-level waste in different forms. This high-level waste contains most of the reactor-produced fission products and actinides, with slight residues of the uranium and plutonium (see Table 1.) These waste products generate sufficient heat to require substantial cooling, and they emit large amounts of potentially hazardous ionizing radiation.

Quantity of waste. The growth of nuclear power in the United States will result in increased quantities of high-level waste. Installed nuclear electrical generating capacity is projected, according to an AEC Office of Planning and Analysis study, to

Table 1. Typical materials in high-level liquid waste

	Grams per metric ton from various reactor types[a]		
Material[b]	Light water reactor[c]	High-temperature gas-cooled reactor[d]	Liquid metal fast breeder reactor[e]
Reprocessing chemicals			
Hydrogen	400	3800	1300
Iron	1100	1500	26,200
Nickel	100	400	3300
Chromium	200	300	6900
Silicon	–	200	–
Lithium	–	200	–
Boron	–	1000	–
Molybdenum	–	40	–
Aluminum	–	6400	–
Copper	–	40	–
Borate	–	–	98,000
Nitrate	65,800	435,000	244,000
Phosphate	900	–	–
Sulfate	–	1100	–
Fluoride	–	1900	–
SUBTOTAL	68,500	452,000	380,000
Fuel product losses[f,g]			
Uranium	4800	250	4300
Thorium	–	4200	–
Plutonium	40	1000	500
SUBTOTAL	4840	5450	4800
Transuranic elements[g]			
Neptunium	480	1400	260
Americium	140	30	1250
Curium	40	10	50
SUBTOTAL	660	1440	1560
Other actinides[g]	<0.001	20	<0.001
Total fission products[h]	28,800	79,400	33,000
TOTAL	103,000	538,000	419,000

SOURCE: From K. J. Schneider and A. M. Platt (eds.), *Advanced Waste Management Studies: High-Level Radioactive Waste Disposal Alternatives*, USAEC Rep. BNWL-1900, May 1974.

[a]Water content is not shown; all quantities are rounded.

[b]Most constituents are present in soluble, ionic form.

[c]U-235 enriched pressurized water reactor (PWR), using 378 liters of aqueous waste per metric ton, 33,000 MWd/MT exposure. (Integrated reactor power is expressed in megawatt-days [MWd] per unit of fuel in metric tons [MT].)

[d]Combined waste from separate reprocessing of "fresh" fuel and fertile particles, using 3785 liters of aqueous waste per metric ton, 94,200 MWd/MT exposure.

[e]Mixed core and blanket, with boron as soluble poison, 10% of cladding dissolved, 1249 liters per metric ton, 37,100 MWd/MT average exposure.

[f]0.5% product loss to waste.

[g]At time of reprocessing.

[h]Volatile fission products (tritium, noble gases, iodine, and bromine) excluded.

increase from about 25,000 MW in 1974 to about 1,200,000 MW by the year 2000. The anticipated volume of solidified high-level waste accumulated from now until the year 2000 is about 13,000 m³, the result of reprocessing almost 200,000 metric tons of fuel, about 80% of which is associated with light water reactor (LWR) plants. If this amount of solid waste were stacked as a solid cube, the cube would be about 25 m on a side. Approximately 150,000 megacuries (5.5×10^{21} disintegrations per second) of radioactivity and 700 MW of heat will be associated with this projected waste inventory in the year 2000. This heat content is equivalent to about one-third of the waste heat rejected from one LWR generating 1000 MW of electricity.

Table 2 shows the projected accumulation of solidified high-level waste in future years, assuming that 0.5% of the fuel product (uranium and plutonium or thorium) is lost to waste during reprocessing, and that all other actinides are in the waste. The toxicity indices in Table 2 are base 10 logarithms of the quantity in cubic meters of air, for the inhalation index, or in cubic meters of water, for the ingestion hazard index, required to dilute radioactive material to limits stipulated in federal regulations. Beyond the year 2000, fission products (primarily strontium) and transplutonium elements (primarily americium) are the chief potential hazards in drinking water up to about 350 years and 2×10^4 years, respectively. Radioactivity from plutonium losses during reprocessing then becomes the main factor until about 10^6 years. Finally, radioactivity remaining as the result of uranium losses during reprocessing becomes the predominant contribution to the ingestion toxicity index.

Alternative waste management concepts.
Scientists are investigating many of the options for separating, treating, and otherwise managing radioactive waste from the time the material is formed in a fission reactor. Key considerations in the route to ultimate disposal or elimination of the material are outlined in the illustration.

Constituents of the waste material are a mix of long- and short-lived radioisotopes. Some have radioactive decay half-lives of no more than tens of years, while others must be isolated from the biosphere for thousands upon thousands of years. By dividing the high-level waste into actinides and fission products (a process called partitioning), the materials can be managed as separate classes.

Present regulations require that liquid high-level waste be converted to a solid material within 5 years after fuel reprocessing. The material is then to be encapsulated and shipped to a federal repository within 10 years of its production for long-term management by the AEC. Solidification processes (known as waste fixation) under current development include methods for incorporating the radioactive waste into glasslike or ceramic materials of low solubility. These silicate solids can be formed within various containments.

Common to all waste management–disposal concepts is the probability of interim storage in a retrievable surface storage facility. Three concepts are under study for the facility to be built by the AEC—a water basin concept, an air-cooled vault concept, and a concept for storage of wastes in sealed casks in the open air. The major differences between these proposals are in radiation shields, containment barriers, heat removal techniques, and relative dependence on utilities and maintenance. The canisters of solidified waste would be retrievable at all times for various waste management options or treatment by future techniques of disposal.

Many short-lived waste components will decay to unimportant radioactivity levels in relatively short periods of time. Their storage in artificial structures can be considered. For the longer-lived

Table 2.   Projected accumulation of solidified high-level waste through end of year, 1975–2000

Fiscal year	Volume[a] of waste, m³	Actinide mass, metric tons	Radio-activity,[b,c] MCi[d]	Thermal power,[b,c] MW	Toxicity indices[b,c]	
					Inhalation	Ingestion
1975	30	3	700	3	18.78	14.04
1980	550	50	10,200	50	20.26	15.38
1985	1720	190	26,300	140	21.30	15.85
1990	3900	410	50,300	250	21.59	16.18
1995	7650	760	90,500	420	21.71	16.48
2000	13,340	1270	149,000	660	21.86	16.70
Time elapsed after year 2000, years						
10^2			5700	20	21.29	15.55
10^3			30	<1	20.19	12.74
10^4			10	<1	19.70	12.14
10^5			4	<1	18.79	12.38
10^6			1	<1	18.60	11.86

SOURCE: From K. J. Schneider and A. M. Platt (eds.), *Advanced Waste Management Studies: High-Level Radioactive Waste Disposal Alternatives*, USAEC Rep. BNWL-1900, May 1974.

[a]Volume based on 0.057, 0.170, and 0.085 m³ of solidified waste per metric ton of heavy metal for LWR, high-temperature gas-cooled reactor (HTGR), and liquid-metal fast breeder reactor (LMFBR) fuels, respectively.

[b]Waste initially generated 150, 365, and 90 days after spent fuel discharged from LWR, HTGR, and LMFBR units, respectively.

[c]All tritium and noble-gas fission products and 99.9% of iodine and bromine fission products excluded.

[d]1 megacurie (MCi) = 3.7×10^{16} disintegrations per second.

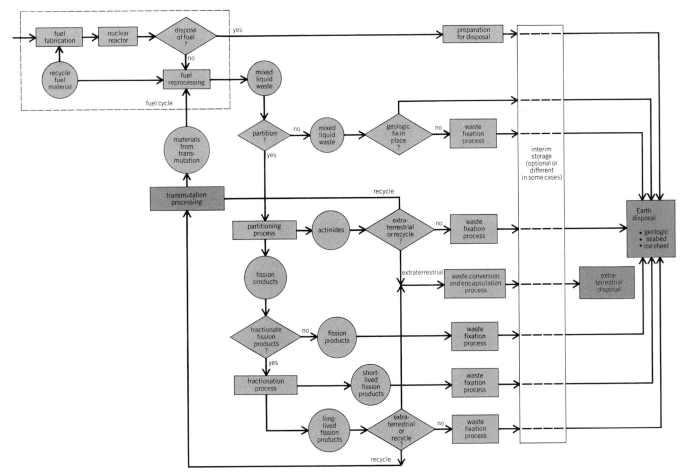

High-level radioactive waste management options. (*K. J. Schneider and A. M. Platt, eds., Advanced Waste Management Studies: High-Level Radioactive Waste Disposal Alternatives, USAEC Rep. BNWL-1900, May 1974*)

and highly toxic actinide fraction of radioactive waste, there appear to be only three basic management options: elimination of waste constituents by transmutation—the conversion to other, less undesirable isotopes by nuclear processes; transport off the Earth; and isolation from the human environment somewhere on Earth for periods of time sufficient to permit natural radioactive decay.

These potential alternative methods for long-term management of high-level radioactive waste provide the framework for a major study by the AEC's Division of Waste Management and Transportation. Included in the comprehensive review is a compilation of information relevant to the technical feasibility; the safety, cost, environmental, and policy considerations; the public response; and research and development needs for various waste management alternatives.

The basic requirement for the suitability of any environment for disposal of radioactive waste is its capability to safely contain and isolate it until decay has reduced the radioactivity to nonhazardous levels. Geologic formations exist which have been physically and chemically stable for millions of years. Ice sheets appear to offer some potential advantages as a disposal medium remote from the human environment. Both are under study as a potential future alternative. In the ice sheet disposal concept, a waste canister would either melt down through the ice sheet to bedrock, or be connected to the surface by cables or chains which would stop its descent through the ice, or be placed in a surface storage facility which would gradually become covered with snow and buried in the ice sheet. Bedrock zones in stable areas of the deep sea floor are the subject of another study concept, as is the process of tectonic plate movement which should carry waste material down into the Earth's mantle from areas known as subduction zones. Also under study is storage in bedrock beneath high-sedimentation-rate areas where major rivers are building deltas into the ocean. Although very high costs per unit of weight would be encountered, an in-depth analysis of extraterrestrial disposal is under way. Also being assessed for possible future applications are nuclear techniques for transmutation of the actinides to isotopes having lower toxicity or shorter half-lives or both.

For background information *see* NUCLEAR FUELS REPROCESSING; RADIOACTIVE WASTE DISPOSAL in the McGraw-Hill Encyclopedia of Science and Technology.   [ALLISON M. PLATT]

Bibliography: *Draft Environmental Statement: Management of Commercial High-Level and Transuranium-Contaminated Radioactive Waste*, USAEC Rep. WASH-1539, September 1974; K. J. Schneider and A. M. Platt (eds.), *Advanced Waste Management Studies: High-Level Radioactive Waste Disposal Alternatives*, USAEC Rep. BNWL-1900, May 1974.

Radiocarbon dating

New developments in radiocarbon (C[14]) dating were reported at the 8th International Conference on Radiocarbon Dating held in New Zealand in October 1972. Noteworthy were expansions into many new fields and the intensification of applications in fields where the process had been used previously. A brief account of the proceedings follows.

Secular variations. Changes in geomagnetism seem to be the major cause of variations in atmospheric C[14], although other factors, such as climatic changes and sunspot activity, must be considered. Major contributions were made in the recalibration of C[14] dates on the basis of precisely dated wood samples reaching to 6200 B.C.

Laboratory improvements. Improvements in analytical techniques include the use of a combustion "bomb" in place of the conventional furnace, solid-state electronic components in place of vacuum tubes, controlled use of solvents to extract organic materials, improved catalysts for scintillation counting, and a mobile archeological C[14] laboratory.

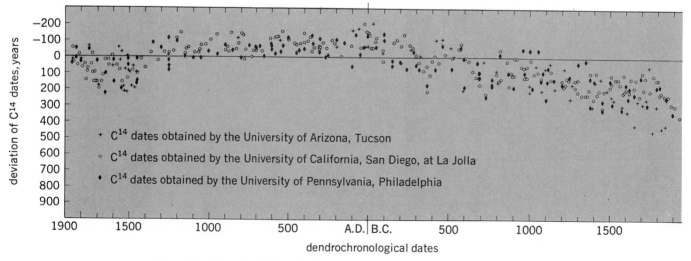

Fig. 1. Deviation of C[14] dates of various wood samples from precise dates obtained by tree-ring chronology. (*From H. N. Michael and E. K. Ralph, Discussion of radiocarbon dates obtained from precisely dated sequoia and bristlecone pine samples, in T. A. Rafter and T. Grant-Taylor, eds., Proceedings of the 8th International Conference on Radiocarbon Dating, 1:27–43, March 1973*)

C¹⁴ and water. An important development concerning C¹⁴ variations in the oceans is the establishment of a Geochemical Ocean Sections Program which, besides providing physical and chemical data on water samples, will establish the time scale of the mixing processes in deep oceans.

C¹⁴ exchange rates between the atmosphere and the ocean have been recalculated and used to estimate exchange times between surface and deep ocean. These were found to be much shorter than thought previously.

The slow decrease in the excess artificial (bomb) C¹⁴ in the atmosphere following the nuclear test ban treaty is being monitored in both hemispheres, as well as the changes in C¹⁴ content of surface ocean waters. Other studies involve the C¹⁴ dating of relatively recent sediments in the western Baltic Sea, the effects of solution and exchange on C¹⁴ dating of sediments and natural waters, and an important report on the differential latitudinal uptake of bomb-produced C¹⁴ by the surface waters of the Pacific.

The C¹⁴ measurements of recent samples (affected by atmospheric nuclear explosions) of water and aqueous plants indicate that these are in equilibrium, with a lag of a few years between atmosphere and water and between water and surface sediment. The latter, however, is influenced by a number of factors.

C¹⁴ activity has served as an indicator of pollution in rivers and lakes. In another study it has helped to determine the age of Hot Springs, AR, waters (4600 years before present) and adjacent cold spring waters (9000 years before present). Geologic variations in permeability along the length of flow paths may explain these age differences.

Major climatic variations occurring, for instance, during the postglacial altithermal or at the onset of the last glaciation are suggested by C¹⁴ dating of accumulations of pedogenic carbonates at different depths. The understanding of pedogenic carbonate formation will greatly enhance knowledge of the dilution factor of groundwaters.

Radiocarbon in soil. The application of the C¹⁴ method to soil development is a new field based upon the increase of atmospheric C¹⁴ from nuclear explosions which is then used to trace the sequence of C¹⁴ enrichment in soils. Climate, vegetation, permeability, amount of carbon in the soil, action of animals—all play a role in determining the chronosequence.

Correction factors. In the years after the 8th International Radiocarbon Conference, a number of studies have been published which deal with the derivation of correction factors for recalibration of radiocarbon dates. For the most part, the correction factors are being derived from C¹⁴ dates of precisely dated wood. In this connection, V. C. LaMarche, Jr., has developed a tree-ring chronology for bristlecone pines independent of that of C. W. Ferguson, who had established a 7500-year bristlecone chronology through cross dating of wood specimens. The two chronologies are exactly parallel (to 3435 B.C.) and confirm the validity of the correction curves and factors.

All of the investigators who have published correction factors for radiocarbon dates recently (P. E. Damon, H. McKerrell, E. K. Ralph and H. N. Michael, C. Renfrew and R. M. Clark, and V. R. Switsur) agree that the results of the three principal radiocarbon laboratories engaged in analyzing precisely dated wood samples are, on the average, in accord. The differences lie in the statistical approaches to the raw data (Fig. 1). Damon and coworkers, after rejecting over 7% of the laboratory data on the bases that they included more than 25 rings, were less than 350 years old and thus subject to the Suess effect, or were anomalously young or old, then grouped the remaining 549 dates into 25-year intervals and computed the mean dendrochronological date for each interval. These were plotted and their trend was computed by curvilinear regression analysis using Chebychev orthogonal polynomials. Standard deviations were also computed for 250-year intervals. The results of

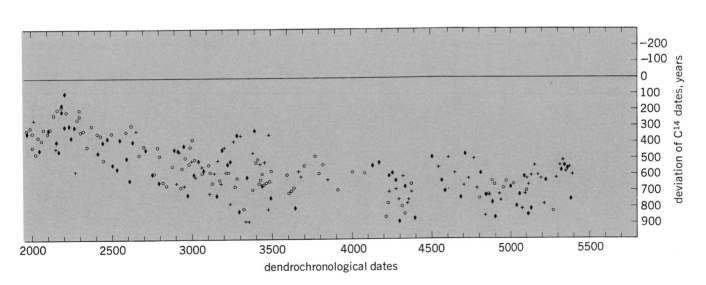

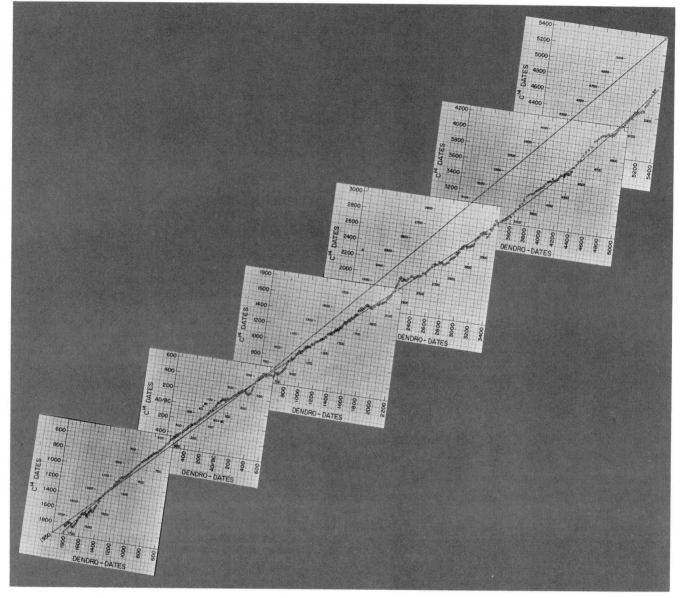

Fig. 2. Plot of C¹⁴ dates of wood samples against precise dendrochronological dates, obtained by using statistical smoothing procedures to remove scatter from raw data. *(From E. K. Ralph, H. N. Michael, and M. C. Han, Radiocarbon dates and reality, MASCA Newslett., 9(1):1–20, 1973)*

Damon's procedure is a smooth cyclic curve from which the correction factors can be read. The curve is also expressed in tabular form.

Ralph and coworkers, after experimenting with numerous statistical approaches, have used a moving nine-cell regression averaging, centered on its midpoint to eliminate some of the scatter in the raw data (Fig. 2). This smoothing procedure has the advantage of preserving all of the major deviations and most of the minor ones expressed in the raw data (Fig. 1). The derivation of this curve and its tabular expression are based on 631 C¹⁴ dates of precisely dated woods which spread over 661 C¹⁴ decades (A.D. 1849 to 4760 B.C.). In 560 (85%) of the decades the correction is determined within a span of 20 to 50 years because the C¹⁴ date crosses the curve only once. The remaining 101 (15%) of the

decades present the problem of the C¹⁴ date crossing the curve more than once with the resultant range of the correction exceeding 50 years. The curve and tables are accompanied by instructions for their use and an assessment of the errors or pitfalls this may involve.

Switsur has combined the results of both Damon and Ralph, thus obtaining a curve which is a compromise of the two; that is, it preserves the major deviations but obscures most of the minor ones. This opens it to criticism, particularly by Suess, who maintains that the minor deviations are real and represent rapid changes of atmospheric C¹⁴ activity.

Two additional variants to calibration curves have been recently introduced. McKerrell has challenged the accuracy of tree-ring-derived correction factors and has attempted to improve correction procedures by use of what he calls "historical" dates — a series of C^{14} dates of samples from the various Egyptian dynasties extending from 3000 to 600 B.C., as well as Minoan and Helladic dates. He derives his historical correction curve from a fourth-order polynomial regression procedure which, in his words, provides a simple graphical relationship for comparison with tree-ring-derived curves. He finds excellent agreement of the two curves between 3000 and 2300 B.C., but poor agreement from there on to 600 B.C.

Clark and Renfrew are critical of McKerrell's use of the "historical" curve and offer a statistical approach to make a comparison of Egyptian historical dates with corresponding radiocarbon dates and bristlecone pine dates with corresponding radiocarbon dates. They conclude that the calibrated Egyptian dates do not differ significantly from the historical dates.

For background information *see* DENDROCHRONOLOGY; LOW-LEVEL COUNTING; RADIOCARBON DATING in the McGraw-Hill Encyclopedia of Science and Technology.   [HENRY N. MICHAEL]

Bibliography: R. M. Clark and C. Renfrew, *Nature*, 243:266–270, June 1, 1973; P. E. Damon et al., *Amer. Antiquity*, 39(2):350–366, 1974; V. C. LaMarche, Jr., and T. P. Harlan, *J. Geophys. Res.*, 78(36):8849–8858, 1974; H. N. Michael and E. K. Ralph, *Radiocarbon*, 16(2):198–218, 1974; T. A. Rafter and T. Grant-Taylor (eds.), *Proceedings of the 8th International Radiocarbon Conference*, March 1973; E. K. Ralph, H. N. Michael, and M. C. Han, *MASCA Newslett.*, 9(1):1–20, 1973; V. R. Switsur, *Antiquity*, 47(186):131–137, 1973.

Reactor, nuclear

The U.S. Atomic Energy Commission's Reactor Safety Research Program includes investigations of safety issues relevant to power reactors, experimental and analytical programs to provide improved capability to predict detailed aspects of the safety of these reactors, and large experiments designed to proof-test the ability to synthesize the detailed information into overall predictions of reactor safety.

Emphasis is given to development of understanding of the many complex phenomena that must be dealt with in reactor safety analysis, over broad ranges of interest. Experimental programs generate data and lay a basis for the development and validation of analytical models. The models are then used to extrapolate understanding from laboratory conditions and laboratory sizes to ranges of interest in light of full-scale reactors. Integral tests (tests where an entire system is represented in order to combine all of the separate effects in proper relation to each other) then are performed to test the validity of the extrapolation. The results of the program are methods of analysis necessary to assess the safety of reactors, and information and methods needed to achieve safe design and operation.

During the past year there have been several significant developments in the safety research program. Three of these are highlighted in the following discussion. Two of them relate to the emergency core cooling system (ECCS), which is one of the backup safety features included in light-water reactors to cool the core in the highly unlikely event of loss of normal reactor cooling water. The third involves the reactor primary vessel.

ECCS acceptance criteria. In January 1972 the AEC began a long public rulemaking hearing on the acceptance criteria for ECCS in light-water reactors. This hearing resulted in a ruling issued by the commission in December 1973 which established new acceptance criteria for ECCS. These criteria are to be utilized by reactor vendors and electric utility companies in the evaluation of proposed reactor plants to obtain appropriate construction and operating licenses. The principal change from the existing interim policy statement was the adoption of two criteria to replace the peak Zircaloy cladding (fuel element surface) temperature of 2300°F (1260°C) calculated as resulting from a loss-of-coolant accident. The peak calculated Zircaloy temperature has been lowered to 2200°F (1204°C), and a limit is now set on the maximum allowed local oxidation. The new acceptance criteria contain a specific implementation schedule which requires compliance by all operating reactors by August 1974, with all licensing action after December 28, 1974, to be based on the new criteria unless variances are requested, justified, and granted.

ECCS and semiscale blowdown. The semiscale blowdown and ECCS project is one of the AEC's major reactor safety research programs which, during the past year, provided an extensive base of experimental data to assess certain broad aspects of the effectiveness of the ECCS. An ECCS is a standby auxiliary core cooling system which would inject subcooled water into the primary system if a postulated loss-of-coolant accident (LOCA) were to occur. Such an accident assumes that one of the inlet cooling lines (referred to as "cold legs") is instantaneously severed and offset, resulting in rapid expulsion of the primary coolant out of the postulated break as the system decompresses (or "blows down") from an initial pressure of 2250 pounds per square inch gage (15.5 megapascals). The ECCS begins injecting water into each of the cold legs when system pressure drops below 600 psig (4.1 MPa). To reach the core, the injected ECC water must proceed from the cold leg down the annular region between the reactor vessel wall and the core barrel (referred to as the "downcomer") to the region beneath the core (referred to as the "lower plenum"). The ECCS is intended to either add to the inventory of water in the lower plenum or force water from the lower plenum into the core and downcomer regions if the lower plenum is already full. The flow rate of ECC water to the lower plenum is dependent upon complex steam-water phenomena occurring in the cold leg, the downcomer, and lower plenum.

The semiscale isothermal system is a small-scale one-dimensional representation of a large pressurized water reactor (PWR) in which basic thermal hydraulic processes, attendant to a LOCA, can be studied. The data on ECCS performance obtained in the semiscale system cannot, however, be used directly to ascertain all aspects of the ECCS performance of a PWR because necessary scaling compromises have, in certain cases, distorted some of the thermal-hydraulic features of semiscale relative to a PWR. Instead, the data obtained from semiscale have been used, and will be used, to evaluate and improve the analytical models developed to predict both system and ECCS performance.

An experimental program was conducted during the past year to investigate the thermal-hydraulic processes associated with ECC injection in the semiscale facility. Three separate but interrelated test programs were aimed at systematically investigating the basic processes postulated to occur following ECC injection. The initial phase of the test program was conducted with a transparent vessel to investigate the interaction of ECC water flowing down the downcomer with gas flowing up the downcomer (referred to as "countercurrent flow") and the possibility that ECC water injected in the unbroken loop cold leg could flow around the core barrel and out the broken loop cold leg. This possibility was explored in experiments in which ECC water was injected in the semiscale downcomer, to determine if the phenomena could be described in terms of existing countercurrent flow correlations. Air and water were used as the fluids for the transparent vessel tests since existing data were limited almost exclusively to these fluids. The second phase of the test program used the semiscale isothermal system vessel to investigate countercurrent flow in a steam-water medium where condensation and evaporation could affect the phenomena. The final portion of the test program was conducted using the 1½-loop isothermal semiscale system to investigate transient integral effects of injecting ECC during a simulated LOCA in a system that resembles a PWR configuration.

Steady-state tests conducted in the transparent vessel were used to determine the relative tendency of the ECC water to flow into the lower plenum or out of the broken cold leg. The data from the air-water tests in the transparent vessel were used to establish a relationship between commonly used countercurrent flow correlations, derived from data based on the use of small tubes or packed beds, and countercurrent flow data obtained with an annular geometry whose size and inlet conditions were typical of the semiscale system. The results of these tests led to modification of the universally used countercurrent flow correlations of Wallis to characterize better the countercurrent flow in annular geometry.

Countercurrent flow tests then were conducted in a steady-state experiment to provide a data base for relating the velocity of steam up the downcomer annulus to the water delivery rate down to the lower plenum. These tests showed that condensation effects in semiscale-sized steam-water countercurrent flow tests overwhelmed the countercurrent flow in the downcomer below a specified steam upflow. Countercurrent flow did not occur in any cases where subcooled water reached the downcomer.

The ability of correlations developed from these steady-state experiments to characterize ECC phenomena in a transient LOCA was assessed in the isothermal blowdown test program employing the 1½-loop isothermal semiscale system. This system consisted of a pressure vessel with simulated steam generator and pump. The facility also contained a pressure-suppression system with a suppression tank and header, and an emergency coolant injection system. Tests were initiated from isothermal conditions of 2250 psig (15.5 MPa) and 540°F (282°C). In contrast to the previous integral semiscale tests employing a single loop (with a heated core), ECC injection directly into the lower plenum was not expelled but accumulated and remained in the lower plenum.

Reactor primary vessel. Another area of research related to reactor safety responds to the need to increase understanding of the reaction of the reactor primary vessel and piping to the operational conditions that will be encountered throughout the reactor plant lifetime. Research is needed to improve the basis for accurately predicting that the reactor pressure vessel and associated piping will not rupture or break during service.

The Heavy Section Steel Technology Program at the Oak Ridge National Laboratory is focused on studies pertinent to the massive pressure vessels used in water reactor systems, with particular emphasis on the effects of flaws and discontinuities on the behavior of the vessel under startup, operating, cooldown, and accident conditions. Recent research has included testing of 6-in. (152 mm) thick intermediate-size pressure vessels

Tests of 6-in. (152 mm) thick intermediate-size pressure vessels in the Heavy Section Steel Technology Program

Vessel	Test temperature, °F (°C)	Flaw dimensions, in. (cm)		Flaw location	Fracture pressure in units of 10^3 psi (10^6 Pa) (design = 9×10^3 psi = 62×10^6 Pa)
		Depth	Length		
V-1	130 (54)	2.56 (6.50)	8.25 (20.95)	Base	28.8 (199)
V-2	32 (0)	2.53 (6.43)	8.30 (21.08)	Base	27.9 (192)
V-3	130 (54)	2.11 (5.36)	8.50 (21.59)	Weld	31.0 (214)
V-4	75 (24)	3.00 (7.62)	8.25 (20.95)	Weld*	26.5 (183)
	75 (24)	3.10 (7.87)	8.10 (20.57)	Base	26.5 (183)
V-5	190 (88)	1.2 (3.0)	2.4 (6.1)	Nozzle† Corner	26.6 (183)
V-6	190 (88)	1.87 (4.75)	5.25 (13.33)	Weld*	31.9 (220)
	190 (88)	1.34 (3.40)	5.20 (13.21)	Base	31.9 (220)
	190 (88)	1.94 (4.93)	5.30 (13.46)	Weld	31.9 (220)

*Flaw causing failure.   †Leak only.

which have had large flaws introduced into them and are then pressurized to failure. The results of these tests have so far confirmed that current design methods provide a substantial margin against failure that might be a consequence of flaws. The table summarizes these results, which are described in greater detail below.

The six intermediate-scale pressure vessels which have been tested to date were all fabricated from A533-B steel plate or from A508 Class-2 steel forgings in accordance with requirements of Section III of the ASME Pressure Vessel Code. The vessels were 6 in. (152 mm) thick, had an outside diameter of 39 in. (991 mm), and a straight cylindrical length of 54 in. (1372 mm), terminating in welded and bolted heads. Several vessels had longitudinal seam welds, and one had a 9-in. (229 mm) inside-diameter nozzle welded into the cylindrical barrel section. All vessels were intentionally flawed by cutting a narrow groove of typical dimensions 2.5 in. (60 mm) deep by 5 to 8 in. (130 to 200 mm) long; the vessel with a nozzle had a 1.2-in. (30 mm) deep by 2.4-in. (61 mm) long flaw in the corner junction between shell and nozzle. All flaws were sharpened either by fatiguing or by electron-beam cutting plus hydrogen charging and cracking. Testing was conducted at various temperatures from just above the 10°F (−12°C) nil-ductility transition (brittle-to-ductile fracture) temperature.

In every case, in testing the intermediate test vessel to destruction, a pressure very near three times the design pressure was required for failure. For the vessel tested just above the nil-ductility transition temperature, no slow crack growth was detected, prior to unstable rapid fracture, despite an overpressure three times the design pressure. For all tests conducted at 75°F (24°C) and above, however, significant slow crack growth occurred during cycling and was positively detected and followed right up to failure. For a test conducted at 130°F (54°C), slow stable crack growth on cycling was observed to reach a depth of 5 in. (130 mm) and a length of 18 in. (450 mm) before onset of rapid crack propagation and failure at a pressure about three times the design value. At the upper shelf temperature, 190°F (88°C), shear lips extended completely across the wall thickness in a full slant fracture, indicating the highest degree of material toughness and resistance to fracture extension. For the nozzle-corner-flaw test at 190°F, failure occurred by formation of a leak, wherein the flaw grew through the steel at the corner junction and penetrated the outer wall prior to becoming a critical size under the applied load of three times design pressure.

These tests have shown quite conclusively that when nuclear-grade vessels of A533-B and A508 Class-2 steel are pressurized under conditions such that upper shelf levels of toughness exist, crack growth occurs initially in a stable fashion, and energy must continue to be put into the system to extend the flaw. The flaw must then become very large relative to the vessel dimensions before failure occurs, and even then gross overpressures are required. In the case of the vessel with the nozzle, the decreasing stress-strain gradient in the nozzle corner provided a condition such that critical flaw size for unstable growth could not be achieved before leakage occurred, thus leading to "leak before break" performance.

For background information *see* NUCLEAR POWER; REACTOR, NUCLEAR in the McGraw-Hill Encyclopedia of Science and Technology.

[HERBERT J. C. KOUTS]

Bibliography: Oak Ridge National Laboratory, *Test of 6 Inch Thick Pressure Vessels—Series 1: Intermediate Test Vessels V-I and V-2*, ORNL-4895, February 1974; Opinion of the Commission in the Matter of Rulemaking Hearing: Acceptance Criteria for Emergency Core Cooling Systems for Light-water-cooled Nuclear Power Reactors, *USAEC Regulatory Adjudication Issuances*, RAI-73-12, December 1973.

Rodentia

Studies of the unusual feeding behavior of the Great Basin, or chisel-toothed, kangaroo rat *(Dipodomys microps)* have shed new light on the ecology, physiology, and evolution of desert rodents. Whereas typical species of kangaroo rats, or other desert rodents, feed largely on dry seeds and can survive without drinking water or eating succulent vegetation, *D. microps* eats the leaves of the spiny saltbush shrub *(Atriplex confertifolia)*, which serves as a year-round source of nutrition and water. The adaptations for extracting useful nutrition and water from the unusual, salty leaves of *A. confertifolia* represent the evolution of a divergent pattern of survival in the desert environment.

Typical desert adaptations. The nocturnal seed-eating rodents are among the most abundant inhabitants of the major desert regions of the world. These desert-adapted species belong to several different families of rodents. The North American rodents of the family Heteromyidae have been the most thoroughly studied of the desert rodents with regard to their ecological, behavioral, and physiological adaptations for survival. The 21 species of kangaroo rats constitute the genus *Dipodomys*. Their weights range from 30 to 120 g, and they are the most conspicuous of the heteromyids in the deserts of southwestern North America. However, their smaller heteromyid relatives, the pocket mice *(Perognathus)*, are also widespread.

Typical kangaroo rats are specialized for surviving on a diet of dry seeds, without any water or succulent food, during the nonreproductive seasons. They emerge only at night to forage through the desert sand for seeds, spending the daytime beneath the ground in their burrows. They must cover relatively large areas of the desert in search of the sparsely distributed food. Exposure of kangaroo rats to the physical elements and to predators is minimized because they utilize efficient, rapid locomotion by bipedal, or "ricochetal" leaping, and because they use their fur-lined external cheek pouches for carrying seeds, thereby making it unnecessary for them to hull or eat the seeds until they return to the burrow. The cheek pouches open on each side of the face lateral to and independent of the mouth cavity.

The physiological adaptations by which kangaroo rats are able to survive on a diet of dry seeds without water or succulent vegetation include sev-

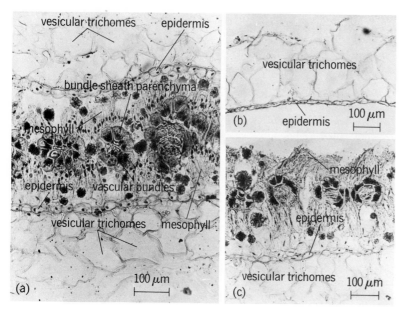

Fig. 1. Cross sections of the leaf of the spiny saltbush (*Atriplex confertifolia*). (a) Whole leaf. (b) Piece of salty surface tissue shaved from the leaf by *Dipodomys microps*. (c) A leaf taken away from a rat after it had removed the outer, salty tissue from one side. (From G. J. Kenagy, *Adaptations for leaf eating in the Great Basin kangaroo rat, Dipodomys microps, Oecologia, 12:383–412, 1973*)

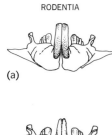

(a)

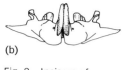

(b)

Fig. 2. Incisors of *Dipodomys*. (a) Incisors of *D. microps* are uniquely specialized: broad, anteriorly flattened, and chisel-shaped. (b) *D. ordii* incisors are typical of those of kangaroo rats as a whole: relatively narrow, rounded, and awl-shaped. (From E. R. Hall, *Mammals of Nevada*, p. 417, 1946)

eral water-conserving mechanisms: the production of highly concentrated urine by the reabsorption of water in the kidney; a reduced loss of water by evaporation from the lungs; and the production of dry feces, by the reabsorption of water in the intestine. Typical desert species of kangaroo rats can survive indefinitely on a diet of nothing more than dry seeds, with no water or succulent plant food. In nature, the typical foraging pattern of such kangaroo rats consists of searching for seeds in the desert soil.

Evolutionary divergence of D. microps. Field observations of *D. microps* show that it differs markedly from the usual pattern just described. *D. microps* has been most intensively studied in the Owens Valley of eastern California, where it occurs together with, and thus can be readily compared with, the well-known and typical species *D. merriami*. Whereas *D. merriami* and other species forage in the sand for seeds, *D. microps* climbs into shrubs and gathers small bunches of leaves from the twigs. The animals stuff the leaves into their external cheek pouches and carry them back to the burrow either to be eaten immediately or to be stored. Amounts of leaves weighing as much as five times the body weight of an animal have been found in the burrows of individual *D. microps*. The leaves of one shrub species, *A. confertifolia*, account for essentially all of the leaves eaten by *D. microps*.

Atriplex is an unusual plant to be the major constituent in the diet of a small rodent. The salt content of *Atriplex* leaves is as great as 40% of the dry weight of the leaves. However, most of the salts are located in the metabolically relatively inactive vesicular trichome tissue, into which they are excreted across the epidermis (Fig. 1a).

The broad, anteriorly flattened, chisel-shaped lower incisors of *D. microps* (Fig. 2a) have been

discovered to be a particular adaptation for removing the superficial salty tissue of the leaves of the spiny saltbush. These lower incisors are different from those of all the other species of *Dipodomys*, which are narrow and rounded anteriorly and used for hulling seeds (Fig. 2b). When eating the saltbush leaves, *D. microps* holds a single leaf, which measures about 7–10 mm in diameter, in its forefeet and draws it over the broad lower incisors, quivering the lower incisors at high frequency and thus shaving off the outer layers of tissue from the downwardly directed side of the leaf (Fig. 1b and c). The leaf is turned over, and the process repeated on the opposite surface. Finally, only the inner tissue, between the two epidermal layers, is eaten.

For a short time in the spring, it is possible for *D. microps* to eat some of the newly developed leaves of *A. confertifolia* wholly, without first removing the surface tissue, because the new leaves have a low salt content. During most of the year, however, *D. microps* must mechanically detoxify its major food source by shaving off the salty superficial tissue of the leaves. The sodium content relative to water in surface tissue from wintertime leaves is 4200 meq/liter, or more than 30 times greater than the 135 meq/liter in the inner tissue, which is the part that is eaten. On the other hand, the overall sodium concentration of the springtime leaves which can be eaten entirely, without surface shaving, is only 250 meq/liter, less than twice the concentration of the interior tissue of wintertime leaves.

By removing the portions of the saltbush leaves that are unfit for consumption, *D. microps* avails itself of the inner leaf tissue, which is high in starch and water throughout the year. Captive *D. microps* can be maintained in healthy condition on an exclusive diet of saltbush leaves. Other kangaroo rat species, such as *D. merriami*, cannot extract the useful nutrients and water from saltbush leaves; they quickly starve if they are offered these leaves exclusively.

From laboratory experiments it is known that typical kangaroo rats, such as *D. merriami*, can survive indefinitely on an exclusive diet of dry seeds, without water or succulent plant foods. Under such conditions, *D. merriami* conserves water by excreting very concentrated urine, about 4700 milliosmol/liter. These capabilities have not evolved in *D. microps*, which loses body weight rapidly and succumbs on an exclusive diet of dry seed. *D. microps* can excrete urine only at a concentration of about 2800 milliosmol/liter under these conditions.

Two, three, and even four species of kangaroo rats are known to occur together in the same habitat. Under such conditions, competition for resources arises among the different species of the same genus, all of which are attempting to "make a living" in very similar ways. Such competition must have been an important selective pressure for the evolution of the unusual life-style of *D. microps*. Another factor may have been that, as this species concentrated its feeding effort on fresh plant materials, the only plants affording a year-round source of leaves were the perennial shrubs associated with certain areas of alkaline soil in the deserts. Because of its dietary specialization, *D. microps* should be able to minimize its dependence on the unpredictable seed crops of desert annuals, on which typical seed-eating species of *Dipodomys* must rely. In habitats where *D. microps* occurs together with other species of *Dipodomys*, the coexistence of *D. microps* should be favored owing to its heavy utilization of a resource essentially unused by other kangaroo rat species. However, the distribution of *D. microps* is generally limited by the distribution of *A. confertifolia*, and thus *D. microps* is found only in the state of Nevada and in nearby localities in the surrounding states. *D. merriami*, on the other hand, is widespread throughout several different types of desert habitats across the Colorado-Sonoran and Mojave deserts, from the central plateau of Mexico to northern Nevada.

Evolution of adaptations. Evolutionary biologists recognize that behavior is one of the most plastic and variable elements of a biological system or organism. It is through the immediacy of a behavioral response that survival can be enhanced in a new or changing environment. Those individuals showing a behavioral response that maximally increases the chances for survival are favored selectively in their chances for producing offspring, which in turn, by the laws of genetics, closely resemble their parents.

How, then, do structural, or "morphological," changes such as the specially adapted lower incisors of *D. microps* come about? It has been recognized that the very behavioral patterns that initially evolve in response to a particular environmental selective pressure do themselves serve as further selective pressures for the evolution by natural selection of structural types that are increasingly more fit for performing the given behavioral pattern. Thus the unique lower incisors of *D. microps* evolved in response to the evolution of patterns of foraging and eating behavior that emphasized the leaves of shrubs as the principal dietary item. Natural selection then favored those individuals in the natural (and slightly variable) population with broader and more flattened lower incisors, because of their greater efficiency in shaving off the hypersaline surface tissues of saltbush leaves.

On a diet of dry seeds, the kidney of *D. microps* has a less efficient performance than that of other species of kangaroo rats. This likely reflects a reduction in selective pressure upon *D. microps* for a greater water-conserving capacity that is afforded by the incorporation of a continuous source of water, the inner tissue of saltbush leaves, into the diet.

For background information *see* RODENTIA in the McGraw-Hill Encyclopedia of Science and Technology.

[G. J. KENAGY]

Bibliography: G. J. Kenagy, *Oecologia*, 12:383–412, 1973.

Rydberg constant

Recent advances in high-resolution spectroscopy with tunable lasers have made it possible to determine a new, more accurate Rydberg constant by measuring the wavelength of optically resolved fine-structure components of the red Balmer line H_α of atomic hydrogen and D_α of deuterium. Doppler broadening was eliminated by a technique of saturation spectroscropy in which a pulsed dye laser was used.

Significance of Rydberg constant. Much attention has been focused in the past few years on the Rydberg constant, which describes the binding energy between the electron and the atomic nucleus. It can be expressed as a combination of electron mass m, electron charge e, Planck's constant h, and light velocity c: $R = 2\pi^2 me^4/h^3 c$. It has traditionally been an important cornerstone in the evaluation of the fundamental constants of physics. The constant is determined from the wavelength of spectral lines of simple hydrogen-like atoms, which allow accurate theoretical calculations. The relationship between the Rydberg constant and the wavelength is given by Bohr's formula, corrected for finite nuclear mass, relativistic effects, and Lamb shifts.

The red Balmer line of hydrogen is perhaps the most extensively studied of all spectral lines. But precise wavelength measurements always presented a peculiar problem, because this line consists of seven closely spaced fine-structure components (Fig. 1a) which always appeared blurred and masked by Doppler broadening to the random motion of the light atoms. This problem is only partly alleviated when Doppler broadening is reduced by operation at cryogenic temperatures and by the use of the heavier isotopes deuterium and tritium. The fine-structure intervals are well known from

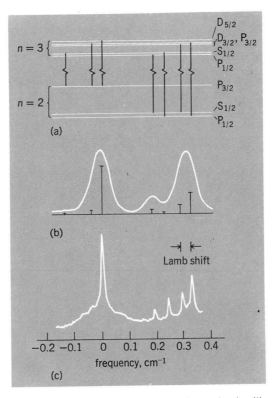

Fig. 1.   Deuterium Balmer line D_α. (a) Energy levels with fine-structure transitions. (b) Emission-line profile of a cooled deuterium gas discharge (temperature 50K) and theoretical fine-structure lines with relative transition probabilities. (From B. P. Kibble et al., J. Phys., B6: 1079, 1973) (c) Saturation spectrum was optically resolved Lamb shift. (From T. W. Hansch et al., Precision measurement of the Rydberg constant by laser saturation spectroscopy of the Balmer α line in hydrogen and deuterium, Phys. Rev. Lett., 32:1336, 1974)

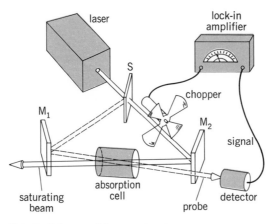

Fig. 2. Scheme of laser saturation spectrometer. A beam splitter S and two mirrors M_1 and M_2 divide the laser output into a weak probe beam and a stronger counterpropagating saturating beam. *(From T. W. Hänsch, in S. J. Smith and G. K. Walters, eds., Atomic Physics, vol. 3, 1973)*

radio-frequency (rf) spectroscopy, but the relative line intensities emitted by a gas discharge follow no simple rule, and the mathematical line fitting of the observed blend of unresolved components has always involved troublesome uncertainties.

In 1970, after a careful analysis, G. W. Series pointed out that the accuracy of the accepted Rydberg value (1 part in 10^7) may well have been optimistically overstated. On the other hand, it became increasingly clear that future consistency tests and adjustments of the fundamental constants would soon call for an accuracy of the Rydberg constant to within a few parts in 10^8. B. N. Taylor pointed out that an uncertainty of a few parts in 10^7 would severely limit the interpretation of several future precision experiments in physics.

Recent conventional measurements. Responding to this situation, several research groups have recently made new efforts to determine a precise Rydberg value by measuring the wavelength of gas-discharge emission lines with modern versions of conventional high-resolution spectroscopy. In 1973 B. P. Kibble and coworkers at the National Physics Laboratory in England reported on a wavelength measurement of the red Balmer line of deuterium and tritium, comparing it directly with the present standard length, a spectral line of Kr^{86} at 606 μm. By cooling an rf discharge tube with liquid helium, they obtained an emission-line profile of D_α, as shown in Fig. 1b. The theoretical fine-structure components with their relative transition probabilities are shown for comparison. The wavelengths were determined with the help of a deconvolution and fitting procedure. A comparison with numerical calculations by G. Erickson (1974) yielded a new Rydberg value, $R_\infty = 109737.326(8)$ cm^{-1}, with a somewhat smaller uncertainty than the previously accepted value, $R_\infty = 109737.312(11)$ cm^{-1}.

In 1973 E. G. Kessler, Jr., at the National Bureau of Standards (NBS) in Washington, D.C., reported on another new Rydberg measurement. He measured the wavelength of the $n = 3-4$ line in ionized helium in terms of a well-known Hg line. The fine structure of this line is considerably larger than that of hydrogen and can be optically resolved. But the ionic line is weak and easily subject to systematic shifts that limit the obtainable accuracy. Kessler's Rydberg value, $R_\infty = 109737.3208(85)$ cm^{-1}, agrees with Kibble's result within the quoted standard deviations.

Saturation spectroscopy. The feasibility of a dramatically improved Rydberg measurement became apparent in 1972, when T. W. Hänsch, I. S. Shahin, and A. L. Schawlow at Stanford University succeeded in resolving the fine structure of the red hydrogen Balmer line, eliminating Doppler broadening by observation in saturated absorption. Using this new nonlinear spectroscopic technique, in 1974 Hänsch and coworkers completed a precision measurement of the Rydberg constant.

Figure 2 shows a scheme of the saturation spectrometer used by the Stanford group. Prerequisite is a narrow-band laser, the wavelength of which can be scanned continuously across the absorption line of interest. The absorbing gas sample is contained in a cell outside the laser resonator. A beam splitter divides the laser output into a weak probe beam and a stronger saturating beam, which are sent in nearly opposite directions through the absorber. When the laser is tuned to the center of the Doppler-broadened absorption profile, both light waves can interact simultaneously with the same atoms — those with essentially zero axial velocity. The saturating beam can then bleach a path for the probe, reducing its absorption. So that small bleaching effects can be detected, the saturating beam is periodically blocked by a chopper, and the resulting probe modulation is detected with a lock-in amplifier. The resolution in the saturation spectrum at low laser intensities is limited only by the natural atomic line width and the laser bandwidth. Earlier versions of saturation spectroscopy have been used in other laboratories to study molecular absorption lines in accidental coincidence with gas laser lines, or to stabilize the frequency of gas lasers. Saturation spectroscopy has become a widely applicable technique since Hänsch, Shahin, and Schawlow demonstrated in 1971 that broadly tunable dye lasers can be made sufficiently monochromatic to allow the study of arbitrary visible atomic absorption lines in saturated absorption. *See* LASER, TUNABLE.

A repetitively pulsed dye laser, pumped by a nitrogen gas laser, was used in the Stanford experiment. A wavelength selective resonator and an external filter interferometer reduced its bandwidth to 0.001 cm^{-1}. The hydrogen or deuterium atoms were excited to the absorbing $n = 2$ state in a simple gas-discharge tube. An electronic switch allowed measurements in the afterflow of a pulsed discharge to minimize Stark shifts and Stark broadening.

A saturation spectrum of the red deuterium Balmer line is shown in Fig. 1c. Single fine-structure components are, for the first time, resolved in the optical spectrum. The relative line intensities are not expected to be exactly the same as the relative transition probabilities. The splitting between the two line components at the outer right is entirely due to radiative corrections (Lamb shifts), as predicted by modern quantum electrodynamics.

The Stanford team compared the wavelengths of the optically resolved Balmer line components interferometrically with the wavelength of a 6333-nm He-Ne laser which was electronically frequency-stabilized to an absorption line of I_2^{129} vapor inside the cavity. The He-Ne laser wavelength was measured by W. G. Schweitzer and coworkers at NBS (1973) in terms of the Kr^{86} standard to within 1.4 parts in 10^9. A major part of the experimental effort was devoted to the determination of possible systematic errors due, for example, to Stark shifts and pressure shifts in the discharge environment. *See* WAVELENGTH STANDARDS.

The experiment yielded a new Rydberg value, $R_\infty = 109737.3143(10)$, with a standard deviation of only 1 part in 10^8. This value agrees well with Kessler's result and is only slightly outside the error limits of Kibble. For the foreseeable future, the new measurement is likely to maintain the distinctive role of the Rydberg constant as one of the best-known constants of physics. Saturation spectroscopy provides much narrower lines than the Kr^{86} lamp, which is presently accepted as standard of length, does, and it seems desirable to define a new, sharper length standard before substantial further improvements in accuracy are attempted.

For background information *see* ATOMIC STRUCTURE AND SPECTRA; RYDBERG CONSTANT in the McGraw-Hill Encyclopedia of Science and Technology.

[THEO W. HÄNSCH]

Bibliography: T. W. Hänsch et al., *Phys. Rev. Lett.*, 32:1336, 1974; E. G. Kessler, Jr., *Phys. Rev.*, A7:408, 1973; B. P. Kibble et al., *J. Phys.*, B6:1079, 1973; G. W. Series, *Contemp. Phys.*, 14:49, 1974.

Scattering experiments, nuclear

During the last few years it has become possible to study nuclear scattering in a new and exciting energy region. This is due to the successful operation of the CERN Intersecting Storage Rings (ISR) in Geneva, Switzerland, and of the Fermi National Accelerator Laboratory (Fermilab) at Batavia, IL. The ISR produce two proton beams, which collide head-on, of up to 31 GeV in energy, while the Fermilab yields a proton beam of up to 400 GeV in energy. This new energy region is of special significance because for the first time scientists have controlled beams to carry out experiments where, in the center-of-mass system, each incoming particle is extremely relativistic. *See* PARTICLE ACCELERATOR.

In a nuclear scattering experiment one of the most important quantities to measure is the total cross section, which is essentially the effective area for the scattering and thus represents the "size" of the particles being studied. In the 1950s and the 1960s it was generally believed that, as functions of energy, the total cross sections had reached an asymptotically constant value. Experimental data from the Brookhaven National Laboratory in New York, CERN, and Serpukhov in the Soviet Union seemed to confirm this belief. Furthermore, since the de Broglie wavelength of an extremely relativistic hadron is small compared with its radius, an asymptotically constant cross section might be expected on the basis of an analog with optics: measurements of the size of this

Yearbook, for example, yield the same result whether red light or violet light is used.

Theoretical predictions. In 1970, however, it was predicted on purely theoretical grounds that this expectation is not so: at sufficiently high energies the total cross section for the scattering of any two hadrons increases with energy. This result is due to the interplay of a number of basic principles in physics, including special relativity (nobody can go faster than the velocity of light), unitarity (one cannot get something out of nothing), and particle production (what can happen does happen). In particular, this last property of the copious production of additional particles is the feature of high-energy scattering processes which is absent in the optical analog presented above.

Experimental confirmation. In 1973 two experimental groups working with the ISR obtained dramatic confirmation of this prediction. When the energy of each of the two beams of the ISR is increased from 11.8 to 26.6 GeV, the total cross section for proton-proton scattering is found to rise by 10%. Since the ISR are the first major colliding-beam facility for protons in the world, many difficulties, expected and unexpected, had to be solved before the successful completion of these experi-

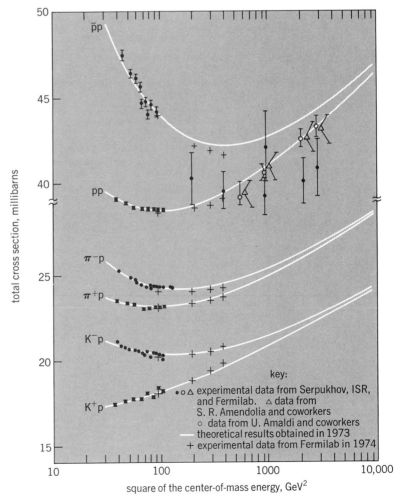

Total cross sections in millibarns (10^{-27} cm^2) as functions of (center-of-mass energy)^2 in GeV^2.

ments. These experimental values for the total cross sections, together with the results of earlier measurements from Serpukhov, ISR, and Fermilab, are shown in the illustration as closed or open circles or as triangles.

More quantitative predictions. At the same time, efforts were under way to make the original qualitative prediction of rising total cross sections more quantitative. The experimental data from the ISR supplied precisely the missing link, and the resulting quantitative phenomenological theory was used in 1973 to predict the behavior of the total cross sections, at and above the energies now available at Fermilab, for antiproton-proton (p^-p), pion-proton (π^+p and π^-p), and kaon-proton (K^+p and K^-p) scatterings. These predictions are shown in the illustration as the solid curves. The realization that the basic mechanism for rising total cross sections is the same for all hadronic scattering processes renders it possible to make this quantitative prediction.

Further experimental confirmation. In 1974 the measurement at Fermilab of all these total cross sections to an extremely high precision of $\frac{1}{2}\%$ confirmed once more the theoretical predictions. These most recent data are shown in the illustration as crosses. It is remarkable that these data taken at incident energies between 50 and 200 GeV are actually more accurate than the corresponding data at lower energies. Plans are being made at Fermilab to extend these measurements up to about 300 GeV for antiproton-proton and kaon-proton scatterings, and up to nearly 400 GeV for proton-proton and pion-proton scatterings. Both this experiment at Fermilab and the two ISR experiments mentioned above must be considered to be among the most beautiful ones in elementary particle physics in recent years.

This development in knowledge of total cross sections illustrates one of the typical ways for physics to progress: (1) A theoretical prediction is made of a qualitative departure from the generally accepted physical picture. (2) The predicted qualitative departure is found experimentally. (3) The experimental result is used to make the original theory more quantitative, and more detailed predictions are derived. (4) Further experimental results are found to be in quantitative agreement with these more detailed predictions. In the case of the rising total cross sections, this development took about 4 years.

For background information *see* ELEMENTARY PARTICLE; MESON; PROTON; SCATTERING EXPERIMENTS, NUCLEAR in the McGraw-Hill Encyclopedia of Science and Technology.   [TAI TSUN WU]

Bibliography: U. Amaldi et al., *Phys. Lett.*, 44B: 112, 1973; S. R. Amendolia et al., *Phys. Lett.*, 44B: 119, 1973; H. Cheng, J. K. Walker, and T. T. Wu, *Phys. Lett.*, 44B:97, 1973; H. Cheng and T. T. Wu, *Phys. Rev. Lett.*, 24:1456, 1970.

Semiconductor

The unique electronic and optical properties of semiconductors are determined by the character of their excited states. A recently discovered form of electronic excitation at cryogenic temperatures in germanium and silicon is referred to as electron hole droplets. The phenomenon may be described as a liquid-gas phase transition of the electronic charge carriers. Interest arises not only because this is a new many-body phenomenon readily accessible to experimental and theoretical investigation, but also because of the general importance of high excitation conditions in solids to the development of laser technology.

In all crystalline solids, the allowed energy levels of electrons occur only within certain ranges termed energy bands. In the ground state of semiconductors, the energy bands are either filled or empty. The highest-energy filled band is termed the valence band, and the lowest-energy empty band is termed the conduction band.

The simplest excitation of a semiconductor, then, is to raise an electron from the valence band to the conduction band by imparting to it some energy greater than the energy gap separating the two bands. The empty state left in the valence band is termed a hole. The response to an electric field of negatively charged electrons and positively charged holes may often be discussed as if they were free particles with effective masses chosen to best describe the semiconductor in question.

Since an electron and hole represent an excitation of a semiconductor, they will eventually recombine. Energy is conserved by the emission of photons or light which may be readily detected. Momentum must also be conserved in recombination, but light carries off little momentum. In those semiconductors described as having an indirect gap, the electrons at the bottom of the conduction band and holes at the top of the valence band differ in momentum so that, in a recombination, phonons or lattice vibrations must also be emitted to conserve momentum. This process is considerably slower than recombination in direct-gap semiconductors and allows excited electrons and holes to come into thermal equilibrium with one another. Germanium and silicon are indirect-gap materials.

Electron hole droplets are the result of the electrostatic interaction between electrons and holes, which follows Coulomb's law modified by the dielectric constant of the material. A single electron hole pair may be bound together in a state termed an exciton in the same fashion as electron and proton bind to form a hydrogen atom. The equilibrium between excitons and free electrons and holes may be accurately described at low pair densities by the usual law of mass action. Excitons predominate at low temperatures. Since excitons are electrically neutral, a gas of excitons should be insulating.

At low temperatures and high pair densities, a description of an excited semiconductor in terms of individual excitons is inaccurate since the Bohr radii of excitons begin to overlap (approximately 14 nanometers in germanium or pair densities of 10^{16} cm^{-3}). The Fermi-Dirac statistics of electrons and holes lead to metallic behavior at high excitation; that is, conduction and valence bands are filled with electrons and holes up to a Fermi level. Metallic electrons and holes should not be bound together and therefore should be conducting.

"Electron hole droplets" is a description of what occurs in germanium and silicon in place of a smooth transition from excitonic to metallic behavior with increasing excitation level. The electrons

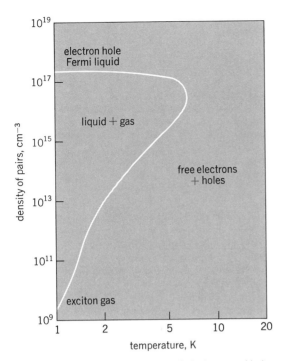

Fig. 1. Schematic phase diagram of electrons and holes in germanium. The labels give the dominant carrier state in each region of temperature and density. The solid line is the liquid-gas coexistence curve.

and holes undergo a liquid-gas phase transition. This possibility was first suggested after some experimental hints by L. V. Keldysh of the Soviet Union, with Ya. Pokrovsky of the Soviet Union foremost among experimenters in confirming this behavior.

A schematic phase diagram for electrons and holes in germanium is shown in Fig. 1. At high temperatures most carriers exist as free electrons and holes. At low temperatures and low densities most electrons and holes are bound together as excitons. At low temperatures and high densities an electron hole Fermi liquid is found. The solid line is termed the liquid-gas coexistence curve. For a temperature and average density inside the line, the carriers in the crystal separate into regions of Fermi liquid at the density of the upper part of the line termed electron hole droplets coexisting with regions of mainly excitonic gas at the density of the lower part of the line. This phenomenon is analogous to what occurs when air becomes supersaturated with water vapor and water droplets condense. The temperature-density where upper and lower branches of the coexistence curve meet is termed the critical point.

Experiments. In most experiments on germanium and silicon, excitation is achieved by the absorption of light from lasers, whose photon energies exceed the band gap. The earliest experiments studied the changes in the recombination radiation as a function of excitation level. Photons emitted during recombination of an electron and hole should have an energy equal to the band gap minus the energy of phonons emitted to conserve momentum plus the energy, whether positive or

negative, due to the interactions of electrons and holes with one another. For excitons the latter energy is simply the exciton Rydberg. Photons arising from recombination in the electron hole liquid are lower in energy than photons which arise from exciton recombination. The energy difference corresponds to the latent heat associated with a liquid-gas transition.

In Fig. 2 photon energy spectra for highly excited silicon are shown. The carrier density of the experiment is outside of the coexistence curve for silicon at $T = 23$ K. Only recombination radiation from excitons at 1.098 ± 0.001 eV is seen. While free electrons and holes are presumably also present in appreciable amounts at this temperature and density, they recombine radiatively by first dropping into an exciton state. As the temperature is lowered to 1.8 K, the experiment drops inside the coexistence curve for silicon, and separation of the carriers into liquid and gas phases occurs. The new peak at 1.082 ± 0.001 eV is due to recombination of electrons and holes in the liquid phase. An exciton peak is still visible but is weak because of the low pair density of the gas phase at this temperature.

The Fermi-Dirac statistics determine the kinetic energy distribution of electrons and holes in the metallic liquid. This is reflected in the energy spectra of the recombination radiation. The chemical potential and density may be determined by fitting these spectra in the effective mass approximation. The results agree well with the T^2 temperature dependence of the chemical potential and

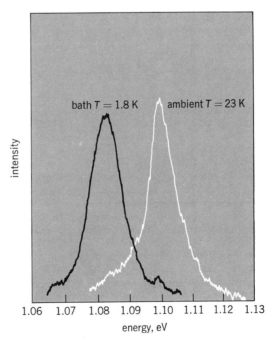

Fig. 2. Recombination radiation spectra from a silicon double-injection device. At 23 K only the peak at 1.098 ± 0.001 eV corresponding to recombination of excitons is seen. At 1.8 K a new peak at 1.082 ± 0.001 eV appears which is due to recombination in the electron hole liquid, while a small peak due to excitons remains. *(From R. B. Hammond et al., Condensation of injected electrons and holes in silicon, Solid State Commun., 15:251, 1974)*

density expected of a Fermi system. From these experiments one may estimate liquid densities at 0 K of 2×10^{17} cm^{-3} for germanium and 3×10^{18} cm^{-3} for silicon.

The metallic character of the liquid phase has been confirmed in a variety of other ways. In a magnetic field the energy bands split into a set of discrete Landau levels separated by an energy equal to Planck's constant times the cyclotron frequency. This is reflected in the recombination radiation in two ways: the change in energy distribution of emitted photons; and the change in free energy of the electron hole liquid which results in oscillations of the recombination radiation intensity periodic in the reciprocal magnetic field.

Another confirmation of the metallic character of the liquid phase has been the observation of absorption and radiation corresponding to the plasma modes of the liquid phase. This also determines a liquid phase density of around 2×10^{17} cm^{-3} for germanium.

The electron hole droplets should scatter light in the same fashion as water droplets result in the opacity of fog. Application of Rayleigh-Gans theory to the angular distribution of scattered light allows one to determine a typical droplet diameter on the order of 10 μ. Droplet sizes of the same magnitude are also determined from shot noise experiments in which a p-n junction is attached to the germanium crystal and back-biased to collect the electrons and holes as droplets drift into the high electric field of the junction. Whereas these experiments confirm the liquid-gas model, the interpretation of measured size distributions remains in question due to uncertainties concerning the nature of condensation centers and the role of transport effects.

Much recent effort has been devoted to mapping out the electron hole phase diagram for germanium. At a fixed temperature the excitation level is increased until some characteristic signal of the liquid phase appears, whether it is the red-shifted recombination radiation, plasma radiation, shot noise in a p-n junction, cyclotron resonance of the liquid, or some other characteristic of the presence of the droplet. A plot of threshold excitation level versus temperature yields the low density side of the phase diagram. Such experiments agree well with the concept of a liquid-gas transition, at least above 2 K, and establish a work function for the electron hole liquid of about 1.5 meV.

On the high-density side of the phase diagram, the density versus temperature relation is determined from the change with temperature of the liquid recombination radiation. By assuming in fitting the line shapes that the liquid remains metallic through the critical point, G. A. Thomas, T. M. Rice, and T. C. Hensel have determined a critical temperature of $T_c = 6.5 \pm 0.1$ K and a critical density of $n_c = (8 \pm 2) \times 10^{16}$ cm^{-3}.

Although the characteristic recombination radiation of the liquid phase was first observed in silicon, considerably less experimental effort has been devoted to this material because of the shorter carrier lifetimes in silicon (2×10^{-7} sec) compared with carrier lifetimes in germanium (4×10^{-5} sec). Most recombination of the liquid phase in silicon is nonradiative, and the excess energy and

momentum of the recombining electron and hole are given up to another electron or hole. This process is called Auger recombination and is the dominant process in silicon.

However, one effect first observed in silicon will probably be of considerable impact to future research on electron hole droplets. In experiments on heavily doped silicon (10^{15} cm^{-3} impurities), Pokrovsky observed a series of narrow peaks in the recombination radiation extending from below the exciton line and merging into the droplet line. Recent extensive studies of the radiation from doped crystals as a function of excitation and impurity levels by R. Sauer and K. Kosai and M. Gershenzon give strong evidence that the new lines arise from multiexciton complexes bound to impurity atoms. Most physicists agree with Pokrovsky's initial speculation that these observations suggest that impurity atoms act as nucleation centers for electron hole condensation, much as seeding a cloud induces rain.

All of the experiments described above employ the absorption of laser light to create electron hole pairs. The light is actually absorbed in the first micron of the surface, and the electrons and holes created must diffuse into the semiconductor crystal. This means that gradients in electron hole density exist in the crystal which complicate the interpretation of many experiments.

At the California Institute of Technology, experiments have begun on a new way to excite germanium and silicon. The electrons and holes are injected electrically into the crystal. In these experiments one side of a crystal is doped with a p-type impurity which is deficient in electrons and therefore acts as a source of holes, and the other side of the crystal is doped with an n-type impurity which has excess electrons and therefore acts as a source of electrons. When this double-injection device is forward-biased, electrons and holes are driven into the undoped region of the crystal, where condensation into droplets occurs. Since electrons enter the crystal from one side and holes from the other, this method involves volume excitation, although density gradients certainly remain.

The recombination radiation from double injection appears to have exactly the same spectral properties as the radiation from laser-excited crystals. This is strong evidence that electron hole condensation is a bulk phenomenon and not simply associated with the semiconductor surface. Experiments on how electron hole condensation depends on current, electric field, and temperature in double-injection devices should be a testing ground for the hypotheses developed to describe laser experiments, as well as a valuable source of new information.

Theory. Attempts to calculate the quantities measured in these experiments have been simplified by the fact that germanium and silicon, because of their technological importance, are among the best-characterized materials. The parameters of the liquid phase at 0 K have been calculated, employing techniques which have had some success when applied to metals. If the anisotropic structure of the energy bands in germanium and silicon is carefully taken into account, good agreement with experimental values for the work function and liquid-phase density is obtained. For nonzero temperatures a mean field model of the phase transition has been developed, and crude estimates of the critical temperature have been obtained by extrapolation from the 0 K calculations. However, most physicists agree that better theoretical descriptions are needed for the transition from excitonic to metallic behavior.

For background information *see* BAND THEORY OF SOLIDS; EXCITON; FERMI-DIRAC STATISTICS; HOLES IN SOLIDS; SEMICONDUCTOR in the McGraw-Hill Encyclopedia of Science and Technology.

[R. N. SILVER; T. C. MCGILL]

Bibliography: L. Keldysh, *Proceedings of the 9th International Conference on Semiconductors*, Moscow, p. 1307, 1968; K. Kosai and M. Gershenzon, *Phys. Rev.*, B9:723, 1974; V. Marrello et al., *Phys. Rev. Lett.*, 31:593, 1973; Ya. Pokrovsky, *Phys. Stat. Sol.*, 11(a):385, 1972; R. Sauer, *Solid State Commun.*, 14:481, 1974; G. A. Thomas, T. M. Rice, and T. C. Hensel, *Phys. Rev. Lett.*, 33:219, 1974.

Semiconductor, organic

Organic semiconductors represent a potentially inexpensive, plentiful source of materials with electrical, mechanical, and thermal properties which can be tailored for specific purposes. Recent advances in the preparation of new materials, theory of transport, and biological and electronic device applications are the subject of this article. The electrical properties of organic semiconductors are diverse, with conductivities ranging from 10^{-7} (ohm·meter)$^{-1}$ to 10^3 (ohm·meter)$^{-1}$. Materials with resistivities higher than 10^7 (ohm·meter) undergo a change in resistivity under the action of light and constitute a class of semiconductors referred to as photoconductors. The transport of charge through such systems is similar to that for a large class of materials with higher conductivities, the main difference being the origin of charge carriers.

In semiconductors the carriers are generated internally from thermal equilibrium between conduction and valence "bands" or levels, or from injection into the valence or conduction levels from charged impurities in the bulk. However, in photoconductors the carriers can be generated internally by photoexcitation, or they may be photoinjected from an external source. A particularly interesting class of materials are the one-dimensional materials. They exhibit large anisotropic conductivities which give them metallic properties in one direction while retaining semiconductor-like properties in the perpendicular direction.

Transport in molecular solids. One of the most important applications of organic semi(photo)conductor technology to date has been in the area of electrophotography. The properties of the polymeric charge-transfer complex poly-*N*-vinylcarbazole-2,4,7-trinitrofluorenone (PVK-TNF) has been widely studied in this regard, and significant progress has recently been made in the understanding of charge transport in these materials. One of the most interesting and difficult-to-explain features of transport in these systems has been the apparent field- and thickness-dependent carrier mobility;

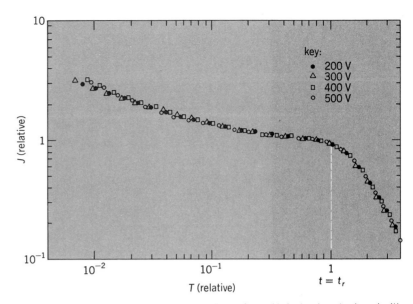

Fig. 1. Logarithmic plot of *J* versus *T* for films of poly-*N*-vinylcarbazole doped with 2,4,7-trinitrofluorenone at a mole ratio of 1 to 1. *J* is the ratio of the photocurrent at time *t* to the photocurrent at time t_r, where t_r is the time marking the exit of the fastest carriers from the film, and *T* is the ratio t/t_r. *(From H. Seki, Field and temperature dependent drift mobility in solids, in J. Stuke and W. Brenig, eds., Amorphous and Liquid Semiconductors, p. 1015, 1974)*

that is, mobility is proportional to *(E/L)*, where *E* is the field and *L* is the thickness.

Another unusual feature of the transport is illustrated in Fig. 1, where the transient response to a short pulse of light in the presence of an electric field was measured at various values of the field. The deviation of the curve from a square-shaped pulse (that is, constant current while the carriers are in transit, zero current when the sheet of carriers reaches the opposite electrode) indicates a dispersion in the velocity of the charge carriers in this system. The striking feature of this plot is the independence of the relative dispersion (the ratio of the dispersion to the change in the peak position of the carrier packet) on the transit time of the drifting carriers. (If the packet were to broaden as a Gaussian as it propagates through the film, the peak position would vary as the elapsed time *t* while the width of the packet would vary as $t^{1/2}$; hence, the relative dispersion would decrease as $t^{-1/2}$). This feature of the transport contains fundamental information on the microscopic aspects of the transport process.

A theory based on a stochastic hopping model has been developed. Carriers injected as a sheet at one surface of a film undergo an electric-field-biased random-walk process until they are absorbed at the other electrode. Essential to the success of such a theory is the proper formulation of the waiting time distribution $\psi(t)$ between hops. In general, $\psi(t) \sim t^{-(1+\alpha)}$, where $0 < \alpha < 1$, accounts for the behavior of the carrier packet over a wide range of transit times. These theoretical insights into the transport process should make it possible to physically optimize electronic and structural properties of new materials for maximum transport efficiency.

One-dimensional materials. Characteristic of one-dimensional materials is the highly anisotropic

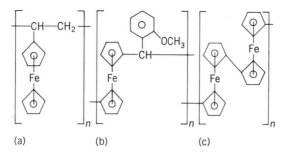

(a)   (b)   (c)

Fig. 2. Structural formulas for (a) polyvinylferrocene, (b) ferrocene-O-anisaldehyde condensation polymer, and (c) polyferrocenylene. The polymers were rendered conductive to various extents by oxidation with 2,3-dichloro-5,6-dicyanoquinone, 3,4,5,6-tetrachloro-1,2-benzoquinone, benzoquinone, or HBF_4.

conductivity with the largest component along the molecular strands formed from stacking of individual molecules or complexes in a crystal. The electrons are localized to a particular strand, but the interactions between neighboring strands are sufficiently large so that the conductivity is only moderately anisotropic. When the electrons are delocalized over a specific strand, the organic systems exhibit metallic-like behavior in one direction. Examples of two types of materials that exhibit this kind of conductivity are the cyanoplatinum complexes and charge-transfer salts of tetracyanoquinodimethanes. These materials, depending on their degree of purity, may exhibit conductivities in the semiconductor-to-metallic range. It is noteworthy that wide ranges of conductivities have been observed for materials which are otherwise very similar in their optical and magnetic properties. The conductivity is a bulk phenomenon which is extremely susceptible to defects that cause resistance to current flow. The defects may arise from cracks or fissures or solvent or impurity occlusion which impedes electron flow. The measured conductivity observed in these materials is to a large extent a measure of their crystalline perfection. These properties of these materials are currently the subject of many investigations. Although they have not yet found commercial appli-

cation, expectation is that the unusual optical, magnetic, and electrical phenomena they exhibit will form the basis for future technologies. See SUPERCONDUCTIVITY.

Mixed-valence polymers. Closely related to the one-dimensional materials are the mixed-valence polymers and salts of ferrocene. In these materials a fraction of the ferrocene moieties are oxidized, and the resulting semiconducting materials exhibit conductivities higher than either the fully oxidized or reduced form. In order to appreciate the potential for mixed-valence organometallic polymers, it is useful to consider briefly the properties of some monomeric charge-transfer salts and in particular the mixed-valence biferrocene {Fe(II)Fe(III)}+ picrate⁻. This compound was shown to have a conductivity 10^6 larger than either its fully bivalent or trivalent counterpart. This high conductivity occurs presumably because of the reduction in Coulomb repulsion for transferring an additional positive charge due to the presence of two Fe centers. The small changes in Fe-cyclopentadienyl bond lengths imply very little reorganizational energy in transferring the electron. This concept was extended to polymeric systems with the synthesis of the three polymers shown in Fig. 2. A maximum conductivity of $[2 \times 10^{-5}$ (ohm·meter)$^{-1}]$ was observed when the polymer in Fig. 2b was 70% oxidized. This observation is consistent with optimal electrical conductivity arising from an electron hopping model where ferrocene is surrounded by all nearest-neighbor ferricenium moieties. The other two polymers exhibited similar maxima in their conductivities. The staggered conformation of Fig. 2c offers a maximum opportunity for π conjugation but exhibits a conductivity several orders of magnitude lower than Fig. 2a or b. This also confirms that hopping occurs via iron moieties and does not take place through the conjugated π system.

Mixed-valence compounds may be particularly important for electron-transfer reactions in biological systems. There are many components of living systems which contain two or more metal atoms in close proximity. These mixed-valence effects may be of importance in determining oxidation-reduction potentials and rates of chemical reactions. Mixed-valence intermediates are involved as redox couples in the electron-transfer chains of the chloroplasts in the mitochondria where a number of metal-containing proteins shuttle electrons between oxidizing and reducing substrates. One such group of proteins are the non-heme iron proteins of the type $(Fe-S)_n$ where $n = 1-8$ such as found in spinach ferredoxin and beef adrenodoxin.

Molecular semiconductors. A new and potentially exciting concept for the use of organic semiconductors in electrical device applications has been described recently. It involves the use of specifically organized donor-acceptor molecules of the proper ionization potential and electron affinity as molecular semiconductors. The concept is based on the idea that electron transfer is highly directional and may permit current flow in only one direction. An example of such a device is shown schematically in Fig. 3. This device will act as a molecular rectifier. Electrons will tunnel from donor to acceptor (left to right) only, and the

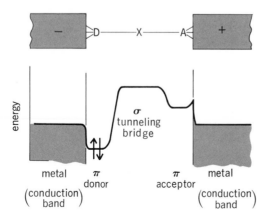

Fig. 3. Schematic representation of a molecular rectifier with corresponding potential energy profile of the metal–π electron donor–π electron acceptor–metal structure. An applied field will cause electrons to flow via tunneling from left to right.

structure will therefore act as a rectifier, a simple device for changing the periodically reversing flow of electrons in alternating current into the one-way flow of direct current. Achieving the precise spacing between donor and acceptor molecules and the electrodes to avoid the molecular version of a short circuit may be difficult in practice, but a new concept in organic semiconductors has been developed which may stimulate considerable activity in the years to come.

For background information *see* SEMICONDUCTOR in the McGraw-Hill Encyclopedia of Science and Technology.   [DAVID J. WILLIAMS]

Bibliography: A. Aviram and M. A. Ratner, *Bull. Amer. Phys. Soc.*, 19:341, 1974; D. O. Cowan et al., *Account. Chem. Res.*, 6:1, 1973; J. S. Miller and A. J. Epstein, *One-dimensional Inorganic Complexes in Progress in Inorganic Chemistry*, vol. 20, in press; H. Scher, in J. Stuke and W. Brenig (eds.), *Amorphous and Liquid Semiconductors*, 1974.

Sewage treatment

Reports of recent research on treatment of sewage and industrial waste waters using dissolved air flotation (DAF) have been concerned with new areas of application, collection of data on process results at established installations, improvement of batch bench-scale DAF test methods, and determination of the gas-dissolving efficiency of commercial pressurization systems. DAF is a liquid-solids separation process wherein the main mechanism of suspended solids removal is a change in the apparent specific gravity of the solids in relation to that of the suspending liquid by attachment of small gas bubbles (formed by release of the dissolved gas) to the solids. DAF continues to be applied to new areas of waste water treatment because of its ability to remove difficult-to-separate substances. Only the lack of application data and techniques, and the lack of a thorough understanding of the process principles by the design engineer, limits its use.

DAF has been applied to liquid-solids separation operations in sewage treatment for primary separation of floatable suspended solids, grease, and oil, for secondary clarification in the activated sludge biological treatment process, and for thickening of waste sludges. Primary treatment using DAF has been practiced when the sewage treatment plant receives a large amount of industrial wastes. These wastes consist primarily of fruit, poultry, or slaughterhouse processing solids, which are readily removed by DAF so that the organic and suspended solids load to the biological treatment section of the plant is decreased. DAF has also been successfully applied as the secondary clarification step following the activated sludge process or for clarification of waste water treated in an algae stabilization pond. Both clarification applications usually require the addition of coagulating chemicals to effect a high degree of suspended solids removal. Waste sludges produced by treatment of the main sewage stream are often thickened before further processing by aerobic or anaerobic digestion, or are dewatered in the final stages of sewage treatment by filtration or centrifugation. Waste-activated sludge discharged from a secondary clarifier at 1 wt % suspended solids can often be thickened to 3–4 wt % suspended solids by DAF.

The use of DAF as the primary treatment unit in the treatment of combined domestic sewage was investigated by R. L. Levy, R. L. White, and T. G. Shea. Data were collected on clarification of chemically treated raw sewage while process parameters, such as the hydraulic loading, recycle ratio, air-to-solids ratio, and the degree of chemical pretreatment, were varied. Levy and coworkers concluded that application of DAF in conjunction with alum pretreatment is a feasible primary treatment step for sewage and that removals of more than 85% suspended solids and 75% biological oxygen demand (BOD_5) were possible at optimum process conditions. The removal of suspended solids increased from 65 to 90% as the hydraulic loading decreased from 4000 to 1000 gpd/ft². The optimum air-to-solids weight ratio was 0.3–0.4; values outside the range of this ratio produced lower suspended-solids removal rates. Advantages cited for DAF over conventional gravity clarification included a more stable process operation over a wide range of hydraulic loading rates and influent suspended-solids concentrations and an increased suspended-solids removal capability.

Industrial waste water treatment. Treatment of industrial waste waters using DAF to produce effluents acceptable for discharge to waterways, to lessen the discharge of pollutants to domestic sewers and the associated surcharges, or for recovery of valuable products or by-products has been practiced for many years. Recovery of fats and proteins from slaughterhouse waste waters is profitable when these materials are used in rendering or in animal feed production. Vegetable oils and fats recovered at food-processing plants are often sold for use in the manufacture of nonedible products. M. G. Biesinger, T. S. Vining, and G. L. Shell collected DAF process data for several industries. They indicated that treatment of poultry-packing waste waters processed by DAF removed 28–46% suspended solids, 31–35% BOD_5, and 44–79% grease and oil. Suspended solids and grease removals of 40% and 73–86% respectively were observed when treating beef-packing waste water; the floated solids were rendered. Treatment of acidified soybean oil waste water from a food-processing plant removed 80% of the suspended solids and 69% of the oil.

DAF is commonly used in the paper and petroleum industries for product recovery and waste water treatment. Paper pulp is recovered from the paper machine white water for reuse. Waste water from de-inking of reclaimed paper is treated with chemicals and clarified by DAF to remove more than 80% of the suspended solids. Oil refineries and tanker terminals apply DAF for treatment of refinery oily waste waters and tanker ballast water to recover oil and produce an effluent acceptable for discharge. Oil removals of 92–96% were observed for these applications by Biesinger and coworkers.

Batch DAF tests. The design of full-scale DAF installations is often based on design criteria obtained from bench-scale batch flotation tests after applying appropriate scale-up factors. Data are usually collected with vessels of several liters' volume to closely simulate the full-scale process conditions. The test methods vary widely, and each equipment manufacturer or researcher has a different test procedure or apparatus. R. F. Wood and R. I. Dick conducted an extensive study on factors influencing batch flotation results. Waste-activated sludge from a continuous laboratory biological treatment system was used during the flotation study to closely control the character of the waste sludge. Batch DAF tests were conducted with varying air-to-solids ratios, feed suspended-solids concentrations, flotation vessel diameters and depths, and pressurization system pressures. The data collected indicated that each of the above process conditions can directly affect the separation rate of the floated solids. Decreased flotation vessel diameter, feed suspended-solids concentration, and pressurization system pressure, as well as increased flotation vessel depth and air-to-solids weight ratio, all increase the separation rate of the floated solids in bench-scale tests. The influence of batch flotation vessel diameter, feed suspended-solids concentration, and air-to-solids weight ratio was known, and the other factors presented had been investigated separately by other researchers, but the overall influence of all of the above factors upon the test results obtained had not been fully investigated until now. It was also noted that continuous full-scale flotation units produce greater float solids concentrations than those observed during batch bench-scale tests. Research to develop a rational approach to batch bench-scale testing for collection of data to design continuous full-scale DAF units and predict process results is continuing.

Pressurization system efficiency. The availability of sufficient dissolved air for precipitation to effect flotation of suspended solids is a primary design criterion. Calculations for the design of pressurization systems to dissolve air in the pressurized liquid stream are based on the dissolving efficiency of a system and on the solubility of air at the system operating conditions of pressure and temperature. Equipment manufacturers claim dissolving efficiencies of 70% to more than 95%. However, the methods used to determine the pressurization system dissolving efficiency are not uniform. Many methods of evaluation use a material balance of air and liquid flows around the pressurization system. The difference in the amount of air fed to the system and that leaving is assumed to be dissolved in the liquid stream; no allowances are made for the small amount of air that leaves the pressurization system with the liquid stream in the form of small entrained air bubbles. K. V. Leininger and D. J. Wall have developed a method to directly measure the amount of air dissolved in the pressurized stream and the dissolved gas composition. Using a series of measurements and calculations involving the partial pressures of oxygen and nitrogen, and other gas-solubility data, gas-dissolving efficiency values are calculated for each component of the air dissolved and the mixture. Data collected on several full-scale pressurization systems indicate air-dissolving efficiencies of 67–84%.

For background information *see* SEWAGE TREATMENT in the McGraw-Hill Encyclopedia of Science and Technology.   [JERRY L. BOYD]

Bibliography: M. G. Biesinger, T. S. Vining, and G. L. Shell, in *Proceedings of the 29th Industrial Waste Conference*, Purdue University, 1974; R. V. Leininger and D. J. Wall, in *Deeds and Data*, supplement to *Highlights of the Water Pollution Control Federation*, D-1–D-7, May 1974; R. L. Levy, R. L. White, and T. G. Shea, *Water Res.*, 6:1487–1500, 1972; R. F. Wood and R. I. Dick, *J. Water Pollut. Control Fed.*, 45(2):304–315, 1973.

Sex determination

In a number of species of *Drosophila*, females captured in nature have been found that produce all or nearly all female progeny as a result of the death of males at some stage in their development. This condition, called the sex-ratio (SR) trait, was first described by C. Malogolowkin in 1958 and has now been found in four related species of *Drosophila* from Puerto Rico, Haiti, Brazil, and Jamaica. There is very little information available regarding the fundamental cellular mechanisms of sex differentiation in any higher organism. Understanding why only the male sex is killed in the SR trait and what kills it could lead to better insights into the basic processes that differentiate males and females.

SR infectivity. The SR condition is normally transmitted from one generation of females to the next generation through the egg. The males that sometimes appear in the progeny are incapable of transmitting the trait when they are mated with normal or wild-type females. The trait is maintained through outcrossing of SR females to males from normal strains of the same species.

Early in the study of the SR trait, Malogolowkin and D. Poulson demonstrated that the cytoplasm from eggs laid by SR females could be transferred with a small glass pipet into the abdomen of normal females. After 10–15 days, these recipient females, mated to normal males, began to produce unisexual (female) progenies. Since it was possible to establish new SR lines from the progeny of these injected females, the fact that some infective agent is involved in the production of the SR trait was demonstrated. When various tissues of adult flies were investigated for the presence of the infective SR agent, hemolymph was found to be the most infective. Hemolymph from SR females has since been used as a source of the SR agent to transfer the SR trait into a number of species and strains of *Drosophila* in which it does not occur naturally. In nearly every case, the SR agent in the new host behaves basically the way it does in the donor host; that is, unisexual (female) progeny and maternal inheritance occur. The high level of SR infectivity in the hemolymph of adult females led to phase-contrast microscopic observations of freshly collected samples of SR hemolymph in which large numbers of a small (4–5 μm × 0.1–0.15 μm) spirochete-like organism were found (see illustration).

Male lethality. The lethal effects of the sex-ratio organism (SRO) can be expressed at any developmental stage of the male from embryo to adult, although, in well-established SR strains, male lethality occurs primarily during the embryonic state. Most attempts to understand why only the males die have dealt with manipulations of the chromosomes of flies carrying and transmitting the SRO. Hemolymph containing SROs was injected into females of a number of special stocks of *D. melanogaster*. Some examples of such studies are the following:

(1) Triploid females produced progeny devoid of males and supermales; females and intersexes were found in the usual frequencies. (2) Attached-X females, which normally possess a Y chromosome, produce only daughters, all of which received the two attached-X chromosomes from their mother and a Y chromosome from their father. The males, which receive their X chromosome from their mother and the Y chromosome from their father, do not survive. This study provides strong evidence that male death is related to the single-X condition rather than to the presence of the Y chromosome. (3) There is a high frequency of gynandromorphs in the progeny of ring-X females, a result of the loss of one of the two X chromosomes at an early stage of female embryogenesis. No males appeared in the progeny of such injected females, although healthy bilateral and one-quarter gynandromorphs were found, all possessing SROs in their hemolymph. The single-X (X0) tissue in these gynandromorphs has a male phenotype; nevertheless, it does not appear to be abnormal and does not affect the survival of the fly itself. It is known from experiments by G. Fink that X0 males do not occur in the progeny of SR females that have been mated to attached-XY males. (4) Finally, in experiments with a laboratory stock of the autosomal recessive gene mutation transformer, in which homozygous females are transformed into phenotypic males, female parents injected with SROs do not produce normal males, although "transformed" males appear in expected numbers, all carrying SROs in their hemolymph.

Male lethality, then, is in no direct way dependent upon the presence of the Y chromosome but, instead, appears to be more directly associated with the very poorly understood primary events in sex determination and differentiation. In *Drosophila* the X chromosomes possess genes that are female determiners, and the autosomes are male determiners. SR males die because they have only one X chromosome; two X chromosomes are needed for survival. It may be possible to localize the genes for female determination, and thus zygote survival, by taking advantage of special stocks that permit the introduction of progressively greater portions of the X chromosome by attached-XY males, which would, at some length of the X chromosome, cause a shift from maleness to femaleness. These experiments have not yet been done.

SRO morphology and taxonomic affinity. In spite of its spirochete-like appearance, the SR organism was shown by electron microscopy of both negatively stained whole specimens and thin sections of fixed and plastic-embedded organisms that it lacks an outer envelope and an axial filament, both of which, along with the inner protoplasmic cylinder, are characteristic structures of spirochetes. The SRO, having only a membrane-bound protoplasmic cylinder and no outer envelope or cell wall, is probably not taxonomically related to the spirochetes. Instead, the latest information available seems to show that it is related to a re-

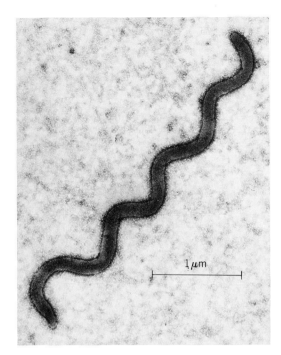

Electron micrograph of a sex-ratio organism fixed and negatively stained.

cently discovered group of spiral-shaped, wall-free microorganisms referred to as spiroplasma. R. E. Davis and coworkers at the Plant Disease Laboratory at the U.S. Department of Agriculture described a spiral-shaped microorganism derived from mycoplasma-like organisms recovered from corn plants afflicted with a stunting disease. P. Saglio and collaborators in France have also described a spiral-shaped microorganism that developed from mycoplasma cultured from diseased citrus plants. Only the citrus organism, named *Spiroplasma citri*, has been successfully cultured in a prepared medium, although very recent results from the laboratory of D. L. Williamson indicate success with media culture of the corn stunt organism. All attempts to grow the SRO outside the fly have not been successful.

Just how closely related these three organisms are, in spite of their similar morphology, is a question currently under investigation. In an attempt to answer the question concerning their relatedness, antibody has been prepared in rabbits against fresh suspensions of each of the three organisms. This kind of serological study is done to determine whether there are antigens in common among the three organisms. The information presently available has been gained from a series of experiments in which antiserum against one organism has been mixed with suspensions of each organism. Although the study has not yet been completed, the data do indicate that the citrus and the corn organisms are weakly related, as are the corn and the SROs, but that the relationship between *S. citri* and SRO is very weak or nonexistent.

Transmission patterns of SRO. When *Drosophila* females are injected with hemolymph containing SROs, the frequency of males in their progeny gradually declines until, after about 5 days, no males appear, and all further progeny are females. As the infection progresses in the injected females, males in their progeny are seen to be eliminated at increasingly earlier stages of their development—normal adults, weak and immature adults, dead pupae, dead larvae, and, finally, dead embryos. Samples of hemolymph from the progeny of these injected females reveal an interesting pattern of transmission of the SROs by these females to their progeny. The early progeny, both males and females, may or may not possess SROs, and when they are present, they are usually rare or very few in number. In subsequent progeny, by the time the males have disappeared, all their female siblings have SROs and in far greater numbers than observed in the earlier progeny. The injected female parents at this point have a dense population of SROs in their hemolymph and will continue to produce unisexual (female) progeny with a high density of SROs in their hemolymph throughout their reproductive life. If females to be used as parents for the next generation are collected from progeny that consist solely of females and have a high density of SROs, the pattern will be repeated, except that male elimination and continuous SRO transmission will occur in earlier progeny.

It has always been assumed that the actual presence of the SRO in the fertilized egg is necessary for male death. SROs have been observed in material extracted from eggs deposited by SR females as well as in hemolymph from each of the three larval stages through which *Drosophila* passes prior to pupation. Occasionally, however, in the first progeny of SR females it is possible to find adult females having no SROs in their hemolymph, even though there may be no males present among the progeny. If the SRO must be present in an egg to cause the male embryo to die, then, since some females emerge without SROs, an equivalent number of males should be expected to appear, also without the SRO. The fact that males do not appear seems to indicate that the male-lethal factor might be produced by the SRO and released to enter the developing egg and cause the death of that embryo if it is a male.

The strongest evidence that male death may occur is the absence of any indication that the SRO has been transmitted through the egg. This evidence comes from studies in which one of the SRO strains was introduced into *D. robusta*. The usual pattern of transmission of SROs to the daughters of infected females is one in which there are, first, few or no SROs in the first progeny, then an increase in the number of organisms transmitted, and finally transmission to all the later progeny. However, when *D. robusta* females are infected with SROs from *D. willistoni*, the highest frequency of transmission (never 100%) of the organism occurs in the early progeny, followed by a marked reduction, even a total cessation, in transmission to the late progeny, with few or no males ever appearing. The most interesting and important observation is that males do not appear even though most of their female siblings do not possess the SRO in their hemolymph. And if the SRO is not entering eggs that develop into females, then it should not be expected to enter eggs that will become males, and the males should become normal

adults. The egg is fertilized just prior to being laid, and the male-lethal factor and the SRO are presumably already present. But whether the SRO could be present in some nonfilamentous form, and thus be overlooked in hemolymph examination, is an unanswered question. However, a female which emerges without filamentous SROs in her hemolymph produces progeny in a normal 1:1 sex ratio. The original injected female parents of such flies possess a very dense population of SROs in their hemolymph but are simply not transmitting them. Nevertheless, whatever factor is responsible for the death of the male is apparently capable of getting into the egg and eventually causing the death of male embryos. The mechanism involved in this peculiar transmission pattern is not at all understood.

Male-lethal factor. The nature of the male-lethal factor remains unknown. The discovery by K. Oishi of a virus associated with the SRO suggested that it might be involved with male death. The SROs of each species of *Drosophila* in which they are found to occur in nature have their own virus. This virus is similar in both its morphology and behavior to the bacteriophages of various species of bacteria. It has a spheroidal head about 45 nm in diameter with a short (1.4-nm) tail. When viruses from one strain of SRO are mixed with SROs from a different species of *Drosophila*, the latter undergo complete lysis, releasing mature viruses into the hemolymph. The interesting result is that lysis of the SRO with concomitant release of mature virus particles into the hemolymph of the host fly results in a "curing" of the SR trait; that is, males reappear in the progeny. Thus a role for the virus in male lethality would seem to be ruled out.

The best hope for understanding the events in male death as they occur in the SR condition appear to lie in two areas. (1) The cultivation of the SRO outside the fly—in some kind of prepared medium—would permit the growth of large numbers of organisms and make it possible to search the medium in which the SROs have grown for some factor that could bring about male death when injected into egg-laying females or even, perhaps, kill adult males. The nature of the factor could be studied along with its mode of action. (2) A search for mutations in the fly that would enable males to survive even in the presence of the SRO or its male-lethal factor, or both, could be carried out. Even though there is usually a large time gap between finding a mutant gene and determining what it does or does not do in an organism, these mutants would be a beginning in the final unraveling of this very unusual and fascinating symbiotic relationship that has become established between this spiroplasma-like organism and the four species of *Drosophila* in which it is found.

For background information *see* CYTOPLASMIC INHERITANCE; GENETICS; SEX DETERMINATION in the McGraw-Hill Encyclopedia of Science and Technology.

[DAVID L. WILLIAMSON]

Bibliography: K. Oishi and D. F. Poulson, *Proc. Nat. Acad. Sci.*, 67:1565, 1971; D. F. Poulson, "Appendix III," in W. J. Burdette (ed.), *Methodology in Basic Genetics*, 1963; D. L. Williamson, *J. Invertebr. Pathol.*, 7:493, 1965; D. L. Williamson, *Japan. J. Genet.*, 44(Suppl. 1):36, 1969.

Ship, ferry

According to the normal designation, the term ferry boats refers only to vessels in other than oceangoing or coastwise service that have provisions only for deck passengers or vehicles or both, that operate frequently on a short run between two points over the most direct water route, and that offer a public service normally provided by a bridge or tunnel.

In the United States there are two notable exceptions to this definition: first, the ferries of the Alaska Marine Highway, operated by the state of Alaska and providing service from Seattle, WA, to the principal ports of southeastern Alaska (a distance of 1200 nautical mi or 2220 km); and, second, the Hydrofoil ferries for the Hawaiian interisland service, provided by Pacific Sea Transportation Company of Hawaii, which uses Boeing 929-100 Jetfoils and was begun early in 1975.

Insofar as normal ferry boat service is concerned, however, special note should be taken of the two new Washington state ferries, M/V *Spokane* and M/V *Walla Walla*, which began operation in 1973, and the three 165-ft (50 m) gas turbine-propelled aluminum-hulled passenger ferries being constructed for the Golden Gate Highway and Transportation District of San Francisco to reestablish commuter ferry service on San Francisco Bay late in 1974.

Alaska Marine Highway. Although the Alaska Marine Highway first started operations in 1963 with three vessels, the M/V *Malaspina*, *Taku*, and *Matanuska*, operating from Prince Rupert, British Columbia, to southeastern Alaska, with the service eventually extended south to Seattle, the most significant addition to the ferry fleet occurred during the summer of 1974, with the addition of the M/V *Columbia* to the system (Fig. 1).

The *Columbia* has been designed as an oceangoing ferry with the capability of crossing the Gulf of Alaska. The vessel has been fitted with 124 modular staterooms to provide sleeping accommodations for 324 passengers and can handle any highway-type vehicle with space on two decks for 184 standard American automobiles.

In order to maintain a 21-knot (39 km/hr) service speed, the *Columbia* is powered by two 9000-hp (6714 kW) diesel engines and is thus the most powerful diesel-driven vessel under the American flag. The *Columbia* is equipped with a bow thrus-

Fig. 1. M/V *Columbia*, built for the Alaska Marine Highway, designed by Nickum & Spaulding Associates, Inc. (*Courtesy of Jim Davis Photography, Des Moines, WA*)

ter driven by a 600-hp (448 kW) electric motor to give lateral thrust to the bow for assistance while making landings. Vehicles are loaded through a watertight door in the stern or through watertight side ports, port and starboard, near the bow of the vessel. The upper car deck, which accommodates automobiles and campers only, is serviced by two vehicle elevators.

In addition to passenger sleeping accommodations, a quiet lounge fitted with 100 reclining aircraft-style chairs has been provided for economy-minded travelers. Two levels of food service are offered: for the cruise-type vacationer, a dining salon with seats for 184 persons; for the budget-sensitive, a cafeteria with seats for 104 persons. The cocktail lounge, which is located on the boat deck and can accommodate 108 persons, is so designed that it can be opened into the observation lounge, more than doubling the capacity should the need arise.

The route of the Alaska Marine Highway

Table 1. Alaska Ferry Fleet*

Name	Length, overall	Length, waterline	Length between perpendiculars	Breadth	Draft	Displacement, long tons	Power, total shaft horsepower	Service speed, knots	Passenger accommodations	Sleeping accommodations	Vehicle capacity
Columbia	418 ft 0 in.	385 ft 0 in.	375 ft 0 in.	85 ft 1 in.	16 ft 0 in.	6700	18,000	21	1000	324	184
Matanuska	408 ft 0 in.	382 ft 0 in.	370 ft 0 in.	73 ft 7 in.	15 ft 4 in.	4774	8000	18	500	264	134
Malaspina	408 ft 0 in.	382 ft 0 in.	370 ft 0 in.	73 ft 7 in.	15 ft 4 in.	4774	8000	18	500	284	134
Taku	352 ft 0 in.	326 ft 0 in.	314 ft 0 in.	73 ft 7 in.	15 ft 0 in.	3585	8000	18	500	100	109
Tustemena	296 ft 0 in.	276 ft 0 in.	266 ft 0 in.	60 ft 6 in.	14 ft 6 in.	2750	3600	16	250	40	58
LeConte	235 ft 0 in.	215 ft 0 in.	210 ft 0 in.	57 ft 4 in.	12 ft 9 in.	1900	3200	15.5	250		47
Bartlett	193 ft 0 in.	172 ft 6 in.	167 ft 6 in.	53 ft 0 in.	12 ft 9 in.	1480	3400	15	165		38
Chilkat	100 ft 0 in.	92 ft 0 in.			36 ft 0 in.		1000	10	59		15

*1 ft = 0.35 m, 1 long ton = 1016 kg, 1 hp = 746 W, 1 knot = 1.85 km/hr.

through the "inside passage" of southeastern Alaska offers some of the most awe-inspiring scenery in the world. Two observation lounges located in the forward part of the deckhouse, one on the cabin deck and the other on the boat deck, accommodate a total of 243 passengers.

For those who enjoy the fresh salt air out of doors, a solarium has been fitted on the sun deck. Reclining deck chairs afford comfortable viewing of the magnificent scenery from within this weather-protected area.

The interior of the vessel has been tastefully decorated throughout with modern durable materials, the motif reflecting Alaskan native art.

The vessels of the ferry fleet presently in service, together with those about to be placed in service (Table 1), represent an investment by the people of Alaska of more $65,000,000. When this cost is spread over the state's population base, each man, woman, and child in the state has a stake of more than $215 in the Alaska Marine Highway.

Pacific Sea Transportation Company. Early in 1975 three Boeing 929-100 Jetfoils will begin Hawaiian interisland service out of Honolulu (Fig. 2). The distance from Honolulu to the island of Kauai is 94 nautical miles (1 nautical mile = 1.85 km); to the island of Maui, 90 mi; and to the island of Hawaii, 127 mi.

The Boeing Jetfoil 929-100 is a hydrofoil with a length of 90 ft (31.5 m), a beam of 31 ft (10.9 m), and a passenger-carrying capacity of 250. Passenger seating is arranged on two decks in a configuration and decor similar to those of wide-body jumbo jets.

The Boeing 929-100 is the most advanced commercial hydrofoil; its foil system is fully submerged, with the hull supported above the surface of the water by streamlined struts when the vessel is in foil-borne mode. The submerged foils are fitted with flaps extending the full length of the trailing edge, and the control system is very similar to that of modern aircraft, with autopilot systems that consist of an array of gyroscopes, accelerometers, and height sensors. As with a conventional rudder, steering is accomplished by rotating the forward foil about a vertical axis, except that, in this case, the rudder is in the bow. The Jetfoil's smooth ride is considered to be a function of the control system and not influenced by surface wave profile.

The vessel is propelled by two axial-flow water-jet pumps, each rated at 22,300 gal (84.4 m³) per minute. Each water-jet pump is driven by a 3780-hp (2820 kW) gas turbine through a reduction gear. The discharge nozzles from the pumps direct two streams of water astern in the go-ahead mode and thereby produce the thrust reaction necessary for propulsion. Conventional propellers are not used.

Each jet nozzle is equipped with a deflecting bucket that is so designed that, when in neutral thrust, the jet stream is directed downward and, when in reverse mode, the jet stream is directed forward, causing the ship to go astern.

In shallow-water operation, the foils are retracted; when the Jetfoil is hull-borne, it can proceed at a maximum speed of 10 knots (18.5 km/hr). A bow thruster is installed in an athwartship trunk to assist in maneuvering when the Jetfoil is hull-borne. The cruising range of the Jetfoil is 4 hr at a speed of 45 knots (83 km/hr).

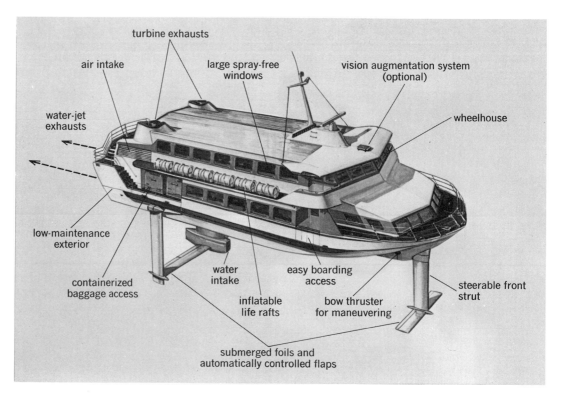

Fig. 2.   Boeing Jetfoil hydrofoil, model 929-100, for Hawaiian interisland service. (*Boeing Aerospace Company*)

Table 2. Washington State ferries*

Name	Length, overall	Breadth	Draft	Power, total shaft horsepower	Propulsion	Service speed, knots	Passenger capacity	Vehicle capacity	Crew complement
Spokane	440 ft 0 in.	86 ft 10 in.	17 ft 0 in.	10,300	Diesel-electric	20	2000	206	15
Walla Walla	440 ft 0 in.	86 ft 10 in.	17 ft 0 in.	10,300	Diesel-electric	20	2000	206	15
Hyak	382 ft 2 in.	73 ft 2 in.	16 ft 6 in.	8000	Diesel-electric	20	2500	160	14
Kaleetan	382 ft 2 in.	73 ft 2 in.	16 ft 6 in.	8000	Diesel-electric	20	2500	160	14
Yakima	382 ft 2 in.	73 ft 2 in.	16 ft 6 in.	8000	Diesel-electric	20	2500	160	14
Elwha	382 ft 2 in.	73 ft 2 in.	16 ft 6 in.	8000	Diesel-electric	20	2500	160	14
Tillikum	310 ft 2 in.	73 ft 2 in.	15 ft 6 in.	2500	Diesel-electric	13	1140	100	9
Klahowya	310 ft 2 in.	73 ft 2 in.	15 ft 6 in.	2500	Diesel-electric	13	1140	100	9
Evergreen State	310 ft 0 in.	73 ft 0 in.	15 ft 6 in.	2500	Diesel-electric	13	1000	100	9
Illahee	256 ft 2 in.	73 ft 10 in.	12 ft 0 in.	1800	Diesel-electric	12	800	75	8
Nisqually	256 ft 0 in.	73 ft 10 in.	12 ft 0 in.	1800	Diesel-electric	12	665	75	8
Klickitat	256 ft 0 in.	73 ft 10 in.	12 ft 0 in.	1800	Diesel-electric	12	800	75	8
Quinault	256 ft 0 in.	73 ft 10 in.	12 ft 0 in.	1800	Diesel-electric	12	665	75	8
Kulshan	242 ft 1½ in.	65 ft 1½ in.	11 ft 6 in.	1200	Diesel-electric	13	350	65	8
Klahanie	240 ft 6 in.	59 ft 6 in.	11 ft 0 in.	1200	Diesel-electric	10	601	50	8
Chetzemoka	239 ft 11 in.	60 ft 3 in.	11 ft 0 in.	1200	Diesel-electric	10	400	50	8
Kehloken	239 ft 8 in.	60 ft 3 in.	11 ft 0 in.	1200	Diesel-electric	10	770	50	8
Rhododendron	225 ft 9 in.	63 ft 0 in.	8 ft 6 in.	1610	Diesel	12	546	65	7
Olympic	207 ft 6 in.	62 ft 0 in.	8 ft 6 in.	1400	Diesel	11	605	55	7
Vashon	200 ft 0 in.	58 ft 0 in.	12 ft 0 in.	925	Diesel	10.5	646	50	8
Hiyu	150 ft 0 in.	63 ft 1 in.	11 ft 3 in.	860	Diesel	10	200	40	4

*1 ft = 0.35 m, 1 hp = 746 W, 1 knot = 1.85 km/hr.

Washington State Ferry System. The Washington State Ferry System operates 21 ferry boats in Puget Sound service (Table 2). These ferries are all conventional double-ended vessels, with a propeller and rudder at each end, and can proceed in either direction, fulfilling the true definition of a ferry in that they operate on a frequent schedule between two points over the most direct water route. The vessels range in size from 150 to 440 ft (52.5 to 154 m) in length.

When in February 1973 the state took delivery of the M/V *Spokane* (Fig. 3), and in April 1973, the M/V *Walla Walla*, the largest and fastest double-ended ferries ever built were placed in service. These vessels offered a new dimension in commuter travel in that great care was given to passenger amenities. All joiner materials and furniture were selected to reduce maintenance to a minimum. Passengers are mainly accommodated on the upper deck above the vehicle space with lounge seating areas, nonsmoking areas, ship's office, first-aid room, public toilets, and baby change room adjacent to the women's lounge. The beautiful scenery of Puget Sound is framed by large picture windows, and a modern two-line cafeteria located in a most attractive dining area with seating for 208 persons serves a varied menu of delicious food. Wool carpeting has been used throughout the enclosed passenger spaces because of its low maintenance cost. Throughout, warm colors have been used to complement the Puget Sound country.

For the "fresh-air" passengers, two solariums have been installed on the sun deck and are fitted with infrared heaters for cold-weather comfort. The solariums give protection during blustering weather, yet afford an unobstructed view for passengers while they travel across Puget Sound.

Each vessel is of welded steel construction with a complete double bottom fitted in way of the engine room. Fuel oil is carried in the double-bottom tanks, and potable water is stored in tanks at either end adjacent to the motor rooms. Isolated sewage holding tanks are provided so that no sewage or waste water is discharged into Puget Sound. Connections are fitted to discharge all sewage ashore to be treated by municipal sewage-treatment plants.

The vehicle deck arrangement provides for four lanes of passenger cars down the center of the vessel between the twin engine-room casings. Suf-

Fig. 3. M/V *Spokane*, designed by Nickum & Spaulding Associates, Inc. (*Courtesy of Darrel Wood, Photographer, Seattle*)

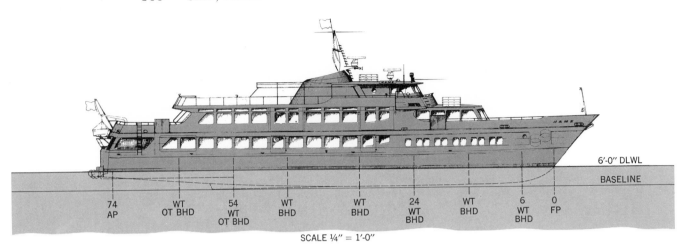

key:
BASELINE = construction reference plane from which
       all vertical dimensions are taken
AP = after perpendicular
FP = forward perpendicular

WT OT BHD = watertight oiltight bulkhead
WT BHD = watertight bulkhead
DLWL = design full-load waterline

Fig. 4. Outboard profile of the Golden Gate ferry. (*Nickum & Spaulding Associates, Inc.*)

ficient headroom has been furnished so that three lanes of trucks or trailers can be accommodated within the same space if necessary. Outboard of the machinery casing port and starboard are two levels that provide two-lane car parking. When the ferries are fully loaded, 12 lanes of cars can be carried, for a total capacity of 206 standard automobiles.

The propulsion plant is diesel electric with four 2875-hp (2145 kW) prime movers each coupled to an ac generator. All equipment—engine generator, heat exchangers, filters, control panel—was factory-mounted on a common base, and all components were prepiped for operation, before delivery to the shipyard for installation. The four ac generators supply current through silicon diode rectifiers to the two double-armature propulsion motors, one located at each end of the vessel.

The control system is so designed that a single hand wheel controls ship motion from the engineer's soundproof control room in the machinery space.

Normal operation is 100% motor power to the pushing propeller and 10% motor power to the pulling propeller, just to overcome its resistance. These two vessels maintain a 20-knot (37 km/hr) schedule on the Seattle-Winslow (Bainbridge Island) run.

Golden Gate ferry system. When the world-famous Golden Gate Bridge was opened to traffic on May 28, 1937, spanning the entrance to San Francisco Bay, it spelled the doom of a ferry system that had been in existence since gold rush days. Through the subsequent years, with the phenomenal growth of daily commuter traffic to San Francisco, the bridge has increasingly become a bottleneck, and traffic at peak hours has built beyond its capacity. Cars have moved at a snail's pace. Public pressure exerted on the California legislature caused that body in 1969 to ask the board of directors of the Golden Gate Bridge to seek a solution to the traffic problem.

Various plans were considered, such as building a second deck on the bridge, or even building a parallel bridge. These plans were strongly opposed by the city of San Francisco, for they would result in greater automobile traffic in San Francisco's already overtaxed streets. Also, there was no more land available for parking space.

Marin County residents, remembering the old efficient ferries, prevailed upon the bridge directors to reestablish a ferry system paralleling the bridge to help relieve the traffic pressure. A small ferry, the M/V *Golden Gate*, was acquired and started operation between the Ferry Building in San Francisco and Sausalito in Marin County in August 1970. The plan was a great success; each year the vessel has carried nearly 1,000,000 passengers.

The bridge district also acquired the Greyhound commuter bus system and, by providing new buses and improved service, has built the traffic to 7000 commuters riding the buses each way each day.

In July 1972 orders were placed for three new aluminum-hulled high-speed commuter ferries that will carry 750 passengers at a 25-knot (46 km/hr) speed (Fig. 4).

In addition to the Sausalito terminal, a new terminal is being constructed at Larkspur, centrally located in the more heavily populated area of Marin County. The Larkspur terminal will have parking for 600 automobiles and is located 11.5 mi (18.5 km) from the Ferry Building in San Francisco.

As the object of the ferry system is to attract as many commuters as possible away from their automobiles, stress has been placed upon speed and passenger comfort. Interior decor and passenger seating will be equivalent to those in the latest jumbo jet aircraft. Large picture windows on both the main deck and upper deck will afford a panoramic view. A snack bar and cocktail lounge are located on both the main deck and the upper deck

Table 3. Characteristics of Golden Gate ferries

Length overall	165 ft 0 in.
Length waterline	150 ft 0 in.
Breadth	33 ft 4 in.
Depth of hull	10 ft 4 in.
Draft	5 ft 8½ in.
Displacement	252 long tons
Registered tonnage	99 gross tons
Total power	7500 shp
Service speed	25 knots
Passenger capacity	750

for food and beverage service. Outside seating will be protected by a wind screen, and a canvas canopy can be added during bad weather.

The hulls are of all-welded-aluminum construction of the single-chine V-bottom semiplaning type. Sewage holding tanks have been built into the hull, and sewage will be pumped ashore at routine intervals in order to prevent environmental contamination.

The most distinguishing feature of these three vessels is that, like the Boeing 929-100 Jetfoil, they will be propelled by gas turbine-driven water jets. This type of propulsion was chosen to ensure reliable performance in debris-laden San Francisco Bay and for shallow-water operation up the mile-long dredged channel to the Larkspur terminal.

Each vessel will have three compact lightweight gas turbine-driven water-jet pumps installed at the stern. Valuable space normally occupied by much larger engines in conventional craft was made available for extra accommodations on the Golden Gate ferries. Also, the lack of engine vibration will permit greater passenger comfort.

Under full power each jet unit will expel 65,000 gal (246 m³) of water per minute. With all three engines at full throttle, developing a total of 7500 hp (5595 kW), they will deliver more than 45,000 lb (200,000 N) of thrust at 25 knots (46 km/hr). The jet pumps are designed for 100% forward thrust and 50% reverse thrust with full power available to the steerable nozzles for ship handling. All controls for operating the ferries are located in the wheelhouse, as the engine room is to be totally unmanned.

The Golden Gate ferries will have the characteristics shown in Table 3.

For background information *see* SHIP, MERCHANT in the McGraw-Hill Encyclopedia of Science and Technology.   [PHILIP F. SPAULDING]

Bibliography: Gas turbine/water jet propulsion for 25-knot San Francisco commuter ferries, *Motor Ship*, March 1973; R. Krantz, Boeing's hydrofoil programs, *Diesel Gas Turbine Progr.*, March 1974; Propulsion by pump will cut draft, save space, *Marine Eng./Log*, July 1973; Spokane, Double-ended vehicle and passenger ferry, *Shipping World Shipbuilder*, April 1973.

Silicon

The important role of electronic surface states in understanding electron conduction of semiconductor devices has been recognized since the time of the invention of the transistor, more than 26 years

ago. The excess charge in occupied surface states gives rise to an electric field (or space-charge region) that extends typically thousands of atomic layers from the surface (or interface), even though the surface charge is localized to a few atom layers at the surface. Most properties of surface states on semiconductors such as silicon have been determined rather indirectly from measurements of electrical properties such as conductivity and capacitance or from surface-sensitive parameters such as the work function and photoelectric threshold. Recently, several spectroscopic techniques have been developed that give much more detailed information (in the form of a spectral curve) than the single-parameter measurements used earlier and hence allow a more detailed comparison between theory and experiment. These techniques include optical absorption and photoconductivity, which are used to measure surface-state optical transitions within the forbidden band-gap of a semiconductor, as well as electron spectroscopic techniques, which are useful over a much wider energy range.

Electron spectroscopy. The very short penetration distance (~10 A, or 1 nm) of low-energy electrons greatly enhances the surface-to-bulk contribution of spectroscopic measurements based on electrons. Two complementary electron experiments are ultraviolet photoemission spectroscopy (UPS) and electron energy loss spectroscopy (ELS). Two typical examples of UPS are shown in Fig. 1a for the atomically clean silicon (111) surface and for the same surface after coverage with a monolayer of hydrogen atoms. The final-state kinetic energies of the measured photoelectrons have been shifted by the photon energy of 21.2 eV so that the energy scale corresponds to that of the initially occupied state. If all initial states were excited with the same photoemission probability, the UPS curves would be proportional to the energy density of occupied states. The four features labeled A_1, B_1, A_2, and A_3 are due to intrinsic surface states on the clean silicon (111) surface that

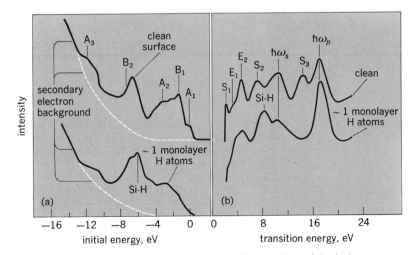

Fig. 1. Comparison of (a) ultraviolet photoemission spectra and (b) electron energy loss spectra for the automatically clean (111) surface of silicon and for the (111) surface covered with a monolayer of atomic hydrogen.

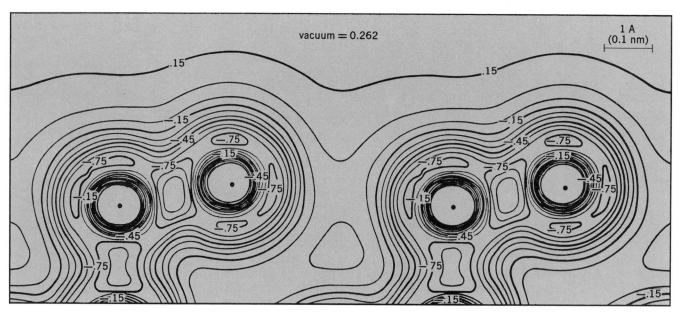

vacuum = 0.262

1 A
(0.1 nm)

Fig. 2.   Contours of constant surface potential are shown plotted on a plane normal to the Si (111) surface and passing through the back-bond line connecting a surface atom with one of its nearest neighbors in the second plane of atoms. Contours are plotted at intervals of 0.1 atomic unit between −0.95 and 0.15 atomic unit. The heavy black dots locate the centers of silicon atoms. *(From D. R. Hamann and J. A. Appelbaum, in Proceedings of the 12th International Conference on the Physics of Semiconductors, publication pending)*

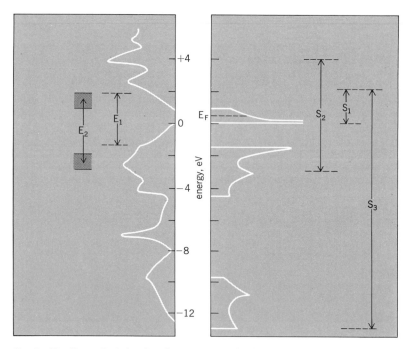

Fig. 3.   The theoretical density-of-states curves for bulk silicon (on the left) and for the (111) surface (on the right) are plotted. The initial and final states are shown for the E_1 and E_2 bulk interband transitions as well as for the S_1, S_2, and S_3 surface interband transitions. E_F is the Fermi energy.

are removed by bonding hydrogen atoms to saturate the dangling bonds of the clean surface. At the same time a new peak appears in the lower UPS curve at −6 eV owing to photoelectrons excited from the silicon-hydrogen bonding level. *See* SURFACE PHYSICS.

In Fig. 1*b* the ELS results are shown for the same two surfaces. This technique measures both transitions between occupied and unoccupied energy levels (interband transitions) and collective excitations such as the bulk plasmon excitation $\hbar\omega_p$ and the surface plasmon excitation $\hbar\omega_s$. Bulk interband transitions labeled E_1 and E_2 have been previously studied by optical reflectance experiments. Surface-state interband transitions are labeled S_1, S_2, and S_3 and are again removed in the lower curve corresponding to ELS from the silicon surface covered with a monolayer of hydrogen atoms. The large number of surface-state features in UPS and ELS are not consistent with the simple chemical picture of dangling-bond levels, which should occur near zero energy with small transition energies such as the A_1 and S_1 features in Fig. 1. This suggests that other surface bonds are involved in producing surface states.

Back bonds and dangling bonds. Although the simple idea of dangling bonds occurs to almost everyone who has looked at ball-and-stick models of crystal lattices, the detailed theoretical calculation of dangling-bond surface-state charge distributions has only recently been performed. J. A. Appelbaum and D. R. Hamann have used self-consistent field methods to determine the surface potential energy function and its associated surface-state charge distribution. They found that, in addition to the surface states associated with dangling bonds, there are surface states associated with strengthened back bonds between the surface atoms and atoms in the second layer. These back-bond surface states are fully occupied and hence do not directly contribute to electrical conductivity. However, they are intimately connected with the structural arrangement of atoms at silicon surfaces and thus indirectly affect the dangling-bond surface states as well.

The presence of both back-bond and dangling-bond surface states is shown in Fig. 2, which displays the surface potential energy contours calculated by Appelbaum and Hamann. A detailed discussion of Fig. 2 is not appropriate here; however, the atomic potential wells around each atom position can be clearly seen. In addition, there are bonding potential wells corresponding to the small closed contours at energies of −0.75 atomic unit (1 atomic unit = 27.6 eV). They are located above the surface atoms in the dangling-bond position as well as in the back-bond position along the nearly horizontal line between the surface atoms and the second-layer atoms. The bulk silicon-silicon bonds are shown between the second- and third-layer atoms and are vertical in Fig. 2. It should be evident that the three types of bonds have different potential contours and thus correspond to different electronic states. The surface atom layer has relaxed toward the second layer by 0.34 Å (0.034 nm) owing to the strengthened back bonds.

Electronic density of states. The fundamental conceptual bridge between spectroscopic experiments and the theoretical potential energy contours discussed above is the density-of-states function. This is shown in Fig. 3 for both bulk energy levels and for surface energy levels. The bulk curve was calculated by E. O. Kane several years ago, and the surface curve is a preliminary result from calculations of Appelbaum and Hamann. The occupied bulk valence band levels occur below the energy zero. The initial- and final-state energies of the E_1 and E_2 interband transitions are also shown. The surface curve consists of three bands of states with the three interband transitions S_1, S_2, and S_3 placed at energies corresponding to the features A_1, A_2, and A_3 observed in UPS. The agreement between theoretical peaks and experimental features is very good, although not every theoretical peak is observed. The S_1 transition corresponds to the dangling-bond surface states, and the S_2 and S_3 transitions correspond to back-bond surface states. Thus the existence of these two types of surface states is confirmed both theoretically and experimentally.

A more detailed theoretical and experimental understanding of these surface states for other semiconductors and other surfaces may lead to improved understanding of interfaces in semiconductor devices (and thus to improved performance). It is also likely that surface states play an important role in many surface chemical reactions such as corrosion and catalysis.

For background information *see* BAND THEORY OF SOLIDS; ELECTRON SPECTROSCOPY; SEMICONDUCTOR; SILICON in the McGraw-Hill Encyclopedia of Science and Technology.

[J. E. ROWE]

Bibliography: J. A. Appelbaum and D. R. Hamann, *Phys. Rev. Lett.*, 31:106, 1973, and 32:225, 1974; D. E. Eastman and W. D. Grobman, *Phys. Rev. Lett.*, 28:1378, 1972; H. Ibach and J. E. Rowe, *Surface Sci.*, 43:481, 1974; J. E. Rowe, *Phys. Lett.*, 46A:400, 1974; J. E. Rowe and H. Ibach, *Phys. Rev. Lett.*, 31:102, 1973, and 32:421, 1974.

Soil

Reports of recent research on soils have been concerned with the fate of fertilizer nitrogen in semiarid grassland, the effect of soluble aluminum in soils upon growth in plants, and salinity effects on crops and soils of the tropics.

Fertilizer in semiarid grasslands. In the semiarid grasslands of temperate regions, lack of available nitrogen often limits production as much as does lack of available water. Consequently, use of nitrogen fertilizer is increasing on millions of acres of grasslands, particularly in the northern Great Plains of the United States and Canada. This practice immediately raises concern about the ecological impact of extensive nitrogen fertilization on pollution of surface and ground waters with nitrate. Results of recent research on the fate of fertilizer nitrogen applied to semiarid grasslands have greatly reduced the uncertainty that has surrounded this subject.

In addition to the nitrogen absorbed and translocated into plant tops, a semiarid grassland ecosystem can immobilize a fairly definite quantity of fertilizer nitrogen in the roots, mulch, residues, and soil organic matter. The quantity of nitrogen immobilized in these pools varies with soil type and texture, water availability, and possibly temperature, but is not influenced greatly by either grass species or most management schemes. Fertilizer nitrogen immobilized in these organic forms may later be mineralized by soil microorganisms and recirculated through the ecosystem. A relatively small quantity (10 to 40 pounds per acre) of fertilizer nitrogen seems to be absorbed directly into the cells of the soil microbes and in a few weeks or months is mineralized and recirculated as successive generations of microbes are produced and die. (One pound per acre equals 1.121 kg per hectare.) Much more fertilizer nitrogen (up to about 200 pounds per acre) is immobilized in grass roots and mulches and seems to be recycled in 3 to 5 years. Typically, up to 350 pounds of fertilizer nitrogen per acre can be immobilized in various organic pools in the soil-plant system.

Nitrogen cycle. The nitrogen cycle in semiarid grassland ecosystems is essentially a closed system; that is, losses of nitrogen from the soil-plant system are relatively low. Ordinarily, no fertilizer nitrogen is leached below the root zone in semiarid grasslands, so leaching losses are generally inconsequential. Losses of fertilizer nitrogen in gaseous form (by ammonia volatilization or denitrification) also seem usually to be relatively small, except perhaps where urea-containing fertilizers are applied to semiarid grasslands at rates exceeding 80 to 100 pounds of nitrogen per acre. In such instances, available data suggest that volatilization losses may be relatively high.

Typical data on the fate of fertilizer nitrogen applied to semiarid grasslands emerged in an experiment in which 80 pounds of nitrogen per acre (as ammonium nitrate) was applied annually for 11 years to mixed prairie (primarily *Agropyron smithii, Stipa viridula,* and *Bouteloua gracilis*) grazed by yearling steers. After 11 years, approximately 35% of the fertilizer nitrogen applied was found in the roots (19%) and vegetative mulch (16%) on the soil surface. A slightly larger quantity remained in the soil as inorganic (ammonium 2%, nitrate 39%) nitrogen, indicating that the fertilizer applied exceeded the nitrogen required by the ecosystem. Less than 3% of the fertilizer nitrogen was physically removed from the pasture in the form of beef.

Fig. 1. Differential Al tolerance of (a) weeping lovegrass and (b) tall fescue grown in nutrient solutions. Left to right: 0,2, and 4 ppm Al added. (*From A. L. Fleming, J. W. Schwartz, and C. D. Foy, Agron. J., 66:715–719, 1974*)

In total, about 82% (including standing tops 2%, crown 1%) of the fertilizer nitrogen applied was accounted for. The 18% not accounted for was immobilized in soil organic matter or lost to the atmosphere as gaseous nitrogen. Other research suggests that the gaseous loss was about 5% of that applied. Therefore, losses from the nitrogen cycle are relatively low, and a major part of the nitrogen applied to grasslands remains in forms that can be recycled and used for plant growth in later years. All of the nitrogen in the inorganic pool plus a major part of that in roots, residues, and mulches, and some in the soil organic nitrogen pool (included in the unaccounted-for fraction), may be recycled.

Plant debris. Research using the ^{15}N isotope shows that within hours after application, the isotope is found primarily in the senescent or dead plant material—mulches and decaying root materials. This suggests that fertilizer nitrogen is absorbed into the cells of the microorganisms as they rapidly multiply after addition of nitrogen fertilizer. The increased microbial population then decomposes the senescent and dead plant materials, mobilizing the nitrogen they contain. Thus, nitrogen immobilized in plant material is recirculated through the nitrogen cycle, illustrating the importance of plant debris both above and below the soil surface as a pool of potential plant-available nitrogen in semiarid grasslands.

[J. F. POWER]

Aluminum toxicity in plants. Aluminum toxicity is an important growth-limiting factor for plants in many acid soils, particularly those having a pH of 5.0 or below. Excess soluble Al is especially harmful in subsoils because it restricts the rooting depths of plants. Shallow rooting means greater susceptibility to drought and less efficient use of subsoil nutrients. Liming the soil to pH 5.5–6.0 will prevent the direct toxicity of Al by reducing its solubility. However, lime applied to the plow layer moves downward very slowly, and mixing lime with the subsoil is mechanically difficult and generally not economically feasible. A promising alternative to subsoil liming is the selection or development of plants having greater resistance to Al toxicity.

Differences in tolerance. Plant species differ widely in tolerance to Al in the growth medium. For example, weeping lovegrass, *Eragrostis curvula* (Schrad.) Nees, is much more tolerant to Al concentrations of 2 and 4 ppm in nutrient solutions than tall fescue, *Festuca arundinacea* Schref. var. Ky. 31 (Fig. 1). Weeping lovegrass also grows well on acid (pH 4.0), Al-toxic mine spoils where tall fescue fails.

Plant varieties within species also differ in tolerance to excess Al in acid soils or nutrient solutions. Recent studies have shown that plant varieties developed in regions of strongly acid soils (surface or subsoils) are generally more tolerant to Al than those varieties developed on less acid, neutral, or alkaline soils. For example, Thorne wheat, *Triticum aestivum* L., developed at Wooster, OH, is much more tolerant to Al in acid soils and nutrient solution than Redcoat wheat, developed at Lafayette, IN (Fig. 2). Findings have been similar for other wheat varieties developed in these two adjacent states.

Genetic control of tolerance. In certain barley (*Hordeum vulgare* L.) populations, Al tolerance is controlled by one major, dominant gene. At least one degree of Al tolerance in certain wheat populations has also been attributed to a single dominant gene; however, recent evidence for other wheat populations indicates that two or three major genes, plus possible modifier genes, are involved (according to a personal communication from H. N. Lafever, Ohio Agricultural Research and Development Center, Wooster).

Physiological basis of tolerance. The exact physiological or biochemical mechanisms by which certain plants tolerate high levels of Al are still debated. However, the effects of Al on plants in general provide clues concerning possible causes of differential tolerance between plant species or varieties. Excess Al has been reported to interfere with cell division in roots, fix phosphorus in less available forms in the soil and on root surfaces, decrease root respiration, and interfere with the uptake and use of water and nutrients, particularly calcium and phosphorus.

In some plants, the symptoms of Al toxicity resemble those of P deficiency (stunting; small, abnormally dark green leaves; purpling of stems, leaves, and leaf veins; and yellowing and death of leaf tips). In other plants, Al injury may appear as an induced Ca deficiency (curling or rolling of young leaves and collapse of growing points or petioles). Aluminum-injured roots are characteristically stubby or swollen; root tips thicken and turn brown or black. The root system as a whole contains many short laterals, but lacks fine root branching. Such roots are inefficient in absorbing both water and nutrients.

Obviously, Al-tolerant plants must be able either to prevent the absorption of excess Al (avoid it in the growth medium) or to tolerate or detoxify the element after it has been absorbed. High Al tolerance in the azalea (*Rhododendron* species) plant has been associated with the entrapment of excess Al in the roots, thereby restricting its transport to plant tops. A similar mechanism has been proposed to explain the superior Al tolerance of certain alfalfa (*Medicago sativa* L.) clones. However, in wheat and barley such selective accumulation of Al by roots appears to be detrimental, rather than beneficial. For example, Al-sensitive barley and wheat varieties generally accumulate higher Al concentrations in their roots, but not in tops when compared with more tolerant varieties. The tea bush (*Camellia sinensis* L.) apparently has a high level of internal tolerance to Al and accumulates very high concentrations in its tops without injury.

Certain varieties of wheat (Thorne in Fig. 2), barley, rice (*Oryza sativa* L.), and corn (*Zea mays* L.) increase the pH of soils or nutrient solutions and thereby reduce the solubility and toxicity of Al. In contrast, the Al-sensitive varieties of the same species (Redcoat wheat in Fig. 2) lower the pH of their root zones and hence increase the solubility and toxicity of Al. Decreasing the pH by only 0.1 unit may double the solubility of Al in the root zone. Thus, plant varieties within a species not only differ in tolerance to initial soil conditions, but also, within limits, can alter soil conditions to their own benefit or detriment. The superior Al tolerance of peanut (*Arachis hypogaea* L.), compared with Al-sensitive cotton (*Gossypium hirsutum* L.), has been attributed to a similar (pH-increasing) mechanism. Similar plant-induced pH changes in root zones are also important in regulating solubility and availability of essential elements.

Recent evidence shows that Al tolerance in some plants is associated with the ability to absorb, transport, and use Ca and P in metabolic processes. For example, certain varieties of wheat and tomato (*Lycopersicon esculentum* Mill.) appear to be more efficient than others in absorbing and using low levels of P in the growth medium, either in the presence or absence of Al. The Al-tolerant corn inbred line (Pa 36) has a higher root phosphatase activity and absorbs P (organic or inorganic) more efficiently at low levels in nutrient solutions, with or without Al, than does the Al-sensitive WH inbred. Superior Al tolerance in certain pasture species has been associated with more efficient uptake and transport of Ca and P. Differential susceptibilities to a leaf-spotting disorder among certain tobacco (*Nicotiana tabacum* L.) strains has been attributed to interactions between Al and P within plant tops. Aluminum tolerance among certain varieties of wheat, barley, and soybean (*Glycine max* L. Merr.) seems to be associated with the ability to resist Al-induced Ca deficiency.

Need for tolerant varieties. Aluminum-tolerant plant varieties are needed for deeper rooting and, hence, greater drought tolerance in acid subsoils; for use in vast regions of acid soils in the tropics

Fig. 2. Contrasting lime responses of tops and roots of two wheat varieties grown on acid, Al-toxic Bladen soil. (*a*) Thorne and Redcoat with no lime (pH 4.3); (*b*) Thorne and Redcoat with 3000 ppm CaCO₃ (pH 5.8). (*From C. D. Foy et al., Agron. J., 66:715–758, 1974*)

where Al toxicity and P fixation are serious growth-limiting factors; for crop rotations in which even the surface soil must be kept acid for disease control (potato scab in a rotation of potatoes, *Solanum tuberosum* L., and barley); and for revegetation of strongly acid mine spoils and other wasteland. The Al-tolerant plant varieties presently available are the indirect result of selecting for crop yield and quality under various climatic, insect, and disease stresses, with little attention to soil properties. A direct effort should be made to breed plant varieties for greater tolerance to specific acid soil stress factors (Al toxicity) that may be impractical to correct.   [CHARLES D. FOY]

Soil salinity. Salinity may be inherent to the soil, due to natural soil genesis and weathering processes, or introduced to it by mismanagement of irrigation water. Regardless of origin, salt build-up may deleteriously affect soils as well as growing crops due to either the total amount of salt present or the types of ions that prevail in it, or both. In the tropics, where certain specialized crops are grown and where highly weathered soils prevail, salinity effects are different from effects on the crops and soils that prevail in arid regions of the temperate zone. Considerable information is now available, and still more is being provided, on the interactions involving salinity, crops, and soils of the tropics. The immediate use for such information will be the formulation of new criteria for judging irrigation water quality and for recommending irrigation water management practices that are more applicable for tropical conditions.

Tolerances of tropical crops. Classical published compilations on salinity effects on plants, none of which is recent, reflect a lack of information on tropical crops. Recent studies have given insight into the salinity tolerances of several cultivars of sugarcane. Differences in tolerance were detected among different cultivars, but sugarcane as a whole may be looked upon as a medium-tolerant plant, tolerating an average salt level in soil solution corresponding to an electric conductance of 5–6 millimhos/cm (at 25°C) with approximately 25% reduction in yield, and thus falling in a class comparable with field corn and grain sorghum. Although rice is also medium in tolerance, it can be grown on relatively more saline soils, since it is normally grown in paddy culture in which the concentration of any salts present is reduced by large volumes of ponded water. Pineapple was recently reported to be of high salt tolerance, particularly when the initial critical months after planting have elapsed. As shown in the table, young plants from slips are most susceptible, and oldest transplants least susceptible, to salt damage. Coconuts appear to resemble date palms in their high tolerance to salinity, particularly when the palms are well established. No sufficient information is currently at hand on the salinity tolerances of casavas, taro, papayas, mangoes, and macadamia nuts.

Tolerances of tropical soils. Large areas of soils in the tropics respond to salinity effects rather similarly to their counterparts in temperate regions. Thus, they tend to accumulate salts and to exhibit unstable structures and reduced permeabilities to water when sodium ions prevail over calcium or magnesium ions. These include the alluvial and dark and black soils of the tropics, commonly called Vertisols, and other soils whose mineralogical and structural make-up reflect an abundance of swelling clays and a lack of intensive weathering. Most of those soils occur as discontinuous patches among other, more weathered soils and are occasionally salt-affected in their natural habitat. On

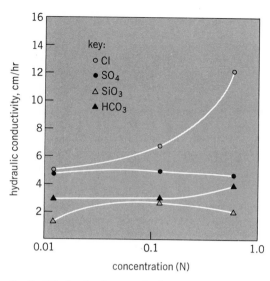

Fig. 3. Effects of salt concentration and anion types on the hydraulic conductivity of the surface horizon of Molokai silty clay, an Oxisol from Hawaii. Soil is sodium-saturated. *(From S. A. El-Swaify, Soil Sci., 115:64–72, 1973)*

the other hand, the more extensive, and productive, soils of the tropics are intensively weathered, rich in nonswelling clays (such as kaolinite) and in oxide minerals (such as oxides and hydroxides of aluminum and of iron), and are characterized by very strong aggregates and stable structures. Typical of such soils are Oxisols, the usually reddish soils occurring on gentle slopes under tropical arid to prehumid climates. Salinity effects on these, and on similar soils, have been shown to differ appreciably from effects on soils of the temperate zone. Their well-developed structural characteristics result in excellent water transmission properties and ensure regular leaching, by frequently occurring tropical rainstorms, of any salts that may have been contained in irrigation water. Such soils, therefore, show little or no tendency to accumulate salts on a long-term basis. It has also been established that these soils have less tendency to accumulate detrimental sodium ions at particle surfaces than do temperate arid region soils. This was attributed to their different mineralogical constitution with a resulting higher soil preference for divalent ions over sodium ions than expected. Studies recently completed have provided equations useful for predicting results of equilibria involving cations in soil-solution competing for adsorption at particle surfaces.

Effect of soil salinity level on weights of pineapple plants*

Age at planting: Salt treatment	Fresh weight, g			Dry weight, g		
	Slips	8 months	12 months	Slips	8 months	12 months
None	180	6865	7441	28	460	1130
Low	173	7140	8408	28	593	1096
Medium	166	7208	9673	25	534	1277
Medium-high	155	6659	8483	25	437	949
High	144	6728	9376	21	414	1220

*From H. Wambiji and S. A. El-Swaify, *Hawaii Agr. Exp. Sta. Dep. Pap. no. 22,* 1974.

The absence of swelling clays from highly weathered tropical soils reduces the potential hazard of adsorbed sodium ions as they prevail in the soil. While sodium/total-ions ratios of 0.5 to 0.15 are considered as upper limits that, if exceeded, will be deleterious to the structures of many temperate zone soils, certain Oxisols have been shown to tolerate full sodium saturation (ratio = 1) with little change in structure or water transmission properties. It was found, on the other hand, that these soils are more sensitive to the types of anions present than are temperate zone soils. Figure 3, for the surface horizon of an important sugarcane Oxisol from Hawaii, shows significant differences among anions prevailing in irrigation water or soil solution on the water permeability of saturated soil. This adds an extra dimension to concepts developed from research findings on temperate zone soils which indicated that hazards of anions are mostly due to toxic effects on plants and that soil structural modifications are mostly controlled by cations.

Implications of above information are that highly weathered tropical soils may tolerate higher salinity levels and sodium proportions relative to other cations in irrigation water, but that restrictions regarding prevailing anions may be necessary when water quality standards are formulated for their irrigation.

For background information *see* NITROGEN CYCLE; SOIL; SOIL CHEMISTRY in the McGraw-Hill Encyclopedia of Science and Technology.

[SAMIR A. EL-SWAIFY]

Bibliography: C. S. Andrew, A. D. Johnson, and R. L. Sandland, *Aust. J. Agr. Res.*, 24:325–340, 1973; F. E. Clark, Partitioning of added isotopic nitrogen in a blue grama grassland, in J. K. Marshall, ed., *The Belowground Ecosystem: A Synthesis of Plant-associated Processes*, in press; R. B. Clark and J. C. Brown, *Crop Sci.*, 14:505–508, 1974; S. A. El-Swaify, *Soil Sci.*, 115:64–72, 1973; C. D. Foy, in E. W. Carson (ed.), *The Plant Root and Its Environment*, pp. 601–642, 1974; R. H. Lowe and C. E. Bortner, *Agron. J.*, 65:263–265, 1973; J. F. Power, *J. Range Manage.*, 27:161–164, 1974; J. O. Reuss and C. V. Cole, Simulation of nitrogen flow in a grassland ecosystem, in *Proceedings of the 1973 Summer Simulation Conference*, Simulation Councils, Inc., La Jolla, CA, 1973; S. Sinanuwong and S. A. El-Swaify, *Soil Sci. Soc. Amer. Proc.*, in press; M. M. Syed and S. A. El-Swaify, *Trop. Agr.*, 50:45–51, 1973; I. Vallis et al., *Aust. J. Agr. Res.*, 24:693–702, 1973; H. Wambiji and S. A. El-Swaify, *Hawaii Agr. Exp. Sta. Dep. Pap. no. 22*, 1974.

Solid waste disposal

The handling and treatment of solid wastes have been dominated by three concerns during the last few years: damage to the environment, rising costs, and shortage and increased cost of energy. A new concern is increasingly becoming the subject of attention: growing shortages of raw materials.

The nationally expressed desire to save the natural environment from damage led to federal support of research and development of new methods of disposing of solid wastes. Many of these new methods have become realistic possibilities only in the last year or two, and others are due to reach commercial viability soon. Among the accepted new processes are high-pressure compaction and shredding. These very different approaches to solid waste treatment enable wastes to be transported long distances more economically than before and to be used as landfill with less possibility of water pollution and with a greatly reduced possibility of disease transmission through vector infestation. Because of these developments, for example, strip mines in Pennsylvania are being successfully reclaimed.

About three-quarters of the cost of domestic solid waste treatment is due to the collection phase, and a large variety of ingenious semiautomated collection trucks have been developed and are being used in suburban and rural areas. In some cases the cost of pickup with trucks employing a driver-controlled bag-pickup scoop or an automatic barrel emptier is half that of the earlier methods, in which three- to five-man crews were employed.

The third concern mentioned above was the energy shortage. Although the total energy content of domestic solid wastes in the United States amounts to only about 3% of the energy consumption, the utilization of at least some of this available energy can make important local contributions and can reduce the costs of waste disposal. An obvious way to recover energy from solid wastes is through heat recovery during incineration. Yet this approach has drawbacks.

The unreliability of supply of solid wastes and their varying combustion characteristics would normally require that standby equipment be used when heat recovered during incineration is used for some purpose external to the incinerator, especially when refuse is burned in the as-received condition. In electricity generation plants in Germany, two separate water-wall combustion chambers, one for refuse and one for conventional fuel, discharge their gases to common superheaters, economizers, air-pollution control system, and stack.

This necessity for duplication of capital plant reduces the attractiveness of incineration heat recovery. An alternative that avoids this duplication is suspension burning of shredded wastes in a common combustion chamber with regular fuel.

Suspension burning. At the Meramec station of Union Electric in St. Louis, refuse that has been shredded to a maximum dimension of 2 in. (5 cm) and air-classified (injected into a rising current of air) to remove most of the inorganic fraction is burned in suspension in a modified combustion chamber with a small grate to burn out any chunks that form or pass through the system. Conventional pulverized-coal burners supply most of the energy (90%) in the same combustion chambers. In this approach the additional capital cost required to convert an existing utility boiler to one burning refuse is small, and the risk to disruption of the normal boiler operation, which is normally an overriding concern, is also small.

Operating problems in St. Louis have been principally the erosion of the pulverized-fuel supply tubes. The basic plant operation and control with combined firing have been quite successful.

This method of burning the air-classified light

fraction of municipal refuse would seem to have wide applications.

Air-classified light fraction as fuel. The average fuel composition of the air-classified light fraction of solid wastes on a dry-weight basis is about 30% ash, 35% carbon, and less than 0.25% sulfur; it has a heating value higher than that of wood and peat, about equal to lignite, and somewhat lower than that of hard coal.

Several companies, such as Browning-Ferris Industries and Combustion Equipment Associates, have begun to offer this light fuel under trade names such as Ecofuel and Thermofluff. The large quantity of ash produced is a disadvantage of this fuel, in comparison with oil and gas in particular. Nevertheless, with the end of the cheap fuel era, there are likely to be abundant applications for this lower-cost energy source.

The air-classified light fraction can also be compressed into cubes and used as a solid fuel. The National Research Corporation of Fort Wayne, IN, has produced cubes of approximately 1½ in. (3.8 cm) that have been successfully burned experimentally in solid-fuel boilers.

Fuel-gas production from solid wastes. When organic materials are allowed to decompose anaerobically (digestion), carbon dioxide and methane are produced in approximately equal volumes. Theoretically, 1 lb (0.37 kg) of convertible waste yields 6.65 ft³ (0.186 m³) of methane, and a like volume of carbon dioxide, at standard conditions of temperature and pressure.

Research on the anaerobic digestion of solid wastes to produce methane has been carried out at the universities of California and Illinois and, more recently, at Dynatech Corporation in Cambridge, MA.

In a controlled digestion process, initial separation of the inorganic fraction is required. The organic fraction is slurried with water, and nutrients

are added. Raw refuse sludge can be used as a nutrient, thus avoiding the costs of purchased nutrients and of sludge disposal.

Uncontrolled digestion of organic wastes occurs in landfills. Some landfills in the Los Angeles area are being tapped to draw off the gases evolved, which are being cleaned and delivered to local homes in a test program.

Pyrolysis. When organic materials are heated in the total or partial absence of oxygen, they break down into combinations of gases, liquids, tars, and solids (ash). The relative proportions of these various constituents change as the temperature is varied between 500 and 1500°F (260 and 816°C), with gas production increasing and liquid production decreasing as the temperature increases. Shredding to 2–4 in. (5–10 cm) maximum size and separation out of the inorganic fraction are required for all processes except for that developed by Union Carbide. The wastes are introduced into a chamber (reactor), and hot inert gas under pressure or a fluid bed such as sand is introduced to heat the wastes. The process is run either on a batch basis, in which case the reactor must be periodically filled and emptied, or on a continuous basis, with approximately steady-flow conditions prevailing throughout the system.

Pyrolysis has a very great advantage over incineration in that there are no gases or liquid products that must be treated before discharge to the environment. The solids that remain after pyrolysis are inert and can be safely used as landfill.

The liquid fuel produced from pyrolysis has an average heating value of about 12,000 Btu/lbm (27.9×10^6 J/kg); the low-sulfur char has a heating value of about 9000 Btu/lbm (20.9×10^6 J/kg). A high-heating-value gas, 600 Btu/ft³ (22.4×10^6 J/m³), can also be produced. At least one of these streams is normally required as a heat input to the process.

An approach to pyrolysis that avoids the expensive shredding process and some of the costs of transferring heat to the refuse in the externally heated systems is to confine solid waste with oxygen sufficient to burn some of the refuse and to produce melting temperatures; the remainder of the refuse is pyrolyzed. The steam and methane undergo a shift reaction to produce carbon monoxide and hydrogen. This approach has been pioneered by Union Carbide (see illustration). The slagging (melting) of the solids greatly reduces the volume and the handling difficulty and produces a glass-like "frit."

Separation processes. Separation technology has followed three main approaches. The most popular is primary size reduction, followed by air classification and subsequent processing of the light and heavy fractions. A second approach is to pulp the incoming solid waste in water and to carry out separation processes on the slurry. A third approach is to separate the solid wastes insofar as possible in the as-received condition.

Air classification. Methods based on air classification have been developed by the National Center for Resource Recovery and the U.S. Bureau of Mines. Solid wastes are shredded and fed to an air classifier. The light organic fraction can be processed by any of the methods described above into a storable fuel, or it can be sorted into plastic and

Oxygen refuse converter. (*Union Carbide*)

paper fractions by a promising electrodynamic technique. The ferrous component of the heavy fraction is magnetically separated, and the remainder is sorted by size. The smaller pieces tend to be glass, which can be fed to optical sorting machines produced by the Sortex Company to produce single-color, higher-value fractions. The larger pieces of the nonmagnetic heavy fraction tend to be nonferrous metals, which are sorted by heavy-media separators. Water elutriation is suggested by the Bureau of Mines to separate aluminum from the heavy organic fraction.

This approach is typical of a branched binary system, in which a relatively large number of sorting devices are strung together, each device separating the flow into two streams.

Water-based systems. The first fully automated central-station solid waste separation plant is the water-based system at Franklin, OH, using the Black Clawson papermaking Hydrapulper as the fundamental treatment unit. Wastes are fed to this pulper without pretreatment, and a variety of screens and cyclones, and a magnet, are used for separation of the usable fibers, the ferrous metals, and the nonferrous metals and glass. The nonferrous metals and glass are sorted optically and magnetically by a multibranch binary system developed by the Sortex Company.

The proportion of solid wastes reclaimed was initially about 15% (into usable fibers) and is increasing to 30% as the glass- and metal-recovery sections come on-stream. Most of the remaining portion is incinerated.

Raw refuse separation. In traditional reclamation plants, of which there is one left (Houston) in the United States, solid wastes are separated in the as-received condition. The wastes are loaded in some manner onto a so-called picking conveyor belt, which in most plants is arranged to take the wastes up an incline to a second-floor level. Workers are positioned by hoppers next to the belt, and each one is responsible for extracting from the flow of refuse passing by a particular class of large, salable items. One person removes newspaper, a second cardboard, a third glass, and a fourth nonferrous metals.

A small prototype automated separation plant of this general type was developed at MIT. The principal features are that the larger pieces of refuse are first sorted out for treatment on an item-by-item basis; these items are examined by a number of sensors in series; a decision is made by a minicomputer as to which category, among perhaps 25, the items should be placed in; and subsequently, switching to that category is accomplished by means of bottom-opening carts which pass over a series of hoppers that feed balers.

Separation of the large items is accomplished by means of a two-deck vibrating screen of perhaps 8-in. (20 cm) and 4-in. (10 cm) mesh sizes. Loose paper and plastic film are sucked off by an overhead fan operating on the inside of an open-mesh belt. A magnet removes ferrous materials. The fines passing through the vibrating screens join the large items that have been rejected as inhomogeneous by the sensing system and are passed to a small hammer mill for further shredding and sorting by new or existing classifiers.

Increasing material shortages guarantee a greatly increased role for separation processes in the future.

For background information *see* FERMENTATION; METHANE; PYROLYSIS in the McGraw-Hill Encyclopedia of Science and Technology.

[DAVID GORDON WILSON]

Bibliography: E. A. Glysson, J. R. Packard, and C. H. Barnes, *The Problem of Solid-Waste Disposal*, University of Michigan, 1972; C. G. Golueke and P. H. McGauhy, *Comprehensive Studies of Solid-Waste Management*, University of California, 1st and 2d Annual Reports, U.S. Pub. Health Serv. Publ. 2039, 1970, and 3d Annual Report, U.S. Environ. Protect. Agency Rep. SW-(Org), 1971; National Center for Resource Recovery, *State-of-the-Art Review of Resource Recovery from Municipal Solid-Waste*, October 1972; U.S. Department of Health, Education, and Welfare, *Rep. no. SW3rg*, 1970, and *Rep. no. SW-105*, 1971; D. G. Wilson, Review of advanced solid-waste processing technology, *American Institute of Chemical Engineers Symposium on Solid Waste Management*, Pap. no. 40a, June 4, 1974.

Somatic hybridization

Although classical genetic analysis in humans is limited by the small numbers of progeny and the long generation time, parasexual systems of genetic analysis that allow fairly fine gene localization are now available. It is quite possible that future technological refinements and innovations will provide the means for high-resolution genetic mapping in humans.

The demonstration that two or more genes are syntenic, that is, are located on the same chromosome, and the assignment of genes or groups of syntenic genes to particular chromosomes can be accomplished in three basic ways. The first and best-established method involves following the segregation of genetic markers in informative families. This approach is limited by ethical barriers to selective matings as well as by the long generation time in humans. The second approach involves in-place annealing to metaphase chromosomes of isolated radioactively labeled mRNA, isolated fractions of labeled DNA, or labeled copied RNA (cRNA) from the isolated DNA. The RNA or DNA preferentially anneals to the region of the chromosome that has the same nucleotide sequence—the corresponding gene. Audioradiography utilizing the radioactive label indicates the chromosome to which the RNA or DNA has attached. This method is currently restricted to genes that are represented by a number of copies in the genome. The third method involves the genetic analysis of interspecific somatic cells, that is, nongerm cells, or hybrids. During the past year or so, analysis of these hybrid cells formed in the laboratory has provided a wealth of data concerning syntenic groups of genes and has made possible assignments of genes to all but six of the human autosomes, and in addition has confirmed the assignments of several X-linked genes.

The map of the human genome that is now rapidly evolving should provide insights into chromosome structure and organization, as well as into the evolution of this structure. Furthermore, this map should be highly useful in experiments involving cellular differentiation and regulation phenom-

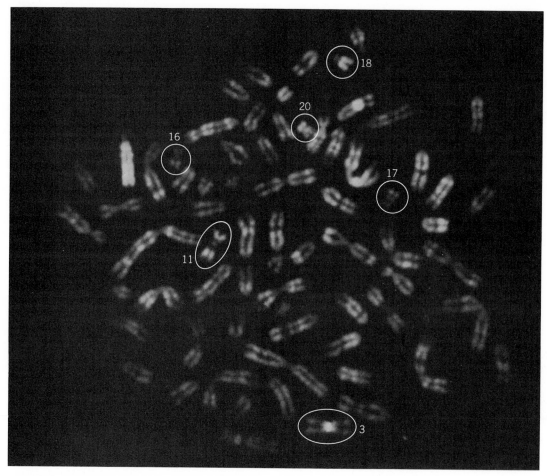

Quinacrine mustard fluorescence photomicrograph of the metaphase chromosomes of a mouse-human hybrid cell. The human-human chromosomes are indicated. The fluorescent banding patterns are characteristic for each particular chromosome.

ena. The future possibilities of genetic engineering, particularly any modification of the basic genetic blueprint, would certainly be aided by a knowledge of the normal organization of the unmodified genome.

The early observations of G. Barski and coworkers established that somatic cells could be fused experimentally and could then form viable, proliferating hybrid cells containing at least part of each parental genome. Agents such as inactivated Sendai virus or lysolecithin, which enhance the formation of hybrid cells, and methods that specifically select for survival of proliferating hybrid cells, as well as staining methods that permit the cytogenetic analysis of the resultant hybrid lines, have provided a system that is useful for genetic analysis.

Special properties of cell hybrids. Interspecific somatic cell hybrids, especially rodent-human hybrids, have proved useful for human genetic analysis because of their several special properties. Human chromosomes are preferentially and apparently randomly lost from these hybrid cells, with a rapid early loss followed by a much slower loss. The slow loss allows the establishment of relatively stable clonal lines, that is, lines derived from a single original hybrid cell, each of which has a complete rodent genome plus different numbers and combinations of human chromosomes.

The presence of particular human chromosomes can be determined by analysis of cells in metaphase. The human metaphase chromosomes can be identified by the characteristic banding patterns revealed by several recently developed staining methods (see illustration).

Expression of several types of human phenotypes can be detected in the hybrid cells. Particularly useful have been enzymes or other proteins that can be differentiated electrophoretically from their mouse homologues. Human surface antigens that are expressed in the hybrid cells have also been useful.

If, in a series of independently derived hybrid clones, two or more human phenotypes are always concordantly present or absent, then it is likely that the genes for these phenotypes are located on the same chromosome, since genes located on the same chromosome are retained or lost as a group. There exists the possibility, however, that two or more chromosomes could be preferentially associated and retained or lost as a group. Alternatively, a chromosome could be broken, with only a part retained or lost.

Cytogenetic analysis of the metaphase chromosomes can determine which of the possibilities mentioned above is actually occurring. If it can be shown that expression of a gene or group of genes correlates with the presence of a single intact

Human gene assignments: A list of phenotype markers*

Chromosome	Marker	Symbol
1	Phosphoglucomutase$_1$	PGM$_1$
	6-Phosphogluconate dehydrogenase	PGD
	Phosphopyruvate hydratase (enolase)	PPH
	Uridine diphosphoglucose pyrophosphorylase	UGPP
	Fumarate hydratase (fumarase)	FH
	Guanylate kinase	GuK
	Peptidase-C	Pep-C
	Adenylate kinase-2	AK-2
2	Isocitrate dehydrogenase (cytoplasmic)	IDH-1
	Malate dehydrogenase (cytoplasmic)	MDH-1
	Acid phosphatase (red cell)	AcP$_1$
	Interferon	If$_1$
3	No assignment	
4 or 5	Formylglycinamide ribotide amidotransferase	Ade$^+$ B
	Esterase activator	Es-Act
5	Interferon	If$_2$
	Hexosaminidase-B	Hex B
	Diphtheria toxin sensitivity	DTS
6	Malic enzyme (cytoplasmic)	ME-1
	Superoxide dismutase (mitochondrial)	SOD-2
	Phosphoglucomutase$_3$	PGM$_3$
	Histocompatibility antigen	HLA
7	Malate dehydrogenase (mitochondrial)	MDH-2
8	Glutathione reductase	GR
9	No assignment	
10	Glutamate oxaloacetate transaminase (cytoplasmic)	GOT-1
	Hexokinase (fibroblast)	HK
11	Lactate dehydrogenase-A	LDH-A
	Esterase-A$_4$	Es-A$_4$
	Acid phosphatase (lysosomal)	AcP$_2$
	Lethal antigen	AL
12	Lactate dehydrogenase-B	LDH-B
	Peptidase-B	Pep-B
	Triose phosphate isomerase	TPI
	Serine hydroxymethylase	Gly$^+$ A
	Citrate synthetase (mitochondrial)	CS
13	Esterase D	EsD
14	Nucleoside phosphorylase	NP
15	Mannose phosphate isomerase	MPI
	Pyruvate kinase (white cell type)	PK-3
	Hexosaminidase-A	HexA
16	Adenine phosphoribosyl-transferase	APRT
17	Thymidine kinase	TK
	Galactokinase	GaK
18	Peptidase-A	Pep-A
19	Glucose phosphate isomerase	GPI
	Polio virus receptor	PVR
20	Adenosine deaminase	ADA
21	Superoxide dismutase-1	SOD-1
	Antiviral protein	AVP
22	No assignment*	
X	Phosphoglycerate kinase	PGK
	α-Galactosidase	α-Gal
	Hypoxanthine-guanine phosphoribosyl-transferase	HPRT
	Glucose-6-phosphate dehydrogenase	G6PD
	Tyrosine aminotransferase regulator	TATr
Y	No assignment	

*The genes for 18S and 28S ribosomal RNA have been assigned by in-place hybridization to the satellite region of chromosomes 13, 14, 15; 21, and 22.

human chromosome, and that the expression of these genes disappears when this particular chromosome is lost, then these genes can be assigned to that chromosome.

The system outlined above has permitted the assignment of a large number of genes to human chromosomes (see table). The extension of this map of the human genome is limited only by the state of development of the methods of detecting expression of human genes in hybrid cells.

Hybrid cell system refinements. The somatic cell hybrid system has been refined, and further methods have been developed that allow assignment of genes not only to particular chromosomes but to regions within the chromosomes. One approach utilizes human cell lines or strains in which naturally occurring chromosome rearrangements have been found. These rearrangements include deletions, in which part of one chromosome is lost, and translocations, in which part of one chromosome is attached to another. For example, if expression of a human gene that has been assigned to chromosome 1 is concordant with a deleted or translocated chromosome involving only part of chromosome 1, localization of the gene is further restricted. A series of clones involving several overlapping regions of one chromosome can restrict localization of the genes on that chromosome to smaller and smaller regions, and can also indicate the order of genes along the chromosome. Estimates of the intrachromosomal intergene distance can be derived in this fashion, and the information can be correlated with data from family studies to establish the relationship of physical distance to the linkage distance expressed in terms of crossover events at meiosis.

Like chromosomal rearrangements in human parental cells, rearrangements involving human chromosomes that originate in the cultured hybrid cells can be used to restrict the localization of genes within chromosomes. Furthermore, the use of such agents as x-rays, which induce chromosome breakage and rearrangement, has proved useful for gene localization.

Facultatively expressed phenotypes. The great majority of the phenotypes whose genes have been assigned to chromosomes are constitutively expressed; that is, if the gene is present, the corresponding phenotype is expressed. Yet the genetics of facultatively expressed phenotypes, such as those found only in certain cell types, is of great interest. A significant class of facultative phenotypes consists of those phenotypes that are expressed during the differentiation of cells. Phenotypes such as albumin, melanin, and hemoglobin production are expressed only in specific cell types such as, respectively, hepatocytes, melanocytes, and erythrocytes, even though strong evidence exists for the presence of their corresponding structural genes in all cell types. Cell differentiation is thus marked by controlled differential expression of subsets of genes from the total cell genome. Somatic cell genetics can contribute to an understanding of the regulatory processes involved in this differential gene expression.

Tumor use in tissue culture. It is now possible to adapt differentiated, "minimal-deviation" tumors to long-term growth in tissue culture. These cell populations are abnormal in many respects, such as chromosomal constitution and acquired neoplastic properties, but more important, they retain the expression of particular specialized functions that are restricted to one or a limited number of cell types. It is possible to use these cell populations as inputs in somatic cell hybrids, in combination with cells of similar or dissimilar differentiation. Furthermore, the hybrids can be constructed so that either both parental chromosome sets are retained or one or the other is segregating. One can thus evaluate the effect of specific chromosomes on the expression of particular differentiated phenotypes. Three kinds of results have been obtained in this type of experiment: extinction of the gene expression, continued expression of specialized functions, and activation of gene expression.

Extinction of gene expression. This process has been demonstrated in a number of specialized gene products in hybrid cells. Hybrids that are formed by fusing pigmented mouse melanoma cells with nonpigmented cells, and that have a 1:1 parental genome ratio, are nearly always nonpigmented. Considerable evidence indicates that an intact set of pigment genes is retained, although the products of this set are not expressed in the hybrids. This result can be partially reversed by producing hybrids that have a ratio of two melanoma genomes to one nonmelanoma genome. About half the hybrids isolated from this cross are pigmented.

An electrophoretically distinct murine esterase (Es-2) has also been used as a differentiated-facultative marker. Es-2 is limited in laboratory experiments to expression in kidney, liver, and large intestine. RAG, a mouse cell line derived from kidney, continues to express Es-2 under experimental conditions. However, hybridization of RAG with human diploid fibroblasts yields many clones that do not express Es-2. It has been possible, though, to recover subclones from Es-2 negative hybrid clones that have regained Es-2 expression. This is a significant finding, for it provides strong evidence for the retention of an unexpressed structural gene for Es-2. These experiments were also consistent with the loss of human chromosomes bearing a possible relationship to the reexpression of the specialized mouse function. Similar results for a number of specialized liver traits have been reported by M. Weiss and coworkers.

Specialized-function continued expression. J. Minna and coworkers and A. McMorris have isolated hybrids of neuroblastoma cells with fibroblastoid cell lines of various types. These hybrids are striking in their continued expression of neuronal phenotypes such as neurite extension, acetylcholinesterase activity, nerve-specific protein, and membrane action potentials. It is not clear why there is continued expression of the neuronal traits, but it may possibly be related to the fact that the neuroblastoma parents have approximately double the chromosome number of the nonneuroblastoma parent. Among other instances of continued expression of differentiated functions in hybrid cells is that of immunoglobulin synthesis.

Gene expression activation. Activation of a phenotype refers to the expression in hybrid cells of a specialized function coded by the genome of the adifferentiated parent (a parent not originally expressing differential functions) but consistent with the phenotype expression of the differentiated parental cell. G. Darlington and H. Bernhard have recently demonstrated the activation of the human albumin phenotype in hybrids formed between human peripheral leukocytes, which do not normally produce albumin, and mouse hepatoma−derived cells, which do produce mouse albumin. Their results suggest that the human gene for albumin has been retained in the hybrid and its phenotype activated. This kind of system provides a possible means of mapping the genes for specialized cell functions. Thus, it may be possible, utilizing hybrids of human leukocytes or fibroblasts with the appropriate differentiated rodent cell, to map genetic functions that regulate the expression of particular differentiated phenotypes.

Although the results to date from hybridization experiments using differentiated cell lines have been varied, they clearly demonstrate the regulation of differentiated phenotype expression in hybrid cells. Thus, an experimental system now exists that makes it possible to regulate differentiated gene phenotypes under controlled conditions. This may represent the first step in gaining insight into specific mechanisms that regulate differentiation.

Further use of all hybrid systems. Further extension of the use of somatic cell hybrid systems will most certainly involve studies of the role of differential gene expression in host-virus interactions as well as attempts to elucidate oncogenic mechanisms.

The methods that have proved so successful for human gene mapping are now being extended to other primates and genetically interesting mammals such as the mouse. The combination of comparative karyology, using chromosome banding techniques, with comparative linkage group analysis should prove to be very useful in deciphering the chromosomal rearrangement processes involved in the generation of present karyotypes.

Somatic cell hybridization is a versatile and powerful addition to the array of methods available for genetic analysis. It has had its greatest impact to date on the construction of a human genetic map, but it is becoming increasingly useful in studies involving differential gene expression.

For background information *see* CHROMOSOME; DEOXYRIBONUCLEIC ACID (DNA); GENE; RIBONUCLEIC ACID (RNA); SOMATIC HYBRIDIZATION in the McGraw-Hill Encyclopedia of Science and Technology.

[RICHARD P. CREAGAN; FRANK H. RUDDLE]

Bibliography: D. Bergsma (ed.), *New Haven Conference, 1973: First International Workshop on Human Gene Mapping*, The National Foundation, 1974; F. H. Ruddle, *Advan. Hum. Genet.*, 3:173−235, 1972; F. H. Ruddle, *Nature*, 242:165−169, 1973; F. H. Ruddle and R. P. Creagan, *Annu. Rev. Genet.*, vol. 9, 1975.

Space flight

The year 1974 saw a lull in manned space flight. The third manned visit to *Skylab* (launched on Nov. 16, 1973, and the last in the Skylab program) splashed down on Feb. 8, 1974, after 84 days in orbit. No further United States manned flights were planned until 1975, when the first launches in the joint American-Soviet Apollo-Soyuz Test Project were to take place. Except for some manned Soyuz test flights, Soviet manned space activity was also uneventful in 1974.

Most space activity consisted of launches of scientific and applications satellites built by the United States, the Soviet Union, the United Kingdom, Italy, and the Netherlands (see table). The fact that space technology provides useful tools for communications engineers and meteorologists was evident in the high proportion of applications satellites. Space science was not forgotten altogether, but budget reductions caused a considerable decrease in the number of scientific flights.

Lunar and planetary probes. With the Apollo program completed, the only Moon flights in the foreseeable future will be unmanned—for example, *Luna 22* in the table. No American lunar or planetary launches were scheduled during 1974, although the German *Helios* solar probe was planned for launch by an American rocket late in 1974.

Two previously launched American planetary probes reached their targets in 1974. *Pioneer 11* emerged undamaged from the asteroid belt on March 20 and headed for a rendezvous with Jupiter on Dec. 5, 1974. Some outstanding photographs of Venus and Mercury were taken by *Mariner 10* when the 1108-lb (502 kg) probe swept past the planets on February 5 and March 29. The photographs of Venus revealed details in its complex cloud structure that are impossible to see from Earth. It was discovered that Mercury has a heavily cratered surface, like those of the Moon, Mars, and, by inference, the much more heavily eroded Earth. *See* SPACE PROBE.

SMS-1. The *SMS-1* (synchronous meteorological satellite) represents a departure from previous meteorological satellites in that it is stationed in a synchronous orbit over a specific spot on the Equator. In contrast, the earlier Tiros and Nimbus weather satellites were injected into inclined orbits at much lower altitudes. Consequently, they could not transmit weather photographs of the same area on a continuous basis—one of the operational features of *SMS-1*.

SMS-1 was launched from Cape Canaveral on May 17, 1974. Its initial orbit was lower than desired, but its on-board hydrazine gas jets were able to boost it to the required altitude of 21,471 mi (34,547 km), where it remains fixed over one spot of the Earth. Its first orbital station was at 45° west longitude, from which it has been returning excellent cloud-cover photographs every 30 min as part of the international Global Atmospheric Research Program (GARP). In September 1974 *SMS-1* was scheduled to be repositioned at 70° west longitude, to become part of the operational meteorological satellite system of the National Oceanic and Atmospheric Administration (NOAA).

The *SMS-1* is only part of an extensive system that includes ground stations and remote scientific stations. The master ground station is at Wallops Island, VA. The spacecraft Operations Control Center and Data Processing Facility is located at Suitland, MD. There are also several field stations at other locations.

The basic payload of the *SMS-1* is a telescope-radiometer called the visible infrared spin-scan

Major nonmilitary space missions through August 1974

Date	Designation and origin	Purpose
February 8	*San Marco 4* (Italy; launched by NASA)	Measurement of density, composition, and temperature in upper atmosphere
March 5	*Meteor 16* (Soviet Union)	Meteorology
March 8	*UK-X4* (United Kingdom; launched by NASA)	Testing of gas-jet attitude-control system and various sensors
April 13	*Westar 1* (United States; Western Union)	Commercial communication
April 20	*Molniya 1/27* (Soviet Union)	Communication
April 24	*Meteor 17* (Soviet Union)	Meteorology
April 26	*Molniya 2/9* (Soviet Union)	Communication
May 17	*Intercosmos 11* (Soviet Union)	Presumably a scientific mission
May 17	*SMS-1* (United States)	Part of a network of meteorological satellites
May 29	*Luna 22* (Soviet Union)	Lunar orbital science
May 30	*ATS-6* (United States)	Provision of basic design information for synchronous applications satellites
June 3	*Hawkeye* or *Explorer 52* (United States)	Study of high-altitude polar magnetosphere
August 30	*Astronomical Netherlands Satellite* (Netherlands; launched by NASA)	X-ray and ultraviolet astronomy

radiometer (VISSR), which provides both infrared imaging and high-resolution photographs in visible light. Complete scans of the Earth's disk are made every 30 min in eight visible channels and one infrared channel. The satellite's synchronous orbit enables the VISSR to follow large storms (hurricanes) over a wide area on a continuous basis. Short-term weather phenomena, such as tornadoes, can also be spotted for warning purposes.

An important feature of the *SMS-1* system is its data-collection capability. Environmental data from as many as 10,000 data-collection platforms (DCPs) on the Earth and in its atmosphere can be received by *SMS-1* and relayed to the station at Wallops Island. The DCPs can send data to the *SMS-1* at regular intervals, or they can be selectively interrogated by signals sent via *SMS-1*. Some typical DCPs are illustrated in Fig. 1.

SMS-1 also transmits weather pictures in a form that can be received by the small automatic picture-transmission (APT) stations set up in many countries for local weather forecasting during the Tiros and Nimbus meteorological satellite programs.

ATS-6. The *ATS-6* (applications technology satellite) is far larger and more complex than its five predecessors. With its large parabolic antenna (Fig. 2) and 500-W power supply, *ATS-6* is the most

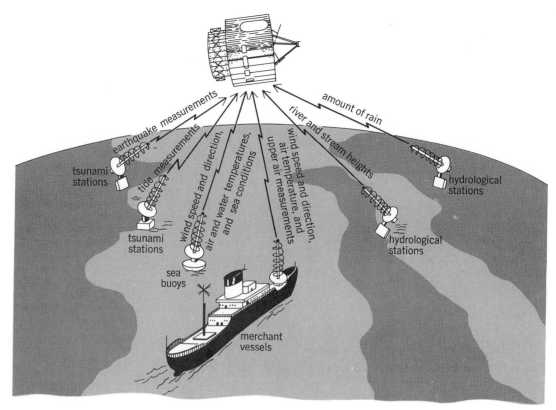

Fig. 1. *SMS-1* data collection from remote scientific stations.

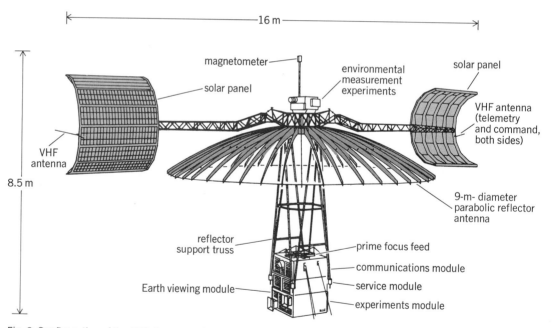

Fig. 2. Configuration of the *ATS-6* spacecraft.

powerful communications satellite ever orbited by NASA.

The spacecraft weighs 1402 kg and is 8 m high. The deployable solar panels and 9-m parabolic antenna dominate the configuration, but most of the spacecraft weight (907 kg) is in the boxlike earth-viewing module under the parabolic antenna. Many of the experiments and most of the spacecraft operating equipment are in this "box."

The unfurlable antenna is a novel design feature. In the launch configuration, its 48 aluminum umbrellalike ribs are wrapped around the antenna hub along with the copper-coated Dacron fabric. The whole assembly is released when a pyrotechnic cable cutter severs restraining cables. In less than 2 sec, the compressed elastic ribs deploy the paraboloid. The spacecraft attitude-control system keeps this high-gain antenna pointed directly at the Earth so that signals can be sent and received efficiently.

ATS-6 was launched into synchronous orbit from Cape Canaveral on May 30, 1974, by a Titan-IIIC rocket. During its first year of operation, it will be stationed at 94° west longitude (over the Galapagos). From this position, its antenna views the entire United States continuously.

More than 20 scientific and technical experiments will be conducted from *ATS-6*. One of these, the health-education telecommunications (HET) experiment, will pioneer the use of communications satellites in educational television and two-way medical teleconferencing. Some of the other experiments are: very-high-resolution radiometer experiment; radio-frequency interference experiment; millimeter-wave propagation experiment; COMSAT propagation experiment; cesium-ion bombardment engine experiment; advanced thermal-control flight experiment; spacecraft attitude precision pointing and slewing adaptive control experiment; radio beacon experiment; environmental measurements experiments; and international magnetospheric relay experiment.

For background information *see* COMMUNICATIONS SATELLITE: METEOROLOGICAL SATELLITES; SATELLITES, APPLICATIONS; SATELLITES, TECHNOLOGY; SPACE FLIGHT in the McGraw-Hill Encyclopedia of Science and Technology.

[WILLIAM R. CORLISS]

Space probe

The most significant recent space probe activity is the opening up of the outer solar system by *Pioneer 10* and *Pioneer 11*. These space probes explored the solar system beyond the orbit of Mars, checked the asteroid belt for hazards to spacecraft, and defined the environment of Jupiter.

Because the outer, giant planets of the solar system are so distant, they are difficult to observe by telescope and are relatively unknown to researchers. Jupiter is 483,000,000 mi (10^6 mi $= 1.609 \times 10^6$ km) from the Sun and never comes closer to Earth than 390,000,000 mi. Saturn, the next-largest planet, never comes closer than 780,000,000 mi, and Uranus is almost 1,000,000,000 mi beyond Saturn. Yet these big planets are important to a full understanding of the solar system and its origin.

Jupiter—uses and hazards. For space probes to travel to the outer planets in reasonable times of years instead of decades, higher velocities are required than those obtainable with available launch vehicles. By using the gravity and orbital motion of Jupiter, however, space probes can be accelerated into more energetic paths and can reach the outer planets relatively quickly.

Using Jupiter in this way to explore the outer solar system presents a major problem. The planet's strong magnetic field traps energetic protons and electrons in radiation belts that extend from Jupiter farther than the distance of the Moon from the Earth. How damaging these belts could be had to be determined by a space probe before the outer solar system could be explored by more sophisticated spacecraft. This exploratory testing became the mission of two space probes—*Pioneer 10* and *Pioneer 11*.

Pioneers 10 and 11. The new probes were extensions of earlier Pioneers that for years have patrolled the inner solar system as solar weather stations. The two Jupiter spacecraft are identical. *Pioneer 10* blazed the trail. If the asteroid belt or Jupiter's environment had destroyed it, *Pioneer 11* would have provided backup. *Pioneer 10* dispelled fears about the hazards of the asteroid belt and of Jupiter. *Pioneer 11* also penetrated the asteroid belt for a December 1974 encounter with Jupiter. The success of *Pioneer 10* at Jupiter in December 1973 permitted retargeting of *Pioneer 11* beyond Jupiter for an encounter with Saturn in 1979.

To reach Jupiter, each spacecraft had to travel at slightly more than 32,000 mi (51,490 km) per hour as it left Earth. Even with the Atlas-Centaur launch vehicle and an additional upper stage, the weight of each space probe still had to be carefully managed. A decision was made early in the program to keep as much system complexity as possible on the ground and avoid using it in the spacecraft. By "flying" the Pioneers from the ground, designers eliminated the weight of on-board computers and memories, but major operations-control hurdles had to be surmounted.

Radio waves take 46 min to travel from Earth to a spacecraft (and vice versa) at the distance of encounter with Jupiter. As a consequence, flying from the ground is not simple. Controllers at Pioneer Mission Operations Center, NASA-Ames Research Center, CA, must be 92 min ahead of the spacecraft, anticipating and correcting problems before they arise. New command techniques were devised to overcome spurious commands generated by Jupiter's radiation belts. Reconfiguration commands, transmitted through the hazardous zone of the encounter, kept critical instruments continually updated, to point where they should be pointing, and at correct gain settings. Thus, when Jupiter's radiation generated a spurious command, it was quickly corrected by a command already on its way from Earth. In this way, only a few images of the many hundreds obtained during the Jupiter flyby were lost.

Communications. Communications with the distant space probe stretched technology to the limit. The amount of energy received at Earth over the radio link from the 8-W spacecraft transmitter is incredibly small. An 85-ft (26 m) antenna would need 16,700,000 years to gather enough of this energy to flash a 7½-W night-light for one-thousandth of a second. Only the advanced data-coding and special signal-modulation techniques, coupled with large ground antennas and supercold receiving devices, allowed the reception of these faint signals from Pioneer.

To conserve weight, the antenna of the spacecraft had to be fixed and directed toward Earth by spin-stabilizing the spacecraft itself. A command system was also devised to keep the spin axis pointing correctly, again with the goal of minimum weight aboard the spacecraft in mind.

Power requirement. Another major engineering problem overcome by Pioneer's designers was how to generate electrical power at great distances from the Sun. At the distance of Jupiter the Sun's radiation is only 1/27 its intensity at Earth's orbit. Moreover, scientists want to hear from Pioneer about the interplanetary medium as far out as the orbit of Uranus, where the Sun's radiation is only 1/368 that at Earth's orbit. Not only are solar cells

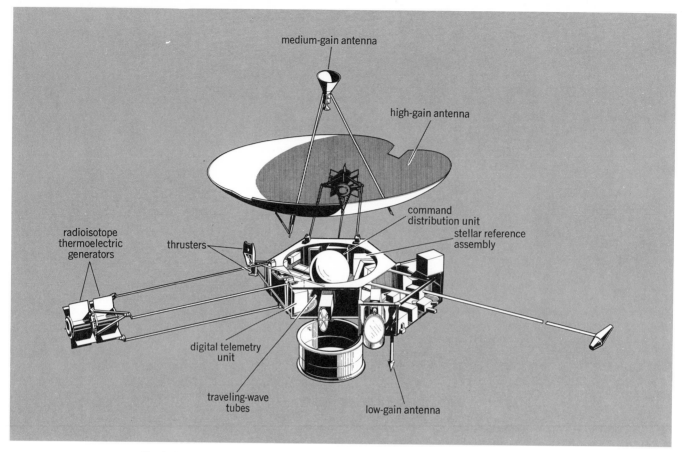

Fig. 1.   Major subsystems of the Pioneer space probe used to study Jupiter. (*NASA*)

impractical from the standpoint of the number needed to gather the required solar energy, but they could not survive the radiation environment of Jupiter.

Pioneer 10 and *Pioneer 11* use a new type of power generator for interplanetary spacecraft—the radioisotope thermoelectric generator (RTG), which converts the heat from the decay of plutonium 238 into electricity. Moreover, by careful selection of materials, engineers made the RTG relatively radiation-clean so that it would not interfere with the extremely sensitive scientific instruments of the Pioneers. The RTGs were also made highly reliable to last for the expected 8–10 years of the mission to the outer solar system. Each Pioneer carries four RTGs.

Subsystems. The Pioneer space probe consists of several distinct subsystems—a lightweight general structure, an attitude-control and propulsion system, a communications system, an electrical power system, a navigation system, and a scientific payload of 11 instruments to measure particles, radiation, and fields and to build up spin-scan images. These systems are shown in Fig. 1.

The flyby of Jupiter proved the efficacy of the engineering design. *Pioneer 10* survived and passed almost unscathed through the radiation belts to demonstrate that Jupiter can be used for gravity-assist trajectories to the outer planets. *Pioneer 10* also proved the feasibility of space probes using RTGs instead of solar cells. It

showed that command and control can be extended to vast distances despite round-trip propagation time delays and that scientific instruments can be designed to withstand the extreme radiation environment of Jupiter and, later, gather data at the outer planets.

Scientific data. Investigation of interplanetary space beyond the orbit of Mars resolved several unknowns about the behavior of the solar wind at great distances from the Sun and the mix of cosmic rays from the Sun and the Galaxy. *Pioneer 10* revealed that peaks and valleys in the solar wind smooth out at the distance of Jupiter, where the wind blows at about the same average velocity as at Earth but is more consistent and at a higher temperature. *Pioneer 10* also confirmed that low-energy cosmic rays from the Galaxy do not penetrate into the solar system—inside the orbit of Jupiter, at least. *See* JUPITER.

Another important discovery is that the asteroid belt does not contain a hazardous amount of small particles that might destroy a spacecraft passing through it.

At Jupiter, the Pioneer space probe investigated the particles, fields, and radiation of the Jovian environment and provided spin-scan images of the planet and some of its satellites. Some of these images (Fig. 2) have better resolution of Jupiter's clouds than Earth-based photographs do, and are at viewing angles, such as a crescent phase, impossible from Earth. They reveal atmospheric circula-

Fig. 2. Jupiter's Red Spot, a shadow of the moon (Io), and Jupiter's cloud structure are shown in this photograph, taken at 11:02 p.m. PST on December 1 as NASA's *Pioneer 10* spacecraft was about 1,580,000 mi (2,500,000 km) from the giant planet. (*NASA*)

tion patterns and suggest that the controversial Great Red Spot is a collection of thunderstorms in a Jovian equivalent of a hurricane.

Intensity of radiation belts of Jupiter proved to be considerably greater than Earth's Van Allen belts, and their shape quite different. The inner belt is doughnut-shaped, somewhat like Earth's, but extending for 20 Jovian radii in the plane of the magnetic equator, offset 11° from the rotational equator. An outer current sheet extends more than 100 Jovian radii parallel to the rotational equator but flops around Jupiter like the brim of a fedora. In addition, *Pioneer 10* revealed that Jupiter is the source of high-energy electrons detected at Earth's orbit but previously classified as being of unknown origin.

As measured from radio signals received at Earth, the motion of the spacecraft provided a new estimate of the mass of Jupiter—heavier than previously thought by 1 lunar mass. Also, it showed the lunar masses of the Galilean satellites as being: Io, 1.22; Europa, 0.67; Ganymede, 2.02; and Callisto, 1.44. Thus the density of these satellites decreases with increasing distance from Jupiter. A spin-scan image of Ganymede reveals a Mars-like object, and an occultation experiment indicates that Io has an extensive ionosphere.

From every engineering standpoint, *Pioneer 10* performed admirably, doing everything it was supposed to do. It proved that space probes can explore Jupiter and the outer planets. It gave an accurate measurement of the environments of the asteroid belt and Jupiter and provided enough new information to whet scientists' appetites for more exploration of the outer planets.

Engineering data coming back from *Pioneer 10* promise that it will still be sending information when it crosses the orbit of Uranus in 1980, the expected limit of communications. Then *Pioneer 10* heads out to the stars carrying a plaque that tells where it came from and who its creators were,

to become humankind's first interstellar emissary.

For background information *see* JUPITER; SPACE PROBE in the McGraw-Hill Encyclopedia of Science and Technology.   [ERIC BURGESS]

Bibliography: R. O. Fimmel, W. Swindell, and E. Burgess, *Pioneer Odyssey*, NASA SP 349, 1974; *J. Geophys. Res.*, Pioneer Special Issue, 1974; *Science*, 183:301–324, Jan. 25, 1974.

Statistical mechanics

The Landau and Curie-Weiss theory of critical points in magnets and the Van der Waals theory of a liquid-gas critical point are both invalid. The renormalization group approach, the ϵ expansion, and the $1/n$ expansion, all recently developed, work better. It is found that Landau theory is correct for space dimension d greater than 4 (for ordinary critical points). The ϵ expansion is an expansion about four dimensions ($\epsilon = 4 - d$). The recent work confirms the earlier scaling hypotheses of B. Widom, L. Kadanoff, and others.

Critical points occur at the onset of a first-order phase transition. A ferromagnet has a critical point at the Curie temperature T_c, where the spontaneous magnetization vanishes. A liquid-gas critical point occurs when the densities of coexisting liquid and gas phases become equal. Critical points also occur in antiferromagnets, binary alloy transitions, superfluid helium transitions, and so on.

Experimentally the behavior of all critical points is rather similar. A common set of critical exponents can be defined for most critical points, and their experimental values vary for different systems by about 10% (see table). The principal theoretical concern is to explain this near-universality of critical behavior and calculate the universal exponents.

Critical points are not of much practical value. First-order transitions involving large jumps in magnetization or density are more useful.

Critical exponents. The spontaneous magnetization M of a magnet behaves as $(T_c - T)^\beta$ near T_c, where the exponent β is experimentally about $\frac{1}{3}$. The magnetic susceptibility above T_c behaves as $(T - T_c)^{-\gamma}$, where γ is about 1.25. In an external field H a more elaborate functional dependence is required. Scaling theory predicts an equation of state of the form

$$H = a\, M^\delta f[\, b(T - T_c)/M^{1/\beta}\,]$$

for T near T_c and small M. Here δ is another critical exponent and $f(x)$ is a function, both universal, while a and b are constants depending on the particular system.

Fluctuations. There are always time-dependent fluctuations on an atomic scale due to motions of the constituent electrons and nuclei. These fluctuations have to be averaged over by the rules of statistical mechanics to obtain time-independent bulk properties of a microscopic system such as a

Values of the exponent β

Substance	β	Theory	β
CO_2	.34	Landau	.5
MnF_2	.34	ϵ expansion	.34
β-brass	.305	3-d Ising	.31

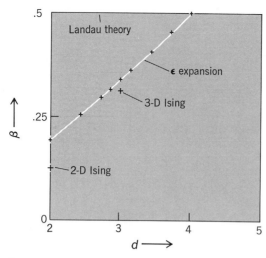

Plot of exponent β versus dimension d. Results are compared from Landau theory, ϵ expansion, and the Ising model. The solution of the Ising model is exact for dimension 2, and approximate for dimension 3.

magnet. Near the critical point very long wavelength fluctuations become important. Near a liquid-gas critical point the fluctuations with wavelengths ~ 100 nm cause critical opalescence (strong light scattering). The maximum wavelength of the fluctuations is called the correlation length ξ. At a critical point, ξ is infinite (for an infinite-size system).

Renormalization group. The new methods are needed to cope with fluctuations on all length scales from 0.1 nm to ξ. The basic idea of the renormalization group method is a generalization of the canonical ensemble. The generalization is to divide a magnet (for example) into cells of an arbitrary size L. An average magnetization M_i is specified for each of these cells. The index i labels different cells. The ensemble comprises all configurations of the atoms of the magnet consistent with these average magnetizations. For each of these ensembles one can compute a free energy $F_L\{M_i\}$ which depends on L and the set of cell magnetizations $\{M_i\}$. An ensemble for cell size $L/2$ is a subset of an ensemble for cell size L. This is true provided each cell of size L is made up of size $L/2$ cells, and provided the average magnetization specified for the larger cell is explicitly the average of the magnetizations specified for the constituent smaller cells. In consequence the free energy F_L can be computed in terms of $F_{L/2}$ without reference to the microscopic Hamiltonian. The calculation involves a sum over all possible choices of the smaller cell magnetizations holding fixed the larger cell magnetization.

Fixed points. At the critical point the functions F_L approach a fixed point for large L, at least for the examples studied to date. A "fixed point" is a function $F^*(M_i)$ independent of L. More precisely one finds $F_L(M_i) \rightarrow F^*(L^x M_i)$ for large L, where x is an exponent. The fixed point F^* must reproduce itself when one calculates F_L from $F_{L/2}$; this requirement determines F^*. It is independent of the initial Hamiltonian.

Universality. Critical exponents and the scaling function $f(x)$ can be determined once the fixed point F^* is known. They are independent of the initial Hamiltonian, hence different systems can show the same critical behavior.

The fixed point is not unique. Different fixed points develop if the magnetization M_i is a vector instead of a scalar quantity. (An example of this is an isotropic ferromagnet.) Models have been discussed where M_i is a vector with n components; there are separate fixed points for each n. In consequence there are different values for all the exponents and a different function $f(x)$ for each n.

The ϵ and $1/n$ expansions. Computing the fixed-point function F^* and the associated exponents can be done only approximately. Three general methods exist for these calculations. Near four dimensions it has been found that F^* is approximately a quadratic form in the arguments M_i, with small but important M_i terms in addition. This fixed point (for any n) can be computed by a Feynman diagram expansion. The result is an expansion for critical exponents and scaling functions in powers of $\epsilon = 4 - d$. The starting point for this expansion is Landau theory; the corrections to Landau theory are of order ϵ, ϵ^2, etc. The results for β, from Landau theory, ϵ expansion, and the Ising model, are shown in the figure. The ϵ expansion seems to be asymptotic only. The best results are obtained by calculating only to order ϵ^2. The results for three dimensions are invariably better than mean field theory and appear to be accurate to 5–10%, to the extent this accuracy can be determined. The exponents β, γ, and so on, the scaling function $f(x)$, and many other effects (for example, dipolar effects in magnets) have been calculated using the ϵ expansion.

The second method of calculation is an expansion in powers of $1/n$, developed by R. Abe following earlier work by E. Stanley. It is less useful for physical values of n (1, 2, or 3) but is helpful for theoretical studies of fixed-point behavior.

The third approach is purely numerical approximate calculations of the fixed point. This field is in its infancy. So far only the two-dimensional Ising model has been studied this way, by T. Niemejer and J. M. J. Van Leeuwen.

It is possible that the whole fixed-point theory is only approximately valid. In particular there remain small and unexplained discrepancies between the exponents for β-brass and for other transitions (see table).

For background information *see* OPALESCENCE; STATISTICAL MECHANICS in the McGraw-Hill Encyclopedia of Science and Technology.

[KENNETH WILSON]

Bibliography: S. K. Ma, *Rev. Mod. Phys.*, 45: 589, 1973; T. Niemejer and J. M. J. Van Leeuwen, *Phys. Rev. Lett.*, 31:1411, 1973; K. Wilson and J. Kogut, *Phys. Rep.* in press.

Stem (botany)

Reflecting the annual course of climatic changes, all trees in the temperate zone alternate between periods of active shoot growth (flush) and rest (dormancy); that is, they show intermittent or rhythmic growth. One might expect that trees growing in tropical regions, which are characterized by rather constant day length, high temperatures, and good moisture supply, or trees growing in plant growth chambers, would grow continuously. However, most tropical trees, like avocado, cacao, mango, rubber, and tea, have been observed to grow rhythmically rather than continuously. Within 1 year, young trees often pass through 8–10 cycles of active shoot growth and rest, but adult trees usually show only one or two growth flushes per year. As rhythmic growth under constant conditions obviously cannot be ascribed to fluctuations in environmental factors, its causes must be sought within, rather than outside, the plant. Viewing trees as growing systems, and applying basic ideas of system analysis to them, R. Borchert recently attempted to construct a model that explains rhythmic shoot growth as resulting from feedback interaction between shoot and root growth.

Rhythmic growth of rubber tree. Rhythmic growth in two representative tropical trees, the cacao *(Theobroma cacao)* and rubber tree *(Hevea brasiliensis)*, has been described in detail by D. Greathouse and F. Hallé respectively. Morphological changes associated with rhythmic growth in the rubber tree are shown in Fig. 1. A comparison between stem and root elongation (Fig. 2) indicates that rhythmic stem growth is accompanied by continuous root growth. Whereas root growth occurs at a fairly constant rate throughout the observation period, the rate of shoot growth varies between 3 cm/day during stage II of the growth cycle and zero during dormancy. During stage III, both stem and leaf growth are gradually arrested. Although there is a good correlation between the two main components of shoot growth, no such correlation is apparent between root and shoot growth.

Root and shoot relationship. Under a given set of environmental conditions, both herbaceous and woody plants maintain a rather constant ratio between their root and shoot systems. If the root-shoot ratio is altered by pruning a root or a shoot, the ratio tends to be restored by the compensatory growth of the severed organ. If plants are transferred from one environment to another, a different root-shoot ratio will be established. The maintenance of a constant root-shoot ratio probably reflects the basic biological fact that any multicellular organism, whether animal or plant, can survive only if its various organs maintain a functional equilibrium. Maintaining such an equilibrium requires an extensive network of feedback mechanisms whereby the functioning of various organs can be continuously correlated and adjusted to that of others. Unlike animals, plants must achieve their functional balance by means of rather slow and insensitive feedback mechanisms which—particularly in large plants like trees—should manifest themselves in distinct feedback oscillations resulting from overshoot. It is assumed here that rhythmic growth in trees is essentially a manifestation of feedback oscillations that reflect the efforts of the tree to achieve a functional balance between the root and shoot systems.

Feedback system. Since rates of shoot growth during flushing in *Hevea* are significantly higher than root growth rates (Fig. 2), a rapid decrease in root-shoot ratio occurs during flushing. To restore the functional balance between root and shoot that existed at the beginning of the flush, the temporary arrest of shoot growth becomes necessary. Thus the questions most pertinent to the control of

Fig. 1. Rhythmic shoot growth in the rubber tree *(Hevea brasiliensis)*. (a) Young tree during its fourth growth flush. (b) Transition from continuous to rhythmic growth. (c) Transition from rhythmic to continuous growth. (d) Experimental induction of continuous growth by reduction of leaf area. (e) Sequence of leaves associated with rhythmic growth. (f–j) Successive stages of shoot development during one flush: (f) bud opening, stage I; (g, h) rapid stem elongation and initial leaf growth, early (stage IIa) and late (stage IIb); (i) leaf maturation and arrest of stem growth, stage III; (j) dormancy, stage IV. *(From F. Hallé and R. Martin, Étude de la Croissance Rhythmique chez l'Hévea brasiliensis Mull.-Arg. Euphorbiacées-Crotonoidées, Adansonia, 8:475–503, 1968)*

rhythmic growth are: How is the temporary arrest of shoot growth achieved; and what is the nature of the feedback system involved?

Basically, the arrest of shoot growth may be caused by deficiencies in any one of the various substances that the growing shoot receives from other parts of the tree—water, minerals, or hormones, usually supplied by the root, or organic nutrients stored in the older parts of root or stem. In the present tentative form of the model, rhythmic growth is assumed to be primarily due to a periodic imbalance in the water economy of the tree, because the observed simultaneous reduction of stem and leaf growth during stage III (Fig. 1*i*) reflects an inhibition of cell expansion in both organs that might be caused by an existing water deficit.

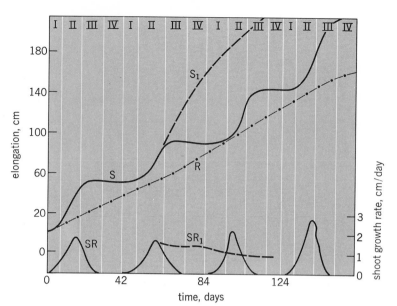

key:

S = stem elongation   SR = rate of stem elongation S_1 = stem elongation during
                                                        experimental reduction
SR_1 = rate of stem elongation during experimental   of leaf area to one-third
        reduction of leaf area to one-third

R = root elongation   I-IV = stages of root growth as given in Fig. 1f-j

Fig. 2. Time course of shoot and root growth in a young rubber tree. *(From F. Hallé and R. Martin, Étude de la Croissance Rhythmique chez l'Hévéa—Hevea brasiliensis Mull.-Arg. Euphorbiacées-Crotonoidées, Adansonia, 8:475–503, 1968)*

A number of basic known or assumed relationships have been formulated mathematically and incorporated into a computer program that describes the growth of a tree, consisting of stem, leaves, and root, under constant, optimal environmental conditions. The calculated time course of the growth of this tree is given in Fig. 3. During the first four time intervals (days), the shoot growth rate increases from zero to its maximum value; root growth takes place at a constant rate; and a new leaf is initiated every second day. The growth rate for each leaf is increased from zero to its maximum value, and leaf growth is arrested once a leaf has attained its genetically determined maximum length. Leaf area is calculated from leaf length; the rate of transpiration is proportional to total leaf area and is reduced by an existing water deficit. The rate of water absorption is proportional to root length. As more and more leaves attain maturity, transpiration exceeds water absorption by the root, and a water deficit begins to develop at day 14. At day 17, the water deficit surpasses a critical value, and shoot and leaf growth rates are gradually reduced to zero. As the flush ends, the development of immature leaves is terminated before they have reached their maximum size. This arrested development explains the frequently observed phenomenon that, in each flush, fully developed leaves are followed by a series of leaves of gradually decreasing size (Fig. 1a and e). After the arrest of shoot and leaf growth, the water deficit gradually disappears because of the continuation of root growth; transpiration reaches its maximum value for a given leaf area; and a new flush begins.

Does evidence exist to support this model? Although the assumed feedback mechanism between shoot and root growth cannot be tested experimentally, the agreement between observed shoot growth patterns and patterns predicted by the model, as seen in Figs. 2 and 3, supports the contention that a feedback mechanism similar to that postulated in the model is operating in trees. Another example is illustrated by Figs. 1b–d, 2, and 4. Under natural conditions, transition from rhythmic to continuous growth, and vice versa, is frequently observed in *Hevea*. Experimentally, continuous growth has been produced by regularly removing about two-thirds of each leaf blade. The same transition from rhythmic to continuous growth is predicted by the model if maximum leaf length is reduced from 28 to 16 cm, which is equivalent to a reduction in leaf area by about 60%. Finally, it follows from the model that a decrease in root growth rate, as imposed on a growing tree by a limited depth of soil or by competition with the root system of neighboring trees, should result in shorter flushes and longer rest periods, that is, in a reduced number of flushes per year. This prediction agrees with the observations described in the introduction.

In conclusion, growth rhythms under constant environmental conditions can be considered endogenous rhythms, that is, self-sustaining oscillations that occur in the absence of periodic changes in the environment. They result from the feedback interaction between potentially continuous processes like shoot or root growth if the slower process is rate-limiting for the faster one. The length

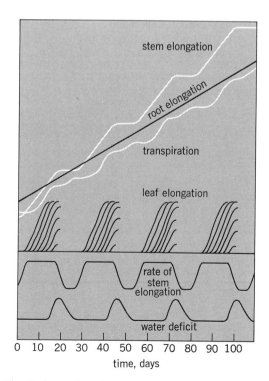

Fig. 3. Computer-calculated time course of rhythmic growth. *(From R. Borchert, Simulation of rhythmic tree growth under constant conditions, Physiol. Plant., 29:173–180, 1973)*

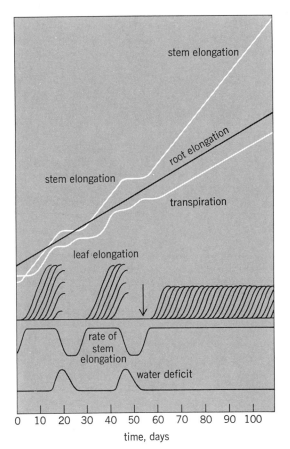

Fig. 4. Computer-calculated time course of shoot growth during transition from rhythmic to continuous growth caused by a reduction of maximum leaf length from 28 to 16 cm at arrow. (*From R. Borchert, Simulation of rhythmic tree growth under constant conditions, Physiol. Plant., 29:173–180, 1973*)

of the periods of growth rhythms depends on the quantitative genetic characters governing rates of shoot, leaf, and root growth, as well as upon the set of environmental factors affecting the growing plant. For instance, *Hevea* trees of the same clone always flush simultaneously, whereas flushing is asynchronous in genetically different trees. There is no basic difference between the control of rhythmic and continuous growth. The latter simply represents a special and relatively rare case of the general, rhythmic growth pattern.

Temperate-zone tree growth. The seasonal variations that occur in most natural habitats superimpose a secondary, exogenous rhythm upon the basic endogenous rhythm. Growth patterns observed in the temperate zone therefore reflect adaptations of the general pattern to the specific annual course of climatic conditions in the temperate zone. This view is supported by observations of growth patterns of tree seedlings in the temperate zone, which under favorable growing conditions usually behave the way their tropical counterparts do. For instance, oak seedlings may flush 3 or 4 times during one summer, and more than 10 times per year in a plant growth chamber. Adult oaks usually produce one or, at most, two short annual growth flushes, but stem sprouts may grow con-

tinuously throughout the growing season. Obviously, the shoot growth patterns of trees in the temperate zone are as variable as those in the tropics, and both appear to be the result of the same type of interaction between internal and environmental factors.

For background information *see* ROOT (BOTANY); STEM (BOTANY) in the McGraw-Hill Encyclopedia of Science and Technology.   [ROLF BORCHERT]

Bibliography: R. Borchert, *Physiol. Plant.*, 29: 173–180, 1973; D. C. Greathouse, W. M. Laetsch, and B. O. Phinney, *Amer. J. Bot.*, 58:281–286, 1971; F. Hallé and R. Martin, *Adansonia*, 8:475–503, 1968; M. H. Zimmermann and C. L. Brown, *Trees, Structure and Function*, 1971.

Stochastic calculus

The evolution of a system in engineering is, by nature, stochastic rather than deterministic because of unpredictable small disturbances; thus it may be described by a stochastic differential equation (1) or equivalently by a stochastic integral

$$dX_t = a_t dt + b_t dW_t \tag{1}$$

equation (2), where $\{W_t,\ t \geq 0\}$ is a Wiener pro-

$$X_t = X_0 + \int_0^t a_s ds + \int_0^t b_s dW_s \tag{2}$$

cess, dW_t represents the random disturbances occurring in the infinitesimal time interval dt, and a_t and b_t are independent of the future disturbances. The second integral is the stochastic integral (often called Itô's integral), which was introduced by K. Itô to construct the sample functions of a general diffusion process from those of a Wiener process. Suppose Eq. (3), where

$$dX_t^i = a_t^i dt + \sum_{\alpha=1}^m b_t^{i\alpha} dW_t^\alpha, i = 1, 2, \ldots, n \tag{3}$$

$\{W_t^\alpha,\ t \geq 0\}$, $\alpha = 1, 2, \ldots, m$ are independent Wiener processes, and let $u(x_1, x_2, \ldots, x_n)$ be a function whose derivatives $\partial_i u$ and $\partial_i \partial_j u$ are continuous. Then the process $U_t = u(X_t^1, X_t^2, \ldots, X_t^n)$ satisfies the stochastic chain rule (often called Itô's formula) in Eq. (4), with the convention expressed in Eqs. (5).

$$dU = \sum_i \partial_i u dX^i + \tfrac{1}{2} \sum_{i,j} \partial_i \partial_j u dX^i dX^i \tag{4}$$

$$(dt)^2 = 0 \qquad dW^\alpha dW^\beta = \partial_{\alpha\beta} dt \tag{5}$$

The quadratic term in Eq. (4) is characteristic of stochastic differentials but looks undesirable. To avoid it, the symmetric stochastic integral (often called Stratonovich's integral) has recently been introduced by R. L. Stratonovich, E. Wong, and others, and E. J. McShane has investigated it elaborately. It is more illuminating to use Stratonovich's integral when one wants to make a stochastic model from a deterministic one. Stochastic calculus contains the mathematical theory of stochastic integrals and differentials and its application to stochastic filtering and control. This article explains the most fundamental results obtained in recent years.

Modern theory of stochastic calculus. D. L. Fisk, P. Courrege, H. Kunita and S. Watanabe, and others extended the stochastic integral $\int bdW$ in Eq. (2) to the case where W_t is more general than a Wiener process. Although most practical problems are formulated in terms of the classical theory, such an extension permits establishment of a unified theory of stochastic calculus. For simplicity it may be assumed that the stochastic processes considered below have continuous sample functions. As a first step several terminologies are introduced. A nonempty class of random events closed under countable unions and complements is called a σ-algebra. Let $F = \{F_t, \ t \geq 0\}$ be an increasing family of σ-algebras which intuitively represents the amount of information increasing with time. A process $\{X_t, \ t > 0\}$ is called an F-process, if the events $\{X_t \leq a\}$ belong to F_t for every t and a; this means intuitively that the value of the process at time t is determined by the information up to time t. A process $\{X_t\}$ is called an F-martingale if the expectation of X_t under F_s equals X_s whenever $s < t$. A process is called a quasi-F-martingale if it is the sum of an F-martingale and an F-process having bounded variation on every finite time interval. Let $\{X_t^{(n)}\}$ denote the process obtained from $\{X_t\}$ by stopping it when it reaches the level n or $-n$. A process $\{X_t\}$ is called a local quasi-F-martingale if the process $\{X_t^{(n)}\}$ is a quasi-F-martingale for each n.

In the same way as for Itô's integral, one can define the stochastic integral of Eq. (6), where

$$Y_t = \int_0^t a_s \, dX_s \tag{6}$$

the process $\{a_t\}$ is an F-process and $\{X_t\}$ is a local quasi-F-martingale. Equation (6) is written in the form of the stochastic differentials of Eq. (7).

$$dY_t = a_t \, dX_t \tag{7}$$

Denoting $d(XY) - X\,dY - Y\,dX$ (X, Y being local quasi-F-martingales) by $dX\,dY$, it can be shown that the stochastic differentials have a very simple algebraic structure; for example, $dX\,dY\,dZ = 0$. The stochastic chain rule for this general case also takes the form of (4); now (5) can be proved rigorously, so it is no longer a convention. To avoid the quadratic term in (4) the operation defined in Eq. (8) is introduced. Then the stochastic chain

$$Y \circ dX = Y\,dX + \tfrac{1}{2}dX\,dY \tag{8}$$

rule can be written in the form of Eq. (9) as desired.

$$du(X^1, X^2, \ldots, X^n) = \sum_{i=1}^{n} \partial_i u \circ dX^i \tag{9}$$

The integral $\int_0^t Y \circ dX$ is called Fisk's symmetric stochastic integral, which is an extension of Stratonovich's.

Stochastic filtering. Let $X = \{X_t, \ t \geq 0\}$ be an m-dimensional process, called a signal process, and $Y = \{Y_t, \ t \geq 0\}$ be an n-dimensional process, called an observed process, and assume that they are determined by stochastic differential equations (10), where W is an $(m+n)$-dimensional Wie-

$$\begin{aligned} dX &= a_t \, dt + b_t \, dW \\ dY &= c_t \, dt + d_t \, dW \end{aligned} \tag{10}$$

ner process and the coefficients a_t, b_t, c_t, and d_t are vector- or matrix-valued processes given as functions of the values of the processes X and Y

up to time t. By E_t one denotes the conditional expectation when the observed process Y is known up to time t. The problem of stochastic filtering is to find the conditional probability law of X_t when the observed process Y is known up to time t, or equivalently to find the random linear functional in Eq. (11) where f moves over a certain class of

$$M_t(f) = E_t(f(X_t)) \tag{11}$$

functions on the n-dimensional space R^n. For the case where the coefficients in Eq. (10) are of the special form of Eqs. (12) (A, B, C and D being de-

$$\begin{aligned} a_t &= A_t X_t & b_t &= B_t \\ c_t &= C_t X_t & d_t &= D_t \end{aligned} \tag{12}$$

terministic matrix processes), there is the famous Kalman-Bucy linear filtering theory. In this case it can be proved that both X_t and Y_t are linear functionals of $(W_s, \ s \leq t)$, so the whole system $\{X_t, Y_t, W_t, \ t \geq 0\}$ is Gaussian; that is, all finite joint distributions of these random vectors are Gaussian. Hence the random functional $M_t(f)$ to be found is completely determined by the conditional expectation vector $\overline{X}_t = E_t(X_t)$ and the conditional variance matrix $P(t) = E_t(X_t - \overline{X}_t)(X_t - \overline{X}_t)'$, and $P(t)$ is deterministic. R. E. Kalman and R. S. Bucy proved that $\overline{X}_t$ is determined by the stochastic differential equation (13), and $P(t)$ is determined by the ordin-

$$d\overline{X} = A\overline{X}\,dt + K(dY - C\overline{X}\,dt) \tag{13}$$
$$(K = (PC' + BD') \ (DD')^{-1})$$

ary differential matrix equation (14). Recent work by T. Kailath provides useful computational methods for solving Eq. (14).

$$\begin{aligned} dP/dt &= AP + PA' + BB' \\ &+ (PC' + BD')(DD')^{-1}(PC' + BD')' \end{aligned} \tag{14}$$

The next significant progress was the Markov filtering theory, due to R. S. Liptzer and A. N. Shiraev, in which the coefficients a_t, b_t, c_t, and d_t may be general functions of the present states X_t and Y_t. The general filtering problem covering non-Markovian cases has recently received much attention; the work by M. Fujisaki, G. Kallianpur, and H. Kunita is most important. Using the modern stochastic calculus, they proved a general fact which implies that under certain general conditions the stochastic functional process $M_t = M_t(f)$ satisfies a stochastic differential equation of form (15), where α and β are certain unbounded func-

$$dM_t = \alpha(M_t)\,dt + \beta(M_t)\,d\tilde{W}_t \tag{15}$$

tionals determined by the coefficients of Eqs. (10), and $\tilde{W}_t$ is a Wiener process (different from the original W_t) called the innovation process. The work done thus far is quite abstract, and it is an open problem to establish a concrete theory comparable with the linear filtering theory.

Stochastic control. To explain the idea of stochastic control one may take a simple example where the controlled process is governed by a stochastic differential equation (16). Here W_t is a

$$dX_t = a(X_t, U(X_t))\,dt + b(X_t, U(X_t))\,dW_t \tag{16}$$

Wiener process and the function $U(x)$ is an arbitrary function called the control function. If $U(x)$ is fixed, this equation with the initial condition

$X_0 = x$ determines a diffusion process. Let T be the first time for the process X_t to leave the interval $0 \leq x \leq 1$. The expected total cost $V(x, U)$ is assumed to be of form (17). It is obvious that Eq. (18) is true. The aim of stochastic control is to

$$V(x, U) = E\left(\int_0^T f(X_t, U(X_t))dt \,|\, X_0 = x\right) \quad (17)$$

$$V(0, U) = V(1, U) = 0 \quad (18)$$

minimize $V(x, U)$ for each x, where U moves over a certain class of functions.

Suppose that the minimum $v(x)$ of $V(x, U)$ is attained by $U = U_0$; that is, U_0 is the optimal control. Under the assumption that $v(x)$ is twice differentiable one can show that $U_0(x)$ and $v(x)$ are determined by conditions (19) and (20), where $L_u v(x) = a(x, u)\, v'(x) + \frac{1}{2} b^2(x, u)\, v''(x)$. Hence $U_0(x)$ is expressed in terms of $v(x)$, $v'(x)$, and $v''(x)$, and $v(x)$ is

$$L_u v(x) + f(x, u)$$

$$\geq [L_u v(x) + f(x, u)]_{u=U_0(x)} = 0 \quad (19)$$

$$v(0) = v(1) = 0 \quad (20)$$

obtained by solving a certain nonlinear ordinary differential equation of the second order (called the Bellman equation) with boundary condition (20), so finally $U_0(x)$ is determined as a function of x. Since it is also shown that if (19) and (20) have solutions $U_0(x)$ and $v(x)$, these give the minimizing function and the minimum value, so the assumption of twice differentiability of $v(x)$ is replaced by that of solvability of the Bellman equation. Since there are many nice conditions for solvability of

ordinary differential equations, this reduction works well to rigorously prove that U_0 is obtained by the above method for the one-dimensional case, but not always for the several-dimensional case for which the Bellman equation is a nonlinear partial differential equation. N. V. Krylov removed this difficulty by directly proving twice differentiability of $v(x)$ for a very large class of stochastic control problems.

For background information *see* STOCHASTIC PROCESS in the McGraw-Hill Encyclopedia of Science and Technology.

[KIYOSI ITÔ]

Bibliography: M. Fujisaki, G. Kallianpur, and H. Kunita, *Osaka J. Math.*, 9(1):19–40, 1972; T. Kailath, *IEEE Trans. Informational Theory*, IT-19, no. 6, pp. 750–760, 1973; N. V. Krylov, *Theory of Probability and Its Applications*, vol. 17, no. 1, pp. 114–131, 1972; E. T. McShane, Stochastic calculus and stochastic model, publication pending.

Storm

Many recent advances in the understanding of severe thunderstorms and in the ability of meteorologists to forecast them flow from developments in the new field of meteorological remote sensing. Radar is an example of an active remote sensor; in storm research, Doppler radars illuminate storms with microwave electromagnetic energy and process the echoes to chart air currents inside storms. Electromagnetic sensors are also used passively to listen to waves that the storms themselves emit. For example, a kind of radio receiver that monitors the "atmospherics" emitted by lightning strokes

Fig. 1. Photograph of a cumulonimbus near Boulder, CO; its top reached 40,000 ft (12,200 m). At the time this photograph was taken, infrasound from the direction of the storm was being recorded by NOAA microbarographs near Boulder.

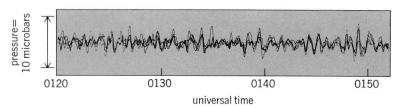

Fig. 2. Superimposed pressure versus time records from four microbarographs at Boulder, CO, during severe storm activity in Oklahoma.

and other electrical activity inside storms is now being developed into a tornado-warning device. Even satellite photography, used for tracking storm activity on a global scale, might be called a passive optical (or, in some cases, infrared) remote-sensing tool.

Still another remote-sensing technique that has been recently used to study severe storms measures their emissions of ultra-low-frequency acoustic waves called infrasound (Fig. 1). At the moment, no one knows why certain storms radiate infrasound and others do not, but scientists at the National Oceanic and Atmospheric Administration (NOAA), who have been observing the waves for more than a decade, are trying to find out what these waves can reveal about the internal dynamics of storms, and whether the emissions have any practical value, specifically as advance indicators of storm severity.

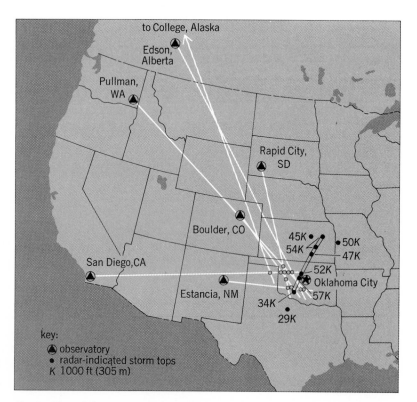

Fig. 3. Map of the western United States showing the intersections of infrasound bearings from seven observatories (the seventh observatory is in College, Alaska) made on June 5, 1973, at 0100 universal time. Locations of thunderstorm radar echoes and their heights are shown in the vicinity of the intersections. Line of radar echoes near Oklahoma City indicates presence of a squall line.

Pressure waves. Infrasonic waves are pressure fluctuations that travel in the atmosphere at essentially the local speed of sound—about 340 m/sec under standard conditions—but their frequencies lie below the nominal 20-Hz limit of human hearing. The infrasound from severe storms typically has wave periods in the tens of seconds; one usually speaks of wave period, the duration of 1 wave cycle, when the frequency of the wave is below 1 Hz. Since atmospheric absorption is much lower at these frequencies than it is for audible sound, infrasound can travel great distances with little loss of strength. Thus, the infrasound from some severe storms has been detected several thousands of kilometers from its source, and waves from more powerful sources, like nuclear bombs, have been detected after several circuits around the Earth.

Because the pressure fluctuations associated with the waves that storms emit are very weak—only about one-millionth of an atmosphere—arrays of very sensitive microphones (called microbarographs), with special filters to reduce the noise caused by wind, are required to detect them. Even then, pressure fluctuations must be cross-correlated between several microphones before the storm's signal is recognizable (Fig. 2).

Ionospheric waves. Acoustic waves from severe thunderstorms can also travel into the upper atmosphere and cause observable effects by moving its layers of electrically charged ions up and down. These ionospheric motions, occurring about 250 km above the Earth, are detectable with certain radio-sounding devices that bounce radio waves off the layers.

In 1967 NOAA scientists first identified certain peculiar wavelike motions in the ionosphere as the effects of acoustic emissions from severe thunderstorms. Since these waves have somewhat longer periods than those of the infrasound observed at ground level—3–5 min compared to tens of seconds—an immediate connection between the two effects was not made. But recent theoretical studies of the frequency-filtering effects of the atmosphere on the two different kinds of propagation path have explained how the two different observations can be just different manifestations of some broad-band emission process. Indeed, detailed case studies of storm events that produced both kinds of effects have lent credibility to the hypothesis of a common emission mechanism.

Both the ionospheric waves and the ground-level pressure fluctuations attributable to severe storms are seen almost exclusively during the late afternoon and early evening of the spring and summer months. The average duration of the emissions is about 2 hr. The wave sources, when identifiable, seem to be predominantly in the Midwest—most frequently in Oklahoma and Texas. Whereas the waves observed at the ground generally contain many superimposed frequencies, those detected in the ionosphere invariably appear as nearly sinusoidal oscillations whose frequencies are confined to the narrow band between 2- and 5-min wave periods.

Source models. Although the exact emission mechanism remains unknown, several reasonable theoretical models have been advanced and are currently being subjected to observational tests. Among them are electrical mechanisms for generating "infrasonic thunder," various kinds of oscillations in latent heat release and of air circulation in storm cells, and the aerodynamic noise of turbulence inside storms. The most promising mechanism, in terms of the detail with which it conforms to the phenomenology of the observed waves, is drawn from the theory of sound radiation from vortex motion. Whereas steady vortex flow emits no sound, vortex flow that contains irregularities, instabilities, or secondary vortexes can be shown to radiate acoustically somewhat like the rotating propeller of a fan. There is ample evidence for the presence of irregular vortex flow and of secondary vortexes within larger vortex flows in the atmosphere, specifically in observations of tornadoes and dust devils. But such observations are rare, and no specific instance has yet been associated with observed infrasound. It seems likely, however, that such visible effects represent only the "tip of the iceberg," in the sense that invisible, yet intense, vortex motion abounds in and around convective storms, particularly the severe ones that occur when squall lines pass through the Midwest.

The most powerful storms emit up to 100,000,000 W of acoustic power, equivalent to the electrical power consumed by a city of 100,000; yet the acoustic emissions still represent an insignificant fraction of the total energy of a storm. Such high power levels present one difficulty in the search for a suitable source model.

Practical value. To find out whether the emissions have any practical value, NOAA conducted tests of the storm-detecting abilities of its sensitive microphones during the 1972 and 1973 storm seasons. During 1972, with only one array of microphones at Boulder, CO, NOAA recorded about 86 infrasonic events that were subsequently identified as storm-related by comparison with independent weather data. More than half of those events were identified with storms that produced confirmed tornadoes or funnel clouds. More than two-thirds of the emitting storms were in Texas, Oklahoma, Kansas, Nebraska, or South Dakota. At least 87% of the detected storms produced some documented severe effects, such as large hail, heavy rains, high winds, and tornadoes. In some instances, when radar indicated a grouping of storms with similar echo characteristics (for example, echo height), infrasound emissions appeared to select the location of most severe effects (large hail, heavy rainfall, tornadoes).

During the 1973 season, tests were conducted with two additional infrasound observatories, one near Albuquerque, NM, and the other near Rapid City, SD, to increase detection reliability and to permit storm triangulation (Fig. 3). Preliminary results indicate that well over a hundred storms were detected and located from bearing intersections of infrasound received by at least two of the observatories. More detailed analysis of these data should provide the information needed to assess the value of infrasound in simulated storm-warning situations.

At least two limitations on such practical uses of infrasound are imposed by the atmosphere itself.

One is that the waves travel at the relatively slow speed of sound, about 1200 km/hr. If the sensors are located too far away, their warning value is obviously diminished. The other limitation is the distortion of the waves' propagation paths by atmospheric winds, which can cause the measured source direction to differ by several degrees from its true direction. Uncorrected bearing intersections can thus be up to tens of miles in error. If atmospheric winds are roughly known, however, bearing corrections can be estimated.

For background information *see* THUNDERSTORM; WEATHER FORECASTING AND PREDICTION in the McGraw-Hill Encyclopedia of Science and Technology.   [T. M. GEORGES]

Bibliography: K. Davies and J. E. Jones, *NOAA Profess. Pap. no. 6*, 1972; T. M. Georges, *Rev. Geophys. Space Phys.*, 11:571–594, 1973.

Superconducting devices

In 1963 B. Josephson predicted that tunnel junctions between bulk superconductors could carry a supercurrent possessing a remarkable nonlinear and sensitive dependence on applied voltage. His prediction was shortly confirmed, and junctions with such properties are called Josephson junctions. They have been widely used in laboratories to construct very sensitive magnetometers and voltmeters. Their major technical use, however, may come in computer and information processing technology, where they possess the attractive qualities of inherent high speed, low power consumption, and small size. A class of devices for this purpose called flux shuttles and based on persistent supercurrent loops in Josephson junctions has recently been proposed and preliminary experimental devices demonstrated. *See* TUNNEL JUNCTION.

Josephson junctions. The tunnel junction consists of two overlapping metal electrodes (usually evaporated thin films) separated by a thin insulator (usually an oxide $\sim$20 Å, or 2 nm, thick). The insulating barrier is sufficiently thin that the quantum-mechanical properties of electrons in the electrodes allow them to penetrate the barrier on occasion, a classically forbidden process called tunneling. Josephson tunnel junctions have electrodes of superconducting metal, for example, Pb at a temperature < 7.2 K. In this case the tunneling current can occur as a supercurrent, a current which

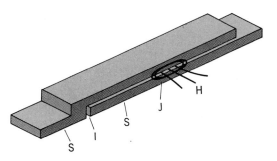

A long, narrow Josephson junction is formed by two overlapping metal electrodes *S* separated by a thin insulator *I*, shown as a gap. A vortex consisting of a current loop *J* supporting a magnetic field *H* extends through the junction between the electrodes.

can flow at a constant value with no accompanying voltage drop, and consequently no dissipation of energy, a property shared by ordinary superconducting metals.

The tunneling supercurrent between the electrodes of a Josephson junction flows through the barrier throughout the area of overlap with density J_s. While a steady J_s flows with no voltage drop V, a change in J_s at some point P, designated $J_s(P)$, requires a momentary nonzero V at that point, $V(P)$. Josephson predicted that $J_s(P)$ would depend sinusoidally upon the time-integrated value of $V(P)$, according to $J_s(P) = J_c(P) \sin \varphi(P)$, where $\varphi(P) = 2\pi \int dt V(P)/\Phi_0$ is called the phase difference across the junction at P, $J_c(P)$ is the maximum value of $J_s(P)$ (determined by the thinness of the insulator at P), and $\Phi_0 = 2.07 \times 10^{-15}$ Wb is the flux quantum, the ratio of Planck's constant and twice the charge of an electron. The supercurrent is thus very sensitive to weak voltages applied for short times; for example, 10^{-9} volt for 5×10^{-7} sec increases J_s from zero to maximum.

The flux shuttle concept makes use of the response of the supercurrent to magnetic fields. This arises from the voltages induced by changes in the field. Since magnetic fields penetrate the superconducting electrodes only to a depth of ~500 A, or 50 nm (Meissner effect), the fields affecting J_s occur in a thin layer inside the junction centered on the insulating barrier. These fields may be generated externally or by the junction currents themselves. From Faraday's law, the voltages induced by introducing a magnetic flux $\Delta\Phi$ into the junction between two points P and Q will cause a change in the phase difference, φ, between these points of $\varphi(P) - \varphi(Q) = 2\pi\Delta\Phi/\Phi_0$. Thus significant changes in J_s are induced by $\Delta\Phi \lesssim 10^{-15}$ Wb.

Vortices. For a long, narrow Josephson junction the important variations in φ and J_s with position are along the long dimension and arise from transverse magnetic fields. If no external currents or magnetic fields are applied to such a junction, the minimum energy state has $J_s = 0$ everywhere. Other states of higher energy, called vortex states, also occur which are central to the flux shuttle. These involve self-generated magnetic fields linking the junction. The simplest is the single-vortex state, in which a magnetic field of flux Φ_0 links the junction over a localized region (see illustration). The field causes φ to increase by 2π along this region, producing a flow of J_s in a closed circular pattern. This current loop in turn generates the magnetic field. Flux and a current loop of the opposite sense could equally well occur. Such current-field patterns are called vortices. They will persist indefinitely once established. This occurs because the ends of the junction beyond the vortex region form with the electrodes a completely superconducting loop, and the magnetic flux linking a superconducting loop will not decay. Thus the vortex is analogous to a persistent current flowing in a loop of superconducting wire. Vortices possess certain particlelike properties which allow them to be used as information bits in the flux shuttle. They can either be stationary or can move along the junction. In motion they possess kinetic energy and inertia. They experience an effective force in the presence of externally applied currents or magnetic fields, and these may be used to control

the position and motion of a vortex. Vortices also interact with nonuniformities in the junction, being attracted to narrow points or regions of low J_c. Several vortices can occur side by side in a junction. Two vortices of the same flux sense repel each other, but only weakly unless they overlap, while two of opposite sense attract each other, and indeed can annihilate each other as no net change in flux linking the junction would result. For this reason flux shuttle designs generally use only one sign of vortex. Annihilation or creation of single vortices can occur only at the ends of the junction.

Flux shuttle. In the flux shuttle, as proposed by P. Anderson, information would be stored by arranging vortices in a pattern of storage sites on a long junction. The presence or absence of a vortex at a site represents a binary one or zero, the entire pattern forming a binary word of information. The sites could be, for example, constrictions in junction width, regions where J_c is small, or regions subjected to localized external magnetic fields. Of major importance, the pattern could be moved along the junction by shifting each vortex to the next adjacent site, giving a shift register. The stored information could then be read out sequentially by a detector of magnetic field located at one of the sites. Related methods for processing the moving information and performing logic have also been proposed. A flux shuttle possesses potentially significant advantages in operating speed and power dissipation. Vortices can move at speeds up to $\bar{c}$, the velocity of electromagnetic waves in the junction, where $\bar{c} \sim 10^7$ m/sec. Since the vortex size can be as small as $\lesssim 10^{-4}$ m, storage sites can be spaced at this distance without excessive repulsion forces between neighboring vortices. Consequently, minimum transfer times $\sim 10^{-11}$ sec seem possible. The energy dissipated in transferring a vortex one site can be less than $I\Phi_0$, where I is the maximum current of the vortex current loop. This energy is typically $\lesssim 10^{-18}$ joule. The power dissipated at one site operating at 10^{11} Hz would then be $\lesssim 10^{-8}$ watt. Such low power is desirable to avoid excessive refrigeration requirements.

At present such devices are in an early experimental stage. The existence of vortices in a long junction is experimentally established. Vortex storage at positions controlled by varying junction width or localized external magnetic fields (magnetic potential wells) has been demonstrated. Controlled vortex motion by small oscillatory motion of an entrapping magnetic potential well at ~ 0.1 MHz and uncontrolled inertial motion at velocities approaching $\bar{c}$ have also been demonstrated. Most recently a rudimentary shift register was operated in which a single vortex was created at one end of a 1-cm-long junction, moved through four magnetic potential wells with ½-msec transfer times, and ultimately was detected at the other end.

For background information *see* SUPERCONDUCTING DEVICES in the McGraw-Hill Encyclopedia of Science and Technology.

[T. A. FULTON]

Bibliography: T. A. Fulton and L. N. Dunkleberger, *Appl. Phys. Lett.*, 22:232–233, 1973; T. A. Fulton, R. C. Dynes, and P. W. Anderson, *Proc. IEEE*, 61:28–35, 1973.

Superconductivity

Recent advances in the field of superconductors include the preparation of a compound, Nb_3Ge, which displays superconductivity at temperatures higher than previously observed, and the prediction and observation of large enhanced conductivities and other phenomena characteristic of superconductors in certain organic materials.

High-T_c Nb_3 Ge. After a lapse of several years the maximum temperature for the occurrence of superconductivity has again been raised. Research performed at the Westinghouse Research laboratories during the past year has shown that Nb_3Ge can be prepared with a superconducting transition temperature T_c of approximately 23 K. This T_c is 2 degrees higher than the previous record holder (an alloy of niobium, aluminum, and germanium) and almost 3 degrees higher than the normal boiling point of liquid hydrogen (20.3 K). This discovery now suggests the real possibility that liquid hydrogen can eventually replace liquid helium as the refrigerant for superconducting devices. Liquid hydrogen cooling is, of course, thermodynamically more efficient than liquid helium. Also, hydrogen is much more readily available and cheaper. However, even if helium continues to be used to cool superconducting devices, the use of higher operating temperatures made possible by materials such as Nb_3Ge will still provide large economic advantages.

Since the discovery of superconductivity in 1911, the successful search for new materials with higher transition temperatures has been an intermittent and at times an agonizingly slow process (Fig. 1). For a time it was believed that the main obstacle to raising T_c was the lack of a fundamental theory to explain the occurrence of superconductivity. In 1957 J. Bardeen, L. Cooper, and J. Schrieffer published their Nobel prize-winning theory (BCS theory), which proposed that the superconducting state results from an interaction of electrons with crystal lattice vibrations (phonons) causing the electrons (at sufficiently low temperatures) to combine in pairs. It has since been shown that the properties of superconductors can be satisfactorily explained on the basis of such electron pairs. However, despite the availability of a valid theory, the discovery of new higher-T_c materials has continued to depend on empirical methods. This is due to the difficulty of calculating, from first principles, the strength of the electron-phonon interaction. Without this knowledge one cannot predict which materials should have high T_c's.

High-T_c materials. The empiricism used to find new high-T_c materials has been developed primarily by B. T. Matthias, J. K. Hulm, T. H. Geballe and their collaborators. They have found that transition metal compounds which crystallize in the A15 (B-W type) crystal structure are especially favorable for high-temperature superconductivity. Such compounds generally have the formula A_3B. In all of the very highest T_c materials (that is, > 15 K) the A element is either niobium or vanadium and the B element is a non-transition-metal element. When using standard bulk melting techniques, these materials sometimes form slightly off stoichiometry, that is, the A-to-B ratio is greater than 3/1. The importance of this fact was first shown by studies

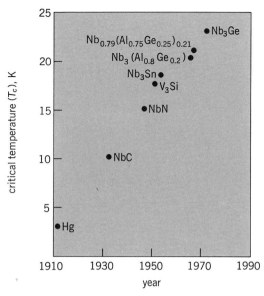

Fig. 1. Plot illustrating the slow pace at which the maximum T_c for superconductivity has been increased.

on the A15 structure compound Nb_3Ge. This compound, when prepared by standard bulk methods, has the off-stoichiometric formula $Nb_{3.3}Ge$ and its T_c in this form is only 6 K. By using a very-high-speed quenching technique, this material was prepared in bulk form with a composition believed close to the desired 3/1 stoichiometry. The onset of superconductivity was now found to be near 17 K. Since this material was inhomogeneous and highly disordered, it was suspected that the T_c for ordered homogeneous Nb_3Ge would be even higher than 17 K. However, for many years following these original experiments, there was no growth technique capable of investigating this possibility. In the experiments performed at the Westinghouse Research Laboratories this problem has now apparently been resolved. By using a specially developed low-energy sputtering technique, Nb_3Ge films have been prepared which are at, or very near to, the stoichiometric 3/1 composition. These films show the presence of superconductivity up to 23 K.

Sputtering. Sputtering is a well-known thin-film growth technique that is used in the electronics industry to prepare high-purity materials in thin-film form. In this technique an inert sputtering gas (typically argon) is ionized by an electric field in a vacuum enclosure. The positively charged ions that are formed are accelerated toward the source material (target) by holding the target at a high negative potential. The resulting collisions dislodge particles which deposit on substrates placed in close proximity to the target. When a two-element target is used, it has been found that the sputtered particles are sufficiently reactive to permit compound formation at temperatures much lower than those possible when using ordinary bulk melting methods. In initial sputtering experiments Nb-Ge films were deposited with T_c's of ~ 17 K. Transition temperatures of 23 K were obtained by optimizing three of the parameters in the sputtering process. These highest-T_c films were de-

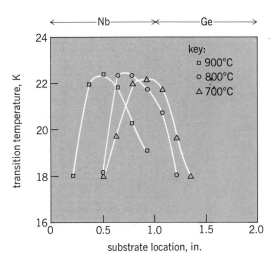

Fig. 2. Transition temperature onsets of Nb-Ge films from deposition experiments at three different temperatures. Films were sputtered from a two-part target as shown above the plot. 1 in. = 25.4 mm. *(From J. R. Gavaler, M. A. Janocko, and C. K. Jones, The preparation and properties of high T_c Nb-Ge films, J. Appl. Phys., July 1974)*

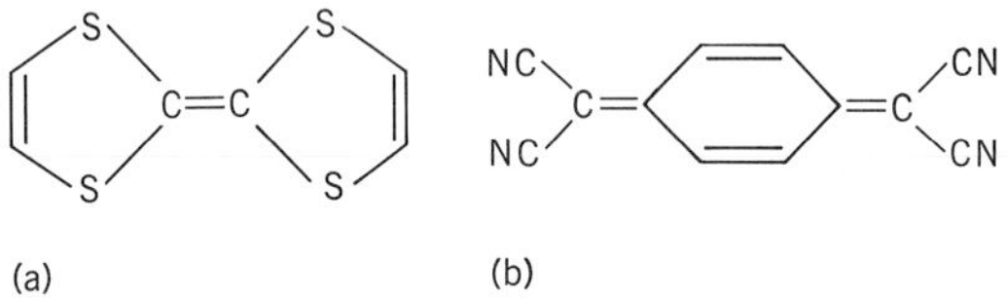

Fig. 3. Molecular structures of *(a)* TTF and *(b)* TCNQ.

posited by using lower sputtering voltages (< 1000 V), higher argon gas pressures (> 0.1 torr), and higher substrate temperatures (700–950°C) than commonly used in sputtering. Under the original sputtering conditions where higher voltages and lower argon pressures were employed, it is theorized that the Nb-Ge compound was formed rapidly and the growth of a disordered material resulted. Also, the reaction of the highly energetic Nb and Ge particles was probably similar to the bulk reaction of these elements at very high temperatures. As discussed, ordinary bulk melting methods produce the more stable nonstoichiometric $Nb_{3.3}Ge$ compound, which has a low T_c. In the new process the low sputtering voltages produce particles with low initial energies. In addition, the high agron pressures cause these particles to encounter many collisions as they travel between the target and the substrate. Under these conditions it is believed that the sputtered particles have only thermal energy on arrival at the substrate surface, thus permitting the formation of the normally unstable, stoichiometric Nb_3Ge phase—probably in a metastable form.

The necessity of using substrate temperatures of 700°C and higher introduced one additional complication with regard to achieving the desired Nb_3Ge composition. At these substrate temperatures the sticking coefficients of the Nb and Ge particles are less than unity, which means that all of the particles arriving at the substrate surface do not remain to react. Choosing the proper composition of the sputtering target thus becomes a problem since the composition of films will not necessarily be the same as the target material. This problem was circumvented by sputtering from a composite target whose surface is half niobium and half germanium. A series of substrates were then positioned beneath this target. In this configuration a series of compounds were prepared which had a wide range of compositions related to their proximity to the two parts of the sputtering target. The T_c's of films from three experiments as a function of their location beneath this sputtering target are shown in Fig. 2. The differing locations of the T_c maxima illustrate the different sticking coefficients of the sputtered particles at the three temperatures used. As expected, x-ray analysis of the films with the highest T_c's, in each case, showed they had the A15 crystal structure and lattice parameters indicating they were at, or very close to, the stoichiometric Nb_3Ge composition.

[JOHN R. GAVALER]

Metallic states in charge transfer salts. The achievement of the metallic state in a class of organic materials known as charge transfer salts has attracted considerable interest.

These salts are usually composed of flat planar molecules which lead to anisotropic crystal structures and therefore to pseudo one-dimensional electronic properties. Conventional molecular crystals are composed of neutral organic molecules held together by van der Waals forces. In contrast, the charge transfer salts have unpaired electrons on an organic electron acceptor molecule (A) or donor (D) or both, due to the electron transfer, $D + A \rightarrow D^+ \cdot A^-$. This strikingly simple result opens up a new area of electronic phenomena in organic solids, for if the unpaired electrons delocalize over all molecular sites, the metallic state results.

Of particular interest are the one-dimensional organic metals based on the acceptor tetracyanoquinodimethan (TCNQ), discovered in the early 1960s at DuPont. *See* SEMICONDUCTOR, ORGANIC.

Mechanism for superconducting effects. Organic metals such as tetrathiofulvalene-tetra-cyanoquinodimethan, TTF-TCNQ (Fig. 3), represent a new class of solids which have many of the properties required for achieving superconductivity. They are narrow-band metallic systems with relatively high electron concentrations ($n \approx 5 \times 10^{21}$ per unit volume) and inherently strong electron-phonon coupling. The electron-electron Coulomb repulsion (which is detrimental at least to conventional BCS superconductivity) can be reduced to a minor role by inclusion of large electronic polarizability through appropriate molecular design. This was first demonstrated in studies of the related compound N-methyl phenazinium-TCNQ and led to the synthesis of metallic TTF-TCNQ.

The one-dimensional metal is unstable to formation of density waves in the underlying ionic lattice as predicted many years ago by R. Peierls. The Peierls distortion need not be static with a fixed phase from chain to chain, but can be dynamic, giving rise to giant density waves in the solid. H. Fröhlich pointed out that coupling of the electrons to these giant density waves in one-dimen-

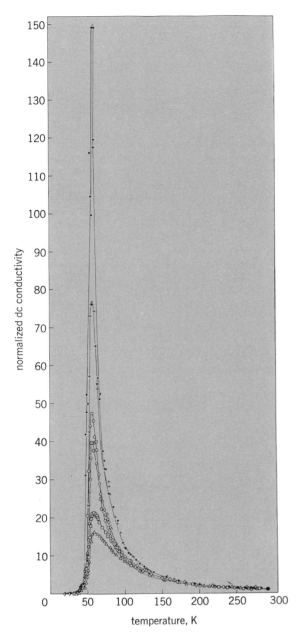

Fig. 4. Normalized dc conductivity (ratio of conductivity to conductivity at room temperature) as a function of temperature for different samples of TTF-TCNQ. (*From Marshall J. Cohen et al., The electrical conductivity of tetrathiofulvalene-tetracyanoquinodimethan, Phys. Rev. B, August 1974*)

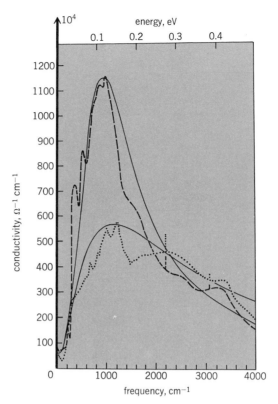

Fig. 5. Conductivity versus frequency of TTF-TCNQ at 65 K (dashed line) and 320 K (dotted line). The solid curves represent theoretical fits to the experimental data. The heavy bars at zero frequency indicate the dc and microwave values. (*From D. B. Tanner et al., Infra-red conductivity of tetrathiofulvalene-tetracyanoquinodimethan films, Phys. Rev. Lett., 32:1301, 1974*)

sional systems could lead to superconducting effects without BCS pairing. In the Fröhlich mechanism one can picture the electrons individually "surf-riding" on a giant lattice density wave. The collective motion of the electrons and the lattice inhibits electron scattering and leads to greatly enhanced electrical conductivity.

Experimental evidence. The first evidence for the possible existence of these phenomena came from measurement of the electrical conductivity of TTF-TCNQ. The conductivity is found to increase from a room temperature value of approximately 1000 ohm^{-1} cm^{-1} (10^5 ohm^{-1} m^{-1}) to more than 100,000 ohm^{-1} cm^{-1} (10^7 ohm^{-1} m^{-1}) at 58 K, where a metal to insulator transition takes place. The magnitude of the conductivity maximum varies from crystal to crystal (Fig. 4) and is associated with the extreme sensitivity of one-dimensional metals to crystalline defects. The associated electrical anisotropy near 58 K is greater than 10^4 so that any defects seriously degrade electrical transport properties. Intrinsic dc conductivity maxima approaching 10^5 ohm^{-1} cm^{-1} (10^7 ohm^{-1} m^{-1}) have been observed in only a few samples. Microscopic crystal perfection remains as one of the outstanding problems in the study of these materials. Further understanding of the intrinsic electrical properties awaits current studies utilizing contactless ac techniques.

In addition to enhanced conductivities, a fundamental property of the Peierls-Fröhlich collective state is the existence of an energy gap in the electronic excitation spectrum. This feature has been observed in the infra-red spectrum of TTF-TCNQ (Fig. 5). The frequency-dependent conductivity $\sigma(\omega)$ is that of an electronic system with an energy gap and a collective mode near zero frequency. These features are qualitatively similar to those observed in infra-red studies of superconductors. The present understanding of the data suggests that TTF-TCNQ is a one-dimensional Fröhlich superconductor.

Prospects for the future. Further investigations of TTF-TCNQ are continuing, as well as synthesis of related one-dimensional conductors. Large enhanced conductivities are expected but not true persistent currents, since long-range order is improbable in these one-dimensional systems, and the Peierls-Fröhlich mechanism is sensitive to dissipative processes. However, recent theory suggests the possibility of a simultaneous Fröhlich-BCS collective state, which motivates continued studies of one-dimensional metals such as the linear-chain TCNQ salts and related systems.

For background information *see* LATTICE VIBRATIONS; SUPERCONDUCTIVITY in the McGraw-Hill Encyclopedia of Science and Technology.

[ALAN J. HEEGER]

Bibliography: D. Allender, J. W. Bray, and J. Bardeen, *Phys. Rev. B*, 9:119, 1974; L. B. Colemann et al., *Solid State Commun.*, 12:1125, 1973; A. J. Epstein et al., *Phys. Rev. B*, 5:952, 1972; J. Ferraris et al., *J. Amer. Chem. Soc.*, 95:948, 1973; A. F. Garito and A. J. Heeger, *Proceedings of the Nobel Symposium*, 24:129, 1973; J. R. Gavaler, *Appl. Phys. Lett.*, 23:480–482, 1973; J. R. Gavaler, M. A. Janocko, and C. K. Jones, *J. Appl. Phys.*, July 1974; D. B. Tanner et al., *Phys. Rev. Lett.*, 32:1301, 1974.

Terrain sensing, remote

Although recent research into the application of remote sensing techniques to the soil sciences has embraced a variety of sensing devices operating throughout the electromagnetic spectrum, most investigations continue to be concerned with the interpretation of panchromatic or color aerial photography and multispectral imagery. The availability of Earth satellite data and the increasing use of mechanical aids to interpretation have been significant. However, the interpretation of the conventional aerial photograph is still the only operational method. So far, the studies at Oxford by P. Beckett and coworkers have been the only attempts to assess the uniformity of soil properties within the mapping units derived by different survey procedures using aerial photograph interpretation. There is a need for a similar fundamental scrutiny of the validity of many remote sensing assumptions such as the multispectral concept.

Visible sector. Methods of semiautomatic interpretation have been employed to aid human interpretation. Photocolors, or the closely correlated data derived by microdensitometer measurement, are analyzed, and areas with surface colors that are either uniform or ranging within specified limits can be delineated on computer printouts. Density-slicing methods, which can also be used to enhance images, are especially valuable when subtle changes in hue and saturation are masked by large differences in brightness; areas of clay pan soils or with erosion limitations have been identified by this method. Another study, using the camera as a photometer, has shown empirically that the ratios between the reflectance of a soil element in blue and red spectral bands can be used to discriminate and delineate patterns of soil moisture and textural variation.

Multispectral sensing. Computer analysis has also aided in the interpretation of the enormous volume of data generated by optical-mechanical scanning devices. Pattern recognition techniques have been devised to classify the surface reflectance of nonvegetated and uniformly cultivated fields, and computer printout maps, showing the areal distribution of soil spectral classes, have been compared with conventional soil surveys. Although several studies have demonstrated that soils cannot be mapped accurately solely on the basis of their spectral response, computer display maps provide additional information on soil distribution and promise to reduce presurvey preparation time and to increase the accuracy and speed of ground mapping.

Thermal infrared. Investigation of a line-scan system in Canada showed that coarse-textured soils could generally be separated from those of medium or fine texture; soil aggregation, rather than texture, appeared to affect the response in loamy or clayey soils. Drainage differences could also be separated, but the response varied according to the moisture content and soil structure near the ground surface. In this study, unlike previous ones, the moisture content of subsurface horizons did not appear to affect the imagery; thus it seems likely that a qualitative indication of soil moisture in the upper 50 cm of bare soil can be obtained with thermal line-scan systems. Under ideal conditions, salinity could also be inferred from the response pattern.

Microwave and radiowave sensing. The potential of imaging radar systems for mapping soils has not yet been widely tested, for the relation between the radar signal and the feature imaged is very complex. This is partly because of the averaging effect of the relatively large area of ground imaged and thus soil separations can be made only at the association level and not at the series level. Such separations appear likely to be more successful in untilled areas in subhumid to arid regions, rather than in cultivated or densely forested areas.

Both active and passive microwave sensors (frequencies 1–100 GHz), however, show much promise for mapping the moisture content of soils, for small differences in moisture content result in large differences in brightness temperature. The use of a combination of short and long wavelengths would perhaps also allow the direct measurement of soil depth and texture, or a distinction between contrasting horizons. Good correlations have been found between data from airborne passive multifrequency microwave radiometers and ground-based soil moisture measurements. The electrical properties of the soil are complex, however, and only partially understood. Further complications also arise because microwave emission or the radar return is scattered at these frequencies by the vegetation cover or terrain irregularities. The depth of penetration of microwaves into the soil is poor and is only several millimeters for moist soils. For this reason attempts have been made to develop radio-frequency sensors; the spectral range between 100 MHz and 2 GHz appears to be the most promising. The lower frequencies (broadcast bands) are required for penetration depths exceeding 1 m. Unfortunately, less is known about this spectral region than about almost any other.

Color combination methods of microwave image discrimination, comparable to multispectral additive viewers, have been developed; they make possible the detection of subtle differences between the different wavelengths and polarizations used. It seems likely that microwave channels will be added to existing multispectral systems. A valuable characteristic of microwave sensors is their all-weather capability, which is especially useful in areas with much cloud cover.

Satellite data. The assessment of imagery from the Earth resources technology satellite (ERTS), Skylab, and Russian satellites is already in progress. Satellite imagery has been found to be a useful means of identifying soil associations, although some workers prefer an identification based on lower-altitude aircraft imagery. The ERTS imagery provides a synoptic view of a 3,000,000-hectare scene, which is large enough so that the effect of climate, topography, and geology on soils can be seen. Most, if not all, of the extent of the association can thus be viewed, and its homogeneity can be checked. Several new soil associations have been reported in the United States, and major soil types have been mapped in countries as diverse as Greece and Kenya. The associations have been recognized mainly by delineating the vegetation cover common to them. Computer printouts of densimetric data have aided the separation of major soil moisture differences. Density values from the visible red band of the multispectral scanner have been found to be the most generally useful. Preliminary investigation of Skylab data suggests that antenna temperatures correlate well with the moisture content of the upper 5 cm of soil.

For background information *see* AERIAL PHOTOGRAPH; SOIL; TERRAIN SENSING, REMOTE in the McGraw-Hill Encyclopedia of Science and Technology.

[D. M. CARROLL]

Bibliography: D. M. Carroll, *Soils Fertil.*, 36: 259–266 and 313–320, 1973; H. L. Mathews et al., *Proc. Soil Sci. Soc. Amer.*, 37:88–93, 1973; W. Michalyna and R. G. Eilers, *Can. J. Soil Sci.*, 53: 445–457, 1973; K. R. Piech and J. E. Walker, *Photogramm. Eng.*, 40:87–94, 1974.

Thermoanalysis

Kinetic titrimetry and peak enthalpimetry are new developments in the field of enthalpimetric analysis. Enthalpimetric analysis is the generic designation for a group of modern thermochemical methodologies that rely on monitoring temperature changes engendered in adiabatic calorimeters by heats of reactions occurring in solution. In contradistinction, classical methods of thermoanalysis (such as thermogravimetry) focus primarily on changes occurring in solid samples in response to externally imposed programmed alterations in temperature. Examples of well-known enthalpimetric methods include thermometric enthalpy titrations (TET), which yield stoichiometric equivalence points, and direct injection enthalpimetry (DIE), in which instantaneous temperature increments (in the case of exothermic reactions) or decrements (in the case of endothermic processes) are measured in the presence of excess reagent.

Kinetic titrimetry. Thermokinetic analysis (TKA) by kinetic titrimetry involves rapid and continuous automatic delivery of a suitable titrant, under judiciously controlled experimental condi-

tions. "Late" end points are obtained in this manner, depending on the time required for the relevant reaction to catch up. Such end points have no direct analytical or stoichiometric significance by themselves. However, mathematical procedures have been devised for calculating valid stoichiometric equivalence points and for determining reaction rate constants as high as 500,000 M^{-1} sec^{-1}. Promising applications to organic functional group analysis have been reported.

Peak enthalpimetry. Peak enthalpimetry (Figs. 1 and 2) is a novel approach that is applicable to biochemical and clinical analysis. The salient feature is rapid mixing of a reagent stream with an isothermal solvent stream into which discrete samples are intermittently injected. The temperature versus time of the resulting product stream is recorded with the aid of a thermistor circuit that has a sensitivity of 0.00001°. The resulting analog plots are peak enthalpograms, the analytic geometry of which approximates Gaussian shapes. Peak enthalpograms exhibit the response characteristics of genuine differential detectors; that is, the instantaneous signal is proportional to concentra-

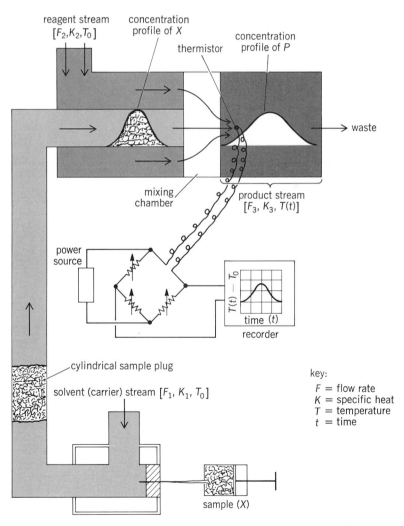

Fig. 1. Schematic drawing of peak enthalpimetry apparatus. (*From A. C. Censullo et al., in R. S. Porter and J. F. Johnson, eds., Analytical calorimetry III, Proceedings of the American Chemical Society Symposium on Analytical Calorimetry, Los Angeles, April 1–4, 1974, Plenum Press, 1974*)

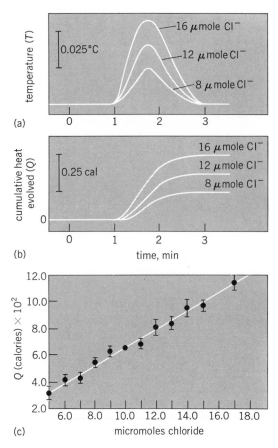

Fig. 2. Principle of chloride determination by peak enthalpimetry. (a) Experimental peak enthalpograms. (b) Corresponding integral plots. (c) Plot of total heats evolved versus amount of chloride. Ordinate represents limiting Qs where curves shown in b level off. (From A. C. Censullo et al., in R. S. Porter and J. F. Johnson, eds., Analytical calorimetry III, Proceedings of the American Chemical Society Symposium on Analytical Calorimetry, Los Angeles, Calif., April 1–4, 1974, Plenum Press, 1974)

tion. Such behavior is similar to that of the thermal conductivity detectors commonly used in gas chromatography. Integrals under peak enthalpograms possess analytical as well as thermochemical significance. The working equation of peak enthalpimetry has the form shown in Eq. (1), where $\Delta T(t) \equiv T(t) - T_0$ is the instantaneous temperature incre-

$$\int_i^f \Delta T(t)\, dt = (\text{const.})\, N = (\text{const.}')\, Q \qquad (1)$$

ment with respect to the initial common temperature T_0 of the solvent and reagent streams prior to mixing; t, N, and Q denote time, number of moles of sample, and heat evolved; and the integration limits i and f refer to initial and final times when $T(t) = T_0$. A typical example of quantitative analysis by peak enthalpimetry is the determination of chloride in blood serum with the aid of the reaction shown in Eq. (2), in which $\Delta H^\circ = -6.7$ kcal

$$2Cl^- + Hg^{++} = HgCl_2 \qquad (2)$$

per mole of Cl^-. When a concentrated aqueous solution of mercuric nitrate is used as the reagent stream, peak enthalpograms with an area (that is,

the integral under the curve) representing a proportional measure of the chloride present can be obtained.

Applications. Unique capabilities of enthalpimetric analysis have become apparent in the field of protein chemistry. For instance, well-defined TET end points were obtained in the alkalimetric study of an egg albumin moiety that contained 277 peptide linkages and whose molecular weight was 45,000. Seventy-two Brønsted acid-base side chains were determined and differentiated into "sets." The carboxyl set contained 46 groups, the ϵ-amino set 19, and the imidazole set 7.

Several interesting biomedical applications of enthalpimetric analysis have been made, including enzymatic, immunological, and hematological determinations. Among these applications is the quantitative estimation of glucose in human plasma, by measuring the heat evolved in the reaction between glucose and adenosinetriphosphate (ATP) in the presence of the enzyme hexokinase, which yields glucose-6-phosphate plus adenosinediphosphate (ADP). Successful enthalpimetric enzyme assays have been reported for glucose oxidase, cholinesterase, alkaline phosphatase, lactic acid dehydrogenase, and ATP-ase. In the area of immunochemistry, antibody-antigen and antibody-hapten reactions have been investigated by enthalpimetric methods.

A remarkable spin-off of instrumental developments devised for enthalpimetric analysis is a blood clot timer invented by W. D. Bostick and P. W. Carr. Their method is based on a thermometric detection system that utilizes a thermistor temperature sensor mechanically coupled to an electromagnetic vibrator. Temperature changes are recorded on a linear time coordinate, as the unbalance potential of a Wheatstone-type thermistor bridge that is fed to the y axis of a strip-chart millivoltmeter whose x axis is driven by a synchronous motor. The coagulation end point is indicated by an abrupt rise in temperature when conversion of the plasma sol to a gel insulates the thermistor, producing a drastic increase in the thermistor temperature owing to a concomitant decrease in the rate of ohmic heat dissipation.

For background information see THERMO-ANALYSIS; THERMOCHEMISTRY; TITRATION in the McGraw-Hill Encyclopedia of Science and Technology.   [JOSEPH JORDAN]

Bibliography: A. E. Beezer, *MIP International Review of Science: Physical Chemistry, Series One,* vol. 13, pp. 71–93, 1973; W. D. Bostick and P. W. Carr, *Amer. J. Clin. Pathol.,* 60:330–336, 1973; P. W. Carr and J. Jordan, *Anal. Chem.,* 45:634–640, 1973; A. C. Censullo et al., *Analytical calorimetry III,* in R. S. Porter and J. F. Johnson (eds.), *Proceedings of the American Chemical Society Symposium on Analytical Calorimetry,* Los Angeles, April 1–4, 1974; R. N. Goldberg and G. T. Armstrong, *Med. Instrum.,* 8:30–36, 1974; G. A. Vaughan, *Thermometric and Enthalpimetric Titrimetry,* 1973.

Toxoplasmosis

Recognition that *Toxoplasma* is an intestinal coccidian of cats and that oocysts are shed in cat feces has reoriented epidemiologic concepts. Recent investigations of the transmission, epidemiology,

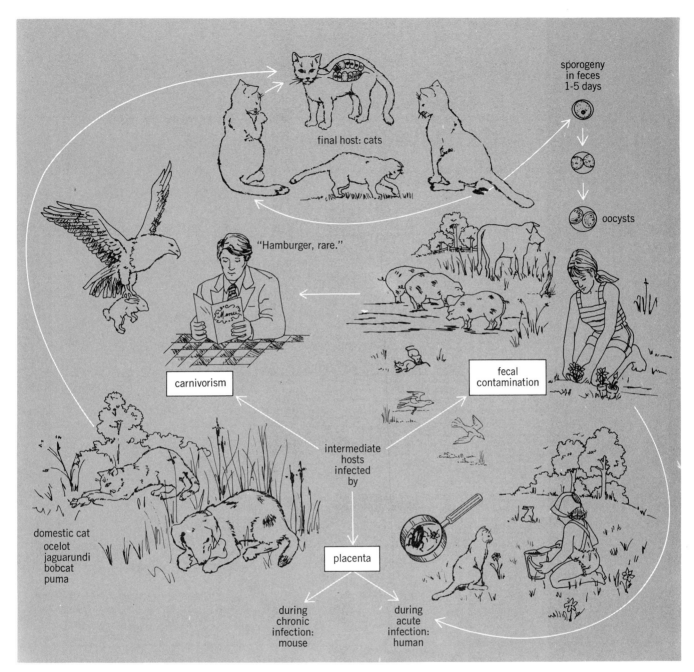

Fig. 1. Postulated transmission of toxoplasmosis. After sporulation, oocysts are infectious to a great variety of hosts by fecal contamination. Carnivorism and transplacental transmission are other important means of transmission. (From R. A. Marcial-Rojas, ed., Pathology of Protozoan and Helminthic Diseases, Williams and Wilkins, 1971)

and immunology of toxoplasmosis have elucidated age-related and cultural factors in the prevalence rates of antibody to *Toxoplasma*.

Millions of oocysts, which are highly persistent, are deposited in soil during 7–10 days with the feces of acutely infected cats. The oocysts form a ready source of infection for mammals, birds, and humans. In addition, carnivores can become infected by eating the flesh of infected animals. Occasionally, transplacental transmission takes place. Figure 1 illustrates the concepts of transmission now being tested epidemiologically.

Evidence for modes of infection. Transplacental transmission was first observed in 1937, when A. Wolf and D. Cowen from Columbia Medical Center in New York City recognized toxoplasmosis as an infection of the newborn. The development in 1948 by A. Sabin and H. Feldman of the dye test, a serologic test based on the lysis of toxoplasma antibody in the presence of an accessory factor, made it possible to relate maternal and fetal infection accurately and to study the disease pictures produced. In the course of surveying thousands of pregnant women, G. Desmonts and J. Couvreur at the Saint Vincent de Paul Hospital in Paris identified 118 women who developed toxoplasma antibody during pregnancy; in 48 cases (40%) the infant also became infected.

Carnivorism was proved to be a mode of transmission in 1954, when D. Weinman studied the infection in pigs and rodents. The frequent findings of toxoplasma cysts in the skeletal muscle of sheep, pigs, and, occasionally, cattle led L. Jacobs, J. S. Remington, and M. L. Melton (1960) to make biological comparisons between the "resting" cyst and the actively multiplying *Toxoplasma*. They found the cyst organisms to be resistant to gastric juices and to be highly infectious orally, whereas the proliferative forms were rarely infectious by mouth. Desmonts suspected that ingestion of undercooked or raw meat might be an important mode of infection in France and proved his theory in 1965 by showing that the acquisition rate of infection could be increased if the quantity of undercooked meat was increased. These observations readily explained the existence of toxoplasmosis in carnivores and in some human populations in which raw meat is eaten customarily, or as a delicacy, or by faddists. However, the common occurrence of infection in some herbivores, such as sheep and rabbits that serve as food to carnivores, remained unexplained. It was clear also that carnivorism alone would not be sufficient to maintain the infection even only in carnivores; since each carnivore is eaten by only one or a few carnivores, a significant multiplying mechanism necessary to compensate for the carnivores not eaten was not apparent. Attempts to show that blood-sucking arthropods could serve as vectors failed consistently.

Oocysts, which are developed in the intestine of infected cats and are shed in the feces, furnished the missing link and the multiplying mechanism in the transmission chain. A single acutely infected cat can produce from 1,000,000 to 15,000,000

oocysts. The feces are buried superficially in soil. In moist and shaded areas oocysts have been found, by A. Ruiz and M. Chinchilla in Costa Rica and J. K. Frenkel in Kansas, to survive from 1 year to 18 months (in the Kansas study, that period included two winters). Oocysts can be spread by earthworms, which in turn are attractive food for birds.

The detailed microepidemiology surrounding a fecal deposit containing oocysts of cats is being studied. It is reasonable that animals feeding on the ground can be infected. Also, human beings digging in soil or children playing in contaminated sand piles can carry the infectious oocysts on their hands. Cat feces can be unrecognizable in soil after 1–2 weeks. The amount of soil that can be found under and around fingernails is sufficient to convey the infection more or less frequently, if the fingers are put into the mouth or eyes or contaminate food.

Epidemiology. It could be postulated that people who have a pet cat might have a greater opportunity to become infected than those who do not. In a survey conducted by D. R. Peterson, E. Tronca, and P. Bonin at the University of Washington in Seattle, toxoplasma antibody was found in 21% of the individuals who possessed a cat but in only 9% of the individuals who had never owned one. In a survey by G. W. Comstock and J. P. Ganley in Maryland, there was no significant difference in antibody prevalence between those "with cats on the premises" and those without. G. Wallace in Hawaii and B. L. Munday in Tasmania compared the presence or absence of toxoplasma antibody with that of cats on isolated Pacific islands and atolls. They found good correlation between the presence of cats and antibody in rats and humans (Wallace) and in sheep (Munday), whereas in the absence of cats such antibodies were rare or absent.

Sand and soil contaminated by infected cat feces should present durable sources of infection that are usually not susceptible to eradication. Oocysts have been isolated repeatedly from garden soil in Costa Rica by Ruiz, L. Cerdas, and Frenkel. Their disappearance coincided with direct sun exposure and drying of the site with soil temperatures exceeding 100°F (38°C).

If transmission is caused by oocysts, one could postulate that young children playing in or close to soil should develop antibody at a high yearly rate, whereas adults should show a lower rate. Two studies of antibody related to age support such relationships (one study was carried out in El Salvador, by J. S. Remington, B. Efron, E. Cavanaugh, H. J. Simon, and A. Trejos; another study covered Central America and was performed by B. C. Walton on sera collected for a nutritional and antibody survey by the Institute of Nutrition of Central America and Panama). Central America is particularly suitable for studies on oocyst transmission, for cats are plentiful and, since the meat consumed by humans is habitually well cooked, transmission by meat would play an unimportant role.

Age-related prevalence rates of antibody to *Toxoplasma* are shown in Fig. 2, in which it is evident that, in central France, antibody is acquired at a lower rate during childhood than in El Salvador

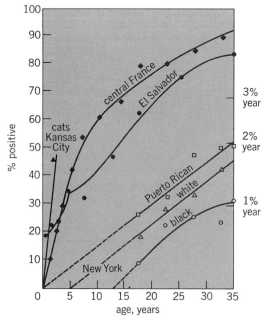

Fig. 2. Prevalence rate of toxoplasma antibody in human populations. Note that cats acquire antibody at a much more rapid rate than humans do. (*From J. K. Frenkel, Toxoplasma in and around us, BioScience, 23:343–352, 1973*)

but that it continues to accumulate at a greater rate during adulthood than in El Salvador. This difference could reasonably be attributed to lesser exposure of French children to contaminated soil and to greater transmission by means of the ingestion of undercooked meat by French adults. In El Salvador, meat is generally well cooked, and the high transmission rate in children is attributed entirely to ingestion of oocysts from contaminated soil or from transport hosts. The antibody transmission rates of three New York populations can be related to the rate at which the habit of eating undercooked meat is culturally acquired; transmission by means of oocysts probably plays a small role. Puerto Rican immigrants to New York City can be expected to have a complex pattern composed of a Salvador-like childhood pattern upon which a North American pattern is superimposed. Figure 2 also shows that cats from Kansas and Iowa that were studied in the Kansas City area may have an average 45% antibody presence at the age of 2. It has been shown by Wallace and J. P. Dubey that antibody begins to appear after cats are old enough to hunt and does not represent congenital infection.

These surveys and statistics are in reasonable agreement with the postulates developed in the laboratory. However, interpretations were made without adequate data on the contact of people with soil. In the surveys concerning the relationship of humans and cats, it is essential to include not only all contact with cats as pets but also all contact with soil contaminated by cats, especially during childhood. The phrase "cats on the premises" does not mean that the association must be a close one.

Prevention. Apart from the clear-cut transmission pattern that can be estimated statistically, situations exist that should be avoided since they increase the chance of transmission to the individual. Pregnant women should be aware of these situations, since unborn children are susceptible to damage, and young children should be protected from them. The precautions include the disposal of feces from cats that hunt birds and mice or are fed raw meat. If a litterbox is used, it should be changed and disinfected daily. Hands should be washed after contact with cats and with soil potentially contaminated with cat feces and after handling raw meat.

Toxoplasmosis in humans. Most toxoplasma infections are asymptomatic. The rare clinical symptoms can be characterized according to the stage of infection during which they occur. Acute infection may be associated with pneumonia, hepatitis, a rash, and lymph node inflammation. In these instances lesions may result from the destruction of many cells that are parasitized by toxoplasma tachyzoites. At the end of the acute infection, one or several lymph nodes may enlarge. The nodes are occasionally removed because a malignant tumor is suspected; however, a characteristic cell multiplication, suggesting an immune process, is present, and few *Toxoplasma* remain.

Subacute infection characterizes infants who are infected while still in the uterus. Probably because these children are partly protected by antibody transferred from their mother, they have a slowly progressing infection. However, since infants do not develop an active immunity as quickly as adults can, the infection tends to be of longer duration and many lesions accumulate. The mothers usually have no symptoms. Infants may be born with hepatitis, jaundice, and anemia, or encephalitis and retinochoroiditis (inflammation of the inner coats of the eye) may develop, often causing partial blindness and mental retardation.

Chronic toxoplasmosis refers to both the asymptomatic infection and the active disease, which is usually characterized by the presence of cysts. When intact, cysts do little damage. However, when cysts disintegrate, an intense inflammatory reaction, attributed to hypersensitivity (allergy), follows. The liberated *Toxoplasma* are destroyed, indicating immunity to be effective. Lesions are usually in the retina of the eye, in the brain, and in the muscles, where most cysts are found.

Recrudescent or relapsing toxoplasmosis is found in immunodeficient individuals in whom lesions develop, usually in brain and eye and occasionally in muscle and lungs. The bradyzoites liberated from cyst rupture enter new cells and begin to multiply as tachyzoites. Although the immune defect occasionally develops as part of the patient's disease, corticosteroids, cyclophosphamide, and a combination of cytostatic drugs most commonly give rise to this form of toxoplasmosis. Recrudescent toxoplasmosis may occur when these agents are used to suppress the immune response in a patient who has received a tissue transplant or who is receiving treatment for certain lymphomas, cancers, and other diseases.

Diagnosis is by identification of *Toxoplasma* in the lesions or circumstantially by antibody tests. Treatment is by certain sulfonamides, which enter the cells in which the parasites grow, and by pyrimethamine. These two drugs interfere with successive steps in the biosynthesis of the parasite and are highly effective in its suppression, but they do not cure infection. Since diagnosis is often delayed, irreparable damage may occur prior to suppression of the parasite. The type of immunity conferred suppresses the parasite only, and chronic infection is associated with immunity. Most mammals and birds studied are not able to eliminate the *Toxoplasma*. This condition is sometimes spoken of as infection-immunity, or premunition.

Nomenclature of stages. An enteroepithelial and an extraintestinal or tissue cycle of *Toxoplasma* can be distinguished. The cycle in the intestinal epithelium is similar to that of other coccidia, consisting of multiplicative stages, the gametocyte stage, and the oocyst stage. The multiplicative stages, however, classified by Dubey and Frenkel as types A, B, C, D, and E, each with several generations, are unlike those in other coccidia, in which each morphologic type appears to correspond to one generation only.

Since the stages of *Toxoplasma* outside the intestine of cats have not been recognized regularly in other coccidia, and since previous terminology was based on fallacious homology and was confusing, several new terms have been suggested to designate each stage. The rapidly multiplying forms of the acute infection are called tachyzoites (from the Greek *tachos*, meaning "speed"); they form groups in the vacuoles of host cells. The slowly multiplying forms of the chronic infection are called bradyzoites (from the Greek *bradys*, meaning "slow"); they usually contain amylopectin. Bradyzoites form cysts surrounded by a definite cyst wall that impregnates characteristically with silver and certain stains. Cats can be regarded as complete hosts, since they support both the enteroepithelial and tissue cycles. Nonfelines are called incomplete or intermediate hosts, since only the tissue cycle takes place in them.

Related organisms. Several genera are related to *Toxoplasma*. Most closely related is *Besnoitia*, which has a similar life cycle but a cyst that surrounds the entire host cell rather than being included within it, as is the *Toxoplasma* cyst. Bradyzoites of both *Toxoplasma* and *Besnoitia* can be subinoculated into another incomplete host in which, first, tachyzoites and, later, bradyzoites develop.

The general morphology of the individual bradyzoites of *Sarcocystis*, an organism that forms cysts in the skeletal muscle of many mammals, birds, and reptiles, and of *Frenkelia*, which forms cysts in the brain and possibly the skeletal muscle of mammals and birds, appears to be similar to that of *Toxoplasma* and *Besnoitia*. However, the bradyzoites of several *Sarcocystis* species studied can be transferred only to a host in which the sexual cycle can take place; transmission thus appears to require a change in host species. The cycle of *Frenkelia* has not been elucidated, but its bradyzoites cannot be transferred directly within the same host species.

Isospora and *Eimeria* are well known only from their enteroepithelial or equivalent cycle. Rodents can serve as intermediary hosts for *I. felis* and *I. rivolta* of cats, and forms apparently similar to tachyzoites and bradyzoites in cysts occur in rodents.

Encephalitozoon is now regarded as a member of the Microsporidia, and it is not biologically or morphologically closely related to *Toxoplasma*.

For background information *see* TOXOPLASMOSIS in the McGraw-Hill Encyclopedia of Science and Technology.   [J. K. FRENKEL]

Bibliography: J. K. Frenkel, *BioScience*, 23: 343–352, 1973; J. K. Frenkel and J. P. Dubey, *J. Infect. Dis.*, 126:664–673, 1972; D. M. Hammond and P. L. Long (eds.), *The Coccidia: Eimeria, Isospora, Toxoplasma, and Related Genera*, 1973; Symposium on Toxoplasmosis, *Bull. N.Y. Acad. Med.*, 50:107–240, 1974.

Transducer

During the past few years there have been widespread scientific and commercial applications of electret transducers. Of particular interest are electret microphones, which in a variety of implementations not only developed into invaluable research tools but also conquered a sizable part of the audio microphone market. Other electret transducers of recent importance are earphones, phonograph cartridges, key transducers, and impact transducers. All such electret devices are self-biased electrostatic or condenser systems. They thus exhibit all the advantages of this transducer class, such as wide dynamic range and flat response over a frequency range of several decades, without requiring the external bias necessary in conventional transducers of this kind.

Foil electret. The basic component of all modern electret transducers is a "foil electret" consisting of a thin film of insulating material that has been electrically charged to produce an external electric field. Strongly insulating materials capable of trapping charge carriers, such as the halocarbon polymers, in particular polyfluoroethylenepropylene (Teflon), are best suited for this purpose. Before charging, the material is either metallized on one side or backed up with a metal electrode. Charging can be achieved in a number of ways, for example, by treatment with a corona discharge or by voltage application by means of a wet-contact electrode. Another charging technique, allowing greater control than other methods, is electron injection with an electron beam having a range less than the film thickness. In all cases, carriers of one polarity are injected into the insulator and trapped. A compensation charge of equal magnitude but opposite sign flows into the back electrode, thus forming an electric double layer. On nonmetallized electrets, the compensation charge is generally transferred to the dielectric by air breakdown when the back electrode is removed. In the presence of electrodes, the electret exhibits an external electric field extending from the electret to the electrodes. Such a foil electret is thus, as far as its external field is concerned, an electrostatic analog of a permanent magnet.

Charge storage on halocarbon polymers is permanent. At charge densities of about 20 nC/cm^2, as required in electret transducers, the time constant of the charge decay of Teflon is about 200 years if measured at room temperature and low relative humidity. This time constant drops to about 10 years at 50°C and 95% relative humidity. However, Teflon has unfavorable mechanical properties because of stress relaxation, which causes a decrease in the mechanical tension of stretched films. As discussed below, this effect can be minimized in transducer applications.

Electret microphones. The most widely used transducer of this kind, the foil-electret microphone, is shown in the cutaway drawing of Fig. 1.

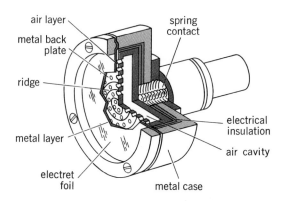

Fig. 1. A cutaway drawing of a foil-electret microphone showing the basic elements. (*From G. M. Sessler and J. E. West, Electret transducers: A review, J. Acoust. Soc. Amer., 53:1589, 1973*)

The diaphragm, typically 12- or 25-μm Teflon metallized on one surface, is charged to 10–20 nC/cm², corresponding to an external bias of about 200 V. The nonmetallized surface of the foil electret is placed next to a backplate, leaving a shallow air layer, the thickness of which (about 10 μm) is controlled by ridges or raised points on the backplate surface.

Since the mechanical tension of the foil is generally kept at a relatively low value (about 10 N/m), the restoring force is determined by the compressibility of the air layer. Controlling the restoring force by the air layer is advantageous because changes in tension due to stress relaxation thus have only a minor effect on the sensitivity, which is largely independent of transducer area. The stiffness of the air layer can be decreased (and thus the sensitivity of the microphone can be improved) by connecting the air layer to a larger cavity by means of small holes through the backplate. The backplate is either a metal disk or a metal-coated dielectric with a thermal expansion coefficient about equal to that of the diaphragm. The electrical output of the microphone is taken between the backplate, which is insulated from the outer case, and the metal side of the foil. The output is fed into a high-impedance preamplifier.

The problem of stress relaxation can be virtually eliminated by using a modified microphone design consisting of a metallic backplate coated with a layer of permanently charged Teflon. A metal (or metallized polyester) diaphragm is stretched over this backplate. In this approach, the excellent electrical properties of the Teflon layer and the good mechanical behavior of the metal or polyester diaphragm are used to advantage.

Under open-circuit conditions, a displacement d of the diaphragm of an electret microphone causes an output voltage given by Eq. (1), where E is the

$$v = Ed = \frac{\sigma D_1 d}{\epsilon_0 (D_1 + \epsilon D_2)} \qquad (1)$$

(constant) electric field in the air layer of the transducer; σ is the surface-charge density of the electret, D_1 and D_2 are the thicknesses of electret film and air layer, respectively; ϵ_0 is the permittivity of free space; and ϵ is the relative dielectric constant of the electret material. As in conventional electrostatic transducers, the displacement is proportional to the applied pressure in a wide frequency band extending from a lower cutoff given by a pressure-equalization leak in the back cavity to an upper cutoff determined by the resonance frequency. The voltage response for constant sound pressure is therefore frequency-independent in this range.

Typical electret microphones designed for the audio-frequency range have constant sensitivities of 1–10 mV/μbar in the frequency range from 20 to 15,000 Hz. Nonlinear distortion is less than 1% for sound-pressure levels below 140 dB, and the impulse response is excellent, owing to the flat amplitude and phase characteristics. Other properties of electret microphones are their low sensitivity to vibration, owing to the small diaphragm mass, and their insensitivity to magnetic fields. Compared with conventional electrostatic transducers, electret microphones have the following

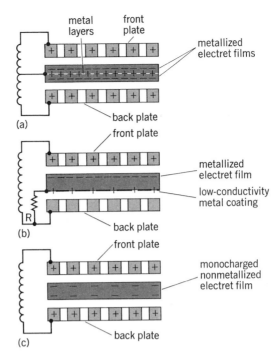

Fig. 2. Schematic cross sections of push-pull electret headphones, showing static charge distributions. (a) Conventional double-electret transducer. (b) Single-electret transducer with metallized conventionally charged electret. (c) Single-electret transducer with nonmetallized monocharged electret.

advantages: they do not require a dc bias; they have three times higher capacitance per unit area, resulting in a better signal-to-noise ratio; and they are not subject to destructive arcing between foil and backplate in humid atmospheres and under conditions of water condensation.

Various electret microphones for operation at infrasonic and ultrasonic frequencies, covering the range from 0.001 Hz to 200 MHz, have been designed by properly positioning the upper and lower cutoff frequencies discussed above. Furthermore, transducers with directional characteristics such as cardioid, bidirectional, toroidal, and second-order unidirectional have been developed.

Electret headphones. Another group of electret transducers of recent interest are electret headphones. Although the above microphone design can be utilized in this case, such an approach has a number of drawbacks when applied to headphones. Among these disadvantages are nonlinear performance due to the quadratic dependence of the force F per unit area, exerted on the diaphragm, on the applied ac voltage v, as can be seen from Eq. (2). Other drawbacks are small voltage

$$F = -\tfrac{1}{2} (D_1 \sigma + \epsilon \epsilon_0 v)^2 / \epsilon_0 (D_1 + \epsilon D_2)^2 \qquad (2)$$

sensitivity and limitations of air-gap thickness due to field considerations. These shortcomings have been overcome by the use of push-pull transducers and monocharge electrets.

The principle of a push-pull transducer is shown in Fig. 2a. A diaphragm consisting of two electrets, each metallized on one side and with these metal layers in contact, is sandwiched between two perforated metal electrodes, forming a symmetrical system. Application of a signal voltage $\bar{v}$ in antiphase to the two electrodes causes the electrodes to exert forces F_1 and F_2 on the diaphragm. These forces are given by Eq. (2) if $\pm\bar{v}$ is substituted for v. The net force $F = F_1 - F_2$ on the diaphragm is determined by Eq. (3), which is linear in $\bar{v}$, indicating the absence of nonlinear distortion.

$$F = -2\bar{v}\sigma\,\epsilon D_1/(D_1 + \epsilon D_2)^2 \qquad (3)$$

This transducer can be simplified by using the scheme shown in Fig. 2b. In this asymmetric system, a single electret coated on one side with a low-conductivity layer is used. The diaphragm holds an excess charge because of the presence of an induction charge on the front electrode. Thus, application of an ac signal causes a net force between diaphragm and plates if the resistivity of the coating (or the resistor R) prevents charge equalization during a period of the applied signal.

An interesting modification of the above push-pull transducers can be achieved by using nonmetallized monocharge electrets, which differ from customary electrets in that they carry only a single-polarity charge and no compensation charge. It is possible to form these electrets by electron injection or by the use of wet-contact charging methods. In the absence of a compensating charge, monocharge electrets have a strong external field that is independent of electrode distance. Thus, if such electrets are used in transducer configurations, as shown in Fig. 2c, large air gaps of the order of 1 mm can be used without loss in field strength. This in turn will result in highly efficient transducers that can operate at large displacement amplitudes.

Electromechanical transducers. Apart from its use in electroacoustic transducers, such as microphones and earphones, the electret principle has recently been applied to electromechanical transducers. Examples are phonograph cartridges, touch or key transducers, and impact transducers.

Two types of phonograph cartridges have been suggested. In one implementation, the stylus is coupled by a cavity to an electret microphone. The cavity serves as an acoustic transformer that converts the large-amplitude stylus vibrations to sound waves sensed by the microphone. Such cartridges have favorably low mass and are capable of high trackability and linearity over a wide frequency range, and yet are immune to magnetic fields. Another design consists essentially of a cantilever, to which a stylus is attached, and two electrets. The electrets, together with the cantilever, form a pair of electret transducers actuated by the vibrations of the cantilever. Advantages of these cartridges are low intermodulation distortion and a dynamic range of 100 dB.

Touch-actuated electret transducers similar in design to electret microphones have also been implemented. These transducers generate output signals on the order of 10–100 V due to direct or key operation resulting in a deflection of the diaphragm. Because of the small diaphragm deflections possible in such a device, tactile feedback is almost totally absent. However, feedback can be provided by actuating a mechanically compliant movable electrode by a mechanical spring.

Impact-sensitive electret transducers have been implemented as more or less conventional systems similar in design to the above-described microphones and as line transducers consisting essentially of a coaxial cable with polarized dielectric. In the line transducers the center conductor and the shield serve as electrodes. Mechanical excitation resulting in a deformation of the shield at any point along the length of such a cable produces an electrical output signal.

Applications. Because of their favorable properties, simplicity, and low cost, electret transducers have recently been used in many applications, both as research tools and in the commercial market. Among the research applications are microphones for use in acousto-optic spectroscopy, applied to the detection of air pollution and to the study of reaction kinetics of gases and optical absorption of solids. Because of the favorable noise performance of electret microphones, the detection threshold for air pollutants has been lowered by more than an order of magnitude. Other applications of electret microphones have been reported in aeronautics and shock-tube studies, in which the low vibration sensitivity of these transducers is crucial. The wide frequency range of electret transducers, discussed above, made possible their application in infrasonic atmospheric studies and in ultrasonic investigations of liquids and solids. In addition, ultrasonic arrays of electret microphones have recently been used in acoustic holography. Research uses of electromechanical electret transducers have been reported in such diverse areas as data transmission, vibration analysis, and leak detection in space stations. In these applications, the simplicity and reliability of electret transducers are of importance.

Of all commercial applications of electret devices, the high-fidelity electret microphone for amateur, professional, studio, and tape recorder use is most prominent. Although the electret microphone was introduced only about 5 years ago, tens of millions of the instruments are now produced annually all over the world, accounting for about one-half of the entire output of high-fidelity microphones. Other uses of electret microphones are in noise dosimeters, and movie cameras, and miniature microphones are used in hearing aids and in headsets used by telephone operators, as noise-canceling (first-order gradient) transducers. The success of the electret microphone in these applications is primarily due to its acoustic quality and low cost. It is noteworthy that, owing to their low vibration sensitivity, foil-electret microphones were the first transducers to be built directly into widely used tape recorders. In addition to electret microphones, push-pull electret earphones and electret phonograph cartridges have been introduced to the market recently.

For background information *see* ELECTRET; MICROPHONE; TRANSDUCER in the McGraw-Hill Encyclopedia of Science and Technology.

[GERHARD M. SESSLER]

Bibliography: R. E. Collins, *AWA Tech. Rev.*, 15:53, 1973; C. W. Reedyk, Electret transducers, in J. Thewlis (ed.), *Encyclopaedic Dictionary of Physics*, suppl. 5, 1974; G. M. Sessler and J. E. West, *J. Acoust. Soc. Amer.*, 53:1589, 1973.

Transfer factor

Reports from several laboratories during the past year have confirmed the efficacy of dialyzable transfer factor in generalized cellular immunodeficiency (certain genetic disorders, for example, the Wiskott-Aldrich syndrome) and of antigen-specific transfer factor in selective cellular immune deficiencies, for example, mucocutaneous candidiasis, a fungus infection severely affecting hands, feet, face, and, in females, the genital tract. Preliminary reports suggest that tumor-specific transfer factor may be an extremely useful adjunct in certain types of human tumors, but that nonspecific transfer factor is of no value in such situations.

Characteristics. Transfer factor (TF), a low-molecular-weight (<20,000) dialyzable moiety (TF_d) obtained from human leukocytes, was first described by S. Lawrence in 1955. Although TF_d activity in other species has been reported, the experimental work has not yet been reproducible. TF transfers positive skin tests (delayed hypersensitivity) from tuberculin-positive donors to tuberculin-negative recipients. Skin tests indicate that the converted recipients remain positive for 6 months. Delayed hypersensitivity from donors positive to other skin test antigens can also be transferred to negative recipients for periods of 6 months.

The mechanism of action of TF is unknown; it may act by way of macrophage cells rather than by way of T-lymphocytes, as has been commonly assumed. Studies to elucidate its mechanism of action and its structure have been hampered because purified TF of different specificities is difficult to obtain, owing to the problems in creating suitable reproducible animal models and laboratory test systems; hence, at present, normal human beings are the test subjects for fractions obtained from the crude dialyzate containing the active material. Studies carried out in several laboratories indicate that TF_d appears to have a molecular weight of 2500–3000 and is composed of a peculiar small double-strand RNA which is joined to a small peptide.

Current clinical use. TF remained primarily a laboratory curiosity until A. S. Levin and coworkers in 1970 reported its first therapeutic use (in a patient with a genetically determined deficiency of systemic cellular immunity, that is, a deficiency in T-cell function, the Wiskott-Aldrich syndrome). In the same report Levin and coworkers also demonstrated for the first time that TF could transfer biologic parameters known to be associated with systemic cellular immunity, for example, ability to produce mediators of cellular immunity such as macrophage in migration inhibitory factor.

Since then, the group of L. E. Spitler, A. S. Levin, and H. H. Fudenberg, at the University of California, San Francisco, have treated more than 150 patients with TF_d, and several independent laboratories have confirmed their findings of the therapeutic usefulness of TF_d in patients with various immunodeficiency disorders. TF is now established as a useful therapeutic modality in treating patients with hereditary T-cell defects. For example, approximately 60% of all patients with Wiskott-Aldrich syndrome benefit markedly from TF injections; eczema clears, splenomegaly disappears, and frequency of infection is markedly diminished for varying periods of time (usually 6 months). Subsequent injections of TF maintain prophylaxis, preventing recurrence of symptoms. With other diseases of cellular immunity, TF must be administered more frequently (the greater the antigenic mass "on board," the greater the amount of TF required).

TF_d also has been used in therapy to treat a variety of infectious diseases, specifically, coccidioidomycosis and chronic mucocutaneous candidiasis in patients with impaired cellular immunity to these organisms despite high levels of serum antibody against them. In each case, antigen-specific TF appears to be capable of increasing cell-mediated immunity, diminished either because the T-cells are overwhelmed by antigen overload or because the T-cells are genetically deficient for only one antigen.

In certain fungal diseases, TF appears to reduce the necessity of large doses of antifungal agents in current use and, in some situations, may even eliminate the need for such toxic drugs. TF is also being used extensively in various types of human cancer. Fudenberg and coworkers reported in 1974 that in 12 osteogenic sarcoma patients treated with osteogenic sarcoma–specific TF, they demonstrated that tumor immunity can be boosted by tumor-specific TF; in contrast, non-tumor-specific TF results in no change, or in a marked decrease in tumor immunity. Suggestive results have been observed in a small number of patients with other types of tumors.

Probable future clinical use. TF has the potential to be useful in treating a variety of defects in T-cell function. There is increasing evidence that "autoimmune phenomena" may be a function of the loss of suppressor T-cell activity. Hence, it is highly likely that TF can enable the host to regain suppressor T-cell function and thereby arrest or reverse symptomatology in such "autoimmune" diseases as rheumatoid arthritis, lupus erythematosus, and multiple sclerosis (the last-mentioned now appears to be due to deficient cell-mediated immunity to measles or related viruses). Different types of TF may well be useful in the future for reducing morbidity and mortality in a variety of viral, fungal, and parasitic diseases, especially those of children and the aged, and should be an extremely helpful agent in clinical practice. Obviously, knowledge of the structure of transfer factor and its mechanism of action must be obtained before its full spectrum of clinical utility can be established.

For background information *see* IMMUNOLOGY; IMMUNOPATHOLOGY in the McGraw-Hill Encyclopedia of Science and Technology.

[H. HUGH FUDENBERG]

Bibliography: H. H. Fudenberg et al., *Hosp. Pract.*, 9:95–104, January 1974; A. S. Levin et al., *Proc. Nat. Acad. Sci.*, 67:821–828, October 1970; A. S. Levin, L. E. Spitler, and H. H. Fudenberg, Transfer Factor I: Methods of therapy, and Transfer Factor II: Results of therapy, in D. Bergsma and R. A. Good (eds.), *Primary Immunodeficiency Diseases in Man*, National Foundation, in press.

Tree diseases

The dwarf mistletoes (family Viscaceae, genus *Arceuthobium*) are the most significant source of tree disease in coniferous forests in North America. They not only cause widespread mortality and growth reduction (Fig. 1) but also reduce seed crops, lower wood quality, and increase the susceptibility of trees to attack by insects and to other diseases.

The dwarf mistletoes occur in millions of acres of westen coniferous forests. The loss in lumber in the United States alone, for example, has been estimated at more than 3,000,000,000 bd ft (7,077,000 m^3) annually. This is equivalent to the amount of wood necessary to construct approximately 300,000 homes. The dwarf mistletoes occur mainly in the Northern Hemisphere and are most abundant

Fig. 2. Shoots of a dwarf mistletoe on a ponderosa pine branch showing nearly mature fruits near the tips of the branches. *(U.S. Forest Service)*

in North America, where they range from Alaska southeast to Newfoundland and New England and south throughout the western United States and Mexico to Central America.

Host-parasite relationship. As the common name implies, the dwarf mistletoes are generally small, mostly under 6 in. high (Fig. 2), and in some species as small as ¼ in. (1 in. = 2.54 cm). At the other extreme are some of the "giant" dwarf mistletoes of southern Mexico and Guatemala, which attain heights of nearly 3 ft (1 ft = 0.3 m). Most genera of conifers are parasitized, but pines are the most commonly affected. The dwarf mistletoes also attack firs, spruce, Douglas fir, hemlock, and larch. Curiously, junipers are not attacked in the New World, although these trees are the most common hosts in the Old World. The dwarf mistletoes generally have very narrow host ranges and usually parasitize only one host tree or a few closely related tree species.

Since the dwarf mistletoes are leafless, they depend on their host trees for nutrients and water, which they obtain through a "root" system in the host bark and wood. Since they manufacture very little of their own carbohydrates, they are much more damaging than the leafy mistletoes, which appropriate mainly water from their host trees.

Seed dispersal. One of the most remarkable features of the dwarf mistletoes is their explosive seed-dispersal mechanism. Several species of plants have explosive fruits (such as witch hazel, castor bean, and violets), but the seed-dispersal system of the dwarf mistletoes is one of the most efficient in the whole plant kingdom. Each dwarf mistletoe fruit contains a single tear-shaped seed 2–3 mm long. At maturity the fruit is severed from the shoot, and the seed is hurled upward (Fig. 3). Studies by F. G. Hawksworth and coworkers on

Fig. 1. Dwarf mistletoe caused damage in a Douglas fir stand in New Mexico. Most trees have been killed by the parasite. Note the distorted branches, or "witches' brooms," which are a common symptom of trees affected by dwarf mistletoe. *(U.S. Forest Service)*

Fig. 3. A dwarf mistletoe seed immediately after expulsion from the fruit. Photograph taken at 0.000005 sec. (*U.S. Forest Service*)

the ballistics of these seeds indicate that they have an initial velocity of 2400 cm/sec or about 60/mph. The maximum distance to which these seeds are hurled is about 50 ft, but the average distance is about 10–15 ft. Seeds produced high in trees may spread for 100 ft or more if they are dispersed during periods of high winds. Another distinctive feature of the seed-dispersal mechanism of the dwarf mistletoe is that the vertical angle of seed discharge is controlled.

Studies by Hawksworth and coworkers indicate that the average vertical angle of discharge is about 45° above the horizontal. Interestingly, this is the optimum angle for maximum horizontal distance by a projectile. Their seed-dispersal mechanism enables dwarf mistletoes to spread upward in trees and also, by hurling seeds outward, to infect nearby trees. Another unusual feature of the dwarf mistletoes is that they are not dependent on birds for seed dispersal, as are most, if not all, of the other 60 genera of mistletoes. Birds may play an incidental role in the distribution of dwarf mistletoes, but the extent of this role has not been determined.

Control methods. Because of their abundance and extreme destructiveness, control of the dwarf mistletoes is necessary for optimum forest production in western North America. Fortunately, these parasites can, in many cases, be controlled with only slight modifications of current timber-cutting practices. The basic idea behind control is to break the chain of infection to safeguard young trees of subsequent generations. By harvesting infected trees and by cutting off infected branches, young stands can be protected.

No biological or chemical controls of the dwarf mistletoes are yet available, but research on the discovery and development of these methods is actively being carried out, both by the U.S. Forest Service and by several universities. Other current areas of major dwarf mistletoe research efforts include basic biology and host-parasite relationships, rates of spread and intensification in trees and stands, extent of host mortality and growth losses, and computer simulation of wood yields in forests infected by the dwarf mistletoe. This kind of computer simulation represents a new area for research, and for the first time for any forest pest it

has been possible to develop means to predict several decades into the future the extent of damage caused by the parasite. By using these methods, the forest manager can determine for each particular stand what yields can be expected if control is or is not undertaken. Such analyses will also help the forest manager spend his appropriations much more efficiently, for he can then concentrate control efforts in the areas where they will be most beneficial.

The dwarf mistletoes, by causing tree mortality and loss of wood growth, are a serious threat to the productivity of North American coniferous forests. Studies are being conducted on the possible use of biological or chemical controls against these pests. At present the only control measures available are the pruning out of infected branches or the removing of infected trees to protect young stands from the ravages of these parasites.

For background information *see* MISTLETOE; TREE DISEASES in the McGraw-Hill Encyclopedia of Science and Technology.

[FRANK G. HAWKSWORTH]

Bibliography: F. G. Hawksworth and C. A. Myers, *USDA Forest Serv. Res. Note RM-237*, 1973; F. G. Hawksworth and D. Wiens, *Biology and Classification of Dwarf Mistletoes (Arceuthobium)*, USDA Agric. Handb. 401, 1972; W. R. Mark and F. G. Hawksworth, *J. Forest.*, 72:146–147, 1974; L. F. Roth, *Phytopathology*, 64:689–692, 1974.

Tundra

The Tundra Biome Program of the International Biological Program (IBP) has been examining the structure and function of circumpolar arctic tundra ecosystems, tundras on subantarctic islands, and alpine tundras of mid-latitudes during the past 5 years in order to obtain a predictive understanding of how tundra ecosystems operate and to provide a data base upon which effects of environmental impacts can be assessed.

Biological productivity. Decomposition processes are slow in cold tundra soils; this restricts the turnover and availability of nutrients necessary for plant growth. Fungi are more abundant than bacteria in tundra soils, and microfauna play a significant role in the decomposition process. Primary production by tundra vegetation, which varies with geographic region from 20 to more than 350 g of dry matter per square meter per year, occurs during a short interval that peaks after the summer solstice. Insect herbivores are largely absent from tundra, but the action of cyclic populations of microtine mammals (lemmings) and roaming herds of ungulates (reindeer, caribou, musk-oxen), not only in consumption but also in trampling and cutting of vegetation, has a marked effect on annual variations in rate of primary production.

Intervention of white population. The human population has been a natural part of the circumpolar tundra ecosystem for thousands of years. Human beings harvested mammals and birds for food, clothing, and building material generally in a density-dependent fashion; that is, populations of primitive native humans were largely controlled by the abundance of populations of seals, walrus, caribou, reindeer, wolves, bears, and other animals that were the objects of the hunter. As the white

Fig. 1. Scarring of the tundra surface through indiscriminate use of tracked vehicles in summer. Note water-filled areas and the long, developing erosion channel. (*Courtesy of Dr. David R. Klein*)

race gradually infiltrated native villages, the subsistence economy of the people steadily declined; now, almost all populations of tundra-inhabiting humans are dependent upon supplies obtained by purchase from the whites' economy. Populations of both natives and whites in tundra regions have therefore increased, since they need not depend on the local populations of native animal species for their subsistence. This increase in population has been aggravated during the past 5 years by the discovery of oil in the Prudhoe Bay field near the arctic coast on the North Slope of Alaska.

Entry of persons from industrially organized society is so recent that the consequences of their actions cannot be assessed. However, initial exploration and development activities have pointed to potential problem areas that must be attacked through research.

Access by road and air. Northern tundras are vast expanses of land that, because of their low productivity, support migratory and transient populations of animals. Therefore, great distances separate native villages, and much of the land surface is unoccupied or seldom visited by humans. No conventional surface access routes exist in most tundras, and people must create roads, employ oversurface vehicles, or fly in order to gain access to land for exploration and development. Although tundra surfaces can for the most part be

safely crossed in winter while frozen under a cushioning layer of snow, in summer, removal or compression of the vegetative mat by tracked vehicles (Fig. 1) or even by successive passes of vehicles with low-pressure tires has a detrimental effect. A decrease in the thickness of the vegetative mat reduces its insulative quality so that the underlying permafrost melts. Over long periods, water channels are created from the melting ice, and if the surfaces are inclined, severe erosion results. Surface disturbance near water results in siltation. Air-cushion vehicles and helicopters appear to be the best methods for crossing summer tundras, but these vehicles have many practical limitations. Helicopters also present a significant harassment potential to large mammals when pilots photograph or observe the animals closely. Caribou or reindeer running from helicopters require added energy. Their winter food demands may exceed the available energy in the food supply, and they may succumb. Rapid intake of cold air for extended periods by vigorously exercising animals may result in respiratory illness. In spring, pregnant females or those with newborn calves are especially susceptible to overexertion caused by harassment.

Detrimental effects of roads. Roads must be built of gravel deposited on the surface so that the permafrost is not disturbed. Although gravel roads protect the integrity of the tundra, they have drawbacks, including the removal of gravel from other areas for their construction, impoundment of water and alteration of normal drainage patterns, increase in amount of dust produced by vehicle traffic, and need for a raised landform on an otherwise relatively flat landscape. In the northern tundras, the principal source of gravel is the beds of streams and rivers. Removal of large quantities of gravel for roads and pads upon which structures are placed may change river courses and cause siltation detrimental to aquatic organisms. Creation of ponds along roads and prevention of water movement alter the distribution of plant and animal life. Road dust blown onto snow results in faster melting in spring and thus an earlier breakup. The increased amount of open water attracts early-spring migrant bird populations, which rest in these areas prior to breeding. Dust settling on plants and on the ground may alter photosynthetic and soil heating rates. Roads that rise above the normal surface constitute a barrier to the normal movements of some animals and may also serve as a concentration point for others (Fig. 2). Caribou find movement easier on roads, and the slight elevation provides the higher wind velocities preferred by caribou under insect attack.

At the end of the road, where camps are set up, disposal of waste becomes an immediate problem. Liquids will not sink into the ground because it is perennially frozen; solid wastes do not decompose. The terrain encourages runoff to adjacent stream channels and lakes; anadromous as well as resident fish populations are affected by this type of contamination. Deposition of waste often attracts carnivores such as the wolf, fox, and bear. These larger predators are not numerous in tundras and, because of their scarcity, are desired by man as trophies. They also often become a nuisance to camps, and since they may be a source of rabies, they are therefore eliminated.

Atmospheric pollution. During periods of intense cold, below −30°C, ice fog conditions commonly develop in arctic areas; the heavier cold air is trapped near the ground in the absence of wind. The most prolific sources of ice fogs, which are composed of frozen droplets of water suspended in air, are combustion of fossil fuels in heating plants and vehicle exhaust. During an ice fog, visibility is limited and gaseous waste products remain suspended in the air; both conditions are detrimental to human safety and health. In addition, flaring of gas from oil production and gaseous emissions released in oil refining may have detrimental effects on humans, other animals, and plants. Lichens are particularly susceptible to sulfur-containing gases, and deleterious effects have been seen in lichens in Scandinavia. Lichens are slow-growing plants that are important in the winter diet of reindeer and caribou. More than 50 years may be necessary to replace lichens that have been destroyed; on the other hand, normal grazing removes only the uppermost portions of the plants, and recovery requires 5–10 years.

Problem of oil spills. Oil discovered in isolated northern tundra regions must be transported to refineries and markets further south, usually by pipeline. Pipelines, like fences and other obsta-

Fig. 2. A small herd of caribou resting on a gravel roadway on the arctic tundra. The simulated gathering pipeline to the left of the roadway constitutes a barrier to the normal movements of the animals. (*Courtesy of Dr. David R. Klein*)

cles, act as barriers to the natural migratory movements of caribou and reindeer. Pilot studies in Alaska and observations in the Scandinavian and Siberian tundras show that the behavior of these animals must be altered so that they will cross these barriers. Also, fears have been expressed over the effects of spillage of oil in tundra regions. Small spills that are contained on tundra surfaces do not appear to be severely detrimental. Much of the oil can be cleaned up, and naturally occurring decomposers break down the oil to nontoxic components. Oil spills that run off into streams or lakes may have more detrimental consequences since clean-up techniques have not been as well developed as those for land spills. Oil spreads more rapidly over water surfaces, and it may be transported away from the site of the spill, making clean-up even more difficult.

Tourism. Finally, the opening up of previously inaccessible tundra regions invites increased tourism, recreation, and associated developments that will perhaps constitute the severest impact on northern ecosystems. Because of its "fragile" nature, and the relative scarcity of game animals, tundra is highly susceptible to the increased pressure of human intervention, and careful safeguards to preserve the tundra ecosystem must be built into any tundra land-use management plan.

For background information *see* TUNDRA in the McGraw-Hill Encyclopedia of Science and Technology.   [GEORGE C. WEST]

Bibliography: M. E. Britton (ed.), *Alaskan Arctic Tundra*, Arctic Inst. N. Amer. Tech. Pap. no. 25, 1973; J. Brown (ed.), *The Tundra Ecosystem: Terrestrial Studies*, 1975; J. Hobbie (ed.), *The Tundra Ecosystem: Aquatic Studies*, 1975; D. R. Klein, in *Petrolio e ambiente: Proceedings of the 3d Interpe-*

trol Congress, pp. 109–121, 1973; B. H. McCown (ed.), *Impact of Oil Resource Development on Northern Plant Communities*, Institute of Arctic Biology, University of Alaska, 1973; J. J. Moore (ed.), *Tundra and Tundra-like Ecosystems*, 1975; National Science Foundation, in *Mosaic*, 5:2–9, 1974.

Tunnel junction

Recent advances have included the experimental observation of resonant tunneling in double- and multiple-barrier structures of semiconductors, and the further progress in applications of the dc and ac Josephson effects in superconducting tunnel junctions.

Tunnel junctions are two-terminal electronic devices in which there exists an extremely thin potential barrier to electron flow. The transport characteristic (the current-voltage curve) is primarily governed by the quantum-mechanical tunneling process, which permits electrons to penetrate from one side to the other through the thin barrier. The barrier would be a forbidden region if the electron were treated as a classical particle.

During the infancy of the quantum theory, L. de Broglie introduced the fundamental hypothesis that matter may be endowed with a dualistic nature—particles such as electrons, α-particles, and so on, may also have the characteristics of waves. This hypothesis found expression in the definite form now known as the Schrödinger wave equation, whereby an electron or an α-particle is represented by a solution to this equation. The nature of such solutions implies an ability to penetrate classically forbidden regions of negative kinetic energy and a probability of tunneling from one classically allowed region to another. The concept of tunneling, indeed, arises from this quantum-mechanical result. The subsequent experimental manifestations of this concept, such as high-field electron emission from cold metels, α-decay, and so on, in the 1920s, can be regarded as one of the early triumphs of the quantum theory.

In the 1930s, attempts were made to understand the mechanism of electrical transport in resistive contacts between metals and rectifying metal-semiconductor contacts in terms of electron tunneling in solids. In the latter case, since a proposed theoretical model did not properly represent the actual situation, the theory predicted the wrong direction of rectification. In many cases, however, conclusive experimental evidence of tunneling was lacking, primarily because of the rudimentary stage of material science.

Tunnel diode. The invention of the transistor in 1947 spurred the progress of semiconductor technology. By the 1950s, materials technology for semiconductors such as Ge and Si was sufficiently advanced to permit the construction of well-defined semiconductor structures. The tunnel diode (also called the Esaki diode) was discovered in 1957 by L. Esaki. This discovery demonstrated the first convincing evidence of electron tunneling in solids, a phenomenon which had been clouded by questions for decades. This device is a version of the semiconductor *p-n* junction diode which is made of a *p*-type semiconductor, containing mobile positive charges called holes (which correspond to the vacant electron sites), and an *n*-type semiconductor, containing mobile electrons (the electron has a negative charge). Esaki succeeded in making the densities of holes and electrons in the respective regions extremely high by doping a large amount of the appropriate impurities with an abrupt transition from one region to the other. Now, in semiconductors, the conduction band for mobile electrons is separated from the valence band for mobile holes by an energy gap, which corresponds to a forbidden region. Therefore, a narrow transition layer from *n*-type to *p*-type, 5 to 15 nm thick, consisting of the forbidden region of the energy gap, provided a tunneling barrier. Since the tunnel diode exhibits a negative incremental resistance with a rapid response, it is capable of serving as an active element for amplification, oscillation, and switching in electronic circuits at high frequencies. The discovery of the diode, however, is probably more significant from the scientific aspect because it has opened up a new field of research—tunneling in solids.

Esaki and colleagues continue to explore negative resistance phenomena in semiconductors which can be observed in novel tunnel structures. One obvious question is: What would happen if two tunnel barriers are placed close together, or if a periodic barrier structure—a series of equally spaced potential barriers—is made in solids? It has been known that there is a phenomenon called the resonant transmission. Historically, resonant transmission was first demonstrated in the scattering of electrons by atoms of noble gases and is known as the Ramsauer effect. In the above-mentioned tunnel structures, it is clear that the resonant tunneling should be observed. Recently, in preparing double tunnel barriers and periodic structures with a combination of semiconductors, the resonant tunneling was experimentally demonstrated and negative resistance effects were observed.

Tunnel junctions between metals. As discussed above, tunneling had been considered to be a possible electron transport mechanism between metal electrodes separated by either a narrrow vacuum or a thin insulating film usually made of metal oxides. In 1960, I. Giaever demonstrated for the first time that, if one or both of the metals were in a superconducting state, the current-voltage curve in such metal tunnel junctions revealed many details of that state. At the time of Giaever's work, the first satisfactory microscopic theory of superconductivity had just been developed by J. Bardeen, L. N. Cooper, and J. R. Schrieffer (BCS theory). Giaever's technique was sensitive enough to measure the most important feature of the BCS theory—the energy gap which forms when the electrons condense into correlated, bound pairs (called Cooper pairs), resulting in superconductivity.

Josephson effects. Giaever's work opened the door to more detailed experimental investigations—it pioneered a new spectroscopy of high accuracy to study the superconducting state. In 1962, B. Josephson made a penetrating theoretical analysis of tunneling between two superconductors by treating the two superconductors and the coupling process as a single system, which would be valid if the insulating oxide were sufficiently thin, say, 20 A (2 nm). His theory predicted, in addition to the Giaever current, the existence of a supercurrent, arising from tunneling of the bound electron pairs.

This led to two startling conclusions: the dc and ac Josephson effects. The dc effect implies that a supercurrent may flow even if no voltage is applied to the junction. The ac effect implies that, at finite voltage V, there is an alternating component of the supercurrent which oscillates at a frequency of 483.6 MHz per microvolt of voltage across the junction, and is typically in the microwave range. The dc Josephson effect was soon identified among existing experimental results, while the direct observation of the ac effect eluded experimentalists for a few years. The effects are indeed quantum phenomena on a macroscopic scale. Extraordinary sensitivity of the supercurrents to applied electric and magnetic fields has led to the development of a rich variety of devices with application in wide areas of science and technology. High-sensitivity magnetometers or galvanometers and low-power and high-speed memory and logic devices are a few examples. Furthermore, the ac Josephson effect is now used to define the volt in terms of frequency in standards laboratories, eliminating the antiquated standard cell. *See* SUPERCONDUCTING DEVICES.

Esaki, Giaever, and Josephson shared the Nobel prize for physics in 1973 for the above-mentioned discoveries in tunnel junctions.

For background information *see* ESAKI TUNNEL DIODE; JOSEPHSON EFFECT; SUPERCONDUCTING DEVICES; SUPERCONDUCTIVITY in the McGraw-Hill Encyclopedia of Science and Technology. [LEO ESAKI]

Bibliography: L. Esaki, *Science*, 183:1149, 1974; I. Giaever, *Science*, 183:1253, 1974; B. D. Josephson, *Science*, 184:527, 1974.

Virus

The 1972 reports of L. S. Diamond, C. F. T. Mattern, and colleagues on the viruses of the human pathogenic protozoan *Entamoeba histolytica* provided the first tangible evidence for the existence of viruses in protozoa. The described agents caused lysis in susceptible (heterologous) ameal strains, passed through 200-nm filters, could be passaged continuously, and possessed morphological properties of known viruses. Prior reports of viruses in protozoa were based solely on electron-microscopic evidence. The phagelike particles associated with *Paramecium aurelia* are entities associated with the bacterial endosymbiont kappa. A similar relationship appears to exist between an endosymbiont and viruslike particles described by F. L. Schuster and T. H. Dunnebacke in the amebo-flagellate *Naegleria gruberi*.

Morphologic types. Viruses have been isolated from healthy axenic (free of other living organisms) cultures of each of nine strains of *E. histolytica* examined to date. Two morphologic types were distinguished, both of which may occur in the same host strain; one is a polyhedral structure having the geometry of an icosahedron; the other, a filamentous (probably helical) form. The former was found in all strains, the latter in three. Each

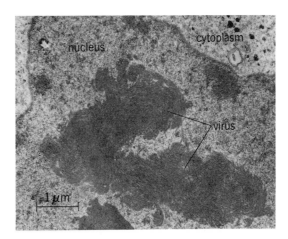

Fig. 1. Filamentous virus V$_{ABRM}$ replicating in large clusters in the nucleus of an HK-9 ameba.

ameal strain was found to be resistant to its indigenous viruses, and the viruses of each strain infected and lysed amebas of one or more of the other eight strains. Serologic study of the icosahedral viruses with neutralizing antiserum produced in rabbits indicated that an antigenic kinship exists among them.

Although viruses can be isolated from apparently normal amebas, they were not revealed in the host cell by electron microscopy, except on two occasions. In these instances, amebas from two different strains that had undergone spontaneous lysis (a common phenomenon observed during the process of axenizing a culture) were found to contain a very few icosahedral particles. Subsequently these strains were shown to produce icosahedral viruses when tested on the appropriate sensitive strains. On the other hand, viruses can be readily observed in experimentally infected sensitive (indicator) strains that are lysed by viral infection. The filamentous virus consisting of multiple clusters of fine filaments (about 10 nm in diameter) is first observed in the nucleus (Fig. 1) and, later, after lysis of the nuclear membrane, in the cytoplasm. Clearly identifiable icosahedral viruses (80 nm in diameter) are seen replicating in the perinuclear cytoplasm. In lysed amebas these particles are characteristically bound to membranous debris (Fig. 2).

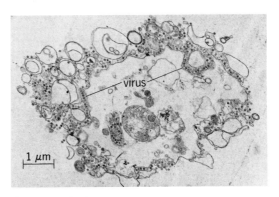

Fig. 2. Icosahedral viruses attached to the membranes of a lysed HK-9 ameba.

Attempts to produce pathology in suckling and adult mice with these agents have failed, as have attempts to induce cytopathology in a variety of vertebrate cell types in tissue culture.

Icosahedral virus. The most recent investigations of the viruses of *E. histolytica* by J. F. Hruska and coworkers have been concerned with identification of some of the biological characteristics of the icosahedral viruses, the possible lysogenic nature of these viruses, their detailed ultrastructure, and the characterization of the nucleic acids of both viral types.

Intensive study of the icosahedral virus designated V_{301} showed it to be highly unstable when frozen and thawed. More than 90% infectivity was lost after a single freezing at $-40°C$ and subsequent thawing; at $-79°C$ the loss was 99.9%. After the initial freeze-thaw there was little loss of infectivity of the remaining fractions upon repeated freezing and thawing. Regarding thermal inactivation, infectivity was lost at the rate of approximately 90% in 24 hr at 37°C and 99.9% per hour at 56°C. The virus was relatively stable over a narrow pH range of 6.5–8.0 but readily inactivated at pH values less than 5.0 and at 9.0.

In amebal cultures lysed after infection with V_{301}, approximately 99% of the infectivity was found in the pellet formed after low-speed centrifugation (2000 g). Electron-microscopic examination of these pellets revealed the virus particles to be bound to membranous debris from the lysed amebas. In contrast, the supernate formed after low-speed centrifugation was relatively noninfectious, although it contained large numbers of membrane-free particles. Whether these particles are mostly defective or have a low efficiency of infection is not known.

Various chemical agents have been employed in an attempt to dissociate the virus-membrane complex, but without success. EDTA and sodium citrate destroyed viral infectivity, but their action could be partially prevented by preincubation with Ca^{++}. Treatment with a variety of enzymes, including chymotrypsin, hyaluronidase, neuraminidase, phospholipase A2, pronase, snake venom, and subtilisin, had no effect on the infectivity of either the viruses of the sediment or the supernate. Deoxycholate, lithium diiodosalycilate, Nonidet P-40, sodium dodecyl sulfate, Triton X, and Tween 80 decreased the infectivity of the pellet in varying degrees but did not increase activity of the supernate. Ethyl ether and chloroform drastically reduced the infectivity of the pellet.

In an attempt to develop a virus-free amebal strain, the host of V_{301} was subcultured 54 consecutive times in the presence of neutralizing antiserum without success. This result, although not the desired one, suggested that the system was lysogenic. Further evidence supporting this view came from the observation that 43 amebal clones representing three generations of cloning were all infected with the virus, and treatment of a low-virus-producing clone with BUDR (5-bromo-2'-deoxyuridine) enhanced virus production.

Nucleic acid studies. Treatment of the icosahedral virus V_{301} and the filamentous virus V_{ABRM} with bromodeoxyuridine, iododeoxyuridine, and cytosine arabinoside, known inhibitors of DNA synthesis, resulted in inhibition of viral replication, suggesting that the nucleic acid of both viruses was DNA. Furthermore, self-hybridization observed in DNA studies with V_{301} and the indicator amebal strain HK-9 suggested that the nucleic acid of the virus was different from amebal DNA and was double-stranded. Likewise, the chartreuse color obtained after acridine orange staining of nuclear inclusions produced by the filamentous virus V_{ABRM} suggested that its DNA was double-stranded.

The arrangement of the nucleic acid in V_{301} was found to be unique, setting this virus apart from certain bacterial and algal viruses that it resembles. It is believed the DNA exists as a folded filament. In cross-section views a central filament is surrounded by 6 filaments, which in turn are surrounded by 12 filaments, all in a hexagonal arrangement. Other views appear to show the S-shaped connection of this folded DNA filament.

Virus universality. Each of the amebal strains studied for virus was derived from a patient with active amebic disease. Whether viruses are present in avirulent strains remains to be discovered. The fact that the patients involved were from widely separated geographic areas of both the Old and New Worlds points to the possible universality of the amebal viruses, at least in virulent strains. Incidentally, a single-strain *E. hartmanni* (another amebal parasite of man) was found to be infected with a polyhedral viral agent.

For background information *see* ANIMAL VIRUS; LYSOGENY; LYTIC REACTION; VIRUS in the McGraw-Hill Encyclopedia of Science and Technology.

[LOUIS S. DIAMOND; CARL F. T. MATTERN]

Bibliography: L. S. Diamond, C. F. T. Mattern, and I. L. Bartgis, *J. Virol.*, 9:326–341, 1972; J. F. Hruska et al., *J. Virol.*, 11:129–136, 1973; J. F. Hruska, C. F. T. Mattern, and L. S. Diamond, *J. Virol.*, 13:205–210, 1974; C. F. T. Mattern, L. S. Diamond, and W. A. Daniel, *J. Virol.*, 9:342–358, 1972; C. F. T. Mattern, J. F. Hruska, and L. S. Diamond, *J. Virol.*, 13:247–249, 1974.

Wavelength standards

At its meeting in October 1973 the Comité International des Poids et Mesures (CIPM) adopted recommended values for the wavelength of light (from two stabilized lasers) and for the speed of light. One of these extremely accurate wavelengths may become the primary standard, replacing the krypton-86 standard of 605.780211 nm (6057.80211 A) as the wavelength of the spectral line in the orange-red in the radiation from a specified hot-cathode lamp containing not less than 99% ^{86}Kr. Since 1960 the legal definition of the meter has been 1,650,763.73 wavelengths of this ^{86}Kr radiation. The specifications were designed to have as the standard as sharp a spectral line as possible within the limits of the technique then available.

Stabilized lasers. In stabilized lasers, the plasma tube, containing perhaps a suitable ^{3}He-^{20}Ne gas mixture, and the absorption cell filled with, say, methane gas or iodine vapor at a proper pressure, are mounted in line in the same cavity. The cavity length is typically about 20 to 30 cm, with the end mirrors in holders; one holder contains a piezoelectric transducer. A servo loop with the proper components supplies power input and stabilization.

When analyzed with an interferometer, the intense, narrow beam of light from an ordinary laser will show a spectral line having Doppler broadening and, quite possibly, magnetic and isotope hyperfine structure. The availability of separated isotopes makes possible a He-Ne laser that is, for example, just ^{3}He-^{20}Ne or just ^{3}He-^{22}Ne. In 1967 P. H. Lee and M. L. Skolnick first used saturated absorption to eliminate Doppler broadening. Since then their technique has been used, especially with either methane or iodine, for laser stabilization and high-resolution spectroscopy. A He-Ne laser has been stabilized to an absorption line in methane at 3.39 μm. In addition, a ^{3}He-^{20}Ne laser has been stabilized to hyperfine components in an absorption line of either ^{127}I$_2$ or ^{129}I$_2$ at 633 nm. A recent National Bureau of Standards (NBS) report by W. G. Schweitzer and coworkers describes the performance of iodine-stabilized lasers at 633 nm, some absolute wavelength measurements of its components, and a comparison with methane-stabilized lasers at 3.39 μm.

Basis for CIPM recommendations. The 1973 recommendations of the CIPM are based on the interferometric measurements at five laboratories of the vacuum wavelength of the light from both the methane- and the iodine-stabilized lasers. These recommended values from the Comité Consultatif pour la Définition du Mètre (CCDM), a committee established by the CIPM, are summarized below.

(1) The wavelength of the light emitted by a He-Ne laser stabilized to the P(7) line in the ν_3 band of the methane molecule is $3,392,231.40 \times 10^{-12}$m. (2) The wavelength emitted by a He-Ne laser stabilized to the "i" component of the R(127) line in the 11-5 band of ^{127}I$_2$ is $632,991.399 \times 10^{-12}$m. (3) Other components of this R(127) line in the 11-5 band of ^{127}I$_2$ or of ^{129}I$_2$ could also be used as wavelength standards, since they could be related to the "i" component by difference-frequency measurements. These calculated wavelengths would therefore be of the same accuracy as the "i" component. (4) Using the value $88,376,181,627 \pm 50$ kHz for the frequency of the methane line specified in recommendation 1, as determined by the National Bureau of Standards using intermediate étalons whose frequency has been confirmed by independent measurement in other laboratories, multiplication with the wavelength in recommendation 1 gives $299,792,458$ m sec^{-1} for the velocity of light in vacuum. The uncertainty in this velocity value and in the wavelengths is four parts in 10^9.

CCDM recommendations. Aiming for the highest accuracy possible for the two important standards, the definition of the meter and the value of the velocity of light, CCDM recommends that there be further research, particularly new measurements of optical frequencies and new comparisons of the wavelengths of radiations from stabilized lasers. There is already a second report from the NBS describing a high-resolution interferometric comparison of an iodine-stabilized laser with a methane-stabilized laser. Details such as pressure broadening, pressure shift to the red, power broadening and power shifts in these laser lines, and the specification of other experimental variables may affect only the last decimal place, but for international standards they are important.

In addition to the ^{86}Kr wavelength standard there is another standard value of the speed of light ($299,792,500 \pm 100$ m sec^{-1}), determined in 1957 by K. D. Froome of the National Physical Laboratory, Teddington, United Kingdom, with a free-space microwave interferometer operating at 70,000 MHz (wavelength of 4 mm) over a path difference of 1000 minima. Froome's value of the speed of light, which agrees, but with an uncertainty greater than that of the ^{86}Kr wavelength standard, with the new CCDM recommended value, has been widely used since 1957 for long-distance measurements.

Advantage of laser-based standard. The principal gain from a shift to the standards based on the stabilized laser sources is the remarkable agreement in the measurements with independently constructed equipment. However, there is still a decision to be made between defining the meter from a wavelength measurement with one of the stabilized lasers and defining it as the distance traveled by electromagnetic radiation in vacuum in a certain fraction of a second. The CCDM recommendation seems preferable.

For background information see ATOMIC STRUCTURE AND SPECTRA; HYPERFINE STRUCTURE; INTERFEROMETRY; ISOTOPE SHIFT; LASER; WAVELENGTH STANDARDS in the McGraw-Hill Encyclopedia of Science and Technology.

[WILLIAM W. WATSON]

Bibliography: H. P. Layer, R. D. Deslattes, and W. G. Schweitzer of NBS, publication pending; P. H. Lee and M. L. Skolnick. *Appl. Phys. Lett.*, 10:303, 1967; W. G. Schweitzer et al., *Appl. Opt.*, 12:2927–2938, 1973.

Weather modification

The past few years have seen several advances in weather modification that point the way toward useful hail-suppression techniques. In northeastern Colorado a comprehensive hail research experiment has been established through which advanced methods of measuring inside hailstorms and new methods for measuring hail fall at the ground have evolved. There has been a clarification of the processes by which hail forms, and advances have been made in the techniques of delivering seeding materials into the storms. There are also new data on the economic and ecological effects of hail-suppression activities and new knowledge about social responses to weather modification.

National Hail Research Experiment. The worldwide agricultural loss due to hail is approximately $1,000,000,000 annually. In the United States alone, the loss is in excess of $500,000,000 per year. Although such economic incentive to reduce damaging hail has long existed, the claims of spectacular success in hail suppression in the Soviet Union during the late 1950s and early 1960s were responsible for much of the recent worldwide interest in hail suppression. Although visiting American scientists found that these claims were impressive, many believed that the verification procedures used were not adequate enough to be convincing. In an effort to provide a definitive experiment on hail suppression, in 1972 the United States initiated the National Hail Research Experiment (NHRE), sponsored by the National Science Foundation and managed by the National Center for Atmospheric Research. In accord with modern-day methods of statistical and information science for extracting meaningful physical relationships from an assortment of data, NHRE is carrying out a statistical seeding experiment as well as coordinated physical measurements and theoretical analyses, all aimed at delineating the mechanisms of hail formation and the techniques for its suppression.

Included in the NHRE program are direct aircraft observations of the dynamical and microphysical properties of the storm, Doppler radar coverage to indicate internal air motion and to estimate hail size spectra, dual-wavelength radar for discriminating between hail and rain within the storms, a dense ground network for recording time-resolved hail fall data, and intensive hailstone collection and analysis for delineating the growth history of the hailstones.

Studying the formation of hail. Possibly the most unique instrument of all, operated by the South Dakota School of Mines and Technology, is the North American T-28 aircraft, which is armored to withstand 8-cm (3-in.) diameter hailstones, stressed for very severe turbulence, and instrumented for measuring hail, rain, and vertical air motions.

Guided by ground-based radar, the aircraft has made well over 100 penetrations into the highly turbulent, hail-forming regions of severe thunderstorms. Multiple updrafts have been found just below the location of the storm's maximum radar reflectivity that contain large quantities of large liquid drops in the cores and a predominance of hailstones in the flanks. The measurements of vertical air velocities, liquid water, and hailstone size show reasonable correlation with the predictions of theoretical models.

Laboratory sections taken from more than 1500 hailstones gathered on the ground show that most hail in northeastern Colorado originates from the freezing of small droplets less than 100 μm in diameter. Most hail, however, comes in the form of smaller hailstones, which are generally not as damaging as the larger ones. The same data show that the majority of the larger hailstones originate from larger frozen drops. This suggests that the more severe storms generate larger drops by drop coalescence more rapidly than the less severe storms do, possibly because of higher liquid water contents in the updrafts. Since larger drops tend to freeze before smaller drops do, the few large drops that do freeze will encounter an abundance of supercooled, smaller liquid drops with which to impact and freeze and thereby begin the process of forming large hailstones.

Studies of the deuterium content, which codes the altitude at which water freezes, show that large and giant hailstones form in a single ascent that is followed by a descent to the ground. This finding invalidates some previous theories which claimed that several up-and-down motions were required to

form large hail, and indicates that the alternating clear and cloudy concentric layers commonly found in hailstones do not result from significant up-and-down recycling motions. The finding is reinforced by radar data that show an absence of recirculating motions among the centers of high radar reflectivity that are approximate indicators of the motion of groups of particles.

Measuring hail fall. It has now become evident that the conclusions reached in a hail-suppression experiment may well depend upon the measure that is used for the hail fall. Recent measurements in South Dakota suggest that the primary effect of seeding a hailstorm may be to reduce the hail size and increase the number of hailstones, leaving the total hail mass relatively unchanged but reducing crop damage.

Three instruments have been developed for measuring hail fall. The first is a hail-rain separator that records hail and rain at 1-min intervals. The second is a hail pad consisting of a styrofoam sheet that is first painted white and then, after the hailstorm, is painted black with a roller so that the dimples caused by the hail are revealed. These depressions have been calibrated and may well become a worldwide, economical standard for assessing hail damage and evaluating hail-suppression efforts. The third instrument consists of a box containing an optical scanning device that is capable of measuring and recording time-resolved hail size distributions.

Seeding experiments. Getting the seeding materials into the right place in the storm is both a practical and a scientific problem. A common technique is to burn the seeding flares from an aircraft that is flying just below cloud base in an updraft area. A new method is to launch a rocket vertically from this aircraft into the higher regions of the storm. Another technique consists of dropping burning flares into the tops of feeder clouds just before they are ingested into the updraft regions of the storm. A refinement of this technique, being used in South Africa by an American company, consists of using a special door to eject the flares from inside a pressurized, high-performance business jet aircraft. Once airborne, this jet vastly increases the ground-to-air response capability and the areal coverage. In addition, the technique has been extended to nighttime operations over mountainous terrain with the use of on-board radar for guidance to the desired portions of the storm.

Impact of suppression programs. Economic studies of the cost of suppressing hail in the Great Plains show that an area of at least 5,000,000 acres is needed for an economically efficient program. Costs would be on the order of 16¢ per planted acre per year. In comparison, the long-term average cost of damage to crops by hail is in the range of $4 per planted acre per year. Thus, only a small percentage of success in a hail-suppression operation would make it cost-effective.

The effect of hail-suppression activities on rainfall is crucial to the usefulness of the operation, for, in the Great Plains, the advantages of a 30% decrease in hail damage can be offset by a 10% decrease in rainfall. Fortunately, all hail-suppression operations, including NHRE, have reported a significant increase in rainfall associated with hail-suppression seeding in correspondence to the predictions of physical and numerical models.

The monitoring of silver concentrations in soils, grasses, water, aquatic sediments, and aquatic plants in the NHRE experimental area has revealed no increases in these concentrations after each seeding season.

NHRE enjoys widespread public support among the local residents, with two-thirds indicating that they would vote to have the project continued, and less than 1 in 10 voicing opposition. The majority, however, believe that an operational suppression program should be run at the local level rather than by the Federal government, and more than two-thirds of the residents indicate that they would be willing to make direct contributions toward the cost of such a program.

In many areas, the public does support operational hail-suppression programs. In the Great Plains, the most successful operational programs, in terms of continued public support and acceptance, are those that include regular evaluation of project operations and effects, extensive participation in policy decisions by public officials at the county level, and substantial financial support through an accepted taxing authority.

For background information *see* CLOUD PHYSICS; PRECIPITATION (METEOROLOGY); WEATHER MODIFICATION in the McGraw-Hill Encyclopedia of Science and Technology.   [EDWIN X. BERRY]

Bibliography: D. J. Musil, W. R. Sand, and R. A. Schleusener, *J. Appl. Meteorol.*, 12:1364–1370, 1973.

Weathering processes

Organic acids have been cited as agents of rock weathering for more than a century, but controlled laboratory experiments simulating weathering in natural systems have been conducted primarily within the past few years. Single, pure organic acids whose properties are chemically well characterized have been used in order to quantify the experiments, and they may logically be followed by work with fulvic acid and more complex reagents.

Reactions of organic acids. Although the process of chelation is the most distinctive reaction of strongly complexing acids, typical hydrogen-ion activity is inherent and available in organic acids (and in inorganic acids) to weather and dissolve rocks and minerals. Such acid properties likewise maintain the hydrolysis reaction between silicates (rock formers) and distilled (rain) water that otherwise would be stopped because of alkalinity built up in the system during hydrolysis.

As mentioned, organic acids and presumably their derivatives attack (weather) rocks because of their ability to chelate or form soluble complexes with such rock-forming elements as Fe and Al. For example, although water alone may dissolve only 20 parts per billion Al from Arkansas bauxite, 0.01 M tartaric or salicylic acid dissolves 80 parts per million, or more. This ratio may exceed the concentration of silica dissolved. Significantly, when Al is transported in solution out of the system, the time-honored order of susceptibility of minerals in silicate rocks to weathering actually may be reversed. Furthermore, instead of laterites and bauxites (hydrated Fe and Al oxides) being

produced as end members of weathering, silica is concentrated to yield podsols or a silica-rich regolith.

A variant of the common laterite composed of hydrated oxides may occur when dissolved Al encounters phosphate ions. Highly insoluble Al-phosphate minerals, with structures similar to that of traditional laterite, are precipitated, thus producing "lateritic phosphates."

Chelation of heavy metals. Some geologic field observations on deposits resulting from weathering suggest that differential or selective dissolution (weathering) between Fe and Al has taken place. In Africa, aluminous bauxites containing relatively little iron oxide may occur under geologic environments whose counterparts produce ferruginous laterites. Part of the Arkansas bauxite occurs beneath lignite layers (a rich source of organic compounds). In a few diaspore deposits in Mis-

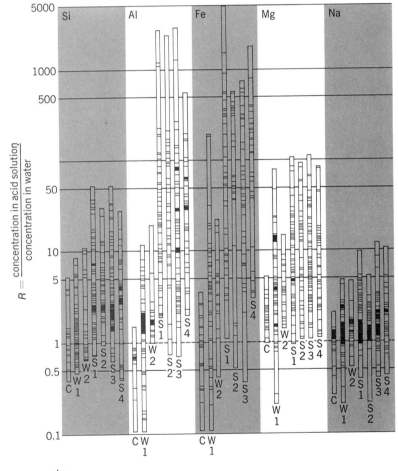

key:

C = water charged with CO_2 (1 atm) S_1 = 0.01 M tartaric acid
W_1 = 0.01 M aspartic acid S_2 = 0.01 M citric acid
W_2 = 0.01 M acetic acid S_3 = 0.01 M salicylic acid
    S_4 = 0.01 M tannic acid

Fig. 1. The ratio of the concentration of each cation dissolved from primary rock-forming silicates and clay minerals in acid solutions to that in water. Unity equates concentrations in water and acids. Each horizontal line within the vertical bars represents one analytical ratio. High density of lines in the bars represents multiplicity of overlapping ratios. (*From W. H. Huang and W. D. Keller, Organic acids as agents of chemical weathering of silicate minerals, Nature Phys. Sci., 239:149–151, 1972*)

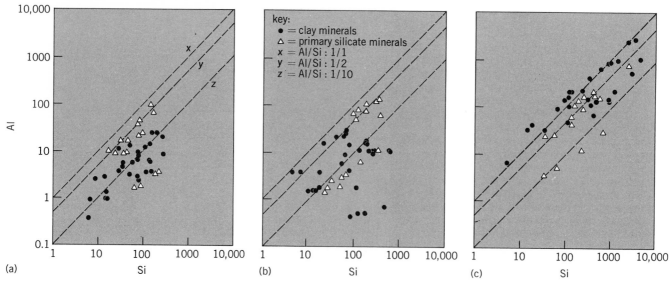

Fig. 2. Al and Si dissolved from primary rock-forming silicates and clay minerals, expressed as μmol liter^{-1}, in (a) deionized water, (b) aspartic acid, and (c) tartaric acid. (*From W. H. Huang and W. D. Keller, Organic acids as agents of chemical weathering of silicate minerals, Nature Phys. Sci., 239:149–151, 1972*)

souri, "iron-band" diaspore may be significant. It is typically made up of a boulder-size core of light-gray, relatively pure diaspore enclosed concretion-wise within hydrated iron oxide rims. Field geologists regularly have postulated that reducing organic solutions have mobilized the iron, but immediately pertinent chemical data that would delineate the mechanisms have not been adduced. Iron oxide–containing bauxite in Hungarian deposits commonly contains bleached, iron-depleted spots alternating with concentrations of iron oxide and thus resembles Missouri iron-band diaspore. Laboratory experiments designed to investigate possible differential solution of iron and aluminum oxides from both geologic and technologic viewpoints are under way, but no results have been reported. Geologic field observations suggest that other common heavy metals may be chelated and mobilized by organic acids.

An auxiliary effect of the removal by chelation of Al or Fe, or both, from a complex silicate mineral is to disrupt the silicate framework structure and thereby facilitate further breakdown and weathering by typical hydrolysis and reaction with CO_2-containing water. Fulvic acid compounds of Al generated during weathering apparently predispose Al to sixfold coordination with OH, thereby implementing the formation of kaolin minerals upon condensation of such a sheet with tetrahedral silica. The enhanced solubility of Al caused by organic acids indicates a possible means whereby, in geologic situations, clay minerals may be dissolved or reprecipitated by the action of considerably less solvent liquid than water alone.

Environment for organic weathering. Organic acids are stable and can act as agents of weathering only when the Eh (oxidation potential) of the environment is low enough for the acids to exist. A high Eh may oxidize the organic reactant. Weathering and dissolution can be reversed to precipitation and deposition by a rise in Eh.

Hence, the work of organic acids is far more sensitive to Eh than that of inorganic acids.

On the other hand, organic acids are far more diverse chemically than inorganic acids are. Organic acids can be aromatic, aliphatic, or both (tannic acid, for example); amino-, chloro-, mono-, or multi-carboxy; mono- or multi-hydroxy, and so forth. Preliminary, incomplete observations further indicate that specific, unique, or preferential reactions may occur between organic acids and certain ions, for example, aspartic acid with Ca and Mg.

Among the large-scale environments dominated by organic weathering are such areas as (1) the northwestern part of the Amazon River basin drained by the huge Río Negro, (2) subtropical humid regions such as the Suwannee River and cypress-inhabited water bodies of the southeastern United States, and (3) cool, humid peat-bog environments in the northern United States, Canada, Scotland, and the northern European mainland. The Río Negro, comparable in size to the Mississippi River, carries water that is relatively clear compared to that of the muddy Amazon into which it flows at Manaus, Brazil, but reflected light makes it look black—hence its name. Actually, the water is a transparent brownish color by transmitted light; it is stained by a rich content of organic acids (compounds) extracted by weathering from its tropical rainforest drainage basin.

Tannic acid, popularly thought to be derived from cypress knees, colors the water brown in some lakes and rivers of the southern and eastern United States. This organic-rich water is a black, strong reflector that yields the famous scenic reflections at Cypress Gardens Park, near Charleston, S.C., and also is effective at Cypress Gardens, Fla. Undoubtedly, residues from various plants other than cypress also contribute organic compounds to water in thickly vegetated swamps, bogs, rivers, and lakes. Ashy-gray podsols formed in peat bog regions are silica-rich soils from which aluminum and iron have been leached, typically by complexing organic acids. The invasion of the surfaces of igneous rocks by algae and lichen observed on lava flows within a few years after eruption, and on otherwise bare granite knobs, accompanies the extraction of nutrient ions from the rocks by reactivity of organic exudates and residues from the primitive plants on the rocks.

Simulated weathering. Experimental dissolution of common rock-forming silicate minerals in dilute organic acids at room temperature is typically incongruent. Figure 1 shows the ratios of concentrations of cations dissolved from common primary rock-forming silicate minerals and clay minerals in various organic acids in relation to the concentration dissolved in water. The results of more than 2000 analyses are included in this diagram. Augite, muscovite, labradorite, microcline, kaolinites, illites, flint clays, and montmorillonites were crushed or dispersed and gently shaken for 102 days in the specified liquids at room temperature. Analyses were made on the clear centrifugate. In some acids, however, certain primary and secondary (clay) minerals may yield dissolved Al and Si in congruent ratios with respect to the parent material (Fig. 2). Alkali and alkaline earth elements are typically dissolved from Al-silicate rocks independently of complexing action, as would be expected because of their solubility characteristics.

For background information *see* WEATHERING PROCESSES in the McGraw-Hill Encyclopedia of Science and Technology.   [WALTER D. KELLER]

Bibliography: A. L. I. Fernandez and J. L. M. Vivaldi, in *Proceedings of the 1972 International Clay Conference*, Madrid, pp. 173–184, 1973; W. H. Huang and W. D. Keller, *Amer. Mineral.*, 56: 1082–1095, 1971; W. H. Huang and W. D. Keller, *Clays and Clay Minerals*, 20:69–74, 1972; W. H. Huang and W. D. Keller, *Nature Phys. Sci.*, 239: 149–151, 1972; A. I. Ragim-Zade, *Gidrokhim. Mater.*, 51:145–152, 1969.

Wood decay

A new concept about how decay begins and develops in wood has emerged in recent years. The decay process is no longer seen as a simple relationship between wood and fungi, but as a complex succession of events that involve chemical reactions, bacteria, different kinds of fungi, and discoloration. Research on this new concept has revealed the unique ways in which a tree reacts to its wounds by sealing off the affected tissues. Even though a tree may be rotten at the core, it may still live on to produce healthy new wood for a long time.

Natural process. Decay of wood is a natural and dynamic process. If wood and other organic matter did not decay, the Earth would soon be covered with dead matter, oxygen would not be released, and the Earth would lack other materials essential for life.

No doubt decay has been known ever since humans first began to climb trees and to use wood for tools and shelter and fuel. And today decay of living trees and wood products is still a problem of worldwide dimensions. Decay causes more damage to trees—and loss of wood fiber—all over the world than all the other destructive forces combined; it is a threat to every product made of wood.

The causes of decay were not understood until the late 1800s. Before that time, it was thought that decay caused fungi. Then Robert Hartig, a German plant pathologist and forester, advanced the theory that it was the other way around: fungi cause decay. Hartig's research set the foundation for the science of forest pathology.

Hartig developed his concept of decay around three major events: a wound, infection of the wound by decay fungi, and breakdown of the wood by the fungi. This classical concept remained essentially unchanged until a few years ago. Now, results of recent research have made it necessary to reexamine and expand upon Hartig's original concept.

Starting point. As in Hartig's concept, the wound is still the starting point (Fig. 1). But it is now known that a complex succession of events takes place in the processes that lead to decay. In living trees, discoloration of the wood usually precedes decay; therefore decay cannot be considered without considering discoloration (Fig. 2).

Wounds that may start the decay process can occur in many ways. A branch may die or break off; insects, birds, or animals may wound the tree; a fire may burn the base; snow or ice may break limbs; frost may crack the stem; or a logging machine may scrape the tree in passing.

When the tree is wounded, some living cells may be killed and others may be injured. The injured cells are exposed to the air. Chemical changes quickly take place in the wood. Phenolic substances in the cells are quickly oxidized. The oxidized phenols then begin to polymerize. Polyphenoloxidase enzyme systems are activated after

Fig. 1.   Severe wound on yellow birch tree 106Y. Wounds start the processes that can lead to decay.

Fig. 2.   Dissection of yellow birch tree 106Y. Decay at the base is associated with the 8-year-old wound. The central column of discolored wood above is associated with the dead branch stubs. The diameter of the column of discoloration was the diameter of the tree when the branches died.

wounding. Slight discoloration of the wood results, owing to the dark materials formed in the living wood cells by the chemical changes. Sometimes the early discoloration is a bleaching of the wood rather than a darkening. Vessel plugging is associated with the bleaching. The materials that plug the vessels come from the living cells that surround the vessels. Some of these parenchyma cells are in contact with the ray parenchyma and the vessels. These "contact cells" are thought to be the principal regulators of changes that take place after wounding. The intense activity of the "contact cells" can be demonstrated by the use of nitroblue tetrazolium.

At this early stage in the process, microorganisms are usually not involved in the discoloration process. These early discolorations of cell contents do not weaken the wood. The process initiated by the wound may stop at this point when the wound heals. Whether it heals or not depends on the severity of the wound, the time of year of wounding, and the vigor of the tree. Wound healing appears to be genetically regulated. Some trees heal wounds rapidly while others of the same species do not. In some trees the tissues surrounding the wound continue to die for several weeks, thus increasing the size of the wound.

When the wound does not heal rapidly, discoloration continues to develop. Then, in time, the cambium—that thin layer of tissue under the bark that produces new wood and bark each year—responds to the wound. If the wound occurs during the dormant period, the cambium responds to the wound as soon as growth begins again in the

spring. If it occurs during the growing period, the cambium responds immediately.

The first cells produced by the cambium after a wounding are different from the cells that are normally produced. They have thicker walls, smaller vessels, more cells with protoplasm, and different orientation. These new and different cells act as a barrier to the discoloration process. They wall off the discolored wood; they compartmentalize the defect. The discoloration can spread up and down inside the tree, within the core sealed off by the barrier cells, but it does not spread outward into the new wood being formed.

The extent and intensity of discoloration depend on the vigor of the tree, the severity of the wound, and time. Discoloration continues to advance as long as the wound is open. If the wound heals, the entire cylinder of wood present when the tree was wounded may not become discolored. Meanwhile, the cambium continues to form new growth rings that are free of discoloration.

Microorganisms. At the same time, some of the microorganisms that first colonized the nutrient-rich wound surface may begin to grow into the tree. Many different microorganisms can be found on the wound surface—most common are fungi in the genera *Penicillium, Alternaria, Hormodendrum, Gliocladium,* and *Mucor.* They compete for nutrients, and many do not survive the intense competition. Of those that do survive, only a few types are able to begin growing into the wood through the wound—only those that can thrive in the discolored wood.

The first microorganisms to invade the tree—the pioneers—usually are bacteria and nondecay fungi. The most aggressive pioneer fungi are those in the genera *Phialophora, Fusarium, Cytospora, Ceratocystis, Graphium, Cephalosporium,* and *Gliocladium.* The principal pioneer bacteria are in the genera *Pseudomonas* and *Bacillus.* In some cases, decay fungi are pioneers. Some of the principal pioneer decay fungi are *Fomes annosus* and *Armillaria mellea.* The pioneers first infect the cells that have been altered by chemical changes in response to the wound. The new tissues formed after the injury still remain free of infection. The tree begins to compartmentalize the pioneer microorganisms.

The infected cells are further altered by the pioneer microorganisms. The discoloration may intensify; the cells may become moister; the mineral content of the cells may increase; and parts of the cell walls may be slightly eroded. Because of these changes, the infected wood in different species of trees is called by many names: "wetwood," "mineral stain," "blue butt," "brownheart," "redheart," "blackheart," and so on. It is not true heartwood. The wound-disease process can still stop at this stage if the tree is vigorous and the wound heals.

In some cases the wood tissues are killed, and decay microorganisms begin to move in. The succession of the microorganisms continues. The decay microorganisms affect those tissues that were altered first by chemical changes and then by the pioneer microorganisms. But still the new growth of wood that continues to form remains free of discoloration and decay.

The wound-disease process continues as long as

the wound remains open. Many species of microorganisms may interact with one another until the dead wood is decomposed. The succession of organisms does not stop when the first decay microorganisms enter; it stops only when the tissues have been completely digested.

The decaying wood is often separated—walled off—from the new whitewood by a band of discolored wood. The pioneer microorganisms may remain in this band. As decay continues, the decay microorganisms slowly digest this disolored band; and only a hard, black rim then separates the (by then) hollow core from the healthy whitewood.

Up to this point the process may take 40 or 50 years or even longer. Healthy white blemish-free new wood will surround the hollow core, unless other wounds are inflicted later.

It is important to note that the processes need not go through to completion. Healing of wounds, antagonism among organisms, unfavorable environments, and other forces may cause the processes to abate in any stage.

Control of decay. Described above is a series of events that follow a single wound at one period in the life of a tree. But a tree is apt to be injured a number of times; and the same process takes place each time.

After a tree dies, or is cut down, a large mass of dead wood—cellulose and lignin—remains. Sometimes, materials impregnated in the walls of wood cells when they were still living make some kinds of wood very resistant to decay long after the tree is cut, and products are made from the wood. But under favorable conditions of moisture and temperature, microorganisms will begin to digest the dead cells in wood products and in cut timber.

As the decay process proceeds in wood products or cut timber, many species of microorganisms—a few at first and many later—grow into the wood; and slowly the wood is digested. Successions of microorganisms occur here also. Some preservative treatments will stall the decay process for a long time; but, given enough time and proper conditions, the microorganisms will succeed in digesting the wood.

In living trees decay can be prevented by avoiding wounds. In wood products and in cut timber, decay can be prevented by keeping moisture low or by using preservatives.

Wounds on living trees can be treated to minimize decay by cutting away dead bark, shaping the wound to form a vertical ellipse, pruning dead and dying branches, and watering and fertilizing to increase tree vigor. Results of recent research show that the commonly used wound dressings do little to stop decay.

The chances for regulating the decay process will increase as more is learned about host response to wounding and compartmentalization and about successions of microorganisms.

For background information see WOOD DECAY in the McGraw-Hill Encyclopedia of Science and Technology.   [ALEX L. SHIGO]

Bibliography: E. M. Sharon, *Can. J. Forest Res.*, 3:83, 1973; A. L. Shigo and W. E. Hillis, *Annu. Rev. Phytopathol.*, 11:197, 1973; W. C. Shortle and A. L. Shigo, *Can. J. Forest Res.*, 3:354, 1973; T. A. Tattar and A. E. Rich, *Phytopathology*, 63:167, 1973.

X-ray star

The past few years have seen unprecedented advances in the knowledge and understanding of cosmic x-ray and gamma-ray sources. In particular, scientists have been able to observe certain details of physical processes involving neutron stars and possibly even the mysterious black holes.

Methods of observation. Much of this new understanding is the direct consequence of the launching of numerous balloons and rockets, and a few satellites, instrumented to study specific problems. Particularly notable is the outstanding success of the first Small Astronomical Satellite, *Uhuru*, built by R. Giacconi and his collaborators at American Science and Engineering to locate cosmic x-ray sources accurately and to study their temporal behavior in the spectral range from approximately 3 keV to approximately 20 keV.

The rest of the universe is directly observable from the ground in only two "windows," the optical (with small extensions into the infrared and near-ultraviolet) and a number of radio bands. Several very important classes of astrophysical processes result in energy being radiated largely in x-rays and gamma rays, and can be studied properly only in those regions. A number of very-high-temperature thermal processes in plasmas—at temperatures of tens of millions of degrees—result largely in x-radiation, and may be very weak or undetectable in the optical band. Nonthermal processes include synchrotron radiation from relativistic electrons spiraling in magnetic fields, or interacting with low-energy (optical) photons, nuclear de-excitation resulting in gamma-ray line radiation, and such processes as positron-electron annihilation and π^0-meson decay. All of these have now been observed in astrophysical processes. To study this region, where there is no "window," any means are employed which can place detectors above most of the atmosphere (balloons) or above all of it (rockets and satellites). For energies below approximately 15 keV, detectors must be out of the atmosphere; the lifetimes of satellites are required to make detailed studies of behavior in time or to map the sources systematically.

Types of sources. The cosmic x-radiation and gamma radiation may be divided into the discrete and the diffuse components, although it must be borne in mind that the diffuse component includes unresolved discrete sources, while the discrete component includes certain extended sources. This article will concentrate on advances in knowledge of discrete sources, since, with some reservations, the integrated effect of all the discrete sources in the universe may account for most of the diffuse component.

The latest *Uhuru* catalog lists some 160 x-ray sources (although perhaps a few dozen were discovered before *Uhuru*). About two-thirds of these are known to be or are suspected of being in the Galaxy, the rest are extragalactic. The figure shows the location of the sources listed in the catalog. The clustering of sources near the galactic center and the concentration along the Milky Way are clearly seen. Extragalactic sources are distributed randomly. The first known and brightest x-ray star, Scorpius X-1, has been studied intensively in

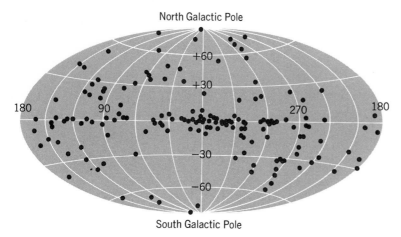

North Galactic Pole

South Galactic Pole

Location of discrete cosmic x-ray sources located and studied by the *Uhuru* satellite and published in the 3U Catalog. New galactic coordinates use the Milky Way as the equator—the central horizontal line. The center of the Milky Way Galaxy is at the center of the figure. (*Herbert Gursky, Smithsonian Observatory*)

recent years. The optical counterpart, a variable ranging from fourteenth to twelfth magnitude, has also been observed carefully. Strangely enough, with all these observations a convincing model of the behavior of Scorpius X-1 is still not available.

Supernova remnants. The Crab Nebula is one of a number of supernova remnants (including Tycho's supernova of 1572, Vela X, Cass A, Puppis A, and the optically beautiful Cygnus Loop) contributing to the cosmic x-radiation. The Crab pulsar, NP0532, has been found to pulse also in the x-ray, gamma-ray, and optical regions, synchronized with the radio pulsing, but thus far is the only one of the nearly 100 known pulsars to do so. Since it is among the youngest (born A.D. 1054) it may be that the x-rays decay quicker than the radio emission.

Transient sources. Three transient sources (Cen X-2, Cen X-4, and Lup X-1) have been observed to behave in x-rays like novae in the optical, appearing suddenly and decaying over several months. No corresponding light emission was detected. All three, at their peak, were the brightest nonsolar objects in the x-ray sky.

Binary systems. Among the most fascinating sources are the close binaries where one component is an invisible, collapsed object such as a neutron star which accretes material from its companion and utilizes the gravitational potential energy thus freed to power its emissions. Many are also eclipsing binaries which provide a wealth of additional data on masses, diameters, and orbital size and shape.

Centaurus X-3 is one of these sources. The neutron star has a 4.8-sec x-ray period and is eclipsed regularly every 2.1 days by the primary. The source lies near the galactic plane, and, probably due to obscuration by dust, its optical counterpart is not yet detected.

Hercules X-1 is another such source. The x-rays pulse with a period of 1.237 sec—the probable rotation period of the neutron star. The primary is a variable star known since the beginning of the century, HZ Herculis. The x-ray source is eclipsed by HZ Her for 6 of every 42 hr, and superimposed on this is still another period, the x-rays being off for

approximately 25 of every 35 days. This behavior, not yet satisfactorily explained, correlates with an optical 35-day period. A further complication is that the optical variation occasionally ceases for years at a time.

Cyg X-3 is still another type, with a 4.8-hr period, possibly due to periodic eclipsing. No neutron star rotation period has been detected. Enormous radio outbursts occurred in the same location in September 1972, with no reflected changes in x-rays. It is possible that they are not connected.

The source presently causing the most excitement is Cygnus X-1. The x-ray emission is variable on time scales from months down to a few milliseconds, yet no real periodicity has emerged. The optical counterpart is known, HDE226868, a ninth-magnitude spectroscopic binary with a 5.5-day period, of very early spectral type, a very bright star of about 30 solar masses. Its distance is about 8000 light-years. The invisible secondary has a mass somewhere between 4 and 10 solar masses, the uncertainty due to the orbital inclination being unknown. Presently accepted theory, developed since about 1960 by J. Wheeler of Princeton and coworkers, is that no neutron star of this mass can exist, and the secondary would need to be a black hole with a gravitational field so strong that neither matter nor radiation could ever escape. A conclusive test is still awaited. *See* GRAVITATIONAL COLLAPSE.

Extragalactic sources. Turning now to extragalactic sources, x-rays have been observed from companion galaxies, the Lesser and Greater Magellanic Clouds, and the Great Andromeda Galaxy. X-ray observations of M87, the galaxy with the famous jet, have been improved. The radio galaxy NGC5128 (known as Cen A) emits x-rays, mainly from a small point in the nucleus. Some, but not all, Seyfert galaxies are very intense emitters of x-radiation, approximately 10^{46} ergs/sec. Finally, some of the rich clusters of galaxies, such as those in Virgo, Coma Berenices, and Perseus, appear to emit x-rays over extended regions, possibly pointing to thermal bremsstrahlung radiation from intergalactic plasma.

Data from SAS-2 satellite. The SAS-2 satellite, successor to *Uhuru*, incorporates a spark chamber sensitive to gamma rays above 30 MeV. Analysis of the data has only begun, but initial results show increased gamma radiation from the central bulge of the Galaxy, without any pronounced point source at the nucleus itself. Elsewhere in the Galaxy, it appears that π^0 production (and decay), from the interaction of cosmic rays confined magnetically to the spiral arms with the material in the arms, suffices to explain observed gamma-ray intensities.

Gamma-ray bursts. A recent, unexpected development has been the discovery in the Vela satellite system data of the so-called gamma-ray bursts—brief, extremely intense blasts of soft gamma rays or hard x-rays. They seem to occur at random time intervals; more than 20 have been recorded in 4 years of data. The peak energy is in the hundreds of kilovolts. Durations range from a tenth of a second to tens of seconds. The sources are widely distributed over the sky, and no conclusive identification has been made with any other known object or occurrence. They may represent a new class of object or extremely unusual behavior in an already known class. Proposed sources include novae and supernovae, several kinds of flaring in magnetic dwarf stars, infall of matter onto neutron stars, or, most recently, instabilities in black hole accretion disks resulting from extra-large mass transfers from a binary companion. *See* GAMMA-RAY ASTRONOMY.

Diffuse radiation. It now appears likely that most of the isotropic, diffuse component of the cosmic x-radiation and gamma radiation can be explained as the integrated flux of innumerable point sources of the kinds described above. One exception could be the apparent enhanced emission in the soft x-rays below 1 keV. Both observational and theoretical work here is in a state of flux.

For background information *see* BINARY STARS; CRAB NEBULA; GALAXY, EXTERNAL; ROCKET ASTRONOMY; SUPERNOVA; X-RAY ASTRONOMY; X-RAY STAR in the McGraw-Hill Encyclopedia of Science and Technology.   [IAN B. STRONG]

Bibliography: H. Friedman, *Science*, 181:395–407, Aug. 3, 1973; R. B. Hoover, R. J. Thomas, and J. H. Underwood, in *Advances in Space Science and Technology*, vol. 11, pp. 1–214, 1972; K. Pinkau, in *Proceedings of the 13th International Cosmic Ray Conference*, University of Denver, vol. 5, pp. 3501–3512, 1973; J. Silk, in *Annual Review of Astronomy and Astrophysics*, vol. 11, pp. 269–308, 1973.

McGRAW-HILL YEARBOOK OF SCIENCE AND TECHNOLOGY

List of Contributors

List of Contributors

A

Abaunza, Dr. Alfred E., Jr. *Medical Center, University of Utah.* LUNG DISORDERS (coauthored).

Allan, Roger. *Associate Editor, IEEE Spectrum Magazine, New York.* INTEGRATED CIRCUITS.

Allen, Dr. Robert C. *Department of Biochemistry, Tulane University, School of Medicine.* PHAGOCYTOSIS.

Anger, Dr. Clifford. *Department of Physics, University of Calgary, Alberta, Canada.* AURORA.

Appella, Dr. Ettore. *Laboratory of Cell Biology, National Institutes of Health, Bethesda.* ANTIGEN.

B

Ball, Dr. L. Andrew. *Microbiology Section, University of Connecticut.* PLANT VIRUS.

Bang, Dr. Frederik B. *School of Hygiene and Public Health, Johns Hopkins University.* INVERTEBRATE PATHOLOGY.

Barnes, Dr. Robert F. *Laboratory Director, U.S. Department of Agriculture, Regional Pasture Research Laboratory, University Park, PA.* FORAGE CROPS (in part).

Beckner, Dr. Everet H. *Director of Physical Research, Sandia Laboratories, Albuquerque.* FUSION, NUCLEAR.

Bemis, Dr. Curtis E., Jr. *Oak Ridge National Laboratory.* ELEMENT 104.

Berger, U. S. *Director, Radio Systems Laboratory, Bell Laboratories, North Andover, MA.* COMMUNICATIONS SYSTEMS (TRAFFIC) DESIGN.

Berry, Dr. Edwin X. *Program Manager for Weather Modification, National Science Foundation, Washington.* WEATHER MODIFICATION.

Beveridge, Prof. David L. *Department of Chemistry, Hunter College.* MOLECULAR ORBITAL THEORY.

Black, Dr. C. C. *Department of Botany, University of Georgia.* PHOTOSYNTHESIS.

Blake, Neal A. *Office of Systems Engineering Management, Federal Aviation Administration, Washington.* AIR-TRAFFIC CONTROL (in part).

Borchert, Prof. Rolf. *Departments of Botany and of Physiology and Cell Biology, University of Kansas.* STEM (BOTANY).

Boucher, Dr. Laurence J. *Associate Professor of Chemistry, Carnegie-Mellon University.* PORPHYRIN (in part).

Boyd, Jerry L. *Director of Technical Services, Eimco BSP Division, Envirotech Corporation, Salt Lake City.* SEWAGE TREATMENT.

Brackett, Prof. Benjamin G. *Department of Clinical Studies, School of Veterinary Medicine, and Department of Obstetrics and Gynecology, School of Medicine, University of Pennsylvania.* MAMMALIAN FERTILIZATION (feature).

Brauman, Prof. John I. *Department of Chemistry, Stanford University.* ACID AND BASE.

Brown, Dr. Charles A. *Assistant Professor of Chemistry, Cornell University.* HYDRIDE, METAL.

Buchsbaum, Dr. Ralph. *Formerly Department of Biology, University of Pittsburgh.* INVERTEBRATE ZOOLOGY.

Buhl, Dr. David. *Astrochemistry Branch, National Aeronautics and Space Administration, Goddard Space Flight Center, Greenbelt, MD.* INTERSTELLAR MATTER.

Burgess, Eric. *Communications Consultant, Science and Technology News Service, Northridge, CA.* SPACE PROBE.

Burke, Prof. Kevin. *Department of Geology, State University of New York at Albany.* EARTH, HEAT FLOW IN (coauthored).

Busch, Dr. K. W. *Department of Chemistry, Cornell University.* FLAME PHOTOMETRY (coauthored).

Bush, Dr. Lowell P. *Department of Agronomy, University of Kentucky.* FORAGE CROPS (in part).

C

Carey, Dr. Frank G. *Woods Hole Oceanographic Institution, Woods Hole, MA.* PISCES (ZOOLOGY).

Carroll, Dr. D. M. *Soil Survey of England and Wales, Yorkshire, England.* TERRAIN SENSING, REMOTE.

Carter, Dr. David L. *Soil Scientist, U.S. Department of Agriculture, Snake River Conservation Research Center, Kimberly, ID.* IRRIGATION OF CROPS (in part).

Chaudhari, Dr. Praveen. *International Business Machines Corporation, Thomas J. Watson Research Center, Yorktown Heights, NY.* ALLOY.

Coats, Dr. Keith H. *Intercomp, Houston.* PETROLEUM RESERVOIR MODELS.

Cocks, Prof. Franklin H. *Department of Mechanical Engineering, Duke University.* CRYOBIOLOGY.

Collins, Prof. J. H. *School of Engineering Science, University of Edinburgh, Scotland.* FILTER, ELECTRIC.

Cook, Prof. David I. *Department of Mechanical Engineering, University of Nebraska.* NOISE CONTROL (coauthored).

Corliss, William R. *Technical Consultant, Glenarm, MD.* SPACE FLIGHT.

Creagan, Dr. Richard P. *Department of Biology, Yale University.* SOMATIC HYBRIDIZATION (coauthored).

Cushman, Robert H. *Special Features Editor, EDN Magazine, Cahners Publishing Company, New York.* MICROPROCESSOR.

D

Davis, Capt. Michael C. *U.S. Navy Surface Effect Ships Project Office, Bethesda.* AIR-CUSHION VEHICLE.

Davis, Dr. Robert E. *U.S. Department of Agriculture, Plant Virology Laboratory, Beltsville, MD.* PLANT DISEASE (in part).

De Carli, Dr. Luigi. *Facoltà di Medicina, Istituto di Biologia Generale, Università degli Studi di Milano, Italy.* HUMAN GENETICS.

Des S. Thomas, Dr. Donovan. *Department of Biology, University of Windsor, Ontario, Canada.* CYTOCHALASINS.

Deutschman, Dr. William. *Assistant Professor of Astronomy, Dickinson College.* COMETS (feature).

Diamond, Dr. Louis S. *Laboratory of Parasitic Diseases, National Institutes of Health, Bethesda.* VIRUS (coauthored).

Dienes, Prof. Andrew. *Department of Electrical Engineering, University of California at Davis.* LASER, TUNABLE.

E

Ellsworth, William M. *Department of the Navy, Naval Ship Research and Development Center, Bethesda.* HYDROFOIL CRAFT.

El-Swaify, Dr. Samir A. *Associate Professor of Soil Science, University of Hawaii at Manoa.* SOIL (in part).

Esaki, Dr. Leo. *International Business Machines Corporation, Thomas J. Watson Research Center, Yorktown Heights, NY.* TUNNEL JUNCTION.

Evans, Dr. M. E. G. *Department of Zoology, University of Manchester, England.* DIPLOPODA.

Evert, Prof. Ray F. *Chairman, Department of Botany, University of Wisconsin.* PHLOEM.

Ewing, Dr. George. *Professor of Chemistry, Indiana University.* INTERMOLECULAR FORCES (in part).

F

Faulkner, Dr. D. John. *Scripps Institution of Oceanography, La Jolla, CA.* ENDOCRINE SYSTEM (INVERTEBRATE).

Fotino, Prof. Mircea. *Supervisor, Laboratory for High-Voltage Electron Microscopy, Department of Molecular, Cellular and Developmental Biology, University of Colorado.* MICROSCOPE, ELECTRON.

Foy, Dr. Charles D. *Plant Physiology Institute, Beltsville Research Center, Beltsville, MD.* SOIL (in part).

Franzini-Armstrong, Dr. Clara. *Department of Physiology, University of Rochester School of Medicine and Dentistry.* MUSCLE (BIOPHYSICS).

Freeman, Prof. T. E. *Plant Pathology Department, Institute of Food and Agricultural Sciences, University of Florida.* PLANT DISEASE (in part).

Freis, Dr. Edward D. *Senior Medical Investigator, Veterans Administration Hospital, Washington.* HYPERTENSION.

Frenkel, Dr. J. K. *Professor of Pathology, University of Kansas Medical Center.* TOXOPLASMOSIS.

Fudenberg, Dr. H. Hugh. *Professor of Medicine, University of California at San Francisco; Professor of Bacteriology and Immunology, University of California at Berkeley.* TRANSFER FACTOR.

Fulton, Dr. T. A. *Bell Laboratories, Murray Hill, NJ.* SUPERCONDUCTING DEVICES.

G

Gardner, Dr. R. B. *Principal Research Engineer, Forestry Sciences Laboratory, Intermountain Forest and Range Experiment Station, Bozeman, MT.* FOREST MANAGEMENT AND ORGANIZATION.

Gascard, Dr. Jean-Claude. *Laboratoire d' Océanographie Physique, Muséum National d'Histoire Naturelle, Paris.* MEDITERRANEAN SEA.

Gavaler, Dr. John R. *Westinghouse Electric Corporation, Research and Development Center, Pittsburgh.* SUPERCONDUCTIVITY (in part).

Geitgey, Duane C. *Senior Vice President, Maynard Research Council Inc., Pittsburgh.* METRIC SYSTEM.

Georges, Dr. T. M. *NOAA Environmental Research Laboratories, Boulder.* STORM.

Goldby, Steven. *President, Dynapol, Palo Alto, CA.* FOOD.

Goldman, Dr. Maurice. *Centre d'Etudes Nucléaires de Saclay, Gif sur Yvette, France.* MAGNETISM.

Gooder, Dr. Harry. *Department of Bacteriology and Immunology, University of North Carolina.* LYSIN.

Gray, Dr. George R. *Technical Consultant, Bellaire, TX.* OIL AND GAS WELL DRILLING.

Gray, Nomer. *Ammann & Whitney Consulting Engineers, New York.* BRIDGE.

Gray, Dr. William R. *Department of Biology, University of Utah.* CONNECTIVE TISSUE.

Grundy, Dr. Scott M. *Associate Professor of Medicine, Veterans Administration Hospital, La Jolla, CA.* GALLSTONES.

Grunes, Dr. D. L. *Soil Scientist, U.S. Department of Agriculture, Plant, Soil and Nutrition Laboratory, Ithaca, NY.* FORAGE CROPS (in part).

Gustine, Dr. David L. *Research Plant Physiologist, U.S. Department of Agriculture, Regional Pasture Research Laboratory, University Park, PA.* FORAGE CROPS (in part).

H

Habeck, Dr. James R. *U.S. Department of Agriculture, Northern Forest Fire Laboratory, Missoula, MT.* FOREST AND FORESTRY (coauthored).

Hambright, Dr. Peter. *Department of Chemistry, Howard University.* PORPHYRIN (in part).

Hamerman, Dr. David. *Professor and Chairman, Department of Medicine, Albert Einstein College of Medicine.* ARTHRITIS.

Hänsch, Prof. Theo W. *Department of Physics, Stanford University.* RYDBERG CONSTANT.

Hansen, Dr. Wilford N. *Department of Physics, Utah State University.* ELECTRODE.

Hawksworth, Dr. Frank G. *Forest Pathologist, U.S. Department of Agriculture, Rocky Mountain Forest and Range Experiment Station, Fort Collins, CO.* TREE DISEASES.

Heeger, Prof. Alan J. *Department of Physics, University of Pennsylvania.* SUPERCONDUCTIVITY (in part).

Hill, Dr. Bridget T. *Imperial Cancer Research Fund Laboratories, London.* CELL DIFFERENTIATION, SENESCENCE AND DEATH.

Hinckley, Dr. C. C. *Department of Chemistry and Biochemistry, Southern Illinois University.* NUCLEAR MAGNETIC RESONANCE (NMR) (in part).

Hodgeson, Dr. J. A. *Supervisory Chemist, National Environmental Research Center, Las Vegas.* AIR-POLLUTION CONTROL.

I

Itô, Prof. Kiyosi. *Department of Mathematics, Cornell University.* STOCHASTIC CALCULUS.

J

Jackson, Dr. Everett D. *U.S. Geologic Survey, Washington.* OCEANIC ISLANDS (coauthored).

Jackson, Dr. Marion L. *Professor of Soil Science, University of Wisconsin.* ATMOSPHERIC POLLUTION.

James, Dr. Brian R. *Department of Chemistry, University of British Columbia, Vancouver, Canada.* KINETICS, CHEMICAL.

Jay, Robert M. *Manager, VP Development, National CSS, Inc., Stamford, CT.* COMPUTER DESIGN.

Jelalian, Albert V. *Manager, Electro-Optics Department, Equipment Division, Raytheon Company, Sudbury, MA.* RADAR.

Jensen, Dr. Marvin E. *Director, U.S. Department of Agriculture, Snake River Conservation Research Center, Kimberly, ID.* IRRIGATION OF CROPS (in part).

Jones, Prof. Lawrence W. *Harrison M. Randall Laboratory of Physics, University of Michigan.* QUARKS.

Jones, Dr. Thony B. *Department of Psychology, University of Massachusetts.* ETHOLOGY.

Jordan, Prof. Joseph. *Department of Chemistry, Pennsylvania State University.* THERMOANALYSIS.

K

Kanner, Dr. Richard E. *Assistant Professor of Medicine, University of Utah Medical Center.* LUNG DISORDERS (coauthored).

Kanury, Dr. A. Murty. *Senior Mechanical Engineer, Stanford Research Institute, Menlo Park, CA.* FIRE ENGINEERING (feature).

Kay, Dr. Marshall. *Department of Geology, Columbia University*. GEOSYNCLINES.

Keller, Dr. Walter D. *Professor Emeritus of Geology, University of Missouri*. WEATHERING PROCESSES.

Kenagy, Dr. G. J. *Physiological Research Laboratory, Scripps Institution of Oceanography, La Jolla, CA*. RODENTIA.

Kenney, Dr. Malcolm E. *Professor of Chemistry, Case Western Reserve University*. NUCLEAR MAGNETIC RESONANCE (NMR) (in part).

Kidd, Dr. W. S. F. *Department of Geology, State University of New York at Albany*. EARTH, HEAT FLOW IN (coauthored).

Klopper, Prof. Arnold. *Department of Obstetrics and Gynaecology, University of Aberdeen, Scotland*. GESTATION PERIOD.

Kohl, Dr. R. A. *Soil Scientist, U.S. Department of Agriculture, Snake River Conservation Research Center, Kimberly, ID*. IRRIGATION OF CROPS (in part).

Koppang, Dr. Nils. *Department of Pathology, Veterinary College of Norway, Oslo*. ONCOLOGY.

Kouts, Dr. Herbert J. C. *Director, Division of Reactor Safety Research, Atomic Energy Commission, Washington*. REACTOR, NUCLEAR.

L

Lamb, Prof. D. Q., Jr. *Department of Physics, University of Illinois at Urbana-Champaign*. GAMMA-RAY ASTRONOMY.

Lefevre, Dr. George, Jr. *Professor and Chairman, Department of Biology, California State University at Northridge*. CHROMOSOME.

Lhermitte, Dr. Roger. *Professor of Physical Meteorology, University of Miami School of Marine and Atmospheric Science*. DOPPLER RADAR.

Lowry, Prof. Ralph A. *Department of Engineering Science and Systems, University of Virginia*. NUCLEAR FUELS.

M

McGill, Dr. T. C. *Associate Professor of Applied Physics, California Institute of Technology*. SEMICONDUCTOR (coauthored).

McLeod, W. R. *Marathon Oil Company, Findlay, OH*. OIL AND GAS, OFFSHORE (coauthored).

Maizels, Dr. Nancy. *Biological Laboratories, Harvard University*. GENE ACTION (in part).

Malm, Duane S. *Technical Consultant, Berwyn, PA*. FOOD ENGINEERING (in part).

Mann, Dr. A. K. *Professor of Physics, University of Pennsylvania*. FORCE, WEAK AND ELECTROMAGNETIC.

Marten, Dr. Gordon C. *Research Agronomist, U.S. Department of Agriculture, Agricultural Research Service; Professor of Agronomy, University of Minnesota*. FORAGE CROPS (in part).

Mattern, Dr. Carl F. T. *Laboratory of Parasitic Diseases, National Institutes of Health, Bethesda*. VIRUS (coauthored).

Mayland, Dr. H. F. *Soil Scientist, U.S. Department of Agriculture, Snake River Conservation Research Center, Kimberly, ID*. FORAGE CROPS (in part).

Meier, Dr. Mark F. *Project Chief—Glaciology, U.S. Geological Survey, Tacoma*. GLACIOLOGY.

Messerschmidt, Harold J. *Graphic Research Director, Mona Industries, Patterson, NJ*. PRINTING PLATE.

Meyerhof, Dr. W. E. *Professor of Physics, Stanford University*. ATOMIC PHYSICS.

Michael, Dr. Henry N. *Research Associate, Applied Center for Archaeology, University of Pennsylvania Museum*. RADIOCARBON DATING.

Milburn, Dr. John A. *Department of Botany, University of Glasgow, Scotland*. PLANT, WATER RELATIONS OF.

Mitchell, Norman. *Product Manager, Versatec, Inc., Cupertino, CA*. COMPOSITION OF TYPE.

Morabito, Dr. J. M. *Bell Telephone Laboratories, Allentown, PA*. ELECTRON SPECTROSCOPY.

Morris, Michael F. *Formerly Department of the Air Force and FEDSIM, Washington*. DIGITAL COMPUTER USAGE.

Morrison, Dr. G. H. *Professor of Chemistry, Cornell University*. FLAME PHOTOMETRY (coauthored).

Morse, N. L. *MTM Product Research and Development Laboratory, Shell Development Company, Wood River, IL*. PETROLEUM PROCESSES.

Mote, Dr. Michael I. *Department of Biology, Temple University*. EYE (INVERTEBRATE).

Müller, Dr. Erwin H. *Professor of Physics, Pennsylvania State University*. FIELD-EMISSION MICROSCOPY.

Mutch, Dr. Robert W. *Research Forester, U.S. Department of Agriculture, Northern Forest Fire Laboratory, Missoula, MT*. FOREST AND FORESTRY (coauthored).

N

Nevins, James L. *Division Leader, Automation and Man-Machine Systems Division, Charles Stark Draper Laboratory, Inc., Cambridge, MA*. SENSORS FOR INDUSTRIAL AUTOMATION (feature).

Nicholson, Dr. Charles. *Department of Physiology and Biophysics, University of Iowa*. BRAIN (VERTEBRATE).

O

Olmsted, Leonard M. *Technical Consultant, South Orange, NJ*. ELECTRICAL UTILITY INDUSTRY.

Olson, Dr. Harry F. *Staff Vice President, Acoustical and Electromechanical Laboratory, RCA Laboratories, Princeton, NJ*. BINAURAL SOUND.

O'Mara, Dr. Michael M. *B. F. Goodrich Chemical Company, Avon Lake, OH*. COMBUSTION.

Opp, Dr. Albert G. *National Aeronautics and Space Administration, Washington*. JUPITER.

P

Phillips, Dr. Paul E. *Assistant Professor of Medicine, Hospital for Special Surgery, New York*. IMMUNOPATHOLOGY.

Pinnell, Dr. Sheldon R. *Associate Professor of Medicine, Dermatology Division, Duke University Medical Center*. CONGENITAL ANOMALY.

Pirie, Dr. N. W. *Rothamsted Experimental Station, Harpenden, Herts., England*. AGRICULTURAL SCIENCE (PLANT).

Platt, Allison M. *Manager, Nuclear Waste Technology Department, Battelle Pacific Northwest Laboratories, Richland, WA*. RADIOACTIVE WASTE DISPOSAL.

Power, Dr. J. F. *Soil Scientist, U.S. Department of Agriculture, Northern Great Plains Research Center, Mandan, ND*. SOIL (in part).

Price, Dr. Richard H. *Assistant Professor of Physics, University of Utah*. GRAVITATIONAL COLLAPSE.

Ptashne, Dr. Mark. *Biological Laboratories, Harvard University*. GENE ACTION (in part).

Putnam, Dr. Frank W. *Professor of Molecular Biology, Zoology, and Biochemistry, Indiana University*. IMMUNOGLOBULIN.

R

Raup, Prof. David M. *Department of Geological Sciences, University of Rochester*. PHYLOGENY.

Reisenauer, Dr. H. M. *Professor of Soil Science, University of California at Davis*. HYDROPONICS.

Ritter, Dr. Rogers C. *Professor of Physics, University of Virginia*. CLINICAL PATHOLOGY.

Robards, Dr. A. W. *Department of Biology, University of York, England.* ENDODERMIS.

Rocap, William A., Jr. *Director of Research and Engineering, Printing Division, Meredith Corporation, Des Moines.* PRINTING PRESS.

Rowe, J. E. *Bell Laboratories, Murray Hill, NJ.* SILICON.

Rubin, Jack. *Avionics Division, International Telephone and Telegraph Corporation, Nutley, NJ.* AIR-TRAFFIC CONTROL (in part).

Ruddle, Dr. Frank H. *Department of Biology, Yale University.* SOMATIC HYBRIDIZATION (coauthored).

S

Sacharow, Stanley. *Packaging Division, Reynolds Metals Company, New York.* FOOD ENGINEERING (in part).

Samter, Dr. Max. *Professor of Medicine, University of Illinois at the Medical Center, Chicago.* ASPIRIN.

Sanford, Dr. James R. *National Accelerator Laboratory, Batavia, IL.* PARTICLE ACCELERATOR (in part).

Sauter, Dr. Jörg J. *Botanisches Institut und Botanischer Garten der Universität, Kiel, West Germany.* BARK.

Saxena, Dr. Satish C. *Professor of Energy Engineering, University of Illinois.* INTERMOLECULAR FORCES (in part).

Scheidt, Dr. Robert. *Department of Chemistry, University of Notre Dame.* PORPHYRIN (in part).

Schneider, William C. *Deputy Associate Administrator for Manned Space Flight, National Aeronautics and Space Administration, Washington.* SKYLAB (feature).

Scholz, Prof. Christopher H. *Lamont-Doherty Geological Observatory of Columbia University.* EARTHQUAKE PREDICTION (feature).

Schoonmaker, G. R. *Vice President—Exploration, Marathon Oil Company, Findlay, OH.* OIL AND GAS, OFFSHORE (coauthored).

Schultz, Prof. R. Jack. *Ecology Section, University of Connecticut.* CYPRINODONTIFORMES.

Sessler, Dr. Gerhard M. *Bell Laboratories, Murray Hill, NJ.* TRANSDUCER.

Shaw, Dr. Herbert R. *U.S. Geologic Survey, Washington.* OCEANIC ISLANDS (coauthored).

Sherr, Sol. *Executive Vice President, North Hills Associates, Glen Cove, NY.* CONTROL SYSTEMS.

Shigo, Dr. Alex L. *Chief Plant Pathologist, Northeastern Forest Experiment Station, Durham, NH.* WOOD DECAY.

Silberberg, Dr. Rein. *Laboratory for Cosmic Ray Physics, Naval Research Laboratory, Washington.* COSMIC RAYS.

Silver, Dr. R. N. *Los Alamos Scientific Laboratory, University of California, Los Alamos, NM.* SEMICONDUCTOR (coauthored).

Simmons, Dr. William. *MODE Executive Officer, MODE-I Scientific Council, Massachusetts Institute of Technology.* OCEAN CURRENTS.

Snavely, Dr. Benjamin B. *Lawrence Livermore Laboratory, Livermore, CA.* ISOTOPE (STABLE) SEPARATION.

Spaulding, Philip F. *Nickum & Spaulding Associates, Inc., Seattle.* SHIP, FERRY.

Stearns, Dr. Mary Beth. *Scientific Research Staff, Ford Motor Company, Dearborn, MI.* FERROMAGNETISM.

Stormont, Dr. Clyde. *Professor of Immunogenetics, School of Veterinary Medicine, University of California at Davis.* BLOOD GROUPS.

Strong, Dr. Ian B. *Los Alamos Scientific Laboratory, University of California, Los Alamos, NM.* X-RAY STAR.

T

Turcotte, Prof. Donald L. *Department of Geological Sciences, Cornell University.* EARTH, INTERIOR OF.

V

Valentine, Prof. James W. *Department of Geology, University of California at Davis.* EVOLUTION, ORGANIC.

Van Haverbeke, Dr. D. F. *Department of Engineering Mechanics, University of Nebraska.* NOISE CONTROL (coauthored).

Veillon, Dr. Claude. *Biophysics Research Laboratory, Harvard Medical School, Peter Bent Brigham Hospital, Boston.* ATOMIC ABSORPTION SPECTROSCOPY.

W

Walker, Dr. Dan B. *Department of Botany, University of Georgia.* FLOWER.

Ward, Dr. William J., III. *Manager of Membrane Projects, General Electric Company Research and Development Center, Schenectady.* MEMBRANE, GAS SEPARATION BY.

Watson, Prof. William W. *Department of Physics, Yale University.* WAVELENGTH STANDARDS.

Weinhouse, Dr. Sidney. *Director, Fels Research Institute, Temple University School of Medicine.* LIVER DISORDERS.

West, Dr. George C. *Acting Director and Professor of Zoophysiology, Institute of Arctic Biology, University of Alaska.* TUNDRA.

Williams, Dr. David J. *Webster Research Center, Xerox Corporation, Webster, NY.* SEMICONDUCTOR, ORGANIC.

Williamson, Dr. David L. *Department of Anatomical Sciences, State University of New York at Stony Brook.* SEX DETERMINATION.

Wilson, Prof. David Gordon. *Department of Mechanical Engineering, Massachusetts Institute of Technology.* SOLID WASTE DISPOSAL.

Wilson, Dr. Kenneth. *Laboratory of Nuclear Studies, Cornell University.* STATISTICAL MECHANICS.

Wilson, Lynn S. *Grumman Data Systems Corporation, Bethpage, NY.* AIRCRAFT TESTING.

Winick, Dr. Herman. *Associate Director for Technical Matters, Stanford Synchrotron Radiation Project, Stanford, CA.* PARTICLE ACCELERATOR (in part).

Wolpert, Prof. Lewis. *Department of Biology as Applied to Medicine, Middlesex Hospital Medical School, London.* ANIMAL MORPHOGENESIS.

Wu, Dr. Tai Tsun. *Division of Engineering and Applied Physics, Harvard University.* SCATTERING EXPERIMENTS, NUCLEAR.

Y

Yochelson, Dr. Ellis L. *U.S. Geological Survey, National Museum of Natural History, Washington.* MOLLUSCA.

Z

Zimmerman, Dr. David W. *Senior Research Associate, Department of Physics, Washington University.* ARCHEOLOGICAL CHEMISTRY.

McGRAW-HILL YEARBOOK OF SCIENCE AND TECHNOLOGY

Index

Index

Physics: atomic, molecular, and nuclear 96–99, 114–117, 148, 178–179, 207–209, 243–246, 255–257, 261–263, 286–289, 303–308, 337–339, 351–353, 353–354, 412–413, 419–421
  cosmic-ray 148
  high-energy 303–308, 337–339, 353–354
  low-temperature 266–267, 354–357, 391–392, 393–396
  Nobel prizes 282
  solid-state 190–193, 261–263, 266–267, 354–357, 357–359, 367–369, 393–396, 410–411
  surface 176–178, 367–369
  theoretical 102–103, 187–188, 188–189, 266–267, 337–339, 351–353, 353–354, 367–369, 383–384, 391–392, 393–396, 410–411
  thin-film electrode 174–176
Physiology: comparative 125–127, 155, 185–187, 280–281, 321–322, 349–351
  general 161–162, 179–180
  plant 155, 317–319, 322–324, 370–371
  Skylab experiments 53–55
Phytohemoagglutinin (chromosome alteration) 229
Phytopathology: plant disease 324–328
  plant virus 328–330
  tree diseases 406–407
  wood decay 417–419
Pi mesons (particle accelerator) 305
Pi (protease inhibitor) system 264
Pickerel weed 328
Pickering, G. 235
Piez, K. A. 145
Piezoelectricity (electric filter) 190–193
Pig: arthritis 109
  blood typing 124
  neonatal isoerythrolysis 125
  Toxoplasma infection 400
Pigment, visual 185–187
Pilafidis, E. J. 61
Pinaceae 119
Pine: bristlecone 345
  dwarf mistletoe 406–407
  Strasburger cells 120
Pineapple (soil salinity tolerance) 372
Pines, D. 217
Pinkau, K. 421
Pinnell, S. 142
Pion: charged 208
  particle accelerator 305
  pion-proton scattering 354
Pioneer program 258–259, 381–383
Pioneer 10 257, 258, 259, 381–383
Pioneer 11 257, 258, 259, 379, 381–383
Pipelines: subsea 298
  tundra regions 409

Pipes, kimberlite 170
Pisces (zoology) 321–322
  heat-exchange mechanism 321–322
  muscle function and features 321
  muscle metabolism 321
Pistia stratiotes 328
Pit fields (endodermis) 181
Pituitary gland (onset of labor) 223–224
Pizzichini, G. 217
Placenta: onset of labor 223–224
  progesterone 224
  toxoplasmosis transmission 399
Placozoa 250, 251
Plainview (AGEH-1) 232
Planet: inner 17
  Jupiter 257–259
  terrestrial 17
Planetary probe 379
Plankton (silica deposition) 113
Planning, urban 283
Plant: aquatic 327–328
  vascular 180–182, 315–316
Plant, mineral nutrition of 253
  aluminum toxicity 370–371
  fertilizer in semiarid grasslands 369–370
  hydroponics 233–235
Plant, water relations of 322–324
  cavitation detection 323
  irrigation of crops 251–255
  pressure bomb measurements 322
  psychrometer and hygrometer techniques 322–323
  shoot growth 386
  summary of developments 323–324
  thermoelectric and electromagnetic techniques 323
Plant anatomy: bark 119–120
  endodermis 180–182
  flower 195–197
  phloem 315–316
  stem 384–387
Plant community, fire-dependent 210
Plant disease 324–328
  mycoplasma-like organisms 324–327
  rhizoctoniosis of aquatic plants 327–328
Plant ecology (tundra) 407–410
Plant growth: optimum temperatures 254–255
  stem 384–387
Plant microclimate (effect of sprinkler irrigation) 253
Plant pathology: plant disease 324–328
  plant virus 328–330
  tree diseases 406–407
  wood decay 417–419
Plant physiology: aluminum tolerance 370–371
  effects of cytochalasins 155
  photosynthesis 317–319
  plant, water relations of 322–324

Plant protein 90–92
Plant temperature (effect of sprinkler irrigation) 253–255
Plant virus 328–330
  cell-free protein synthesis 329
  translation of BMV RNA 329–330
  translation of STNV RNA 329
  translation of TMV RNA 330
Plasma: laser fusion 214
  magnetic confinement fusion 214
Plasma, interplanetary 12
Plasma membrane (cytochalasins) 154
Plasmalemma (muscle fiber) 280
Plasmodesmata: endodermis 181
  sieve areas 316
Plastic-forming processes 60, 63–64
Plate: lithospheric 20, 166, 167
  oceanic 292
  surface of Earth 169, 170
Plate, printing 335
Plate tectonics 21, 167, 168
  earthquake risk evaluation 24–25
  eugeosynclinal belts 223
  geosynclinal studies 222–223
  hot spots 166
  kinematic models 292–294
Platform, offshore drilling 296
Platform drilling rig, submersible 296
Platinum-rhenium catalyst 309
Platt, R. 237
Platycerium bifurcatum 315, 316
Plaut, A. G. 239
Plectronoceras 279, 280
Plume: hypothesis 293
  mantle 170, 293–294
  thermal 295
Plummer, E. W. 188
Pluto (comet formation) 17
Plutonium: disposal as waste 341
  radioactive waste 342
Plutonium-242 178
Pneumococcal autolysin 265
POC detectors *see* Products-of-combustion detectors
Pocket calculator, electronic 273
Podsols 415
Poecilia 152
Poecilia formosa 152, 153
Poecilia latipinna 152
Poecilia mexicana 152
Poeciliopsis 152, 153, 154
Poeciliopsis latidens 153
Poeciliopsis lucida 153, 154
Poeciliopsis monacha 153, 154
Poeciliopsis monacha-latidens 153
Poeciliopsis monacha-lucida 153, 154
Poeciliopsis monacha-occidentalis 153
Poeciliopsis occidentalis 153
Points, critical 383–384
Pokrovsky, Ya. 355, 356

Polar body (activated egg) 3
Polarization, nuclear 266
Poljak, R. 239
Pollution: atmospheric 96–99, 111–113, 172, 263, 409
  fertilizer nitrogen 369
  radiocarbon analysis 345
  sewage treatment 359–360
  solid waste disposal 373–375
  water 172, 409
Pollution (printing): ink 336
  magnesium photoengraving 335
Pollution, audio 282–284
Polyarteritis 239, 240
POLYATOM (computer program) 278
Polyatomic gas: kinetic theory 243
  thermal conductivity 244
  van der Waals molecules 244
Polyatomic molecular structure 278
Polycarbonate 135
Polyester 135
Polyethylene 135
Polyferrocenylene 358
Polyfluoroethylenepropylene (Teflon) 402–403
Polyimide 135
Polymer: antioxidants 198
  charge-transfer complex 357
  combustion analyses 135
  drilling fluids 299–300
  food additives 197–199
  halocarbon 402
  ink 336
  mixed-valence 358
  organometallic 358
  solvent-castable 270
  supported catalysts 260
Polymethacrylonitrile 135
Polymorphism, antigenic 107
Polymorphonuclear leukocyte: microbicidal metabolism 314
  phagocytosis 313–315
Polymyositis 239, 240
Polyoma virus 107
Polyphenylene oxide 135
Polyploidy (unisexual vertebrates) 152–153
Polypodium schraderi 315, 316
Polypodium vulgare 315, 316
Polypropylene 135
Polyspermy 3, 7
Polystyrene 135
Polystyrene pallet 199
Polysulfane 135
Polytene chromosomes (bands) 132, 133
Polyurethane 135
Poly-*N*-vinylcarbazole-2,4,7-trinitrofluorenone (PVK-TNF) 357
Polyvinyl chloride 135, 136
Polyvinylferrocene 358
Pontederia lanceolata 328
Pople, J. A. 278
POPOP (scintillator dye) 261
Population genetics (mass extinctions) 184–185
Pores (sieve areas) 316
Porifera 251
Porphin 330
Porphine reagents 287

XYZ